Organico's
Income Statement
For Month Ended March 31, 2020

Revenues:		
Food services revenue	$3,800	
Teaching revenue	300	
Total revenues		$4,100
Operating expenses:		
Rent expense	$1,000	
Salaries expense	700	
Total operating expenses		1,700
Profit		$2,400

Organico
Statement of Changes in Equity
For Month Ended March 31, 2020

Hailey Walker, capital, March 1		$ -0-
Investments by owner	$10,000	
Profit	2,400	12,400
Total		$12,400
Less: Withdrawals by owner		600
Hailey Walker, capital, March 31		$11,800

Organico
Balance Sheet
March 31, 2020

Assets		Liabilities	
Cash	$ 8,400	Accounts payable	$ 200
Supplies	3,600	Notes payable	6,000
Equipment	6,000	Total liabilities	$ 6,200
		Equity	
		Hailey Walker, capital	11,800
Total assets	$18,000	Total liabilities and equity	$18,000

Organico
Statement of Cash Flows
For Month Ended March 31, 2020

Cash flows from operating activities		
Cash received from clients	$ 4,100	
Cash paid for supplies	(3,400)	
Cash paid for rent	(1,000)	
Cash paid to employee	(700)	
Net cash used by operating activities		$(1,000)
Cash flows from investing activities		-0-
Cash flows from financing activities		
Investment by owner	$10,000	
Withdrawal by owner	(600)	
Net cash provided by financing activities		9,400
Net increase in cash		$ 8,400
Cash balance, March 1		-0-
Cash balance, March 31		$ 8,400

The arrows are provided for education purposes only to emphasize the link between statements.

Differentiating the Financial Statements

Fundamental Accounting Principles uses a colour scheme to help students differentiate among the four key financial statements.

Sixteenth Canadian Edition

FUNDAMENTAL
ACCOUNTING
PRINCIPLES

VOLUME 1

Kermit D. Larson
University of Texas—Austin

Heidi Dieckmann
Kwantlen Polytechnic University—British Columbia

Mc
Graw
Hill
Education

Fundamental Accounting Principles
Volume 1
Sixteenth Canadian Edition

The Internet addresses listed in the text were accurate at the time of publication. The inclusion of a website does not indicate an endorsement by the authors or McGraw-Hill Ryerson, and McGraw-Hill Ryerson does not guarantee the accuracy of the information presented on these sites.

ISBN-13: 978-1-25-965465-7
ISBN-10: 1-25-965465-6

5 6 7 8 M 23 22 21

Printed and bound in Canada.

Care has been taken to trace ownership of copyright material contained in this text; however, the publisher will welcome any information that enables them to rectify any reference or credit for subsequent editions.

Product Director: Rhondda McNabb
Senior Portfolio Manager: Alwynn Pinard
Senior Marketing Manager: Loula March
Content Developer: Shalini Khanna
Senior Portfolio Associate: Stephanie Giles
Supervising Editor: Jessica Barnoski
Photo/Permissions Editor: Karen Hunter
Copy Editor: Kelli Howey
Plant Production Coordinator: Michelle Saddler
Manufacturing Production Coordinator: Jason Stubner
Cover Design: Michelle Losier
Cover Image: Rachel Idzerda
Interior Design: Liz Harasymczuk
Page Layout: Aptara®, Inc.
Printer: Marquis Book Printing

About the Authors

KERMIT D. LARSON, UNIVERSITY OF TEXAS–AUSTIN

Kermit D. Larson is the Arthur Andersen & Co. Alumni Professor of Accounting Emeritus at the University of Texas at Austin. He served as chair of the University of Texas, Department of Accounting, and was visiting associate professor at Tulane University. His scholarly articles have been published in a variety of journals, including *The Accounting Review, Journal of Accountancy*, and *Abacus*. He is the author of several books, including *Financial Accounting* and *Fundamentals of Financial and Managerial Accounting,* both published by Irwin/McGraw-Hill.

Professor Larson is a member of the American Accounting Association, the Texas Society of CPAs, and the American Institute of CPAs. His positions with the AAA have included vice president, southwest regional service president, and chair of several committees, including the Committee of Concepts and Standards. He was a member of the committee that planned the first AAA doctoral consortium and served as its director.

HEIDI DIECKMANN, KWANTLEN POLYTECHNIC UNIVERSITY–BRITISH COLUMBIA

Heidi Dieckmann graduated from Simon Fraser University in Burnaby, BC with a BBA in Accounting and carried on her studies in the Masters of Professional Accountancy Program at the University of Saskatchewan. Heidi attained her CA designation while working in public practice at KPMG in Burnaby before beginning her career in education as an accounting instructor at Kwantlen Polytechnic University. While at KPU, Heidi has served as Department Chair and has sat on several committees. Her major initiatives at KPU included spearheading the Accounting Society of Kwantlen, an impressive accounting student club that has created opportunities for students to network with professional accountants in industry and public practice. She was also actively involved in the redesign of KPU's new BBA program and managed the detailed competency mapping for the transition to the CPA designation. She is also currently involved as a CPA Mentor, coaching upcoming CPAs through the new CPA education and experience requirements.

Heidi has a keen interest in providing students with real-world relevance and preparing students for ethical issues they will come across in the workplace. She has a passion for maximizing student engagement and learning outcomes and is inspired by Eric Mazur's research on the Flipped Classroom and Peer Instruction, and Dee Fink's research in Creating Significant Learning Experiences. Heidi focusses her research on engagement and motivation strategies to reach today's generation of technology-immersed students. She has an interest in online student engagement with a focus on creating a seamless transition into online learning and providing resources to assist teams to collaborate in a virtual environment.

Heidi is a member of the Canadian Academic Accounting Association's Education Committee and has presented at the CAAA annual conference for her work in student engagement through online education and top strategies to reach millennial learners. She has been inspired to embrace international education through participating in the award-winning Canadian Academics Studying Europe conference led by Catherine Vertesi and Robert Buttery; visiting the European Union and the Council of Europe; and studying Swiss banking at the University of Zurich, and political and education systems at the University of Applied Sciences and Arts Northwestern Switzerland. In her spare time Heidi enjoys volunteering through teaching art and STEM classes at her children's school. She loves to explore nutrition through creating new flavours, travel, take art classes at a local gallery, analyze real estate investment opportunities, and most of all spend time with her husband Andrew, her two children Nolan and Hailey, and her close family and friends.

Brief Contents

Contents

CONTENTS

CHAPTER 6
Inventory Costing and Valuation 396

CHAPTER 7
Internal Control and Cash 468

CHAPTER 8
Receivables 538

CHAPTER 9
Property, Plant, and Equipment and Intangibles 604

APPENDIX I
Payroll Liabilities A-1

APPENDIX II
Accounting Information Systems A-34

APPENDIX III
Financial Statement Information A-35

APPENDIX IV
Chart of Accounts A-94

Preface

A Note About Our Cover

The cover of the Sixteenth Canadian Edition is the work of Rachel Idzerda. Rachel's playful illustration spotlights many of the companies, entrepreneurs, and organizations featured in *Fundamental Accounting Principles'* chapter-opening vignettes. See if you can spot the images representing Zane Caplansky's Deli (Chapter 1), Amazon's drones (Chapter 6), Betterwith Ice Cream (Chapter 7), and the Vancouver Airport Authority (Chapter 9). Rachel is a freelance illustrator specializing in editorial illustration and portraiture. She works with her husband and lives with him and their two dogs just outside of Toronto.

INSIDE THE CHAPTERS

As educators, instructors strive to create an environment that fosters learning and provides students with the tools they need to succeed. The Sixteenth Canadian Edition continues to meet and surpass the high standards the market expects from *Fundamental Accounting Principles*. We continue to put learning first, with student-centred pedagogy and critical thinking lessons throughout the text.

All the pedagogical tools are carefully designed for ease of use and understanding, helping the instructor teach and giving the students what they need to succeed.

PEDAGOGY

Student Success Cycle

Student success at the post-secondary level is measured not by how much knowledge a student has acquired, but rather by how well a student can *use* knowledge. The Student Success Cycle, illustrated by a circular icon, reinforces decision-making skills by highlighting key steps toward understanding and critically evaluating the information the student has just read. **Read–Do–Check–Apply** reinforces active learning rather than passive learning. This tool is integrated throughout the text, including the chapter opening page, Checkpoint questions, Demonstration Problems, and end-of-chapter material.

Critical Thinking Challenge

An essential element of critical thinking is the ability to ask questions while reading (or listening or speaking). These exercises are designed to help students develop the skills related to questioning. Suggested answers are posted on **Connect**.

> **CRITICAL THINKING CHALLENGE**
> Why is assessing customer credit critical to the overall success of businesses like WN Pharmaceuticals?

IFRS AND ASPE—THE DIFFERENCES		
Difference	International Financial Reporting Standards (IFRS)	Accounting Standards for Private Enterprises (ASPE)
Recording adjusting entries	• Requires that financial statements be presented at least annually[a]; therefore, adjustments would be prepared at least annually. However, for publicly listed companies, securities commissions law requires publicly listed companies to present quarterly financial statements, which in turn would require that adjusting entries be prepared at least quarterly.	• Unlike IFRS, ASPE does not explicitly require that financial statements be presented at least annually although it is implied given that financial statements must be presented in a timely manner[b] and items must be presented consistently from period to period.[c] Financial statements are prepared at least annually for tax purposes and, for example, to meet any banking requirements.
	• Both public and private enterprises may prepare adjusting entries more frequently, such as monthly, to enhance the accuracy of information required for decision making.	
Depreciation vs. amortization	• Uses the term *depreciation*[d] (although it uses *amortization* for intangible assets).[e]	• Uses the term *amortization*.[f]

a. IFRS 2018, IAS 1 para. 36.
b. ASPE, Accounting Standards, Section 1000.17(b).
c. ASPE, Accounting Standards, Section 1000.19-20.
d. IFRS 2018, IAS 16 para. 6.
e. IFRS 2018, IAS 38 para. 8.
f. ASPE, Accounting Standards, Section 3061.16.

IFRS and ASPE—The Differences

This box appears at the end of every chapter to highlight any differences or important points about reporting and terminology as they relate to the financial accounting course. The chapter content is IFRS 2018 compliant for Volumes I and II; references are provided where appropriate.

Real-World Focus

The Sixteenth Canadian Edition has increased the use of real business examples to reflect the most current information available. This continues the text's strong ties to the real world of accounting, be it through detailed interviews with business-

A **business** is an entity represented by one or more individuals selling products or services for profit. Products sold include anything from athletic apparel (**CCM, Bauer, Lululemon Athletica, Nike, Reebok**) to electronic devices (**Apple, Dell, Hewlett-Packard, Samsung**) and clothing (**Abercrombie & Fitch, The Gap, Zara**). Service providers such as data communication providers (**Bell, Rogers, Telus**), food services (**McDonald's, Starbucks, Tim Hortons**), and Internet services (**Google, Twitter, Skype, Facebook, Instagram**) make our lives more connected. A business can be as small as an in-home tutoring business or as large as **George Weston Limited**, the food processing company known for its President's Choice and No Name brands, owner of the clothing label Joe Fresh, and holder of a significant investment in the supermarket chain **Loblaw Companies Limited**. Nearly 100,000 new businesses are started in Canada each year, with most of them being founded by people who want freedom from ordinary jobs, a new challenge in life, or the potential of earning extra money.

people for the chapter-opening vignettes, examples of ethical standards and treatments, or annual reports for both in-chapter example disclosures and end-of-chapter material. The first time an actual business is used, its name is highlighted in **bold magenta** for emphasis. This integration with real-world companies helps engage students while they read.

Food Truck Frenzy

Across the country, major urban centres are experiencing an industry trend to go to the street to entice customers with a wide range of fresh, made-to-order food options. In Canada, the street vendor industry is in the growth phase of its industry life cycle according to IBISWorld, a global market research firm. IBISWorld estimates the market for street vendors in Canada will continue to grow over the next five years. Revenues are expected to reach $335 million with an expected annualized growth rate of 1.7% by 2023. The market is dominated by new market entrants—in most cases, individual owners operating as sole proprietors. The most successful street vendors will take advantage of effective marketing and branding toward health-conscious consumers looking for unique dining options.

Thunderin' Thelma made her debut on CBC's *Dragons' Den* when owner Zane Caplansky decided to expand his famous downtown Toronto brick-and-mortar deli and enter the trendy urban food truck business. After being labelled "insane Zane" by Kevin O'Leary, and seeing the other Dragons balk at the 15% ownership interest at a proposed cost of $350,000, Zane decided to continue his new business venture on his own. A year later, Caplansky returned to *Dragons' Den* and boasted achieving profit margins between 30 and 40% and achieving $110,000 in sales in his first six months of operation. Caplansky's business continues to thrive, with its latest location at the Toronto Pearson International Airport. According to Zane, "persistence, hard work and integrity" are key to achieving success in new business initiatives.

Sources: https://www.ibisworld.ca/industry/street-vendors.html, accessed September 15, 2017; http://www.torontolife.com/daily-dish/people-dish/2011/11/03/zane-caplansky-on-dragons-den, accessed April 19, 2014; http://www.postcity.com/Eat-Shop-Do/Eat/November-2013/Weekly-Restaurant-Recap-Harvest-Kitchen; CBC *Dragons' Den*, Season 7, Episode 11, aired January 7, 2013; On the Journey Towards a Perfect Sandwich: Zane Caplansky at TEDxQueensU, https://youtu.be/cN_8HMMnNFk accessed September 14, 2017.

Video Links: http://www.cbc.ca/dragonsden/pitches/caplanskys-deli and https://youtu.be/cN_8HMMnNFk.

Video Links

This text features interactive digital links directing students and instructors to helpful videos to provide students with real-world application of the chapter content and enhance student exposure to valuable online resources.

A Look Back, A Look at This Chapter

In these brief paragraphs, students are directed to reflect on their learning from previous chapters and are provided with a high-level summary of the current chapter. These helpful learning summaries assist students in understanding how their chapter by chapter learning ties into the big-picture learning objectives.

Receivables

A Look Back

Chapter 7 provides an introduction to internal control and cash with a detailed analysis of internal control guidelines, banking activities, accounting for petty cash funds, and reconciling the differences between cash reported in the bank account and cash in the company's accounting records.

A Look at This Chapter

This chapter takes a look at accounting for customer accounts receivable and short-term notes receivable, specifically investigating tools such as initial recognition of the receivables and subsequent measurement at the end of the accounting period. Valuation is assessed through methods to estimate bad debts, including the benefits of an A/R aging report, and using the accounts receivable turnover ratio and days' sales uncollected ratios to evaluate financial statements.

Learning Objectives

Learning Objectives have long been a standard in the Larson textbook. By giving students a head start on what the following material encompasses, the text readies them for the work ahead.

Checkpoints

This series of questions within the chapter reinforces the material presented immediately before it. These questions allow students to "Do" problem material by referencing what they have just learned. Answers at the end of each

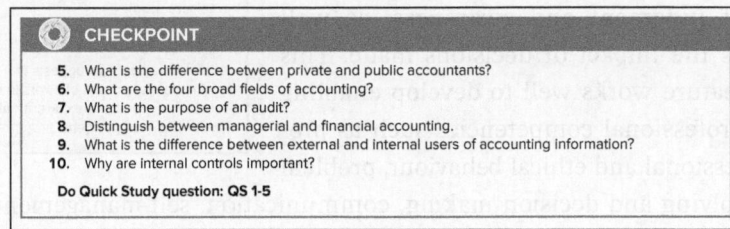

chapter will then allow them to "Check" their work, further supporting the Student Success Cycle. Under each set of Checkpoints is a reference to the Quick Study questions (single-topic exercises) available at the end of each chapter. Students can go ahead and try them at this point. Checkpoint solutions are at the end of the chapter. Quick Study solutions are available on **Connect**.

Important Tip:

Ensure you know the following rules as illustrated in Exhibit 2.7 before reading Chapter 3. For a helpful learning tool, review the following video by Colin Dodds, an educational music video enthusiast.

Video Link: https://youtu.be/7EuxfW76BWU

Important Tips

Important tip boxes have been incorporated throughout the text to direct students' attention to critical concepts that students often miss in their initial reading of the text.

Ethical Impact

Ethics continues to be a critical foundation-level concern to prepare students to understand and apply ethical values in their day-to-day decisions. This new feature helps develop students to reach toward CPA-enabling competencies such as professional and ethical behaviour, problem solving and decision making,

communication, self-management, teamwork, and leadership skills. It will be an excellent tool instructors can utilize to provide real-world relevance and develop these critical skills for students as they work toward developing professional competencies.

Each scenario is designed to strengthen each student's professional competencies as they approach ethical dilemmas that have been developed from current, real-world Canadian and global business scenarios. Each box is designed with a concise scenario and provides open-ended questions to enable effective classroom discussions. Encourage students to use the framework presented in Chapter 1 Decision Insight on Resolving Ethical Dilemmas to help them develop a compass to guide them through alternative courses of action.

Decision Insight

Social responsibility is a key concern for today's generation of socially conscious students. Through the Decision Insight feature, accounting's role in ethics and social responsibility is

described by both reporting and assessing its impact. Relating theory to a real-life situation piques interest and reinforces active learning.

Decision Maker

This feature requires students to make accounting and business decisions by using role-playing to show the interaction of judgment and awareness, as well as the impact of decisions made. This feature works well to develop enabling professional competencies such as professional and ethical behaviour, problem

Guidance Answer to DECISION MAKER

Analyzing Results

Yes, you are concerned about the absence of a depreciation adjustment on the manufacturing equipment. Equipment does lose value as it is used in the business, and financial statements must recognize this occurrence. Its absence suggests an error or a misrepresentation (there is also the possibility that equipment is fully utilized and should have been completely depreciated or that it was scrapped).

Analyst

A current ratio of 1.2 suggests that current assets are sufficient to cover current liabilities, but it implies a minimal buffer in case of errors in measuring current assets or current liabilities. Removing the past due receivable reduces the current ratio to 0.7. Your assessment is that the bakery will have some difficulty meeting its loan payments.

solving and decision making, communication, self-management, teamwork, and leadership skills. These boxes work well in conjunction with the new Ethical Impact box. Guidance answers are available at the end of each chapter.

Extend Your Knowledge (EYK)

Supplementary material has been developed to explore some topics in more detail than the textbook can allow. A list of EYKs relevant to each chapter is presented at the end of the chapter, alerting students to visit **Connect** if they choose to delve deeper into the material.

For further study on some topics of relevance to this chapter, please see the following Extend Your Knowledge supplements:

EYK 4-1 Work Sheet Demonstration
EYK 4-2 Corporate Supplement
EYK 4-3 Summary of Business Activities
EYK 4-4 Examples of Classified Balance Sheets

Financial Statements

Features and assignments that highlight companies such as **Spin Master** (a successful Canadian toy innovator and children's entertainment company) and **WestJet** (a company that provides services) show accounting in a modern and global context. Because students go directly to the financial statements of real companies, they remain engaged in the active learning process. The audited annual financial statement section of these annual reports (with notes to the financial statements), as well as those of **Telus** and **Indigo Books & Music** (with weblinks provided to access the notes), are reproduced at the end of Volume 1. In Volume 2, the annual audited financial statements are presented without notes, and weblinks are provided for student access to the full set of Annual Reports.

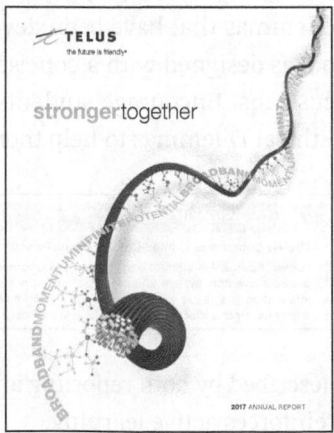

End-of-Chapter Material

Fundamental Accounting Principles sets the standard for quantity and quality of end-of-chapter material.

Summary

Each chapter includes a Summary of the chapter by Learning Objective, to reinforce what students have just learned.

SUMMARY

LO1 **Explain the accounting cycle.** The accounting cycle includes the steps in preparing financial statements for users that are repeated each reporting period.

LO2 **Describe an account, its use, and its relationship to the ledger.** An account is a detailed record of increases and decreases in a specific asset, liability, or equity item. Information is taken from accounts, analyzed, summarized, and presented in useful reports and financial statements for users.

LO3 **Define debits and credits and explain their role in double-entry accounting.** Debit refers to left, and credit refers to right. The following table summarizes debit and credit effects by account type:

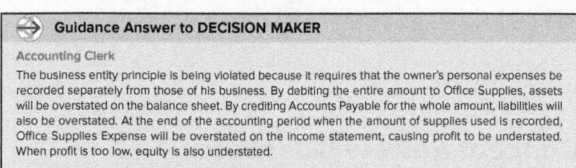

Guidance Answer to DECISION MAKER

Accounting Clerk

The business entity principle is being violated because it requires that the owner's personal expenses be recorded separately from those of his business. By debiting the entire amount to Office Supplies, assets will be overstated on the balance sheet. By crediting Accounts Payable for the whole amount, liabilities will also be overstated. At the end of the accounting period when the amount of supplies used is recorded, Office Supplies Expense will be overstated on the income statement, causing profit to be understated. When profit is too low, equity is also understated.

Guidance Answers to Decision Maker

These discuss the Decision Maker boxes presented earlier in the chapter, and reinforce the need for decision making and critical thinking skills. This feature fits into the Student Success Cycle by reinforcing the "Apply" step.

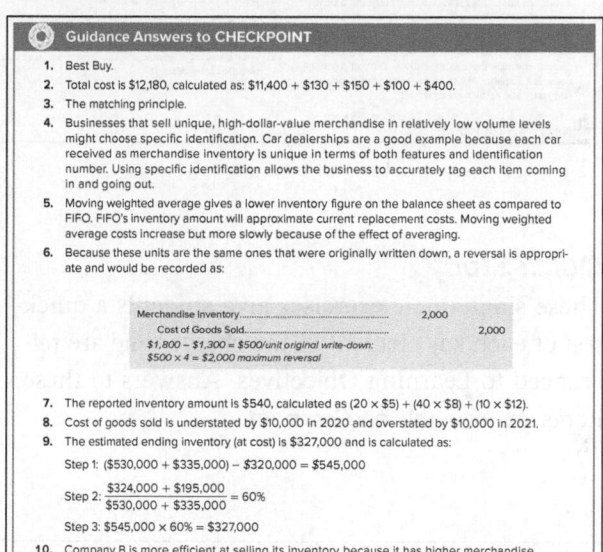

Guidance Answers to CHECKPOINT

1. Best Buy.
2. Total cost is $12,180, calculated as: $11,400 + $130 + $150 + $100 + $400.
3. The matching principle.
4. Businesses that sell unique, high-dollar-value merchandise in relatively low volume levels might choose specific identification. Car dealerships are a good example because each car received as merchandise inventory is unique in terms of both features and identification number. Using specific identification allows the business to accurately tag each item coming in and going out.
5. Moving weighted average gives a lower inventory figure on the balance sheet as compared to FIFO. FIFO's inventory amount will approximate current replacement costs. Moving weighted average costs increase but more slowly because of the effect of averaging.
6. Because these units are the same ones that were originally written down, a reversal is appropriate and would be recorded as:

| Merchandise Inventory | 2,000 | |
| Cost of Goods Sold | | 2,000 |

$1,800 − $1,300 = $500/unit original write-down:
$500 × 4 = $2,000 maximum reversal

7. The reported inventory amount is $540, calculated as (20 × $5) + (40 × $8) + (10 × $12).
8. Cost of goods sold is understated by $10,000 in 2020 and overstated by $10,000 in 2021.
9. The estimated ending inventory (at cost) is $327,000 and is calculated as:

Step 1: ($530,000 + $335,000) − $320,000 = $545,000

Step 2: $\frac{\$324,000 + \$195,000}{\$530,000 + \$335,000} = 60\%$

Step 3: $545,000 × 60% = $327,000

10. Company B is more efficient at selling its inventory because it has higher merchandise turnover.

Guidance Answers to Checkpoint

The Checkpoint material throughout the chapter allows students to pause and check their progress. This feature reinforces the "Do," "Check," and "Apply" steps of the Student Success Cycle.

GLOSSARY

Consignee One who receives and holds goods owned by another party for the purpose of acting as an agent and selling the goods for the owner. The consignee gets paid a fee from the consignor for finding a buyer.

Consignor An owner of inventory goods who ships them to another party who will then find a buyer and sell the goods for the owner. The consignor retains title to the goods while they are held offsite by the consignee.

Consistency principle The accounting requirement that a company use the same accounting policies period after

period so that the financial statements of succeeding periods will be comparable.

Days' sales in inventory A financial analysis tool used to estimate how many days it will take to convert the inventory on hand into accounts receivable or cash; calculated by dividing the ending inventory by cost of goods sold and multiplying the result by 365.

Faithful representation The accounting principle that requires information to be complete, neutral, unbiased, and free from error.

Glossary

All terms highlighted in the chapter are included.

PROBLEM MATERIAL

Demonstration Problems

These problems reinforce the chapter material and further bolster the Student Success Cycle.

Demonstration Problem

This Demonstration Problem is based on the same facts as the Demonstration Problem at the end of Chapter 1 except for two additional items: (b) August 1 and (k) August 18.

The following activities occurred during the first month of Joanne Cardinal's new haircutting business called The Cutlery:

a. On August 1, Cardinal put $16,000 cash into a chequing account in the name of The Cutlery. She also invested $10,000 of equipment that she already owned.

b. On August 1, Cardinal paid $2,400 for six months of insurance effective immediately.

c. On August 2, she paid $2,000 cash for furniture for the shop.

d. On August 3, she paid $3,200 cash to rent space in a strip mall for August.

e. On August 4, she furnished the shop by installing the old equipment and some new equipment that she bought on credit for $21,000. This amount is to be repaid in three equal payments at the end of August, September, and October.

Analysis Component

An analysis component is included in each Mid- and End-of-Chapter Demonstration Problem, as well as several Exercises, Problems, and Focus on Financial Statements questions. These promote critical thinking and give students opportunities to practise their analytical skills.

> **Analysis Component:**
> Refer to The Cutlery's August 31, 2020, financial statements. What do each of *equity* and *liabilities* represent?

CONCEPT REVIEW QUESTIONS

1. What tasks are performed with the work sheet?

2. What two purposes are accomplished by recording closing entries?

3. What are the four closing entries?

4. Daniel is having trouble determining whether withdrawals, owner's capital, interest income, and prepaid insurance are temporary or permanent accounts. Explain to him the difference between a temporary and a permanent account in accounting and classify the accounts into each category.

5. Alexis believes that temporary account information is deleted through the closing entries. Do you agree or disagree? Explain. What is the relationship between temporary and permanent accounts?

6. Describe the similarities and differences between adjusting and closing entries.

7. What is the purpose of the Income Summary account? How is it different from the Income Statement?

8. Explain whether an error has occurred if a post-closing trial balance includes a Depreciation Expense, Building account.

9. Refer to Spin Master's income statement in Appendix III at the end of the book. What journal entry was recorded as of December 31, 2017 to close the revenue account?

10. What is a company's operating cycle?

11. Why is a classified balance sheet more useful to financial statement users than a non-classified balance sheet?

12. What classes of assets and liabilities are shown on a typical classified balance sheet?

Concept Review Questions

These short-answer questions reinforce the chapter content by Learning Objective.

Quick Study

These single-topic exercises give students a quick test of each key element in the chapter and are referenced to Learning Objectives. Answers to these items are available on **Connect**.

QUICK STUDY

QS 6-1 Inventory ownership LO1

1. At year-end Carefree Company has shipped, FOB destination, $500 of merchandise that is still in transit to Stark Company. Which company should include the $500 as part of inventory at year-end?

2. Carefree Company has shipped goods to Stark and has an arrangement that Stark will sell the goods for Carefree. Identify the consignor and the consignee. Which company should include any unsold goods as part of inventory?

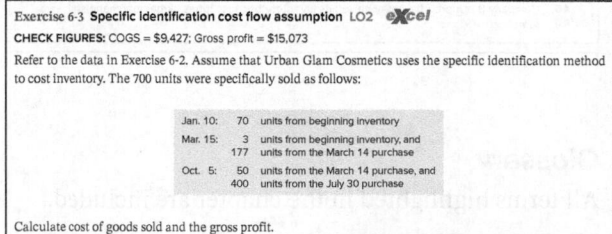

Exercise 6-3 **Specific identification cost flow assumption** LO2 eXcel

CHECK FIGURES: COGS = $9,427; Gross profit = $15,073

Refer to the data in Exercise 6-2. Assume that Urban Glam Cosmetics uses the specific identification method to cost inventory. The 700 units were specifically sold as follows:

Jan. 10:	70	units from beginning inventory
Mar. 15:	3	units from beginning inventory, and
	177	units from the March 14 purchase
Oct. 5:	50	units from the March 14 purchase, and
	400	units from the July 30 purchase

Calculate cost of goods sold and the gross profit.

Exercises

Exercises provide students with an additional opportunity to reinforce basic chapter concepts by Learning Objective. **Note:** Selected end-of-chapter exercises and problems are marked with this icon: **eXcel**. These have Excel templates located on **Connect**.

Problems

Problems typically incorporate two or more concepts. There are two groups of problems: A problems and Alternate or B problems. B Problems mirror the A problems to help improve understanding through repetition.

PROBLEMS

Problem 1-1A Identifying type of business organization LO2

Complete the chart below by placing a check mark in the appropriate column.

| Characteristic | Type of Business Organization | | |
	Sole Proprietorship	Partnership	Corporation
Limited liability			
Unlimited liability			
Owners are shareholders			
Owners are partners			
Taxed as a separate legal entity			

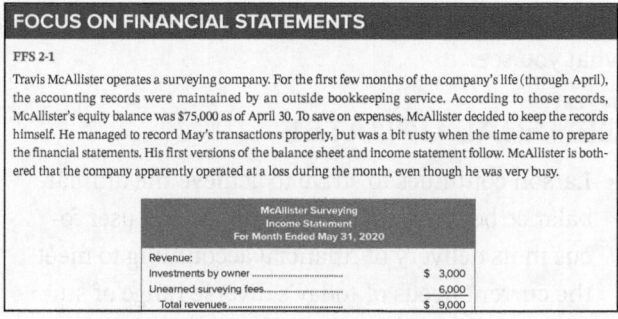

ETHICS CHALLENGE

EC 5-1

Claire Phelps is a popular high school student who attends approximately four dances a year at her high school. Each dance requires a new dress and accessories that necessitate a financial outlay of $100 to $200 per event. Claire's parents inform her that she is on her own with respect to financing the dresses. After incurring a major hit to her savings for the first dance in her second year, Claire developed a different approach. She buys the dress on credit the week before the dance, wears it to the dance, and returns the dress the next week to the store for a full refund on her charge card.

Required

1. Comment on the ethics exhibited by Claire and possible consequences of her actions.
2. How does the store account for the dresses that Claire returns?

Ethics Challenge

Each chapter includes at least one Ethics Challenge to reinforce critical thinking skills for students and open up discussion about various ethical topics.

Focus on Financial Statements

Each chapter includes two technical and analytical questions that incorporate into the financial statements all major topics covered up to that point. Additional questions are available online on **Connect**.

FOCUS ON FINANCIAL STATEMENTS

FFS 2-1

Travis McAllister operates a surveying company. For the first few months of the company's life (through April), the accounting records were maintained by an outside bookkeeping service. According to those records, McAllister's equity balance was $75,000 as of April 30. To save on expenses, McAllister decided to keep the records himself. He managed to record May's transactions properly, but was a bit rusty when the time came to prepare the financial statements. His first versions of the balance sheet and income statement follow. McAllister is bothered that the company apparently operated at a loss during the month, even though he was very busy.

McAllister Surveying Income Statement For Month Ended May 31, 2020	
Revenue:	
Investments by owner	$ 3,000
Unearned surveying fees	6,000
Total revenues	$ 9,000

CRITICAL THINKING MINI CASE

Prairie Insurance sells life insurance, disability insurance, vehicle insurance, crop insurance, and homeowners' insurance. You are employed by Prairie Insurance and have been promoted to sales division manager for the Western Canadian division. You will be supervising approximately 25 salespeople, along with five administrative assistants at various locations. The salespeople travel extensively and submit expense reports along with sales information monthly. A sample expense report for September shows:

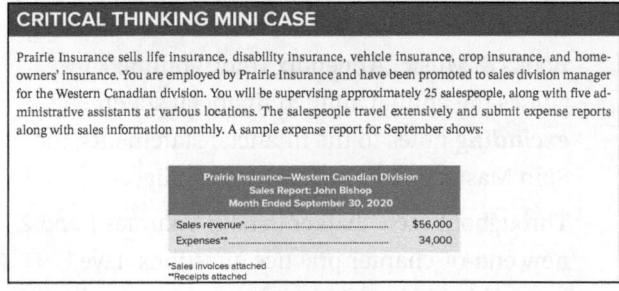

Prairie Insurance—Western Canadian Division Sales Report: John Bishop Month Ended September 30, 2020	
Sales revenue*	$56,000
Expenses**	34,000

*Sales invoices attached
**Receipts attached

Critical Thinking Mini Cases

These cases give students the opportunity to apply critical thinking skills to concepts learned in the chapter, thus further reinforcing the "Apply" step of the Student Success Cycle.

Help Me Solve It

New *Help Me Solve It* tutorials are available on **Connect** for Larson's *Fundamental Accounting Principles*. The tutorials guide students through one or two of the more challenging end-of-chapter problems per chapter, providing them with an engaging visual and audio walk-through of the problem.

What's New

The Accounting Standard

We listened! Through extensive reviewing and consultations with the market, we have heard the issues and concerns instructors like you have about the materials you use to teach introductory financial accounting. Here you will find a list of new changes to specific chapters that our author has made to ensure the content of Larson's *Fundamental Accounting Principles* remains current and fresh. Whether you are new to using *Fundamental Accounting Principles* or new to this edition, you can see that McGraw-Hill Education and Larson/Dieckmann are setting the accounting standard in *Fundamental Accounting Principles*. We know you'll like what you see.

GENERAL UPDATES

- Larson continues to strive to achieve the ultimate balance between the preparer focus and user focus in its delivery of financial accounting to meet the current needs of today's diverse range of students. A strong preparer focus provides students with the tools to understand what is happening at the individual transaction level to the financial statements, providing a strong foundation for a career in accounting, as an entrepreneur, or as a savvy business professional. These skills are essential for students to develop to accurately understand the numbers behind key decisions they will face in their careers. In addition, each chapter provides several real-world company business scenarios, an increased focus on ethical issues, financial statement excerpts, and financial statement analysis tools to prepare students to be an effective decision maker in any career path they choose.

- Increased emphasis on global perspectives, bringing ethical issues and examples to students from around the world.

- New Knowledge Check-Up (KCU) questions are ten single-topic, multiple-choice questions designed to assess initial comprehension of the key chapter learning objectives. These reading readiness assessments have been written by the author to provide students with a quick and easy test as to whether they achieved the critical comprehension concepts in each chapter before moving on to more comprehensive review problems. These can be used as a quick mini quiz at the beginning of each lecture to encourage students to complete chapter readings before class. Answers are provided on **Connect** under the instructor resources tab.

- Appendix III for Volume 1 includes the complete annual audited financial statements, including notes to the financial statements, for Spin Master and WestJet, as well as the audited financial statements *without* the notes for Telus and Indigo Books & Music. Appendix II for Volume 2 includes the annual audited financial statements, *excluding* notes to the financial statements, for Spin Master, WestJet, Telus, and Indigo.

- Throughout each chapter in both Volumes 1 and 2, new end-of-chapter practice questions have been added in targeted areas, based on feedback from the market, where students would benefit from additional practice opportunities. Approximately 25% of the exercises and problems have been refreshed in terms of numbers and/or business scenarios. Existing company scenarios have been expanded and updated to provide students with more information and updated examples to enhance student engagement. Volume 1 and 2 end-of-chapter content was revised by Laura Dallas of Kwantlen Polytechnic University.

- The chapter content is IFRS 2018 compliant throughout Volume 1 and Volume 2; references are included where appropriate. New updates include coverage of IFRS 16 Leases in Chapter 14 and conceptual framework integrated throughout. IFRS and ASPE differences are identified at the end of each chapter.

- The Sixteenth Canadian Edition includes three exciting *new* chapter-opening vignettes, and significant updates to the remaining 14 featuring a range of engaging topics and including inspiring stories from company startups to success stories of well-known businesses and not-for-profit organizations. Nearly all of the vignettes include relevant video links for students to broaden their real-world exposure to critical business decisions.

- Seventeen new *Ethical Impact* boxes have been crafted to highlight an ethical dilemma for each chapter based on a real-world example linked directly to issues within the chapter learning objectives. Instructors can take a moment to help students develop these critical professional skills.

- Real-world relevance is provided with actual businesses used as examples with several financial statement excerpts throughout Volumes 1 and 2, including issues relating to financial statement presentation and disclosure. These real company names are bolded and highlighted in magenta at first mention to emphasize integration of accounting concepts with actual business practice.

- New important tip boxes have been added and are incorporated throughout the text to direct students' attention to critical concepts that students often miss in their initial reading of the text.

- Chapter 9 on property, plant, and equipment is now included in both Volume 1 and Volume 2 to offer flexibility to instructors, depending on institutional course design.

- Chapter 14 includes a more integrated approach to bond pricing that includes instructional tips on how to use a financial calculator, with helpful hints and examples provided for students to follow along during their chapter reading.

CHAPTER-BY-CHAPTER UPDATES

Chapter 1

- Updated chapter-opening vignette "Food Truck Frenzy" featuring entrepreneur Zane Caplansky, founder of Caplansky's Deli and the food truck

"Thunderin' Thelma" as featured on CBC's *Dragons' Den*.

- New *Ethical Impact* box on an $18.7 million maple syrup heist that helps students to assess how they would handle identified irregularities.

- Updated Exhibit 1.5 charting average annual salaries for accounting positions.

- Updated section on professional certification in Canada.

- New *Ethical Impact* box on resolving ethical dilemmas.

- New *Decision Insight* on evaluating charitable organizations.

- Updated section on the measurement principle, highlighting current cost, fair value, and value in use terminology

- Updated Exhibit 1.12 summarizing the elements of financial statements, including updating the definition of an asset and a liability.

- Ten new *Knowledge Check-Up* questions to help students assess their reading readiness and to identify any initial learning hurdles.

Chapter 2

- New *Important Tips* boxes added to provide extra support in topic areas where students typically struggle; new box on unearned revenue to emphasize this common learning hurdle for students.

- New *Decision Insight* on Cara Operations to help students understand the real-world applicability of this chapter's concepts relating to financial reporting.

- Updated presentation and approach to mid-chapter demonstration problem makes the transaction analysis section easier to follow.

- Updated Exhibit 2.8 presentation of revenue and expenses in relation to equity.

- New presentation of recording and posting transactions, based on reviewer feedback to improve student connections of material.

- New *Ethical Impact* box on International Ethics: Corporate Corruption vs. Cross Cultural Management to expose students to real-world issues relating to factors impacting their decision making.

- Ten new *Knowledge Check-Up* questions to help students assess their reading readiness and to identify any initial learning hurdles.

Chapter 3

- Exciting new chapter-opening vignette featuring a project run by Cities Foundation called *Wasted* that provides digital coins to incentivize its residents in Amsterdam's Noord district to recycle. Includes an engaging new video link to help students understand the program.

- New vignette also introduces students to the concept of cryptocurrencies and provides an overview of the organization Recereum, which is a blockchain-based platform that aims to provide money in the form of cryptocurrency coins for "every single recycled bottle."

- Updated wording to introduction to the purpose of adjusting to help students understand the purpose of the adjusting process.

- New *Ethical Impact* box for MagnaChip, which is a South Korea–based semiconductor company that is publicly traded in the United States and was recently under investigation by the SEC for engaging in unethical/improper conduct. MagnaChip was charged by the SEC with artificially increasing revenue, delaying or avoiding expenses, avoiding reductions in revenue, smoothing gross margins, and hiding delays in receivables collections.

- Updated *Decision Maker* box with a focus on revenue recognition. Students assume a small publishing company signed basketball superstar LeBron James to write a book. The company paid LeBron $500,000 today and will pay future book royalties.

- Updated Exhibit 3.20, Summary of Adjustments and Financial Statement Impact, to clarify "need to know" journal entries for students.

- Ten new *Knowledge Check-Up* questions to help students assess their reading readiness and to identify any initial learning hurdles.

Chapter 4

- Updated chapter-opening vignette featuring founders of the BC startup Cupcakes, as featured on their reality series *The Cupcake Girls* on W, We TV, and the Oprah Network (OWN).

- Expanded *Decision Maker* on a vitamin manufacturing company with a concern over its depreciation expense adjustment.

- Updated Exhibit 4.15 featuring example presentation of current assets for Apple Inc.

- New *Ethical Impact* box putting students in the role of a junior accountant working for a local building supply store. The CFO asks them to capitalize a number of small items for which they do not understand the long-term future benefit.

- New *Decision Insight* highlighting examples of how companies are maintaining high levels of their most liquid asset—cash.

- Updated *Decision Maker* regarding a commercial loan manager's analysis of a local bakery's current ratio.

- Ten new *Knowledge Check-Up* questions to help students assess their reading readiness and to identify any initial learning hurdles.

Chapter 5

- Updated chapter-opening vignette featuring Mountain Equipment Co-op (MEC), including a new video link to review MEC's financial results.

- New chapter feature company Lifetime Equipment Co-op to help students understand typical journal entries in a merchandising business.

- New *Ethical Impact* box relating to the role of marketing manager and a concern over revenue recognition and channel stuffing.

- Updated Exhibit 5.18 providing a gross margin snapshot for a number of different types of businesses to help students understand the financial statement user perspective.

- Updated Appendix 5B discussion on PST, GST, and HST.

- Updated Exhibit 5B.1 summarizing zero-rated and exempt products for GST/HST.

- Updated Exhibit 5B.2 organizing sales tax rates for rate changes and restructured into a more student-friendly format.

- Ten new *Knowledge Check-Up* questions to help students assess their reading readiness and to identify any initial learning hurdles.

Chapter 6

- Updated chapter-opening vignette featuring inventory innovation at Amazon.com, including video links outlining Amazon's warehouse operations and demonstrating its Kiva robots.

- New *Important Tip* box summarizing the incidental costs that are to be added to inventory.

- New chapter demonstration company, Lifetime Equipment Co-op, continued from Chapter 5.

- Updated real-world examples providing accounting policy disclosures for Amazon.com Inc., Lululemon Athletica, Procter & Gamble Co., and Tiffany & Co., illustrating examples of companies that use the various inventory costing alternatives.

- New *Ethical Impact* box featuring the example of Fair Beans Coffee, an ethical roaster that obtains organic beans from Nicaragua. Students, in the role of manager of accounting, consider how they would handle a concern over inventory valuation.

- Updated note disclosure for TJX Companies Inc. illustrating both the retail method of inventory and disclosure over inventory shrinkage.

- Ten new *Knowledge Check-Up* questions to help students assess their reading readiness and to identify any initial learning hurdles.

Chapter 7

- Exciting new chapter-opening vignette featuring Lori Joyce, founder of Betterwith Foods—a new Vancouver-based ice cream brand with a focus on delivering high-quality, clean and simple ice cream from farm-fresh traceable dairy. A video link is included providing Lori's perspective on the business.

- Updated section on the fraud triangle and the drivers of fraud (includes two new exhibits).

- New *Ethical Impact* box, involving a manager, the director of finance, demonstrating some warning signs of fraud, including modifying the

control environment and making significant lifestyle changes. Students are asked if they have any concerns and what they would do.

- Two new *Important Tip* boxes have been added to the chapter to simplify adjustments to the book balance and adjustments to the bank balance for students when preparing a bank reconciliation.

- Additional new *Important Tip* box on types of adjusting entries required after preparing a bank reconciliation.

- New *Decision Insight* developed from a previous chapter-opening vignette, featuring an analysis of "What Is Cash?" investigating today's payment options in Canada, and outlining the important role of the Canadian Payments Association. A video link is provided for students who want to learn more about how the complex payment system functions in Canada.

- Updates in the Financial Statement Analysis section for the quick ratio highlight differences with current ratio for WestJet.

- Ten new *Knowledge Check-Up* questions to help students assess their reading readiness and to identify any initial learning hurdles.

Chapter 8

- Updated chapter-opening vignette discussing BC-based WN Pharmaceuticals, providing a valuable perspective to students in understanding a risk-based approach to the management of customer receivables.

- Updated Exhibit 8.1, Accounts Receivable Analysis for Selected Companies as a Percentage of Total Assets.

- Updated *Decision Insight* box covers a recent application from Rogers Communications and the development of a wholly owned subsidiary, Rogers Bank.

- New *Ethical Impact* box featuring a real-world example from an organization that discovered millions in fraudulent loans in a subsidiary company. The box asks students what they would do if they were asked to falsify invoices to help their business obtain a bank loan.

- Updated control considerations for customer payments.

- New *Decision Insight* providing students with an understanding of payment securities; this feature is linked directly to learning concepts highlighted in the chapter-opening vignette.

- New *Important Tip* box highlighting the logic behind recording only the note receivable and not the interest income on a dishonoured note.

- Updated Exhibit 8.21, Comparison of Accounts Receivable Turnover and Days' Sales Uncollected for High Liner Foods Inc. and Maple Leaf Foods Inc.

- Ten new *Knowledge Check-Up* questions to help students assess their reading readiness and to identify any initial learning hurdles.

Chapter 9

- Updated chapter-opening vignette featuring Vancouver International Airport and its latest collaborative innovation CHECKiTXPRESS, which is an innovative and user-friendly bag drop for travellers.

- This chapter has a number of up-to-date examples of PPE items drawn from a variety of public companies.

- Updated language under Cost of PPE to refer to capital expenditures as betterments and revenue expenditure as repairs and maintenance expense to align more closely with industry practice.

- Updated presentation under Cost of PPE of types of expenses that can be capitalized are summarized now in bulleted form to assist in student comprehension and retention.

- New *Ethical Impact* box on a fictitious scenario involving an ethical issue that a junior accountant comes across in their new role managing the property, plant, and equipment subledger for the Bermuda Airport Authority.

- Updated financial statement excerpts featuring presentation of Indigo Books & Music Inc.'s accounting policy and depreciation schedule for property, plant, and equipment and Microsoft's presentation and disclosure over intangible assets.

- New *Decision Insight* identifying fixed asset tracking and the related depreciation of the underlying assets as a critical role in business.

- New Exhibit 9.23, World's Most Valuable Brands, presented in an easy to understand and engaging display.

- Ten new *Knowledge Check-Up* questions to help students assess their reading readiness and to identify any initial learning hurdles.

Appendix I

- All rates (i.e., EI, CPP, provincial tax, federal tax) updated to 2018.

Appendix II

- Responding to reviewer feedback this former online appendix, Accounting Information Systems, is now included in the body of the textbook.

Appendix III

- Volume 1 includes annual audited financial statements (including notes to the financial statements) for Spin Master and WestJet and annual audited financial statements (excluding notes to the financial statements) for Telus Corporation and Indigo Books & Music.

- Volume 2 includes annual audited financial statements (*excluding* notes to the financial statements) for Spin Master, WestJet, Telus Corporation, and Indigo Books & Music.

Appendix IV

- Sample chart of accounts updated to reflect textbook content.

Market Leading Technology

connect

LEARN WITHOUT LIMITS

McGraw-Hill Connect® is an award-winning digital teaching and learning platform that gives students the means to better connect with their coursework, with their instructors, and with the important concepts that they will need to know for success now and in the future. With Connect, instructors can take advantage of McGraw-Hill's trusted content to seamlessly deliver assignments, quizzes and tests online. McGraw-Hill Connect is the only learning platform that continually adapts to each student, delivering precisely what they need, when they need it, so class time is more engaging and effective. Connect makes teaching and learning personal, easy, and proven.

CONNECT KEY FEATURES:

Smartbook®

As the first and only adaptive reading experience, SmartBook is changing the way students read and learn. SmartBook creates a personalized reading experience by highlighting the most important concepts a student needs to learn at that moment in time. As a student engages with SmartBook, the reading experience continuously adapts by highlighting content based on what each student knows and doesn't know. This ensures that he or she is focused on the content needed to close specific knowledge gaps, while it simultaneously promotes long-term learning.

Connect Insight®

Connect Insight is Connect's one-of-a-kind visual analytics dashboard—available for instructors—that provides at-a-glance information regarding student performance, which is immediately actionable. By presenting assignment, assessment, and topical performance results together with a time metric that is easily visible for aggregate or individual results, Connect Insight gives the instructor the ability to take a just-in-time approach to teaching and learning, which was never before available. Connect Insight presents data that and helps instructors improve class performance in a way that is efficient and effective.

Simple Assignment Management

With Connect, creating assignments is easier than ever, so instructors can spend more time teaching and less time managing.

- Assign SmartBook learning modules
- Instructors can edit existing questions and create their own questions
- Draw from a variety of text specific questions, resources, and test bank material to assign online
- Streamline lesson planning, student progress reporting, and assignment grading to make classroom management more efficient than ever

Smart Grading

When it comes to studying, time is precious. Connect helps students learn more efficiently by providing feedback and practice material when they need it, where they need it.

- Automatically score assignments, providing students immediate feedback on their work and comparisons with correct answers
- Access and review each response, manually change grades, or leave comments for students to review

- Track individual student performance—by question or assignment, or in relation to the class overall—with detailed grade reports.
- Reinforce classroom concepts with practice tests and instant quizzes.
- Integrate grade reports easily with Learning Management Systems including Blackboard, D2L, and Moodle.

Mobile Access

Connect makes it easy for students to read and learn using their smartphones and tablets. With the mobile app, students can study on the go—including reading and listening using the audio functionality—without constant need for Internet access.

Instructor Library

The Connect Instructor Library is a repository for additional resources to improve student engagement in and out of the class. It provides all the critical resources instructors need to build their course. Instructors can

- Access Instructor resources
- View assignments and resources created for past sections
- Post their own resources for students to use

Instructor Resources
Instructor supplements are available within **Connect**.

Solutions Manual

Fundamental Accounting Principles continues to set the standard for accuracy of its problem material. The Solutions Manual has been revised by Laura Dallas, Kwantlen Polytechnic University. Additional accuracy check was conducted by Rhonda Heninger, SAIT Polytechnic. Available in both Microsoft Word and PDF format, solutions for all problem material are included.

Computerized Test Bank

The test bank has been revised and technically checked for accuracy to reflect the changes in the Sixteenth Canadian Edition. Sarah Magdalinski, Northern Alberta Institute of Technology, revised the test bank for this edition. Grouped according to Learning Objective, difficulty level, and by level of Bloom's Taxonomy, the questions in the computerized test bank include true/false, multiple choice, matching, short essay, and problem material.

PowerPoint® Presentations

These presentation slides, revised by Lise Wall, Red River College, are fully integrated with the text to visually present chapter concepts.

Instructor's Manual

The Instructor's Manual, revised by Milena Ceglie, Durham College, cross-references assignment materials by Learning Objective and also provides a convenient chapter outline.

Focus on Financial Statements

These include technical and analytical questions that incorporate major topics covered. These, and accompanying solutions, have been revised by Laura Dallas, Kwantlen Polytechnic University. Additional Focus on Financial Statement exercises for each chapter are included on **Connect**.

Extend Your Knowledge

This supplemental material has been developed to delve into more detail for specific topics.

Excel Template Solutions

Solutions to the problems using Excel templates are available for instructors. These have been revised by Heather Cornish, Northern Alberta Institute of Technology.

Image Bank

All exhibits and tables displayed in the text are available for your use, whether for creating transparencies or handouts, or customizing your own PowerPoint presentations.

Other Supplements for Students

Working Papers

Available for purchase by students, printed Working Papers for Volumes 1 and 2 match the end-of-chapter material. They include papers that can be used to solve all of the Quick Study questions, Exercises, and A and B Problem sets. The Working Papers for the Sixteenth Canadian Edition have been revised by Laura Dallas, Kwantlen Polytechnic University. Additional technical checking was completed by Rhonda Heninger, Southern Alberta Institute of Technology.

Superior Learning Solutions and Support

The McGraw-Hill Education team is ready to help instructors assess and integrate any of our products, technology, and services into your course for optimal teaching and learning performance. Whether it's helping your students improve their grades, or putting your entire course online, the McGraw-Hill Education team is here to help you do it. Contact your Learning Solutions Consultant today to learn how to maximize all of McGraw-Hill Education's resources.

For more information, please visit us online: http://www.mheducation.ca/he/solutions.

Developing a Market-Driven Text

The success of this text is the result of an exhaustive process, which has gone beyond the scope of a single edition. Hundreds of instructors and educators across the country have been involved in giving their feedback to help develop the most successful accounting fundamentals text in the country. We owe thanks to all of those who took the time to evaluate this textbook and its supplemental products. *In preparation for the 16th edition, the following reviewers provided us with invaluable feedback based on the 15th edition:*

REVIEWERS

Treena Burns	*Seneca College*	Darlene Lowe	*MacEwan University*
Milena Celgie	*Durham College*	Heather Martin	*Nova Scotia Community College*
Barb Chapple	*St. Clair College*	Michelle Nicholson	*Okanagan College*
Heather Cornish	*Northern Alberta Institute of Technology*	Dal Pirot	*MacEwan University*
		James Reimer	*Lethbridge College*
John Currie	*Humber College*	Joe Toste	*Centennial College*
Samuel Kiragu	*Nova Scotia Community College*	Shawn West	*Mount Saint Vincent University*

Fundamental Accounting Principles continues to set the bar in terms of its leading-edge approach to educating today's students to both excel as users of financial accounting as well as having outstanding technical understanding through a commitment to relevance, quality, accuracy, and state-of-the-art supplemental resources.

This has been possible only because of the outstanding efforts and contributions of a dedicated team of exceptional individuals. I owe many thanks to their expertise and commitment as it was extensively drawn upon during the process of writing this textbook. Particular thanks go out to Maria Belanger, Shannon Butler, Cheryl Wilson, Sarah Magdalinski, Rhonda Heninger, Milena Ceglie, Lise Wall, Heather Cornish, and Amy Hoggard. A big thanks to the many entrepreneurs, financial experts, and business owners that devoted their precious time to making our chapter opening-vignettes compelling and captivating. Thanks also to our brilliant illustrator, Rachel Idzerda (www.rachelidzerda.com), for sharing our vision and for her tireless efforts in crafting our cover illustration with creativity and vibrant energy. A special thanks to my close friend and colleague Laura Dallas for committing to developing a leading-edge product that is technically strong, relevant, and an effective learning tool for introductory accounting students. Laura's outstanding dedication ensured the end-of-chapter questions are accurate, logical, and easy for students to understand. I am thankful to McGraw-Hill Ryerson's exceptional team, including Rhondda McNabb, Joy Armitage Taylor, Loula March, Alwynn Pinard, Jessica Barnoski, Kelli Howey, Karen Hunter, and Shalini Khanna, who have been exceptionally responsive, supportive, and dedicated to producing a top-tier product.

I am incredibly appreciative to my colleagues, passionate and forward thinking educators, current and past students, the phenomenal group of entrepreneurs and outstanding professional accountants across Canada who have inspired enhancements for this edition. Their knowledge and expertise in identifying student learning hurdles in the classroom and suggestions for enhancing student comprehension are invaluable in our continuous improvement initiative to maintain this textbook as the industry standard.

With heartfelt appreciation,
Heidi Dieckmann

CHAPTER 1

Accounting in Business

A Look at This Chapter

Whether you are embarking on a new career, are managing an investment account, or have an entrepreneurial spirit like Zane Caplansky from our opening vignette, a clear understanding of accounting will provide you with the tools to make effective decisions. Accounting is the system of recording and interpreting financial information to make relevant decisions. In this chapter, we discuss the significant role of accounting in organizations today and describe its many users and uses.

Andrew Francis Wallace/Toronto Star/Getty Images

LEARNING OBJECTIVES

LO1	Describe the purpose and importance of accounting.
LO2	Describe forms of business organization.
LO3	Identify users and uses of accounting and opportunities in accounting.
LO4	Identify and explain why ethics and social responsibility are crucial to accounting.
LO5	Identify, explain, and apply accounting principles.
LO6	Identify and explain the content and reporting aims of financial statements.
LO7	Analyze business transactions by applying the accounting equation.
LO8	Prepare financial statements reflecting business transactions.

Food Truck Frenzy

Across the country, major urban centres are experiencing an industry trend to go to the street to entice customers with a wide range of fresh, made-to-order food options. In Canada, the street vendor industry is in the growth phase of its industry life cycle according to IBISWorld, a global market research firm. IBISWorld estimates the market for street vendors in Canada will continue to grow over the next five years. Revenues are expected to reach $335 million with an expected annualized growth rate of 1.7% by 2023. The market is dominated by new market entrants—in most cases, individual owners operating as sole proprietors. The most successful street vendors will take advantage of effective marketing and branding toward health-conscious consumers looking for unique dining options.

Thunderin' Thelma made her debut on CBC's *Dragons' Den* when owner Zane Caplansky decided to expand his famous downtown Toronto brick-and-mortar deli and enter the trendy urban food truck business. After being labelled "insane Zane" by Kevin O'Leary, and seeing the other Dragons balk at the 15% ownership interest at a proposed cost of $350,000, Zane decided to continue his new business venture on his own. A year later, Caplansky returned to *Dragons' Den* and boasted achieving profit margins between 30 and 40% and achieving $110,000 in sales in his first six months of operation. Caplansky's business continues to thrive, with its latest location at the Toronto Pearson International Airport. According to Zane, "persistence, hard work and integrity" are key to achieving success in new business initiatives.

Sources: https://www.ibisworld.ca/industry/street-vendors.html, accessed September 15, 2017; http://www.torontolife.com/daily-dish/people-dish/2011/11/03/zane-caplansky-on-dragons-den, accessed April 15, 2014; http://www.postcity.com/Eat-Shop-Do/Eat/November-2013/Weekly-Restaurant-Recap-Harvest-Kitchen/; CBC *Dragons' Den*, Season 7, Episode 11, aired January 7, 2013; On the Journey Towards a Perfect Sandwich: Zane Caplansky at TEDxQueensU, https://youtu.be/cN_8HMMnNFk, accessed September 14, 2017.

Video Links: http://www.cbc.ca/dragonsden/pitches/caplanskys-deli and https://youtu.be/cN_8HMMnNFk.

CRITICAL THINKING CHALLENGE

What questions might Zane Caplansky need to answer in order to get a loan from a bank? Who else might require accounting information from Caplansky's business?

↑ An essential element of critical thinking is the ability to ask questions while reading (or listening or speaking). This exercise is designed to help students develop the skills related to questioning. Suggested answers are available on Connect.

CHAPTER PREVIEW

↑ A chapter preview introduces the importance and relevance of the material, and also links these materials to the opening article to help you understand how what you are learning in the chapter relates to the real world through practical examples.

Accounting information pulsates throughout an organization, feeding decision makers with key details needed to make important decisions and navigate through today's competitive business environment. Whether your future role is in accounting, human resources, finance, operations, marketing, or strategy, you will find the study of financial accounting integral to your ability to make relevant decisions. Understanding accounting terms such as revenue, expenses, assets, liabilities, and profitability is critical to effectively analyzing the financial performance of any business. Through your study of this book, you will learn key accounting concepts and develop an ability to interpret financial information that is essential for making sound business decisions.

Student Success *Cycle*

This first chapter accomplishes three goals in your journey toward understanding financial accounting. First, it introduces the subject of accounting and helps you to deepen your understanding of the role of accounting in business, including the importance of ethics and social responsibility in producing trustworthy financial reports.

Second, it demonstrates how accounting information is created and communicated in the form of *financial statements*, which report on the financial performance and condition of an organization. Chapter concepts are illustrated through an in-depth demonstration of how a young entrepreneur, Hailey Walker, handles financial information as she pursues the initial start-up phase in her new food truck business, Organico. Her goal is to capitalize on the increasing consumer demand for healthier options in the fast food market by specializing in fresh, organic, Mexican burritos. The illustration begins with Walker registering her business name and commencing her first month of operations on March 1, 2020.

Third, this chapter introduces you to each of the learning features found in most chapters. For example, a note above explains the purpose of the chapter preview, and three additional features—learning objectives, boldfaced key terms, and real company names—are described below. Some of the features refer to Connect, located on the Web. Take the time in this chapter to explore and learn the value of these additional resources.

What Is Accounting?

LO1 Describe the purpose and importance of accounting.

↑ Each chapter is separated into chunks of information called learning objectives (LO). Each LO tells you what needs to be mastered in that section of reading.

Accounting knowledge is a powerful tool; it provides you with essential information to make critical business decisions. How does accounting knowledge give you power? What exactly is the focus of accounting? This section answers these fundamental questions.

POWER OF ACCOUNTING

Accounting is an information system that identifies, measures, records, and communicates *relevant* information that *objectively and correctly represents* an organization's economic activities,[1] as shown in Exhibit 1.1. Its objective is to help people make better decisions. It also helps people better assess opportunities, products,

EXHIBIT 1.1

Accounting Activities

(left) © Diane Diederich/istockphoto.com; (centre) © JGI/Tom Gril/Blend Images LLC; (right) © shironosov/istockphoto.com

---

1   When information makes a difference in the decisions made by users, it is *relevant*. For information to possess the quality of *faithful representation,* it must be complete, neutral, and free from error (IFRS 2018, "The conceptual framework for financial reporting," para. QC5-QC6, QC 12). These primary qualitative characteristics of useful accounting information will be discussed in more detail later in this chapter.

investments, and social and community responsibilities. In addition to reporting on the performance of a business, what the business owns, and what it owes, accounting opens our eyes to new and exciting possibilities. Put more simply, accounting involves collecting relevant information, recording it, and then reporting it to various decision makers. In the chapter-opening story, for example, **Caplansky's Deli** collects and records accounting information so that it can be reported to Zane Caplansky, the business owner, and other investors, to help them make important decisions—such as those involved in setting selling prices for his deli sandwiches, and developing an effective expansion strategy.

↑ Boldfaced words or phrases represent new terminology that is explained here and defined in the glossary at the end of the chapter.

Real company names are printed in bold magenta the first time they are mentioned in each chapter.

FOCUS OF ACCOUNTING

Accounting for our personal finances enables us to better manage and plan for our future. Examples of common personal points of contact with financial accounting include applying for credit approvals, opening bank accounts, filling out student loan forms, and making decisions regarding whether to purchase a new or a used car. These experiences often focus on the *recordkeeping* (or *bookkeeping*) parts of accounting. **Recordkeeping**, or **bookkeeping**, is the recording of financial transactions, either manually or electronically, for the purpose of creating a bank of data that is complete, neutral, and free from error. Accounting *involves* the recordkeeping process but *is* much more.

Accounting also involves designing information systems to provide useful reports that provide relevant information in monitoring and controlling an organization's activities. In order to use the reports effectively, decision makers must be able to interpret the information. The skills needed to understand and interpret accounting information are developed through building a foundation in accounting concepts and developing an understanding of recording transactions through the recordkeeping process. The use of technology in recordkeeping reduces the time, effort, and cost of accounting while improving accuracy. As technology has changed the way we store, process, and summarize masses of data, financial analysis tools have improved, resulting in improved decision making. Consulting, planning, and other financial services are now closely linked to accounting. These services require sorting through data, interpreting their meaning, identifying key factors, and analyzing their implications. Because accounting is part of so much that we do in business and our everyday lives, you can enjoy greater opportunities if you understand and are able to use accounting information effectively.

 CHECKPOINT

1. What is the major objective of accounting?
2. Distinguish between accounting and recordkeeping.

Do Quick Study questions: QS 1-1, QS 1-2

↑ A series of Checkpoint questions in the chapter reinforce the immediately preceding materials. These questions give you feedback on your comprehension before you go on to new topics. Answers to these Checkpoint questions are available for you at the end of each chapter.

↑ Answers to the Quick Study (QS) questions are available on Connect.

Forms of Organization

LO2 Describe forms of business organization.

A **business** is an entity represented by one or more individuals selling products or services for profit. Products sold include anything from athletic apparel (**CCM, Bauer, Lululemon Athletica, Nike, Reebok**) to electronic devices (**Apple, Dell, Hewlett-Packard, Samsung**) and clothing (**Abercrombie & Fitch, The Gap, Zara**). Service providers such as data communication providers (**Bell, Rogers, Telus**), food services (**McDonald's, Starbucks, Tim Hortons**), and Internet services (**Google, Twitter, Skype, Facebook, Instagram**) make our lives more connected. A business can be as small as an in-home tutoring business or as large as **George Weston Limited**, the food processing company known for its President's Choice and No Name brands, owner of the clothing label Joe Fresh, and holder of a significant investment in the supermarket chain **Loblaw Companies Limited**. Nearly 100,000 new businesses are started in Canada each year, with most of them being founded by people who want freedom from ordinary jobs, a new challenge in life, or the potential of earning extra money.

Most organizations engage in economic activities such as the business activities of purchasing materials and labour, and selling products and services. They can also involve activities for non-business organizations, more commonly referred to as not-for-profit organizations, such as government, schools, and health care and charities. Non-business organizations do not plan and operate for profit, but rather for other goals such as health, education, and cultural and social activities. A common feature in all organizations, both business and non-business, is the reliance on reported financial information to successfully run the organization.

BUSINESS ORGANIZATIONS

When a business is initially established, the owner(s) need to select one of the three legal business structures: sole proprietorship, partnership, or corporation.

Sole Proprietorship

A **sole proprietorship**, or *single proprietorship*, is a business owned by one person. Initial setup of a sole proprietorship is relatively easy and inexpensive. No special legal requirements must be met in order to start this form of business, other than to file for a business licence and register the business name. While it is a separate entity[2] for accounting purposes, it is *not* a separate legal entity from its owner. This means, for example, that a court can order an owner to sell personal belongings to pay a proprietorship's debt. An owner is even responsible for debts that are greater than the resources of the proprietorship; this is known as **unlimited liability**. This unlimited liability is a clear disadvantage of a sole proprietorship, because tax authorities do not separate a proprietorship from its owner; the profits of the business are reported and taxed on the owner's personal income tax return. Small retail stores and service businesses often are organized as proprietorships.

Partnership

A **partnership**[3] is owned by two or more persons called *partners*. Similar to a proprietorship, no special legal requirements must be met in order to start a partnership, other than to register the business name and obtain a business licence. To run the business together, the partners need an oral or written agreement that usually

---

2 The *business entity principle* is one of a group of accounting rules, the *generally accepted accounting principles (GAAP),* which are discussed later in this chapter. This principle states that each economic entity or business of the owner must keep accounting records and reports separate from the owner and any other economic entity of the owner.

3 Partnerships are discussed in greater detail in Chapter 11 in Volume 2 of the textbook.

indicates how profits and losses are to be shared, referred to as a partnership agreement. A partnership, like a proprietorship, is not legally separate from its owners; therefore, each partner's share of profits is reported and taxed on that partner's tax return. Partners are usually subject to *unlimited liability*, meaning they are personally responsible for the debts of the business.

Corporation

A **corporation**[4] is a business that is set up as a separate legal entity chartered (or *incorporated*) under provincial or federal laws. A corporation is responsible for its actions and any debts incurred. It can enter into its own contracts, and it can buy, own, and sell property. It can also sue and be sued. Separate legal status not only gives a corporation an unlimited life, but also entitles the corporation to conduct business with the rights, duties, and responsibilities of a person. As a result, a corporation files a tax return and pays tax on its profits. A corporation acts through its managers, who are its legal agents. Separate legal status also means that the shareholders are not personally liable for corporate acts and debts. Shareholders are legally distinct from the business and their loss is limited to whatever resources they have invested. This **limited liability** is a key to why corporations can raise resources from shareholders who are not active in managing the business. Ownership, or equity, of all corporations is divided into units called **shares**. Owners of shares are called **shareholders** (another term for shares is *stock* and for shareholders, *stockholders*). A shareholder can sell or transfer shares to another person without affecting the operations of a corporation. When a corporation issues (or sells) only one class of shares, we call them **common shares**. A corporation that sells its shares to the public is called a **publicly accountable enterprise (PAE)**. The **public sale of shares** refers to the trading of shares in an organized stock market such as the Montreal or Toronto stock exchanges. A **private enterprise (PE)** is a corporation that does not offer its shares for public sale. **Canadian Tire Corporation** is an example of a publicly accountable enterprise. Its shares are available on the Toronto Stock Exchange, and as of December 31, 2016, Canadian Tire had issued a total of 68.51 million common shares to the public. This means that Canadian Tire Corporation's ownership is divided into 68.51 million units. **McCain Foods** is a Canadian corporation that is a private enterprise. McCain's shares are held by a small group of individuals and are not for sale to the public.

Exhibit 1.2 lists some of the characteristics of each business form.

EXHIBIT 1.2
Characteristics of Business Organizations

	Sole Proprietorship	Partnership	Corporation
Separate business entity	yes	yes	yes
Separate legal entity	no	no	yes
Limited owner liability	no	no	yes
Unlimited life	no	no	yes
Business profit is taxed separate from owner(s)	no	no	yes
One owner allowed	yes	no	yes

---

4   Corporations are discussed in greater detail in Chapter 12 in Volume 2 of the textbook.

CHECKPOINT

1. Identify examples of non-business organizations.
2. What are the three common forms of business organization?

Do Quick Study questions: QS 1-3, QS 1-4

Users of Accounting Information

LO3 Identify users and uses of accounting and opportunities in accounting.

Accounting is a service activity that serves the decision-making needs of *external* and *internal* users, as shown in Exhibit 1.3.

EXTERNAL INFORMATION USERS

External users of accounting information are any party outside the company that relies on the company's reported accounting information to make financial decisions. These users often hold a financial interest in the company but are not involved in day-to-day operations. They include existing and potential shareholders, lenders such as banks, and other creditors such as suppliers and bondholders. Each external user has special information needs that depend on the kind of decisions to be made. To make decisions, these individuals do not have access to internal records of the company but rely on information presented in financial reports, known widely as financial statements.

External Reporting

Financial accounting is the area of accounting aimed at providing information to external users. Its primary objective is to provide external reports called *financial statements* to help users analyze an organization's operations and assess performance. Because external users have limited access to an organization's information, their own success depends on getting external reports that communicate relevant information that is truthfully represented. Some governmental and regulatory agencies have the power to get reports in specific forms,

EXHIBIT 1.3

Users of Accounting Information

External users

- Lenders
- Shareholders
- Governments
- Consumer groups
- External auditors
- Customers

© Photolink/Getty Images

Internal users

- Officers
- Managers
- Internal auditors
- Sales staff
- Budget officers
- Controllers

© Yuri_Arcurs/istockphoto.com

but most external users must rely on *general purpose financial statements*. The term "general purpose" refers to the broad range of purposes for which external users rely on these statements. *Generally accepted accounting principles (GAAP)* are important in increasing the usefulness of financial statements to users. GAAP are the underlying concepts that make up acceptable accounting practices. GAAP for public companies in Canada follow International Financial Reporting Standards (IFRS). IFRS are the "accounting laws" that must be applied by accountants to public companies in Canada when recording and reporting accounting information. We discuss GAAP and IFRS along with the financial statements in more detail later.

INTERNAL INFORMATION USERS

Internal users of accounting information are those individuals directly involved in making decisions in an organization's day-to-day activities. The internal role of accounting is to provide information to help internal users improve the efficiency and effectiveness of an organization in delivering products or services.

Internal Reporting

Managerial accounting is the area of accounting aimed at serving the decision-making needs of internal users. Managerial accounting provides special-purpose reports customized to meet the information needs of internal users. An example of such a report is a monthly sales report for each **David's Tea** location to be used to monitor performance of the store's managers in leading their team. Another example would be a report showing a detailed listing of suppliers owed money by David's Tea for food purchases. Internal reports aim to answer questions such as

- What are the manufacturing expenses per unit of product?
- What is the most profitable mix of goods and/or services?
- What level of revenues is necessary to show profit income?
- Which expenses increase with an increase in revenues?

This book will help you to learn the skills needed to record accounting information effectively to provide answers to questions like these and others.

Internal Operating Functions

The responsibilities and duties of internal users extend to every function of an organization including human resources, sales, marketing, purchasing, production, distribution, and research and development. Accounting is essential to the smooth operation of each aspect of an organization.

 ETHICAL IMPACT

$18.7 Million Maple Syrup Theft

On July 30, 2012, Micheal Gavreau arrived at a warehouse to audit $30 million worth of inventory at the Global Strategic Maple Syrup Reserve. To his surprise, several of the barrels were discovered to be empty; others had their contents replaced with water. It was the "largest theft investigated by the Sûreté du Québec in its history." The leader of the heist was found guilty of fraud, theft, and trafficking stolen goods and was sentenced to eight years in prison and fined $9.4 million. This situation occurred because of inadequate internal controls. In Chapter 7 we will introduce you to the concept of internal controls and the critical role they play in maintaining corporate assets.

What would you do if you noticed unusual activities or discrepancies at your audit client or place of work, such as boxes that looked like they had been tampered with? Would you turn a blind eye or would you take the time to investigate?

Video Link: Follow this link to view a video summary of the full story of "The Sweetest Heist": https://youtu.be/adCQ9cwYA8o.

To monitor operating functions, managers rely on **internal controls**—procedures set up to protect assets (like cash, equipment, and buildings); ensure that accounting reports are free from error, neutral, and complete; promote efficiency; and ensure that company policies are followed. For example, certain actions require verification, such as a manager's approval before materials enter production. Internal controls are crucial if accounting reports are to provide relevant and trustworthy information.

Accounting Opportunities

Exhibit 1.4 identifies some of the countless job opportunities in accounting by classifying accountants according to the kind of work that they perform. In general, accountants work in four broad fields:

- Financial
- Managerial
- Taxation
- Accounting related

Another way to classify accountants is to identify the kinds of organizations in which they work. Most accountants are **private accountants** and work for a single employer, which is often a business. **Public accountants** are licensed and regulated by their professional accounting bodies in the provinces in which they work. For example, the Chartered Professional Accountants of Ontario provides licensing and regulation over CPAs working in Ontario. Exhibit 1.5 shows the average annual salaries for various accounting groups.

FINANCIAL ACCOUNTING

Financial accounting serves the needs of external users by providing standardized financial reports referred to as financial statements. Public companies are required to issue annual financial reports that are audited by a professional accountant. An **audit** is an independent review of an organization's accounting systems and records; it is performed to add credibility to the financial statements. **External auditors** perform the audit at the request of the board of directors to protect investor interests.

EXHIBIT 1.4
Opportunities in Practice

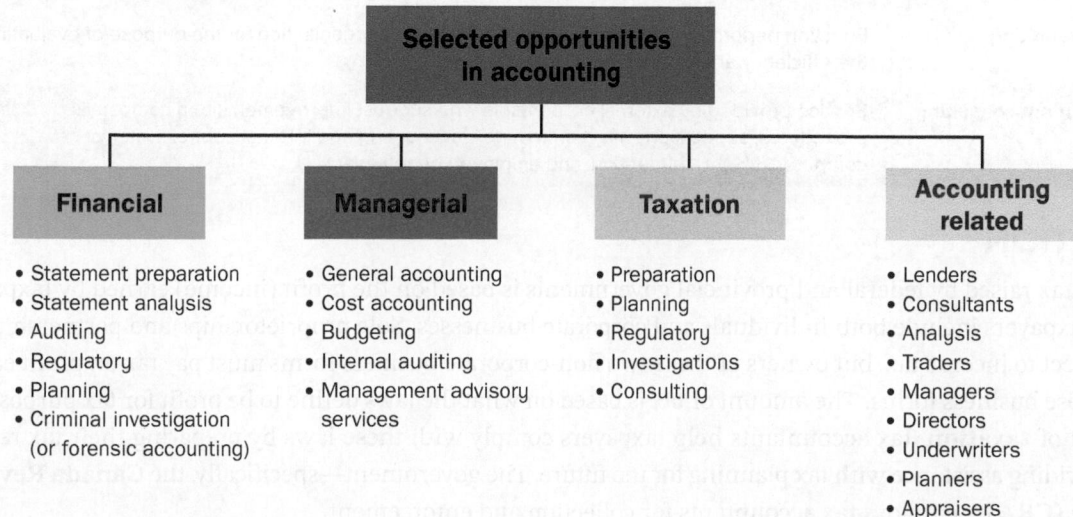

EXHIBIT 1.5

Average Annual Salaries for Accounting Positions

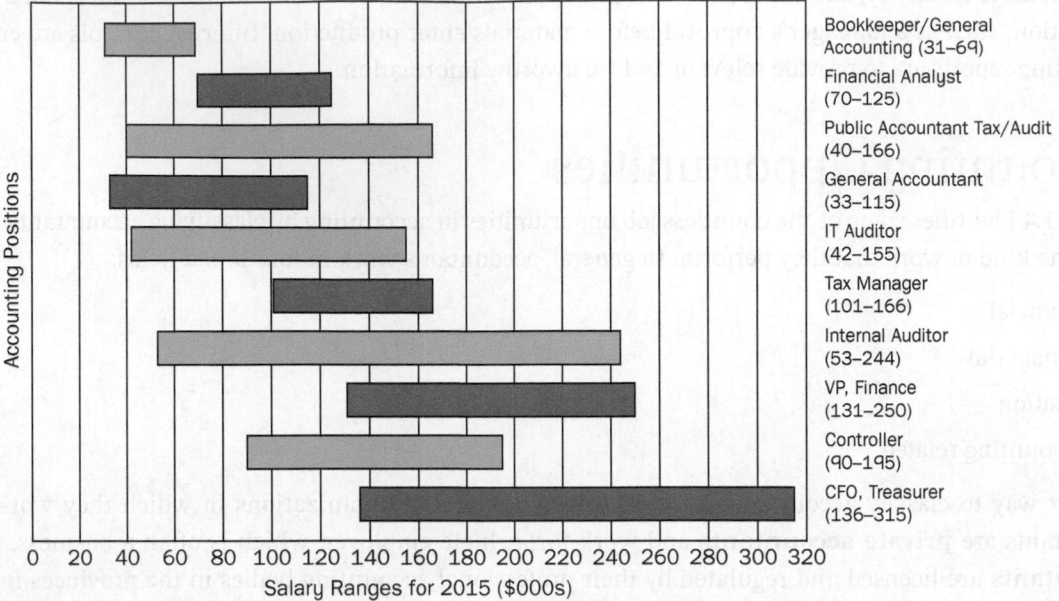

*These values do not include benefits/bonuses.

Source: 2018 Robert Half Salary Guide for Accounting and Finance.

MANAGERIAL ACCOUNTING

Managerial accounting serves the needs of internal users by providing special-purpose reports. These special-purpose reports are the result of general accounting, cost accounting, budgeting, internal auditing, and management consulting.

General accounting	The task of recording transactions, processing the recorded data, and preparing reports for members of the management team such as the **controller** (the chief accounting officer of an organization).
Cost accounting	The process of accumulating the information that managers need about the various **costs** within the organization.
Budgeting	The process of developing formal plans for an organization's future activities.
Internal auditing	Function performed by auditors employed within the organization for the purpose of evaluating the efficiency and effectiveness of procedures.
Management consulting	Service provided by external accountants who suggest improvements to a company's procedures; suggestions may concern new accounting and internal control systems, new computer systems, budgeting, and employee benefit plans.

TAXATION

Income tax raised by federal and provincial governments is based on the profit (income) earned by taxpayers. These taxpayers include both individuals and corporate businesses. Sole proprietorships and partnerships are not subject to income tax, but owners of these two non-corporate business forms must pay tax on profit earned from these business forms. The amount of tax is based on what the laws define to be profit for tax purposes. In the field of **taxation**, tax accountants help taxpayers comply with these laws by preparing their tax returns and providing assistance with tax planning for the future. The government—specifically, the **Canada Revenue Agency (CRA)**—employs tax accountants for collection and enforcement.

PROFESSIONAL CERTIFICATION

Accounting is a profession, like law and medicine, because accountants have special access to confidential matters and the responsibility to adhere to the rules of the profession. The professional status of an accountant is often indicated by one or more professional certifications. In Canada, Chartered Professional Accountants of Canada **(CPA Canada)** is the national organization that has been established to train and monitor its highly qualified professionals to navigate through today's complex and dynamic business climate while demonstrating a commitment to its core values. The CPA certification program is designed to provide students with a pathway to gain the necessary skills and experience that lead to earning the CPA credential.[5] CPA Canada also provides an alternative credential: the Advanced Certificate in Accounting and Finance (ACAF) program. This nationally recognized certificate is geared toward individuals pursuing roles in accounting and finance functions who are interested in obtaining a credential and job-ready skills, but not as a qualified CPA.

> For detailed information regarding professional accounting education programs, refer to the following website: www.cpacanada.ca

The preceding discussions illustrate how critical the accounting function is for all organizations. You can be certain that wherever your future career path leads you, an understanding of accounting will be critical because it is integrated deeply into the language of business. A study of this text will help you to develop the foundational skills required to succeed in using this new language and to consider how it relates to your future career.

 CHECKPOINT

5. What is the difference between private and public accountants?
6. What are the four broad fields of accounting?
7. What is the purpose of an audit?
8. Distinguish between managerial and financial accounting.
9. What is the difference between external and internal users of accounting information?
10. Why are internal controls important?

Do Quick Study question: QS 1-5

Ethics and Social Responsibility

LO4 Identify and explain why ethics and social responsibility are crucial to accounting.

Ethics and ethical behaviour are important to the effectiveness of the accounting profession and to those who use accounting information. If trust is missing in the accounting profession, shareholders lose confidence in the financial markets and will refrain from investing in businesses. This will make it very difficult for businesses to grow, survive, and be successful in Canada. An important goal of accounting is to provide useful information for decision making. For information to be useful it must be trusted; this demands ethics in accounting. Closely related to ethics is social responsibility. Both are discussed in this section.

UNDERSTANDING ETHICS

Ethics are beliefs based on our value system that enable us to differentiate right from wrong. Business ethics involves producing safe, quality products and treating customers responsibly, understanding the impact of

---

5   https://www.cpacanada.ca/en/the-cpa-profession, and https://www.cpacanada.ca/en/become-a-cpa, accessed September 2017.

one's actions to the environment, society, and the employees of the company. An ethical dilemma occurs when an individual comes across a situation and needs to make a decision about a right or wrong course of action. Factors impacting the individual making the decision include society's legal framework, the individual's personal value and belief system, and his or her ability to see the impact of a decision on all individuals that are affected by the decision. Companies can encourage employees to uphold corporate values by ensuring employees are properly trained and that their compensation systems are aligned with these values. Examples of ethical issues in the world of business include:

- Proper labelling of products for consumers to make informed decisions (such as "organic" or "genetically modified," and accurate nutrition and ingredient labelling).
- Recording sales made to customers in the appropriate year. GAAP require companies to follow principles in determining when to recognize revenue as earned from the customer.
- Publicly funded charities utilizing their resources for the end benefit of their stated purpose. The charity directors would need to develop a policy against utilization of charity funds for personal uses such as vacations, personal gifts, etc.
- Companies specifically designing products to break down some time after the elapsed warranty period to require customers to replace the product.
- Universities redirecting monies donated for scholarships and bursaries for capital expansion or employee compensation.

Identifying the optimal ethical decision can be very difficult. Considering how your decisions impact others is a key aspect of choosing the best path when confronted with a difficult decision. The preferred ethical path is to decide on a course of action that maximizes the benefit to the largest number of stakeholders and one that enables you to sleep at night.

Organizational Ethics

Organizational ethics are influenced through management example and leadership and are reinforced through the design of compensation systems. Companies that are concerned about their public image in the area of sustainability report their annual performance in a sustainability report. This report is geared to communicate company initiatives in the area of social, environmental, and corporate governance programs to external and internal users. A growing body of research indicates that there is a strong link between companies that adopt sustainable business practices and their financial performance.[6] Companies like **PepsiCo**, **Kinross Gold**, **L'Oréal**, **Intel**, and Canadian Tire were recognized as part of *Maclean's* magazine's Top 50 Socially Responsible Companies for 2015.[7]

Ethical practices build trust, which promotes loyalty and long-term relationships with customers, suppliers, employees, and investors. Good ethics add to an organization's reputation and its success.

Accounting Ethics

A high commitment to ethics is crucial in the field of accounting due to the confidential nature of information accountants are exposed to and the massive financial and social impact if ethics are neglected. If accounting information is fraudulently presented, shareholders, employees, and many other parties can experience significant consequences. Misleading information can result in many people losing their life's savings when they make investment decisions based on falsified information.

---

6 http://www.cga-canada.org/en-ca/ResearchReports/ca_rep_2011-12_informed-view.pdf, accessed April 2014.

7 http://www.macleans.ca/economy/business/canadas-top-50-most-socially-responsible-companies/.

ETHICAL IMPACT

Resolving Ethical Dilemmas

The Chartered Professional Accountants of Ontario's Rules of Professional Conduct—Approach to Ethical Conflict Resolution state that as part of the resolution process members should consider:

- Relevant facts;
- Ethical issues involved;
- Fundamental principles and rules applicable to the matter in question;
- Established internal procedures; and
- Alternative courses of action.

After considering the above issues, an appropriate course of action needs to be considered that is consistent with the key principles and rules identified as being relevant. The accountant should also assess the consequences of each possible course of action. If the accountant is having difficulty determining the right course of action, the member should consult with other appropriate persons within the firm or employing organization for help. Where a matter involves a conflict with, or within, an organization, the accountant should also consider consulting with those responsible for the governance of the organization, such as the board of directors or the audit committee.

Source: Used with permission of the Chartered Professional Accountants of Ontario. https://media.cpaontario.ca/cpa-members/pdfs/20928_Revision%2020160226.pdf, accessed September 20, 2017.

Professional accountants have ethical obligations in at least four general areas: they are expected to maintain a high level of professional competence, to treat sensitive information as confidential, to exercise personal integrity, and to be objective in matters of financial disclosure. These expectations are outlined in a formal code of ethics that is established and monitored by the provincial professional accounting bodies of the provincial chartered professional accountants. The CPA Code of Professional Conduct requires members to comply with the Code of Ethics of Chartered Professional Accountants, which outlines that accountants have a responsibility to society; describes their obligations to clients, employers, and colleagues; and obliges the following of sound and fair accounting and business practices. This code can help guide accountants when confronted with ethical dilemmas, including concerns that they must not be associated with deceptive information.

Ethics codes are also useful when one is dealing with confidential information. For example, auditors have access to confidential salaries and an organization's strategies. Organizations can be harmed if auditors pass this information to others. To prevent this, Canadian professional accounting bodies require all accountants to maintain confidentiality of information about their client or employer.

 DECISION INSIGHT

Ranking Charitable Organizations?

Millennials as a generation are committed to giving back, but how can those donated dollars be made to count for those who truly need them? *MoneySense* magazine has developed a rating system based on program spending efficiency, fundraising costs, governance, and reserve fund size. Companies were investigated based on the information reported in three consecutive years in their Canada Revenue Agency T3010 information returns. Organizations are ranked by type in categories such as Fundraising, Environment, Health, Hospital, Religion, and Social Services. Based on the 2017 survey, some of the top rated charities include the United Way in both the Calgary area and Ottawa region, the Nature Conservancy of Canada, and WE Charity.

Sources: http://www.moneysense.ca/save/financial-planning/2016-charity-100-methodology/, accessed September 25, 2017; and http://www.moneysense.ca/save/financial-planning/2017-charity-100-canadas-top-rated-charities/, accessed September 25, 2017.

Ethical Challenge

In our lives, we encounter many situations requiring ethical decisions. We need to remember that accounting and other business activities must be practised ethically to maintain the value of the financial reporting process, and we must always ensure that our actions and decisions are ethical.

SOCIAL RESPONSIBILITY

Social responsibility is a concern for the impact of our actions on society as a whole. It requires that an organization identify issues, analyze options, and make socially responsible decisions.

Socially conscious employees, customers, investors, and others see to it that organizations follow claims of social awareness with action, by placing significant pressure on organizations to contribute positively to society. Organizations such as **WestJet** and Loblaw Companies take social responsibility seriously. WestJet invests in the community through WestJet Cares, a program that supports ten national charities including the Boys and Girls Clubs of Canada, Big Brothers Big Sisters of Canada, Hope Air, Make-A-Wish Canada, Missing Children Society of Canada, Ronald McDonald House Charities Canada, David Foster Foundation, and WE Charity.

Appendix III at the end of the text includes four sets of real-life financial statements to provide you with a frame of reference.

CHECKPOINT

11. What are the guidelines to use in making ethical and socially responsible decisions?
12. Why are ethics and social responsibility valuable to organizations?
13. Why is ethics crucial to accounting?

Do Quick Study question: QS 1-6

Generally Accepted Accounting Principles (GAAP)

LO5 Identify, explain, and apply accounting principles.

As has already been stated, the goal of accounting is to provide useful information for decision making. For information to be useful, it must be relevant and trustworthy. The accounting profession has created a framework and set of principles to ensure accounting is valuable and can be relied on when making important decisions. The underlying concepts that make up acceptable accounting practices are referred to as **generally accepted accounting principles (GAAP)**.

GAAP FOR PUBLIC VS. PRIVATE ENTERPRISES

Canada currently has two main sets of accounting standards. Publicly accountable enterprises (PAEs), including companies that have shares trading on Canadian stock exchanges, are required to meet **International Financial Reporting Standards (IFRS)**. Additionally, the **Accounting Standards Board (AcSB)**, the body that originally governed accounting standards in Canada, has issued a set of "made in Canada" **Accounting Standards for Private Enterprises (ASPE)**.

	Publicly Accountable Enterprises (PAEs)	Private Enterprises (PEs)
GAAP to be used	IFRS	ASPE or IFRS

Why IFRS? Although professional accountants around the world all follow GAAP, how GAAP are interpreted and applied in the recording and reporting of accounting information differs from country to country. These differences can prevent investors, creditors, and other users of global accounting information from making the most informed decisions possible. To improve the comparability of accounting information, the **International Accounting Standards Board (IASB)** was established to try to achieve global agreement on the use of a common set of accounting standards, namely IFRS.

Why ASPE? Private enterprises are privately owned and so have some different reporting needs than public enterprises. For example, a small sole proprietorship might incur significant costs if it had to comply with the complexities of the related IFRS. The AcSB developed ASPE to meet the need for simplification in areas where the adoption of IFRS might have caused significant cost/benefit concerns for private enterprises. Private enterprises can choose whether to follow ASPE or IFRS.

Although these two sets of standards—ASPE and IFRS—are developed by different standard setters, the underlying accounting principles and framework upon which the standards have been developed have many similarities. The differences, within the scope of an introductory financial accounting textbook, are identified and briefly discussed in the "IFRS and ASPE—The Differences" section at the end of each chapter. This textbook focuses on GAAP as they relate to IFRS, and we begin emphasizing these in the early chapters of this book.

Purpose of GAAP

The primary purpose of GAAP is to ensure the usefulness of financial information for external users. The main objective of financial reporting is to provide useful information to external users including existing and potential investor groups, banks, and other lenders to make decisions about providing the entity with resources. For financial information to be useful, it must possess the fundamental qualitative characteristics of *relevance* and *faithful representation*.[8] Information that has **relevance** helps users predict future performance or confirm previous predictions or understandings.[9] Information that has **faithful representation** is complete, neutral, and free from error.[10] Information is neutral when prudence (caution) is exercised to ensure assets, liabilities, income, or expenses are not overstated or understated. Usefulness is enhanced when the financial information is *comparable*, *verifiable*, *timely*, and *understandable*. If companies use a similar framework for accounting, users are able to compare the performance of two different companies or compare the company's performance in different fiscal years, enhancing **comparability**.[11] **Verifiability** means that different knowledgeable individuals would reach consensus that the numbers represented in the financial statements are reasonable.[12] Information has **timeliness** if it is available to decision makers in time to influence their decisions.[13] Presenting information clearly and concisely gives it **understandability**.[14]

---

8 IFRS 2018, "The conceptual framework for financial reporting," para. QC5. This information has been updated to reflect the revised IFRS Conceptual Framework issued March 2018.

9 IFRS 2018, "The conceptual framework for financial reporting," para. QC6. This information has been updated to reflect the revised IFRS Conceptual Framework issued March 2018.

10 IFRS 2018, "The conceptual framework for financial reporting," para. QC12. This information has been updated to reflect the revised IFRS Conceptual Framework issued March 2018.

11 IFRS 2018, "The conceptual framework for financial reporting," para. QC20. This information has been updated to reflect the revised IFRS Conceptual Framework issued March 2018.

12 IFRS 2018, "The conceptual framework for financial reporting," para. QC26. This information has been updated to reflect the revised IFRS Conceptual Framework issued March 2018.

13 IFRS 2018, "The conceptual framework for financial reporting," para. QC29. This information has been updated to reflect the revised IFRS Conceptual Framework issued March 2018.

14 IFRS 2018, "The conceptual framework for financial reporting," para. QC30. This information has been updated to reflect the revised IFRS Conceptual Framework issued March 2018.

EXHIBIT 1.6
Summary Model of GAAP Framework

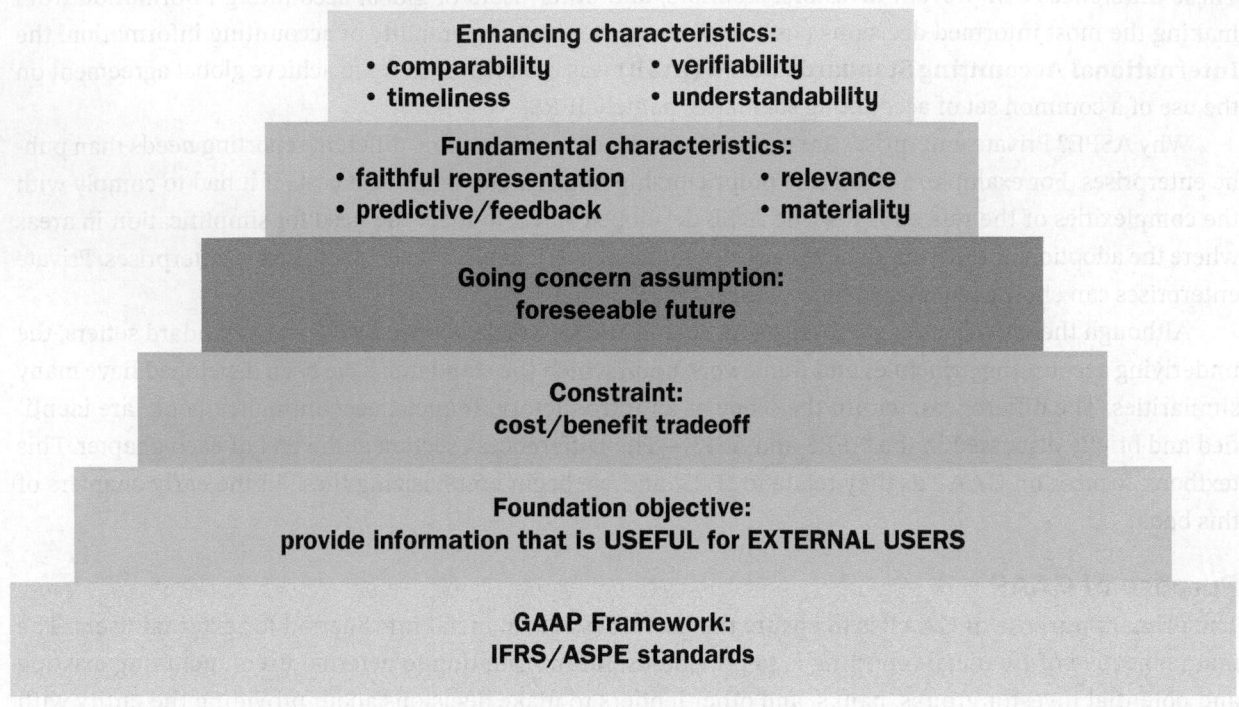

Enhancing characteristics:
- comparability
- timeliness
- verifiability
- understandability

Fundamental characteristics:
- faithful representation
- predictive/feedback
- relevance
- materiality

Going concern assumption:
foreseeable future

Constraint:
cost/benefit tradeoff

Foundation objective:
provide information that is USEFUL for EXTERNAL USERS

GAAP Framework:
IFRS/ASPE standards

Note: Trade-offs between elements require professional judgment to achieve appropriate balance.

In the next section of the chapter, we highlight some of the fundamental accounting principles that all companies must follow.

Fundamental Building Blocks of Accounting

The following discussion and Exhibit 1.6 summarize the core accounting principles that form the framework of GAAP.[15] Note that the primary objective of GAAP is to provide financial information that is useful for external users. Professional judgment is often required to achieve the right balance in satisfying the various elements of the framework with the focus on meeting the needs of external users.

Business Entity Principle

The **business entity principle** requires that each separate economic entity or business of the owner must keep accounting records apart from those of the owner and any other company owned by the owner. To maximize the usefulness of information presented, users want information about the performance of a specific entity.

Example: Zane Caplansky, owner of Caplansky's Deli from the chapter-opening vignette, must not include personal expenses, such as personal clothing, vacations, and the cost of going to the movies, as expenses of his business.

Cost Constraint

The **cost constraint** indicates that the benefits of providing information need to justify the costs incurred in reporting financial statement information to external users.

---

15 Based on IFRS 2018, "The conceptual framework for financial reporting." This information has been updated to reflect the revised IFRS Conceptual Framework issued March 2018.

Going Concern Assumption

According to the **going concern assumption**, financial statement users can safely assume that the statements reflect a business that is going to continue its operations at least 12 months into the future unless clearly notified. Therefore, assets are maintained in the accounting records at original cost and not reduced to a liquidation value as if the business were being bought or sold. Companies are required to inform users about material uncertainties that cast significant doubt on their ability to continue on in the foreseeable future.[16]

Example: It is assumed from a review of Organico's financial statements that the business is continuing its operations, because there is no information presented in the audited statements notifying the users that the company is experiencing financial hardships.

Currency

Transactions are to be expressed using units of money in the **currency** of the country in which the company primarily operates[17] as the common denominator. It is assumed that the monetary unit is stable; therefore, a transaction is left at its originally recorded cost and is not later adjusted for changes in currency value or inflation. The greater the changes in currency value and inflation, the more difficult it is to use and interpret financial statements across time.

Example: Assume that in August 2020 Organico, a Canadian company, purchased equipment from a supplier in the United States at a total cost of $1,000 (US), or $950 (Cdn) ($1,000/1.0526 exchange rate). If the exchange rate changes several months later to 1.0256, Organico does not restate the value of the equipment to $975 ($1,000/1.0256 current exchange rate). The equipment remains in the accounting records at $950 (Cdn).

Revenue Recognition Principle

The **revenue recognition principle** requires that revenue be recorded at the time that it is earned (generally triggered when the service is performed or product has been delivered), regardless of whether cash or another asset has been exchanged.[18] The amount of revenue to be recorded is the cash received plus the cash equivalent value (market value) of any other assets received.

Example: Assume that on April 3, Organico delivers lunch for a sales meeting at Telus in the amount of $600. Telus does not pay the $600 invoice until May 15. Organico records revenue in the amount of $600 when the work was performed on April 3, at the point in time when the food was delivered. It also reports an asset of $600, representing the balance receivable from Telus. Alternatively, if Organico received $1,000 on April 15 in advance for work to be done next month, revenue is *not* recorded until the work is performed in May. The amount collected represents a future obligation of the company—unearned revenue.

Measurement

Within the accounting standards there are four key methods used to determine the dollar value at which to capture/record a transaction in the financial accounting records[19]:

1. **Historical cost.** Historical cost is the *most commonly adopted method* to record accounting transactions. It requires that all transactions be recorded based on the actual cash amount received or paid. In the absence of cash, the cash equivalent amount of the exchange is recorded.[20]

---

16 IFRS 2018, IAS 1, para. 25.

17 IFRS 2018, IAS 21, para. 9.

18 IFRS 2018, IAS 18, para. 9–34; "The conceptual framework for financial reporting," para. 4.37–4.39; IFRS 2018, IFRS 15, para. 9 and 31.

19 IFRS 2018, "The conceptual framework for financial reporting," para. 4.54-4.56. Note the measurement basis was revised by the IASB in March 2018 and is effective for preparers who develop a new accounting policy based on the Conceptual Framework for annual periods beginning on or after January 1, 2020. This new basis of measurement has been included in this section of the chapter. Source: http://www.ifrs.org/issued-standards/list-of-standards/conceptual-framework/.

20 IFRS 2018, IAS 16, para. 23.

Example: If Organico purchased used equipment for $5,000 cash, it is recorded in the accounting records at $5,000. It makes no difference if Hailey Walker thinks that the value of the equipment is $7,000.

2. **Current value measurement basis:**

   • **Current cost.** Current cost indicates the amount of cash required to acquire that asset or received to take on an equivalent liability today. For example, investments in actively traded corporate stock are reported at their fair value at the year-end date.

   • **Fair value.** The asset or liability is reported at the amount of cash that would be received by selling the asset or paying off the liability in the normal course of business. For example, inventory is reported at the lower of historical cost and realizable value.

   • **Value in use (assets)/fulfillment value (liabilities).** Assets are reported at the present value of future expected cash flows, after discounting to reflect the time value of money in terms of expected interest/inflation. For example, long-term debt instruments (corporate bonds) sold are reported at the present value of future cash payments, as described in Chapter 14.

Unless otherwise indicated, assume the measurement method used is *historical cost*, which is the amount paid/payable or the amount collected/collectible. In future chapters you will be informed of the specific measurement method to be used for specific assets or liabilities.

 CHECKPOINT

14. Why is the business entity principle important?
15. Describe the historical cost measurement method and explain why it might be considered verifiable.
16. A customer pays cash today for a product that is to be delivered to her next month. When should revenue be recognized?

Do Quick Study questions: QS 1-7, QS 1-8

Communicating Through Financial Statements

LO6 Identify and explain the content and reporting aims of financial statements.

Financial statements are an organization's primary means of financial communication and are the end result of a process, or cycle, that begins with a business transaction like a sale. These transactions are recorded, classified, sorted, and summarized in order to produce the statements.

PREVIEWING FINANCIAL STATEMENTS

We will begin our study of the four major financial statements—the income statement, statement of changes in equity, balance sheet, and statement of cash flows—with a brief description of each. Exhibit 1.7 shows how these statements are linked. Examples of financial statements are illustrated in the following pages using Organico.

Note: Flexibility is permitted in the naming of financial statements. For example, the *statement of financial position* is another name for the *balance sheet*. In Appendix III at the end of the textbook, notice that WestJet uses the term *statement of financial position*, while **Indigo** uses *balance sheet*. The *statement of profit and loss (P&L), statement of earnings,* and other names are used instead of *income statement*. For consistency, the financial statements will be named throughout this textbook as introduced in Exhibit 1.7.

EXHIBIT 1.7

Links Among the Financial Statements

Transactions occur over a period of time, or during the accounting period, and are reported on the income statement, statement of changes in equity, and statement of cash flows. These transactions result in a new balance sheet at the end of the period.

A balance sheet reports on an organization's financial position at a *point in time.* The income statement, statement of changes in equity, and statement of cash flows report on performance over a *period of time.*

Selection of a reporting period is up to preparers and users (including regulatory agencies). A one-year, or annual, reporting period is common, as are semi-annual, quarterly, and monthly periods. The one-year reporting period is also known as the accounting or **fiscal year**. Businesses whose reporting period follows the **calendar year** begin on January 1 and end on December 31. Many companies choose a fiscal year based on their **natural business year** that ends when sales and inventories are low. For example, Lululemon Athletica's fiscal year-end is the Sunday closest to January 31, after the holiday season, reporting operating results as at January 29, 2017, January 31, 2016, and February 1, 2015, respectively.[21]

Income Statement

The purpose of an **income statement** (statement of profit or loss) is to measure and summarize the results of a business's operating activities over a period of time.

Revenues are the value of assets exchanged for products and services provided to customers as part of a business's main operations. Assets are economic resources controlled by a business and include cash, equipment, buildings, and land. They reflect a right of ownership that has the potential to produce economic benefits such as income. Later in the chapter, we will define assets more precisely. The income statement for Organico's first month of operations is shown in Exhibit 1.8. It shows that Organico earned total revenues of $4,100 during March: $3,800 from food services revenue plus $300 from teaching revenue.

Expenses reflect the using up of assets or the incurrence of liabilities that result in decreases in equity (other than direct distributions to owners or shareholders). The income statement in Exhibit 1.8 shows that Organico used up some of its assets in paying for rented space. The $1,000 expense for rental space is reported in the income statement as rent expense. Organico also paid for an employee's salary at a cost of $700. This is

Revenues	–	Expenses	=	Profit or Loss
For example:				
$100 Revenues	–	$75 Expenses	=	$25 Profit
		OR		
$300 Revenues	–	$360 Expenses	=	$60 Loss

21   Lululemon Athletica Inc. Form 10-K Annual Report, for the period ending 01/29/17, Note 1, para. 3, Nature of Operations and Basis of Presentation.

EXHIBIT 1.8
Income Statement for Organico

Organico Income Statement For Month Ended March 31, 2020		
Revenues:		
Food services revenue	$3,800	
Teaching revenue	300	
Total revenues		$4,100
Operating expenses:		
Rent expense	$1,000	
Salaries expense	700	
Total operating expenses		1,700
Profit		$2,400

EXHIBIT 1.9
Statement of Changes in Equity for Organico

Organico Statement of Changes in Equity For Month Ended March 31, 2020		
Hailey Walker, capital, March 1		$ -0-
Investments by owner	$10,000	
Profit	2,400	12,400
Total		$12,400
Less: Withdrawals by owner		600
Hailey Walker, capital, March 31		$11,800

EXHIBIT 1.10
Balance Sheet for Organico

Organico Balance Sheet March 31, 2020			
Assets		**Liabilities**	
Cash	$ 8,400	Accounts payable	$ 200
Supplies	3,600	Notes payable	6,000
Equipment	6,000	Total liabilities	$ 6,200
		Equity	
		Hailey Walker, capital	11,800
Total assets	$18,000	Total liabilities and equity	$18,000

EXHIBIT 1.11
Statement of Cash Flows for Organico

Organico Statement of Cash Flows For Month Ended March 31, 2020		
Cash flows from operating activities		
Cash received from clients	$ 4,100	
Cash paid for supplies	(3,400)	
Cash paid for rent	(1,000)	
Cash paid to employee	(700)	
Net cash used by operating activities		$(1,000)
Cash flows from investing activities		-0-
Cash flows from financing activities		
Investment by owner	$10,000	
Withdrawal by owner	(600)	
Net cash provided by financing activities		9,400
Net increase in cash		$ 8,400
Cash balance, March 1		-0-
Cash balance, March 31		$ 8,400

The arrows are provided for education purposes only to emphasize the link between statements.

reported on the income statement as salaries expense. The income statement heading in Exhibit 1.8 identifies the business, the type of statement, and the time period covered. Knowledge of the time period is important for us in judging whether the $2,400 profit earned in March is satisfactory.

Profit, or *income*, means that revenues are more than expenses. A **loss** means that expenses are more than revenues.

An income statement lists the types and amounts of both revenues and expenses to help users understand and predict company performance. This detailed information is more useful for making decisions than a simple profit or loss number would be.

Statement of Changes in Equity

Equity is equal to total assets minus total liabilities; it represents how much of the assets *belong* to the owner. Equity increases with *owner investments* and profit and decreases with *owner withdrawals* and losses. **Owner investments** occur when the owner transfers personal assets, such as cash, into the business. Since owner investments do not result from the sale of a product or service, they are *not* revenue and *not* reported on the income statement. **Owner withdrawals**, or **withdrawals**, occur when the owner takes cash or other assets from the business. Withdrawals represent a distribution of profit to the owner. Since withdrawals do not help to create revenue, they are *not* expenses and therefore are not reported on the income statement.

The purpose of the **statement of changes in equity** is to measure and report on changes in the equity position of a business over the reporting period. This statement starts with beginning equity and adjusts it for transactions that (1) increase it (investments by the owner and profit), and (2) decrease it (owner withdrawals and losses).

The statement of changes in equity for Organico's first month of operations is shown in Exhibit 1.9. This statement describes transactions that changed equity during the month. It shows $10,000 of equity created by Hailey Walker's initial investment. It also shows $2,400 of profit earned during the month. The statement also reports the owner's $600 withdrawal. Organico's equity balance at the end of the month is $11,800.

Balance Sheet

The purpose of the **balance sheet**, or **statement of financial position**, is to report the resources owned and the claims on resources of a business at a point in time. This statement is usually prepared at the end of a month, quarter or year. It describes financial position by listing the types and dollar amounts of *assets*, *liabilities*, and *equity*. **Assets** are the properties or economic resources controlled by a business as a result of past events. A common characteristic of assets is their ability to provide future benefits to the company.[22] Cash is an asset that businesses can easily exchange for goods and services. **Accounts receivable** is an asset created by selling products or services to customers on credit, meaning in advance of collecting cash from the customer. It reflects amounts owed to a business by its credit customers. Customers that owe money for services performed are called **debtors**. Other common assets include merchandise inventory held for sale, **supplies**, **equipment**, buildings, and land. Discussed in Chapter 4 are other assets having intangible rights, such as those granted by a patent or copyright.

Liabilities are debts or obligations of a business to transfer cash or another economic resource as a result of past events. These existing obligations represent a dollar value of claims of others, against the assets of the business. A common characteristic of liabilities is they represent a future obligation to settle with no practical

---

22 IFRS 2018, "The conceptual framework for financial reporting," para. 4.8. Updated to reflect the revised Conceptual Framework issued by the IASB, March 2018.

ability to avoid, reducing future assets or requiring future services or products.[23] Typical liabilities include *accounts payable* and *notes payable*. An **account payable** is a liability created by buying products or services on credit. It reflects amounts owed to others. A **note payable** is a liability expressed by a written promise to make a future payment at a specific time. Other common liabilities are salaries and wages owed to employees, interest payable, and money collected from customers in advance of providing a service called unearned revenues (further described in Chapter 2). Individuals and organizations that own the right to receive payments from a business are called its **creditors**.

One entity's payable is another entity's receivable. If a business fails to pay its obligations, the law gives creditors a right to force sale of its assets to obtain the money to meet their claims. When assets are sold under these conditions, creditors are paid first but only up to the amount of their claims. Any remaining money goes to the owner(s) of the business. Creditors often compare the amounts of liabilities and assets on a balance sheet to help them decide whether to lend money to a business. A loan is less risky if liabilities are small in comparison to assets, because there are more resources than claims on resources. A loan is more risky if liabilities are large compared to assets.

Equity is the owner's claim on the assets of a business. It represents the assets that remain after deducting liabilities,[24] also called **net assets**. We explained that income is the difference between revenues and expenses of a business over a period of time. Income on the income statement results in an increase in equity on the balance sheet due to profitable operating activities over a period of time. An operating loss on the income statement results in a decrease in equity on the balance sheet in an accounting period. In this way, the income statement links to the balance sheet at the end of a reporting period. Changes in equity are reported in the statement of changes in equity, and give us the ending balance of equity that is reported in the balance sheet.

Exhibit 1.12 provides a brief summary of the elements of the financial statements.[25]

Exhibit 1.10 shows the balance sheet as of March 31, 2020. The balance sheet heading lists the business name, the statement, and the specific date on which assets and liabilities are identified and measured. The amounts in the balance sheet are measured as of the close of business on that specific date.

The balance sheet for Organico shows that it has three different assets at the close of business on March 31, 2020. The assets are cash, supplies, and equipment, for a total dollar amount of $18,000. The balance sheet also shows total liabilities of $6,200. Equity is $11,800. Equity is the difference between assets and liabilities. The statement is named a *balance sheet* because (1) the total amounts on both sides of the statement are equal; and (2) the reporting of assets, liabilities, and equity is in *balance*.

Statement of Cash Flows

The **statement of cash flows** describes the sources and uses of cash for a reporting period. It also reports the amount of cash at both the beginning and the end of a period. The statement of cash flows is organized by a company's major activities: operating, investing, and financing. Since a company must carefully manage cash if it is to survive and prosper, cash flow information is important.

As an example, the statement of cash flows for Organico is shown in Exhibit 1.11 (notice that Organico shows both operating and financing activities but it had no investing activities during March). To fully appreciate this financial statement, a solid understanding of some basic accounting concepts is required. Therefore, a detailed discussion has been left to Chapter 16.

---

23 IFRS 2018, "The conceptual framework for financial reporting," para. 4.15. Updated to reflect the IASB's revised conceptual framework issued March 2018.

24 IFRS 2018, "The conceptual framework for financial reporting," para. 4.20.

25 IFRS 2018, "The conceptual framework for financial reporting," ch. 4, 6. Updated to reflect the IASB's Conceptual Framework, revised March 2018.

EXHIBIT 1.12
Elements of Financial Statements Summary

Element of F/S	Definition	Characteristics	Example
Assets	Economic resources controlled by a business that has the potential to produce economic benefits.	The resource: 1) Will result in a future financial benefit 2) Is owned by the business 3) Transaction/exchange to acquire the item has occurred.	By purchasing a food truck, Organico acquires an asset that will provide a future benefit. It will enable Organico to make and distribute its burritos to customers.
Liabilities	Debts or obligations of a business	Present obligation to transfer an economic resource resulting from a past event that the entity has no practical ability to avoid.	Organico purchases $1,100 of biodegradable food packaging supplies from CanFood Supply Co. and agrees to pay cash for the items in 30 days.
Equity/Net Assets	The owner's claim on the assets of the business.	Represents the residual interest of the owner(s) in the assets of the company after deducting liabilities.	Hailey Walker has $11,800 of equity/capital at the end of the first month of operations (Exhibit 1.9).
Profit	The difference between revenues and expenses of a business during a specific period of time.	Increase in assets or decreases in liabilities, resulting in increases in equity other than those relating to contributions from owners.	Organico earns $2,400 in its first month of operations (Exhibit 1.8).
Expenses	Costs incurred or the using up of assets as a result of the operations of the business.	Represents decreases in assets or increases in liabilities that result in decreases in equity other than distributions to owners.	Organico pays for fuel to operate its food truck.
Revenue	The value of assets received or receivable as a result of selling goods or services to customers.	Must be: 1) *Earned*, meaning the asset/service has been transferred/provided to the customer. 2) Expect to *collect* from the customer. 3) Able to quantify or *measure* the transaction in terms of value expected from the sale/service based on the terms of the contract with the customer.	Organico sells a burrito to a customer.

Learning Summary: Changes to Equity	
Increases in equity are caused by:	**Decreases in equity are caused by:**
• Owner investments	• Owner withdrawals
• Profit (excess revenue over expenses)	• Losses (expenses exceed revenue)

Ending Owner's Equity = Beginning Owner's Equity + Owner Investments + Profit − Withdrawals by Owner

Financial Statements and Forms of Organization

Earlier in the chapter, three different forms of business organization were described: sole proprietorships, partnerships, and corporations. Exhibit 1.13 summarizes key differences among these three forms of business ownership. While many differences exist, financial statements for these three types of organizations are very similar.

EXHIBIT 1.13

Financial Statement Differences Based on Type of Business Organization

Difference	Type of Business Organization		
	Sole Proprietorship	Partnership	Corporation
Equity on the balance sheet belongs to:	Sole owner	Partners	Shareholders
Distributions to owners are called:	Withdrawals	Withdrawals	Dividends
When managers are also owners, their salaries are:	Not an expense	Not an expense	Expense

The emphasis in the early chapters of this book is on sole proprietorships. This allows us to focus on important measurement and reporting issues in accounting without getting caught up in the complexities of additional forms of organization. We do discuss other forms of organization, however, and provide examples when appropriate. Chapters 11 and 12 return to this topic and provide additional detail about the financial statements of partnerships and corporations.

 CHECKPOINT

17. What are the four major financial statements?
18. Describe revenues and expenses.
19. Explain assets, liabilities, and equity.
20. What are three differences in financial statements for different forms of organization?

Do Quick Study question: QS 1-9

The Accounting Equation

LO7 Analyze business transactions by applying the accounting equation.

Notice in Exhibit 1.10 that there are two main sections of the balance sheet: assets on one side and liabilities and equity on the other side. Observe that the total assets of $18,000 equal the total liabilities and equity of $18,000. This equality is known as the *accounting equation*. This equation is based on relationships fundamental to accounting.

When an organization invests in assets, it is the result of an equal amount of financing. This relationship is expressed in the following equation:

$$Investing = Financing$$

Since invested amounts are referred to as *assets*, and financing is made up of owner and non-owner financing, we can also express this equality as:

$$Assets = Non\text{-}Owner\ Financing + Owner\ Financing$$

Non-owners are creditors. Creditors and owners hold claims or rights in the assets. Creditors' claims are called *liabilities* and the owner's claim is called *equity*. The equation can be rewritten as shown in Exhibit 1.14.

EXHIBIT 1.14
The Accounting Equation

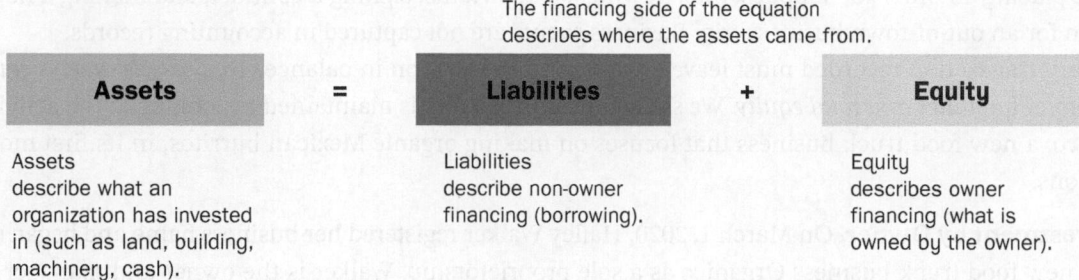

The financing side of the equation describes where the assets came from.

Assets	=	Liabilities	+	Equity

Assets describe what an organization has invested in (such as land, building, machinery, cash).

Liabilities describe non-owner financing (borrowing).

Equity describes owner financing (what is owned by the owner).

The **accounting equation** describes the relationship between a company's assets, liabilities, and equity. To demonstrate, assume you want to buy a car that costs $25,000. The bank lends you $15,000 and you pay $10,000 out of your personal savings account.

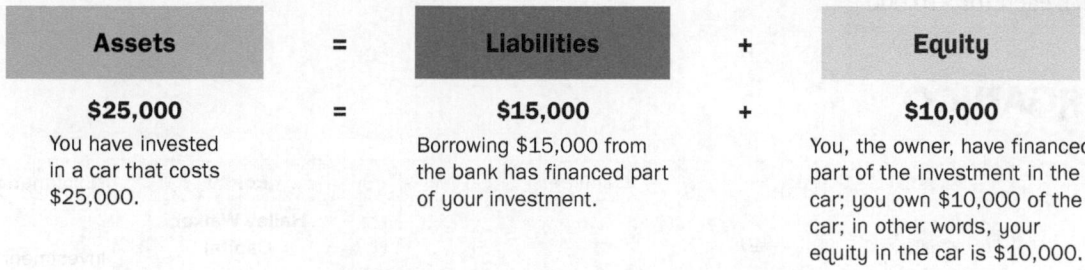

Assets	=	Liabilities	+	Equity
$25,000	**=**	**$15,000**	**+**	**$10,000**

You have invested in a car that costs $25,000.

Borrowing $15,000 from the bank has financed part of your investment.

You, the owner, have financed part of the investment in the car; you own $10,000 of the car; in other words, your equity in the car is $10,000.

The accounting equation can be changed by moving liabilities to the left side of the equation:

$$\underbrace{\text{Assets} - \text{Liabilities}}_{\text{Net assets}} = \text{Equity}$$

Assets less liabilities equals *net assets*, another name for equity.

 CAUTION: The illustration of transaction analysis on the following pages is a learning tool to demonstrate the effects of transactions on the accounting equation. How transactions are recorded in the real world is the topic of Chapter 2.

TRANSACTION ANALYSIS

Business activities can be described in terms of *transactions* and *events*. A **business transaction** is an exchange of *economic consideration* between two parties that causes a change in assets, liabilities, or equity. An **economic consideration** is something of value, and examples include products, services, money, and rights to collect money. These transactions cause changes in the accounting equation. **Source documents** identify and describe transactions entering the accounting process. They are the *source* of accounting information, and can be in either paper or electronic form. Source documents, especially if obtained from outside the organization, provide objective evidence about transactions and their amounts, making information more reliable and useful. Examples of source documents are sales invoices, cheques, purchase orders, charges to customers, bills from suppliers, employee earnings records, and bank statements.

Not all business activities are transactions. **Business events** are activities that do not involve an exchange of economic consideration between two parties and therefore do not affect the accounting equation. Examples include placing an order for supplies, interviewing job applicants, signing a contract, and making a hotel reservation for an out-of-town business trip. Business events are not captured in accounting records.

Every transaction recorded must leave the accounting equation in balance. *Total assets always equal the sum of total liabilities and total equity.* We show how this equality is maintained by looking at the activities of Organico, a new food truck business that focuses on making organic Mexican burritos, in its first month of operations.

1. Investment by Owner. On March 1, 2020, Hailey Walker registered her business name and began setting up her new food truck business Organico as a sole proprietorship. Walker is the owner and manager of the business. The marketing plan for Organico is to focus primarily on providing fresh, organic, Mexican fast food with a focus on quality and taste. Walker invests $10,000 cash in the new company, which she deposits in a bank account opened under the name Organico. By moving her personal money into the business an exchange of resources has taken place, so this is classified as a transaction. Transactions affect the accounting equation. As shown, this transaction affects both Organico's cash (an asset) and equity (called *Hailey Walker, Capital*), each for $10,000.

	Assets	=	Liabilities	+	Equity	Explanation
	Cash	=			Hailey Walker, Capital	Investment by Owner
(1)	+$10,000	=			+$10,000	

This specific increase in equity is identified as an investment by the owner, differentiating it from other transactions affecting equity.

2. Purchase Supplies for Cash. Organico uses $2,500 of its cash to purchase organic food supplies. This is a transaction because it involves an exchange of cash, an asset, for another kind of asset, supplies. The transaction produces no expense because no value is lost. The decrease in cash is exactly equal to the increase in supplies. The equation remains in balance.

	Assets			=	Liabilities	+	Equity	Explanation
	Cash	+	Supplies	=			Hailey Walker, Capital	
Old Bal.	$10,000			=			$10,000	
(2)	–$ 2,500		+$2,500					Purchased Supplies
New Bal.	$ 7,500	+	$2,500	=			$10,000	
		$10,000		=		$10,000		

3. Purchase Equipment and Supplies on Credit. Hailey Walker finds a used food truck from a supplier that specializes in restaurant equipment supplies, CanFood Supply Co. Walker is able to negotiate a deal with the same supplier on biodegradable food packaging supplies; these purchases total $7,100. As we see from the accounting equation in (2) above, however, Organico has only $7,500 in cash. Concerned that these purchases would use nearly all of Organico's cash, Walker arranges to purchase the items on credit from CanFood Supply Co. This is a transaction because an exchange has occurred: Organico has acquired items in exchange for a promise to pay for them later. Supplies cost $1,100, and the equipment costs $6,000. The total liability to CanFood Supply is $7,100. Organico will pay for the supplies in 30 days, but has arranged to pay for the equipment by signing an agreement called a *note*. The effects of this transaction on the accounting equation are:

	Assets					=	Liabilities			+	Equity	Explanation
	Cash	+	Supplies	+	Equipment	=	Accounts Payable	+	Notes Payable	+	Hailey Walker, Capital	
Old Bal.	$7,500		$2,500								$10,000	
(3)			+$1,100	+	+$6,000		+$1,100	+	+$6,000			Purchased Supplies and Equipment
New Bal.	$7,500	+	$3,600	+	$6,000	=	$1,100	+	$6,000	+	$10,000	
			$17,100						$17,100			

This purchase increases assets by $7,100, while liabilities (called *accounts payable* and *notes payable*) increase by the same amount. Both of these payables are promises by Organico to repay its debt, where the note payable reflects a more formal written agreement. We will discuss these liabilities in detail in later chapters.

4. Services Rendered for Cash. A primary objective of a business is to increase its owner's wealth. This goal is met when a business produces a profit, also called *income*. Profit is reflected in the accounting equation as an increase in equity. Organico earns revenue by selling fresh, organic Mexican burritos and providing cooking demonstrations. On March 10, Organico provides catering services for a corporate sales training event for Whole Foods and sells $2,200 worth of burritos for cash. This is a transaction since an exchange of resources has taken place. When revenue is earned in exchange for cash, it affects the accounting equation by increasing cash and equity. Organico's cash increases by $2,200 and equity also increases by $2,200, identified in the far right column as revenue.

	Assets					=	Liabilities			+	Equity	Explanation
	Cash	+	Supplies	+	Equipment	=	Accounts Payable	+	Notes Payable	+	Hailey Walker, Capital	
Old Bal.	$7,500		$3,600		$6,000		$1,100		$6,000		$10,000	Food Services
(4)	+$2,200			+		=		+			+$ 2,200	March 10 Revenue
New Bal.	$9,700	+	$3,600	+	$6,000	=	$1,100	+	$6,000	+	$12,200	
			$19,300						$19,300			

5. and 6. Payment of Expenses in Cash. On March 10, Organico pays its landlord rent on its downtown parking space at a cost of $1,000 for March. Since an exchange has taken place, this is a transaction and affects the accounting equation as shown below in line (5). On March 14, Organico pays the $700 salary of the business's only employee—Nolan. This is also a transaction because an exchange has occurred, and it is therefore reflected in the accounting equation in line (6).

	Assets			=	Liabilities			+	Equity	Explanation
	Cash	+ Supplies	+ Equipment	=	Accounts Payable	+	Notes Payable	+	Hailey Walker, Capital	
Old Bal.	$9,700	+ $3,600	+ $6,000	=	$1,100	+	$6,000	+	$12,200	
(5)	−$1,000								−$ 1,000	Rent Expense
Bal.	$8,700	+ $3,600	+ $6,000	=	$1,100	+	$6,000	+	$11,200	
(6)	−$ 700								−$ 700	Salaries Expense
New Bal.	$8,000	+ $3,600	+ $6,000	=	$1,100	+	$6,000	+	$10,500	
		$17,600				$17,600				

Both (5) and (6) produce expenses for Organico as noted in the far right column. They use up cash for the purpose of providing services to clients. Unlike the asset purchase in (2), the cash payments in (5) and (6) acquire services. The benefits of these services do *not* last beyond the end of this month. The accounting equation remains in balance, and shows that both transactions reduce cash and Walker's equity.

7. Service Contract Signed for April. On March 11, the accounting club at the local university and Hailey Walker sign a $2,700 contract that requires Organico to provide food for a group of graduating students at a CPA recruitment event. Organico has agreed to attend the event to be held next month.

	Assets			=	Liabilities			+	Equity	Explanation
	Cash	+ Supplies	+ Equipment	=	Accounts Payable	+	Notes Payable	+	Hailey Walker, Capital	
Old Bal.	$8,000	+ $3,600	+ $6,000	=	$1,100	+	$6,000		$10,500	
(7)										
New Bal.	$8,000	+ $3,600	+ $6,000	=	$1,100	+	$6,000	+	$10,500	
		$17,600				$17,600				

This is a business event and *not* a business transaction because there was no economic exchange (nothing has yet been received by Organico *and* nothing has been provided to the club (the customer) as of March 11). Therefore, this has no effect on the accounting equation.

8. Services and Rental Revenues Rendered for Credit. On March 17, Organico taught a Mexican cooking class as a team-building exercise for a group of HR professionals for $300 and sold an additional $1,600 in food services at the HR conference. The group's coordinator is billed for $1,900 for both activities. This is a transaction because an exchange has occurred: Organico provided services to a customer and in exchange received an asset, an account receivable, from the customer. The $1,900 increase in assets produces an equal increase in equity. Notice that the increase in equity is identified as two revenue components in the far right column of the accounting equation:

	Assets				=	Liabilities			+	Equity	Explanation
	Cash	+ Receivable	+ Supplies	+ Equipment	=	Accounts Payable	+	Notes Payable	+	Hailey Walker, Capital	
Old Bal.	$8,000		+ $3,600	+ $6,000	=	$1,100	+	$6,000	+	$10,500	Food Services Revenue
(8)		+$1,900								+$1,600	
					=		+		+	+$ 300	Teaching Revenue
New Bal.	$8,000	+ $ 1,900	+ $3,600	+ $6,000		$1,100		$6,000		$12,400	
		$19,500					$19,500				

9. Receipt of Cash on Account. The amount of $1,900 is received from the client on March 27, ten days after the billing for services in (8). This exchange between Organico and the customer represents a transaction and therefore affects the accounting equation. This transaction does not change the total amount of assets and does not affect liabilities or equity. It converts the receivable to cash and *does not* create new revenue. Revenue was recognized when Organico provided the services on March 17. Therefore, revenue is *not* recorded on March 27 when the cash is collected. The new balances are:

	Assets					=	Liabilities			+	Equity	Explanation
	Cash	+	Accounts Receivable	+ Supplies	+ Equipment	=	Accounts Payable	+	Notes Payable	+	Hailey Walker, Capital	
Old Bal.	$8,000	+	$1,900	+ $3,600	+ $6,000	=	$1,100	+	$6,000	+	$12,400	Collected Payment
(9)	+$1,900		−$1,900									
New Bal.	$ 9,900	+	$ -0-	+ $3,600	+ $6,000	=	$1,100	+	$6,000	+	$12,400	
				$19,500					$19,500			

10. Payment of Accounts Payable. Organico pays $900 to CanFood Supply on March 27. This is a transaction since an exchange has occurred between Organico and CanFood Supply. It therefore affects the accounting equation. The $900 payment is for the earlier $1,100 purchase of supplies from CanFood, leaving $200 unpaid. The $6,000 amount due to CanFood for equipment remains unpaid. The accounting equation shows that this transaction decreases Organico's cash by $900 and decreases its liability to CanFood Supply by the same amount. As a result, equity does not change. It is important to note that this transaction does not create an expense, even though cash flows out of Organico.

	Assets					=	Liabilities			+	Equity	Explanation
	Cash	+	Accounts Receivable	+ Supplies	+ Equipment	=	Accounts Payable	+	Notes Payable	+	Hailey Walker, Capital	
Old Bal.	$9,900		$ -0-	+ $3,600	+ $6,000	=	$1,100	+	$6,000	+	$12,400	Paid Supplier
(10)	−$ 900						−$ 900					
New Bal.	$ 9,000	+	$ -0-	+ $3,600	+ $6,000	=	$ 200	+	$6,000	+	$12,400	
				$18,600					$18,600			

11. Withdrawal of Cash by Owner. Walker withdraws $600 in cash from Organico for personal living expenses. This is not a business expense, but a removal of equity from the business by the owner. An exchange has taken place between the owner and the business, so this is a transaction and affects the accounting equation. Notice that this transaction does not affect profit.

	Assets					=	Liabilities			+	Equity	Explanation
	Cash	+	Accounts Receivable	+ Supplies	+ Equipment	=	Accounts Payable	+	Notes Payable	+	Hailey Walker, Capital	
Old Bal.	$9,000	+	$ -0-	+ $3,600	+ $6,000	=	$ 200	+	$6,000	+	$12,400	Withdrawal by Owner
(11)	−$600										−$ 600	
New Bal.	$8,400	+	$ -0-	+ $3,600	+ $6,000	=	$ 200	+	$6,000	+	$11,800	
				$18,000					$18,000			

SUMMARY OF TRANSACTIONS

Summarized in Exhibit 1.15 are the effects of all of Organico's March transactions using the accounting equation. From the summary below five key points should be noted.

1. The accounting equation remains in balance after every transaction.

2. Transactions can be analyzed by their effects on components of the accounting equation. For example, total assets and equity increase by equal amounts in (1), (4), and (8). In (2) and (9), one asset increases while another decreases by an equal amount. For (3), we see equal increases in assets and liabilities. Both assets and equity decrease by equal amounts in (5), (6), and (11). In (10), we see equal decreases in an asset and a liability.

3. Transactions cause assets, liabilities, or equity to change. Notice in Exhibit 1.15 that (1)–(6) and (8)–(11) caused changes to the accounting equation because each transaction involved an exchange; (7) did not involve an exchange and so did not affect the accounting equation.

EXHIBIT 1.15

Summary Analysis of Organico's Transactions Using the Accounting Equation

		Assets			=	Liabilities		+	Equity	Explanation of Equity Transaction
	Cash	+ Accounts Receivable +	Supplies +	Equipment =		Accounts Payable +	Notes Payable +		Hailey Walker, Capital	
(1)	$10,000								$10,000	Investment by Owner
(2)	– 2,500		+$2,500							Purchased Supplies
Bal.	$ 7,500		$2,500						$10,000	Purchased Supplies and Equipment
(3)			+1,100	+$6,000		+ 1,100	+$6,000			
Bal.	$ 7,500		$3,600	$6,000		$1,100	$6,000		$10,000	Food Services Revenue
(4)	+ 2,200								+ 2,200	
Bal.	$ 9,700		$3,600	$6,000		$1,100	$6,000		$12,200	
(5)	– 1,000								– 1,000	Rent Expense
Bal.	$ 8,700		$3,600	$6,000		$1,100	$6,000		$11,200	
(6)	– 700								– 700	Salaries Expense
Bal.	$ 8,000		$3,600	$6,000		$1,100	$6,000		$10,500	
(7)	No entry*									Food Services Revenue
(8)		+$1,900							+ 1,600	
									+ 300	Teaching Revenue
Bal.	$ 8,000	$ 1,900	$3,600	$6,000		$1,100	$6,000		$12,400	
(9)	+ 1,900	– 1,900								Collected Payment
Bal.	$ 9,900	$ -0-	$3,600	$6,000		$1,100	$6,000		$12,400	
(10)	– 900					– 900				Paid Supplier
Bal.	$ 9,000	$ -0-	$3,600	$6,000		$ 200	$6,000		$12,400	
(11)	– 600								– 600	Withdrawal by Owner
Bal.	$ 8,400 +	$ -0- +	$3,600 +	$6,000 =		$ 200 +	$6,000 +		$11,800	

$18,000 $18,000

*Note: (7) did not involve an economic transaction between two parties, so it is an event and does not affect the accounting equation.

4. The format of the preceding analysis was used to demonstrate the effects of transactions on the components of the accounting equation; transactions in the real world are not recorded in this manner.

5. The equality of effects in the accounting equation is fundamental to the *double-entry accounting system* that is discussed in the next chapter.

It is important to recognize that the accounting equation is a representation of the balance sheet. Therefore, we can take the information in Exhibit 1.15 and prepare financial statements for Organico. This will be done in the next section.

 CHECKPOINT

21. How can a transaction *not* affect liability and equity accounts?
22. Describe a transaction that increases equity and one that decreases it.
23. Identify a transaction that decreases both assets and liabilities.
24. When is the accounting equation in balance, and what does it mean?
25. Explain the difference between a transaction and an event.
26. Identify examples of accounting source documents.
27. Explain the importance of source documents.

Do Quick Study questions: QS 1-10, QS 1-11, QS 1-12, QS 1-13, QS 1-14

Mid-Chapter Demonstration Problem

↑ All chapters have a Mid-Chapter and End-of-Chapter Demonstration Problem to illustrate and reinforce important topics.

Part A

Jeremy Delgado founded a new moving company as a proprietorship on May 1. The accounting equation showed the following *balances* after each of the company's first five transactions. Analyze the equations and describe each of the five transactions with their amounts.

Transaction	Cash	+	Accounts Receivable	+	Office Supplies	+	Truck	+	Office Furniture	=	Accounts Payable	+	Jeremy Delgado, Capital
1	$10,000		$ -0-		$-0-		$45,000		$ -0-		$ -0-		$55,000
2	9,000		-0-		-0-		45,000		1,000		-0-		55,000
3	9,000		-0-		-0-		45,000		6,000		5,000		55,000
4	9,000		3,000		-0-		45,000		6,000		5,000		58,000
5	11,000		1,000		-0-		45,000		6,000		5,000		58,000

Part B

During June, Jeremy Delgado's second month of operations, transactions occurred resulting in a $68,000 balance in the column Jeremy Delgado, Capital. Calculate the profit or loss for June under each of the following independent situations:

1. Jeremy made no investments or withdrawals during June.
2. Jeremy invested $15,000 during June and made no withdrawals.
3. Jeremy withdrew a total of $5,000 during June and made no additional investments.
4. Jeremy invested $5,000 during June and made withdrawals of $3,000.

Analysis Component: Several activities cause equity to change. Of those activities, which one will help build equity over the long term?

SOLUTION

Part A

1. Started the business by investing $10,000 cash and a $45,000 truck.
2. Purchased $1,000 of office furniture by paying cash.
3. Purchased $5,000 of office furniture on account.
4. Billed a customer $3,000 for services performed.
5. Collected $2,000 from a credit customer.

Part B

1.

Assets	=	Liabilities	+	Equity	
$63,000		$5,000		$58,000	Beginning assets, liabilities, and capital on June 1
				+ 0	Plus owner investments during June
				− 0	Less owner withdrawals during June
				+ 10,000	**Plus profit (less loss) realized during June**
				= $68,000	Equals ending capital on June 30

Calculations: $68,000 − $58,000 = $10,000 profit

2.

Assets	=	Liabilities	+	Equity	
$63,000		$5,000		$58,000	Beginning assets, liabilities, and capital on June 1
				+ 15,000	Plus owner investments during June
				− 0	Less owner withdrawals during June
				− 5,000	**Plus profit (less loss) realized during June**
				= $68,000	Equals ending capital on June 30

Calculations: $68,000 − $15,000 − $58,000 = $5,000 loss

3.

Assets	=	Liabilities	+	Equity	
$63,000		$5,000		$58,000	Beginning assets, liabilities, and capital on June 1
				+ 0	Plus owner investments during June
				− 5,000	Less owner withdrawals during June
				+ 15,000	**Plus profit (less loss) realized during June**
				= $68,000	Equals ending capital on June 30

Calculations: $68,000 + $5,000 − $58,000 = $15,000 profit

4.

Assets	=	Liabilities	+	Equity	
$63,000		$5,000		$58,000	Beginning assets, liabilities, and capital on June 1
				+ 5,000	Plus owner investments during June
				− 3,000	Less owner withdrawals during June
				+ 8,000	**Plus profit (less loss) realized during June**
				= $68,000	Equals ending capital on June 30

Calculations: $68,000 + $3,000 − $5,000 − $58,000 = $8,000 profit

Analysis Component: Equity increases because of owner investments and profit (when revenues are greater than expenses) and decreases because of owner withdrawals and losses (when expenses are greater than revenues). Recurring profit will help build (or grow) equity over the long term.

Financial Statements

LO8 Prepare financial statements reflecting business transactions.

We illustrated financial statements earlier in this chapter. These statements are required under GAAP. In this section, we describe how the financial statements shown in Exhibits 1.8 to 1.10 were prepared from the business transactions summarized in Exhibit 1.15. The analysis of the statement of cash flows, Exhibit 1.11, is left to Chapter 16.

INCOME STATEMENT

Organico's income statement is shown on the right side of Exhibit 1.16. It was prepared using revenue and expense information taken from the equity column in Exhibit 1.15, copied in Exhibit 1.16 on the left side.

Revenues of $4,100 are reported first and include food services revenues of $3,800 ($2,200 + $1,600) plus teaching revenue of $300. Expenses follow revenues, and can be listed in different ways. For convenience in this chapter, we list larger amounts first. Rent of $1,000 and salaries expenses of $700 result in total operating expenses of $1,700. Profit is reported at the bottom and is the amount earned during March. Owner's investments and withdrawals are *not* part of measuring profit; they are shown on the statement of changes in equity.

STATEMENT OF CHANGES IN EQUITY

The second report in Exhibit 1.16 is the statement of changes in equity for Organico. Its heading lists the month as March 2020 because this statement describes transactions that happened during that month. The beginning balance of equity is measured as of the start of business on March 1. It is zero because Organico did not exist before then. An existing business reports the beginning balance as of the end of the prior reporting period. Organico's statement shows that $10,000 of equity is created by Hailey Walker's initial investment. It also shows the $2,400 of profit earned during the month. This item links the income statement to the statement of changes in equity as shown in Exhibit 1.16. The statement also reports the owner's $600 withdrawal and Organico's $11,800 equity balance at the end of the month.

EXHIBIT 1.16
Organico's Financial Statements

Equity	Explanation of Equity Transaction	
Hailey Walker, Capital		
$10,000	Investment by Owner	
_____		
$10,000		
_____		
$10,000		
+ 2,200	Food Services Revenue	
$12,200		
− 1,000	Rent Expense	
$11,200		
− 700	Salaries Expense	
$10,500		
+ 1,600	Food Services Revenue	
+ 300	Teaching Revenue	
$12,400		
_____		
$12,400		
_____		
$12,400		
− 600	Withdrawal by Owner	
$11,800		

Organico
Income Statement
For Month Ended March 31, 2020

Revenues:		
Food Services revenue...	$3,800	
Teaching revenue...	300	
Total revenues..		$4,100
Operating expenses:		
Rent expense...	$1,000	
Salaries expense	700	
Total operating expenses....................................		1,700
Profit...		$2,400

Organico
Statement of Changes in Equity
For Month Ended March 31, 2020

Hailey Walker, capital, March 1..................................		$ -0-
Investments by owner...	$10,000	
Profit..	2,400	12,400
Total...		$12,400
Less: Withdrawals by owner.......................................		600
Hailey Walker, capital, March 31		$11,800

Organico
Balance Sheet
March 31, 2020

Assets		Liabilities	
Cash............................	$ 8,400	Accounts payable........................	$ 200
Supplies	3,600	Notes payable	6,000
Equipment..................	6,000	Total liabilities.............................	$ 6,200
		Equity	
		Hailey Walker, capital	11,800
Total assets	$18,000	Total liabilities and equity.........	$18,000

Note: Arrows in the exhibit are for educational purposes only.

BALANCE SHEET

The balance sheet in Exhibit 1.16 is the same statement that we described in Exhibit 1.10. Its heading tells us that the statement refers to Organico's financial position at the close of business on March 31, 2020. *Notice that the amounts appearing on the balance sheet came from the column totals summarized in Exhibit 1.15.*

The left side of the balance sheet lists Organico's assets: cash, supplies, and equipment. The right side of the balance sheet shows that Organico owes $6,200 to creditors, an amount made up of $200 for accounts payable and $6,000 for notes payable. The equity section shows an ending balance of $11,800. Note the link between the ending balance from the statement of changes in equity and the equity balance of the capital account. Also, note that the balance sheet equation, Assets = Liabilities + Equity, is still true ($18,000 = $6,200 + $11,800).

The financial statements for Organico can be useful to both internal and external users for making decisions.

DECISION MAKER

Answer—End of chapter

Extending Credit

You open a wholesale business selling entertainment equipment to retail outlets and online retailers such as **Amazon.ca**, **Best Buy Canada**, and Canadian Tire. You find that most of your customers demand to buy on credit. How can you use the balance sheets of these customers to help you decide which ones are worthy of credit?

CHECKPOINT

28. Explain the link between a profit statement and the statement of changes in equity
29. Describe the link between a balance sheet and the statement of changes in equity.

Do Quick Study questions: QS 1-15, QS 1-16, QS 1-17, QS 1-18

CRITICAL THINKING CHALLENGE

Refer to the Critical Thinking Challenge questions at the beginning of the chapter. Compare your answers to those suggested on Connect.

IFRS AND ASPE—THE DIFFERENCES

Differences	International Financial Reporting Standards (IFRS)	Accounting Standards for Private Enterprises (ASPE)
Financial statements	• Refers to the financial statements as: statement of financial position (or balance sheet), statement of income, statement of changes in equity, and statement of cash flows.*	• Refers to the financial statements as: balance sheet, income statement, statement of retained earnings (or statement of changes in equity), and cash flow statement.†
GAAP	• Publicly accountable enterprises must use IFRS.	• Private enterprises can choose between ASPE and IFRS, but once the choice is made it must be applied consistently.
	• Does not use the terms *reliability* and *conservatism*.**	• Includes conservatism as a measure of reliability.‡

*IFRS 2018, IAS 1, para. 10.
**IFRS 2018, "The conceptual framework for reporting entities," para. 4.1-4.39.
†ASPE, Accounting Standards, General Accounting, Section 1000.04 and Section 1400.10.
‡ASPE, Accounting Standards, Section 1000.18(d).

↑ Each chapter identifies the primary differences between IFRS and ASPE at the introductory level of accounting.

A Look Ahead

Chapter 2 describes and analyzes business transactions. We explain the analysis and recording of transactions, the ledger and trial balance, and the double-entry system. More generally, Chapters 2 through 4 use the accounting cycle to show how financial statements reflect business activities.

For further study on some topics of relevance to this chapter, please see the following Extend Your Knowledge supplements:

EYK 1-1 External Accounting Information Needs

EYK 1-2 Internal Operating Functions

EYK 1-3 Applying the 4-Way Test

EYK 1-4 Corporate Governance—Example

EYK 1-5 Return and Risk

EYK 1-6 Corporate Supplement

EYK 1-7 Examples of Source Documents

EYK 1-8 Case Study: Transaction Analysis Using Source Documents

SUMMARY

↓ Each chapter includes a summary of the chapter by learning objective.

LO1 Describe the purpose and importance of accounting. Accounting is an information and measurement system that aims to identify, measure, record, and communicate relevant information that faithfully represents an organization's economic activities. It helps us better assess opportunities, products, investments, and social and community responsibilities. The greatest benefits of understanding accounting often come to those outside accounting, because an improved understanding of accounting helps us to compete better in today's globally focused and technologically challenging world.

LO2 Describe forms of business organization. Organizations can be classified either as businesses or as non-businesses. Businesses are organized for profit, while non-businesses or not-for-profit organizations serve us in ways not always measured by profit. Businesses take one of three forms: sole proprietorship, partnership, or corporation. These forms of organization have characteristics that hold important implications for legal liability, taxation, continuity, number of owners, and legal status.

LO3 Identify users and uses of accounting and opportunities in accounting. There are both internal and external users of accounting. Some users and uses of accounting include (a) management for control, monitoring, and planning; (b) lenders for making decisions regarding loan applications; (c) shareholders for making investment decisions; (d) directors for overseeing management; and (e) employees for judging employment opportunities. Opportunities in accounting encompass traditional financial and managerial accounting, and taxation, but also include accounting-related fields such as lending, investing, consulting, managing, and planning.

LO4 Identify and explain why ethics and social responsibility are crucial to accounting. The goal of accounting is to provide useful information for decision making. For information to be useful, it must be trusted. This demands ethics and socially responsible behaviour in accounting. Without these, accounting information loses its reliability.

LO5 Identify, explain, and apply accounting principles. Accounting principles aid in producing relevant information that faithfully represents an organization's economic activities. The general principles described in this chapter include business entity, historical cost, going concern, currency, and revenue recognition. We will discuss others in later chapters. The **business entity principle** requires that a business be accounted for separately from its owners. The **historical cost principle** requires that financial statements be based on actual costs incurred in business transactions. The **going concern principle** requires that financial statements reflect an assumption that the business is expected continue operating for the foreseeable future. The **currency principle** assumes that transactions can be captured in money terms in the disclosed currency and that the monetary unit is stable over time. The **revenue recognition principle** assumes that revenue is recognized when earned, assets received from selling products and services do not have to be in cash, and revenue recognized is measured by cash received plus the cash equivalent (market) value of other assets received.

LO6 Identify and explain the content and reporting aims of financial statements. The major financial statements are the income statement (shows a company's profitability determined as revenues less expenses equals income or loss), statement of changes in equity (explains how equity changes from the beginning to the end of a period), balance sheet (reports on a company's financial position, including assets, liabilities, and equity), and statement of cash flows (identifies all cash inflows and outflows for the period). The differences in financial statements across forms of business organization are (1) the equity on the balance sheet belongs to the sole owner in a sole proprietorship, to the partners in a partnership, and to the shareholders in a corporation; (2) distributions of assets to the owner(s) are called withdrawals for both a sole proprietorship and a partnership, and dividends for a corporation; and (3) when the owner of a proprietorship or partnership is its manager, no salary expense is reported, while in a corporation, salaries paid to managers who are also shareholders are reported as expenses.

LO7 **Analyze business transactions by applying the accounting equation.** Investing activities are funded by an organization's financing activities. An organization's assets (investments) must equal its financing (from liabilities and from equity). This basic relation gives us the accounting equation: Assets = Liabilities + Equity. A transaction is an exchange of economic consideration between two parties and affects the accounting equation. The equation is always in balance when business transactions are properly recorded. An economic consideration is something of value; examples include products, services, money, and rights to collect money. Source documents are the source of accounting information. An event does not involve an economic exchange; it has no effect on the accounting equation.

LO8 **Prepare financial statements reflecting business transactions.** Using the accounting equation, business transactions can be summarized and organized so that we can readily prepare the financial statements. The balance sheet uses the ending balances in the accounting equation at a point in time. The statement of changes in equity and the income statement use data from the equity account for the period.

 Guidance Answer to DECISION MAKER

Extending Credit

You can use the accounting equation (Assets = Liabilities + Equity) to help identify risky customers to whom you would likely not want to extend credit. A balance sheet provides amounts for each of these key components. A low percentage of equity compared to total assets means the business has little value that does not already have creditor claims to it. The lower a customer's equity is relative to liabilities, the less likely you would be to extend credit.

 Guidance Answers to CHECKPOINT

1. Accounting is an information and measurement system that identifies, measures, records, and communicates relevant and faithfully representative information to people that helps them in making better decisions. It helps people in business to identify and react to investment opportunities, and to better assess opportunities, products, investments, and social and community responsibilities.

2. Recordkeeping is the recording of financial transactions and events, either manually or electronically. While recordkeeping is essential to ensuring data are complete, free from error, and neutral, accounting is this and much more. Accounting includes identifying, measuring, recording, reporting, and analyzing economic events and transactions. It involves interpreting information, and designing information systems to provide useful reports that monitor and control an organization's activities.

3. Non-business organizations may include public airports, libraries, museums, religious institutions, municipal governments, law enforcement organizations, postal services, colleges, universities, highways, shelters, parks, hospitals, and schools.

4. The three common forms of business organization are sole proprietorships, partnerships, and corporations.

5. Private accountants work for a single employer, which is often a business. A public accountant is available to the public, which means that services are provided to many different clients.

6. The four broad fields of accounting are financial, managerial, taxation, and general accounting.

7. The purpose of an audit is to add credibility to the financial statements.
8. Managerial accounting is for internal users, while financial accounting is for external users.
9. External users of accounting information are existing and potential investors, banks/lenders and other creditors and are not involved in internal business decisions. Internal users of accounting information are those individuals directly involved in managing and operating an organization.
10. Internal controls are procedures set up to protect assets; ensure that accounting reports are complete, free from error, and neutral; promote efficiency; and encourage adherence to company policies. Internal controls are crucial if accounting reports are to provide relevant and trustworthy information.
11. The guidelines for ethical and socially responsible decisions are threefold: (1) identify the ethical and/or social issue; (2) analyze options, considering both good and bad consequences for all individuals affected; and (3) make an ethical/socially responsible decision, choosing the best option after weighing all consequences.
12. Ethics and social responsibility are important for people because without them existence is more difficult, lacks satisfaction, and is generally unpleasant. They are equally important to organizations for the same reason. In addition, they often translate into higher profits, greater employee satisfaction, and a better working environment.
13. Accounting aims to provide useful information for decision making. For information to be useful, it must be trusted. Trustworthiness of information demands ethics in accounting.
14. The business entity principle is important to the usefulness of accounting. Users desire information about the performance of a *specific* entity. If information is mixed between two or more entities, its usefulness decreases. It is imperative that the business entity principle be followed.
15. The historical cost principle determines that financial statements are based on actual costs incurred in business transactions. Information prepared using the historical cost principle is considered verifiable because it can be confirmed and is not subject to arbitrary manipulation.
16. Revenue should be recognized next month when the product is delivered, according to the revenue recognition principle. This principle states that revenue is recognized when the product has been provided or performance of the contractual agreement has taken place. This does not necessarily relate to the point at which the cash payment has been received. In this case, the business has received the cash from the customer without providing the product. Therefore, the business has not realized revenue but instead has incurred a liability; it owes the customer the product.
17. The four major financial statements are income statement, statement of changes in equity, balance sheet, and statement of cash flows.
18. Revenues are the value of assets received in exchange for products or services provided to customers as part of a business's main operations. Expenses are costs incurred or the using up of assets that results from providing products or services to customers. Expenses also can arise from increases in liabilities.
19. Assets are the economic resources controlled by a business as a result of past events with the potential to produce economic benefits. Liabilities are a present obligation of a business, to transfer an economic resource as a result of a past event that the entity has no reasonable ability to avoid. Equity is the owner's claim on the assets of the business. It is the assets of a business that remain after deducting liabilities.
20. Three differences in financial statements for different forms of organization are (1) A proprietorship's equity belongs to one owner. A partnership's equity belongs to the partners. A corporation's equity belongs to the shareholders. (2) Distributions of cash or other assets to owners of a proprietorship or partnership are called withdrawals. Distributions of cash or other assets to owners of a corporation are called dividends. (3) When the owner of a sole proprietorship is also its manager, no salary expense is reported on the income statement. The same is true for a partnership. In a corporation, however, salaries paid to all employees, including managers who are shareholders, are reported as expenses.

21. A transaction such as (2) that involves changing the form of one asset for another asset would *not* affect any liability and equity accounts.
22. Performing services for a customer, such as in (4), increases the equity (and assets). Incurring expenses while servicing clients, such as in (5) and (6), decreases the equity (and assets). Other examples include owner investments, such as (1) those that increase equity, and owner withdrawals, such as (11) those that decrease equity.
23. Payment of a liability with an asset reduces both asset and liability totals. An example is (10), where an account payable is settled by paying cash.
24. The accounting equation is Assets = Liabilities + Equity. It is in balance when the sum of the assets is equal to the sum of the liabilities and equity accounts. This equation is always in balance, both before and after every transaction. Balance refers to the equality in this equation, which is always maintained.
25. Business transactions are exchanges between two parties and affect the accounting equation. Events do not involve an exchange and therefore do not affect the accounting equation.
26. Examples of source documents are sales invoices, cheques, purchase orders, charges to customers, bills from suppliers, employee earnings records, and bank statements.
27. Source documents serve many purposes, including recordkeeping and internal control. Source documents, especially if obtained from outside the organization, provide evidence about transactions and their amounts for recording. Evidence is important because it makes information more reliable and useful.
28. An income statement describes a company's revenues and expenses along with the resulting profit or loss. A statement of changes in equity describes changes in equity that *include* profit or loss. Also, both statements report transactions occurring over a period of time.
29. A balance sheet describes a company's financial position (assets, liabilities, and equity) at a point in time. The equity account in the balance sheet is obtained from the statement of changes in equity.

Demonstration Problem

After several months of planning, Joanne Cardinal started a haircutting business called The Cutlery. The following business activities occurred during its first month, August 2020:

a. On August 1, Cardinal put $16,000 cash into a chequing account in the name of The Cutlery. She also invested $10,000 of equipment that she already owned.

b. On August 2, she paid $2,000 cash for furniture for the shop.

c. On August 3, she paid $3,200 cash to rent space in a strip mall for August.

d. On August 4, she equipped the shop by installing the old equipment and some new equipment that she bought on credit for $21,000. This amount is to be repaid in three equal payments at the end of August, September, and October.

e. On August 5, The Cutlery opened for business. Receipts from services provided for cash in the first week and a half of business (ended August 15) were $1,100.

f. On August 15, Cardinal provided haircutting services on account for $750.

g. On August 17, Cardinal received a $750 cheque in the mail for services previously rendered on account.

h. On August 17, Cardinal paid wages of $250 to an assistant for working during the grand opening.

i. On August 18, Cardinal interviewed a job applicant. The applicant was successful in getting the position and will receive $750 per week for part-time work starting in September.

j. Cash receipts from services provided during the second half of August were $1,950.

k. On August 31, Cardinal paid an instalment on the account payable created in (d).

l. On August 31, the August hydro bill for $450 was received. It will be paid on September 14.

m. On August 31, Cardinal withdrew $500 cash for her personal use.

Required

1. Arrange the following asset, liability, and equity titles in a table similar to the one in Exhibit 1.15: Cash; Accounts Receivable; Furniture; Store Equipment; Accounts Payable; and Joanne Cardinal, Capital. Show the effects of each transaction on the equation. Explain each of the changes in equity.

2. Prepare an income statement for August.

3. Prepare a statement of changes in equity for August.

4. Prepare a balance sheet as of August 31.

Analysis Component:

a. Identify how much of the assets held by The Cutlery are owned by the owner, Joanne Cardinal.

b. How much of the total assets are financed by equity? By debt? Explain what it means to "finance assets by equity" and to "finance assets by debt."

Planning the Solution

- Set up a table with the appropriate columns, including a final column for describing the transactions that affect equity.

- Identify and analyze each transaction and show its effects as increases or decreases in the appropriate columns. Be sure that the accounting equation remains in balance after each transaction.

- To prepare the income statement, find the revenues and expenses in the Explanation of Equity Transaction column. List those items on the statement, calculate the difference, and label the result as *profit* or *loss*.

- Use the information in the Explanation of Equity Transaction column to prepare the statement of changes in equity.

- Use the information in the last row of the table to prepare the balance sheet.

- Prepare an answer to each part of the analysis component question.

SOLUTION

1.

	Assets				= Liabilities +	Equity	Explanation of Equity Transaction
	Cash	+ Accounts Receivable +	Furniture +	Store Equipment =	Accounts Payable +	Joane Cardinal, Capital	
a.	$16,000			$10,000		$26,000	Investment by Owner
b.	− 2,000		+$2,000				
Bal.	$14,000		$2,000	$10,000		$26,000	
c.	− 3,200					− 3,200	Rent Expense
Bal.	$10,800		$2,000	$10,000		$22,800	
d.				+21,000	+$21,000		
Bal.	$10,800		$2,000	$31,000	$21,000	$22,800	
e.	+ 1,100					+ 1,100	Haircutting Services Revenue
Bal.	$11,900		$2,000	$31,000	$21,000	$23,900	
f.		+ $750				+ 750	Haircutting Services Revenue
Bal.	$11,900	$750	$2,000	$31,000	$21,000	$24,650	
g.	+ 750	− 750					
Bal.	$12,650	$ -0-	$2,000	$31,000	$21,000	$24,650	
h.	− 250					− 250	Wages Expense
Bal.	$12,400		$2,000	$31,000	$21,000	$24,400	
i.	No entry*						
j.	+ 1,950					+ 1,950	Haircutting Services Revenue
Bal.	$14,350		$2,000	$31,000	$21,000	$26,350	
k.	− 7,000				− 7,000		
Bal.	$ 7,350		$2,000	$31,000	$14,000	$26,350	
l.					+ 450	− 450	Hydro Expense
Bal.	$ 7,350		$2,000	$31,000	$14,450	$25,900	
m.	− 500					− 500	Withdrawal by Owner
Bal.	$ 6,850 +	$ -0- +	$2,000 +	$31,000 =	$14,450 +	$25,400	

= $39,850   = $39,850

*Note: (i) does not involve an economic exchange between two parties; therefore, it does not affect the accounting equation.

2.

The Cutlery Income Statement For Month Ended August 31, 2020		
Revenues:		
Haircutting services revenue..		$ 3,800
Operating expenses:		
Rent expense..	$3,200	
Hydro expense...	450	
Wages expense...	250	
Total operating expenses.....................................		3,900
Loss..		$ 100

3.

The Cutlery Statement of Changes in Equity For Month Ended August 31, 2020		
Joanne Cardinal, capital, August 1..		$ –0–
Investments by owner...		26,000
Total		$26,000
Less: Withdrawals by owner..	$500	
Loss	100	600
Joanne Cardinal, capital, August 31		$25,400

4.

The Cutlery Balance Sheet August 31, 2020			
Assets		**Liabilities**	
Cash...	$ 6,850	Accounts payable....................................	$14,450
Furniture	2,000		
Store equipment..................	31,000	**Equity**	
		Joane Cardinal, capital	25,400
Total assets	$39,850	Total liabilities and equity.....................	$39,850

The arrows are imaginary but they emphasize the link between statements.

Analysis Component:

a. $25,400 or 64% ($25,400/$39,850 × 100% = 63.74% or 64%) of the total assets are owned by the owner, Joanne Cardinal.

b. $25,400 or 64% ($25,400/$39,850 × 100% = 63.74% or 64%) of the total assets are financed by equity. $14,450 or 36% ($14,450/$39,850 × 100% = 36.26% or 36%) of the total assets are financed by debt.

To *finance assets by equity* means that the equity transactions of owner investment, plus profit (or less loss) and less owner withdrawals, resulted in a portion of the assets. In the case of The Cutlery, 64% of the assets at August 31, 2020, resulted from these equity transactions.

To *finance assets by debt* (or liabilities) means that a portion of the assets resulted from borrowings. In the case of The Cutlery, 36% of the assets at August 31, 2020 resulted from, specifically, accounts payable.

GLOSSARY

↓ The glossary includes terms and phrases explained in the chapter.

Accounting An information system that identifies, measures, records, and communicates relevant information that faithfully represents an organization's economic activities.

Accounting equation A description of the relationship between a company's assets, liabilities, and equity; expressed as Assets = Liabilities + Equity.

Accounting Standards Board (AcSB) Prior to Canada's adoption of IFRS, the AcSB was the authoritative body that set accounting standards for Canada. With IFRS being set by the IASB, the AcSB's new role is evolving.

Accounting Standards for Private Enterprises (ASPE) Rules created by the Accounting Standards Board to govern accounting for Canadian private enterprises.

Account payable A liability created by buying goods or services on credit.

Accounts receivable Assets created by selling products or services on credit.

AcSB See *Accounting Standards Board*.

ASPE See *Accounting Standards for Private Enterprises*.

Assets Properties or economic resources controlled by the business; more precisely, resources with an ability to provide future economic benefits to the business, results from a past event.

Audit An independent, external check of an organization's accounting systems and records.

Balance sheet A financial statement that reports the financial position of a business at a point in time; lists the types and dollar amounts of assets, liabilities, and equity as of a specific date; also called the *statement of financial position*.

Bookkeeping The part of accounting that involves recording economic transactions electronically or manually; also called *recordkeeping*.

Budgeting The process of developing formal plans for future activities, which often serve as a basis for evaluating actual performance.

Business One or more individuals selling products or services for profit.

Business activities All of the transactions and events experienced by a business.

Business entity principle The principle that requires every business to be accounted for separately from its owner or owners. It is based on the goal of providing relevant information about each business to users.

Business events Activities that do not involve an exchange of economic consideration between two parties and therefore do not affect the accounting equation.

Business transaction An exchange of economic consideration between two parties that causes a change in assets, liabilities, or equity. Examples of economic considerations include products, services, money, and rights to collect money.

Calendar year An accounting year that begins on January 1 and ends on December 31.

Canada Revenue Agency (CRA) The federal government agency responsible for the collection of tax and enforcement of tax laws.

Common shares The name for a corporation's shares when only one class of share capital is issued.

Comparability Similarity; ability to be compared with other information.

Controller The chief accounting officer of an organization.

Corporation A business that is a separate legal entity under provincial or federal laws with owners who are called shareholders.

Cost accounting A managerial accounting activity designed to help managers identify, measure, and control operating costs.

Cost constraint The accounting standard that requires the benefits obtained from financial statement information to be justifiable based on costs incurred in financial reporting.

Costs The expenses incurred to earn revenues (or sales).

CPA Canada Chartered Professional Accountants of Canada, the newly formed accounting body with a mandate to merge the three legacy accounting designations (CA, CMA, CGA).

Creditors Individuals or organizations entitled to receive payments from a company.

Currency Transactions are to be expressed in money units based on the main currency used in operations; examples include units such as the Canadian dollar, American dollar, peso, and pound sterling.

Debtors Individuals or organizations that owe amounts to a business.

Economic consideration Something of value (e.g., products, services, money, and rights to collect money).

Equipment Tangible asset intended to be used in the business with an expected life of more than one year.

Equity The owner's claim on the assets of a business; more precisely, the assets of an entity that remain after deducting its liabilities. Equity increases with owner investments and profit and decreases with owner withdrawals and losses, also called *net assets*.

Ethics Beliefs that differentiate right from wrong.

Events See *business events*.

Expenses Decreases in assets or increases in liabilities, resulting in decreases in equity other than distributions to owners.

External auditors Accountants outside the company who examine and provide assurance that financial statements are prepared according to generally accepted accounting principles (GAAP).

External users Existing and potential investors, banks/lenders, and other creditors that rely on financial reports to make decisions. They are not directly involved in the running of the organization.

Faithful representation A quality of information that is complete, neutral (neither allows overstatement or understatement of assets, liabilities, income or expenses), and is free from error.

Financial accounting The area of accounting that reports on the financial performance and condition of an organization. It is aimed at serving external users.

Financial statements The products of accounting that report on the financial performance and condition of an organization. They include the income statement, statement of changes in equity, balance sheet, and statement of cash flows.

Fiscal year A one-year (12-month) reporting period.

GAAP See *generally accepted accounting principles*.

General accounting The task of recording transactions, processing data, and preparing reports for managers; includes preparing financial statements for disclosure to external users.

Generally accepted accounting principles (GAAP) The underlying concepts adopted by the accounting profession that make up acceptable accounting practices for the preparation of financial statements.

Going concern assumption The rule that requires financial statements to reflect the assumption that the business will continue operating instead of being closed or sold, unless evidence shows that it will not continue.

IASB See *International Accounting Standards Board*.

IFRS See *International Financial Reporting Standards*.

Income Another name for *profit*.

Income statement The financial statement that shows, by subtracting expenses from revenues, whether the business earned a profit; it lists the types and amounts of revenues earned and expenses incurred by a business over a period of time. Also known as the statement of profit or loss.

Internal auditing Function performed by employees within organizations who assess whether managers are following established operating procedures and evaluates the efficiency of operating procedures.

Internal controls Procedures set up to protect assets, ensure reliable accounting reports, promote efficiency, and encourage adherence to company policies.

Internal users Persons using accounting information who are directly involved in managing and operating an organization; examples include managers and officers.

International Accounting Standards Board (IASB) The body responsible for setting IFRS.

International Financial Reporting Standards (IFRS) The standards for financial reporting in Canada for all publicly accountable entities.

Liabilities The present obligations of a business that require future economic resources, resulting from a past transaction that the entity has no practical ability to avoid.

Limited liability The owner's liability is limited to the amount of investment in the business.

Loss The excess of expenses over revenues for a period.

Management consulting Activity in which suggestions are offered for improving a company's procedures; the suggestions may concern new accounting and internal control systems, new computer systems, budgeting, and employee benefit plans.

Managerial accounting The area of accounting aimed at serving the decision-making needs of internal users.

Natural business year A 12-month period that ends when a company's sales activities are at their lowest point.

Net assets Assets minus liabilities; another name for *equity*.

Note payable A liability expressed by a written promise to make a future payment at a specific time.

Owner investments The transfer of an owner's personal assets to the business.

Owner withdrawals See *withdrawals*.

Partnership A business owned by two or more people that is not organized as a corporation.

Private accountants Accountants who work for a single employer other than the government or a public accounting firm.

Private enterprise (PE) A corporation that does not offer its shares for public sale.

Profit The excess of revenues over expenses for a period; also called *income*.

Public accountants Accountants licensed and regulated by their professional accounting bodies in the provinces in which they work. They provide professional services such as audit, tax, and consulting to many different clients.

Publicly accountable enterprise (PAE) A corporation that sells its shares to the public.

Public sale of shares The issuance of shares by a corporation in an organized stock exchange.

Recordkeeping The recording of financial transactions manually or electronically; also called *bookkeeping*.

Relevance Information must make a difference in the decision-making process.

Revenue recognition principle Provides guidance on when revenue should be reflected on the income statement; the rule states that revenue is recorded at the time it is earned regardless of whether cash or another asset has been exchanged.

Revenues The value of assets received or receivable as a result of selling goods or services to customers.

Shareholders The owners of a corporation; also known as *stockholders*.

Shares Units of ownership in a corporation; also known as *stocks*.

Social responsibility A commitment by an organization to consider the impact and being accountable for the effects that actions might have on society.

Sole proprietorship A business owned by one person that is not organized as a corporation; also called a *single proprietorship*.

Source documents Original documents that identify and describe transactions within the organization. These documents provide information to be recorded in the accounting information system and can be in paper or electronic form. An example of a source document is an invoice used to record a sale of merchandise to a customer.

Statement of cash flows A financial statement that describes the sources and uses of cash for a reporting period, i.e., where a company's cash came from (receipts) and where it went during the period (payments); the cash flows are arranged by an organization's major activities: operating, investing, and financing activities.

Statement of changes in equity A financial statement that reports the changes in equity over the reporting period; beginning equity is adjusted for increases such as owner investment or profit and for decreases such as owner withdrawals or a loss.

Statement of financial position See *balance sheet*.

Supplies Consumable items that are purchased by the business to carry out its recurring activities. Examples include stationary, printer ink, flour used by a bakery, milk/coffee beans purchased by a café, nails purchased by a carpenter. Classified as a current asset. Consumed supplies become supplies expense.

Taxation The field of accounting that includes preparing tax returns and planning future transactions to minimize the amount of tax paid; involves private, public, and government accountants.

Timeliness A characteristic of accounting information that ensures it is available to decision makers in time to influence their decisions.

Transaction See *business transaction*.

Understandability A quality of information that is useful to users with reasonable knowledge of accounting and business and economic activities.

Unlimited liability When the debts of a sole proprietorship or partnership are greater than its resources, the owner(s) is (are) financially responsible.

Verifiability A quality of information that different knowledgeable users could agree was faithfully represented.

Withdrawals The distributions of cash or other assets from a proprietorship or partnership to its owner or owners.

KNOWLEDGE CHECK-UP

↓ Knowledge Check-Up questions are ten single-topic, multiple-choice questions designed to assess initial comprehension of the key chapter learning objectives. Answers to the Knowledge Check-Up (KCU) questions are available on Connect.

1. The form of business organization that enables limited owner liability is:
    a. Sole proprietorship
    b. Partnership
    c. Business entity
    d. Corporation

2. Accounting involves designing:
    a. Information systems to provide useful reports to monitor and control an organization's activities
    b. An efficient warehouse to enable free flow of goods
    c. An effective transportation system to deliver products efficiently to customers
    d. Marketing programs to help manage customer demands and anticipate future inventory requirements

3. The professional association CPA Canada requires its members to maintain a commitment to:
    a. Environmental sustainability reporting
    b. Ethical decision making to benefit the largest number of stakeholders

    c. Human resource programs that provide gender neutral equal opportunities and pay
    d. Providing mentor opportunities for new accountants to develop skills and experience

4. Ethics is defined as:
    a. Compliance requirements that can be established by the local government or trade association
    b. Beliefs based on our value system that enable us to differentiate right from wrong
    c. Functions performed by auditors employed within the organization with the purpose of evaluating the efficiency of procedures
    d. Opportunities to give back to society through engaging in volunteer activities

5. Examples of ethical issues in the world of business include:
    a. Properly labelling products for customers to make informed decisions
    b. Selling products to customers at the lowest price possible

c. Providing a guarantee to customers that products will last for a specified amount of time

d. Building products with high-quality components to ensure durability

6. Social responsibility is defined as:

a. Decisions made to maximize the health and well being of children

b. Engaging in a commitment to minimize waste

c. A concern for the impact of our actions on society as a whole

d. Ensuring the costs incurred in reporting financial statement information must not outweigh the benefits received from the value of the reported information to external users

7. The business entity principle requires that:

a. All businesses must define their scope and establish a corporate vision

b. Financial statement users can safely assume the statements reflect a business that is going to continue its operations at least 12 months into the future

c. Information presented by a business must be comparable, verifiable, timely, and understandable

d. Each separate economic entity or business of the owner must keep accounting records apart from those of the owner and any company owned by the owner

8. The revenue recognition principle requires that:

a. Revenue is recorded at the time it is earned

b. Revenue is recorded in the currency in which the company primarily operates

c. Different knowledgeable individuals would reach consensus that the number represented in the financial statements is reasonable

d. Revenue is reported at the amount of cash it would cost to purchase the asset today

9. The three key methods to determine the dollar value to record a transaction at its current value accounting records are:

a. Current cost, fair value, value in use

b. Historical cost, future cost, realizable value

c. Present cost, future value, present value

d. Historical cost, current cost, realizable value

10. Another acceptable term for the income statement is:

a. Statement of Cash Flows

b. Statement of Financial Position

c. Statement of Earnings

d. Statement of Changes in Equity

CONCEPT REVIEW QUESTIONS

↓ Short-answer questions reinforce key chapter concepts in order of learning objectives.

1. The chapter's opening vignette describes Zane Caplansky's success with his food truck, Thunderin' Thelma. Explain why accounting is critical for Caplansky's business and for his expansion strategy.

2. Think about the businesses that you encounter in your everyday life. Identify three real product-based businesses and specify the product that each provides. Name three real service-based businesses and specify the service that each provides.

3. Your friends are studying marketing and human resources and another is undecided on his major. They say, "This accounting course is a waste of my time when I don't even want to be an accountant!" Explain to your friends how accounting is important and relevant to all students, including those studying marketing and human resources.

4. You have decided to start a business. What will you sell? Identify the three forms of business organization you could choose and describe their characteristics. Which form of business is best for your business and why?

5. Review Organico's financial statements presented in the chapter for the month ended March 31, 2020. Review the balance sheet and determine the business form Hailey Walker has chosen to organize her business.

6. Identify two organizations for which accounting information is available in Appendix III at the end of the book.

7. Identify three types of organizations that can be formed as either profit-oriented businesses, government entities, or not-for-profit organizations.

8. Identify four external and internal users and their uses of accounting information.

9. Describe the internal role of accounting for organizations.

10. Tyler is considering a career in accounting, but is not sure what career options are available. Help Tyler with his decision by identifying three main areas of accounting for accounting professionals. For each accounting area, identify three accounting-related career opportunities.

11. Identify the auditing firm that audited the financial statements of WestJet in Appendix III.

12. What is the purpose of accounting in society?

13. What ethical issues might accounting professionals face in dealing with confidential information?

14. Why does the user of an income statement need to know the time period that it covers?

15. Why is the revenue recognition principle needed? What does it require?

16. Identify four financial statements that a proprietorship presents to its owner and other users.

17. Jordan thinks the income statement and the balance sheet look the same. Explain to Jordan what information is presented on the income statement and what is presented on the balance sheet.

18. Assets are resources that the organization has control over that provide future benefit to a business as a result of a past transaction. Explain how cash, accounts receivable, and supplies provide future benefit to a business.

19. Rachel believes that the terms *accounts receivable* and *accounts payable* can be used interchangeably. Rachel says,

"They both show up on the balance sheet and they both are in the accounting equation." Do you agree with Rachel? Explain.

20. In the first year of selling frozen yogurt, the owner of Swirl invested $10,000 into the business and sold $5,000 of frozen yogurt. The accountant has recorded $15,000 of revenue. What do accountants mean by the term *revenue*? Has the accountant at Swirl recorded revenue correctly or incorrectly? Explain.

21. What transactions increase and decrease equity?

22. Your favourite celebrity has asked you to prepare a personal balance sheet for her. Define (a) assets, (b) liabilities, and (c) equity. Identify some of her personal assets and liabilities. Explain to her what her equity represents.

23. Why is it important to prepare the financial statements (statement of changes in equity, balance sheet, income statement, and statement of cash flows) in a specific order? Identify the specific order. Identify how the financial statements are interrelated.

QUICK STUDY

↓ Quick Study questions are single-topic exercises that give the reader a brief test of each key element in the chapter. Answers to the Quick Study (QS) questions are available on Connect.

↓ Each Quick Study, Exercise, and Problem is referenced to a learning objective in the chapter.

QS 1-1 Uses of accounting LO1

You have just graduated from the finance program at a local post-secondary institution. An opportunity to become the marketing manager for a medium-sized florist chain is available to you. You are concerned because you know that accounting plays a major role in the successful execution of this role and accounting was not your best subject. Identify at least two questions or issues for which the marketing manager would require accounting information.

QS 1-2 Determining when to record accounting transactions LO1

Determine whether each of the following events should be recorded in the accounting records.

a. Meeting with the mechanical staff to determine new machine requirements for next year.

b. Receiving the company's utility bill detailing usage for the past month.

c. Analyzing last year's sales report to determine if the discount policy is effective in getting customers to buy in multiple quantities.

d. Downloading the online bank statements and identifying customer payments.

e. Interviewing and then hiring an employee for an accounting position.

QS 1-3 Business vs. non-business organizations LO2

Identify whether each of the following represents a business or non-business organization.

Hint: Enhance your research skills and check the Internet to confirm your answers.

a. Highlands United Church   **d.** University of Toronto

b. Royal Alexandra Hospital   **e.** Loblaw Companies Limited

c. Toronto-Dominion Bank   **f.** World Vision

QS 1-4 Financial statements and forms of organization LO2

SP – Sole proprietorship

P – Partnership

C – Corporation

Identify the type of business organization based on the following independent financial statement findings:

_____ **1.** The equity section of the balance sheet has one capital account.

_____ **2.** The owners receive dividends, a distribution of earnings, in the form of cash.

_____ **3.** There are two capital accounts: Tara Davis, Capital, and Sheila Kelton, Capital.

_____ **4.** The one owner receives distributions of earnings in the form of withdrawals.

_____ **5.** A manager, also the owner of the business, is paid a salary that is recorded as an expense.

_____ **6.** The equity on the balance sheet is held by shareholders.

_____ **7.** The five owners receive distributions of earnings in the form of withdrawals.

QS 1-5 Describing accounting responsibilities LO3

Many accounting professionals work in one of the following three areas:

a. Financial accounting

b. Managerial accounting

c. Taxation accounting

For each of the following responsibilities, identify the area of accounting that most likely involves that responsibility:

_____ **1.** Auditing financial statements

_____ **2.** Planning transactions to minimize taxes paid

_____ **3.** Cost accounting

_____ **4.** Preparing financial statements

_____ **5.** Reviewing financial reports for compliance with provincial securities commissions requirements

_____ **6.** Budgeting

_____ **7.** Internal auditing

_____ **8.** Investigating violations of tax laws

QS 1-6 Ethics in Accounting: Applying the Chartered Professional Accountants of Ontario's Rules of Professional Conduct—Approach to Ethical Conflict Resolution LO4

You are a student taking an introductory accounting course. During week two of the course, your girlfriend broke up with you. You missed the lecture on debits and credits and were lost in week three. You did not pass your midterms and desperately need to pass the final. During the final, you go to the bathroom where you take a look at the accounting notes you "threw away" in the garbage. You remember your professor's speech on academic dishonesty. You have always valued honesty, but this situation is your ex-girlfriend's fault. Using Ontario's Rules of Professional Conduct, determine whether your behaviour is ethical.

QS 1-7 Identifying accounting principles LO5

Identify which GAAP most directly describes each of the following correct practices:

_____ 1. Tracy Regis owns two businesses, Second Time Around Clothing and Antique Accents, both of which are sole proprietorships. In having financial statements prepared for the antique store, Regis should be sure that the revenue and expense transactions of Second Time Around are excluded from the statements of Antique Accents.

_____ 2. In December 2019, Classic Coverings received a customer's order to install carpet and tile in a new house that would not be ready for completion until March 2020. Classic Coverings should record the revenue for the order in March 2020, not in December 2019.

_____ 3. If $30,000 cash is paid to buy land, the land should be reported on the purchaser's balance sheet at $30,000 although the purchaser was offered $35,000 the following week.

QS 1-8 Identifying accounting principles LO5

For each of the following, identify which GAAP, if any, has been violated.

_____ 1. A customer called and made arrangements for Jay's Plumbing to provide $6,000 of services _next month_. Jay, the owner, recorded revenue of $6,000 _this month_. No cash was exchanged.

_____ 2. Land was purchased for $50,000. The bank appraised it for loan purposes at $68,000. Therefore, the owner of the land recorded it on the balance sheet at $68,000.

_____ 3. The owner of Dallas Pizza and Don's Deli combines all transactions by keeping only one set of accounting records for both businesses.

_____ 4. The owner of Miko Japanese Eatery has become ill suddenly and is unable to continue the business. The owner's spouse, in need of cash to finance growing personal expenses, took the business's most recent financial statements to the bank and was granted a loan. She did not inform the bank of her husband's inability to work.

_____ 5. Dale's Consulting Services completed a contract with an organization located overseas. Dale included the revenue on the income statement without converting the foreign currency to Canadian dollars.

QS 1-9 Identifying accounting principles LO5

For each of the following, identify which GAAP was violated by Delco Consulting. In cases where more than one GAAP applies, name the primary GAAP that was not followed.

_____ 1. Delco performed work for a client located in China and collected 8,450,000 RMB (renminbi, the Chinese currency), the equivalent of about $1,320,000 Canadian. Delco recorded it as 8,450,000.

_____ 2. Delco collected $180,000 from a customer on December 20, 2020, for work to be done in February 2021. The $180,000 was recorded as revenue during 2020. Delco's year-end is December 31.

_____ 3. Delco's December 31, 2020, balance sheet showed total assets of $840,000 and liabilities of $1,120,000. The income statements for the past six years have shown a trend of increasing losses.

_____ 4. Included in Delco's assets was land and a building purchased for $310,000 and reported on the balance sheet at $470,000.

_____ 5. Delco's owner, Tom Del, consistently buys personal supplies and charges them to the company.

QS 1-10 Applying the accounting equation LO7

Determine the missing amount for each of the following equations:

	Assets	=	Liabilities	+	Equity
a.	$ 75,000		$ 40,500		?
b.	$300,000		?		$85,500
c.	?		$187,500		$95,400

QS 1-11 Applying the accounting equation LO7

Use the accounting equation to determine:

a. The equity in a business that has $374,700 of assets and $252,450 of liabilities.

b. The liabilities of a business having $150,900 of assets and $126,000 of equity.

c. The assets of a business having $37,650 of liabilities and $112,500 of equity.

QS 1-12 Applying the accounting equation LO7

The balance sheet is a more detailed presentation of the accounting equation. The income statement and statement of changes in equity are linked to the balance sheet (by the accounting equation). Calculate the missing amounts below.

a.

All-In Servicing Income Statement For Month Ended April 30, 2020	
Revenues...	$300
Expenses	?
Profit (loss)...	?

All-In Servicing Statement of Changes in Equity For Month Ended April 30, 2020		
Tim Allin, capital, April 1		$ 50
Investments by owner	$30	
Profit	?	?
Total..		$255
Less: Withdrawals by owner.............		?
Tim Allin, capital, April 30		?

All-In Servicing Balance Sheet April 30, 2020			
Assets		**Liabilities**	
Cash......................	$ 60	Accounts payable	$ 25
Equipment...........	?	**Equity**	
		Tim Allin, capital	?
		Total liabilities	
Total assets	$265	and equity.............	?

b.

All-In Servicing Income Statement For Month Ended May 31, 2020	
Revenues...	?
Expenses	$ 85
Profit (loss)...	?

All-In Servicing Statement of Changes in Equity For Month Ended May 31, 2020		
Tim Allin, capital, May 1		?
Investments by owner	$ 60	
Profit	?	$110
Total..		?
Less: Withdrawals by owner.............		75
Tim Allin, capital, May 31		?

All-In Servicing Balance Sheet May 31, 2020			
Assets		**Liabilities**	
Cash......................	$120	Accounts payable	$ 45
Equipment...........	?	**Equity**	
		Tim Allin, capital	?
		Total liabilities	
Total assets	?	and equity.............	?

QS 1-13 Applying the accounting equation LO7

Using the accounting equation provided, calculate:

1. Beginning capital on January 1, 2020, and
2. Ending capital at December 31, 2020.

Assets	=	Liabilities	+	Equity	
$20,000		$15,000		?	Beginning capital on January 1, 2020
				+3,000	Plus owner investments during the year
				+8,000	Plus profit earned during the year
				−4,000	Less owner withdrawals during the year
				?	Equals ending capital on December 31, 2020

Hint: Review Part B of the Mid-Chapter Demonstration Problem before trying this question.

QS 1-14 Transaction analysis LO7

For each transaction described, identify which component of the accounting equation increases and/or decreases. The first one is done as an example.

Example: Services were performed for a client on credit.

a. A credit customer paid his account.

b. Supplies were purchased on credit.

c. The balance owing regarding the supplies purchased in part (b) was paid.

d. Last month's telephone bill was received today. It will be paid on the due date, which is 10 days from now.

e. Paid the employees their weekly wage.

Assets	=	Liabilities	+	Equity
Example: Increase				*Increases*
a.				
b.				
c.				
d.				
e.				

QS 1-15 Identifying financial statement items LO5, 8

Tim Roadster began Roadster Servicing on April 1, 2020, and showed the following items after the first month of operations. Match each of these items with the financial statement or statements on which it should be presented. Indicate your answer by writing the letter or letters for the correct statement(s) in the blank space next to each item.

a. Income statement   b. Statement of changes in equity   c. Balance sheet

_____	1. Supplies	$10	_____	8. Utilities expense	$10
_____	2. Supplies expense	22	_____	9. Furniture	20
_____	3. Accounts receivable	25	_____	10. Revenue	70
_____	4. Accounts payable	12	_____	11. Rent revenue	35
_____	5. Equipment	40	_____	12. Salaries expense	45
_____	6. Tim Roadster's withdrawals in April	35	_____	13. Tim Roadster's investments in April	60
_____	7. Notes payable	30	_____	14. Profit	?

QS 1-16 Calculating financial statement elements LO5, 8

Using the information provided in QS 1-15, calculate each of the following financial statement elements.

1. Total revenues
2. Total operating expenses
3. Profit
4. Total assets

5. Total liabilities
6. Tim Roadster, capital (April 30, 2020)
7. Total liabilities and equity

QS 1-17 Balance sheet LO5, 8

Paul Sangha began Sangha Consulting on May 1, 2020 and reported the items below at May 31, 2020. Match each numbered item with the part of the balance sheet on which it should be presented. If the item does not appear on the balance sheet, choose (d) and identify on which financial statement(s) the item would appear.

a. Asset   b. Liability   c. Equity   d. Does not appear on the balance sheet

_____	1. Loss	$?	_____	8. Repair supplies	$ 5
_____	2. Rent expense	22	_____	9. Notes payable	25
_____	3. Rent payable	6	_____	10. Paul Sangha's withdrawals in May	5
_____	4. Accounts receivable	14	_____	11. Truck	15
_____	5. Paul Sangha's investments in May	30	_____	12. Consulting revenue	18
_____	6. Interest income	2	_____	13. Paul Sangha, capital, May 31, 2020	?
_____	7. Paul Sangha, capital, May 1, 2020	0	_____	14. Cash	20

QS 1-18 Calculating financial statement elements LO5, 8

Using the information in QS 1-17, prepare an income statement and statement of changes in equity for the month ended May 31, 2020, and a balance sheet at May 31, 2020.

EXERCISES

↓ Exercises provide you with an additional opportunity to reinforce basic chapter concepts.

Exercise 1-1 Distinguishing business organizations LO2

Presented below are descriptions of several different business organizations. Determine whether the situation described refers to a sole proprietorship, partnership, or corporation.

a. Ownership of Cola Corp. is divided into 1,000 shares.

b. Text Tech is owned by Kimberly Fisher, who is personally liable for the debts of the business.

c. Jerry Forrentes and Susan Montgomery own Financial Services, a financial and personal services provider. Neither Forrentes nor Montgomery has personal responsibility for the debts of Financial Services.

d. Nancy Kerr and Frank Levens own Runners, a courier service. Both Kerr and Levens are personally liable for the debts of the business.

e. MRS Consulting Services does not have a separate legal existence apart from the one person who owns it.

f. Biotech Company has one owner and does not pay income taxes.

g. Torby Technologies has two owners and pays its own income taxes.

Exercise 1-2 Users of accounting information LO3

You are working part-time at Starbucks while you are taking an introductory accounting course. You have learned that accounting information is useful to many users. Identify four external and four internal users for Starbucks' financial information. For each user, describe what decisions accounting information can help them make specific to Starbucks.

Exercise 1-3 Accounting and accounting-related opportunities LO3

You have decided to pursue a career in accounting. However, you do not know what area of accounting you want to focus on. Based on your readings and performing some additional research online (job postings, accounting firm websites, and other resources), describe what you think a typical day would be like for (1) an external auditor, (2) a controller, and (3) a tax specialist.

Exercise 1-4 Applying the Chartered Professional Accountants of Ontario's Rules of Professional Conduct—Approach to Ethical Conflict Resolution LO4

Required For each situation described below, apply the Chartered Professional Accountants of Ontario's Rules of Professional Conduct—Approach to Ethical Conflict Resolution as identified earlier in the chapter to determine whether the behaviour is ethical or not.

a. In performing your job, you and a colleague often need to use your cell phones to make long distance calls to suppliers. Your employer allows you to submit business calls for reimbursement. Your colleague has mentioned that he likes the perk of getting the company to pay for a few of his personal long distance calls.

b. You and a friend go to the movie theatre and purchase tickets. As you and your friend approach the ticket-taker, you both notice that the three people ahead of you have no tickets. The group and the ticket-taker, who appear to know each other, have a brief conversation and the group is admitted without having purchased tickets.

c. To use the facilities at the local fitness centre, clients can pay a $5 drop-in fee each visit or they can purchase an annual pass for unlimited access. The cashier collects the $5 from drop-in clients and provides them with a cash register receipt only if they ask.

Exercise 1-5 Accounting principles LO5

Match each of these numbered descriptions with the term it best describes. Indicate your answer by writing the letter for the correct principle/standard in the blank space next to each description.

a. Historical cost accounting standard   **c.** Revenue recognition principle

b. Business entity principle   **d.** Going concern assumption

_____ **1.** Requires every business to be accounted for separately from its owner or owners.

_____ **2.** Requires financial statement information to be based on costs incurred in transactions.

_____ **3.** Requires financial statements to reflect the assumption that the business will continue operating instead of being closed or sold.

_____ **4.** Requires revenue to be recorded only when the earnings process is complete.

Exercise 1-6 Classifying accounts LO6

Kate is having a difficult time differentiating all of the account names. "My head is spinning when all the accounts sound the same to me! Does unearned revenue belong on the income statement or the balance sheet?" Create a study sheet by categorizing all of the following accounts into a table with the following headings. Some accounts may be used more than once.

Accounts Payable	Prepaid Rent	Supplies	Equipment
Accounts Receivable	Vehicle Expenses	Wages Expense	Maintenance Expense
Advertising Expense	Furniture	Fuel Expense	Land
Insurance Expense	Salaries Expense	Notes Payable	Unearned Revenue
Owner's Capital, Ending Balance	Service Revenue	Merchandise Inventory	Rent Revenue
Interest Payable	Other Expenses	Utilities Expense	Supplies Expense
Prepaid Expenses	Interest Income	Vehicles	Interest Receivable
Interest Expense	Cash	Salaries Payable	Rent Expense
Withdrawals	Telephone Expense	Building	
Owner's Capital, Beginning Balance	Investment by Owner	Profit/Loss	

Balance Sheet			Income Statement		Statement of Changes in Equity
Assets	Liabilities	Owner's Equity	Revenues	Expenses	

Exercise 1-7 Determining profit LO6

CHECK FIGURE: d. $24,000 net loss

Profit (loss), owner withdrawals, and owner investment cause equity to change. We also know that revenues less expenses equals profit (loss). Using the following information, calculate profit (loss) for each independent situation.

a. The business earned revenues of $540,000 and had expenses of $504,000.

b. The business showed expenses of $300,000 and revenues of $177,000.

c. The equity at the beginning of the month was $44,000. During the month, the owner made no investments or withdrawals. At the end of the month, equity totalled $110,000.

d. The equity at the beginning of the month was $60,000. During the month, the owner made an investment of $52,000 but made no withdrawals. Equity at the end of the month totalled $88,000.

Exercise 1-8 Missing information LO6 eXcel

This symbol means that an Excel template is available on Connect to help you solve this question. ↑

CHECK FIGURE: e. $102,000

Referring to Exhibit 1.9, calculate the amount of the missing item in each of the following independent cases:

	a	b	c	d	e
Equity, January 1	$ -0-	$ -0-	$ -0-	$ -0-	$?
Owner's investments during the year.................	60,000	?	31,500	37,500	140,000
Profit (loss) for the year...........................	15,750	30,500	(4,500)	?	(8,000)
Owner's withdrawals during the year	?	(27,000)	(20,000)	(15,750)	(63,000)
Equity, December 31................................	56,000	49,500	?	32,000	171,000

Exercise 1-9 Income statement LO6

CHECK FIGURE: Profit = $11,110

On November 1, 2020, Jean Higgins started a wedding planning company, Extraordinary Studios. On November 30, 2020, the company's records showed the following items. Use this information to prepare a November income statement for the business, similar to Exhibit 1.8.

Cash	$16,000	Owner's withdrawals	$ 3,360
Accounts receivable	17,000	Wedding consulting revenue	22,000
Office supplies	5,000	Rent expense	2,550
Automobiles	36,000	Salaries expense	6,000
Office equipment	25,250	Telephone expense	1,680
Accounts payable	7,500	Utilities expenses	660
Owner's investments	84,000		

Exercise 1-10 Statement of changes in equity LO6

CHECK FIGURE: Jean Higgins, Capital, November 30 = $91,750

Use the facts in Exercise 1-9 to prepare a November statement of changes in equity for Extraordinary Studios, similar to Exhibit 1.9.

Analysis Component: What activities caused equity to increase during the month of November 2020?

Exercise 1-11 Balance sheet LO6

CHECK FIGURE: Total assets = $99,250

Use the facts in Exercise 1-9 to prepare a November 30 balance sheet for Extraordinary Studios, similar to Exhibit 1.10.

Analysis Component: Identify how much of the assets held by Extraordinary Studios are financed by the owner, Jean Higgins.

Exercise 1-12 Income statement LO6

CHECK FIGURE: Loss = $420

On July 1, 2020, Academic Learning Services entered its second month of operations. On July 31, 2020, Breanne Allarie, the owner, finalized the company's records that showed the following items. Use this information to prepare a July income statement similar to Exhibit 1.8.

Accounts payable	$2,500	Owner's investments during July 2020	$3,200
Accounts receivable	4,000	Owner's withdrawals	3,000
Cash	3,600	Supplies	2,080
Computer equipment	4,200	Textbook rental revenue	500
Furniture	3,800	Tutoring revenue	6,200
Breanne Allarie, capital, June 30, 2020*	15,400	Tutors' wages expense	1,740
Office rent expense	4,500	Utilities expense	880

Hint: The ending capital balance for one period is the beginning capital balance for the next period.

Exercise 1-13 Statement of changes in equity LO6

CHECK FIGURE: Breanne Allarie, Capital, July 31 = $15,180

Use the facts in Exercise 1-12 to prepare a July statement of changes in equity for Academic Learning Services, similar to Exhibit 1.9.

Analysis Component: Identify those activities that caused equity to decrease during July 2020.

Exercise 1-14 Balance sheet LO6

CHECK FIGURE: Total assets = $17,680

Use the facts in Exercise 1-12 to prepare a July 31 balance sheet for Academic Learning Services, similar to Exhibit 1.10.

Analysis Component: Identify how much of the assets held by Academic Learning Services are financed by debt.

Exercise 1-15 Determining profit LO6, 7

CHECK FIGURE: b. $86,000 profit

A business had the following amounts of assets and liabilities at the beginning and end of a recent year:

	Assets	Liabilities
Beginning of the year...	$ 75,000	$30,000
End of the year..	$120,000	$46,000

Determine the profit earned or loss incurred by the business during the year under each of the following unrelated assumptions:

a. The owner made no additional investments in the business and withdrew no assets during the year.

b. The owner made no additional investments in the business during the year but withdrew $4,750 *per month* to pay personal living expenses.

c. The owner withdrew no assets during the year but invested an additional $80,000 cash.

d. The owner withdrew $3,500 *per month* to pay personal living expenses and invested an additional $75,000 cash in the business.

Hint: Review the Mid-Chapter Demonstration Problem before trying this question.

Exercise 1-16 Accounting equation LO7

CHECK FIGURE: b. Equity Aug. 31, 2020 = $6,000

In the following table, the accounting equation is applied to Business A:

	Assets	=	Liabilities	+	Equity
At August 1, 2020.............................	?		$10,000		?
At August 31, 2020...........................	$25,000		?		?

Calculate the missing amounts assuming that:

a. Assets decreased by $15,000 during August, and

b. Liabilities increased by $9,000 during August.

Exercise 1-17 Effects of transactions on the accounting equation LO5, 7 eXcel

CHECK FIGURE: Total assets = $41,450

Digital Protection Servicing provides support to customers in the area of ecommerce. Using the format provided, show the effects of the activities listed in (a) through (f).

a. Katie Copp, the owner, invested cash of $36,000 into the business.

b. The owner purchased office supplies on credit; $1,150.

c. Digital Protection Servicing did work for a client and received $8,100 cash.

d. Completed an application form for a $15,500 government grant.

e. The owner paid her assistant's salary; $5,600 cash.

f. Completed work for a customer on credit; $1,800.

Exercise 1-18 Effects of transactions on the accounting equation LO6, 7 eXcel

CHECK FIGURE: Total assets = $30,600

DigiCom repairs laptops. Using the format provided below, show the effects of the activities listed in (a) through (i).

a. Stacey Comeau, owner of DigiCom, invested cash of $29,000 into her business.

b. DigiCom paid $4,000 to cover rent for the current month.

c. DigiCom purchased supplies on credit; $1,550.

d. DigiCom completed work for a client on credit; $4,900.

e. DigiCom purchased a new piece of equipment by paying cash of $2,700.

f. DigiCom hired a technician, to start next month, who will get paid $6,500 per month.

g. DigiCom paid for the supplies purchased in (c).

h. DigiCom performed work for a client and received cash of $4,900.

i. DigiCom paid the administrative assistant's salary of $4,200.

Exercise 1-19 Analyzing the accounting equation LO6, 7

Elena Bellisario began a new consulting firm on January 3. The accounting equation showed the following transactions. Analyze the equation and describe each of the transactions with their amounts. Transaction (a) has been done as an example for you.

Transaction	Assets Cash	+	Accounts Receivable	+	Office Supplies	+	Office Furniture	=	Liabilities Accounts Payable	+	Equity Elena Bellisario, Capital
Beginning Balances	-0-		-0-		-0-		-0-		-0-		-0-
a.	+15,000										+15,000
b.	− 500				+500						
c.	− 8,000						+8,000				
d.			+1,000								+ 1,000
e.					+400				+400		
f.	− 250								−250		
g.	+ 750		− 750								
Totals	7,000		250		900		8,000		150		16,000

Description of transaction (a):

a. *The owner invested $15,000 cash into the business.*

Exercise 1-20 Effects of transactions on the accounting equation LO6, 7 eXcel

CHECK FIGURE: Mailin Moon, Capital = $13,650

Mailin Moon is a freelance writer who submits articles to various magazines and newspapers. She operates out of a small office where she employs one administrative assistant. The following activities occurred during March 2020, her first month of business:

a. Moon invested $2,500 worth of equipment into her business along with $3,000 cash.

b. Submitted a series of articles to *The Globe and Mail* and received $6,500 cash.

c. Purchased supplies on credit; $600.

d. Paid the part-time administrative assistant's salary of $1,450.

e. Moon ordered $3,000 of office equipment from the IKEA catalogue. It is scheduled to arrive in April or May.

f. Paid the rent for the first month; $1,400.

g. Submitted an article to *Report on Business*; will receive $4,500 next month.

Using the format provided below, show the effects of the activities listed in (a) through (g). For each transaction that affects equity, include a brief description beside it (owner investment, owner withdrawal, revenue, rent expense, and salaries expense).

Assets Cash	+	Accounts Receivable	+	Supplies	+	Equipment	=	Liabilities Accounts Payable	+	Equity Mailin Moon, Capital	Explanation of Equity Transaction

Exercise 1-21 Financial statements LO8 eXcel

CHECK FIGURES: Profit = $8,150; Total assets = $14,250

Using your answer from Exercise 1-20, prepare an income statement, a statement of changes in equity, and a balance sheet using the formats provided.

Mailin Moon—Freelance Writing
Income Statement
For Month Ended March 31, 2020

Revenues:
  Freelance writing revenue...
Operating expenses:
  Salaries expense...
  Rent expense...   ————
    Total operating expenses..   ————
Profit...   ════

Mailin Moon—Freelance Writing
Statement of Changes in Equity
For Month Ended March 31, 2020

Mailin Moon, capital, March 1 ....
  Investments by owner ....
  Profit...   ————
Mailin Moon, capital, March 31...   ════

Mailin Moon—Freelance Writing
Balance Sheet
March 31, 2020

Assets		Liabilities	
Cash..............................		Accounts payable............................	
Accounts receivable......................			
Supplies		**Equity**	
Equipment		Mailin Moon, capital..........................	
Total assets	————	Total liabilities and equity...............	————
	════		════

Analysis Component: Identify which assets were financed by:

a. Liabilities   **b.** Owner investment   **c.** Profit

Also identify the amount(s) for each.

Exercise 1-22 Effects of transactions on the accounting equation LO6, 7 e**X**cel

CHECK FIGURE: Accounts payable, March 31, 2020 = $2,350

a. Ali Omar invested $4,300 cash and $15,000 of equipment to start his business, Omar's Yard Care.

b. Purchased various supplies on account; $1,600.

c. Bought supplies on credit; $950.

d. Omar signed a $4,000 contract to do yard work beginning in May.

e. Did work for a client on account; $550.

f. Performed services for a customer on credit; $600.

g. Paid $200 for the supplies purchased in (c).

h. Paid $250 for advertising online.

i. Collected the amount owed from the customer in (f).

Using the format provided below, show the effects of the activities listed in (a) through (i). For each transaction that affects equity, include a brief description beside it (owner investment, owner withdrawal, revenue, expense).

Assets					=	Liabilities	+	Equity	
Cash	+ Accounts Receivable	+ Supplies	+ Equipment		=	Accounts Payable	+	Ali Omar, Capital	Explanation of Equity Transaction

Exercise 1-23 Financial statements LO8

CHECK FIGURE: Ali Omar, Capital, March 31, 2020 = $20,200

Using your answer from Exercise 1-22, prepare an income statement, statement of changes in equity, and balance sheet for March 2020.

Analysis Component: Review Omar's income statement. Does the profit of $900 represent $900 of cash? Explain.

Exercise 1-24 Effects of transactions on the accounting equation LO6, 7

CHECK FIGURE: Natalie Gold, Capital, July 31, 2020 = $11,550

Natalie Gold is the owner of the marketing agency Vivid Voice. The company focuses on online consulting services, such as online marketing campaigns and blog services. The June transactions for Vivid Voice resulted in totals at June 30, 2020, as shown in the following accounting equation format:

Assets					=	Liabilities	+	Equity	
Cash	+ Accounts Receivable	+ Supplies	+ Equipment		=	Accounts Payable	+	Natalie Gold, Capital	Explanation of Equity Transaction
$6,000	+ $1,200	+ $1,900	+ $6,500		=	$4,000	+	$11,600	

During July, the following occurred:

a. Collected $800 from a credit customer.

b. Paid $2,500 for equipment purchased on account in June.

c. Did work for a client and collected cash; $1,100.

d. Paid a part-time consultant's wages; $950.

e. Paid the July rent; $1,200.

f. Paid the July utilities; $600.

g. Performed services for a customer on credit; $1,600.

h. Called an information technology consultant to fix the agency's photo editing software in August; it will cost $350.

Using the format provided above, show the effects of the activities listed in (a) through (h). For each transaction that affects equity, include a brief description beside it (owner investment, owner withdrawal, revenue, expense).

Exercise 1-25 Financial statements LO8

CHECK FIGURES: Loss = $50; Total assets = $13,050

Using your answer from Exercise 1-24, prepare an income statement, a statement of changes in equity, and a balance sheet for July 2020.

Analysis Component: Review Gold's balance sheet. How much of the assets are financed by Gold? How much of the assets are financed by debt?

PROBLEMS

↓ Problems typically incorporate two or more concepts. There are two groups of problems: A problems and Alternate or B problems. B problems mirror the A problems to help you improve your understanding through repetition.

Problem 1-1A Identifying type of business organization LO2

Complete the chart below by placing a check mark in the appropriate column.

	Type of Business Organization		
Characteristic	Sole Proprietorship	Partnership	Corporation
Limited liability			
Unlimited liability			
Owners are shareholders			
Owners are partners			
Taxed as a separate legal entity			

Problem 1-2A Understanding assets LO6

You are an accountant at Bright Consulting. The CEO tells his employees, "People are our greatest assets." When you show him the financial statements, he becomes very angry and demands, "Why do we not have our employees on this balance sheet? You better fix these statements or you are fired!"

Required Write an email to the CEO explaining whether employees should be recorded as assets on the balance sheet. Ensure you explain your reasoning based on the definition of an asset.

Problem 1-3A Financial statements: analysis of statement of changes in equity LO6

CHECK FIGURE: Profit 2019 = $60,000

Blue Water Kayak began operations on January 1, 2019. The owner invested $10,000 during the first year and was able to withdraw cash of $42,000 after a successful first year.

During 2020, the second year of operations, the business reported profit of $175,000, owner withdrawals of $78,000, and no owner investments.

In 2021, the third year, Blue Water Kayak incurred a loss of $5,000. The owner made no withdrawals and no owner investments during this period. At the end of 2021, owner's capital was $120,000.

Required Calculate the profit or loss for 2019.

Problem 1-4A Financial statements LO6

CHECK FIGURES: Profit = $35,700; Total assets = $108,900

On August 1, 2019, Cross Fitness entered its second year of operations. Cross Fitness provides high-performance group and personal training courses that have been derived from scientific research and exercises used by professional athletes. On July 31, 2020, Jay Grey, the owner, finalized the company's records, which showed the following items.

Accounts payable	$ 10,900		Prepaid rent	$ 5,500
Accounts receivable	57,000		Rent expense	21,500
Jay Grey, capital, July 31, 2019*	80,800		Personal training revenue	5,500
Jay Grey, withdrawals	53,500		Group training revenue	153,500
Cash	7,100		Supplies	3,900
Furniture	14,700		Supplies expense	17,400
Interest expense	3,600		Utilities expense	11,300
Notes payable	35,000		Wages expense	69,500
Workout equipment	20,700			

Hint: The ending capital balance for one period is the beginning capital balance for the next period. There were no owner investments during the year ended July 31, 2020.

Required Prepare an income statement and statement of changes in equity for the year ended July 31, 2020, and balance sheet at July 31, 2020, similar to Exhibits 1.8, 1.9, and 1.10.

Analysis Component: Analyze the balance sheet and calculate what percentage of the assets at July 31, 2020, were financed by (a) debt and (b) equity.

Problem 1-5A Financial statements LO6

CHECK FIGURES: Profit = $50,100; Ending capital = $80,200

On January 1, 2019, Dance Training Co entered its second year of operations. Dance Training Co provides elite personal training courses to dancers who want to work on cruise ships. On December 31, 2020, Jordan Ryan, the owner, finalized the company's records, which showed the following items.

Accounts payable	$ 10,200		Jordan Ryan, withdrawals	$50,000
Accounts receivable	50,000		Notes payable	28,000
Cash	26,400		Prepaid rent	4,800
Choreography revenue	24,100		Rent expense	18,000
Dance studio equipment	20,000		Supplies	3,200
Dance training revenue	143,000		Supplies expense	16,700
Furniture	14,000		Utilities expense	10,600
Interest expense	2,900		Wages expense	68,800
Jordan Ryan, capital, December 31, 2019*	80,100			

Hint: The ending capital balance for one period is the beginning capital balance for the next period. There were no owner investments during the year ended December 31, 2020.

Required Prepare an income statement and statement of changes in equity for the year ended December 31, 2020, and balance sheet at December 31, 2020, similar to Exhibits 1.8, 1.9, and 1.10.

Analysis Component: Analyze the balance sheet and calculate what percentage of the assets at December 31, 2020, were financed by (a) debt and (b) equity.

Problem 1-6A Calculating and interpreting profit and preparing a balance sheet LO6, 7, 8

This icon indicates that there is a video tutorial available on Connect to assist you with completing this question. ↑

CHECK FIGURES: 1. Total assets 2019 = $138,750; Total assets 2020 = $235,200

The accounting records of LeClaire Delivery Services show the following assets and liabilities as of the end of 2020 and 2019:

	December 31	
	2020	**2019**
Cash..	$ 9,375	$26,250
Accounts receivable..	11,175	14,250
Office supplies	1,650	2,250
Trucks	27,000	27,000
Office equipment...	73,500	69,000
Land	22,500	
Building	90,000	
Accounts payable..	18,750	3,750
Notes payable..	52,500	

During December 2020 the owner, Jess LeClaire, purchased a small office building and moved the business from rented quarters to the new building. The building and the land it occupies cost $112,500. The business paid $60,000 in cash and a note payable was signed for the balance. LeClaire had to invest $17,500 cash in the business to enable it to pay the $60,000. The business earned a profit during 2020, which enabled LeClaire to withdraw $1,500 per month from the business for personal expenses.

Required

1. Prepare balance sheets for the business as of the end of 2019 and the end of 2020.
2. Prepare a calculation to show how much profit was earned by the business during 2020.

Analysis Component: Assets increased from $138,750 at December 31, 2019, to $235,200 at December 31, 2020. Using numbers wherever possible, explain how these assets were financed.

Problem 1-7A Missing information LO7   *eXcel*

The following financial statement information is known about five unrelated companies:

	Company A	Company B	Company C	Company D	Company E
December 31, 2019:					
Assets..	$106,000	$121,000	$74,000	$168,000	$262,000
Liabilities..	46,000	53,000	36,000	92,000	?
December 31, 2020:					
Assets..	112,000	98,000	?	266,000	241,000
Liabilities..	?	63,000	46,000	136,000	158,000
During 2020:					
Owner investments.....................	26,000	35,000	23,500	?	10,600
Profit (loss)	(24,000)	?	19,600	32,000	37,600
Owner withdrawals......................	6,600	7,600	10,150	-0-	19,600

Required

1. Answer the following questions about Company A:

   a. What was the equity on December 31, 2019?

   b. What was the equity on December 31, 2020?

   c. What was the amount of liabilities owed on December 31, 2020?

2. Answer the following questions about Company B:

   a. What was the equity on December 31, 2019?

   b. What was the equity on December 31, 2020?

   c. What was the profit (loss) for 2020?

3. Calculate the amount of assets owned by Company C on December 31, 2020.

4. Calculate the amount of owner investments in Company D made during 2020.

5. Calculate the amount of liabilities owed by Company E on December 31, 2019.

Problem 1-8A Analyzing transactions and preparing financial statements LO6, 7, 8 eXcel

CHECK FIGURES: 2. George Littlechild, Capital, March 31, 2020 = $175,100; 3. Loss = $1,300; Total assets = $743,100

George Littlechild started a new kitchen and bath design business called Littlechild Enterprises. The following activities occurred during its first month of operations, March 2020:

a. Littlechild invested $160,000 cash and office equipment valued at $20,000 in the business.

b. Purchased a small building for $600,000 to be used as an office. Paid $100,000 in cash and signed a note payable promising to pay the balance over several years.

c. Purchased $3,000 of office supplies for cash.

d. Purchased $72,000 of office equipment on credit.

e. Littlechild made reservations at a hotel hosting a kitchen and bath design conference in August 2020. He will send a $1,000 deposit on July 1, 2020.

f. Completed a project on credit and billed the client $5,200 for the work.

g. Paid a local online newspaper $3,500 for an announcement that the office had opened.

h. Completed a project for a client and collected $4,000 cash.

i. Made a $4,000 payment on the equipment purchased in (d).

j. Received $2,500 from the client described in (f).

k. Paid $7,000 cash for the office secretary's wages.

l. Littlechild withdrew $3,600 cash from the company bank account to pay personal living expenses.

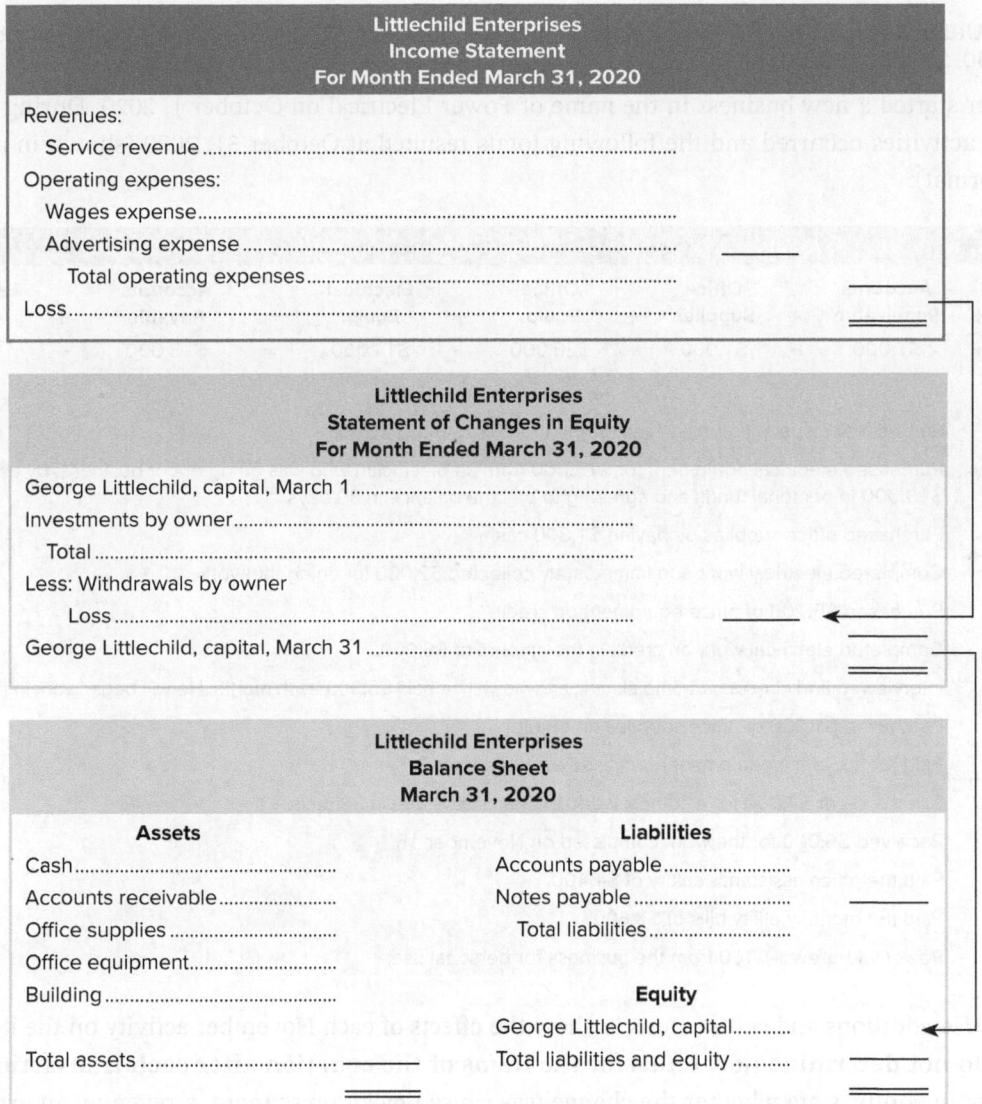

Littlechild Enterprises
Income Statement
For Month Ended March 31, 2020

Revenues:

   Service revenue ....

Operating expenses:

   Wages expense...

   Advertising expense ....

      Total operating expenses..

Loss..

Littlechild Enterprises
Statement of Changes in Equity
For Month Ended March 31, 2020

George Littlechild, capital, March 1...

Investments by owner...

   Total ....

Less: Withdrawals by owner

     Loss ....

George Littlechild, capital, March 31 ....

Littlechild Enterprises
Balance Sheet
March 31, 2020

Assets	Liabilities
Cash...	Accounts payable..........................
Accounts receivable.......................	Notes payable ....
Office supplies	Total liabilities............................
Office equipment..............................	
Building	**Equity**
	George Littlechild, capital.............
Total assets .... _____	Total liabilities and equity ....

Required

1. Create a table like the one in Exhibit 1.15, using the following headings for the columns: Cash; Accounts Receivable; Office Supplies; Office Equipment; Building; Accounts Payable; Notes Payable; and George Littlechild, Capital. Leave space for an Explanation of Equity Transaction column to the right of the Capital column. Identify revenues and expenses by name in the Explanation of Equity Transaction column.

2. Use additions and subtractions to show the transactions' effects on the elements of the equation. **Do not determine new totals for the items of the equation after each transaction.** Next to each change in equity, state whether the change was caused by an investment, a revenue, an expense, or a withdrawal. Determine the final total for each item and verify that the equation is in balance.

3. Prepare an income statement, a statement of changes in equity, and a balance sheet using the formats provided.

Analysis Component: Littlechild Enterprises' assets are financed 76% by debt. What does this mean? As part of your answer, include an explanation of how the 76% was calculated.

Problem 1-9A Analyzing transactions LO5, 7 e**X**cel

CHECK FIGURES: Accounts payable balance, November 30, 2020 = $27,000; Larry Power, Capital balance, November 30, 2020 = $69,100

Larry Power started a new business in the name of Power Electrical on October 1, 2020. During October, a number of activities occurred and the following totals resulted at October 31, 2020 (shown in accounting equation format):

Assets									=	Liabilities	+	Equity
Cash	+	Accounts Receivable	+	Office Supplies	+	Office Equip.	+	Electrical Equip.	=	Accounts Payable	+	Larry Power, Capital
$30,000	+	$7,000	+	$1,900	+	$28,000	+	$14,000	=	$18,000	+	$62,900

Nov.	1	Rented office space and paid cash for the month's rent of $7,200.
	3	Purchased electrical equipment for $18,000 from an electrician who was going out of business, by using $10,000 in personal funds and agreeing to pay the balance in 30 days.
	5	Purchased office supplies by paying $1,800 cash.
Nov.	6	Completed electrical work and immediately collected $2,000 for doing the work.
	8	Purchased $5,200 of office equipment on credit.
	15	Completed electrical work on credit in the amount of $6,000.
	16	Interviewed and hired a part-time electrician who will be paid $5,300 each month. He will begin work in three weeks.
	18	Purchased $1,000 of office supplies on credit.
	20	Paid for the office equipment purchased on November 8.
	24	Billed a client $4,800 for electrical work; the balance is due in 30 days.
	28	Received $6,000 for the work completed on November 15.
	30	Paid the office assistant's salary of $4,400.
	30	Paid the monthly utility bills of $3,600.
	30	Power withdrew $1,400 from the business for personal use.

Required Use additions and subtractions to show the effects of each November activity on the items in the equation. **Do not determine new totals for the items of the equation after each transaction.** Next to each change in equity, state whether the change was caused by an investment, a revenue, an expense, or a withdrawal. Determine the final total for each item and verify that the equation is in balance.

Analysis Component: Revenue is not recorded on November 28. Explain, using your understanding of GAAP.

Problem 1-10A Preparing financial statements LO8

CHECK FIGURES: Loss = $2,400; Total assets = $96,100

Required Using your answer to Problem 1-9A, prepare an income statement, a statement of changes in equity, and a balance sheet.

Analysis Component: Assets are financed by debt and equity. Profit is a component of equity. Therefore, profit helps to finance assets. Explain how/if profit helped to finance assets for Power Electrical for the month ended November 30, 2020.

Problem 1-11A **Identifying the effects of transactions on the financial statements** LO7, 8

Identify how each of the following transactions affects the company's financial statements. For the balance sheet, identify how each transaction affects total assets, total liabilities, and equity. For the income statement, identify how each transaction affects profit. If there is an increase, place a "+" in the column or columns. If there is a decrease, place a "−" in the column or columns. If there is both an increase and a decrease, place a "+/−" in the column or columns. The line for the first transaction is completed as an example.

		Balance Sheet			Income Statement
	Transaction	Total Assets	Total Liabilities	Equity	Profit
1	Owner invests cash	+		+	
2	Sell services for cash				
3	Acquire services on credit				
4	Pay wages with cash				
5	Owner withdraws cash				
6	Borrow cash with note payable				
7	Sell services on credit				
8	Buy office equipment for cash				
9	Collect receivable from (7)				
10	Buy asset with note payable				

ALTERNATE PROBLEMS

Problem 1-1B **Identifying type of business organization** LO2

a. Refer to Appendix III at the end of the book. Determine if WestJet is a sole proprietorship, partnership, or corporation.

b. Refer to Appendix III at the end of the book. Determine if **Spin Master** is a sole proprietorship, partnership, or corporation.

Problem 1-2B **Understanding assets** LO6

You are the accountant at Global Consulting. The marketing manager is excited about the success of their new marketing campaign. She boasts, "We spent $1 million on marketing in 2019 and we have already seen an increase in sales of 5% this year!" When you show her the financial statements, she exclaims, "You have made a big mistake! I want to see $1 million recorded under assets for our investment in marketing!"

Required Write an email to the marketing manager explaining whether money spent on marketing should be recorded as an asset on the balance sheet. Be sure to explain your reasoning based on the definition of an asset.

Problem 1-3B **Financial statements: analysis of statement of changes in equity** LO6

CHECK FIGURE: 2019 loss = $31,000

Dublin Window Cleaners began operations on January 1, 2019. The owner invested $400,000 during the first year and made no withdrawals.

During 2020, the business reported profit of $192,000, owner withdrawals of $104,000, and zero owner investments.

In 2021, Dublin Window Cleaners earned profit of $366,000. The owner withdrew $218,000 during 2021 and made no investments. Owner's capital at December 31, 2021, was $605,000.

Required Calculate the profit or loss for the year 2019.

Problem 1-4B Financial statements LO6

CHECK FIGURE: Wes Gandalf, Capital, Dec. 31, 2020 = $192,000

On January 1, 2020, Fireworks Fantasia entered its third year of operations. On December 31, 2020, Wes Gandalf, the owner, finalized the company's records that showed the following items.

Accounts payable	$58,000	Office supplies	$ 3,000
Accounts receivable	14,000	Office supplies expense	3,600
Advertising expense	9,000	Rent revenue	66,000
Building	81,000	Service Revenue	140,000
Cash	8,000	Tools	18,000
Fireworks supplies	49,000	Utilities expense	25,100
Fireworks supplies expense	77,500	Wages expense	92,000
Land	63,000	Wes Gandalf, capital, December 31, 2019*	175,200
Office equipment	14,000	Wes Gandalf, withdrawals	12,000

***Hint:** The ending capital balance for one period is the beginning capital balance for the next period. The owner made investments of $30,000 during the year ended December 31, 2020.*

Required Prepare an income statement and statement of changes in equity for the year ended December 31, 2020, and a December 31, 2020, balance sheet, similar to Exhibits 1.8, 1.9, and 1.10.

Analysis Component: Analyze the balance sheet and calculate what percentage of the assets at December 31, 2020, were financed by (a) debt and (b) equity.

Problem 1-5B Financial statements LO6

CHECK FIGURES: Profit = $39,700; Ending capital = $65,000

On January 1, 2019, Dog Obedience Training Co entered its second year of operations. This year the business expanded to include doggy daycare because many customers requested the service. On December 31, 2020, the owner Tim Oram finalized the company's records, which showed the following items.

Accounts payable	$ 11,400	Prepaid rent	$ 6,000
Accounts receivable	62,000	Rent expense	24,000
Cash	7,600	Doggy daycare revenue	46,500
Dog kennel equipment	21,200	Obedience training revenue	121,000
Tim Oram, capital, December 31, 2019*	81,300	Supplies	4,400
Tim Oram, withdrawals	56,000	Supplies expense	17,900
Vehicle	15,200	Utilities expense	11,800
Interest expense	4,100	Wages expense	70,000
Notes payable	40,000		

***Hint:** The ending capital balance for one period is the beginning capital balance for the next period. There were no owner investments during the year ended December 31, 2020.*

Required Prepare an income statement and statement of changes in equity for the year ended December 31, 2020, and balance sheet at December 31, 2020, similar to Exhibits 1.8, 1.9, and 1.10.

Analysis Component: Analyze the balance sheet and calculate what percentage of the assets at December 31, 2020, were financed by (a) debt and (b) equity.

Problem 1-6B Calculating and interpreting profit and preparing a balance sheet LO6, 7, 8

CHECK FIGURES: 1. Total assets 2019 = $279,000; Total assets 2020 = $936,000

The accounting records of Carmen Creek Gourmet Meats show the following assets and liabilities as of the end of 2020 and 2019:

	December 31	
	2020	2019
Cash	$ 20,000	$ 28,000
Accounts receivable	60,000	50,000
Office supplies	25,000	20,000
Office equipment	120,000	120,000
Machinery	61,000	61,000
Land	130,000	
Building	520,000	
Accounts payable	30,000	10,000
Notes payable	520,000	

During 2020, Carmen Munch, the owner, purchased a small office building and moved the business from rented quarters to the new building. The building and the land it occupies cost $650,000. The business paid $130,000 in cash and a note payable was signed for the balance. Munch had to invest an additional $50,000 to enable it to pay the $130,000. The business earned a profit during 2020, which enabled Munch to withdraw $2,000 per month from the business for personal use.

Required

1. Prepare balance sheets for the business as of the end of 2019 and the end of 2020.

2. Prepare a calculation to show how much profit was earned by the business during 2020.

Analysis Component: Assets increased from $279,000 at December 31, 2019, to $936,000 at December 31, 2020. Using numbers wherever possible, explain how these assets were financed.

Problem 1-7B Missing information LO7 eXcel

The following financial statement information is known about five unrelated companies:

	Company V	Company W	Company X	Company Y	Company Z
December 31, 2019:					
Assets	$165,000	$70,000	$121,500	$82,500	$124,000
Liabilities	30,000	50,000	58,500	50,000	?
December 31, 2020:					
Assets	192,000	90,000	136,500	?	160,000
Liabilities	26,000	?	55,500	72,000	52,000
During 2020:					
Owner investments	60,000	10,000	?	38,100	40,000
Profit (loss)	?	30,000	16,500	(46,000)	32,000
Owner withdrawals	4,500	2,000	-0-	18,000	6,000

Required

1. Answer the following questions about Company V:

   a. What was the equity on December 31, 2019?

   b. What was the equity on December 31, 2020?

   c. What was the profit (loss) for 2020?

2. Answer the following questions about Company W:

   a. What was the equity on December 31, 2019?

   b. What was the equity on December 31, 2020?

   c. What was the amount of liabilities owed on December 31, 2020?

3. Calculate the amount of owner investments in Company X made during 2020.

4. Calculate the amount of assets owned by Company Y on December 31, 2020.

5. Calculate the amount of liabilities owed by Company Z on December 31, 2019.

Problem 1-8B Analyzing transactions and preparing financial statements LO6, 7, 8 eXcel

CHECK FIGURES: 2. Cash balance, December 31, 2020 = $43,800; 3. Profit = $5,700; Total assets = $324,200

Lily Zhang started a new business on January 1, 2020, called Zhang Consulting. She develops financial investment plans for young adults. During the business's first year of operations, the following activities occurred:

a. Zhang invested $120,000 cash and office equipment valued at $10,000 in the business.

b. Purchased a small building for $240,000 to be used as an office. Paid $50,000 in cash and signed a note payable promising to pay the balance over several years.

c. Purchased $18,000 of office equipment for cash.

d. Purchased $4,000 of office supplies and $6,400 of office equipment on credit.

e. Paid a local online newspaper $4,500 for an announcement that the office had opened.

f. Completed a financial plan on credit and billed the client $6,000 for the service.

g. Designed a financial plan for another client and collected an $8,000 cash fee.

h. Zhang withdrew $5,500 cash from the company bank account to pay personal expenses.

i. Zhang signed a $20,000 contract for the office to be painted in February 2021. A deposit of $6,000 will be paid on January 15, 2021.

j. Received $4,000 from the client described in (f).

k. Paid for the equipment purchased in (d).

l. Paid $3,800 cash for the administrative assistant's wages.

Required

1. Create a table like the one presented in Exhibit 1.15, using the following headings for the columns: Cash; Accounts Receivable; Office Supplies; Office Equipment; Building; Accounts Payable; Notes Payable; and Lily Zhang, Capital. Leave space for an Explanation of Equity Transaction column to the right of the Capital column. Identify revenues and expenses by name in the Explanation column.

2. Use additions and subtractions to show the effects of the above transactions on the elements of the equation. **Do not determine new totals for the items of the equation after each transaction.** Next to

each change in equity, state whether the change was caused by an investment, a revenue, an expense, or a withdrawal. Determine the final total for each item and verify that the equation is in balance.

3. Prepare an income statement, a statement of changes in equity, and a balance sheet for 2020 using the formats provided.

Zhang Consulting
Income Statement
For Year Ended December 31, 2020

Revenues:	
Consulting services revenue	
Operating expenses:	
Wages expense..	
Advertising expense	_____
Total operating expenses..	_____
Profit..	════════

Zhang Consulting
Statement of Changes in Equity
For Year Ended December 31, 2020

Lily Zhang, capital, January 1..	
Investments by owner..	
Profit...	_____
Total	_____
Less: Withdrawals by owner..	_____
Lily Zhang, capital, December 31	════════

Zhang Consulting
Balance Sheet
December 31, 2020

Assets		**Liabilities**	
Cash..		Accounts payable..........................	
Accounts receivable.......................		Notes payable	_____
Office supplies		Total liabilities	
Office equipment............................			
Building		**Equity**	
		Lily Zhang, capital..........................	
Total assets	_____	Total liabilities and equity	_____
	════════		════════

Analysis Component: Zhang's assets are financed 60% by debt. What does this mean? As part of your answer, include an explanation of how the 60% was calculated.

Problem 1-9B **Analyzing transactions** **LO5, 7** e**X**cel

CHECK FIGURE: Cash balance, July 31 = $20,000

Beyond Music provides DJ services for events such as high school dances, weddings, and corporate events. Michael Cantu started the business on June 1, 2020. The June activities resulted in totals at June 30, 2020, as follows (illustrated in accounting equation format):

Assets					=	Liabilities	+	Equity
Cash	+ Accounts Receivable	+ Office Supplies	+ Event Equip.	+ Sound System Equip.	=	Accounts Payable	+	Michael Cantu, Capital
$12,000 +	$4,600 +	$1,560 +	$9,600 +	$24,000	=	$6,200	+	$45,560

During July, the following occurred:

July	1	Cantu invested $20,000 cash in the business.
	1	Rented office space and paid the month's rent of $1,000.
	1	Purchased sound system equipment for $8,000 by paying $3,000 in cash and agreeing to pay the balance in 30 days.
	6	Purchased office supplies by paying $1,000 cash.
	8	Provided DJ services for three weddings and immediately collected $4,400 in total for completing the services.
	10	Purchased $7,600 of projectors and screens on credit.
	15	Completed DJ services for a customer on credit in the amount of $4,800.
	17	Purchased $3,840 of office supplies on credit.
	23	Paid for the event equipment purchased on July 10.
	25	Billed a large corporate customer $6,000 for DJ services and $4,000 for the rental of event equipment; the balance is due in 30 days.
	28	Received $4,800 for the work completed on July 15.
	31	Paid DJ wages of $4,500.
	31	Paid the monthly utility bills of $1,700.
	31	Cantu withdrew $2,400 cash from the business to pay personal expenses.

Required Use additions and subtractions to show the effects of each July transaction on the items in the equation. **Do not determine new totals for the items of the equation after each transaction.** Next to each change in equity, state whether the change was caused by an investment, a revenue, an expense, or a withdrawal. Determine the final total for each item and verify that the equation is in balance.

Analysis Component: Identify which GAAP guides your treatment of the July 15 transaction. Explain your answer.

Problem 1-10B Preparing financial statements LO8

CHECK FIGURES: Profit = $12,000; Total assets = $90,200

Required Using your answer to Problem 1-9B, prepare an income statement, a statement of changes in equity, and a balance sheet.

Analysis Component: Assets are financed by debt and equity. Owner investment is a component of equity. Therefore, owner investment helps to finance assets. Explain how/if owner investment helped to finance assets for Beyond Music for the month ended July 31, 2020.

Problem 1-11B Identifying the effects of transactions on the financial statements LO7, 8

Identify how each of the following transactions affects the company's financial statements. For the balance sheet, identify how each transaction affects total assets, total liabilities, and equity. For the income statement, identify how each transaction affects profit. If there is an increase, place a "+" in the column or columns. If there is a decrease, place a "−" in the column or columns. If there is both an increase and a decrease, place "+/−" in the column or columns. The line for the first transaction is completed as an example.

		Balance Sheet			Income Statement
	Transaction	Total Assets	Total Liabilities	Equity	Profit
1	Owner invests cash	+		+	
2	Pay wages with cash				
3	Acquire services on credit				
4	Buy store equipment for cash				
5	Borrow cash with note payable				
6	Sell services for cash				
7	Sell services on credit				
8	Pay rent with cash				
9	Owner withdraws cash				
10	Collect receivable from (7)				

ANALYTICAL AND REVIEW PROBLEMS

A & R Problem 1-1

CHECK FIGURE: Total assets = $89,775

Jack Tasker opened his Auto Repair Shop in November 2020. The balance sheet at November 30, 2020, prepared by an inexperienced part-time bookkeeper, is shown below.

Required Prepare a correct balance sheet.

Tasker Auto Repair Shop
Balance Sheet
November 30, 2020

Assets		Liabilities and Equity	
Cash..	$ 6,300	Parts and supplies......................................	$14,175
Accounts payable.......................................	34,650	Accounts receivable...............................	47,250
Equipment...	22,050	Mortgage payable....................................	28,350
Jack Tasker, capital...................................	26,775		
Total income...	$89,775	Total equities..	$89,775

A & R Problem 1-2

CHECK FIGURES: Profit = $5,880; Total liabilities and equity = $17,430

Susan Huang began the practice of law October 1, 2020, with an initial investment of $10,500 in cash. She made no withdrawals during the month. After completing the first month of practice, the financial statements were prepared by Ryan Player, the secretary/bookkeeper Ms. Huang had hired. Ms. Huang almost burst out laughing when she saw them. She had completed a course in legal accounting in law school and knew the statements prepared by Player left much to be desired. Consequently, she asked you to revise the statements. The Player version is presented as follows:

Susan Huang, Lawyer Balance Sheet October 31, 2020			
Assets		**Liabilities and Equity**	
Cash	$ 3,780	Susan Huang, capital	$10,500
Furniture	2,100		
Supplies expense	420		
Accounts payable	1,050		
Rent expense	2,100		
Supplies	1,050		
	$10,500		$10,500

Susan Huang, Lawyer Income Statement For Month Ended October 31, 2020		
Revenues:		
Legal revenue	$11,550	
Accounts receivable	2,100	$13,650
Expenses:		
Salaries expense	$ 2,940	
Telephone expense	210	
Law library	8,400	11,550
Profit		$ 2,100

Required Prepare the corrected financial statements for Susan Huang.

A & R Problem 1-3

For each of the following activities, identify the effect on each component of the income statement and balance sheet. The first one has been done as an example for you.

1. $14,000 of services were provided to clients on credit today.

Income Statement		Balance Sheet		
Revenues	**Expenses**	**Assets**	**Liabilities**	**Equity**
1. ⬆ $14,000		⬆ $14,000		⬆ $14,000

2. $5,000 cash was collected for services performed on credit last month.
3. $25,000 cash was borrowed from the bank.
4. $500 of advertising was done in the local newspaper today on account.
5. $500 was paid regarding the advertising in (4) above.
6. The owner invested an additional $10,000 cash into the business.
7. The owner withdrew $5,000 of cash from the business.
8. The owner took $200 worth of office supplies home for personal use.

9. A new computer was purchased for $2,000 cash.

10. A one-year insurance policy costing $12,000 was purchased today.

11. Purchased $45 of fuel for the van; paid cash.

12. Collected $900 from a client for work performed today.

ETHICS CHALLENGE

EC 1-1

Sue Santos is a new entry-level accountant for a snowboard manufacturer. At the end of the fiscal period, Santos is advised by a supervisor to include as revenue for the period any orders that have been submitted online, but have not yet been shipped. Santos is also advised to include as revenue any orders where payment has already been received but where shipment is still pending.

Required

1. Identify relevant accounting principles that Santos should be aware of in view of the supervisor's instructions.

2. What are the ethical factors in this situation?

3. Would you recommend that Santos follow the supervisor's directives?

4. What alternatives might be available to Santos if she decides not to follow the supervisor's directions?

FOCUS ON FINANCIAL STATEMENTS

FFS 1-1 e**X**cel

CHECK FIGURES: 3. Cash, June 30, 2020 = $15,000; Total assets, June 30, 2020 = $23,000; Cash, July 31, 2020 = $12,500; Total assets, July 31, 2020 = $23,800

Glenrose Servicing began operations on June 1, 2020. The transactions for the first two months follow:

	2020	
June	1	The owner, Diane Towbell, invested $20,000 cash and office equipment with a value of $6,000.
	5	Glenrose Servicing performed $3,000 of services for a client on account.
	7	Paid rent for June in the amount of $1,500.
	9	Collected $1,000 from the customer of June 5.
	15	Paid $5,000 of mid-month wages to part-time employees.
	17	Provided $2,000 of services to a client and collected the cash immediately.
	29	Received the $300 June utilities bill. It will be paid in July.
	30	Paid $1,500 in wages to part-time employees.
July	5	Did work for a customer on account; $3,500.
	8	Collected $2,000 from credit customers.
	9	Paid $1,500 rent for July.
	12	Purchased $1,800 of additional office equipment on account.
	14	Paid $1,000 of the amount owing regarding July 12.
	15	Paid mid-month wages to part-time staff; $2,500.
	17	Performed services for a customer and immediately collected $4,800.
	25	Paid $300 in utilities for the month of July plus the balance owing from June.
	31	Paid $1,700 in wages to part-time employees.
	31	The owner withdrew cash of $2,000 for personal use.

Required

1. Create two tables like the one in Exhibit 1.15 for each of June and July using the following headings for the columns: Cash; Accounts Receivable; Office Equipment; Accounts Payable; Diane Towbell, Capital; and Explanation of Equity Transaction.

2. Use additions and subtractions to show the effects of the above transactions on the elements of the equation for each of June and July.

3. Prepare an income statement and statement of changes in equity for each of the months ended June 30 and July 31, 2020. Also prepare a balance sheet at June 30, 2020, and July 31, 2020.

Analysis Component: Answer each of the following questions:

1. Assets increased by $800 from June 30, 2020 to July 31, 2020. How was this increase financed?

2. Which financial statement reports on a company's

   a. performance?

   b. financial position?

   Explain what is meant by each of these terms.

3. Explain how Glenrose Servicing's July income statement, statement of changes in equity, and balance sheet are linked.

FFS 1-2

Part A:

1. Refer to Appendix III at the end of the textbook for the December 31, 2017, balance sheet for WestJet, a Canadian airline based in Calgary. What types of assets does WestJet have?

2. To what level of significance are the dollar amounts rounded on the financial statements?

3. Prove the accounting equation for WestJet at December 31, 2017.

4. Assume that the personal home of one of the owners of WestJet (a shareholder) is valued at over $2,000,000. Should it be included as an asset on the balance sheet for WestJet? Why or why not?

5. Identify a potential internal user who would be interested in WestJet's statements and explain his or her interest.

Part B:

6. Refer to Appendix III at the end of the textbook for the December 31, 2017, balance sheet for Spin Master, a Canadian global toy and entertainment company based in Toronto. Identify the following for Spin Master at December 31, 2017:

   a. Total assets

   b. Total net assets

   Prove the accounting equation for Spin Master at December 31, 2017.

7. Notice that the balance sheet provides data for two years. Why do you think information has been presented for both December 31, 2017 and December 31, 2016?

8. Identify a potential external user who would be interested in Spin Master's statements and explain his or her interest.

CRITICAL THINKING MINI CASE

You have worked with Gaming Consulting as the marketing manager for a number of years. Each of your salespeople must submit a monthly report detailing money they spent while conducting business on behalf of Gaming Consulting. Each item on the monthly report must be coded as to the effect on assets, liabilities, and equity. As marketing manager, one of your duties is to review the monthly reports. One salesperson's report for September shows the following:

Date	Description of Transaction	Amount of Transaction	Effect on Assets	Effect on Liabilities	Effect on Equity
Aug. 28	Delivered market strategy report for a key customer	$150,000	Increased cash	No effect	Increased revenue
Sept. 10	Purchased new desk for office to be paid in October	$1,500	No effect	Increased accounts payable	Increased office expense
Sept. 2–30	Took clients for lunch and paid cash	$680	Decreased cash		Increased owner investments
Oct. 5	Paid for September cell phone usage	$130	Decreased cash		Increased expenses

Required Using the elements of the critical thinking model described on the inside front cover, respond, focusing on the following key areas:

1. What problems are identified in the September report?
2. What is the goal of the monthly report and what is the purpose of your review?
3. What assumptions have been made and what principles need to be considered in presenting the transactions?
4. What are the key facts and how do we rely on the facts to identify errors in the report?
5. How will you address with the salesperson the issues you have found?

Analyzing and Recording Transactions

A Look Back

Chapter 1 defined accounting and introduced financial statements. We described forms of organizations and identified users and uses of accounting. We defined the accounting equation and applied it to transaction analysis.

A Look at This Chapter

This chapter focuses on the accounting process. We describe transactions and source documents, and we explain the analysis and recording of transactions. The accounting equation, T-account, general ledger, trial balance, and debits and credits are key tools in the accounting process.

© Jonathan Hayward/The Canadian Press

LEARNING OBJECTIVES

LO1 Explain the accounting cycle.

LO2 Describe an account, its use, and its relationship to the ledger.

LO3 Define debits and credits and explain their role in double-entry accounting.

LO4 Describe a chart of accounts and its relationship to the ledger.

LO5 Analyze the impact of transactions on accounts, record transactions in a journal, and post entries to a ledger.

LO6 Prepare and explain the use of a trial balance.

Accounting in Action

Alexandre Bilodeau is the first athlete to win back-to-back Olympic gold medals in any freestyle skiing discipline. Alexandre dominated the men's moguls event in freestyle skiing in both the Vancouver 2010 and Sochi 2014 Olympic games. His commitment and thirst for success motivated Bilodeau to push himself to the next level in his sport, breaking down previously established barriers. Because the conditions are constantly changing, Alexandre needed to be incredibly adaptable and maintain a high degree of precision, skiing 11.5 metres per second while landing impressive jumps with rock-solid stability. In Sochi, conditions were especially challenging on the slushy Rosa Khutor Extreme Park course in the medal round.

The athlete faced a huge setback in his pursuit of gold at the 2006 Turin Olympics when a landing error put him in 11th place. He later said, "It was a reality check for me ... I did a perfect downhill sprint but a single landing error in the final jump cost me three points." But he learned determination and perseverance were the keys to success. "I promised myself to give it everything and then to have no regrets. And how do you avoid regrets? You do what you have to do. You don't skip training one day just because you don't feel like it. You don't make excuses. That's an attitude I now carry with me in everything I do."

Right after Sochi, Alexandre announced he was leaving the competitive sport to study accounting at Concordia University. From the age of 12, Alexandre has fond memories of accompanying his father, a tax accountant at KPMG, on visits to clients. He plans to keep his options open in the field of accounting. "Many opportunities present themselves to me, but I want to prove myself ... Accounting is so vast, it's a launch pad that can lead to so many things." For career options as a professional accountant, visit your provincial CPA recruiting website.

In business, the customer, political, technological, and social environments are constantly changing. Accountants and business professionals need to be prepared to navigate through challenging and often unfamiliar situations. The best leaders will maintain rock-solid stability while responding quickly to changes impacting the organization. How will you make a difference in your future career?

Sources: https://www.cpacanada.ca/en/connecting-and-news/cpa-magazine/articles/2014/June/bumps-spins-and-spectacular-wins; accessed September 2014; http://www.thestar.com/sports/sochi2014/skiing/2014/02/10/sochi_olympics_all_four_canadians_advance_to_mens_moguls_final.html; accessed May 2015; http://espn.go.com/olympics/winter/2014/freestyleskiing/story/_/id/10432528/2014-winter-olympics-canada-alex-bilodeau-repeats-gold-medalist-men-moguls, accessed May 2015; and http://olympic.ca/team-canada/alexandre-bilodeau, accessed May 2015.

Video Link: http://nsb.com/speakers/alexandre-bilodeau.

CRITICAL THINKING CHALLENGE

What can we take away from Alexandre Bilodeau's determination in the face of challenges?

CHAPTER PREVIEW

The accounting process identifies business transactions and events, analyzes and records their effects, and summarizes and presents information in reports and financial statements. These reports and statements are used for making investing, lending, and other business decisions. The steps in the accounting process that focus on *analyzing and recording* transactions and events are shown in Exhibit 2.1.

Student Success *Cycle*

Read the material

Apply your critical thinking skills

Do the exercises

Check your answers

Business transactions and events are the starting points as inputs into the accounting system. The transactions and events are analyzed using the accounting equation to understand how they affect company performance and financial position. These effects are recorded in accounting records using the related source documents, such as sales invoices and purchase invoices. Additional steps such as posting and then preparing a trial balance help summarize and classify the effects of transactions and events. Ultimately, the accounting process provides information in useful reports or financial statements to decision makers. Student success in mastering this cycle requires commitment to read the material, do the exercises, check the appropriate answers, and apply critical thinking skills in analyzing conclusions.

The Accounting Cycle

LO1 Explain the accounting cycle.

The **accounting cycle** refers to the series of steps required to prepare a set of financial statements for users. These steps are referred to as a cycle because they are repeated each time financial statements are prepared for that company, also known as a reporting period. Exhibit 2.1 illustrates the required steps in the accounting

EXHIBIT 2.1
Accounting Cycle

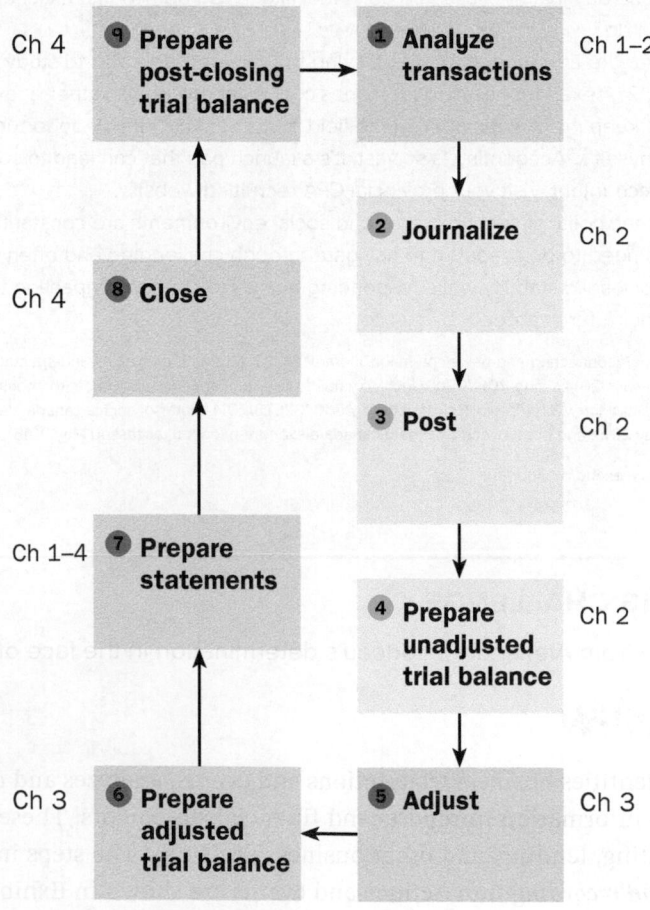

Ch 4   **⑨ Prepare post-closing trial balance** → **① Analyze transactions**   Ch 1–2

② Journalize   Ch 2

Ch 4   **⑧ Close**

③ Post   Ch 2

Ch 1–4   **⑦ Prepare statements**

④ Prepare unadjusted trial balance   Ch 2

Ch 3   **⑥ Prepare adjusted trial balance** ← **⑤ Adjust**   Ch 3 cycle. Chapter 1 introduced transaction analysis, the first step in the accounting cycle. Chapter 2 will focus on the next three steps of the accounting cycle. Step 7, the preparation of financial statements, was introduced in Chapter 1 and is reinforced in Chapters 2 through 4.

Accounts

LO2 Describe an account, its use, and its relationship to the ledger.

This section explains the importance of an account to accounting and business. We also describe several crucial elements of an accounting system, including ledgers, T-accounts, debits and credits, double-entry accounting, and the chart of accounts.

THE ACCOUNT

An **account** is a detailed record of increases and decreases in a specific asset, liability, or equity item. Information is taken from accounts, analyzed, summarized, and presented in useful reports and financial statements for users. Separate accounts[1] are kept for each type of asset, liability, and equity item. Exhibit 2.2 shows examples of the different types of accounts used by Organico.

EXHIBIT 2.2

Types of Accounts for Organico

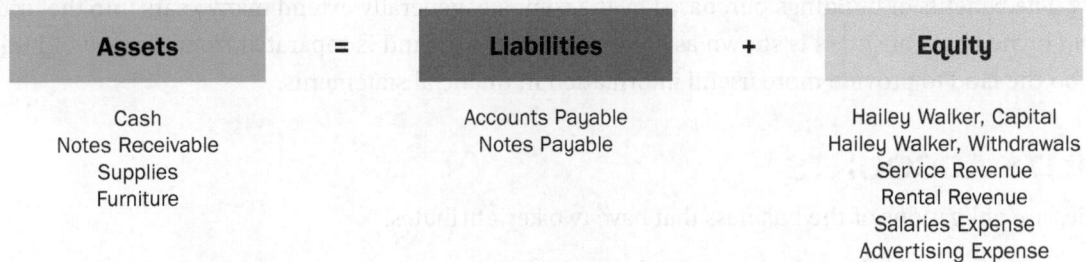

Assets	=	Liabilities	+	Equity
Cash		Accounts Payable		Hailey Walker, Capital
Notes Receivable		Notes Payable		Hailey Walker, Withdrawals
Supplies				Service Revenue
Furniture				Rental Revenue
				Salaries Expense
				Advertising Expense

A **ledger** is the term used to describe a record containing all individual accounts used by a business. A ledger is typically maintained electronically and summarizes the final balances in each account after being entered in the journal. Each company will have its own unique set of accounts to suit its type of operation. The following section introduces accounts that are most commonly used by businesses today.

ASSET ACCOUNTS

Assets are properties or economic resources held by a business with three key attributes:

1. The transaction to acquire the asset has occurred.
2. The company has control over the asset (owns/has title to the asset).
3. A future benefit exists for the company as it is used in operations.[2]

Assets have value and are used in the operations of the business to create revenue. For example, airplanes are assets held by **WestJet** for the purpose of creating revenue in current and future periods. A separate account is maintained for each asset category.

Cash increases and decreases are recorded in a separate Cash account. Examples are coins, currency, cheques, money orders, and chequing account balances. Each bank account used by the company will have a

---

1 As an example of an account, Exhibit 2.5 shows the Cash account as one of several asset accounts used by Organico.
2 IFRS 2018, "Framework," para. 4.44.

separate account number. *Receivables* are amounts that the business is expecting to receive or collect in the future. Types of receivables include:

- **Accounts receivable** are created when services are performed for or goods are sold to customers in return for a commitment from the customer to pay in the future, instead of settling in cash today. These transactions are said to be on credit or *on account*. Accounts receivable are *increased* as services are performed or goods are sold on credit and *decreased* when customers make payments.

- **Notes receivable** (or **promissory notes**) are a formal contract signed by the customer or another party that owes a specific sum of money to the company. The contract provides details regarding the total dollar value of the commitment, when the payment is due, and any interest required to be paid.

Prepaid expenses occur when a company pays in advance for a service or goods for which the benefit extends beyond the current accounting period. Examples include Office Supplies, Store Supplies, Prepaid Rent, and Prepaid Insurance. As these assets are used up, the costs of the used assets become expenses. This account supports the *matching principle* introduced in Chapter 1. Because the benefits of these goods/services are used in future periods, they should be matched to the revenue in future periods. A prepaid cost can be initially recorded as an expense *if* it is used up before the end of the period.

Equipment includes assets such as vehicles, machinery, computers, printers, desks, chairs, display cases, and cash registers. These assets are used in the operations of a business for more than one accounting period.

Buildings are assets owned by an organization that can provide space for a store, an office, a warehouse, or a factory. The benefits of buildings purchased by the company generally extend many years into the future.

Land owned by a business is shown as an asset. The cost of land is separated from the cost of buildings located on the land to provide more useful information in financial statements.

LIABILITY ACCOUNTS

Liabilities are obligations of the business that have two key attributes:

1. They are a present obligation as a result of a past event
2. The company has an outstanding obligation to pay via a transfer of assets or provision of services in the future[3]

An organization often has several different liabilities, each of which is represented by a separate account that shows amounts owed to each creditor. The more common liability accounts are described here.

Payables are promises by a business to pay later for an asset or service already received. Types of payables include:

- **Accounts payable** occur with the purchase of merchandise, supplies, equipment, or services made with a commitment to pay later

- **Notes payable** occur when an organization formally recognizes a promise to pay by signing a contract referred to as a promissory note

Unearned revenues result when customers pay in advance for products or services. Because cash from these transactions is received before revenues are earned, the seller considers them unearned, as they do not meet the requirements of the revenue recognition principle introduced in Chapter 1. Unearned revenue is a liability because a service or product is *owed* to a customer. It will be earned when the service or product is delivered in the future. Examples of unearned revenue include magazine subscriptions collected in advance by a publisher, sales of gift certificates by stores, airline tickets sold in advance, and rent collected in advance by a landlord.

---

3   IFRS 2018, "Framework," para. 4.46.

> **Important Tip:**
>
> Unearned Revenue is not a revenue account but is recorded as a liability. It occurs when cash has already been received by the company for work that has not yet been performed. This account appears as a current liability on the balance sheet, as an obligation exists to perform the service or provide the goods.

WestJet reported *advance ticket sales* of $695,111,000 on December 31, 2017. See Appendix III.

Other liabilities include wages payable, taxes payable, and interest payable. Each of these is often recorded in a separate liability account. If they are not large in amount, two or more of them may be added and reported as a single amount on the balance sheet.

The liabilities section of WestJet's balance sheet at December 31, 2017, included accounts payable and accrued liabilities of $549,844,000. See Appendix III.

EQUITY ACCOUNTS

We described in the previous chapter four types of transactions that affect equity: (1) investments by the owner, (2) withdrawals by the owner, (3) revenues, and (4) expenses. In Chapter 1, we entered all equity transactions in a single column under the owner's name, as copied in Exhibit 2.3. When we later prepared the income statement and the statement of changes in equity, we had to review the items in that column to classify them properly in financial statements.

A preferred approach is to use separate accounts, as illustrated under the Equity heading in Exhibit 2.2.

Owner Capital records owner investments. The capital account is identified by including the owner's name. The owner's capital account includes transactions in addition to owner investments, as discussed in the following two paragraphs.

Owner withdrawals are recorded in an account with the name of the owner and the word *Withdrawals*. This account is also sometimes called the owner's *Personal* account or *Drawing* account.

Revenues and expenses incurred for a period must be known to decision makers. Businesses use a variety of accounts to report revenues earned and expenses incurred on the income statement. Examples of revenue accounts are Sales, Commissions, Consulting Revenue, Rent Revenue, Subscription Revenue, and Interest Income. WestJet uses the simple term *Revenue* to report its airline revenue and breaks down its revenue into two revenue categories "Guest" and "Other." WestJet reported $3.8 billion in guest revenue and $680 million in other revenue in fiscal 2017. Examples of expense accounts include Advertising Expense, Store Supplies Expense, Office Salaries Expense, Office Supplies Expense, Rent Expense, Utilities Expense, and Insurance Expense.

EXHIBIT 2.3

Equity Transactions as Analyzed in Chapter 1

Equity	Explanation
Hailey Walker, Capital	
$10,000	Investment by Owner
$10,000	
$10,000	
+ 2,200	Food Services Revenue
$12,200	
− 1,000	Rent Expense
$11,200	
− 700	Salaries Expense
$10,500	
+ 1,600	Food Services Revenue
+ 300	Teaching Revenue
$12,400	
$12,400	
$12,400	
− 600	Withdrawal by Owner
$11,800	

> **Important Tip:**
>
> Turn to Appendix IV to find detailed information relating to accounts used within the book. It will help you tremendously to study this Appendix to familiarize yourself with common account names and the categories of accounts they fall under. For example, terminology for several types of expense accounts are listed. The accounts listed will be needed to solve some of the exercises and problems in this book.[4]

 CHECKPOINT

1. Explain the accounting cycle.
2. Classify the following accounts as either assets, liabilities, or equity: (1) Prepaid Rent, (2) Rent Expense, (3) Unearned Rent, (4) Rent Revenue, (5) Buildings, (6) Owner Capital, (7) Wages Payable, (8) Wages Expense, (9) Office Supplies, and (10) Owner Withdrawals.
3. What is the difference among the accounts Rent Earned, Rent Revenue, and Earned Rent?

Do Quick Study question: QS 2-1

T-ACCOUNTS

A **T-account** is a helpful learning tool that represents an account in the ledger. It shows the effects of individual transactions on specific accounts. The T-account is so named because it looks like the letter T. It is shown in Exhibit 2.4.

The format of a T-account includes (1) the account title on top, (2) a left or debit side, and (3) a right or credit side. Debits and credits are explained in the next section. A T-account provides one side for recording increases in the item and the other side for decreases. As an example, the T-account for Organico's Cash account after recording the transactions in Chapter 1 is in Exhibit 2.5.

EXHIBIT 2.4
The T-Account

Account Title	
(Left side)	(Right side)
Debit	*Credit*

EXHIBIT 2.5
Calculating the Balance of a T-Account

Cash			
Investment by owner	10,000	2,500	Purchase of supplies
Received from providing food services	2,200	1,000	Payment of rent
		700	Payment of salary
Collection of account receivable	1,900	900	Payment of account payable
		600	Withdrawal by owner
Total increases	14,100	5,700	Total decreases
Less decreases	−5,700		
Balance	8,400		

T-accounts are used throughout this text to help illustrate debits and credits and to solve accounting problems. *This form of account is a learning tool and is typically not used in actual accounting systems. However, many professional accountants often find T-accounts useful for analytical purposes.*

---

4 Different companies can use account titles different from those listed in Appendix III. For example, a company might use *Interest Revenue* instead of *Interest Earned*, or *Subscription Fees Revenue* or *Subscription Fees Earned* instead of *Earned Subscription Fees*, or *Rental Expense* instead of *Rent Expense*. It is only important that an account title describes the item it represents. We must use our good judgment when reading financial statements since titles can differ even within the same industry.

BALANCE OF AN ACCOUNT

An **account balance** is the difference between the increases and decreases recorded in an account. To determine the balance, we:

1. Calculate the total increases shown on one side (including the beginning balance)
2. Calculate the total decreases shown on the other side
3. Subtract the sum of the decreases from the sum of the increases, and
4. Calculate the account balance.

The total increases in Organico's Cash account are $14,100, the total decreases are $5,700, and the account balance is $8,400. The T-account in Exhibit 2.5 shows how we calculate the $8,400 balance.

DEBITS AND CREDITS

LO3 Define debits and credits and explain their role in double-entry accounting.

The left side of a T-account is always called the **debit** side, often abbreviated Dr. The right side is always called the **credit** side, abbreviated Cr.[5] We enter amounts on the left side of an account to *debit* the account. We enter amounts on the right side of the T-account to *credit* the account. The difference between total debits and total credits for an account is the account balance. When the sum of debits exceeds the sum of credits, the account has a *debit balance* as is demonstrated with the following example:

Office Supplies		
	100	60
	300	200
Balance	140	

Total debits = 100 + 300 = 400
Total credits = 60 + 200 = 260
Balance = 400 − 260 = $140 debit balance

A T-account has a *credit balance* when the sum of credits exceeds the sum of debits, as is illustrated next:

Accounts Payable		
350	400	
500	600	
	150	Balance

Total debits = 350 + 500 = 850
Total credits = 400 + 600 = 1,000;
Credits are greater than debits, so the
Balance = 850 − 1,000 = $150 credit balance

When the sum of debits equals the sum of credits, the account has a zero balance. This dual method of recording transactions as debits and credits is an essential feature of *double-entry accounting*, and is the topic of the next section.

DOUBLE-ENTRY ACCOUNTING

Double-entry accounting means every transaction affects and is recorded in at least two accounts. *For the accounting records to be accurate, every time a transaction is recorded the total amount debited must equal the total amount credited.* Therefore, the sum of the debits recorded must equal the sum of the credits for each economic event captured in the accounting records. As well, the sum of debit account balances in the ledger must equal the sum of credit account balances. The only reason that the sum of debit balances would not

---

5   These abbreviations are remnants of 18th-century English recordkeeping practices in which the terms *Debitor* and *Creditor* were used instead of *debit* and *credit*. The abbreviations use the first and last letters of these terms where **Dr** resulted from **D**ebito**r** and **Cr** from **C**redito**r**, just as we still do for *Saint* (St) and *Doctor* (Dr).

equal the sum of credit balances is if an error had occurred. Double-entry accounting helps to prevent errors by ensuring that debits and credits for each transaction are equal.

$$\text{Debits} = \text{Credits}$$

The system for recording debits and credits follows from the accounting equation in Exhibit 2.6.

EXHIBIT 2.6
Accounting Equation

Assets are on the left side of this equation. Liabilities and equity are on the right side. Like any mathematical equation, increases or decreases on one side have equal effects on the other side. For example, the net increase in assets must be accompanied by an identical net increase in the liabilities and equity side. Some transactions affect only one side of the equation. This means that two or more accounts on one side are affected, but their net effect on this one side is zero.

The debit and credit effects for asset, liability, and equity accounts are captured in Exhibit 2.7.

EXHIBIT 2.7
Debit and Credit Effects for Accounts

Debits are always on the left and credits are always on the right.

Important Tip:

Ensure you know the following rules as illustrated in Exhibit 2.7 before reading Chapter 3. For a helpful learning tool, review the following video by Colin Dodds, an educational music video enthusiast.

Video Link: https://youtu.be/7EuxfW76BWU

Three important rules for recording transactions in a double-entry accounting system follow from Exhibit 2.7.

1. Increases in assets are debited to asset accounts. Decreases in assets are credited to asset accounts.

2. Increases in liabilities are credited to liability accounts. Decreases in liabilities are debited to liability accounts.

3. Increases in equity are credited to equity accounts. Decreases in equity are debited to equity accounts.

CAUTION: Do not assume the terms *debit* and *credit* mean increase or decrease. For asset accounts debit means increase and credit means decrease. When liabilities and equity are increased the related account is credited and when they are decreased the related account is debited.

EXHIBIT 2.8

Debit and Credit Effects for Accounts

Profit: Only adjusts owner's capital after financial statement preparation to prepare owner's capital for next period.

We explained in Chapter 1 how equity increases with owner investments and revenues, and decreases with expenses and owner withdrawals. Please note that revenues and expenses impact equity through the profit (loss) recognized on the income statement. The equity adjustment of recording the profit (loss) to the owner's capital account is not made until after the financial statements have been prepared. The closing process is covered in Chapter 4 (refer to Exhibit 4.5 outlining the recording and posting of closing entries). We can therefore expand the accounting equation and debit and credit effects as shown in Exhibit 2.8 and summarize them in Exhibit 2.9.

Important Tip:

Profit (loss) is booked to the Owner's Capital account only after financial statements have been prepared, during the closing process discussed in Chapter 4. It is added to equity in the statement of owner's equity, as is shown in the end-of-chapter Demonstration Problem featuring The Cutlery.

EXHIBIT 2.9
The Debit and Credit Summary

Debit and Credit Summary	
Debits Record	**Credits Record**
Assets	Liabilities
Expenses/Losses	Revenues/Profit
Withdrawals	Owner's Capital $\Longrightarrow$ Investments
Debits Decrease:	**Credits Decrease:**
Existing Liabilities	Existing Assets

EXHIBIT 2.10
Normal Account Balances

Normal Account Balances	
Debit	**Credit**
Assets	Liabilities
Withdrawals	Owner's Capital*
Expenses	Revenue

*Used to record owner investments profit closing entry after f/s preparation.

Exhibit 2.10 highlights the *normal balance* of each type of account.[6] The **normal balance** refers to the debit or credit side when *increases* are recorded and in most cases where the balance in the account should rest. For example, the normal balance for an asset account would be a debit because a debit balance indicates that the company has something that will provide a future benefit. The normal balance for a revenue account would be a credit because revenues are increased by credits and result in an increase in equity.

Important Tip:

The following video* highlights a "Hand Game," presenting a quick way to remember your debits and credits:

Video Link: https://www.youtube.com/watch?v=onq8AfjxjRo

*Thanks to Leanne Vig, MBA, CGA, Accounting Instructor, Red Deer College for sharing this helpful learning tool.

Increases in owner's capital or revenues *increase* equity. Increases in owner's withdrawals or expenses *decrease* equity. These important relations are reflected in the following four additional rules:

4. Investments in the company made by the owner are credited to owner's capital because they increase equity.

5. Revenues are credited to revenue accounts because they increase equity, as they increase profit.

6. Expenses are debited to expense accounts because they decrease equity, as they decrease profit.

7. Withdrawals made by the owner are debited to owner's withdrawals because they decrease equity.

Our understanding of these diagrams and rules is crucial to analyzing and recording transactions. This also helps us to prepare and analyze financial statements.[7]

---

6 The Owner's Capital account is also used to record end of period profit (loss); however, entries are not made to the capital account until the financial statements are prepared. Refer to the closing process for a proprietorship covered in Chapter 4, Exhibit 4.5.

7 We can use good judgment to our advantage in applying double-entry accounting. For example, revenues and expenses often (but not always) accumulate in a growing business. This means they increase and rarely decrease over the course of an accounting period. Accordingly, we should be alert to unexpected decreases in these accounts (debit revenues or credit expenses) as a sign of potential errors.

CHART OF ACCOUNTS

LO4 Describe a chart of accounts and its relationship to the ledger.

Recall that the collection of all accounts in a company's accounting information system is called a *ledger*. The number of accounts needed in the ledger is affected by a company's size and diversity of operations. A small company may have as few as 20 accounts, while a large company may need several thousand.

The **chart of accounts** is a list of all accounts used in the ledger by a company. The chart includes an identification number assigned to each account. The chart of accounts in Appendix IV of the text uses the following numbering system for its accounts:

101–199	$\longrightarrow$	Asset accounts
201–299	$\longrightarrow$	Liability accounts
301–399	$\longrightarrow$	Owner capital and withdrawals accounts
401–499	$\longrightarrow$	Revenue accounts
501–599	$\longrightarrow$	Cost of sales expense accounts
601–699	$\longrightarrow$	Operating expense accounts

The numbers provide a three-digit code that is useful in recordkeeping. In this case, the first digit assigned to asset accounts is 1, while the first digit assigned to liability accounts is 2, and so on. The first digit of an account's number also shows whether the account appears on the balance sheet or the income. The second and subsequent digits may also relate to the accounts' categories. The numerical basis of a chart of accounts is a fundamental component of a computerized accounting system. A partial chart of accounts for Organico follows.[8]

Account Number	Account Name	Account Number	Account Name
101	Cash	301	Hailey Walker, Capital
106	Accounts Receivable	302	Hailey Walker, Withdrawals
125	Supplies	403	Food Services Revenue
128	Prepaid Insurance	406	Teaching Revenue
167	Equipment	622	Salaries Expense
201	Accounts Payable	641	Rent Expense
236	Unearned Teaching Revenue	690	Utilities Expense
240	Notes Payable		

 CHECKPOINT

4. What is the relationship of an account to the ledger and chart of accounts?
5. What is the normal balance for assets, liabilities, revenue, expenses, withdrawals, and capital accounts?

Do Quick Study questions: QS 2-2, QS 2-3, QS 2-4, QS 2-5

---

8 Organico does not use accounts 501–599. These accounts are used by merchandisers, a topic discussed in Chapter 5.

DECISION INSIGHT

Cara Operations Limited owns several popular Canadian restaurant brands including Swiss Chalet, Harvey's, Montana's, and Milestones. Its income statement for the year ended December 31, 2017, showed total revenues of $463 million. On the December 31, 2017, balance sheet, there were total assets of $1.3 billion, total liabilities of $736 million, and total equity of $607 million. Although the details of Cara Operations' chart of accounts can not be seen on its financial statements, it likely has hundreds of accounts to track its wide range of transactions.

Source: http://cara.investorroom.com/index.php?s=120, accessed September 4, 2018.

Recording and Posting Transactions

LO5 Analyze the impact of transactions on accounts, record transactions in a journal, and post entries to a ledger.

We next walk you through the first four big-picture steps of the accounting cycle: analyzing transactions, journalizing, posting, and preparing an unadjusted trial balance. The first four steps of the accounting cycle are illustrated in Exhibit 2.11.

The *first step* in the accounting cycle is identifying a business transaction, as was highlighted in the Chapter 1 discussion of transaction analysis.

The *second step* of recording the journal entry is covered in the next section. We first introduce you to the concept of a journal entry and then demonstrate how a journal entry is recorded using proper presentation.

The *third step* of **posting** an entry to the ledger is illustrated through examining six key components of a posted journal entry. The chapter demonstrates how the entry is recorded in the general journal and how it is then is broken up into the individual ledger accounts.

We have broken *steps two and three* into six micro steps, which are illustrated in detail with Organico's first 15 transactions later in the chapter.

Step four of the accounting cycle, *preparing a trial balance*, is explained later in the chapter.

EXHIBIT 2.11

Four Big-Picture Steps of the Accounting Cycle

JOURNAL ENTRY ANALYSIS

A **journal** is a record where journal entries are posted in chronological order. Recording all journal entries in a journal helps to prevent errors and enables us to identify mistakes effectively. A journal gives us a complete record of each transaction entered in the accounting information system. A **journal entry** refers to an individual transaction that has been entered in the journal, and provides information regarding the date the transaction is entered, which accounts are debited, which accounts are credited, and the corresponding transaction amounts. The process of recording transactions in a journal is called **journalizing**. The **general journal** is flexible in that it can be used to record any economic transaction not captured in a special journal, and is typically used in practice to record non-routine transactions. Special journals are used to capture journal entries relating to similar types of transactions. Examples of special journals include sales journal, cash receipts journal, cash disbursements journal, purchases journal, and the payroll journal.

A journal entry includes the following information about each transaction:

1. Date of transaction
2. Titles of affected accounts with corresponding account number
3. Dollar amount of each debit and credit
4. Explanation of transaction

Exhibit 2.12 shows how the first three transactions of Organico are recorded chronologically using a general journal. Although businesses use computerized systems, this textbook will demonstrate the processes of journalizing and posting using a manual system to ensure you have a strong foundation in accounting processes. Computerized journals and ledgers all operate on the same basic principles and processes as manual systems.

The third entry in Exhibit 2.12 uses four accounts. There are debits to the two assets purchased, Supplies and Equipment. There are also credits to the two sources of payment, Accounts Payable and Notes Payable. A transaction affecting two accounts is called a **simple journal entry**. A transaction affecting three or more accounts is called a **compound journal entry**.

EXHIBIT 2.12
Partial General Journal for Organico

GENERAL JOURNAL				Page 1
Date	Account Titles and Explanation	PR	Debit	Credit
2020 Mar. 1	Cash...		10,000	
	Hailey Walker, Capital...			10,000
	Investment by owner...			
1	Supplies...		2,500	
	Cash..			2,500
	Purchased store supplies for cash.			
1	Supplies...		1,100	
	Equipment..		6,000	
	Accounts Payable...			1,100
	Notes Payable			6,000
	Purchased supplies and equipment on credit.			

RECORDING JOURNAL ENTRIES

Important Tip:

Ensure total debits equal total credits—in other words, that the journal entry balances—before moving on to the next transaction.

The **posting reference (PR) column** is left blank when a transaction is initially recorded. Individual account numbers are later entered into the PR column when entries are posted to the ledger.

Computerized accounting software programs include error-checking routines that ensure that debits equal credits for each entry. Shortcuts often allow recordkeepers to enter account numbers instead of names, and to enter account names and numbers with pull-down menus.

POSTING JOURNAL ENTRIES

To ensure that the ledger is up to date, entries are posted as soon as possible. This might be daily, weekly, or monthly. Electronic journal entries entered in computerized accounting software are posted each time a journal entry is recorded. All entries must be posted to the ledger by the end of a reporting period. Updating account balances in a timely manner to reflect current values is especially important when financial statements are prepared. The ledger is the final destination for individual transactions; as such, it is referred to as the *book of final entry*.

To demonstrate the posting process, Exhibit 2.13 demonstrates the six key steps to post a manual journal entry from the general journal to the individual ledger accounts. When posting manual entries to the ledger, the debits in journal entries are copied into ledger accounts as debits (as illustrated using the Cash ledger

EXHIBIT 2.13
Posting a Manual Journal Entry to the Ledger Accounts

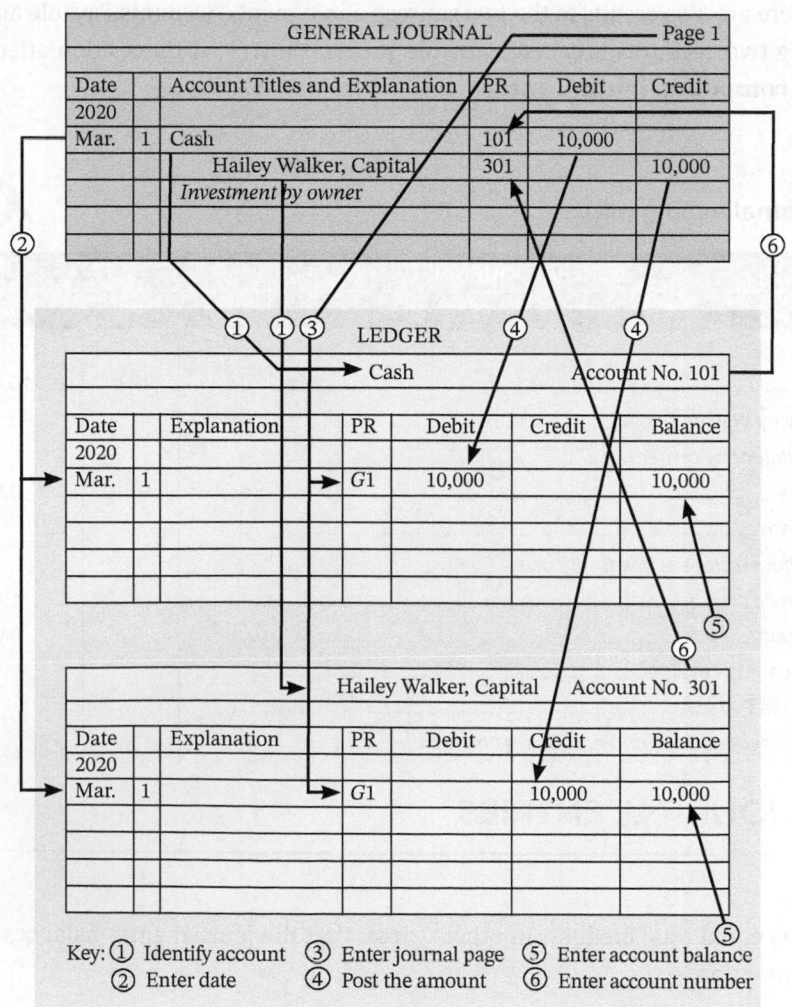

account below), and credits are copied into the ledger as credits (as illustrated using the Hailey Walker, Capital ledger account below). This process of recording the journal entry into the individual ledger accounts is covered automatically in a computerized accounting system.

Posting occurs after debits and credits for each transaction are entered into a journal. This process leaves a helpful trail that can be followed in checking for accuracy. T-accounts are a useful tool to demonstrate the posting of journal entries to the ledger accounts and determining the impact of a transaction on the account balance.

For each journal entry, the usual process is to post debit(s) and then credit(s).

Six-Step Process to Post a Manual Journal Entry to the Ledger

① Identify the ledger account that was debited in the journal entry.

② Enter the date of the journal entry in this ledger account.

③ Enter the source of the debit in the PR column, both the journal and page. The letter G shows it came from the general journal.*

④ Enter the amount debited from the journal entry into the Debit column of the ledger account.

⑤ Calculate and enter the account's new balance in the Balance column.

⑥ Enter the ledger account number in the PR column of the journal entry.

*Other journals are identified by their own letters. We discuss other journals later in the book.

Repeat the six steps for credit amounts and Credit columns. Notice that posting does not create new information; posting simply transfers (or copies) information from the general journal to the appropriate account in the ledger.

Step six in the posting process for both debit and credit amounts of an entry inserts the account number in the journal's PR column. This creates a cross-reference between the ledger and the journal entry for tracing an amount from one record to another.

T-Accounts

T-accounts are used to demonstrate the impact of posting the transactions to the general ledger accounts. Refer to Exhibit 2.4 and Exhibit 2.5 for an explanation of T-accounts.

Remember that in a double-entry accounting system we always have a minimum of two accounts included in each journal entry posted and we need to ensure that the journal entry is balanced, meaning the total dollar value of debits equals the total dollar value of credits.

Computerized Systems

Computerized systems require no added effort to post journal entries to the ledger. These systems automatically transfer debit and credit entries from the journal to the individual ledger accounts in the database. Journal entries are posted directly to ledger accounts. Many systems have controls built into the software that test the reasonableness of a journal entry and the account balance when recorded. For example, a payroll program might alert a preparer to hourly wage rates that are greater than $100. They also will prevent the user from posting an unbalanced journal entry.

Financial Statement Impact of Transaction

It is helpful to assess overall what the big-picture impact is to the accounting equation after posting the transactions to T-accounts. This process serves as a double-check that the entry we recorded is keeping the accounting equation in balance. We need to determine which elements of the accounting equation are increasing and which are decreasing. For example, if assets increase then either a corresponding asset decreased or liabilities or owner's equity must have increased. To illustrate, when a company purchases new supplies, it either pays cash (resulting in a decrease to assets) or incurs a liability for future payment, referred to as accounts payable (increasing a liability). This is illustrated in the following section.

$$\text{Assets} = \text{Liabilities} + \text{Owner's Equity}$$

 CHECKPOINT

6. Assume Maria Sanchez, the owner of a new business called La Casa de Cafe, invested $15,000 cash and equipment with a market value of $23,000. Assume that La Casa de Cafe also took responsibility for an $18,000 note payable issued to finance the purchase of equipment. Prepare the journal entry to record Sanchez's investment.
7. Explain what a compound journal entry is.
8. Why are posting reference numbers entered in the journal when entries are posted to accounts?

Accounting Transactions in Action

We return to the first activities of Organico as Hailey Walker launches the food truck business to show how debit and credit rules and double-entry accounting are useful in analyzing and processing transactions. We analyze Organico's transactions and demonstrate how these entries are journalized and posted to T-accounts using the following six micro steps:

- *Step one* analyzes a transaction.
- *Step two* applies double-entry accounting to identify the effect of a transaction on account balances.
- *Step three* analyzes the journal entry required to record the transaction.
- *Step four* records the journal entry, and includes a description of the journal entry. In step four it is critical that you ensure your total debits equal your total credits.
- *Step five* uses T-accounts to post the transaction to ledger accounts and identifies the effect of a transaction on account balances.
- *Step six* determines the big-picture financial statement impact of the transaction on Assets, Liabilities, and Equity.

We should study each transaction thoroughly before proceeding to the next transaction. The first 11 activities are familiar to us from Chapter 1. We expand our analysis of these items and consider four new transactions (numbered 12 through 15) of Organico.

1. Investment by owner.

Transaction. Hailey Walker invested $10,000 in Organico on March 1, 2020.

Analysis. Assets increase as business receives cash. Equity increases due to owner investment.

Journal Entry Analysis. **Assets increased**, debit cash $10,000. **Equity increased**, credit Hailey Walker, Capital account for $10,000.

Journal Entry. Debit the Cash asset account for $10,000. Credit the Hailey Walker, Capital account in equity for $10,000.

Mar. 1	Cash..	10,000	
	Hailey Walker, Capital.....		10,000
	Investment by owner.		

Post to Ledger.

Cash		101
(1)	10,000	

Hailey Walker, Capital		301
	10,000	(1)

Financial Statement Impact.
A = L + E*
↑   ↑

*The effect of each transaction on the accounting equation is repeated here from Chapter 1 to help you transition to debits and credits.

94

2. Purchase supplies for cash.

Transaction. March 1, Organico purchases supplies by paying $2,500 cash.

Analysis. **Assets increase** as supplies are brought in. **Assets decrease** as cash is spent. This changes the composition of assets, but does not change the total amount of assets.

Journal Entry Analysis. Assets increased, debit the Supplies asset account for $2,500. Assets decreased, credit the Cash asset account for $2,500.

Journal Entry.

Mar. 1	Supplies	2,500	
	Cash		2,500
	Purchased store supplies for cash.		

Financial Statement Impact.
A = L + E
↑↓

Post to Ledger.

Supplies		125
(1)	2,500	

	Cash	301
10,000	2,500	(2)

3. Purchase equipment and supplies on credit.

Transaction. March 4, Organico purchases $1,100 of supplies and $6,000 of equipment on credit. Organico signs a promissory note, agreeing to pay for the $6,000 of equipment at a future date.

Analysis. **Assets increase** as equipment and supplies are brought into the company for use. **Liabilities increase** as the company purchases on a short-term credit arrangement for supplies and a longer-term credit arrangement for the equipment.

Journal Entry Analysis. Assets increased for equipment and supplies, debit Supplies for $1,100 and debit Equipment for $6,000. Liabilities increase; credit Accounts Payable for $1,100 and credit Notes Payable for $6,000.

Journal Entry.

March 4	Supplies	1,100	
	Equipment	6,000	
	Accounts Payable		1,100
	Notes Payable		6,000
	Purchased supplies and equipment on credit.		

Financial Statement Impact.
A = L + E
↑   ↑

Post to Ledger.

Supplies		125
(2)	2,500	
(3)	1,100	

Equipment		167
(3)	6,000	

Accounts Payable		201
	1,100	(3)

Notes Payable		240
	6,000	(3)

4. Services rendered for cash.

Transaction. On March 10, Organico sets up the truck outside a concert facility before a sold-out venue and sells $2,200 worth of burritos for cash.

Journal Entry.

Mar. 10	Cash	2,200	
	Food Services Revenue.		2,200
	Food truck sales for cash.		

Financial Statement Impact.
A = L + E
↑   ↑

Analysis. **Assets increase** as cash is collected. **Equity increases** from earned Revenue.

Journal Entry Analysis. Assets increase; debit the Cash asset account for $2,200. Equity increases; credit the Food Services Revenue account for $2,200.

Post to Ledger.

Cash			125
(1)	10,000	2,500	(2)
(4)	2,200		

Food Services Revenue			403
		2,200	(4)

5. Payment of expense in cash.

Transaction. On March 10, Organico pays $1,000 cash for March rent.

Analysis. **Assets decrease** as payment for rent is made out of cash. **Equity decreases** due to Expense incurred.

Journal Entry Analysis. Equity decreases, debit the Rent Expense account for $1,000 (this decreases equity). Assets decrease; credit the Cash asset account for $1,000.

Journal Entry.

Mar. 10	Rent Expense	1,000	
	Cash		10,000
	Payment of March rent.		

Financial Statement Impact.
A = L + E
↓   ↓

Post to Ledger.

Rent Expense			641
(5)	1,000		

Cash			101
(1)	10,000	2,500	(2)
(4)	2,200	1,000	(5)

6. Payment of expense in cash.

Transaction. On March 10, Organico pays $700 cash for employee's salary for the pay period ending on March 14.

Analysis. **Assets decrease** to due cash payment. **Equity decreases** due to Expense incurred.

Journal Entry Analysis. Equity decreases due to expense incurred, debit the Salaries Expense account for $700. Assets decrease; credit the Cash asset account for $700.

Journal Entry.

Mar. 10	Salaries Expense	700	
	Cash		700
	Payment of employee salaries.		

Financial Statement Impact.
A = L + E
↓   ↓

Post to Ledger.

Salaries Expense			622
(6)	700		

Cash			101
(1)	10,000	2,500	(2)
(4)	2,200	1,000	(5)
		700	(6)

7. Service contract signed for April.

Event. On March 11, the accounting club at the local university and Hailey Walker sign a $2,700 contract that requires Organico to provide food for a group of graduating students at a CPA recruitment event. Organico has agreed to attend the event to be held in April.

Analysis. There has been no economic exchange between two parties (the services have not been provided and Organico did not receive any assets); therefore, this has no effect on the accounting equation.

8. Services and rental revenues rendered on credit.

Transaction. On March 17, Organico provided catering for a corporate event for $1,600 and taught a fresh Mexican cooking class for $300. The customer is billed $1,900 for the services and Organico expects to collect this money in the near future.

Analysis. **Assets increase** as customer is billed for services provided. **Equity increases** due to earned Revenue.

Journal Entry Analysis. Assets increase; debit the Accounts Receivable asset account for $1,900. Equity increases; credit two revenue accounts: Food Services Revenue for $1,600 (this increases equity) and Teaching Revenue for $300 (this increases equity).

Journal Entry.

Mar. 1	Accounts Receivable....................................	1,900	
	Food Services Revenue......................		1,600
	Teaching Revenue...............................		300
	Customer billed for services provided		

Post to Ledger.

Financial Statement Impact.
$A = L + E$
↑   ↑

Accounts Receivable		106
(8)	1,900	

Food Services Revenue		403
	2,200	(4)
	1,600	(8)

Teaching Revenue		406
	300	(8)

9. Receipt of cash on account.

Transaction. On March 27, an amount of $1,900 is received from the customer in Transaction 8.

Analysis. **Assets increase** as cash is received. **Assets decrease**, as customer obligation to pay is no longer outstanding. This changes the composition of assets, but does not change the total amount of assets.

Journal Entry Analysis. Debit the Cash asset account for $1,900. Credit the Accounts Receivable asset account for $1,900.

Journal Entry.

Mar. 27	Cash..	1,900	
	Accounts Receivable......		1,900
	Collection of cash from customer.		

Post to Ledger.

Financial Statement Impact.
$A = L + E$
↓↑

Cash			101
(1)	10,000	2,500	(2)
(4)	2,200	1,000	(5)
(9)	1,900	700	(6)

Accounts Receivable			106
(8)	1,900	1,900	(9)

10. Partial payment of accounts payable.

Transaction. On March 27, Organico pays CanFood Supply $900 cash toward the account payable of $1,100 owed from the purchase of supplies in Transaction 3.

Analysis. **Assets decrease** as cash is paid. **Liabilities decrease** as $900 of the obligation is settled.

Journal Entry Analysis. Liabilities decrease; debit the Accounts Payable liability account for $900. Assets decrease; credit the Cash asset account for $900.

Journal Entry.

Mar. 27	Accounts Payable.....................	900	
	Cash....................................		900
	Cash payment to supplier.		

Post to Ledger.

Financial Statement Impact.
$A = L + E$
↓   ↓

Accounts Payable			201
(10)	900	1,100	(3)

	Cash		101
(1)	10,000	2,500	(2)
(4)	2,200	1,000	(5)
(9)	1,900	700	(6)
		900	(10)

11. Withdrawal of cash by owner.

Transaction. On March 28, Hailey Walker withdraws $600 from Organico for personal living expenses.

Analysis. **Equity decreases** as owner extracts equity from the business. **Assets decrease** as cash is withdrawn.

Journal Entry Analysis. Equity decreases; debit the Hailey Walker, Withdrawals account for $600. Assets decrease, credit the Cash asset account for $600.

Journal Entry.

Mar. 28	Hailey Walker, Withdrawals.............	600	
	Cash		600
	Withdrawal of cash by owner.		

Financial Statement Impact.
A = L + E
↓   ↓

Post to Ledger.

Hailey Walker, withdrawals		302
(11)	600	

	Cash		101
(1)	10,000	2,500	(2)
(4)	2,200	1,000	(5)
(9)	1,900	700	(6)
		900	(10)
		600	(11)

12. Receipt of cash for future services.

Transaction. On March 29, Organico enters into (signs) a contract with a local advertising agency to provide food for a series of Tuesday "Train the Trainer" ski/snowboard instructor training events at a local ski hill called Mount Mundy. Organico receives $3,000 cash in advance of the event.

Analysis. **Assets increase** as cash is received. **Liabilities increase** as accepting the $3,000 cash obligates Organico to provide food services for the event next month, classified for accounting purposes as unearned revenue. No revenue is earned until services are provided.

Journal Entry Analysis. Assets increase, debit the Cash asset account for $3,000. Liability incurred, credit Unearned Food Services Revenue this is a *liability* account for $3,000.

Journal Entry.

Mar. 29	Cash..	3,000	
	Unearned Food Services Revenue		3,000
	Collection of payment for future services.		

Financial Statement Impact.
A = L + E
↑   ↑

Post to Ledger.

	Cash		101
(1)	10,000	2,500	(2)
(4)	2,200	1,000	(5)
(9)	1,900	700	(6)
(12)	3,000	900	(10)
		600	(11)

Unearned Food Services Revenue		236
	3,000	(12)

13. Payment of cash for future insurance coverage.

Transaction. On March 30, Organico pays $2,400 cash (premium) for a two-year insurance policy. Coverage begins on May 1.

Analysis. Assets increase as company benefits from having insurance coverage for the next two years. Assets decrease as cash is expended. This changes the composition of assets from cash to a "right" of insurance coverage. Expense will be incurred monthly as the benefit of the insurance coverage is utilized through the passage of time.

Journal Entry Analysis. Asset increases, debit the Prepaid Insurance asset account for $2,400. Asset decreases, credit the Cash asset account for $2,400.

Journal Entry.

Mar. 30	Prepaid Insurance............................	2,400	
	Cash..		2,400
	Payment for insurance coverage.		

Financial Statement Impact
A = L + E
↑↓

Post to Ledger.

Prepaid Insurance		128
(11)	2,400	

Cash			101
(1)	10,000	2,500	(2)
(4)	2,200	1,000	(5)
(9)	1,900	700	(6)
(12)	3,000	900	(10)
		600	(11)
		2,400	(13)

14. Payment of expense in cash.

Transaction. On March 31, Organico pays $230 cash for March Internet/phone connectivity/usage.

Analysis. **Assets decrease** as cash is expended. **Equity decreases** due to Expense incurred.

Journal Entry Analysis. Equity decreases, debit the Communications Expense account for $230 (this decreases equity). Asset decreases, credit the Cash asset account for $230.

Journal Entry.

Mar. 31	Communications Expense............	230	
	Cash..		230
	Payment of March Communications.		

Financial Statement Impact
A = L + E
↓   ↓

Post to Ledger.

Communications Expense		690
(14)	230	

Cash			101
(1)	10,000	2,500	(2)
(4)	2,200	1,000	(5)
(9)	1,900	700	(6)
(12)	3,000	900	(10)
		600	(11)
		2,400	(13)
		230	(14)

15. Payment of expense in cash.

Transaction. On March 31, Organico pays $700 cash for employee's salary for the two-week pay period ending on March 28.

Analysis. **Assets decrease** as cash is expended. **Equity decreases** through Expenses incurred.

Journal Entry Analysis. Equity decreases, debit the Salaries Expense account for $700. Assets decrease; credit the Cash asset account for $700.

Journal Entry.

Mar. 31	Salaries Expense................................	700	
	Cash..		700
	Payment of employee wages.		

Financial Statement Impact
A = L + E
↓   ↓

Post to Ledger.

Salaries Expense	622		
(6)	700		
(15)	700		

Cash			101
(1)	10,000	2,500	(2)
(4)	2,200	1,000	(5)
(9)	1,900	700	(6)
(12)	3,000	900	(10)
		600	(11)
		2,400	(13)
		230	(14)
		700	(15)

Accounting Equation Analysis

Exhibit 2.14 shows Organico's accounts in the ledger after all March transactions are recorded and the balances calculated. For emphasis, the accounts are grouped into three major columns representing the terms in the accounting equation: assets, liabilities, and equity.

 DECISION MAKER   Answer—End of chapter

Accounting Clerk

Congratulations! You recently got a job as a part-time accounting clerk for a local coffee shop to earn money while you attend school. Today, your employer, the owner of the business, made some purchases and instructed you to debit Office Supplies and credit Accounts Payable for the entire amount. He tells you that the invoice is for a few office supplies but mainly for some items that he needed for personal use at home. Explain which GAAP is being violated, and the impact of this error on the financial statements of the business.

Exhibit 2.14 highlights three important points.

1. The totals for the three columns show that the accounting equation is in balance

Assets $20,070	=	Liabilities $9,200	+	Equity $10,870

2. The owner's investment is recorded in the capital account and the withdrawals, revenue, and expense accounts reflect the transactions that change equity. Their ending balances make up the statement of changes in equity.

3. The revenue and expense account balances are summarized and reported in the income statement.

 CHECKPOINT

9. Does "debit" always mean increase and "credit" always mean decrease?
10. What kinds of transactions increase equity? What kinds decrease equity?
11. Why are most accounting systems called double entry?
12. Double-entry accounting requires that (select the best answer):
    a. All transactions that create debits to asset accounts must create credits to liability or equity accounts.
    b. A transaction that requires a debit to a liability account also requires a credit to an asset account.
    c. Every transaction must be recorded with total debits equal to total credits.

    Do Quick Study questions: QS 2-6, QS 2-7, QS 2-8, QS 2-9, QS 2-10, QS 2-11, QS 2-12, QS 2-13, QS 2-14

EXHIBIT 2.14

Ledger for Organico at March 31, 2020

Assets				=	Liabilities				+	Equity			

Cash 101

(1)	10,000	2,500	(2)
(4)	2,200	1,000	(5)
(9)	1,900	700	(6)
(12)	3,000	900	(10)
		600	(11)
		2,400	(13)
		230	(14)
		700	(15)

Balance 8,070

Accounts Receivable 106

(8)	1,900	1,900	(9)

Balance 0

Supplies 125

(2)	2,500		
(3)	1,100		

Balance 3,600

Prepaid Insurance 128

(13)	2,400		

Balance 2,400

Equipment 167

(3)	6,000		

Balance 6,000

Accounts Payable 201

(10)	900	1,100	(3)
		200	Balance

Unearned Food Services Revenue 236

		3,000	(12)
		3,000	Balance

Notes Payable 240

		6,000	(3)
		6,000	Balance

Hailey Walker, Capital 301

		10,000	(1)
		10,000	Balance

Hailey Walker, Withdrawals 302

(11)	600		
Balance	600		

Food Services Revenue 403

		2,200	(4)
		1,600	(8)
		3,800	Balance

Teaching Revenue 406

		300	(8)
		300	Balance

Salaries Expense 622

(6)	700		
(15)	700		
Balance	1,400		

Rent Expense 641

(5)	1,000		
Balance	1,000		

Accounts in the white area reflect increases and decreases in equity. Their balances are reported on the income statement or the statement of changes in equity

Communications Expense 690

(14)	230		
Balance	230		

TOTALS:	$20,070*	=	$9,200**	+	$10,870†

* $8,070 + $0 + $3,600 + $2,400 + $6,000 = $20,070
** $200 + $3,000 + $6,000 = $9,200
† $10,000 − $600 + $3,800 + $300 − $1,400 − $1,000 − $230 = $10,870

Mid-Chapter Demonstration Problem

Kara Morris founded her dream business, called Kara's Kiteboarding Adventures. The following transactions occurred during June 2020, her first month of operations.

a. Kara invested $15,000 cash into the business on June 1.

b. Kara's Kiteboarding paid $400 to cover insurance for the month of June.

c. June 3, Kara's Kiteboarding purchased $12,000 worth of kiteboarding equipment on credit.

d. June 6, the business rented additional kiteboarding equipment for $1,500 on account.

e. June 9, the business provided lessons to a group of clients for $3,500 on account.

f. June 14, the business collected $2,000 from its credit customers.

g. The kiteboarding equipment purchased June 3, on credit was paid for June 28.

Required

    1. Open the following T-accounts: Cash; Accounts Receivable; Equipment; Accounts Payable; Kara Morris, Capital; Teaching Revenue; Insurance Expense; Equipment Rental Expense.

    2. Post the June entries directly into the T-accounts.

Analysis Component:

Using your answer in Part 2, prove that the accounting equation balances at the end of June.

SOLUTION

1 and 2.

Cash				Accounts Receivable				Equipment		Accounts Payable			
(a)	15,000	400	(d)	(e)	3,500	2,000	(f)	(b)	12,000	(g)	12,000	12,000	(b)
(f)	2,000	12,000	(g)									1,500	(c)
(Bal.)	4,600			(Bal.)	1,500							1,500	(Bal.)

Kara Morris, Capital			Teaching Revenue			Insurance Expense			Equipment Rental Expense	
	15,000	(a)		3,500	(e)	(d)	400		(c)	1,500

Analysis Component:

Total assets	=	Cash 4,600 + Accounts Receivable 1,500 + Equipment 12,000 = 18,100
Total liabilities	=	Accounts Payable 1,500
Total equity	=	Kara Morris, Capital 15,000 + Teaching Revenue 3,500 − Insurance Expense 400 − Equipment Rental Expense 1,500 = 16,600
Assets 18,100	=	Liabilities 1,500 + Equity 16,600
18,100	=	18,100

LEDGERS

As highlighted previously, T-accounts are a simple and direct learning tool to show how the accounting process works. They allow us to omit less relevant details and concentrate on calculating the balance in a specific account. Once journal entries are recorded in the appropriate journal, transaction details need to be posted to the appropriate ledger. Ledgers contain financial statement activity for each specific account. A **general ledger** summarizes each financial statement account, providing a total balance in each account used in the organization's chart of accounts. Detailed information on account activity is required to be maintained in subsidiary ledgers; the control account in the general ledger contains the total balance for each account. The accounts receivable subsidiary ledger, for example, maintains specific information regarding each customer's account history, including sales invoice details and information regarding customer cash payments. Exhibit 2.15 provides an example of the cash control account detail in the general ledger for Organico.

EXHIBIT 2.15
Cash Control Account in General Ledger

Cash						Account No. 101
Date		Explanation	PR	Debit	Credit	Balance
2020						
Mar.	1		G1	10,000		10,000
	1		G1		2,500	7,500
	10		G1	2,200		9,700

The T-account was derived from the ledger account format and it too has a column for debits and a column for credits. Look at the imaginary T-account superimposed over Exhibit 2.15. The ledger account is different from a T-account because it includes a transaction's date and explanation and has a third column with the balance of the account after each entry is posted. This means that the amount on the last line in this column is the account's current balance. For example, Organico's Cash account in Exhibit 2.15 is debited on March 1 for the $10,000 investment by Hailey Walker. The account then shows a $10,000 debit balance. The account is also credited on March 1 for $2,500, and its new $7,500 balance is shown in the third column. The Cash account is debited for $2,200 on March 10, and its balance increases to a $9,700 debit.

Abnormal Balance

Unusual transactions can sometimes give an abnormal balance to an account. An *abnormal balance* refers to a balance on the side where decreases are recorded. For example, a customer might mistakenly overpay a bill. This gives that customer's account receivable an abnormal credit balance.[9] It is helpful to be alert for abnormal balances as they may be as a result of an error in recording a journal entry.

Zero Balance

A zero balance for an account is usually shown by writing zeros or a dash in the Balance column. This practice avoids confusion between a zero balance and one omitted in error.

TRIAL BALANCE

LO6 Prepare and explain the use of a trial balance.

Double-entry accounting records every transaction with equal debits and credits. An error exists if the sum of debit entries in the ledger does not equal the sum of credit entries. The sum of debit account balances must always equal the sum of credit account balances.

Step four of the accounting cycle shown in Exhibit 2.1 requires the preparation of a trial balance to check whether debit and credit account balances are equal. A **trial balance** is a list of accounts and their balances

---

9 Assume a customer overpaid an account, causing an abnormal balance. To highlight this, brackets can be used as illustrated below or the value could be shown in red.

Accounts Receivable						Account No. 106
Date		Explanation	PR	Debit	Credit	Balance
2020						
May	1		G1	100		100
	15		G6		125	(25)

EXHIBIT 2.16
Trial Balance

Acct. No.	Account	Debit	Credit
	Organico		
	Trial Balance		
	March 31, 2020		
101	Cash..	$ 8,070	
106	Accounts receivable...	-0-	
125	Supplies..	3,600	
128	Prepaid insurance..	2,400	
167	Equipment..	6,000	
201	Accounts payable		$ 200
236	Unearned food services revenue..		3,000
240	Notes payable...		6,000
301	Hailey Walker, capital..		10,000
302	Hailey Walker, withdrawals..	600	
403	Food Services revenue		3,800
406	Teaching revenue		300
622	Salaries expense...	1,400	
641	Rent expense...	1,000	
690	Communications expense...	230	
	Totals...	$23,300	$23,300

at a point in time. Account balances are reported in the debit or credit column of the trial balance. Exhibit 2.16 shows the trial balance for Organico after the entries described earlier in the chapter are posted to the ledger.

Another use of the trial balance is as an internal report for preparing financial statements. Preparing statements is easier when we can take account balances from a trial balance instead of searching the ledger. The preparation of financial statements using a trial balance is illustrated in the end-of-chapter Demonstration Problem. We expand on this process in Chapter 3.

Preparing a Trial Balance

Preparing a trial balance involves five steps:

1. Identify each account balance from the ledger.
2. List each account and its balance (in the same order as in the Chart of Accounts). Debit balances are entered in the Debit column and credit balances are entered in the Credit column.[10]
3. Calculate the total of debit balances.
4. Calculate the total of credit balances.
5. Verify that total debit balances equal total credit balances.

Notice that the total debit balance equals the total credit balance for the trial balance in Exhibit 2.16. If these two totals were not equal, we would know that one or more errors exist. Equality of these two totals does *not* guarantee the absence of errors.

---

10   If an account has a zero balance, it can be listed in the trial balance with a zero in the column for its normal balance.

Using a Trial Balance

We know that one or more errors exist when a trial balance does not *balance* (when its columns are not equal). When one or more errors exist, they often arise from one of the following five steps in the accounting process:

1. Preparing journal entries
2. Posting entries to the ledger
3. Calculating account balances
4. Copying account balances to the trial balance
5. Totalling the trial balance columns

When a trial balance does balance, the accounts are likely free of the kinds of errors that create unequal debits and credits. Yet errors can still exist. One example is when a debit or credit of a correct amount is made to a wrong account. This can occur when either journalizing or posting. The error would produce incorrect balances in two accounts but the trial balance would balance. Another error is to record equal debits and credits of an incorrect amount. This error produces incorrect balances in two accounts but again the debits and credits are equal. We give these examples to show that when a trial balance does balance, it does not prove that all journal entries are recorded and posted correctly.

In a computerized accounting system, the trial balance would *always* balance. Accounting software is such that unbalanced entries would not be accepted by the system. However, errors as described in the last paragraph can still exist in a computerized system.

 ETHICAL IMPACT

International Ethics: Corporate Corruption vs. Cross Cultural Management

According to Transparency International, "68% of countries worldwide have a serious corruption problem, and not one single country worldwide is corruption free."

Consider the following business scenario: you work for a water distribution firm and recently won a contract to set up a new pump system in a small village in East Africa. The dollar value of the contract is $20 million and is going to be funded by a U.S. charity. How would you respond if you were asked by the local East African government to contribute $500,000 to help build a new hospital to support that region? What would you do?

Guilu/Dreamstime.com

Jeffrey Fadiman, in his article "A Traveller's Guide to Gifts and Bribes," suggests that it is important to understand the culture of the region with which you engage in business in order to understand how to manage these types of requests. It would be prudent to understand the viewpoint of the government and circumstances behind the request that is made, as well as Canadian laws regarding foreign payments of this nature to determine the appropriate action to take.

Sources: https://hbr.org/1986/07/a-travelers-guide-to-gifts-and-bribes; and https://www.transparency.org/cpi2015.

Searching for Errors

When performing accounting manually, if the trial balance does not balance, the error (or errors) must be found and corrected before financial statements are prepared. To search for the error, we check the journalizing, posting, and trial balance preparation process in *reverse order*. Otherwise, we would need to look at every transaction until the error was found. The steps involved are:

1. Verify that the trial balance columns are correctly added. If this fails to show the error, then
2. Verify that account balances are accurately copied from the ledger.
3. Determine if a debit or credit balance is mistakenly listed in the trial balance as a credit or debit. Look for this when the difference between total debits and total credits in the trial balance equals twice the amount of the incorrect account balance.
4. Recalculate each account balance. If the error remains, then
5. Verify that each journal entry is properly posted to ledger accounts.
6. Verify that the original journal entry has equal debits and credits.

One frequent error is called a **transposition error**, in which two digits are switched or transposed within a number (e.g., 619 instead of 691). Another type of error, a **slide**,[11] occurs when adding or deleting a zero (or zeros) in a value (e.g., 32 instead of 320). If transposition or a slide is the only error, then the difference between the totals of the trial balance columns will be *evenly divisible by 9*. For example, to find a transposition error:

1. Subtract total debits in the trial balance from total credits.

   Based on the transposition given above, the difference between total debits and credits is $72 ($691 − $619)

2. Divide the difference by 9.

   $72 ÷ 9 = 8

3. The quotient equals the difference between the two transposed numbers.

   8 is the difference between 9 and 1 in both 91 of 691 and 19 of 619.

4. The number of digits in the quotient tells us the location of the transposition.

   The quotient of 8 is only one digit, so the transposition can be found by checking the first digit from the right in each number.[12]

Formatting Conventions

Dollar signs are *not* used in journals and ledgers. They *do* appear in financial statements and other reports, including trial balances, to identify the kind of currency being used. This book follows the usual practice of putting a dollar sign beside the first amount in each column of numbers and the first amount appearing after a ruled line that indicates that an addition or subtraction has been performed. The financial statements in Exhibit 1.16 demonstrate how dollar signs are used in this book. Different companies use various conventions for dollar signs.

When amounts are entered manually in a formal journal, ledger, or trial balance, commas are not needed to indicate thousands, millions, and so forth. Also, decimal points are not needed to separate dollars and cents. If an amount consists of even dollars without cents, a convenient shortcut uses a dash in the cents column instead of two zeros. However, commas and decimal points are used in financial statements and other reports. An exception is when this detail is not important to users.

---

[11] To find a slide error, follow steps 1 and 2 for a transposition error. The quotient resulting from Step Two identifies the correct value (the incorrect value +/− the correct zeros).

[12] Consider another example, where a transposition error involves posting $961 instead of the correct $691. The difference in these numbers is $270, and its quotient is $30 ($270/9). Because the quotient has two digits, it tells us to check the second digits from the right for a transposition of two numbers that have a difference of 3.

It is common for companies to round amounts to the nearest dollar, and to an even higher level for certain accounts. WestJet is typical of many companies in that it rounds its financial statement amounts to the nearest thousand dollars.

 CHECKPOINT

13. If a $4,000 debit to Equipment in a journal entry is incorrectly posted as a $4,000 credit to the Equipment account in the ledger, what is the effect of this error on the trial balance column totals, assuming no other errors?

14. When are dollar signs typically used in accounting reports?

Do Quick Study questions: QS 2-15, QS 2-16, QS 2-17, QS 2-18

CRITICAL THINKING CHALLENGE

Refer to the Critical Thinking Challenge questions at the beginning of the chapter. Compare your answers to those suggested on Connect.

IFRS AND ASPE—THE DIFFERENCES

Difference	International Financial Reporting Standards (IFRS)	Accounting Standards for Private Enterprises (ASPE)
Financial statement elements	• The level of account detail for expenses must allow the income statement to show the nature and/or function of expenses incurred for the purpose of providing relevant information to financial statement users.* The nature vs. function of an expense is discussed in greater detail in Chapter 5.	• No minimum level of account detail is prescribed for expenses under ASPE.

*IFRS 2018, IAS 1, para. 99-105.

A Look Ahead

Chapter 3 extends our focus on processing information. We explain the importance of adjusting accounts and the procedures in preparing financial statements.

For further study on some topics of relevance to this chapter, please see the following Extend Your Knowledge supplements:

EYK 2-1 Chapter 2 Corporate Supplement

EYK 2-2 How Banks Account for Cash

EYK 2-3 Preparing Financial Statements

EYK 2-4 Recording and Posting Transactions

EYK 2-5 Case: Journalizing Based on Source Documents, Posting, and Preparing a Trial Balance

---

SUMMARY

LO1 **Explain the accounting cycle.** The accounting cycle includes the steps in preparing financial statements for users that are repeated each reporting period.

LO2 **Describe an account, its use, and its relationship to the ledger.** An account is a detailed record of increases and decreases in a specific asset, liability, or equity item. Information is taken from accounts, analyzed, summarized, and presented in useful reports and financial statements for users.

LO3 **Define debits and credits and explain their role in double-entry accounting.** Debit refers to left, and credit refers to right. The following table summarizes debit and credit effects by account type:

	Assets	=	Liabilities	+			Equity		
					Owner's Capital	Owner's Withdrawals	Revenues	Expenses
Increases	Debits		Credits		Credits	Debits	Credits	Debits
Decreases	Credits		Debits		Debits	Credits	Debits	Credits

Double-entry accounting means that every transaction affects at least two accounts. The total amount debited must equal the total amount credited for each transaction. The system for recording debits and credits follows from the accounting equation. The debit side is the normal balance for assets, owner's withdrawals, and expenses, and the credit side is the normal balance for liabilities, owner's capital, and revenues.

LO4 **Describe a chart of accounts and its relationship to the ledger.** A ledger is a record that contains all accounts used by a company. This is what is referred to as *the books*. The chart of accounts is a listing of all accounts and usually includes an identification number that is assigned to each account.

LO5 **Analyze the impact of transactions on accounts, record entries in a journal, and post entries to a ledger.** We analyze transactions using the concepts of double-entry accounting. This analysis is performed by determining a transaction's effects on accounts. We record transactions in a journal to give a record of their effects. Each entry in a journal is posted to the accounts in the ledger. This provides information in accounts that are used to produce financial statements. General ledger accounts are widely used and include columns for debits, credits, and the account balance after each entry.

LO6 **Prepare and explain the use of a trial balance.** A trial balance is a list of accounts in the ledger showing their debit and credit balances in separate columns. The trial balance is a convenient summary of the ledger's contents and is useful in preparing financial statements. It reveals errors of the kind that produce unequal debit and credit account balances.

 ## Guidance Answer to DECISION MAKER

Accounting Clerk

The business entity principle is being violated because it requires that the owner's personal expenses be recorded separately from those of his business. By debiting the entire amount to Office Supplies, assets will be overstated on the balance sheet. By crediting Accounts Payable for the whole amount, liabilities will also be overstated. At the end of the accounting period when the amount of supplies used is recorded, Office Supplies Expense will be overstated on the income statement, causing profit to be understated. When profit is too low, equity is also understated.

 ## Guidance Answers to CHECKPOINT

1. The accounting cycle represents the steps followed in each reporting period for the purpose of preparing financial statements.
2. Assets   Liabilities   Equity
   1, 5, 9   3, 7   2, 4, 6, 8, 10
3. The difference among the three accounts is in the name only; they are variations of a revenue account for rent.
4. An account is a record in the ledger where increases and decreases in a specific asset, liability, or equity item are recorded and stored. A ledger is a collection of all accounts used by a business. A chart of accounts is a numerical list of the accounts in the ledger. The numbers represent whether the account is an asset, liability, or type of equity.
5. The normal balance for assets, expenses, and withdrawals is a debit balance. The normal balance for revenue, liabilities, and capital accounts is a credit balance.
6. The entry is:

Cash..	15,000	
Equipment..	23,000	
Notes Payable.....................................		18,000
Maria Sanchez, Capital...................		20,000

7. A compound journal entry is one that affects three or more accounts.
8. Posting reference numbers are entered in the journal when posting to the ledger as a control over the posting process. They provide a cross-reference that allows the bookkeeper or auditor to trace debits and credits from journals to ledgers and vice versa.
9. No. Debit and credit both can mean increase or decrease. The particular meaning depends on the type of account.
10. Equity is increased by revenues and owner's investments in the company. Equity is decreased by expenses and owner's withdrawals.
11. The name *double-entry* is used because all transactions affect and are recorded in at least two accounts. There must be at least one debit in one account and at least one credit in another.
12. c
13. This error, if uncorrected, will cause the trial balance's debit column total to be understated by $8,000.
14. Dollar signs are used in financial statements and other reports to identify the kind of currency being used in the reports. At a minimum, they are placed beside the first and last numbers in each column. Some companies place dollar signs beside any amount that appears after a ruled line to indicate that an addition or subtraction has taken place.

Demonstration Problem

This Demonstration Problem is based on the same facts as the Demonstration Problem at the end of Chapter 1 except for two additional items: (b) August 1 and (k) August 18.

The following activities occurred during the first month of Joanne Cardinal's new haircutting business called The Cutlery:

a. On August 1, Cardinal put $16,000 cash into a chequing account in the name of The Cutlery. She also invested $10,000 of equipment that she already owned.

b. On August 1, Cardinal paid $2,400 for six months of insurance effective immediately.

c. On August 2, she paid $2,000 cash for furniture for the shop.

d. On August 3, she paid $3,200 cash to rent space in a strip mall for August.

e. On August 4, she furnished the shop by installing the old equipment and some new equipment that she bought on credit for $21,000. This amount is to be repaid in three equal payments at the end of August, September, and October.

f. On August 5, The Cutlery opened for business. Cash receipts from haircutting services provided in the first week and a half of business (ended August 15) were $1,100.

g. On August 15, Cardinal provided haircutting services on account for $750.

h. On August 17, Cardinal received a $750 cheque in the mail for services previously rendered on account.

i. On August 17, Cardinal paid $250 to an assistant for working during the grand opening.

j. On August 18, Cardinal interviewed a job applicant. The applicant was successful in getting the position and will receive $750 per week for part-time work starting in September.

k. On August 18, a regular customer paid $500 for services to be provided over the next three months.

l. Cash receipts from haircutting services provided during the second half of August were $1,950.

m. On August 31, Cardinal paid an installment on the account payable created in (e) above.

n. On August 31, the August hydro bill for $450 was received. It will be paid on September 14.

o. On August 31, she withdrew $500 cash for her personal use.

Required

1. Prepare general journal entries for the preceding transactions.

2. Open the following accounts: Cash, 101; Accounts Receivable, 106; Prepaid Insurance, 128; Furniture, 161; Store Equipment, 165; Accounts Payable, 201; Unearned Haircutting Services Revenue, 236; Joanne Cardinal, Capital, 301; Joanne Cardinal, Withdrawals, 302; Haircutting Services Revenue, 403; Wages Expense, 623; Rent Expense, 640; and Hydro Expense, 690.

3. Post the journal entries to the ledger accounts.

4. Prepare a trial balance as of August 31, 2020.

5. Prepare an income statement and a statement of changes in equity for the month ended August 31, 2020, and a balance sheet at August 31, 2020.

Analysis Component:

Refer to The Cutlery's August 31, 2020, financial statements. What do each of *equity* and *liabilities* represent?

Planning the Solution

• Analyze each activity to determine if it is a transaction.

• For each transaction, identify the accounts affected and the amount of each effect.

• Use the debit and credit rules to prepare a journal entry for each transaction.

• Post each debit and each credit in the journal entries to the appropriate ledger accounts and cross-reference each amount in the Posting Reference columns in the journal and account.

• Calculate each account balance and list the accounts with their balances on a trial balance.

• Verify that the total debits in the trial balance equal total credits.

• Prepare an income statement, statement of changes in equity, and balance sheet using the information in the trial balance.

• Prepare an answer to each part of the *analysis component* question.

SOLUTION

1. General journal entries:

Date	General Journal — Account Titles and Explanations	PR	Debit	Page G1 — Credit
2020				
Aug. 1	Cash	101	16,000	
	Store Equipment	165	10,000	
	Joane Cardinal, Capital	301		26,000
	Owner's initial investment.			
1	Prepaid Insurance	128	2,400	
	Cash	101		2,400
	Purchased six months of insurance.			

Continued

| General Journal | | | | Page G1 |
Date	Account Titles and Explanations	PR	Debit	Credit
2	Furniture..	161	2,000	
	Cash	101		2,000
	Purchased furniture for cash.			
3	Rent Expense..	640	3,200	
	Cash	101		3,200
	Paid rent for August.			
4	Store Equipment..	165	21,000	
	Accounts Payable...	201		21,000
	Purchased additional equipment on credit.			
15	Cash	101	1,100	
	Haircutting Services Revenue............................	403		1,100
	Cash receipts from 10 days of operations.			
15	Accounts Receivable..	106	750	
	Haircutting Services Revenue............................	403		750
	To record revenue for services provided on account.			
17	Cash	101	750	
	Accounts Receivable...	106		750
	To record cash received as payment on account.			
17	Wages Expense	623	250	
	Cash	101		250
	Paid wages to assistant.			
18	No entry required since there has been no economic exchange.			
18	Cash	101	500	
	Unearned Haircutting Services Revenue..........	236		500
	To record payment in advance.			
31	Cash...	101	1,950	
	Haircutting Services Revenue............................	403		1,950
	Cash receipts from second half of August.			
31	Accounts Payable...	201	7,000	
	Cash	101		7,000
	Paid an instalment on accounts payable.			
31	Hydro Expense...	690	450	
	Accounts Payable...	201		450
	August hydro to be paid by Sept. 14.			
31	Joane Cardinal, Withdrawals...	302	500	
	Cash	101		500
	Owner withdrew cash from the business.			

2. and 3. Accounts in the ledger:

		Cash				Account No. 101
Date		Explanation	PR	Debit	Credit	Balance
2020						
Aug.	1		G1	16,000		16,000
	1		G1		2,400	13,600
	2		G1		2,000	11,600
	3		G1		3,200	8,400
	15		G1	1,100		9,500
	17		G1	750		10,250
	17		G1		250	10,000
	18		G1	500		10,500
	31		G1	1,950		12,450
	31		G1		7,000	5,450
	31		G1		500	4,950

		Accounts Receivable				Account No. 106
Date		Explanation	PR	Debit	Credit	Balance
2020						
Aug.	15		G1	750		750
	17		G1		750	-0-

		Prepaid Insurance				Account No. 128
Date		Explanation	PR	Debit	Credit	Balance
2020						
Aug.	1		G1	2,400		2,400

		Furniture				Account No. 161
Date		Explanation	PR	Debit	Credit	Balance
2020						
Aug.	2		G1	2,000		2,000

		Store Equipment				Account No. 165
Date		Explanation	PR	Debit	Credit	Balance
2020						
Aug.	1		G1	10,000		10,000
	4		G1	21,000		31,000

		Accounts Payable				Account No. 201
Date		Explanation	PR	Debit	Credit	Balance
2020						
Aug.	4		G1		21,000	21,000
	31		G1	7,000		14,000
	31		G1		450	14,450

Note: The T-account has been superimposed on each general ledger account for illustrative purposes only. It emphasizes that using T-accounts will produce identical balances to the balance column ledger account but in a shortened form. This shortened form is what makes the T-account a convenient tool.

2. and 3.

		Unearned Haircutting Services Revenue				Account No. 236	
Date		**Explanation**		**PR**	**Debit**	**Credit**	**Balance**
2020 Aug.	18			G1		500	500

		Joanne Cardinal, Capital				Account No. 301	
Date		**Explanation**		**PR**	**Debit**	**Credit**	**Balance**
2020 Aug.	1			G1		26,000	26,000

		Joanne Cardinal, Withdrawals				Account No. 302	
Date		**Explanation**		**PR**	**Debit**	**Credit**	**Balance**
2020 Aug.	31			G1	500		500

		Haircutting Services Revenue				Account No. 403	
Date		**Explanation**		**PR**	**Debit**	**Credit**	**Balance**
2020 Aug.	15			G1		1,100	1,100
	15			G1		750	1,850
	31			G1		1,950	3,800

		Wages Expense				Account No. 623	
Date		**Explanation**		**PR**	**Debit**	**Credit**	**Balance**
2020 Aug.	17			G1	250		250

		Rent Expense				Account No. 640	
Date		**Explanation**		**PR**	**Debit**	**Credit**	**Balance**
2020 Aug.	3			G1	3,200		3,200

		Hydro Expense				Account No. 690	
Date		**Explanation**		**PR**	**Debit**	**Credit**	**Balance**
2020 Aug.	31			G1	450		450

4.   5.

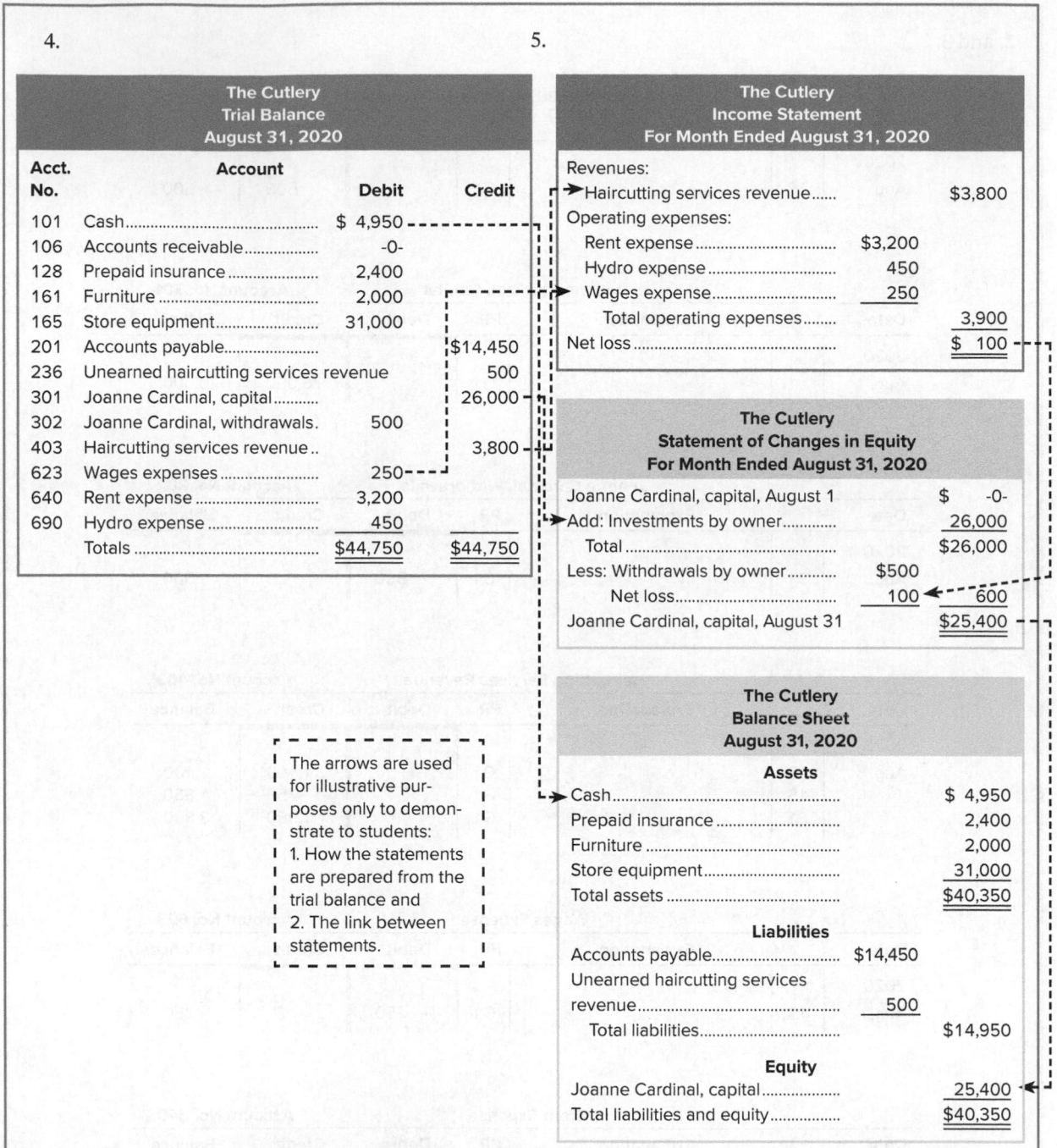

The Cutlery
Trial Balance
August 31, 2020

Acct. No.	Account	Debit	Credit
101	Cash	$ 4,950	
106	Accounts receivable	-0-	
128	Prepaid insurance	2,400	
161	Furniture	2,000	
165	Store equipment	31,000	
201	Accounts payable		$14,450
236	Unearned haircutting services revenue		500
301	Joanne Cardinal, capital		26,000
302	Joanne Cardinal, withdrawals	500	
403	Haircutting services revenue		3,800
623	Wages expenses	250	
640	Rent expense	3,200	
690	Hydro expense	450	
	Totals	$44,750	$44,750

The Cutlery
Income Statement
For Month Ended August 31, 2020

Revenues:		
Haircutting services revenue		$3,800
Operating expenses:		
Rent expense	$3,200	
Hydro expense	450	
Wages expense	250	
Total operating expenses		3,900
Net loss		$ 100

The Cutlery
Statement of Changes in Equity
For Month Ended August 31, 2020

Joanne Cardinal, capital, August 1		$ -0-
Add: Investments by owner		26,000
Total		$26,000
Less: Withdrawals by owner	$500	
Net loss	100	600
Joanne Cardinal, capital, August 31		$25,400

The arrows are used for illustrative purposes only to demonstrate to students:
1. How the statements are prepared from the trial balance and
2. The link between statements.

The Cutlery
Balance Sheet
August 31, 2020

Assets		
Cash		$ 4,950
Prepaid insurance		2,400
Furniture		2,000
Store equipment		31,000
Total assets		$40,350

Liabilities		
Accounts payable	$14,450	
Unearned haircutting services revenue	500	
Total liabilities		$14,950

Equity		
Joanne Cardinal, capital		25,400
Total liabilities and equity		$40,350

Analysis Component:

Equity represents how much of the total assets are owned (or financed) by the owner of the business. In the case of The Cutlery, the owner, Joanne Cardinal, owns $25,400 of the total $40,350 in assets or 63% ($25,400/$40,350 × 100% = 62.949% or 63%). Most of her equity in the business is a result of her $26,000 investment at start-up. The original $26,000 investment was decreased during the month by a $100 loss and a $500 withdrawal by the owner.

    Liabilities represent how much of the total assets have been financed by debt. In the case of The Cutlery, $14,950 or 37% of the total assets are financed by liabilities ($14,950/$40,350 × 100% = 37.051% or 37%).

GLOSSARY

Account A record within an accounting system in which the increases and decreases in a specific asset, liability, or equity are recorded and stored. Also referred to as ledger account. Examples of individual ledger accounts include asset accounts such as Cash and Accounts Receivable and liability accounts such as Accounts Payable and Unearned Revenue.

Account balance The total for a specific account. It is calculated by determining the difference between the increases (including the beginning balance) and decreases recorded in an account over a period.

Accounting cycle The steps repeated each reporting period for the purpose of preparing financial statements for users.

Accounts payable Obligations that arise when the company promises to pay a supplier/service provider in the future for purchases of merchandise, supplies, or equipment.

Accounts receivable An asset representing the amount owed to the company from their customers. *Accounts receivable* are created when services are performed for or goods are sold to customers in return for promises to pay in the future. These transactions are said to be *on credit* or *on account*. Accounts receivable are *increased* by services performed or goods sold on credit and *decreased* by customer payments.

Chart of accounts A list of all accounts used by a company; includes the identification number assigned to each account.

Compound journal entry A journal entry that affects at least three accounts.

Credit An entry that decreases asset, expense, and owner's withdrawals accounts or increases liability, owner's capital, and revenue accounts; recorded on the right side of a T-account.

Debit An entry that increases asset, expense, and owner's withdrawals accounts or decreases liability, owner's capital, and revenue accounts; recorded on the left side of a T-account.

Double-entry accounting An accounting system where every transaction affects and is recorded in at least two accounts; the sum of the debits for all entries must equal the sum of the credits for all entries.

General journal The most flexible type of journal; typically used to record non-recurring transactions.

General ledger A complete summary of each financial statement account, providing a total balance in each account used in the organization's chart of accounts. T-Accounts are often utilized for learning purposes to represent the individual general ledger accounts.

Journal A record where transactions are recorded before they are recorded in ledger accounts; transaction amounts are posted from the journal to the ledger; special journals are used to group recurring transactions of a similar nature.

Journal entry An individual transaction that has been entered in the journal. It includes information regarding the dated the transaction is entered, which accounts are debited, which accounts are credited and the corresponding transaction amounts.

Journalizing Recording transactions in a journal.

Ledger A record containing all accounts used by a business.

Normal balance The debit or credit side on which a specific account increases. For example, assets increase with debits, therefore the normal balance for an asset is a debit. Revenues increase with credits; therefore, a credit is the normal balance for a revenue account. Liabilities and Equity have a default credit balance; expense accounts have a default debit balance.

Notes payable Obligations that arise when an organization formally recognizes a promise to pay by signing a promissory note.

Notes receivable Unconditional written promises to pay a definite sum of money on demand or on a defined future date(s); also called *promissory notes*. They represent an asset, signalling a future benefit on a company's balance sheet.

Posting Transferring journal entry information to ledger accounts.

Posting reference (PR) column A column in *journals* where individual account numbers are entered when entries are posted to the ledger. A column in *ledgers* where journal page numbers are entered when entries are posted.

Prepaid expenses Items that are paid for in advance of receiving their benefits. These are assets.

Promissory notes Unconditional written promises to pay a definite sum of money on demand or on a defined future date(s); also called *notes receivable*.

Simple journal entry A journal entry that impacts only two accounts.

Slide An error that results from adding or deleting a zero (or zeros) in a value.

T-account A simple characterization of an account form used as a helpful tool in showing the effects of transactions on specific accounts.

Transposition error Error due to two digits being switched or transposed within a number.

Trial balance A list of accounts and their balances at a point in time; the total debit balances should equal the total credit balances.

Unearned revenues Liabilities created when customers pay in advance for products or services; created when cash is received before revenues are earned. Revenue is earned and the liability is relieved when the products or services are delivered/provided in the future.

KNOWLEDGE CHECK-UP

1. An account is defined as a:

   a. Detailed record of increases or decreases in a specific asset, liability, or equity item

   b. Financial statement record that maintains customer information for a business entity

   c. Double-entry accounting system

   d. Transaction that is recorded to report financial statements to users

2. Asset accounts are properties or economic resources held by a business with three key attributes:

   a. The transaction to acquire the asset will be settled within 30 days, the company has a pre-established delivery date, and a future benefit exists for the company

   b. A present obligation of a past event, requires future settlement, and the company maintains legal title to the asset

   c. The transaction to acquire the asset has occurred, the company has legal title to the asset, and a future benefit exists for the company as it is used in operations

   d. Represents investments made by the owner, requires future settlement, and the company maintains legal title to the asset

3. The balance of the following T-account is:

Cash	
6,500	2,200
	1,000
	600

   a. 2,700 debit balance

   b. 2,700 credit balance

   c. 3,800 credit balance

   d. 2,900 debit balance

4. Double-entry accounting means:

   a. All accounting records need to be recorded twice to ensure appropriate backup of data

   b. All accounting transactions need to be entered twice in the system to ensure accuracy of data

   c. Every time a transaction is recorded, the total amount debited must equal the total amount credited

   d. The increases in an account must always equal the decreases in the same account

5. An important rule in a double-entry accounting system includes:

   a. Increases in equity accounts always result in a decrease to a liability account

   b. Equity accounts and liability accounts are always credited, assets are always debited

   c. Liabilities are always decreased through a debit to equity

   d. Increases in assets are debited to asset accounts, decreases in assets are credited to asset accounts

6. Profit is adjusted to owner's capital accounts only after:

   a. The fiscal year-end financial statements have been audited

   b. The financial statements have been prepared and the closing process has begun

   c. The closing process has been completed and the balance sheet has been prepared

   d. The total revenue for the accounting period exceeds the total cost of goods sold

7. The primary purpose of recording journal entries is:

   a. To list all accounts in a general ledger

   b. To see the increases and decreases in a specific account

   c. To determine the overall financial performance of the company by having detailed financial records and enable the production of financial reports

   d. To identify the source of recorded transactions

8. The term *debit* means:

   a. Increase

   b. An entry that increases asset, expense, and owner's equity accounts

   c. A transaction that is recorded in a journal

   d. An entry to transfer a journal entry to ledger accounts

9. On March 10, One Eleven Music Studio purchases a new student drum kit for $1,500 and receives an invoice from Pearl to be paid within 30 days. The following entry is booked:

   a. Debit Equipment 1,500 and credit Accounts Payable 1,500

   b. Debit Supplies 1,500 and credit Accounts Payable 1,500

   c. Debit Asset 1,500 and credit Cash 1,500

   d. Credit Accounts Payable $1,500 and credit Supplies 1,500

10. On March 1, One Eleven Music Studio collects $125 from each of its 40 students taking drum lessons to pay for lessons for the month of March. Record the required journal entry to book the transaction:

    a. No entry is required until the end of the month

    b. Debit Cash $5,000 and credit Revenue $5,000

    c. Debit Revenue $5,000 and credit Cash $5,000

    d. Debit Cash $5,000 and credit Unearned Revenue $5,000

CONCEPT REVIEW QUESTIONS

1. You are an accounting manager training a co-op student at the **Lululemon Athletica** head office. Explain to the student the fundamental steps in the accounting process. Why is the accounting cycle important for Lululemon?

2. What is the difference between an account receivable and a note receivable?

3. Review the **Spin Master** balance sheet for fiscal year-end December 31, 2017, in Appendix III. Identify four different asset accounts and three different liability accounts.

4. Ted says, "This debit and credit stuff is easy! Debits increase an account and credits decrease an account!" You do not agree with Ted. Give three examples of accounts where a debit decreases an account and a credit increases an account.

5. Review the WestJet balance sheet for fiscal year-end December 31, 2017, in Appendix III. Identify three accounts on the balance sheet that would carry debit balances and three accounts on the balance sheet that would carry credit balances.

6. Explain the concept of Accounts Receivable and Revenue. What are the differences between these two accounts in terms of (1) type of account, (2) normal balance, (3) the financial statement the account is recorded on, and (4) the time period each balance represents?

7. Explain the concept of owner's withdrawals and expenses and give an example of each. What are the differences between these two accounts in terms of (1) type of account, (2) normal balance, and (3) the financial statement the account is recorded on?

8. Are debits or credits listed first in general journal entries? Are the debits or the credits indented?

9. Should a transaction be recorded first in a journal or the ledger? Why?

10. Julia says, "I heard that companies use software to do their accounting. Why do we need to learn how to draw T-accounts and prepare trial balances manually?" Explain why knowing the basics of accounting is important.

11. Nicholas wants to save time by not preparing a trial balance. What are the risks of skipping this step?

12. Examine the financial statements shown in Chapter 1. What three things must be included in the title? Where are dollar signs used? Why are some numbers indented? Do indentations represent debits and credits?

QUICK STUDY

QS 2-1 Identifying accounts LO2

Identify the account as an asset, liability, or equity by entering the letter of the account type beside the account name. If the item is an equity account, indicate the type of equity account.

A = Asset
L = Liability

OE = Owner's Capital (Equity)
W = Owner's Withdrawals (Equity)

R = Revenues (Equity)
E = Expenses (Equity)

_____ 1. Buildings
_____ 2. Building Repair Expense
_____ 3. Wages Expense
_____ 4. Wages Payable
_____ 5. Notes Receivable
_____ 6. Notes Payable
_____ 7. Prepaid Advertising
_____ 8. Advertising Expense
_____ 9. Advertising Payable
_____ 10. Unearned Advertising

_____ 11. Advertising Revenue
_____ 12. Interest Income
_____ 13. Interest Expense
_____ 14. Interest Payable
_____ 15. Subscription Revenue
_____ 16. Unearned Subscription Revenue
_____ 17. Prepaid Subscription Fees
_____ 18. Supplies
_____ 19. Supplies Expense
_____ 20. Rent Revenue

_____ 21. Unearned Rent Revenue
_____ 22. Prepaid Rent
_____ 23. Rent Payable
_____ 24. Service Revenue
_____ 25. Jessica Vuong, Withdrawals
_____ 26. Jessica Vuong, Capital
_____ 27. Salaries Expense
_____ 28. Salaries Payable
_____ 29. Furniture
_____ 30. Equipment

QS 2-2 Identifying normal balance as a debit or credit LO3

Indicate whether the normal balance of each of the following accounts is a debit or a credit:

a. Equipment
b. Land
c. Amrit Sandhu, Withdrawals
d. Rent Expense
e. Interest Income

f. Prepaid Rent
g. Accounts Receivable
h. Office Supplies
i. Notes Receivable
j. Notes Payable

k. Amrit Sandhu, Capital
l. Rent Revenue
m. Rent Payable
n. Interest Expense
o. Interest Payable

QS 2-3 Analyzing debit or credit by account LO3

Identify whether a debit or credit entry would be made to record the indicated change in each of the following accounts:

a. To increase Notes Payable
b. To decrease Accounts Receivable
c. To increase Owner, Capital
d. To decrease Unearned Revenue
e. To decrease Prepaid Insurance
f. To decrease Cash
g. To increase Utilities Expense
h. To increase Revenue

i. To increase Store Equipment
j. To increase Owner, Withdrawals
k. To decrease Rent Payable
l. To decrease Prepaid Rent
m. To increase Supplies
n. To increase Supplies Expense
o. To decrease Accounts Payable

QS 2-4 Linking credit or debit with normal balance LO3

Indicate whether a debit or credit is necessary to *decrease* the normal balance of each of the following accounts:

a. Buildings
b. Interest Income
c. Bob Norton, Withdrawals
d. Bob Norton, Capital
e. Prepaid Insurance

f. Interest Payable
g. Accounts Receivable
h. Salaries Expense
i. Office Supplies
j. Repair Services Revenue

k. Interest Expense
l. Unearned Revenue
m. Salaries Payable
n. Furniture
o. Interest Receivable

QS 2-5 Developing a chart of accounts LO4

Using the chart of accounts numbering system, develop a chart of accounts that assigns an account number to each of the following accounts:

a. Buildings
b. Interest Income
c. Matthew Lee, Withdrawals
d. Matthew Lee, Capital
e. Prepaid Insurance

f. Interest Payable
g. Accounts Receivable
h. Salaries Expense
i. Office Supplies
j. Repair Services Revenue

k. Interest Expense
l. Unearned Revenue
m. Salaries Payable
n. Furniture
o. Interest Receivable

QS 2-6 Analyze the impact of transactions on accounts LO5

Douglas Malone started CityBnB, which is a bed and breakfast in Vancouver. CityBnB offers accommodations and breakfast to travellers exploring the city. The following are the transactions for the month of August.

a. On August 1, purchased an IKEA bed for $400 cash.

b. On August 7, discussed the prices of staying at CityBnB with a customer over the phone.

c. On August 13, rented a room to a family and billed them $600 on credit.

d. On August 14, purchased and used cleaning services for $300 on credit.

e. On August 31, invested $25,000 cash into the business.

Required For each transaction, complete the **analysis** and determine the **journal entry analysis**. Use the template below. The first transaction has been completed for you.

a.	**Analysis**	Assets increase. Assets decrease.
	Journal entry analysis	Debit the furniture account for $400. Credit the cash account for $400.
		Continue...

QS 2-7 Preparing general journal entries LO5

Using the information and analysis prepared in QS 2-6, prepare the journal entries for the month of August. Use the following template. Ensure to include the **date**, the **account descriptions**, the **debit and credit amount**, and a **description of the journal entry**. The first transaction has been completed for you.

	Date	**Account Titles and Explanation**		**Debit**	**Credit**
a.	Aug. 1	Furniture		400	
		Cash			400
		To record purchase of furniture			
		Continue...			

QS 2-8 Posting entries to T-accounts LO5

CityBnB's records showed the following beginning balances on July 31, 2020. Using the information provided and the analysis completed in QS 2-6 and QS 2-7, complete the following:

1. Post the journal entries to the general ledger using T-accounts. Include the date of each transaction next to your posting.

2. Calculate the balance in each T-account.

3. Prove the accounting equation (Assets = Liabilities + Equity).

Cash		
Jul 31	25,000	

Accounts Receivable		
Jul 31	1,500	

Furniture		
Jul 31	5,000	

Accounts Payable		
	500	Jul 31

Douglas Malone, Capital		
	28,000	Jul 31

Revenue		
	4,500	Jul 31

Cleaning Expense		
Jul 31	1,500	

QS 2-9 Analyzing and recording journal entries LO5

Dee Bell Company had the following transactions in the month of May.

May	2	Dee Bell transferred her personal car valued at $8,000 into the business.
	10	Did $4,000 of work for a customer on account.
	12	Collected $10,000 from a customer for work to be done in July 2020.
	15	Paid wages of $6,000.
	16	Collected $4,000 from the customer of May 10.
	22	Paid $3,000 of the outstanding accounts payable.

Required For each transaction, **(1) complete the analysis, (2) determine the journal entry analysis**, and **(3) record the journal entry**. Use the template below. The first transaction on May 2 has been completed for you.

May 2	Analysis	Assets increase. Equity increases.		
	Journal entry analysis	Debit the Car account for $8,000. Credit the Dee Bell, Capital account for $8,000.		
	Journal Entry			
	Date	Account Titles and Explanation	Debit	Credit
	May 2	Car	8,000	
		Dee Bell, Capital		8,000
		To record investment by owner.		
May 10		Continue...		

QS 2-10 Posting entries to T-accounts LO5

Dee Bell Company's records showed the following April 30, 2020, account balances:

Cash
Apr 30 15,000

Accounts Receivable
Apr 30 3,200

Car

Accounts Payable
6,000 Apr 30

Unearned Revenue
1,800 Apr 30

Dee Bell, Capital
8,900 Apr 30

Revenue
3,000 Apr 30

Wages Expense
Apr 30 1,500

Required

1. Using the chart of accounts numbering system, assign an account number to each account.
2. Using the information provided and the analysis performed in QS 2-9, post the May transactions into the general ledger using T-accounts.
3. Calculate the May 31 balance in each T-account and prove the accounting equation.

QS 2-11 Calculating account balances LO5

Calculate the account balance for each of the following:

Accounts Receivable	
1,000	650
400	920
920	1,500
3,000	

Accounts Payable	
250	250
900	1,800
650	1,400
	650

Service Revenue	
	13,000
	2,500
	810
	3,500

Utilities Expense	
610	
520	
390	
275	

Cash	
3,900	2,400
17,800	3,900
14,500	21,800
340	

Notes Payable	
4,000	50,000
8,000	

QS 2-12 Preparing journal entries LO3, 5

Prepare journal entries for the following transactions that occurred during 2020:

May	1	Purchased equipment on account; $500.
	2	Paid for the equipment purchased on May 1.
	3	Purchased supplies for cash; $100.
	4	Paid wages to employees; $2,000.
	5	Performed services for a client and collected cash; $750.
	6	Did work for a customer on credit; $2,500.
	7	Collected the amount owing from the customer of May 6.

QS 2-13 Preparing journal entries LO3, 5

Prepare journal entries for the following transactions that occurred during January 2020:

January	3	Stan Adams opened a landscaping business by investing $60,000 cash and equipment having a $40,000 fair value.
	4	Purchased office supplies on credit for $340.
	6	Received $5,200 for providing landscaping services to a customer.
	15	Paid $200 regarding the office supplies purchase of January 4.
	16	Purchased $700 of office supplies on account.
	30	Paid the balance owing regarding the office supplies purchase of January 4.

QS 2-14 Posting entries in T-accounts LO5

a. Set up the following general ledger accounts (use the balance column format as illustrated in Exhibit 2.12: Cash (101), Office Supplies (124), Equipment (163), Accounts Payable (201), Stan Adams, Capital (301), and Landscaping Services Revenue (403).

b. Post the journal entries from QS 2-13 to the general ledger accounts and enter the balance after each posting.

QS 2-15 Preparing a trial balance LO6

Using the account information shown below, prepare a trial balance at January 31, 2020.

Vahn Landscaping
General Ledger

Cash	101
5,000	6,000
2,000	4,000
3,000	1,000
8,000	

Equipment	163
9,000	

Unearned Revenue	233
	2,000

Brea Vahn, Capital	301
	14,000

Brea Vahn, Withdrawals	302
1,000	

Revenue	401
	3,000
	8,000

Rent Expense	640
6,000	

Utilities Expense	690
4,000	

QS 2-16 Identifying a posting error LO3, 5, 6

A trial balance has total debits of $21,000 and total credits of $25,500. Which one of the following errors would create this imbalance? Explain.

a. A $4,500 debit to Salaries Expense in a journal entry was incorrectly posted to the ledger as a $4,500 credit, leaving the Salaries Expense account with a $750 debit balance.

b. A $2,250 credit to Teaching Revenue in a journal entry was incorrectly posted to the ledger as a $2,250 debit, leaving the Teaching Revenue account with a $6,300 credit balance.

c. A $2,250 debit to Rent Expense in a journal entry was incorrectly posted to the ledger as a $2,250 credit, leaving the Rent Expense account with a $3,000 debit balance.

QS 2-17 Identifying a transposition error LO6

Identify the transposition error in the following trial balance, assuming this is the only error.

	Be Fabulous Flowers		
	Trial Balance		
	September 30, 2020		
Acct. No.	**Account**	**Debit**	**Credit**
101	Cash..	$ 9,800	
165	Equipment...	10,350	
201	Accounts payable		$ 750
301	Tracy Rumanko, Capital.........................		3,800
403	Consulting revenue		17,000
640	Rent expense	4,100	
	Totals	$24,250	$21,550

QS 2-18 Identifying a slide error LO6

Identify the slide error in the following trial balance, assuming this is the only error.

Body Boot Camp Trial Balance April 30, 2020		
Cash	$330	
Supplies	38	
Notes payable		$ 25
Michelle Jackson, capital		100
Revenue		378
Wages expense	360	
Totals	$728	$503

EXERCISES

Exercise 2-1 Classifying accounts LO2, 3

The following accounts are from Yoojin Chang's interior design company, Big Apple Design. For each account, complete the following. The first one has been completed for you as an example.

(1) The **basic account** category (asset, liability, owner's capital, withdrawal, revenue, or expense)

(2) The **financial statement** the account is recorded on (Income Statement, Statement of Changes in Equity, or Balance Sheet).

(3) The **normal balance** (debit or credit).

(4) The **effect of a debit** to the account (increase or decrease).

(5) The **effect of a credit** (increase or decrease).

a. Cash
b. Supplies
c. Accounts payable
d. Yoojin Chang, Capital Account
e. Yoojin Chang, Withdrawals
f. Design Revenue
g. Salaries Expense
h. Accounts Receivable
i. Notes Payable
j. Prepaid Insurance

	(1) Basic Account	(2) Financial Statement	(3) Normal Balance	(4) Effect of a Debit	(5) Effect of a Credit
a. Cash	Asset	Balance Sheet	Debit	Increase	Decrease

Exercise 2-2 Analyzing transactions LO3, 5

Christina Reis is a photographer who owns Lola Lemon Photography. This is the first month of operations. The following are the transactions for the month of September.

a. On September 1, Reis invested $15,000 cash into her new business.

b. On September 12, purchased $2,000 of equipment (cameras) on credit.

c. On September 13, purchased $500 of equipment (lighting), paying cash.

d. On September 18, photographed an engagement session for $1,000; collected cash.

e. On September 21, photographed a family session for $700 on credit.

f. On September 26, paid $1,000 regarding (b).

g. On September 29, collected $300 regarding (e).

Required For each transaction, complete the **analysis** and determine the **journal entry analysis**. Use the template below. The first transaction has been completed for you.

a.	**Analysis**	Assets increase. Equity increases.
	Journal entry analysis	Debit the cash account for $15,000. Credit the Christina Reis, Capital account in equity for $15,000
		Continue...

Exercise 2-3 **Journalizing general journal entries** LO5

Using the analysis prepared in Exercise 2-2, prepare the journal entries for the month of September. Use the following template. Ensure to include the **date**, the **account descriptions**, the **debit and credit amount**, and a **description of the journal entry**. The first transaction has been completed for you.

	Date	Account Titles and Explanation	Debit	Credit
a.	Sept. 1	Cash...	15,000	
		Christina Reis, Capital......................................		15,000
		Investment by owner.		
		Continue...		

Exercise 2-4 **Posting entries to T-accounts** LO5

Using the information provided in Exercise 2-2 and the analysis prepared in Exercise 2-3, complete the following:

1. Post the journal entries to the general ledger using T-accounts. Include the letter of each transaction next to your posting.

2. Calculate the balance in each T-account.

3. Prove the accounting equation (Assets = Liabilities + Equity).

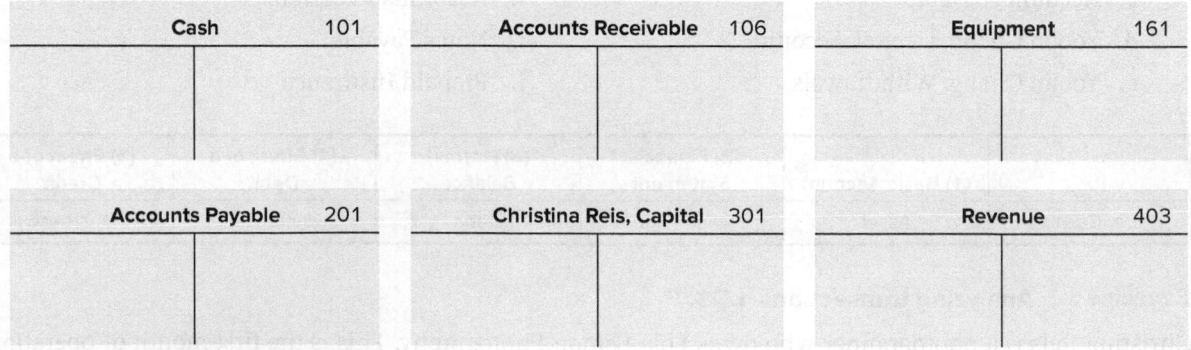

Exercise 2-5 **Analyzing transactions** LO3, 5

William Curtis is a personal finance expert and owns Much Money Consulting. This is his first month of operations and William has hired you to do his accounting. The following transactions are for the month of October.

a. On October 2, William Curtis invested $32,600 cash into his business.

b. On October 4, purchased $925 of office supplies for cash.

c. On October 6, purchased $13,600 of office equipment on credit.

d. On October 10, received $3,000 cash as revenue for being a guest on the TV show *CityTalk*.

e. On October 12, paid for the office equipment purchased in transaction (c).

f. On October 16, billed a customer $5,400 for delivering a corporate workshop on smart investing.

g. On October 18, paid October's rent for the downtown office with $3,500 cash.

h. On October 26, collected all cash for the account receivable created in transaction (f).

i. On October 31, withdrew $5,000 cash from the business for a trip to Hawaii.

Required For each transaction, **(1) complete the analysis, (2) determine the journal entry analysis,** and **(3) record the journal entry.** Use the template below. Transaction (a) has been completed for you.

a.	Analysis	Assets increase. Equity increases.			
	Journal entry analysis	Debit the Cash account for $32,600. Credit the William Curtis, Capital account for $32,600.			
	Journal Entry				
	Date	Account Titles and Explanation		Debit	Credit
	Oct. 2	Cash..		32,600	
		William Curtis, Capital..			32,600
		Investment by owner.			
b.		**Continue...**			

Exercise 2-6 Posting transactions to the general ledger LO3, 5

Use the information given and the analysis completed in Exercise 2-5.

Required

1. Set up the following general ledger accounts using T-accounts: Cash; Accounts Receivable; Office Supplies; Office Equipment; Accounts Payable; William Curtis, Capital; William Curtis, Withdrawals; Revenue; and Rent Expense.

2. Post the journal entries from Exercise 2-5 into the T-accounts. Include the letter of the transaction next to your posting.

3. Determine the balance of each account.

Exercise 2-7 Analyzing and journalizing revenue transactions LO3, 5

Examine the following transactions and identify those that created revenues for TI Servicing, a sole proprietorship owned by Todd Iver. Prepare general journal entries to record those transactions and explain why the other transactions did not create revenues.

a. Invested $76,500 cash in the business.

b. Provided $2,700 of services on credit.

c. Received $3,150 cash for services provided to a client.

d. Received $18,300 from a client in payment for services to be provided next year.

e. Received $9,000 from a client in partial payment of an account receivable.

f. Borrowed $300,000 from the bank by signing a promissory note.

Exercise 2-8 Analyzing and journalizing expense transactions LO3, 5

Myra Sharma owns and operates a yoga studio, Green Yoga. Examine the following transactions and identify those that created expenses for Green Yoga. Prepare journal entries to record those transactions and explain why the other transactions did not create expenses.

a. Paid $14,100 cash for office supplies purchased 30 days previously.

b. Paid the $1,125 salary of the receptionist.

c. Paid $45,000 cash for yoga studio equipment.

d. Paid utility bill with $930 cash.

e. Withdrew $5,000 from the business account for personal use.

Exercise 2-9 Journalizing, posting, preparing a trial balance, and financial statements LO3, 5, 6

CHECK FIGURES: 4. Total debits = $25,470; 5. Total assets = $17,530

Manny Gill is an entrepreneur who started West Secure, a business that provides a number of security guard services. West Secure incurred the following transactions during July 2020, its first month of operations:

July	1	The owner, Manny Gill, invested $5,200 cash.
	10	Purchased $2,700 worth of security equipment on credit.
	12	Performed security services for a sold-out concert and received $12,000 cash from the client.
	14	Paid for expenses; $3,700.
	15	Completed security services for a graduation event and sent the client a bill for $1,600.
	31	The owner withdrew $270 cash for personal use.

Required

1. Set up the following general ledger accounts using either the T-account format or the balance column format: Cash, 101; Accounts Receivable, 106; Equipment, 150; Accounts Payable, 201; Manny Gill, Capital, 301; Manny Gill, Withdrawals, 302; Revenue, 401; Expenses, 501.

2. Record the journal entries for the month of July.

3. Post the July journal entries into your general ledger accounts. Include the date next to each number posted. Determine the balances.

4. Prepare a trial balance using the balances in your general ledger accounts.

West Secure			
Trial Balance			
July 31, 2020			
Acct. No.	Account Title	Debit	Credit

5. Prepare an income statement, statement of changes in equity, and balance sheet based on your trial balance.

West Secure
Income Statement
For Month Ended July 31, 2020

Revenue.. _____

Expenses..

Profit.. _____

West Secure
Statement of Changes in Equity
For Month Ended July 31, 2020

Manny Gill, capital, July 1...

Investments by owner..

Profit... _____

Total ....

Less: Withdrawals by owner..

Manny Gill, capital, July 31 .... _____

West Secure
Balance Sheet
July 31, 2020

Assets	Liabilities
Cash..	Accounts payable.......................... _____
Accounts receivable......................	
Equipment....................................	**Equity**
	Manny Gill, capital ....
	Total liabilities and equity............
Total assets .... _____	_____

Analysis Component: Assets are financed by debt and equity transactions, a concept reinforced by the accounting equation: $A = L + E$. Since accounts receivable are an asset, are they financed by debt and/or equity? Explain.

Exercise 2-10 Chart of accounts LO4

Aaron Paquette has given the following guide regarding the chart of accounts for Paquette Advisors:

100–199	Assets
200–299	Liabilities
300–399	Equity
400–499	Revenues
500–599	Expenses

Required Using the account information from Exercise 2-11, develop a chart of accounts for Paquette Advisors.

Exercise 2-11 Journalizing, posting, preparing a trial balance, and financial statements LO3, 5, 6

CHECK FIGURES: 4. Profit = $21,700; 6. Total assets = $35,400

After its first month of operations, Paquette Advisors showed the following account balances in its general ledger accounts (T-accounts) as at January 31, 2020.

Cash	
15,000	

Accounts Receivable	
3,800	

Office Equipment	
22,500	

Accounts Payable	
	8,000

Unearned Revenue	
	2,600

Aaron Paquette, Capital	
	9,500

Aaron Paquette, Withdrawals	
2,000	

Consulting Revenues	
	41,700

Salaries Expense	
10,000	

Rent Expense	
7,500	

Utilities Expense	
1,000	

During February, the following transactions occurred:

Feb.	1	Performed work for a client and received cash of $8,500.
	5	Paid $5,000 regarding outstanding accounts payable.
	10	Received cash of $3,600 for work to be done in March.
	12	Called FasCo Rentals to book the use of some equipment next month. The $400 rental fee will be paid in full when the equipment is returned.
	17	The owner withdrew cash of $3,000 for personal use.
	28	Paid salaries of $10,000.

Required
1. Record the journal entries for the month of February.
2. Post the journal entries to the general ledger (T-accounts above). Include the date next to each posting.
3. Prepare a trial balance based on the balances in your T-accounts.
4. Prepare an income statement for the two months ended February 28, 2020.
5. Prepare a statement of changes in equity for the two months ended February 28, 2020.
6. Prepare the balance sheet as at February 28, 2020.

Analysis Component: Paquette Advisors shows Unearned Revenue on its February 28, 2020, balance sheet. Explain what Unearned Revenue is. As part of your answer, be sure to address why Unearned Revenue is reported as a liability.

Exercise 2-12 Analyzing transactions from T-accounts LO3, 5

Prepare journal entries for each of the seven transactions posted to the following T-accounts. Provide a short description of each transaction. The first description is done as an example.

(a) *The owner invested cash, an automobile, and equipment in the business.*

		Cash		
(a)	7,000	3,600	(b)
(e)	2,500	600	(c)
		2,400	(f)
		700	(g)

		Office Supplies	
(c)		600	
(d)		200	

		Prepaid Insurance	
(b)		3,600	

		Equipment	
(a)		5,600	
(d)		9,400	

		Automobiles	
(a)		11,000	

		Accounts Payable		
(f)	2,400	9,600	(d)

		Jerry Steiner, Capital	
		23,600	(a)

		Delivery Services Revenue	
		2,500	(e)

		Gas and Oil Expense	
(g)		700	

Exercise 2-13 General Journal Entries LO3, 5

Precision Laser Centres showed the following selected activities during the month of April 2020. Record the journal entries for the following transactions.

April	5	Performed surgery on a customer today and collected $5,200 cash.
	8	Purchased surgical supplies on credit; $19,600.
	10	Contacted a client's lawyer today regarding a complaint about the surgery. The client is planning to sue for $100,000.
	18	Paid salaries; $47,000.
	20	Performed six surgeries today, all on credit; $4,400 each.
	21	Paid for the surgical supplies purchased on April 8.
	22	Paid the April utilities bill today; $2,100.
	29	Collected from four of the credit customers of April 20.

Exercise 2-14 Posting from the general journal to the general ledger LO5

CHECK FIGURE: b. Jan. 31, 2020, Cash balance = $3,600

Sato Inspection Services is in its second month of operations. You have been given the following journal entries regarding its January 2020 transactions.

Required

a. Set up the following accounts (use the balance column format) entering the opening balances brought forward from the end of last month, December 31, 2019: Cash (101) $850; Accounts Receivable (106) $300; Equipment (167) $1,500; Accounts Payable (201) $325; Toshi Sato, Capital (301) $2,325; Toshi Sato, Withdrawals (302) $300; Revenue (401) $1,800; and Salaries Expense (622) $1,500.

b. Post the journal entries to the accounts and enter the balance after each posting.

General Journal					Page 1
Date	Account Titles and Explanation	PR	Debit	Credit	
2020					
Jan. 1	Cash..		3,500		
	Toshi Sato, Capital..			3,500	
	Additional owner investment.				
12	Accounts Receivable..		9,000		
	Revenue..			9,000	
	Performed work for a customer on account.				
20	Equipment..		12,000		
	Accounts Payable...			10,000	
	Cash			2,000	
	Purchased equipment by paying cash and the balance on credit.				
31	Cash..		5,000		
	Accounts Receivable..			5,000	
	Collected cash from credit customer.				

Analysis Component: The accounting cycle requires that transactions be journalized in the general journal and then posted in the general ledger. This seems to indicate that we are recording the same information in two different places. Why can't we eliminate journalizing or posting?

Exercise 2-15 Preparing journal entries LO3, 5

Prepare journal entries to record the following August 2020 transactions of a new business called For the Love of Pixels.

Aug.	1	Joseph Eagle, the owner, invested $20,000 cash and photography equipment with a fair value of $42,000.
	1	Rented a studio, paying $12,000 for the next three months in advance.
	5	Purchased office supplies for $1,800 cash.
	20	Received $9,200 in photography revenue.
	31	Paid $1,400 for August utilities.

Exercise 2-16 General ledger accounts and the trial balance LO3, 5, 6

CHECK FIGURE: Trial balance total debits = $71,200

Set up the following accounts (use the balance column format): Cash (101); Office Supplies (124); Prepaid Rent (131); Photography Equipment (167); Joseph Eagle, Capital (301); Photography Revenue (401); and Utilities Expense (690). Then, using your journal entries from Exercise 2-15, post to the general ledger (balance column format). Finally, prepare the August 31, 2020, trial balance.

Analysis Component: Joseph Eagle wanted to buy a building for his business and took the August 31, 2020, trial balance to his bank manager. Is the trial balance used for external reporting? Explain.

Exercise 2-17 T-accounts and the trial balance LO3, 5, 6

Follow the instructions in Exercise 2-16, but instead of using a balance column format for the accounts, use T-accounts. Include the date next to each posting.

Exercise 2-18 Preparing financial statements from a trial balance LO6

CHECK FIGURES: Loss = $19,000; Total assets = $93,300

Extreme Hockey trains top-level hockey players with on-ice and off-ice programs. Extreme Hockey aims to maximize every hockey player's full potential. The company showed the following trial balances for its first year just ended December 31, 2020:

Account Title	Debit	Credit
Cash..	$ 18,000	
Accounts receivable....................................	5,200	
Prepaid rent...	13,000	
Machinery...	57,100	
Accounts payable...		$ 17,300
Notes payable..		47,000
Ryan Roy, capital...		50,000
Ryan Roy, withdrawals................................	2,000	
Training revenue..		18,000
Wages expense...	29,000	
Rent expense..	8,000	
Totals..	$132,300	$132,300

Required Use the information provided to complete an income statement, statement of changes in equity, and balance sheet.

Analysis Component: If Extreme Hockey continues to experience losses, what alternatives are available to prevent assets from decreasing?

Exercise 2-19 Preparing financial statements from a trial balance LO6

CHECK FIGURES: Profit = $770; Total assets = $3,170

Cycle Travel Tours showed the following trial balance information (in alphabetical order) for its first month just ended March 31, 2020:

Account	Debit	Credit
Accounts payable...		$ 430
Accounts receivable....................................	$1,880	
Cash...	430	
Equipment...	630	
Interest expense..	10	
Francois Laneuv, capital.............................		1,980
Francois Laneuv, withdrawals....................	1,430	
Notes payable..		1,030
Prepaid insurance.......................................	230	
Salaries expense..	730	
Service revenue...		1,510
Unearned service revenue.........................		390
Totals..	$5,340	$5,340

Required Use the information provided to complete an income statement, statement of changes in equity, and balance sheet.

Exercise 2-20 Preparing financial statements from a trial balance LO6

CHECK FIGURES: Loss = $27,000; Total assets = $237,000

Media Marketing Services has been operating for several years. It showed the following trial balance information (in alphabetical order) for the month just ended March 31, 2020:

Account	Debit	Credit
Accounts payable..		$ 46,000
Accounts receivable.....................................	$ 3,000	
Building...	80,000	
Cash..	17,000	
Revenue..		126,000
Sam Smith, capital*.....................................		122,000
Sam Smith, withdrawals...............................	18,000	
Land..	84,000	
Machinery...	50,000	
Notes payable..		114,000
Office supplies...	3,000	
Office supplies expense..............................	7,000	
Wages expense..	146,000	
Totals..	$408,000	$408,000

*The $122,000 balance includes $35,000 invested by the owner during March.

Required Using the information provided, prepare an income statement and a statement of changes in equity for the month ended March 31, 2020, and a balance sheet at March 31, 2020.

Exercise 2-21 Effects of posting errors on the trial balance LO3, 5, 6

Complete the following table by filling in the blanks. For each of the listed posting errors:

1. Enter in column (1) the amount of the difference that the error would create between the two trial balance columns (show a zero if the columns would balance).
2. Identify if there would be a difference between the two columns, and identify in column (2) the trial balance column that would be larger.
3. Identify the account(s) affected in column (3).
4. Identify the amount by which the account(s) is (are) under- or overstated in column (4). The answer for the first error is provided as an example.

	Description	(1) Difference Between Debit and Credit Columns	(2) Column With the Larger Total Stated	(3) Identify Account(s) Incorrectly Understated	(4) Amount That Account(s) Is (Are) Over- or Understated
a.	A $2,400 debit to Rent Expense was posted as a $1,590 debit.	$810	Credit	Rent Expense	Rent Expense is understated by $810
b.	A $42,000 debit to Machinery was posted as a debit to Accounts Payable.				
c.	A $4,950 credit to Services Revenue was posted as a $495 credit.				
d.	A $1,440 debit to Store Supplies was not posted at all.				
e.	A $2,250 debit to Prepaid Insurance was posted as a debit to Insurance Expense.				
f.	A $4,050 credit to Cash was posted twice as two credits to the Cash account.				
g.	A $9,900 debit to the owner's withdrawals account was debited to the owner's capital account.				

Exercise 2-22 Analyzing the trial balance LO3, 5, 6

During March, Salma Ahmad, the owner of Doan Cleaning Services, had trouble keeping her debits and credits equal. The following errors were noted:

a. Ahmad did not post the entry to record $3,500 of services performed on account.

b. In posting a $300 payment on account, debited Cash and credited Accounts Payable.

c. In posting a cash payment, correctly debited Accounts Payable for $425 but incorrectly credited Cash for $245.

d. In posting a cash receipt of $750, debited Cash but forgot to post the credit to Accounts Receivable.

e. In posting the purchase of $1,000 of equipment on credit, debited Accounts Payable and credited Equipment.

Required For each of the errors described, indicate:

1. Whether debits equal credits on the trial balance, and
2. Which account(s) have incorrect balances.

Exercise 2-23 Transposition and slide errors on the trial balance LO6

Required Identify the single transposition or slide error in each of the following independent trial balances.

	Case A		Case B		Case C	
Cash..	$ 120		$ 3,900		$ 59	
Accounts receivable...............................	260		1,900		46	
Equipment..	3,170		12,900		791	
Accounts payable.....................................		$ 190		$ 2,350		$ 72
Capital		1,100		16,150		229
Withdrawals	850		7,000		-0-	
Revenue...		3,000		9,600		641
Wages expense..	610		8,700		10	
Totals..	$5,010	$4,290	$34,400	$28,100	$906	$942

PROBLEMS

Problem 2-1A Analyzing transactions and recording journal entries LO3, 5

Tobias Eaden started a sole proprietorship named Sky High Ads. A customer's message can be displayed on an airplane banner across the city. Sky High Ads had the following business activities during the month of November 2020:

Nov	1	Invested $200,000 cash and aircraft equipment with a $50,000 fair value in a new sole proprietorship named Sky High Ads.
	3	Purchased land and a small office building. The land was worth $400,000, and the building was worth $100,000. The purchase price was paid with $125,000 cash and a long-term note payable for the balance.
	7	Eaden transferred title of his personal airplane to the business. The airplane had a value of $200,000 and was to be used exclusively in the business.
	9	Purchased $5,000 of supplies on credit.
	13	Provided services to a customer for a marriage proposal and collected $16,000 on credit.
	17	Paid $3,000 wages to a pilot.
	21	Signed an advertising contract to commence in January. A deposit of $250 must be paid by December 15.
	23	Paid for half of the account payable from the November 9 transaction.
	27	Purchased $20,000 of new aircraft equipment by paying $15,000 cash and trading in old aircraft equipment with a recorded cost of $5,000.
	30	Withdrew $3,200 cash from the business for personal use.

Required For each transaction, **(1) complete the analysis, (2) determine the journal entry analysis,** and **(3) record the journal entry.** Use the template below.

Nov 1	Analysis				
	Journal entry analysis				
	Journal Entry				
	Date	Account Titles and Explanation		Debit	Credit
Nov 3					

Problem 2-2A Posting journal entries to T-accounts LO5

CHECK FIGURE: 2. Cash balance, Nov. 30, 2020 = $51,300

Refer to the scenario described in Problem 2-1A.

Required

1. Set up the following general ledger accounts using T-accounts: Cash; Accounts Receivable; Supplies; Airplane; Aircraft Equipment; Building; Land; Accounts Payable; Long-Term Notes Payable; Tobias Eaden, Capital; Tobias Eaden, Withdrawals; Revenue; and Wages Expense.

2. Post the journal entries into the T-accounts. Identify the date next to each posting. Determine the balance in each account.

3. Prove the accounting equation.

Problem 2-3A Preparing general journal entries LO3, 5

Bruce Ibach owns Biotech Fitness Centre, which showed the following selected transactions for the month ended May 31, 2020:

May	1	Purchased new equipment, paying cash of $14,700 and signing a 90-day note payable for the balance of $39,000.
	2	Purchased 12 months of insurance to begin May 2; paid $28,200.
	3	Completed a fitness contract for a group of clients today and received $6,700.
	4	Purchased office supplies on account; $4,100.
	6	Returned to the supplier $820 of defective office supplies purchased on May 4.
	10	Provided services to a client today on account; $12,200.
	15	Paid for the May 4 purchase less the return of May 6.
	20	Received payment from the client of May 10.
	25	Received cash of $3,200 from a client for work to be done in June.
	31	Paid month-end salaries of $54,000.
	31	Paid the May telephone bill today; $2,600.
	31	Received the May electrical bill today; $3,800. It will be paid on June 15.

Required Prepare journal entries for each of the above transactions.

Problem 2-4A Preparing general journal entries LO3, 5

Abe Factor opened a new accounting practice called X-Factor Accounting and completed these activities during March 2020:

Mar.	1	Invested $50,000 in cash and office equipment that had a fair value of $12,000.
	1	Prepaid $9,000 cash for three months' rent for an office.
	3	Made credit purchases of used office equipment for $6,000 and office supplies for $1,200.
	5	Completed work for a client and immediately received $6,200 cash.
	9	Completed a $4,000 project for a client, who will pay within 30 days.
	11	Paid the account payable created on March 3.
	15	Paid $3,000 cash for the annual premium on an insurance policy.
	20	Received $1,500 as partial payment for the work completed on March 9.
	22	Placed an order with a supplier for $4,800 of supplies to be delivered April 7. They must be paid for within 15 days of being received.
	23	Completed work for another client for $2,850 on credit.
	27	Abe Factor withdrew $3,600 cash from the business to pay some personal expenses.
	30	Purchased $650 of additional office supplies on credit.
	31	Paid $860 for the month's utility bill.

Required Prepare journal entries to record the transactions.

Problem 2-5A Posting, preparing a trial balance LO4, 5, 6

CHECK FIGURE: 3. Total Dr. = $75,700

Required Using the journal entries prepared in Problem 2-4A, complete the following:

1. Set up the following accounts (use the balance column format or T-accounts): Cash (101); Accounts Receivable (106); Office Supplies (124); Prepaid Insurance (128); Prepaid Rent (131); Office Equipment (163); Accounts Payable (201); Abe Factor, Capital (301); Abe Factor, Withdrawals (302); Accounting Revenue (401); and Utilities Expense (690).

2. Post the entries to the accounts and enter the balance after each posting.

3. Prepare a trial balance as of the end of the month.

Problem 2-6A Preparing financial statements from a trial balance LO6

CHECK FIGURES: Profit = $12,190; Total assets = $71,240

Using the trial balance prepared for X-Factor Accounting in Part 3 of Problem 2-5A, prepare an income statement and statement of changes in equity for the month ended March 31, 2020, and a balance sheet at March 31, 2020.

Problem 2-7A Preparing and posting journal entries; preparing a trial balance LO3, 4, 5, 6

CHECK FIGURE: 4. Total Dr. = $176,230

Elizabeth Wong has strong problem-solving skills and loves to work with people. After becoming a Certified Human Resources Professional (CHRP) and working for several companies, she opened her own business, HR Solutions. She completed the following transactions during May 2020:

May	1	Invested $78,000 in cash and office equipment that had a fair value of $51,000 in the business.
	1	Prepaid $15,300 cash for three months' rent for an office.
	2	Made credit purchases of office equipment for $25,500 and office supplies for $5,100.
	6	Completed a report on hiring solutions for a client and collected $8,300 cash.
	9	Completed a $16,300 project implementing a training program for a client, who will pay within 30 days.
	10	Paid half of the account payable created on May 2.
	19	Paid $7,800 cash for the annual premium on an insurance policy.
	22	Received $13,100 as partial payment for the work completed on May 9.
	25	Developed a performance review process for another client for $5,580 on credit.
	25	Paid wages for May totalling $35,500.
	31	Withdrew $5,300 cash from the business to take a trip to Paris in June.
	31	Purchased $1,750 of additional office supplies on credit.
	31	Paid $1,430 for the month's utility bill.

Required

1. Prepare journal entries to record the transactions. Use page 1 for the journal.

2. Set up the following accounts (use the balance column format or T-accounts): Cash (101); Accounts Receivable (106); Office Supplies (124); Prepaid Insurance (128); Prepaid Rent (131); Office Equipment

(163); Accounts Payable (201); Elizabeth Wong, Capital (301); Elizabeth Wong, Withdrawals (302); Services Revenue (403); Wages Expense (623); and Utilities Expense (690).

3. Post the entries to the accounts and enter the balance after each posting.

4. Prepare a trial balance at May 31, 2020.

Analysis Component: Utilities Expense, Services Revenue, and Elizabeth Wong, Withdrawals are equity accounts. Explain why.

Problem 2-8A   Preparing financial statements from a trial balance   LO6

CHECK FIGURES: Loss = $6,750; Total assets = $134,000

Using the trial balance prepared for HR Solutions in Part 4 of Problem 2-7A, prepare an income statement and statement of changes in equity for the month ended May 31, 2020, and a balance sheet at May 31, 2020.

Problem 2-9A   Preparing financial statements from a trial balance   LO6

CHECK FIGURES: Profit = $7,580; Total assets = $73,800

	Hipster Optical Trial Balance May 31, 2020		
Acct. No.	**Account Title**	**Debit**	**Credit**
101	Cash	$19,500	
106	Accounts receivable	9,480	
124	Office supplies	7,400	
128	Prepaid insurance	10,820	
163	Office equipment	26,600	
201	Accounts payable		$ 1,700
230	Unearned service revenue		8,800
301	Peeta Black, capital		57,300
302	Peeta Black, withdrawals	1,580	
403	Services revenue		30,380
623	Wages expense	16,000	
640	Rent expense	5,300	
690	Utilities expense	1,500	
	Totals	$98,180	$98,180

Required Using the trial balance provided above, prepare an income statement and statement of changes in equity for the first month ended May 31, 2020, and a balance sheet at May 31, 2020.

Analysis Component: Prepare two different journal entries, including explanations, that might have created the May 31, 2020, balance in Utilities Expense of $1,500. Use May 31, 2020, as the date for your entries.

Problem 2-10A   Journalizing, posting, preparing a trial balance   LO3, 4, 5, 6

CHECK FIGURE: 4. Total Dr. = $658,740

Binbutti Engineering, a sole proprietorship, completed the following transactions during July 2020, the third month of operations:

July	1	Bob Binbutti, the owner, invested $300,000 cash, office equipment with a value of $12,000, and $90,000 of drafting equipment in the business.
	2	Purchased land for an office. The land was worth $108,000, which was paid with $10,800 cash and a long-term note payable for $97,200.
	3	Purchased a portable building with $150,000 cash and moved it onto the land.
	5	Paid $12,000 cash for the premiums on two one-year insurance policies.
	7	Completed and delivered a set of plans for a client and collected $1,400 cash.
	9	Purchased additional drafting equipment for $45,000. Paid $21,000 cash and signed a long-term note payable for the $24,000 balance.
	10	Completed $4,000 of engineering services for a client. This amount is to be paid within 30 days.
	12	Purchased $4,500 of additional office equipment on credit.
	15	Completed engineering services for $7,000 on credit.
	16	Received a bill for rent on equipment that was used on a completed job. The $13,800 rent must be paid within 30 days.
	17	Collected $400 from the client of July 10.
	19	Paid $12,000 wages to the drafting assistants.
	22	Paid the account payable created on July 12.
	25	Paid $1,350 cash for some repairs to an item of drafting equipment.
	26	Binbutti withdrew $800 cash from the business for personal use.
	30	Paid $12,000 wages to the drafting assistants.
	31	Paid $6,000 cash for advertising in the local newspaper during July.

Required

1. Prepare journal entries to record the transactions. Use page 1 for the journal.

2. Set up the following general ledger accounts (use the balance column format or T-accounts), entering the balances brought forward from June 30, 2020: Cash (101) $26,000; Accounts Receivable (106) $3,000; Prepaid Insurance (128) $500; Office Equipment (163) $1,700; Drafting Equipment (167) $1,200; Building (173) $42,000; Land (183) $28,000; Accounts Payable (201) $1,740; Long-Term Notes Payable (251) $24,000; Bob Binbutti, Capital (301) $54,000; Bob Binbutti, Withdrawals (302) $1,000; Engineering Revenue (401) $29,600; Wages Expense (623) $4,000; Equipment Rental Expense (645) $1,000; Advertising Expense (655) $640; and Repairs Expense (684) $300.

3. Post the entries to the general ledger accounts and enter the balance after each posting.

4. Prepare a trial balance at July 31, 2020.

Problem 2-11A Preparing financial statements from a trial balance LO6

CHECK FIGURES: Loss = $9,090; Total assets = $605,850

Using the trial balance prepared for Binbutti Engineering in Part 4 of Problem 2-10A, prepare an income statement and statement of changes in equity for the three months ended July 31, 2020, and a balance sheet at July 31, 2020.

Problem 2-12A Journalizing, posting, preparing a trial balance and financial statements LO1, 3, 4, 5, 6

CHECK FIGURES: 4. Dr. = $66,200; 5. Profit = $11,350; Total assets = $16,050

Taylor Smith is a singer who has experienced international success in her career. On May 1, 2020, Taylor started her business, Glitter and Gold Studio, where she teaches singing. The following activities occurred during July, the third month of operations:

July	1	Purchased supplies including sheet music on credit for $100.
	2	Collected $4,000 in advance for singing lessons to be delivered in August.
	3	Collected $2,000 for teaching singing lessons in July.
	4	Paid $3,000 to rent her music studio for the month of July.
	5	Paid $500 for supplies purchased on account last month.
	15	Taylor Smith withdrew cash of $500 to do some personal shopping on the weekend.
	20	Paid her assistant wages of $1,300.
	31	Purchased new microphone equipment on credit for $300.

Required

1. Prepare journal entries to record the July transactions.

2. Set up the following general ledger accounts using T-accounts, entering the balances brought forward from June 30, 2020: Cash (101) $6,000; Supplies (126) $950; Equipment (161) $8,000; Accounts Payable (201) $1,500; Unearned Teaching Revenue (233) $9,800; Taylor Smith, Capital (301) $3,000; Taylor Smith, Withdrawals (302) $13,000; Teaching Revenue (401) $46,000; Wages Expense (623) $26,350; and Rent Expense (640) $6,000.

3. Post the entries to the T-accounts; calculate the ending balance in each account.

4. Prepare a trial balance at July 31, 2020.

5. Use the trial balance to prepare an income statement and statement of changes in equity for the three months ended July 31, 2020, as well as a balance sheet at July 31, 2020.

Problem 2-13A **Journalizing, posting, preparing a trial balance and financial statements** LO1, 3, 4, 5, 6

CHECK FIGURES: 4. Dr. = $68,100; 5. Profit = $11,250; Total assets = $16,900

Ranjeet Gill is a wedding planner who is one of the best known in her area; she has a high presence at wedding shows and works closely with a wedding dress boutique. On January 1, 2020, Ranjeet started her business called Everything Wedding Planning. The following activities occurred during March, the third month of operations:

March	1	Purchased supplies for organizing files on credit for $200.
	2	Collected $4,400 in advance for a wedding in May.
	3	Collected the final payment of $2,200 for the Singh wedding happening this weekend.
	4	Paid $3,200 to rent the hall for the Singh wedding.
	5	Paid $600 for supplies purchased on account last month.
	15	Ranjeet withdrew cash of $450 to do some personal shopping on the weekend.
	20	Paid her assistant wages of $1,500.
	31	Purchased new punch bowl equipment on credit for $400.

Required

1. Prepare journal entries to record the July transactions.

2. Set up the following general ledger accounts using T-accounts, entering the balances brought forward from February 29, 2020: Cash (101) $6,200; Supplies (126) $1,050; Equipment (161) $8,200; Accounts Payable (201) $1,700; Unearned Wedding Planning Revenue (233) $10,000; Ranjeet Gill, Capital (301) $3,200; Ranjeet Gill, Withdrawals (302) $13,200; Wedding Planning Revenue (401) $46,600; Wages Expense (623) $26,650; and Rent Expense (640) $6,200.

3. Post the entries to the T-accounts; calculate the ending balance in each account.

4. Prepare a trial balance at March 31, 2020.

5. Use the trial balance to prepare an income statement and statement of changes in equity for the three months ended March 31, 2020, as well as a balance sheet at March 31, 2020.

Problem 2-14A **Preparing financial statements from a trial balance** LO6

CHECK FIGURES: Loss = $2,700; Total assets = $388,500

	Feline Pet Care Trial Balance July 31, 2020		
Acct. No.	**Account Title**	**Debit**	**Credit**
101	Cash...	$ 22,800	
106	Accounts receivable..	11,400	
128	Prepaid insurance...	12,300	
163	Equipment..	18,000	
173	Building..	190,000	
183	Land..	134,000	
201	Accounts payable		$ 14,240
230	Unearned revenue...		91,000
301	Dwight Turnbull, capital...		290,760
302	Dwight Turnbull, withdrawals................................	4,800	
401	Revenue..		111,900
623	Wages expense...	56,000	
645	Equipment rental expense......................................	32,000	
655	Advertising expense	9,000	
684	Pet food expense..	17,600	
	Totals	$507,900	$507,900

Required Using the trial balance provided above, prepare an income statement and statement of changes in equity for the first year ended July 31, 2020, and a balance sheet at July 31, 2020.

Analysis Component: Prepare two different journal entries, including explanations, that might have created the July 31, 2020, balance in Revenue of $111,900. Use July 31, 2020, as the date for your entries.

Problem 2-15A **Analyzing trial balance errors** LO3, 5, 6

CHECK FIGURE: Total Dr. = $118,400

Wilm Schmidt, the owner of Wilm's Window Washing Services, had difficulty getting the debits to equal credits on the January 31, 2020, trial balance.

	Wilm's Window Washing Services Trial Balance January 31, 2020	
	Debit	**Credit**
Cash...	$ 11,600	
Accounts receivable..	9,240	
Prepaid insurance...	2,400	
Equipment..	24,000	
Accounts payable		$ 5,400
Wilm Schmidt, capital...		45,000
Wilm Schmidt, withdrawals...	8,960	
Service revenues		60,400
Salaries expense..	32,000	
Insurance expense	5,200	
Maintenance expense	13,000	
Utilities expense..	5,200	
Totals	$111,600	$110,800

The following errors were discovered:

a. Schmidt did not post a $4,000 purchase of equipment on credit.

b. In posting a $1,400 collection from a credit customer, Schmidt debited Accounts Receivable and credited Cash.

c. In posting a cash receipt, Schmidt correctly debited Cash for $2,660 but incorrectly credited Accounts Receivable for $6,260.

d. In posting a $4,400 payment on account, Schmidt debited Accounts Payable but forgot to post the credit to Cash.

e. In posting the entry for services of $3,600 performed for a customer on credit, Schmidt debited Accounts Receivable but credited Maintenance Expense.

Required Prepare a corrected trial balance.

ALTERNATE PROBLEMS

Problem 2-1B Analyzing transactions and recording journal entries LO3, 5

Peters Consulting completed these transactions during June 2020:

June	2	Trevor Peters, the sole proprietor, invested $46,000 cash and office equipment with a $24,000 fair value in the business.
	4	Purchased land and a small office building. The land was worth $268,000 and the building was worth $66,000. The purchase price was paid with $30,000 cash and a long-term note payable for $304,000.
	8	Transferred title of his personal automobile to the business. The automobile had a value of $7,000 and was to be used exclusively in the business.
	10	Purchased $600 of office supplies on credit.
	14	Completed $2,400 of services for a client. This amount is to be paid within 30 days.
	18	Paid $1,800 salary to an assistant.
	22	Paid the account payable from the transaction on June 10.
	24	Purchased $4,000 of new office equipment by paying $2,400 cash and trading in old equipment with a recorded cost of $1,600.
	28	Received $1,000 payment on the receivable created from the transaction on June 14th.
	30	Withdrew $1,050 cash from the business for personal use.

Required For each transaction, **(1) complete the analysis, (2) determine the journal entry analysis,** and **(3) record the journal entry.** Use the template below.

June 2	Analysis			
	Journal entry analysis			
	Journal Entry			
	Date	Account Titles and Explanation	Debit	Credit
June 4				

Problem 2-2B Posting general journal entries to T-accounts LO5

CHECK FIGURE: 2. Cash balance June 30, 2020 = $11,150

Using the information in Problem 2-1B, complete the following:

Required

1. Set up the following general ledger accounts using T-accounts: Cash; Accounts Receivable; Office Supplies; Vehicle; Office Equipment; Building; Land; Accounts Payable; Long-Term Notes Payable; Trevor Peters, Capital; Trevor Peters, Withdrawals; Revenue; and Salaries Expense.

2. Post the journal entries into the T-accounts. Identify the date next to each posting. Determine the balance in each account.

3. Prove the accounting equation.

Problem 2-3B Preparing general journal entries LO3, 5

Atlas Advertising showed the following selected transactions for the month ended March 31, 2020:

Mar.	1	Purchased a new portable building, paying cash of $75,000 and signing a five-year note payable for the balance of $300,000.
	1	Purchased six months of insurance to begin March 1; paid $5,700.
	2	Made a hotel reservation by phone regarding a business meeting to be held on March 28. The full payment of $240 will be required upon arrival at the hotel.
	4	Purchased cleaning supplies on account; $450.
	15	Paid for the March 4 purchase.
	19	Performed advertising work for a client today on account; $35,000.
	20	Collected cash of $8,000 from a customer. The advertising work will be done in April.
	28	Registered at the hotel booked on March 2 and paid the bill. Attended the out-of-town business meeting and returned to the office the next day.
	29	Provided advertising services to the local botanical garden society; collected $5,000.
	30	Paid month-end salaries of $25,600.
	30	Received the March telephone bill today; $1,300. It will be paid April 14.
	30	Collected half of the amount owed by the customer of March 19.

Required Prepare journal entries for each of the above transactions.

Problem 2-4B Preparing general journal entries LO3, 5

Francis Dhami, Public Accountant, completed these activities during September 2020, the first month of operations:

Sept.	1	Began a public accounting practice by investing $48,000 in cash and office equipment having a $11,800 fair value.
	1	Prepaid cash for three months' rent in advance on suitable office space, $8,700.
	2	Purchased on credit used office equipment, $5,800, and office supplies, $1,180.
	4	Completed accounting work for a client and immediately received payment of $6,000 cash.
	8	Completed accounting work on credit for Frontier Bank, $3,800.
	10	Paid for the items purchased on credit on September 2.
	14	Paid the annual $2,800 premium on an insurance policy.
	15	Registered to attend an all-day seminar, costing $800 on October 20 regarding ethical accounting practices and will pay when attending.
	18	Received $1,400 from Frontier Bank for the work completed on September 8.
	24	Completed accounting work on credit for Travis Realty, $2,750.
	28	Withdrew $3,400 cash from the practice to pay personal expenses.
	29	Purchased additional office supplies on credit, $630.
	30	Paid the September utility bills, $840.

Required Prepare journal entries to record the transactions.

Problem 2-5B Posting, preparing a trial balance LO4, 6

CHECK FIGURE: 3. Total Dr. = $72,980

Required Using the general journal entries prepared in Problem 2-4B, complete the following:

1. Set up the following accounts (use the balance column format or T-accounts): Cash (101); Accounts Receivable (106); Office Supplies (124); Prepaid Insurance (128); Prepaid Rent (131); Office Equipment (163); Accounts Payable (201); Francis Dhami, Capital (301); Francis Dhami, Withdrawals (302); Accounting Revenue (401); Professional Development Expense (680); and Utilities Expense (690).

2. Post the entries to the general ledger accounts and enter the balance after each posting.

3. Prepare a trial balance as of September 30, 2020.

Problem 2-6B Preparing financial statements from a trial balance LO6

CHECK FIGURES: Profit = $11,710; Total assets = $68,740

Using the trial balance prepared in Part 3 of Problem 2-5B, prepare an income statement and statement of changes in equity for the month ended September 30, 2020, and a balance sheet at September 30, 2020.

Problem 2-7B Preparing and posting general journal entries; preparing a trial balance LO3, 4, 5, 6

CHECK FIGURE: 4. Total Dr. = $96,300

WiCom Servicing completed these transactions during November 2020, its first month of operations:

Nov.	1	Tait Unger, the owner, invested $62,000 cash and office equipment that had a fair value of $19,000 in the business.
	2	Prepaid $21,000 cash for three months' rent for an office.
	4	Made credit purchases of used office equipment for $9,000 and office supplies for $1,650.
	8	Completed work for a client and immediately received $5,200 cash.
	12	Completed a $4,800 project for a client, who will pay within 30 days.
	13	Paid the account payable created on November 4.
	19	Paid $3,750 cash as the annual premium on an insurance policy.
	22	Received $2,000 as partial payment for the work completed on November 12.
	24	Completed work for another client for $3,600 on credit.
	28	Withdrew $5,300 from the business for personal use.
	29	Purchased $1,700 of additional office supplies on credit.
	30	Paid $19,000 in wages.
	30	Paid $1,650 for the month's utility bill.

Required

1. Prepare journal entries to record the transactions. Use general journal page 1.

2. Set up the following general ledger accounts (use the balance column format or T-accounts): Cash (101); Accounts Receivable (106); Office Supplies (124); Prepaid Insurance (128); Prepaid Rent (131); Office Equipment (163); Accounts Payable (201); Tait Unger, Capital (301); Tait Unger, Withdrawals (302); Service Revenue (401); Wages Expense (680); and Utilities Expense (690).

3. Post the entries to the general ledger accounts, and enter the balance after each posting.

4. Prepare a trial balance at November 30, 2020.

Analysis Component: Is the November 29 purchase of office supplies recorded as a debit to an asset or an expense account? Explain.

Problem 2-8B Preparing financial statements from a trial balance LO6

CHECK FIGURES: Loss = $7,050; Total assets = $70,350

Using the trial balance prepared in Part 4 of Problem 2-7B, prepare an income statement and statement of changes in equity for the month ended November 30, 2020, and a balance sheet at November 30, 2020.

Problem 2-9B Preparing financial statements from a trial balance LO6

CHECK FIGURES: Loss = $3,120; Total assets = $135,680

	Rush Innovations Trial Balance November 30, 2020		
Acct. No.	**Account Title**	**Debit**	**Credit**
101	Cash	$ 23,480	
106	Accounts receivable	7,000	
124	Office supplies	5,800	
128	Prepaid insurance	10,400	
131	Prepaid rent	21,000	
163	Office equipment	68,000	
201	Accounts payable		$ 3,400
301	Jay Rush, capital		146,000
302	Jay Rush, withdrawals	10,600	
401	Service Revenue		15,800
680	Wages expense	16,000	
690	Utilities expense	2,920	
	Totals	$165,200	$165,200

Required Use the trial balance provided above to prepare an income statement and statement of changes in equity for the first month ended November 30, 2020, and a balance sheet at November 30, 2020.

Analysis Component: Prepare two journal entries, including explanations: one that would have caused Accounts Receivable to increase, and one that would have caused it to decrease. Use November 30, 2020, as the date for your entries.

Problem 2-10B Journalizing, posting, preparing a trial balance LO3, 4, 5, 6

CHECK FIGURE: 4. Total Dr. = $271,500

At the beginning of June 2020, Brett Wilson created a moving company called Frog Box Company. The company had the following transactions during July, its second month of operations:

July	1	Purchased office equipment for $9,000 and a truck for $56,000 by signing a long-term note payable.
	2	Purchased land for an office. The land was worth $124,000, which was paid with $40,800 cash and a long-term note payable for the balance.
	3	Purchased a used portable building with $21,000 cash and moved it onto the land.
	5	Paid $9,600 cash for the premiums on two one-year insurance policies.
	9	Provided services to a client and collected $3,200 cash.
	12	Purchased additional office equipment for $6,500. Paid $700 cash and signed a long-term note payable for the balance.
	15	Completed $3,750 of services for a client. This amount is due within 30 days.
	20	Completed another hauling job for $9,200 on credit.
	21	Received a bill for rent on a specialized hauling truck that was used to complete the job done on July 20. The $1,300 rent must be paid within 30 days.
	22	Collected $5,000 from the client described in the transaction on July 20.
	23	Paid $1,600 wages to an assistant.
	24	Paid the account payable created in the transaction of July 21.
	25	Paid $1,425 cash for some repairs to the truck.
	26	Wilson withdrew $3,875 in cash from the business for personal use.
	27	Paid $1,600 wages to an assistant.
	28	Paid $800 cash for advertising in the local newspaper during July.
	29	Received $1,400 from a client for services to be performed in August.

Required

1. Prepare journal entries to record the transactions. Use page 1 for the journal.

2. Set up the following general ledger accounts (use the balance column format or T-accounts), entering the balances brought forward from June 30, 2020: Cash (101) $75,000; Accounts Receivable (106) $950; Prepaid Insurance (128) $275; Trucks (153) $20,800; Office Equipment (163) $1,200; Building (173) $-0-; Land (183) $-0-; Accounts Payable (201) $725; Unearned Revenue (233) $-0-; Long-Term Notes Payable (251) $7,000; Brett Wilson, Capital (301) $83,825; Brett Wilson, Withdrawals (302) $600; Revenue (401) $8,400; Wages Expense (623) $780; Truck Rental Expense (645) $230; Advertising Expense (655) $75; and Repairs Expense (684) $40.

3. Post the entries to the general ledger accounts and enter the balance after each posting.

4. Prepare a trial balance as of the end of the month.

Problem 2-11B Preparing financial statements from a trial balance LO6

CHECK FIGURES: Profit = $16,700; Total assets = $259,175

Using the trial balance prepared in Part 4 of Problem 2-10B, prepare an income statement and statement of changes in equity for the two months ended July 31, 2020, and a balance sheet at July 31, 2020.

Problem 2-12B **Journalizing, posting, preparing a trial balance and financial statements**
LO1, 3, 4, 5, 6

CHECK FIGURES: 4. Dr. = $137,000; 5. Profit = $3,750; Total assets = $86,750

Ike Petrov started a tour company, Tour-Along, on October 1, 2020. The following activities occurred during November, the second month of operations:

Nov.	1	Paid $10,000 regarding purchases made on account during October.
	2	Purchased a $34,000 photocopier, paying $6,000 cash and signing a note payable for the balance.
	3	Purchased office supplies for cash; $800.
	4	Signed a $200,000 contract with RBC to arrange travel for its employees beginning January 1, 2021.
	14	Paid wages of $6,000.
	20	Collected $14,000 for clients travelling in November.
	25	Ike Petrov withdrew $2,000 cash for personal use.
	30	Paid interest on the notes payable; $150.

Required

1. Prepare journal entries to record the November transactions.

2. Set up the following T-accounts, entering the balances brought forward from October 31, 2020: Cash (101) $26,000; Office Supplies (124) $900; Office Equipment (163) $36,000; Accounts Payable (201) $43,000; Notes Payable (205) $20,000; Ike Petrov, Capital (301) $8,000; Ike Petrov, Withdrawals (302) $4,000; Travel Revenue (401) $34,000; Wage Expense (623) $38,000; and Interest Expense (633) $100.

3. Post the entries to the T-accounts; calculate the ending balance in each account.

4. Prepare a trial balance at November 30, 2020.

5. Use the trial balance to prepare an income statement and statement of changes in equity for the two months ended November 30, 2020, as well as a balance sheet at November 30, 2020.

Analysis Component: Part 2 of the *Required* states that the account Ike Petrov, Capital had a balance of $8,000 at October 31, 2020. Explain what this balance represents.

Problem 2-13B **Journalizing, posting, preparing a trial balance and financial statements** LO1, 3, 4, 5, 6

CHECK FIGURES: 4. Dr. = $100,500; 5. Profit = $32,000; Total assets = $43,350

Tom Keenan is a vacation planner who specializes in outback adventures; he has a high presence at outdoor shows and gets most of his business from there. On May 1, 2020, Tom started his business called Epic Adventures. The following activities occurred during July, the third month of operations:

July	1	Purchased camping supplies on credit for $400.
	2	Collected $7,000 in advance for a trip in August.
	3	Collected the final payment of $13,500 for this month's trip.
	4	Paid $4,500 to rent a van for this month's trip.
	5	Paid $700 for supplies purchased on account last month.
	15	Tom withdrew cash of $650 to do some personal shopping on the weekend.
	20	Paid his assistant wages of $1,400.
	31	Purchased new camera equipment on credit for $1,000.

Required

1. Prepare journal entries to record the July transactions.

2. Set up the following general ledger accounts using T-accounts, entering the balances brought forward from June 30, 2020: Cash (101) $17,500; Supplies (126) $1,700; Equipment (161) $9,500; Accounts Payable (201) $3,000; Unearned Travel Deposit Revenue (233) $11,300; Tom Keenan, Capital (301) $4,500; Tom Keenan, Withdrawals (302) $14,500; Travel Planning Revenue (401) $60,500; Wages Expense (623) $28,600; and Rent Expense (640) $7,500.

3. Post the entries to the T-accounts; calculate the ending balance in each account.

4. Prepare a trial balance at July 31, 2020.

5. Use the trial balance to prepare an income statement and statement of changes in equity for the three months ended July 31, 2020, as well as a balance sheet at July 31, 2020.

Problem 2-14B Preparing financial statements from a trial balance LO6

CHECK FIGURES: Loss = $33,680; Total assets = $120,670

	Lincoln Landscaping Trial Balance July 31, 2020		
Acct. No.	**Account Title**	**Debit**	**Credit**
101	Cash	$ 23,720	
106	Accounts receivable	18,600	
128	Prepaid insurance	13,750	
167	Equipment	64,600	
201	Accounts payable		$ 37,500
233	Unearned revenue		2,800
251	Long-term notes payable		58,000
301	Brielle Lincoln, capital		65,000
302	Brielle Lincoln, withdrawals	8,950	
401	Revenue		29,100
623	Wages expense	59,000	
645	Rental expense	1,100	
655	Advertising expense	1,750	
684	Repairs expense	930	
	Totals	$192,400	$192,400

Required Using the trial balance provided above, prepare an income statement and a statement of changes in equity for the first three months ended July 31, 2020, and a balance sheet at July 31, 2020.

Analysis Component: Analyze the balance sheet and calculate what percentage of the assets is financed by (a) debt and (b) equity.

Problem 2-15B Analyzing trial balance errors LO3, 4, 6

CHECK FIGURE: Total Dr. = $49,860

On January 1, 2020, Paula Fernandes started a new business called Wicked Dance. Near the end of the year, she hired a new bookkeeper without checking references or requesting an academic transcript. As a result, a number of mistakes have been made in preparing the following trial balance:

Wicked Dance Trial Balance December 31, 2020		
	Debit	Credit
Cash...	$ 5,500	
Accounts receivable...		$ 7,900
Office supplies...	2,650	
Office equipment	20,500	
Accounts payable...		9,465
Paula Fernandes, Capital...	16,745	
Services revenue		22,350
Wages expense...		6,000
Rent expense..		4,800
Advertising expense		1,250
Totals	$45,395	$52,340

Paula's analysis of the situation has uncovered these errors:

a. The sum of the debits in the Cash account is $37,175 and the sum of the credits is $30,540.

b. A $275 payment from a credit customer was posted to Cash but was not posted to Accounts Receivable.

c. A credit purchase of office supplies for $400 was not posted at all.

d. A transposition error occurred in copying the balance of the Services Revenue account to the trial balance. The correct amount was $23,250.

Other errors were made in placing account balances in the wrong trial balance columns and in taking the totals of the columns.

Required Prepare a corrected trial balance.

ANALYTICAL AND REVIEW PROBLEMS

A & R Problem 2-1

Carlos Young started an engineering firm called Young Engineering. He began operations in March 2020 and completed seven transactions, including his initial investment of $17,000 cash. After these transactions, the ledger included the following accounts with their normal balances:

Cash...	$26,660
Office Supplies...	660
Prepaid Insurance	3,200
Office Equipment...	16,500
Accounts Payable...	16,500
Carlos Young, Capital...	17,000
Carlos Young, Withdrawals..	3,740
Engineering Revenue...	24,000
Rent Expense	6,740

Required
Preparation Component: Prepare a trial balance for the business.

Analysis Component: Analyze the accounts and balances and prepare narratives that describe each of the seven most likely transactions and their amounts.

A & R Problem 2-2

Designer Dry Cleaning showed the following information for its first and second months just ended, March and April of 2020:

Account Title	April 30, 2020	March 31, 2020
Cash...	7,000	3,000
Cleaning supplies..	3,500	900
Prepaid rent..	12,000	16,000
Equipment...	76,000	30,000
Accounts payable...	700	500
Notes payable...	40,000	15,000
Christopher Dior, capital*..	?	?

*Christopher Dior made a $10,000 investment during March and had withdrawals of $1,000 in March and $25,100 in April.

Required Use the information provided to complete a statement of changes in equity and a balance sheet for each of March and April 2020. *Note:* Prepare the statements on a comparative[13] basis similar to the statements for Spin Master and WestJet in Appendix III at the end of the textbook.

Analysis Component:

a. Liabilities increased by $25,200 from March 31, 2020, to April 30, 2020. Review the balance sheet and identify why liabilities increased.

b. Equity increased by $34,400 during March and by $23,400 during April, yet profit was much higher in April. Explain.

ETHICS CHALLENGE

EC 2-1

You are a cashier at a retail convenience store. When you were hired, the owner explained to you the policy of immediately ringing up each sale. Recently, lunch hour traffic has increased dramatically and the manager asks you to take customers' cash and make change without ringing up sales to avoid delays. The manager says she will add up cash and ring up sales equal to the cash amount after lunch. She says that in this way the register will always be accurate when the owner arrives at 3:00 p.m.

Required

1. Identify the advantages and disadvantages of the manager's suggestion.

2. Identify the ethical dilemma and evaluate at least two courses of action you might consider and why.

---

[13] Preparing statements on a comparative basis means to have numbers for at least two periods side by side. This kind of presentation provides decision makers with something meaningful against which the current period can be compared.

FOCUS ON FINANCIAL STATEMENTS

FFS 2-1

Travis McAllister operates a surveying company. For the first few months of the company's life (through April), the accounting records were maintained by an outside bookkeeping service. According to those records, McAllister's equity balance was $75,000 as of April 30. To save on expenses, McAllister decided to keep the records himself. He managed to record May's transactions properly, but was a bit rusty when the time came to prepare the financial statements. His first versions of the balance sheet and income statement follow. McAllister is bothered that the company apparently operated at a loss during the month, even though he was very busy.

McAllister Surveying Income Statement For Month Ended May 31, 2020		
Revenue:		
Investments by owner		$ 3,000
Unearned surveying fees		6,000
Total revenues		$ 9,000
Operating expenses:		
Rent expense	$3,100	
Telephone expense	600	
Surveying equipment	5,400	
Advertising expense	3,200	
Utilities expense	300	
Insurance expense	900	
Withdrawals by owner	6,000	
Total operating expenses		19,500
Profit (loss)		$(10,500)

McAllister Surveying Balance Sheet May 31, 2020				
Assets			**Liabilities**	
Cash	$ 3,900		Accounts payable	$ 2,400
Accounts receivable	2,700		Surveying fees earned	18,000
Prepaid insurance	1,800		Short-term notes payable	48,000
Prepaid rent	4,200		Total liabilities	$ 68,400
Office supplies	300			
Buildings	81,000		**Equity**	
Land	36,000		Travis McAllister, capital	64,500
Salaries expense	3,000			
Total assets	$132,900		Total liabilities and equity	$132,900

Required Using the information contained in the original financial statements, prepare corrected statements, including a statement of changes in equity, for the month of May.

Analysis Component: The owner, Travis McAllister, made a withdrawal during May. Withdrawals cause equity to decrease. Why would the owner intentionally cause equity to decrease by making a withdrawal?

FFS 2-2

1. Refer to WestJet's income statement in Appendix III at the end of the textbook.

   a. Total *Guest revenues* for 2017 were $3,822,045 (thousand).

      (i) Prepare two possible journal entries that might have been recorded to create this result.

      (ii) What effect do revenues have on the balance sheet?

      (iii) What assurances do we have that the revenues appearing on the income statement are for the year 2017? *Hint:* Which GAAP?

   b. Total *Finance costs* for 2017 were $53,710 (thousand).

      (i) Prepare a possible journal entry that might have recorded the interest expense.

      (ii) Do expenses affect the balance sheet? Explain.

2. Refer to WestJet's balance sheet in Appendix III at the end of the textbook. Find the line showing *Advance ticket sales* of $695,111 (thousand).

   a. Explain what you think the account *Advance ticket sales* represents.

   b. Prepare the journal entry that might have recorded this account balance.

CRITICAL THINKING MINI CASE

Prairie Insurance sells life insurance, disability insurance, vehicle insurance, crop insurance, and home-owners' insurance. You are employed by Prairie Insurance and have been promoted to sales division manager for the Western Canadian division. You will be supervising approximately 25 salespeople, along with five administrative assistants at various locations. The salespeople travel extensively and submit expense reports along with sales information monthly. A sample expense report for September shows:

Prairie Insurance—Western Canadian Division Sales Report: John Bishop Month Ended September 30, 2020	
Sales revenue*	$56,000
Expenses**	34,000

*Sales invoices attached
**Receipts attached

The former manager was dismissed because division results have been deteriorating. The consolidated sales report for the past three months shows the following:

Prairie Insurance—Western Canadian Division Sales Report Month Ended			
	September 30, 2020	August 31, 2020	July 31, 2020
Sales revenue	$680,000	$510,000	$440,000
Expenses	544,000	382,500	321,200
Profit	$136,000	$127,500	$118,800

You learn that the company has one revenue account called Sales Revenue and one expense account called Expenses. You proceed to prepare a brief memo to the company's accountant requesting information that is needed to help you analyze the situation.

Required Using the elements of critical thinking described on the inside front cover, respond to the following:

1. What are the main problems you need to address in your memo to the company's accountant?
2. What are your goals as division manager in addressing your main concerns?
3. What principles need to be considered in order to improve the reporting at Prairie Insurance?
4. What are the key facts you need to consider in improving the reporting at Prairie Insurance?
5. What will you do about your concerns to improve the reporting at Prairie Insurance?

CUMULATIVE COMPREHENSION PROBLEM: ECHO SYSTEMS

(This comprehensive problem starts in this chapter and continues in Chapters 3, 4, and 5. Because of its length, this problem is most easily solved if you use the Working Papers[14] that accompany this text.)

On October 1, 2020, Mary Graham organized a computer service company called Echo Systems. Echo is organized as a sole proprietorship and will provide consulting services, computer system installations, and custom program development. Graham has adopted the calendar year for reporting, and expects to prepare the company's first set of financial statements as of December 31, 2020. The initial chart of accounts for the accounting system includes these items:

Account Number	Account Name	Account Number	Account Name
101	Cash	301	Mary Graham, Capital
106	Accounts Receivable	302	Mary Graham, Withdrawals
126	Computer Supplies	403	Computer Services Revenue
128	Prepaid Insurance	623	Wages Expense
131	Prepaid Rent	655	Advertising Expense
163	Office Equipment	676	Mileage Expense
167	Computer Equipment	684	Repairs Expense, Computer
201	Accounts Payable	699	Charitable Donations Expense

Part A:

CHECK FIGURES: 4. Total Dr. = $159,450; Profit = $8,920; Total assets = $145,720

Required

1. Set up balance column accounts based on the chart of accounts provided.
2. Prepare journal entries to record each of the following October transactions.
3. Post the October entries.
4. Prepare a trial balance at October 31, 2020.
5. Prepare an income statement and a statement of changes in equity for the month ended October 31, 2020, as well as a balance sheet at October 31, 2020.

---

14 If students have not purchased the Working Paper package, the Working Papers for the Serial Problem are available on Connect.

Oct.	1	Graham invested $90,000 cash, a $36,000 computer system, and $18,000 of office equipment in the business.
	2	Paid rent in advance of $9,000.
	3	Purchased computer supplies on credit for $2,640 from Abbott Office Products.
	5	Paid $4,320 cash for one year's premium on a property and liability insurance policy.
	6	Billed Capital Leasing $6,600 for installing a new computer.
	8	Paid for the computer supplies purchased from Abbott Office Products.
	10	Hired Carly Smith as a part-time assistant for $200 per day, as needed.
	12	Billed Capital Leasing another $2,400 for computer services rendered.
	15	Received $6,600 from Capital Leasing on its account.
	17	Paid $1,410 to repair computer equipment damaged when moving into the new office.
	20	Paid $3,720 for an advertisement in the local newspaper.
	22	Received $2,400 from Capital Leasing on its account.
	28	Billed Decker Company $6,450 for services.
	31	Paid Carly Smith for seven days' work.
	31	Withdrew $7,200 cash from the business for personal use.

Part B:

CHECK FIGURES: 8. Total Dr. = $184,950; 9. Profit = $27,920; Total assets = $161,120

Required

6. Prepare journal entries to record each of the following November transactions.

7. Post the November entries.

8. Prepare a trial balance at November 30, 2020.

9. Prepare an income statement and a statement of changes in equity for the two months ended November 30, 2020, as well as a balance sheet at November 30, 2020.

Nov.	1	Reimbursed Graham's business automobile expense for 1,000 kilometres at $1.00 per kilometre.
	2	Received $9,300 cash from Elite Corporation for computer services rendered.
	5	Purchased $1,920 of computer supplies for cash from Abbott Office Products.
	8	Billed Fostek Co. $8,700 for computer services rendered.
	13	Notified by Alamo Engineering Co. that Echo's bid of $7,500 for an upcoming project was accepted.
	18	Received $3,750 from Decker Company against the bill dated October 28.
	22	Donated $1,500 to the United Way in the company's name.
	24	Completed work for Alamo Engineering Co. and sent a bill for $7,500.
	25	Sent another bill to Decker Company for the past due amount of $2,700.
	28	Reimbursed Graham's business automobile expense for 1,200 kilometres at $1.00 per kilometre.
	30	Paid Carly Smith for 14 days' work.
	30	Withdrew $3,600 cash from the business for personal use.

Adjusting Accounts for Financial Statements

A Look Back

Chapter 2 explained the analysis and recording of transactions. We showed how to apply and interpret company accounts, ledgers, T-accounts, double-entry accounting, postings, and trial balances.

A Look at This Chapter

This chapter explains the timing of reports and the need to adjust accounts. Adjusting accounts is important for recognizing revenues and expenses in the proper period. We describe the adjusted trial balance and how it is used to prepare financial statements.

Source: Nattanan23/Pixabay.com

LEARNING OBJECTIVES

LO1 Describe the purpose of adjusting accounts at the end of a period.

LO2 Explain how the timeliness, matching, and revenue recognition principles affect the adjusting process.

LO3 Explain accrual accounting and cash basis accounting and how accrual accounting adds to the usefulness of financial statements.

LO4 Prepare and explain adjusting entries for prepaid expenses, depreciation, unearned revenues, accrued expenses, and accrued revenues.

LO5 Explain how accounting adjustments link to financial statements.

LO6	Explain and prepare an adjusted trial balance.
LO7	Prepare financial statements from an adjusted trial balance.
***Appendix 3A**	
LO8	Explain and prepare correcting entries.
***Appendix 3B**	
LO9	Identify and explain an alternative in recording prepaid assets and unearned revenues.

An asterisk (*) identifies appendix material.

Global Profiles: Turning Waste into Currency

Governments promote recycling through public collection programs, deposit refund schemes, municipal laws, and product standards requiring a specified minimum percentage of recycled material. Recently, there has been a movement to embrace unique methods of incentivizing recycling.

Amsterdam's Noord district has implemented an exciting way to incentivize its residents to embrace recycling in a profound way. The non-profit Amsterdam-based organization Cities Foundation has piloted a project called *Wasted* that provides digital coins stored in their app to individuals who bring in a bag full of recycling (plastics, paper, cardboard, small household appliances, batteries, lights, latex paint, and textiles). The coins provide a real value for the act of recycling as they can be exchanged for discounts and products and services offered by local businesses such as a free cup of coffee, piece of cake, or workshops. Since its inception in 2015 approximately 800 households have signed up with 50 businesses acting as rewarders, and many involved in the program have cut back their usage of plastic and have significantly improved their recycling habits. In the meantime the Wasted design club has invented a building block made out of the recycled plastic that can be used in the community to build items such as chairs, tables, or plant boxes.

In an effort to overcome barriers that prevent individuals from recycling and to help the markets for recyclable materials function better, the Ukrainian organization Recereum was launched in 2017 as a blockchain-based platform that aims to provide money in the form of cryptocurrency coins for "every single recycled bottle, battery, piece of old equipment or electronics" to each household that engages in waste sorting. These coins can then be used to pay for services of an official partner of the program. An app has been developed to make it easy for users to track account balances, receive coins, and scan QR codes. They use blockchain to ensure security of the financial transactions. Recereum is providing a franchising model to enable others to get involved in the business of recycling. Other companies with a similar program are:

- Swachhcoin—households are rewarded with digital tokens called "Swachhcoin."
- Agora Tech Lab—blockchain-based digital tokens are provided as rewards for recycling and can be redeemed for public services.
- Dutch Ministry for Infrastructure—has an additional goal beyond improving recycling rates to improve accountability and visibility into waste while in transit.

Cryptocurrencies like blockchain are generating a lot of attention among accounting professionals. The Securities and Exchange Commission (the regulatory board for investing in the United States) has made regulatory matters for initial coin offerings a priority for its 2018 agenda. Cryptocurrencies are not accepted as legal tender and therefore do not meet the accounting definition of cash or cash equivalents. A key issue will be for companies involved and accounting regulators to determine how to account for these different forms of currency as digital credits are paid out and received.

Sources: https://www.pawsandpines.com/zero-waste-amsterdam/; http://hemispheres.ink-live.com/html5/reader/production/default. aspx?pubname=&edid=d7c8a68d-9945-4ad8-b2f1-88ddfd86d6de; https://wastedlab.nl/en/concept/; https://www.nasdaq.com/article/reducing-waste-introducing-garbage-collection-to-blockchain-technology-cm960317; http://www.abnewswire.com/pressreleases/recereum-solving-the-global-waste-problem-using-blockchain-technology_174731.html; https://recereum.com/; and https://www.pwc.com/us/en/cfodirect/publications/point-of-view/cryptocurrency-bitcoin-accounting.html.

Video Link: Check out the following video link for an outline of the Wasted program: https://youtu.be/A3X0lEyUo7E.

CRITICAL THINKING CHALLENGE

Why are cryptocurrencies and digital coins not considered to be cash and cash equivalents under GAAP?

CHAPTER PREVIEW

Financial statements reflect revenues when earned and expenses when incurred. This is known as *accrual basis accounting*. Accrual basis accounting is achieved by following the steps of the accounting cycle. We described the first four of these steps in Chapter 2.

An important part of the accounting cycle is the adjustment of account balances. The adjusted account balances are what is reported in the financial statements that are prepared according to generally accepted accounting principles. Adjustment of accounts is necessary so that financial statements at the

end of a reporting period reflect the effects of all transactions. This chapter emphasizes Steps 5 and 6 of the accounting cycle as highlighted in Exhibit 3.1. Preparation of financial statements, Step 7 of the accounting cycle, is reinforced in this chapter, with an emphasis on how *adjusting entries* impact the financial statements. Companies like the ones introduced in the chapter-opening vignette use adjusting entries to ensure their financial statements are fairly stated. To illustrate the adjusting process, we continue with the example of Organico used in previous chapters.

EXHIBIT 3.1

Steps in the Accounting Cycle Introduced in Chapter 3

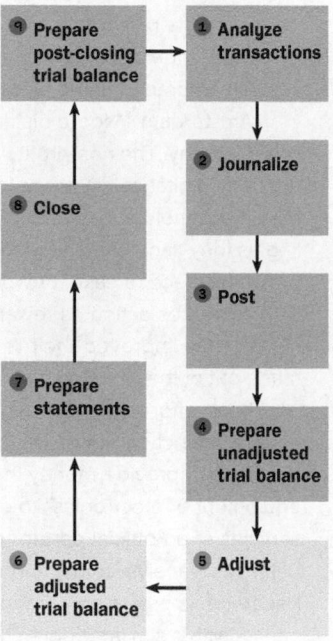

Purpose of Adjusting

LO1 Describe the purpose of adjusting accounts at the end of a period.

During an accounting period the primary focus is to record *external transactions*. **External transactions** are exchanges between two parties; these were the focus of Chapters 1 and 2. After external transactions are recorded, several accounts in the ledger need adjustment for their balances to appear in financial statements. This need arises because *internal transactions* remain unrecorded. **Internal transactions** represent exchanges and usage of resources within an organization that affect the accounting equation and are the focus of this chapter.

The purpose of adjusting accounts at the end of an accounting period is to ensure the financial records reflect the true financial position of the business at a specific date. The cost of certain assets expire or are used up as time passes and at the month end or year end date we are concerned the balances reported in the financial statements reflect assets used up, revenues earned and costs incurred. For example, the following accounts often need to be adjusted at the end of an accounting period:

1. Prepaid Insurance
2. Supplies

3. Prepaid Rent

4. Depreciation

5. Unearned Revenues

6. Interest Expense

7. Salaries Expense

8. Services Revenue

9. Accrued Interest Income

As an example, Organico's trial balance (Exhibit 3.2) shows Prepaid Insurance with a balance of $2,400. This amount is the premium for two years of insurance protection beginning on March 1, 2020. By March 31, 2020, because one month's coverage is used up, the $2,400 is no longer the correct account balance for Prepaid Insurance. The Prepaid Insurance account balance must be reduced by one month's cost, or $100 ($2,400/24 months). The income statement must report this $100 cost as insurance expense for March.

EXHIBIT 3.2
Trial Balance

Organico		
Trial Balance		
March 31, 2020		
	Debit	**Credit**
Cash..	$ 8,070	
Accounts receivable..	-0-	
Prepaid insurance...	2,400	
Supplies..	3,600	
Equipment..	6,000	
Accounts payable...		$ 200
Unearned food services revenue..		3,000
Notes payable..		6,000
Hailey Walker, capital..		10,000
Hailey Walker, withdrawals...	600	
Food services revenue...		3,800
Teaching revenue...		300
Rent expense..	1,000	
Salaries expense..	1,400	
Utilities expense...	230	
Totals..	$23,300	$23,300

Another example is the $3,600 balance in Supplies. Part of this balance includes the cost of supplies that were used in March. The cost of the supplies used must be reported as an expense in March. The balances of both the Prepaid Insurance and Supplies accounts must be *adjusted* before they are reported on the March 31 balance sheet.

Another adjustment necessary for Organico relates to one month's usage of equipment. The balances of the Unearned Food Services Revenue, Food Services Revenue, and Salaries Expense accounts often also need adjusting before they appear on the statements. We explain *why* this adjusting process is carried out in the next section.

GAAP and the Adjusting Process

LO2 Explain how the timeliness, matching, and revenue recognition principles affect the adjusting process.

The adjusting process is based on three generally accepted accounting principles: the timeliness principle, the matching principle, and the revenue recognition principle. In this section, we explain how GAAP contribute to the usefulness of financial statements.

THE ACCOUNTING PERIOD

The adjusting process is often linked to timeliness of information. Information must reach decision makers frequently and on a timely basis; therefore, accounting systems need to prepare periodic reports at regular intervals. This results in an accounting process impacted by the timeliness principle.[1] The **timeliness principle** assumes that an organization's activities can be divided into specific time periods such as a month, a three-month quarter, or a year, as illustrated in Exhibit 3.3. It requires that statements be presented at least annually.

EXHIBIT 3.3

Accounting Periods—For Year-End Adjusting Entries TIMING IS EVERYTHING!

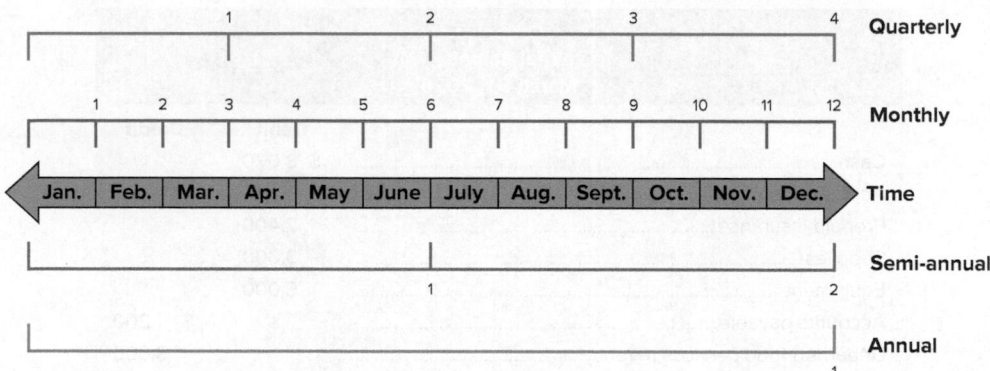

Time periods covered by statements are called **accounting periods** (or **reporting periods**). Reports covering a one-year period are known as *annual financial statements*. Recall that a company can adopt a *fiscal year* based on the *calendar year* or its *natural business year*. Many organizations also prepare **interim financial reports** covering one, three (quarterly), or six (semi-annual) months of activity.

The annual reporting period is not always a calendar year ending on December 31. An organization can adopt a fiscal year consisting of any 12 consecutive months. It is also acceptable to adopt an annual reporting period of 52 weeks. For example, **The Gap**'s fiscal year consistently ends the final week of January or the first week of February each year.

Companies with little seasonal variation in sales often choose the calendar year as their fiscal year. For example, **Facebook, Inc.** uses calendar-year reporting. However, the financial statements of **The Kellogg Company** (which controls characters such as Tony the Tiger, Snap, Crackle and Pop, and the Keebler Elves) reflect a fiscal year that ends on the Saturday nearest December 31. Companies experiencing seasonal variations in sales often choose a natural business year-end, which is when sales activities are at their lowest level for the year. The natural business year for retailers such as **Walmart**, **Target**, and **Macy's** usually ends

---

1   IFRS 2018, IAS 1, para. 36; "Framework," para. QC29.

around January 31, after the holiday season. **Lululemon Athletica** has opted for a floating year-end that falls on the Sunday closest to January 31 of the following year. **Mountain Equipment Co-op** recently changed from a December 31 year-end to a March–February cycle to enable "better inventory management and planning.[2]

RECOGNIZING REVENUES AND EXPENSES

Because it is critical for external users to understand how the company performed financially compared to previous years, accounting standard-setting bodies developed a set of principles to clarify the appropriate level of revenue and expense to report. Two main generally accepted accounting principles are used in the adjusting process: the *matching principle* and the *revenue recognition principle*. The **matching principle** aims to report or *match* expenses in the same accounting period as the revenues they helped to earn.[3] For example, assume that as part of an upcoming catering event Organico is to supply a customized menu and event plan to a corporate customer in May. Hailey agreed on a price of $500 with her customer for the menu/event plan. In the process of earning this $500 in revenue, Organico will use $150 of office supplies that were purchased and paid for in April. The $150 of office supplies used in May is an expense that will be reported on the May income statement even though the supplies were purchased and paid for in April. The $150 of office supplies used in May must be *matched* against the $500 of May revenues in accordance with the matching principle. Financial statements will reflect accurate information about the profit actually earned during the period only if expenses are properly matched against the revenues they helped to create.

To illustrate *revenue recognition*, we will look at two situations. First, assume that Organico teaches a healthy cooking class for a fee of $500 to a Foodie club at a local college and collects the cash from the students immediately in the month of May. The $500 of revenue is earned in May and is reported on the May income statement in accordance with the revenue recognition principle. Second, assume that Organico collected $1,000 cash in May for a cooking class to be taught in June. The $1,000 of revenue will be earned in June and will therefore be reported on the June income statement; the $1,000 will *not* be reported as revenue in May because it has not yet been earned. A major goal of the adjusting process is to have revenue *recognized* (reported) in the time period when it is *earned* regardless of when the cash is actually received. This concept is the foundation on which the *accrual basis of accounting* was developed.

ACCRUAL BASIS COMPARED TO CASH BASIS

LO3 Explain accrual accounting and cash basis accounting and how accrual accounting adds to the usefulness of financial statements.

Accrual basis accounting is founded on the revenue recognition principle, where revenues and expenses are *recognized* or recorded when earned or incurred regardless of when cash is received or paid. The word *accrual* and its root word *accrue* mean *to accumulate* or *to add*. So accrual basis accounting means that revenues and expenses must be *added* or *matched* to the *time period* in which they actually happened; when cash was received or paid is irrelevant to the recording of revenues and expenses. Accrual basis accounting, then, is based on the three GAAP of *timeliness*, *matching*, and *revenue recognition*.

Accrual Basis Accounting

Revenues (= when earned)
– Expenses (= when incurred)
Profit

Cash Basis Accounting

Revenues (= cash receipts)
– Expenses (= cash payments)
Profit

---

2   MEC Annual Report, 2016-2017, page 3, http://meccms.wpengine.com/wp-content/uploads/2017/06/MEC_2016-17_Annual-Report_digital_EN.pdf.
3   IFRS 2018, IAS 18, para. 19; "Framework," para. 4.50.

In contrast, **cash basis accounting** recognizes revenues and expenses when *cash* is received or paid. Cash basis accounting for the income statement, balance sheet, and statement of changes in equity is *not* permitted under generally accepted accounting principles. It is commonly held that accrual basis accounting provides a better indication of business performance than information about current cash receipts and payments. Accrual basis accounting also increases the comparability of financial statements from one period to another. Information about cash flows is also useful, which is why companies also include a cash flow statement, discussed in Chapter 16.

> **Important Tip:**
>
> The cash basis of accounting is not an acceptable method for use in financial reporting. IFRS and Canadian ASPE standards require companies to use the accrual basis of accounting. CRA also requires companies to adopt the accrual basis of accounting.

 ETHICAL IMPACT

MagnaChip is a South Korea–based semiconductor company that has been publicly traded in the United States since its initial public offering in 2011. The company was recently under investigation by the SEC for engaging in unethical/improper conduct over the period from 2011 to December 2013. These practices included artificially increasing revenue, delaying or avoiding expenses, avoiding reductions in revenue, smoothing gross margins, and hiding delays in receivables collections. MagnaChip also engaged in a practice called "channel stuffing," which means they negotiated side agreements with distributors, offering incentives to take products earlier than needed to enable the company to meet sales targets. The company's falsified records misled investors and resulted in increasing their stock price by 69% over the period.

A red flag that signalled the Board and Audit Committee that a problem existed occurred when they recognized accounts receivable balances were increasing. These prudent board members pursued an investigation into the company's accounting practices that resulted in a subsequent restatement of their financial statements in 2015, reducing previously recognized revenue by $121 million. Consequently, the company's 2011 reported net profit was changed to a net loss and a correction to its previously recognized increasing trend of more than 5% revenue growth each quarter, "when in fact it was declining." After the restatement announcement, MagnaChip's stock price dropped by 50%. The SEC imposed monetary fines of $3 million for the company, and the chief financial officer was ordered to pay a fine of $135,000. The CFO was a CPA (US), and is no longer able to work for a public company in an accounting capacity or as an officer or director.

MagnaChip's executives were known to set aggressive revenue and gross margin targets and insisted employees meet their prescribed targets. This resulted in employees throughout the sales, finance, and manufacturing organizations engaging in improper acts leading to fraudulent financial reporting. If you were hired as a junior accountant into a company that was engaging in similar practices, what would you do?

Source: Exchange Act Release No. 80,564; https://www.sec.gov/litigation/admin/2017/33-10352.pdf.

 CHECKPOINT

1. Describe a company's annual reporting period.
2. Why do companies prepare interim financial statements?
3. What accounting principles most directly lead to the adjusting process?
4. Is cash basis accounting consistent with generally accepted accounting principles?

Do Quick Study questions: QS 3-1, QS 3-2, QS 3-3

Adjusting Accounts

The process of adjusting accounts is similar to our process of analyzing and recording transactions in Chapter 2. We must analyze each account balance and the transactions that affect it to determine any needed adjustments. An **adjusting entry** is recorded at the *end* of the accounting period to bring an asset or liability account balance to its proper amount. This entry also updates the related expense or revenue account and is necessary to prepare the financial statements. Adjustments are journalized in the general journal and then posted to accounts in the ledger—this is the same process described in Chapter 2 for routine transactions. This next section demonstrates how to handle common adjusting entries and their relationship to the adjusted trial balance and period-end financial statements.

FRAMEWORK FOR ADJUSTMENTS

LO4 Prepare and explain adjusting entries for prepaid expenses, depreciation, unearned revenues, accrued expenses, and accrued revenues.

Exhibit 3.4 identifies the five main adjustments, each of which is detailed in the following sections. As you navigate through each example, pay close attention to the logic behind which accounts are debited/credited and why the adjusting entry is required at period-end. Each entry requires consideration of the timing of cash receipt or payment in comparison to when the revenue is earned or the matched expense has been incurred.

EXHIBIT 3.4
Framework for Adjustments

ADJUSTING PREPAID EXPENSES

Prepaid expenses[4] refers to costs *paid for* in advance of receiving their benefits. Don't be fooled by the name—*prepaid expenses are assets.* As these assets are used, their costs become expenses. Three common prepaid expenses are insurance, rent payments made in advance, and supplies purchased for use in the business. When the payment is initially made, it is important for businesses to capture these costs as assets—labelled as prepaid expenses. In general, the benefits of prepaid expenses are utilized within a year, thus they are classified as current assets. The adjusting entry comes into effect at period-end when these assets have been depleted through direct usage or usage due to the passing of time.

Adjusting entries for prepaids involve increasing (debiting) expenses and decreasing (crediting) prepaid assets as shown in Exhibit 3.5.

EXHIBIT 3.5
Adjusting for Prepaid Expenses

---

4 Prepaids are also called *deferrals* because the recognition of the expense or revenue on the income statement is *deferred* to a future accounting period.

Prepaid Insurance

We illustrate prepaid insurance using Organico's payment of $2,400 for two years of insurance protection beginning on March 1, 2020. The following entry records the purchase of the insurance:

Mar.	1	Prepaid Insurance	2,400	
		Cash		2,400
		To record purchase of insurance for 24 months.		

By March 31, one month's insurance coverage is used, causing a portion of the asset Prepaid Insurance to become an expense. This expense is $100 ($2,400 × 1/24). Our adjusting entry to record this expense and reduce the asset is:

Adjustment (a)

Mar.	31	Insurance Expense	100	
		Prepaid Insurance		100
		To record expired insurance.		

A = L + E*
↓   ↓
*Recall that expenses cause equity to decrease.

Posting this adjusting entry affects the accounts shown in Exhibit 3.6:

EXHIBIT 3.6

Insurance Accounts After Adjusting for Prepaids

Prepaid Insurance					Insurance Expense		
Mar. 1	2,400	100	Mar. 31		Mar. 31	100	
Balance	2,300						

After posting, the $100 balance in Insurance Expense and the $2,300 balance in Prepaid Insurance are ready for reporting in the financial statements. If the adjustment is *not* made at March 31, then (a) expenses are *understated* by $100 and profit is *overstated* by $100 for the March income statement, and (b) both Prepaid Insurance and equity are overstated by $100 in the March 31 balance sheet.

An **understated account** is too low. For example, if Revenue has a balance of $100 and it is understated by $20, the correct balance is $120. An **overstated account** is too high. For example, if Equipment has a balance of $450 and it is overstated by $40, the correct balance is $410.

Supplies

Organico purchased $3,600 of supplies in March and used some of them during this month. Daily usage of supplies is not generally recorded for accounting purposes because of the difficulty of tracking each miscellaneous item used (each piece of paper, pen, pencil, etc.). When we report account balances in financial statements at the end of a month, making only one adjusting entry at that time can reduce recordkeeping costs. This entry needs to record the total cost of all supplies used in the month.

The cost of supplies used during March must be determined to recognize supplies expense. Organico calculates ("takes inventory of") the remaining unused supplies. The cost of the remaining supplies is then deducted from the cost of the purchased supplies (plus any supplies left over from the prior month) to calculate the amount used for March. Organico has **$2,550** of supplies remaining out of the **$3,600** ($2,500 + $1,100) purchased in March. The $1,050 difference between these two amounts is the cost of the supplies used.

This amount is March's Supplies Expense. Our adjusting entry to record this expense and reduce the Supplies asset account is:

Adjustment (b)

A = L + E
↓   ↓

	Mar.	31	Supplies Expense...	1,050	
			Supplies...		1,050
			To record supplies used.		

Posting this adjusting entry affects the accounts shown in Exhibit 3.7:

EXHIBIT 3.7

Supplies Ledger Accounts After Adjusting for Prepaids

Supplies				Supplies Expense		
Mar. 1	2,500	1,050	Mar. 31	Mar. 31	1,050	
1	1,100					
Balance	2,500					

The balance of the Supplies account is $2,550 after posting and equals the cost of remaining unused supplies. If the adjustment is *not* made at March 31, then (a) expenses are understated by $1,050 and profit is overstated by $1,050 for the March income statement, and (b) both Supplies and equity are overstated by $1,050 in the March 31 balance sheet.

Other Prepaid Expenses

There are other prepaid expenses (including Prepaid Rent), which are accounted for in exactly the same manner as Insurance and Supplies above. We should also note that some prepaid expenses are both paid for and fully used up within a single accounting period. One example is when a company pays monthly rent on the first day of each month. The payment creates a prepaid expense on the first day of each month that fully expires by the end of the month. In these special cases, we can record the cash paid with a debit to the expense account instead of an asset account.

 DECISION MAKER   Answer—End of chapter

Investor

Assume a small publishing company signed the basketball superstar LeBron James to write a book. The company paid LeBron $500,000 today and will pay future book royalties. A note to the company's financial statements indicates "prepaid expenses include $500,000 in author signing fees to be matched against future expected sales." Is this accounting for the signing bonus acceptable? How might it affect your analysis as an investor in the publishing company?

 CHECKPOINT

   5. If the entry to adjust Prepaid Insurance was not recorded, what effect would this have on each of the three components of the accounting equation (Assets, Liabilities, and Equities)?

   Do Quick Study questions: QS 3-4, QS 3-5, QS 3-6

ADJUSTING FOR DEPRECIATION[5]

Property, plant, and equipment (PPE) are assets owned and controlled by the business as a result of past transactions and used within the business to produce and sell products and services. PPE also includes **intangible assets** (such as patents). Both of these asset groups are expected to provide benefits for more than one accounting period. Examples of property, plant, and equipment assets are land, buildings, machines, vehicles, and furniture. Because these assets (except for land) wear out or decline in usefulness as they are used, an expense must be recorded to match the cost of the asset over the time the asset helped earn revenues. **Depreciation** is the process of calculating expense from matching (or allocating) the cost of plant and equipment assets over their expected useful lives. Businesses that have significant dollars invested in plant and equipment can have large amounts of depreciation appearing on the income statement. For example, **Air Canada** reported buildings and equipment at a value of $8.5 billion with $617 million of corresponding depreciation in its December 31, 2016, financial statements. **WestJet**, on its December 31, 2016 statements, reported its property, plant, and equipment at a value of $4.04 billion with depreciation expense of $335 million.

Organico uses equipment in earning revenue. This equipment's cost must be depreciated to match the cost of the equipment over the time that the equipment helps earn revenue. Recall that Organico purchased its food truck for $6,000 on March 1. Hailey Walker expects the equipment to have a useful life (benefit period) of two years. Hailey expects to sell the truck for about $1,200 at the end of two years. This means that the *net cost* expected to expire over the estimated useful life is $4,800 (= $6,000 − $1,200).

Monthly Straight-Line Depreciation

Calculated as:

$$\frac{\text{Cost of asset} - \begin{array}{c}\text{Estimated value} \\ \text{at end of} \\ \text{estimated} \\ \text{useful life}\end{array}}{\text{Estimated useful life in months}}$$

There are several methods that we can use to allocate this $4,800 net cost to expense. Organico uses *straight-line depreciation*.[6] The **straight-line depreciation method** allocates equal amounts of an asset's net cost over its estimated useful life. When the $4,800 net cost is divided by the asset's useful life of 24 months (2 years × 12 months per year), we get an average monthly cost of $200 ($4,800/24). Our adjusting entry to record monthly depreciation expense is:

Calculation:

$$= \frac{\$6,000 - \$1,200}{24 \text{ months}} = \underline{\$200} \text{ per month}$$

Adjustment (c)

A = L + E	Mar.	31	Depreciation Expense, Equipment..	200	
↓	↓		Accumulated Depreciation, Equipment......................		200
			To record monthly depreciation on equipment		

Posting this adjusting entry affects the accounts shown in Exhibit 3.8:

EXHIBIT 3.8

Accounts After Depreciation Adjustments

Equipment			Accumulated Depreciation, Equipment			Depreciation Expense, Equipment		
Mar. 1	6,000							
Bal.	6,000			200	Mar. 31	Mar. 31	200	

---

5 Prior to 2011, the term *amortization* was used instead of *depreciation*. IFRS uses the terminology *depreciation* for plant and equipment (IFRS 2018, IAS 16, para. 43). *Amortization* will continue to be used for intangible assets (IFRS 2018, IAS 38, para. 97). Intangible assets include items such as copyrights, patents, and trademarks and are introduced in Chapter 4. Amortization for intangible assets is discussed in more detail in Chapter 9.

6 We investigate the different types of *depreciation* methods in Chapter 9. We briefly describe the straight-line method here to help you understand the adjusting process.

Accumulated depreciation is recorded in a *contra asset account.* A **contra account** is an account that is linked with another account and has an opposite normal balance to its counterpart. It is reported at the net amount, after subtracting the contra account from the normal account balance. On Organico's balance sheet, the balance in the contra asset account, *Accumulated Depreciation, Equipment,* will be subtracted from the Equipment account balance as shown in Exhibit 3.10. The cost of an asset less its accumulated depreciation is the net **book value of an asset**. The **fair value of an asset**, also known as the **market value of an asset**, is the amount it can be sold for. It is important to note that market value and book values do not agree because book values are based on historical costs less residual and depreciation will not match perfectly with swings in the current market values.

After posting the adjustment, the *Equipment* account less its *Accumulated Depreciation, Equipment* account equals the March 31 balance sheet amount for this asset. The balance in the Depreciation Expense, Equipment account is the expense reported in the March income statement. If the adjustment is *not* made at March 31, then (1) expenses are understated by $200 and profit is overstated by $200 for the March income statement, and (2) both assets and equity are overstated by $200 in the March 31 balance sheet.

The use of the contra asset account Accumulated Depreciation allows balance sheet readers to know both the cost of assets and the total amount of depreciation charged to expense to date. The title of the contra account to the Equipment asset account is *Accumulated Depreciation*. This means that the account includes *total* depreciation expense for all prior periods when the assets were being used. Organico's Equipment and Accumulated Depreciation, Equipment accounts would appear on May 31, 2020, as shown in Exhibit 3.10, after the three monthly adjusting entries detailed in Exhibit 3.9.

EXHIBIT 3.9

Accounts After Three Months of Depreciation Adjustments

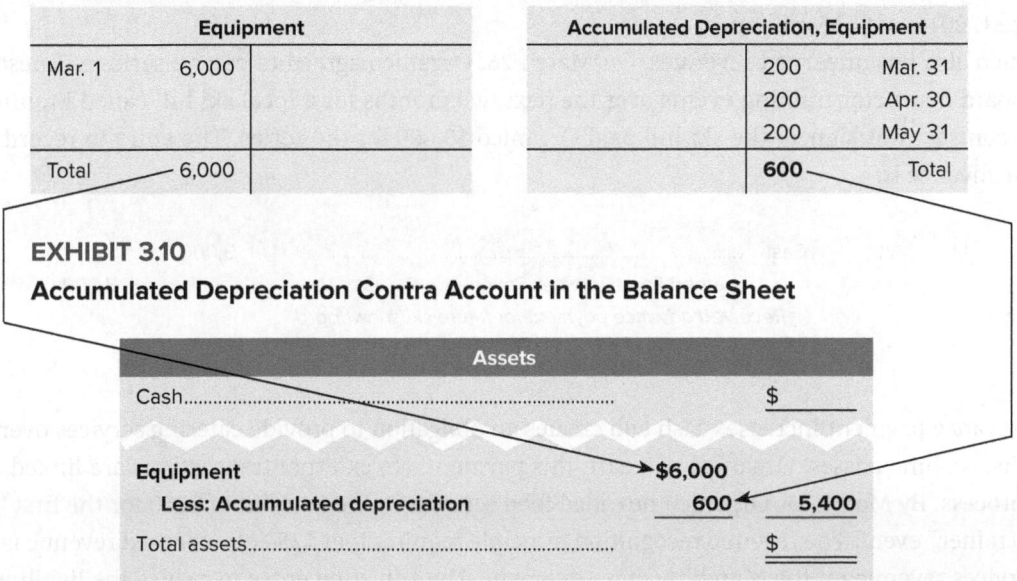

EXHIBIT 3.10

Accumulated Depreciation Contra Account in the Balance Sheet

Assets		
Cash...	$ _____	
Equipment	$6,000	
Less: Accumulated depreciation	600	5,400
Total assets...	$ _____	

 CHECKPOINT

6. If the year-end adjusting entry to record depreciation expense were not recorded, what effect would this have on each component of the accounting equation?

7. Explain what a contra account is.

Do Quick Study questions: QS 3-7, QS 3-8

DECISION MAKER Answer—End of chapter

Small Business Owner

You are preparing to make an offer to purchase a small family-run restaurant. The manager gives you a copy of her depreciation schedule for the restaurant's building and equipment. It shows costs of $75,000 and accumulated depreciation of $55,000. This leaves a net total for building and equipment of $20,000. Is this information valuable in deciding on a purchase offer for the restaurant?

ADJUSTING UNEARNED REVENUES

Unearned revenues refer to cash received in advance of providing products and services. Unearned revenues, also known as *deferred revenues*, are a *liability*. When cash is accepted, an obligation to provide products and services is also accepted. As products and services are provided, the amount of unearned revenues becomes *earned* revenues. Adjusting entries for unearned revenues involve increasing (crediting) revenues and decreasing (debiting) unearned revenues as shown in Exhibit 3.11. These adjustments reflect economic events (including passage of time) that impact unearned revenues.

EXHIBIT 3.11

Adjusting for Unearned Revenues

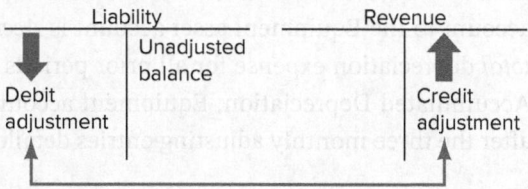

We see an example of unearned revenues in **Telus**'s 2016 annual report. Telus reports unearned revenue of $737 million on its balance sheet that includes customer deposits and amounts received related to services to be provided in the future. Another example is WestJet, which reports advance (unearned) ticket sales at December 31, 2016, of $626 million.

Organico also has unearned revenues. On March 26, Organico agreed to cater a series of Tuesday night ski/snowboard instructor training events over the next two months for a local ski hill called Mount Mundy. When the contract was signed, the ski hill paid Organico $3,000 for the series. The entry to record the cash received in advance is:

Mar. 26	Cash..	3,000	
	Unearned Food Services Revenue.............................		3,000
	Received advance payment for future ski/snowboard catering services for Mount Mundy.		

This advance payment increases cash and creates an obligation to provide catering services over the next two months. As time passes, Organico will earn this payment. No external transactions are linked with this earnings process. By March 31, Organico provided food services in the amount of $250 for the first "Tuesday Train the Trainer" event. The revenue recognition principle requires that $250 of unearned revenue is reported as food services revenue on the March income statement. The adjusting entry to reduce the liability account and recognize earned revenue is:

Adjustment (d)

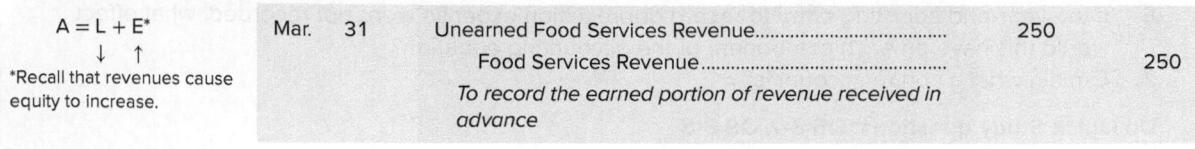

$A = L + E^*$

↓ ↑

Recall that revenues cause equity to increase.

Mar. 31	Unearned Food Services Revenue..	250	
	Food Services Revenue..		250
	To record the earned portion of revenue received in advance		

The accounts look as shown in Exhibit 3.12 after posting the adjusting entry.

EXHIBIT 3.12
Unearned Revenue and Revenue Accounts After Adjustments

Unearned Food Services Revenue				Food Services Revenue		
Mar. 31	**250**	3,000	Mar. 26		2,200	Mar. 10
					1,600	15
					250	31
		2,750	Balance		4,050	Total

The adjusting entry transfers $250 out of Unearned Food Services Revenue (a liability account) to a revenue account. If the adjustment is *not* made, then (a) revenue and profit are understated by $250 in the March income statement, and (b) Unearned Food Services Revenue is overstated and equity understated by $250 on the March 31 balance sheet.

 CHECKPOINT

8. AltaCo credited Unearned Revenue for $20,000 received on November 3, 2020, for work to be done just prior to year-end. The work was completed as scheduled. If Unearned Revenue is not adjusted at year-end to reflect the completion of the work, which GAAP will be violated and why?

9. Describe how unearned revenue arises. Give an example.

Do Quick Study questions: QS 3-9, QS 3-10

ADJUSTING ACCRUED EXPENSES

Accrued expenses refer to costs incurred in a period that are both unpaid and unrecorded prior to adjustment. Generally they relate to expenses incurred for services provided or products received for which the company has yet to be billed. For example, Telus Corporation reported $2.3 billion of accounts payable and accrued liabilities on its December 31, 2016, balance sheet. Accrued expenses are part of expenses and reported on the income statement. Adjusting entries for recording accrued expenses involve increasing (debiting) expenses and recording the required accounts payable, crediting liabilities as shown in Exhibit 3.13.

EXHIBIT 3.13
Adjusting for Accrued Expenses

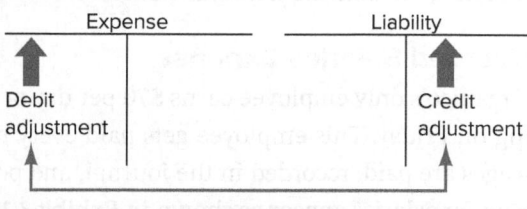

Common examples of accrued expenses are interest, salaries, rent, and taxes. We use interest and salaries to show how to adjust accounts for accrued expenses.

Accrued Interest Expense

It is common for companies to have accrued interest expense on notes payable, certain accounts payable, and other debt at the end of an accounting period. Interest expense is incurred with the passage of time. Unless interest is paid on the last day of an accounting period, we need to adjust accounts for interest expense incurred but not yet paid.

Interest of $35 has accrued on Organico's $6,000, 7%, six-month note payable for the month of March.[7] The journal entry is:

Adjustment (e)

A = L + E	Mar.	31	Interest Expense..	35	
↑ ↓			Interest Payable		35
			To record accrued interest.		

After the adjusting entry is posted, the expense and liability accounts appear as shown in Exhibit 3.14.

EXHIBIT 3.14

Notes Payable and Interest Accounts After Accrual Adjustments

Notes Payable			Interest Payable			Interest Expense		
	6,000	Mar. 1		35	Mar. 31	35		Mar. 31

This means that $35 of interest expense is reported on the income statement and that $35 interest payable is reported on the balance sheet. Notice that the Notes Payable account is *not* affected by recording interest. If the interest adjustment is not made, then (a) Interest Expense is understated and profit overstated by $35 in the March income statement, and (b) Interest Payable is understated and equity overstated by $35 on the March 31 balance sheet.

Accrued Interest Expense
Calculated as:
Interest = Principal of the note × Annual interest rate × Time expressed years OR $i = Prt$
Where the term of the note is in days,
$$\text{Interest} = \text{Principal} \times \text{Rate} \times \frac{\text{Exact days}}{365}.$$

The $6,000 principal and total interest of $210 ($6,000 × 7% × 6/12 = $210) will be paid six months from March 1, the date the note was issued.[8]

Accrued Salaries Expense

Organico's only employee earns $70 per day or $350 for a five-day workweek beginning on Monday and ending on Friday. This employee gets paid every two weeks on Friday. On the 13th and the 27th of March, the wages are paid, recorded in the journal, and posted to the ledger. The *unadjusted* Salaries Expense and Cash paid for salaries appear as shown in Exhibit 3.15.

---

7 Interest on the $6,000, 7%, six-month note payable was calculated using the above formula. Therefore, $6,000 × 7% × 1/12 = $35. Interest is discussed in greater detail in Chapter 9.

8 When the note payable and accrued interest are paid to the lender on September 1, six months after the date of issue on March 1, the entry would be (assuming interest expense of $35 per month has accrued):

Sept.	1	Notes Payable..	6,000	
		Interest Payable..	210	
		Cash..		6,210
		To record payment of note payable and accrued interest.		

EXHIBIT 3.15
Salary and Cash Accounts Before Adjusting

	Cash				Salaries Expense	
	700	Mar. 13		Mar. 13	700	
	700	27		27	**700**	

The calendar in Exhibit 3.16 shows two working days after the March 27 payday (March 30 and 31). This means that the employee earns two days' salary by the close of business on Tuesday, March 31. While this salary expense is incurred, it is not yet paid or recorded by the company. The period-end adjusting entry to account for accrued salaries is:

Adjustment (f)

Mar.	31	Salaries Expense..	140		$A = L + E$
		Salaries Payable..		140	↑ ↓
		To record one day's accrued salary; 2 × $70.			

EXHIBIT 3.16
Salary Accrual Period and Paydays

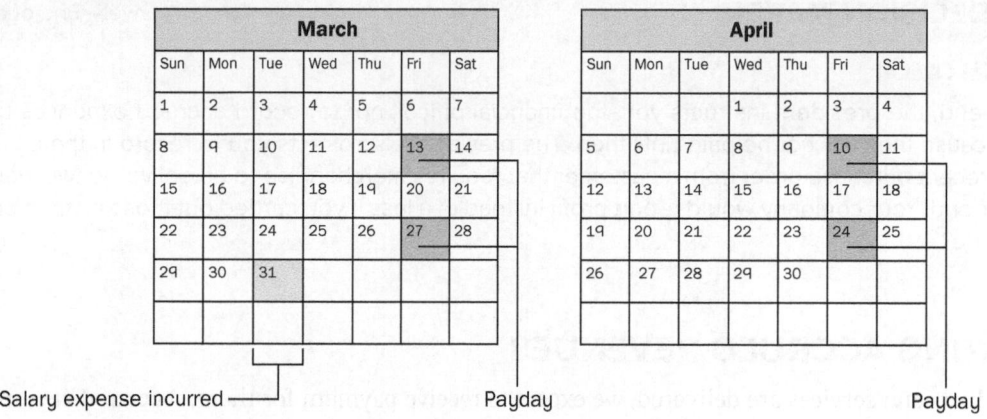

Salary expense incurred ⸺ ⎦   Payday   Payday

After the adjusting entry is posted, the expense and liability accounts appear as shown in Exhibit 3.17.

EXHIBIT 3.17
Salary Accounts After Accrual Adjustments

	Salaries Expense				Salaries Payable	
Mar. 13	700				140	**Mar. 31**
27	700					
31	**140**					
Total	1,540					

This means that $1,540 of salaries expense is reported on the income statement and that $140 in salaries payable (liability) is reported in the balance sheet. If the adjustment is *not* made, then (1) Salaries Expense is understated and net profit overstated by $140 in the March income statement, and (2) Salaries Payable is understated and equity overstated by $140 on the March 31 balance sheet.

The accrued salaries are paid on the first payday of the next biweekly period, which occurs on Friday, April 10. The entry includes the added salaries expense for the eight days worked in April:

Apr.	10	Salaries Payable	140	
		Salaries Expense	560	
		Cash		700
		Paid two weeks' salary including two days accrued		
		in March (1 day at $70; 8 days at $140 = $560).		

CHECKPOINT

10. In error, the May utility bill for $6,900 was not included in the May 31 adjusting entries. What effect would this error have on the components of the accounting equation?

11. What is an accrued expense? Give an example.

12. Digitalworld.com, an Internet-based music store, records $1,000 of accrued salaries on December 31. Five days later on January 5 (the next payday), salaries of $7,000 are paid. What is the January 5 entry?

Do Quick Study questions: QS 3-11, QS 3-12, QS 3-13

DECISION MAKER

Answer—End of chapter

Financial Officer

At year-end, the president instructs you, the financial officer, not to record accrued expenses until next year because they will not be paid until then. The president also directs you to record in the current-year sales a recent purchase order from a customer that requires merchandise to be delivered two weeks after the year-end. Your company would report profit instead of a loss if you carried out these instructions. What will you do?

ADJUSTING ACCRUED REVENUES

When products and services are delivered, we expect to receive payment for them. **Accrued revenues** refer to revenues earned in a period that are both unrecorded and not yet received in cash (or other assets). Accrued revenues are part of revenues and must be reported on the income statement. The adjusting entries increase (debit) assets and increase (credit) revenues as shown in Exhibit 3.18.

Common examples of accrued revenues are fees for services and products, interest income, and rent revenue. We use service fees and interest income to show how to adjust accounts for accrued revenues.

EXHIBIT 3.18
Adjusting for Accrued Revenues

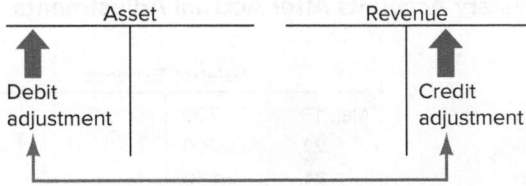

Accrued Services Revenue

Accrued revenue is revenue that is earned but not yet recorded because either the customer has not paid for them or the seller has not yet billed the customer. Organico provides us with an example of accrued revenue. In the second week of March, Organico agrees to provide daily lunch catering services at 11:00 a.m. to a local builder on a residential building project for a fixed fee of $2,700 per month to feed the staff for the period from March 11 to April 10, or 30 days of service. The client agrees to pay $2,700 cash to Organico on April 10, 2020, when the catering service period is complete.

At March 31, 2020, 20 days of catering services are already provided to the client. Since the contracted services are not yet entirely provided, the client is not yet billed nor has Organico recorded the services already provided. Organico has earned $1,800 (= $2,700 × 20/30). The *revenue recognition principle* requires that we report the $1,800 on the March income statement because it is earned in March. The balance sheet also must report that this client owes Organico $1,800. The adjusting entry to account for accrued teaching services revenue is:

Adjustment (g)

Mar.	31	Accounts Receivable..	1,800		A = L + E
		Food Services Revenue...		1,800	↑ ↑
		To record 20 days' accrued revenue.			

After the adjusting entry is posted, the affected accounts look as shown in Exhibit 3.19.

EXHIBIT 3.19

Receivable and Revenue Accounts After Accrual Adjustments

Accounts Receivable					Food Services Revenue	
Mar. 15	1,900	1,900	Mar. 25		2,200	Mar. 10
31	**1,800**				1,600	15
Balance	1,800				250	31
					1,800	**31**
					5,850	Total

Accounts receivable are reported on the balance sheet at $1,800, and $5,850 of revenues are reported on the income statement. If the adjustment is *not* made, then (1) both Food Services Revenue and profit are understated by $1,800 in the March income statement, and (2) both Accounts Receivable and equity are understated by $1,800 on the March 31 balance sheet.

When the catering fee is received from the builder on April 10, Organico makes the following entry to remove the accrued asset (accounts receivable) and recognize the added 10 days of revenue earned in April:

Apr.	10	Cash..	2,700	
		Accounts Receivable..		1,800
		Food Services Revenue..		900
		Received cash for accrued asset and earned		
		teaching revenue; $900 = $2,700 × 10/30		

Accrued Interest Income

In addition to the accrued interest expense we described earlier, interest can yield accrued revenue when a company is owed money (or other assets) by a debtor. If a company is holding notes or accounts receivable that produce interest income, we must adjust the accounts to record any earned and yet uncollected interest income. The adjusting entry is recorded as a debit to Interest Receivable (asset) and a credit to Interest Income (equity). The approach to calculate interest income is the same as was discussed previously to calculate interest payable on a note.

 CHECKPOINT

13. An adjusting entry to record $6,000 of accrued interest income was omitted due to an oversight. What effect would this error have on the components of the accounting equation?

Do Quick Study question: QS 3-14

Adjustments and Financial Statements

LO5 Explain how accounting adjustments link to financial statements.

Exhibit 3.20 lists the five major types of transactions requiring adjustment. Understanding this exhibit is important to understanding the adjusting process and its link to financial statements. Remember that each adjusting entry affects both income statement accounts and balance sheet accounts.

EXHIBIT 3.20

Summary of Adjustments and Financial Statement Impact

Type	Before Adjusting		Adjusting Entry	
	Balance Sheet Account	Income Statement Account		
Prepaid Expense	Asset and equity overstated	Expense understated	Dr. _____ Expense XX Cr. _____ Prepaid Asset e.g., Supplies......................... XX	where XX = how much of the prepaid was used during the period

Depreciation/ Amortization	Asset and equity overstated	Expense understated	Dr. Depreciation
			   Expense _____...................... XX
			Cr. Accumulated
			   Depreciation_____............... XX
				where XX = how much of the asset's cost was matched as an expense to the period

Unearned Revenues	Liability overstated; equity understated	Revenue understated	Dr. Unearned _____ Revenue... XX Cr. _____ Revenue XX	where XX = how much of the liability was earned during the period
Accrued Expenses	Liability understated; equity overstated	Expense understated	Dr. _____ Expense................... XX Cr. _____ Liability (e.g., Salaries Payable)....... XX	where XX = the amount of the unpaid and unrecorded expense for the period
Accrued Revenues	Asset and equity understated	Revenue understated	Dr. _____ Asset e.g., Accts Receivable........ XX Cr. _____ Revenue XX	where XX = the amount of the uncollected and unrecorded revenue for the period

> **Important Tip:**
>
> *Note that adjusting entries related to the framework in Exhibit 3.20 never affect cash.*[9] In the case of prepaid assets and unearned revenues, cash has already been correctly recorded; it is the prepaid asset and unearned revenues account balances that need to be *fixed* or adjusted. In the case of accrued revenues and expenses, cash will be received or paid in the future and is not to be accounted for until that time; it is the revenue or expense account balance that needs to be fixed or adjusted. Depreciation is a non-cash transaction and therefore does not affect cash.

A common error made by students learning to prepare adjusting entries is either to debit or to credit cash.

Exhibit 3.21 summarizes the adjusting entries of Organico on March 31. The posting of adjusting entries to individual ledger accounts was shown when we described the transactions above and is not repeated here. Adjusting entries are often set apart from other journal entries with the caption *Adjusting Entries*, as shown in Exhibit 3.21.

---

9   Adjusting entries related to bank reconciliations affect cash but these adjustments are excluded from the framework in Exhibit 3.20 and will be discussed in Chapter 7.

EXHIBIT 3.21
Journalizing Adjusting Entries of Organico

ORGANICO

GENERAL JOURNAL				Page 2
Date	**Account Titles and Explanations**	**PR**	**Debit**	**Credit**
2020	*Adjusting Entries*			
Mar. 31	Insurance Expense		100	
	Prepaid Insurance			100
	To record expired insurance; $2,400/24.			
31	Supplies Expense..		1,050	
	Supplies			1,050
	To record supplies used; $3,600 − $2,550.			
31	Depreciation Expense, Equipment.......................................		200	
	Accumulated Depreciation, Equipment...........................			200
	To record monthly depreciation on equipment;			
	$6,000 − $1,200 = $4,800/24.			
31	Unearned Food Services Revenue		250	
	Food Services Revenue..			250
	To record earned revenue received in advance.			
31	Interest Expense..		35	
	Interest Payable			35
	To record one month of accrued interest.			
31	Salaries Expense..		140	
	Salaries Payable...			140
	To record two day's accrued salary; 2 × $70 = $140.			
31	Accounts Receivable...		1,800	
	Food Services Revenue..			1,800
	To record 20 days of accrued revenue; $2,700 × 20/30.			

 CHECKPOINT

14. Explain how adjusting entries are linked to the components of the accounting equation.

Do Quick Study questions: QS 3-15, QS 3-16, QS 3-17

Mid-Chapter Demonstration Problem

The owner of a landscape company prepares *annual* financial statements.

Part A

Prepare the appropriate adjusting entries for July 31, 2020, based on the following information available at the end of July.

a. An annual insurance policy amounting to $1,200 was purchased on May 1, 2020. The Prepaid Insurance account was debited and Cash credited on the same date.

b. The landscape company's lawn tractor was purchased for $3,200 in 2018. The salvage value of the lawn tractor at the end of its four-year useful life is estimated to be $800. Calculate the annual depreciation for the year ended July 31, 2020, and record the corresponding adjusting journal entry.

c. On April 1, 2020, a customer paid for a six-month lawn service plan to begin June 1, 2020. The journal entry credited the Unearned Service Revenue account when the $3,000 payment was received. The monthly fee is $500.

d. The last weekly salary of $1,400 was paid to employees on Friday, July 25. Employees are paid based on a five-day workweek. Salaries for July 28, 29, 30, and 31 have accrued.

e. Service fees of $1,800 were earned by July 31 but not recorded.

Part B

Refer to (d) above. Prepare the entry to pay the salaries on Friday, August 1.

Analysis Component:

Assume a business were to falsify its earnings by understating them for tax purposes. Omitting which of the adjustments in Part A would accomplish this? What are the repercussions for doing so?

SOLUTION

Part A	a. July 31	Insurance Expense...	300	
		Prepaid Insurance..		300
		To record insurance for May, June, and July; calculated as: $1,200/12 = $100 \times 3 = $300.		
	b. 31	Depreciation Expense, Lawn Tractor	600	
		Accumulated Depreciation, Lawn Tractor..............		600
		Annual depreciation, calculated as $3,200 - $800 = $2,400/4 years = $600/year.		
	c. 31	Unearned Service Fees..	1,000	
		Service Fee Revenue..		1,000
		To record service fees earned for June and July; calculated as $500 \times 2 = $1,000.		
	d. 31	Salaries Expense...	1,120	
		Salaries Payable..		1,120
		To record salaries for the last two days of July, calculated as $1,400/5 = $280/day \times 4 days = $1,120.		
	e. 31	Accounts Receivable...	1,800	
		Service Fee Revenue..		1,800
		To record accrued service revenue for July.		
Part B	Aug. 1	Salaries Payable	1,120	
		Salaries Expense	280	
		Cash		1,400
		To record payment of weekly salaries; where salaries expense is calculated as $1,400/5 = $280/day \times 1 day = $280.		

Analysis Component:

Omitting adjustments (c) and (e) would cause revenues to be understated; hence, profit would also be understated. CRA could audit the company's reported taxable earnings and fine the company with interest penalties for not recording earnings correctly.

Adjusted Trial Balance

LO6 Explain and prepare an adjusted trial balance.

An **unadjusted trial balance** is a listing of accounts and balances prepared *before* adjustments are recorded. An **adjusted trial balance** is a list of accounts and balances prepared *after* adjusting entries are recorded and posted to the ledger. Exhibit 3.22 shows the unadjusted and adjusted trial balances for Organico at March 31, 2020, using an electronic spreadsheet. Electronic spreadsheet software such as Excel allows us to compile and adjust the relevant numbers efficiently.

EXHIBIT 3.22

Unadjusted and Adjusted Trial Balance for Organico

	Unadjusted Trial Balance		Adjustments		Adjusted Trial Balance	
	Dr.	Cr.	Dr.	Cr.	Dr.	Cr.
Cash	$ 8,070				$ 8,070	
Accounts receivable			(g) $1,800		1,800	
Supplies	3,600			(b) $1,050	2,550	
Prepaid insurance	2,400			(a) 100	2,300	
Equipment	6,000				6,000	
Accumulated depreciation, equipment				(c) 200		$ 200
Accounts payable		$ 200				200
Interest payable				(e) 35		35
Salaries payable				(f) 140		350
Unearned food services revenue		3,000	(d) 250			2,750
Notes payable		6,000				6,000
Hailey Walker, capital		10,000				10,000
Hailey Walker, withdrawals	600				600	
Food services revenue		3,800		(d) 250 (g) 1,800		5,850
Teaching revenue		300				300
Depreciation expense, equipment			(c) 200		200	
Salaries expense	1,400		(f) 140		1,540	
Interest expense			(e) 35		35	
Insurance expense			(a) 100		100	
Rent expense	1,000				1,000	
Supplies expense			(b) 1,050		1,050	
Utilities expense	230				230	
Totals	$23,300	$23,300	$3,575	$3,575	$25,475	$25,475

In Exhibit 3.22, notice several new accounts arising from the adjusting entries. The listing of accounts is also slightly changed to match the order listed in the Chart of Accounts in Appendix IV at the end of the book.

Preparing Financial Statements

LO7 Prepare financial statements from an adjusted trial balance.

We prepare financial statements directly from information in the *adjusted* trial balance. An adjusted trial balance includes all balances appearing in financial statements. We know that a trial balance summarizes information in the ledger by listing accounts and their balances. This summary is easier to work from than the entire ledger when preparing financial statements.

Exhibit 3.23 shows how Organico's revenue and expense balances are transferred from the adjusted trial balance to (1) the income statement, and (2) the statement of changes in equity. Note how we use the profit as reported on the income statement and the end-of-year balance in the withdrawals account to prepare the statement of changes in equity.

> **Important Tip:**
> Notice how the balance in the capital account in Exhibit 3.23 cannot be used as the opening capital balance in the statement of changes in equity. You always need to deduct owner investments made during the year from the *balance* in the Capital account to determine the owner's capital account balance at the beginning of the period.

Exhibit 3.23 also shows how Organico's asset and liability balances on the adjusted trial balance are transferred to the balance sheet. The ending equity is determined on the statement of changes in equity and transferred to the balance sheet. There are different formats for the balance sheet. The **account form balance sheet**, which has been demonstrated previously, lists assets on the left and liabilities and equity on the right side of the balance sheet. Its name comes from its link to the accounting equation, *Assets = Liabilities + Equity*. The balance sheet in Exhibit 1.16 is in account form. The **report form balance sheet** lists items vertically, as shown in Exhibit 3.23. Both forms are widely used and are considered equally helpful to users. For consistency, we will use the report form in the preparation of financial statements from this point forward.

We usually prepare financial statements in the order shown: income statement, statement of changes in equity, and balance sheet. This order makes sense since the balance sheet uses information from the statement of changes in equity, which in turn uses information from the income statement.

CHECKPOINT

15. Jordan Air Company has the following information in its unadjusted and adjusted trial balances:

	Unadjusted		Adjusted	
	Debit	Credit	Debit	Credit
Prepaid insurance	$6,200		$5,900	
Salaries payable		$ -0-		$1,400

What are the adjusting entries that Jordan Air likely recorded?

16. What types of accounts are taken from the adjusted trial balance to prepare an income statement?

17. In preparing financial statements from an adjusted trial balance, what statement is usually prepared first? second? third? Explain why.

Do Quick Study question: QS 3-18

EXHIBIT 3.23
Preparing the Income Statement, Statement of Changes in Equity, and Balance Sheet from the Adjusted Trial Balance

ORGANICO

Organico
Adjusted Trial Balance
March 31, 2020

Acct. No.	Account Title	Debit	Credit
101	Cash	$ 8,070	
106	Accounts receivable	1,800	
125	Supplies	2,550	
128	Prepaid insurance........................	2,300	
167	Equipment	6,000	
168	Accumulated depreciation, equipment		$ 200
201	Accounts payable		200
203	Interest payable		35
209	Salaries payable		140
236	Unearned food services revenue..........		2,750
240	Notes payable..............................		6,000
301	Hailey Walker, capital		10,000*
302	Hailey Walker, withdrawals	600	
403	Food services revenue		5,850
406	Teaching revenue		300
614	Depreciation expense, equipment.......	200	
622	Salaries expense..........................	1,540	
633	Interest expense	35	
637	Insurance expense	100	
641	Rent expense...............................	1,000	
651	Supplies expense	1,050	
690	Utilities expense	230	
	Totals	$25,475	$25,475

*Recall that this balance is the result of a $10,000 investment by Hailey Walker during March 2020.

Step One   Prepare income statement

Organico
Income Statement
For Month Ended March 31, 2020

Revenues:		
Food services revenue	$5,850	
Teaching revenue	300	
Total revenues		$6,150
Operating expenses:		
Salaries expense	$1,540	
Supplies expense	1,050	
Rent expense	1,000	
Utilities expense	230	
Depreciation expense, equipment	200	
Insurance expense	100	
Interest expense	35	
Total operating expenses		$4,155
Profit		$1,995

Step Two   Prepare statement of changes in equity

Organico
Statement of Changes in Equity
For Month Ended March 31, 2020

Hailey Walker, capital, March 1		$ -0-
Investments by owner	$10,000	
Profit	$1,995	11,995
Total		$11,995
Less: Withdrawal by owner		600
Hailey Walker, capital, March 31		$11,395

Step Three   Prepare balance sheet

Organico
Balance Sheet
March 31, 2020

Assets		
Cash		$ 8,070
Accounts receivable		1,800
Supplies		2,550
Prepaid insurance		2,300
Equipment	$ 6,000	
Less: Accumulated depreciation	200	5,800
Total assets		$ 20,520

Liabilities		
Accounts payable	$ 200	
Interest payable	35	
Salaries payable	140	
Unearned food services revenue	2,750	
Notes payable	6,000	
Total liabilities		$ 9,055

Equity		
Hailey Walker, capital		11,395
Total liabilities and equity		$ 20,520

CRITICAL THINKING CHALLENGE

Refer to the Critical Thinking Challenge questions at the beginning of the chapter. Compare your answers to those suggested on Connect.

IFRS AND ASPE—THE DIFFERENCES

Difference	International Financial Reporting Standards (IFRS)	Accounting Standards for Private Enterprises (ASPE)
Recording adjusting entries	• Requires that financial statements be presented at least annually[a]; therefore, adjustments would be prepared at least annually. However, for publicly listed companies, securities commissions law requires publicly listed companies to present quarterly financial statements, which in turn would require that adjusting entries be prepared at least quarterly.	• Unlike IFRS, ASPE does not explicitly require that financial statements be presented at least annually although it is implied given that financial statements must be presented in a timely manner[b] and items must be presented consistently from period to period.[c] Financial statements are prepared at least annually for tax purposes and, for example, to meet any banking requirements.
	• Both public and private enterprises may prepare adjusting entries more frequently, such as monthly, to enhance the accuracy of information required for decision making.	
Depreciation vs. amortization	• Uses the term *depreciation*[d] (although it uses *amortization* for intangible assets).[e]	• Uses the term *amortization*.[f]

a. IFRS 2018, IAS 1 para. 36.
b. ASPE, Accounting Standards, Section 1000.17(b).
c. ASPE, Accounting Standards, Section 1000.19-20.
d. IFRS 2018, IAS 16 para. 6.
e. IFRS 2018, IAS 38 para. 8.
f. ASPE, Accounting Standards, Section 3061.16.

A Look Ahead

Chapter 4 highlights the completion of the accounting cycle. We explain the important final steps in the accounting process. These include closing procedures, the post-closing trial balance, and reversing entries.

For further study on some topics of relevance to this chapter, please see the following Extend Your Knowledge supplements:

EYK 3-1 Using the Trial Balance as a Framework for Adjustments

EYK 3-2 Subsequent Payment/Collection of Accruals

SUMMARY

LO1 Describe the purpose of adjusting accounts at the end of a period. After routine daily transactions are recorded, several accounts need adjusting for their balances to be correct, as several transactions relating to revenues/expenses are triggered simply due to the passage of time. The purpose of adjusting accounts at the end of a period is to recognize unrecorded revenues and expenses.

LO2 Explain how the timeliness, matching, and revenue recognition principles affect the adjusting process. The value of information is often linked to its timeliness. Accounting systems deliver timely financial information by preparing periodic reports at regular intervals such as each month, every three-month quarter, or, at minimum, once a year. Adjustments are made so that revenues and expenses are recognized as they occur and matched to the proper period.

LO3 Explain accrual accounting and cash basis accounting and how accrual accounting adds to the usefulness of financial statements. Accrual accounting recognizes revenue when earned and expenses when incurred, not necessarily when cash inflows and outflows occur. The accrual basis of accounting requires adjusting entries to be posted at the end of the period to reflect the economic reality of the company's true financial position. Cash basis accounting recognizes revenues when cash is received and expenses when cash is paid; it is not in accordance with IFRS or ASPE standards.

LO4 Prepare and explain adjusting entries for prepaid expenses, depreciation, unearned revenues, accrued expenses, and accrued revenues. Prepaid expenses, an asset, refers to items paid for in advance of receiving their benefits. As this asset is used, its cost becomes an expense.

Dr. Expense xx
    Cr. Prepaid xx
To adjust prepaid for amount used.

Depreciation is the expense created by spreading the cost of plant and equipment assets over the periods these assets are used. Accumulated Depreciation, a contra asset account, is credited to track the total amount of the plant and equipment asset used.

Dr. Depreciation Expense............................ xx
    Cr. Accumulated Depreciation............. xx
To adjust for depreciation.

Unearned revenues, a liability, refers to cash received in advance of providing products and services. As products and services are provided, the amount of unearned revenues becomes earned revenues.

Dr. Unearned Revenue.................................. xx
    Cr. Revenue xx
To adjust for unearned revenue that is earned.

Accrued expenses are costs incurred in a period that are unpaid by the company and have not yet been recorded.

Dr. Expense xx
    Cr. Liability... xx
To adjust for unrecorded and unpaid expenses.

Accrued revenues are revenues earned in a period and not yet collected from the customer/client.

Dr. Receivable.. xx
    Cr. Revenue xx
To adjust for unrecorded revenues not yet collected.

LO5 Explain how accounting adjustments link to financial statements. Accounting adjustments bring an asset or liability account balance to its correct amount and update related expense or revenue accounts. Every adjusting entry affects one or more income statement *and* balance sheet accounts. An adjusting entry never affects cash. Adjustments are necessary for transactions that extend over more than one period. Exhibit 3.20 summarizes financial statement links by type of adjustment.

LO6 Explain and prepare an adjusted trial balance. An adjusted trial balance is a list of accounts and balances prepared after adjusting entries are recorded and posted to the ledger. Financial statements are often prepared from the adjusted trial balance.

LO7 Prepare financial statements from an adjusted trial balance. We can prepare financial statements directly from the adjusted trial balance that includes all account balances. Revenue and expense balances are transferred to the income statement and statement of changes in equity. Asset, liability, and equity balances are transferred to the balance sheet. We usually prepare statements in the following order: income statement, statement of changes in equity, and balance sheet (statement of financial position).

 Guidance Answer to DECISION MAKER

Investor

Prepaid expenses are items paid for in advance of receiving their benefits. They are assets and are expensed as they are used up. The publishing company's treatment of the signing bonus is acceptable provided future book sales can at least match the $500,000 expense. As an investor, you are concerned about the risk of future book sales. The more uncertain future book sales are, the more likely your analysis is to treat the $500,000, or a portion of it, as an expense in the current accounting period, not a prepaid expense (an asset on the balance sheet).

Small Business Owner

We know that depreciation is a process of cost allocation, not asset valuation. Knowing the depreciation schedule of the restaurant is not especially useful in your estimation of what the restaurant's building and equipment are currently worth, as they do not reflect current market values. Your assessment of the age,

(Continued)

quality, and usefulness of the building and equipment is much more important. Also, you would use the current market values of similar assets as a benchmark in estimating the value of this restaurant's building and equipment.

Financial Officer

Omitting accrued expenses and recognizing revenue early can mislead financial statement users and lead to fraudulent financial reporting. One action is to request a second meeting with the president so you can explain that accruing expenses when incurred and recognizing revenue when earned are requirements that need to be followed due to both the revenue recognition and matching principles. If the president persists, you might discuss the situation with legal counsel and any auditors involved. Your ethical action might cost you this job, but the potential pitfalls for falsification of statements, reputation and personal integrity loss, and other costs are too great.

 Guidance Answers to CHECKPOINT

1. An annual reporting (or accounting) period covers one year and refers to the preparation of annual financial statements. The annual reporting period can follow the calendar year or a fiscal year. The fiscal year can follow the business's natural business year.
2. Interim (less than one year) financial statements are prepared to provide decision makers with information frequently and promptly.
3. The revenue recognition principle, the timeliness principle, and the matching principle lead most directly to the adjusting process.
4. No. Cash basis accounting is not consistent with generally accepted accounting principles.
5. If Prepaid Insurance is not adjusted, assets and equity will be overstated.
6. If the adjusting entry to record depreciation were not recorded, assets and equity would be overstated.
7. A contra account is an account that is subtracted from the balance of a related account. Use of a contra account often provides more complete information than simply reporting a net amount.
8. The revenue recognition principle will be violated because revenues earned have not been recognized. The matching principle will also be violated because revenues earned will not be assigned to the correct accounting period—the period in which the expenses related to the revenues were incurred.
9. Unearned revenue arises when cash is (or other assets are) received from a customer before the services and products are delivered to the customer. Magazine subscription receipts in advance are one example.
10. The omission of the $6,900 interest expense accrual will cause liabilities to be understated by $6,900 and equity to be overstated by $6,900.
11. An accrued expense refers to costs incurred in a period that are both unpaid and unrecorded prior to adjusting entries. One example is salaries earned by employees but not yet paid at the end of a period.
12. The January 5 entry to settle the accrued salaries and pay for added salaries is:

Jan. 5	Salaries Payable	1,000	
	Salaries Expense	6,000	
	Cash		7,000
	Paid salary including accrual from December.		

13. The omission of an adjusting entry to record $6,000 of accrued interest would cause assets and equity to be understated by $6,000 each.

14. The various adjusting entries are linked to the accounting equation as follows: (a) adjustment to account for prepaid assets and the recording of depreciation cause assets and equity to decrease; (b) adjustment of unearned amounts causes liabilities to decrease and equity to increase; (c) accrual of revenues causes assets and equity to increase; and (d) accrual of expenses causes liabilities to increase and equity to decrease.
15. The probable adjusting entries of Jordan Air are:

Insurance Expense	300	
Prepaid Insurance		300
To record insurance expired.		

Salaries Expense	1,400	
Salaries Payable		1,400
To record accrued salaries.		

16. Revenue accounts and expense accounts.
17. The income statement is usually prepared first, followed by the statement of changes in equity because profit (loss) from the income statement flows into the statement of changes in equity. The balance sheet is then prepared since the ending capital balance from the statement of changes in equity flows into the equity section of the balance sheet. This is illustrated in Exhibit 3.23.

Demonstration Problem

The following information continues with The Cutlery, featured in the Chapter 1 and 2 Demonstration Problems. After the first month of business, The Cutlery's August 31, 2020, unadjusted trial balance appeared as follows:

The Cutlery
Trial Balance
August 31, 2020

Account	Debit	Credit
Cash	$ 4,950	
Accounts receivable	-0-	
Prepaid insurance	2,400	
Furniture	2,000	
Store equipment	31,000	
Accounts payable		$14,450
Unearned haircutting services revenue		500
Joanne Cardinal, capital		26,000
Joanne Cardinal, withdrawals	500	
Haircutting services revenue		3,800
Wages expense	250	
Rent expense	3,200	
Hydro expense	450	
Totals	$44,750	$44,750

The following additional information is available for the *month* just ended:

a. Depreciation of $100 per month will be taken on the furniture.

b. It is estimated that the store equipment will have a $1,000 value at the end of its estimated five-year (or 60-month) useful life. Joanne Cardinal will record a full month of depreciation for August.

c. It was determined that the balance in unearned haircutting services revenue at August 31 should be $420.

d. The prepaid insurance represents six months of insurance beginning August 1.

e. On August 31, The Cutlery provided $130 of services to a client who will pay in September.

f. On August 31, Joanne Cardinal received the business's August cell phone bill totalling $50. It will be paid in September.

Required

1. Prepare the adjusting entries needed on August 31, 2020, to record the previously unrecorded items.

2. Prepare T-accounts for accounts affected by the adjusting entries. Post the adjusting entries to the T-accounts.

3. Prepare an adjusted trial balance.

4. Prepare an income statement, a statement of changes in equity, and a balance sheet.

Analysis Component:

Calculate the net effect of the adjusting entries on the balance sheet. Is profit positively or negatively affected by these adjusting entries overall? Could the opposite effect be achieved? If so, how?

Planning the Solution

- Analyze the information for each situation to determine which accounts need to be updated with an adjustment.

- Calculate the dollar amount of each adjustment and prepare the necessary journal entries.

- Show the amount entered by each adjustment in the designated accounts and determine the adjusted balance.

- Determine each entry's effect on profit for the year and on total assets, total liabilities, and equity at the end of the year.

- Using the adjusted balances, prepare an adjusted trial balance.

- Using the adjusted trial balance, prepare the income statement, statement of changes in equity, and balance sheet.

- Analyze the adjusting entries and calculate the effect on each component of the accounting equation.

SOLUTION

1. Adjusting journal entries.

a.	Aug. 31	Depreciation Expense, Furniture	100	
		Accumulated Depreciation, Furniture		100
		To record depreciation expense for the month of August for the furniture.		

b.	31	Depreciation Expense, Store Equipment............................	500	
		Accumulated Depreciation, Store Equipment		500
		To record depreciation expense for the month; ($31,000 − $1,000)/60 months = $500/month.		

c.	31	Unearned Haircutting Services Revenue............................	80	
		Haircutting Services Revenue.......................................		80
		To recognize haircutting services revenue earned;		
		$500 − $420 = $80.		

d.	31	Insurance Expense..	400	
		Prepaid Insurance..		400
		To adjust for the expired portion of prepaid insurance;		
		$2,400/6 months = $400/month.		

e.	31	Accounts Receivable...	130	
		Haircutting Services Revenue.......................................		130
		To record revenue earned.		

f.	31	Phone Expense..	50	
		Accounts Payable...		50
		To record August cell phone bill.		

2.

Accounts Receivable		
(e)	130	

Prepaid Insurance			
Balance	2,400	400	(d)
Balance	2,000		

Accumulated Depreciation, Furniture		
		100	(a)

Accumulated Depreciation, Store Equipment		
		500	(b)

Accounts Payable			
		14,450	Balance
		50	(f)
		14,500	Balance

Unearned Haircutting Services Revenue			
(c)	80	500	Balance
		420	Balance

Haircutting Services Revenue		
	3,800	Balance
	80	(c)
	130	(e)
	4,010	Balance

Depreciation Expense, Furniture		
(a)	100	

Depreciation Expense, Store Equipment		
(b)	500	

Insurance Expense		
(d)	400	

Phone Expense		
(f)	50	

3.

The Cutlery Adjusted Trial Balance August 31, 2020		
Account	**Debit**	**Credit**
Cash..	$ 4,950	
Accounts receivable	130	
Prepaid insurance...	2,000	
Furniture..	2,000	
Accumulated depreciation, furniture............................		$ 100
Store equipment	31,000	
Accumulated depreciation, store equipment...............		500
Accounts payable..		14,500
Unearned haircutting services revenue		420
Joanne Cardinal, capital		26,000
Joanne Cardinal, withdrawals	500	
Haircutting services revenue...		4,010
Depreciation expense, furniture	100	
Depreciation expense, store equipment......................	500	
Wages expense..	250	
Insurance expense..	400	
Rent expense..	3,200	
Hydro expense...	450	
Phone expense	50	
Totals..	$45,530	$45,530

4.

The Cutlery Income Statement For Month Ended August 31, 2020		
Revenues:		
Haircutting services revenue......................		$4,010
Operating expenses:		
Rent expense...	$3,200	
Depreciation expense, store equipment....	500	
Hydro expense...	450	
Insurance expense	400	
Wages expense..	250	
Depreciation expense, furniture	100	
Phone expense..	50	
Total operating expenses..................		4,950
Loss		$ 940

The Cutlery Statement of Changes in Equity For Month Ended August 31, 2020		
Joanne Cardinal, capital, August 1..		$ -0-
Add: Investments by owner		26,000
Total		$26,000
Less: Withdrawals by owner	$500	
Loss...	940	1,440
Joanne Cardinal, capital, August 31		$24,560

The Cutlery Balance Sheet August 31, 2020		
Assets		
Cash		$ 4,950
Accounts receivable		130
Prepaid insurance...		2,000
Furniture..	$ 2,000	
Less: Accumulated depreciation...............	100	1,900
Store equipment	$31,000	
Less: Accumulated depreciation...............	500	30,500
Total assets..		$39,480
Liabilities		
Accounts payable	$14,500	
Unearned haircutting services revenue	420	
Total liabilities....................................		$14,920
Equity		
Joanne Cardinal, capital		24,560
Total liabilities and equity		$39,480

Reminder: The loss on the income statement flows into the statement of changes in equity. The August 31 balance in capital on the statement of changes in equity is reported on the balance sheet.

Analysis Component:

The net effect of the adjustments on assets, liabilities, and equity is detailed below.

Entry	a.	b.	c.	d.	e.	f.	Net effect
Assets	$100 ↓	$500 ↓	No effect	$400 ↓	$130 ↑	No effect	$870 ↓
Liabilities	No effect	No effect	$80 ↓	No effect	No effect	$50 ↑	$ 30 ↓
Equity	$100 ↓	$500 ↓	$80 ↑	$400 ↓	$130 ↑	$50 ↓	$840 ↓

Equity decreased by $840 as a result of the adjusting entries. All of the adjustments that affected equity were income statement items (revenues or expenses); therefore, profit was negatively affected by the adjusting entries (a net decrease in income of $840).

The opposite effect could have been achieved if accrued revenues (Dr. Receivables and Cr. Revenues) plus the adjustment of unearned amounts (Dr. Unearned Revenues and Cr. Revenues) were greater than the adjustment for prepaid assets (Dr. Expense and Cr. Prepaid) plus depreciation (Dr. Depreciation Expense and Cr. Accumulated Depreciation) and accrued expenses (Dr. Expense and Cr. Payable).

Correcting Errors

LO8 Explain and prepare correcting entries.

Correcting entries, as the term implies, account for the correction of errors, and are not to be confused with adjusting entries.

If an error in a journal entry is discovered before the error is posted, it can be corrected in a manual system by drawing a line through the incorrect information. The correct information is written above it to create a record of change for the auditor. Many computerized systems allow the operator to replace the incorrect information directly.

When an error in a journal entry is *not* discovered until after it is posted, the usual practice is to correct the error by creating *another* journal entry.[10] This *correcting entry* removes the amount from the wrong account and records it to the correct account. For example, suppose we recorded a purchase of office supplies with an incorrect debit to Office Equipment as follows:

Oct.	14	Office Equipment..	1,600	
		Cash		1,600
		To record the purchase of office supplies.		

Once posted, the Office Supplies account balance is understated by $1,600 and the Office Equipment account balance is overstated by the same amount. When we discover the error three days later, a correcting entry is made using either one or two entries as shown below:

	17	Office Supplies...	1,600	
		Office Equipment..		1,600
		To correct the entry of October 14 that incorrectly debited Office Equipment instead of Office Supplies.		

OR

	17	Cash...	1,600	
		Office Equipment..		1,600
		To reverse the incorrect entry.		

	17	Office Supplies...	1,600	
		Cash		1,600
		To journalize the purchase of office supplies correctly.		

In the approach to the left, the credit removes the error and the debit correctly records supplies. Alternatively, the two entries on the right could be used: the first entry reverses the incorrect entry *entirely*, and the second entry records the transaction as it should have been. Both methods achieve the same final results.

---

10 For tracking purposes, correcting entries must be referenced to the incorrect entry and any calculations are to be documented.

Computerized systems often use similar correcting entries. The exact procedure depends on the system used and management policy. Yet nearly all systems include controls to show when and where a correction is made.

 CHECKPOINT

18. On March 14, Accounts Receivable was debited for $4,100 and Service Revenue was credited for $4,100. At the end of the month, it was discovered that the March 14 entry should have been credited to Rent Revenue. What correcting entry is required?

Do Quick Study questions: *QS 3-19, *QS 3-20

An Alternative in Recording Prepaid Assets and Unearned Revenues

LO9 Identify and explain an alternative in recording prepaid assets and unearned revenues.

This section explains an alternative in recording prepaid expenses and unearned revenues.

Recording Prepaid Expenses in Expense Accounts

We explained that prepaid expenses are assets when they are purchased and are recorded with debits to asset accounts. Adjusting entries transfer the used amounts to expense accounts at the end of an accounting period.

There is an acceptable alternative practice of recording *all* prepaid expenses with debits to expense accounts. If any prepaid assets remain unused at the end of an accounting period, then adjusting entries transfer the unused portions from expense accounts to asset accounts. The financial statements are identical under either procedure, but the adjusting entries are different.

To illustrate, let's look at Organico's cash payment for 24 months of insurance coverage beginning on March 1. Organico recorded that payment with a debit to an asset account, but alternatively it could have been recorded as a debit to an expense account. Exhibit 3B.1 shows the two approaches.

EXHIBIT 3B.1

Initial Entry for Prepaid Expenses for Two Approaches

				Payment Recorded As an Asset	Payment Recorded As an Expense
Mar.	1	Prepaid Insurance		2,400	
		Cash			2,400	
	1	Insurance Expense			2,400
		Cash				2,400

On March 31, insurance protection for one month is used up. This means $100 ($2,400/24) is the expense for March. Exhibit 3B.2 shows that the adjusting entry depends on how the original payment is recorded:

EXHIBIT 3B.2

Adjusting Entry for Prepaid Expenses for Two Approaches

				Payment Recorded As an Asset	Payment Recorded As an Expense
Mar.	31	Insurance Expense		100	
		Prepaid Insurance			100	
	31	Prepaid Insurance			2,300
		Insurance Expense				2,300

When these entries are posted, we can see in Exhibit 3B.3 that these two approaches give identical adjusted account balances at March 31.

EXHIBIT 3B.3

Account Balances Under Two Approaches for Recording Prepaid Expenses

Payment Recorded as Asset			
Prepaid Insurance			
Mar. 1	2,400	100	Mar. 31
Balance	2,300		

Insurance Expense			
Mar. 31	100		

Payment Recorded as Expense			
Prepaid Insurance			
Mar. 31	2,300		

Insurance Expense			
Mar. 1	2,400	2,300	Mar. 31
Balance	100		

RECORDING UNEARNED REVENUES IN REVENUE ACCOUNTS

Unearned revenues are liabilities requiring delivery of products and services and are recorded as credits to liability accounts when cash and other assets are received. Adjusting entries at the end of an accounting period transfer to revenue accounts the earned portion of unearned revenues.

An acceptable alternative is to record *all* unearned revenues with credits to revenue accounts. If any revenues are unearned at the end of an accounting period, then adjusting entries transfer the unearned portions from revenue accounts to unearned revenue accounts. While the adjusting entries are different for these two approaches, the financial statements are identical.

To illustrate, let's look at Organico's March 26 receipt of $3,000 for catering food services covering the period for the Mount Mundy ski hill. Organico recorded this transaction with a credit to a liability account. The alternative, shown in Exhibit 3B.4, is to record it with a credit to a revenue account as follows:

EXHIBIT 3B.4

Initial Entry for Unearned Revenues for Two Approaches

			Receipt Recorded As a Liability	Receipt Recorded As Revenue
Mar.	26	Cash...	3,000	
		Unearned Food Services Revenue..	3,000	
	26	Cash...		3,000
		Food Services Revenue....................		3,000

By the end of the accounting period (March 31), Organico earns $250 of this revenue. This means that $250 of the liability is satisfied. Depending on how the initial receipt is recorded, Exhibit 3B.5 shows the adjusting entry:

EXHIBIT 3B.5

Adjusting Entry for Unearned Revenues for Two Approaches

			Receipt Recorded As a Liability	Receipt Recorded As Revenue
Mar.	31	Unearned Food Services Revenue	250	
		Food Services Revenue......................	250	
	31	Food Services Revenue.............................		2,750
		Unearned Food Services Revenue..		2,750

After adjusting entries are posted, the two approaches give identical adjusted account balances at March 31 as shown in Exhibit 3B.6.

EXHIBIT 3B.6

Account Balances Under Two Approaches for Recording Unearned Revenues

Receipt Recorded as Liability			
Unearned Food Services Revenue			
Mar. 31	250	3,000	Mar. 26
		2,750	Balance

Food Services Revenue		
	250	Mar. 31

Receipt Recorded as Revenue		
Unearned Food Services Revenue		
	2,750	Mar. 31

Food Services Revenue			
Mar. 31	2,750	3,000	Mar. 26
		250	Balance

 CHECKPOINT

19. Miller Company records cash receipts of unearned revenues and cash payments of prepaid expenses in balance sheet accounts. Bud Company records these items in income statement accounts. Explain any difference in the financial statements of these two companies from their different ways of recording prepaid assets.

Do Quick Study question: *QS 3-21

SUMMARY OF APPENDIX 3A AND APPENDIX 3B

LO8 **Explain and prepare correcting entries.** A correcting entry is required when an error in a journal entry is not discovered until after it has been posted. The correcting entry can be done in one of two ways: the incorrect portion of the entry can be corrected, or the entire incorrect entry can be reversed and the correct entry recorded; both methods accomplish the same result.

LO9 **Identify and explain an alternative in recording prepaid assets and unearned revenues.** It is acceptable to charge all prepaid expenses to expense accounts when they are purchased. When this is done, adjusting entries must transfer any unexpired amounts from expense accounts to asset accounts. It is also acceptable to credit all unearned revenues to revenue accounts when cash is received. In this case the adjusting entries must transfer any unearned amounts from revenue accounts to unearned revenue accounts.

 Guidance Answers to CHECKPOINT

18. The correcting entry can be done in one of two ways:

31	Service Revenue	4,100	
	Rent Revenue		4,100
	To correct the March 14 entry.		

OR

31	Service Revenue	4,100	
	Accounts Receivable		4,100
	To reverse the incorrect March 14 entry.		
31	Accounts Receivable	4,100	
	Rent Revenue		4,100
	To enter the correct entry for March 14.		

19. When adjusting entries are correctly prepared, the financial statements of these companies will be identical under both approaches.

GLOSSARY

Account form balance sheet A balance sheet that lists assets on the left and liabilities and equity on the right side of the balance sheet.

Accounting periods Time frames covered by financial statements and other reports; also called *reporting periods*.

Accrual basis accounting The approach to preparing financial statements that uses the adjusting process to recognize revenues when earned and expenses when incurred, not when cash is paid or received; the required approach for generally accepted accounting principles.

Accrued expenses Costs incurred in a period that are unpaid and unrecorded; adjusting entries for recording accrued expenses involve increasing (debiting) expenses and increasing (crediting) liabilities.

Accrued revenues Revenues earned in a period that are both unrecorded and not yet received in cash (or other assets); adjusting entries for recording accrued revenues involve increasing (debiting) assets and increasing (crediting) revenues.

Adjusted trial balance A listing of accounts and balances prepared after adjustments are recorded and posted to the ledger.

Adjusting entry A journal entry at the end of an accounting period to bring an asset or liability account balance to its proper amount while also updating the related expense or revenue account.

Amortization The expense created by allocating the cost of intangible assets to the periods in which they are used; represents the expense of using these assets.

Book value of an asset The cost of the asset less its accumulated depreciation. It represents the reported value of the asset on the balance sheet.

Cash basis accounting Revenues are recognized when cash is received, and expenses are recorded when cash is paid.

This method ignores the matching principle and revenue recognition principle and is not acceptable under GAAP.

Contra account An account linked with another account and having an opposite normal balance; reported as a subtraction from the other account's balance, at the net amount. Example: Accumulated Depreciation Equipment is the contra account for the Equipment account.

Correcting entries Accounting entries made in order to correct errors.

Depreciation The expense created by allocating the cost of plant and equipment to the periods in which they are used; represents the expense of using the associated assets.

External transactions Exchanges between the entity and some other person or organization.

Fair value of an asset The amount that would be received to sell an asset or settle a liability in a transaction with independent parties. Also known as the market value of an asset or liability.

Intangible assets Long-lived assets that have no physical substance, but provide a right to produce or use a product or process.

Interim financial reports Financial reports covering less than one year; usually based on one-, three- or six-month periods. Publicly listed companies report financial statements every three months, also referred to as quarterly.

Internal transactions Exchanges within an organization that can also affect the accounting equation.

Market value of an asset Amount an asset can be sold for today. Market value is not tied to the book value of an asset.

Matching principle The GAAP principle that requires expenses to be recorded in the same period as the associated revenues are recognized.

Overstated account An account that is listed at an amount that is higher than the correct balance.

Prepaid expenses Items that are paid for in advance of receiving their benefits. These are assets.

Property, plant, and equipment (PPE) Tangible long-lived assets used to produce goods or services.

Report form balance sheet A balance sheet that lists items vertically with assets above the liabilities and equity.

Reporting periods See *accounting periods*.

Straight-line depreciation method Allocates equal amounts of an asset's cost to depreciation expense during its useful life.

Timeliness principle A broad principle that assumes that an organization's activities can be divided into specific time periods such as in months, quarters, or years.

Unadjusted trial balance A listing of accounts and balances prepared before adjustments are recorded and posted to the ledger.

Understated account An account that is listed at an amount lower than the correct balance.

Unearned revenues Liabilities created when customers pay in advance for products or services; created when cash is received before revenues are earned; satisfied by delivering the products or services in the future.

KNOWLEDGE CHECK-UP

1. At the end of an accounting period, financial statements need to be adjusted for the following reasons:
   a. The accrual basis of accounting is a requirement of GAAP
   b. The cash basis of accounting is not an acceptable method for use in financial reporting
   c. The timeliness principle, the revenue recognition principle and the matching principle
   d. All of the above.

2. Prepaid expenses refer to:
   a. Assets that are paid for in cash
   b. Expenses that are incurred immediately when the item is purchased
   c. Costs paid for in advance of receiving their benefits
   d. Adjusting entries that debit cash and credit expense when recognized

3. Depreciation is:
   a. The cost of storing inventory and supplies
   b. The process of calculating expenses to match the cost of plant and equipment assets over their expected useful lives
   c. Calculated by dividing the asset cost by 10 years
   d. Items that are paid for in advance of receiving their benefits

4. It is determined that One Eleven Music Studios has $500 worth of supplies left at the end of March out of the $2,200 purchased in March. The entry to record the month-end adjustment is:
   a. Debit Supplies Expense $500 and credit Supplies $500
   b. Debit Purchases $2,200 and credit Supplies Expense $2,200
   c. Debit Supplies Expense $1,700 and credit Supplies $1,700
   d. None of the above.

5. Straight-line depreciation is calculated as:
   a. The estimated value of an asset at the end of its useful life divided by the number of years the asset has been in use
   b. The cost of an asset minus the estimated value of the asset at the end of its useful life
   c. The estimated value of an asset divided by its estimated useful life
   d. All of the above.

6. Interest of $15 has been accrued on One Eleven's $3,000, 6% six-month note payable. Select the appropriate journal entry:
   a. Debit Interest Asset $15, credit Interest Expense $15
   b. Debit Interest Payable $180, credit interest expense $180
   c. Debit Interest Expense $15, credit Interest Payable $15
   d. Debit Interest Income $180, credit Interest Payable $180

7. The revenue recognition principle requires that One Eleven Music Studio report $5,000 on the March Income Statement for student tuition revenue that was collected March 1 and earned over the month. Select the appropriate journal entry:
   a. Debit Unearned Revenue $5,000, credit Revenue $5,000
   b. Debit Income $5,000, credit Cash $5,000
   c. Debit Accounts Receivable $5,000, credit Revenue $5,000
   d. Debit Cash $5,000, credit Revenue $5,000

8. At the end of March, One Eleven Music Studio had $200 outstanding relating to employee salaries that were earned in March but not yet paid. Select the appropriate journal entry:
   a. Debit Salaries Payable $200, credit Salaries Expense $200
   b. Debit Salaries Expense $200, credit Salaries Payable $200

c. Debit Supplies Asset $200, credit Supplies Payable $200

d. Debit Salaries Expense $200, credit Cash $200

9. Which of the following is correct about adjusting entries?

a. Adjusting entries never affect cash

b. Adjusting entries always affect cash

c. Both A and B are true.

d. Neither A nor B are true.

10. When preparing financial statements from an accrued trial balance, which of the following financial statements should be prepared first?

a. Statement of Changes in Equity

b. Balance Sheet

c. Cash Flow Statement

d. Income Statement

CONCEPT REVIEW QUESTIONS

1. What is the difference between the cash basis and accrual basis of accounting? Why is the accrual basis of accounting preferred over the cash basis?

2. Your friend is a graphic designer who started his own business. He asks you "How do I record revenue and expenses correctly?" Explain when to record revenue and expenses based on the accrual basis of accounting. Give one example for revenue and one example for expenses to show your point.

3. Hannah is preparing an income statement for homework. She identifies revenues as service revenue, rent revenue, and unearned revenue. She identifies expenses as advertising expense, prepaid expense and rent expense. Check Hannah's work and explain any errors.

4. In your personal life, when do you need to prepay for products or services? Why do you think companies want you to prepay instead of paying later?

5. After reviewing the financial statements, the marketing department will finalize its decision on launching a new advertising campaign and the human resources

department will finalize how many employees to hire. The accounting department is very busy and has decided not to post the year-end adjusting entries. What are the potential consequences of not posting adjusting entries?

6. What contra account is used when recording and reporting the effects of depreciation? Why is it used?

7. What is an accrued revenue? Give an example.

8. Review the consolidated balance sheet of **Spin Master** in Appendix III. Identify an asset account that requires adjustment before annual financial statements can be prepared. What would be the effect on the income statement if this asset account were not adjusted?

9. Review the income statement of WestJet in Appendix III. How much depreciation was recorded in the adjusting entry for depreciation at the end of 2017? What types of assets would WestJet need to depreciate?

*10. If a company initially records prepaid expenses with debits to expense accounts, what type of account is debited in the adjusting entries for prepaid expenses?

QUICK STUDY

QS 3-1 **GAAP and adjusting entries** LO2

For each of the following, identify the primary GAAP that has been violated and explain why.

1. Delta Company prepared its first set of financial statements for the three years ended July 31, 2020.

2. Allard Consulting purchased $9,800 of supplies on September 30, 2020, and debited Office Supplies Expense. Allard's year-end is September 30.

3. On May 3, 2020, Nikos Car Wash collected $3,000 in advance from a new limousine company to begin operating June 1, 2020. Nikos credited a revenue account for the $3,000.

4. On November 20, 2020, Scooter Town rented equipment for $1,500. Scooter Town is not recording the transaction until it pays (payment is required 15 days from the rental date).

An asterisk (*) identifies assignment material based on Appendix 3A or Appendix 3B.

QS 3-2 Accrual accounting LO3

Based on the accrual basis of accounting, determine when the following independent companies should recognize revenue.

1. **Starbucks** sells you a $25 gift card for your friend's birthday in February. Your friend spends the gift card on coffee and baked goods in March.

2. You paid your university tuition in September for the Fall semester that runs from September to December.

QS 3-3 Accrual and cash accounting LO3

In its first year of operations, Harris Construction earned $39,000 in revenues and received $33,000 cash from customers. The company incurred expenses of $22,500, but had not paid for $2,250 of them at year-end. In addition, Harris prepaid $3,750 for expenses that would be incurred the next year.

1. Calculate the first year's profit under the cash basis.

2. Calculate the first year's profit under the accrual basis.

3. What is the difference?

QS 3-4 Preparing adjusting entries (annual)—prepaid expense LO4

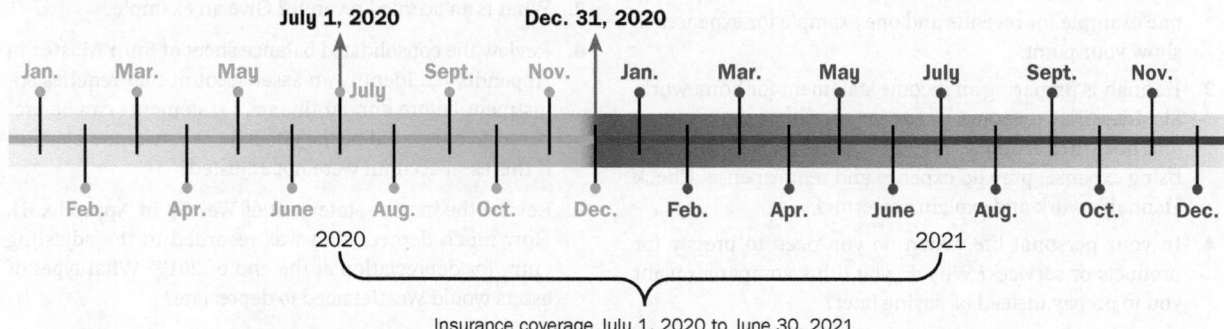

Stud Muffin Bakery prepares financial statements on an annual basis and has a December 31, 2020 year-end. On July 1, 2020, the bakery purchased a one-year insurance policy for $12,000 cash. The insurance policy covers July 1, 2020 to June 30, 2021.

a. How much does the insurance policy cost per month?

b. How many months are between July 1, 2020 and December 31, 2020?

c. Record the journal entry on July 1, 2020.

d. In order to prepare the annual financial statements, record the adjusting journal entry on December 31, 2020.

QS 3-5 Preparing adjusting entries (annual)—supplies LO4

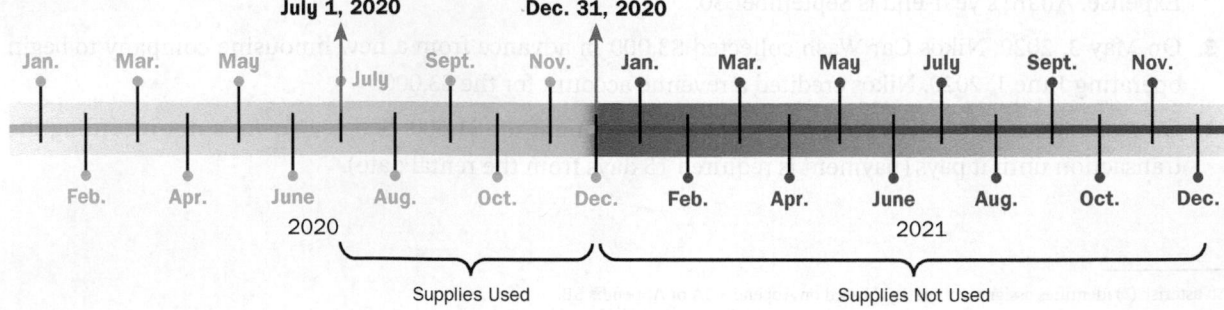

Organic Market, a grocery store, purchased supplies for $12,000 cash on July 1, 2020. As of December 31, 2020, $7,000 had been used and $5,000 of supplies had not been used. Organic Market prepares financial statements on an annual basis and has a December 31 year-end.

a. Record the journal entry on July 1, 2020.

b. In order to prepare the annual financial statements, record the adjusting journal entry to reflect the amount of supplies used as of December 31, 2020.

c. On January 1, 2021, what amount in supplies does Organic Market have?

QS 3-6 Preparing adjusting entries (annual)—prepaid expense LO4

Kiss the Chef Co., a cooking school, purchased a two-year insurance policy on April 1, 2020, paying cash of $7,680. Its year-end is December 31.

a. Record the journal entry on April 1, 2020.

b. How many months are between April 1, 2020 and December 31, 2020? Record the adjusting entry on December 31, 2020.

c. How many months are between January 1, 2021 and December 31, 2021? Record the adjusting entry on December 31, 2021.

d. How many months of the insurance policy are left in 2022?

QS 3-7 Preparing adjusting entries (annual)—depreciation LO4

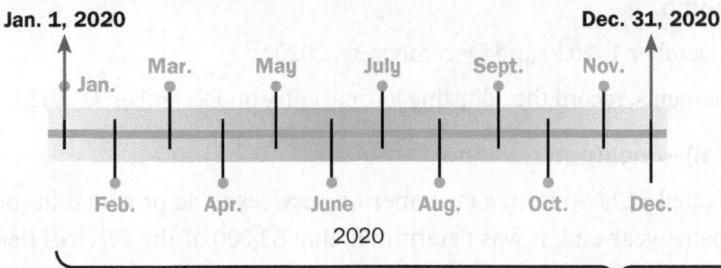

Equipment will last five years (2020–2024)

On January 1, 2020, Taco Taqueria, a Mexican restaurant, purchased equipment for $12,000 cash. Taco Taqueria estimates that the equipment will last five years (useful life). The restaurant expects to sell the equipment for $2,000 at the end of five years. Taco Taqueria prepares financial statements on an annual basis and has a December 31 year-end.

a. Record the journal entry on January 1, 2020.

b. What is the formula to calculate straight-line depreciation?

c. Using the straight-line depreciation method, calculate the annual depreciation for 2020 (Jan. 1 to Dec. 31, 2020).

d. In order to prepare the annual financial statements, record the adjusting journal entry for depreciation on December 31, 2020.

QS 3-8 Preparing adjusting entries (annual)—depreciation expense LO4

Gold Co. purchased a vehicle on March 1, 2020, for cash of $32,000. It will be used by the president for business purposes for four years and then sold for an estimated amount of $8,000. Gold Co.'s year-end is December 31.

a. Record the journal entry on March 1, 2020.

b. Using the straight-line depreciation method, calculate the depreciation expense for March 1, 2020 to December 31, 2020.

c. To prepare the 2020 annual financial statements, record the adjusting entry for December 31, 2020.

d. Using the straight-line depreciation method, calculate the depreciation expense for January 1, 2021 to December 31, 2021.

e. To prepare the 2021 annual financial statements, record the adjusting entry for December, 31, 2021.

QS 3-9 Preparing adjusting entries (annual)—unearned revenue LO4

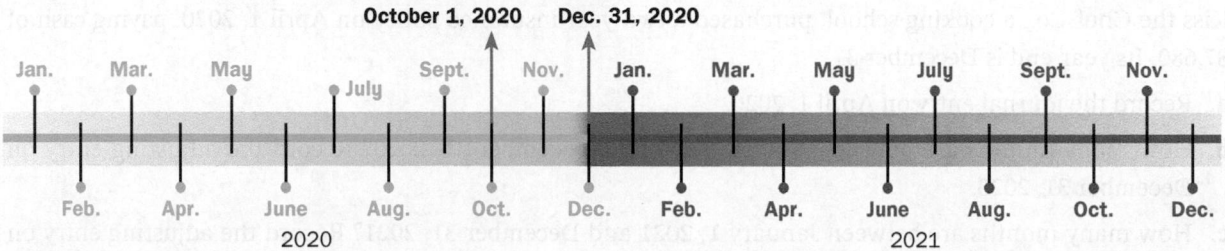

Club 17X Fitness prepares financial statements on an annual basis and has a December 31 year-end. On October 1, 2020, Club 17X sells a one-year prepaid gym membership for $300 cash.

a. Record the journal entry on October 1, 2020.

b. How much is the gym membership per month?

c. How many months have passed between October 1, 2020 and December 31, 2020?

d. In order to prepare the annual financial statements, record the adjusting journal entry on December 31, 2020.

QS 3-10 Preparing adjusting entries (annual)—unearned revenue LO4

On November 1, 2020, Race Car Repairs collected $12,000 from a customer for services to be provided in the future. On December 31, 2020, Race Car Repairs' year-end, it was determined that $3,000 of the services had not been provided (unearned).

a. Record the journal entry on November 1, 2020.

b. How much revenue was earned as of December 31, 2020?

c. To prepare the 2020 annual financial statements, record the adjusting entry for December 31, 2020.

QS 3-11 Preparing adjusting entries (annual)—accrued interest expense LO4

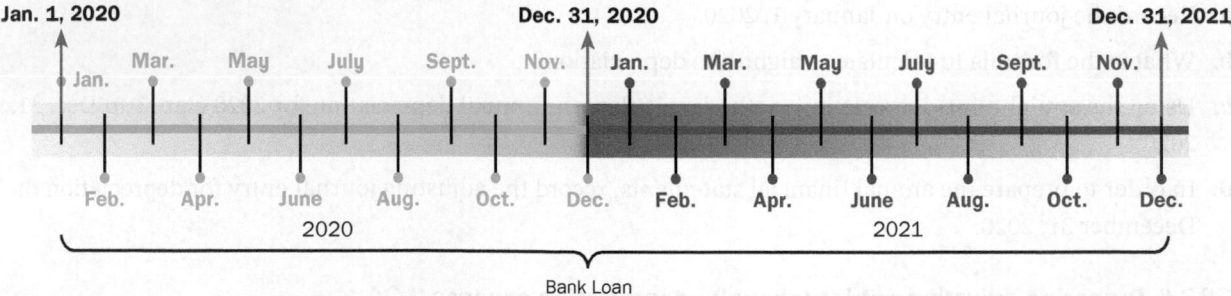

Rise and Shine Ice Cream prepares annual financial statements and has a December 31 year-end. As of March 1, 2020, Rise and Shine Ice Cream took out a bank loan for $12,000 with an interest rate of 8%. Interest is incurred on a monthly basis and needs to be paid on December 31, 2021.

a. What is the formula to calculate interest expense?

b. How many months of interest expense have been incurred at December 31, 2020?

c. In order to prepare the annual financial statements, record the adjusting journal entry on December 31, 2020.

QS 3-12 Preparing adjusting entries (annual)—accrued salaries expense LO4

December 2020

December						
Sun	Mon	Tue	Wed	Thu	Fri	Sat
		1	2	3	4	5
6	7	8	9	10	11	12
13	14	15	16	17	18	19
20	21	22	23	24	25	26
27	28	29	30	31		

January 2021

January						
Sun	Mon	Tue	Wed	Thu	Fri	Sat
					1	2
3	4	5	6	7	8	9
10	11	12	13	14	15	16
17	18	19	20	21	22	23
24	25	26	27	28	29	30
31						

Salary expense incurred   Payday Salary expense incurred

Yara Clothing (Yara), a retail store at the mall, hires a number of employees to work 7 days a week. Yara owes its employees wages for the period of December 27, 2020 to January 9, 2021 (14 days) for $5,600. The wages owed are equal each day and the employees will be paid on January 11, 2021. Yara prepares annual financial statements and has a December 31 year-end.

a. How much does Yara owe its employees per day?

b. How many days are between December 27, 2020 and December 31, 2020?

c. In order to prepare the annual financial statements, record the adjusting journal entry on December 31, 2020.

d. Record the payment of wages on January 11, 2021.

QS 3-13 Preparing adjusting entries (annual)—accrued expenses LO4

On December 31, 2020, Beautiful Brows Salon received the business cell phone bill for December (Dec. 1 to Dec. 31) usage of $2,000. It must be paid by January 15, 2021.

a. To prepare the 2020 annual financial statements, record the adjusting entry on December 31, 2020.

b. Record the payment of the cell phone bill on January 15, 2021.

QS 3-14 Preparing adjusting entries (monthly)—accrued revenues LO4

Tiger Computer provided $17,000 of services to customers in the month of March 2020. On March 31, 2020, Tiger Computer has not yet billed or collected payment for the $17,000. On April 16, $12,000 of these were collected.

a. Using the accrual basis of accounting, explain whether Tiger Computer earned revenue of $17,000 as of March 31, 2020.

b. Record the adjusting journal entry on March 31, 2020.

c. Record the journal entry on April 16, 2020.

QS 3-15 Preparing adjusting entries LO4

Stark Company records prepayments of expenses in asset accounts and receipts of unearned revenues in liability accounts. Using the list of accounts provided, identify the debit and credit entry required for each of the annual adjustments described in (a) through (e). The first one is done as an example.

1. Cash	**7.** Depreciation Expense
2. Prepaid Advertising	**8.** Accumulated Depreciation—Equipment
3. Advertising Payable	**9.** Equipment
4. Advertising Expense	**10.** Services Revenue
5. Accounts Receivable	**11.** Unearned Services Revenue
6. Equipment Expense	

	Debits	**Credits**
Example: Accrual of uncollected and unrecorded services revenue.	*5*	*10*

a. Accrual of unpaid and unrecorded advertising that was used by Stark Company.   _____ _____

b. Adjustment of Unearned Services Revenue to recognize earned revenue.   _____ _____

c. Recorded revenue for work completed this accounting period; the cash will be received in the next period.   _____ _____

d. The cost of Equipment was matched to the time periods benefited.   _____ _____

e. Adjustment of Prepaid Advertising to recognize the portion used.   _____ _____

QS 3-16 Recording and analyzing adjusting entries LO4, 5

Adjusting entries affect one balance sheet account and one income statement account. For the entries listed below, identify the account to be debited and the account to be credited. Indicate which of the two accounts is the income statement account and which is the balance sheet account.

a. Entry to record annual depreciation expense.

b. Entry to show wages earned by employees but not yet paid.

c. Entry to show revenue earned that was previously received as cash in advance.

d. Entry to show expiration of prepaid insurance.

e. Entry to show revenue earned but not yet billed.

QS 3-17 Linking adjustments to financial statements LO5

For each type of adjustment in (a) through (e), indicate the effect on profit (overstated or understated) if the adjustment is not recorded.

	If adjustment is not recorded:			
Type of Adjustment	**Profit will be overstated, under-stated, or no effect**	**Assets will be overstated, under-stated, or no effect**	**Liabilities will be overstated, under-stated, or no effect**	**Equity will be over-stated, understated, or no effect**
a. Prepaid Expenses				
b. Depreciation				
c. Unearned Revenues				
d. Accrued Expenses				
e. Accrued Revenues				

QS 3-18 Interpreting adjusting entries LO4, 6

The following information has been taken from Out Loud Comedy Club's unadjusted and adjusted trial balances at October 31, 2020.

	Unadjusted		Adjusted	
	Debit	Credit	Debit	Credit
Prepaid insurance...	$3,100		$2,350	
Interest payable...		$ -0-		$750
Insurance expense	-0-		750	
Interest expense...	-0-		750	

Given this trial balance information, prepare the adjusting journal entries.

*QS 3-19 Correcting entries LO8

The following entry was recorded on November 14.

Nov.	14	Salaries Expense	14,800	
		Cash		14,800
		To record supplies expense.		

At month-end, it was discovered that *Supplies Expense* should have been debited on November 14 instead of *Salaries Expense*. Prepare the correcting entry required on November 30.

*QS 3-20 Correcting entries LO8

The following entry was recorded on January 10.

Jan.	10	Office Furniture..	25,000	
		Accounts Payable..		25,000
		To record purchase of computer equipment by borrowing from the bank.		

At month-end, it was discovered that on January 10, computer equipment was purchased for $25,000 by borrowing from the bank. Prepare the correcting entry required on January 31.

*QS 3-21 Recording prepaids and unearned amounts as expenses and revenues LO9

Foster Company initially records prepaid and unearned items in income statement accounts. Given Foster Company's practices, what is the appropriate adjusting entry for each of the following at November 30, 2020, the end of the company's first accounting period?

a. There are unpaid salaries of $3,000.

b. Unused office supplies of $800 were counted at year-end. There was no beginning balance in office supplies.

c. Earned but unbilled consulting revenue of $2,300 was discovered.

d. It was determined that there was unearned revenue of $4,200.

An asterisk (*) identifies assignment material based on Appendix 3A or Appendix 3B.

EXERCISES

Exercise 3-1 Recognizing revenue LO3

The following are independent situations. Based on the accrual basis of accounting, explain when the companies should recognize revenue.

a. You order a leather jacket from **Aritzia** online. You submit your credit card information, submit the order, and receive the shipment in 14 days.

b. Telus sends your cell phone bill for the month of March. Your bill shows the invoice date as March 31, 2020 and the payment is due April 15, 2020.

c. The **Toronto Transit Commission (TTC)** sells monthly bus passes. The September bus passes can be purchased in August. The bus pass then provides access to the TTC in September.

Exercise 3-2 Identifying adjusting entries LO4

For each entry (1) to (12) below, enter the letter of the explanation that describes it in the blank space to the left. You can use some letters more than once.

a. To record depreciation expense.

b. To record an accrued expense.

c. To record the use of a prepaid expense.

d. To record accrued revenue.

e. To record the earning of previously unearned revenue.

f. Not an adjusting entry.

___ 1. Depreciation Expense 3,000		
Accumulated Depreciation		3,000
___ 2. Unearned Professional Revenue... 2,000		
Professional Revenue.................		2,000
___ 3. Rent Expense 1,000		
Prepaid Rent................................		1,000
___ 4. Interest Expense 4,000		
Interest Payable		4,000
___ 5. Prepaid Rent................................ 3,500		
Cash		3,500
___ 6. Salaries Expense............................ 5,000		
Salaries Payable...........................		5,000

___ 7. Insurance Expense........................... 6,000		
Prepaid Insurance.........................		6,000
___ 8. Salaries Payable............................... 1,500		
Cash		1,500
___ 9. Cash.. 6,500		
Unearned Professional Revenue		6,500
___10. Cash.. 9,000		
Interest Receivable.......................		9,000
___11. Interest Receivable........................... 7,000		
Interest Income.............................		7,000
___12. Cash.. 8,000		
Accounts Receivable....................		8,000

Exercise 3-3 Preparing adjusting entries (annual)—prepaid expense LO4

Dr. Erica Chan, MD owns EC Health Clinic. She prepares annual financial statements and has a December 31, 2020 year-end.

a. On October 1, 2020, Dr. Chan prepaid $8,000 for four months of rent.

b. On November 1, 2020, Dr. Chan prepaid $480 to renew the clinic's magazine subscriptions. The subscription is for one year.

c. On December 1, 2020, Dr. Chan pays $3,000 for supplies. At the end of the year, $2,000 of supplies had not been used.

Required For each transaction, record the initial journal entry and the adjusting entry required on December 31, 2020.

Exercise 3-4 **Preparing adjusting entries (annual)—depreciation** LO4

Mean Beans, a local coffee shop, has the following assets on January 1, 2020. Mean Beans prepares annual financial statements and has a December 31, 2020 year-end. The company's depreciation policy is to use the straight-line method to depreciate its assets.

a. On January 1, 2020, purchase equipment costing $15,000 with an estimated life of five years. Mean Beans will scrap the equipment after five years for $0.

b. On July 1, 2020, purchase furniture (tables and chairs) costing $12,000 with an estimated life of ten years. Mean Beans estimates that it can sell the furniture for $2,000 after ten years.

c. On January 1, 2018, Mean Beans had purchased a car costing $25,000 with an estimated life of eight years. Mean Beans estimates that it can sell the car for $5,000 after eight years.

Required

1. For each transaction, calculate the annual depreciation expense and record the adjusting entry on December 31, 2020.

2. For the car, determine the accumulated depreciation as of December 31, 2020.

3. For the car, determine the carrying amount as of December 31, 2020.

Exercise 3-5 **Preparing adjusting entries (annual)—unearned revenue** LO4

Splish Splash Art is a centre that offers children's music and dance lessons. Splish Splash prepares annual financial statements and has a December 31, 2020, year-end.

a. On September 1, Splish Spash Art collects $15,000 cash for dance lessons running from September 1, 2020 to December 31, 2020.

b. On October 1, Splish Splash Art collects $5,000 cash in advance from the Music Box Inc. ($2,500 per month) to rent its performance stage for the full month of December 2020 and January 2021.

c. On October 1, 2020, Splish Splash Art collects $5,000 cash for four months of music lessons for a local private school. The lessons run from October 1, 2020 to January 31, 2021.

Required For each transaction, record the **initial journal entry** and the **adjusting entry** required on December 31, 2020.

Exercise 3-6 **Preparing adjusting entries (annual)—accrued expenses and revenue** LO4

Jurassic Jumpers Co. (JJ Co.) offers bungee jumping for those looking for an extreme outing. JJ Co. prepares annual financial statements and has a December 31, 2020 year-end.

a. On April 1, 2020, JJ Co. took out a five-year, $500,000 bank loan with an interest rate of 3%. Interest expense is paid on the first day of each month.

b. On July 1, 2020, JJ Co. issued a two-year, $50,000 Note Receivable with an interest rate of 4%. Interest income will be collected on January 1 and July 1 of each year.

c. On December 15, 2020, JJ Co. took a university student club bungee jumping for $2,000. The student club was invoiced on December 31, 2020 and paid JJ Co. on January 15, 2021.

Required Record the adjusting journal entries at December 31, 2020.

Exercise 3-7 **Adjusting entries (annual)** LO4

On January 1, you started a tutoring business called Brain Worx and charge $30 an hour for tutoring. The following are your transactions for 2020. Assume Brain Worx uses the straight-line method to depreciate its assets.

a. On January 1, you purchased a computer from **Apple Inc.** for $1,500 cash. You estimate that your computer will last three years. After that time, you will give the computer to your sister as a gift.

b. On February 1, you paid $1,200 cash for one year of insurance coverage.

c. On March 1, you purchased supplies including paper, pens, and notebooks for $650 cash at **Staples**. At the end of the year, you had $230 of supplies left.

d. On November 1, Charlotte, a student, pays cash for eight hours of tutoring per month for November 2020, December 2020, and January 2021.

e. You tutor George four hours in December. However, George was away for Christmas and has promised to pay you January 2021.

f. On December 31, 2020, Telus sends your December business cell phone bill for $65. The bill is due January 15, 2021.

Required

1. For transactions (a) to (d), record the initial journal entry during the year.

2. For transactions (a) to (f), record the adjusting entries on December 31, 2020.

Exercise 3-8 Adjusting entries (annual) LO4

EnviroWaste's year-end is December 31. The information in (a) to (e) is available at year-end for the preparation of adjusting entries:

a. Of the $18,500 balance in Unearned Revenue, $3,050 remains unearned.

b. The annual building depreciation is $14,600.

c. The Spare Parts Inventory account shows an unadjusted balance of $1,200. A physical count reveals a balance on hand of $980.

d. Unbilled and uncollected services provided to customers totalled $14,600.

e. The utility bill for the month of December was received but is unpaid; $2,100.

Required Prepare *t*he required adjusting entries at December 31, 2020, for (a) to (e) and the subsequent cash entries required for (f) and (g).

f. The accrued revenues of $14,600 recorded in (d) were collected on January 4, 2021.

g. The $2,100 utility bill accrued in (e) was paid on January 14, 2021.

Exercise 3-9 Adjusting entries—different accounting periods LO4

Queen & Ace Games (Q&A Games) runs its business from January 1 to December 31 (year-end). On January 1, 2020, Q&A Games pays $12,000 for a one-year insurance policy that covers January 1, 2020 to December 31, 2020. Record the journal entries for the following:

1. Record the initial entry on January 1, 2020, when Q&A Games pays for the insurance policy.

2. The following are independent situations. Assume Q&A Games reports using the following accounting periods.

    a. Monthly (1 month)—Assume Q&A Games reports on a monthly basis. Record the adjusting journal entry on **January 30, 2020.**

b. Quarterly (3 months)—Assume Q&A Games reports on a quarterly basis. Record the adjusting journal entry on **March 30, 2020**.

c. Semi-annual (6 months)—Assume Q&A Games reports on a semi-annual basis. Record the adjusting journal entry on **June 30, 2020**.

d. Annual (12 months)—Assume Q&A Games reports on an annual basis. Record the adjusting journal entry on **December 31, 2020**.

Exercise 3-10 Adjusting entries (monthly) LO4

After winning the TV show competition *Star Chef*, Adriana started a cooking school, Adriana's Apron. Adriana's Apron prepares monthly financial statements. The following are the transactions for the month of September 2020.

a. On January 1, 2020, Adriana took out a bank loan for $60,000 with an interest rate of 5%. Interest is payable on the first day of each following month.

b. Students paid $30,000 in advance for cooking classes. At the end of the month, Adriana finished teaching $10,000 worth of cooking classes.

c. During the month, Adriana purchased supplies for her cooking classes such as meats and cheese for $5,000. At the end of the month, a physical count shows that $1,000 of supplies are left.

d. On September 1, Adriana purchased a refrigerator costing $2,400. This equipment will be used for 5 years and then donated to the food bank.

e. Adriana was hired to teach at a food festival. She taught the "Secrets to Italian Cooking" on September 30 and sent the festival organizers an invoice for $9,350. The invoice was paid in full on October 15, 2020.

f. Adriana will pay salaries of $3,360 for two weeks (14 days) on October 9, 2020. At the end of the month, nine days of salaries are unpaid and unrecorded.

Required For transactions (a) to (f), help Adriana prepare the adjusting entries on September 30, 2020.

Exercise 3-11 Unearned and accrued revenues LO4

Landmark Properties owns and operates an apartment building and prepares annual financial statements based on a March 31 fiscal year-end.

Required Journalize the adjusting entry for each of (a) and (b) and the subsequent entry required in (c).

a. The tenants of one of the apartments paid five months' rent in advance on November 1, 2019. The monthly rental is $2,200 per month. The journal entry credited the Unearned Rent account when the payment was received. No other entry had been recorded prior to March 31, 2020. Give the adjusting journal entry that should be recorded on March 31, 2020.

b. On January 1, 2020, the tenants of another apartment moved in and paid the first month's rent. The $2,650 payment was recorded with a credit to the Rent Revenue account. However, the tenants have not paid the rent for February or March. They have agreed to pay it as soon as possible. Give the adjusting journal entry that should be recorded on March 31, 2020.

c. On April 22, 2020, the tenants described in (b) paid $7,950 rent for February, March, and April. Give the journal entry to record the cash collection.

Exercise 3-12 Identifying adjusting entries LO4

Selected information in T-account format is presented below. Journalize the most likely adjustments that caused the balances to change.

a. Accounts Receivable	
Unadjusted Bal. 7,900 Dec. 31/20	
Adjusted Bal. 9,650 Dec. 31/20	

b. Prepaid Rent	
Unadjusted Bal. 31,000 Dec. 31/20	
Adjusted Bal. 25,500 Dec. 31/20	

c. Accumulated Depreciation, Machinery	
	9,050 Unadjusted Bal. Dec. 31/20
	12,500 Adjusted Bal. Dec. 31/20

d. Unearned Revenue	
	7,200 Unadjusted Bal. Dec. 31/20
	3,150 Adjusted Bal. Dec. 31/20

e. Salaries Expense	
Unadjusted Bal. 61,000 Dec. 31/20	
Adjusted Bal. 64,100 Dec. 31/20	

Exercise 3-13 Missing data in supplies expense calculations LO4, 5

Determine the missing amounts in each of these four independent situations:

	a	b	c	d
Supplies on hand, January 1...........................	$ 210	$ 810	$ 1,700	?
Supplies purchased during the year.............	2,000	2,200	?	$77,900
Supplies on hand, December 31	1,100	?	2,400	8,200
Supplies expense for the year.......................	?	750	25,100	85,100

Exercise 3-14 Adjusting and subsequent cash entries for accrued expenses LO4

MODERN is a store with trendy and affordable furniture. MODERN has five part-time employees, each of whom earns $210 per day. They are normally paid on Fridays for work completed on Monday through Friday of the same week. They were all paid in full on Friday, December 25, 2020. The next week, all five of the employees worked only four days because New Year's Day was an unpaid holiday. Show the adjusting entry that would be recorded on Thursday, December 31, 2020, MODERN's year-end, and the journal entry that would be made to record paying the employees' wages on Friday, January 1, 2021.

Exercise 3-15 Adjustments and subsequent cash entries for accrued expenses LO4

The following three situations require adjusting journal entries to prepare financial statements as of April 30, 2020. For each situation, present the adjusting entry and the entry that would be made to record the payment of the accrued liability during May 2020.

a. The company has a $370,000 note payable that requires 0.3% interest to be paid each month on the 20th of the month. The interest was last paid on April 20 and the next payment is due on May 20.

b. The total weekly salaries expense for all employees is $13,600. This amount is paid at the end of the day on Friday of each week with five working days. April 30 falls on a Thursday this year, which means that the employees had worked four days since the last payday. The next payday is May 1.

c. On April 1, the company retained a lawyer at a flat monthly fee of $3,600. This amount is payable on the 12th of the following month.

Exercise 3-16 Identifying the effects of adjusting entries LO4, 5 eXcel

Following are two income statements for Javelin Company for the month ended December 31, 2020. Column B was prepared before any adjusting entries were recorded and column D includes the effects of adjusting entries. The company records cash receipts and disbursements related to unearned and prepaid items in balance sheet accounts. Analyze the statements and prepare the adjusting entries that must have been recorded. (*Note:* Of the $12,000 increase in *Revenue*, 30% represents additional revenue but not billed. The other 70% was earned by performing services that the customers had paid for in advance.)

	A	B	C	D
		Javelin Company		
		Income Statements		
		For Month Ended December 31, 2020		
4		**Before**		**After**
5		**Adjustments**	**Adjustments**	**Adjustments**
6	Revenues:			
7	Service revenue	$ 48,000		$ 60,000
8	Commissions revenue	85,000		85,000
9	Total revenues	$133,000		$145,000
10	Operating expenses:			
11	Depreciation expense, computers	$ -0-		$ 3,000
12	Depreciation expense, office furniture	-0-		3,500
13	Salaries expense	25,000		29,900
14	Insurance expense	-0-		2,600
15	Rent expense	9,000		9,000
16	Office supplies expense	-0-		960
17	Advertising expense	6,000		6,000
18	Utilities expense	2,500		2,640
19	Total operating expenses	$ 42,500		$ 57,600
20	**Profit**	$ 90,500		$ 87,400

Analysis Component: Identify and explain which GAAP requires that adjusting entries be recorded. By how much would revenues, expenses, and profit be overstated/understated if adjustments were *not* recorded at December 31, 2020, for Javelin Company?

Exercise 3-17 Adjusting entries LO4, 6 eXcel

CHECK FIGURE: Adjusted trial balance, debits = $511,500

Nuna Music Trial Balances.xlsx

Home   Insert   Page Layout   Formulas   Data   Review   View

P18   fx

		Unadjusted Trial Balance		Adjustments		Adjusted Trial Balance	
		Dr.	Cr.	Dr.	Cr.	Dr.	Cr.
7	Cash	$ 14,000					
8	Accounts receivable	32,000					
9	Prepaid insurance	16,800					
10	Equipment	102,000					
11	Accumulated depreciation, equipment		$ 23,000				
12	Accounts payable		19,000				
13	Abraham Nuna, capital		213,000				
14	Abraham Nuna, withdrawals	102,000					
15	Revenues		214,000				
16	Depreciation expense, equipment	-0-					
17	Salaries expense	187,700					
18	Insurance expense	14,500					
19	**Totals**	$ 469,000	$ 469,000				

Rows 1–3: **Nuna Music / Trial Balances / February 28, 2020**

Additional information:

a. Annual depreciation of the equipment; $11,500.

b. $12,000 of the Prepaid Insurance balance has expired.

c. Unbilled and unrecorded revenues at year-end totalled $31,000.

Required Referring to Exhibit 3.22, use the information provided to complete the columns.

Exercise 3-18 Preparing financial statements LO7

CHECK FIGURES: Profit = 19,300; Total assets = $149,300

Using the completed adjusted trial balance columns from Exercise 3-17, prepare an income statement, a statement of changes in equity, and a balance sheet for the year ended February 28, 2020. Assume that the owner made no investments during the year.

Analysis Component: Which GAAP requires the preparation of financial statements?

***Exercise 3-19 Journalizing correcting entries LO8**

For each of the following incorrect entries, journalize the appropriate correcting entry (or entries).

a. The purchase of office supplies on credit for $1,800 was recorded as:

Office Supplies 1,800
    Cash.. 1,800

b. A credit customer paid her account in full: $4,500. This was recorded as:

Cash.. 4,500
    Revenue.. 4,500

An asterisk (*) identifies assignment material based on Appendix 3A or Appendix 3B.

c. The owner withdrew cash of $1,500. This was recorded as:

Salaries Expense...	1,500	
Cash..		1,500

d. Work was performed for a customer today and cash of $750 was received. This was recorded as:

Cash..	750	
Accounts Receivable.............................		750

Analysis Component: If the error in (b) is not corrected, what is the effect on the income statement and balance sheet?

*Exercise 3-20 **Entering adjustments for prepaid items recorded in expense and revenue accounts** LO9

Classic Customs began operations on December 1, 2020. In setting up the bookkeeping procedures, the company decided to debit expense accounts when the company prepays its expenses and to credit revenue accounts when customers pay for services in advance. Prepare journal entries for items (a) through (c) and adjusting entries as of December 31, 2020, for items (d) through (f):

a. Supplies were purchased on December 1 for $8,000.

b. The company prepaid insurance premiums of $3,200 on December 2.

c. On December 15, the company received an advance payment of $16,100 from one customer for remodelling work.

d. By counting the supplies on December 31, Classic Customs determined that $1,450 was on hand.

e. An analysis of the insurance policies in effect on December 31 showed that $800 of insurance coverage had expired.

f. As of December 31, it was determined that $8,500 of the amount received in advance on December 15 had been earned.

*Exercise 3-21 **Alternative procedures for revenues received in advance** LO9

Pavillion Company experienced the following events and transactions during July:

July	1	Received $4,000 in advance of performing work for Andrew Renking.
	6	Received $16,800 in advance of performing work for Matt Swarbuck.
	12	Completed the job for Andrew Renking.
	18	Received $15,000 in advance of performing work for Drew Sayer.
	27	Completed the job for Matt Swarbuck.
	31	The job for Drew Sayer has not been started.

a. Give journal entries (including any adjusting entry as of the end of the month) to record these items using the procedure of initially crediting the Unearned Revenue account when a payment is received from a customer in advance of performing services.

b. Give journal entries (including any adjusting entry as of the end of the month) to record these items using the procedure of initially crediting the Revenue account when a payment is received from a customer in advance of performing services.

c. Under each method, determine the amount of earned revenue that should be reported on the income statement for July and the amount of unearned revenue that should appear on the balance sheet as of July 31.

An asterisk (*) identifies assignment material based on Appendix 3A or Appendix 3B.

PROBLEMS

Problem 3-1A **Preparing adjusting entries (monthly)—prepaid expenses** LO4

Willow Window Washing Services prepares adjustments monthly and shows the following selected accounts on its December 31, 2020, unadjusted trial balance:

Account	Debit	Credit
Prepaid insurance	$ 3,720	
Prepaid office rent	23,000	
Prepaid subscriptions	1,300	
Prepaid equipment rental	26,320	

Required Prepare the required monthly adjusting entries at December 31, 2020, based on the following additional information:

a. The remaining balance in Prepaid Insurance was for a six-month insurance policy purchased for $7,440 and in effect on September 1, 2020.

b. $5,200 of the balance in Prepaid Office Rent had not been used as at December 31, 2020.

c. $1,140 of the balance in Prepaid Subscriptions had been used as at December 31, 2020.

d. The company paid $33,840 on April 1, 2020, to rent equipment for a three-year period beginning April 1, 2020.

Analysis Component: If the above adjustments were not recorded, identify the types of accounts that would be affected and if they would be over- or understated.

Problem 3-2A **Preparing adjusting entries (annual)—depreciation expense** LO4

Details regarding Leroux Steel's purchases of plant and equipment items during 2020 follow:

	Date of Purchase	Plant and Equipment Item	Cost	Estimated Useful Life	Estimated Sales Value at End of Estimated Useful Life
a.	Jan. 1	Machine A	$102,000	5 years	$ -0-
b.	Apr. 1	Machine B	61,000	4 years	3,400
c.	Nov. 1	Machine C	30,500	2 years	2,900

Required Prepare the annual adjusting entry at December 31, 2020, Leroux's year-end, for each plant and equipment item. Assume Leroux Steel uses the straight-line method to depreciate its assets.

Analysis Component: What is the purpose of recording depreciation? If depreciation is not recorded, how would the income statement be affected?

Problem 3-3A **Preparing adjusting entries (monthly)—unearned revenues** LO4

Helping Hand Outdoor Services pre-sells yard maintenance packages for the gardening season. During October, the company collects cash from clients for Christmas trees to be delivered in December. Snow removal services are also provided. Helping Hand prepares adjusting entries monthly. The following selected accounts appear on the November 30, 2020, unadjusted trial balance:

Account	Debit	Credit
Unearned lawn services...................................		$102,000
Unearned garden services.............................		36,400
Unearned snow removal services................		11,800
Unearned Christmas tree sales.....................		21,200

Required Prepare the monthly adjusting journal entries at November 30, 2020, using the following additional information.

a. $86,000 of the Unearned Lawn Services account represents payments received from customers for the 2021 season. The remainder represents fall lawn services actually performed during November 2020.

b. $31,950 of the Unearned Garden Services account had been earned by November 30, 2020.

c. $9,200 of the Unearned Snow Removal Services account remained unearned at November 30, 2020.

d. Helping Hand arranges with its customers to deliver trees from December 5 to December 20. As a result, the Unearned Christmas Tree Sales account will be earned in total by December 20.

Analysis Component: If the Unearned Lawn Services of $102,000 had been recorded as a revenue when received instead of as a liability, what would the effect have been on the November 30, 2020, financial statements assuming no adjustment was made on November 30, 2020?

Problem 3-4A Preparing adjusting (monthly) and subsequent cash entries—accrued expenses LO4

Envirocan Resources prepares adjusting entries monthly. In reviewing the accounts on March 31, Envirocan Resources discovered the following:

a. Interest of $1,080 had accrued on the note payable as at March 31. It is to be paid on April 2.

b. Unpaid and unrecorded salaries at March 31 totalled $33,150. The $33,150 plus salaries of $22,200 for the first four days of April were paid on April 4.

c. The March telephone bill for $470 is unpaid and unrecorded at March 31. It is to be paid on April 15.

d. Envirocan normally pays rent in three-month installments. At March 31, rent of $4,500 per month had not been paid for February, March, or April. Rent of $4,500 was correctly accrued at the end of February. The balance owing plus rent for May, June, and July was paid on April 26.

e. Envirocan pays commissions to the technicians at the rate of 4% of services performed. During March, total services performed were $440,000. Commissions are unrecorded and unpaid at March 31. Commissions are paid on the 15th of the following month.

Required Using the information provided above, prepare the monthly adjusting journal entries at March 31 along with the appropriate subsequent cash entries.

Problem 3-5A Preparing adjusting and subsequent cash entries (annual)—accrued revenues LO4

In reviewing the accounts on March 31 for the year just ended, DigiTech discovered the following:

a. DigiTech owns the building that it occupies. Part of the building is rented to E-Quip Company for $4,150 per month. E-Quip had not paid the March rent as at March 31. On April 3, DigiTech collected the rent accrued on March 31.

b. Services performed but unrecorded at March 31 totalled $8,400. This amount was collected on April 7.

c. Interest for the month of March had accrued on a note receivable in the amount of $640. The interest accrued on March 31 was collected on April 1.

d. On February 1, DigiTech signed a $34,500 six-month contract to perform services for a client. DigiTech has been providing the services but as of March 31 no cash had been received. On April 2, DigiTech collected the revenue accrued on March 31.

Required Using the information provided above, prepare the annual adjusting journal entries at March 31 along with the appropriate subsequent cash entries.

Problem 3-6A Adjusting entries (annual); adjusted trial balance LO4, 6 eXcel

CHECK FIGURE: 2. Adjusted Trial Balance, debits = $572,520

PacRim Careers provides training to individuals who pay tuition directly to the business. The business also offers extension training to groups in off-site locations. Additional information available at the December 31, 2020, year-end follows:

a. An analysis of the company's policies shows that $1,250 of insurance coverage has expired.

b. An inventory shows that teaching supplies costing $450 are on hand at the end of the year.

	PacRim Careers Trial Balances.xlsx						
	Home Insert Page Layout Formulas Data Review View						
	P18 fx						
	A	B	C	D	E	F	G
1	**PacRim Careers**						
2	Trial Balances						
3	December 31, 2020						
4		Unadjusted				Adjusted	
5		Trial Balance		Adjustments		Trial Balance	
6	**Account**	Dr.	Cr.	Dr.	Cr.	Dr.	Cr.
7	Cash	$ 18,000					
8	Accounts receivable	-0-					
9	Teaching supplies	6,500					
10	Prepaid insurance	1,400					
11	Prepaid rent	7,200					
12	Professional library	60,000					
13	Accumulated depreciation, professional library		$ 18,000				
14	Equipment	96,000					
15	Accumulated depreciation, equipment		32,000				
16	Accounts payable		2,500				
17	Salaries payable		-0-				
18	Unearned extension revenue		6,300				
19	Karoo Ashevak, capital		229,000				
20	Karoo Ashevak, withdrawals	92,000					
21	Tuition revenue		196,000				
22	Extension revenue		72,500				
23	Depreciation expense, equipment	-0-					
24	Depreciation expense, professional library	-0-					
25	Salaries expense	206,000					
26	Insurance expense	-0-					
27	Rent expense	44,000					
28	Teaching supplies expense	-0-					
29	Advertising expense	14,000					
30	Utilities expense	11,200					
31	**Totals**	$ 556,300	$ 556,300				

c. The estimated annual depreciation on the equipment is $8,000.

d. The estimated annual depreciation on the professional library is $4,500.

e. The school offers off-campus services for specific employers. On November 1, the company agreed to do a special six-month course for a client. The contract calls for a monthly fee of $950, and the client paid the first five months' revenue in advance. When the cash was received, the Unearned Extension Revenue account was credited.

f. On October 15, the school agreed to teach a four-month class for an individual for $1,200 tuition per month payable at the end of the class. The services to date have been provided as agreed, but no payment has been received.

g. The school's two employees are paid weekly. As of the end of the year, three days' wages have accrued at the rate of $120 per day for each employee.

h. The balance in the Prepaid Rent account represents the rent for three months: December, January, and February.

Required

1. Prepare the necessary annual adjusting journal entries at December 31, 2020, based on (a) to (h) above.

Analysis Component:

2. Refer to the format presented in Exhibit 3.22 and complete the adjusted trial balance using the information in (a) through (h) above.

3. If the adjustments were *not* recorded, calculate the over- or understatement of income.

4. Is it ethical to ignore adjusting entries?

Problem 3-7A   Adjusting entries (monthly)   LO4

Wedona Energy Consultants prepares adjusting entries monthly. Based on an analysis of the unadjusted trial balance at January 31, 2020, the following information was available for the preparation of the January 31, 2020, month-end adjusting entries:

a. Equipment purchased on November 1 of this accounting period for $21,600 is estimated to have a useful life of three years. After three years of use, it is expected that the equipment will be scrapped due to technological obsolescence.

b. Of the $11,400 balance in Unearned Consulting Revenue, $8,700 had been earned.

c. The Prepaid Rent account showed a balance of $13,500. This was paid on January 1 of this accounting period and represents six months of rent commencing on the same date.

d. Accrued wages at January 31 totalled $18,500.

e. One month of interest had accrued at the rate of 4% per year on a $42,000 note payable.

f. Unrecorded and uncollected consulting revenues at month-end were $6,150.

g. A $3,510 insurance policy was purchased on April 1 of the current accounting period and debited to the Prepaid Insurance account. Coverage began April 1 for 18 months.

h. The monthly depreciation on the office furniture was $625.

i. Repair revenues accrued at month-end totalled $3,400.

j. The Store Supplies account had a balance of $800 at the beginning of January. During January, $1,780 of supplies were purchased and debited to the Store Supplies account. At month-end, a count of the supplies revealed a balance of $650.

Required Prepare adjusting journal entries for the month ended January 31, 2020, based on the above. Assume Wedona Energy uses the straight-line method to depreciate its assets.

Problem 3-8A Adjusting (annual) and subsequent cash journal entries LO4

The following information concerns the adjusting entries to be recorded on November 30, 2020, for RaiLink's year just ended.

a. The Office Supplies account started the year with a $4,800 balance. During 2020, the company purchased supplies at a cost of $24,800, which was added to the Office Supplies account. The inventory of supplies on hand at November 30 had a cost of $6,300.

b. An analysis of the company's insurance policies provided these facts:

Policy	Date of Purchase	Years of Coverage	Total Cost
1	March 1, 2019	2	$ 5,760
2	March 1, 2020	3	22,320
3	July 1, 2020	1	3,780

The total premium for each policy was paid in full at the purchase date, and the Prepaid Insurance account was debited for the full cost. *Appropriate adjusting entries have been made to November 30, 2019.*

c. The company has 15 employees who earn a total of $4,800 in salaries for every working day. They are paid each Wednesday for their work in the five-day workweek ending on the preceding Friday. All 15 employees worked November 23 to 27 inclusive. They will be paid salaries for five full days on Wednesday, December 2, 2020.

d. The company purchased a building on July 1, 2020. The building cost $306,000 and is expected to have a $25,000 residual value at the end of its predicted 30-year life.

e. Because the company is not large enough to occupy the entire building, it arranged to rent some space to a tenant at $3,100 per month, starting on October 1, 2020. The rent was paid on time on October 1, and the amount received was credited to the Rent Revenue account. However, the tenant has not paid the November rent. The company has worked out an agreement with the tenant, who has promised to pay both November's and December's rent in full on December 15.

f. On October 1, the company also rented space to another tenant for $3,650 per month. The tenant paid five months' rent in advance on that date. The payment was recorded with a credit to the Unearned Rent account.

Required

1. Use the information to prepare the annual adjusting entries as of November 30, 2020. Assume RaiLink uses the straight-line method to depreciate its assets.

2. Prepare journal entries to record the subsequent cash transactions in December 2020 described in parts (c) and (e).

Problem 3-9A Adjusting entries (annual) LO4

Rainmaker Environmental Consultants is just finishing its second year of operations. The company's unadjusted trial balance at October 31, 2020, follows.

Rainmaker prepares adjustments each October 31. The following additional information is available on October 31, 2020.

a. It was determined that $12,000 of the unearned consulting revenue had not yet been earned.

b. It was discovered that $14,000 of the balance in the Consulting Revenue account was for services to be performed in November.

c. The balance in the Prepaid Rent account represents three months of rent beginning September 1, 2020.

d. Accrued wages at October 31 totalled $6,800.

e. The office furniture was purchased on March 1, 2019, and has an estimated useful life of two years. After two years of use, it is expected that the furniture will be worthless.

f. Accrued consulting revenue at year-end totalled $4,200.

g. Interest of $85 had accrued on the note receivable for the month of October.

h. The balance in the Prepaid Insurance account represents the remaining balance of a two-year policy purchased on April 1, 2019.

i. A count of the supplies on October 31 revealed a balance remaining of $620.

	Rainmaker Environmental Consultants Unadjusted Trial Balance October 31, 2020		
Acct. No.	**Account**	**Debit**	**Credit**
101	Cash	$ 26,000	
106	Accounts receivable	61,000	
109	Interest receivable	-0-	
111	Notes receivable	50,000	
126	Supplies	5,300	
128	Prepaid insurance	3,400	
131	Prepaid rent	27,000	
161	Office furniture	84,000	
162	Accumulated depreciation, office furniture		$ 28,000
201	Accounts payable		18,000
210	Wages payable		-0-
233	Unearned consulting revenue		26,000
301	Jeff Moore, capital		223,000
302	Jeff Moore, withdrawals	28,000	
401	Consulting revenue		232,020
409	Interest income		480
601	Depreciation expense, office furniture	-0-	
622	Wages expense	192,000	
637	Insurance expense	-0-	
640	Rent expense	44,000	
650	Supplies expense	6,800	
	Totals	$527,500	$527,500

Required Prepare the annual adjusting journal entries for October 31, 2020, based on the above. Assume Rainmaker Environmental uses the straight-line method to depreciate its assets.

Problem 3-10A Posting, adjusted trial balance, and preparing financial statements LO6, 7

CHECK FIGURES: 3. Adjusted trial balance, debits = $580,585; 4. Loss = $79,895

Required Using the information in Problem 3-9A, complete the following:

1. Set up balance column accounts for Rainmaker Environmental Consultants and enter the balances listed in the unadjusted trial balance.

2. Post the adjusting entries prepared in Problem 3-9A to the accounts.

3. Prepare an adjusted trial balance.

4. Use the adjusted trial balance to prepare an income statement, a statement of changes in equity, and a balance sheet. Assume that the owner, Jeff Moore, made no owner investments during the year.

Analysis Component: Assume that total revenues and expenses reported for the year ended October 31, 2019, were $189,000 and $157,600, respectively. Compare the business's financial performance for the years ended October 31, 2019 and 2020.

Note

For Part 1, your instructor may ask you to set up T-accounts instead of balance column accounts. The solution is available in both formats.

Problem 3-11A Adjusting entries (monthly) LO4 Help Me SOLVE IT

Arrow Hospitality prepares adjustments monthly and showed the following at September 30, 2020:

	Arrow Hospitality Trial Balances.xlsx						
	Arrow Hospitality Trial Balances September 30, 2020						
		Unadjusted Trial Balance		Adjustments		Adjusted Trial Balance	
Account		Dr.	Cr.	Dr.	Cr.	Dr.	Cr.
7 Cash		$ 6,000					
8 Accounts receivable		11,200					
9 Repair supplies		2,200					
10 Prepaid rent		14,000					
11 Office furniture		26,000					
12 Accounts payable			$ 8,000				
13 Notes payable			21,600				
14 Eli Arrow, capital			67,758				
15 Eli Arrow, withdrawals		5,000					
16 Hospitality revenues			128,000				
17 Salaries expense		144,000					
18 Wages expense		16,958					
19 **Totals**		$ 225,358	$ 225,358				

Additional information available for the month ended September 30, 2020:

a. Interest of $162 had accrued on the notes payable for the month of September.

b. The office furniture was acquired on September 1, 2020, and has an estimated four-year life. The furniture will be sold for about $2,000 at the end of its four-year life.

c. A count of the Repair Supplies revealed a balance on hand of $700.

d. A review of the Prepaid Rent account showed that $10,000 had been used during September.

e. Accrued wages of $2,800 had not been recorded at month-end.

f. The September Internet bill for $100 had been received and must be paid by October 14.

g. Accrued revenues of $6,200 were not recorded at September 30.

Required Prepare adjusting entries for the month ended September 30, 2020, for each of (a) through (g) above.

Problem 3-12A **Preparation of financial statements** LO6, 7 e**X**cel

CHECK FIGURES: 1. Adjustments columns = $21,262; Adjusted trial balance columns = $235,120; 2. Loss = $41,820

Required

1. Using the format presented in Problem 3-11A, complete the adjusted trial balance by including the adjusting entries prepared in Problem 3-11A.

2. Prepare an income statement, a statement of changes in equity, and a balance sheet based on the adjusted trial balance completed in Part 1. Assume that the owner, Eli Arrow, made an investment during September of $3,600.

Analysis Component: Assume that total assets reported at August 31, 2020, were $76,900. Determine what total liabilities and equity were on that date and comment on the change in the financial position from August to September.

Problem 3-13A **Preparing financial statements from the adjusted trial balance** LO7

CHECK FIGURES: a. Profit = $84,925; c. Total assets = $264,500

This alphabetized adjusted trial balance is for GalaVu Entertainment as of its December 31, 2020, year-end:

	Debit	Credit
Accounts payable		$ 44,000
Accounts receivable	$ 18,700	
Accumulated depreciation, automobiles		69,000
Accumulated depreciation, equipment		20,500
Advertising expense	9,000	
Automobiles	140,000	
Cash	11,000	
Depreciation expense, automobiles	13,200	
Depreciation expense, equipment	4,100	
Equipment	65,000	
Revenue		240,000
Interest income		150
Interest expense	3,500	
Interest payable		75
Interest receivable	300	
John Conroe, capital		23,000
John Conroe, withdrawals	19,000	
Land	35,000	
Long-term notes payable		115,000
Notes receivable (due in 90 days)	80,000	
Office supplies	4,000	
Office supplies expense	13,000	
Repairs expense, automobiles	8,400	
Salaries expense	76,225	
Salaries payable		5,500
Unearned revenue		11,000
Wages expense	27,800	
Totals	$528,225	$528,225

Required Use the information in the trial balance to prepare:

1. The income statement for the year ended December 31, 2020.

2. The statement of changes in equity for the year ended December 31, 2020, assuming that the owner made additional investments of $15,000 during the year.

3. The balance sheet as of December 31, 2020.

Analysis Component: The owner, John Conroe, is very pleased with the change in the business's financial position. Specifically, he noted that his equity increased. "My banker told me that as long as equity is increasing, my business is doing great." Comment.

Problem 3-14A Journalizing, posting, adjusted trial balance, adjusting entries (monthly), financial statements LO4, 5, 6, 7

CHECK FIGURES: 3. Cash balance, Aug. 31, 2020 = $3,240; 6. Dr. = $15,803; 7. Profit = $412

On August 1, 2020, Mark Diamond began a tour company in the Northwest Territories called Millennium Arctic Tours. The following occurred during the first month of operations:

Aug.	1	Purchased office furniture on account; $4,700.
	1	Mark Diamond invested $6,100 cash into his new business.
	2	Collected $2,550 in advance for a three-week guided caribou watching tour beginning later in August.
	3	Paid $4,650 for six months' rent for office space effective August 1.
	4	Received $2,100 for a four-day northern lights viewing tour just completed.
	7	Paid $1,050 for hotel expenses regarding the August 4 tour.
	15	Mark withdrew cash of $600 for personal use.
	22	Met with a Japanese tour guide to discuss a $100,000 tour contract.
	31	Paid wages of $1,210.

Required

1. Prepare general journal entries to record the August transactions.

2. Set up the following T-accounts: Cash (101); Prepaid Rent (131); Office Furniture (161); Accumulated Depreciation, Office Furniture (162); Accounts Payable (201); Unearned Revenue (233); Mark Diamond, Capital (301); Mark Diamond, Withdrawals (302); Revenue (401); Depreciation Expense, Office Furniture (602); Wages Expense (623); Rent Expense (640); Telephone Expense (688); and Hotel Expenses (696).

3. Post the entries to the accounts; calculate the ending balance in each account.

4. Prepare an unadjusted trial balance at August 31, 2020.

5. Use the following information to prepare and post adjusting entries on August 31:

   a. The office furniture has an estimated life of three years and a $272 residual value. Use the straight-line method to depreciate the furniture.

   b. Two-thirds of the August 2 advance has been earned.

   c. One month of the Prepaid Rent has been used.

   d. The August telephone bill was not received as of August 31 but amounted to $230.

6. Prepare an adjusted trial balance.

7. Prepare an income statement, a statement of changes in equity, and a balance sheet.

Analysis Component: When a company shows revenue on its income statement, does this mean that cash equal to revenues was received during the period in which the revenues were reported?

*Problem 3-15A Correcting entries LO8

The accountant for Karma Counselling Services found several errors in reviewing the unadjusted trial balance on September 30. You are to prepare correcting entries based on the following information:

a. The Counselling Revenue account included an entry debiting cash for $7,000 that should have been debited to Accounts Receivable.

b. Utilities Expense was debited $1,680 that should have been recorded as Telephone Expense.

c. The Office Supplies account shows a credit of $2,800 regarding the use of Cleaning Supplies.

d. A transaction involving $19,600 of service revenue performed on account was incorrectly recorded as a debit to Accounts Payable and a credit to Unearned Service Revenue.

e. Equipment was incorrectly debited for $1,200 with a corresponding credit to Accounts Payable regarding supplies that were sold to a neighbouring store on credit.

Required Journalize the correcting entries required on September 30.

Analysis Component: The error in (b) shows that an incorrect expense account was debited. Since the net effect on the financial statements is nil after recording the correction, is it necessary to prepare a correcting entry for this type of error?

*Problem 3-16A Recording prepaid expenses and unearned revenues LO9

CHECK FIGURE: Adjusted trial balance, debits = $136,400

Willis Consulting follows the approach of recording prepaid expenses as expenses and unearned revenues as revenues. Willis's unadjusted trial balance follows for the year ended March 31, 2020.

	Willis Consulting Trial Balances.xlsx						
	Home Insert Page Layout Formulas Data Review View						
	P18 fx						
	A	B	C	D	E	F	G
1	Willis Consulting						
2	Trial Balances						
3	March 31, 2020						
4		Unadjusted				Adjusted	
5		Trial Balance		Adjustments		Trial Balance	
6	Account	Dr.	Cr.	Dr.	Cr.	Dr.	Cr.
7	Cash	$ 32,000					
8	Accounts receivable	63,000					
9	Prepaid rent	-0-					
10	Prepaid insurance	-0-					
11	Accounts payable		$ 16,000				
12	Unearned consulting revenue		-0-				
13	Bruce Willis, capital		38,400				
14	Consulting revenue		82,000				
15	Rent expense	38,990					
16	Insurance expense	2,410					
17	**Totals**	$ 136,400	$ 136,400				

An asterisk (*) identifies assignment material based on Appendix 3A or Appendix 3B.

Additional information:

a. A review of the Consulting Revenue account showed that $6,400 of the balance has not yet been earned.

b. The balance in the Rent Expense account was paid on January 15, 2020, and represents seven months of rent beginning February 1, 2020.

c. It was determined that $1,900 of the balance in the Insurance Expense account was used by March 31, 2020.

Required Refer to Exhibit 3.22 and use the information provided to complete the columns above.

*Problem 3-17A Recording prepaid expenses and unearned revenues LO4, 9

The following events occurred for a company during the last two months of its fiscal year ended December 31, 2020:

Nov.	1	Paid $4,500 for future newspaper advertising.
	1	Paid $7,800 for insurance through October 31 of the following year.
	30	Received $6,600 for future services to be provided to a customer.
Dec.	1	Paid $5,850 for the services of a consultant, to be received over the next three months.
	15	Received $12,100 for future services to be provided to a customer.
	31	Of the advertising paid for on November 1, $1,780 worth had not yet been published by the newspaper.
	31	Part of the insurance paid for on November 1 had expired.
	31	Services worth $1,650 had not yet been provided to the customer who paid on November 30.
	31	One-third of the consulting services paid for on December 1 had been received.
	31	The company had performed $2,750 of the services that the customer had paid for on December 15.

Required

1. Prepare the November and December entries for the above activities under the approach that records prepaid expenses as assets and records unearned revenues as liabilities. Also, prepare adjusting entries at the end of the year.

2. Prepare the November and December entries under the approach that records prepaid expenses as expenses and records unearned revenues as revenues. Also, prepare adjusting entries at the end of the year.

Analysis Component: Explain why the alternative sets of entries in requirements 1 and 2 do not result in different financial statement amounts.

ALTERNATE PROBLEMS

Problem 3-1B Preparing adjusting entries (annual)—prepaid expenses LO4

Camillo's Cleaning Services is gathering information for its year-end, April 30, 2020. Selected accounts on the April 30, 2020, unadjusted trial balance are reproduced below:

Account	Debit	Credit
Prepaid equipment rental	$24,750	
Prepaid warehouse rental	8,800	
Prepaid insurance	9,160	
Cleaning supplies	4,100	

An asterisk (*) identifies assignment material based on Appendix 3A or Appendix 3B.

Required Prepare the required annual adjusting entries at April 30, 2020, based on the following additional information:

a. The balance in the Prepaid Equipment Rental account is for 18 months of equipment rental that began December 1, 2019.

b. $6,000 of the balance in the Prepaid Warehouse Rental account had been used as of April 30, 2020.

c. The balance in the Prepaid Insurance account represents six months of insurance effective February 1, 2020.

d. A count of the cleaning supplies revealed that $2,850 had been used.

Analysis Component: Which GAAP require the recording of adjusting entries and why?

Problem 3-2B Preparing adjusting entries (monthly)—depreciation expense LO4

Zebra Consulting prepares adjusting entries and financial statements monthly. Details regarding Zebra Consulting's plant and equipment items follow:

	Date of Purchase	Plant and Equipment Item	Cost	Estimated Useful Life	Estimated Sales Value at End of Estimated Useful Life
a.	Dec. 1, 2019	Furniture	$ 36,000	3 years	$ -0-
b.	Mar. 1, 2020	Equipment	187,000	10 years	25,000
c.	Nov. 1, 2020	Building	491,000	15 years	131,000

Required Prepare the monthly adjusting entry to record depreciation for each plant and equipment item at November 30, 2020.

Analysis Component: What is the purpose of recording depreciation? If depreciation is not recorded, how would each of the components of the accounting equation be affected?

Problem 3-3B Preparing adjusting entries (annual)—unearned revenues LO4

Blackfeather Tours sells scuba diving and kayaking excursions, along with a number of unique sightseeing packages. The company requires a 50% payment from the customer at the time of booking. The following selected accounts appear on Blackfeather's January 31, 2020, year-end unadjusted trial balance:

Account	Debit	Credit
Unearned heli-tour revenue............................		$ 38,000
Unearned tour package revenue..................		652,000
Unearned scuba diving revenue..................		290,000
Unearned kayaking tour revenue.................		116,000

Required Prepare the annual adjusting journal entries at January 31, 2020, using the following additional information:

a. Blackfeather Tours has custom helicopter packages in which groups are flown in and out of island retreats. The balance in this unearned account is for a group scheduled for early March 2020.

b. Three-quarters of the Unearned Tour Package Revenue account had been earned by January 31, 2020.

c. $72,000 of the Unearned Scuba Diving Revenue account remained unearned at January 31, 2020.

d. $15,500 of the Unearned Kayaking Tour Revenue account represents payments received from customers for February and March 2020. The balance in the account is for tours provided in January 2020.

Analysis Component: Using your understanding of GAAP, explain how and why unearned revenues are adjusted at the end of the accounting period.

Problem 3-4B Preparing adjusting (annual) and subsequent cash entries—accrued expenses LO4

In reviewing the accounts on September 30, 2020, for the year just ended, Geek Designers discovered the following:

a. The September cell phone bill for $465 was unpaid and unrecorded at September 30. It will be paid on October 5.

b. Accrued wages at September 30 totalled $82,500. On October 9, the first biweekly payday of October, $115,000 was paid to employees representing the seven days accrued on September 30 plus the first three working days in October.

c. On September 30, $1,650 of cable charges were accrued regarding the past two months of usage that were not recorded or paid. This amount was paid on October 2.

d. Interest of $1,220 had accrued on the bank loan as at September 30. It is to be paid on October 2.

e. $1,675 of property taxes covering September were accrued on September 30. This amount was paid on October 15.

Required Using the information provided above, prepare the annual adjusting journal entries at September 30 along with the appropriate subsequent cash entries.

Problem 3-5B Preparing adjusting (monthly) and subsequent cash entries—accrued revenues LO4

WonderWeb prepares adjusting entries monthly. In reviewing the accounts on March 31, 2020, WonderWeb discovered the following:

a. Interest of $450, representing 25 days in March, had accrued on the note receivable as of March 31. The accrual of $450 plus an additional five days in April was collected on April 5.

b. Accrued consulting revenue totalling $5,600 was not recorded on March 31. This amount was collected on April 6.

c. Web design work totalling $8,750 was completed on March 31 but not recorded. This amount was collected on April 13.

d. WonderWeb rents the basement of its building to a student. The student has not paid the March rent of $950 as at March 31. On April 27, the March rent plus the rent for April was collected.

Required Using the information provided above, prepare the March 31 month-end adjusting journal entries along with the appropriate subsequent cash entries.

Problem 3-6B Adjusting entries (monthly); adjusted trial balance LO4, 6 *eXcel*

CHECK FIGURE: 2. Adjusted Trial Balance, debits = $588,570

Fawcett Institute provides one-on-one training to individuals who pay tuition directly to the business and also offers extension training to groups in off-site locations. Fawcett prepares adjusting entries monthly. Additional information available on December 31, 2020:

a. An analysis of the company's policies shows that $31,000 of insurance coverage has expired.

b. An inventory shows that teaching supplies costing $13,400 are on hand at the end of the month.

c. The estimated monthly depreciation on the equipment is $650.

d. The estimated monthly depreciation on the professional library is $320.

e. The school offers off-campus services for specific operators. On December 1, the company agreed to do a special four-month course for a client. The contract calls for a $5,400 monthly fee, and the client paid the first two months' revenue in advance. When the cash was received, the Unearned Extension Revenue account was credited.

f. On December 15, the school agreed to teach a four-month class to an individual for $1,600 tuition per month payable at the end of the class. The services have been provided as agreed, and no payment has been received.

g. The school's only employee is paid weekly. As of the end of the month, wages of $1,200 have accrued.

h. The balance in the Prepaid Rent account represents the rent for December, January, February, and March.

	Fawcett Institute Trial Balance.xlsx						
Home Insert Page Layout Formulas Data Review View							
P18	*fx*						
	A	B	C	D	E	F	G
1	Fawcett Institute						
2	Trial Balance						
3	December 31, 2020						
4		Unadjusted				Adjusted	
5		Trial Balance		Adjustments		Trial Balance	
6	Account	Dr.	Cr.	Dr.	Cr.	Dr.	Cr.
7	Cash	$ 25,000					
8	Accounts receivable	-0-					
9	Teaching supplies	107,200					
10	Prepaid insurance	36,000					
11	Prepaid rent	11,600					
12	Professional library	20,000					
13	Accumulated depreciation, professional library		$ 3,000				
14	Equipment	141,400					
15	Accumulated depreciation, equipment		32,000				
16	Accounts payable		24,400				
17	Salaries payable		-0-				
18	Unearned extension revenue		55,200				
19	Jay Fawcett, capital		62,000				
20	Jay Fawcett, withdrawals	40,000					
21	Tuition revenue		285,000				
22	Extension revenue		124,000				
23	Depreciation expense, equipment	-0-					
24	Depreciation expense, professional library	-0-					
25	Salaries expense	143,600					
26	Insurance expense	-0-					
27	Rent expense	-0-					
28	Teaching supplies expense	-0-					
29	Advertising expense	36,000					
30	Utilities expense	24,800					
31	**Totals**	$ 585,600	$ 585,600				

Required

1. Prepare the necessary December 31, 2020, month-end adjusting journal entries based on (a) through (h) above.

Analysis Component:

2. Refer to the format presented in Exhibit 3.22 and prepare an adjusted trial balance using the information in (a) through (h) above.

3. If the adjustments were *not* recorded, calculate the over- or understatement of income.

4. Is it ethical to ignore adjusting entries?

Problem 3-7B Adjusting entries (annual) LO4

Kazz Industries' year-end is May 31. Based on an analysis of the unadjusted trial balance at May 31, 2020, the following information was available:

a. Machinery costing $77,500 was acquired on September 1 of this accounting period. It is estimated to have a useful life of six years. The machinery is estimated to have a $5,500 value at the end of its six-year life.

b. Accrued revenues at year-end totalled $24,300.

c. The Prepaid Insurance account showed a balance of $23,040. This was paid and takes effect on March 1 of this accounting period and represents a two-year policy.

d. Accrued salaries at year-end were $21,500.

e. One month of interest had accrued at a rate of 3.5% on the $144,000 note payable.

f. The annual depreciation on the office equipment was $8,100.

g. $6,480 worth of advertising was prepaid on January 1 of the current accounting period and debited to the Prepaid Advertising account. This covered four months of advertising beginning on the same date.

h. It was determined that $4,500 of completed work was included in the $9,200 Unearned Revenue account balance at year-end.

i. Interest income accrued at year-end totalled $570.

j. The Office Supplies account had a balance of $4,000 at the beginning of the accounting period. During the year, $29,500 of supplies were purchased and debited to the Office Supplies account. At year-end, a count of the supplies revealed that $28,400 had been used.

Required Prepare adjusting journal entries for the year ended May 31, 2020, based on the above.

Problem 3-8B Identifying adjusting (monthly) and subsequent cash journal entries LO4

Valor Ventures prepares adjusting entries monthly. The following information concerns the adjusting entries that need to be recorded on October 31, 2020, for the month just ended.

a. The Office Supplies account had a $1,000 balance on October 1. During October, the company purchased supplies at a cost of $9,100, which was added to the Office Supplies account. The inventory of supplies on hand at October 31 had a cost of $600.

b. An analysis of the company's insurance policies provided these facts:

Policy	Date of Purchase	Years of Coverage	Total Cost
1	April 1, 2019	2	$8,400
2	April 1, 2020	3	6,660
3	August 1, 2020	1	1,500

The total premium for each policy was paid in full at the purchase date, and the Prepaid Insurance account was debited for the full cost. *Appropriate adjusting entries have been made to September 30, 2020.*

c. The company has 10 employees who earn a total of $3,250 for every working day. They are paid each Monday for their work in the five-day workweek ending on the preceding Friday. October 31, 2020, falls on a Saturday, and all 10 employees worked the five days that week. They will be paid salaries for five full days on Monday, November 2, 2020.

d. The company purchased a building on August 1, 2018. The building cost $250,000, and is expected to have a $40,000 residual value at the end of its predicted 25-year life.

e. Because the company is not large enough to occupy the entire building, it arranged to rent some space to a tenant at $2,600 per month, starting on September 1, 2020. The rent was paid on time on September 1, and the amount received was credited to the Rent Revenue account. However, the tenant has not paid the October rent. The company has worked out an agreement with the tenant, who has promised to pay both October's and November's rent in full on November 15.

f. On October 1, the company also rented space to another tenant for $2,350 per month. The tenant paid five months' rent in advance on that date. The payment was recorded with a credit to the Unearned Rent account.

Required

1. Use the information to prepare the October 31, 2020, month-end adjusting entries.

2. Prepare journal entries to record the subsequent cash transactions described in items (c) and (e).

Problem 3-9B Adjusting journal entries (monthly) LO4

Ben Hallmark, the owner of Hallmark Surveying Services, has been in business for two years. The unadjusted trial balance at December 31, regarding the month just ended, follows.

The following additional information is available on December 31, 2020:

a. Depreciation on the equipment for the month was $430.

b. $9,600 of the balance in Unearned Surveying Revenue is unearned at December 31.

c. The balance in Prepaid Rent is for six months of rent beginning December 1.

d. Accrued wages at month-end were $12,400.

e. December's interest in the amount of $120 had accrued on the notes payable.

f. Accrued surveying revenue at month-end totalled $21,800.

g. The balance in Prepaid Advertising covers four months of advertising beginning December 15.

h. A count of the supplies on December 31 showed $1,320 had been used.

i. The December electricity bill for $2,340 was received on December 31. It is unrecorded and unpaid.

Required Prepare adjusting journal entries for the month ended December 31, 2020, based on the above.

Analysis Component: Explain the differences between *Accumulated Depreciation* and *Depreciation Expense.*

Hallmark Surveying Services Unadjusted Trial Balance December 31, 2020			
Acct. No.	**Account**	**Debit**	**Credit**
101	Cash...	$ 15,600	
106	Accounts receivable......................................	29,200	
126	Supplies	1,640	
128	Prepaid advertising......................................	1,280	
131	Prepaid rent	17,880	
167	Surveying equipment	58,000	
168	Accumulated depreciation, surveying equipment		$ 7,348
201	Accounts payable...		13,800
203	Interest payable...		-0-
210	Wages payable...		-0-
233	Unearned surveying revenue		14,800
251	Notes payable		36,000
301	Ben Hallmark, capital....................................		28,652
302	Ben Hallmark, withdrawals............................	24,300	
401	Surveying revenue...		170,948
601	Depreciation expense, surveying equipment....	-0-	
622	Salaries expense	56,000	
623	Wages expense	39,726	
633	Interest expense..	-0-	
637	Insurance expense...	6,000	
640	Rent expense..	-0-	
650	Supplies expense...	2,958	
655	Advertising expense.......................................	-0-	
671	Gas and oil expense......................................	6,564	
684	Repairs expense	12,400	
690	Utilities expense	-0-	
	Totals..	$271,548	$271,548

Problem 3-10B Posting, adjusted trial balance, and preparing financial statements LO6, 7

CHECK FIGURES: 3. Adjusted trial balance, debits = $308,638; 4. Profit = $54,550

Required Using the information in Problem 3-9B, complete the following:

1. Set up balance column accounts for Hallmark Surveying Services and enter the balances listed in the unadjusted trial balance.

2. Post the adjusting entries prepared in Problem 3-9B to the balance column accounts.

3. Prepare an adjusted trial balance.

4. Use the adjusted trial balance to prepare an income statement, a statement of changes in equity, and a balance sheet. Assume that the owner, Ben Hallmark, made owner investments of $4,000 during the month.

Analysis Component: At December 31, 2020, how much of the business's assets are financed by the owner? by debt? Assuming total assets at the end of the previous month totalled $84,200, did equity financing increase or decrease during December? Generally speaking, is this a favourable or unfavourable change?

Note

For Part 1, your instructor may ask you to set up T-accounts instead of balance column accounts. The solution is available in both formats.

Problem 3-11B Adjusting entries (annual) LO4

B52 Skate Training prepares adjustments annually and showed the following on its June 30, 2020, year-end:

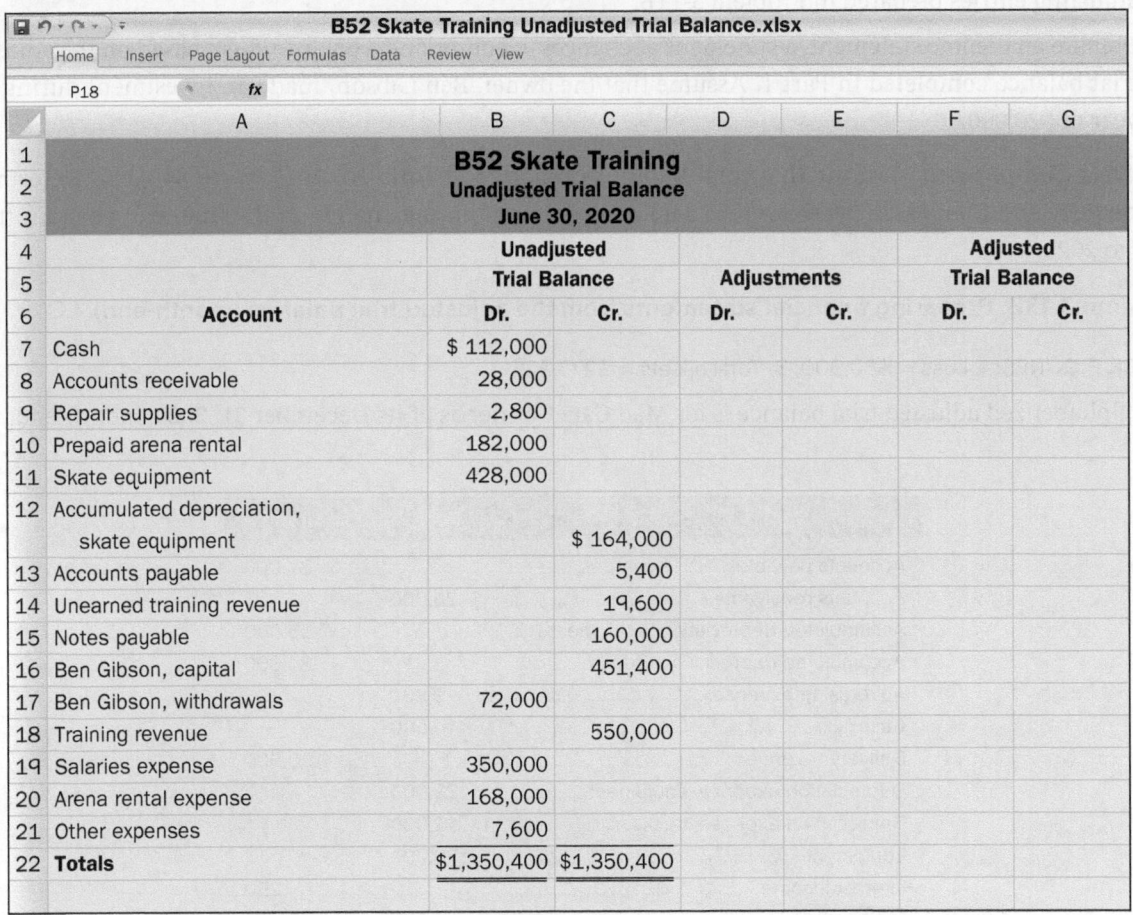

Account	Unadjusted Trial Balance Dr.	Cr.	Adjustments Dr.	Cr.	Adjusted Trial Balance Dr.	Cr.
Cash	$ 112,000					
Accounts receivable	28,000					
Repair supplies	2,800					
Prepaid arena rental	182,000					
Skate equipment	428,000					
Accumulated depreciation, skate equipment		$ 164,000				
Accounts payable		5,400				
Unearned training revenue		19,600				
Notes payable		160,000				
Ben Gibson, capital		451,400				
Ben Gibson, withdrawals	72,000					
Training revenue		550,000				
Salaries expense	350,000					
Arena rental expense	168,000					
Other expenses	7,600					
Totals	$1,350,400	$1,350,400				

Additional information available at year-end:

a. The Prepaid Arena Rental of $182,000 was paid on February 1, 2020. It represents seven months of rent on the arena.

b. A count of the Repair Supplies at year-end revealed that $1,900 had been used.

c. Annual depreciation of the skate equipment was $82,000.

d. A review of the Unearned Training Revenue account at year-end showed that included in the balance was $12,600 that had not yet been earned.

e. Accrued salaries of $58,000 had not been recorded at year-end.

f. Interest of $1,800 had accrued regarding the Notes Payable.

g. On June 5, 2020, cash of $92,000 was received for 2020/2021 training sessions (lessons begin in October). This amount is included in the Training Revenue balance.

Required Prepare the annual adjusting entries on June 30, 2020, for each of (a) through (g) above.

Problem 3-12B Preparation of financial statements LO6, 7 e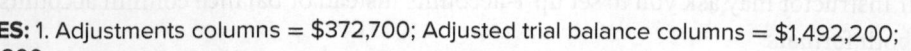cel

CHECK FIGURES: 1. Adjustments columns = $372,700; Adjusted trial balance columns = $1,492,200;
2. Loss = $334,300

Required

1. Using the format presented in Problem 3-11B, complete the adjusted trial balance by including the adjusting entries prepared in Problem 3-11B.

2. Prepare an income statement, a statement of changes in equity, and a balance sheet based on the adjusted trial balance completed in Part 1. Assume that the owner, Ben Gibson, made an investment during the year of $20,000.

Analysis Component: Assume that total liabilities reported at June 30, 2019, were $90,000. Determine what equity and total assets were on that date and comment on the change in the financial position from 2019 to 2020.

Problem 3-13B Preparing financial statements from the adjusted trial balance (month-end) LO7

CHECK FIGURES: 1. Loss = $80,900; 3. Total assets = $273,925

This alphabetized adjusted trial balance is for Mad Catz Courier as of its December 31, 2020, month-end:

	Debit	Credit
Accounts payable..		$ 37,000
Accounts receivable.......................................	$ 25,000	
Accumulated depreciation, equipment........		95,000
Accumulated depreciation, trucks...............		24,000
Advertising expense......................................	9,800	
Cash...	14,000	
Delivery revenue		190,000
Depreciation expense, equipment...............	23,000	
Depreciation expense, trucks.......................	12,000	
Equipment..	130,000	
Interest income..		250
Interest expense..	650	
Interest payable...		325
Interest receivable	125	
Land...	60,000	
Long-term notes payable..............................		100,000
Madison Catz, capital....................................		152,500
Madison Catz, withdrawals...........................	5,000	
Notes receivable (due in 90 days)................	100,000	
Office supplies	1,800	
Office supplies expense................................	5,400	
Repairs expense..	17,300	
Salaries expense...	41,000	
Salaries payable		15,000
Trucks..	62,000	
Unearned delivery revenue...........................		55,000
Wages expense	162,000	
Totals..	$669,075	$669,075

Required Use the information in the trial balance to prepare:

1. The income statement for the month ended December 31, 2020.

2. The statement of changes in equity for the month ended December 31, 2020, assuming the owner invested $127,000 during December.

3. The balance sheet as of December 31, 2020.

Problem 3-14B Journalizing, posting, adjusted trial balance, adjusting entries (monthly), financial statements (quarterly) LO4, 5, 6, 7

CHECK FIGURES: 3. Cash balance, July 31, 2020 = $3,400; 4. Dr. = $45,820; 6. Dr. = $50,100; 7. Profit = $7,550

On July 1, 2020, Melanie Thornhill began her third month of operating an electronics repair shop called MT Repairs out of her dad's garage. The following occurred during the third month of operations:

July	1	Collected $3,600 as a deposit for work to be done at the local college in the fall.
	1	Melanie Thornhill withdrew $4,000 cash for personal expenses.
	2	Paid $2,200 for repair supplies purchased on account last month.
	3	Did work for a client and immediately collected $1,400.
	4	Performed services for a customer and collected $3,600.
	7	Hired a new technician to start next week on a casual basis at $400 per day.
	15	Melanie withdrew cash of $1,000 for personal use.
	22	Purchased repair supplies for cash; $1,600.
	31	Paid wages of $2,800.

Required

1. Prepare general journal entries to record the July transactions.

2. Set up the following T-accounts with June 30 adjusted balances: Cash (101), $6,400; Repair Supplies (131), $3,000; Tools (161), $16,800; Accumulated Depreciation, Tools (162), $560; Accounts Payable (201), $3,200; Unearned Revenue (233), $700; Melanie Thornhill, Capital (301) $?; Melanie Thornhill, Withdrawals (302), $0; Revenue (401), $25,800; Depreciation Expense, Tools (602), $560; Wages Expense (623), $1,960; Rent Expense (640), $8,000; and Repair Supplies Expense (696), $2,700.

3. Post the entries to the accounts; calculate the ending balance in each account.

4. Prepare an unadjusted trial balance at July 31, 2020.

5. Use the following information to prepare and post adjusting entries for the month of July:

   a. The tools have an estimated life of five years with no residual value.

   b. One-quarter of the repair supplies balance remained on hand at July 31.

   c. Accrued the July rent expense of $4,000; it will be paid in August.

   d. $3,800 of the unearned revenues remained unearned as at July 31.

6. Prepare an adjusted trial balance.

7. Prepare an income statement and a statement of changes in equity for the three months ended July 31, 2020, and a July 31, 2020 balance sheet.

Analysis Component: When a company shows expenses on its income statement, does this mean that cash equal to the expenses was paid during the period in which the expenses were reported?

*Problem 3-15B Correcting entries LO8

As the accountant for Jasper's Telemarketing Services, you discovered the following errors in the May 31 unadjusted trial balance that require correction:

a. Advertising Expense was debited and Accounts Receivable was credited on May 17 for $16,200 of repairs paid for by Jasper's.

b. On May 18, Computer Equipment was debited and Accounts Payable was credited, each for $8,100 regarding the purchase of office furniture in exchange for a promissory note.

c. On May 28, Cash was debited and Telemarketing Revenue was credited for $15,000 cash received in advance from a client.

d. The Telephone Expense account included $6,300 of delivery expense.

e. The Telemarketing Revenue account was credited for $1,200 of interest income.

Required Journalize the correcting entries required on May 31.

Analysis Component: The error in (e) shows that an incorrect revenue account was credited. Since the net effect on the financial statements is nil after recording the correction, is it necessary to prepare a correcting entry for this type of error?

*Problem 3-16B Recording prepaid expenses and unearned revenues LO9   eXcel

CHECK FIGURE: Adjusted trial balance, debits = $110,850

Rainbow Janitorial Services follows the approach of recording prepaid expenses as expenses and unearned revenues as revenues. Rainbow's unadjusted trial balance for the year ended October 31, 2020, follows.

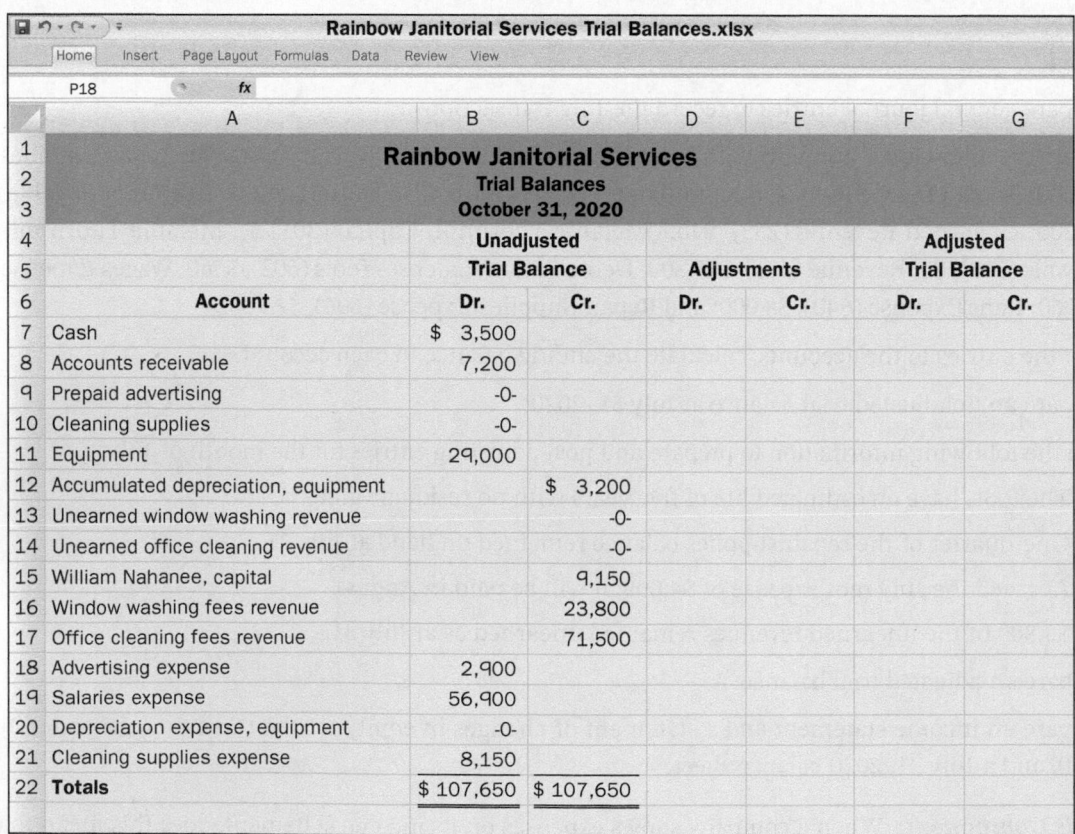

	Rainbow Janitorial Services Trial Balances.xlsx						
	Home Insert Page Layout Formulas Data Review View						
	P18 fx						
	A	B	C	D	E	F	G
1	**Rainbow Janitorial Services**						
2	Trial Balances						
3	October 31, 2020						
4		**Unadjusted**				**Adjusted**	
5		**Trial Balance**		**Adjustments**		**Trial Balance**	
6	**Account**	**Dr.**	**Cr.**	**Dr.**	**Cr.**	**Dr.**	**Cr.**
7	Cash	$ 3,500					
8	Accounts receivable	7,200					
9	Prepaid advertising	-0-					
10	Cleaning supplies	-0-					
11	Equipment	29,000					
12	Accumulated depreciation, equipment		$ 3,200				
13	Unearned window washing revenue		-0-				
14	Unearned office cleaning revenue		-0-				
15	William Nahanee, capital		9,150				
16	Window washing fees revenue		23,800				
17	Office cleaning fees revenue		71,500				
18	Advertising expense	2,900					
19	Salaries expense	56,900					
20	Depreciation expense, equipment	-0-					
21	Cleaning supplies expense	8,150					
22	**Totals**	**$ 107,650**	**$ 107,650**				

An asterisk (*) identifies assignment material based on Appendix 3A or Appendix 3B.

Additional information:

a. On October 31, a physical count revealed cleaning supplies on hand of $6,150.

b. Annual depreciation on the equipment is $3,200.

c. It was determined that $6,900 of the balance in Office Cleaning Revenue had not yet been earned as of October 31.

d. A review of the Window Washing Revenue account showed that only $21,400 had been earned as of October 31.

e. $1,500 of the total recorded in the Advertising Expense account had not yet been used.

Required Refer to Exhibit 3.22 and use the information provided to complete the columns above.

*Problem 3-17B Recording prepaid expenses and unearned revenues LO4, 9

The following occurred for a company during the last two months of its fiscal year ended May 31, 2020:

Apr.	1	Paid $7,200 for future consulting services.
	1	Paid $1,920 for insurance through March 31 of the following year.
	30	Received $7,500 for future services to be provided to a customer.
May	1	Paid $1,200 for future newspaper advertising.
	23	Received $9,200 for future services to be provided to a customer.
	31	Of the consulting services paid for on April 1, $5,000 worth had been received.
	31	Part of the insurance paid for on April 1 had expired.
	31	Services worth $7,200 had not yet been provided to the customer who paid on April 30.
	31	Of the advertising paid for on May 1, $340 worth had not been published yet.
	31	The company had performed $9,000 of the services that the customer had paid for on May 23.

Required

1. Prepare entries for April and May under the approach that records prepaid expenses and unearned revenues in balance sheet accounts. Also, prepare adjusting entries at the end of the year.

2. Prepare entries for April and May under the approach that records prepaid expenses and unearned revenues in income statement accounts. Also, prepare adjusting entries at the end of the year.

Analysis Component: Explain why the alternative sets of entries in requirements 1 and 2 do not result in different financial statement amounts.

ANALYTICAL AND REVIEW PROBLEM

A & R Problem 3-1

The Salaries Payable account of James Bay Company Limited appears below:

Salaries Payable			
		22,520	Bal. Jan. 1, 2020
Entries during 2020	398,120	388,400	Entries during 2020

The company records the salary expense and related liability at the end of each week and pays the employees on the last Friday of the month.

An asterisk (*) identifies assignment material based on Appendix 3A or Appendix 3B.

Required

1. What was the salary expense for 2020?

2. How much was paid to employees in 2020 for work done in 2019?

3. How much was paid to employees in 2020 for work done in 2020?

4. How much will be paid to employees in 2021 for work done in 2020?

ETHICS CHALLENGE

EC 3-1

Jackie Houston is a new accountant for Seitzer Company. She is learning on the job from Bob Welch, who has already worked several years for Seitzer. Jackie and Bob are preparing the year-end adjusting entries. Jackie has calculated that depreciation expense for the fiscal year should be recorded as:

Depreciation Expense, Equipment..............	123,546	
Accum. Dep., Equipment.......................		123,546

Bob is rechecking the numbers and says that he agrees with her computation. However, he says that the credit entry should be made directly to the Equipment account. He argues that while accumulated depreciation is taught in the classroom, "It is easier to ignore the contra account and just credit the Equipment account directly for the annual depreciation. Besides, the balance sheet shows the same amount for total assets under both methods."

Required

1. How should depreciation be recorded? Do you support Jackie or Bob?

2. Evaluate the strengths and weaknesses of Bob's reasons for preferring his method.

3. Indicate whether the situation faced by Jackie is an ethical problem.

FOCUS ON FINANCIAL STATEMENTS

FFS 3-1 e**X**cel

You have been given the following information for RPE Consulting for the year ended July 31, 2020.

	A	B	C	D	E	F	G

RPE Consulting Trial Balances.xlsx

Home Insert Page Layout Formulas Data Review View

P18 fx

	A	B	C	D	E	F	G
1		**RPE Consulting**					
2		Trial Balances					
3		July 31, 2020					
4		Unadjusted				Adjusted	
5		Trial Balance		Adjustments		Trial Balance	
6	**Account**	Dr.	Cr.	Dr.	Cr.	Dr.	Cr.
7	Accounts payable		$ 9,300				$ 10,200
8	Accounts receivable	$ 12,000				$ 22,460	
9	Accumulated depreciation, office equipment		12,000				18,000
10	Advertising expense	13,800				14,700	
11	Cash	27,000				27,000	
12	Consulting revenue		156,000				168,160
13	Depreciation expense, office equipment	-0-				6,000	
14	Insurance expense	-0-				2,440	
15	Interest expense	1,400				2,200	
16	Interest payable		-0-				800
17	Notes payable		44,000				44,000
18	Office equipment	92,000				92,000	
19	Office supplies	18,000				3,000	
20	Office supplies expense	-0-				15,000	
21	Prepaid insurance	7,320				4,880	
22	Ray Edds, capital		28,420				28,420
23	Ray Edds, withdrawals	10,000				10,000	
24	Rent expense	13,200				13,200	
25	Salaries expense	71,000				77,600	
26	Salaries payable		-0-				6,600
27	Unearned consulting revenue		16,000				14,300
28	**Totals**	$ 265,720	$ 265,720			$ 290,480	$ 290,480

Required

1. Prepare the company's income statement, statement of changes in equity, and balance sheet. Assume that the owner, Ray Edds, invested $20,000 during the year ended July 31, 2020.

Analysis Component:

2. Analyze the unadjusted and adjusted trial balances and identify the adjustments that must have been made by inserting them in the two middle columns. Label each entry with a letter.

3. If the adjustments had not been recorded, identify the net overstatement/understatement of each component of the accounting equation.

FFS 3-2

Part 1

Refer to WestJet's income statement in Appendix III at the end of the textbook.

a. Prepare two possible adjusting entries that would have caused 2017 guest revenues to increase.

b. Prepare two possible adjusting entries that would have caused 2017 aircraft fuel expenses to increase.

Part 2

Refer to WestJet's balance sheet in Appendix III at the end of the textbook.

c. Prepare a possible adjusting entry that could have caused the December 31, 2017, balance in Prepaid expenses, deposits, and other to decrease.

d. Prepare a possible adjusting entry that could have caused the December 31, 2017, balance in Accounts payable and accrued liabilities to increase.

CRITICAL THINKING MINI CASE

It's a week before **Frogbox**'s October 31, 2020, year-end. You are the personnel director and are reviewing some financial information regarding the March 1, 2018, purchase of office furniture for the Western Region offices totalling $700,000 ($300,000 was paid in cash and the balance was financed over four years at 4% annual interest with annual principal payments of $100,000). The useful life of the furniture was estimated to be five years with a projected resale value at that time of $20,000. Insurance was purchased on the furniture at a cost of $8,000 annually, payable each March 1. You leave the office for the day wondering what needs to be considered regarding these items in preparation for year-end.

Required

1. Identify the relevant facts.

2. Describe what principles need to be considered.

3. Outline the goal of financial reporting.

4. Recommend an appropriate accounting policy and describe the impact to the year-end financial statements.

CUMULATIVE COMPREHENSION PROBLEM: ECHO SYSTEMS

(This comprehensive problem was introduced in Chapter 2 and continues in Chapters 4 and 5. If the Chapter 2 segment has not been completed, the assignment can begin at this point. You need to use the facts presented in Chapter 2. Because of its length, this problem is most easily solved if you use the Working Papers[11] that accompany this book.)

After the success of its first two months, Mary Graham has decided to continue operating Echo Systems. (The transactions that occurred in these months are described in Chapter 2.) Before proceeding in December, Graham adds these new accounts to the chart of accounts for the ledger:

Account	No.
Accumulated Depreciation, Office Equipment................................	164
Accumulated Depreciation, Computer Equipment	168
Wages Payable	210
Unearned Computer Services Revenue	236
Depreciation Expense, Office Equipment......................................	612
Depreciation Expense, Computer Equipment...............................	613
Insurance Expense	637
Rent Expense	640
Computer Supplies Expense...	652

Required

1. Prepare journal entries to record each of the following transactions for Echo Systems. Post the entries to the accounts in the ledger.

Dec.	3	Paid $2,100 to the Lakeshore Mall for the company's share of mall advertising costs.
	3	Paid $1,200 to repair the company's computer.
	4	Received $7,500 from Alamo Engineering Co. for the receivable from the prior month.
	10	Paid Carly Smith for six days' work at the rate of $200 per day.
	14	Notified by Alamo Engineering Co. that Echo's bid of $12,000 on a proposed project was accepted. Alamo paid an advance of $3,000.
	17	Purchased $2,310 of computer supplies on credit from Abbott Office Products.
	18	Sent a reminder to Fostek Co. to pay the fee for services originally recorded on November 8.
	20	Completed a project for Elite Corporation and received $11,250 cash.
	24–28	Took the week off for the holidays.
	31	Received $5,700 from Fostek Co. on its receivable.
	31	Reimbursed Mary Graham's business automobile expenses of 600 kilometres at $1.00 per kilometre.*
	31	Graham withdrew $3,600 cash from the business.

2. Prepare adjusting entries to record the following additional information collected on December 31, 2020. Post the entries to the accounts in the ledger.

   a. The December 31 inventory of computer supplies was $1,440.

   b. Three months have passed since the annual insurance premium was paid.

   c. As of the end of the year, Carly Smith has not been paid for four days of work at the rate of $200 per day.

   d. The computer is expected to have a four-year life with no residual value.

   e. The office equipment is expected to have a three-year life with no residual value.

   f. Prepaid rent for three of the four months has expired.

3. Prepare an adjusted trial balance as of December 31, 2020.

4. Prepare an income statement and statement of changes in equity for the three months ended December 31, 2020.

5. Prepare a balance sheet as of December 31, 2020.

Completing the Accounting Cycle and Classifying Accounts

A Look Back

Chapter 3 explained the timing of reports. We described why adjusting accounts is key for recognizing revenues and expenses in the proper period. We prepared an adjusted trial balance and used it to prepare financial statements.

A Look at This Chapter

This chapter emphasizes the final steps in the accounting process and reviews the entire accounting cycle. We explain the closing process, including accounting procedures and the use of a post-closing trial balance. We show how a work sheet aids in preparing financial statements.

Source: Courtesy of Heather White and Lori Joyce, Cupcakes

LEARNING OBJECTIVES

LO1	Describe and prepare a work sheet and explain its usefulness.
LO2	Describe the closing process and explain why temporary accounts are closed each period.
LO3	Prepare closing entries.
LO4	Explain and prepare a post-closing trial balance.
LO5	Complete the steps in the accounting cycle.

LO6 Explain and prepare a classified balance sheet.

LO7 Calculate the current ratio and debt to equity ratios, and describe what they reveal about a company's financial condition.

*Appendix 4A

LO8 Prepare reversing entries and explain their purpose.

Sweet Dreams

Heather White and Lori Joyce met when they were only 15 years old working in retail in Victoria, BC, and the two often dreamed of the day when they would start a business together. After high school they parted ways, but kept in touch and reconnected in 2001 when they found themselves working together selling an industrial product in New York City (NYC). They were working at Ground Zero a couple of weeks after the terrorist attack on the World Trade Center, witnessing the massive cleanup efforts, including the sombre retrieval of bodies from the wreckage. According to Lori, at that time "the hustle and bustle of the City was gone, the City was eerie and silent, people slowed down and were kind, opening doors for each other." To get a break from the intensity Lori took Heather to her favourite bakery in the city, Magnolia, which was located in the heart of NYC. Over delicious cupcakes, Heather dreamed up their next initiative, a trendy cupcake shop.

Three months later, the friends were jogging in Vancouver's popular West End on Denman Street when Lori had an epiphany as they came upon an empty shop that appeared to be the perfect location for the bakery they had imagined that afternoon in NYC. Heather and Lori saw this as the perfect time in their lives to take action and pursue their dream of running their own company. They wanted their company to be "fresh, fun and a reminder of simpler and innocent times." Without any previous experience in food services or baking, in April 2002 the dynamic duo took a leap of faith and co-founded their first urban bakery—Cupcakes.

Heather and Lori have proven creativity and an acute business sense can be successfully combined. They meet customer demand through maximizing usage of their bakeries with a focus on wholesome, fresh ingredients and a commitment to quality, and by presenting themselves as a "sweet escape" from the everyday. By focusing on maximizing each other's strengths and building the brand reputation of their business, Cupcakes has had an incredible 16 years.

Their fresh approach to business and willingness to share their experiences has been highlighted by their own reality series on W, We TV, and the Oprah Network (OWN)—which has sold to 95 countries worldwide—called *The Cupcake Girls.* Throughout the episodes they openly expose their business experiences via behind-the-scenes views of the challenges of executing their strategy with time constraints and real-world mishaps. Lori recently embraced a philosophy from the Canadian owner of Boston Pizza and *Dragons' Den* investor Jim Treliving. In his book *Decisions* he advises people to "make decisions about work with their heart, decisions about money with their head and decisions about people with their gut."

Understanding the importance of paying attention to a balance of customer needs and profitability, they have found that in order for business to be successful, "Financials need to be organized and relevant—it is essential that they are up to date and current to make appropriate decisions. It is important to be able to understand an income statement and a balance sheet." Lori encourages future business leaders: "Once you understand the language of accounting it is less intimidating, and you can leverage that and turn it into power. Knowledge is power. Reading monthly P&Ls put us in control of the business. For any business decision first the numbers have to make sense, then go beyond the numbers, as many other variables need to be considered—even factors such as culture of the location, luck and timing can drive the success of a store."

In 2017, Cupcakes underwent a branding rejuvenation, from "Cupcakes by Heather & Lori" to "Cupcakes & Other Good Stuff," to expand their portfolio into other sweet desires such as cookies, cakes, ice creams, and coffee drinks. Heather has moved with her family out of the Vancouver area. Lori has hired a CEO to run Cupcakes and manage the day-to-day operations of the franchisees and their eight locations in the Vancouver area with an additional location on

(Continued)

Vancouver Island. Lori maintains her commitment to the brand's reputation as the president and owner of the company, but for now is focusing her attention on her new start-up—Betterwith Foods. Her advice to future entrepreneurs: "If you trust your gut and you trust you're disciplined to put in the required effort to make your business succeed, take the leap. Trust your gut instinct! You can't be risk averse to be an entrepreneur."

Sources: http://cupcakesonline.com; interview with Lori Joyce, January 23, 2018.

Video Link: Find Season 1 of *The Cupcake Girls* at https://www.youtube.com/playlist?list=PLesO1cn-vYHeDy7Nr19XlDV4fCyBfZpgr.

CRITICAL THINKING CHALLENGE

What type of external users might Cupcakes have for its financial statements? If your job was to review bank loan applications for a bank, what financial statement information would you examine (and why) if Cupcakes submitted a loan application to open a new bakery to supply their stores?

CHAPTER PREVIEW

Student Success *Cycle*

Read the material

Apply your critical thinking skills

Do the exercises

Check your answers

Many of the important steps leading to financial statements were explained in earlier chapters. We described how transactions and events are analyzed, journalized, and posted. This chapter begins with an introduction to the work sheet, which is a useful tool for these final steps and in preparing financial statements. Steps 8 and 9 of the accounting cycle are now demonstrated. Steps 8 and 9 (see Exhibit 4.1) involve the closing process that prepares revenue, expense, and withdrawal accounts for the next reporting period and updates the capital account. It also explains how accounts are classified on a balance sheet to increase their usefulness to decision makers. These tools for managing data are the kind used by Lori Joyce of Cupcakes (in the chapter-opening vignette) to make important decisions such as whether to expand their franchise into new markets or to consider hiring a new store manager.

Completing the Accounting Cycle

Work Sheet

- Benefits of a work sheet
- Use of a work sheet

Closing Process

- Temporary and permanent accounts
- Closing entries
- Post-closing trial balance

Accounting Cycle

- Definition of accounting cycle
- Review of accounting cycle

EXHIBIT 4.1

Steps in the Accounting Cycle Introduced in Chapter 4

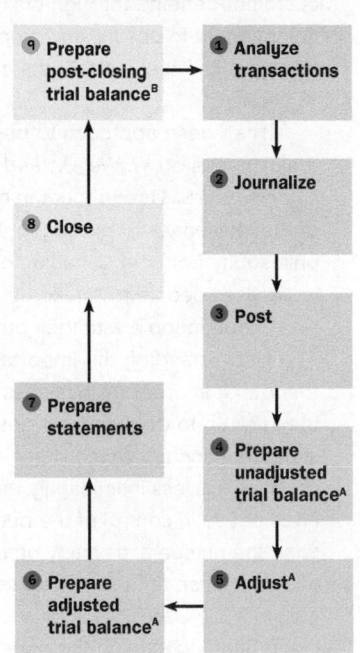

⁹ Prepare post-closing trial balance[B]

① Analyze transactions

② Journalize

⑧ Close

③ Post

⑦ Prepare statements

④ Prepare unadjusted trial balance[A]

⑥ Prepare adjusted trial balance[A]

⑤ Adjust[A]

[A]Steps 4, 5, and 6 can be done on a *work sheet*.
[B]*Reversing entries* are optional and, if prepared, are done between Steps 9 and 1. Reversing entries are covered in Appendix 4A.

Classified Balance Sheet

- Classification structure
- Classification categories

Work Sheet as a Tool

LO1 Describe and prepare a work sheet and explain its usefulness.

When compiling the financial statements, accountants prepare several reports and informal documents to help them understand, summarize, and evaluate the numbers presented. These informal documents, called **working papers**, are important tools for accountants to ensure the financial statements are appropriately presented. The **work sheet** is an *optional* working paper that can simplify the accountant's efforts in preparing financial statements. It is an internal document that is not generally distributed to decision makers. The work sheet gathers information about the accounts, the needed adjustments, and the financial statements. When it is finished, the work sheet contains information that is recorded in the journal and then presented in the statements.

BENEFITS OF A WORK SHEET (SPREADSHEET)

Computerized accounting systems prepare financial statements without the need for a work sheet. Yet there are several potential benefits to using a manual or electronic work sheet:

1. It is useful in preparing interim (monthly or quarterly) financial statements when journalizing and posting adjusting entries are postponed until the year-end.

2. It captures the entire accounting process, linking economic transactions to their effects in financial statements.

3. Auditors of financial statements often use a work sheet for planning and organizing the audit. It can also be used to reflect any additional adjustments necessary as a result of the audit.

4. It helps preparers to avoid errors when working with a lot of information in accounting systems involving many accounts and adjustments.

⚖ DECISION INSIGHT

Benefits of Spreadsheets to Produce Work Sheets

Electronic work sheets using spreadsheet software such as Excel make it easy to change numbers, assess the impact of alternative strategies, and prepare financial statements quickly and at less cost. This can also increase the time available for analysis and interpretation. Several of the end-of-chapter exercises and problems include the symbol shown here, which means that an Excel template is available to help in the preparation of a solution.

EXHIBIT 4.2

Preparing the Work Sheet at the End of the Accounting Period

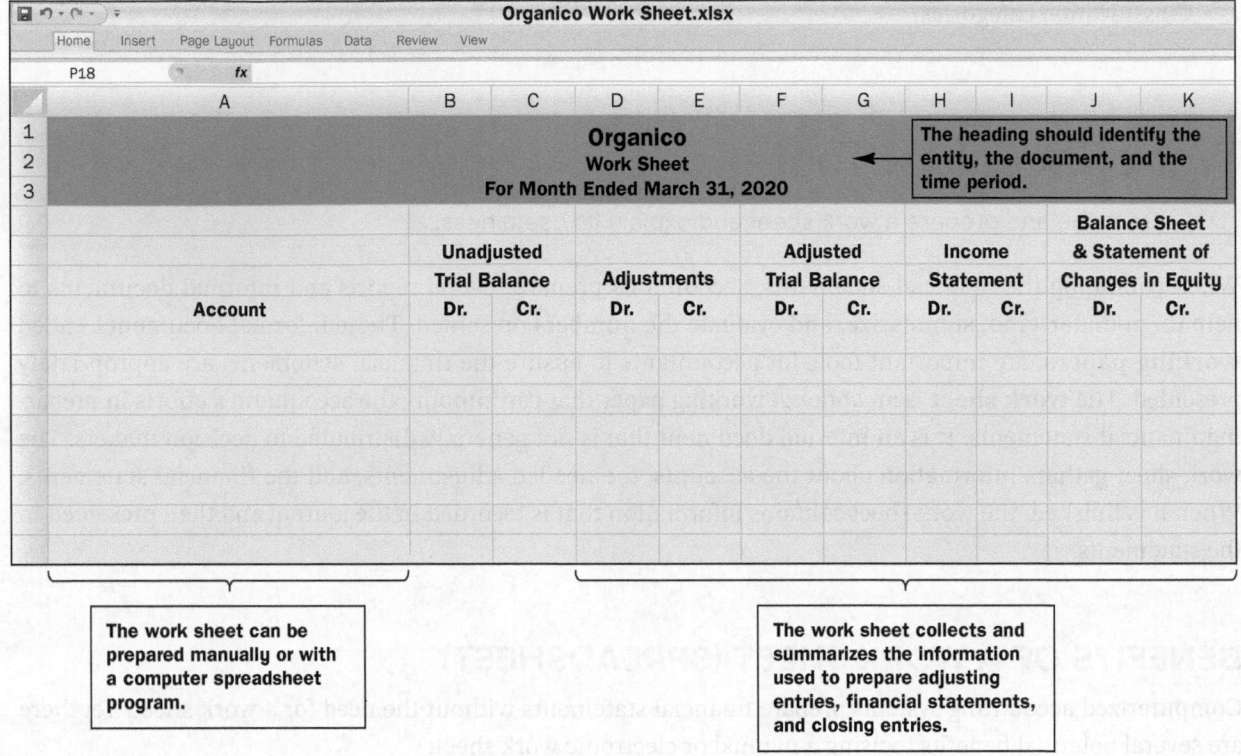

USING A WORK SHEET

Exhibit 4.2 shows a blank work sheet. Notice that it has five sets of double columns for the:

> 1. Unadjusted trial balance.
>
> 2. Adjustments.
>
> 3. Adjusted trial balance.
>
> 4. Income statement.
>
> 5. Balance sheet and statement of changes in equity.

The purpose of double columns is to accommodate both debits and credits. Because the statement of changes in equity includes only a few items, they are simply listed with the balance sheet items.

The work sheet can be completed by following five steps.

Enter Unadjusted Trial Balance

Step 1 requires us to list the number and title of each account from the ledger along with the account's unadjusted debit or credit balance, as shown in Exhibit 4.3.[1] We use the financial information of Organico to demonstrate the function of the work sheet.

---

1 In practice, accounts with a zero balance that are likely to require an adjusting entry would also be listed.

EXHIBIT 4.3
Work Sheet

Note: The steps for completing a work sheet are colour coded and correspond to the described steps.

ORGANICO

Organico Work Sheet.xlsx

Home | Insert | Page Layout | Formulas | Data | Review | View

P18 | fx

Organico
Work Sheet
For Month Ended March 31, 2020

	Account	Unadjusted Trial Balance Dr.	Cr.	Adjustments Dr.	Cr.	Adjusted Trial Balance Dr.	Cr.	Income Statement Dr.	Cr.	Balance Sheet & Statement of Changes in Equity Dr.	Cr.
101	Cash	8,070				8,070				8,070	
125	Supplies	3,600			b) 1,050	2,550				2,550	
128	Prepaid insurance	2,400			a) 100	2,300				2,300	
167	Equipment	6,000				6,000				6,000	
168	Accumulated depreciation, equipment				c) 200		200				200
201	Accounts payable		200				200				200
236	Unearned food services revenue		3,000	d) 250			2,750				2,750
240	Notes payable		6,000				6,000				6,000
301	Hailey Walker, capital		10,000				10,000				10,000
302	Hailey Walker, withdrawals	600				600				600	
					d) 250						
403	Food services revenue		3,800		g) 1,800		5,850		5,850		
406	Teaching revenue		300				300		300		
622	Salaries expense	1,400		f) 140		1,540		1,540			
641	Rent expense	1,000				1,000		1,000			
690	Utilities expense	230				230		230			
	Totals	23,300	23,300								
637	Insurance expense			a) 100		100		100			
651	Supplies expense			b) 1,050		1,050		1,050			
614	Depreciation expense, equipment			c) 200		200		200			
209	Salaries payable				f) 140		140				140
633	Interest expense			e) 35		35		35			
203	Interest payable				e) 35		35				35
106	Accounts receivable			g) 1,800		1,800				1,800	
	Totals			3,575	3,575	25,475	25,475	4,155	6,150	21,320	19,325
	Profit							1,995			1,995
	Totals							6,150	6,150	21,320	21,320

③

① When entering the unadjusted trial balances, include all accounts that have balances or that are expected to have balances after adjustments.

② Adjustments may create the need for additional accounts. Add new accounts to the existing list as required.

Add two new lines for the profit (or loss) and the totals.

These two columns must show equal totals.

Enter the drafts of the adjusting entries and find the total debits and credits.

These two columns must show equal totals.

Sum the unadjusted trial balance accounts with the adjustments, and enter them in the adjusted trial balance.

These two columns must show equal totals.

Extend revenues and expenses from the adjusted trial balance columns to these columns.

The totals are not equal because the debit and the credit balances in the revenue and expense accounts are not equal.

Extend assets, liabilities, and the owner's capital and withdrawals from the adjusted trial balance columns to these columns.

The totals are not equal because the profit component of equity is missing.

④

⑤

Enter the profit amount as the difference between the debits and the credits in the income statement columns.

Also enter the profit amount in the credit column to include in equity the change caused by net income.

Enter Adjustments

Step 2 begins with the entry of adjustments in the adjustments columns. The adjustments shown in Exhibit 4.3 are the same as those discussed in Chapter 3. They are as follows:

 a. Expiration of $100 of prepaid insurance.

 b. Used $1,050 of supplies.

 c. Depreciation on equipment of $200.

 d. Earned $250 of revenue received in advance.

 e. Accrued interest of $35 on the note payable.

 f. Accrued $140 of salaries owed to an employee.

 g. Accrued $1,800 of revenue owed by a customer.

To help you correctly match the debit and credit of each adjusting entry, notice that an identifying letter is used for each adjustment. In entering adjustments, we sometimes find additional accounts that need to be inserted on the work sheet. Additional accounts are inserted below the initial list. ***After entering adjustments on a work sheet, we still must enter adjusting entries in the journal and post them to the ledger.***

Prepare Adjusted Trial Balance

Step 3 prepares the adjusted trial balance by combining the adjustments with the unadjusted balances for each account. As an example, in Exhibit 4.3, the Supplies account has a $3,600 debit balance in the Unadjusted Trial Balance columns. This $3,600 debit is combined with the $1,050 credit in the Adjustments columns to give Supplies a $2,550 debit in the Adjusted Trial Balance columns. The totals of the Adjusted Trial Balance columns confirm the equality of debits and credits.

Extend Adjusted Trial Balance Amounts to Financial Statement Columns

Step 4 involves sorting adjusted amounts to their proper financial statement columns. Expense items go to the Income Statement Debit column, and revenues to the Income Statement Credit column. Assets and withdrawals go to the Balance Sheet and Statement of Changes in Equity Debit column. Liabilities and owner's capital go to the Balance Sheet and Statement of Changes in Equity Credit column. At this point it is essential that you know your account titles and to which financial statement each account belongs. These concepts were covered in Chapter 1. Each statement column is totalled. Notice in Exhibit 4.3 that for this step the debits do not equal the credits (explained in Step 5).

Enter Profit (or Loss) and Balance the Financial Statement Columns

Step 5 calculates the difference between the Debit and Credit totals of the Income Statement columns to determine the profit or loss. If the Credit total exceeds the Debit total, there is a profit. If the Debit total exceeds the Credit total, there is a loss. In Exhibit 4.3, Organico's work sheet shows the Credit total to exceed the Debit total, resulting in profit of $1,995. The difference is added to the *Income Statement* and *Balance Sheet & Statement of Changes in Equity* columns for balancing. In the case of Organico where a profit of $1,995 has been calculated, the $1,995 is listed as a *debit* in the Income Statement columns. It is also listed in the Balance Sheet & Statement of Changes in Equity columns, but as a *credit*.

The *new totals* are entered for both sets of columns, showing that the Income Statement columns and Balance Sheet & Statement of Changes in Equity columns now *balance*. If they do not balance, an error has occurred in the completion of the work sheet.[2] The term *profit* (or *loss*) is listed in the Account column to label the $1,995. Adding profit to the last Credit column implies that it is to be added to owner's capital. If a loss occurs, it is listed in the last Debit column, implying that it is to be subtracted from owner's capital.

Prepare Financial Statements Using a Work Sheet

In *Step 6* the completed work sheet is used to prepare the financial statements. It is important to note that a work sheet is not a substitute for financial statements, it is a tool to help us prepare the financial statements.

Calculate the ending balance of owner's capital, as it does not appear in the last two columns as a single amount.

> Owner's capital = Owner's capital account balance + profit (or minus loss) − Withdrawals account balance

The opening capital balance for the period used for the Statement of Changes in Equity can be calculated by subtracting any owner investments made during the period from the owner's capital account balance, as shown in the last credit column on the work sheet. Exhibit 4.4 shows the statements for Organico as prepared from the work sheet.[3]

DECISION MAKER

Answer—End of chapter

Analyzing Results

You own a vitamin manufacturing business that customizes vitamin and supplement plans for individuals. You prepare a printout of the electronic work sheet used to prepare financial statements. There is no depreciation adjustment, yet the business owns a large amount of expensive manufacturing equipment. Does the absence of a depreciation adjustment concern you?

CHECKPOINT

1. Where do we get the amounts entered in the Unadjusted Trial Balance columns of a work sheet?
2. What are the advantages of using a work sheet to prepare adjusting entries?
3. What are the benefits of a work sheet?

Do Quick Study questions: QS 4-1, QS 4-2, QS 4-3, QS 4-4

---

2 If the columns balance, an error(s) could still be present. For example, the columns would still balance if Accounts Payable were listed as a credit, but in the Income Statement columns. Profit would be incorrect, but the columns would still balance.

3 Notice that the $21,320 balance of the last two columns in the work sheet in Exhibit 4.3 does not agree with the balance of $20,520 on the balance sheet; there is a difference of $800 (= $21,320 − $20,520). *This is not an error!* Notice that accumulated depreciation of $200 is subtracted on the balance sheet to arrive at total assets; it is *added* in the last Credit column on the work sheet. Also, withdrawals of $600 are *subtracted* on the statement of changes in equity to arrive at ending capital; on the work sheet, they are *added* in the last Debit column. These two items account for the difference of $800 (= $200 + $600).

EXHIBIT 4.4

Step 6—Prepare Financial Statements Using a Work Sheet

Organico Income Statement For Month Ended March 31, 2020		
Revenues:		
Food Services revenue	$5,850	
Teaching revenue	300	
Total revenues		$6,150
Operating expenses:		
Salaries expense	$1,540	
Supplies expense	1,050	
Rent expense	1,000	
Utilities expense	230	
Depreciation expense, equipment	200	
Insurance expense	100	
Interest expense	35	
Total operating expenses		4,155
Profit		$1,995

Organico Statement of Changes in Equity For Month Ended March 31, 2020		
Hailey Walker, capital, March 1		$ -0-
Investments by owner	$10,000	
Profit	1,995	11,995
Total		$11,995
Less: Withdrawals by owner		600
Hailey Walker, capital, March 31		$11,395

Organico Balance Sheet March 31, 2020		
Assets		
Cash		$ 8,070
Accounts receivable		1,800
Supplies		2,550
Prepaid insurance		2,300
Equipment	$6,000	
Less: Accumulated depreciation	200	5,800
Total assets		$20,520
Liabilities		
Accounts payable	$ 200	
Interest payable	35	
Salaries payable	70	
Unearned food services revenue	2,750	
Notes payable	6,000	
Total liabilities		$ 9,125
Equity		
Hailey Walker, capital		11,395
Total liabilities and equity		$20,520

Closing Process

LO2 Describe the closing process and explain why temporary accounts are closed each period.

The **closing process** is an important step of the accounting cycle that is performed at the end of an accounting period after financial statements are prepared. The purpose of this essential step is to prepare accounts for recording transactions in the next accounting period. Accounting software automatically performs this step; however, it is important for us to understand the process.

An income statement aims to report revenues earned and expenses incurred during one accounting period. We know that the profit (or loss) from the income statement is shown on the statement of changes in equity, along with withdrawals, to show the change caused to the owner's capital account during one period. Because revenues, expenses, and withdrawals are a part of equity, their balances need to be transferred to the owner's capital account at the end of the period. This transfer of account balances is accomplished by using **closing entries**.

Therefore, closing entries are a necessary step because we want the:

1. Revenue, expense, and withdrawals accounts to begin with zero balances to measure the results from the period just ending.

2. Owner's capital account to reflect:

   a. Increases from profit (or decreases from losses), and

   b. Decreases from withdrawals from the period just ending.

In the closing process, we must:

1. Identify accounts for closing,

2. Record and post the closing entries, and

3. Prepare the post-closing trial balance.

IDENTIFY ACCOUNTS FOR CLOSING— TEMPORARY AND PERMANENT ACCOUNTS

Temporary accounts accumulate data related to one accounting period. They include all income statement accounts, withdrawals accounts, and the *Income Summary account.* They are temporary because the accounts are opened at the beginning of a period, used to record transactions for that period, and then closed at the end of the period by transferring their balances to the owner's capital account. They are *temporary* because the accounts describe transactions or changes that have occurred rather than the financial position that exists at the end of the period.

Important Tip:

Only temporary accounts are closed, resulting in a reset to zero for the next accounting period. Permanent account balances carry into the next accounting period.

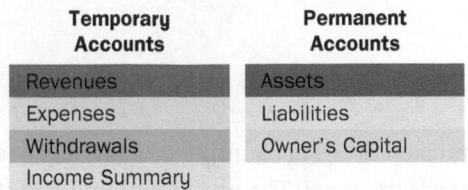

Temporary Accounts	Permanent Accounts
Revenues	Assets
Expenses	Liabilities
Withdrawals	Owner's Capital
Income Summary	

Permanent accounts report on transactions related to one or more future accounting periods. They carry their ending balances into the next period, and include all balance sheet accounts. *Asset, liability, and owner's capital accounts are not closed* as long as a company continues to own the assets, owe the liabilities, and have equity. They are permanent because they reflect the existing financial position.

RECORDING AND POSTING CLOSING ENTRIES

LO3 Prepare closing entries.

Recording and posting closing entries transfers the end-of-period balances in the revenue, expense, and withdrawals to the permanent owner's capital account.

To close revenue and expense accounts, we transfer their balances first to an account called *income summary*. **Income summary** is a temporary account that contains a credit for the sum of all revenues and a debit for the sum of all expenses. Its balance equals profit or loss, and is transferred to the owner's capital account. Next, we transfer the withdrawals account balance to the owner's capital account. After these closing entries are posted, the revenue, expense, income summary, and withdrawals accounts have zero balances. These accounts are then said to be closed or cleared. The four-step closing process is illustrated in Exhibit 4.5.

Organico's adjusted trial balance on March 31, 2020, is shown in Exhibit 4.6. Exhibit 4.7 shows the four closing entries necessary to close Organico's revenue, expense, income summary, and withdrawals accounts. We explain each of these four entries.

Entry 1: **Close Temporary Accounts with Credit Balances to Income Summary**

The first closing entry in Exhibit 4.7 transfers credit balances in revenue accounts to the Income Summary account. We get accounts with credit balances to zero by debiting them as shown in Exhibit 4.8. This prepares

EXHIBIT 4.5

Closing Process for a Proprietorship

Four-Step Closing Process

① Close temporary accounts with credit balances to income summary account.

② Close temporary accounts with debit balances to income summary account.

③ Close Income Summary account to Owner's Capital account.

④ Close Withdrawals account to Owner's Capital account.

EXHIBIT 4.6
Adjusted Trial Balance

Organico Adjusted Trial Balance March 31, 2020		
	Debit	**Credit**
Cash..	$ 8,070	
Accounts receivable..	1,800	
Supplies...	2,550	
Prepaid insurance..	2,300	
Equipment...	6,000	
Accumulated depreciation, equipment..		$ 200
Accounts payable		200
Interest payable..		35
Notes payable..		6,000
Salaries payable..		140
Unearned food services revenue...		2,750
Hailey Walker, capital..		10,000
Hailey Walker, withdrawals...	600	
Food services revenue...		5,850
Teaching revenue		300
Depreciation expense, equipment..	200	
Salaries expense...	1,540	
Interest expense	35	
Insurance expense	100	
Rent expense	1,000	
Supplies expense	1,050	
Utilities expense...	230	
Totals..	$25,475	$25,475

each account to record new revenues for the next period. The Income Summary account is created and used only for the closing process. The $6,150 total credit balance in Income Summary equals the total revenues for the year.

Entry 2: **Close Temporary Accounts with Debit Balances to Income Summary**

The second closing entry in Exhibit 4.7 transfers debit balances in expense accounts to the Income Summary account. We get the debit balances in the expense accounts to zero by crediting them as shown in Exhibit 4.8. This prepares each account for expense entries for the next period. The entry makes the balance of income summary equal to March's profit of $1,995. All debit and credit balances related to expense and revenue accounts have now been collected in the Income Summary account.

Entry 3: **Close Income Summary to Owner's Capital**

The third closing entry in Exhibit 4.7 transfers the balance of the Income Summary account to the owner's capital account. As illustrated in Exhibit 4.8, the Income Summary account has a zero balance after posting this entry. It continues to have a zero balance until the closing process occurs at the end of the next period. The owner's capital account has now been increased by the amount of profit. Since we know that the normal balance of owner's capital is a credit, increases to owner's capital from profit are credits.

EXHIBIT 4.7

Closing Entries for Organico

Entry 1:	**Close temporary accounts with credit balances to Income Summary**			
Mar. 31	Food Services Revenue..	5,850	
	Teaching Revenue...	300	
	Income Summary		6,150
	To close the revenue accounts.		
Entry 2:	**Close temporary accounts with debit balances to Income Summary**			
31	Income Summary..	4,155	
	Depreciation Expense, Equipment............		200
	Salaries Expense..		1,540
	Interest Expense		35
	Insurance Expense		100
	Rent Expense..		1,000
	Supplies Expense		1,050
	Utilities Expense..		230
	To close expense accounts.		
Entry 3:	**Close Income Summary to Owner's Capital**			
31	Income Summary..	1,995	
	Hailey Walker, Capital		1,995
	To close the Income Summary account.		
Entry 4:	**Close Withdrawals Account to Owner's Capital**			
31	Hailey Walker, Capital..	600	
	Hailey Walker, Withdrawals		600
	To close the withdrawals account.		

Entry 4: Close Withdrawals Account to Owner's Capital

The fourth closing entry in Exhibit 4.7 transfers any debit balance in the withdrawals account to the owner's capital account (withdrawals *is not* closed to the Income Summary account). This entry gives the withdrawals account a zero balance, and the account is ready to accumulate next period's payments to the owner. As illustrated in Exhibit 4.8, this entry reduces the Hailey Walker, Capital account balance to $11,395, the amount reported on the balance sheet.

Sources of Closing Entry Information

We can identify the accounts that need to be closed and the amounts in the closing entries by looking to individual revenue, expense, and withdrawals accounts in the ledger.[4] If we prepare an adjusted trial balance after the adjusting process, the information for closing entries is available on the trial balance as illustrated in Exhibit 4.6.

Exhibit 4.9 highlights the posting of closing entries of Exhibit 4.7 in the ledger accounts for Organico. Notice that all of the temporary accounts (revenues, expenses, and withdrawals) have a zero balance. The closing process transferred the balances of the temporary accounts to the Hailey Walker, Capital account. The capital account balance of $11,395 includes owner investment of $10,000 and profit of $1,995, less withdrawals of $600.

4　When accounting software is in use, closing entries are done automatically.

EXHIBIT 4.8
Closing Entries of Organico

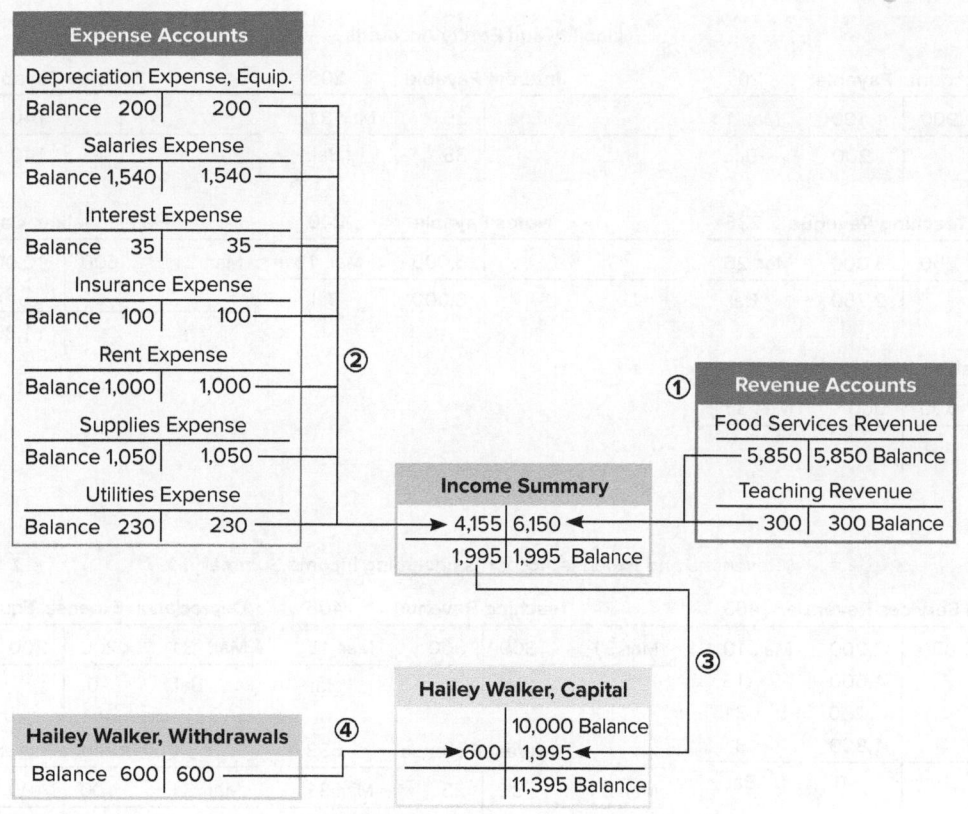

EXHIBIT 4.9
Ledger After the Closing Process for Organico

Ledger
Asset Accounts

		Cash	101			Accounts Receivable	106				Supplies	125	
Mar. 1	10,000	2,500	Mar. 1		Mar. 15	1,900	1,900	Mar. 25		Mar. 1	2,500	1,050	Mar. 31
10	2,200	2,400	1		31	1,800		·		1	1,100		
25	1,900	1,000	10		Bal.	1,800				Bal.	2,550		
26	3,000	700	14										
		900	25			Prepaid Insurance	128				Equipment	167	
		600	26		Mar. 1	2,400	100	Mar. 31		Mar. 1	6,000		
		230	26		Bal.	2,300				Bal.	6,000		
		700	28										
Bal.	8,070												

	Accumulated		
	Depreciation, Equipment	168	
		200	Mar. 31
		200	Bal.

(Continued)

EXHIBIT 4.9 (continued)

Ledger After the Closing Process for Organico

Liability and Equity Accounts

Accounts Payable 201

Mar. 25	900	1,100	Mar. 1
		200	Bal.

Interest Payable 203

		35	Mar. 31
		35	Bal.

Salaries Payable 209

		140	Mar. 31
		140	Bal.

Unearned Teaching Revenue 236

Mar. 31	250	3,000	Mar. 26
		2,750	Bal.

Notes Payable 240

		6,000	Mar. 1
		6,000	Bal.

Hailey Walker, Capital 301

Mar. 31	600	10,000	Mar. 1
		1,995	31
		11,395	Bal.

Hailey Walker, Withdrawals 302

Mar. 26	600	600	Mar. 31
Bal.	-0-		

Revenues and Expense Accounts (including Income Summary)

Food Services Revenue 403

Mar. 31	5,850	2,200	Mar. 10
		1,600	15
		250	31
		1,800	31
		-0-	Bal.

Teaching Revenue 406

Mar. 31	300	300	Mar. 15
		-0-	Bal.

Depreciation Expense, Equipment 614

Mar. 31	200	200	Mar. 31
Bal.	-0-		

Salaries Expense 622

Mar. 14	700	1,540	Mar. 31
28	700		
31	140		
Bal.	-0-		

Interest Expense 633

Mar. 31	35	35	Mar. 31
Bal.	-0-		

Insurance Expense 637

Mar. 31	100	100	Mar. 31
Bal.	-0-		

Supplies Expense 651

Mar. 31	1,050	1,050	Mar. 31
Bal.	-0-		

Utilities Expense 690

Mar. 26	230	230	Mar. 31
Bal.	-0-		

Rent Expense 641

Mar. 10	1,000	1,000	Mar. 31
Bal.	-0-		

Income Summary 901

Mar. 31	4,155	6,150	Mar. 31
31	1,995	1,995	Bal.
		-0-	Bal.

 CHECKPOINT

4. What are the four major closing entries?
5. Why are revenue and expense accounts called temporary? Are there other temporary accounts?

Do Quick Study questions: QS 4-5, QS 4-6, QS 4-7, QS 4-8

PREPARING A POST-CLOSING TRIAL BALANCE

LO4 Explain and prepare a post-closing trial balance.

A **post-closing trial balance** is a list of permanent accounts and their balances from the ledger after all closing entries are journalized and posted. It is a list of balances for accounts not closed. These accounts are a company's assets, liabilities, and equity at the end of a period. They are identical to those in the balance sheet. The aim of a post-closing trial balance is to verify that (1) total debits equal total credits for permanent accounts, and (2) all temporary accounts have zero balances.

Organico's post-closing trial balance is shown in Exhibit 4.10 and is the last step in the accounting process. The post-closing trial balance in Exhibit 4.10 was created by listing the account balances found in Exhibit 4.9. Like the trial balance, the post-closing trial balance does not prove that all transactions are recorded or that the ledger is correct.

EXHIBIT 4.10

Post-Closing Trial Balance

Organico Post-Closing Trial Balance March 31, 2020		
	Debit	**Credit**
Cash	$ 8,070	
Accounts receivable	1,800	
Supplies	2,550	
Prepaid insurance	2,300	
Equipment	6,000	
Accumulated depreciation, equipment		$ 200
Accounts payable		200
Interest payable		35
Salaries payable		140
Unearned food services revenue		2,750
Notes payable		6,000
Hailey Walker, capital		11,395
Totals	$20,720	$20,720

Closing Entries After Period-End Date

We are not usually able to make closing entries on the last day of each period. This is because information about certain transactions that require *adjusting* is not always available until several days or even weeks later. Because some adjusting entries are recorded later, closing entries are recorded later, but both are dated as of the last day of the period. Financial statements therefore reflect what is known on the date they are prepared instead of what was known as of the last day of the period.

One example is a company that receives a utility bill on February 4 for costs incurred for the month of January. In preparing the January financial statements, the company's accountant identifies the utility bill as a required accrual and records the expense and the payable as of January 31. The January income statement then reflects expenses incurred in January and the January 31 balance sheet includes the payable, even though the amounts are not actually known on January 31.

CHECKPOINT

6. What accounts are listed on the post-closing trial balance?

Do Quick Study question: QS 4-9

Completing the Accounting Cycle

LO5 Complete the steps in the accounting cycle.

We have now completed the steps in the accounting cycle that have been the focus in this and the previous chapters. Let's now briefly summarize these steps in Exhibit 4.11 to emphasize their importance in providing users with information for decision making.

EXHIBIT 4.11

Summary of Steps in the Accounting Cycle

1. Analyze transactions	Analyze transactions in preparation for journalizing.
2. Journalize	Record debits and credits with explanations in a journal.
3. Post	Transfer debits and credits from journal entries to the ledger accounts.
4. Unadjusted trial balance*	Summarize ledger accounts and amounts.
5. Adjust*	Record adjustments to bring account balances up to date; journalize and post adjusting entries to the accounts.
6. Adjusted trial balance	Summarize adjusted ledger accounts and amounts.
7. Prepare statements	Use adjusted trial balance to prepare: income statement, statement of changes in equity, balance sheet, and statement of cash flows (details of preparing the statement of cash flows are in Chapter 16).
8. Close	Journalize and post entries to close temporary accounts (revenue, expense, and withdrawals) and update the owner's capital account.
9. Post-closing trial balance**	Test clerical accuracy of adjusting and closing steps.

*Steps 4, 5, and 6 can be done on a work sheet.
**Reversing entries* are optional and, if prepared, are done between Steps 9 and 1. Reversing entries are covered in Appendix 4A.

 CHECKPOINT

7. What steps in the accounting cycle are optional?

Do Quick Study question: QS 4-10

The closing process just demonstrated using account information for Organico was a case where revenues were greater than expenses, thus creating profit. The closing process is applied in an identical manner when a loss occurs, as illustrated in the following Mid-Chapter Demonstration Problem.

Mid-Chapter Demonstration Problem

Using the account information in the following adjusted trial balance for Melodie's Piano School:

1. Prepare the closing entries for December 31, 2020.
2. Post the closing entries.
3. Prepare the post-closing trial balance at December 31, 2020.

Analysis Component:

Rather than closing temporary accounts, it would be more efficient to record all transactions affecting temporary accounts (revenues, expenses, and owner withdrawals) directly into capital. Explain why this would be problematic.

Melodie's Piano School Adjusted Trial Balance December 31, 2020		
	Debit	**Credit**
Cash..	$ 7,000	
Accounts receivable...	3,000	
Piano..	31,000	
Accumulated depreciation, piano..		$27,000
Salaries payable..		700
Melodie Martin, capital		17,200
Melodie Martin, withdrawals	2,300	
Teaching revenue		38,000
Salaries expense...	30,000	
Depreciation expense, piano..	5,000	
Utilities expense...	4,600	
Totals..	$82,900	$82,900

Planning the Solution

1. Journalize the four closing entries.
2. Post the closing entries.
3. Prepare the post-closing trial balance.
4. Prepare a response to the analysis question.

SOLUTION

Part 1

	Entry 1:	**Close the revenue account:**		
	Dec. 31	Teaching Revenue...	38,000	
		Income Summary...		38,000
		To close the revenue account.		

(Continued)

Entry 2: **Close the expense accounts:**

31	Income Summary	39,600	
	Salaries Expense		30,000
	Depreciation Expense, Piano		5,000
	Utilities Expense		4,600
	To close the expense accounts.		

Entry 3: **Close Income Summary to owner's capital:**

31	Melodie Martin, Capital	1,600	
	Income Summary		1,600
	To close the loss in the Income Summary account to capital.		

Entry 4: **Close withdrawals account to owner's capital:**

31	Melodie Martin, Capital	2,300	
	Melodie Martin, Withdrawals		2,300
	To close the withdrawals account.		

Part 2

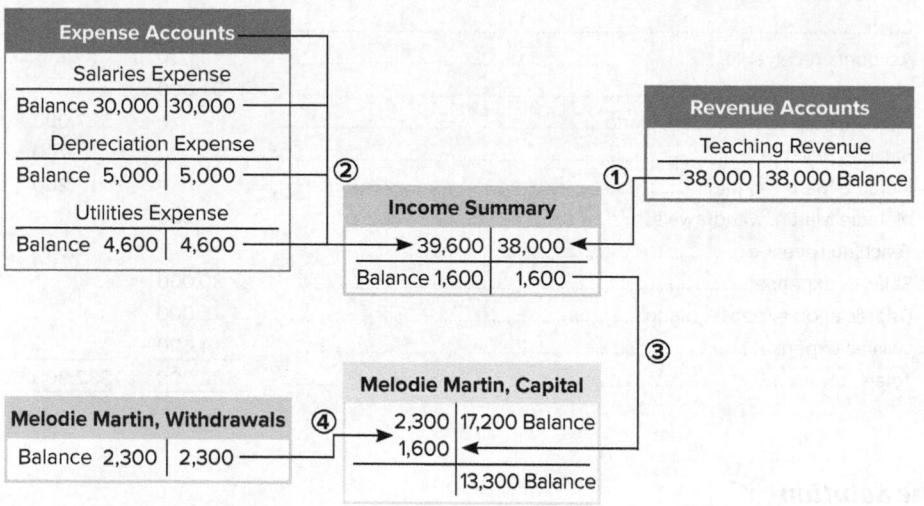

Part 3

Melodie's Piano School Post-Closing Trial Balance December 31, 2020		
	Debit	**Credit**
Cash	$ 7,000	
Accounts receivable	3,000	
Piano	31,000	
Accumulated depreciation, piano		$27,000
Salaries payable		700
Melodie Martin, capital		13,300
Totals	$41,000	$41,000

Analysis Component:

It might be more efficient to record all transactions affecting temporary accounts directly in capital, but the result would be that the information needed by decision makers regarding the business's performance would be *hidden* within the capital account balance. The purpose of using temporary accounts is to have revenues and expenses appear on the income statement to detail the business's performance for the period. The resulting profit or loss is then combined with owner withdrawals and owner investments as part of capital to show the business's equity position at a specific point in time.

Classified Balance Sheet

LO6 Explain and prepare a classified balance sheet.

Our discussion to this point has been limited to unclassified financial statements. An **unclassified balance sheet** is one in which items are broadly grouped into assets, liabilities, and equity. One example is Organico's balance sheet in Exhibit 4.4. A **classified balance sheet** organizes assets and liabilities into important subgroups to provide users with more useful information for making decisions. One example is information to differentiate liabilities that are due in the near future from those not due within the next fiscal year. Information in this case helps financial statement users assess a company's ability to meet liabilities when they come due.

CLASSIFICATION SCHEME

There is no required layout for a classified balance sheet.[5] Yet a classified balance sheet often contains common groupings, including those shown in Exhibit 4.12:

One of the more important classifications is the separation between current and non-current items for both assets and liabilities. Current items are those that are expected to come due within the longer of one year or the company's normal *operating cycle*. An **operating cycle** is the average length of time between (1) paying employees who perform services and receiving cash from customers (for a service company) or (2) paying for merchandise and receiving cash from customers (for a company that sells goods).[6]

EXHIBIT 4.12

Sections of a Classified Balance Sheet

Assets	Liabilities and Equity
Current Assets	Current Liabilities
Non-current Investments*	Non-current Liabilities
Property, Plant, and Equipment*	Equity
Intangible Assets*	
*Non-current assets	

---

5   IFRS 2018, IAS 1, Presentation of Financial Statements, para. 57.
6   IFRS 2018, IAS 1, Presentation of Financial Statements, para. 68.

EXHIBIT 4.13

Operating Cycles for a Service Company and a Merchandising Company

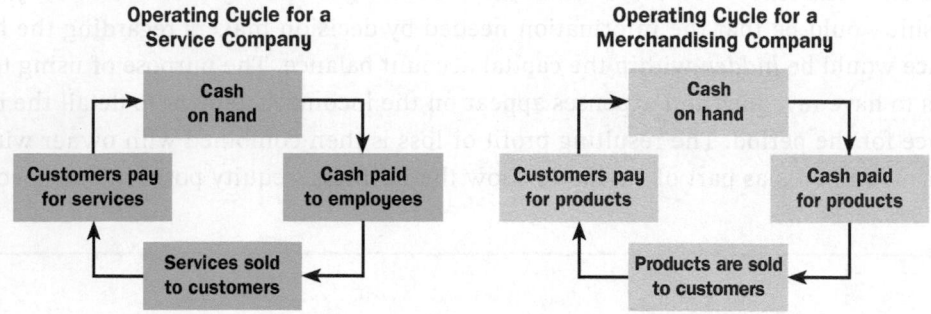

Exhibit 4.13 shows the steps of an operating cycle for both service and merchandising companies.

Most operating cycles are less than one year. This means that most companies use a one-year period in deciding which assets and liabilities are current. Yet there are companies with an operating cycle that is longer than one year. One example is a company that routinely allows customers to take more than one year to pay for purchases. Another example is a producer of distilled beverages and other products that require aging for several years. Understanding the operating cycle of a business is critical, as it must be managed effectively to balance cash resources and maintain sufficient cash to support operations. Companies use their operating cycle in deciding which balance sheet items are classified under the current assets category.[7]

In most cases, companies present their balance sheet items with current assets before long-term assets, and current liabilities before non-current liabilities. This highlights to users assets that are most easily converted to cash, and liabilities that are shortly coming due. Items in the current group are usually listed in the order of how quickly they could be converted to or paid in cash, which is referred to as a company's liquidity.

CLASSIFICATION EXAMPLE

The balance sheet for Elite Boardshop is shown in Exhibit 4.14. It shows the most commonly used groupings. Its assets are classified into (1) current assets, (2) equity investments, (3) property, plant, and equipment, and (4) intangible assets. Its liabilities are classified as either current or non-current. Not all companies use the same categories of assets and liabilities on their balance sheets. For example, **Apple Inc.**'s September 30, 2017, balance sheet lists six asset classes: current assets; long-term marketable securities; property, plant, and equipment; goodwill; acquired intangible assets, net; and other non-current assets.

CLASSIFICATION GROUPS

Current Assets

Assets classified under the **current assets** category include all assets such as cash and other resources that are expected to be sold, collected, or used within the longer of *one year of the company's balance sheet date* or the company's operating cycle.[8] Examples are cash, short-term investments, accounts receivable, notes receivable, goods for sale to customers (called *merchandise inventory* or *inventory*), and prepaid expenses. Notes receivable expected to be collected after a year or operating cycle would be classified under non-current assets. As of September 30, 2017, Apple Inc.'s current assets were reported as shown in Exhibit 4.15.

---

7 In these uncommon situations, companies provide supplemental information about their current assets and liabilities to allow users to compare them with other companies.

8 IFRS 2018, IAS 1, para. 66.

EXHIBIT 4.14

A Classified Balance Sheet

Elite Boardshop Balance Sheet* January 31, 2020		
Assets		
Current assets:		
Cash	$ 6,500	
Short-term investments	2,100	
Accounts receivable	4,400	
Merchandise inventory	29,000	
Prepaid expenses	2,400	
Total current assets		$ 44,400
Non-current investments:		
Notes receivable, due March 31, 2022	$ 18,000	
Land not currently used in operations	48,000	
Total investments		66,000
Property, plant, and equipment:		
Land	$ 73,200	
Buildings	$170,000	
Less: Accumulated depreciation	45,000	125,000
Store equipment	$ 33,200	
Less: Accumulated depreciation	8,000	25,200
Total property, plant, and equipment		223,400
Intangible assets:		
Trademark		10,000
Total assets		$343,800
Liabilities		
Current liabilities:		
Accounts payable	$ 15,300	
Wages payable	3,200	
Notes payable	3,000	
Current portion of non-current liabilities	7,500	
Total current liabilities		$ 29,000
Non-current liabilities:		
Notes payable (less current portion)	150,000	
Total liabilities		$179,000
Equity		
Nolan Jacobsen, capital		164,800
Total liabilities and equity		$343,800

*The classified balance sheet is labelled "Balance Sheet"; it is *not* labelled "Classified Balance Sheet," a common error made by students.

Short-term marketable securities is the terminology used to describe the company's equity or debt investments for which an active trading market exists and those that management intends to sell in the next fiscal year. Deferred tax assets relates to a future benefit the company can utilize to reduce future taxes.

EXHIBIT 4.15

Example Presentation: Current Assets—Apple Inc. as at September 30, 2017

Apple Inc. Consolidated Balance Sheets	
Current assets (in millions of US dollars)	
Cash and equivalents	$ 20,289
Short-term marketable securities	53,892
Accounts receivable, less allowance of $58	17,874
Inventories	4,855
Vendor non-trade receivables..	17,799
Other current assets...	13,936
Total current assets	$128,645

Vendor non-trade receivables is a result of Apple's selling raw materials to its manufacturing subcontractors, which assemble either subcomponents or final products for which Apple expects to collect in the future. Other current assets include items such as the company's prepaid expenses and are usually small compared to other assets, and are often combined and shown as a single item. It is likely that other current assets in Exhibit 4.15 include items such as prepaid insurance, prepaid rent, office supplies, and store supplies.

Non-Current Investments

Non-current investments include all investments management intends to hold to maturity. The distinction between current and non-current classification is determined largely by management's strategic intent to keep the instrument to maturity. Examples of non-current investments in debt instruments include bonds, loans outstanding, and non-current notes receivable. Non-current equity investments generally relate to significant equity ownership in another company usually held for strategic purposes. Non-current investments also can include land that is not being used in operations.

Property, Plant, and Equipment (PPE)

Property, plant, and equipment (PPE) are tangible assets of which the company has legal ownership as a result of a past business transaction and can use for more than one accounting period to produce or sell products and services.[9] Examples of PPE include machinery, vehicles, computer hardware, buildings, and land. All PPE items are expected to be used in the business to carry out its operations and are not intended to be sold.

Intangible Assets

Intangible assets are resources that lack physical form and have benefits that flow to the company for more than one accounting period,[10] result from a past transaction for which the company has the legal right, and are expected to provide future benefits. These intangibles add value to the company and are used to produce or sell products and services. Examples include patents, trademarks, copyrights, and franchise rights. Their value comes from the privileges or rights granted to or held by the owner. Apple Inc. lists intangible assets at September 30, 2017, as shown in Exhibit 4.16.

---

9 IFRS 2018, IAS 16, para. 6-7.

10 IFRS 2018, IAS 38, para. 8-12. Intangible assets are subject to *amortization* in a way similar to how plant and equipment are depreciated. *Amortization* is discussed in Chapter 9.

EXHIBIT 4.16

Example Presentation: Intangible Assets—Apple Inc., as at September 30, 2017

(presented in US$) Apple Inc. (in millions)	
Acquired intangible assets, net..	$2,298

 ETHICAL IMPACT

Dilemma

You are a junior accountant working for a local building supply store. The CFO asks you to capitalize (record on the balance sheet as property, plant, and equipment) a number of small items (light bulbs, stationery, industrial cleaners, etc.) for which you do not understand the long-term future benefit. When you ask about the depreciation policy the CFO tells you that "They are just a bunch of small items—we won't worry about depreciating them." You do not agree with the CFO and know that these items do not belong in the property, plant, and equipment accounting records. You also happen to overhear the CFO and CEO talking about the president planning to put the store up for sale. What will you do?

Current Liabilities

Current liabilities are obligations due to be paid or settled within the longer of one year of the company's balance sheet date or its normal operating cycle. They are usually settled by paying out current assets. Current liabilities include accounts payable, notes payable, wages payable, taxes payable, interest payable, and unearned revenues. Any portion of a non-current liability due to be paid within the longer of one year or the operating cycle is classified as a current liability. Exhibit 4.14 shows how the current portion of long-term liabilities is usually reported. Unearned revenues are current liabilities when they will be settled by delivering products or services within the longer of the year or the operating cycle. While practice varies, current liabilities are often reported in the order of those that are due to be settled first.

Non-Current Liabilities

Non-current liabilities are obligations due beyond the longer of one year or the company's normal operating cycle. Common non-current liabilities include notes payable, mortgages payable, bonds payable, and lease obligations. If a portion of a non-current liability is due to be paid within the year immediately following the balance sheet date, it must be separated and shown as a current liability on the balance sheet. For example, assume the Notes Payable account at December 31, 2020, shows a balance of $150,000. We know that $25,000 of this amount will be paid during 2021. On the December 31, 2020 balance sheet, the $25,000 current portion is disclosed as a current liability and the balance of $125,000 ($150,000 − $25,000) is listed as a non-current liability as follows:

Liabilities	
Current liabilities:	
Current portion of notes payable...	$ 25,000
Non-current liabilities:	
Notes payable (less current portion)..	125,000

Equity

Equity is the owner's claim on the assets of a company. In a sole proprietorship, it is reported in the equity section with an owner's capital account. The equity sections of a partnership and corporation are discussed in detail in later chapters.

CHECKPOINT

8. Identify which of the following assets are classified as (1) current assets, (2) property, plant, and equipment, or (3) intangible assets: (a) land used in operations; (b) office supplies; (c) receivables from customers due in ten months; (d) insurance protection for the next nine months; (e) trucks used to provide services to customers; (f) trademarks used in advertising the company's services.
9. Name two examples of assets classified as non-current investments on the balance sheet.
10. Explain an operating cycle for a service company, and identify its importance to the classified balance sheet.

Do Quick Study questions: QS 4-11, QS 4-12, QS 4-13

Financial Statement Analysis

LO7 Calculate the current ratio and debt to equity ratios, and describe what they reveal about a company's financial condition.

CURRENT RATIO

Financial statements are important tools for helping decision makers to determine a company's ability to pay its debts in the near future.

The **current ratio** is one important measure used to evaluate a company's ability to pay its short-term obligations. The *ability to pay* day-to-day obligations (current liabilities) with existing *liquid assets* is commonly referred to as **liquidity**. **Liquid assets** are those that can easily be converted to cash or used to pay for services or obligations. Cash is the most liquid asset. The current ratio is useful for decision making and is a widely used tool in making decisions like whether or not to lend money to a company or allow a customer to buy on credit. The current ratio is calculated as current assets divided by current liabilities, as shown in Exhibit 4.17.

Using information from the financial statements of **Brick Brewing Co. Limited** (Brick Brewing), we calculate and compare its current ratios at January 31, 2017, and January 31, 2016 (rounded to two decimal places):

January 31, 2017	January 31, 2016
$\frac{16,080,182}{11,140,597} = 1.44$	$\frac{10,216,245}{6,854,613} = 1.49$

Brick Brewing's current ratio at January 31, 2017, can also be expressed as 1.44:1, meaning that there are $1.44 of current assets available to cover each $1.00 of current debt. This tells us that Brick Brewing's current ratio has dropped slightly in 2017; however, the company is still in a good position to pay its day-to-day obligations. Back in 2013 Brick Brewing's ratio was a low 0.92:1, indicating that in that year the company did not have sufficient liquid assets to cover its current obligations. Notice how through effective strategies the company has been able to improve its current ratio in recent years.

EXHIBIT 4.17
Current Ratio

$$\text{Current ratio} = \frac{\text{Current assets}}{\text{Current liabilities}}$$

EXHIBIT 4.18
Quick Ratio

$$\text{Quick Ratio} = \frac{\text{Cash} + \text{Equivalents} + \text{Marketable Securities} + \text{Accounts Receivable}}{\text{Current Liabilities}}$$

Although it varies between industries, generally speaking a healthy (favourable) current ratio falls between 1.5 and 2.0. When the current ratio is less than this, a company could face challenges in paying for its current obligations. A current ratio greater than 2:1 may signal that an excess of current assets exists. More information would be needed to understand why management is holding on to liquid assets instead of using funds to grow the business. Excessive current assets could represent an inefficient use of assets.

QUICK RATIO

The quick ratio (Exhibit 4.18) is a simple modification from the current ratio, and is a more robust measure of liquidity. The current ratio includes under-the-numerator-only assets that are easily converted into cash, including cash and marketable securities, short-term investments, and receivables. It measures the dollar value of liquid assets available to settle current liabilities. It excludes items such as inventory and prepaid assets to focus on assets that more easily convert to cash. A quick ratio of greater than one is important.

 DECISION INSIGHT

Stashes of Cash

According to *Global Finance* magazine, companies are still maintaining high levels of their most liquid asset—cash. "Increased geopolitical risks coupled with memories of the recent (US) recession are keeping corporate decision makers cautious." Other companies are building up cash reserves to be able to engage in mergers and acquisitions. Another reason to maintain higher levels of cash is to improve their credit ratings, which enable more cost-effective borrowing in the future. The article states that according Moody, US corporate cash has reached $1.3 trillion. The top 5 Global Public Companies by Cash on the Balance Sheet are as follows*:

Company	Cash (in Millions $US)	Country	Industry
Microsoft	113,239	US	Technology
Apple	67,155	US	Technology
Oracle	66,078	US	Automotive
Cisco Systems	65,756	US	Technology
Toyota Motor	48,129	Japan	Technology

*https://www.gfmag.com/magazine/september-2017/cash-piles-keep-growing, accessed January 2018.

DEBT TO EQUITY RATIO

The debt to equity ratio (Exhibit 4.19) is another calculation that is important for understanding financial statements as it indicates the risk position of a company. Debt financing can be costly for companies, as interest is required to be paid to the bank in conjunction with principal repayments. Investors and external users typically like to assess debt to equity to determine the riskiness of the company in relation to the risk of default on its outstanding loans, as too high of a debt load can lead to bankruptcy. It is important to determine what is normal for the industry when assessing debt to equity ratios as some industries will naturally have higher

EXHIBIT 4.19
Debt to Equity Ratio

$$\text{Debt to Equity Ratio} = \frac{\text{Total Debt}}{\text{Total Equity}}$$

debt loads—such as airlines, which need to finance new aircraft. Automotive manufacturers, food services establishments, and accommodations establishments have higher ratios. The high-tech sector, including computer and electronic manufacturing, typically has lower debt to equity ratios. A lower number is more favourable; the higher the number, the higher the risk associated with the potential for bankruptcy. Refer to Statistics Canada's debt to equity ratio by industry at http://www.statcan.gc.ca for more information on industry trends.

We return to the financial statements of Brick Brewing to calculate and compare its debt to equity ratios at January 31, 2017, and January 31, 2016 (rounded to two decimal places):

2017	2016
$= \dfrac{17,915,020}{37,836,101} = 0.47$	$= \dfrac{13,314,897}{35,525,579} = 0.37$

The fiscal 2017 increase in the debt to equity ratio over 2016 signals an unfavourable change. In 2017 Brick Brewing Co. increased its debt and decreased its ownership interest (equity). Accounts payable and accrued liabilities increased significantly from $4.9 million to $9.7 million. Revenue increased from $37.6 million in fiscal 2016 to $45.1 million in fiscal 2017. It is important to perform a comprehensive financial analysis of the company to understand the overall impact of the change.

 CHECKPOINT

11. If a company misclassifies a portion of liabilities as non-current when they are current how does this affect its current ratio?

Do Quick Study questions: QS 4-14, QS 4-15, QS 4-16

 DECISION MAKER   Answer—End of chapter

Analyst

You are a commercial loans manager for RBC and are analyzing the financial condition of a local bakery business to assess its ability to meet upcoming loan payments. You calculate its current ratio as 1.2. You also find that a major portion of accounts receivable is due from one company that has not paid your client for a major catering event and has not made any payments in the past 12 months. Removing this receivable from current assets lowers the current ratio to 0.7. What do you conclude?

CRITICAL THINKING CHALLENGE

Refer to the Critical Thinking Challenge questions at the beginning of the chapter. Compare your answers to those suggested on Connect.

IFRS AND ASPE—THE DIFFERENCES

Difference	International Financial Reporting Standards (IFRS)	Accounting Standards for Private Enterprises (ASPE)
Depreciation vs. amortization	• Uses the term *depreciation** (although they use *amortization* for intangible assets**)	• Uses the term *amortization*[†]

*IFRS 2018, IAS 16, para. 6.
**IFRS 2018, IAS 38, para. 8.
[†]ASPE, Accounting Standards, Section 3061.16.

A Look Ahead

Chapter 5 looks at accounting for merchandising activities. We describe the sale and purchase of merchandise and their implications for preparing and analyzing financial statements.

For further study on some topics of relevance to this chapter, please see the following Extend Your Knowledge supplements:

EYK 4-1 Work Sheet Demonstration

EYK 4-2 Corporate Supplement

EYK 4-3 Summary of Business Activities

EYK 4-4 Examples of Classified Balance Sheets

SUMMARY

LO1 **Describe and prepare a work sheet and explain its usefulness.** A work sheet is optional and can be a useful tool when preparing and analyzing financial statements. It is helpful at the end of a period for preparing adjusting entries, an adjusted trial balance, and financial statements. A work sheet often contains five pairs of columns for an unadjusted trial balance, the adjustments, an adjusted trial balance, an income statement, and the balance sheet and statement of changes in equity.

LO2 **Describe the closing process and explain why temporary accounts are closed each period.** The closing process is the final step of the accounting cycle; it closes temporary accounts at the end of each accounting period: (1) to update the owner's capital account for revenue, expense, and withdrawals transactions recorded for the period; and (2) to prepare revenue, expense, and withdrawals accounts for the next reporting period by giving them zero balances.

LO3 **Prepare closing entries.** Closing entries involve four steps: (1) close credit balances in revenue accounts to Income Summary, (2) close debit balances in expense accounts to Income Summary, (3) close Income Summary to Owner's Capital, and (4) close the Withdrawals account to Owner's Capital.

LO4 **Explain and prepare a post-closing trial balance.** A post-closing trial balance is a list of permanent accounts and their balances after all closing entries are journalized and posted. Permanent accounts are asset, liability, and equity accounts. The

purpose of a post-closing trial balance is to verify that (1) total debits equal total credits for permanent accounts and (2) all temporary accounts have zero balances.

LO5 **Complete the steps in the accounting cycle.** The accounting cycle consists of nine steps: (1) analyze transactions, (2) journalize, (3) post, (4) prepare unadjusted trial balance, (5) adjust, (6) prepare adjusted trial balance, (7) prepare statements, (8) close, and (9) prepare post-closing trial balance. If a work sheet is prepared, it covers Steps 4 to 6. Reversing entries are an optional step that is done between Steps 9 and 1.

LO6 **Explain and prepare a classified balance sheet.** Classified balance sheets usually report four groups of assets: current assets; non-current investments; property, plant, and equipment; and intangible assets. Also, they include at least two groups of liabilities: current and non-current. The equity section on the balance sheet for a proprietorship reports the capital account balance.

LO7 **Calculate the current ratio and debt to equity ratios, and describe what they reveal about a company's financial condition.** A company's current ratio is defined as current assets divided by current liabilities. We use it to evaluate a company's ability to pay its current liabilities out of current assets. A company's debt to equity ratio is calculated as total debt divided by total equity and is used to determine whether the company is at higher risk of bankruptcy.

Guidance Answer to DECISION MAKER

Analyzing Results

Yes, you are concerned about the absence of a depreciation adjustment on the manufacturing equipment. Equipment does lose value as it is used in the business, and financial statements must recognize this occurrence. Its absence suggests an error or a misrepresentation (there is also the possibility that equipment is fully utilized and should have been completely depreciated or that it was scrapped).

Analyst

A current ratio of 1.2 suggests that current assets are sufficient to cover current liabilities, but it implies a minimal buffer in case of errors in measuring current assets or current liabilities. Removing the past due receivable reduces the current ratio to 0.7. Your assessment is that the bakery will have some difficulty meeting its loan payments.

 Guidance Answers to CHECKPOINT

1. Amounts in the Unadjusted Trial Balance columns are taken from account balances in the ledger.
2. A work sheet offers the advantage of listing on one page all of the necessary information to make adjusting entries.
3. A work sheet can help in (a) preparing interim financial statements, (b) linking transactions and events to their effects in financial statements, (c) showing adjustments for audit purposes, (d) avoiding errors, and (e) showing effects of proposed or "what-if" transactions.
4. The four major closing entries consist of closing (1) credit balances in revenue accounts to Income Summary, (2) debit balances in expense accounts to Income Summary, (3) Income Summary to Owner's Capital, and (4) Withdrawals account to Owner's Capital.
5. Revenue and expense accounts are called temporary because they are opened and closed every reporting period. The Income Summary and owner's withdrawals accounts are also temporary accounts.
6. Permanent accounts are listed on the post-closing trial balance. These accounts are the asset, liability, and equity accounts.
7. Making reversing entries is an optional step in the accounting cycle. Also, a work sheet is an optional tool for completing Steps 4 to 6.
8. Current assets: b, c, d. Property, plant, and equipment: a, e. Intangible assets: f.
9. Notes receivable, land not currently used in business operations.
10. An operating cycle for a service company is the average time between (1) paying employees who do the services and (2) receiving cash from customers. Knowing the operating cycle allows current versus long-term assets and liabilities to be disclosed appropriately on the balance sheet.
11. Since the current ratio is defined as current assets divided by current liabilities, then ignoring a portion of current liabilities (1) decreases the reported amount of current liabilities and (2) increases the current ratio because current assets are now divided by a smaller number.

Demonstration Problem

The partial adjusted trial balance for The Cutlery shows the following account balances as at December 31, 2020.

			Debit	Credit
_____	101	Cash..	$ 15,000	
_____	106	Accounts receivable...	22,665	
_____	124	Spare parts supplies	5,800	
_____	128	Prepaid insurance..	8,700	
_____	141	Notes receivable[A]	36,900	
_____	163	Office equipment	12,510	
_____	164	Accumulated depreciation, office equipment.........		$ 2,825
_____	173	Building..	129,000	
_____	174	Accumulated depreciation, building.......................		33,000
_____	183	Land..	55,000	
_____	191	Patent...	11,500	
_____	193	Franchise..	26,000	
_____	201	Accounts payable		16,500
_____	209	Salaries payable..		26,300
_____	230	Unearned revenue		7,600
_____	251	Long-term notes payable[B]...................................		142,000
_____	301	Joanne Cardinal, capital[C]...................................		104,000
_____	302	Joanne Cardinal, withdrawals...............................	72,000	

[A]The note receivable is due to be collected May 1, 2022.
[B]$22,000 of the December 31, 2020, balance in notes payable will be paid during 2021.
[C]Joanne Cardinal, the owner, invested $5,000 during the accounting period.

Required Using the information provided above for The Cutlery,

1. Prepare a classified balance sheet at December 31, 2020. For simplicity, The Cutlery lists accounts on the balance sheet in account order.

2. Prepare a statement of changes in equity for the year ended December 31, 2020.

Analysis Component: Has Joanne Cardinal, the owner of The Cutlery, financed growth by reinvesting profits? Explain.

Planning the Solution

1. Prepare a classified balance sheet by first listing all of the classification headings under assets and liabilities. Then, sort the accounts by listing them under the appropriate heading. *Hint: Place an X in the column provided to the left of the account number column on the adjusted trial balance as you transfer account information from the adjusted trial balance to the balance sheet. This process will help you determine whether all of the appropriate accounts have been transferred to the balance sheet.*

2. Prepare a statement of changes in equity. *Hint: Revenue and expense information has not been provided from which to calculate profit or loss. However, you will be able to determine what the profit or loss was by taking into consideration the balance sheet prepared in Step 1 and the other elements of equity that have been provided.*

3. Review the information and prepare an answer to the analysis component question.

SOLUTION

1. Prepare a classified balance sheet.

The Cutlery Balance Sheet December 31, 2020		
Assets		
Current assets:		
Cash	$ 15,000	
Accounts receivable	22,665	
Spare parts supplies	5,800	
Prepaid insurance	8,700	
Total current assets		$ 52,165
Non-current investments:		
Notes receivable		36,900
Property, plant, and equipment:		
Land	$ 55,000	
Building	$129,000	
Less: Accumulated depreciation	33,000	96,000
Office equipment	$ 12,510	
Less: Accumulated depreciation	2,825	9,685
Total property, plant, and equipment		160,685
Intangible assets:		
Patent	$ 11,500	
Franchise	26,000	
Total intangible assets		37,500
Total assets		$287,250
Liabilities		
Current liabilities:		
Accounts payable	$ 16,500	
Salaries payable	26,300	
Unearned revenue	7,600	
Current portion of long-term notes payable	22,000	
Total current liabilities		$ 72,400
Non-current liabilities:		
Long-term notes payable (less current portion)	120,000	
Total liabilities		$192,400
Equity		
Joanne Cardinal, capital		94,850
Total liabilities and equity		$287,250

2. Prepare a statement of changes in equity.

The Cutlery Statement of Changes in Equity For Year Ended December 31, 2020		
Joanne Cardinal, capital December 31, 2019..		$ 99,000[1]
Investment by owner	$ 5,000	
Profit..	$62,850[3]	67,850[4]
Total..		$166,850[2]
Less: Withdrawals by owner...		72,000
Joanne Cardinal, capital, December 31, 2020.......................................		$ 94,850

[1]Adjusted capital balance on December 31, 2020 = $104,000; $104,000 − $5,000 owner investment during 2020 = $99,000 capital balance on December 31, 2019.
[2]$94,850 post-closing balance per December 31, 2020, balance sheet + $72,000 owner withdrawals = $166,850.
[3]$166,850 − $5,000 − $99,000 = $62,850
[4]$62,850 + $5,000 = $67,850

3. Joanne Cardinal is not reinvesting profits. This is evident from the amount of her withdrawals, $72,000, which represents 115% of the profit earned ($72,000/$62,850 × 100% = 115%). Reinvesting profits occurs when assets are retained by the business for the purpose of growth of the business rather than being taken out through withdrawals, which depletes assets.

APPENDIX 4A

Reversing Entries

Reversing Entries

LO8 Prepare reversing entries and explain their purpose.

Reversing entries are optional entries used to simplify recordkeeping. They are prepared on the first day of the new accounting period. Reversing entries are prepared for those adjusting entries that created accrued assets and liabilities (such as interest receivable and salaries payable).

Exhibit 4A.1 shows how reversing entries work for Organico. The top of the exhibit shows the adjusting entry recorded by Organico on March 31, 2020, for earned but unpaid salary. The entry recorded one day's salary to increase March's total salary expense to $1,470. The entry also recognized a liability of $70. The expense is reported on March's income statement and the expense account is closed. As a result, the ledger on April 1, 2020, reflects a $70 liability and a zero balance in the Salaries Expense account. At this point, April 1, the company would make the choice to use reversing entries or not.

ACCOUNTING WITHOUT REVERSING ENTRIES

The path down the left side of Exhibit 4A.1 is described in Chapter 3. That is, when the next payday occurs on April 1, we record payment with a compound entry that debits both the expense and liability accounts. Posting that entry creates a $630 balance in the expense account and reduces the liability account balance to zero because the debt has been settled.

The disadvantage of this approach is the complex entry required on April 1. Paying the accrued liability means that this entry differs from the routine entries made on all other paydays. To construct the proper entry on April 1, we must recall the effect of the adjusting entry. Reversing entries overcome this disadvantage.

ACCOUNTING WITH REVERSING ENTRIES

The right side of Exhibit 4A.1 shows how a reversing entry on April 1 overcomes the disadvantage of the complex April 11 entry. The reversing entry is the exact opposite of the adjusting entry recorded on March 31. The Salaries Payable liability is debited for $70, meaning that this account now has a zero balance after the entry is posted. Technically, the Salaries Payable account now understates the liability, but this is not a problem since financial statements are not prepared before the liability is settled on April 11. The credit to the Salaries Expense account is unusual because it gives the account an *abnormal credit balance*.

Because of the reversing entry, the April 11 entry to record payment is simple. This entry debits the Salaries Expense account for the full $700 paid. It is the same as all other entries made to record 10 days' salary for the employee.

After the payment entry is posted, the expense and liability accounts have exactly the same balances whether reversing entry is made or not.

 CHECKPOINT

12. How are financial statements affected by a decision to make reversing entries?

Do Quick Study question: *QS 4-17

EXHIBIT 4A.1

Reversing Entries for Accrued Expenses

Accrue salaries expense on March 31, 2020:

Salaries Expense 70
    Salaries Payable 70

Salaries Expense

Mar. 12	700
26	700
31	**70**

Salaries Payable

	70 Mar. 31

No reversing entry recorded on April 1, 2020:

Salaries Expense

Salaries Payable

	70 Mar. 31

Reversing entry recorded on April 1, 2020:

Salaries Payable 70
    Salaries Expense 70

Salaries Expense

	70 Apr. 1

Salaries Payable

Apr. 1	70	70 Mar. 31
		-0- Balance

Pay the accrued and current salaries on April 11, the first payday in April 2020:

Salaries Expense 630
Salaries Payable 70
    Cash 700

Salaries Expense

Apr. 11	630

Salaries Payable

Apr. 11	70	70 Mar. 31
		-0- Balance

Salaries Expense 700
    Cash 700

Salaries Expense

Apr. 11	700	70 Apr. 1
Balance	630	

Salaries Payable

Apr. 1	70	70 Mar. 31
		-0- Balance

SUMMARY OF APPENDIX 4A

LO8 Prepare reversing entries and explain their purpose. Reversing entries are an optional step. They are applied to accrued assets and liabilities.

The purpose of reversing entries is to simplify subsequent journal entries. Financial statements are unaffected by the choice to use reversing entries or not.

 Guidance Answer to CHECKPOINT

12. Financial statements are unchanged by the choice of using reversing entries or not.

GLOSSARY

Classified balance sheet A balance sheet that presents the assets and liabilities in relevant subgroups.

Closing entries Journal entries recorded at the end of each accounting period that transfer the end-of-period balances in revenue, expense, and withdrawals accounts to the permanent owner's capital account in order to prepare for the upcoming period and update the owner's capital account for the period just finished.

Closing process A step at the end of the accounting period that prepares accounts for recording the transactions of the next period.

Current assets Cash or other assets that are expected to be sold, collected, or used within the longer of one year or the company's operating cycle.

Current liabilities Obligations due to be paid or settled within the longer of one year or the operating cycle.

Current ratio A ratio that is used to evaluate a company's ability to pay its short-term obligations, calculated by dividing current assets by current liabilities.

Equity The owner's claim on the assets of a company.

Income summary A temporary account used only in the closing process to which the balances of revenue and expense accounts are transferred; its balance equals profit or loss and is transferred to the owner's capital account.

Intangible assets Long-lived assets that lack physical form and are used to produce or sell products or services.

Liquid assets Assets that can easily be converted to cash or used to pay for services or obligations; cash is the most liquid asset.

Liquidity The ability to pay day-to-day obligations (current liabilities) with existing liquid assets.

Non-current investments Assets not used in day-to-day operating activities that are held for more than one year or the operating cycle, such as a non-current note receivable.

Non-current liabilities Obligations that are not due to be paid within the longer of one year or the operating cycle.

Operating cycle For a business, the average time between paying cash for employee salaries or merchandise and receiving cash from customers.

Permanent accounts Accounts that are used to report on activities related to one or more future accounting periods; their balances are carried into the next period, and include all balance sheet accounts; permanent account balances are not closed as long as the company continues to own the assets, owe the liabilities, and have equity.

Post-closing trial balance A list of permanent accounts and their balances from the ledger after all closing entries are journalized and posted; a list of balances for all accounts not closed.

PPE See *property, plant, and equipment.*

Property, plant, and equipment (PPE) Long-lived tangible assets used to produce or sell products and services; abbreviated *PPE.*

Reversing entries Optional entries recorded at the beginning of a new period that prepare the accounts for simplified journal entries subsequent to accrual adjusting entries.

Temporary accounts Accounts that are used to describe revenues, expenses, and owner's withdrawals for one accounting period; they are closed at the end of the reporting period.

Unclassified balance sheet A balance sheet that broadly groups the assets, liabilities, and equity.

Working papers Internal documents that are used to assist the preparers in doing the analyses and organizing the information for reports to be presented to internal and external decision makers.

Work sheet A 10-column spreadsheet used to draft a company's unadjusted trial balance, adjusting entries, adjusted trial balance, and financial statements; an optional step in the accounting process.

KNOWLEDGE CHECK-UP

1. Which of the following statements is true about work sheets:
   a. They are required and must be prepared by all companies that produce financial statements
   b. They are optional working papers that can simplify the accountant's efforts in producing financial statements
   c. They are produced without the use of a computer
   d. They do not show the adjustments made to produce the adjusted trial balance

2. The closing process is:
   a. A required step at the end of the accounting period after the financial statements are prepared
   b. An optional step used to analyze the financial statements at the end of an accounting period
   c. Performed at the beginning of the accounting period to close inactive customer accounts
   d. Performed to close the accounting system at the end of the business day

3. In the closing process temporary accounts are used for which of the following reasons:

   a. To record transactions temporarily, preparing for adjusting entries

   b. To keep track of one-time-only or unique transactions

   c. To close all accounts that are reset to zero to prepare for the next accounting period

   d. To manage period-end adjustments

4. An example of a permanent account is:

   a. Withdrawals

   b. Revenue

   c. Utilities Expense

   d. Cash

5. The Income Summary account is used for the following purpose:

   a. To transfer the permanent accounts to the owner's capital account at the end of an accounting period

   b. To keep track of the profitability of an organization during the accounting period

   c. To transfer the credit balances and debit balances in temporary accounts and to transfer the net balance to the owners' capital account

   d. To ensure the accounting software package is summarizing financial information correctly during the accounting period

6. The purpose of a post-closing trial balance is:

   a. To list all permanent accounts and their balances after all closing entries are posted

   b. To list all temporary accounts and their balances after all closing entries are posted

   c. To record all year-end balances of accounts at the end of an accounting period

   d. To prepare financial statements at the end of an accounting period

7. A classified balance sheet involves:

   a. Grouping assets and liabilities into current and non-current assets and liabilities

   b. Providing more detailed information regarding a company's existing assets and liabilities

   c. Presenting the balance sheet in a specific format, based on the standard by industry

   d. Organizing the revenue and expense line items from largest to smallest

8. An operating cycle is

   a. The average time it takes to produce a product for a manufacturing-based company

   b. The average time it takes a company to pay off operating expenses during a fiscal year

   c. The average length of time between paying employees (for a service-based organization) or purchasing inventory (for a merchandising company) and receiving cash from customers

   d. The average length of time between investing in R&D and the time to product development for a company

9. An example of a current asset is:

   a. Intangible assets

   b. Property, plant, and equipment

   c. Accounts payable

   d. Merchandise inventory

10. The current ratio provides information to users of financial statements regarding:

    a. Ability to pay for existing assets with day-to-day obligations

    b. Ability to pay day-to-day obligations with existing liquid assets

    c. The amount of debt outstanding compared to total equity in a business

    d. The amount of cash currently available to pay for all outstanding obligations of a business

CONCEPT REVIEW QUESTIONS

1. What tasks are performed with the work sheet?

2. What two purposes are accomplished by recording closing entries?

3. What are the four closing entries?

4. Daniel is having trouble determining whether withdrawals, owner's capital, interest income, and prepaid insurance are temporary or permanent accounts. Explain to him the difference between a temporary and a permanent account in accounting and classify the accounts into each category.

5. Alexis believes that temporary account information is deleted through the closing entries. Do you agree or disagree? Explain. What is the relationship between temporary and permanent accounts?

6. Describe the similarities and differences between adjusting and closing entries.

7. What is the purpose of the Income Summary account? How is it different from the Income Statement?

8. Explain whether an error has occurred if a post-closing trial balance includes a Depreciation Expense, Building account.

9. Refer to **Spin Master**'s income statement in Appendix III at the end of the book. What journal entry was recorded as of December 31, 2017 to close the revenue account?

10. What is a company's operating cycle?

11. Why is a classified balance sheet more useful to financial statement users than a non-classified balance sheet?

12. What classes of assets and liabilities are shown on a typical classified balance sheet?

13. What are the characteristics of property, plant, and equipment?

14. Refer to the December 31, 2017, balance sheet for **WestJet** in Appendix III at the end of the book. What amount of WestJet's long-term debt is coming due before December 31, 2018?

*15. How do reversing entries simplify a company's accounting efforts?

*16. If a company had accrued unpaid salaries expense of $500 at the end of a fiscal year, what reversing entry could be made? When would it be made?

QUICK STUDY

QS 4-1 Applying a work sheet LO1

In preparing a work sheet, indicate the financial statement debit column to which a normal balance of each of the following accounts should be extended. Use *IS* for the Income Statement Debit column and *BS* for the Balance Sheet or Statement of Changes in Equity Debit column.

1. Equipment
2. Owner, withdrawals
3. Insurance expense

4. Prepaid insurance
5. Accounts receivable
6. Depreciation expense, equipment

QS 4-2 Completing a work sheet LO1

Enter the following unadjusted trial balance and adjustment information onto a work sheet. Complete the work sheet.

	Trial Balance.xlsx				
	Home Insert Page Layout Formulas Data Review View				
	P18 fx				
	A	B	C	D	E
1	Trial Balance				
2					
3		Unadjusted			
4		Trial Balance		Adjustments	
5	Account	Dr.	Cr.	Dr.	Cr.
6	Cash	15			
7	Accounts receivable	22			
8	Supplies	25			8
9	Ed Wolt, capital		40		
10	Ed Wolt, withdrawals	12			
11	Service revenue		48		
12	Supplies expense	14		8	
13	**Totals**	88	88	8	8

An asterisk (*) identifies assignment material based on Appendix 4A.

QS 4-3 Work sheet information LO1

The following information is from the work sheet for Pursley Company as of December 31, 2020. Using this information, determine the amount that should be reported for Alice Pursley, Capital on the December 31, 2020, balance sheet.

	Income Statement		Balance Sheet and Statement of Changes in Equity	
	Debit	Credit	Debit	Credit
Cash...			7,000	
Alice Pursley, capital				50,000
Alice Pursley, withdrawals			32,000	
Totals	125,000	184,000		

QS 4-4 Interpreting a work sheet LO1

The following information is from the work sheet for Hascal Company as of December 31, 2020. Using this information, determine the amount for Sam Hascal, Capital that should be reported on the December 31, 2020, balance sheet.

	Income Statement		Balance Sheet and Statement of Changes in Equity	
	Debit	Credit	Debit	Credit
Cash...			4,500	
Sam Hascal, capital				165,000
Sam Hascal, withdrawals			32,000	
Totals	115,000	74,000		

QS 4-5 Classifying temporary and permanent accounts LO2

You are the accountant at Stephos Greek Taverna. After completing the December 31, 2020 financial statements, you need to post the closing entries to prepare for the 2021 year. Start the process by completing the following table.

Required

1. Identify whether the following accounts are temporary or permanent with a "✓" and
2. Determine what financial statement(s) each account is recorded on (income statement, balance sheet, or statement of changes in equity). Note that some accounts may be recorded on more than one financial statement.

Account	(1) Temporary?	(1) Permanent?	(2) Financial Statement?
a. Accounts Payable			
b. Insurance Expense			
c. Delivery Vehicle			
d. Interest Income			
e. Unearned Revenue			
f. Accumulated Depreciation			
g. Stephos Petridis, Capital			
h. Depreciation Expense			
i. Stephos Petridis, Withdrawals			
j. Wages Payable			
k. Prepaid Insurance			
l. Utility Expense			
m. Building			
n. Supplies Expense			

QS 4-6 Effects of closing entries LO2, 3

Jontil Co. began the current period with a $14,000 balance in the Peter Jontil, Capital account. At the end of the period, the company's adjusted account balances include the following temporary accounts with normal balances:

Service revenue..	$35,000
Salaries expense..	19,000
Depreciation expense..	4,000
Interest income..	3,500
Peter Jontil, withdrawals	6,000
Utilities expense...	2,300

a. After closing the revenue and expense accounts, what will be the balance of the Income Summary account?

b. After all of the closing entries are journalized and posted, what will be the balance of the Peter Jontil, Capital account?

QS 4-7 Closing entries LO3

Pure Plant Beauty is a sole proprietorship that has a developed a new line of skin care and makeup that uses natural and organic ingredients. The company showed the following adjusted account balances on April 30, 2020. Prepare and post the closing entries.

Assets		Liabilities		Capital	
250			30		200

Withdrawals		Revenue		Expenses	
20			100	60	

Income Summary	

QS 4-8 Closing entries LO3

Warden Repairs showed the following adjusted account balances on October 31, 2020. Prepare and post the closing entries.

Assets		Liabilities		Capital	
250			110		200

Withdrawals		Revenue		Expenses	
20			100	140	

Income Summary	

QS 4-9 Post-closing trial balance LO4

Silver Star Automotive showed the following account balances at October 31, 2020, after posting the closing entries. Prepare the post-closing trial balance.

Cash		Accounts Receivable		Unearned Revenue	
Bal.	40	Bal.	20	10	Bal.

Capital		Withdrawals		Revenues	
	5 40		5 5		23 23
	15	Bal.	-0-		-0- Bal.
	50 Bal.				

Expenses	
	8 8
Bal.	-0-

QS 4-10 Explaining the accounting cycle LO5

List the following steps of the accounting cycle in the proper order:

a. Preparing the unadjusted trial balance.

b. Preparing the post-closing trial balance.

c. Journalizing and posting adjusting entries.

d. Journalizing and posting closing entries.

e. Preparing the financial statements.

f. Journalizing transactions.

g. Posting the transaction entries.

h. Completing the work sheet.

QS 4-11 Classifying balance sheet items LO6

The following are categories on a classified balance sheet:

a. Current assets

b. Non-current investments

c. Property, plant, and equipment

d. Intangible assets

e. Current liabilities

f. Non-current liabilities

For each of the following items, select the letter that identifies the balance sheet category in which the item should appear.

_____ 1. Store equipment

_____ 2. Wages payable

_____ 3. Cash

_____ 4. Notes payable (due in three years)

_____ 5. Land not currently used in business operations

_____ 6. Accounts receivable

_____ 7. Trademarks

QS 4-12 Balance sheet classifications LO6

In the blank space beside each numbered balance sheet item, enter the letter of its balance sheet classification. If the item should not appear on the balance sheet, enter an *h* in the blank.

a. Current assets

b. Non-current investments

c. Property, plant, and equipment

d. Intangible assets

e. Current liabilities

f. Non-current liabilities

g. Equity

h. Does not appear on balance sheet

_____ 1. Depreciation expense, trucks

_____ 2. Lee Hale, capital

_____ 3. Interest receivable

_____ 4. Lee Hale, withdrawals

_____ 5. Automobiles

_____ 6. Notes payable (due in three years)

_____ 7. Accounts payable

_____ 8. Prepaid insurance

_____ 9. Land not currently used in business operations

_____ 10. Unearned services revenue

_____ 11. Accumulated depreciation, trucks

_____ 12. Cash

_____ 13. Building

_____ 14. Brand name

_____ 15. Office equipment

_____ 16. Land (used in operations)

_____ 17. Repairs expense

_____ 18. Prepaid property taxes

_____ 19. Notes payable (due in two months)

_____ 20. Notes receivable (due in two years)

QS 4-13 Classifying liabilities LO6

Use the following March 31, 2020, year-end adjusted balances to prepare Jardine Servicing's liabilities section on its March 31, 2020, classified balance sheet.

Accounts payable...	$ 14,000
Unearned revenue...	26,000
Notes payable, due February 1, 2021	45,000
Mortgage payable*	115,000

*$56,000 of this amount will be paid by March 31, 2021.

QS 4-14 Calculating current ratio LO7

Calculate Tucker Company's current ratio given the following information about its assets and liabilities (round to two decimal places), and compare it to the industry average current ratio of 2.2.

Accounts receivable...................................	$15,000	Long-term notes payable*.......................................	$20,000
Accounts payable......................................	10,000	Office supplies	1,800
Buildings...	42,000	Prepaid insurance	2,500
Cash...	6,000	Unearned services revenue...................................	4,000

*Due in three years.

QS 4-15 Calculating quick ratio LO7

Using the information in QS 4-14, calculate Tucker Company's quick ratio (round to two decimal places).

QS 4-16 Calculating debt to equity ratio LO7

The following is selected financial information from WestJet's Balance Sheet as at December 31, 2017 and 2016. Calculate the debt to equity ratio for 2017 and 2016 (round to two decimal places). Comment on the change.

(Numbers in thousands)	2017	2016
Current liabilities	1,726,954	1,621,333
Non-current liabilities	2,560,362	2,482,261
Shareholders' equity	2,212,524	2,060,702

*QS 4-17 Reversing entries LO8

On December 31, 2020, Ace Management Co. prepared an adjusting entry to accrue $9,800 of earned but un-recorded rent revenue. On January 20, 2021, Ace received rent payments in the amount of $15,500. Assuming Ace uses reversing entries, prepare the 2021 entries pertaining to the rent transactions.

EXERCISES

Exercise 4-1 Extending adjusted account balances on a work sheet LO1

These accounts are from the Adjusted Trial Balance columns in a company's 10-column work sheet. In the blank space beside each account, write the letter of the appropriate financial statement column to which a normal account balance should be extended.

a. Debit column for the income statement.

b. Credit column for the income statement.

_____
An asterisk (*) identifies assignment material based on Appendix 4A.

c. Debit column for the balance sheet and statement of changes in equity.

d. Credit column for the balance sheet and statement of changes in equity.

_____ **1.** Roberta Jefferson, withdrawals	_____ **9.** Cash
_____ **2.** Interest income	_____ **10.** Office supplies
_____ **3.** Accumulated depreciation, machinery	_____ **11.** Roberta Jefferson, capital
_____ **4.** Service revenue	_____ **12.** Wages payable
_____ **5.** Accounts receivable	_____ **13.** Machinery
_____ **6.** Rent expense	_____ **14.** Insurance expense
_____ **7.** Depreciation expense, machinery	_____ **15.** Interest expense
_____ **8.** Accounts payable	_____ **16.** Interest receivable

Exercise 4-2 Extending accounts in the work sheet LO1 eXcel

CHECK FIGURE: Loss = $8,150

The Adjusted Trial Balance columns of a 10-column work sheet for Webber Co. follow. Complete the work sheet by extending the account balances into the appropriate financial statement columns and by entering the amount of profit or loss for the reporting period.

	Webber Co. Work Sheet.xlsx		
Home Insert Page Layout Formulas Data Review View			
P18	fx		
	A	B	C
1	**Webber Co.**		
2	**Work Sheet**		
3	**December 31, 2020**		
4		**Adjusted**	
5		**Trial Balance**	
6	**Account**	**Debit**	**Credit**
7	101 Cash	$ 21,000	
8	106 Accounts receivable	8,200	
9	153 Trucks	48,000	
10	154 Accumulated depreciation, trucks		$ 31,250
11	193 Franchise	6,500	
12	201 Accounts payable		13,000
13	209 Salaries payable		14,600
14	233 Unearned revenue		2,450
15	301 Bo Webber, capital		37,750
16	302 Bo Webber, withdrawals	7,200	
17	401 Plumbing revenue		31,600
18	611 Depreciation expense, trucks	12,100	
19	622 Salaries expense	17,800	
20	640 Rent expense	6,000	
21	677 Miscellaneous expense	3,850	
22	**Totals**	**$ 130,650**	**$ 130,650**

Exercise 4-3 Preparing a work sheet LO1

CHECK FIGURE: 3. Adjusted trial balance columns = $358,200

The December 31, 2020, unadjusted trial balance for Musical Sensations after its second year of operations follows:

	Musical Sensations Work Sheet.xlsx		
	Home Insert Page Layout Formulas Data Review View		
	P18 fx		
	A	B	C
1	**Musical Sensations**		
2	**Work Sheet**		
3	**December 31, 2020**		
4		**Unadjusted**	
5		**Trial Balance**	
6	**Account**	**Debit**	**Credit**
7	Cash	$ 7,500	
8	Accounts receivable	14,200	
9	Office supplies	790	
10	Musical equipment	125,000	
11	Accumulated depreciation, musical equipment		$ 21,600
12	Accounts payable		4,200
13	Unearned performance revenue		12,400
14	Jim Daley, capital		154,300
15	Jim Daley, withdrawals	52,000	
16	Performance revenue		138,000
17	Salaries expense	86,000	
18	Travelling expense	45,010	
19	**Totals**	**$ 330,500**	**$ 330,500**

Required

1. Enter the unadjusted trial balance onto a work sheet.

2. Using the following additional information, enter the adjustments into the work sheet:

   a. A review of the Unearned Performance Revenue account revealed a balance remaining of $9,225.

   b. Annual depreciation on the musical equipment is $21,600.

   c. Accrued salaries at December 31 totalled $6,100.

   d. It was determined that $650 of the balance in the Office Supplies account had been used.

3. Complete the work sheet.

4. Calculate the balance in the capital account as it would appear on the December 31, 2020, balance sheet.

Exercise 4-4 Work sheet interpretation and closing entries LO1, 3

Below are excerpts from the work sheets of two businesses as at March 31, 2020. Those rows that calculate totals are at the bottom of the last two sets of columns.

Required Do the following for each business:

1. Identify the profit or loss for the year ended March 31, 2020.

2. Prepare the entry to close the Income Summary account to capital.

3. Calculate the post-closing balance in capital at March 31, 2020.

a.

Income Statement		Balance Sheet and Statement of Changes in Equity	
Debit	Credit	Debit	Credit
263,700	300,500	357,300	320,500
36,800			36,800
300,500	300,500	357,300	357,300

The adjusted balances in withdrawals and capital were $17,000 and $63,000, respectively.

b.

Income Statement		Balance Sheet and Statement of Changes in Equity	
Debit	Credit	Debit	Credit
540,000	480,000	945,000	1,005,000
	60,000	60,000	
540,000	540,000	1,005,000	1,005,000

The adjusted balances in withdrawals and capital were $0 and $114,000, respectively.

Exercise 4-5 Completing the income statement columns and preparing closing entries LO1, 3

These partially completed Income Statement columns from a 10-column work sheet are for the Winston Sail'em Boat Rental Company for the year ended December 31, 2020. Use the information to determine the amount that should be entered on the profit line of the work sheet. In addition, prepare closing entries for the company. The owner's name is Carl Winston, and the pre-closing balance of the withdrawals account is $17,700.

	Debit	Credit
Rent revenue		97,000
Salaries expense	35,000	
Insurance expense	4,100	
Dock rental expense	11,700	
Boat supplies expense	5,920	
Depreciation expense, boats	21,200	
Totals		
Profit		
Totals		

Exercise 4-6 Preparing closing entries and the post-closing trial balance LO2, 3, 4

CHECK FIGURE: Post-closing trial balance columns = $49,700

The adjusted trial balance at April 30, 2020, for Zhang Co. follows.

		Debit	Credit
101	Cash	$ 3,400	
106	Accounts receivable	8,300	
153	Trucks	25,000	
154	Accumulated depreciation, trucks		$ 8,050
193	Franchise	13,000	
201	Accounts payable		9,400
209	Salaries payable		3,000
233	Unearned revenue		1,300
301	Angel Zhang, capital		28,100
302	Angel Zhang, withdrawals	9,400	
401	Plumbing revenue		41,050
611	Depreciation expense, trucks	4,700	
622	Salaries expense	17,600	
640	Rent expense	2,800	
677	Advertising expense	6,700	
901	Income summary		
	Totals	$90,900	$90,900

Required

1. Prepare the four closing entries.

2. Prepare a post-closing trial balance.

Exercise 4-7 Closing entries LO2, 3

Following is the adjusted trial balance, with accounts in alphabetical order, for TRN Magazine as at January 31, 2020:

	Debit	Credit
Accounts receivable...	$ 21,400	
Accumulated depreciation, equipment..................		$ 12,400
Cash...	8,900	
Depreciation expense, equipment.........................	1,700	
Equipment...	19,400	
Interest income...		490
Rent expense	17,900	
Salaries expense..	61,400	
Subscription revenues...		71,400
Trish Norris, capital		46,810
Trish Norris, withdrawals	19,800	
Unearned subscription revenue.............................		19,400
Totals..	$150,500	$150,500

Required Prepare the closing entries.

Exercise 4-8 Closing entries LO2, 3

Improv Club (IC) features entertaining improvisational theatre performances. The theatre features a range of shows and talented performers. IC prepares financial statements on an annual basis. The following year-end accounts as of December 31, 2020 are listed in alphabetical order and have normal balances.

Account	Amount	Account	Amount
Accumulated depreciation, equipment.................	$ 13,000	Prepaid insurance..	$ 6,500
Cash...	40,000	Rent expense	61,000
Depreciation expense, equipment.........................	4,000	Salaries expense...	42,000
Equipment...	46,000	Supplies	4,000
Insurance expense	3,000	Supplies expense..	8,600
Nick Stilz, capital...	110,100	Ticket revenue..	131,000
Nick Stilz, withdrawals..................................	43,000	Unearned revenue...	4,000

Required

1. Prepare an adjusted trial balance as at December 31, 2020. Will Nick Stilz's capital account of $110,100 appear on the balance sheet as at December 31, 2020? Explain.

2. Prepare the closing entries for the company.

3. What is the ending balance of Nick Stilz's capital account as at December 31, 2020?

Exercise 4-9 Preparing and posting closing entries LO2, 3

CHECK FIGURE: Post-closing balance, Marcy Jones, Capital = $91,000

Set up the following general ledger accounts using T-accounts for Jones Consulting with the balances provided. Prepare closing entries at December 31, 2020, and post them to the T-accounts.

Assets	
Dec. 31 142,000	

Liabilities	
	51,000 Dec. 31

Marcy Jones, Capital	
	71,800 Dec. 31

Rent Expense	
Dec. 31 9,100	

Marcy Jones, Withdrawals	
Dec. 31 38,000	

Salaries Expense	
Dec. 31 27,000	

Income Summary	

Insurance Expense	
Dec. 31 1,500	

Services Revenue	
	103,000 Dec. 31

Depreciation Expense	
Dec. 31 8,200	

Exercise 4-10 Post-closing trial balance LO4

Required Using your answer from Exercise 4-9, prepare a post-closing trial balance.

Exercise 4-11 Post-closing trial balance LO2, 3, 4

Jozef's Roofing Services showed the following post-closing trial balance after the posting of the closing entries on June 30, 2020:

	Debit	Credit
Cash	$ 21,000	
Accounts receivable	36,000	
Equipment	59,500	
Accumulated depreciation, equipment		$ 12,000
Trucks	138,000	
Accumulated depreciation, trucks		66,000
Accounts payable		19,200
Jozef Jones, capital		216,200
Jozef Jones, withdrawals	59,900	
Interest income		1,150
Other expenses	150	
Totals	$314,550	$314,550

Required

1. Identify the error(s) in the post-closing trial balance.
2. What entry is required to correct the error(s)?
3. Calculate the correct balance at June 30, 2020, for Jozef Jones, Capital.

Exercise 4-12 Post-closing trial balance LO2, 3, 4

CHECK FIGURE: b. = $200,150

The March 31, 2020, adjusted trial balance for Amusement Park Repair is shown below with accounts in alphabetical order.

		Debit	Credit
_____	Accounts payable		$ 31,000
_____	Accounts receivable..	$ 48,000	
_____	Accumulated depreciation, equipment............................		9,000
_____	Accumulated depreciation, truck.....................................		21,000
_____	Cash..	14,400	
_____	Depreciation expense..	3,800	
_____	Equipment..	19,000	
_____	Franchise..	21,000	
_____	Gas and oil expense...	7,500	
_____	Intangible asset	7,000	
_____	Interest expense..	450	
_____	Interest payable...		750
_____	Land not currently used in business operations..............	148,000	
_____	Long-term notes payable[1]		35,000
_____	Notes payable, due February 1, 2021		7,000
_____	Notes receivable[2]..	6,000	
_____	Prepaid rent...	14,000	
_____	Rent expense	51,000	
_____	Repair revenue		266,000
_____	Repair supplies	13,100	
_____	Repair supplies expense..	29,000	
_____	Truck...	26,000	
_____	Unearned repair revenue		12,600
_____	Vic Sopik, capital...		74,900
_____	Vic Sopik, withdrawals...	49,000	
_____	Totals	$457,250	$457,250

[1]$5,000 of the long-term note payable is due during the year ended March 31, 2021.
[2]$2,000 of the notes receivable will be collected by March 31, 2021.

Required

Preparation Component:

a. Place an X in the space provided beside each *account balance* that would *not* appear on the post-closing trial balance.

b. Calculate the post-closing balance in the owner's capital.

Analysis Component: Explain why the account balances identified in part (a) would not appear on the post-closing trial balance.

Exercise 4-13 Classified balance sheet LO6

CHECK FIGURE: i. = $286,500

Using the information in Exercise 4-12, calculate each of the following:

a. Current assets

b. Property, plant, and equipment

c. Intangible assets

d. Non-current investments

e. Total assets

f. Current liabilities

g. Non-current liabilities

h. Total liabilities

i. Total liabilities and equity

Exercise 4-14 Preparing a classified balance sheet LO6 eXcel

Sunshine Sushi, a Japanese restaurant, has the following adjusted trial balance with accounts listed in alphabetical order. Using the template provided, prepare a classified balance sheet for the year ended December 31, 2020. For the bank loan, $60,550 is due in 2021. For Notes receivable, $41,500 will be collected in 2021.

Account Title	Debit	Credit
Accounts payable		$ 41,625
Accumulated depreciation, equipment		99,700
Accumulated depreciation, furniture		38,250
Bank loan		501,000
Cash	$115,000	
Equipment	373,875	
Operating expenses	38,150	
Furniture	102,000	
Merchandise inventory	34,250	
Natsuki Miyakawa, capital		28,500
Natsuki Miyakawa, withdrawal	11,300	
Notes receivable	115,500	
Revenue		50,750
Wages payable		30,250
Total	$790,075	$790,075

Sunshine Sushi
Balance Sheet
December 31, 2020

Assets			
Current assets:			
Total current assets			
Non-current investments:			
Property, plant, and equipment:			
Total assets			
Liabilities			
Current liabilities:			
Total current liabilities			
Non-current liabilities:			
Total liabilities			
Equity			
Total liabilities and equity			

Exercise 4-15 **Preparing a classified balance sheet** LO6

CHECK FIGURE: Total assets = $122,150

A partial alphabetized list of adjusted account balances is shown for Dover Pacific Tours as at November 30, 2020 (all accounts have normal balances). Pat Dover, the owner, uses the following account classification system:

101–149	Current assets		190–199	Non-current investments
150–169	Property, plant, and equipment		201–249	Current liabilities
170–189	Intangible assets		250–299	Non-current liabilities

Acct. No.	Account Title	Adjusted Account Balance
201	Accounts payable	$41,000
106	Accounts receivable	19,000
155	Accumulated depreciation, office furniture	4,100
153	Accumulated depreciation, vehicles	15,800
101	Cash	7,200
172	Copyright	9,000
240	Notes payable A	14,000
270	Notes payable B[1]	21,600
195	Notes receivable[2]	20,500
154	Office furniture	6,500
110	Prepaid insurance	4,600
112	Prepaid rent	9,000
205	Salaries payable	12,100
118	Supplies	2,250
206	Unearned touring revenue	23,000
152	Vehicles	64,000

[1]$10,000 of note payable B is to be paid by November 30, 2021.
[2]$7,500 of the notes receivable is to be collected by November 30, 2021.

Required Prepare a classified balance sheet for year ended November 30, 2020.

Exercise 4-16 **Preparing a classified balance sheet** LO6

CHECK FIGURE: Total assets = $444,700

Use the following adjusted trial balance of Hanson Trucking Company to prepare a classified balance sheet as of December 31, 2020.

Account Title	Debit	Credit
Cash	$ 13,000	
Accounts receivable	29,600	
Office supplies	3,100	
Trucks	170,000	
Accumulated depreciation, trucks		$ 46,000
Land	275,000	
Accounts payable		31,000
Interest payable		400
Long-term notes payable (due in 4 years)		152,000
Stanley Hanson, capital		206,200
Stanley Hanson, withdrawals	19,000	
Trucking revenue		168,000
Depreciation expense, trucks	22,500	
Salaries expense	58,000	
Office supplies expense	6,500	
Repairs expense, trucks	6,900	
Total	$603,600	$603,600

Exercise 4-17 Comprehensive accounting cycle LO2, 3, 4, 6

CHECK FIGURES: c. Total debits = $38,000; e. Total debits = $40,000; f. Profit = $3,400; Total assets = $18,000; h. Total debits = $30,000

After five years of operations, Svenson's Tutoring Clinic showed the following post-closing balances at December 31, 2019.

Cash	Accounts Receivable	Prepaid Rent	Office Equipment
2,000	5,000	3,000	20,000

Accumulated Depreciation, Office Equipment	Unearned Revenue	Leda Svenson, Capital	Leda Svenson, Withdrawals
10,000	2,900	17,100	-0-

Tutoring Revenue	Rent Expense	Depreciation Expense	Advertising Expense
-0-	-0-	-0-	-0-

Required

Analysis Component:

a. Explain why Leda Svenson, Withdrawals, Tutoring Revenue, Rent Expense, Depreciation Expense, and Advertising Expense have zero balances.

Preparation Component:

b. Journalize and post the following transactions that occurred during 2020.

Jan 15	Provided $8,000 of tutoring services on account.
Feb. 20	Paid $2,000 for advertising that appeared in today's newspaper.
Jul. 7	Collected $9,000 from credit customers.
Dec. 10	The owner withdrew $3,000 cash for personal use.

c. Prepare an unadjusted trial balance as at December 31, 2020.

d. Journalize and post the adjusting entries on December 31, 2020, based on the following additional information:
- Annual depreciation on the office equipment is $2,000.
- $2,400 of the balance in unearned revenue has been earned.
- The entire balance in prepaid rent has expired.

e. Prepare an adjusted trial balance at December 31, 2020.

f. Prepare an income statement, statement of changes in equity, and classified balance sheet.

g. Journalize and post the closing entries.

h. Prepare a post-closing trial balance.

Exercise 4-18 Complete accounting cycle (monthly) LO2, 3, 5, 6

Emily Lee grew up in Vancouver and loves to be a tourist in her own city. In order to make money to pay for university, she opened a walking tour company, Very Vancouver. The following are transactions for the month of May 2020, the first month of operations.

May 2	Emily moved $5,500 from her personal bank account to a business bank account at TD Bank. She also invested a laptop worth $900 into the business.
May 3	Purchased supplies, including a microphone, and brochures for $600 cash.
May 4	Purchased a printer for $360 on account.
May 5	Purchased a one-year insurance policy for $2,400 cash.
May 6	Emily withdrew $200 for a Mother's Day gift.
May 8	Interviewed and hired one employee to assist with leading tours.
May 10	Emily launched a social media campaign of Very Vancouver on Facebook. As a result, she received $1,920 of cash for future tour bookings.
May 15	Led three tours of Stanley Park and received $600 cash.
May 25	Led four tours of Granville Island for $1,000. The customers on this tour had prepaid on May 10.

The following information is known at May 31, 2020.

- The laptop has an estimated life of three years.
- The printer has an estimated life of three years.
- There are $200 of supplies that are not used.
- A portion of the insurance policy has expired.
- Wages of $500 were unpaid and unrecorded.

Required

1. Prepare journal entries for the May transactions.
2. Post the journal entries to the general ledger accounts using T-accounts.
3. Prepare and post all required adjusting entries to the T-accounts.
4. Prepare an income statement, statement of changes in equity, and classified balance sheet.
5. Prepare the journal entries for the closing entries and post them to the T-accounts.
6. Prepare a post-closing trial balance.

Exercise 4-19 Calculating the current ratio LO7

Calculate (to two decimal places) the current ratio in each of the following cases and indicate whether it is *Favourable* (F) or *Unfavourable* (U) (assuming that the current ratio for the industry is an average of 1.1):

	Case 1	Case 2	Case 3	Case 4
Current Assets	$78,000	$104,000	$44,000	$84,500
Current Liabilities	31,000	75,000	48,000	80,600

Exercise 4-20 Calculating the current ratio and quick ratio LO7

The following is selected simplified information from Organic Catering's balance sheet as at December 31, 2020 and December 31, 2021. You, business analyst at Organic Catering, have been asked to calculate the current ratio and the quick ratio (round to two decimal places). Provide your manager with comments on the ratios and the change from 2020 to 2021.

(Numbers in thousands)	2021	2020
Cash	$ 6,501	$ 3,880
Accounts receivable	4,368	4,616
Notes receivable (current)	220	265
Inventories	123	137
Prepaid expenses and other (current) assets	190	695
Current liabilities	11,061	10,649
Total liabilities	31,376	31,980
Shareholders' equity	45,964	56,700

Exercise 4-21 Calculating the debt to equity ratio LO7

Refer to the information in Exercise 4-20. You, business analyst at Organic Catering, have been asked to calculate the debt to equity ratio (round to two decimal places). Provide your manager with comments on the ratio and the change from 2020 to 2021.

*Exercise 4-22 Reversing entries LO8

Breaker Corporation records prepaid assets and unearned revenues in balance sheet accounts. The following information was used to prepare adjusting entries for Breaker Corporation as of August 31, 2020, the end of the company's fiscal year:

a. The company has earned $5,000 of unrecorded service revenue.

b. The expired portion of prepaid insurance is $2,700.

c. The earned portion of the Unearned Revenue account balance is $1,900.

d. Depreciation expense for the office equipment is $2,300.

e. Employees have earned but have not been paid salaries of $2,400.

Required Prepare the appropriate reversing entries that would simplify the bookkeeping effort for recording subsequent cash transactions related to these adjustments.

*Exercise 4-23 Reversing entries LO8

The following conditions existed for Maxit Co. on October 31, 2020, the end of its fiscal year:

a. Maxit rents a building for $3,200 per month. By a prearrangement, the company delayed paying October's rent until November 5. On this date, the company paid the rent for both October and November.

b. Maxit rents space in a building it owns to a tenant for $750 per month. By prearrangement, the tenant delayed paying the October rent until November 8. On this date, the tenant paid the rent for both October and November.

Required

1. Prepare the adjusting entries that Maxit should record for these situations as of October 31.

2. Assuming that Maxit does not use reversing entries, prepare journal entries to record Maxit's payment of rent on November 5 and the collection of rent on November 8 from Maxit's tenant.

3. Assuming that Maxit does use reversing entries, prepare those entries and the journal entries to record Maxit's payment of rent on November 5 and the collection of rent on November 8 from Maxit's tenant.

An asterisk (*) identifies assignment material based on Appendix 4A.

PROBLEMS

Problem 4-1A Completing a work sheet LO1 eXcel

CHECK FIGURE: 3. Adjusted trial balance columns = $646,265

The March 31, 2020, unadjusted trial balance for Silva Rentals after its first year of operations is shown below:

			Silva Rentals Trial Balance.xlsx		
			Home Insert Page Layout Formulas Data Review View		
			P18 fx		
			A	B	C
1			**Silva Rentals**		
2			**Unadjusted Trial Balance**		
3			**March 31, 2020**		
4				**Unadjusted**	
5				**Trial Balance**	
6	**No.**		**Account**	**Dr.**	**Cr.**
7	101	Cash		$ 7,000	
8	110	Rent receivable		31,000	
9	124	Office supplies		2,250	
10	141	Notes receivable, due 2023		46,000	
11	161	Furniture		16,000	
12	173	Building		216,000	
13	183	Land		41,000	
14	191	Patent		9,600	
15	201	Accounts payable			$ 13,750
16	252	Long-term note payable			175,000
17	301	Stephen Silva, capital			90,250
18	302	Stephen Silva, withdrawals		92,000	
19	406	Rent revenue			328,800
20	620	Office salaries expense		52,000	
21	633	Interest expense		5,250	
22	655	Advertising expense		14,600	
23	673	Janitorial expense		41,000	
24	690	Utilities expense		34,100	
25		**Totals**		$ 607,800	$ 607,800

Required

1. Enter the unadjusted trial balance onto a work sheet.

2. Using the following additional information, enter the adjustments into the work sheet (the Chart of Accounts in Appendix IV may be useful when additional accounts are required):

   a. It was determined that the balance in the Rent Receivable account at March 31 should be $36,000.

   b. A count of the office supplies showed $1,830 of the balance had been used.

   c. Annual depreciation on the building is $25,000 and $3,500 on the furniture.

   d. The two part-time office staff members each get paid $1,600 biweekly. The last biweekly pay period ended Friday, March 20. At March 31, six days' salary had accrued.

e. A review of the balance in Advertising Expense showed that $2,400 was for advertisements to appear in the April issue of *Canadian Business* magazine.

f. Accrued utilities at March 31 totalled $2,620.

g. March interest of $425 on the long-term note payable is unrecorded and unpaid as of March 31.

3. Complete the work sheet.

Problem 4-2A Completing a work sheet LO1 eXcel

CHECK FIGURE: 3. Adjusted trial balance columns = $67,380

The June 30, 2020, unadjusted trial balance for Trenton Consulting after its first year of operations follows:

	Trenton Consulting Trial Balance.xlsx		
Home Insert Page Layout Formulas Data Review View			
P18	fx		
	A	B	C
1	**Trenton Consulting**		
2	**Unadjusted Trial Balance**		
3	**June 30, 2020**		
4		**Unadjusted**	
5		**Trial Balance**	
6	**Account**	**Dr.**	**Cr.**
7	Cash	680	
8	Accounts receivable	2,900	
9	Prepaid rent	3,660	
10	Equipment	9,600	
11	Accounts payable		1,730
12	Toni Trenton, capital		26,650
13	Toni Trenton, withdrawals	6,880	
14	Consulting revenue		30,200
15	Wages expense	24,920	
16	Insurance expense	1,620	
17	Rent expense	8,320	
18	**Totals**	58,580	58,580

Required

1. Enter the unadjusted trial balance onto a work sheet.

2. Using the following additional information, enter the adjustments onto the work sheet:

   a. Annual depreciation on the equipment is $1,500.

   b. The balance in the Prepaid Rent account is for six months of rent commencing March 1, 2020.

   c. Unpaid and unrecorded wages at June 30 totalled $3,200.

   d. Accrued revenues at June 30 totalled $4,100.

3. Complete the work sheet.

4. Calculate the balance in the capital account as it would appear on the June 30, 2020, balance sheet.

Analysis Component: What effect does a loss have on the accounting equation?

Problem 4-3A LO1, 6 eXcel

CHECK FIGURES: 1. Adjusted trial balance columns = $447,890; 3. Profit = $64,130; Total assets = $130,300

This unadjusted trial balance is for Challenger Construction at the end of its fiscal year, September 30, 2020. The beginning balance of the owner's capital account was $46,000 and the owner invested another $25,000 cash in the company during the year.

		Challenger Construction Trial Balance.xlsx		
		Home Insert Page Layout Formulas Data Review View		
		P18	fx	
	A		B	C
1	**Challenger Construction**			
2	**Unadjusted Trial Balance**			
3	**September 30, 2020**			
4			Unadjusted	
5			Trial Balance	
6	**No.**	**Account**	**Dr.**	**Cr.**
7	101	Cash	$ 22,000	
8	126	Supplies	17,200	
9	128	Prepaid insurance	9,600	
10	149	Land not currently used in operations	50,000	
11	167	Equipment	106,000	
12	168	Accumulated depreciation, Equipment		$ 40,500
13	191	Copyright	6,000	
14	201	Accounts payable		8,100
15	203	Interest payable		-0-
16	210	Wages payable		-0-
17	251	Long-term notes payable		50,000
18	301	Chris Challenger, capital		71,000
19	302	Chris Challenger, withdrawals	68,000	
20	401	Construction revenue		255,620
21	612	Depreciation expense, equipment	-0-	
22	623	Wages expense	96,000	
23	633	Interest expense	1,200	
24	637	Insurance expense	-0-	
25	640	Rent expense	26,400	
26	652	Supplies expense	-0-	
27	683	Business taxes expense	10,000	
28	684	Repairs expense	5,020	
29	690	Utilities expense	7,800	
30		**Totals**	**$ 425,220**	**$ 425,220**

Required

1. Prepare a 10-column work sheet for fiscal 2020, starting with the unadjusted trial balance and including these additional facts:

   a. The inventory of supplies at the end of the year had a cost of $3,200.

   b. The cost of expired insurance for the year is $8,400.

   c. Annual depreciation of the equipment is $17,600.

d. The September utilities expense was not included in the trial balance because the bill arrived after it was prepared. Its $750 amount needs to be recorded.

e. The company's employees have earned $4,200 of accrued wages.

f. The interest expense of $120 for September has not yet been paid or recorded.

2. Use the work sheet to prepare the adjusting and closing entries.

3. Prepare an income statement, a statement of changes in equity, and a classified balance sheet. $16,000 of the long-term note payable is to be paid by September 30, 2021.

Analysis Component: Analyze the following potential errors and describe how each would affect the 10-column work sheet. Explain whether the error is likely to be discovered in completing the work sheet and, if not, the effect of the error on the financial statements.

a. The adjustment to record used supplies was credited to Supplies for $3,200 and debited the same amount to Supplies Expense.

b. When completing the adjusted trial balance in the work sheet, the $22,000 cash balance was incorrectly entered in the Credit column.

Problem 4-4A Closing entries LO2, 3, 4

CHECK FIGURE: 2. Post-closing trial balance = $122,000

MY Autobody's adjusted trial balance on December 31, 2020, appears in the work sheet as follows:

No.	Account	Debit	Credit
101	Cash	$ 28,000	
124	Shop supplies	1,800	
128	Prepaid insurance	4,200	
167	Equipment	88,000	
168	Accumulated depreciation, equipment		$ 7,500
201	Accounts payable		19,000
210	Wages payable		8,860
301	Mike Yang, capital		140,000
302	Mike Yang, withdrawals	36,000	
401	Repair revenue		157,630
612	Depreciation expense, equipment	8,500	
623	Wages expense	104,500	
637	Insurance expense	1,900	
640	Rent expense	52,350	
650	Office supplies expense	4,800	
690	Utilities expense	2,940	
	Totals	$332,990	$332,990

Required

1. Prepare closing entries.

2. Prepare the post-closing trial balance at December 31, 2020.

Problem 4-5A Financial statements LO6

CHECK FIGURES: Loss = $17,360; Total assets = $114,500

Using the information from Problem 4-4A, prepare an income statement and a statement of changes in equity for the year ended December 31, 2020, and a classified balance sheet at December 31, 2020. There were no investments by the owner during the year.

Analysis Component: MY Autobody experienced a loss during 2020. If you were one of the business's creditors, should this loss cause you to be concerned about being paid in 2021?

Problem 4-6A Closing entries LO2, 3

The adjusted trial balance for Lloyd Construction as of December 31, 2020, follows:

No.	Account	Debit	Credit
101	Cash	$ 15,300	
104	Current investments	20,300	
126	Supplies	6,900	
149	Notes receivable	38,500	
167	Equipment	71,000	
168	Accumulated depreciation, equipment		$ 34,500
173	Building	253,000	
174	Accumulated depreciation, building		137,500
183	Land	82,500	
193	Franchise	27,500	
201	Accounts payable		16,300
203	Interest payable		120
233	Unearned professional revenue		26,300
251	Long-term notes payable		125,000
301	Amar Lloyd, capital		85,640
302	Amar Lloyd, withdrawals	2,300	
401	Professional revenue		199,480
406	Rent revenue		22,500
606	Depreciation expense, building	19,300	
612	Depreciation expense, equipment	7,300	
623	Wages expense	63,300	
633	Interest expense	540	
637	Insurance expense	17,300	
652	Supplies expense	12,100	
688	Telephone expense	3,700	
690	Utilities expense	6,500	
	Totals	$647,340	$647,340

An analysis of other information reveals that Lloyd Construction is required to make a $41,500 payment on the long-term notes payable during 2021. The notes receivable are due May 1, 2022. Also, Amar Lloyd invested $68,000 cash early in 2020.

Required Prepare the closing entries made at the end of the year.

Problem 4-7A Financial statements LO6

CHECK FIGURES: Profit = $91,940; Total assets = $343,000

Using the adjusted trial balance in Problem 4-6A, prepare the income statement and statement of changes in equity for the year ended December 31, 2020, and the classified balance sheet at December 31, 2020.

Analysis Component: Why must liabilities be separated on the balance sheet between *current* and *non-current*? What effect would it have had on Lloyd's balance sheet if the long-term note were not separated?

Problem 4-8A Adjusting entries and closing entries LO2, 3, 5

Adventure Elements provides outdoor activities including ropes courses, rock climbing, and zip-lining. The company offers a unique experience for team building activities, camps for youth, and anyone seeking outdoor adventure.

No.	Account	Debit	Credit
201	Accounts payable and accrued liabilities..................................		$ 4,500
103	Accounts receivable	$ 6,200	
168	Accumulated depreciation, equipment....................................		6,250
300	Becky Brenner, capital..		44,300
301	Becky Brenner, withdrawals...	40,300	
101	Cash	10,750	
194	Copyright	11,350	
167	Equipment..	23,400	
633	Insurance expense...	2,660	
623	Interest expense	525	
233	Long-term notes payable...		18,500
141	Notes receivable, due January 1, 2023...................................	10,900	
610	Rent expense..	9,800	
402	Revenues..		74,070
126	Supplies..	475	
637	Supplies expense...	2,580	
652	Telephone expense..	2,980	
203	Unearned revenues		13,800
688	Utilities expense...	2,500	
612	Wages expense...	37,000	
	Totals...	$161,420	$161,420

You are the accounting manager. Your staff submitted the following trial balance for the year ended March 31, 2020. In your review, you discover the following additional information that has not been included in the trial balance.

a. On April 2, you received the telephone bill for the month of March for $365.

b. On March 31, Adventure Element took a university student club zip-lining. An invoice had been sent to the student club for $4,250 due April 30.

c. On March 31, the company held a teen's camp for $1,840. All tickets had been prepaid two weeks in advance.

d. The equipment has an estimated useful life of 20 years. If you need to create a new account, use account number 606.

Required

1. Prepare the missing adjusting entries for transactions a–d.

2. Prepare an adjusted trial balance.

3. Based on your adjusted trial balance, prepare the closing entries.

Problem 4-9A Financial statements LO6

CHECK FIGURES: Profit = $20,580; Total assets = $59,905

Based on the adjusted trial balance prepared in Problem 4-8A, prepare an income statement and a statement of changes in equity for the year ended March 31, 2020, and a classified balance sheet at March 31, 2020. The owner made an additional investment during the year of $12,000. A $3,800 payment on the long-term notes payable will be made during the year ended March 31, 2021.

Analysis Component: Why might Adventure Elements be tempted to report the notes receivable as a current asset on the March 31, 2020, balance sheet?

Problem 4-10A Analyzing closing entries LO2, 3, 4

CHECK FIGURE: 1. Profit = $60,230

The following closing entries were prepared for Apex Architectural Designs regarding its year just ended June 30, 2020:

2020				
June	30	Design Revenue...	135,000	
		Income Summary		135,000
		To close the revenue account.		
	30	Income Summary..	74,770	
		Depreciation Expense, Office Equipment..................		1,700
		Depreciation Expense, Office Furniture.....................		840
		Insurance Expense		1,190
		Interest Expense		340
		Supplies Expense		2,100
		Telephone Expense..		1,550
		Utilities Expense..		2,650
		Salaries Expense..		64,400
		To close expense accounts.		
June	30	Income Summary	60,230	
		Nolan Apex, Capital...		60,230
		To close Income Summary to capital.		
	30	Nolan Apex, Capital	34,500	
		Nolan Apex, Withdrawals...		34,500
		To close withdrawals to capital.		

Required

1. Prepare an income statement based on the information provided.

2. Calculate the post-closing balance in the capital account at June 30, 2020, given that the adjusted balance on June 30, 2019, was $85,500.

Problem 4-11A Preparing financial statements LO6

CHECK FIGURES: Loss = $62,020; Total assets = $226,720

The adjusted trial balance for Impressions Dance School has been provided for the year ended September 30, 2020. The new bookkeeper alphabetized the accounts.

Account	Debit	Credit
Accounts payable		$ 22,480
Accounts receivable	$ 13,300	
Accumulated depreciation, automobiles		39,160
Accumulated depreciation, building		163,000
Alisha Bjorn, capital		164,960
Alisha Bjorn, withdrawals	10,000	
Automobiles	70,000	
Brand name	8,600	
Building	234,000	
Cash	11,400	
Copyright	6,700	
Dance lesson revenue		153,680
Depreciation expense, automobiles	6,900	
Depreciation expense, building	28,200	
Gas, oil, and repairs expense	29,400	
Land	32,700	
Land for future expansion	48,000	
Notes payable*		88,000
Rent revenue		20,800
Salaries expense	172,000	
Store supplies	4,180	
Unearned revenue		23,300
Totals	$675,380	$675,380

*The notes payable plus interest are due in 18 months.

Required Prepare an income statement and a statement of changes in equity for the year ended September 30, 2020, plus a September 30, 2020, classified balance sheet. The owner made no investments during the year.

Analysis Component: Alisha Bjorn wants to buy a new car for the business. As her bank manager, what do you advise?

Problem 4-12A Preparing a classified balance sheet LO6, 7

CHECK FIGURES: 1. Capital = $520,775; 2. Total assets = $895,400

An alphabetical list of the adjusted trial balance accounts for North Country Rentals after its first year of operations ending March 31, 2020, is shown below:

Account	Adjusted Account Balance*
Accounts payable	$ 9,100
Accumulated depreciation, building	25,000
Accumulated depreciation, furniture	3,500
Advertising expense	16,200
Brand name	3,000
Building	591,000
Cash	17,000
Depreciation expense, building	25,000
Depreciation expense, furniture	3,500
Furniture	42,800
Interest expense	10,260
Interest payable	900
Janitorial expense	41,000
Land	110,000
Long-term notes payable	362,000
Notes receivable, due 2023	143,000
Office salaries expense	126,625
Office supplies	700
Office supplies expense	6,100
Prepaid advertising	400
Rent revenue	398,400
Rent receivable	16,000
Salaries payable	2,625
Utilities expense	36,720
Wyett North, capital	415,780
Wyett North, withdrawals	28,000

*Assume all accounts have a normal balance.

Required

1. Calculate the capital balance as it would appear on the March 31, 2020, balance sheet.
2. Prepare a classified balance sheet. Assume that $215,000 of the Long-Term Notes Payable will be paid during the year ended March 31, 2021. Also, $55,000 of the notes receivable will be collected by March 31, 2021.
3. Calculate the current ratio and the debt to equity ratio (round to two decimal places).

Analysis Component: North Country shows an adjusted balance in the *Long-Term Notes Payable* account of $362,000 at March 31, 2020. Review the balance sheet just prepared and make a reasonable assumption about what the $362,000 was most logically used for by North Country. Explain whether or not this is generally considered a good use of borrowed funds and why.

Problem 4-13A **Performing the steps in the accounting cycle** LO2, 3, 4, 5, 6

CHECK FIGURES: 4. Loss = $1,070; Total assets = $102,100; 6. Post-closing trial balance = $104,150

On June 1, 2020, Sam Near created a new travel agency called Tours-For-Less. These activities occurred during the company's first month:

June	1	Near created the new company by investing $40,000 cash, $5,000 of furniture, and computer equipment worth $60,000.
	2	The company rented furnished office space by paying $3,200 rent for the first month.
	3	The company purchased $2,400 of office supplies for cash.
	10	The company paid $7,200 for the premium on a one-year insurance policy.
	14	The owner's assistant was paid $3,600 for two weeks' salary.
	24	The company collected $13,600 of commissions from airlines on tickets obtained for customers.
	28	The assistant was paid another $3,600 for two weeks' salary.
	29	The company paid the month's $3,500 phone bill.
	30	The company repaired its computer for $700 on account.
	30	The owner withdrew $2,850 cash from the business for personal use.

The company's chart of accounts included these accounts:

101	Cash		302	Sam Near, Withdrawals
106	Accounts Receivable		405	Commissions Revenue
124	Office Supplies		610	Depreciation Expense, Furniture
128	Prepaid Insurance		612	Depreciation Expense, Computer Equipment
160	Furniture		622	Salaries Expense
161	Accumulated Depreciation, Furniture		637	Insurance Expense
167	Computer Equipment		640	Rent Expense
168	Accumulated Depreciation, Computer Equipment		650	Office Supplies Expense
201	Accounts Payable		684	Repairs Expense
209	Salaries Payable		688	Telephone Expense
301	Sam Near, Capital		901	Income Summary

Required

1. Set up each of the listed accounts. *Note: Your instructor will tell you to use either the balance column format or T-accounts.*

2. Prepare journal entries to record the transactions for June and post them to the accounts.

3. Use the following information to journalize and post the adjustments for the month:

   a. Two-thirds of one month's insurance coverage was consumed.

   b. There were $1,600 of office supplies on hand at the end of the month.

   c. Depreciation on the computer equipment was estimated to be $1,650 and $400 on the furniture.

   d. The assistant had earned $320 of unpaid and unrecorded salary.

   e. The company had earned $3,500 of commissions that had not yet been billed.

4. Prepare an income statement, a statement of changes in equity, and a classified balance sheet.

5. Prepare journal entries to close the temporary accounts and post them to the accounts.

6. Prepare a post-closing trial balance.

Problem 4-14A Calculating current, quick, and debt to equity ratios LO7

You are the accountant at **Indigo**. Refer to Appendix III for Indigo's Consolidated Balance Sheet as at March 31, 2018. Your manager has assigned you the following tasks.

a. Calculate the current ratio, quick ratio, and debt to equity ratios for 2017 and 2018. Round your answer to two decimal places.

b. Comment on the ratios, the change between 2017 and 2018, and what additional information you would want to know to get a better picture of Indigo's financial performance.

*Problem 4-15A Adjusting, reversing, and subsequent cash entries LO8

The unadjusted trial balance for Lewis Fitness Centre as of December 31, 2020, follows:

Account	Debit	Credit
Cash	$ 22,000	
Accounts receivable	-0-	
Supplies	9,000	
Equipment	300,000	
Accumulated depreciation, equipment		$ 30,000
Interest payable		-0-
Salaries payable		-0-
Unearned membership revenue		48,000
Notes payable		100,000
Bev Lewis, capital		116,500
Bev Lewis, withdrawals	60,000	
Membership revenue		180,000
Depreciation expense, equipment	-0-	
Salaries expense	76,000	
Interest expense	7,500	
Supplies expense	-0-	
Totals	$474,500	$474,500

Information necessary to prepare adjusting entries is as follows:

a. As of December 31, employees have earned $1,600 of unpaid and unrecorded wages. The next payday is January 8, and the total wages to be paid will be $2,400.

b. The cost of supplies on hand at December 31 is $3,600.

c. The note payable requires an interest payment to be made every three months. The amount of unrecorded accrued interest at December 31 is $2,500, and the next payment is due on January 15. This payment will be $3,000.

d. An analysis of the unearned membership revenue shows that $32,000 remains unearned at December 31.

e. In addition to the membership revenue included in the revenue account, the company has earned another $24,000 in revenue that will be collected on January 21. The company is also expected to collect $14,000 on the same day for new revenue during January.

f. Depreciation expense for the year is $30,000.

An asterisk (*) identifies assignment material based on Appendix 4A.

Required

1. Prepare adjusting journal entries.

2. Prepare journal entries to reverse the effects of the adjusting entries that involve accruals.

3. Prepare journal entries to record the cash payments and collections that are described for January.

ALTERNATE PROBLEMS

Problem 4-1B Completing a work sheet LO1 eXcel

CHECK FIGURE: 3. Adjusted trial balance columns = $99,307

The July 31, 2020, unadjusted trial balance for Daimler Tours after its first month of operations is shown below:

			Daimler Tours Trial Balance.xlsx		
			Daimler Tours		
			Unadjusted Trial Balance		
			July 31, 2020		
				Unadjusted	
				Trial Balance	
	No.	**Account**		**Dr.**	**Cr.**
7	101	Cash		$ 9,100	
8	106	Accounts receivable		18,700	
9	111	Notes receivable, due Feb. 2021		16,000	
10	128	Prepaid insurance		5,100	
11	161	Furniture		6,750	
12	201	Accounts payable			$ 6,925
13	230	Unearned tour revenue			12,430
14	301	Jan Rider, capital			60,975
15	302	Jan Rider, withdrawals		-0-	
16	403	Tour revenue			16,700
17	623	Wages expense		41,380	
18		Totals		$ 97,030	$ 97,030

Required

1. Enter the unadjusted trial balance onto a work sheet.

2. Using the following additional information, enter the adjustments into the work sheet (the Chart of Accounts in Appendix IV may be useful when additional accounts are required):

a. Interest of $40 had accrued on the note receivable by month-end.

b. The July utility bill for $175 was received in the mail on July 31. It is unpaid and unrecorded.

c. Depreciation on the furniture for the month of July is $210.

d. The balance in Prepaid Insurance is from a six-month policy that went into effect on July 1, 2020.

e. The company has two part-time employees, each of whom gets paid $315 every other Friday for a five-day part-time workweek. July 31 falls on a Friday, however two days of accrued wages need to be recorded for each employee.

f. At July 31, it was determined that $4,900 of the balance in Unearned Tour Revenue was not yet earned.

g. Accrued tour revenue of $1,600 was unrecorded and uncollected at July 31.

3. Complete the work sheet.

Problem 4-2B Completing a work sheet—profit LO1 eXcel

CHECK FIGURE: 3. Adjusted trial balance columns = $83,310

The December 31, 2020, unadjusted trial balance for Tucker Photographers after the first month of operations is shown below:

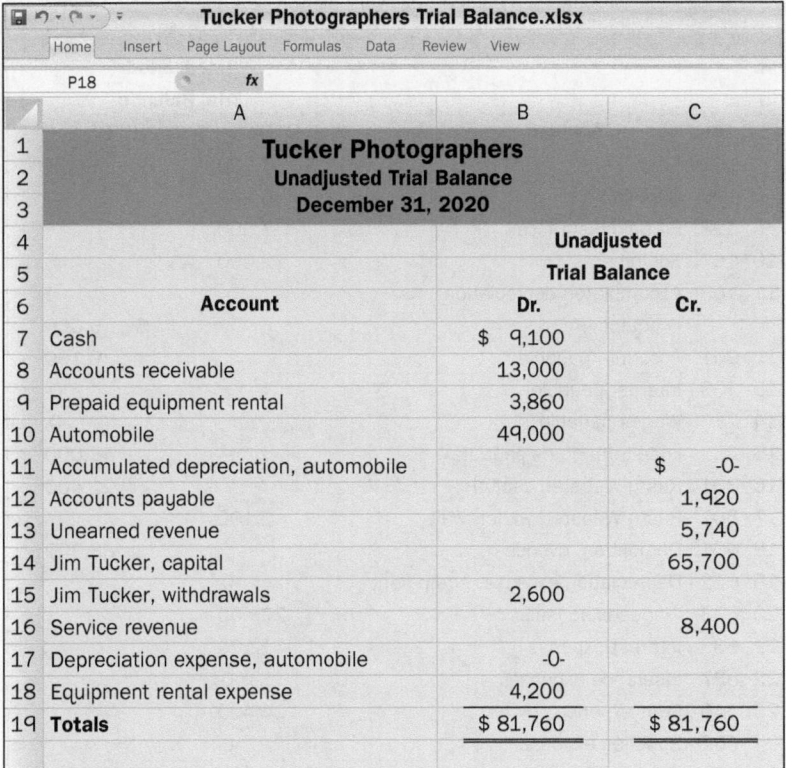

		Unadjusted Trial Balance	
Account		Dr.	Cr.
Cash		$ 9,100	
Accounts receivable		13,000	
Prepaid equipment rental		3,860	
Automobile		49,000	
Accumulated depreciation, automobile			$ -0-
Accounts payable			1,920
Unearned revenue			5,740
Jim Tucker, capital			65,700
Jim Tucker, withdrawals		2,600	
Service revenue			8,400
Depreciation expense, automobile		-0-	
Equipment rental expense		4,200	
Totals		$ 81,760	$ 81,760

Tucker Photographers / Unadjusted Trial Balance / December 31, 2020

Required

1. Enter the unadjusted trial balance onto a work sheet.

2. Using the following additional information, enter the adjustments into the work sheet.

   a. It was determined that $2,000 of the balance in the Prepaid Equipment Rental account had been used during December.

   b. Depreciation on the automobile for the month of December was $610.

   c. Accrued utilities expense of $940 was unrecorded at December 31.

   d. $460 of the Unearned Revenue account had been earned by December 31.

3. Complete the work sheet.

4. Calculate the balance in the capital account as it would appear on the December 31, 2020, balance sheet.

Analysis Component: What effect does a profit have on the balance sheet?

Problem 4-3B Work sheet, journal entries, financial statements LO1, 6 e**X**cel

CHECK FIGURES: 1. Adjusted trial balance columns = $174,085; 3. Loss = $3,835; Total assets = $71,150

Presented below is the unadjusted trial balance of Webster Demolition Company as of June 30, 2020, the end of its fiscal year. The owner invested $17,500 cash in the company during the year.

		Webster Demolition Company Trial Balance.xlsx		
		Home Insert Page Layout Formulas Data Review View		
		P18	fx	
		A	B	C
1		**Webster Demolition Company**		
2		**Unadjusted Trial Balance**		
3		**June 30, 2020**		
4			**Unadjusted**	
5			**Trial Balance**	
6	No.	Account	Dr.	Cr.
7	101	Cash	$ 4,500	
8	126	Supplies	8,200	
9	128	Prepaid insurance	7,300	
10	167	Equipment	72,000	
11	168	Accumulated depreciation,		
		equipment		$ 5,000
12	201	Accounts payable		9,100
13	203	Interest payable		-0-
14	210	Wages payable		-0-
15	251	Long-term notes payable		45,000
16	301	Rusty Webster, capital		21,400
17	302	Rusty Webster, withdrawals	2,100	
18	401	Demolition revenue		83,300
19	612	Depreciation expense, equipment	-0-	
20	623	Wages expense	27,400	
21	633	Interest expense	1,100	
22	637	Insurance expense	-0-	
23	640	Rent expense	24,400	
24	652	Supplies expense	-0-	
25	683	Business tax expense	4,200	
26	684	Repairs expense	4,200	
27	690	Utilities expense	8,400	
28		**Totals**	$ 163,800	$ 163,800

Required

Preparation Component:

1. Prepare a 10-column work sheet for 2020, starting with the unadjusted trial balance and including these additional facts:

   a. The inventory of supplies at the end of the year had a cost of $6,800.

   b. The cost of expired insurance for the year is $5,750.

   c. Annual depreciation on the equipment is $8,700.

   d. The June utilities expense of $375 was not included in the trial balance because the bill arrived after it was prepared. The $375 amount owed needs to be recorded.

e. The company's employees have earned $1,100 of accrued wages.

f. Interest of $110 for June has not yet been paid or recorded. In addition, the company is required to make a $2,000 payment on the note on August 30, 2020.

2. Use the work sheet to journalize the adjusting and closing entries.

3. Prepare an income statement, a statement of changes in equity, and a classified balance sheet.

Analysis Component: Analyze the following independent errors and describe how each would affect the 10-column work sheet. Explain whether the error is likely to be discovered in completing the work sheet and, if not, the effect of the error on the financial statements.

a. The adjustment for consumption of the insurance coverage credited the Prepaid Insurance account for $1,550 and debited the same amount to the Insurance Expense account.

b. When completing the adjusted trial balance in the work sheet, the $4,200 Repairs Expense account balance was extended to the Debit column for the balance sheet.

Problem 4-4B Closing entries LO2, 3, 4

CHECK FIGURE: 2. Post-closing trial balance = $86,800

The adjusted trial balance for Dillan's Tailoring Services on December 31, 2020, appears as follows:

No.	Account	Debit	Credit
101	Cash	$ 15,500	
125	Store supplies	6,500	
128	Prepaid insurance	3,800	
167	Equipment	61,000	
168	Accumulated depreciation, equipment		$ 19,700
201	Accounts payable		39,400
210	Wages payable		6,400
301	Vy Dillan, capital		23,300
302	Vy Dillan, withdrawals	32,000	
401	Sewing revenue		109,920
612	Depreciation expense, equipment	5,400	
623	Wages expense	61,200	
637	Insurance expense	2,200	
640	Rent expense	4,800	
651	Store supplies expense	2,600	
690	Utilities expense	3,720	
	Totals	$198,720	$198,720

Required

1. Prepare closing entries.

2. Prepare a post-closing trial balance.

Problem 4-5B Financial statements LO6

CHECK FIGURES: Profit = $30,000; Total assets = $67,100

Using the information from Problem 4-4B, prepare an income statement and a statement of changes in equity for the year ended December 31, 2020, and a classified balance sheet at December 31, 2020. The owner made no investments during the year.

Analysis Component: Dillan's Tailoring Services experienced a profit during 2020. If you were one of the business's creditors, would you conclude that because of this profit Dillan's Tailoring will pay its obligations in 2021?

Problem 4-6B Closing entries LO2, 3

The adjusted trial balance for Destination Wedding Photo as of December 31, 2020, follows:

No.	Account	Debit	Credit
101	Cash	$ 16,800	
104	Current investments	21,800	
126	Supplies	8,400	
149	Notes receivable, due May 1, 2022	46,000	
167	Equipment	66,000	
168	Accumulated depreciation, equipment		$ 22,000
173	Building	168,000	
174	Accumulated depreciation, building		45,000
183	Land	90,000	
193	Franchise	35,000	
201	Accounts payable		17,800
203	Interest Payable		120
233	Unearned professional revenue		27,800
251	Long-term notes payable		140,000
301	David Sale, capital		99,290
302	David Sale, withdrawals	3,800	
401	Photography revenue		214,000
406	Interest income		480
605	Depreciation expense, building	20,800	
606	Depreciation expense, equipment	8,800	
612	Wages expense	34,800	
623	Interest expense	690	
633	Insurance expense	18,800	
637	Supplies expense	13,600	
652	Telephone expense	5,200	
688	Utilities expense	8,000	
	Totals	$566,490	$566,490

An analysis of other information reveals that Destination Wedding Photo is required to make a $49,000 payment on the long-term notes payable during 2021. Also, David Sale invested $83,000 cash early in the year.

Required Prepare the closing entries made at the end of the year.

Problem 4-7B Financial statements LO6

CHECK FIGURES: Profit = $103,790; Total assets = $385,000

Using the adjusted trial balance in Problem 4-6B, prepare the income statement, statement of changes in equity, and classified balance sheet.

Analysis Component: Why must liabilities be separated on the balance sheet between *current* and *non-current*? What effect would it have had on Sale's balance sheet if the non-current notes were not separated?

Problem 4-8B Adjusting entries and closing entries LO2, 3, 5

Bullseye Market Research Company (BMRC) specializes in conducting focus groups for businesses launching a new product. BMRC analyzes customer likes and dislikes to ensure new products will be successful.

No.	Account	Debit	Credit
201	Accounts payable		$ 100
108	Accounts receivable	$2,000	
168	Accumulated depreciation, equipment		7,250
184	Accumulated depreciation, office furniture		3,100
101	Cash	1,500	
302	Consulting revenue		44,000
194	Copyright	4,200	
251	Dan Eagle, capital		24,715
301	Dan Eagle, withdrawals	3,500	
606	Depreciation expense, office furniture	700	
167	Equipment	16,000	
633	Insurance expense	600	
401	Interest income		70
623	Interest expense	30	
233	Long-term notes payable		4,000
145	Notes receivable	5,000	
183	Office furniture	5,100	
104	Short-term investments	4,000	
126	Supplies	750	
637	Supplies expense	2,150	
652	Telephone expense	470	
203	Unearned consulting revenue		3,375
688	Utilities expense	3,230	
612	Wages expense	37,380	
	Totals	$86,610	$86,610

You are the accounting manager. Your staff submitted the above trial balance for December 31, 2020. In your review, you discover the following additional information that has not been included in the trial balance.

a. The equipment has an estimated useful life of 16 years. If you need to create a new account, use account number 604.

b. Employees were paid $3,100 for 10 days of work. This payroll included 2 days of payroll in December that were not recorded at year-end. If you need to add an account, use account number 202.

c. On December 31, BMRC completed a focus group for a client on handbags. An invoice was sent to the company for $5,000 due January 31, 2021.

d. On December 31, the company completed a market research report for a client. The client had prepaid $3,000 for this service in November.

Required

1. Prepare the missing adjusting entries for transactions a–d.
2. Prepare an adjusted trial balance.
3. Based on your adjusted trial balance, prepare the closing entries.

Problem 4-9B Financial statements LO6

CHECK FIGURES: Profit = $5,890; Total assets = $32,200

Using the information in Problem 4-8B, prepare an income statement and a statement of changes in equity for the year ended December 31, 2020, and a classified balance sheet at December 31, 2020. The owner made no additional investments during the year. A $2,500 payment on the long-term notes payable will be made during 2021. Also, $1,500 of the notes receivable will be collected by December 31, 2021.

Analysis Component: Bullseye Market Research Company's equity increased by $2,390 during 2020. What effect does an increase in equity have on the other major components of the balance sheet?

Problem 4-10B Analyzing closing entries LO2, 3, 4

CHECK FIGURE: 1. Total operating expenses = $177,290

The following closing entries were prepared for Greenway Gardening Services regarding the year ended October 31, 2020:

2020				
Oct.	31	Service Revenue...	136,000	
		Income Summary		136,000
		To close the revenue account.		
	31	Income Summary..	177,290	
		Depreciation Expense, Gardening Equipment..........		9,950
		Depreciation Expense, Vehicles...............................		10,600
		Insurance Expense		6,900
		Interest Expense		340
		Supplies Expense		24,800
		Telephone Expense..		1,700
		Utilities Expense..		1,800
		Fuel Expense..		9,200
		Wages Expense..		112,000
		To close expense accounts.		
Oct.	31	Grant Greenway, Capital..	41,290	
		Income Summary		41,290
		To close the Income Summary to capital.		
	31	Grant Greenway, Capital..	10,000	
		Grant Greenway, Withdrawals		10,000
		To close withdrawals to capital.		

Required

1. Prepare an income statement based on the information provided.

2. Calculate the post-closing balance in the capital account at October 31, 2020, given that the adjusted balance on October 31, 2019, was $76,000.

Problem 4-11B Preparing financial statements LO6

CHECK FIGURES: Profit = $35,680; Total assets = $136,580

Required Using the adjusted trial balance below, for FairQuest Equipment Servicing for the year ended August 31, 2020, prepare an income statement, statement of changes in equity, and classified balance sheet. The owner made a $50,000 investment into the business during the year. The investment in Nova shares is expected to be held for the long term.

No.	Account	Debit	Credit
101	Cash	$ 7,500	
106	Accounts receivable	16,000	
109	Interest receivable	280	
124	Office supplies	1,700	
141	Investment in Nova shares	35,000	
161	Furniture	81,000	
162	Accumulated depreciation, furniture		$ 21,400
193	Franchise	16,500	
201	Accounts payable		4,300
205	Notes payable, due in 7 months		3,200
230	Unearned servicing revenue		5,000
251	Long-term notes payable*		31,000
301	Jade Fairquest, capital		61,400
302	Jade Fairquest, withdrawals	4,000	
403	Equipment servicing revenue		171,080
409	Interest income		2,600
601	Depreciation expense, furniture	2,060	
623	Wages expense	116,000	
637	Insurance expense	16,680	
688	Telephone expense	2,800	
690	Utilities expense	460	
	Totals	$299,980	$299,980

*An $18,000 payment will be made on the long-term notes payable during the year ended August 31, 2021.

Analysis Component: Why might FairQuest Equipment Servicing be tempted to report the investment in Nova shares as a current asset on the August 31, 2020, balance sheet?

Problem 4-12B Preparing a classified balance sheet LO6, 7

CHECK FIGURES: 1. Capital = $84,484; 2. Total assets = $133,100

An alphabetical list of the adjusted trial balance accounts at July 31, 2020, for Delta Tours after its first month of operations is shown below:

Account	Adjusted Account Balance*
Accounts payable	$ 27,000
Accounts receivable	21,300
Accumulated depreciation, furniture	700
Cash	25,300
Depreciation expense, furniture	700
Furniture	29,000
Insurance expense	5,250
Interest receivable	100
Interest income	700
Jan Delta, capital	95,434
Jan Delta, withdrawals	10,700
Notes receivable (due in 6 months)	56,000
Prepaid insurance	2,100
Tour revenue	146,000
Unearned tour revenue	19,600
Utility expense	1,300
Wages expense	139,700
Wages payable	2,016

*Assume all accounts have a normal balance.

Required

1. Calculate the capital balance as it would appear on the July 31, 2020 balance sheet.

2. Prepare a classified balance sheet.

3. Calculate the current ratio and the debt to equity ratio (round to two decimal places).

Problem 4-13B Performing the steps in the accounting cycle LO2, 3, 4, 5, 6

CHECK FIGURES: 4. Profit = $5,140; Total assets = $604,000; 6. Post-closing trial balance = $606,400

On July 1, 2020, Amy Young created a new self-storage business called Young Co. These events occurred during the company's first month:

July	1	Young invested $40,000 cash and land and buildings worth $320,000 and $240,000, respectively.
	2	Rented equipment by paying $3,600 rent for the first month.
	5	Purchased $4,600 of office supplies for cash.
	10	Paid $10,800 for the premium on a one-year insurance policy effective today.
	14	Paid an employee $1,800 for two weeks' salary.
	24	Collected $17,600 of storage revenue from customers.
	28	Paid another $1,800 for two weeks' salary.
	29	Paid the month's $600 phone bill.
	30	Repaired leaking roof for $1,700 on account.
	31	Young withdrew $3,200 cash from the business for personal use.

The company's chart of accounts included these accounts:

101	Cash	302	Amy Young, Withdrawals
106	Accounts Receivable	401	Storage Revenue
124	Office Supplies	606	Depreciation Expense, Buildings
128	Prepaid Insurance	622	Salaries Expense
170	Land	637	Insurance Expense
173	Buildings	640	Equipment Rental Expense
174	Accumulated Depreciation, Buildings	650	Office Supplies Expense
201	Accounts Payable	684	Repairs Expense
209	Salaries Payable	688	Telephone Expense
301	Amy Young, Capital	901	Income Summary

Required

1. Set up each of the listed accounts. *Note: Your instructor will tell you to use either the balance column format or T-accounts.*

2. Prepare journal entries to record the transactions for July and post them to the accounts. Record prepaid and unearned items in balance sheet accounts.

3. Use the following information to journalize and post the adjustments for the month:

   a. Two-thirds of one month's insurance coverage was used.

   b. $3,100 of office supplies were on hand at the end of the month.

   c. Depreciation on the buildings was estimated to be $2,400 per month.

d. The employee had earned $360 of unpaid and unrecorded salary.

e. The company had earned $1,900 of storage revenue that had not yet been billed.

4. Prepare an income statement, a statement of changes in equity, and a classified balance sheet.

5. Prepare journal entries to close the temporary accounts and post them to the accounts.

6. Prepare a post-closing trial balance.

Problem 4-14B Calculating current ratios and debt to equity ratios LO7

You are the accountant at Spin Master. Refer to Appendix III for Spin Master's Consolidated Balance Sheets as at December 31, 2017. Your manager has asked you to do the following:

a. Calculate the current ratio, quick ratio, and debt to equity ratios for 2016 and 2017 (round to two decimal places).

b. Comment on the ratios, the change between 2016 and 2017 and what additional information you would want to know to get a better picture of Spin Master's financial performance.

*Problem 4-15B Adjusting, reversing, and subsequent cash entries LO8

Smart Resource Company's unadjusted trial balance on December 31, 2020, the end of its annual accounting period, is as follows:

Account	Debit	Credit
Cash	$ 73,725	
Note receivable	37,500	
Office supplies	4,200	
Land	45,000	
Unearned service revenue		$ 18,000
Note payable		90,000
Justin Chambers, capital		37,500
Justin Chambers, withdrawals	60,000	
Service revenue		267,000
Interest income		2,550
Rent revenue		12,375
Salaries expense	193,500	
Insurance expense	4,950	
Interest expense	8,550	
Totals	$427,425	$427,425

Information necessary to prepare adjusting entries is as follows:

a. Employees, who are paid $7,500 every two weeks, have earned $5,250 since the last payment. The next payment of $7,500 will be on January 4.

b. Smart Resource has earned but not recorded revenue for $8,250 for services provided to a customer who will pay for the work on January 24. At that time, the customer will also pay $3,100 for services Smart Resource will perform in early January.

An asterisk (*) identifies assignment material based on Appendix 4A.

c. Smart Resource rents office space to a tenant who has paid only $450 of the $1,125 rent for December. On January 12, the tenant will pay the remainder along with the rent for January.

d. An inventory of office supplies discloses $675 of unused supplies.

e. Premiums for insurance against injuries to employees are paid monthly. The $450 premium for December will be paid January 12.

f. Smart Resource owes $90,000 on a note payable that requires quarterly payments of accrued interest. The quarterly payments of $2,700 each are made on the 15th of January, April, July, and October.

g. An analysis of Smart Resource's service contracts with customers shows that $6,300 of the amount customers have prepaid remains unearned.

h. Smart Resource has a $37,500 note receivable on which interest of $175 has accrued. On January 22, the note and the total accrued interest of $575 will be repaid to Smart Resource.

Required

1. Prepare adjusting journal entries.

2. Prepare reversing entries.

3. Prepare journal entries to record the January 2021 cash receipts and cash payments identified in the above information.

ANALYTICAL AND REVIEW PROBLEMS

A & R Problem 4-1   eXcel

The owner of Dynamo Stores has come to you for assistance because his bookkeeper has just moved to another city. The following is the only information his bookkeeper left him.

1. Balance sheets as of December 31, 2020 and 2021.

2. The owner withdrew $105,000 in 2021 for his personal use.

3. The business incurred total expenses of $168,000 for 2021, of which $126,000 was for wages and $42,000 was for advertising.

	2021	2020
Assets	$168,000	$210,000
Liabilities	$ 42,000	$ 63,000
Capital	126,000	147,000
	$168,000	$210,000

Required

1. Calculate the profit and total revenue for 2021.

2. Prepare closing entries for 2021.

A & R Problem 4-2   eXcel

The partially completed work sheet for the current fiscal year of Sandy's Delivery Service appears below:

		Sandy's Delivery Service Work Sheet.xlsx									

Home   Insert   Page Layout   Formulas   Data   Review   View

P18   fx

	A	B	C	D	E	F	G	H	I	J	K
1		**Sandy's Delivery Service**									
2		**Work Sheet**									
3		**For the Year Ended December 31, 2020**									
4										**Balance Sheet**	
5		**Unadjusted**				**Adjusted**		**Income**		**& Statement of**	
6		**Trial Balance**		**Adjustments**		**Trial Balance**		**Statement**		**Changes in Equity**	
7	**Account**	**Dr.**	**Cr.**	**Dr.**	**Cr.**	**Dr.**	**Cr.**	**Dr.**	**Cr.**	**Dr.**	**Cr.**
8	Cash	10,650									
9	Accounts receivable	7,000				9,000					
10	Supplies	4,200								1,600	
11	Prepaid insurance	2,400									
12	Prepaid rent	1,800									
13	Delivery trucks	40,000				40,000					
14	Accounts payable		3,130				3,130				
15	Unearned delivery revenue		4,500								2,000
16	Sandra Berlasty, capital		50,000								
17	Sandra Berlasty, withdrawals	3,000									
18	Delivery service revenue		18,500								
19	Advertising expense	600									
20	Gas and oil expense	680	.								
21	Salaries expense	5,600									
22	Utilities expense	200									
23	**Totals**	76,130	76,130								
24	Insurance expense					800					
25	Rent expense					900					
26	Supplies expense										
27	Dep. expense, delivery trucks										
28	Accumulated dep., delivery trucks										2,000
29	Salaries payable										400
30	Profit										

Required

1. Complete the work sheet.

2. Journalize the adjusting and closing entries (omit narratives).

ETHICS CHALLENGE

EC 4-1

On January 20, 2020, Jennifer Nelson, the staff accountant for Newby Enterprises, is feeling pressure to complete the preparation of the annual financial statements. The president of the company has said he needs up-to-date financial statements to share with several bankers on January 21 at a dinner meeting that has been called to discuss the possibility of Newby's obtaining loan financing for a special building project. Jennifer knows that she won't be able to gather all the needed information in the next 24 hours to prepare the entire set of adjusting entries that must be posted before the financial statements will accurately portray the company's performance and financial position for the fiscal period just ended December 31, 2019. Jennifer ultimately decides to estimate several expense accruals at the last minute. When deciding on estimates for the expenses, Jennifer uses low estimates as she doesn't want to make the financial statements look worse than they possibly are in reality. Jennifer finishes the financial statements before the deadline and gives them to the president without mentioning that several accounts could be only estimated as to their balance on December 31, 2019.

Required

1. List several courses of action that Jennifer could have taken instead of the one on which she ultimately decided.

2. If you had been in Jennifer's situation, what would you have done? Briefly justify your response.

FOCUS ON FINANCIAL STATEMENTS

FFS 4-1

CHECK FIGURES: 1. Profit = $70,575; Total assets = $95,850; 3. Post-closing trial balance = $121,350

Sarda Electrical Servicing began operations two years ago. Its adjusted account balances at December 31, 2020, are listed alphabetically below. The owner, Nymeth Sarda, made a $20,000 investment early in the year just ended December 31, 2020.

Required

1. Prepare an income statement, statement of changes in equity, and classified balance sheet based on the information provided.

2. Prepare the closing entries.

3. Prepare the post-closing trial balance.

Account	Account Balance*
Accounts payable	$ 21,000
Accounts receivable	10,500
Accumulated depreciation, tools	4,500
Accumulated depreciation, truck	21,000
Cash	5,000
Copyright	5,100
Depreciation expense, tools	2,250
Depreciation expense, truck	3,600
Electrical revenue	126,600
Electrical supplies	19,000
Insurance expense	1,275
Interest expense	900
Notes receivable**	12,000
Nymeth Sarda, capital	27,825
Nymeth Sarda, withdrawals	61,500
Notes payable, due August 31, 2022	27,000
Notes payable, due June 1, 2021	2,550
Prepaid insurance	1,050
Prepaid rent	7,200
Rent expense	21,000
Salaries expense	27,000
Salaries payable	3,150
Tools	21,000
Truck	40,500
Unearned electrical revenue	5,250

*Assume all account balances are normal.
**$2,000 of the note is due September 15, 2021.

Analysis Component: Cupcakes owners Lori and Heather, featured in the chapter-opening vignette, have financed a significant portion of their growth by reinvesting profits. Is Nymeth Sarda, the owner of Sarda Electrical Servicing, following a similar practice? Explain.

FFS 4-2

GolfLink is a golf course company with clubs in ten provinces. Listed here is part of the comparative balance sheet at December 31, 2021, showing the following assets and liabilities, in alphabetical order:

(thousands of dollars)	2021	2020
Accounts payable and accrued liabilities..........................	20,706	17,755
Accounts receivable...	3,743	3,238
Cash..	1,567	1,447
Current borrowings..	25,817	24,839
Current portion of mortgage...	1,411	61
Customer deposits and prepaid dues..............................	10,965	6,037
Income taxes receivable...	1,322	176
Inventories and prepaid expenses...................................	5,848	5,289
Mortgage payable..	8,669	7,432
Property Plant & Equipment...	18,715	14,977

Required

Part 1

a. Calculate total current assets at December 31, 2020, and December 31, 2021.

b. Calculate total current liabilities at December 31, 2020, and December 31, 2021.

Part 2

c. Calculate the current ratio for December 31, 2020 and December 31, 2021 (round to two decimal places).

d. Explain the meaning of GolfLink's current ratio results calculated in part (c). Also indicate whether the change in the ratio was favourable or unfavourable.

CRITICAL THINKING MINI CASE

The owner of Delton Property Rentals, Teal Delton, has requested an emergency meeting with you, a representative from the bank. "Our accountant has been on leave for the past several months and her replacement has resigned suddenly. I'm told we can't pay our employees this month and your bank won't lend us any money. I don't understand. We have lots of assets that can be used to pay expenses, as you can see from our balance sheet."

Delton Property Rentals Balance Sheet March 31		
	2020	**2019**
Assets...	$2,850,000	$750,000
Liabilities..	2,780,000	240,000
Equity...	70,000	510,000

You explain to Mr. Delton that you will need to obtain some additional information. He faxes you the following:

Delton Property Rentals Post-Closing Trial Balance March 31		
	2020	**2019**
Accounts payable	$ 340,000	$ 7,000
Accounts receivable	75,000	215,000
Accumulated depreciation, buildings	165,000	150,000
Accumulated depreciation, equipment	35,000	30,000
Buildings	2,112,000	430,000
Cash	15,000	40,000
Equipment	45,000	45,000
Land	675,000	150,000
Notes payable*	2,440,000	204,000
Notes receivable, due Nov. 30, 2021	120,000	-0-
Supplies	8,000	50,000
Teal Delton, capital**	70,000	510,000
Unearned revenue	-0-	29,000

*$200,000 principal is due annually each February 1.
**No withdrawals were made during 2019 or 2020.

Required Using the elements of critical thinking described on the inside front cover, outline how you will respond to Teal Delton.

CUMULATIVE COMPREHENSION PROBLEM: ECHO SYSTEMS

CHECK FIGURE: 2. Total credits in post-closing trial balance = $155,720

(The first two segments of this comprehensive problem were in Chapters 2 and 3, and the final segment is presented in Chapter 5. If the Chapter 2 and 3 segments have not been completed, the assignment can begin at this point. It is recommended that you use the Working Papers[11] that accompany this book because they reflect the account balances that resulted from posting the entries required in Chapters 2 and 3.)

The transactions of Echo Systems for October through December 2020 have been recorded in the problem segments in Chapters 2 and 3, as well as the year-end adjusting entries. Prior to closing the temporary accounts for 2020, the accounting system is modified to include the Income Summary account, which is given the number 901.

Required

1. Record and post the appropriate closing entries.

2. Prepare a post-closing trial balance.

---

11   If students have not purchased the Working Papers package, the Working Papers for the serial problem are available on Connect.

CHAPTER 5

Accounting for Merchandising Activities

A Look Back

Chapters 3 and 4 focused on the final steps of the accounting process. We explained the importance of proper revenue and expense recognition, and described the adjusting and closing processes. We also prepared financial statements.

A Look at This Chapter

This chapter emphasizes merchandising activities. We explain how reporting merchandising activities differs from reporting service activities. We also analyze and record merchandise purchases and sales transactions, and explain the adjustments and financial statement presentation for merchandisers.

© Olichel/Pixabay.com

LEARNING OBJECTIVES

LO1 Describe merchandising, and identify and explain the important income statement and balance sheet components for a merchandising company.

LO2 Describe both perpetual and periodic inventory systems.

LO3	Analyze and record transactions for merchandise purchases and sales using a perpetual system.
LO4	Prepare adjustments for a merchandising company.
LO5	Define, prepare, and analyze merchandising income statements.
LO6	Calculate gross margin and markup on inventory cost.

*Appendix 5A

LO7	Record and compare merchandising transactions using both periodic and perpetual inventory systems.

*Appendix 5B

LO8	Explain and record Provincial Sales Tax (PST), Goods and Services Tax (GST), and Harmonized Sales Tax (HST).

Sustainable Gear for Outdoor Enthusiasts

Mountain Equipment Co-op, more commonly referred to as MEC, is Canada's leading retailer of outdoor merchandise including clothing and gear for self-propelled sports like cycling, hiking, paddling, and climbing. MEC was founded in 1971 in Vancouver by six individuals interested in providing mountain climbers in Canada with reasonably priced, quality wilderness gear. MEC is a members-only cooperative, and before you can buy or rent from MEC you have to purchase a $5 membership that is good for your lifetime. This investment in the store hasn't put people off, and in fact the idea of membership is obviously appealing to many: membership at the end of fiscal 2017 stood at approximately 4.5 million, and sales for the year totalled $465 million.* In 2018, in addition to its online store at http://www.mec.ca, MEC has 22 stores in six provinces, with its latest opening in Vancouver's Olympic Village.

MEC carries a huge variety of merchandise inventory, and to minimize its ecological impact it promotes sustainable products. This means in part that MEC-brand contract manufacturing centres are required to follow MEC's Social Compliance Program, designed to improve the human condition in factories. Also, to the greatest extent possible, the components of MEC's products are organic (cotton), recycled (polyester), and PVC-free.

Clearly, implementing the many facets of MEC's philosophy in such a massive business is no simple task. But MEC seeks simplicity wherever it can be found, and inventory management is one such area. MEC's public affairs manager Tim Southam says, "Continually balancing supply against demand is the crux of MEC's inventory management practices. A perpetual inventory system allows us to replenish stock in a timely manner to best meet the needs of our members. It also enables us to respond quickly to discrepancies and gives us a high level of control over our inventory. At any given time—in real time—we are able to access the current inventory levels in our stores and our distribution centre." A perpetual inventory system updates each time an item is purchased from a supplier or sold to a customer, resulting in up-to-date inventory records.

MEC will celebrate its 50th year of operation in 2021. As a member of 1% for the Planet and through its community grants program, MEC is widely recognized for its commitment to sustainable outdoor recreation and environmental initiatives. MEC has made more than $37 million in community investments in support of outdoor recreation and conservation in Canada. In 2017, it partnered with the Vancouver Aquarium to fund $50,000 in research to study specific sources of microplastic pollution in marine environments on Canada's west coast. MEC truly has raised the bar in terms of how a business can meet social and environmental goals and have a significant community impact.

*MEC recently changed its fiscal year-end from December 31 to the end of February; reported financial information includes 14 months due to this change.

Source: http://www.mec.ca.

Video Links: Our Co-op Roots: https://youtu.be/XwHdLwHen4U; MEC Fiscal 2017 Summary: https://youtu.be/tXaLkDONmcc.

CRITICAL THINKING CHALLENGE

Why would MEC choose a perpetual inventory system over a periodic inventory system? Is the periodic inventory system acceptable under GAAP?

CHAPTER PREVIEW

Our emphasis in previous chapters was on the accounting and reporting activities of companies providing services. This chapter emphasizes merchandising, a major part of modern business. Consumers expect a wealth of products, discount prices, inventory on demand, and high quality. This chapter introduces us to the business and accounting practices used by companies engaged in merchandising activities. These companies buy products and then resell them to customers. We show how financial statements capture merchandising transactions. The new financial statement elements created by merchandising transactions are demonstrated using a fictional example company, Lifetime Equipment Co-op, that has similar business operations to MEC, the company introduced in the chapter-opening vignette. We also analyze and record merchandise purchases and sales, and explain adjusting entries and the closing process for merchandising companies. An understanding of these important topics is, as MEC knows, critical to ensure continued success.

Student Success *Cycle*

Read the material

Do the exercises

Check your answers

Apply your critical thinking skills

Merchandising Activities

LO1 Describe merchandising, and identify and explain the important income statement and balance sheet components for a merchandising company.

A merchandising company's activities are different from those of a service company. A **merchandiser** earns profit by buying and selling merchandise. **Merchandise** consists of products that a company acquires for the purpose of reselling them to customers. The cost of these goods is an expense presented on the income statement as **cost of goods sold (COGS)**.[1]

Merchandisers are often identified as either *wholesalers* or *retailers*. A **wholesaler** is a company that buys products from manufacturers or other wholesalers and sells them to retailers or other wholesalers. Wholesalers include companies such as **General Mills, Webber Naturals** pharmaceuticals, **Western Family Foods**, and **Westfair Foods**. A **retailer** is an *intermediary* that buys products from manufacturers or wholesalers and sells them to consumers. Examples of retailers include **Roots Canada, Lululemon Athletica, Amazon.ca, Canadian Tire**, and **The Gap**. Some retailers, such as **Bell Canada**, sell a combination of products and services.

REPORTING FINANCIAL PERFORMANCE

Profit to a merchandiser results when revenue from selling merchandise exceeds both the cost of merchandise sold to customers and the cost of other operating expenses for the period (see Exhibit 5.1). The usual accounting term for revenues from selling merchandise is *sales*. **Net sales** refers to the result of subtracting *sales discounts* and *sales returns and allowances*[2] from total or gross sales. The term used for the cost of

---

1 Cost of goods sold is also commonly called *cost of sales*.

2 Sales discounts and sales returns and allowances are discussed in more detail later in this chapter.

EXHIBIT 5.1

Calculating Profit for Both a Service Company and a Merchandising Company

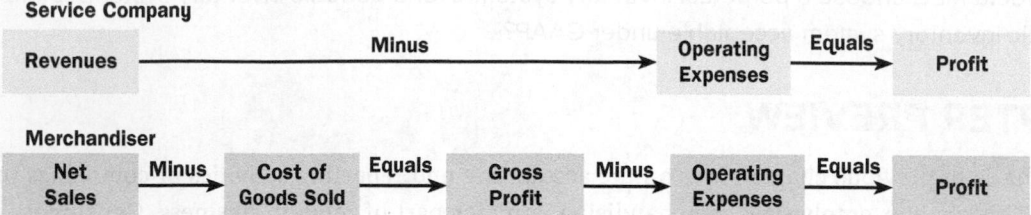

merchandise sold to customers is an expense called *cost of goods sold.*[3] A merchandiser's other expenses are often called *operating expenses.*

The summarized illustrative income statement information for Lifetime Equipment Co-op (LEC) in Exhibit 5.2 shows us how net sales, gross profit, and profit are related. This statement shows that LEC sold products to customers for $314,700. LEC acquired these goods at a cost of $230,400. This yields an $84,300 gross profit. **Gross profit**, also called **gross margin**, equals net sales less cost of goods sold. Changes in gross profit often greatly impact a merchandiser's operations since gross profit must cover all other expenses and yield a return for the owner. LEC, for instance, used gross profit to cover $68,960 of operating and other revenues and expenses. This left $15,340 in profit for the fiscal year ended February 23, 2020.

EXHIBIT 5.2

Summarized Income Statement Information for a Merchandiser

Lifetime Equipment Co-op Summarized Income Statement Information For Year Ended February 28, 2020	
Net sales...	$314,700
Cost of goods sold...	230,400
Gross profit from sales..	$ 84,300
Total operating expenses and other revenues and expenses	68,960
Profit...	$ 15,340

REPORTING FINANCIAL POSITION

A merchandising company's balance sheet includes an item not on the balance sheet of a service company. This item is a current asset called *merchandise inventory*. **Merchandise inventory**, or **inventory**, refers to products a company owns for the purpose of selling to customers. Exhibit 5.3 shows an example of what a classified balance sheet would look like for a retailer like LEC; note that merchandise inventory is presented at $21,000. The cost of this asset includes the cost incurred to buy the goods, ship them to the store, and otherwise get them ready for sale. Although companies usually hold inventories of other items such as supplies, *most companies simply refer to merchandise inventory as inventory*. We will use both terms in reference to merchandise inventory.

---

3 When preparing the income statement using the "function of expense" method per IFRS 2018, IAS 1, para. 103, cost of goods sold must be shown separately from other expenses.

EXHIBIT 5.3

Classified Balance Sheet for a Merchandiser

Lifetime Equipment Co-op Balance Sheet February 28, 2020			
Assets			
Current assets:			
Cash..		$ 8,200	
Accounts receivable..		11,200	
Merchandise inventory		**21,000**	
Prepaid expenses		1,100	
Total current assets...			$41,500
Plant and equipment:			
Office equipment..	$ 4,200		
Less: Accumulated depreciation....................	1,400	$ 2,800	
Store equipment...	$30,000		
Less: Accumulated depreciation....................	6,000	24,000	
Total plant and equipment			26,800
Total assets...			$68,300
Liabilities			
Current liabilities:			
Accounts payable..		$16,000	
Salaries payable		800	
Total liabilities..			$16,800
Equity			
David Sale, capital..			51,500
Total liabilities and equity..............................			$68,300

OPERATING CYCLE

A merchandising company's operating cycle[4] begins with the purchase of merchandise and ends with the collection of cash from the sale of merchandise.

Exhibit 5.4 graphically shows an operating cycle for a merchandiser with (1) cash sales and (2) credit sales. Credit sales delay the receipt of cash until the account receivable balance is paid by the customer. Company assets tied up in the form of inventory or receivables are not enhancing the company's value, but are a required part of business. Merchandise inventory is not productive (earning profit) until it is sold and any outstanding receivables are collected. Supply chain management (SCM) is a field that attempts to maximize value from the sourcing of the product to final delivery to the customer. A shorter operating cycle is desirable so that the resulting cash from the sale of inventory can be used in the business to earn profit. The length of an operating cycle differs across the types of businesses.

Car manufacturers such as **BMW Group**, **Honda Motor Company**, and **Ford Motor Company** typically have a longer operating cycle, as they need to purchase materials and manufacture the vehicle, ship the vehicle to a dealership, and sell it to the end consumer. Department stores such as **Hudson's Bay Company** commonly have operating cycles of three to five months, but operating cycles for grocery merchants such as **Real Canadian Superstore** and **IGA** usually range from one to two months. Obsolescence

---

4   IFRS 2018, IAS 1, para. 68.

EXHIBIT 5.4

Operating Cycle of a Merchandiser

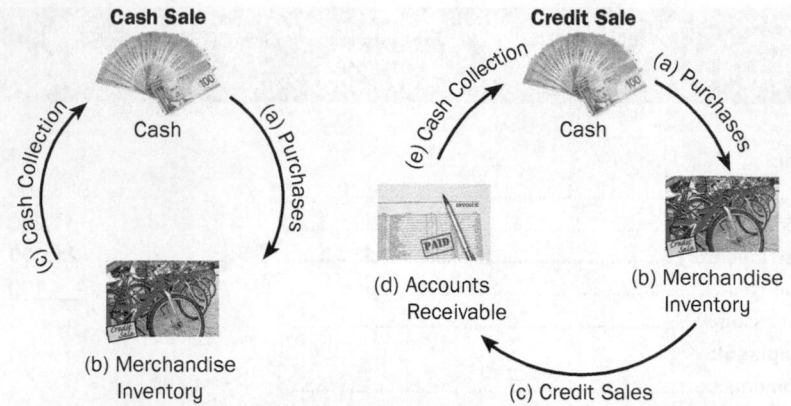

(E5.4a): Feng Yu/Alamy Images; (E5.4b): © Swinnerrr/Dreamstime.com/GetStock.com;
(E5.4d): © Ragsac19/Dreamstime.com/GetStock.com

is a concern for inventory that is subject to expiry or rapid technological advancement; as such, these companies attempt to minimize inventories held at their warehouse and aim to find the right balance to meet customer demands.

INVENTORY SYSTEMS

Exhibit 5.5 shows that a company's merchandise available for sale is a combination of what it begins with (beginning inventory) and what it purchases (net cost of purchases). The merchandise available is either sold (cost of goods sold) or kept for future sales (ending inventory).

Two types of inventory accounting systems are used to collect information about cost of goods sold and cost of inventory on hand: perpetual and periodic. Both inventory systems are permitted under both IFRS and ASPE; therefore, companies have a choice and must disclose their policy to account for inventory in their financial statement notes. We now describe these two inventory accounting options in more detail.

EXHIBIT 5.5

Merchandising Cost Flow

Perpetual Inventory System

LO2 Describe both perpetual and periodic inventory systems.

A **perpetual inventory system** provides an up-to-date record of the amount of inventory on hand. Have you noticed at some retail stores it is possible for the store to determine through a quick computer search whether the specific product you are looking for is available at another location? This is because they are using a perpetual inventory system that updates the inventory records continually each time a purchase or sale of inventory is made. When a purchase is made under a perpetual inventory system, the inventory account is debited for the cost of each purchase and a corresponding accounts payable account is credited, as items are received from the supplier.

Purchase of Inventory

Dr. Inventory xxx
    Cr. Accounts Payable xxx
Purchased merchandise on credit.

Important Tip:

When a sale occurs in a perpetual inventory system, two key journal entries are booked. First, the sale to the customer is recorded, with a debit to accounts receivable and a credit to sales. Second, the cost of the inventory is recorded as a debit to cost of goods sold (COGS) and the item is removed from the inventory account by crediting the inventory account.

---

1) Sales transaction:

Dr. Accounts Receivable xxx
    Cr. Sales xxx
Sold merchandise on credit.

2) Perpetual inventory adjustment:

Dr. Cost of Goods Sold xxx
    Cr. Inventory... xxx
Record the cost of the sale of merchandise and the reduction of inventory.

With a perpetual system, we can find out the cost of merchandise on hand at any time by looking at the balance of the inventory account. The company can also determine the up-to-date dollar amount of cost of goods sold by looking up the balance in the Cost of Goods Sold account. A detailed illustration of the perpetual inventory system is demonstrated using an example from LEC later in the chapter.

Before advancements in IT infrastructures, a perpetual system was often limited to businesses making a small number of daily sales, such as automobile dealers and major appliance stores. Today, with widespread use of computerized data management software, the use of a perpetual system has dramatically grown to include merchandisers with high-volume sales, such as **Walmart**, Canadian Tire, Real Canadian Superstore, **Staples**, The Gap, and **London Drugs**. Because perpetual inventory systems give users more timely information and are widely used in practice, our discussion in this chapter emphasizes a perpetual system.

Merchandise Inventory (MI)	
Beginning MI 10	LESS
PLUS	COGS COGS
Purchases 50	55···→55
EQUALS	
Ending MI 5	

Under a perpetual system, the MI account is updated continually for purchases and goods sold. The balance in MI and COGS is always up to date.

Periodic Inventory System

A **periodic inventory system** requires updating the inventory account only at the *end of a period* to reflect the quantity and cost of both goods on hand and goods sold. It does not require continual updating of the inventory account.

Important Tip:

A periodic inventory system records the cost of all new inventory in a temporary expense account called Purchases.

Purchase of Inventory

Dr. Purchases xxx
    Cr. Accounts Payable xxx
Purchased merchandise on credit.

> **Important Tip:**
>
> Under the periodic method only one journal entry is booked at the time of sale, debiting A/R and crediting Sales. No adjustment to inventory or COGS is made until the end of the accounting period.

When merchandise is sold, revenue is recorded but the cost of the merchandise sold is *not* recorded as a cost at this time.

Sales transaction:

Dr. Accounts Receivable	xxx	
Cr. Sales		xxx
Sold merchandise on credit.		

Merchandise Inventory (MI)	
Beginning MI 10	
PLUS	
Purchases	
Purchases 50	
LESS	
Ending MI (per a physical count)	
5	
EQUALS	
COGS	
55	

Under a periodic system, the MI account is updated when a physical count is performed. COGS is calculated once ending MI is known.

Determining Ending Inventory and Cost of Goods Sold

When financial statements are prepared, the company takes a *physical count of inventory* by counting the quantities of merchandise on hand. The accuracy of the inventory count is critical because it determines both the dollar value of the asset "Inventory" on the balance sheet at period end, as well as the "Cost of Goods Sold" on the income statement. Cost of merchandise on hand is determined by relating the quantities on hand to records showing each item's original cost. This cost of merchandise on hand is used to calculate cost of goods sold as shown to the right. The Merchandise Inventory account and Cost of Goods Sold is then updated to reflect end-of-period balances through booking a closing entry to reflect the amount from the physical count of inventory.[5]

Historically, periodic systems were used by companies such as hardware, drug, grocery, and department stores that sold large quantities of low-value items. Before computers and scanners, it was not feasible for accounting systems to track small items such as nails, pencils, paper clips, soap, and apples through inventory and into customers' hands. The next section highlights accounting for merchandising transactions using the perpetual inventory method. *We provide a comparison of recording of merchandising transactions using both periodic and perpetual inventory systems in Appendix 5A.*

 DECISION INSIGHT

Loblaw Companies Limited Converts from Periodic to Perpetual

Loblaw Companies Limited began a process of converting its corporate-owned grocery stores from a periodic inventory system to a perpetual inventory system that was completed in 2014. The improved information is a result of an upgrade to its IT infrastructure, enabling the stores to integrate costing information more effectively for items held in inventory.

Sources: http://www.newswire.ca/en/story/1390772/loblaw-companies-limited-reports-a-65-1-increase-in-adjusted-operating-income-2-for-the-second-quarter-of-2014-1, accessed October 12, 2014; http://www.loblaw.ca/files/4.%20Investor%20Centre/Financial%20Reports/2014/Annual/AIF-English.pdf, accessed June 26, 2015; *Loblaw Companies Limited 2014 Annual Report,* http://www.loblaw.ca/files/4.%20Investor%20Centre/Financial%20Reports/2015/Annual/655210_Eng_LR_v001_h33m0e.pdf.

---

5   Refer to the Appendix 5A section on Closing Entries for a detailed illustration demonstrating the closing entry adjustments.

CHECKPOINT

1. Describe what a company's cost of goods sold is and where the value comes from.
2. What is gross profit for a merchandising company?
3. Explain why use of the perpetual inventory system has grown dramatically.

Do Quick Study questions: QS 5-1, QS 5-2, QS 5-3, QS 5-4

Accounting for Merchandise Transactions— Perpetual Inventory System

LO3 Analyze and record transactions for merchandise purchases and sales using a perpetual system.

Recording merchandise transactions involves issues regarding the purchase and sale of merchandise inventory. In this first section, we will examine purchase transactions and associated items. Then, in the next section, transactions related to sales will be examined.

ACCOUNTING FOR MERCHANDISE PURCHASES— PERPETUAL INVENTORY SYSTEM

With a perpetual inventory system, the cost of merchandise bought for resale is recorded in the Merchandise Inventory account. LEC records a $1,200 credit purchase of merchandise on November 2 with this entry:

Nov.	2	Merchandise Inventory..	1,200	
		Accounts Payable..		1,200
		Purchased merchandise on credit.		

The invoice for this merchandise is shown in Exhibit 5.6. The buyer usually receives the original, while the seller keeps a copy. This single source document serves as the purchase invoice of LEC (buyer) and the sales invoice for Trex (seller). The costs that can be included in inventory include all costs incurred in acquiring the goods and bringing them to the purchaser's warehouse and any costs incurred to get them ready for sale to the final customer. Specifically, we can include in merchandise inventory all purchase costs, shipping fees, duties, and any other costs necessary to get the products ready for sale.

Important Tip:

To calculate the total cost of merchandise inventory purchases, we must adjust the invoice cost as follows:

(1) Subtract the cost of any returns and allowances for unsatisfactory items received from a supplier;
(2) Subtract discounts given to a purchaser by a supplier for early payment; and
(3) Add required freight costs if paid by the purchaser.

This section explains these items in more detail.

Accounting for Sales Taxes

In Canada, sales taxes include **Provincial Sales Tax (PST)**, **Goods and Services Tax (GST)**, and the **Harmonized Sales Tax (HST)**. HST is a combination of PST and GST that has been adopted by several provinces in Canada.

EXHIBIT 5.6
Invoice

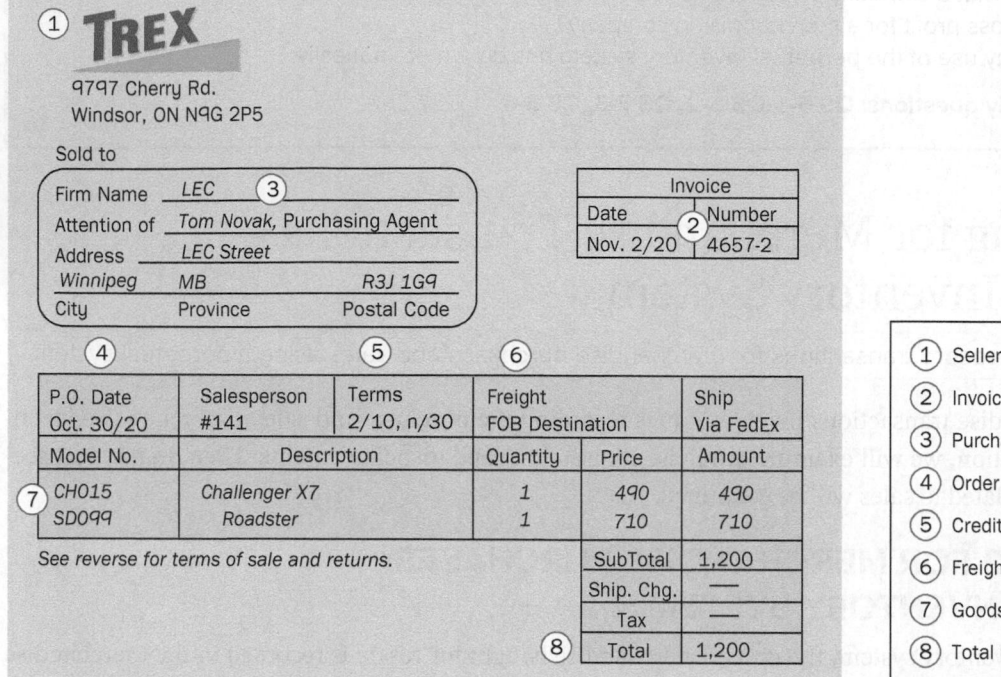

In most provinces, inventory acquired by a merchandising business with the purpose of resale to an end consumer is excluded from PST. Merchandisers can apply for a PST exemption certificate/tax exemption number, which is to be provided to vendors so they are not charged PST on purchases of goods solely for resale. In Canada it is intended for PST to be paid only by the final consumer.[6] As a result, PST is *not included* in the cost of acquiring inventory.

GST and HST paid on the acquisition of goods is *recoverable* from collections of GST and HST from the end customer, and therefore is also *not included* in the cost of inventory.

Appendix 5B provides a high-level overview of accounting for sales taxes in Canada under both perpetual and periodic inventory systems. Additional information relating to accounting for sales tax is provided in Chapter 10.

Purchase Returns and Allowances

Purchase returns are merchandise received by a purchaser and subsequently returned to the supplier. Reasons for returns can vary. The merchandise received may have been the wrong colour or size. A *purchase allowance* is a reduction in the cost of defective merchandise received by a purchaser from a supplier. Purchasers will often keep defective merchandise that is still saleable if the supplier grants an acceptable reduction in the price, providing a sufficient allowance. For example, assume that the merchandise received by the purchaser was furniture scratched during shipment. The purchaser may decide to keep the furniture and pay to repair the furniture if the supplier provides a discount on the original price.

The purchaser informs the supplier of any returns and allowances. This is often through written communication, initiated by the purchaser to inform the supplier of a debit made to the supplier's account,

---

6   An example exemption certificate for BC can be found at https://www2.gov.bc.ca/gov/content/taxes/sales-taxes/pst/forms. In Saskatchewan the vendor licence issued by the Ministry of Finance provides exemption on goods purchased for resale; see http://www.saskatchewan.ca/business/taxes-licensing-and-reporting/provincial-taxes-policies-and-bulletins/provincial-sales-tax.

including the reason for a return or allowance. This communication can be in a formal document called a debit memo.

To illustrate how a buyer accounts for an allowance, we assume that the Roadster mountain bike purchased by LEC on November 2 was discovered to be defective when received on November 5. The November 5 entry by LEC for the purchase allowance is:

Nov.	5	Accounts Payable..	300	
		Merchandise Inventory..................................		300
		Purchase allowance re debit memo		
		dated November 5.		

The entry reduces the Merchandise Inventory account to reflect the allowance. The Accounts Payable account is debited to reduce the liability to the supplier, hence the term *debit memo*.

If this had been a return, then the recorded cost[7] of the defective merchandise would be entered. If there is a refund of cash, then the Cash account is debited for $300 instead of Accounts Payable.

Trade Discounts—Provided for Volume Purchases

When a manufacturer or wholesaler prepares a catalogue of items that it has for sale, each item is usually given a **list price**, also called a **catalogue price**. Often the intended selling price equals list price minus a given percentage called a **trade discount**. The amount of trade discount usually depends on the quantities purchased and on whether a buyer is a wholesaler, retailer, or final consumer. For example, a wholesaler buying 50,000 pens might be granted a 35% trade discount, while a retailer purchasing 500 pens might be granted a 5% trade discount.

Trade discounts are commonly used by manufacturers and wholesalers to change selling prices without republishing their catalogues. When a seller wants to change selling prices, it can notify its customers merely by sending them a new table of trade discounts that they can apply to catalogue prices.

Because a list price is not intended to reflect the actual selling price of merchandise, a buyer records the net amount of list price minus the expected trade discount rather than accounting separately for the discount. For example, on November 2, LEC purchased clothing for resale from The North Place that was listed at $2,000 in the catalogue. Since LEC receives a 40% trade discount, the company records the transaction at $1,200 [= $2,000 – (40% × $2,000)].

Nov.	2	Merchandise Inventory...	1,200	
		Accounts Payable..		1,200
		Purchase of inventory from The North Place.		

Purchase Discounts—Provided for Early Payment

The purchase of goods on credit requires a clear statement of the *credit terms* to avoid misunderstanding. **Credit terms** are a listing of the amounts and timing of payments between a buyer (customer) and seller (supplier). In some industries, purchasers expect terms requiring full or "net" payment within 10 days after the end of a month in which purchases occur. These credit terms are entered on sales invoices or tickets as "n/10 EOM." The **EOM** refers to "end of month." In other industries, invoices are due and payable 30 calendar days after the invoice date. These credit terms are entered as "n/30," meaning "net amount due in 30 days." The 30-day period is called the **credit period**. Credit terms may include a **cash discount**. A buyer views a cash discount as a **purchase discount**. If cash discounts for early payment exist, they are described in the

---

7 Recorded cost is the cost reported in a Merchandise Inventory account minus any discounts.

EXHIBIT 5.7
Credit Terms Illustration—2/10, n/30

credit terms on an invoice. Referring to point 5 in Exhibit 5.6, notice that LEC's November 2 credit purchase was on terms of 2/10, n/30. This should be read "there is a 2% discount if paid within 10 days; the net balance is due within 30 days." The seller allows LEC to deduct 2% of the invoice amount from the payment if it is paid within 10 days of the invoice date. Sellers do this to encourage early payment, improving their operating cycle as described previously. The 10 days are the **discount period**, the period in which the reduced payment can be made. Exhibit 5.7 explains these credit terms.

When LEC takes advantage of the discount and pays the amount due on November 12, the entry to record payment is:

Nov.	12	Accounts Payable..	900	
		Merchandise Inventory..................................		18
		Cash		882
		Paid for the purchase of November 2 less		
		the allowance of November 5 and the		
		discount; $1,200 – $300 = $900;		
		2% × $900 = $18; $900 – $18 = $882.		

Important Tip:

Notice that this entry shows that when goods are returned within the discount period, a buyer will take the discount only on the remaining balance of the invoice.

LEC's Merchandise Inventory account now reflects the net cost of merchandise purchased. Its Accounts Payable account also shows the debt to be satisfied.

Merchandise Inventory					Accounts Payable				
Nov. 2	1,200	300	Nov. 5		Nov. 5	300	1,200	Nov. 2	
		18	Nov. 12		Nov. 12	900			
Balance	882						-0-	Balance	

Managing Discounts

A buyer's failure to pay within a discount period is often quite expensive. If LEC does not pay within the 10-day discount period, it delays the payment by 20 more days. This delay costs LEC an added 2%. Most buyers try to take advantage of purchase discounts. For LEC's terms of 2/10, n/30, missing the 2% discount for an additional 20 days is equal to an annual interest rate of 36.5%, calculated as (365 days ÷ 20 days × 2%).

Most companies set up a system to pay invoices with favourable discounts within the discount period. Careful cash management means that no invoice is paid until the last day of a discount period. Computerized systems achieve this goal by using a code that identifies the last date in the discount period. When that date occurs, the system automatically identifies accounts to be paid.[8]

 DECISION MAKER   Answer—End of chapter

Accounts Payable Manager

You are the new accounts payable manager for a trendy merchandising company that purchases its merchandise on credit. You are trained for your new job by the outgoing employee. You are to oversee payment of payables to maintain the company's credit standing with suppliers and to take advantage of favourable cash discounts. The outgoing employee explains that the computer system is programmed to prepare cheques for amounts net of favourable cash discounts, and cheques are dated the last day of the discount period. You are told that cheques are not mailed until five days later, however. "It's simple," this employee explains. "Our company gets free use of cash for an extra five days, and our department looks better. When a supplier complains, we blame the computer system and the mail room." Your first invoice arrives with a 10-day discount period for a $10,000 purchase. This transaction occurs on April 9 with credit terms of 2/10, n/30. Do you mail the $9,800 cheque on April 19 or April 24? What are your concerns in following the current approach? What are the benefits? Outline your options and the consequences of your possible decisions.

Transfer of Ownership

The point where ownership of merchandise inventory transfers from the buyer to the seller must be identified on the invoice because it determines who pays transportation costs and other incidental costs of transit such as insurance. The party responsible for paying shipping costs is also responsible for insuring the merchandise during transport. The point of transfer is called the **FOB** point, where FOB stands for *free on board* or *freight on board*.

Exhibit 5.8 identifies two alternative points of transfer. *FOB shipping point*, also called *FOB factory*, means the buyer accepts ownership at the seller's place of business. The buyer is then responsible for paying shipping costs and bears the risk of damage or loss when goods are in transit. The seller records the revenue as soon as

---

8   Companies that automatically take advantage of favourable discounts use the *net method* to record merchandise purchases as opposed to using the gross invoice amount when debiting Merchandise Inventory and crediting Accounts Payable (as illustrated in the textbook; known as the *gross method*). Under the net method, both Merchandise Inventory and Accounts Payable are debited/credited for the gross purchase amount less the discount. If payment is not made within the discount period, the payment would debit Accounts Payable for the net amount originally recorded, debit *Discounts Lost* for the amount of the lost discount, and credit Cash for the gross amount of the invoice. The gross method more strictly adheres to the revenue recognition principle than the net method, hence its inclusion in the textbook.

EXHIBIT 5.8

Identifying Transfer of Ownership

FOB Shipping Point
(Buyer Pays Transportation)
→
Carrier
→
FOB Destination
(Seller Pays Transportation)

	Ownership transfers when goods:	Transportation costs paid by:
FOB Shipping Point	**Leave the seller's warehouse**	**Buyer**
FOB Destination	**Arrive at buyer's warehouse**	**Seller**

DreamPictures/Shannon Faulk/Blend Images, © Alamy Images, and © Sean Pavone/Alamy

the items leave their warehouse. The goods are part of the buyer's inventory when they are in transit since ownership has transferred to the buyer.

FOB destination means ownership of the goods transfers to the buyer at the buyer's place of business. The seller is responsible for paying shipping charges and bears the risk of damage or loss in transit. The seller does not record revenue from this sale until the goods arrive at the destination because this transaction is not complete before that point.

There are situations when the party not responsible for shipping costs pays the carrier/transportation agency. In these cases, the party paying these costs either bills the party responsible or, more commonly, adjusts its account payable or receivable with the other party.

ETHICAL IMPACT

You are hired as a marketing manager for the high-tech firm Innovate Inc., located in Toronto. Yesterday you overheard a conversation in the elevator between the VP of sales and the vice president of the company. The VP of sales indicated that she also was disappointed in the current projections and will approach distributors to provide them with an incentive to take extra inventory to help improve the overall sales, improving the end-of-year results and management bonuses.

You remember learning about a concept during your undergrad referred to as "channel stuffing," which recognizes revenue early by having an intermediary company (such as a distributor) act to purchase and sell products between the manufacturing company and the end customer. You are wondering if boosting sales by asking distributors to take additional products is approved of by generally accepted accounting principles. You know that it is normal industry practice to use distributors to reach smaller customers with their more standardized computer chips. What are the benefits to Innovate Inc. if they choose to send more products to distributors? What are the risks? Do you have any concerns with this method of engaging in business?

Transportation Costs

Shipping costs on purchases are called **transportation-in** or **freight-in** costs. LEC's $1,200 purchase on November 2 is on terms of FOB destination. This means that LEC is not responsible for paying transportation costs.

A different situation arises when a company is responsible for paying transportation costs. The cost principle requires these transportation costs to be included as part of the cost of merchandise inventory. This means that a separate entry is necessary when they are not listed on the invoice. For example, LEC's entry to record a $75 freight charge to an independent carrier for merchandise purchased FOB shipping point is:

Nov.	2	Merchandise Inventory..	75	
		Cash		75
		Paid freight charges on purchased merchandise.		

Important Tip:

The cost of shipping goods to customers is different from transportation-in costs. **Transportation-out** or **freight-out** costs for the shipping of goods to customers are debited to the *Delivery Expense* account when the seller is responsible for these costs, and are reported as a *selling expense* in the income statement.

 CHECKPOINT

4. Locate the sample invoice in Exhibit 5.6. When the merchandise inventory is shipped by Trex to LEC, identify at what point ownership of the product transfers to LEC.
5. How long are the credit and discount periods when credit terms are 2/10, n/60?
6. Identify which of the following items are subtracted from the list amount when calculating purchase price: (a) freight-in, (b) trade discount, (c) purchase discount, (d) purchase return and/or allowance.

Do Quick Study questions: QS 5-5, QS 5-6, QS 5-7, QS 5-8

Recording Purchases Information

We have explained how purchase returns and allowances, purchase discounts, and transportation-in are included in calculating the total cost of merchandise inventory. An example presentation of LEC's 2020 net cost of merchandise purchases is summarized in Exhibit 5.9 and is presented for illustrative purposes only.

ACCOUNTING FOR MERCHANDISE SALES— PERPETUAL INVENTORY SYSTEM

Merchandising companies also must account for sales, sales discounts, sales returns and allowances, and cost of goods sold. A merchandising company such as LEC reports these items in an income statement, as shown in Exhibit 5.10.

EXHIBIT 5.9

Net Cost of Merchandise Purchases Calculation—Perpetual

Merchandise Inventory

February 24, 2019, balance.................. 19,000		
Reflects entries to record **purchases of merchandise** during fiscal 2020.................................. 235,800	Reflects entries to record **purchase discounts** 4,200 ....during fiscal 2020	Net Cost of Purchases during fiscal 2020 = $232,400
Reflects **transportation-in** costs incurred during fiscal 2020....... 2,300	Reflects entries to record **purchase returns and** 1,500 ....**allowances** during fiscal 2020	

EXHIBIT 5.10
Gross Profit Section of Income Statement

Lifetime Equipment Co-op Calculation of Gross Profit For Year Ended February 23, 2020		
Sales..		$321,000
Less: Sales discounts..	$4,300	
Sales returns and allowances......................................	2,000	6,300
Net sales..		$314,700
Cost of goods sold..		230,400
Gross profit from sales..		$ 84,300

This section explains how information in this calculation is derived from transactions involving sales, sales discounts, and sales returns and allowances.

Sales Transactions

Accounting for a sales transaction for a seller of merchandise involves capturing information about two related parts:

1. Receiving revenue in the form of an asset from a customer, and
2. Recognizing the cost of merchandise sold to a customer.

As an example, LEC sold $2,400 of merchandise on credit on November 3. The revenue part of this transaction is recorded as:

Nov.	3	Accounts Receivable...	2,400	
		Sales..		2,400
		Sold merchandise on credit.		

This entry reflects an increase in LEC's assets in the form of an account receivable. It also shows the revenue from the credit sale. If the sale is for cash, the debit is to Cash instead of Accounts Receivable.

The expense or cost of the merchandise sold by LEC on November 3 is $1,600. We explain in Chapter 6 how the cost of this merchandise is calculated. The entry to record the cost part of this sales transaction (under a perpetual inventory system) is:

Nov.	3	Cost of Goods Sold...	1,600	
		Merchandise Inventory..................................		1,600
		To record the cost of Nov. 3 sale and reduce inventory.		

This entry records the cost of the merchandise sold as an expense and reduces the Merchandise Inventory account to reflect the remaining balance of inventory on hand.

Sales Discounts

When sellers offer credit terms that include a cash discount, the cash discount is referred to as a **sales discount**. Sales discounts can encourage prompt payments to customers for early payment, improve cash flow, and also reduce future efforts and costs of billing customers.

A seller does not know whether a customer will pay within the discount period and take advantage of a cash discount at the time of a credit sale, so a sales discount is usually not recorded until a customer pays within the discount period. As an example, LEC completed a credit sale for $1,000 on November 12, subject to terms of 2/10, n/60 (the cost of the inventory sold was $600). The entry to record this sale is:

Nov.	12	Accounts Receivable...	1,000	
		Sales...		1,000
		Sold merchandise under terms of 2/10, n/60.		
	12	Cost of Goods Sold...	600	
		Merchandise Inventory...............................		600
		To record the cost of the Nov. 12 sale and reduce inventory.		

This entry records the receivable and the revenue as if the full amount will be paid by the customer.

The customer has two options. One option is to wait 60 days until January 11 and pay the full $1,000. In this case, LEC records the payment as:

Jan.	11	Cash..	1,000	
		Accounts Receivable		1,000
		Received payment for November 12 sale.		

The customer's second option is to pay $980 within a 10-day period that runs through November 22. If the customer pays on or before November 22, LEC records the payment as:

Nov.	22	Cash..	980	
		Sales Discounts...	20	
		Accounts Receivable		1,000
		Received payment for November 12 sale less the discount; $1,000 × 2% = $20.		

Sales discounts are recorded in a *contra revenue* account called Sales Discounts. This is so management can monitor sales discounts to assess their effectiveness and cost. The Sales Discounts account is deducted from the Sales account when calculating a company's net sales (refer to Exhibit 5.10). While information about sales discounts is useful internally, it is seldom reported on income statements distributed to external users.

Sales Returns and Allowances

Sales returns refers to merchandise that customers return to the seller after a sale. Customers return merchandise for a variety of reasons, such as having received an incorrect item or one of poor quality. Many companies allow customers to return merchandise for a full refund. *Sales allowances* refer to reductions in the selling price of merchandise sold to customers. This can occur with damaged merchandise that a customer is willing to purchase if the selling price is decreased. **Sales returns and allowances** involve dissatisfied customers and the possibility of lost future sales. To monitor these problems, managers need detailed information, so many accounting systems record returns and allowances in a separate contra revenue account.

Recall LEC's sale of merchandise on November 3. As already recorded, the merchandise is sold for $2,400 and cost $1,600, but what if the customer returns part of the merchandise on November 6, when returned items sell for $800 and cost $600? The revenue part of this transaction must reflect the decrease in sales from the customer's return:

Nov.	6	Sales Returns and Allowances..............................	800	
		Accounts Receivable		800
		Customer returned merchandise.		

LEC can record this return with a debit to the Sales account instead of Sales Returns and Allowances. This method provides the same net sales, but does not provide information needed by managers to monitor returns and allowances. By using the Sales Returns and Allowances contra account, this information is available. Published income statements usually omit this detail and show only net sales.

If the merchandise returned to LEC is not defective and can be resold to another customer, then LEC returns these goods to its inventory. The entry necessary to restore the cost of these goods to the Merchandise Inventory account is:

Nov.	6	Merchandise Inventory..	600	
		Cost of Goods Sold..		600
		Returned goods to inventory.		

If the merchandise returned is defective, however, the seller may discard the returned items. In this case, the cost of returned merchandise is not restored to the Merchandise Inventory account. Instead, most companies leave the cost of defective merchandise in the Cost of Goods Sold account.[9]

Another possibility is that $800 of the merchandise sold by LEC on November 3 is defective but the customer decides to keep it because LEC grants the customer a price reduction of $500. The only entry that LEC must make in this case is one to reflect the decrease in revenue:

Nov.	6	Sales Returns and Allowances............................	500	
		Accounts Receivable		500
		To record sales allowance.		

Some companies require the seller to prepare a **credit memo** to confirm a customer's return or allowance. A credit memo informs a customer of a credit to his or her account receivable, hence the term *credit memo*.

The information in a credit memo is similar to that of a **debit memo**. The following table summarizes what debit and credit memos are and why they arise:

Inventory Adjustment for Purchaser (Debit Memo)	Vendor Sales Adjustment (Credit Memo)
• Document prepared by the purchaser to "debit" or reduce the purchaser's account payable and "credit" the inventory account.	• Document prepared by the seller to "credit" or reduce the customer's account receivable and "debit" sales returns and allowances.
Why is a debit memo issued?	Why is a credit memo issued?
• To reduce the purchaser's account payable because of:	• To reduce the seller's account receivable because of:
1. Return of unsatisfactory goods	1. Return of unsatisfactory goods
2. Allowance	2. Allowance
3. Error	3. Error

CHECKPOINT

7. Why are sales discounts and sales returns and allowances recorded in contra revenue accounts instead of directly in the Sales account?
8. Under what conditions are two entries necessary to record a sales return?
9. When merchandise is sold on credit and the seller notifies the buyer of a price reduction, does the seller send a credit memo or a debit memo?

Do Quick Study questions: QS 5-9, QS 5-10, QS 5-11, QS 5-12

---

9 When managers want to monitor the cost of defective merchandise, a more informative method is to remove the cost from Cost of Goods Sold and charge it to a *Loss from Defective Merchandise* account.

Mid-Chapter Demonstration Problem

Thorsten Company, a trendy clothing retailer, had the following transactions in March:

March	2	Purchased merchandise from Sabine Company under the following terms: $1,800 invoice price, 2/15, n/60, FOB factory. (The cost of the merchandise to Sabine Company was $990.)
	3	Paid UBS Shipping $125 for shipping charges on the purchase of March 2.
	4	Returned to Sabine Company unacceptable merchandise that had an invoice price of $300 (and a cost to Sabine of $165). Sabine returned the merchandise to inventory.
	17	Sent a cheque to Sabine Company for the March 2 purchase, net of the discount and the returned merchandise.

Required

Assuming both Thorsten and Sabine use a perpetual inventory system:

a. Present the journal entries Thorsten Company should record for these transactions.

b. Present the journal entries Sabine Company should record for these transactions.

Analysis Component:

Who should be insuring the merchandise during shipping: Thorsten or Sabine? Explain.

SOLUTION

a.

Thorsten Company (the buyer)

March 2	Merchandise Inventory	1,800	
	Accounts Payable—Sabine Company		1,800
	Purchased merchandise on credit.		
3	Merchandise Inventory	125	
	Cash		125
	Paid shipping charges on purchased merchandise		
4	Accounts Payable— Sabine Company	300	
	Merchandise Inventory		300
	Returned unacceptable merchandise.		
17	Accounts Payable—Sabine Company	1,500	
	Merchandise Inventory		30
	Cash		1,470
	Paid balance within the discount period and took a 2% discount.		

b.

Sabine Company (the seller)

	Accounts Receivable—Thorsten Company	1,800	
	Sales		1,800
	Sold merchandise under terms 2/15, n/60.		
	Cost of Goods Sold	990	
	Merchandise Inventory		990
	Recorded cost of sales.		
	No entry		
	Sales Returns and Allowances	300	
	Accounts Receivable—Thorsten Company		300
	Customer returned merchandise.		
	Merchandise Inventory	165	
	Cost of Goods Sold		165
	Merchandise returned to inventory.		
	Cash	1,470	
	Sales Discounts	30	
	Accounts Receivable—Thorsten Company		1,500
	Received payment for March 2 sale less the return and discount.		

Analysis Component:

Thorsten should be insuring the merchandise during shipping because the terms *FOB factory* transfers ownership to Thorsten Company the moment the merchandise leaves Sabine Company.

MERCHANDISING INVENTORY JOURNAL ENTRIES SUMMARY—PERPETUAL			
PURCHASES		**SALES**	
Transaction	Journal Entry	Transaction	Journal Entry

Purchase inventory on credit	Merchandise Inventory xxx
	    Accounts Payable xxx
		Sell inventory on credit	**Revenue on sale of goods:**
			Accounts Receivable xxx
			    Sales xxx
			Recording transfer of inventory and COGS on sale:
			Cost of Goods Sold xxx
			    Merchandise Inventory xxx

Return unacceptable merchandise to supplier	Accounts Payable xx
	    Merchandise Inventory xx
		Merchandise returned by customer	**Adjustment to customer's account for return of goods:**
			Sales Returns and Allowances xxx
			    Accounts Receivable xxx
			If items are returned in a saleable condition need to reinstate inventory:
			Merchandise Inventory xxx
			    Cost of Goods Sold xxx

Purchase allowances provided by supplier for defective merchandise[1]	**If supplier provides a discount on the defective goods and the goods are kept for resale:**
	Accounts Payable xx
	    Merchandise Inventory xx
		Sales allowances provided to customer[2]	**If customer keeps defective product and an allowance is provided:**
			Sales Returns and Allowances xx
			    Accounts Receivables xx

Pay freight/shipping charges (FOB Shipping Point)	Merchandise Inventory xx
	    Cash xx
		Pay shipping charges (FOB Destination)	Delivery expense xxx
			    Cash xxx

Pay supplier within discount period	Accounts Payable xxx
	    Merchandise Inventory* xx
	Cash** xxx
	
	*discount = % discount * AP balance
	**cash paid = AP balance − discount
		Receive balance from customer within discount period	Cash## xxx
			Sales Discounts# xx
			    Accounts Receivable xxx
			
			#discount = % discount * AR balance
			##cash received = AR balance − discount

Pay supplier after discount period	Accounts Payable xxx
	    Cash xxx
		Receive balance from customer after discount period	Cash xxx
			    Accounts Receivable xxx

[1] Note: The same journal entry is booked as a return of goods if vendor provides a discount on the goods, except adjustment to A/P is for a lesser amount.

[2] Note: The same journal entry as a return of goods is booked if customer is provided a discount on the goods, except adjustment to A/P is for a lesser amount.

Additional Merchandising Issues— Perpetual Inventory System

This section identifies and explains how merchandising activities affect other accounting processes. We address preparing adjusting entries, and relationships between important accounts.

ADJUSTING ENTRIES

LO4 Prepare adjustments for a merchandising company.

Most adjusting entries are the same for merchandising companies and service companies and involve prepaid expenses, unearned revenues, depreciation, accrued expenses, and accrued revenues.

A merchandising company using a perpetual inventory system needs one additional adjustment to update the Merchandise Inventory account for any losses of merchandise referred to as **shrinkage**. Merchandising companies can lose merchandise in several ways, including theft by employees and customers, accounting errors such as input errors or inventory counting errors, and damage.

Perpetual inventory systems track all goods as they move into and out of the company; however, they do not capture inventory losses due to shrinkage. Since inventory is a high-dollar-value item for a merchandising company, nearly all retailers perform a regular detailed count of their inventory. Some companies will perform regular cycle counts of portions of their inventory (daily, weekly, or monthly) and others will choose to do one thorough detailed count once a year. Shrinkage is calculated by comparing the recorded quantities of inventory in the accounting system with quantities recorded during the physical inventory count. Most companies record any necessary adjustment due to shrinkage by charging it to Cost of Goods Sold, assuming that shrinkage is not abnormally large.

As an example, consider a situation where LEC's Merchandise Inventory account at the end of 2020 had an unadjusted balance of $21,250, but a physical count of inventory revealed only $21,000 of inventory on hand. The adjusting entry to record this $250 shrinkage is:

Dec.	31	Cost of Goods Sold...	250	
		Merchandise Inventory.....................................		250
		To adjust for $250 shrinkage determined		
		by physical count of inventory.		

 DECISION INSIGHT

A PWC Canadian Retail Consumer Security Survey (2012) revealed the following facts about Canadian retailers:

- It is estimated that Canadian retailers are losing over $4 billion per year due to shrinkage, which is approximately $10.8 million per shopping day or approximately $115 per Canadian citizen.

- Items most commonly impacted (in order) are alcohol, ladies' apparel, and cosmetics and fragrances.

- Internal theft was up from 19% in the 2008 study to 33.4% in 2012, signalling a need for strengthened internal loss prevention policies and procedures, and investment in resources to aid in reducing such occurrences.

- 88% of employees who had engaged in theft were charged criminally and 94% were dismissed with cause; 65% of customers engaging in theft were charged criminally.

- 76% of respondents perform either annual or semiannual inventory counts; only 6% of respondents did not perform regular inventory counts.

- The most common loss prevention controls implemented by retail stores include alarm systems, closed-circuit TV/DVR recording systems, armored car deposit/pick-ups, merchandise alarms, exception reporting systems, and safes.

Source: https://www.pwc.com/ca/en/retail-consumer/publications/pwc-security-survey-2012-10-29-en.pdf

 CHECKPOINT

10. When a merchandising company uses a perpetual inventory system, why is it often necessary to adjust the Merchandise Inventory balance with an adjusting entry?

Do Quick Study question: QS 5-13

SUMMARY OF MERCHANDISING COST FLOWS

The Merchandise Inventory account balance at the end of one period is the amount of beginning inventory in the next period.

To summarize the effects of merchandising transactions on the Merchandise Inventory and Cost of Goods Sold accounts, LEC's merchandising activities during 2020 are illustrated in Exhibit 5.11. Most amounts in these T-accounts are summary representations of several entries during the year 2020. Notice that the Cost of Goods Sold balance of $230,400 is the amount reported in the income statement information in Exhibit 5.2. The Merchandise Inventory balance of $21,000 is the amount reported as a current asset on the balance sheet in Exhibit 5.3. These amounts also appear on LEC's adjusted trial balance in Exhibits 5.12 and 5.18.

EXHIBIT 5.11

T-Account Summary of LEC's Merchandising Activities for 2020 (for illustrative purposes only)

Merchandise Inventory

February 24, 2019, balance.................. 19,000	
Net cost of purchases { Reflects entries to record **purchases of merchandise** during fiscal 2020...................................... 235,800	Reflects entries to record **purchase discounts** ....during fiscal 2020 — 4,200
Reflects **transportation-in** costs incurred during fiscal 2020 2,300	Reflects entries to record **purchase returns and** ....**allowances** during fiscal 2020 — 1,500
Reflects entries to record **merchandise returned by customers** and restored to inventory during fiscal 2020 1,400	Reflects **cost of sales** ...... transactions during fiscal 2020 — 231,550
February 23, 2020, unadjusted balance............................... 21,250	February 23, 2020, ... adjustment for **shrinkage** — 250
February 23, 2020, adjusted balance..... 21,000	

Cost of Goods Sold

Cost of goods sold transferred from inventory account.

{ Reflects entries to record the **cost of sales** for 2020...................... 231,550	Reflects entries to record **merchandise returned** by customers and restored to .... inventory during fiscal 2020 — 1,400
February 23, 2020, unadjusted balance 230,150	
February 23, 2020, adjustment for **shrinkage**....................... 250	
February 23, 2020 adjusted balance..................................... 230,400	

Adjusted Trial Balance for a Merchandising Company—Perpetual Inventory System

When using a perpetual system, adjusting entries are similar for merchandising companies and service companies.

The year-end adjustments required for LEC include the following entries:

a. Expiration of $600 of prepaid insurance.

b. Use of $1,200 of store supplies.

c. Use of $1,800 of office supplies.

d. Depreciation of store equipment for $3,000.

e. Depreciation of office equipment for $700.

f. Accrual of $300 of unpaid office salaries and $500 of unpaid store salaries.

g. Physical count of merchandise inventory revealed $21,000 on hand.

Accounts unique to a merchandiser are bolded in the adjusted trial balance in Exhibit 5.12 and include Sales, Sales Discounts, Sales Returns and Allowances, and Cost of Goods Sold.

EXHIBIT 5.12
Adjusted Trial Balance

	Lifetime Equipment Co-op Adjusted Trial Balance February 23, 2020	
	Debit	**Credit**
Cash	$ 8,200	
Accounts receivable	11,200	
Merchandise inventory	21,000	
Office supplies	550	
Store supplies	250	
Prepaid insurance	300	
Office equipment	4,200	
Accumulated depreciation, office equipment		$ 1,400
Store equipment	30,000	
Accumulated depreciation, store equipment		6,000
Accounts payable		16,000
Salaries payable		800
David Sale, capital		40,160
David Sale, withdrawals	4,000	
Rent revenue		2,800
Sales		**321,000**
Sales returns and allowances	**2,000**	
Sales discounts	**4,300**	
Cost of goods sold	**230,400**	
Depreciation expense, store equipment	3,000	
Depreciation expense, office equipment	700	
Office salaries expense	25,300	
Sales salaries expense	18,500	
Interest expense	360	
Insurance expense	600	
Rent expense, office space	900	
Rent expense, selling space	8,100	
Office supplies expense	1,800	
Store supplies expense	1,200	
Advertising expense	11,300	
Totals	$388,160	$388,160

Notice the temporary accounts unique to a merchandiser highlighted on the left. These accounts will need to be closed to income summary using a similar process to that illustrated in Chapter 4.

The accounts unique to a merchandiser are highlighted below.

 DECISION INSIGHT

From Periodic to Perpetual to Virtual Inventory Systems

"Traditional models . . . are going away," according to Keyur Patel, a KPMG partner. Web businesses are changing the way inventory is managed and accounted for. Rather than risk having too little or too much in inventory along with all of the related costs, e-businesses are turning to the manufacturers to package and ship products direct to consumers. The result is that these merchants maintain no inventory balances. Instead, they take customer orders and transmit that information directly to the respective manufacturer, who fulfills the distribution obligation to the customer. Therefore, for these merchants, discussion of an inventory costing system has become redundant.

Income Statement Formats— Perpetual Inventory System

LO5 Define, prepare, and analyze merchandising income statements.

Companies have flexibility as to what format can be used for the presentation of financial statements. As a result, there will be many different formats in practice. However, minimum classification requirements exist regarding how expenses are to be shown on the income statement. The first part of this section looks at formulating a draft income statement through the preparation of a work sheet. The second part of this section describes the classification requirements for expenses and illustrates three presentation formats using LEC's data.

EXPENSE CLASSIFICATION REQUIREMENTS

Expenses are to be shown on an income statement for companies reporting under IFRS based on either their *nature* or their *function*.[10] In previous chapters, expenses were listed on the income statement based on their *nature*. The **nature of an expense** is determined by the type of expense, which is organized based on the basic characteristics of reported expenses. For example, when expenses are identified on the income statement as depreciation, rent, property tax, and salaries, the nature of each expense is being identified.

The **function of an expense** describes the grouping of expenses based on their purpose or what they relate to. For example, an income statement that shows cost of goods sold, *selling expenses*, and *general and administrative expenses* has grouped expenses by their function. When expenses are grouped by function, additional information must be *disclosed* to show the nature of expenses within each group.[11]

ASPE standards provide the opportunity for flexibility in presenting expenses on the income statement. The **full disclosure principle** is the generally accepted accounting principle that requires financial statements to report all relevant information about the operations and financial position of the entity. Information that is relevant but not included in the body of the statements is provided in **notes to financial statements** such as those for **WestJet** in Appendix III of the textbook.

---

10 IFRS 2018, IAS 1, paras. 99–105.

11 IFRS 2018, IAS 1, para. 104. Although students at the introductory level should understand the concept of disclosure, the actual preparation of notes is left to a more advanced accounting course.

MULTIPLE-STEP INCOME STATEMENT

There are two general types of multiple-step income statements: the *classified multiple-step* format and the *multiple-step* format. Both formats can be used in either a perpetual or periodic inventory system.

Classified Multiple-Step Format (for Internal Reporting)

Exhibit 5.13 shows a **classified multiple-step income statement** using data generated for illustrative purposes only for LEC. This format is useful for internal reporting because of the detail it includes, such as the calculation of net sales. The difference between net sales and cost of goods sold is LEC's gross profit.

Exhibit 5.13 shows operating expenses, a broad function or category. Operating expenses are divided into two additional functions: *selling expenses* and *general and administrative expenses*. **Selling expenses** include the expenses of promoting sales through displaying and advertising merchandise, making sales, and delivering goods to customers. In Exhibit 5.13, the selling expenses are disclosed within the body of the statement by providing detailed information on the nature of expenses, including sales salaries, advertising, rent expense allocated to selling, depreciation on the store equipment, and store supplies. **General and administrative expenses**

EXHIBIT 5.13

Classified Multiple-Step Income Statement—Perpetual Inventory System

Lifetime Equipment Co-op
Income Statement
For Year Ended February 23, 2020

Sales			$321,000
Less: Sales discounts		$ 4,300	
Sales returns and allowances		2,000	6,300
Net sales			$314,700
Cost of goods sold			230,400
Gross profit from sales			$ 84,300
Operating expenses:			
Selling expenses:			
Sales salaries expense	$18,500		
Advertising expense	11,300		
Rent expense, selling space	8,100		
Depreciation expense, store equipment	3,000		
Store supplies expense	1,200		
Total selling expenses		$42,100	
General and administrative expenses:			
Office salaries expense	$25,300		
Office supplies expense	1,800		
Rent expense, office space	900		
Depreciation expense, office equipment	700		
Insurance expense	600		
Total general and administrative expenses		29,300	
Total operating expenses			71,400
Profit from operations			$ 12,900
Other revenues and expenses:			
Rent revenue		$ 2,800	
Interest expense		360	2,440
Profit			$ 15,340

Note: Rent revenue is added
Interest expense is subtracted
to get total *Other revenues and expenses*.

support the overall operations of a company and include expenses related to accounting, human resource management, and financial management. In Exhibit 5.13, the general and administrative expenses section provides detail on the nature of these expenses by including office salaries, office supplies, rent expense allocated to the general and administrative category, depreciation on the office equipment, and insurance expense.

Notice that an expense may be divided among categories when it contributes to more than one activity. For example, Exhibit 5.13 shows that LEC allocates rent expense of $9,000 for its store building between two categories: $8,100 is a selling expense, while $900 is listed as a general and administrative expense based on relative rental values.[12]

Revenues and expenses that are *not* part of normal operating activities are reported under the functional heading *Other revenues and expenses* of the income statement. LEC's main operating activity is merchandising; therefore, rent revenue—not a merchandising activity—is added under *Other revenues and expenses*. Another example, interest expense, arises because of a financing (or borrowing) activity and not because of LEC's merchandising (or operating) activities. It is subtracted under *Other revenues and expenses* as highlighted in Exhibit 5.13. Other examples of *Other revenues and expenses* include dividend income and gains and losses on the sale of property, plant, and equipment assets.

Multiple-Step Format (for External Reporting)

Exhibit 5.14 shows a multiple-step income statement format that can be used in external reports. In comparison to Exhibit 5.13, a multiple-step statement leaves out the detailed calculation of net sales. The functional categories of *selling expenses* and *general and administrative expenses* are not included on a multiple-step income statement; operating expenses are listed by nature only on a multiple-step income statement.

EXHIBIT 5.14

Multiple-Step Income Statement—Perpetual Inventory System

Lifetime Equipment Co-op Income Statement For Year Ended February 23, 2020		
Net sales..		$314,700
Cost of goods sold..		230,400
Gross profit from sales...		$ 84,300
Operating expenses:		
Salaries expense..	$43,800	
Advertising expense..	11,300	
Rent expense..	9,000	
Depreciation expense..	3,700	
Supplies expense..	3,000	
Insurance expense...	600	
Total operating expenses...		71,400
Profit from operations..		$ 12,900
Other revenues and expenses:		
Rent revenue...	$ 2,800	
Interest expense...	360	2,440
Profit..		$ 15,340

---

[12] These expenses can be recorded in a single ledger account or in two separate accounts. If they are recorded in one account, we allocate its balance between the two expenses when preparing statements.

SINGLE-STEP INCOME STATEMENT

A **single-step income statement** is another format for external reporting. It shows items based on their function only and is shown in Exhibit 5.15 for LEC. This simple format includes cost of goods sold as an operating expense and shows only one subtotal for total expenses. Because operating expenses are highly summarized on a single-step income statement, additional information regarding the nature of expenses included in each function must be disclosed in the notes to the financial statements.

EXHIBIT 5.15

Single-Step Income Statement—Perpetual Inventory System

Lifetime Equipment Co-op Income Statement For Year Ended February 23, 2020		
Revenues:		
Net sales...	$314,700	
Rent revenue...	2,800	
Total revenues..		$317,500
Expenses:		
Cost of goods sold	$230,400	
Selling expenses..	42,100	
General and administrative expense...........................	29,300	
Interest expense	360	
Total expenses		302,160
Profit..		$ 15,340

Companies can use formats that combine features of both the single- and multiple-step statements for external reporting. As long as income statement items are shown sensibly and minimum requirements are satisfied, management can choose the presentation format.

 CHECKPOINT

11. What income statement format shows detailed calculations for net sales? What format gives no subtotals except total expenses?

Do Quick Study question: QS 5-14

FINANCIAL STATEMENT ANALYSIS TOOLS FOR INVENTORY

LO6 Calculate gross margin and markup on inventory cost.

Gross Profit Margin

Gross profit margin, also called gross margin or gross profit ratio, is an important ratio as it identifies the percentage of sales dollars left over after covering cost of goods sold. Competitors pay close attention to gross margins, as a company with higher margins is either able to achieve better pricing on its inventory or is able to convince customers to pay a premium for its product. Companies compare their margins achieved in the current year to prior years to assess their performance from one year to the next. Industry benchmarks, competitor performance, and historical margins achieved are all helpful tools in determining whether the gross margins achieved are reasonable. A merchandising company needs sufficient gross profit to cover operating expenses or it will not be able to remain competitive.

The **gross profit margin ratio** is defined as shown in Exhibit 5.16. The higher the gross profit margin, the better the company is at achieving a combination of good pricing on its products and managing its costs of inventory.

EXHIBIT 5.16
Gross Profit Margin

$$\text{Gross Profit Margin} = \frac{\text{Net Sales} - \text{Cost of Goods Sold}}{\text{Net Sales}}$$

Exhibit 5.17 shows the gross profit ratios of LEC based on fictitious data for the years 2018, 2019, and 2020.

EXHIBIT 5.17
LEC's Gross Profit Ratio

	2020	2019	2018
Units sold	214,000	160,000	100,000
Gross profit from sales	$ 84,300	$ 69,440	$ 46,400
Net sales	$314,700	$248,000	$160,000
Gross profit ratio	26.8%	28.0%	29.0%

This ratio represents the gross profit in each dollar of sales. For example, Exhibit 5.17 shows that LEC's gross profit ratio in 2018 was 29.0%. This means that each $1 of sales yielded 29¢ in gross profit to cover all other expenses. Exhibit 5.17 shows that LEC's gross profit ratio decreased from 2018 to 2020, reflecting an unfavourable trend. How is this possible given that net sales and gross profit in dollars are both increasing? If net sales are increasing but at a slower rate than the increase in cost of goods sold, gross profit on sales will grow but at a decreasing rate.[13] Success for companies such as LEC depends on a gross profit that adequately covers operating expenses.

---

13 A more detailed analysis of the information in Exhibit 5.17 shows that net sales are increasing but at a slower rate than the increases in cost of goods sold. This has caused gross profit to shrink as a percentage of sales (an unfavourable trend). This conclusion is supported by the following:

	2020	% Change	2019	% Change	2018
Units sold	214,000	33.8	160,000	60.0	100,000
Net sales	$314,700	26.9	$248,000	55.0	$160,000
COGS	230,400	29.0	178,560	57.2	113,600
Gross profit from sales	$ 84,300	21.4	$ 69,440	49.7	$ 46,400
Gross profit ratio	26.8%	-4.3	28.0%	-3.4	29.0%

Exhibit 5.18 highlights a snapshot of gross margins of several Canadian and US public companies. Notice the differences in gross margins achieved by the different companies. Loblaw Companies Limited is largely a grocery chain; its margins are lower than a retail chain like Lululemon Athletica and **Apple Inc. Costco Wholesale Corporation** has relatively low gross margins at 11%; however, its sales for fiscal 2017 reached in excess of $126.2 billion, with profit of $2.68 billion compared to Loblaw with sales of over $46 billion and profit of $990 million for the year ended December 31, 2016. In order to get a snapshot of overall company performance, you would also need to look at net profit margins, which is calculated by dividing profit by net revenue to assess overall profitability, as gross margin ignores all operating expenses.

EXHIBIT 5.18
Gross Margin Snapshot by Company

	Year End	GM%	Prior Year	GM%	Change
Lululemon Athletica Inc.	29-Jan-17	51%	31-Jan-16	48%	+3%
Canadian Tire Corporation Limited	31-Dec-17	35%	2-Jan-17	34%	+1%
Loblaw Companies Limited	31-Dec-16	28%	2-Jan-16	28%	0%
Costco Wholesale Corporation	3-Sept-17	11%	28-Aug-16	11%	0%
Apple Inc.	30-Sep-17	38%	24-Sep-16	40%	−2%
Amazon.com Inc.	31-Dec-16	35%	31-Dec-15	33%	2%

Source: Company annual reports.

Markup on Inventory Cost

A **markup percentage** is the average increase in selling price of a product over the cost. If your product cost is $10 and your retail selling price is $15, your markup is $5, or 5/10 = 50%. A company that has a set markup percentage can determine selling price for a specific item through the formula presented below.

$$\text{Selling Price} = \text{Cost} \times (1 + \text{Markup \%}) = 10 \times (1 + 0.50) = \$15$$

In some industries the selling price is set by the manufacturer to achieve standardized pricing. It can be helpful for businesses to calculate their markup percentage to determine the profitability of the different products they sell. For example, imagine you work for **Best Buy Canada** as a sales director for the Apple product line. You have been asked to determine how much each iPad Mini sale contributes to gross profit. The selling price set by Apple is $319. Assume Apple Inc. charges Best Buy $269 for each iPad Mini it purchases. What is the markup percentage on the product?

$$\text{Markup Percentage} = \frac{\text{Selling Price} - \text{Cost}}{\text{Cost}} = \frac{319 - 269}{269} = 18.6\%$$

Target gross margin is a fixed percentage markup that is concerned with gross margin achieved on a specific product based on the final selling price. If you know that your cost is $10 and you know you must achieve a gross margin of 50%, the required selling price can be calculated using the following formula:

$$\text{Selling Price} = \frac{\text{Cost}}{(1 - \text{Target Margin percentage})} = \frac{10}{(1 - 0.50)} = \$20$$

Consider an example where Lululemon Athletica acquires a new line of men's athletic running jackets and wants to ensure the pricing that is set will contribute equivalently to the bottom line as the company's other product mix. Lululemon has established a target product gross margin percentage of 55%. The manufacturing cost of the jackets is determined to be $45. At what price should the company sell the product? Selling price is $100 calculated as $45 ÷ (1 − 0.55).

When setting pricing, it is also important to pay attention to customer demand, competitor pricing, and potential substitute products. Many marketers perform detailed market research to ensure the pricing they set finds the optimum balance between company profitability and ability to attract customers to a given product.

 CHECKPOINT

12. Surf's Up Merchandising shows gross profit ratios of 39%, 39.5%, and 41% for 2019, 2020, and 2021, respectively. Assuming that all other factors have remained constant, does this reflect a favourable (good) or unfavourable (bad) trend?

Do Quick Study questions: QS 5-15, QS 5-16, QS 5-17, QS 5-18, QS 5-19

CRITICAL THINKING CHALLENGE

Refer to the Critical Thinking Challenge questions at the beginning of the chapter. Compare your answers to those suggested on Connect.

IFRS AND ASPE—THE DIFFERENCES

Difference	International Financial Reporting Standards (IFRS)	Accounting Standards for Private Enterprises (ASPE)
Expense classification	• Must be classified by nature or by function	• Can be classified in way most useful for the company

A Look Ahead

Chapter 6 extends our analysis of merchandising activities and focuses on the valuation of inventory. Topics include the items in inventory, costs assigned, costing methods used, and inventory estimation techniques.

For further study on some topics of relevance to this chapter, please see the following Extend Your Knowledge supplements:

EYK 5-1 PST/GST Comprehensive Exercises
EYK 5-2 Comprehensive Merchandising Problems—Perpetual

SUMMARY

LO1 Describe merchandising, and identify and explain the important income statement and balance sheet components for a merchandising company. Operations of merchandising companies involve buying products and reselling them. A merchandiser's costs on an income statement include an amount for cost of goods sold. Gross profit, or gross margin, equals net sales minus cost of goods sold. The current assets section of the balance sheet includes merchandise inventory, which refers to the products a merchandiser sells and has on hand at the balance sheet date.

LO2 Describe both perpetual and periodic inventory systems. A perpetual inventory system continuously tracks the cost of goods on hand and the cost of goods sold. A periodic system accumulates the cost of goods *purchased* during the period and does not compute the amount of inventory on hand or the cost of goods sold until the end of a period

LO3 Analyze and record transactions for merchandise purchases and sales using a perpetual system. For a perpetual inventory system, purchases net of volume purchase discounts are added (debited) to the Merchandise Inventory account. Purchase discounts and purchase returns and allowances are subtracted from (credited to) Merchandise Inventory, and transportation-in costs are added (debited) to Merchandise Inventory. A merchandiser records sales at list price less any volume purchase discounts. The cost of items sold is transferred from Merchandise Inventory to Cost of Goods Sold. Refunds or credits given to customers for unsatisfactory merchandise are recorded (debited) in Sales Returns and Allowances, a contra account to Sales. If merchandise is returned and restored to inventory, the cost of this merchandise is removed from Cost of Goods Sold and transferred back to Merchandise Inventory. When cash discounts from the sales price are offered and customers pay within the discount period, the seller records (debits) discounts in Sales Discounts, a contra account to Sales. Debit and credit memos are documents sent between buyers and sellers to communicate that the sender is either debiting or crediting an account of the recipient.

LO4 Prepare adjustments for a merchandising company. With a perpetual inventory system, it is often necessary to make an adjustment for inventory shrinkage. This is calculated by comparing a physical count of inventory with the Merchandise Inventory account balance. Shrinkage is normally charged to Cost of Goods Sold.

LO5 Define, prepare, and analyze merchandising income statements. Multiple-step income statements show items by both function and nature. Classified multiple-step income statements are usually limited to internal use; they show the calculation of net sales and report expenses by function—such as selling and general and administrative—supported by a list of expenses by nature. The format of income statements published for external parties is flexible and includes the multiple-step or single-step format. The single-step format shows expenses by function with supporting note disclosure about the nature of the expenses.

LO6 Calculate gross margin and markup on inventory cost. The gross profit ratio is calculated as gross profit divided by net sales. It is an indicator of a company's profitability before deducting operating expenses. A gross profit ratio must be large enough to cover operating expenses and give an adequate profit. Markup on inventory cost is used by retailers to determine how much to set the selling price of inventory items when a specific gross margin percentage is targeted.

 Guidance Answer to DECISION MAKER

Accounts Payable Manager

Your decision is whether to comply with prior policy or create a new policy not to abuse discounts offered by suppliers. Your first step should be to meet with your superior to find out if the automatic late payment policy is the actual policy and, if so, its rationale. It is possible that the prior employee was reprimanded because of this behaviour. If it is the policy to pay late, then you must apply your own sense of right and wrong.

(Continued)

One point of view is that the late payment policy is unethical. A deliberate plan to make late payments means that the company lies when it pretends to make purchases within the credit terms. There is the potential that your company could lose its ability to get future credit.

Another view is that the late payment policy is an acceptable business practice. There may exist markets in which attempts to take discounts through late payments are accepted as a continued phase of price negotiation. Also, your company's suppliers can respond by billing your company for the discounts not accepted because of late payments. This is a questionable viewpoint, especially given the old employee's proposal to cover up late payments as computer or mail problems, and given that some suppliers have previously complained.

Guidance Answers to CHECKPOINT

1. Cost of goods sold is the total cost of merchandise sold to customers during a period. In a perpetual inventory system the cost of goods sold amount is determined from the cost of inventory each time a sale is made. In a periodic system total cost of goods sold is calculated (Beginning Inventory + Purchases − Ending Inventory = COGS).

2. Gross profit is the difference between net sales and cost of goods sold.

3. Widespread use of computing and related technology has dramatically increased use of the perpetual inventory system in practice.

4. The invoice indicates that the shipping terms are FOB destination, which means that Trex maintains ownership until the merchandise inventory reaches LEC. Trex must therefore bear the freight costs and is responsible for insuring the merchandise inventory during transport.

5. Under credit terms of 2/10, n/60, the credit period is 60 days and the discount period is 10 days.

6. b

7. Recording sales discounts and sales returns and allowances separately from sales gives useful information to managers for internal monitoring and decision making.

8. When a customer returns merchandise and the seller restores the merchandise to inventory, two entries are necessary. One entry records the decrease in revenue and credits the customer's account. The second entry debits inventory and reduces cost of goods sold.

9. There will be a credit memo showing the *credit* to the seller's account receivable.

10. Merchandise Inventory balance may need adjusting to reflect shrinkage.

11. Classified multiple-step income statement. Single-step income statement.

12. All other factors remaining constant, this reflects a favourable trend because Surf's Up is showing an increase in gross profit per $1 of net sales over time (from 39¢ of gross profit per $1 of net sales in 2019 to 41¢ of gross profit per $1 of net sales in 2021). This indicates that Surf's Up is generating more gross profit to cover operating expenses, which appears to be favourable.

Demonstration Problem

Use the following adjusted trial balance and additional information to complete the requirements:

Paddle Boards Inc. Adjusted Trial Balance December 31, 2020		
Cash..	$ 19,300	
Merchandise inventory..	50,000	
Store supplies	1,000	
Equipment...	44,600	
Accumulated depreciation, equipment.................................		$ 16,500
Accounts payable		8,000
Salaries payable..		1,000
Dee Rizzo, capital		69,000
Dee Rizzo, withdrawals	8,000	
Interest income...		300
Sales...		325,000
Sales discounts...	6,000	
Sales returns and allowances...	5,000	
Cost of goods sold	148,000	
Depreciation expense, store equipment..............................	4,000	
Depreciation expense, office equipment.............................	1,500	
Sales salaries expense...	28,000	
Office salaries expense..	32,000	
Insurance expense	12,000	
Rent expense (70% is store, 30% is office)...........................	24,000	
Store supplies expense..	6,000	
Advertising expense	30,400	
Totals	$419,800	$419,800

Paddle Boards Inc. showed the following additional information regarding merchandising activities for 2020:

Invoice cost of merchandise purchases...	$140,000
Purchase discounts	3,500
Purchase returns and allowances	2,600
Transportation-in	4,000

Required

1. Use the additional information to calculate the total cost of merchandise purchases.

2. Prepare a 2020 classified multiple-step income statement for internal use similar to Exhibit 5.13.

3. Present a single-step income statement for 2020 similar to the one in Exhibit 5.15.

Analysis Component:

Calculate the gross profit ratio for Paddle Boards Inc. and compare to the gross profit margin presented for Canadian Tire Corp in Exhibit 5.18. Round calculations to two decimal places. Can you compare the gross profit ratios for these two companies? Explain.

Planning the Solution

• Calculate the total cost of merchandise purchases.

• Calculate net sales. Subtract cost of goods sold from net sales to get gross profit. Then classify the operating expenses as selling expenses and general and administrative expenses.

- To prepare the single-step income statement, begin with the net sales and interest income. Then subtract the cost of goods sold and operating expenses.

- The first closing entry debits all temporary accounts with credit balances and opens the Income Summary account. The second closing entry credits all temporary accounts with debit balances. The third entry closes the Income Summary account to the owner's capital account, and the fourth closing entry closes the withdrawals account to the capital account.

- Prepare an answer to the analysis component.

SOLUTION

1.

Invoice cost of merchandise purchases	$140,000
Less: Purchase discounts	3,500
Purchase returns and allowances	2,600
Add: Transportation-in	4,000
Total cost of merchandise purchases	$137,900

2. Classified, multiple-step income statement

Paddle Boards Inc.
Income Statement
For Year Ended December 31, 2020

Sales			$325,000
Less: Sales discounts		$ 6,000	
Sales returns and allowances		5,000	11,000
Net sales			$314,000
Cost of goods sold			148,000
Gross profit from sales			$166,000
Operating expenses:			
Selling expenses:			
Advertising expense	$30,400		
Sales salaries expense	28,000		
Rent expense, selling space	16,800		
Store supplies expense	6,000		
Depreciation expense, store equipment	4,000		
Total selling expenses		$85,200	
General and administrative expenses:			
Office salaries expense	$32,000		
Insurance expense	12,000		
Rent expense, office space	7,200		
Depreciation expense, office equipment	1,500		
Total general and administrative expenses		52,700	
Total operating expenses			137,900
Income from operations			$ 28,100
Other revenues and expenses:			
Interest income			300
Profit			$ 28,400

3. Single-step income statement

Paddle Boards Inc. Income Statement For Year Ended December 31, 2020		
Revenues:		
Net sales		$314,000
Interest income		300
Total revenues		$314,300
Expenses:		
Cost of goods sold	$148,000	
Selling expenses	85,200	
General and administrative expense	52,700	
Total expenses		285,900
Profit		$ 28,400

Analysis Component:

The gross profit ratio for Paddle Boards Inc. is 52.87% ($166,000 / $314,000 × 100%) and 35% for Canadian Tire Corporation Limited for the year ended December 31, 2016, as shown in Exhibit 5.18. You can expect deviations in the company's gross margins because Canadian Tire has a more diversified product base and Paddle Boards Inc. sells one main niche product that is currently a fitness and recreation trend—paddle boards.

Periodic and Perpetual Inventory Systems Compared

Accounting Comparisons

LO7 Record and compare merchandising transactions using both periodic and perpetual inventory systems.

Recall that under a perpetual system, the Merchandise Inventory account is updated after each purchase and each sale. The Cost of Goods Sold account is also updated after each sale so that during the period the account balance reflects the period's total cost of goods sold to date. At the end of the period, a physical count of the merchandise inventory is performed to adjust Merchandise Inventory and Cost of Goods Sold.

Under a periodic inventory system, the Merchandise Inventory account is updated only once each accounting period. This update occurs at the *end* of the period based on a physical count of the merchandise inventory. During the next period, the Merchandise Inventory balance remains unchanged. It reflects the beginning inventory balance until it is updated again at the end of the period. In a periodic inventory system, cost of goods sold is *not* recorded as each sale occurs. Instead, the total cost of goods sold during the period is calculated at the end of the period.

Recording Merchandise Transactions

Under a perpetual system, each purchase, purchase return and allowance, purchase discount, and transportation-in transaction is recorded in the Merchandise Inventory account. Under a periodic system, a separate temporary account is set up for each of these items. At the end of a period, each of these temporary accounts is closed and the Merchandise Inventory account is updated. To illustrate the differences, we use parallel columns to show journal entries for the most common transactions using both periodic and perpetual inventory systems (we drop explanations for simplicity).

Purchases

LEC purchases merchandise for $1,200 on credit with terms of 2/10, n/30, and records this purchase as:

Periodic		
Purchases..	1,200	
Accounts Payable........................		1,200

Perpetual		
Merchandise Inventory....................	1,200	
Accounts Payable........................		1,200

The periodic system debits all merchandise purchases to an expense account called *Purchases*.

Purchase Returns and Allowances

LEC returns merchandise because of defects. If the recorded cost[14] of the defective merchandise is $300, LEC records the return with this entry:

Periodic	
Accounts Payable	300
Purchase Returns and	
Allowances	300

Perpetual	
Accounts Payable	300
Merchandise Inventory	300

This entry is the same if LEC is granted a price reduction (allowance) instead of returning the merchandise. In the periodic system, the entry credits a contra expense account called **Purchase Returns and Allowances** that accumulates the cost of all returns and allowances transactions during a period. Because Purchase Returns and Allowances is a contra expense account related to the Purchases account, it is subtracted from Purchases when determining net purchases as shown in Exhibit 5A.1.

EXHIBIT 5A.1

Calculation of Net Purchases and Cost of Goods Purchased Under a Periodic Inventory System

Purchases...		$235,800
Less: Purchase discounts...	$4,200	
Purchase returns and allowances...	1,500	5,700
Net purchases...		$230,100
Add: Transportation-in		2,300
Cost of goods purchased		$232,400

Purchase Discount

When MEC pays the supplier for the previous purchase within the discount period, the required payment is $882 (= $1,200 − $300 = $900 × 98% = $882) and is recorded as:

Periodic	
Accounts Payable	900
Purchase Discounts	18
Cash	882

Perpetual	
Accounts Payable	900
Merchandise Inventory	18
Cash	882

The periodic system credits a contra expense account called *Purchase Discounts* that accumulates discounts taken on purchase transactions during the period. Purchase Discounts, like Purchase Returns and Allowances, is subtracted from the Purchases account balance as shown in Exhibit 5A.1. If payment is delayed until after the discount period expires, the entry under both the periodic and perpetual methods is to debit Accounts Payable and credit Cash for $900 each.

Transportation-In

LEC paid a $75 freight charge to haul merchandise to its store. In the periodic system, this cost is charged to an expense account known as *Transportation-In*. Transportation-in is included as part of the $232,400 total cost of merchandise purchased as shown in Exhibit 5A.1.

---

14 Recorded cost is the cost recorded in the account after any discounts.

Periodic		
Transportation-In	75	
Cash		75

Perpetual		
Merchandise Inventory	75	
Cash		75

Sales

LEC sold $2,400 of merchandise on credit and LEC's cost of this merchandise is $1,600:

Under the periodic system, the cost of goods sold is *not* recorded at the time of sale. We later show how the periodic system calculates total cost of goods sold at the end of a period.

Periodic		
Accounts Receivable	2,400	
Sales		2,400

Perpetual		
Accounts Receivable	2,400	
Sales		2,400
Cost of Goods Sold	1,600	
Merchandise Inventory		1,600

Sales Returns

A customer returns part of the merchandise from the previous transaction, where returned items sell for $800 and cost $600. LEC restores the merchandise to inventory and records the return as:

Periodic		
Sales Returns and Allowances	800	
Accounts Receivable		800

Perpetual		
Sales Returns and Allowances	800	
Accounts Receivable		800
Merchandise Inventory	600	
Cost of Goods Sold		600

The periodic system records only the revenue reduction.

 CHECKPOINT

13. Identify those accounts included in a periodic system that are not included in a perpetual system.
14. The perpetual system has a Cost of Goods Sold account. Explain why the periodic system does not have a Cost of Goods Sold account.

Do Quick Study questions: *QS 5-20, *QS 5-21

Adjusting Entries

The adjusting entries recorded under a periodic and a perpetual inventory system are identical except for the treatment of merchandise inventory. Under a perpetual inventory system, recall that the adjusting entry shown below was recorded to reflect shrinkage of $250 (the difference between the $21,250 unadjusted balance in Merchandise Inventory and the $21,000 physical count). Under a periodic inventory system, there is no corresponding adjustment to update the $19,000 unadjusted balance in Merchandise Inventory. Instead, we use closing entries to update the Merchandise Inventory account. We show the closing entry approach to update Merchandise Inventory in the next section.

Periodic
No entry

Perpetual		
Cost of Goods Sold	250	
Merchandise Inventory		250

MERCHANDISING INVENTORY JOURNAL ENTRIES SUMMARY—PERIODIC			
PURCHASES		**SALES**	
Transaction	Journal Entry	Transaction	Journal Entry

Purchase inventory on credit	Purchases................................ xxx
	    Accounts Payable............. xxx
		Sell inventory on credit[1]	**Revenue on sale of goods:**
			Accounts Receivable........................ xxx
			    Sales... xxx
			No adjustment to inventory

Return unacceptable merchandise to supplier	Accounts Payable.................. xx
	    Purchase Returns and
	    Allowances xx
		Merchandise returned by customer	**Adjustment to customer's account for return of goods:**
			Sales Returns and Allowances xxx
			    Accounts Receivable xxx
			No adjustment to inventory

Purchase allowances provided by supplier for defective merchandise[2]	If supplier provides a discount on the defective goods and the goods are kept for resale:
	Accounts Payable.................. xx
	    Purchase Returns and
	    Allowances xx
		Sales allowances provided to customer[3]	**If customer keeps defective product and an allowance is provided:**
			Sales Returns and Allowances xx
			    Accounts Receivables xx

Pay freight/shipping charges (FOB Shipping Point)	Transportation-In xx
	    Cash....................................... xx
		Pay shipping charges (FOB Destination)	Delivery expense xxx
			    Cash.. xxx

Pay supplier within discount period	Accounts Payable.................. xx
	    Purchase Discounts* xxx
	    Cash**................................... xxx
	*discount = % discount * AP balance
	**cash paid = AP balance − discount
		Receive balance from customer within discount period	Cash##.. xxx
			Sales Discounts#.............................. xx
			    Accounts Receivable xxx
			#discount = % discount * AR balance
			##cash received = AR balance − discount

Pay supplier after discount period	Accounts Payable.................. xxx
	    Cash....................................... xxx
		Receive balance from customer after discount period	Cash xxx
			    Accounts Receivable xxx

[1]Note: Under periodic inventory systems, the Inventory account is not adjusted for the sales of inventory; instead, an adjusting entry is recorded at the end of the period based on a physical inventory count of the goods on hand.

[2]Note: The same journal entry is booked as a return of goods if vendor provides a discount on the goods, except adjustment to A/P is for a lesser amount.

[3]Note: The same journal entry as a return of goods is booked if customer is provided a discount on the goods, except adjustment to A/P is for a lesser amount.

An Income Statement for a Merchandising Company—Periodic Inventory

Exhibit 5A.2 presents an income statement for a merchandising company that uses the periodic inventory system. Recall that cost of goods sold is calculated as:

Beginning merchandise inventory	$ 19,000
Plus: Net cost of purchases...	232,400
Less: Ending merchandise inventory..................................	21,000
Equals: Cost of goods sold..	$230,400

The adjustments in the financial statements presented below reflect the following:

a. Expiration of $600 of prepaid insurance.

b. Use of $1,200 of store supplies.

c. Use of $1,800 of office supplies.

d. Depreciation of the store equipment for $3,000.

e. Depreciation of the office equipment for $700.

f. Accrual of $300 of unpaid office salaries and $500 of unpaid store salaries.

Once the adjusted amounts are extended into the financial statement columns, the accountant uses the information to develop the company's financial statements.

The classified multiple-step income statement under a periodic inventory system is shown in Exhibit 5A.2.

EXHIBIT 5A.2

Classified Multiple-Step Income Statement—Periodic

	Lifetime Equipment Co-op Income Statement For Year Ended December 31, 2020		
Sales			$321,000
Less: Sales discounts		$ 4,300	
Sales returns and allowances		2,000	6,300
Net sales			$314,700
Cost of goods sold			
Merchandise inventory, Dec. 31, 2019		$ 19,000	
Purchases	$235,800		
Less: Purchase returns and allowances	$1,500		
Purchase discounts	4,200	5,700	
Net purchases		$230,100	
Add: Transportation-in		2,300	
Cost of goods purchased		232,400	
Goods available for sale		$251,400	
Less: Merchandise inventory, Dec. 31, 2020		21,000	
Cost of goods sold			230,400
Gross profit from sales			$ 84,300
Operating expenses:			
Selling expenses:			
Sales salaries expense		$ 18,500	
Advertising expense		11,300	
Rent expense, selling space		8,100	
Depreciation expense, store equipment		3,000	
Store supplies expense		1,200	
Total selling expenses		$ 42,100	
General and administrative expenses			
Office salaries expense		$ 25,300	
Office supplies expense		1,800	
Rent expense, office space		900	
Depreciation expense, office equipment		700	
Insurance expense		600	
Total general and administrative expense		29,300	
Total operating expenses			71,400
Profit from Operations			$ 12,900
Other revenues and expenses:			
Rent revenue		$ 2,800	
Interest expense		360	2,440
Profit			$ 15,340

Credited to Income Summary in the first closing entry:	
Merchandise Inventory (ending balance)..................................	$ 21,000
Purchase Discounts	4,200
Purchase Returns and Allowances	1,500
Debited to Income Summary in the second closing entry:	
Merchandise Inventory (beginning balance)..........................	(19,000)
Purchases	(235,800)
Transportation-in..	(2,300)
Net effect on Income Summary	$(230,400)

This $230,400 effect on Income Summary is the cost of goods sold amount. This figure is confirmed as follows:

Beginning inventory		$ 19,000
Purchases................................	$235,800	
Less: Purchase discounts.................	4,200	
Less: Purchase returns and allowances............................	1,500	
Add: Transportation-in	2,300	
Net cost of goods purchased		232,400
Cost of goods available for sale		$251,400
Less: Ending inventory......................		21,000
Cost of goods sold.............................		$230,400

EXHIBIT 5A.3

Merchandising Cost Flows Across Periods

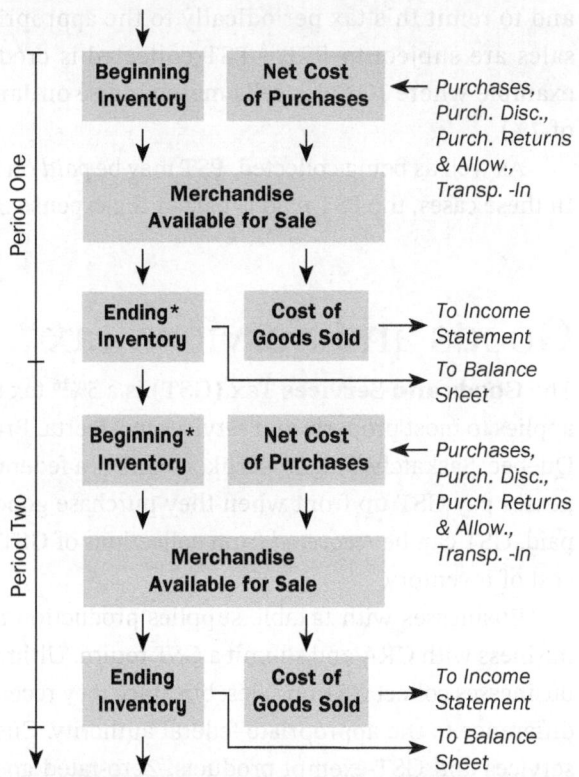

*One period's ending inventory is the next period's beginning inventory.

The periodic system transfers cost of goods sold to the Income Summary account but does not use a Cost of Goods Sold account. Exhibit 5A.3 shows the relation among inventory, purchases, and cost of goods sold across periods.

The periodic system does not measure shrinkage. Instead, it calculates cost of goods available for sale, subtracts the cost of ending inventory, and defines the difference as cost of goods sold, which includes shrinkage.

Sales Tax

LO8 Explain and record Provincial Sales Tax (PST), Goods and Services Tax (GST), and Harmonized Sales Tax.

This section looks at the additional issue of recording sales tax. Most provinces and the federal government require retailers to collect sales tax from customers and to send these taxes periodically to the appropriate agency.

Provincial Sales Tax

Provincial Sales Tax (PST) is a tax applied on sales to the final consumers of products and/or services.

All provinces except Alberta (and the territories) require retailers to collect PST from their customers and to remit this tax periodically to the appropriate provincial authority. It should be noted that not all sales are subject to PST.[15] PST collected is credited to a separate account, as shown in the following example where JC Sales sells merchandise on January 5 costing $600 for $900 on account (assuming PST of 7%).

As well as being collected, PST may be *paid* on items purchased for use or on non-current assets acquired. In these cases, the PST paid is part of the expense or asset cost associated with the purchase.

Goods and Services Tax

The **Goods and Services Tax (GST)** is a 5%[16] tax on almost all goods and services provided in Canada. GST applies to most property and services in Alberta, British Columbia, Manitoba, Northwest Territories, Nunavut, Quebec, Saskatchewan, and Yukon. GST is a federal tax on the end consumer. However, unlike the PST, businesses pay GST up front when they purchase goods but generally receive a full credit or refund for all GST paid. GST can be *recovered* from collections of GST from the end customer; therefore, it is *not included* in the cost of inventory.

Businesses with taxable supplies production at a cost of $30,000 or more are required to register their business with CRA and submit a GST return. Ultimately, only the final consumer pays this tax. This is because businesses collect GST on sales, but since they receive full credit for GST paid on purchases they remit only the difference to the appropriate federal authority. Customers are not charged any GST on zero-rated goods and services and GST-exempt products. Zero-rated goods and services sold to customers enable the supplier to claim input tax credits to recover the GST paid on products purchased and used within the business, even though they did not charge customers GST. GST-exempt products sold to customers do not allow suppliers to claim input credits on goods or services acquired to supply the exempt product. Refer to Exhibit 5B.1 for a combined summary of zero-rated and exempt products for GST and HST.

---

15 A detailed discussion of the liabilities created by PST and GST is found in Chapter 10.
16 Effective since January 1, 2008.

EXHIBIT 5B.1

Summary of Zero-Rated and Exempt Products for GST/HST

GST/HST Zero-Rated Goods and Services	GST/HST Exempt Products
Basic groceries (milk, bread, vegetables)	Music lessons
Prescription drugs and dispensing fees	Educational services that lead to certificate or diploma
Fishery products	Childcare services
Agricultural products (grain, wool)	Most services provided by financial institutions
Exports to foreign countries	Medical devices
Issuing insurance policies	

For a full list of zero-rated goods and services and GST exempt supplies refer to: https://www.canada.ca/en/revenue-agency/services/forms-publications/publications/rc4022/general-information-gst-hst-registrants.html#H2_205

Harmonized Sales Tax

The **Harmonized Sales Tax (HST)** is a combined GST and PST rate applied to taxable supplies. At the time of writing, New Brunswick, Nova Scotia, Newfoundland and Labrador, Prince Edward Island, and Ontario apply HST in lieu of PST and GST. HST can be *recovered* from collections of HST from the end customer, therefore it is *not included* in the cost of inventory. In most cases, HST applies to the same property and services as GST.

PST and GST are accounted for under both perpetual and periodic inventory systems. To illustrate, assume JC Sales, a merchandiser located in Manitoba, purchases $600 of merchandise inventory on January 3 with terms n/10. These items are then sold for $900 on January 5 with terms of n/15. JC Sales records these transactions as follows:[17]

Jan.	3	Merchandise Inventory	600	
		GST Receivable*	30	
		Accounts Payable		630
		To record the purchase of merchandise on account; $600 × 5% = $30 GST.		
Jan.	5	Accounts Receivable	1,017	
		Sales		900
		PST Payable		72
		GST Payable		45
		To record the sale of merchandise on account; $900 × 8% = $72 PST; $900 × 5% = $45 GST; $900 + $72 + $45 = $1,017.		
	5	Cost of Goods Sold	600	
		Merchandise Inventory		600
		To record the cost of sales.		

*Some businesses will debit GST Payable instead of GST Receivable because they use only one account for GST. In such a case, when the account has a credit balance, cash must be paid to the Receiver General for Canada. When the account has a debit balance, a refund is applied for.

PST and GST are calculated as a percentage of the selling price. It should also be noted that while GST is a 5% federal tax, and thus is uniform in all of the provinces, PST is a provincial tax and differs in percentage from province to province. The detailed rates for each province are provided in Exhibit 5B.2.

---

[17] Assume that all amounts here and in related end-of-chapter materials are before PST and GST.

EXHIBIT 5B.2

Sales Tax Rates, Effective January 1, 2018

	PST Rate	GST Rate	HST Rate*
Regions with GST Only			
Alberta..	-0-	5%	—
Northwest Territories...	-0-	5%	—
Nunavut	-0-	5%	—
Yukon	-0-	5%	—
Regions with GST and PST			
British Columbia	7%	5%	—
Manitoba..	8%	5%	—
Quebec..	9.975%	5%	—
Saskatchewan...	5%	5%	—
Regions with HST			
New Brunswick...	—	—	15%
Newfoundland and Labrador...	—	—	15%
Nova Scotia	—	—	15%
Ontario	—	—	13%
Prince Edward Island	—	—	15%

*A Harmonized Sales Tax (HST) is applied in place of PST and GST. HST is the combination of the PST with the GST for a total sales tax. For example, for Ontario the PST rate of 8% is combined with the GST of 5%, resulting in an overall HST of 13%. For New Brunswick, the PST rate of 10% is combined with the GST of 5%, resulting in an overall HST of 15%.

To continue the example, assume the January 3 purchase is paid on January 13 and the sale of January 5 is collected on January 20. Assuming no other purchases and sales during the month, the January sales taxes are paid to the appropriate government bodies on February 28. The entries to record these transactions are:

Jan.	13	Accounts Payable..	630	
		Cash..		630
		To record payment of January 3 purchase.		
	20	Cash	1,017	
		Accounts Receivable.....................................		1,017
		To record collection of January 5 sale.		
Feb.	28	PST Payable..	72	
		Cash..		72
		To record payment of PST to provincial government authority.		
	28	GST Payable	45	
		Cash..		15
		GST Receivable..		30
		To record payment of GST to Receiver General for Canada.		

Examples demonstrating PST/GST for each region in Canada can be found online in Extend Your Knowledge 5-1, along with reinforcement exercises.

 CHECKPOINT

18. What are the differences among PST, GST, and HST?

  Do Quick Study questions: *QS 5-24, *QS 5-25, *QS 5-26, *QS 5-27

SUMMARY OF APPENDIX 5A AND APPENDIX 5B

LO7 **Record and compare merchandising transactions using both periodic and perpetual inventory systems.** Transactions involving the sale and purchase of merchandise are recorded and analyzed under both inventory systems. Adjusting and closing entries for both inventory systems are also illustrated and explained.

LO8 **Explain and record Provincial Sales Tax (PST), Goods and Services Tax (GST), and Harmonized Sales Tax.** PST is a tax applied on sales to final consumers that varies in percent among provinces. GST is a 5% tax collected on most sales but full credit is received for GST paid by a GST registrant (business). Harmonized Sales Tax (HST) is a combined GST and PST rate applied to taxable supplies.

 ## Guidance Answers to CHECKPOINT

13. The beginning Merchandise Inventory balance is included on the periodic unadjusted trial balance and not the perpetual along with Purchases, Purchase Discounts, Purchase Returns and Allowances, and Transportation-In.

14. Cost of Goods Sold is calculated under the periodic system using the account balances of Merchandise Inventory (beginning inventory balance), Purchases, Purchase Discounts, Purchase Returns and Allowances, Transportation-In, and subtracting the ending inventory amount determined through a physical count.

15. The Merchandise Inventory account on the periodic unadjusted trial balance represents the balance at the beginning of the period. The Merchandise Inventory account on the perpetual unadjusted trial balance has been adjusted regularly during the accounting period for all transactions affecting inventory, such as purchases, returns, discounts, transportation-in, and cost of sales, and therefore represents the balance at the end of the period.

16. Cost of Goods Sold.

17. Under a periodic inventory system, the cost of goods sold is determined at the end of an accounting period by adding the net cost of goods purchased to the beginning inventory and subtracting the ending inventory.

18. PST is Provincial Sales Tax and varies across Canada. GST is the Goods and Services Tax of 5% that is constant across Canada. HST is Harmonized Sales Tax that is a combination of the Provincial Sales Tax applicable in the jurisdictions and the 5% Goods and Services Tax.

GLOSSARY

Cash discount A reduction in the price of merchandise that is granted by a seller to a purchaser in exchange for the purchaser paying within a specified period of time called the *discount period*.

Catalogue price See *list price*.

Classified multiple-step income statement An income statement format that shows intermediate totals between sales and profit and detailed computations of net sales and cost of goods sold and is used primarily for internal reporting.

Cost of goods sold (COGS) The cost of merchandise sold to customers during a period; also commonly referred to as *cost of sales*.

Cost of sales See *cost of goods sold*.

Credit memo A notification that the sender has entered a credit in the recipient's account maintained by the sender.

Credit period The time period that can pass before a customer's payment is due.

Credit terms The description of the amounts and timing of payments that a buyer agrees to make in the future.

Debit memo A notification that the sender has entered a debit in the recipient's account maintained by the sender.

Discount period The time period in which a cash discount is available and a reduced payment can be made by the buyer.

EOM The abbreviation for *end of month*, used to describe credit terms for some transactions.

FOB The abbreviation for *free on board/freight on board*, the designated point at which ownership of goods passes to the buyer; *FOB shipping point* (or *factory*) means that the buyer pays the shipping costs and accepts ownership of the goods at the seller's place of business; *FOB destination* means that the seller pays the shipping costs and the ownership of the goods transfers to the buyer at the buyer's place of business.

Freight-in See *transportation-in*.

Freight-out See *transportation-out*.

Full disclosure principle The generally accepted accounting principle that requires financial statements to report all relevant information about the operations and financial position of the entity; disclosure of items not contained in the body of financial statements is often accomplished by providing notes to financial statements such as those for WestJet in Appendix III of the text.

Function of an expense A method of classifying or grouping expenses based on their purpose or what the expenses relate to, such as cost of goods sold, selling expenses, and general and administrative expenses; this method must also provide additional information to show the nature of expenses within each group.

General and administrative expenses Expenses that support the overall operations of a business and include the expenses of activities such as providing accounting services, human resource management, and financial management.

Goods and Services Tax (GST) A federal tax on almost all goods and services provided in Canada.

Gross margin The difference between net sales and the cost of goods sold; also called *gross profit*.

Gross profit The difference between net sales and the cost of goods sold; also called *gross margin*.

Gross profit margin ratio Gross profit from sales (net sales minus cost of goods sold) divided by net sales; also called *gross margin ratio*.

Harmonized Sales Tax (HST) A combined GST and PST rate applied to taxable goods and services.

Inventory See *merchandise inventory*.

List price The catalogue price of an item before any trade discount is deducted.

Markup percentage The average increase in selling price of a product over the unit cost.

Merchandise Products, also called *goods*, that a company acquires for the purpose of reselling them to customers.

Merchandise inventory Products that a company owns for the purpose of selling them to customers. Also called *inventory*.

Merchandiser Earns profit by buying and selling merchandise.

Nature of an expense A method of classifying an expense based on its basic characteristics or what it is. For example, when expenses are identified on the income statement as depreciation, rent, property tax, and salaries, the nature of the expense is being identified.

Net sales Calculated as gross sales less sales discounts and sales returns and allowances.

Notes to financial statements An integral part of financial statements that provides relevant information about the operations and financial position of the entity in addition to that contained in the financial statements; providing notes complies with the full disclosure principle; for an example, see the notes for WestJet in Appendix III of the text.

Periodic inventory system A method of accounting that records the cost of inventory purchased but does not track the quantity on hand or sold to customers; the records are updated at the end of each period to reflect the results of physical counts of the items on hand.

Perpetual inventory system A method of accounting that maintains continuous records of the cost of inventory on hand and the cost of goods sold.

Provincial Sales Tax (PST) A tax applied on sales to the final consumers of products and/or services.

Purchase discount A term used by a purchaser to describe a cash discount granted to the purchaser for paying within the discount period.

Purchase Returns and Allowances A contra expense account used when a periodic inventory system is in place in which purchase returns and/or purchase allowances are recorded.

Retailer An intermediary that buys products from manufacturers or wholesalers and sells them to consumers.

Sales discount A term used by a seller to describe a cash discount granted to customers for paying within the discount period.

Sales returns and allowances A contra revenue account in which sales returns and/or sales allowances are recorded.

Selling expenses The expenses of promoting sales by displaying and advertising the merchandise, making sales, and delivering goods to customers.

Shrinkage Inventory losses that occur as a result of theft or deterioration.

Single-step income statement An income statement format that includes cost of goods sold as an operating expense and shows only one subtotal for total expenses.

Trade discount A reduction below a list or catalogue price that may vary in amount for wholesalers, retailers, and final consumers.

Transportation-in The cost to the purchaser to transport merchandise purchased to the purchaser; transportation-in is part of Cost of Goods Sold.

Transportation-out The cost to the seller to transport merchandise sold to the customer; transportation-out is a selling expense.

Wholesaler A company that buys products from manufacturers or other wholesalers and sells them to retailers or other wholesalers.

KNOWLEDGE CHECK-UP

1. A merchandiser reports gross profit on its income statement to demonstrate which of the following:

   a. How much the company earns after deducting the direct cost of the goods purchased (cost of goods sold/cost of sales) from the net sales (gross sales less sales discounts, sales returns, and allowances) of the merchandise sold

   b. How much the company earns after deducting both the direct cost of goods purchased and operating expenses from net sales

   c. How much the company earns after deducting all expenses, including income taxes, from net sales

   d. All of the above.

2. The main difference between a periodic inventory system and a perpetual inventory system is:

   a. The length of time it takes to sell an item in inventory

   b. The frequency of receipt of goods by the receiving department

   c. The frequency with which the accounting records are updated to reflect the receipt of goods into inventory

   d. The length of time it takes to receive goods into inventory

3. Under a periodic inventory system, which of the following journal entries are booked at the time goods with a purchase price of $200 are sold to the customer for $500:

   a. Dr. Purchases $500
      Cr. Sales $500

   b. Dr. A/R $500
      Cr. Inventory $500

   c. Dr. A/R $500
      Cr. Sales $500

   d. Dr. A/R $500
      Cr. Sales $500

   e. Dr. Inventory $200
      Cr. Cost of Goods Sold $200

4. Trade discounts are provided by a manufacturer or a wholesaler for the following purpose:

   a. A specific percentage discount provided to encourage the customer to engage in early payment of invoices

   b. A specific percentage discount provided to customers based on the quantities/volume of goods purchased

   c. A specific percentage discount provided to customers based on a specific industry benchmark

   d. A credit discount offered based on returned merchandise

5. Purchase discounts are provided by a manufacturer or wholesaler for the following reason:

   a. Volume of goods purchased during the period

   b. Volume of goods returned during the period

   c. To encourage early payment of invoices

   d. To encourage payment of overdue invoices

6. FOB destination is a term used to indicate the following:

   a. Ownership of goods transfers to the buyer when goods reach the buyer's place of business.

   b. Ownership of goods transfers to the buyer when goods leave the shipping dock of the seller and goods are in transit.

   c. Freight charges are paid for by the buyer.

   d. The buyer bears the risk of damage or loss of goods in transit.

7. Sales discounts are provided for the following reason:

   a. To provide a volume discount for goods purchased

   b. To encourage early payment of invoices

   c. As a promotional discount provided by a sales rep

   d. All of the above.

8. The Sk8 Shop sold 10 skateboards to a local summer adventure camp for $135 each at a cost of $95. After five days, the summer camp decided to return two of the unused skateboards and limit the class size to eight students. The Sk8 Shop uses a perpetual inventory system. Which of the following journal entries is correct to record the customer's return:

   a. Dr. Sales Returns and Allowances $135
         Cr. Accounts Receivable $135

   b. Dr. Sales Returns and Allowances $270
         Cr. Accounts Receivable $270

   c. Dr. Merchandise Inventory $190
         Cr. Cost of Goods Sold $190

   d. Dr. Cash $270
         Cr. Sales Discounts $270

   e. Dr. Sales Returns and Allowances $190
         Cr. Accounts Receivable $190

9. The purpose of a classified multiple-step format income statement is:

   a. To provide a detailed income statement for external reporting purposes, including the cost of goods sold and gross profit as well as other revenues and expenses

   b. For external reporting purposes, organizing items by function and showing one total for all expenses

   c. To provide additional detail regarding the merchandise inventory balances as well as sales discounts provided

   d. To provide additional detail regarding the dollar value of sales discounts, sales returns and allowances, and selling expenses and general and administrative expenses for internal decision-making purposes

10. Gross profit margin is calculated as follows:

a. $\dfrac{\text{Net Sales} - \text{Cost of Goods Sold}}{\text{Net Sales}}$

b. $\dfrac{\text{Selling Price} - \text{Cost}}{\text{Cost}}$

c. $\dfrac{\text{Cost of Goods Sold}}{\text{Net Sales}}$

d. $\dfrac{\text{Profit}}{\text{Revenue}}$

CONCEPT REVIEW QUESTIONS

1. Refer to the income statement for WestJet in Appendix III. Is WestJet a merchandiser?

2. Refer to the income statement for **Spin Master** in Appendix III. Is a detailed calculation of the cost of goods sold presented?

3. In comparing the accounts of a merchandising company with those of a service company, what additional accounts would the merchandising company be likely to use, assuming it employs a perpetual inventory system?

4. What items appear in the financial statements of merchandising companies but not in the statements of service companies?

5. You are studying for your accounting exam with Mason and he says, "If a company has positive gross profit, then the company also has positive profit." Tell Mason whether you agree or disagree with him and explain why.

6. Distinguish between volume purchase discounts (trade discounts) and early payment discounts (cash discounts). Is the amount of a trade discount on purchased merchandise recorded in the accounts?

7. The manager exclaims, "Why do we have so many purchase returns?" The accountant asks, "Why does it matter if our suppliers offer unlimited returns?" Explain why the manager is concerned.

8. What is the difference between FOB shipping point and FOB destination? Draw a diagram to clearly illustrate your explanation. Explain the concept to another student using your diagram.

9. Spin Master needs to be skillful in negotiating purchase contracts with suppliers. What shipping terms should Spin Master negotiate to minimize its shipping costs?

10. Does the sender of a debit memo record a debit or a credit in the account of the recipient? Which does the recipient record?

11. What is the difference between a sales discount and a purchase discount?

12. Briefly explain why a company's manager would want the accounting system to record a customer's return of unsatisfactory goods in the Sales Returns and Allowances account instead of the Sales account. In addition, explain whether the information would be useful for external decision makers.

13. How does a company that uses a perpetual inventory system determine the amount of inventory shrinkage?

14. What is the difference between single-step and multiple-step income statement formats?

15. George believes that a 50% markup percentage is the same as a 50% target gross margin. Do you agree or disagree with George? Explain and provide a calculation to prove your point using a cost of $20 as an example.

QUICK STUDY

QS 5-1 Components of income for a merchandiser LO1

Referring to the format presented in Exhibit 5.2, calculate gross profit and the profit or loss for each of the following.

	A	B	C	D	E
Net sales	$14,000	$102,000	$68,000	$540,000	$398,000
Cost of goods sold	8,000	64,000	31,000	320,000	215,000
Operating expenses	9,000	31,000	22,000	261,000	106,000

QS 5-2 Contrasting periodic and perpetual systems LO2

For each description below, identify the inventory system as either periodic or perpetual.

a. Requires a physical count of inventory to determine the amount of inventory to report on the balance sheet.

b. Records the cost of goods sold each time a sales transaction occurs.

c. Provides more timely information to managers.

d. Was traditionally used by companies such as drug and department stores that sold large quantities of low-valued items.

e. Requires an adjusting entry to record inventory shrinkage.

QS 5-3 Perpetual and periodic inventory systems LO2

For each situation given, calculate cost of goods sold and identify whether the information provided reflects a perpetual or periodic inventory system.

a.

Merchandise Inventory			Cost of Goods Sold		
Beginning Inventory	150	?		?	?
Purchases	340				
Ending Inventory	60				

b.

Merchandise Inventory*			Purchases		
Beginning Inventory	150				?
				340	

*A physical inventory count at year-end showed a balance on hand of $60.

QS 5-4 Perpetual and periodic inventory systems LO2

For each situation given, calculate cost of goods sold and identify whether the information provided reflects a perpetual or periodic inventory system.

a. Merchandise Inventory shows a balance at January 1, 2020, of $170, the Purchases account has a balance of $700 at December 31, 2020, and a physical count of merchandise inventory on the same date reveals a balance of $120 on hand.

b. Merchandise Inventory shows a $200 balance at January 1, 2020, purchases during the period of $1,000, and a balance of $75 at December 31, 2020, after the adjustment for shrinkage.

QS 5-5 Purchase discounts—perpetual LO3

You are the accounts payable clerk at Liszt Music. The manager asks you to pay an invoice from the supplier Schumann Co. The date of purchase and the date of the invoice is October 15, 2020, for $5,000 of Taylor Swift and Beyoncé Knowles sheet music. The payment terms are 3/15, n/30.

a. What do the purchase terms mean?

b. Calculate the discount amount available.

c. If today is October 28, 2020, calculate the number of days from the date of purchase to the date of payment. Record the journal entry.

d. If today is November 1, 2020, calculate the number of days from the date of purchase to the date of payment. Record the journal entry.

QS 5-6 Merchandise purchase transactions—perpetual LO3

Journalize each of the following transactions assuming a perpetual inventory system.

May	1	Purchased $1,200 of merchandise inventory; terms 1/10, n/30.
	14	Paid for the May 1 purchase.
	15	Purchased $3,000 of merchandise inventory; terms 2/15, n/30.
	30	Paid for the May 15 purchase, less the applicable discount.

QS 5-7 Merchandise purchase: allowance—perpetual LO3

Journalize each of the following transactions assuming a perpetual inventory system.

Aug.	2	Purchased $14,000 of merchandise inventory; terms 1/5, n/15.
	4	Received a credit memo from the supplier confirming a $1,500 allowance regarding the August 2 purchase.
	17	Paid for the August 2 purchase, less the allowance.

QS 5-8 Merchandise purchase: trade discount, return—perpetual LO3

Prepare journal entries to record each of the following transactions of a merchandising company. Show any supporting calculations. Assume a perpetual inventory system.

Mar.	5	Purchased 500 units of product with a list price of $5 per unit. The purchaser was granted a trade discount of 20% and the terms of the sale were 2/10, n/60.
	7	Returned 50 defective units from the March 5 purchase and received full credit.
	15	Paid the amount due resulting from the March 5 purchase, less the return on March 7 and applicable discount.

QS 5-9 Sale of merchandise: trade discount—perpetual LO3

As a co-op student, you are working as an accounts receivable clerk at Asian Foods. The controller asks you to record a customer payment from Liu and Li Co. The sales invoice is dated October 1, 2020 for $3,000 of tea and tapioca pearls. The payment terms are 4/20, n/60.

a. Determine the beginning and end date of the discount period.

b. Calculate the discount amount available.

c. If today is October 20, record the journal entry.

d. If today is October 23, record the journal entry.

QS 5-10 Sale of merchandise transactions—perpetual LO3

Journalize each of the following transactions assuming a perpetual inventory system.

Sept.	1	Sold merchandise to JenAir for $6,000 (cost of sales $4,200); terms 2/10, n/30.
	14	Collected the amount owing regarding the September 1 sale to JenAir.
	15	Sold merchandise costing $1,500 to Dennis Leval for $1,800; terms 2/10, n/30.
	25	Collected the amount owing from the September 15 sale to Dennis Leval, less the applicable discount.

QS 5-11 Sale of merchandise: allowance—perpetual LO3

Journalize each of the following transactions assuming a perpetual inventory system.

Oct.	15	Sold merchandise to Leslie Garth for $900 (cost of sales $600); terms 1/5, n/20.
	16	Issued a $100 credit memo to Leslie Garth regarding an allowance on the October 15 sale.
	25	Collected the amount owing regarding the October 15 sale to Leslie Garth, less the allowance granted on October 16.

QS 5-12 Sale of merchandise: return—perpetual LO3

Prepare journal entries to record each of the following transactions of a merchandising company. Show any supporting calculations. Assume a perpetual inventory system.

Apr.	1	Sold merchandise for $2,000, granting the customer terms of 2/10, EOM. The cost of the merchandise was $1,400.
	4	The customer in the April 1 sale returned merchandise and received credit for $500. The merchandise, which had cost $350, was returned to inventory.
	11	Received payment for the amount due resulting from the April 1 sale, less the return and applicable discount, on April 4.

QS 5-13 Shrinkage LO4

Beamer Company's unadjusted ledger on July 31, the end of the fiscal year, includes the following accounts, which have normal balances (assume a perpetual inventory system):

Merchandise inventory	$ 34,800
Joy Beamer, capital	115,300
Joy Beamer, withdrawals	4,000
Sales	157,200
Sales discounts	1,700
Sales returns and allowances	3,500
Cost of goods sold	102,000
Depreciation expense	7,300
Salaries expense	29,500
Miscellaneous expenses	2,000

A physical count of the inventory discloses that the cost of the merchandise on hand is $32,900. Prepare the entry to record this information and calculate gross profit.

QS 5-14 Classified multi-step vs. single-step income statements LO5

Use the following adjusted trial balance information for JetCo's December 31, 2020, year-end to prepare (a) a classified multi-step income statement, and (b) a single-step income statement.

Account	Debit	Credit
Advertising expense	$ 6	
Assets	120	
Cost of goods sold	60	
Interest income		$ 5
Liabilities		90
Lisa Jet, capital		31
Lisa Jet, withdrawals	8	
Office salaries expense	10	
Office supplies expense	3	
Sales		100
Sales discounts	4	
Sales salaries expense	15	

QS 5-15 **Profitability** LO1, 3, 5, 6

Using a format similar to Exhibit 5.11, calculate net sales, gross profit from sales, and the gross profit ratio (round to two decimal places).

	a	b	c	d
Sales	$130,000	$512,000	$35,700	$245,700
Sales discounts	4,200	16,500	400	3,500
Sales returns and allowances	17,000	5,000	5,000	700
Cost of goods sold	76,600	326,700	21,300	125,900

QS 5-16 **Gross profit ratio** LO6

Willaby Company had net sales of $248,000 and cost of goods sold of $114,080. Calculate and interpret the gross profit ratio, assuming the gross profit ratio for the industry is an average of 53%.

QS 5-17 **Markups** LO6

Your parents own a grocery store and you need to determine the selling price of fruit. It costs $0.81/kg for non-organic bananas and $1.21/kg for organic bananas. You decide to sell the non-organic produce at a markup percentage of 55% and the organic produce at a markup percentage of 75%. Determine the selling price for non-organic and organic bananas. Round your answer to two decimal places.

QS 5-18 **Markups** LO6

Assume it costs a manufacturer $80 to produce a pair of sunglasses. The manufacturer sells the sunglasses to a fashion designer for $100. The fashion designer puts its brand name on the sunglasses and sells them to optical retail stores for $160. The optical retail stores then sell the sunglasses to the end customers at $320.

Required

1. What is the markup percentage between the following:
    a. Manufacturer and fashion designer?
    b. Fashion designer and optical retail store?
    c. Optical retail store and end customer?
2. What is the total markup from the manufacturer to the end customer?

QS 5-19 **Markups** LO6

You work at a clothing store. Determine the selling price of jeans with a target gross margin of 40% and tops with a markup percentage of 40%. Assume that the jeans and tops both have a cost of $30.

*QS 5-20 **Merchandise purchase transactions—periodic** LO7

Using the information in QS 5-6 through QS 5-8, prepare journal entries to record each of the transactions of the merchandising companies assuming a periodic inventory system.

*QS 5-21 **Sale of merchandise transactions—periodic** LO7

Using the information in QS 5-10 through QS 5-12, prepare journal entries to record each of the transactions of the merchandising companies assuming a periodic inventory system.

An asterisk (*) identifies assignment material based on Appendix 5A or Appendix 5B.

*QS 5-22 Cost of goods sold—periodic LO7

Using the following information, calculate cost of goods sold for the year ended December 31, 2020.

Merchandise inventory (January 1, 2020	$ 40,000
Kay Bondar, capital	102,000
Kay Bondar, withdrawals	65,000
Sales	450,000
Sales returns and allowances	27,000
Purchases	180,000
Purchase discounts	1,400
Transportation-in	14,000
Merchandise inventory (December 31, 2020	22,000
Salaries expense	120,000
Depreciation expense	31,000

*QS 5-23 Profitability—periodic LO5, 6, 7

Calculate net sales, cost of goods sold, gross profit, and the gross profit ratio (round to two decimal places) in each of the following situations.

	a	b	c	d
Sales	$130,000	$512,000	$35,700	$245,700
Sales discounts	4,200	16,500	400	3,500
Merchandise inventory, Jan. 1, 2020	8,000	21,000	1,500	4,300
Purchases	120,000	350,000	29,000	131,000
Purchase returns and allowances	4,000	14,000	750	3,100
Merchandise inventory, Dec. 1, 2020	7,500	22,000	900	4,100

*QS 5-24 Sales tax on purchases—perpetual LO3, 8

On March 1, Dolomite Sales purchased $5,000 of merchandise on account. Record the entry on March 1 including 5% GST. Assume a perpetual inventory system.

*QS 5-25 Sales tax on sales—perpetual LO3, 8

On March 17, Dolomite Sales sold merchandise on credit for $5,800 (cost of sales $5,000). Assuming 7% PST and 5% GST, record the entries on March 17. Assume a perpetual inventory system.

*QS 5-26 Sales tax on purchases—periodic LO7, 8

On March 1, Dolomite Sales purchased $5,000 of merchandise on account. Record the entry on March 1 including 5% GST. Assume a periodic inventory system.

*QS 5-27 Sales tax on sales—periodic LO7, 8

On March 17, Dolomite Sales sold merchandise on credit for $5,800 (cost of sales $5,000). Assuming 7% PST and 5% GST, record the entry on March 17. Assume a periodic inventory system.

An asterisk (*) identifies assignment material based on Appendix 5A or Appendix 5B.

EXERCISES

Exercise 5-1 Calculating income statement components LO1

Referring to Exhibit 5.2, calculate the missing amounts.

	a	b	c	d	e
Net sales..............................	$208,800	$165,000	$73,800	$?	$?
Cost of goods sold..............	?	?	41,600	303,000	205,600
Gross profit from sales.......	108,200	?	?	?	75,200
Operating expenses............	91,600	93,000	?	106,000	?
Profit (loss)...........................	?	(31,000)	(5,900)	57,000	(28,400)

Exercise 5-2 Recording journal entries for merchandise purchase transactions—perpetual LO3

Journalize each of the following transactions assuming a perpetual inventory system.

Feb.	1	Purchased $17,100 of merchandise inventory; terms 2/10, n/30.
	5	Purchased for cash $8,300 of merchandise inventory.
	6	Purchased $22,100 of merchandise inventory; terms 3/15, n/45.
	9	Purchased $1,950 of office supplies; terms n/15.
	10	Contacted a major supplier to place an order for $210,000 of merchandise in exchange for a 25% trade discount to be shipped on April 1 FOB destination.
	11	Paid for the merchandise purchased on February 1.
	24	Paid for the office supplies purchased on February 9.
Mar.	23	Paid for the February 6 purchase.

Exercise 5-3 Recording journal entries for merchandise purchase transactions—perpetual LO3

Jaleh Mehr is the owner of the retail store 151 Jeans. She purchases jeans from a number of manufacturers to bring great style and fit to her customers. Prepare journal entries for March 2020 to record the following transactions. Assume a perpetual inventory system.

Mar.	2	Purchased jeans from Paige Denim under the following terms: $4,200 invoice price, 2/15, n/60, FOB shipping point.
	3	Paid $350 for shipping charges on the purchase of March 2.
	4	Returned to Paige Denim unacceptable merchandise that had an invoice price of $400.
	17	Sent a cheque to Paige Denim for the March 2 purchase, net of the returned merchandise and applicable discount.
	18	Purchased jeans from J Brand under the following terms: $9,600 invoice price, 2/10, n/30, FOB destination.
	21	After brief negotiations, received from J Brand a $2,100 allowance on the purchase of March 18.
	28	Sent a cheque to J Brand paying for the March 18 purchase, net of the discount and the allowance.

Exercise 5-4 Recording journal entries for merchandise sales transactions—perpetual LO3

Journalize each of the following transactions assuming a perpetual inventory system. You are not required to identify the account number in your journal entries.

April	5	Sold merchandise to a customer for $6,400; terms 3/10, n/30 (cost of sales $3,680).
	7	Made a cash sale of $4,700 of merchandise to a customer today (cost of sales $2,660).
	8	Sold merchandise for $12,000; terms 3/10, n/30 (cost of sales $7,040).
	15	Collected the amount owing from the credit customer of April 5.
May	4	The customer of April 8 paid the balance owing.

The company's chart of accounts include the following:

101	Cash
106	Accounts Receivable
119	Merchandise inventory
201	Accounts Payable
401	Sales
414	Sales returns and allowances
415	Sales discounts
500	Cost of goods sold

Exercise 5-5 Recording journal entries for merchandise sales transactions—perpetual LO3

Journalize each of the following transactions assuming a perpetual inventory system.

Feb.	1	Sold merchandise with a cost of $1,500 for $2,100; terms 2/10, n/30, FOB destination.
	2	Paid $225 to ship the merchandise sold on February 1.
	3	The customer of February 1 returned half of the amount purchased because it was the incorrect product; it was returned to inventory.
	4	Sold merchandise to a customer for $3,800 (cost of sales $2,280); terms 2/10, n/30, FOB destination.
	11	Collected the amount owing from the customer of February 1.
	23	Sold merchandise to a customer for cash of $1,200 (cost of sales $720).
	28	The customer of February 4 paid the amount owing.

Exercise 5-6 Recording merchandise transactions: purchase and sale discounts—perpetual LO3

Chad Funk is a hair stylist who opened a business selling hair products. He imports products from around the world and sells to salons in Canada.

Oct.	1	Purchased $1,400 of hair spray from Orbit Pro; terms 3/10, n/30, FOB shipping point. The appropriate party paid the shipping cost of $200.
	5	Sold shampoo costing $420 to Barber & Co. for a price of $600 with terms of 2/10, n/30, FOB shipping point. The appropriate party paid the shipping cost of $80.
	7	Returned $500 of inventory to Orbit Pro due to an error in the October 1 order.
	10	Paid Orbit Pro for the purchase on October 1.
	14	Barber & Co. returned $100 of inventory from the sale on October 5. The inventory had a cost of $70.
	22	Received the payment from Barber & Co. on the October 5 sale.
	23	Purchased $2,000 of hair conditioner from Keratin Hair; terms 2/10, n/30, FOB shipping point. The appropriate party paid the shipping cost of $300.
	25	Sold hair gel to Styling Room for an invoice price of $1,000, terms 2/10, n/30, FOB destination. The hair gel had a cost of $700. The appropriate party paid the shipping cost of $150.
	26	Paid for the purchase on October 23.
	31	Received the payment from Styling Room on the October 25 sale.

Required Record the journal entries for the month of October.

Exercise 5-7 Analyzing and recording merchandise transactions—perpetual LO3

On May 11, 2020, Wilson Purchasing purchased $23,000 of merchandise from Happy Sales; terms 2/10, n/90, FOB Happy Sales. The cost of the goods to Happy was $18,000. Wilson paid $1,300 to Express Shipping Service for the delivery charges on the merchandise on May 11. On May 12, Wilson returned $3,600 of goods to Happy Sales, which restored them to inventory. The returned goods had cost Happy $2,800. On May 20, Wilson mailed a cheque to Happy for the amount owed on that date. Happy received and recorded the cheque on May 21.

Required

a. Present the journal entries that Wilson Purchasing should record for these transactions. Assume that Wilson uses a perpetual inventory system.

b. Present the journal entries that Happy Sales should record for these transactions. Assume that Happy uses a perpetual inventory system.

Analysis Component: Assume that the buyer, Wilson Purchasing, borrowed enough cash to pay the balance on the last day of the discount period at an annual interest rate of 4% and paid it back on the last day of the credit period. Calculate how much the buyer saved by following this strategy. *Use a 365-day year and round all calculations to the nearest whole cent.*

Exercise 5-8 Merchandising terms LO1, 2, 3

Insert the letter for each term in the blank space beside the definition that it most closely matches:

a. Early payment discount   **e.** FOB shipping point   **h.** Volume purchase discount

b. Credit period   **f.** Gross profit   **i.** Sales discount

c. Discount period   **g.** Merchandise inventory   **j.** Trade discount

d. FOB destination

_____ **1.** An agreement that ownership of goods is transferred at the buyer's place of business.

_____ **2.** The time period in which a cash discount is available.

_____ **3.** The difference between net sales and the cost of goods sold.

_____ **4.** A reduction in a receivable or payable that is granted if it is paid within the discount period.

_____ **5.** A purchaser's description of an early payment discount received from a supplier of goods.

_____ **6.** An agreement that ownership of goods is transferred at the seller's place of business.

_____ **7.** A reduction below a list or catalogue price that is negotiated in setting the selling price of goods.

_____ **8.** A seller's description of a cash discount granted to customers in return for early payment.

_____ **9.** The time period that can pass before a customer's payment is due.

_____ **10.** The goods that a company owns and expects to sell to its customers.

Exercise 5-9 Effects of merchandising activities on the accounts—perpetual LO3, 4

The following amounts summarize Transeer Company's merchandising activities during 2020. Set up T-accounts for Merchandise Inventory and Cost of Goods Sold (see Exhibit 5.13). Then record the activities directly in the accounts and calculate the account balances.

Cost of merchandise sold to customers in sales transactions	$180,000
Merchandise inventory balance, Dec. 31, 2019	35,000
Invoice cost of merchandise purchases	186,000
Shrinkage determined on Dec. 31, 2020	31,000
Cost of transportation-in	1,900
Cost of merchandise returned by customers and restored to inventory	2,200
Purchase discounts received	1,600
Purchase returns and allowances received	4,100

Analysis Component: You are the inventory manager and have reviewed these numbers. Comment on the shrinkage.

Exercise 5-10 Calculating expenses and cost of goods sold—perpetual LO1, 3, 5, 6

Westlawn Company discloses the following for the year ended May 31, 2020:

Sales..	$486,000
Sales discounts...	5,000
Sales returns...	12,100
Gross profit from sales...	115,000
Loss...	23,500

Required Calculate (a) net sales, (b) total operating expenses, (c) cost of goods sold, and (d) gross profit ratio (round to two decimal places).

Analysis Component: Refer to your answer in part (d). Westlawn experienced a gross profit ratio for the year ended May 31, 2019, of 22%. Is the change in the ratio favourable or unfavourable?

Exercise 5-11 Calculating income statement components LO1, 5

Referring to Exhibit 5.15, calculate the missing amounts (round to two decimal places).

	Company A		Company B	
	2020	2019	2020	2019
Sales..	$263,000	$187,000	$?	$48,500
Sales discounts...............................	2,630	?	1,200	570
Sales returns and allowances........	?	16,700	6,200	?
Net sales..	?	168,950	?	45,500
Cost of goods sold.........................	157,100	?	57,700	?
Gross profit from sales..................	51,700	?	49,100	22,100
Selling expenses.............................	18,620	19,700	25,700	?
Administrative expenses................	26,300	?	30,400	9,700
Total operating expenses...............	?	47,400	?	?
Profit (loss)......................................	?	15,100	?	2,700
Gross profit ratio............................	?	?	?	?

Analysis Component: Company A and Company B are in similar industries. Comment on their comparative performances.

Exercise 5-12 Preparing an income statement—perpetual LO5

CHECK FIGURE: a. Profit = $7,815

The following is account information listed in alphabetical order for Compu-Soft for the month ended November 30, 2020.

Required Prepare a multiple-step income statement for the month ended November 30, 2020.

		Adjusted Trial Balance	
	Account	**Debit**	**Credit**
201	Accounts payable...		$ 750
106	Accounts receivable...	$ 1,200	
166	Accumulated depreciation, store equipment....................		4,600
101	Cash...	2,100	
502	Cost of goods sold..	14,800	
612	Depreciation expense, store equipment..........................	120	
301	Peter Delta, capital...		1,935
302	Peter Delta, withdrawals...	4,600	
406	Rent revenue..		2,500
413	Sales..		29,400
415	Sales discounts..	45	
414	Sales returns and allowances..	720	
165	Store equipment..	7,200	
690	Utilities expense..	2,100	
623	Wages expense..	6,300	
	Totals	$39,185	$39,185

Analysis Component: Assume that for the month ended October 31, 2020, net sales were $32,000, cost of goods sold was $19,200, and income from operations was $8,000. Calculate and compare the company's gross profit ratios for October and November.

Exercise 5-13 Adjusting entries and income statement—perpetual LO5

CHECK FIGURES: a. Balance sheet columns = $64,200; b. Profit = $8,500

The following list of accounts is taken from the December 31, 2020, unadjusted trial balance of Perdu Sales, a business that is owned by Eldon Perdu.

	Debit	**Credit**
Cash...	$ 8,000	
Merchandise inventory..	9,800	
Prepaid selling expense..	8,000	
Store equipment...	40,000	
Accumulated depreciation, store equipment.............		$ 9,800
Accounts payable...		14,840
Salaries payable		-0-
Eldon Perdu, capital...		25,360
Eldon Perdu, withdrawals...	3,600	
Sales		858,000
Sales returns and allowances..	33,000	
Sales discounts...	8,000	
Cost of goods sold..	431,000	
Sales salaries expense..	94,000	
Utilities expense, store	12,600	
Other selling expenses..	70,000	
Other administrative expenses..	190,000	

Additional information: Accrued sales salaries amount to $3,200. Prepaid selling expenses of $5,200 have expired. Depreciation for the period is $2,500.

Required Assuming a perpetual inventory system, complete the following:

a. Journalize the adjusting journal entries.

b. Prepare a classified multiple-step income statement for the year ended December 31, 2020.

Analysis Component: Assume that for the year ended December 31, 2019, net sales were $600,000; operating expenses were $344,000; and there was a loss of $14,000. Calculate and compare the company's gross profit ratios for 2019 and 2020.

Exercise 5-14 Markups—perpetual LO6

Kim works at a sports store and needs to determine the selling price for running shoes. The running shoes have a cost of $40. The manager asked Kim to price the running shoes with a 60% target gross margin. Kim has priced the running shoes with a 60% markup percentage.

Required

1. What selling price does the manager want?
2. What selling price has Kim calculated?
3. If there are 50 running shoes, how much will the store lose in sales if the price is not corrected?

*Exercise 5-15 Calculating cost of goods sold LO2, 7

Refer to Exhibit 5A.2 and determine each of the missing numbers in the following situations:

	a	b	c
Purchases.	$92,000	$158,000	$120,000
Purchase discounts.	4,000	?	2,600
Purchase returns and allowances.	3,000	6,000	4,400
Transportation-in	?	14,000	16,000
Beginning inventory	5,000	?	34,000
Cost of goods purchased.	89,400	156,000	?
Ending inventory.	4,400	30,000	?
Cost of goods sold.	?	166,400	136,520

*Exercise 5-16 Calculating expenses and income LO2, 7

Referring to Exhibit 5A.2, fill in the following blanks. Identify any losses by putting the amount in brackets.

	Company A		Company B	
	2020	2019	2020	2019
Sales	$110,000	$178,000	$90,000	$?
Cost of goods sold:				
Merchandise inventory (beginning)	8,700	27,300	8,875	6,000
Net cost of merchandise purchases	82,000	?	?	26,100
Merchandise inventory (ending)	?	(22,000)	(8,920)	(9,875)
Cost of goods sold	82,300	106,000	?	?
Gross profit from sales.	?	?	39,545	19,775
Operating expenses.	26,000	54,000	27,000	?
Profit (loss).	1,700	18,000	?	6,275
Gross profit ratio.	?	?	?	?

An asterisk (*) identifies assignment material based on Appendix 5A or Appendix 5B.

Analysis Component: Company A and Company B are in similar industries. Comment on their gross profit ratios.

*Exercise 5-17 Components of cost of goods sold LO1, 2, 7

Referring to Exhibit 5A.2, use the data provided to determine each of the missing numbers in the following situations:

	a	b	c
Invoice cost of merchandise purchases............................	$44,000	$21,000	$16,250
Purchase discounts...	2,000	?	325
Purchase returns and allowances......................................	1,500	750	550
Cost of transportation-in...	?	1,750	2,000
Merchandise inventory (beginning of period).................	4,500	?	3,500
Net cost of merchandise purchases	44,700	19,750	?
Merchandise inventory (end of period)............................	2,200	3,750	?
Cost of goods sold...	?	20,800	17,065

*Exercise 5-18 Journal entries to contrast the periodic and perpetual systems—perpetual and periodic LO2, 7

Journalize the following merchandising transactions for Scout Systems assuming (a) a periodic system, and (b) a perpetual system.

Nov.	1	Scout Systems purchases merchandise for $4,400 on credit with terms of 2/10, n/30.
	5	Scout Systems pays for the previous purchase.
	7	Scout Systems receives payment for returned defective merchandise of $500 that was purchased on November 1.
	10	Scout Systems pays $400 to transport merchandise to its store.
	13	Scout Systems sells merchandise for $6,500 on account. The cost of the merchandise was $4,200.
	16	A customer returns merchandise from the November 13 transaction. The returned item sold for $1,200 and cost $780. The item will be returned to inventory.

*Exercise 5-19 Recording journal entries for merchandise purchase transactions—periodic LO7

Using the information in Exercise 5-2, prepare journal entries to record the transactions assuming a periodic inventory system.

*Exercise 5-20 Recording journal entries for merchandise purchase transactions—periodic LO7

Using the information in Exercise 5-3, prepare journal entries to record the March transactions assuming a periodic inventory system.

*Exercise 5-21 Recording journal entries for merchandise sales transactions—periodic LO7

Using the information in Exercise 5-4, prepare journal entries to record the transactions assuming a periodic inventory system. You are not required to identify the account number in your journal entries.

The company's chart of accounts is below:

101	Cash	415	Sales discounts
106	Accounts Receivable	501	Purchases
119	Merchandise inventory	502	Purchase returns and allowances
201	Accounts Payable	503	Purchase discounts
401	Sales	504	Transportation-in
414	Sales returns and allowances	663	Delivery expense

An asterisk (*) identifies assignment material based on Appendix 5A or Appendix 5B.

*Exercise 5-22 Recording journal entries for merchandise sales transactions—periodic LO7

Using the information in Exercise 5-5, prepare journal entries to record the transactions assuming a periodic inventory system.

*Exercise 5-23 Analyzing and recording merchandise transactions and discounts—periodic LO7

Using the information in Exercise 5-6, and assuming instead a periodic inventory system, record the journal entries.

*Exercise 5-24 Analyzing and recording merchandise transactions and returns—periodic LO7

Using the information in Exercise 5-7:

a. Present the journal entries that Wilson Purchasing should record for these transactions assuming a periodic inventory system.

b. Present the journal entries that Happy Sales should record for these transactions assuming a periodic inventory system.

*Exercise 5-25 Calculating expenses and cost of goods sold—periodic LO7

CHECK FIGURE: c. $16,100

Friar Company discloses the following information for the year ended October 31, 2020:

Sales	$363,000
Sales discounts	6,300
Sales returns	14,800
Merchandise inventory (beginning of period)	31,800
Invoice cost of merchandise purchases	182,000
Purchase discounts	4,400
Purchase returns and allowances	6,800
Cost of transportation-in	11,800
Gross profit from sales	143,600
Profit	65,800

Required Calculate (a) total operating expenses, (b) cost of goods sold, (c) merchandise inventory (end of period), and (d) gross profit ratio (round to two decimal places).

Analysis Component: Assuming that the gross profit ratio for the year ended October 31, 2019, was 47%, compare Friar Company's performance from 2019 to 2020.

*Exercise 5-26 Preparing an income statement—periodic LO7

CHECK FIGURE: c. Loss = $1,183

The following is John's Electronics' adjusted account information listed in alphabetical order for the month ended April 30, 2020. A physical count on April 30, 2020, revealed a merchandise inventory balance actually on hand of $2,550.

An asterisk (*) identifies assignment material based on Appendix 5A or Appendix 5B.

	Account	Debit	Credit
201	Accounts payable		$ 2,208
154	Accumulated depreciation, trucks		16,500
101	Cash	$ 2,050	
611	Depreciation expense, delivery trucks	730	
633	Interest expense	130	
301	John Yu, capital		27,225
302	John Yu, withdrawals	9,650	
119	Merchandise inventory	6,600	
507	Purchase discounts		37
506	Purchase returns and allowances		110
505	Purchases	17,040	
413	Sales		38,200
414	Sales returns and allowances	1,830	
688	Telephone expense, office	150	
689	Telephone expense, store	430	
508	Transportation-in	470	
153	Trucks	30,500	
623	Wages expense, office	5,800	
624	Wages expense, selling	8,900	
	Totals	$84,280	$84,280

Required

a. Calculate net sales.

b. Calculate cost of goods sold.

c. Prepare a classified multiple-step income statement for the month ended April 30, 2020.

*Exercise 5-27 Sales taxes—perpetual LO3, 8

Journalize each of the following transactions assuming a perpetual inventory system and PST at 8% along with 5% GST.

June	1	Purchased $2,000 of merchandise; terms 1/10, n/30.
	5	Sold $1,000 of merchandise for $1,400; terms n/15.

*Exercise 5-28 Sales taxes—periodic LO7, 8

Journalize each of the transactions in Exercise 5-27 assuming a periodic inventory system and PST at 8% along with 5% GST.

PROBLEMS

Problem 5-1A Journal entries for merchandising activities—perpetual LO3

CHECK FIGURE: 2c. $5,960

Part 1

Prepare general journal entries to record the following perpetual system merchandising transactions of Belton Company. *Use a separate account for each receivable and payable; for example, record the sale on June 1 in Accounts Receivable—Avery & Wiest.*

An asterisk (*) identifies assignment material based on Appendix 5A or Appendix 5B.

June	1	Sold merchandise to Avery & Wiest for $9,500; terms 2/5, n/15, FOB destination (cost of sales $6,650).
	2	Purchased $4,900 of merchandise from Angolac Suppliers; terms 1/10, n/20, FOB shipping point.
	4	Purchased merchandise inventory from Bastille Sales for $11,400; terms 1/15, n/45, FOB Bastille Sales.
	5	Sold merchandise to Gelgar for $11,000; terms 2/5, n/15, FOB destination (cost of sales $7,700).
	6	Collected the amount owing from Avery & Wiest regarding the June 1 sale.
	12	Paid Angolac Suppliers for the June 2 purchase.
	20	Collected the amount owing from Gelgar regarding the June 5 sale.
	30	Paid Bastille Sales for the June 4 purchase.

Part 2

Based on the information provided above, calculate (a) net sales, (b) cost of goods sold, and (c) gross profit for the month ended June 30, 2020.

Problem 5-2A Journal entries for merchandising activities—perpetual LO3

Prepare general journal entries to record the following perpetual system merchandising transactions of Belton Company. *Use a separate account for each receivable and payable; for example, record the purchase July 1 in Accounts Payable—Jones Company.* Do the analysis component.

July	1	Purchased merchandise from Jones Company for $14,800 under credit terms of 1/15, n/30, FOB factory.
	2	Sold merchandise to Terra Co. for $2,600 under credit terms of 2/10, n/60, FOB shipping point. The merchandise had cost $1,950.
	3	Paid $450 for freight charges on the purchase of July 1.
	8	Sold merchandise that cost $3,825 for $5,100 cash.
	9	Purchased merchandise from Keene Co. for $9,100 under credit terms of 2/15, n/60, FOB destination.
	12	Received a $1,500 credit memo acknowledging the return of merchandise purchased on July 9.
	12	Received the balance due from Terra Co. for the credit sale dated July 2.
	13	Purchased office supplies from EastCo on credit, $960, n/30.
	16	Paid the balance due to Jones Company.
	19	Sold merchandise that cost $2,850 to Urban Co. for $3,800 under credit terms of 2/15, n/60, FOB shipping point.
	21	Issued a $300 credit memo to Urban Co. for an allowance on goods sold on July 19.
	22	Received a debit memo from Urban Co. for an error that overstated the total invoice by $200.
	29	Paid Keene Co. the balance due.
	30	Received the balance due from Urban Co. for the credit sale dated July 19.
	31	Sold merchandise that cost $7,500 to Terra Co. for $10,000 under credit terms of 2/10, n/60, FOB shipping point.

Analysis Component: As the senior purchaser for Belton Company, you are concerned that the purchase discounts you have negotiated are not being taken advantage of by the accounts payable department. Calculate the total dollar value impact to Belton Company of paying the July 9 purchase from Keene Co. after the discount period. Consider both the lost early payment discount and the cost of capital for the period after the discount period elapsed to the date Belton Company made the payment (assume a 6% interest rate; round calculations to four decimal places). Draft an email to the accounts payable department explaining the overall dollar value impact of paying the invoice after the discount period and how Belton Company can better take advantage of purchase discounts going forward.

Problem 5-3A Journal entries for merchandising activities—perpetual LO3

The Jewel Box purchases jewellery from around the world and sells to local retailers in Canada. Prepare general journal entries to record the following perpetual system merchandising transactions of The Jewel Box. *Use a separate account for each receivable and payable; for example, record the purchase on August 1 in Accounts Payable—Luu Company.*

Aug.	1	Purchased necklaces from Luu Company for $4,000 under credit terms of 1/10, n/30, FOB destination.
	4	At Luu Company's request, paid $350 for freight charges on the August 1 purchase, reducing the amount owed to Luu.
	5	Sold rings to Green Ruby for $3,800 under credit terms of 2/10, n/60, FOB destination. The merchandise had cost $2,470.
	8	Purchased bracelets from Jane Co. for $5,200 under credit terms of 1/10, n/45, FOB shipping point.
	9	Paid $325 shipping charges related to the August 5 sale to Green Ruby.
	10	Green Ruby returned the rings purchased from the August 5 sale that had cost $440 and been sold for $800. The merchandise was restored to inventory.
	12	After negotiations with Jane Co. concerning problems with the merchandise purchased on August 8, received a credit memo from Jane granting a price reduction of $400.
	15	Received balance due from Green Ruby for the August 5 sale.
	17	Purchased office equipment from WestCo on credit, $6,000, n/45.
	18	Paid the amount due Jane Co. for the August 8 purchase.
	19	Sold earrings to Chic Jewellery for $1,800 under credit terms of 1/10, n/30, FOB shipping point. The merchandise had cost $990.
	22	Chic Jewellery requested a price reduction on the August 19 sale because the merchandise did not meet specifications. Sent Chic Jewellery a credit memo for $300 to resolve the issue.
	29	Received Chic Jewellery's payment of the amount due from the August 19 purchase.
	30	Paid Luu Company the amount due from the August 1 purchase.

Problem 5-4A Adjusting entries and multi-step income statement—perpetual LO5

CHECK FIGURE: 2. Profit = $4,855

Information from the unadjusted trial balance of Electric Bike on December 31, 2020, the end of the annual accounting period, is as follows:

	Debit	Credit
Cash..	$ 8,200	
Accounts receivable..	22,765	
Merchandise inventory..	34,700	
Store supplies	2,465	
Office supplies...	785	
Prepaid insurance	3,355	
Equipment..	75,590	
Accumulated depreciation, equipment....................................		$ 13,755
Accounts payable...		8,100
Salaries payable		-0-
Braeden Li, capital		170,715
Braeden Li, withdrawals	62,500	
Interest income..		320
Sales..		529,500
Sales returns and allowances...	5,170	
Cost of goods sold...	381,260	
Salaries expense..	96,400	
Rent expense	29,200	
Supplies expense...	-0-	
Depreciation expense, equipment...	-0-	
Insurance expense	-0-	
Totals...	$722,390	$722,390

Required

1. Record adjusting entries for the following information.

   a. The records show that the equipment was estimated to have a total estimated useful life of 10 years with a resale value at the end of its life of $14,590.

   b. The balance in the Prepaid Insurance account was reviewed and it was determined that $260 was unused at December 31, 2020.

   c. A review of the store supplies on December 31, 2020, revealed a balance on hand of $2,030; a similar examination of the office supplies showed that $645 had been used.

   d. Accrued salaries payable, $1,850.

   e. A count of the merchandise inventory revealed a balance on hand December 31, 2020, of $33,890.

2. Using adjusted trial balance numbers, prepare a multiple-step income statement showing the expenses in detail.

Analysis Component: Explain why Interest income is shown under Other revenues and expenses on the multiple-step income statement.

Problem 5-5A Income statement calculations and formats—perpetual LO5

CHECK FIGURE: 1. Income from operations = $55,000

The following amounts appeared on Davison Company's adjusted trial balance as of October 31, 2020, the end of its fiscal year:

	Debit	Credit
Merchandise inventory	$ 16,000	
Other assets	256,800	
Liabilities		$ 78,400
Brenda Davison, capital		203,280
Brenda Davison, withdrawals	65,000	
Interest income		1,120
Sales		424,000
Sales discounts	6,500	
Sales returns and allowances	28,000	
Cost of goods sold	169,300	
Sales salaries expense	52,000	
Rent expense, selling space	19,000	
Store supplies expense	5,000	
Advertising expense	29,400	
Office salaries expense	53,000	
Rent expense, office space	5,200	
Office supplies expense	1,600	
Totals	$706,800	$706,800

Required

1. Prepare a classified multiple-step income statement for internal use (see Exhibit 5.13) that lists the company's net sales, cost of goods sold, and gross profit, as well as the components and amounts of selling expenses and general and administrative expenses.

2. Present a condensed single-step income statement (see Exhibit 5.15) that lists these costs: cost of goods sold, selling expenses, and general and administrative expenses.

Problem 5-6A Markups LO5

Leah Wells, a yoga instructor, started a company that sells athletic yoga clothing. You are Leah's marketing manager. Round your answers to two decimal places.

a. After assessing the competitors, you determine that Leah needs to price her products with a markup percentage of 60%. The cost of her tank tops is $20 and her pullovers is $30. Determine the selling price for each of Leah's clothing items.

b. Leah is ready to launch her yoga pants. You have determined that she should set her price 30% below her competitor's price of $100. Leah's cost to produce yoga pants is $40 per unit. Determine the markup percentage on Leah's yoga pants.

c. Calculate the gross profit margin for tank tops, pullovers, and yoga pants.

d. After a year, you determine that Leah should set a standard target margin percentage of 45% on all products. Determine the new prices for tank tops, pullovers, and yoga pants.

Problem 5-7A Income statements—perpetual LO5

CHECK FIGURE: 1. Income from operations = $13,590

The following amounts appeared on Plymouth Electronics' adjusted trial balance as of December 31, 2020.

	Debit	Credit
Merchandise inventory	$ 19,500	
Other assets	487,785	
Liabilities		$ 312,370
Celine Plymouth, capital		247,605
Celine Plymouth, withdrawals	67,000	
Sales		942,000
Sales discounts	14,580	
Sales returns and allowances	5,715	
Interest income		720
Cost of goods sold	719,000	
Sales salaries expense	79,200	
Office salaries expense	56,500	
Rent expense, selling space	33,000	
Rent expense, office space	3,000	
Store supplies expense	1,620	
Office supplies expense	735	
Depreciation expense, store equipment	8,910	
Depreciation expense, office equipment	2,760	
Insurance expense	3,390	
Totals	$1,502,695	$1,502,695

Required

1. Prepare a 2020 classified multiple-step income statement for Plymouth Electronics, like Exhibit 5.13.

2. Prepare a single-step income statement, like Exhibit 5.15.

Analysis Component: The gross profit ratio for Plymouth Electronics' year ended December 31, 2019, was 32%. Calculate this ratio for the year ended December 31, 2020, and compare it to the prior year, commenting on whether the change was favourable or unfavourable.

Problem 5-8A Income statements—perpetual LO5

CHECK FIGURE: 1. Operating expenses = $141,800; Profit = $73,200

The following adjusted trial balance for Bell Servicing was prepared at the end of the fiscal year, December 31, 2020:

		Debit	Credit
101	Cash	$ 8,000	
119	Merchandise inventory	16,200	
125	Supplies	10,000	
128	Prepaid insurance	4,000	
165	Store equipment	51,000	
166	Accumulated depreciation, store equipment		$ 46,800
167	Office equipment	69,000	
168	Accumulated depreciation, office equipment		34,200
201	Accounts payable		16,000
301	Jonah Bell, capital		29,000
302	Jonah Bell, withdrawals	41,000	
413	Sales		291,800
415	Sales discounts	2,000	
505	Cost of goods sold	74,800	
612	Depreciation expense, store equipment	5,200	
613	Depreciation expense, office equipment	3,800	
622	Sales salaries expense	46,000	
623	Office salaries expense	32,000	
637	Insurance expense, store	2,000	
638	Insurance expense, office	1,600	
640	Rent expense, office space	13,000	
641	Rent expense, selling space	17,000	
651	Office supplies expense	1,200	
652	Store supplies expense	2,400	
655	Advertising expense	17,600	
	Totals	$417,800	$417,800

Required

1. Prepare a classified multiple-step income statement that would be used by the business's owner (like Exhibit 5.13).

2. Prepare a multiple-step income statement that would be used by external users (like Exhibit 5.14).

3. Prepare a single-step income statement that would be provided to decision makers outside the company (like Exhibit 5.15).

Analysis Component: If you were a decision maker external to Bell Servicing, which income statement format would you prefer and why, if you had a choice? Which income statement format(s) could you expect as an external user? Why?

*Problem 5-9A Journal entries for merchandising activities—periodic LO7

Using the information provided in Part 1 of Problem 5-1A, journalize each of the transactions assuming a periodic inventory system.

An asterisk (*) identifies assignment material based on Appendix 5A or Appendix 5B.

*Problem 5-10A Journal entries for merchandising transactions—periodic LO7

Prepare general journal entries to record the following periodic system merchandising transactions for Safety Merchandising. *Use a separate account for each receivable and payable:*

Oct.	1	Purchased merchandise from Zeon Company on credit, terms 2/10, n/30, $15,800.
	2	Sold merchandise for cash, $2,100.
	7	Purchased merchandise on credit from Billings Co., terms 2/10, n/30, $11,600, FOB the seller's factory.
	7	Paid $450 cash for freight charges on the merchandise shipment of the previous transaction.
	8	Purchased delivery equipment from Finlay Supplies on credit, $24,000.
	12	Sold merchandise on credit to Comry Holdings, terms 2/15, 1/30, n/60, $5,800.
	13	Received a $1,500 credit memo for merchandise purchased on October 7 and returned for credit.
	13	Purchased office supplies on credit from Staples, $620, n/30.
	15	Sold merchandise on credit to Tom Willis, terms 2/10, 1/30, n/60, $4,650.
	15	Paid for the merchandise purchased on October 7.
	16	Received a credit memo for unsatisfactory office supplies purchased on October 13 and returned, $120.
	19	Issued a $420 credit memo to the customer who purchased merchandise on October 15 and returned a portion for credit.
	25	Received payment for the merchandise sold on October 15.
	29	The customer of October 12 paid for the purchase of that date.
	31	Paid for the merchandise purchased on October 1.

*Problem 5-11A Income statement calculations and formats—periodic LO7

CHECK FIGURES: 3. $34,580; 4. Loss from operations = $17,215; Loss = $17,030

The following amounts appeared on the Mendelstein Company's adjusted trial balance as of October 31, 2020, the end of its fiscal year:

	Debit	Credit
Merchandise inventory	$ 1,750	
Other assets	47,000	
Liabilities		$ 43,340
Joe Mendelstein, capital		37,690
Joe Mendelstein, withdrawals	3,700	
Interest income		185
Sales		103,400
Sales returns and allowances	8,200	
Sales discounts	1,195	
Purchases	44,200	
Purchase returns and allowances		2,500
Purchase discounts		970
Transportation-in	5,400	
Sales salaries expense	18,500	
Rent expense, selling space	9,900	
Store supplies expense	3,900	
Advertising expense	9,700	
Office salaries expense	22,700	
Rent expense, office space	8,300	
Office supplies expense	3,640	
Totals	$188,085	$188,085

A physical count shows that the cost of the ending inventory is $13,300.

An asterisk (*) identifies assignment material based on Appendix 5A or Appendix 5B.

Required

1. Calculate the company's net sales for the year.

2. Calculate the company's cost of goods purchased for the year.

3. Calculate the company's cost of goods sold for the year.

4. Present a multiple-step income statement that lists the company's net sales, cost of goods sold, and gross profit from sales.

5. Present a condensed single-step income statement that lists these expenses: cost of goods sold, selling expenses, and general and administrative expenses.

*Problem 5-12A Classified multiple-step income statement—periodic LO5, 6 eXcel

CHECK FIGURE: 1. Profit = $60,515

Information from the December 31, 2020, year-end unadjusted trial balance of Woodstock Store is as follows:

	Debit	Credit
Cash...	$ 3,500	
Merchandise inventory...	31,400	
Store supplies	1,715	
Office supplies	645	
Prepaid insurance...	3,960	
Store equipment..	57,615	
Accumulated depreciation, store equipment...................		$ 6,750
Office equipment..	13,100	
Accumulated depreciation, office equipment...................		6,550
Accounts payable...		4,000
Zen Woodstock, capital..		52,000
Zen Woodstock, withdrawals..	31,500	
Rental revenue...		14,600
Sales...		501,520
Sales returns and allowances...	2,915	
Sales discounts..	5,190	
Purchases..	331,315	
Purchase returns and allowances..		2,140
Purchase discounts...		4,725
Transportation-in	3,690	
Sales salaries expense	34,710	
Rent expense, selling space..	24,000	
Advertising expense..	6,400	
Store supplies expense..	-0-	
Depreciation expense, store equipment	-0-	
Office salaries expense..	27,630	
Rent expense, office space	13,000	
Office supplies expense...	-0-	
Insurance expense	-0-	
Depreciation expense, office equipment	-0-	
Totals..	$592,285	$592,285

An asterisk (*) identifies assignment material based on Appendix 5A or Appendix 5B.

Additional information:

a. The balance on January 1, 2020, in the Store Supplies account was $480. During the year, $1,235 of store supplies were purchased and debited to the Store Supplies account. A physical count on December 31, 2020, shows an ending balance of $180.

b. The balance on January 1, 2020, in the Office Supplies account was $50. Office supplies of $595 were purchased in 2020 and added to the Office Supplies account. An examination of the office supplies at year-end revealed that $590 had been used.

c. The balance in the Prepaid Insurance account represents a policy purchased on September 1, 2020; it was valid for 12 months from that date.

d. The store equipment was originally estimated to have a useful life of 12 years and a residual value of $3,615.

e. When the office equipment was purchased, it was estimated that it would last four years and have no residual value.

f. Ending merchandise inventory, $29,000.

Required Analyze and determine the impact of the adjustments from (a) to (f) on the unadjusted trial balance numbers. Prepare a classified multiple-step income statement like Exhibit 5A.2 using your adjusted trial balance numbers.

*Problem 5-13A Sales taxes—perpetual LO3, 7

Journalize each of the following transactions assuming a perpetual inventory system and PST at 8% along with 5% GST. *Note: Any available cash discount is taken only on the sale price before taxes.*

Aug.	1	Purchased $2,000 of merchandise for cash.
	2	Purchased $6,800 of merchandise; terms 2/10, n/30.
	5	Sold merchandise costing $3,600 for $5,200; terms 1/10, n/30.
	12	Paid for the merchandise purchased on August 2.
	15	Collected the amount owing from the customer of August 5.
	17	Purchased $6,000 of merchandise; terms n/15.
	19	Recorded $7,000 of cash sales (cost of sales $5,800).

*Problem 5-14A Sales taxes—periodic LO7, 8

Journalize each of the transactions in Problem 5-13A assuming a periodic inventory system and PST at 7% along with 5% GST.

ALTERNATE PROBLEMS

Problem 5-1B Journal entries for merchandising activities—perpetual LO3

CHECK FIGURE: 2c. = $5,911

Part 1

Prepare general journal entries to record the following perpetual system merchandising transactions of Laser Supply Company. *Use a separate account for each receivable and payable; for example, record the sale on March 2 in Accounts Receivable—Tessier & Welsh.*

An asterisk (*) identifies assignment material based on Appendix 5A or Appendix 5B.

Mar.	1	Purchased $48,000 of merchandise from Johnson Suppliers paying cash.
	2	Sold merchandise for $9,450 to Tessier & Welsh; terms 2/15, n/30, FOB destination (cost of sales $6,600).
	4	Purchased merchandise from Janz Company for $11,300; terms 2/15, n/45, FOB shipping point.
	5	Paid $1,540 shipping costs regarding the purchase of March 1.
	6	Sold merchandise for $10,900 to Parker Company; terms 3/5, n/eom, FOB destination (cost of sales $7,650).
	10	Purchased $18,000 of merchandise from Delton Suppliers; terms 2/10, n/45, FOB destination.
	16	Collected the balance owing from Tessier & Welsh regarding the March 2 sale.
	17	Paid for the March 4 purchase from Janz Company.
	30	Paid for the March 10 purchase from Delton Suppliers.
	31	Collected the balance owing from Parker Company regarding the sale of March 6.

Part 2

Based on the information provided above, calculate (a) net sales, (b) cost of goods sold, and (c) gross profit for the month ended March 31, 2020.

Problem 5-2B Journal entries for merchandising activities—perpetual LO3

Prepare general journal entries to record the following perpetual system merchandising transactions of Baby Supply Company. *Use a separate account for each receivable and payable; for example, record the purchase on May 2 in Accounts Payable—Mobley Co.*

May	2	Purchased merchandise from Mobley Co. for $18,000 under credit terms of 1/15, n/30, FOB factory.
	4	Sold merchandise to Cornerstone Co. for $3,400 under credit terms of 2/10, n/60, FOB shipping point. The merchandise had cost $2,100.
	4	Paid $750 for freight charges on the purchase of May 2.
	9	Sold merchandise that cost $3,600 for $5,200 cash.
	10	Purchased merchandise from Richter Co. for $7,300 under credit terms of 2/15, n/60, FOB destination.
	12	Received a $600 credit memo acknowledging the return of merchandise purchased on May 10.
	14	Received the balance due from Cornerstone Co. for the credit sale dated May 4.
	15	Sold for cash a piece of office equipment at its original cost, $1,200.
	17	Paid the balance due to Mobley Co.
	18	Purchased $1,750 of cleaning supplies from A & Z Suppliers; terms n/15.
	20	Sold merchandise that cost $2,700 to Harrill Co. for $3,900 under credit terms of 2/15, n/60, FOB shipping point.
	22	Issued a $500 credit memo to Harrill Co. for an allowance on goods sold on May 20.
	23	Received a debit memo from Harrill Co. for an error that overstated the total invoice by $150.
	25	Paid Richter Co. the balance due.
	31	Received the balance due from Harrill Co. for the credit sale dated May 20.
	31	Sold merchandise that cost $10,200 to Cornerstone Co. for $15,000 under credit terms of 2/10, n/60, FOB shipping point.

Analysis Component: You are working in Baby Supply's accounts payable department and have been instructed to pay the Richter account on the last day of the discount period even though the money will have to be borrowed at 6% interest. Why would the company borrow to pay within the discount period? Show your calculations (round to two decimal places).

Problem 5-3B Journal entries for merchandising activities—perpetual LO3

Amuse Me Co. buys and sells new and used equipment for amusement parks, carnivals, parks, and zoos. Prepare general journal entries to record the following perpetual system merchandising transactions of Amuse Me Co. *Use a separate account for each receivable and payable; for example, record the purchase on July 3 in Accounts Payable—CMP Corp.*

July	3	Purchased bumper cars from CMP Corp. for $32,000 under credit terms of 1/10, n/30, FOB destination.
	4	At CMP's request, paid $1,500 for freight charges on the July 3 purchase, reducing the amount owed to CMP.
	7	Sold cotton candy machines to West Coast Zoo for $21,000 under credit terms of 2/10, n/60, FOB destination. The merchandise had cost $17,500.
	10	Purchased snow cone machines from Cimarron Corporation for $29,300 under credit terms of 1/10, n/45, FOB shipping point.
	11	Paid $1,200 shipping charges related to the July 7 sale to West Coast Zoo.
	12	West Coast Zoo returned merchandise from the July 7 sale that had cost $2,500 and been sold for $3,500. The merchandise was restored to inventory.
	14	After negotiations with Cimarron Corporation concerning problems with the merchandise purchased on July 10, received a credit memo from Cimarron granting a price reduction of $4,100.
	17	Received balance due from West Coast Zoo for the July 7 sale.
	18	Sold for cash a piece of vacant land for its original cost of $62,000.
	19	Purchased a used van for the business, $28,000; paid cash of $10,000 and borrowed the balance from the bank.
	20	Paid the amount due Cimarron Corporation for the July 10 purchase.
	21	Sold a climbing wall to Canadian National Exhibition for $18,000 under credit terms of 1/10, n/30, FOB shipping point. The merchandise had cost $13,100.
	24	Canadian National Exhibition requested a price reduction on the July 21 sale because the merchandise did not meet specifications. Sent Canadian National Exhibition a credit memo for $3,000 to resolve the issue.
	31	Received Canadian National Exhibition's payment of the amount due from the July 21 purchase.
	31	Paid CMP Corp. the amount due from the July 3 purchase.

Analysis Component: Regarding the July 24 transaction, what alternative is there to granting a credit memo? Be sure to identify and explain an advantage and disadvantage of the alternative.

Problem 5-4B Adjusting entries and income statements—perpetual LO5

CHECK FIGURES: 1. Income statement columns = $435,000; 2. Loss = $44,000

The following information is from the unadjusted trial balance for Journey's End Company prepared at October 31, 2020, the end of the fiscal year:

	Debit	Credit
Cash	$ 12,800	
Merchandise inventory	41,500	
Store supplies	16,700	
Prepaid insurance	5,700	
Store equipment	167,600	
Accumulated depreciation, store equipment		$ 60,000
Accounts payable		34,700
Dallas End, capital		172,100
Dallas End, withdrawals	12,000	
Sales		391,000
Sales discounts	3,500	
Sales returns and allowances	8,000	
Cost of goods sold	149,600	
Depreciation expense, store equipment	-0-	
Salaries expense	144,000	
Interest expense	800	
Insurance expense	-0-	
Rent expense	56,000	
Store supplies expense	-0-	
Advertising expense	39,600	
Totals	$657,800	$657,800

Rent and salaries expense are equally divided between the selling and administrative functions. Journey's End Company uses a perpetual inventory system.

Required

1. Record adjusting entries for the following information:

    a. Store supplies on hand at year-end amount to $6,600.

    b. The balance in the Prepaid Insurance account represents 12 months of insurance that was in effect starting November 1, 2019.

    c. The store equipment was purchased several years ago, when it was estimated to have a 20-year useful life and a resale value at the end of its life of $47,600.

    d. A physical count of the ending merchandise inventory shows $29,800 of goods on hand.

2. Using adjusted trial balance numbers, prepare a multiple-step income statement (see Exhibit 5.14).

Analysis Component: Explain why Interest Expense is shown under Other revenues and expenses on the multiple-step income statement.

Problem 5-5B **Income statement calculations and formats—perpetual** LO5

CHECK FIGURE: 1. Profit = $10,050

The following amounts appeared on Excel Company's adjusted trial balance as of May 31, 2020, the end of its fiscal year:

	Debit	Credit
Merchandise inventory	$ 21,000	
Other assets	385,200	
Liabilities		$ 105,000
Reena Excel, capital		339,150
Reena Excel, withdrawals	48,000	
Sales		636,000
Sales discounts	9,750	
Sales returns and allowances	42,000	
Cost of goods sold	296,000	
Sales salaries expense	87,000	
Rent expense, selling space	30,000	
Store supplies expense	7,500	
Advertising expense	54,000	
Office salaries expense	79,500	
Rent expense, office space	17,800	
Office supplies expense	2,400	
Totals	$1,080,150	$1,080,150

Required

1. Present a classified multiple-step income statement for internal users (see Exhibit 5.13) that lists the company's net sales, cost of goods sold, and gross profit, as well as the components and amounts of selling expenses and general and administrative expenses.

2. Present a condensed single-step income statement (see Exhibit 5.15) that lists these costs: cost of goods sold, selling expenses, and general and administrative expenses.

Problem 5-6B Markups LO5

Nikki designed a line of environmentally friendly handbags under the brand Nik & Mik. You are the marketing manager. Round all numbers to two decimal places.

a. After assessing the competitors, Nikki needs to price her products with a markup percentage of 40%. The cost is $50 for the small handbags and $60 for the medium handbags. Determine the selling price for each type of handbag.

b. Nik & Mik is ready to launch their large handbags. You determine that Nikki should set her price 25% below her competitor's price of $160. Nikki's cost to produce the large handbags is $70 per unit. Determine the markup percentage.

c. Calculate the gross profit margin for small, medium, and large handbags.

d. After a year of operations, you determine that Nikki should set a standard target gross margin percentage of 40% on all of Nikki's products. Determine the new prices for the small, medium, and large handbags.

Problem 5-7B Income statements—perpetual LO5

CHECK FIGURE: 1. Total operating expenses = $98,484

The following account information appeared on Ucore Sales' adjusted trial balance as of December 31, 2020. The accounts are listed in alphabetical order.

	Debit	Credit
Cost of goods sold	$129,964	
Depreciation expense, office equipment	690	
Depreciation expense, store equipment	3,204	
Insurance expense	1,240	
Liabilities		84,000
Lyle Ucore, capital		46,547
Lyle Ucore, withdrawals	20,500	
Merchandise inventory	3,400	
Other assets	102,952	
Rent expense (80% sales)	19,950	
Salaries expense (70% sales)	71,000	
Sales		226,500
Sales discounts	278	
Sales returns and allowances	1,469	
Supplies expense (35% sales)	2,400	
Totals	$357,047	$357,047

Required

1. Prepare a classified multiple-step income statement for Ucore Sales, like Exhibit 5.13.
2. Prepare a single-step income statement, like Exhibit 5.15.

Analysis Component: The gross profit ratio for Ucore Sales' year ended December 31, 2019, was 28%. Calculate this ratio for the year ended December 31, 2020, and compare it to the prior year, commenting on whether the change was favourable or unfavourable (round to two decimal places).

Problem 5-8B Income statements—perpetual LO5

CHECK FIGURES: 1. Operating expenses = $134,050; 2. Loss = $1,650

The following adjusted trial balance information was taken from the end of the July 31, 2020, fiscal year for Brilliant Sales:

		Debit	Credit
101	Cash	$ 6,500	
119	Merchandise inventory	12,220	
125	Supplies	2,400	
128	Prepaid insurance	1,150	
165	Store equipment	29,400	
166	Accumulated depreciation, store equipment		$ 7,500
167	Office equipment	15,600	
168	Accumulated depreciation, office equipment		8,100
201	Accounts payable		6,400
301	Ty Brilliant, capital		107,920
302	Ty Brilliant, withdrawals	61,000	
413	Sales		395,400
415	Sales discounts	1,200	
505	Cost of goods sold	261,800	
612	Depreciation expense, store equipment	1,500	
613	Depreciation expense, office equipment	1,250	
622	Sales salaries expense	39,000	
623	Office salaries expense	32,000	
637	Insurance expense, store	4,100	
638	Insurance expense, office	2,800	
640	Rent expense, office space	13,100	
641	Rent expense, selling space	21,000	
651	Office supplies expense	2,600	
652	Store supplies expense	1,800	
655	Advertising expense	14,900	
	Totals	$525,320	$525,320

Brilliant Sales uses a perpetual inventory system.

Required

1. Prepare a classified multiple-step income statement for use by internal users (like Exhibit 5.13).

2. Prepare a multiple-step income statement for external users (like Exhibit 5.14).

3. Prepare a single-step income statement (like Exhibit 5.15).

*Problem 5-9B Journal entries for merchandising activities—periodic LO7

Using the information provided in Part 1 of Problem 5-1B, journalize each of the transactions assuming a periodic inventory system.

An asterisk (*) identifies assignment material based on Appendix 5A or Appendix 5B.

*Problem 5-10B Journal entries for merchandising transactions—periodic LO7

Prepare general journal entries to record the following periodic system transactions of Inter-Cap Merchandising. *Use a separate account for each receivable and payable.*

March	1	Purchased merchandise on credit from Zender Holdings, terms 1/10, n/15, $40,000.
	2	Sold merchandise for cash, $5,100.
	7	Purchased merchandise on credit from Red River Co., terms 2/10, n/30, $29,500, FOB the seller's factory.
	8	Incurred freight charges for $1,750 on credit to Dan's Shipping regarding the merchandise shipment of the previous transaction.
	12	Sold merchandise on credit to Bev Dole, terms 2/10, n/45, $26,000.
	13	Received a $1,000 credit memo for merchandise purchased on March 7 and returned for credit.
	14	Purchased furniture for the office on credit from Wilson Supplies, $3,200.
	15	Sold merchandise on credit to Ted Smith, terms 2/10, n/45, $24,000.
	16	Paid for the merchandise purchased on March 7.
	17	Issued a credit memo to the customer of March 15 granting an allowance of $2,000 due to damage during shipment.
	19	The supplier issued a credit memo for $1,500 regarding unsatisfactory furniture purchased on March 14 and returned.
	24	Received payment for the merchandise sold on March 15.
	27	The customer of March 12 paid for the purchase of that date.
	31	Paid for the merchandise purchased on March 1.

*Problem 5-11B Income statement calculations and formats—periodic LO7

CHECK FIGURES: 3. $119,150; 4. Income from operations = $16,300

The following amounts appeared on the Mullen Company's adjusted trial balance in alphabetical order as of November 30, 2020, the end of its fiscal year:

	Debit	Credit
Advertising expense	$ 3,000	
Interest expense	350	
Liabilities		$ 31,000
Merchandise inventory	5,600	
Mitsy Mullen, capital		113,800
Mitsy Mullen, withdrawals	10,000	
Other assets	144,650	
Purchase discounts		1,150
Purchase returns and allowances		4,050
Purchases	120,000	
Rent expense (75% selling)	38,000	
Salaries expense (60% selling)	62,000	
Sales		276,000
Sales discounts	2,350	
Sales returns and allowances	28,500	
Supplies expense (80% selling)	6,700	
Transportation-in	4,850	
Totals	$426,000	$426,000

A physical count shows that the cost of the ending inventory is $6,100.

An asterisk (*) identifies assignment material based on Appendix 5A or Appendix 5B.

Required

1. Calculate the company's net sales for the year.

2. Calculate the company's cost of goods purchased for the year.

3. Calculate the company's cost of goods sold for the year.

4. Present a multiple-step income statement (like Exhibit 5.16) that lists the company's net sales, cost of goods sold, and gross profit, as well as the components and amounts of selling expenses and general and administrative expenses.

5. Present a single-step income statement (like Exhibit 5.17) that lists these expenses: cost of goods sold, selling expenses, general and administrative expenses, and interest expense.

*Problem 5-12B Classified multiple-step income statement—periodic LO5

CHECK FIGURE: 1. Loss = $28,630

Information from the March 31, 2020, year-end unadjusted trial balance of The Online Store is as follows:

	Debit	Credit
Cash...	$ 7,000	
Merchandise inventory	39,500	
Supplies	1,600	
Prepaid rent	19,200	
Store equipment...	60,000	
Accumulated depreciation, store equipment...........................		$ 14,000
Office equipment..	23,000	
Accumulated depreciation, office equipment		6,500
Accounts payable...		16,000
Lucy Baker, capital		134,600
Lucy Baker, withdrawals	34,000	
Sales		506,750
Sales returns and allowances...	13,800	
Sales discounts..	6,000	
Purchases...	346,000	
Purchase returns and allowances...		4,600
Purchase discounts..		7,150
Transportation-in	16,000	
Salaries expense (60% selling, 40% office).............................	58,000	
Rent expense (80% selling space; 20% office space)...........	49,000	
Advertising expense...	7,000	
Supplies expense (30% selling supplies; 70% office supplies)...........	9,500	
Depreciation expense, store equipment	-0-	
Depreciation expense, office equipment	-0-	
Totals..	$689,600	$689,600

Additional information:

a. Supplies inventory at year-end, $920.

b. The balance in the Prepaid Rent account represents a six-month contract effective November 1, 2019.

c. Depreciation on the store equipment, $1,600.

An asterisk (*) identifies assignment material based on Appendix 5A or Appendix 5B.

d. The useful life and trade-in value of the office equipment were originally estimated to be 7 years and $250, respectively.

e. Ending merchandise inventory, $19,200.

Required Analyze and determine the impact of the adjustments from (a) to (e) on the unadjusted trial balance numbers. Prepare a classified multiple-step income statement (like Exhibit 5A.2) using your adjusted trial balance numbers.

*Problem 5-13B Sales taxes—perpetual LO3, 7, 8

Journalize each of the following transactions assuming a perpetual inventory system and PST at 8% along with 5% GST. *Note: Any available cash discount is taken only on the sale price before taxes.*

Sept.	2	Recorded $9,000 of cash sales (cost of sales $6,200).
	3	Purchased $11,000 of merchandise inventory for cash.
	7	Purchased $6,500 of merchandise; terms 1/10, n/45.
	8	Sold merchandise costing $13,200 for $16,200; terms 2/10, n/30.
	17	Paid for the merchandise purchased on September 7.
	18	Collected the amount owing from the customer of September 8.

*Problem 5-14B Sales taxes—periodic LO6, 7, 8

Journalize each of the transactions in Problem 5-13B assuming a periodic inventory system and PST at 8% along with 5% GST.

ANALYTICAL AND REVIEW PROBLEM

A & R Problem 5-1—perpetual

The following income statement was prepared by an office clerk hired for July. As the accounting supervisor, you recognize that it is incorrect and prepare a corrected multi-step income statement.

Demo Sales Income Statement For Month Ended July 31, 2020		
Sales		$562,140
Accounts receivable		37,000
Unearned sales		18,000
Net sales		$617,140
Operating expenses:		
Accumulated depreciation, equipment	$ 30,000	
Advertising expense	14,000	
Cost of goods sold	394,000	
Depreciation expense, equipment	3,000	
Insurance expense	2,500	
Interest expense	1,700	
Interest payable	250	
Jen Conway, withdrawals	14,000	
Office supplies	9,000	
Prepaid insurance	14,000	
Prepaid rent	25,000	
Rent expense	5,000	
Salaries payable	175,000	
Sales discounts	2,800	690,250
Loss		$ 73,110

An asterisk (*) identifies assignment material based on Appendix 5A or Appendix 5B.

ETHICS CHALLENGE

EC 5-1

Claire Phelps is a popular high school student who attends approximately four dances a year at her high school. Each dance requires a new dress and accessories that necessitate a financial outlay of $100 to $200 per event. Claire's parents inform her that she is on her own with respect to financing the dresses. After incurring a major hit to her savings for the first dance in her second year, Claire developed a different approach. She buys the dress on credit the week before the dance, wears it to the dance, and returns the dress the next week to the store for a full refund on her charge card.

Required

1. Comment on the ethics exhibited by Claire and possible consequences of her actions.
2. How does the store account for the dresses that Claire returns?

FOCUS ON FINANCIAL STATEMENTS

FFS 5-1

CHECK FIGURES: Loss = $154; Total current assets = $430; Total assets = $562; Total current liabilities = $74

Colombia Textiles began operations several years ago. Its post-closing trial balance at December 31, 2020, is shown below (with accounts listed in alphabetical order):

Account	Account Balance[1] ($000s)
Accounts payable	34
Accounts receivable	106
Accumulated depreciation, office furniture	38
Accumulated depreciation, store fixtures	61
Brandy Colombia, capital[2]	291
Cash	48
Franchise	62
Merchandise inventory	236
Notes payable[3]	225
Notes receivable[4]	14
Office furniture	52
Office supplies	5
Prepaid rent	32
Store fixtures	106
Unearned revenue	12

[1]Assume all accounts have a normal balance.
[2]The owner, Brandy Colombia, made no investments during 2020.
[3]$180,000 of the note is due after December 31, 2021.
[4]$3,000 of the notes receivable will be collected during 2021.

Additional information: The following closing entries were recorded on December 31, 2020, for the year just ended.

2020				
Dec.	31	Sales..	640	
		Interest Income...	2	
		Income Summary		642
		To close temporary credit balance accounts to the		
		Income Summary account.		
	31	Income Summary..	796	
		Depreciation Expense, Office Furniture....................		13
		Depreciation Expense, Store Fixtures.......................		6
		Cost of Goods Sold		459
		Delivery Expense		21
		Interest Expense		4
		Office Salaries Expense		63
		Office Supplies Expense...		17
		Rent Expense, Office...		21
		Rent Expense, Sales..		46
		Sales Discounts...		7
		Sales Returns and Allowances..................................		19
		Sales Salaries Expense		120
		To close temporary debit balance accounts to the		
		Income Summary account.		
	31	Brandy Colombia, Capital...	154	
		Income Summary		154
		To close the Income Summary account to Capital.		
	31	Brandy Colombia, Capital...	78	
		Brandy Colombia, Withdrawals.................................		78
		To close Withdrawals to Capital.		

Required Using the information provided, prepare a single-step income statement, statement of changes in equity, and classified balance sheet.

Analysis Component: Refer to Spin Master's December 31, 2017, balance sheet in Appendix III at the back of the textbook. Compare Spin Master's liabilities to those of Colombia Textiles. Ignoring the balance sheet dates, which company has the stronger balance sheet? *(A balance sheet is considered to be stronger the fewer liabilities it has as a percentage of total assets.)*

FFS 5-2

Required Answer the following questions.

a. Based on a review of the income statement for Spin Master in Appendix III at the end of the textbook, determine if Spin Master sells products or services. Explain your answer.

b. Based on a review of WestJet's income statement in Appendix III at the end of the textbook, determine if WestJet sells products or services. Explain your answer.

c. The income statement for Spin Master shows a gross profit of $800,456 (thousand) for the year ended December 31, 2017. Explain what this gross profit represents.

d. Did Spin Master have sufficient gross profit to cover operating expenses for the year ended December 31, 2017?

e. Is the income statement format used by Spin Master a classified multiple-step, a multiple-step, or a single-step? (Compare the income statement for Spin Master to those in Exhibits 5.13, 5.14, and 5.15.)

f. Refer to the balance sheets for Spin Master and WestJet in Appendix III at the end of the textbook. Both balance sheets include Inventory. Explain how Inventory is unique for each of these companies.

CRITICAL THINKING MINI CASE

You have just graduated with a business diploma in management and have been hired as the inventory manager for a local sporting goods store. Your first task is to review and assess the following information:

	2020	2019
Cost of merchandise sold to customers in sales transactions...	$480,000	$320,000
Merchandise inventory balance, beginning of year..	?	84,000
Invoice cost of merchandise purchases..	510,000	240,000
Shrinkage determined at end of year..	2,500	14,000
Cost of transportation-in...	25,500	12,000
Cost of merchandise returned by customers and restored to inventory........................	115,000	22,400
Purchase discounts received..	5,100	2,400
Purchase returns and allowances received..	2,550	1,200

Required Using the elements of critical thinking described on the inside front cover, comment.

CUMULATIVE COMPREHENSION PROBLEM: ECHO SYSTEMS

Echo Systems—perpetual or periodic

Note: Solutions are available for both perpetual and periodic.

(The first three segments of this comprehensive problem were presented in Chapters 2, 3, and 4. If those segments have not been completed, the assignment can begin at this point. However, you should use the Working Papers[18] that accompany this text because they reflect the account balances that resulted from posting the entries required in Chapters 2, 3, and 4.)

CHECK FIGURES: 4. Profit = $23,198; 6. Total current assets = $162,358; Total assets = $208,858

Earlier segments of this problem have described how Mary Graham created Echo Systems on October 1, 2020. The company has been successful, and its list of customers has started to grow. To accommodate the growth, the accounting system is ready to be modified to set up separate accounts for each customer. The following list of customers includes the account number used for each account and any balance as of the end of 2020. Graham decided to add a fourth digit with a decimal point to the 106 account number that had been used for the single Accounts Receivable account. This modification allows the existing chart of accounts to continue being used. The list also shows the balances that two customers owed as of December 31, 2020:

Customer Account	No.	Dec. 31 Balance
Alamo Engineering Co...	106.1	-0-
Buckman Services...	106.2	-0-
Capital Leasing	106.3	-0-
Decker Co.	106.4	$2,700
Elite Corporation...	106.5	-0-
Fostek Co.	106.6	$3,000
Grandview Co.	106.7	-0-
Hacienda Inc.	106.8	-0-
Images Inc.	106.9	-0-

---

18   If students have not purchased the Working Papers package, the Working Papers for the Serial Problem are available on Connect.

In response to frequent requests from customers, Graham has decided to begin selling computer software. The company will extend credit terms of 1/10, n/30 to customers who purchase merchandise. No cash discount will be available on consulting revenue. The following additional accounts were added to the general ledger to allow the system to account for the company's new merchandising activities:

Account (Perpetual)	No.
Merchandise Inventory	119
Sales	413
Sales Discounts	414
Sales Returns and Allowances	415
Cost of Goods Sold	502

OR

Account (Periodic)	No.
Merchandise Inventory	119
Sales	413
Sales Discounts	414
Sales Returns and Allowances	415
Purchases	505
Purchase Returns and Allowances	506
Purchase Discounts	507
Transportation-In	508

Because the accounting system does not use reversing entries, all revenue and expense accounts have zero balances as of January 1, 2021.

Required

1. Prepare journal entries to record each of the following transactions for Echo Systems, assuming either a perpetual system or a periodic system.

	2021	
Jan.	4	Paid Carly Smith for five days at the rate of $200 per day, including one day in addition to the four unpaid days from the prior year.
	5	Mary Graham invested an additional $48,000 cash in the business.
	7	Purchased $11,200 of merchandise from Shephard Corp. with terms of 1/10, n/30, FOB shipping point.
	9	Received $3,000 from Fostek Co. as final payment on its account.
	11	Completed five-day project for Alamo Engineering Co. and billed them $9,000, which is the total price of $12,000 less the advance payment of $3,000.
	13	Sold merchandise with a retail value of $8,400 and a cost of $6,720 to Elite Corporation with terms of 1/10, n/30, FOB shipping point.
	15	Paid $1,400 for freight charges on the merchandise purchased on January 7.
	16	Received $6,000 cash from Grandview Co. for computer services.
	17	Paid Shephard Corp. for the purchase on January 7.
	20	Elite Corporation returned $800 of defective merchandise from its purchase on January 13. The returned merchandise, which had a cost of $640, was scrapped.
	22	Received the balance due from Elite Corporation.
	24	Returned defective merchandise to Shephard Corp. and accepted credit against future purchases. Its cost, net of the discount, was $792.
	26	Purchased $16,000 of merchandise from Shephard Corp. with terms of 1/10, n/30, FOB destination.
	26	Sold merchandise with a cost of $9,280 for $11,600 on credit to Hacienda Inc.
	29	Received a $792 credit memo from Shephard Corp. concerning the merchandise returned on January 24.
	31	Paid Carly Smith for 10 days' work at $200 per day.
Feb.	1	Paid $6,750 to the Lakeshore Mall for another three months' rent in advance.
	3	Paid Shephard Corp. for the balance due.
	5	Paid $1,600 to the local newspaper for advertising.
	11	Received the balance due from Alamo Engineering Co. for revenue billed on January 11.
	15	Mary Graham withdrew $9,600 cash for personal use.
	23	Sold merchandise with a cost of $5,120 for $6,400 on credit to Grandview Co.; terms 1/10, n/30.
	26	Paid Carly Smith for eight days' work at $200 per day.
	27	Reimbursed Mary Graham's business automobile expenses for 600 km at $1.00 per kilometre.

Mar.	8	Purchased $4,800 of computer supplies from Abbott Office Products on credit.
	9	Received the balance due from Grandview Co. for merchandise sold on February 23.
	11	Repaired the company's computer paying cash of $1,720.
	16	Received $8,520 cash from Images Inc. for computing services.
	19	Paid the full amount due to Abbott Office Products, including amounts created on December 17 and March 8.
	24	Billed Capital Leasing for $11,800 of computing services.
	25	Sold merchandise with a cost of $2,004 for $3,600 on credit to Buckman Services.
	30	Sold merchandise with a cost of $2,200 for $4,440 on credit to Decker Company.
	31	Reimbursed Mary Graham's business automobile expenses for 400 km at $1.00 per kilometre.

2. Post the journal entries to the accounts in the company's general ledger. (Use asset, liability, and equity accounts that start with balances as of December 31, 2020.)

3. Prepare a partial work sheet consisting of the first six columns showing the unadjusted trial balance, the March 31 adjustments described in (a) through (g) below, and the adjusted trial balance. *Do not prepare closing entries and do not journalize the adjusting entries or post them to the ledger.*

   a. The March 31 computer supplies on hand is $4,230.

   b. Three more months have passed since the company purchased the annual insurance policy at the cost of $4,320.

   c. Carly Smith has not been paid for seven days of work.

   d. Three months have passed since any prepaid rent cost has been transferred to expense. The monthly rent is $2,250.

   e. Depreciation on the computer for January through March is $2,250.

   f. Depreciation on the office equipment for January through March is $1,500.

   g. The March 31 inventory of merchandise is $1,960.

4. Prepare an interim single-step income statement for the three months ended March 31, 2021. List all expenses without differentiating between selling expenses and general and administrative expenses.

5. Prepare an interim statement of changes in equity for the three months ended March 31, 2021.

6. Prepare an interim classified balance sheet as of March 31, 2021.

Inventory Costing and Valuation

A Look Back

Chapter 5 focused on the final steps of the accounting process. We explained how reporting merchandising activities differs from reporting service activities. We also analyzed and recorded merchandise purchases and sales transactions, and explained the adjustments and financial statement presentation for merchandisers.

A Look at This Chapter

This chapter extends our analysis of merchandising activities, emphasizing concepts such as costing and valuation. Topics include the items in inventory, costs assigned, costing methods used, and inventory estimation techniques.

dpa picture alliance/Alamy Stock Photo

© Bloomberg/Getty Images

LEARNING OBJECTIVES

LO1	Identify the components and costs included in merchandise inventory.
LO2	Calculate cost of goods sold and merchandise inventory using specific identification, moving weighted average, and FIFO—perpetual.
LO3	Analyze the effects of the costing methods on financial reporting.
LO4	Calculate the lower of cost and net realizable value of inventory.
LO5	Analyze the effects of inventory errors on current and future financial statements—perpetual.
LO6	Apply both the gross profit and retail inventory methods to estimate inventory.
LO7	Assess inventory management using both inventory turnover and days' sales in inventory.
Appendix 6A	
LO8	Calculate cost of goods sold and merchandise inventory using FIFO—periodic, weighted average, and specific identification.
LO9	Analyze the effects of inventory errors on current and future financial statements—periodic.

Amazon.com: A Leader in Retail Innovation

Jeff Bezos, founder and CEO of Amazon.com, is known for his innovation and outside-the-box thinking when it comes to meeting customer needs and standing out from the competition. He is committed to having the largest selection of items and the best pricing, and is dedicated to providing engaged customer service. The company's many technological initiatives includes introducing new products and aligning with Amazon's mission to be "Earth's most customer-centric company where people can find and discover anything they want to buy online." These advances include products such as Fire TV, Amazon Fire Phone, and Amazon Kindle Fire tablets. The company's recent acquisitions of Ring, a video doorbell, and Twitch, a game service, further broaden its product scope. Amazon is demonstrating to customers that it is a one-stop shop for everything they can dream of. This mega online retailer has several pop-up kiosks in major cities to feature its technical product offerings, and in 2018 opened its first brick-and-mortar convenience store called Amazon Go in Seattle, with no cashiers or checkout lines. Customers just download the app, pick up their items, and walk out of the store. The store's inventory is updated and the customer is billed automatically through the Amazon Go app as they exit the store.

Amazon acquired the robotics company Kiva Systems in March 2012 with the intent to improve warehouse efficiency and tighten delivery timelines for customers. With the deployment of 10,000 robots in fiscal 2014, workers are better able to focus their time and efforts on packing goods and expediting them to the customer. Amazon workers used to walk many kilometres each day to fulfill customer orders, with over 150 million inventory items to manage and a 500,000-square-foot warehouse (refer to the YouTube video below illustrating the warehouse functionality, "Inside One of Amazon's Busiest Days," presented by CNN). According to Amazon executive Dave Clark, "Kiva robots have cut operating expenses by about 20%"; Clark indicates that this "would translate to roughly $22 million in cost savings for each fulfillment center." This savings was derived by improving the efficiency of the warehouses. Kiva robots resulted in reduced inventory cycle times from 60 to 75 minutes to approximately 15 minutes, and inventory storage grew 50% due to more efficient use of space.

With the new Kiva robots all inventory is stored on "pods," which function like a portable shelf. When merchandise inventory is received each item is scanned, assigned a location in inventory, and stored in the up to-date perpetual inventory records. When a customer executes an online purchase, the inventory item's location is retrieved digitally and used to direct the Kiva robot to the item in the warehouse. Upon arriving at the appropriate pod storing the item, the robot connects itself to the shelf and delivers the shelf to human workers who pack the items in boxes and send them off for shipment. The YouTube video linked below, "High-Speed Robots Part 1: Meet BettyBot in 'Human Exclusion Zone' Warehouses—The Window—WIRED," demonstrates how these Kiva robots navigate through a complex warehouse to bring products to the packer for packing and shipping.

The company has expanded same-day delivery with "get it today" capabilities on over a million eligible items. Amazon Prime usage is expanding, with customers benefiting from free two-day delivery and access to free movies, games, and TV episodes for an annual membership fee of $99. Amazon Prime Air is the company's latest R&D initiative that has developed drones called octocopters (shown in the accompanying photo) to pick up products in small yellow buckets at Amazon's warehouse and deliver them to customers in as little as 30 minutes after purchase at Amazon.com. And, in a move to expand its offering of market-fresh groceries, Amazon made a $13.7 billion acquisition of Whole Foods Markets.

Amazon is currently waiting for the Federal Aviation Administration to grant approval for the drones and develop regulations for unmanned aerial vehicles. In March 2014, Amazon was granted approval to test the drone delivery system in highly monitored conditions, and the US Patent and Trademark Office has published Amazon's patent application for the drone delivery system. In the meantime, Amazon continues to impress consumers with its incredible selection of online goods, competitive pricing, and quick delivery options. In its 2017 annual report, Amazon had $4.9 billion in inventory and discloses that it accounts for its inventory using the first-in, first-out inventory costing method, which assumes that inventory is sold in the order it is acquired; this method is demonstrated later in this chapter.

Sources: http://www.amazon.com/b?node=8037720011; www.amazon.com; http://www.kivasystems.com/amazon-press/; Amazon.com 2013 annual report; Amazon.com 2014 annual report; http://www.cnn.com/2015/05/12/politics/amazon-patent-drone-delivery/; http://www.businessinsider.com/kiva-robots-save-money-for-amazon-2016-6; https://www.bloomberg.com/news/articles/2017-06-22/amazon-vision-of-deliveries-by-drone-gets-boost-in-faa-measure; and https://www.geekwire.com/2017/amazons-13-7b-whole-foods-deal-close-monday-prime-integrated-checkout-system/

Video Links: "Inside One of Amazon's Busiest Days," presented by CNNMoney, demonstrates the inventory management required to fulfill a customer order before the Kiva robots. https://www.youtube.com/watch?v=Z2Bs0nqVyqs

The Kiva robots' assistance in warehouse management is presented in the YouTube video "High-Speed Robots Part 1: Meet BettyBot in 'Human Exclusion Zone' Warehouses—The Window—WIRED." https://www.youtube.com/watch?v=8gy5tYVR-28

> **CRITICAL THINKING CHALLENGE**
>
> Would **Amazon** have a merchandise turnover similar to **Lululemon Athletica**'s? Explain why or why not. What does "inventory demand planning" refer to? What would the effect be of cost-saving strategies on the weighted average cost of inventory?

CHAPTER PREVIEW

In the previous chapter, we developed an understanding of how critical inventory management is to a merchandiser and gained an understanding of how both purchases and sales of merchandise are recorded in the accounting records and the related financial statement presentation. In this chapter, we extend our study and analysis of inventory by identifying the items that are included in the cost of inventory and we determine how purchase costs are applied to inventory. We will also consider the impact to financial statements when declines occur in the market values of inventory. We also explain methods used to assign costs to merchandise inventory and to cost of goods sold. The principles and methods we describe are used in department stores, grocery

Student Success *Cycle*

Read the material

Apply your critical thinking skills

Do the exercises

Check your answers

stores, and many other merchandising companies that purchase products for resale. These principles and methods affect reported amounts of profit, assets, and equity. Understanding these fundamental concepts of inventory accounting increases our ability to analyze and interpret financial statements. As is the case for Amazon in the opening article, an understanding of these topics also helps in managing and tracking inventory.

A major goal in accounting for inventory is matching relevant costs against revenues. This is important in order to calculate profit appropriately.[1] We use the matching principle when accounting for inventory to decide how much of the cost of the goods available for sale is assigned to cost of goods sold, matching with current period sales and how much is carried forward as inventory, and matching against future sales. Management must make this decision and several others when accounting for inventory, including the following items:

- Items included in inventory and their costs
- Costing method (specific identification, moving weighted average, or FIFO)
- Inventory system (perpetual or periodic)
- Use of net realizable value or other estimates.

These selections affect the reported amounts for inventory, cost of goods sold, gross profit, profit, current assets, and other accounts. This chapter discusses all of these important issues and their reporting effects.

Inventory Items and Costs

ITEMS IN MERCHANDISE INVENTORY

LO1 Identify the components and costs included in merchandise inventory.

Merchandise inventory includes all goods owned by a company and held for sale in the ordinary course of business.[2] This rule holds regardless of where goods are located at the time inventory is counted. Most inventory items are easy to identify when applying this rule, but certain items require special attention. These include goods in transit, goods on consignment, and goods damaged or obsolete.

---

1 IFRS 2018, IAS 2, para. 1.

2 IFRS 2018, IAS 2 para. 6 includes other items such as those in production to be later sold as inventory and materials or supplies used in the production process.

Goods in Transit

Do we include in inventory goods that are in transit from a supplier? Our answer depends on whether the rights and risks of ownership have passed from the supplier to the purchaser: whether the goods are FOB shipping point or FOB destination. If ownership has passed to the purchaser, they are included in the purchaser's inventory. Recall from Chapter 5 that items purchased FOB shipping point must be included in the purchaser's inventory from the point they leave the supplier's shipping docks. Items purchased FOB destination will be included in inventory until the time they reach the purchaser's receiving department. If it is not clear, it can be helpful to ask: if the goods were damaged in transit, which company's insurance policy would cover the loss? If the company's policy would cover the loss, it likely has title to the goods.

Goods on Consignment

Goods on consignment are goods shipped by their owner, called the **consignor**, to another party called the **consignee**. A consignee is to sell goods for the owner without ever having legal title to the goods. Consigned goods are owned by the consignor and are reported in the consignor's inventory. The consignee acts as an agent to attempt to sell the item for the consignor. The consignee collects a commission on the sale when it finds a buyer for the item(s).

Goods Damaged or Obsolete

Damaged goods and obsolete (or expired) goods are not counted in inventory if they are not in a saleable condition. If these goods can be sold at a reduced price, they are included in inventory at their *net realizable value*. **Net realizable value (NRV)** is expected selling price (**retail price**) minus the cost of making the sale. The period when damage or obsolescence (or deterioration) occurs is the period where the loss is reported. This is consistent with the GAAP relevance principle, as obsolete goods would result in overvalued inventory.

COSTS OF MERCHANDISE INVENTORY

Costs included in merchandise inventory include all expenditures necessary, directly or indirectly, to bringing an item to a saleable condition and location.[3] This means the cost of an inventory item includes:

```
  Purchase price
– Discounts provided by supplier (trade discounts/rebates)
+ Additional costs necessary to put inventory in a place and condition for sale
  Cost of Inventory
```

Important Tip:

The following are examples of additional (incidental) costs that are to be added to inventory:

- Import duties
- Transportation-in (freight costs)
- Storage
- Insurance
- Handling costs
- Costs incurred in an aging process where the aging contributes to the value of the product produced (for example, aging of wine and cheese).

---

3   IFRS 2018, IAS 2, paras. 10-22.

Accounting principles imply that incidental costs are assigned to every unit purchased. This is so that all inventory costs are properly matched against revenue in the period when inventory is sold. The **materiality principle**[4] states that an amount may not be ignored if its effect on the financial statements could impact the decisions of financial statement users. The *materiality principle* is relied on by some companies as the reason some incidental costs are not allocated to inventory. These companies argue either that incidental costs are immaterial or that the effort in assigning these costs to inventory outweighs the benefits. Such companies price inventory using invoice prices only. When this is done, the incidental costs are allocated to cost of goods sold in the period when they are incurred.

PHYSICAL COUNT OF MERCHANDISE INVENTORY

The purpose of a **physical inventory count** is to help determine the dollar amount of inventory included on financial statements by confirming the number of units on hand at period end. This often is performed as close as possible to the end of the fiscal year. Accuracy of inventory records at a company's fiscal year-end is important, as it is a significant current asset on a merchandising company's balance sheet.

The physical count is used to adjust the Merchandise Inventory account balance to the actual inventory on hand. In a perpetual inventory system inventory units can be different than the number of items recorded in the system due to errors, shrinkage, and obsolescence issues. A physical count enables companies to update their accounting records to reflect the true quantity of items available to be sold as inventory.

If the units counted in inventory are lower than the quantity in the accounting records, Cost of Goods Sold is debited and Merchandise Inventory is credited for the total value of inventory that was missing. If the inventory count identifies more inventory than the inventory records show, the entry is the opposite. Differences occur because of events including theft, loss, damage, and errors. If a periodic system is used the inventory count is mandatory, as it determines how much merchandise inventory is on hand. Any differences automatically get booked to Cost of Goods Sold (remember, under periodic systems Beginning Inventory + Purchases − Ending Inventory = COGS).

When performing a physical count of inventory, *internal controls* should be followed to minimize errors. **Internal controls**, discussed in more detail in Chapter 7, are the policies and procedures used to protect assets, ensure reliable accounting, promote efficient operations, and urge adherence to company policies. To improve inventory management controls some companies perform cycle counts, adopting an approach of regularly counting different sections of their inventory throughout the fiscal year. An important control is restricting movement of inventory during the count, which is critical to ensure the accuracy of the count. An example of an internal control technique is the use of pre-numbered inventory tickets, one for each product on hand, to reduce the risk of items being counted more than once or omitted. We show a typical inventory ticket in Exhibit 6.1. By multiplying the number of units counted for each product by its unit cost, we get the dollar amount for each product in inventory. The sum total of all products is the dollar amount reported for inventory on the balance sheet.

In lieu of inventory tickets, the merchandise inventory items of many businesses are labelled with UPC (Universal Product Code) bar codes. The UPC bar codes are used not only for the pricing and costing of sales but also to make physical counts easier, as items can be scanned using handheld scanners and can be tracked electronically.

---

4   IFRS 2018, "Framework," para. QC 11.

EXHIBIT 6.1
Inventory Ticket

Lakeside/Dreamstime.com/GetStock.com

 DECISION INSIGHT

If you look at any grocery product, you will find a UPC bar code printed on the package. Universal Product Codes were created in 1973 to assist in the checkout and inventory process of grocery stores, and UPC bar codes have since spread to nearly every item in the retail world. The Uniform Code Council (UCC) is responsible for issuing the manufacturer's portion of the code. The manufacturer's UPC coordinator assigns the next digits as the item number. The retailer can then assign a price to each individual UPC along with costing information. In this way, inventory and sales records can be updated instantly when the bar code is scanned.

 CHECKPOINT

1. If SodaStream sells goods to Best Buy with terms FOB SodaStream's factory, does SodaStream or Best Buy report these goods in its inventory when they are in transit?
2. The Vancouver Art Gallery purchases a painting for $11,400. Additional costs in obtaining and offering the artwork for sale include $130 for transportation-in, $150 for import duties, $100 for insurance during shipment, $180 for advertising, $400 for framing, and $800 for sales salaries. For calculating inventory cost, what is assigned to the painting?

Do Quick Study questions: QS 6-1, QS 6-2, QS 6-3, QS 6-4

Assigning Costs to Inventory

LO2 Calculate cost of goods sold and merchandise inventory using specific identification, moving weighted average, and FIFO—perpetual.

One of the most important decisions in accounting for inventory is determining how the per-unit costs will be assigned to inventory items. When all units are purchased at the same unit cost, this process is simple, but when identical items are purchased at different costs, a question arises as to what amounts are recorded in cost of goods sold when sales occur and what dollar value should remain in inventory.

Important Tip:

When using a perpetual inventory system, we must record inventory transactions both at the time of purchase as a debit to inventory and as sales occur, updating cost of goods sold and crediting inventory.

Recall that a periodic inventory system determines cost of goods sold and inventory amounts at the end of a period based on a physical count. How we assign these costs to inventory and cost of goods sold affects the reported amounts for both systems. Inventory costing for periodic inventory systems is demonstrated later in Exhibit 6A.5.

The three key methods you need to know that are used in assigning costs to inventory and cost of goods sold under a perpetual inventory system are:

- First-in, first-out (FIFO)
- Moving weighted average
- Specific identification.

Each method assumes a particular pattern for how costs flow through inventory. All three methods are accepted under GAAP and are described in this section.[5] The last-in, first-out (LIFO) method is another way to assign costs to inventory and is popular in the United States, but it is not permitted under GAAP or the Canadian *Income Tax Act*.

If a business has inventory items that are alike and are interchangeable, either the FIFO or moving weighted average method would be most appropriate. A business is required to use the specific identification method for inventory items that are individually unique.[6] Examples of inventory where the specific identification method is appropriate include items such as custom furniture where each piece produced is different, or cars at an automobile dealership each with a unique serial number and unique options. Another example is custom jewellery where each item has a unique gemstone weight, cut, and quality, along with a unique gold carat value and weight. **Loblaw Companies Limited** uses the weighted average costing method for its retail stores and distribution centres; its **Shoppers Drug Mart** stores use FIFO as per their 2017 annual report, and Lululemon Athletica and **Procter & Gamble Co.** use FIFO according to those companies' 2017 annual reports. **Tiffany & Co.** discloses in its 2017 annual report that it uses specific item costing for certain diamond and gemstones and average costing for its remaining inventory.

---

5   Physical flow of goods depends on the type of product and the way it is used. Perishable goods such as fresh fruit demand that a business attempt to sell them in a first-in, first-out pattern. Other products such as canned food can often be sold in a random pattern.

6   IFRS 2018, IAS 2, paras. 23-25.

Amazon.com, Inc. discloses the following under its accounting policy over inventory in its December 31, 2016, annual report:

Inventories, consisting of products available for sale, are primarily accounted for using the first-in, first-out method, and are valued at the lower of cost or market value. This valuation requires us to make judgments, based on currently available information, about the likely method of disposition, such as through sales to individual customers, returns to product vendors, or liquidations, and expected recoverable values of each disposition category.

We provide Fulfillment by Amazon services in connection with certain of our sellers' programs. Third-party sellers maintain ownership of their inventory, regardless of whether fulfillment is provided by us or the third-party sellers, and therefore these products are not included in our inventories.

Lululemon Athletica Inc. discloses the following under its significant accounting policy over inventory in its January 29, 2017, annual report:

Inventories, consisting of finished goods, inventories in transit, and raw materials, are stated at the lower of cost and market value. Cost is determined using weighted-average costs. For finished goods, market is defined as net realizable value, and for raw materials, market is defined as replacement cost. Cost of inventories includes all costs incurred to deliver inventory to the Company's distribution centers including freight, non-refundable taxes, duty and other landing costs.

Procter & Gamble Co. discloses the following combination of costing methods it applies to different segments of its inventory in its June 30, 2017, annual report:

Inventories are valued at the lower of cost or market value. Product-related inventories are maintained on the first-in, first-out method. The cost of spare part inventories is maintained using the average-cost method.

Tiffany & Co. discloses its accounting policy for inventory in its January 31, 2017, annual report as follows:

Inventories are valued at the lower of cost or market using the average cost method except for certain diamond and gemstone jewelry which uses the specific identification method.

We extend the example using information from Lifetime Equipment Co-op (LEC), the fictitious sporting goods store introduced in Chapter 5, to illustrate the three methods. Among its many products, assume LEC carries one type of mountain bike. Its mountain bike ("unit") inventory at the beginning of August 2020 and its purchases during August are shown in Exhibit 6.2.

EXHIBIT 6.2
Cost of Goods Available for Sale

			Units		Cost Per Unit		Total Cost
Aug.	1	Beginning inventory	10	@	$ 91	=	$ 910
	3	Purchased	15	@	$106	=	$1,590
	17	Purchased	20	@	$115	=	$2,300
Total goods available for sale			45 Units available for sale				$4,800 Total cost of goods that were available for sale

LEC had two sales of mountain bikes to two different biking clubs in August, as shown in Exhibit 6.3. LEC ends August with 11 bikes in inventory (45 units available for sale less 34 units sold).

In this section, we will determine how much of the cost of goods available for sale is to be assigned to cost of goods sold and to ending merchandise inventory using the three different cost flow assumptions.

We explained in the last chapter how use of a perpetual inventory system is increasing dramatically due to advances in accounting software, management information systems, and other related technology.

EXHIBIT 6.3
Retail Sales of Goods

			Units		Selling Price Per Unit		Total Sales
Aug. 14	Sales		20	@	$133	=	$2,660
28	Sales		14	@	$150	=	$2,100
			34 Units				$4,760

Widespread use of electronic scanners, point-of-sale systems, and product bar codes further encourages its use having the ability to read bar codes and easily track movement of goods. The focus of the next section is assignment of costs to cost of goods sold and merchandise inventory in a perpetual system. The assignment of costs to inventory using a periodic system is discussed in Appendix 6A.

FIRST-IN, FIRST-OUT

The **first-in, first-out (FIFO)** method of assigning costs to inventory and to goods sold assumes that inventory items are sold in the order acquired. When sales occur, costs of the earliest units purchased are charged to cost of goods sold. This leaves the costs from the most recent purchases in inventory. Use of FIFO for LEC means the costs of mountain bikes are assigned to inventory and goods sold as shown in Exhibit 6.4.

EXHIBIT 6.4
FIFO Calculations—Perpetual

Transaction		Purchases			Sales (at cost)			Inventory Balance		
Transaction	Date	Units	Unit Cost	Total Cost	Units	Unit Cost	Cost of Goods Sold	Units	Unit Cost	Total Cost
Purchase	Aug. 1	Beginning inventory 10 @ $91 =		$910				10 @	$91 =	$910
Purchase	Aug. 3	15 @	$106 =	$1,590				10 @ 15 @	$91 = $106 =	$910 $1,590
Sale	Aug. 14				10 @ 10 @	$91 = $106 =	$910 $1,060	5 @	$106 =	$530
Purchase	Aug. 17	20 @	$115 =	$2,300				5 @ 20 @	$106 = $115 =	$530 $2,300
Sale	Aug. 28				5 @ 9 @	$106 = $115 =	$530 $1,035	11 @	$115 =	$1,265
Totals		45		$4,800	34		$3,535	11		$1,265

Cost of goods available for sale = Cost of goods sold + Ending inventory

① Under FIFO, units are assumed to be sold in the order acquired; therefore, of the 20 units sold on August 14, the first 10 units come from beginning inventory.

② The remaining 10 units sold on August 14 come from the next purchase, August 3.

③ All of the units from beginning inventory have been sold but 5 units remain from the August 3 purchase.

LEC's cost of goods sold on the income statement is $3,535 (= $910 + $1,060 + $530 + $1,035) and its ending inventory reported on the balance sheet is $1,265.

MOVING WEIGHTED AVERAGE

The **moving weighted average** inventory costing method under a perpetual inventory system requires calculating the average cost per unit of merchandise inventory at the time of each purchase. The average is calculated by dividing the cost of goods available for sale by the units on hand. Using the moving weighted average method for LEC means the costs of mountain bikes are assigned to inventory and goods sold as shown in Exhibit 6.5.

EXHIBIT 6.5
Moving Weighted Average Calculations—Perpetual

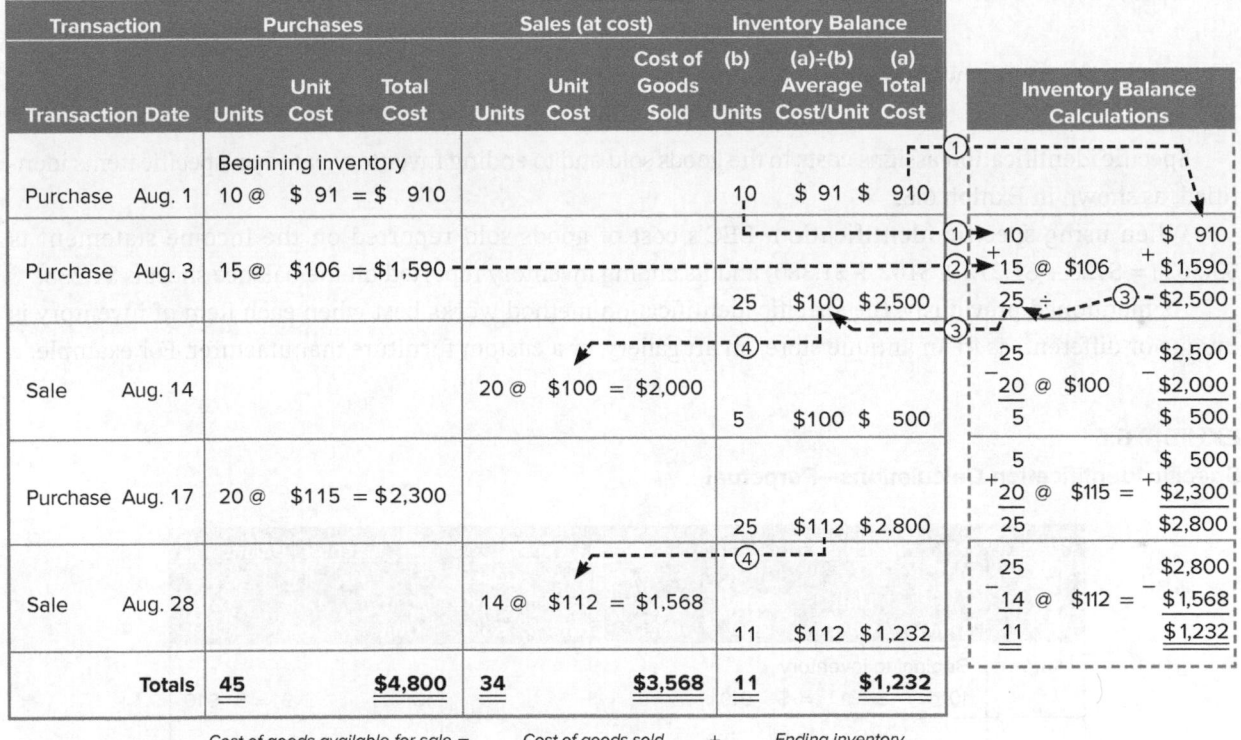

Transaction	Purchases			Sales (at cost)			Inventory Balance				Inventory Balance Calculations
Transaction Date	Units	Unit Cost	Total Cost	Units	Unit Cost	Cost of Goods Sold	(b) Units	(a)÷(b) Average Cost/Unit	(a) Total Cost		
Purchase Aug. 1	Beginning inventory 10 @ $91 = $910						10	$91	$910		
Purchase Aug. 3	15 @ $106 = $1,590						25	$100	$2,500		10 $910 + 15 @ $106 + $1,590 25 ÷ = $2,500
Sale Aug. 14				20 @ $100 = $2,000			5	$100	$500		25 $2,500 − 20 @ $100 − $2,000 5 $500
Purchase Aug. 17	20 @ $115 = $2,300						25	$112	$2,800		5 $500 + 20 @ $115 = + $2,300 25 $2,800
Sale Aug. 28				14 @ $112 = $1,568			11	$112	$1,232		25 $2,800 − 14 @ $112 = − $1,568 11 $1,232
Totals	**45**		**$4,800**	**34**		**$3,568**	**11**		**$1,232**		

Cost of goods available for sale =   Cost of goods sold   +   Ending inventory

① August 1 beginning inventory in units and dollars.
② August 1 beginning inventory is added to the purchase of August 3 to determine the total cost of the units in inventory on August 3.
③ The total cost of all units, at $2,500, is divided by the total number of units, 25 units, to get the average cost per unit of $100 on August 3.
④ The most current weighted average cost is assigned as the cost per unit sold.

Under the moving weighted average method (MWA) LEC's cost of goods sold reported on the income statement is $3,568 (= $2,000 + $1,568) and its ending inventory reported on the balance sheet is $1,232. (Refer to Exhibit 6.7 for a comparison of the methods.) The inventory balance is lower using the MWA method compared to FIFO in this example. Notice how the cost of goods sold is higher using MWA compared to FIFO.

> **Important Tip:**
> The moving weighted average perpetual system often raises a rounding problem in the calculations because the currency figures are limited to two decimal places. The typical solution is to adjust or "plug" the cost of goods sold figure after calculating the inventory balance at the moving weighted average cost.

SPECIFIC IDENTIFICATION

The **specific identification** method applies best when each item sold and remaining in inventory can be directly identified with a unique identifier, as costs can then be tracked and assigned to each item sold. LEC's internal documents indicate the following details regarding purchases made in August:

August 1, 10 red LEC brand 16″ boys bikes were purchased at a cost of $91

August 3, 15 green LEC brand 16″ limited edition boys bikes were purchased at a cost of $106

August 17, 20 silver LEC brand 16″ anniversary edition boys bikes were purchased at a cost of $115

LEC's internal documents reveal the following items were sold during August:

August 14, 20 units were sold:	8 red LEC brand 16″ bikes
	12 green LEC brand 16″ limited edition boys bikes
August 28, 14 units were sold:	2 red LEC brand 16″ bikes
	12 silver anniversary edition LEC brand 16″ boys bikes

Specific identification assigns costs to the goods sold and to ending inventory based on specific items identified, as shown in Exhibit 6.6.

When using specific identification, LEC's cost of goods sold reported on the income statement is $3,562 (= $728 + $1,272 + $182 + $1,380) and its ending inventory reported on the balance sheet is $1,238.

As mentioned previously, the specific identification method works best when each item of inventory is unique or different, as in an antique store, an art gallery, or a custom furniture manufacturer. For example, a

EXHIBIT 6.6
Specific Identification Calculations—Perpetual

Date	Purchases			Sales (at cost)			Inventory Balance		
	Units	Unit Cost	Total Cost	Units	Unit Cost	Cost of Goods Sold	Units	Unit Cost	Total Cost
Aug. 1	Beginning inventory 10 @ $91 = $ 910						10 @	$ 91 = $ 910	
3	15 @ $106 = $ 1,590						10 @ 15 @	$ 91 = $ 910 $106 = $ 1,590	
14				8 @ 12 @	$ 91 $106	= $ 728 = $1,272	2 @ 3 @	$ 91 = $ 182 $106 = $ 318	
17	20 @ $115 = $ 2,300						2 @ 3 @ 20 @	$ 91 = $ 182 $106 = $ 318 $115 = $2,300	
28				2 @ 12 @	$ 91 $115	= $ 182 = $1,380	3 @ 8 @	$106 = $ 318 $115 = $ 920	
Totals	45		$4,800	34		$3,562	11		$1,238

Cost of goods available for sale = Cost of goods sold + Ending inventory

① Of the 10 units from beginning inventory, 8 were specifically identified as the red LEC brand 16″ boys bike being sold.

② Of the 10 units from beginning inventory, 2 red LEC brand 16″ bikes remain in ending inventory.

③ Of the 15 units purchased on August 3, 12 green LEC brand 16″ bikes were specifically identified as being sold.

④ Of the 15 units purchased on August 3, 3 green LEC brand 16″ bikes remain in ending inventory.

EXHIBIT 6.7
Comparison of Inventory Methods

	FIFO		Moving Weighted Average		Specific Identification	
	Units	$	Units	$	Units	$
Cost of Goods Sold (or Cost of Sales)..............	34	$3,535	34	$3,568	34	$3,562
Ending Inventory.......................................	11	1,265	11	1,232	11	1,238
Goods Available for Sale.........................	45	$4,800	45	$4,800	45	$4,800

car dealership would use specific identification because each car has a unique serial number, known as the vehicle identification number (VIN). In all cases where specific identification is used, each inventory item needs to be identified separately.

When inventory items are similar (such as bags of sugar, pallets of concrete blocks, or loaves of bread), specific units being purchased and sold cannot be easily traced; large quantities are often purchased at different times, possibly with different costs. When the cost is greater than the benefit of tracking the sale of individual units that are similar, either the moving weighted average or the FIFO method would be more appropriate.

Notice in Exhibit 6.7 that the total units and cost of the goods available for sale are the same regardless of the method used. What is different is the dollar amount assigned to the ending inventory and the cost of goods sold. In this example, the FIFO method would result in the higher gross profit and profit. FIFO also provided LEC a higher inventory value on the balance sheet. Once an inventory costing accounting policy is selected, companies are expected to consistently apply the same policy year after year.

INVENTORY COSTING AND TECHNOLOGY

A perpetual inventory system can be kept in either electronic or manual form. A manual form is often too costly for businesses, especially those with many purchases and sales or many units in inventory. Advances in information technology and accounting software systems have greatly reduced the cost of an electronic perpetual inventory system, and many companies are now asking whether they can afford not to have one. This is because timely access to information is being used strategically by companies to gain a competitive advantage. Scanned sales data, for instance, can reveal crucial information on buying patterns, and can also help companies target promotional and advertising activities. These and other applications have greatly increased the use of the perpetual system.

 DECISION INSIGHT

Loblaw's Corporate Grocery Stores Go Perpetual

Loblaw Companies Limited identifies its upgrade of its IT infrastructure as a positive move to enable the company to develop a more precise estimate through a "system-generated average cost." The company estimates "the impact of this inventory measurement and other conversion differences associated with implementation of a perpetual inventory system to be a $190 million decrease to the value of the inventory."

Sources: http://www.loblaw.ca/English/Media-Centre/news-releases/news-release-details/2014/Loblaw-Companies-Limited-Reports-a-651-Increase-in-Adjusted-Operating-Income2-for-the-Second-Quarter-of-20141/default.aspx; http://www.marketwatch.com/story/loblaw-companies-limited-reports-a-651-increase-in-adjusted-operating-income2-for-the-second-quarter-of-20141-2014-07-24; http://www.retailingtoday.com/article/loblaw-embarks-its-next-chapter; and http://www.prnewswire.com/news-releases/loblaw-companies-limited-reports-a-651-increase-in-adjusted-operating-income2-for-the-second-quarter-of-20141-268417412.html.

CHECKPOINT

3. What fundamental accounting principle relates most closely with the cost allocations of cost of goods available for sale between ending inventory and cost of goods sold?

Do Quick Study questions: QS 6-5, QS 6-6, QS 6-7, QS 6-8

Mid-Chapter Demonstration Problem

Graphic Artz Co. uses a perpetual inventory system and had the following beginning inventory and purchases during January 2020:

Date			Units		Unit Cost		Total Cost
					Item X		
Jan.	1	Inventory..	300	@	$14	=	$ 4,200
	16	Purchase...	200	@	15	=	3,000
	20	Purchase...	300	@	16	=	4,800
		Total units and cost of goods available for sale.............	800				$12,000

Sales of units were as follows (all on credit):

Jan.	15	200 units at $30
	28	460 units at $35
	Total units sold...........................	660

Additional data for use in applying the specific identification method:
    The specific units sold were:

Jan.	15	200 units from the January 1 units on hand
	28	75 units from the January 1 units on hand
		150 units from the January 16 purchase, and
		235 units from the January 20 purchase

Required

1. Calculate the ending inventory and the cost of goods sold under a perpetual inventory system by applying each of the three different methods of inventory costing:
   a. FIFO
   b. Moving weighted average
   c. Specific identification

2. Using your calculations from Part 1, record the purchase on January 16 and the sale on January 28 for each of:
   a. FIFO
   b. Moving weighted average
   c. Specific identification

Analysis Component:

A new supplier has approached Graphic Artz Co., offering to supply the merchandise inventory at a cost of $11 per unit. What should the company consider when deciding whether or not to change to the new supplier?

Planning the Solution

- Prepare a perpetual FIFO schedule showing the composition of beginning inventory and how the composition of inventory changes after each purchase of inventory and after each sale.

- Make a schedule of purchases and sales, recalculating the average cost of inventory after each purchase to arrive at the moving weighted average cost of ending inventory. Add up the average costs associated with each sale to determine the cost of goods sold using the moving weighted average method.

- Prepare a schedule showing the calculation of the cost of goods sold and ending inventory using the specific identification method. Use the information provided to determine the cost of the specific units sold and which specific units remain in inventory.

- Journalize the purchase on January 16 and the sale on January 28 by taking the relevant information from the schedules prepared in Part 1 for each method.

- Prepare an answer to the analysis question.

SOLUTION

1a. FIFO Perpetual

Date	Purchases			Sales (at cost)			Inventory Balance		
	Units	Unit Cost	Total Cost	Units	Unit Cost	Cost of Goods Sold	Units	Unit Cost	Total Cost
Jan. 1	Beginning inventory								
	300 @	$14 =	$ 4,200	①			300 @	$14 =	$4,200
								②	
15				200 @	$14 =	$2,800	100 @	$14 =	$1,400
							100 @	$14 =	$1,400
16	200 @	$15 =	$ 3,000				200 @	$15 =	$3,000
							100 @	$14 =	$1,400
				③			200 @	$15 =	$3,000
20	300 @	$16 =	$ 4,800		③	③	300 @	$16 =	$4,800
28				100 @	$14 =	$ 1,400	④		
				200 @	$15 =	$3,000			
				160 @	$16 =	$2,560	140 @	$16 =	$2,240
Totals	800		$12,000	660		$9,760	140		$2,240

Cost of goods available for sale = Cost of goods sold + Ending inventory

① Under FIFO, units are assumed to be sold in the order acquired; therefore, the 200 units sold on January 15 come from beginning inventory.

② The 100 units remaining in inventory after the January 15 sale are from beginning inventory.

③ The 460 units sold on January 28 are assumed to be the 100 units from beginning inventory, plus the 200 units purchased on January 16, plus 160 units from the January 20 purchase.

④ All of the units remaining in inventory after the January 28 sale are from the January 20 purchase.

1b. Moving Weighted Average Perpetual

Date		Purchases			Sales (at cost)			Inventory Balance			Inventory Balance Calculations	
	Units	Unit Cost	Total Cost	Units	Unit Cost	Cost of Goods Sold	(b) Units	(a) ÷ (b) Average Cost/Unit	(a) Total Cost			
Jan. 1	Beginning inventory 300 @ $14 = $4,200							300 @ $14.00 = $4,200.00				
15				200 @ $14.00 = $2,800.00			①			300	$4,200.00	
						100 @ $14.00 = $1,400.00				➔ 200 @ $14.00 = ➔ $2,800.00		
										➔ 100	$1,400.00	
16	200 @ $15 = $3,000						③			100	$1,400.00	
										+ 200 @ $15.00 = + $3,000.00		
						300 @ $14.67 = $4,400.00				300	$4,400.00	
20	300 @ $16 = $4,800									300	$4,400.00	
										+ 300 @ $16.00 = + $4,800.00		
						600 @ $15.33 = $9,200.00				600	$9,200.00	
28				460 @ $15.33 = $7,053.80						600	$9,200.00	
										460 @ $15.33 = 7,053.80*		
						140 @ $15.33 = $2,146.20				140	$2,146.20	
Totals	**800**		**$12,000**	**660**		**$9,853.80**	**140**		**2,146.20**			

Cost of goods available for sale = Cost of goods sold + Ending inventory

*Cost of goods sold changed due to rounding $9,200 − 2,148.20 = 7,053.80

① The most current average cost per unit is assigned to the units sold.

② The beginning balance less the units sold equals the remaining inventory.

③ The total cost remaining in inventory divided by the total units remaining equals the average unit cost. Notice that the average unit cost does not change because of a sale.

1c. Specific Identification

Date		Purchases			Sales (at cost)			Inventory Balance	
	Units	Unit Cost	Total Cost	Units	Unit Cost	Cost of Goods Sold	Units	Unit Cost	Total Cost
Jan. 1	Beginning inventory 300 @ $14 = $4,200			①			300 @	$14 =	$4,200
15				200 @	$14 =	$2,800	100 @	$14 =	$1,400
16	200 @	$15 =	$3,000				100 @	$14 =	$1,400
							200 @	$15 =	$3,000
						②	100 @	$14 =	$1,400
						②	200 @	$15 =	$3,000
20	300 @	$16 =	$4,800			②	300 @	$16 =	$4,800
28				75 @	$14 =	$1,050	25 @	$14 =	$350
				150 @	$15 =	$2,250	50 @	$15 =	$750
				235 @	$16 =	$3,760	65 @	$16 =	$1,040
Totals	**800**		**$12,000**	**660**		**$9,860**	**140**		**$2,140**

Cost of goods available for sale = Cost of goods sold + Ending inventory

① 200 of the beginning inventory units were specifically identified as being sold on January 15. Therefore, the 100 units remaining on January 15 are identified as units from beginning inventory.

② The units sold on January 28 are specifically identified. The units sold determines exactly which units are remaining.

		a.		b.		c.	
		FIFO		**Moving Weighted Average**		**Specific Identification**	
2020							
Jan. 16	Merchandise Inventory...............................	3,000		3,000		3,000	
	Accounts Payable.....................................		3,000		3,000		3,000
	To record purchase of merchandise on credit.						
28	Accounts Receivable	16,100		16,100		16,100	
	Sales		16,100		16,100		16,100
	To record credit sales; 460 units × $35 – $16,100.						
28	Cost of Goods Sold	6,960		7,052*		7,060	
	Merchandise Inventory.........................		6,960		7,052*		7,060
	To record the sale of merchandise.						

*Rounded to nearest whole dollar for simplicity

Analysis Component:

Graphic Artz Co. should consider the following (as well as other possibilities):

- The quality of the merchandise inventory offered by the new supplier
- Whether the new supplier can meet the company's merchandise inventory quantity needs
- Whether the new supplier will deliver merchandise when required (dependable)
- The payment/delivery terms
- What kind of service the new supplier provides (customer support)
- Whether the new supplier can provide references (from satisfied customers; reputation)
- The duration of the $11 per unit offer and potential price increases

Financial Reporting and Inventory

LO3 Analyze the effects of the costing methods on financial reporting.

The purpose of this section is to review the financial reporting issues related to inventory, including inventory disclosure, consistency, and prudence. As well, we look at the effects of inventory errors.

FINANCIAL REPORTING

In our analysis of financial statements, it is important to know and understand inventory costing methods because the method used can have a material impact on the income statement and balance sheet, as illustrated in Exhibit 6.8. For this reason, the company's policy over inventory costing, including a description of the method used, must be *disclosed* in the notes to the financial statements as demonstrated previously for Amazon.com, Inc., Lululemon Athletica Inc., Procter & Gamble Co., and Tiffany & Co.

When purchase prices do not change, the choice of an inventory costing method is unimportant. All methods assign the same cost amounts when prices remain constant. When purchase prices are rising or falling, however, the methods are likely to assign different cost amounts.

Because LEC's purchase prices rose in August, FIFO assigned the least amount to cost of goods sold. This led to the highest gross profit and the highest profit. This result will always occur in times of rising prices because the most recent and therefore most costly units are in ending inventory, assigning the least expensive units to cost of goods sold.[7]

---

7 The moving weighted average amount can be higher or lower than the FIFO amount depending on whether prices steadily increase or decrease.

EXHIBIT 6.8

Income Statement and Balance Sheet Effects of Inventory Costing Methods

	FIFO	Moving Weighted Average	Specific Identification
Lifetime Equipment Co-op			
Income Statement—Mountain Bikes			
For Month Ended August 31, 2020			
Sales...	$4,760	$4,760	$4,760
Cost of goods sold*...	3,535	3,568	3,562
Gross profit from sales....................................	$1,225	$1,192	$1,198
Operating expenses...	374	374	374
Profit from operations.....................................	$ 851	$ 818	$ 824

*From Exhibit 6.7

Partial Balance Sheet

	FIFO	Moving Weighted Average	Specific Identification
Assets			
Current assets:			
Merchandise inventory*...........................	$1,265	$1,232	$1,238

*From Exhibit 6.7

Ethics and Inventory Management

Next to cash reserves, inventory is one of the most liquid assets held within a merchandising business and, as seen with Amazon in the chapter-opening vignette, it is often one of the most significant in terms of dollar value of assets held. Fraudsters often target inventory either to generate schemes to take inventory for personal use, resell inventory on a secondary market, or attempt to modify inventory pricing through elaborate schemes. *The Wall Street Journal* reports that bar code scams, where consumers change the bar code to modify the cost of goods purchased, and store gift card scams are two ways that technology has negatively impacted the retail space.[8]

Corporations do well to ensure appropriate security measures and policies are in place to prevent theft of goods from the retail store as well as the shipping/receiving docks. To reduce the risk of fraud, employees who have access to the physical goods in the warehouse and retail space should not have access to modify the accounting records or authorize purchase orders. Chapter 7 further discusses appropriate measures to strengthen the organization's control environment.

Companies should adopt the inventory costing method that best represents the actual cost flow of goods being brought in and sold out of inventory. Because the selection of inventory-costing methods can materially affect amounts on financial statements, some managers may want to adopt the method that provides the most favourable results. For example, if management's bonus plans were based on profit, managers might pick the method that results in the highest bonus each period. If managers were allowed to change methods each period, it would be even more difficult for users of financial statements to compare a company's financial statements from one period to the next. If profit increased, for instance, a user may believe it is due to successful operations and not realize it was due to the accounting method change. Fortunately, accounting standards prevent such questionable activities from occurring.

The **consistency principle** requires a company to use the same accounting methods period after period so that the financial statements are comparable across periods.[9] The consistency principle applies to all accounting methods.

The consistency principle *does not* require a company to use one method exclusively. It can use different methods to value different categories of inventory. **Bombardier Inc.**, the Canadian aerospace and

---

8   http://www.wsj.com/articles/SB116174264881702894, accessed June 2015.
9   IFRS 2018, IAS 1, para. 45.

transportation company, uses two methods (specific identification and weighted average) to assign costs to various types of inventory. The consistency principle also does not mean that a company can never change from one accounting method to another. Instead, it means a company must argue that the method to which it is changing will improve its financial reporting. Under this circumstance, a change is acceptable; yet, when such a change is made, the full disclosure principle requires that the notes to the statements report the type of change, its justification, and its effect on profit.[10] A change in accounting policy of this type would also require restating prior period financial statements, demonstrating the overall impact of the change to prior years' reported results.

Investors and banks track the working capital ratio of a company very closely and corporate debt covenants often require adherence to a specific working capital ratio (for example, a minimum of 2:1 current assets to current liabilities) or the outstanding principal on the debt becomes immediately due. Inventory balances need to be accurately reported and closely monitored.

 DECISION MAKER Answer—End of chapter

Inventory Manager—Ethical Dilemma

You are the inventory manager for a trendy urban retail inventory merchandiser. Your compensation includes a bonus plan based on the amount of gross profit reported in the financial statements. Your supervisor comes to you and asks your opinion about changing the inventory costing method from moving weighted average to FIFO. Since costs have been rising and are expected to continue to rise, your superior predicts the company will be more attractive to investors because of the reported higher profit using FIFO. You realize this proposed change will likely increase your bonus as well. What do you recommend?

Exhibit 6.9 summarizes advantages and disadvantages for the cost flow assumptions discussed.

EXHIBIT 6.9

Advantages and Disadvantages of Cost Flow Assumptions

	FIFO	Moving Weighted Average	Specific Identification
Advantages:	Most current values are on the balance sheet as ending inventory	Smooths out purchase price changes	Exactly matches costs and revenues
	Matches the flow of goods for many businesses that attempt to sell older inventory first, such as a grocery retailer	Matches the flow of goods for businesses that have a large volume of small items that don't expire, such as a landscape centre selling stones/gravel	Works well for companies that sell differentiated products with a higher dollar value, such as a jewellery store
Disadvantages:	Cost of goods sold does not reflect current costs, so does not accurately match expenses to revenue	Averaging does not accurately match expenses to revenues	Relatively more costly to implement and maintain

 CHECKPOINT

4. Give examples of types of businesses that might use specific identification despite the disadvantage indicated in Exhibit 6.9. Explain why these businesses might choose to use specific identification.

5. When costs and prices are rising, what effect does moving weighted average have on a balance sheet compared to FIFO?

Do Quick Study question: QS 6-9

---

10 IFRS 2018, IAS 8, paras. 14-18 and 28-31.

LOWER OF COST AND NET REALIZABLE VALUE (LCNRV)

LO4 Calculate the lower of cost and net realizable value of inventory.

The cost of inventory is not necessarily the amount always reported on a balance sheet. The *principle of faithful representation* provides the guidance in reporting inventory at the amount expected to be received on the sale of the inventory item, referred to as net realizable value, if it is lower than the cost of the item in inventory.[11] Merchandise inventory is then reported on the balance sheet at the **lower of cost and net realizable value (LCNRV)**. **Faithful representation** requires that information be complete, neutral, and free from error so that assets and profit are not overstated and liabilities and expenses are not understated.[12]

For example, assume that on September 10 **Apple Inc.** announces the upcoming releases of its newest iPhone to be rolled out October 15. Immediately after the announcement, sales of the previous edition begin to plummet as consumers anticipate the new device has an improved feature set. Apple subsequently lowers the price of the older model in order to sell the items. As a result, inventory has to be written down from $50 million and reported at its new NRV of $20 million to ensure assets and profit are not overstated at year-end.

If the NRV of the inventory were to recover after the balance sheet date, the inventory write-down would be reversed. The reversal is limited to the amount of the write-down to ensure that inventory is always reported at the lower of cost and NRV. The concept of inventory write-downs and reversals will be demonstrated in the next section.

Notice that Amazon.com, Inc., Lululemon Athletica Inc., Procter & Gamble Co., and Tiffany & Co. all reported in their accounting policy notes listed earlier in the chapter that they value inventory at the lower of cost and NRV.

Calculating the Lower of Cost and Net Realizable Value (LCNRV)

The decline in merchandise inventory from cost to NRV is recorded in an adjusting entry at the end of the period. LCNRV is applied in one of two ways:

1. Usually item by item, or, when not practicable,
2. To groups of similar or related items.[13]

We show in Exhibit 6.10 how LCNRV is applied to the ending inventory of LEC.

EXHIBIT 6.10
LCNRV Calculations

Inventory Items	No. of Units	Cost/ Unit	Total Cost	NRV/ Unit	Total NRV	LCNRV applied to: Items	LCNRV applied to: Groups
Bicycles:							
Roadster..................................	25	$ 750	$ 18,750	$ 790	$19,750	$ 18,750	
Sprint...	60	1,100	66,000	1,100	66,000	66,000	
Group subtotal......................			$ 84,750		$85,750		$ 84,750
Kayaks:							
A1 Series	21	$1,800	$ 37,800	$1,300	$27,300	$ 27,300	
Trax-4..	29	2,200	63,800	2,250	65,250	63,800	
Group subtotal......................			$101,600		$92,550		$ 92,550
Total inventory......................			$186,350			$175,850	$177,300

---

11 IFRS 2018, IAS 2, para. 28.
12 IFRS 2018, "Framework," para. QC 12.
13 IFRS 2018, IAS 2, para. 29.

Using the information in Exhibit 6.10 to demonstrate the application of LCNRV on an item-by-item basis, we see that total LCNRV is $175,850. Therefore, $175,850 must be reported on the balance sheet. To achieve this, inventory needs to be reduced by $10,500, which is the difference between the total cost of $186,350 and total LCNRV of $175,850. The entry is:

Cost of Goods Sold...	10,500	
Merchandise Inventory..		10,500
To write inventory down to LCNRV:		
$186,350 − $175,850 = $10,500.		

After posting this entry, merchandise inventory would appear on the balance sheet as:

Current assets:	
Cash	$ x,xxx
Accounts receivable	x,xxx
Merchandise inventory, net..	175,850

Assume that the A1 Series kayaks in Exhibit 6.10 are still on hand at the end of the next accounting period. There is evidence that their NRV has increased to $1,450 per unit. The original write-down can be reversed (but is limited to the amount of the original write-down).[14] The entry is:

Merchandise Inventory	3,150	
Cost of Goods Sold..		3,150
To reverse the inventory write-down:		
$1,450 − $1,300 = $150;		
$150 × 21 units = $3,150.		

Although international standards prefer the application of LCNRV on an item-by-item basis, in certain circumstances accounting standards permit the application of LCNRV to groups.

To demonstrate the application of LCNRV to groups, refer to the information in Exhibit 6.10. The entry to write inventory down to LCNRV applied to groups is:

Cost of Goods Sold...	9,050	
Merchandise Inventory..		9,050
To write inventory down to LCNRV:		
$186,350 − $177,300 = $9,050.		

🌐 ETHICAL IMPACT

You were recently hired as a manager of accounting by a national coffee bean distributor, Fair Beans Coffee, that supplies local roasters with organic, fair-trade beans. You notice that a large shipment of coffee beans has been delivered that does not have the typical fair-trade packaging and is not labelled with the "organic" stamp that is on the other inventory on hand.

You talk to the purchasing department and find out they have switched providers, as the cost of their ethically sourced Nicaraguan beans had increased significantly due to not only a disease that has impacted a significant amount of the crops but also political unrest

acekreations/Pixabay.com

(Continued)

14   IFRS 2018, IAS 2, para. 33.

in the region that has impacted the transportation of goods. You are concerned that your roasters are expecting a consistent product and have marketed their coffee as organic and fair-trade.

In talking to the warehouse manager, you find out there was a significant quality issue with the most recent batch of inventory that was received from Nicaragua and he does not feel it should be sold to local roasters. When you look up the invoice for this inventory you notice it is for $30,000 and was paid in cash at the time it was picked up at the grower's farm.

You propose to the president of Fair Beans that the company needs to record a current period valuation adjustment for $30,000 debiting cost of goods sold to recognize the loss on inventory and credit inventory, decreasing it by the dollar value of the quality write-down.

The President informs you that he is hopeful the beans will be salable and he is concerned about getting approval for an upcoming bank loan on a warehouse expansion project. At this time he will not support writing off the inventory, but will consider it in the new fiscal year. What, if any, concerns do you have over the impact to the year end financial statements? As a manager in the accounting department, how would you handle this situation?

 CHECKPOINT

6. Refer to the information in Exhibit 6.10. Assume that LCNRV was applied to inventory on an item-by-item basis. In the next accounting period, the NRV of the A1 Series kayaks increased to $1,900 per unit because the factory burned down, causing a shortage in the marketplace. LEC had four of the previously written-down A1 Series kayaks left in ending inventory a year after the original write-down. What entry, if any, is required in applying LCNRV to the remaining four units?

7. A company's ending inventory includes the following items:

Product	Units on Hand	Unit Cost	NRV Per Unit
A	20	$ 6	$ 5
B	40	9	8
C	10	12	15

Using LCNRV applied separately to individual items, calculate the reported amount for inventory.

Do Quick Study question: QS 6-10

ERRORS IN REPORTING INVENTORY

LO5 Analyze the effects of inventory errors on current and future financial statements—perpetual.

Companies must take care in calculating and taking a physical count of inventory. If inventory is reported in error, it causes misstatements of cost of goods sold, gross profit, profit, current assets, and equity. It also means misstatements will exist in the next period's statements. This is because ending inventory of one period is the beginning inventory of the next. An error carried forward causes misstatements of the next period's cost of goods sold, gross profit, and profit. Since the inventory amount often is large, misstatements can reduce the usefulness of financial statements.

Income Statement Effects

The income statement effects of an inventory error are evident when looking at the components of cost of goods sold in each of the alternative presentations in Exhibit 6.11.

EXHIBIT 6.11

Cost of Goods Sold Components—Periodic

or, stated another way:

Merchandise Inventory		
Beginning Inventory		
Cost of Goods Purchased	Cost of Goods Sold ⟶	
Ending Inventory		

Cost of Goods Sold	
Cost of Goods Sold	

The effect of an inventory error on cost of goods sold is determined by calculating the inventory correctly and comparing the result to the result of the calculation when using the incorrect amount, as in Exhibit 6.12.

Exhibit 6.12 assumes that $2,000 of merchandise sold but awaiting delivery was incorrectly included in ending inventory on December 31, 2020. This ending inventory error carries over to the next period as a beginning inventory error yielding a reverse effect. We can see that overstating ending inventory will understate cost of goods sold. An understatement of cost of goods sold yields an overstatement of profit. We can do the same analysis with understating ending inventory and for an error in beginning inventory. Exhibit 6.13 shows the effects of inventory errors on the current period's income statement amounts.

EXHIBIT 6.12

Effects of $2,000 Overstatement in Ending Inventory for 2020 on Three Periods' Income Statement Information—Perpetual

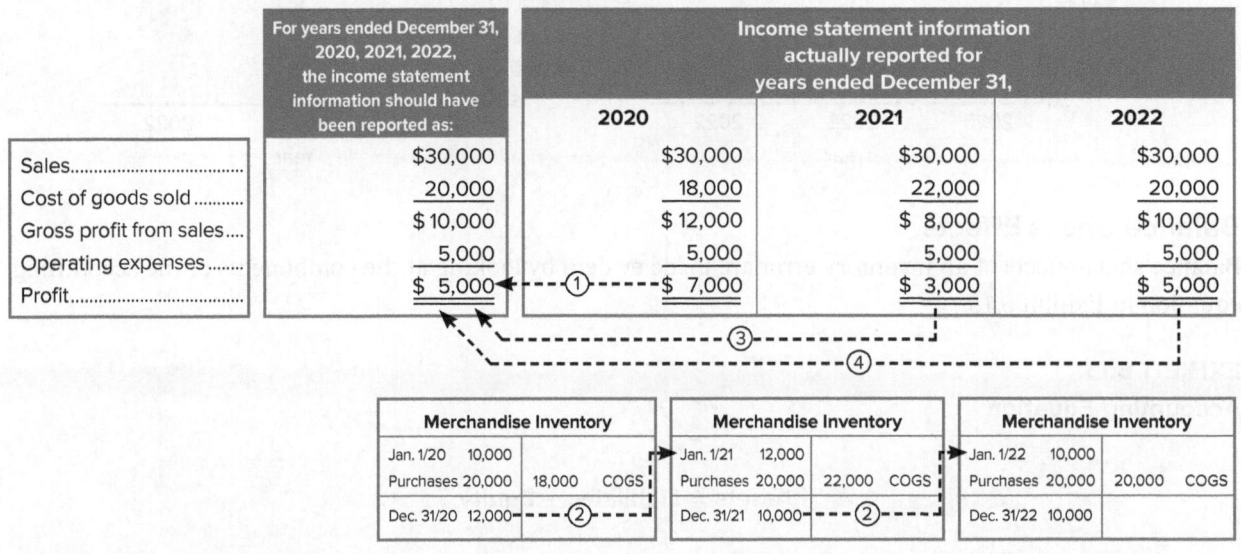

	For years ended December 31, 2020, 2021, 2022, the income statement information should have been reported as:	Income statement information actually reported for years ended December 31,		
		2020	**2021**	**2022**
Sales......................................	$30,000	$30,000	$30,000	$30,000
Cost of goods sold	20,000	18,000	22,000	20,000
Gross profit from sales....	$ 10,000	$ 12,000	$ 8,000	$ 10,000
Operating expenses	5,000	5,000	5,000	5,000
Profit......................................	$ 5,000	$ 7,000	$ 3,000	$ 5,000

Merchandise Inventory		
Jan. 1/20 10,000		
Purchases 20,000	18,000	COGS
Dec. 31/20 12,000		

Merchandise Inventory		
Jan. 1/21 12,000		
Purchases 20,000	22,000	COGS
Dec. 31/21 10,000		

Merchandise Inventory		
Jan. 1/22 10,000		
Purchases 20,000	20,000	COGS
Dec. 31/22 10,000		

① 2020 profit and gross profit are overstated (too high) and cost of goods sold is understated (too low) when ending inventory is overstated (too high).

② Ending inventory for one period becomes the beginning inventory for the next period, carrying forward any errors that existed.

③ 2021 profit and gross profit are understated (too low) and cost of goods sold is overstated (too high) when beginning inventory is overstated (too high). Notice that the error has reversed itself in 2021, the second year.

④ An inventory error in the year 2020 does not affect 2022.

EXHIBIT 6.13

Effect of Inventory Errors on This Period's Income Statement

Inventory Error	Cost of Goods Sold	Profit
Understate ending inventory	Overstated	Understated
Understate beginning inventory	Understated	Overstated
Overstate ending inventory	Understated	Overstated
Overstate beginning inventory	Overstated	Understated

> **Important Tip:**
>
> Notice that inventory errors yield opposite effects in cost of goods sold and profit.

Because an inventory error causes an offsetting error in the next period, it is sometimes said to be *self-correcting*. Do not think, however, that this makes inventory errors less serious. Managers, lenders, owners, and other users make important decisions on changes in profit and cost of goods sold. Imagine how a lender's decision would be affected by each of the graphs presented in Exhibit 6.14. Inventory errors must be avoided.

EXHIBIT 6.14

Graphing the Effects of Inventory Errors on Profit

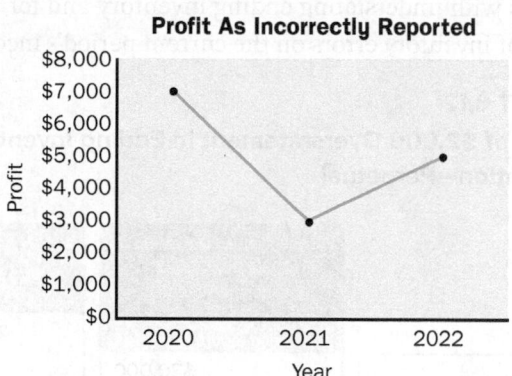

Balance Sheet Effects

Balance sheet effects of an inventory error are made evident by looking at the components of the accounting equation in Exhibit 6.15.

EXHIBIT 6.15

Accounting Equation

Assets = Liabilities + Equity

We can see, for example, that understating ending inventory will understate both current and total assets. An understatement of ending inventory also yields an understatement in equity because of the understatement of profit. We can do the same analysis with overstating ending inventory. Exhibit 6.16 shows the effects of inventory errors on the current period's balance sheet amounts.

EXHIBIT 6.16

Effects of Inventory Errors on This Period's Balance Sheet

Inventory Error	Assets	Equity
Understate ending inventory	Understated	Understated
Overstate ending inventory	Overstated	Overstated

Errors in beginning inventory do not yield misstatements in the balance sheet, but they do affect the end-of-period income statement, as the error results in a higher cost of goods sold and lower profit (illustrated in the year 2021 in Exhibit 6.12).

 CHECKPOINT

8. During 2021, a company discovered that the merchandise inventory reported on the 2020 balance sheet was overstated by $10,000. Did this error cause cost of goods sold to be overstated or understated in 2020? in 2021? By how much?

Do Quick Study question: QS 6-11

Estimating Inventory

This section describes methods to estimate inventory. Knowledge of these methods is important for preparers and users in understanding and analyzing financial information.

GROSS PROFIT METHOD

LO6 Apply both the gross profit and retail inventory methods to estimate inventory.

The **gross profit method** estimates the cost of ending inventory by applying the *gross profit ratio* to net sales (at *retail*). Recall from Chapter 5 that the **gross profit ratio** measures how much of each sales dollar is gross profit. A need for the gross profit estimate can arise when inventory is destroyed, lost, or stolen. These cases need an estimate of inventory so a company can file a claim with its insurer. Users also apply this method to see if inventory amounts from either management or a physical count are reasonable. This method uses the historical relationship between cost of goods sold and net sales to estimate the proportion of cost of goods sold making up current sales. This cost of goods sold estimate is then subtracted from cost of goods available for sale to give us an estimate of ending inventory at cost.

To illustrate, assume the following in March of 2020 when the company's inventory is destroyed by fire:

Sales	$31,500
Sales returns	1,500
Inventory, January 1, 2020	12,000
Net cost of goods purchased	20,500
Gross profit ratio	30%

EXHIBIT 6.17

Calculating Inventory Using the Gross Profit Method

In Step 1 we use income statement relationships to calculate the dollar value of the estimated cost of goods sold.
 	
In Step 2 we use our understanding of the cost of goods sold components as described earlier in Exhibit 6.11 to determine the estimated March inventory.
	Step 1:
	
	Sales $31,500
	  Less: Sales returns..... 1,500
	Net sales........................... $30,000
	  Less: COGS* **21,000**
	Gross profit from sales 30%
	                  or $9,000
		Step 2:
		
		Inventory, January 1, 2020............................ $ 12,000
		  Add: Net cost of goods purchased............. 20,500
		→ Less: COGS.. **21,000**
		
		Estimated March inventory $11,500

*If gross profit equals 30% of net sales or $9,000 (30% × $30,000), then COGS must equal 70% of net sales or $21,000 (70% × $30,000).

To estimate the inventory loss, we first need to recognize that each dollar of net sales is made up of gross profit and cost of goods sold. If this company's gross profit ratio is 30% as given, then 30% of each net sales dollar is gross profit and 70% is cost of goods sold. We show in Exhibit 6.17 how this 70% is used to estimate lost inventory.

For companies using a perpetual system, an important control policy includes having offsite data storage of its accounting records in the event of a fire or natural disaster, to ensure all company records are not destroyed. Some companies are moving to storage on the cloud through an Internet connection to a remote database managed by a third party. Offsite storage is helpful to access detailed inventory records, which would provide a more accurate picture of inventory balances at the point of the disaster than an estimation through the gross profit method. Companies using the periodic inventory system would have to rely on the gross profit method to estimate destroyed inventory.

Important Tip:

Quick Method to Estimate Ending Inventory Using the Gross Profit Method

Step 1: Calculate Cost of Goods Available for Sale: = Inventory + Purchases = 12,000 + 20,500 = 32,500

Step 2: Deduct Cost of Goods Sold: = Net Sales × COGS% = 30,000*(1 − 0.30) = 21,000 Difference = Estimated Ending Inventory = 32,500 − 21,000 = 11,500

RETAIL INVENTORY METHOD

Many companies prepare financial statements on a quarterly or monthly basis. The cost of goods sold information needed to prepare these interim financial reports is readily available if a perpetual inventory system is used. A periodic system, however, requires a physical inventory to determine cost of goods sold. To avoid the time-consuming and expensive process of taking a physical inventory each month or quarter, some companies use the **retail inventory method** to estimate cost of goods sold and ending inventory. Some companies even use the retail inventory method to prepare the annual statements since it is acceptable for income tax purposes. **TJX Companies Inc.** is the parent company for Winners, HomeSense, Marshalls, T.J. Maxx, HomeGoods, and online retailer Sierra Trading Post. They operate in Canada, the United States, and Europe. The group reports in its January 28, 2017, annual report:

TJX Companies Inc. January 28, 2017 Annual Report Excerpt

Significant Accounting Policies Note F/S Note

Merchandise Inventories:

Inventories are stated at the lower of cost or market. TJX uses the retail method for valuing inventories at all of its businesses, except Sierra Trading Post (STP), and Trade Secret. The businesses that utilize the retail method have some inventory that is initially valued at cost before the retail method is applied as it has not been fully processed for sale (e.g. inventory in transit and unprocessed inventory in our distribution centers). Under the retail method, TJX utilizes a permanent markdown strategy and lowers the cost value of the inventory that is subject to markdown at the time the retail prices are lowered in the stores. TJX accrues for inventory obligations at the time title transfers, which is typically at the time when inventory is shipped. As a result, merchandise inventories on TJX's balance sheet include an accrual for in-transit inventory of $641.9 million at January 28, 2017 and $690.3 million at January 30, 2016. Comparable amounts were reflected in accounts payable at those dates.

Calculating the Retail Inventory Estimate

When the retail inventory method is used to estimate inventory, we need to gather information on the following data points:

- Amount of inventory a company had at the beginning of the period in both *cost* and *retail* amounts. Retail amount of inventory refers to its dollar amount measured using selling prices of inventory items.

- Net amount of goods purchased (minus returns, allowances, and discounts) during the period, both at cost and at retail.

- Dollar value of net sales at retail

A three-step process is used to estimate ending inventory after we calculate the amount of goods available for sale during the period both at cost and at retail. This process is demonstrated in Exhibit 6.18.

EXHIBIT 6.18
Inventory Estimation Using Retail Inventory Method

The reasoning behind the retail inventory method is that if we can get a good estimate of the cost to retail ratio, then we can multiply ending inventory at retail by this ratio to estimate ending inventory at cost. Assume TJX Group of Companies has identified the following information in its information system. Exhibit 6.19 illustrates how TJX Group can apply these steps to estimate ending inventory.

EXHIBIT 6.19

Example Calculation of Ending Inventory Using the Retail Inventory Method at TJX Group of Companies

		At Cost	At Retail
	Goods available for sale:		
	Beginning inventory..	$20,500	$ 34,500
	Cost of goods purchased...	39,500	65,500
	Goods available for sale..	$60,000	$100,000
Step 1:	Less: Net sales at retail...		70,000
	Ending inventory at retail..		$ 30,000
Step 2:	Cost to retail ratio: ($60,000 ÷ $100,000).................		× 60%
Step 3:	Estimated ending inventory at cost.............................		$ 18,000

Estimating Physical Inventory at Cost

Items for sale by retailers like those in the TJX Group of Companies usually carry price tags listing selling prices. When a retailer takes a physical inventory, it commonly totals inventory using selling prices of items on hand. It then reduces the dollar total of this inventory to a cost basis by applying the cost to retail ratio. This is done because selling prices are readily available and using the cost to retail ratio eliminates the need to look up invoice prices of items on hand.

Let's assume that the TJX Group in Exhibit 6.19 estimates its inventory by the retail method and takes a physical inventory using selling prices. If the retail value of this physical inventory is $29,600, then we can calculate the cost of this inventory by applying its cost to retail ratio as follows: $29,600 × 60% = $17,760. The $17,760 cost figure for ending physical inventory is an acceptable number for annual financial statements. It is also acceptable to CRA for tax reporting.

Estimating Inventory Shortage at Cost

The inventory estimate in Exhibit 6.19 is an estimate of the amount of goods on hand (at cost). Since it is calculated by deducting sales from goods available for sale (at retail), it does not reveal any shrinkage due to breakage, loss, or theft. However, we can estimate the amount of shrinkage by comparing the inventory calculated in Exhibit 6.19 with the amount from taking a physical inventory. In Exhibit 6.19, for example, we estimated ending inventory at retail as $30,000, but a physical inventory revealed only $29,600 of inventory on hand (at retail). The company has an inventory shortage (at retail) of $400, calculated as $30,000 − $29,600. The inventory shortage (at cost) is $240, calculated as $400 × 60%. The following excerpt outlines how TJX Companies Inc. handles the issue of shrinkage.

TJX Companies Inc. January 28, 2017 Annual Report MD&A Excerpt

Management Discussion and Analysis: Critical Accounting Policies F/S Note

Inventory Valuation:

Inventory shrinkage requires estimating a shrinkage rate for interim periods, but we take a full physical inventory near the fiscal year-end to determine shrinkage at year-end.

CHECKPOINT

9. The following data pertain to a company's inventory during 2020:

	Cost	Retail
Beginning inventory	$324,000	$530,000
Cost of goods purchased	195,000	335,000
Net sales		320,000

Using the retail method, estimate the cost of ending inventory.

Do Quick Study questions: QS 6-12, QS 6-13, QS 6-14, QS 6-15

Financial Statement Analysis—Assess Inventory Management

LO7 Assess inventory management using both inventory turnover and days' sales in inventory.

INVENTORY TURNOVER AND DAYS' SALES IN INVENTORY

This section describes how we use information about inventory to assess a company's near-term liquidity and its management of inventory. Two measures useful for these assessments are defined and explained in this section.

Inventory Turnover

A company's ability to pay its near-term obligations depends, in part, on how quickly it sells its merchandise inventory. The **inventory turnover** is one ratio used to help analyze liquidity. It is also used to assess whether management is doing a good job of controlling the amount of inventory on hand. The inventory turnover is calculated as shown in Exhibit 6.20.

EXHIBIT 6.20
Inventory Turnover

$$\text{Inventory turnover} = \frac{\text{Cost of goods sold}}{\text{Average merchandise inventory}}$$

Average merchandise inventory is calculated by adding beginning and ending inventory and dividing the total by 2. If a company's sales vary within the year, it is often better to take an average of inventory amounts at the end of each quarter or month.

The inventory turnover ratio tells us how many *times* a company turns its inventory over during a period. For example, Exhibit 6.21 shows the merchandise turnover for Loblaw Companies Limited for its year ended December 31, 2017, in comparison to Lululemon Athletica Inc. for its year ended January 29, 2017.

As Exhibit 6.21 illustrates, Loblaws' turnover ratio suggests that the amount of inventory on hand is low and that it is sold more quickly than that of Lululemon. However, Loblaws sells foodstuffs, and is a different type of business than Lululemon. Loblaws is part of the grocery industry, where it is critical to move merchandise quickly because of its perishable nature. Lululemon is in an industry where merchandise turnovers of 4.40 times per year for specialty retailers are typical. Ratio comparisons such as the preceding must be based

EXHIBIT 6.21

Merchandise Turnovers Compared for Loblaw Companies Limited and Lululemon Athletica Inc.

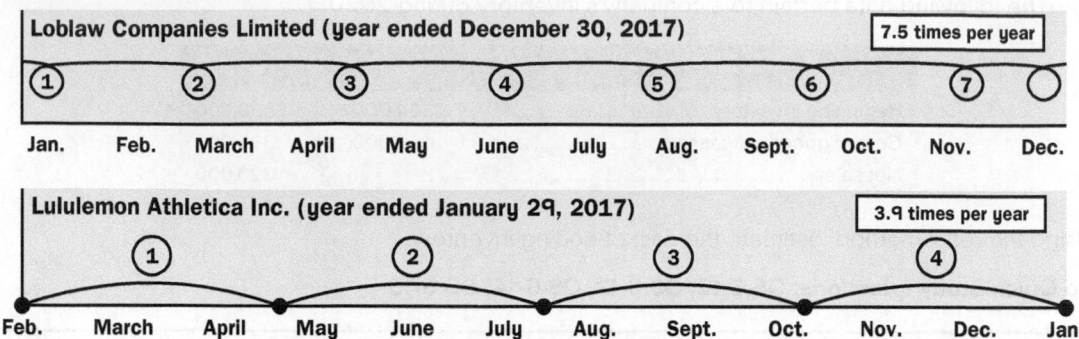

on companies that are similar in order to be meaningful. There is no simple rule with merchandise turnover, except to say that a high ratio is preferable provided inventory is adequate to meet demand. It is imperative to look at comparisons to previous years' results for a particular company and analyze results against companies in a similar industry in order to perform an effective financial statement analysis.

Days' Sales in Inventory

To better interpret merchandise turnover, many users want a measure to determine if inventory levels can meet sales demand. **Days' sales in inventory** is a ratio that estimates how many days it will take to convert inventory on hand into accounts receivable or cash. Days' sales in inventory is calculated as shown in Exhibit 6.22.

EXHIBIT 6.22

Days' Sales in Inventory

$$\text{Days' sales in inventory} = \frac{\text{Ending inventory}}{\text{Cost of goods sold}} \times 365$$

Notice the different focuses of days' sales in inventory and merchandise turnover. Days' sales in inventory focuses on ending inventory, whereas merchandise turnover focuses on average inventory. When looking at year-over-year comparatives for the same company or comparing results with a competitor company, a lower number of days in inventory is better.

 CHECKPOINT

10. Company A and Company B sell similar merchandise. Company A has a merchandise turnover of 4.8, while this same ratio is 5.2 for Company B. Which company is more efficient at selling its inventory?

Do Quick Study questions: QS 6-16, QS 6-17

CRITICAL THINKING CHALLENGE

Refer to the Critical Thinking Challenge questions at the beginning of the chapter. Compare your answers to those suggested on Connect.

IFRS AND ASPE—THE DIFFERENCES

Difference	International Financial Reporting Standards (IFRS)	Accounting Standards for Private Enterprises (ASPE)
There are no significant differences between IFRS and ASPE related to this chapter.		

A Look Ahead

Chapter 7 takes a look at internal control and cash with an introduction to the concept of internal controls, banking activities, accounting for petty cash funds, and reconciling the differences between cash reported in the bank account and cash in the company's accounting records.

SUMMARY

LO1 Identify the components and costs included in merchandise inventory. Merchandise inventory comprises goods owned by a company and held for resale. Goods in transit are reported in inventory of the company that holds ownership rights. Goods out on consignment are reported in inventory of the consignor; the consignee acts as an agent to sell the goods. Goods damaged or obsolete are reported in inventory at a conservative estimate of their net realizable value, calculated as sales price minus the selling costs. Costs of merchandise inventory include expenditures necessary, directly or indirectly, in bringing an item to a saleable condition and location (in other words, the invoice price minus any discount, plus any added or incidental costs necessary to put it in a place and condition for sale).

LO2 Calculate cost of goods sold and merchandise inventory using specific identification, moving weighted average, and FIFO—perpetual. Costs are assigned to the cost of goods sold account each time that a sale occurs in a perpetual system. Specific identification assigns cost by referring to the actual cost of the specific unit sold. Moving weighted average assigns a weighted average cost per unit calculated by taking the current balance in the merchandise inventory account and dividing it by the total items available for sale to determine the weighted average cost per unit. FIFO assigns cost assuming units purchased earliest are the first units sold.

LO3 Analyze the effects of the costing methods on financial reporting. When purchase prices are rising or falling, the inventory methods are likely to assign different cost amounts. Specific identification exactly matches costs and revenues. Moving weighted average smooths out price changes. FIFO assigns an amount to inventory closely approximating current replacement cost. The method(s) used must be disclosed in the notes to the financial statements and be consistent from period to period.

LO4 Calculate the lower of cost and net realizable value of inventory. Inventory is reported at net realizable value (NRV) when NRV is lower than cost. This is called the lower of cost and net realizable value (LCNRV) of inventory. LCNRV can be applied by item or by categories of similar or related items.

LO5 Analyze the effects of inventory errors on current and future financial statements—perpetual. An error in the amount of ending inventory affects assets (inventory), profit (cost of goods sold), and equity of that period. Since ending inventory is next period's beginning inventory, an error in ending inventory affects next period's cost of goods sold and profit. The financial statement effects of errors in one period are offset (reversed) in the next.

LO6 Apply both the gross profit and retail inventory methods to estimate inventory. The gross profit method involves two calculations: (1) net sales at retail multiplied by the gross profit ratio gives estimated cost of goods sold; and (2) goods available at cost minus estimated cost of goods sold gives estimated ending inventory at cost. The retail inventory method involves three calculations: (1) goods available at retail minus net sales at retail gives ending inventory at retail; (2) goods available at cost divided by goods available at retail gives the cost to retail ratio; and (3) ending inventory at retail is multiplied by the cost to retail ratio to give estimated ending inventory at cost.

LO7 Assess inventory management using both inventory turnover and days' sales in inventory. A high inventory turnover is preferred provided inventory is not out of stock and customers are not being turned away. We use days' sales in inventory to assess the likelihood of inventory being out of stock. Together, these ratios help us assess inventory management and evaluate a company's near-term liquidity.

Guidance Answer to DECISION MAKER

Inventory Manager—Ethical Dilemma

Your recommendation is a difficult one. Increased profits may attract investors but they will also increase your bonus. The question becomes one of motivation. That is, would the change really be better for the investors, or would the change take place only because your bonus would increase? This presents the classic conflict of interest. Another problem is that profits can be manipulated by changing accounting methods, and if this were the motivation the profession would frown on the change.

 Guidance Answers to CHECKPOINT

1. Best Buy.

2. Total cost is $12,180, calculated as: $11,400 + $130 + $150 + $100 + $400.

3. The matching principle.

4. Businesses that sell unique, high-dollar-value merchandise in relatively low volume levels might choose specific identification. Car dealerships are a good example because each car received as merchandise inventory is unique in terms of both features and identification number. Using specific identification allows the business to accurately tag each item coming in and going out.

5. Moving weighted average gives a lower inventory figure on the balance sheet as compared to FIFO. FIFO's inventory amount will approximate current replacement costs. Moving weighted average costs increase but more slowly because of the effect of averaging.

6. Because these units are the same ones that were originally written down, a reversal is appropriate and would be recorded as:

Merchandise Inventory...	2,000	
Cost of Goods Sold...		2,000
$1,800 − $1,300 = $500/unit original write-down:		
$500 × 4 = $2,000 maximum reversal		

7. The reported inventory amount is $540, calculated as (20 × $5) + (40 × $8) + (10 × $12).

8. Cost of goods sold is understated by $10,000 in 2020 and overstated by $10,000 in 2021.

9. The estimated ending inventory (at cost) is $327,000 and is calculated as:

Step 1: ($530,000 + $335,000) − $320,000 = $545,000

Step 2: $\dfrac{\$324,000 + \$195,000}{\$530,000 + \$335,000} = 60\%$

Step 3: $545,000 × 60% = $327,000

10. Company B is more efficient at selling its inventory because it has higher merchandise turnover.

Demonstration Problem

Part 1

Assume the accounting department at **Swatch**, the Swiss watch company, prepared the following schedule comparing the total cost and NRV of its December 31, 2020, ending inventory:

	Total Cost	Total NRV	LCNRV applied to: Products	Group*
Product A	$ 29,000	$ 28,000		
Product B	46,000	36,000		
Product C	17,000	17,000		
Product D	31,000	30,000		
Product E	3,000	7,000		
Totals	$126,000	$118,000		

*Assume that all products are similar.

Required

a. Calculate the merchandise inventory value that should appear on Swatch's December 31, 2020, balance sheet. Apply LCNRV to each product and to inventory as a group by completing the schedule provided.

b. Based on your calculations in part (a), prepare the appropriate adjusting entry at year-end assuming LCNRV is applied to inventory as a group.

Analysis Component:

Assuming the adjustment in part (b) is not recorded, identify the over- or understatement of profit, assets, and equity.

Part 2

Assume Swiss Company, a competitor to Swatch, had $435,000 of sales during each of three consecutive years, and it purchased merchandise costing $300,000 during each of the years. It also maintained a $105,000 inventory from the beginning to the end of the three-year period. However, $15,000 of merchandise inventory purchased FOB shipping point on December 31, 2020, was accidentally excluded from the December 31, 2020, inventory. This error caused the company's ending 2020 inventory to appear on the statements at $90,000 rather than at the correct $105,000.

Required

1. Calculate the actual amount of the company's gross profit in each of the years.

2. Prepare a comparative income statement like Exhibit 6.12 to show the effect of this error on the company's cost of goods sold and gross profit in 2020, 2021, and 2022.

SOLUTION

Part 1

a.

	Total Cost	Total NRV	LCNRV applied to: Products	Group*
Product A	$ 29,000	$ 28,000	$ 28,000	
Product B	46,000	36,000	36,000	
Product C	17,000	17,000	17,000	
Product D	31,000	30,000	30,000	
Product E	3,000	7,000	3,000	
Totals	$126,000	$118,000	$114,000	$118,000

*Assume that all products are similar.

b.

2020			
Dec. 31	Cost of Goods Sold..	8,000	
	Merchandise Inventory..		8,000
	To write inventory down to LCNRV.		

Analysis Component:

If the adjusting entry in part (b) is not recorded, profit would be overstated, assets would be overstated, and equity would also be overstated, each by $8,000.

Part 2

1. $435,000 − ($105,000 + $300,000 − $105,000) = $135,000

2.

For years ended December 31, 2020, 2021, 2022, the income statement information should have been reported as:	Income statement information actually reported for years ended December 31,		
	2020	2021	2022
Sales.................................... $435,000	$435,000	$435,000	$435,000
Cost of goods sold.......... 300,000	315,000	285,000	300,000
Gross profit from sales..... $135,000	$120,000	$150,000	$135,000

Merchandise Inventory				Merchandise Inventory				Merchandise Inventory			
Jan. 1/20	105,000			Jan. 1/21	90,000			Jan. 1/22	105,000		
Purchases	300,000	315,000	COGS	Purchases	300,000	285,000	COGS	Purchases	300,000	300,000	COGS
Dec. 31/20	90,000			Dec. 31/21	105,000			Dec. 31/22	105,000		

Assigning Costs to Inventory and Inventory Errors—Periodic System

LO8 Calculate cost of goods sold and merchandise inventory using FIFO—periodic, weighted average, and specific identification.

The aim of the periodic system is the same as the perpetual system: to assign costs to the inventory and the goods sold. The same three methods are used in assigning costs: first-in, first-out; weighted average; and specific identification. We use information from LEC to describe how we assign costs using these three methods with a periodic system. Data for sales and purchases are reported in the chapter in Exhibits 6.2 and 6.3 and are not repeated here.

First-In, First-Out

The first-in, first-out (FIFO) method of assigning cost to inventory and goods sold using the periodic system is shown in Exhibit 6A.1.

EXHIBIT 6A.1
FIFO Calculations—Periodic

Total cost of 45 units available for sale..	$4,800
Less: Ending inventory priced using FIFO:	
11 units from August 17 purchase at $115 each	1,265
Cost of goods sold	$3,535

LEC's ending inventory reported on the balance sheet is $1,265 and its cost of goods sold reported on the income statement is $3,535. The assignment of costs to cost of goods sold and inventory using FIFO is the same for both the perpetual and periodic systems, as summarized in Exhibit 6A.4. This will always occur because the most recent purchases are in ending inventory under both systems.

Weighted Average

The **weighted average** inventory costing method involves three important steps, as illustrated in Exhibits 6A.2 and 6A.3. First, we multiply the unit cost for beginning inventory and each particular purchase by their corresponding number of units. Second, we add these amounts and divide by the total number of units available for sale to find the *weighted average cost per unit*.

EXHIBIT 6A.2

Weighted Average Cost per Unit—Periodic

Step 1:						
Aug. 1	Beginning inventory	10 units	@	$ 91	=	$ 910
3	Purchased	15 units	@	106	=	1,590
17	Purchased	20 units	@	115	=	2,300
		45 units available for sale				$4,800 Total cost of goods available for sale

Step 2: $4,800/45 = $106.67 weighted average cost per unit

The third step is to use the weighted average cost per unit to assign costs to inventory and to units sold:

EXHIBIT 6A.3

Weighted Average Calculations—Periodic

Step 3:

Total cost of 45 units available for sale..	$4,800
Less: Ending inventory priced on a weighted average cost basis:	
11 units at $106.67 each	1,173*
Cost of goods sold (= 34 units × $106.67)..	$3,627*

45 units available for sale − 11 units in ending inventory = 34 units sold during the period

*Rounded to nearest whole dollar.

The assignment of costs to cost of goods sold and inventory using weighted average usually gives different results depending on whether a perpetual or periodic system is used, as shown in Exhibit 6A.4. This is because weighted average under a perpetual system recalculates the unit cost at the time of each item purchased. The periodic inventory system determines an average cost at the end of the period based on all items that were available for sale during the year and applies the cost to the number of items counted in ending inventory.

> **Important Tip:**
>
> Note that under the periodic inventory method, we do not recalculate the unit cost each time an item is purchased. Average cost is determined at the end of the period and is applied to the number of units in ending inventory (based on the year-end inventory count) and cost of goods sold.

EXHIBIT 6A.4

Comparison of Inventory Methods—Periodic and Perpetual

	FIFO		Weighted Average		Specific Identification	
	Perpetual	Periodic	Perpetual	Periodic*	Perpetual	Periodic
COGS...	$3,535	$3,535	$3,568	$3,627	$3,562	$3,562
Ending Inventory.....................................	1,265	1,265	1,232	1,173	1,238	1,238
Cost of Goods Available for Sale........	$4,800	$4,800	$4,800	$4,800	$4,800	$4,800

*Rounded to the nearest whole dollar for simplicity

Specific Identification

The amounts of cost assigned to inventory and cost of goods sold are the same under the perpetual and periodic systems, as detailed in Exhibit 6A.4. This is because specific identification precisely defines which units are in inventory and which are sold.

Exhibit 6A.4 compares the inventory methods for both the periodic and perpetual systems.

Exhibit 6A.4 shows that the figures for specific identification and FIFO are identical under periodic and perpetual systems. However, the figures for weighted average will differ between the perpetual and periodic systems, as explained above.

 CHECKPOINT

11. A company uses a periodic inventory system and reports the following beginning inventory and purchases (and ends the period with 30 units on hand):

	Units	Cost Per Unit
Beginning Inventory	100	$10
Purchases #1	40	12
#2	20	14

    a. Calculate ending inventory using FIFO

    b. Calculate cost of goods sold using weighted average.

Do Quick Study question: *QS 6-18

ERRORS IN REPORTING INVENTORY

LO9 Analyze the effects of inventory errors on current and future financial statements—periodic.

Exhibits 6.11 and 6.12 were based on a perpetual inventory system. Those exhibits are reflected below under the assumption of a periodic inventory system.

Income Statement Effects of Inventory Errors

The income statement effects of an inventory error are evident when looking at the components of cost of goods sold in Exhibit 6A.5.

EXHIBIT 6A.5

Cost of Goods Sold Components—Periodic

The effect of an inventory error on cost of goods sold is determined by calculating the inventory correctly and comparing it to the result of the calculation when using the incorrect amount, as in Exhibit 6A.6.

EXHIBIT 6A.6

Effects of $2,000 Overstatement in Ending Inventory for 2020 on Three Periods' Income Statement Information—Periodic

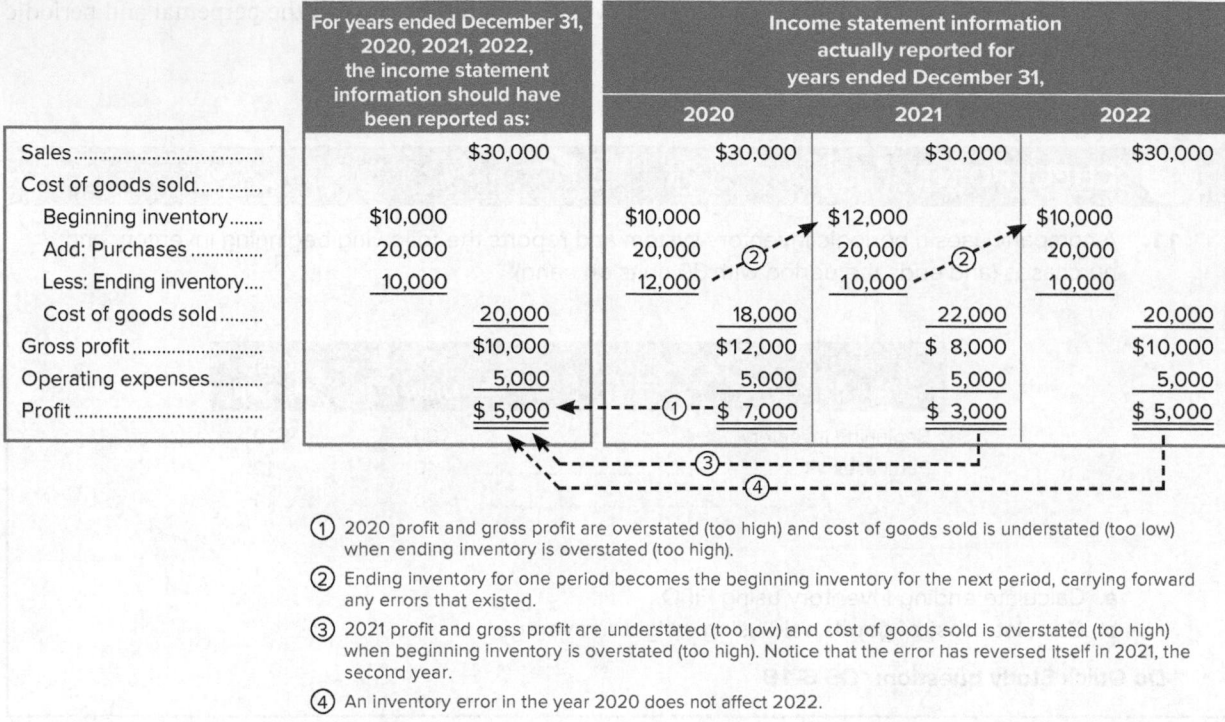

	For years ended December 31, 2020, 2021, 2022, the income statement information should have been reported as:	Income statement information actually reported for years ended December 31,		
		2020	2021	2022
Sales......................................	$30,000	$30,000	$30,000	$30,000
Cost of goods sold..............				
Beginning inventory.......	$10,000	$10,000	$12,000	$10,000
Add: Purchases..............	20,000	20,000	20,000	20,000
Less: Ending inventory....	10,000	12,000	10,000	10,000
Cost of goods sold.........	20,000	18,000	22,000	20,000
Gross profit..........................	$10,000	$12,000	$ 8,000	$10,000
Operating expenses...........	5,000	5,000	5,000	5,000
Profit...................................	$ 5,000	$ 7,000	$ 3,000	$ 5,000

① 2020 profit and gross profit are overstated (too high) and cost of goods sold is understated (too low) when ending inventory is overstated (too high).

② Ending inventory for one period becomes the beginning inventory for the next period, carrying forward any errors that existed.

③ 2021 profit and gross profit are understated (too low) and cost of goods sold is overstated (too high) when beginning inventory is overstated (too high). Notice that the error has reversed itself in 2021, the second year.

④ An inventory error in the year 2020 does not affect 2022.

Exhibit 6A.6 assumes that $2,000 of merchandise sold but awaiting delivery was incorrectly included in ending inventory on December 31, 2020.

Demonstration Problem

Abercrombie Company uses a periodic inventory system and had the following beginning inventory and purchases during January 2020:

		Units		Cost per Unit		Total Cost
Jan. 1	Beginning inventory...................	300	@	$14	=	$ 4,200
16	Purchased.....................................	200	@	15	=	3,000
20	Purchased.....................................	300	@	16	=	4,800
Total goods available for sale........................		800				$12,000

Sales of units were as follows:

Jan. 15	200	units at $30
28	460	units at $35
Total units sold	660	

Additional data for use in applying the specific identification method:
    The specific units sold were:

Jan.	15	200 units from the January 1 units on hand
	28	5 units from the January 1 units on hand
		150 units from the January 16 purchase, and
		235 units from the January 20 purchase

Required

Using the preceding information, calculate the ending inventory and the cost of goods sold for Abercrombie Company under a periodic inventory system by applying each of the three different methods of inventory costing:

a. FIFO

b. Weighted average, and

c. Specific identification

Planning the Solution

• Prepare a periodic FIFO schedule similar to Exhibit 6A.1 (recall that although the calculations differ, the results are the same under each of the periodic and perpetual systems for FIFO).

• Prepare a periodic weighted average schedule similar to Exhibits 6A.2 and 6A.3.

• Prepare a specific identification schedule similar to Exhibit 6.6 (recall that specific identification is calculated in the same manner under each of the perpetual and periodic systems for specific identification).

SOLUTION

a. FIFO

Cost of goods available for sale	$12,000
Less: Ending inventory of 140 units:	
140 @ $16 =	2,240
Equals: Cost of goods sold	$ 9,760

b. Weighted Average

Cost of goods available for sale	$12,000
Less: Ending inventory of 140 units:	
140 × $15 avg. cost/unit*	2,100
Equals: Cost of goods sold	$ 9,900
*$12,000 ÷ 800 units = $15/unit avg. cost	

c. Specific Identification

Cost of goods available for sale..	$12,000
Less: Ending inventory of 140 units:	
25 @ $14 = $ 350	
50 @ $15 = 750	
65 @ $16 = 1,040......................................	2,140
Equals: Cost of goods sold..	$ 9,860

SUMMARY OF APPENDIX 6A

LO8 **Calculate cost of goods sold and merchandise inventory using FIFO—periodic, weighted average, and specific identification.** Periodic systems allocate the cost of goods available for sale between cost of goods sold and ending inventory *at the end of a period*. Specific identification and FIFO give identical results whether the periodic or perpetual system is used. Weighted average cost calculates cost per unit by taking the total cost of both beginning inventory and net purchases and dividing by the total number of units available. It then multiplies

cost per unit by the number of units sold to give cost of goods sold.

LO9 **Analyze the effects of inventory errors on current and future financial statements—periodic.** An error in the amount of ending inventory affects assets (inventory), profit (cost of goods sold), and equity of that period. Since ending inventory is next period's beginning inventory, an error in ending inventory affects next period's cost of goods sold and profit. The financial statement effects of errors in one period are offset (reversed) in the next.

Guidance Answer to CHECKPOINT

11. **a.** Ending inventory = (20 × $14) + (10 × $12) = $400

    b. Cost of goods sold

    = [(100 × $10) + (40 × $12) + (20 × $14)]/160 × 30

    = $11 × 30

    = $330

GLOSSARY

Consignee One who receives and holds goods owned by another party for the purpose of acting as an agent and selling the goods for the owner. The consignee gets paid a fee from the consignor for finding a buyer.

Consignor An owner of inventory goods who ships them to another party who will then find a buyer and sell the goods for the owner. The consignor retains title to the goods while they are held offsite by the consignee.

Consistency principle The accounting requirement that a company use the same accounting policies period after

period so that the financial statements of succeeding periods will be comparable.

Days' sales in inventory A financial analysis tool used to estimate how many days it will take to convert the inventory on hand into accounts receivable or cash; calculated by dividing the ending inventory by cost of goods sold and multiplying the result by 365.

Faithful representation The accounting principle that requires information to be complete, neutral, unbiased, and free from error.

First-in, first-out (FIFO) The pricing of an inventory under the assumption that inventory items are sold in the order acquired; the first items received are the first items sold.

Gross profit method An estimate used for determining ending inventory in the event inventory is destroyed. The company's determined gross profit rate is used to estimate cost of goods sold, which is then subtracted from the cost of goods available for sale to determine the estimated ending inventory.

Gross profit ratio Measures how much of net sales is gross profit (net sales-cost of goods sold); calculated as gross profit divided by net sales; also known as the *gross margin ratio*.

Internal controls The policies and procedures used to protect assets, ensure reliable accounting, promote efficient operations, and urge adherence to company policies.

Inventory turnover A financial statement analysis tool used to determine the number of times a company's average inventory was sold during an accounting period, calculated by dividing cost of goods sold by the average merchandise inventory balance; also called *inventory turnover*.

Lower of cost and net realizable value (LCNRV) The required method of reporting merchandise inventory in the balance sheet where net realizable value is reported when net realizable value is lower than cost. This rule ensures inventory is not recorded at a higher value on the balance sheet than what the company can sell the item for.

Materiality principle This GAAP states that an amount may be ignored if its effect on the financial statements is not important to their users. Financial statement preparers need to assess whether the item would impact the decision of a user.

Moving weighted average A perpetual inventory pricing system in which the unit cost in inventory is recalculated at the time of each purchase by dividing the total cost of goods available for sale at that point in time by the corresponding total units available for sale. The most current moving weighted average cost per unit is multiplied by the units sold to determine cost of goods sold.

Net realizable value (NRV) The expected sales price of an item minus the cost of making the sale.

Physical inventory count To count merchandise inventory for the purpose of reconciling goods actually on hand to the inventory control account in the general ledger; also called *taking an inventory*.

Retail price The selling price of merchandise inventory.

Retail inventory method A method used by retailers to estimate an ending inventory cost based on the ratio of the amount of goods for sale at cost to the amount of goods for sale at marked selling prices.

Specific identification The pricing of an inventory where the purchase invoice of each item in the ending inventory is identified and used to determine the cost assigned to the inventory.

Weighted average A periodic inventory pricing system in which the total cost of goods available for sale is divided by the total units available for sale. The resulting weighted average unit cost is multiplied by the units in ending inventory and then by the units that were sold.

KNOWLEDGE CHECK-UP

1. The following items should be included in merchandise inventory:
   a. Goods in transit with sales terms FOB destination
   b. Additional costs necessary to put inventory in a place and condition for sale
   c. Goods held by a consignee
   d. All of the above.

2. Under both a perpetual and a periodic inventory system goods must be counted at the end of the accounting period for the following reason:
   a. Items that are damaged or obsolete can be identified through the count
   b. Merchandise inventory can be adjusted to reflect the actual inventory on hand at the end of the accounting period
   c. Lost or stolen items can be removed from the balance of inventory
   d. All of the above.

3. Costing methods are an important accounting policy choice for the following reasons:
   a. Once selected, companies must restate financial statements if they decide to change their accounting policy.
   b. The costing method used in a period of changing unit costs will impact ending inventory balances and cost of goods sold.
   c. In a period of rising prices, FIFO has a higher per unit cost held in ending inventory.
   d. All of the above.

4. Under the first-in, first-out inventory costing method:
   a. Inventory items are assumed to be sold in the order they are acquired.
   b. Inventory items are assumed to be purchased in the order they are acquired.
   c. Items in ending inventory do not reflect the most recent purchases.
   d. Average cost per unit is calculated after each sale of goods.

5. Under the moving weighted average costing method:

    a. Costs are assigned to inventory as goods are sold.

    b. Average cost per unit is calculated by dividing total cost of goods available by units on hand and is updated at the time of each purchase.

    c. Average cost is calculated at the end of the reporting period.

    d. None of the above.

6. Which of the following is an example of an inventory item that would best suit the specific identification inventory method:

    a. Pile of bird's-eye gravel at the local gravel pit

    b. Cartons of specialty ice cream produced by a local high-end food manufacturer

    c. Custom-made guitars with unique features produced for established musicians

    d. Individual 2×4 pine wood boards at the local lumber yard

7. Which accounting principle requires that a company use the same accounting methods period after period?

    a. Revenue recognition principle

    b. Lower of cost and net realizable value principle

    c. Business entity principle

    d. Consistency principle

8. The lower of cost and net realizable value principle involves:

    a. Recording the revenue on sale of merchandise inventory at the market price of an inventory item

    b. Writing inventory down to the lower amount of the inventory cost and the amount expected to be received upon sale of the goods

    c. Writing inventory up to the higher of inventory cost and the current market price

    d. None of the above.

9. If inventory is understated at the end of the accounting period, the effect will be which of the following:

    a. Cost of goods sold will be overstated and profit will be understated

    b. Cost of goods sold will be understated and profit will be overstated

    c. Cost of goods sold will be overstated and profit will be overstated

    d. Cost of goods sold will be understated and profit will be understated

10. Marshall Inc. has $500,000 in cost of goods sold and an average inventory balance of $210,000 for fiscal 2020. Inventory turnover for 2020 is:

    a. 1.50 times per year

    b. 0.42 times per year

    c. 2.20 times per year

    d. 2.38 times per year

CONCEPT REVIEW QUESTIONS

1. Caps Co., a store that sells baseball hats, received a shipment of inventory. The purchase price of inventory is $2,000, a bulk discount of 40% off was received, the shipping charges were $200, and the import duties were $140. What is the total cost of inventory?

2. Give the meanings of the following when applied to inventory: (a) FIFO, and (b) cost.

3. If prices are falling, will the moving weighted average or the FIFO method of inventory valuation result in the lower cost of goods sold?

4. Where is merchandise inventory disclosed in the financial statements?

5. May a company change its inventory pricing method each accounting period?

6. Does the accounting principle of consistency disallow any changes from one accounting method to another?

7. What effect does the full disclosure principle have if a company changes from one acceptable accounting method to another?

8. What guidance for accountants is provided by faithful representation?

9. What is the usual meaning of NRV as it is used in determining the LCNRV for merchandise inventory?

10. What is meant when it is said that inventory errors correct themselves?

11. If inventory errors correct themselves, why be concerned when such errors are made?

12. Refer to **WestJet**'s financial statements in Appendix III. On December 31, 2017, what percentage of WestJet's assets was represented by what would be WestJet's inventory? Is this merchandise inventory?

13. Refer to **Spin Master**'s financial statements in Appendix III. What costs are included in inventory value? In what part of the Notes to Financial Statements did you find the answer?

QUICK STUDY

QS 6-1 Inventory ownership LO1

1. At year-end Carefree Company has shipped, FOB destination, $500 of merchandise that is still in transit to Stark Company. Which company should include the $500 as part of inventory at year-end?

2. Carefree Company has shipped goods to Stark and has an arrangement that Stark will sell the goods for Carefree. Identify the consignor and the consignee. Which company should include any unsold goods as part of inventory?

QS 6-2 Inventory ownership LO1

Say It Loud Cards, a distributor of fun and witty cards, operates out of owner Scott Arlen's home. At the end of the accounting period, Arlen has 1,500 units of products in his basement, 30 of which were damaged by water leaks and cannot be sold. He also has another 250 units in his van, ready to deliver to fill a customer order, terms FOB destination, and another 70 units out on consignment to a friend who owns a stationery store. How many units should be included in the end-of-period inventory?

QS 6-3 Inventory costs LO1

A car dealer acquires a used car for $3,000. Additional costs in obtaining and offering the car for sale include $150 for transportation-in, $200 for import duties, $50 for insurance during shipment, $25 for advertising, and $250 for sales staff salaries. For calculating inventory, what cost is assigned to the used car acquired?

QS 6-4 Inventory costs LO1

The owner of 555 Antiques, an antiques dealer, purchased an estate including a rare collection of superhero comic books for a bid price of $37,500. The terms of the purchase were FOB shipping point, and the cost of transporting the goods to the 555 Antiques warehouse was $1,200. 555 Antiques insured the shipment at a cost of $150. Prior to placing the goods in the store, they cleaned and refurbished some merchandise at a cost of $490 for labour and parts. Determine the cost of the inventory acquired in the purchase of the estate's contents.

QS 6-5 Calculating cost of goods available for sale LO2

A company has beginning inventory of 10 units at $50. Every week for four weeks an additional 10 units are purchased at respective costs of $51, $52, $55, and $60. Thirty-eight units were sold for $72 each. Calculate the total cost of goods that were available for sale and the total units that were available for sale.

QS 6-6 Inventory costing methods—perpetual LO2

A company had the following beginning inventory and purchases during January for a particular item. On January 28, 345 units were sold. What is the cost of the 140 units that remain in the ending inventory, assuming the following?

a. FIFO

b. Moving weighted average

Round numbers to the nearest cent. Assume a perpetual inventory system.

	Units	Unit Cost	Total Cost
Beginning inventory on January 1	310	$3.00	$ 930.00
Purchase on January 9	75	3.20	240.00
Purchase on January 25	100	3.35	335.00
Total available for sale	485		$1,505.00

QS 6-7 Specific identification inventory method LO2

Refer to the information in QS 6-6. Recall that 345 units were sold on January 28. The units specifically sold were:

- 250 units from beginning inventory
- 50 units from the January 9 purchase
- 45 units from the purchase on January 25

Calculate cost of goods sold and the cost of ending inventory.

QS 6-8 Inventory costing methods—perpetual LO2

Bishr Company uses the moving weighted average method for inventory costing. You are to complete the following inventory sheet regarding Product XJ23789 (round calculations to two decimal places):

Date		Purchases/Transportation-In/ (Purchase Returns/Discounts)			Cost of Goods Sold/ (Returns to Inventory)			Balance in Inventory		
		Units	Cost/Unit	Total $	Units	Cost/Unit	Total $	Units	Avg Cost/Unit	Total $
Jan.	1		Brought Forward					10	$15.00	$150.00
	3				6					
	7	25	$18.50	$462.50						
	8			50.00						
	17			(46.25)						
	18				14					

Note: January 8 reflects transportation costs regarding the January 7 purchase. The $46.25 on January 17 represents the discount taken regarding payment of the January 7 purchase within the discount period.

QS 6-9 Contrasting inventory costing methods LO3

Identify the inventory costing method most closely related to each of the following statements, assuming a period when the cost per unit is increasing:

a. Current cost of inventory not reflected on income statement

b. Results in a balance sheet inventory closest to replacement costs

c. Is best when each unit of product has unique features that affect cost

QS 6-10 Applying LCNRV to inventories LO4

Thrifty Trading Co. has the following products in its ending inventory at December 31, 2020:

Product	Quantity	Per Unit Cost	Per Unit NRV
Aprons	9	$6.00	$5.50
Bottles	12	3.50	4.25
Candles	25	8.00	7.00

a. Calculate LCNRV for the inventory as a whole, if applicable.

b. Calculate LCNRV applied separately to each product.

c. Prepare the appropriate adjusting entry, if any, assuming your calculations in (b).

QS 6-11 Inventory errors LO5, 9

The Weston Company performed a physical inventory count at the end of 2020. It was later determined that certain units were counted twice. Explain how this error affects the following:

a. 2020 cost of goods sold

b. 2020 gross profit

c. 2020 profit

d. 2021 profit

e. The combined two-year income

f. Income in years after 2021

QS 6-12 Estimating inventories—gross profit method LO6

The inventory of Sixth Avenue Department Store was destroyed by a fire on September 10, 2020. The following 2020 data were found in the accounting records:

Jan. 1 inventory	$180,000
Jan. 1–Sept. 10 purchases (net)	$342,000
Jan. 1–Sept.10 sales	$675,000
2020 estimated gross profit rate	42%

Estimate the cost of the inventory destroyed in the fire using the gross profit method.

QS 6-13 Estimating inventories—gross profit method LO6

During the past two months, management of Wallace Lake Computing Supplies was closely watching inventory levels due to suspected shrinkage caused by unknown factors. The physical count on July 31, the end of the current month, shows $48,000 of merchandise actually on hand. The accounting records for prior periods indicate that gross profit should be 30% of the $565,000 net sales for July. Inventory at June 30 was actually $65,000 and July purchases were $385,500. Calculate the estimated:

a. Ending inventory

b. Shrinkage

QS 6-14 Estimating ending inventory—retail method LO6

Best Stereo Centre showed the following selected information on August 31, 2020:

	Cost	Retail
Cost of goods available for sale	$67,600	$104,000
Net sales		82,000

Using the retail method, estimate the cost of the ending inventory.

QS 6-15 Estimating ending inventory—retail method LO6

Complete the following schedule by using the retail method to estimate ending inventory for September and October.

		September		October	
	Cost	Retail	Cost	Retail
Beginning inventory...	$ 74,950	$112,000		
Cost of goods purchased	395,000	611,000	461,590	674,000
Goods available for sale...............................				
Less: Net sales at retail..................................		614,000		700,000
Ending inventory at retail............................				
Cost to retail ratio..				
Estimated ending inventory				

QS 6-16 Inventory turnover LO7

Huff Company and Puff Company are similar firms that operate within the same industry. The following information is available.

	Huff			Puff		
	2020	2019	2018	2020	2019	2018
Inventory turnover	23.2	20.9	16.1	13.5	12.0	11.6

Required Based on the information provided, which company is managing inventory more efficiently? Explain.

QS 6-17 Inventory turnover and days' sales in inventory LO7

Mixon Company showed the following selected information for the years ended December 31, 2020, 2019, and 2018:

	2020	2019	2018
Cost of goods sold..	$410,225	$344,500	$312,600
Merchandise inventory (December 31)................	56,195	82,500	111,500

For the years ended 2020 and 2019, calculate:

a. Days' sales in inventory

b. Inventory turnover

Indicate if the change in the ratio from 2019 to 2020 is generally considered to be favourable (good) or unfavourable (not good). Round calculations to two decimal places.

*QS 6-18 Inventory costing methods—periodic LO8

Refer to the information in QS 6-6. Determine the cost of the 140 units that remain in ending inventory, assuming:

a. FIFO

b. Weighted average

Round numbers to the nearest cent and use a periodic inventory system.

An asterisk (*) identifies assignment material based on Appendix 6A.

EXERCISES

Exercise 6-1 **Inventory ownership** LO1

You are in charge of the year-end inventory count for OMG Luggage's December 31, 2020 year-end. OMG Luggage is known for its crazy luggage colours and designs. Assume the company uses a perpetual inventory system. Determine whether to include or exclude the following items and explain why. If OMG Luggage should include the inventory, determine the correct inventory cost.

a. On December 25, 2020, OMG Luggage purchased neon green luggage, FOB shipping from Baggage Co. The order had a purchase price of $2,500, shipping charges of $400, import duties of $300, and shipping insurance of $133. The products have not yet arrived at OMG Luggage, but Baggage Co. confirmed that the company shipped the order on December 27, 2020.

b. On December 31, 2020, OMG Luggage shipped leopard print luggage to a customer for a retail price of $777. This luggage had a cost of $500 and was shipped FOB destination. The shipping charges of $55 were paid by the appropriate party. Assume the products are delivered to the customer in the first week of January.

c. During the year, OMG luggage shipped inventory with a cost of $5,000 to a retailer on consignment. On December 31, 2020, the consignment store had sold $3,000 of the inventory and had paid OMG Luggage for the inventory sold.

d. On December 30, 2020, OMG Luggage sold yellow luggage to a customer with a price of $2,222 and a cost of $1,111. The customer paid for the luggage and arranged to pick up the inventory in person on January 4, 2021. As the inventory was still at the warehouse on December 31, 2020, the staff included this inventory in the final inventory listing.

Exercise 6-2 **Alternative cost flow assumptions—perpetual** LO2 e**X**cel

CHECK FIGURES: COGS a. $9,400.00; b. $9,417.90

Urban Glam Cosmetics made purchases of lipstick in the current year as follows:

Jan. 1	Beginning inventory	75 units	@	$12.00	=	$ 900
Mar. 14	Purchased	250 units	@	$13.00	=	3,250
July 30	Purchased	500 units	@	$14.00	=	7,000
	Units available for sale	825 units				
	Cost of goods available for sale					$11,150

Urban Glam Cosmetics made sales on the following dates at a selling price of $35 per unit:

Jan. 10	70 units
Mar. 15	180 units
Oct. 5	450 units
Total	700 units

Required The business uses a perpetual inventory system. Determine the costs that should be assigned to the ending inventory and to goods sold under:

a. FIFO

b. Moving weighted average (round to the nearest whole cent)

Also calculate the gross profit under each method.

Exercise 6-3 Specific identification cost flow assumption LO2 eXcel

CHECK FIGURES: COGS = $9,427; Gross profit = $15,073

Refer to the data in Exercise 6-2. Assume that Urban Glam Cosmetics uses the specific identification method to cost inventory. The 700 units were specifically sold as follows:

Jan. 10:	70	units from beginning inventory
Mar. 15:	3	units from beginning inventory, and
	177	units from the March 14 purchase
Oct. 5:	50	units from the March 14 purchase, and
	400	units from the July 30 purchase

Calculate cost of goods sold and the gross profit.

Exercise 6-4 Alternative cost flow assumptions—perpetual inventory system LO2 eXcel

Sport Box sells a wide variety of sporting equipment. The following is information on the purchases and sales of their top selling hockey stick. The hockey stick sells for $125.

	Description	Units	Unit Cost
Mar. 1	Beginning Inventory	15	$40
Mar. 3	Purchase	60	$45
Mar. 6	Purchase	110	$50
Mar. 17	Sale	55	
Mar. 23	Purchase	50	$50
Mar. 31	Sale	140	

Required Calculate the cost of goods sold and ending inventory under the perpetual inventory system using

a. FIFO

b. Moving weighted average. (Do not round your "Unit Cost" answers. Round all other intermediate and final answers to nearest whole dollar.)

Exercise 6-5 Alternative cost flow assumptions—perpetual inventory system LO2 eXcel

CHECK FIGURES: 3. COGS a. $5,527 b. $5,476

Car Armour sells car wash cleaners. Car Armour uses a perpetual inventory system and made purchases and sales of a particular product in 2020 as follows:

Jan.	1	Beginning inventory	110 units	@	$7.00	=	$	770
Jan.	10	Sold	80 units	@	$15.50	=		1,240
Mar.	7	Purchased	300 units	@	$6.30	=		1,890
Mar.	15	Sold	130 units	@	$15.50	=		2,015
July	28	Purchased	550 units	@	$6.10	=		3,355
Oct.	3	Purchased	500 units	@	$6.00	=		3,000
Oct.	5	Sold	670 units	@	$15.50	=		10,385

Required

1. Calculate the total goods available for sale (in units and cost).

2. Calculate the number of units sold and units remaining in ending inventory.

3. Determine the share of the cost of goods available for sale calculated in Part 1 that should be assigned to ending inventory and to goods sold under:

   a. FIFO

   b. Moving weighted average

Exercise 6-6 Specific identification cost flow assumption LO2 e**X**cel

CHECK FIGURE: COGS = $4,529.50

Use the information in Exercise 6-5. Assume that Car Armour specifically sold the following units:

Jan. 10:	80	units from beginning inventory
Mar. 15:	10	units from beginning inventory, and
	120	units from the March 7 purchase
Oct. 5:	200	units from the July 28 purchase, and
	470	units from the October 3 purchase

Calculate cost to be assigned to ending inventory and cost of goods sold.

Exercise 6-7 Income statement effects of alternative cost flow assumptions LO3

Use the data in Exercises 6-5 and 6-6 to construct comparative income statements for Car Armour (year-end December 31, 2020), similar to those shown in Exhibit 6.8 in the chapter. Assume that operating expenses are $1,250.

1. Which method results in the highest profit?

2. If costs were rising instead of falling, which method would result in the highest profit?

Exercise 6-8 Alternative cost flow assumptions—perpetual inventory system LO2 e**X**cel

CHECK FIGURES: 3. COGS a. $11,388 b. $11,484

Head Smart sells bicycle helmets for $130 in a large mall. Head Smart uses a perpetual inventory system and made purchases and sales in July as follows:

July 1	Beginning inventory		21 units	@	$46
July 3	Purchase		66 units	@	$51
July 6	Purchase		116 units	@	$56
July 17	Sale		61 units		
July 23	Purchase		62 units	@	$56
July 31	Sale		152 units		

Required

1. Calculate the total goods available for sale (in units and cost).

2. Calculate the number of units sold and units remaining in ending inventory.

3. Determine the share of the cost of goods available for sale calculated in Part 1 that should be assigned to ending inventory and to goods sold under:

   a. FIFO

   b. Moving weighted average

Exercise 6-9 Moving weighted average cost flow assumption—perpetual LO2, 3

Telamark Company uses the moving weighted average method for inventory costing. The following incomplete inventory sheet regarding Product W506 is available for the month of March 2020:

Date		Units	Cost/Unit	Total $	Units	Cost/Unit	Total $	Units	Avg Cost/Unit	Total $
		Purchases/Transportation-In/ (Purchase Returns/Discounts)			Cost of Goods Sold/ (Returns to Inventory)			Balance in Inventory		
Mar.	1		Brought Forward					60	$94.00	$5,640.00
	2	35	$96.00							
	3				22					
	4				(2)					
	7				65					
	17	40	97.00							
	28				43					

Note: March 4 reflects a return made by a customer of incorrect items shipped on March 3; these items were returned to inventory.

Required Complete the inventory sheet. Round all calculations to two decimal places.

Analysis Component: The gross profit realized on the sale of Product W506 during February 2020 was 36.16%. The selling price was $148 during both February and March. Calculate the gross profit ratio for Product W506 for March 2020 and determine whether the change is favourable or unfavourable from February. Identify the most probable cause of the change.

Exercise 6-10 Lower of cost and net realizable value LO4

CHECK FIGURES: a. $16,171; b. $15,527

Showtime Company's ending inventory at December 31, 2020, includes the following items:

Product	Units on Hand	Unit Cost	Net Realizable Value per Unit
BB	27	$115	$120
FM	10	150	143
MB	41	191	177
SL	45	83	97

Calculate LCNRV for the inventory:

a. As a whole (assuming the items are similar), and

b. Applied separately to each product.

c. Prepare the appropriate adjusting entry, if required, based on your calculations in (b).

Exercise 6-11 Analysis of inventory errors LO5, 9

Assume that Volleyball Pro Equipment had $900,000 of sales during each of three consecutive years, and it purchased merchandise costing $500,000 during each of the years. It also maintained a $200,000 inventory from the beginning to the end of the three-year period. However, it made an error at the end of the first year, 2020, that caused its ending 2020 inventory to appear on its statements at $180,000 rather than the correct $200,000.

Required

1. Calculate the actual amount of the company's gross profit in each of the years.

2. Prepare a comparative income statement like Exhibit 6.12 (or Exhibit 6A.6) to show the effect of this error on the company's cost of goods sold and gross profit in 2020, 2021, and 2022.

Exercise 6-12 Estimating ending inventory—gross profit method LO6

On January 1, The Parts Store had a $370,000 inventory at cost. During the first quarter of the year, it purchased $1,510,000 of merchandise, returned $19,100, and paid freight charges on purchased merchandise totalling $33,600. During the past several years, the store's gross profit on sales has averaged 30%. Under the assumption the store had $1,920,000 of sales during the first quarter of the year, use the gross profit method to estimate its inventory at the end of the first quarter.

Exercise 6-13 Estimating ending inventory—retail method LO6

CHECK FIGURE: $71,941.68

During 2020, Harmony Co. sold $520,000 of merchandise at marked retail prices. At the end of 2020, the following information was available from its records:

	At Cost	At Retail
Beginning inventory	$127,600	$256,800
Net purchases	231,240	393,600

Use the retail method to estimate Harmony's 2020 ending inventory at cost. Round all calculations to two decimal places.

Exercise 6-14 Reducing physical inventory to cost—retail method LO6

Assume that in addition to estimating its ending inventory by the retail method, Harmony Co. of Exercise 6-13 also took a physical inventory at the marked selling prices of the inventory items at the end of 2020. Assume further that the total of this physical inventory at marked selling prices was $109,200.

a. Determine the amount of this inventory at cost.

b. Determine Harmony's 2020 inventory shrinkage from breakage, theft, or other causes at retail and at cost. Round all calculations to two decimal places.

Exercise 6-15 Inventory turnover and days' sales in inventory LO7

From the following information for Russo Merchandising Co., calculate inventory turnover for 2021 and 2020 and days' sales in inventory at December 31, 2021 and 2020. Round answers to one decimal place.

	2021	2020	2019
Cost of goods sold	$643,825	$426,650	$391,300
Merchandise inventory (December 31)	96,400	86,750	91,500

Comment on Russo's efficiency in using its assets to support increasing sales from 2020 to 2021.

*Exercise 6-16 Alternative cost flow assumptions—periodic LO8

CHECK FIGURE: a. COGS = $12,672

Paddington Gifts made purchases of a particular product in the current year as follows:

Jan.	1	Beginning inventory	240 units	@	$6.00	=	$ 1,440
Mar.	7	Purchased	500 units	@	$5.60	=	2,800
July	28	Purchased	1,000 units	@	$5.00	=	5,000
Oct.	3	Purchased	900 units	@	$4.40	=	3,960
		Totals	2,640 units				$13,200

Required The business uses a periodic inventory system. Ending inventory consists of 120 units. Calculate the costs to be assigned to the ending inventory and to goods sold under:

a. FIFO

b. A weighted average cost basis

Which method provides the lower profit and why?

*Exercise 6-17 Alternative cost flow assumptions—periodic LO8

CHECK FIGURE: b. Ending inventory = $350.30

Jasper & Williams made purchases of a particular product in the current year as follows:

Jan.	1	Beginning inventory	120 units	@	$2.10	=	$ 252
Mar.	7	Purchased	250 units	@	$2.20	=	550
July	28	Purchased	500 units	@	$2.30	=	1,150
Oct.	3	Purchased	60 units	@	$2.45	=	147
		Totals	930 units				$2,099

Required Ending inventory consists of 155 units. Assuming a periodic system, determine the costs to be assigned to cost of goods sold and ending inventory under:

a. FIFO

b. Weighted average cost basis

Which method provides the lower profit, and why?

*Exercise 6-18 Specific identification cost flow assumption—periodic LO8

CHECK FIGURE: COGS = $1,761.20

Use the information in Exercise 6-17. Assume that the specific identification method is used to assign costs to cost of goods sold ending inventory. The units in ending inventory were specifically identified as follows:

- 80 units from beginning inventory
- 27 units from the March 7 purchase
- 48 units from the July 28 purchase

Required Determine the cost to be assigned to ending inventory and cost of goods sold.

An asterisk (*) identifies assignment material based on Appendix 6A.

PROBLEMS

Problem 6-1A Inventory ownership—perpetual LO1

On December 31, 2020, Jen & Mink Clothing (J&M) performed the inventory count and determined the year-end ending inventory value to be $75,500. It is now January 8, 2021, and you have been asked to double-check the year-end inventory listing. J&M uses a perpetual inventory system. **Note:** Only relevant items are shown on the inventory listing.

		Jen & Mink Clothing Inventory Listing December 31, 2020			
#	Inventory Number	Inventory Description	Quantity (units)	Unit Cost ($)	Total Value ($)
1	7649	Blue jackets	100	20	2,000
2	10824	Black pants	500	10	5,000
...					...
				Total Inventory	$75,500

The following situations have been brought to your attention:

a. On January 3, 2021, J&M received a shipment of 100 blue jackets, for $2,000 (Item #7649). The inventory was purchased December 23, 2020, FOB destination from Global Threads. This inventory was included in J&M's inventory count and inventory listing.

b. On December 29, 2020, J&M sold scarves (Item #5566) to a customer with a sale price of $700 and cost of $500, FOB shipping. The order was shipped on December 30, 2020. J&M has not included this inventory.

c. Red Blazers (Item #6193) were purchased and shipped from International Co. on December 30, 2020, for $3,300, FOB shipping. The shipment arrived January 5, 2021, and the appropriate party paid for the shipping charges of $320. Additional costs were $220 for import duties and $60 for insurance during shipment. J&M has not included this inventory.

d. At year-end, J&M is holding $5,000 of black pants (Item #10824) on consignment for designer Duke Co. This inventory was included in J&M's inventory count and inventory listing.

e. On December 31, 2020, J&M shipped white shirts (Item #4291), FOB destination costing $1,000 to a customer. The customer was charged $1,400 and the customer received the goods on January 3, 2021. J&M has not included this inventory.

Required

1. In situations (a) to (e) determine whether inventory should be included or excluded in inventory at December 31, 2020, and explain why. If the inventory should be included, determine the correct inventory cost.

2. Determine the correct ending inventory value at December 31, 2020. Starting with the unadjusted inventory value of $75,500, add or subtract any errors based on your analysis in Part 1. Assume all items that are not shown in the inventory listing or discussed in situations (a) to (e) are recorded correctly.

Problem 6-2A Alternative cost flows—perpetual LO2 e𝕏cel

CHECK FIGURES: 1. Ending inventory; a. $35,750; b. $35,107.80; 2. Ending inventory = $35,395.00

The Stilton Company has the following inventory and credit purchases during the fiscal year ended December 31, 2020.

Beginning	640 units	@	$75/unit
Feb. 10	350 units	@	$72/unit
Aug. 21	230 units	@	$85/unit

Stilton Company has two credit sales during the period. The units have a selling price of $135.00 per unit.

Sales	
Mar. 15	430 units
Sept. 10	335 units

Stilton Company uses a perpetual inventory system.

Required

1. Calculate the dollar value of cost of goods sold and ending inventory using:

    a. FIFO

    b. Moving weighted average. Round to two decimal places.

2. Calculate the dollar value of cost of goods sold and ending inventory using specific identification, assuming the sales were specifically identified as follows:

Mar. 15:	230	units from beginning inventory
	200	units from the February 10 purchase
Sept. 10:	225	units from beginning inventory
	40	units from the February 10 purchase
	70	units from the August 21 purchase

3. Using information from your answers in Parts 1 and 2, journalize the credit purchase on February 10 and the credit sale on September 10 for each of:

    a. FIFO

    b. Moving weighted average

    c. Specific identification.

*Problem 6-3A Alternative cost flows—periodic LO8

CHECK FIGURES: Cost of goods sold: a. $57,000.00; b. $58,160.90

Use the data from Problem 6-2A and do Part 1, assuming Stilton Company uses a periodic inventory costing system. Round calculations to two decimal places.

Problem 6-4A Gross profit comparisons and cost flow assumptions—perpetual LO2, 3 e**X**cel

CHECK FIGURES: 1. Ending inventory: a. $9,600.00; b. $10,982.30

Gale Company has the following inventory and purchases during the fiscal year ended December 31, 2020.

Beginning inventory	280 units	@	$80/unit
Feb. 10 purchased	195 units	@	$84/unit
Feb. 20 sold	360 units	@	$160/unit
Mar. 13 purchased	290 units	@	$78/unit
Sept. 5 purchased	255 units	@	$64/unit
Oct. 10 sold	510 units	@	$160/unit

Gale Company employs a perpetual inventory system.

Required

1. Calculate the dollar value of ending inventory and cost of goods sold using:

   a. FIFO

   b. Moving weighted average. Round all unit costs to two decimal places.

2. Using your calculations from Part 1, complete the following schedule:

	FIFO	Moving Weighted Average
Sales...		
Cost of goods sold...		
Gross profit..		

Analysis Component: How would the gross profits calculated in Part 2 above change if Gale Company had been experiencing increasing prices in the acquisition of additional inventory?

*Problem 6-5A Alternative cost flows—periodic LO8

CHECK FIGURES: 1. Cost of goods sold; a. $68,120; b. $66,290

Use the data from Problem 6-4A and do Part 1 assuming Gale Company uses a periodic inventory costing system.

Problem 6-6A Alternative cost flows—perpetual LO2, 3

Case Defence sells smartphone cases and uses the perpetual inventory system. The following is information on the purchases and sales of "Defender Box" cases. On October 1, Case Defence had 28 units with a unit cost of $22.

| | Purchases | | Sales | |
Date	Units	Unit Cost	Units	Unit Price
Oct. 3	18	23		
Oct. 6			23	$58
Oct. 12	28	25		
Oct. 19			28	$58
Oct. 23	38	27		
Oct. 30			33	$58
Oct. 31	23	28		

Required

1. Calculate the dollar value of cost of goods sold and ending inventory for the month of October using the following methods.

   a. FIFO

   b. Moving weighted average. Round all unit costs to two decimal places and round all other numbers to the nearest dollar.

An asterisk (*) identifies assignment material based on Appendix 6A.

2. Using the calculations in Part 1, complete the following table:

	FIFO	Moving Weighted Average
Sales...		
Cost of goods sold..		
Gross profit		

3. Does using FIFO or moving weighted average produce

    a. A higher gross profit?

    b. A higher ending inventory balance?

4. Calculate the gross profit percentage for FIFO and moving weighted average for the month of October. Round to the nearest percentage.

Problem 6-7A Gross profit comparisons and cost flow assumptions—perpetual LO2, 3 eXcel

CHECK FIGURES: 1. Ending inventory: a. $10,184.00; b. $11,590.60

Ontario Skateboard Company has the following inventory and purchases during the fiscal year ended December 31, 2020.

Beginning inventory	295 units	@	$83/unit
March 10 purchased	210 units	@	$87/unit
March 20 sold	375 units	@	$163/unit
May 13 purchased	277 units	@	$81/unit
August 5 purchased	260 units	@	$67/unit
September 10 sold	515 units	@	$163/unit

Ontario Skateboard Company employs a perpetual inventory system.

Required

1. Calculate the dollar value of ending inventory and cost of goods sold using:

    a. FIFO

    b. Moving weighted average. Round all unit costs to two decimal places.

2. Using your calculations from Part 1, complete the following schedule:

	FIFO	Moving Weighted Average
Sales..		
Cost of goods sold...		
Gross profit		

Analysis Component: How would the gross profits calculated in Part 2 above change if Ontario Skateboard Company had been experiencing increasing prices in the acquisition of additional inventory?

Problem 6-8A **Income statement comparisons and cost flow assumptions—perpetual** LO2, 3

CHECK FIGURE: a. Profit, FIFO = $194,750

During 2020, Fresh Express Company sold 2,410 units of its product on September 20 and 2,550 units on December 22, all at a price of $81 per unit. Incurring operating expenses of $11 per unit sold, it began the year with and made successive purchases of the product as follows:

January 1 beginning inventory...	510 units	@	$26 per unit
Purchases:			
February 20...	1,410 units	@	$28 per unit
May 16	610 units	@	$32 per unit
December 11..	3,210 units	@	$33 per unit
Total	5,740 units		

Required Prepare a comparative income statement for the company, showing in adjacent columns the profits earned from the sale of the product, assuming the company uses a perpetual inventory system and prices its ending inventory on the basis of:

a. FIFO

b. Moving weighted average cost. Round all unit costs to two decimal places.

Analysis Component: If the manager of Fresh Express Company earns a bonus based on a percentage of gross profit, which method of inventory costing will she prefer?

*Problem 6-9A **Income statement comparisons and cost flow assumptions—periodic** LO8

CHECK FIGURE: Profit weighted average = $193,221

Use the data from Problem 6-8A and do the question assuming Fresh Express Company uses a periodic inventory costing system.

Problem 6-10A **Analysis of inventory errors** LO5, 9

Shockley Co. reported the following amounts in its financial statements:

	Financial Statements for Year Ended December 31		
	2020	**2021**	**2022**
(a) Cost of goods sold	$ 715,000	$ 847,000	$ 770,000
(b) Profit...	220,000	275,000	231,000
(c) Total current assets........................	1,155,000	1,265,000	1,100,000
(d) Equity...	1,287,000	1,430,000	1,232,000

An asterisk (*) identifies assignment material based on Appendix 6A.

In making the physical counts of inventory, the following errors were made:

- Inventory on December 31, 2020: understated $70,000
- Inventory on December 31, 2021: overstated $32,000

Required For each of the preceding financial statement items—(a), (b), (c), and (d)—prepare a schedule similar to the following and show the adjustments that would have been necessary to correct the reported amounts.

	2020	2021	2022
Cost of goods sold:			
Reported..			
Adjustments: Dec. 31/20 error..............................			
Dec. 31/21 error			
Corrected			

Analysis Component: What is the error in the aggregate profit for the three-year period that resulted from the inventory errors? Explain why this result occurs. Also explain why the understatement of inventory by $70,000 at the end of 2020 resulted in an understatement of equity by the same amount that year.

Problem 6-11A Analysis of inventory errors LO5, 9

While performing a detailed review of its financial records, Doors Unlimited noted the following ending inventory errors:

2020	2021	2022
Understated $52,000	Overstated $14,000	No errors

	2020	2021	2022
Ending inventory as reported	$ 345,000	$ 420,000	$ 392,000
Cost of goods sold as reported	1,300,000	1,750,000	2,100,000
Profit as reported	340,000	516,000	652,000

Required Calculate the corrected ending inventory and cost of goods sold amounts for each year by completing the following schedule:

	2020	2021	2022
Corrected ending inventory......................................			
Corrected cost of goods sold...................................			
Corrected profit..			

Problem 6-12A **Lower of cost and net realizable value** LO4

CHECK FIGURES: 1a. $536,273; 1b. $527,895

The following information pertains to the physical inventory of Electronics Unlimited taken at December 31:

	Units on Hand	Per Unit	
Product		Cost	NRV
Audio equipment:			
Wireless audio receivers....................................	332	$199	$188
Touchscreen MP3 players	247	203	223
Audio mixers...	313	193	177
Audio stands	191	85	103
Video equipment:			
Televisions	467	253	298
5GB video cards..	278	171	183
Satellite video recorders...................................	199	613	618
Car equipment:			
GPS navigators	172	171	145
Double-DIN Car Deck with iPod/iPhone Control and Aux Input............................	157	213	198

Required

1. Calculate the LCNRV for the:
   a. Inventory by major group
   b. Inventory, applied separately to each product.
2. Prepare the appropriate entry, if any, for (a) and (b).

Problem 6-13A **Estimating ending inventory—gross profit method** LO6

CHECK FIGURE: $188,176

Quebec Traffic Company had a fire on March 10, 2020, that destroyed a major portion of its inventory. The salvaged accounting records contained the following information:

Sales, January 1 to March 10..	$ 355,600
Net merchandise purchased January 1 to March 10....................................	187,400
Additional information was determined from the 2019 annual report:	
Income statement:	
Sales...	$3,300,000
Cost of goods sold	1,782,000
Balance sheet:	
Merchandise inventory..	299,100
Quebec Traffic was able to salvage inventory with a cost of $106,300.	

Required Determine the amount of inventory lost by Quebec Traffic as a result of the fire. Quebec Traffic has a December 31 year-end. *Round the gross profit ratio to the nearest whole percentage point.*

Problem 6-14A Gross profit method LO6

CHECK FIGURE: $660,274

Sporting Pro wants to prepare interim financial statements for the first quarter of 2020 but would like to avoid making a physical count of inventory. During the last five years, the company's gross profit rate has averaged 47%. The following information for the year's first quarter is available from its records:

January 1 beginning inventory.............................	$ 350,260
Purchases...	995,200
Purchase returns	14,050
Transportation-in	7,900
Sales	1,291,150
Sales returns..	9,950

Required Use the gross profit method to prepare an estimate of the company's March 31 inventory.

Problem 6-15A Retail inventory method LO6

CHECK FIGURE: 2. Loss at cost = $40,698

The records of Earthly Goods provided the following information for the year ended December 31, 2020.

	At Cost	At Retail
January 1 beginning inventory.............................	$ 521,350	$ 977,150
Purchases...	4,138,245	6,448,700
Purchase returns	62,800	129,350
Sales		5,595,700
Sales returns..		49,600

Required

1. Prepare an estimate of the company's year-end inventory by the retail method. Round all calculations to two decimal places.

2. Under the assumption the company took a year-end physical inventory at marked selling prices that totalled $1,685,800, prepare a schedule showing the store's loss from theft or other causes at cost and at retail.

Problem 6-16A Retail inventory method LO6

CHECK FIGURE: 2. $76,875

Pet Emporium had a robbery on the weekend in which a large amount of inventory was taken. The loss is covered completely by insurance. A physical inventory count determined that the cost of the remaining merchandise is $58,500. The following additional information is available:

	At Cost	At Retail
Beginning merchandise inventory........................	$ 75,000	$ 93,750
Purchase returns and allowances........................	15,000	20,000
Purchases...	1,275,000	1,731,250
Transportation-in	18,750	
Sales		1,642,500
Sales returns and allowances		18,000

Required

1. Prepare an estimate of ending merchandise inventory using the retail method.

2. Calculate the cost of the stolen inventory.

Problem 6-17A Inventory ratios LO7

Using the **Indigo** financial statements in Appendix III, calculate the following ratios for the year ended April 1, 2017 and March 31, 2018. Comment on the change and consider whether the ratios make sense given the nature of the company's operations.

a. Inventory turnover ratio (round to two decimal places)

b. Days' sales in inventory (round to the nearest day)

*Problem 6-18A Alternative cost flows—periodic LO8

CHECK FIGURES: 2. Cost of goods sold; a. $1,191,500; b. $1,231,250

Synergy Company began 2020 with 19,000 units of Product X in its inventory that cost $7.50 per unit, and it made successive purchases of the product as follows:

Mar. 7	26,000 units	@	$ 9.00 each
May 25	31,000 units	@	$11.00 each
Aug. 1	21,500 units	@	$12.00 each
Nov. 10	31,000 units	@	$13.50 each

The company uses a periodic inventory system. On December 31, 2020, a physical count disclosed that 15,000 units of Product X remained in inventory.

Required

1. Prepare a calculation showing the number and total cost of the units available for sale during 2020.

2. Prepare calculations showing the amounts that should be assigned to the 2020 ending inventory and to cost of goods sold, assuming:

   a. FIFO

   b. Weighted average cost basis (round the average cost per unit to two decimal places).

ALTERNATE PROBLEMS

Problem 6-1B Inventory ownership—perpetual LO1

On November 30, 2020, York + Robin Shoes (Y+R) performed the annual inventory count and determined the year-end ending inventory value to be $49,222. It is now December 3, 2020, and you have been asked to double-check the inventory listing. Y+R uses a perpetual inventory system. **Note:** Only relevant items are shown on the inventory listing.

		York + Robin Shoes Inventory Listing Year-Ended November 30, 2020			
#	Inventory Number	Inventory Description	Quantity (units)	Unit Cost ($)	Total Value ($)
1	A20	Men's brown dress shoes	74	$50	$ 3,700
2	B30	Women's black boots	50	30	1,500
. . .					. . .
				Total Inventory	$49,222

An asterisk (*) identifies assignment material based on Appendix 6A.

The following situations have been brought to your attention:

a. On November 28, 2020, Y+R received a customer order for men's sneakers (Item # D50) with a sale price of $1,000 and cost of $600, FOB shipping. The order was shipped on November 30, 2020. Y+R did not include this inventory.

b. On December 2, 2021, Y+R received a shipment of $1,500 women's black boots (Item # B30). The inventory was purchased November 22, 2020, FOB destination from Global Threads. This inventory was included in Y+R's inventory count and inventory listing.

c. Women's sandals (Item # C40) were purchased and shipped from International Sole Co. on November 30, 2020 for $2,300, FOB shipping. The shipment arrived December 5, 2020 and the appropriate party paid for the shipping charges of $230. Additional costs were $161 for import duties and $86 for insurance during shipment.

d. On November 30, 2020, Y+R shipped women's flip flops (Item #E60) to a customer for $2,520, FOB destination. The inventory cost $1,800 and the customer received the goods on December 3, 2020. Y+R has not included this inventory.

e. Y+R had been holding $3,700 of men's brown dress shoes (Item #A20) on consignment for designer Blue Co. as at November 30, 2020. This inventory was included in Y+R's inventory count and inventory listing.

Required

1. In situations (a) to (e), determine whether each of the following should be included or excluded in inventory as at November 30, 2020 and explain why. If the inventory should be included, determine the inventory cost.

2. Determine the correct ending inventory value at November 30, 2020. Starting with the unadjusted inventory value of $49,222, add or subtract any errors based on your analysis in Part 1. Assume all items that are not shown in the inventory listing or discussed in situations (a) to (e) are recorded correctly.

Problem 6-2B Alternative cost flows—perpetual LO2 eXcel

CHECK FIGURES: 1. Ending inventory: a. $35,345.00; b. $34,760.75; 2. Ending inventory = $35,020.00

The Obama Company has the following inventory purchases during the fiscal year ended December 31, 2020.

Beginning	619 units	@	$78/unit
Feb. 13	335 units	@	$75/unit
Aug. 5	215 units	@	$88/unit

Obama Company has two sales during the period. The units have a selling price of $138 per unit.

Sales	
Feb. 15	415 units
Aug. 10	320 units

Obama Company uses a perpetual inventory system.

Required

1. Calculate the dollar value of cost of goods sold and ending inventory using

   a. FIFO

   b. Moving weighted average method (round the average cost per unit to two decimal places)

2. Calculate the dollar value of cost of goods sold and ending inventory using specific identification assuming the sales were specifically identified as follows:

Feb. 15:	221	units from beginning inventory
	194	units from the February 13 purchase
Aug. 10:	216	units from beginning inventory
	37	units from the February 13 purchase
	67	units from the August 5 purchase

3. Using information from your answers in Parts 1 and 2, journalize the credit sale on February 15, and the credit purchase on August 5 for each of:

   a. FIFO

   b. Moving weighted average

   c. Specific identification

*Problem 6-3B Alternative cost flows—periodic LO8

CHECK FIGURES: Cost of goods sold: a. $56,982.00; b. $58,049.68

Use the data from Problem 6-2B and do Part 1, assuming Obama Company uses a periodic inventory costing system. Round calculations to two decimal places.

Problem 6-4B Gross profit comparisons and cost flow assumptions—perpetual LO2, 3

CHECK FIGURES: 1. Ending inventory; a. $875; b. $960

The Manson Company has the following sales, inventory, and purchases during the fiscal year ended December 31, 2020.

Beginning inventory	180 units	@	$30/unit
Feb. 20 sold	145 units	@	$40/unit
Apr. 30 purchased	315 units	@	$29/unit
Oct. 5 purchased	225 units	@	$25/unit
Oct. 10 sold	540 units	@	$40/unit

Manson Company uses a perpetual inventory system.

Required

1. Calculate the dollar value of ending inventory and cost of goods sold using:

   a. FIFO

   b. Moving weighted average method. Round all unit costs to two decimal places.

2. Using your calculations from Part 1, complete the following schedule:

	FIFO	Moving Weighted Average
Sales		
Cost of goods sold		
Gross profit		

An asterisk (*) identifies assignment material based on Appendix 6A.

Analysis Component: How would the gross profits calculated in Part 2 above change if Manson Company had been experiencing increasing prices in the purchase of additional inventory?

*Problem 6-5B Alternative cost flows—periodic LO8

CHECK FIGURES: Cost of goods sold: a. $19,285; b. $19,180

Use the data from Problem 6-4B and do Part 1 assuming Manson Company uses a periodic inventory costing system. Round calculations to two decimal places.

Problem 6-6B Alternative cost flows—perpetual LO2, 3

Tool Depot sells the latest selection of power tools and uses a perpetual inventory system. The following is information on the purchases and sales of the power drills, "M1500." On November 1, Tool Depot had 150 units with a unit cost of $49.

Date	Purchases		Sales	
	Units	Unit Cost	Units	Unit Price
Nov. 4			100	$100
Nov. 6	200	47		
Nov. 16	350	45		
Nov. 20			275	$100
Nov. 24	150	40		
Nov. 28			250	$110
Nov. 30			100	$110

Required

1. Calculate the cost of goods sold and ending inventory using the following methods.

   a. FIFO

   b. Moving weighted average. Round all unit costs to two decimal places and round all other numbers to the nearest dollar.

2. Using your calculations from Part 1, complete the following schedule:

	FIFO	Moving Weighted Average
Sales		
Cost of goods sold		
Gross profit		

3. Does using FIFO or moving weighted average produce

   a. A higher gross profit?

   b. A higher ending inventory balance?

4. Calculate the gross profit percentage for both methods for the month of November. Round to the nearest percentage.

An asterisk (*) identifies assignment material based on Appendix 6A.

Problem 6-7B **Gross profit comparisons and cost flow assumptions—perpetual** LO2, 3 e**X**cel

CHECK FIGURES: 1. Ending inventory; a. $9,966.00; b. $11,367.90

The Singh Bamboo Company has the following sales, inventory, and purchases during the fiscal year ended December 31, 2020.

Beginning inventory	290 units	@	$ 82/unit
March 10 purchased	205 units	@	$ 86/unit
March 20 sold	370 units	@	$162/unit
April 30 purchased	281 units	@	$ 80/unit
July 5 purchased	255 units	@	$ 66/unit
September 15 sold	510 units	@	$162/unit

Singh Bamboo Company uses a perpetual inventory system.

Required

1. Calculate the dollar value of ending inventory and cost of goods sold using:

   a. FIFO

   b. Moving weighted average method. Round all unit costs to two decimal places.

2. Using your calculations from Part 1, complete the following schedule:

	FIFO	Moving Weighted Average
Sales		
Cost of goods sold		
Gross profit		

Analysis Component: How would the gross profits calculated in Part 2 above change if Singh Bamboo Company had been experiencing increasing prices in the purchase of additional inventory?

Problem 6-8B **Income statement comparisons and cost flow assumptions—perpetual** LO2, 3 e**X**cel

CHECK FIGURE: a. Profit, FIFO = $51,130

During 2020, The Blizzard Company sold 1,350 units of its product on May 20 and 1,700 units on October 25, all at a price of $51 per unit. Incurring operating expenses of $7 per unit in selling the units, it began the year with, and made successive purchases of, units of the product as follows:

January 1 Beginning inventory	610 units costing $29 per unit		
Purchases:			
April 2	810 units	@	$28 per unit
June 14	320 units	@	$27 per unit
Aug. 29	1,340 units	@	$26 per unit
Total	3,080 units		

Required Prepare a comparative income statement for the company for 2020, showing in adjacent columns the profits earned from the sale of the product, assuming the company uses a perpetual inventory system and prices its ending inventory on the basis of:

a. FIFO

b. Moving weighted average cost. Round unit costs to two decimal places.

Analysis Component: If The Blizzard Company's manager earns a bonus based on a percentage of gross profit, which method of inventory costing will she prefer?

*Problem 6-9B Income statement comparisons and cost flow assumptions—periodic LO8

CHECK FIGURE: Profit, weighted average = $51,166.60

Use the data from Problem 6-8B and do the question assuming Blizzard Company uses a periodic inventory costing system.

Problem 6-10B Analysis of inventory errors LO5, 9

Fireplace Company reported the following amounts in its financial statements:

	Financial Statements for Year Ended December 31		
	2020	2021	2022
(a) Cost of goods sold	$102,600	$106,400	$ 98,015
(b) Profit	87,400	105,635	91,955
(c) Total current assets	133,000	138,250	131,475
(d) Equity	152,000	158,000	168,000

In making the physical counts of inventory, the following errors were made:

- Inventory on December 31, 2020: overstated $8,100
- Inventory on December 31, 2021: understated $10,800

Required For each of the preceding financial statement items—(a), (b), (c), and (d)—prepare a schedule similar to the following and show the adjustments that would have been necessary to correct the reported amounts.

	2020	2021	2022
Cost of goods sold:			
Reported			
Adjustments: Dec. 31/20 error			
Dec. 31/21 error			
Corrected			

Analysis Component: What is the error in the aggregate profit for the three-year period that resulted from the inventory errors?

Problem 6-11B Analysis of inventory errors LO5, 9

	Incorrect Income Statement Information For Years Ended December 31				Corrected Income Statement Information For Years Ended December 31			
	2020	%	2021	%	2020	%	2021	%
Sales	$ 671,000	100	$835,000	100				
Cost of goods sold	402,600	60	417,500	50				
Gross profit	$268,400	40	$ 417,500	50				

In comparing income statement information for the years ended December 31, 2020 and 2021, the owner noticed an increase in the gross profit. He was puzzled because he knew that inventory costs were increasing.

A detailed review of the records showed the following:

a. Goods with a cost of $37,500 were on consignment at another location. Through an error, they were not included in the inventory of December 31, 2020.

b. $16,000 of merchandise inventory purchased on December 25, 2021, was shipped FOB shipping point and received on January 6, 2022. It was not included in inventory on December 31, 2021, in error.

c. While performing the physical inventory count on December 31, 2021, a calculation error was discovered that caused inventory on hand to be overstated by $24,500.

Required

1. Using the information provided, complete the schedule showing the corrected income statement information (round percentages to the nearest whole number).

2. Does the new gross profit information reflect the owner's knowledge of increasing inventory costs?

Problem 6-12B Lower of cost and net realizable value LO4

CHECK FIGURES: 1a. $602,546; 1b. $579,744

The following information pertains to the physical inventory of Geo Furniture Company taken at December 31:

Product	Units on Hand	Per Unit Cost	Per Unit NRV
Office furniture:			
Desks	430	$261	$305
Credenzas	290	227	256
Chairs	585	49	43
Bookshelves	320	93	82
Filing cabinets:			
Two-drawer	215	81	70
Four-drawer	400	135	122
Lateral	178	104	118
Office equipment:			
Fax machines	415	168	200
Copiers	544	317	288
Typewriters	355	125	117

Required

1. Calculate the LCNRV for the:
   a. Inventory by major category
   b. Inventory, applied separately to each product.

2. Prepare the appropriate entry, if any, for (a) and (b).

Problem 6-13B Estimating ending inventory—gross profit method LO6

CHECK FIGURE: $81,380.50

The Zeon Company had a flood on July 5, 2020, that destroyed all of its inventory. The salvaged accounting records contained the following information:

Sales, January 1 to July 5	$ 737,650
Net merchandise purchased Jan. 1 to July 5	414,900
Additional information was determined from the 2019 annual report:	
Income statement:	
Sales	$2,122,550
Cost of goods sold	1,337,175
Balance sheet:	
Merchandise inventory	131,200

Zeon was unable to salvage any usable inventory after the water subsided.

Required Determine the amount of inventory lost by Zeon as a result of the flood. Zeon has a December 31 year-end. Round the gross profit ratio to the nearest whole percentage point.

Problem 6-14B Gross profit method LO6

CHECK FIGURE: $183,637.50

Belle Equipment Co. wants to prepare interim financial statements for the first quarter of 2020. The company uses a periodic inventory system but would like to avoid making a physical count of inventory. During the last five years, the company's gross profit rate has averaged 30%. The following information for the year's first quarter is available from its records:

January 1 beginning inventory	$ 376,440
Purchases	1,066,050
Purchase returns	19,185
Transportation-in	32,950
Sales	1,855,125
Sales returns	37,100

Required Use the gross profit method to prepare an estimate of the company's March 31, 2020, inventory.

Problem 6-15B Retail inventory method LO6

CHECK FIGURE: 2. Loss at cost = $2,040.27

The records of The Wilke Co. provided the following information for the year ended December 31, 2020:

	At Cost	At Retail
January 1 beginning inventory	$ 40,835	$ 57,305
Purchases	251,945	383,530
Purchase returns	5,370	7,665
Sales		393,060
Sales returns		2,240

Required

1. Prepare an estimate of the company's year-end inventory by the retail method. Round all calculations to two decimal places.

2. Under the assumption the company took a year-end physical inventory at marked selling prices that totalled $39,275, prepare a schedule showing the store's loss from theft or other causes at cost and at retail.

Problem 6-16B Retail inventory method LO6

CHECK FIGURE: Loss = $40,200

Poundmaker Company just had a fire in its warehouse that destroyed all of its merchandise inventory. The insurance company covers 80% of the loss. The following information is available regarding the year ended March 31, 2020:

	At Cost	At Retail
Beginning merchandise inventory	$ 75,000	$ 125,000
Purchases..	1,050,000	1,750,000
Purchase returns and allowances	125,000	200,000
Transportation-in	5,000	
Sales		1,357,500
Sales returns and allowances.........................		17,500

Required Prepare an estimate of the company's loss using the retail method.

Problem 6-17B Inventory Ratios LO7

Using the Spin Master financial statements in Appendix III, calculate the following ratios for the years ended December 31, 2016, and December 31, 2017. At December 31, 2015, Spin Master had an ending inventories balance of $49,140,000 and cost of sales of $420,486,000. Comment on the change.

a. Inventory turnover ratio (round to two decimal places)

b. Days' sales in inventory (round to the nearest day)

*Problem 6-18B Alternative cost flows—periodic LO8

CHECK FIGURES: 2. COGS: a. $2,565,900; b. $2,487,060

Bonaire Co. began 2020 with 6,300 units of Product B in its inventory that cost $68 each, and it made successive purchases of the product as follows:

Jan. 4.....................................	10,500 units	@	$65 each
May 18.....................................	13,000 units	@	$62 each
July 9.....................................	12,000 units	@	$59 each
Nov. 21.....................................	15,500 units	@	$56 each

The company uses a periodic inventory system. On December 31, 2020, a physical count disclosed that 16,500 units of Product B remained in inventory.

Required

1. Prepare a calculation showing the number and total cost of the units available for sale during the year.

2. Prepare calculations showing the amounts that should be assigned to the ending inventory and to cost of goods sold assuming:

   a. FIFO

   b. Weighted average cost basis (round the average unit cost to two decimal places).

An asterisk (*) identifies assignment material based on Appendix 6A.

ANALYTICAL AND REVIEW PROBLEM

A & R Problem 6-1

The records of Thomas Company as of December 31, 2020, show the following:

	Net Purchases	Profit	Accounts Payable	Inventory
Balance per company's books	$325,000	$25,000	$31,000	$18,400
(a)				
(b)				
(c)				
(d)				
(e)				
Correct balances				

The accountant of Thomas Company discovers in the first week of January 2021 that the following errors were made by his staff.

a. Goods costing $4,500 were in transit (FOB shipping point) and were not included in the ending inventory. The invoice had been received and the purchase recorded.

b. Damaged goods (cost $4,100) that were being held for return to the supplier were included in inventory. The goods had been recorded as a purchase and the entry for the return of these goods had also been made.

c. Inventory items costing $3,900 were incorrectly excluded from the final inventory. These goods had not been recorded as a purchase and had not been paid for by the company.

d. Goods that were shipped FOB destination had not yet arrived and were not included in inventory. However, the invoice had arrived on December 30, 2020, and the purchase for $2,700 was recorded.

e. Goods that cost $2,400 were segregated and not included in inventory because a customer expressed an intention to buy the goods. The sale of the goods for $4,200 had been recorded in December 2020.

Required Using the format provided above, show the correct amount for net purchases, profit, accounts payable, and inventory for Thomas Company as at December 31, 2020.

ETHICS CHALLENGE

EC 6-1

Diversion Inc. is a retail sports store carrying primarily women's golf apparel and equipment. The store is at the end of its second year of operations and, as new businesses often do, is struggling a bit to be profitable. The cost of inventory items has increased just in the short time the store has been in business.

In the first year of operations the store accounted for inventory costs using the moving weighted average method. A loan agreement the store has with Dollar Bank, its prime source of financing, requires that the store maintain a certain gross profit and current ratio.

The store's owner, Cindy Foor, is looking over Diversion's annual financial statements after year-end inventory has been taken. The numbers are not very favourable and the only way the store can meet the required financial ratios agreed upon with the bank is to change from the moving weighted average to the FIFO method of inventory.

Cindy originally decided upon moving weighted average for inventory costing because she felt that moving weighted average yielded a better matching of costs to revenues. Cindy recalculates the ending inventory using FIFO and submits her income statement and balance sheet to the loan officer at the bank for the required bank review of the loan.

As Cindy mails the financial statements to the bank, she gratefully reflects on the latitude she has as manager in choosing an inventory costing method.

Required

1. Why does Diversion's use of FIFO improve the gross profit ratio and current ratio?

2. Is the action by Diversion's owner ethical?

FOCUS ON FINANCIAL STATEMENTS

FFS 6-1

CHECK FIGURES: 2a. Profit = $75,000; 2b. Profit = $79,000

The owner of Fardan Stereo Sales showed the following adjusted trial balance at December 31, 2020:

Account	Account Balance*
Cash..	16,000
Accounts receivable..	27,000
Merchandise inventory..	?
Prepaid rent..	36,000
Store fixtures...	117,000
Accumulated depreciation, store fixtures..............	82,000
Trademark..	3,000
Accounts payable..	18,000
Unearned sales revenue...	4,000
Notes payable, due in 2023......................................	22,000
Mikel Fardan, capital..	61,000
Mikel Fardan, withdrawals.......................................	44,000
Sales..	449,000
Sales discounts..	6,000
Cost of goods sold...	?
Delivery expense...	5,000
Rent expense..	92,000
Salaries expense..	109,000
Interest expense..	2,000
Depreciation expense...	8,000

*Assume normal account balances.

The owner, Mikel Fardan, is analyzing the effect of the various merchandise inventory costing methods on his financial statements and has prepared the following schedule:

	FIFO	Moving Weighted Average
Merchandise inventory, December 31, 2019	12,000	12,000
Purchases...	159,000	159,000
Merchandise inventory, December 31, 2020	?	?
Cost of goods sold..	152,000	148,000

Required

1. Calculate the merchandise inventory values at December 31, 2020, under each inventory costing method shown in the schedule above.

2. Prepare a single-step income statement (showing one line each for net sales, cost of goods sold, operating expenses, and interest expense) for the year ended December 31, 2020, along with a balance sheet at December 31, 2020, assuming:

   a. FIFO

   b. Moving weighted average

Analysis Component:

3. Does the schedule above reflect rising costs for merchandise inventory or falling costs? Explain how you know.

4. Based on your results in Part 2, which method should the owner use if he wants to:

   a. Maximize profit?

   b. Maximize assets?

FFS 6-2

Required Answer the following questions.

a. What are the two categories of inventory that Spin Master has? (Refer to the notes to Spin Master's financial statements in Appendix III at the end of the textbook.)

b. Refer to Notes for the balance sheet for WestJet in Appendix III at the end of the textbook and determine the types of inventory WestJet has.

c. For WestJet and Spin Master both balance sheets include Inventory. Explain how Inventory is unique for each of these companies.

d. How does Spin Master handle its purchase discounts, rebates, import duties, taxes, and transportation costs? Where did you find this information in the financial statements?

e. Did the balance in Inventory for Spin Master increase or decrease from December 31, 2016, to December 31, 2017?

CRITICAL THINKING MINI CASE

The former CEO of Benton Beverages retired and you have been hired in her place. In reviewing the selected financial data shown below, you are puzzled given that industry information clearly shows that the cost of beverages has been on the rise. As you walk about the warehouse area for the first time, you observe that, as pallets of beverages are being moved to the loading dock, empty areas appear behind various rows. You question the forklift driver, who says that the CEO told him always to leave alternating empty rows when stacking pallets. You climb a ladder to get a better view of the inventory layout, gasp, climb down, and determine that an emergency report to the board of directors is required.

| | Years Ended December 31, | | | | | | | |
	2020		2019		2018		2017	
Sales	$900,000	100%	$750,000	100%	$690,000	100%	$640,000	100%
Cost of goods sold	459,000	51%	390,000	52%	372,600	54%	352,000	55%

Merchandise Inventory		Merchandise Inventory		Merchandise Inventory		Merchandise Inventory	
85,000[1]		73,000[1]		63,000[1]		45,000[1]	
345,000[2]	396,000[3]	306,000[2]	342,000[3]	312,600[2]	337,600[3]	330,000[2]	332,000[3]
63,000[4]		48,000[4]		35,000[4]		20,000[4]	
97,000[5]		85,000[5]		73,000[5]		63,000[5]	

1. Beginning inventory
2. Purchases during the period
3. Cost of goods sold
4. Year-end adjusting entry
5. Ending inventory

Required Incorporating the elements of critical thinking on the inside front cover, comment.

CHAPTER 7

Internal Control and Cash

A Look Back

Chapter 5 and Chapter 6 focused on how reporting merchandising activities differs from reporting service activities. We also analyzed and recorded merchandise purchases and sales transactions, explaining the adjustments and financial statement presentation for merchandisers. Concepts included which items are included in inventory, specific costs assigned, costing methods used, inventory valuation, and inventory estimation techniques.

A Look at This Chapter

This chapter provides an introduction to internal control and cash with a detailed analysis of internal control guidelines, banking activities, accounting for petty cash funds, and reconciling the differences between cash reported in the bank account and cash in the company's accounting records.

All photos courtesy of Lori Joyce and Betterwith Ice Cream

LEARNING OBJECTIVES

LO1	Define, explain the purpose of, and identify the principles of internal control.
LO2	Define cash and explain how it is reported.
LO3	Apply internal control to cash.
LO4	Explain and record petty cash fund transactions.
LO5	Explain and identify banking activities and the control features they provide.
LO6	Prepare a bank reconciliation and journalize any resulting adjustment(s).
LO7	Calculate the quick ratio and explain its use as an indicator of a company's liquidity.

A Taste for Success

Lori Joyce was raised on an organic farm in Victoria, BC, by her hardworking Croatian immigrant parents. After having two boys of her own she became committed to ensuring she fed them quality food, and she began paying more attention to reading labels and ingredients listings. She realized that the ice cream brands in the supermarket had many preservatives and other stabilizers, and learned that the brand she had been buying had to be labelled "frozen dessert" because it didn't have sufficient cream; to be called ice cream, a product needs to have a minimum amount of 10% butterfat. After successfully launching and growing Cupcakes (as featured in the Chapter 4 opening vignette) with her life-long best friend Heather White, she was inspired to launch Betterwith Foods—with a focus on delivering high-quality, clean and simple ice cream from farm-fresh traceable dairy.

Lori's focus on sourcing traceable dairy led her on a two-year mission to find the optimal farm to supply her with local, farm-fresh cream. She firmly believes that happy cows lead to better dairy, and found a top-quality small farming operation led by a farmer who has the same vision. She has traceable cream to supply Betterwith Foods with the best foundation for her premium ice cream, with 19% butterfat. Lori worked with the owner of her favourite ice cream shop—who became her close friend and mentor—to develop the best recipe possible with a clean ingredient listing: no artificial colours, or flavours, or preservatives. Betterwith Foods custom selects every ingredient, from "local Totem strawberries to single-source Tumaco chocolate to the perfect blend of Tahitian and Madagascan vanilla beans."

Lori relies heavily on gut instinct to direct her in nearly every business decision. "I definitely don't respond to financial decisions with a gut reaction, nor any legal commitments." There she insists on doing her research to make optimal decisions. Cash management is a critical aspect of managing her new start-up. Lori has strict supplier payment requirements, including the cost to process the dairy into ice cream at a local processing facility. "Suppliers are not willing to take on the risk of a start-up business and want to make sure they get paid." Managing the cash flow demands of sourcing, processing, and storing the ice cream in inventory is a key process impacting the success of her business during the start-up phase. Betterwith Foods sells its ice cream at a fixed price to distributors; the distributors then manage getting the ice cream on the shelves of local grocers. Cash management is critical to a new business. Lori is highly focused, motivated, and determined to reach big and grow her concept into a recognized Canadian brand known for its honest and quality ingredients.

Sources: http://betterwith.com/wp-content/uploads/2018/01/MompreneurMag-V2-2-COVER-LORI-JOYCE.jpg; http://betterwith.com/about/; and personal interview with Lori Joyce, January 23, 2018.

Video Link: https://www.youtube.com/watch?v=MoA5Phk9Txw&feature=youtu.be

CRITICAL THINKING CHALLENGE

If a debit card is used instead of currency to purchase a $10 item, would the journal entry for the buyer/seller be affected? Explain.

CHAPTER PREVIEW

As individuals, we are frequently reminded through media reports and personal experiences that we need to safeguard our personal assets from theft and our personal identity from fraud. We take advantage of security measures such as password protection, securing our wallets, cell phones and laptops, locking our doors and vehicles, installing alarm systems and video cameras, and monitoring suspicious activity around us.

Businesses like **Betterwith**, as featured in the chapter-opening vignette, also need to develop systems and safeguards in order to effectively protect and manage their physical and technological assets (such as physical inventory and online bank account information). Many retailers offer online sales opportunities and have access to their customers' personal credit card information. Hackers and cybercriminals can attempt to access these data, requiring the development and continuous monitoring of the company's firewall, which is its network security system that functions to protect corporate data from outsiders.

Small companies can be the most vulnerable to occurrences of fraud, as they tend to have fewer formalized controls and procedures. For private companies, it is the owner's responsibility to set up policies and procedures to safeguard a company's assets, which is especially imperative for assets such as cash. It is critical that owners and employees understand and apply established policies and procedures of internal control to adequately safeguard the company's core resources, including both physical and technological assets. This chapter provides you with a foundation in internal control concepts and will enable you to identify instances of control weaknesses and deficiencies. If you apply principles taught in the chapter to your current work environment, you will be able to add value to the organization by identifying weaknesses and recommending improvement areas.

Cash is the most liquid asset and, as such, has the highest risk of theft. Common controls to protect cash resources are presented, including accounting for petty cash funds and reconciling bank accounts. Our understanding of these controls and procedures strengthens security in carrying out business. Security with respect to cash receipts and payments is crucial to protect the financial lifeline of both businesses and consumers.

Internal Control

This section introduces internal control and its fundamental principles. We also discuss the impact of computing technology on internal control and the limitations of control procedures.

PURPOSE OF INTERNAL CONTROL

LO1 Define, explain the purpose of, and identify the principles of internal control.

Owners of small businesses often have their eyes, ears, and physical presence in the entire operation. They participate in all activities from hiring and managing employees to signing all cheques. These owners know from personal contact and observation whether the business is actually receiving the assets and services being paid for. Many of these owners have a clear picture of how much cash is in the bank on a daily basis and monitor their cash needs carefully. The larger the operation, the more senior management must delegate responsibilities and rely on formal procedures rather than personal contact in controlling and knowing all operations of the business.

These executives place a high priority on internal control systems to monitor and control operations. This is because a well-developed control system can prevent avoidable losses, help managers plan operations, and monitor company and human performance. An **internal control system** is all policies and procedures used to:

- Protect assets
- Ensure reliable accounting
- Promote efficient operations
- Encourage adherence to company policies

DECISION INSIGHT

Corporate Governance Promotes Corporate Good

Ethical companies are said to have excellent **corporate governance**, the mechanism by which individuals in a company, in particular the board of directors, are motivated to align their behaviours with the overall corporate good. Since the demise of corporations like Enron and WorldCom, caused by fraudulent accounting activities, corporate governance is in the spotlight. Companies with strong corporate governance develop a formal set of policies that their board of directors and executives/employees of the companies will adhere to. Goldcorp, a Canadian gold mining company, with its headquarters in Vancouver and mining operations throughout North and South America, has among its corporate governance guidelines an environment and sustainability policy detailing Goldcorp's commitment to life, health, and the environment, an excerpt of which follows:

> Environmental sustainability is . . . central to our overall strategy. Our ongoing diligence in environmental stewardship is essential to our ability to maintain local relationships and to be accepted into new communities. And, of course, it is simply good business for us, and for any company in the extractive industries, to be a responsible member of the global community.

Source: *2016 Sustainability Report: Responsible Mining.* Goldcorp. 2016. https://s22.q4cdn.com/653477107/files/doc_downloads/corporate_citizenship/0_0_goldcorp_csr_2016_full.pdf accessed October 2018.

Important Tip:

Remember the CAR principle. Attributes of a strong control system can be broken into an easily remembered acronym: CAR. This stands for Custody, Authorization, and Recording of assets. These three duties must always be performed by separate individuals to strengthen the control environment and reduce the potential for errors and reduce opportunities for fraud to take place. A control weakness can be identified when two or more of these tasks are performed by the same or related individuals.

PRINCIPLES OF INTERNAL CONTROL

The purpose of internal control policies and procedures is to help prevent or detect an error from occurring. The types of controls selected to be used in a particular business depends on the nature and size of the organization. The fundamental **principles of internal control** are the following:

1. Establish a Separation of Duties

A **separation of duties** involves dividing responsibility for related transactions between two or more individuals or departments. Specifically the *custody*, *authorization*, and *recording* of assets should be performed by different individuals.

- *Authorization and custody of assets* need to be separate to prevent theft of goods. Having an independent person check incoming goods for quality and quantity encourages more care and attention to detail than when they are checked by the person who placed the order and helps to ensure items received are not stolen and the original order is not modified to hide the theft. Requiring two signatures on cheques also works to verify that disbursements comply with policies and procedures.

- *Recordkeeping* should be separated from the *custody of assets* to ensure a person who controls or has access to an asset is not responsible for maintaining that asset's accounting records. The risk of theft or waste is reduced since the person with control over the asset knows that records are kept by another person. The recordkeeper does not have access to the asset and has no reason to falsify records. In situations where recordkeeping is separate from the custody of assets, *collusion* is necessary to hide theft from the records. **Collusion** is not likely because it means two or more people must agree to commit a fraud.

- Authorization and recordkeeping, if performed by the same individual, can lead to misappropriation of assets. For example, an individual could authorize a purchase transaction from a fictitious vendor and process a payment for goods that were never received. Better control is maintained if, for instance, the person designing and programming the IT system does not serve as the operator. Cheque-writing activities should not be controlled by a computer operator in order to avoid risk of fraud.

2. Ensure Transactions and Activities Are Authorized

Establish responsibilities for each task clearly for each position in the company. Approvals must be made by authorized individuals. When two salesclerks share access to the same cash register, for instance, neither clerk can prove or disprove any alleged shortage. Assigning responsibility for a separate cash drawer for each clerk provides a better opportunity to monitor misappropriation of cash. Having a manager review employee timesheets helps to ensure accuracy and prevents paying employees for hours not worked.

3. Maintain Records

Maintain adequate records to help protect assets by ensuring that employees use prescribed procedures. When detailed records of manufacturing equipment and tools are kept, for instance, lost or stolen items are readily noticed. Similarly, the use of a chart of accounts encourages the correct recording of transactions that improves the accuracy of reports.

Preprinted forms are an important control to ensure required information is tracked and help to ensure employees do not miss recording important information. For example, when sales receipts are prenumbered and automatically generated by the cash register, a salesperson is not able to pocket cash by making a sale and destroying the sales slip. Computerized point-of-sale systems achieve the same control results.

4. Insure Assets and Bond Key Employees

Insure assets and bond key employees to reduce risk of loss from casualty and theft. To **bond** an employee is to purchase an insurance policy, or a bond, against losses from theft by that employee. Bonding reduces the risk of loss suffered from theft in addition to discouraging theft by the bonded employee.

5. Apply Technological Controls

Cash registers with a locked-in tape or electronic file make a record of each cash sale. A time clock registers the exact time an employee arrives at and departs from the job. Passwords limit access to sensitive information. Change and currency counting machines can quickly and accurately count amounts. Personal identification scanners, such as iris scanners or fingerprint scanners, can limit access to only those individuals who are authorized. All of these and other technological controls are effective parts of many internal control systems. For example, gold and gem mines incorporate security measures including cameras, X-ray machines, and body searches to prevent theft of their inventory.

6. Perform Internal and External Audits

Perform regular and independent reviews to ensure that internal control procedures are followed. No internal control system is entirely effective, for various reasons such as employee turnover, human error, and intentional circumventing of controls. Reviews are preferably done by internal auditors who are employees not directly involved in operations and who report directly to senior management or the audit committee of the board of directors. An independent evaluation of the controls ensures the established policies and procedures are being followed.

Many companies also pay for audits by independent external auditors who are professional accountants. These external auditors are required to document the controls for every financial statement line item and test existing controls. The auditors perform a detailed analysis of the company's financial records and give an opinion as to whether the company's financial statements are presented fairly in accordance with the applicable set of generally accepted accounting principles. In the process of their evaluation, they often identify internal controls that need improvement.

Important Tip:

Solving problems related to controls. To ensure you provide a full analysis of a control issue it is helpful to remember the acronym WIR. First identify the *weakness* (could be due to a CAR issue), then explain the *implication* of how the weak control will cause issues/errors, and provide a *recommendation* to resolve the identified weakness.

THREE DRIVERS OF FRAUD

The following diagram highlights a standard framework developed for fraud investigators in the 1950s by criminologist Dr. Donald Cressey that, despite over half a century of technological advancement, has proven to be a useful tool for today's leading forensic investigators.

A 2016 KPMG study, "Global Profiles of the Fraudster: Technology Enables and Weak Controls Fuel the Fraud" revealed the following regarding the components of the fraud triangle:

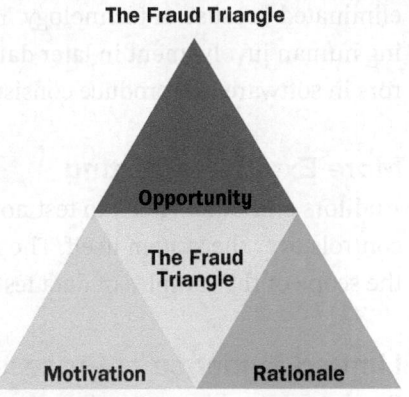

Opportunity:

- 61% of the frauds committed were facilitated by weak internal controls, with 47% of frauds involving misappropriation of assets.
- 22% of frauds were related to fraudulent financial reporting.
- Frauds were found to frequently occur because of a failure to have a basic control in place, such as checking supporting documentation before authorizing a transaction.
- Capability: the more senior the executive position held by the fraudster, the greater ability he or she has to get past the controls. Management's ability to override controls is a key area of risk. The 2016 study also emphasized technology as a key enabler for 24% of fraudsters, who took the opportunity to post a journal entry to camouflage a misappropriation.
- Deterrent: A focus on fraud prevention is key; continuously evaluating the controls in place and strengthening identified weaknesses (including adequate supervision of employees and technologies such as data analytics to identify unusual transactions) will help prevent several of the occurrences.

Motivation:

- Out of 750 fraudsters surveyed, 66% claimed to be motivated by greed, financial gain, and financial difficulty. Approximately 12% were motivated to meet business targets to receive a bonus.
- Deterrent: More and more companies are increasing the linkage between management compensation and their company's financial performance and decreasing the portion of their fixed salary.

Rationale:

- Fraudsters were found to have a sense of superiority, indicating fraudsters likely felt they were above the rules regulating the workplace.

- Deterrent: KPMG International indicated "technological advances provide more-powerful tools in strengthening companies' defenses against fraud."

The similar 2013 study commented with respect to the fraud triangle that "people commit fraud when the three elements occur simultaneously, the perfect storm; motivation, opportunity, and ability to rationalize the act." Key characteristics of the fraudsters who participated in the 2016 study include the following:

- 79% of fraudsters were male
- 68% were between ages 36 and 55
- 38% worked for the business more than 6 years
- 34% were executives or directors and 32% were managers

Reduced Processing Errors

Provided the software and data entries are correct, the risk of mechanical and mathematical errors is nearly eliminated because of technology. Yet mistakes happen, and one must be alert to that possibility. The decreasing human involvement in later data processing can cause data entry errors to go undiscovered. Similarly, errors in software can produce consistent erroneous processing of transactions.

More Extensive Testing

Auditors and others need to test not only samples of data from the electronic accounting system but also the controls over the system itself. The results of the review of the controls over the accounting system will affect the scope of the samples of data tested.

Limited Evidence of Processing

Because many data processing steps are increasingly done by computer, fewer "hard copy" items of documentary evidence are available for review. Yet technologically advanced systems can store additional evidence. They can, for instance, record information such as who made the entries, the date and time, and the source of their entry. Technology can also be designed to require use of passwords or other identification before access to the system is granted. This means that internal control depends more on the design and operation of the information system and less on analysis of the documents left behind by the system.

Increased Ecommerce

Technology has encouraged the growth of ecommerce. **Amazon** and **Kijiji** are examples of companies that have successfully exploited ecommerce, and most companies today have at least some ecommerce transactions. All such transactions involve at least three risks. (1) *Credit card number theft* is a risk of using, transmitting, and storing such data online. This increases the cost of ecommerce. (2) *Computer viruses* are malicious programs that attach themselves to innocent files for purposes of infecting and harming other files and programs. (3) *Impersonation* online can result in charges of sales to bogus accounts, purchases of inappropriate materials, and the inadvertent surrender of confidential information to hackers. To combat some of these risks, companies use both firewalls (points of entry to a system that require passwords to continue) and encryption (a mathematical process to rearrange contents that cannot be read without the process code).

ETHICAL IMPACT

Warning Signs

There are clues to internal control violations. Warning signs from accounting include (1) an increase in customer refunds (could be fake), (2) missing documents (could be used for fraud), (3) differences between bank deposits and cash receipts (could be embezzled cash), (4) delayed recording (could reflect fraudulent records), and (5) increase in customer or supplier complaints. Warning signs from employees include (1) lifestyle changes (could be embezzlement), (2) too close with suppliers (could signal fraudulent transactions), and (3) failure to leave job, even for vacations (could conceal fraudulent activities).

Consider what you would do if you noticed over the past few months some unusual activities with respect to your manager, the director of finance. She began to modify the control requirements, bypassing previously established organizational requirements to eliminate redundancy and to create efficiencies. She also recently informed you that she is going to take over all sign-offs, and from now on everything is to go through her for approval. In addition, you overhear her talking to a coworker about her recent high-end sports car purchase and her new home overlooking Lake Ontario. What concerns, if any, do you have? What would you do?

LIMITATIONS OF INTERNAL CONTROL

All internal control policies and procedures have limitations. Probably the most serious source of these limitations is the human element that we can categorize as either (1) human error, or (2) human fraud.

Human error is a factor whenever internal control policies and procedures are carried out by people. Human error can occur from negligence, fatigue, misjudgment, lack of training, or confusion. *Human fraud* involves intent by people to defeat internal controls for personal gain. This human element highlights the importance of establishing an *internal control environment* that conveys management's attitude and commitment to internal control.

Another important limitation of internal control is the *cost–benefit trade-off.* This means the costs of internal controls must not exceed their benefits. Analysis of costs and benefits must consider all factors, including the impact on morale. Most companies, for instance, have a legal right to read employees' email. Yet companies seldom exercise that right unless confronted with evidence of potential harm to the company. The same holds for drug testing, phone tapping, and hidden cameras. The bottom line is that no internal control system is perfect and that managers must establish internal control policies and procedures with a net benefit to the company.

The preceding discussion is an introduction to internal controls. The study of *auditing* takes a detailed look at internal controls.

DECISION INSIGHT

Cybercriminals Hit ATMs—A Massive $45M Modern-Day Bank Heist

An organized group of criminals recently executed "one of the most sophisticated cyberattacks on bank machines ever conducted." A crime ring of hackers withdrew $45 million from ATMs from 21 countries around the world prior to being arrested. According to *The Globe and Mail*, prosecutors labelled the crime a "massive 21st-century bank heist that reached across the Internet and stretched around the globe." How did they do it? The criminals "allegedly hacked into prepaid debit-card networks, boosted balances, then successfully erased daily withdrawal limits, giving them the ability to drain money from the accounts." This is another reason why companies need to be constantly working to defend themselves from hackers and organized crime; today's bank robbers are able to hide behind laptops and no longer show up with a pistol and a mask. The accompanying video link demonstrates how the hackers were able to accomplish the robbery.

Video Link: http://money.cnn.com/2013/05/09/technology/security/cyber-bank-heist/
Sources: http://www.theglobeandmail.com/report-on-business/eight-men-charged-in-massive-worldwide-atm-heist/article11844090/, accessed October 20, 2014; http://www.nbcnews.com/tech/security/6-arrested-45-million-global-atm-bank-cyberheist-f2D11617858, accessed June 23, 2015; http://www.forbes.com/sites/josephsteinberg/2013/05/13/a-message-for-every-business-owner-from-criminals-who-stole-45-million/, accessed June 23, 2015.

DECISION MAKER   Answer—End of chapter

Campaign Manager

You are leading a campaign to influence the government to improve the health care system. Your funding is limited and you try hiring people who are committed to your cause and will work for less. A systems analyst recently volunteered her services and put together a Web strategy to attract supporters. She also strongly encouraged you to have a mandatory-compliance policy that all employees take at least one week of vacation per year. Why does she feel so strongly about a "forced vacation" policy?

 CHECKPOINT

1. Fundamental principles of internal control state that (choose the correct statement):
   a. Responsibility for a series of related transactions (such as placing orders for, receiving, and paying for merchandise) should be assigned to one person.
   b. Responsibility for all tasks should be shared by two or more employees so that one serves as a check on the other.
   c. Employees who handle cash and negotiable assets are bonded.
2. What are some impacts of computing technology on internal control?

Do Quick Study question: QS 7-1

Cash

LO2 Define cash and explain how it is reported.

Cash is the most important asset companies need to manage. It is not only the most liquid asset, but also the most fraudulently misappropriated. Companies need to maintain adequate cash levels to pay off upcoming current liabilities, as was presented in Chapter 4 with our analysis of the current ratio, also referred to as working capital ratio. Due to the high risk of theft, it is essential that companies implement effective controls over cash handling, cheque processing, and electronic payments. Good accounting systems support both goals by managing how much cash is on hand and controlling who has access to it.

CASH DEFINED

The financial statement line item **cash** includes items such as currency, coins, amounts on deposit in bank accounts, chequing accounts, and most cash savings accounts.[1] Cash also includes items that are acceptable for deposit in these accounts, such as customers' cheques, cashier's cheques, certified cheques, money orders, ecurrency, and deposits made through electronic funds transfer (EFT).

Many companies invest idle cash in short-term investments called *cash equivalents* to increase earnings. Because cash equivalents are similar to cash, many companies combine them with cash as a single item on the balance sheet. Amazon.com, Inc., for instance, reports the following on its December 31, 2016, balance sheet:

Cash and cash equivalents $19,334 (Million)

---

[1] IFRS 2018, IAS 7, para. 6.

Amazon.com, Inc. discloses its accounting policy over the category Cash and Cash Equivalents in its 2016 annual report as:

> *Cash and Cash Equivalents*
>
> We classify all highly liquid instruments with an original maturity of three months or less as cash equivalents.

Liquidity

Cash is the usual means of payment when paying for other assets, services, or liabilities. **Liquidity** refers to how easily an asset can be converted into another asset or used in paying for services or obligations. Cash and cash equivalents are called **liquid assets** because they are converted easily into other assets or used in paying for services or liabilities. A company must maintain a certain level of liquid assets so it has the capacity to pay bills on time and can make cash purchases when necessary.

Quotable Quotes:

"Cash is king. No matter how many good opportunities come your way, do not invest all your cash. If you run out of reserves, the smallest or foolish of things may bring you down. Companies with millions in assets have gone bankrupt because they cannot make a $25,000 payment."

—Mauricio Chaves Mesén
12 Laws of Great Entrepreneurs

CONTROL OF CASH

LO3 Apply internal control to cash.

It is important that we apply principles of good internal control to cash. Cash is the most liquid of all assets and is easily hidden and transported. A good system of internal control for cash provides adequate procedures for protecting both cash receipts and cash disbursements. Because cash is the most liquid of assets, specific controls need to be in place over the handling (custody) of cash. These procedures should meet three basic guidelines:

1. **Separate handling of cash from recordkeeping of cash.** When duties are separated, it requires two or more people to collude for cash to be stolen and the theft to be concealed in the accounting records. (**C**ustody and **R**ecording)

2. **Deposit cash receipts promptly (daily) in a bank.** Immediate (daily) deposits of all cash receipts produces a timely independent test of the accuracy of the count of cash received. It also reduces cash theft or loss, and it reduces the risk of an employee personally using the money before depositing it. (**C**ustody and **R**ecording)

3. **Make cash disbursements by cheque.** Paying expenses by cheque, when possible, develops a bank record of cash disbursements. This guideline also reduces the risk of cash theft. If possible it is best if two signatures are required to ensure that legitimate invoices are being paid. (**A**uthorization and **R**ecording)

One exception to the third guideline is to allow small disbursements of currency and coins from a petty cash fund, as described later in this chapter. Another important point is that the deposit of cash receipts and the use of cheques for cash disbursements allow a company to use bank records as a separate external record of cash transactions. We then explain how using externally prepared bank records enables a company to confirm the accuracy of its internal records using an effective control tool called a bank reconciliation.

CONTROL OF CASH RECEIPTS

Internal control of cash receipts ensures that all cash received is accurately recorded and deposited. Cash receipts arise from many transactions, including cash sales, collections of customers' accounts, receipts of interest and rent, bank loans, sale of assets, and owners' investments. This section explains internal control over two important types of cash receipts: over-the-counter and mail.

Over-the-Counter Cash Receipts

For purposes of internal control, over-the-counter cash sales should be recorded on a cash register at the time of each sale for internal control. To help ensure that correct amounts are entered, each register should be positioned so customers can read the amounts entered. The design of each cash register should provide a permanent, locked-in record of each transaction. Many software programs facilitate point-of-sale cash register transactions and enter them in accounting records. Less technology-dependent registers simply print a record of each transaction on a paper tape or electronic file locked inside the register.

Custody over cash should be separate from its recordkeeping; therefore, the clerk who has access to cash in the register should not have access to modify its locked-in record. The register should open only when a sale is recorded to prevent employees from accessing the till between transactions. Exhibit 7.1 summarizes the cash receipt controls that help to protect cash.

At the end of the clerk's work period, the clerk should count the cash in the register, record the amount, and turn over the cash and a record of the cash balance to an employee in the cashier's office. The employee in the cashier's office, like the clerk, has access to the cash as he or she prepares the bank deposit and should not have access to modify accounting records (or the register tape or file). A third employee compares the record of total register transactions (or the register tape or file) with a copy of the deposit slip and cash receipts summary reported by the cashier's office. This record (or register tape or file) is the basis for a journal entry recording over-the-counter cash sales.

EXHIBIT 7.1
Cash Receipt Controls

Cash register —————————————→ Cashier —————————————→ Computer

© Zavgsg/Dreamstime.com/GetStock.com   © Mario Beauregard/The Canadian Press   © Ds011photo/Dreamstime.com/GetStock.com

Note that the third employee has access to the records for cash but not to the actual cash. The clerk and the employee from the cashier's office have access to cash but not to the accounting records. This means the accuracy of cash records and amounts is automatically checked. The process described above significantly reduces the risk of error or diversion of cash without the difference being revealed.

Cash Over and Short

Sometimes errors in making change are discovered when there is a difference between the cash in a cash register and the record of the amount of cash sales. This difference is reported in the **Cash Over and Short account**. This income statement account, included under general and administrative expenses, records the effects of cash overages and cash shortages to profit from errors in making change and missing petty cash receipts. The journal entries to record cash over and short are illustrated later in this chapter.

Cash Receipts by Mail

Control of cash receipts[2] that arrive through the mail starts with the person who opens the mail. In a large business, two people are assigned the task and are present when opening the mail. The person opening the mail makes a list of money received. This list should contain a record of each sender's name, the amount, invoice number, and an explanation for what purpose the money is sent. Copies of the list are sent with the money to the cashier to prepare the bank deposit, and to the accounting department to adjust the customer accounts and record the cash receipt. The cashier deposits the money in the bank, and the recordkeeper records amounts received in the accounting records. In a small business, the owner should assume responsibility for cash.

CONTROL OF CASH DISBURSEMENTS

Control of cash disbursements is especially important for companies. Most large thefts occur from payments of fictitious invoices. The key to controlling cash disbursements is to require that all expenditures be made by cheque, with two signatures if possible when not signed by the owner. The **three-way match** is a good control for cash disbursements. A copy of the approved purchase order, receiving report, and invoice must be "matched" or present before any cash disbursement is approved. The only exception is for small payments from petty cash. Another key is that when the authority to sign cheques is assigned to a person other than the owner, that person must not have access to modify the accounting records. This separation of duties helps prevent an employee from hiding fraudulent disbursements in the accounting records. It is best to have two signatories on all cheques if possible to prevent a single person from writing him- or herself a cheque.

The manager of a small business often signs cheques and knows from personal contact that the items being paid for are actually received. This arrangement is impossible in large businesses. Instead, internal control procedures must be substituted for personal contact. These controls are achieved through a *voucher system*. Briefly, the voucher system of control requires that a number of procedures be performed and documents collected to support the validity of each disbursement. These procedures are designed to assure the cheque signer that the obligations recorded were properly incurred and should be paid.

The exact procedures used to achieve control over cash vary across companies. They depend on factors such as company size, number of employees, volume of cash transactions, and sources of cash. We must therefore view the procedures described in this section as illustrative of those in practice today.

---

2   Cash receipts by mail are normally in the form of cheques. Cheques are equivalent to cash and would therefore be recorded as cash.

⚖️ DECISION INSIGHT

The Bank of Canada is charged with the issuance of currency and is responsible for the design, issuance, and distribution of Canadian bank notes (bills). The image below identifies the security measures incorporated into the design of the Canadian bills printed by the Bank of Canada. Why do you think the bank develops currency with such a wide range of security measures? In supplying bank notes, the Bank ensures

they are difficult to counterfeit and easy to authenticate, ensuring businesses can easily identify true Canadian currency. As counterfeiters work to reproduce currency, banks need to incorporate more and more security into the manufacture of the notes to prevent fraud. Follow the video link below to view a presentation by the Bank of Canada summarizing the features of the new polymer notes and demonstrating how to handle situations when you identify counterfeit currency.

Video Link: http://www.bankofcanada.ca/multimedia/counterfeit-prevention/
Photo Source: © Bank of Cananda. http://www.bankofcanada.ca/banknotes/image-gallery/

🔄 CHECKPOINT

3. Good internal control procedures for cash receipts imply that (choose one):
   a. All cash disbursements, other than those for very small amounts, are made by cheque.
   b. An accounting employee should count cash received from sales and promptly deposit receipts.
   c. Cash receipts by mail should be opened by an accounting employee who is responsible for recording and depositing receipts.

   Do Quick Study questions: QS 7-2, QS 7-3

Petty Cash System of Control

 LO4 Explain and record petty cash fund transactions.

A basic principle for controlling cash disbursements is that all payments are made by cheque. An exception to this rule is made for petty cash disbursements. Petty cash disbursements are the *small amount* payments required in most companies for items such as postage, courier fees, repairs, and supplies. The purpose of setting up a petty cash fund is to prevent companies from having to write cheques for small amounts. Once a business sets up a petty cash fund, the cash maintained in this fund can be used to make small payments.

Operating a Petty Cash Fund

Establishing a petty cash fund requires estimating the total amount of small payments likely to be made during a short period such as a week or month. A cheque is then drawn by the company cashier's office for an amount slightly in excess of this estimate. To illustrate, assume that a trendy messenger bag company, Demano, established a petty cash fund on November 1, 2020, in the amount of $75. A $75 cheque was drawn, cashed, and its proceeds turned over to Milani Taylor, an office employee designated as the *petty cashier* or *petty cash custodian*. The **petty cashier** is responsible for safekeeping of the cash, for making payments from this fund, and for keeping accurate records. The entry to record the setting up of this petty cash fund is:

Nov.	1	Petty Cash	75	
		Cash		75
		To establish a petty cash fund.		

This entry transfers $75 from the regular Cash account to the Petty Cash account. After the petty cash fund is established, the *Petty Cash account is not debited or credited again unless the size of the total fund is changed.*

The petty cashier should keep petty cash in a locked box in a safe place. As each disbursement is made, the person receiving payment signs a *petty cash receipt* or *petty cash ticket* as illustrated in Exhibit 7.2.

EXHIBIT 7.2
Petty Cash Receipt

Petty Cash Receipt		No. 6
For _____ Delivery charges _____	Date _____ Nov.18, 2020 _____	
Charge to _____ Delivery expense _____	Amount _____ $5.00 _____	
Approved by _____ *Jim Gibbs* _____	Received by _____ *Dick Fitch* _____	

The petty cash receipt is then placed in the petty cash box with the remaining money. When the cash is nearly gone, the fund should be reimbursed. When it is time to reimburse the petty cash fund, the petty cashier should sort the receipts by type and prepare a summary as shown in Exhibit 7.3.

EXHIBIT 7.3
Petty Cash Payments Report

DEMANO Petty Cash Payments Report November 2020			
Receipts:			
Office maintenance			
Nov. 2 Washing windows	$10.00		
17 Washing windows	10.00		
27 Computer repairs	26.50	$46.50	
Transportation-in			
Nov. 5 Delivery of merchandise purchased	$ 6.75		
20 Delivery of merchandise purchased	8.30	15.05	
Delivery expense			
Nov. 28 Customer's package delivered.........		5.00	
Office supplies			
Nov. 15 Purchased office supplies.........		4.75	
Total receipts.........			$71.30
Fund total.........		$75.00	
Less: Cash remaining		2.20	
Equals: Cash required to replenish petty cash.........			$72.80
Cash over/(short)			($ 1.50)

This summary and all petty cash receipts are presented to the company's cashier. The company's cashier stamps all receipts paid so they cannot be reused, files them for record-keeping, records the reimbursement, and gives the petty cashier a cheque for a sum *equal to the fund size less the cash remaining*. In our example, Jim Gibbs had only $2.20 cash remaining in the fund at the end of November. Therefore, the reimbursement cheque is for $72.80 (= $75.00 − $2.20). Notice that Exhibit 7.3 shows total receipts for $71.30. The difference between the total receipts and the reimbursement cheque represents a cash shortage of $1.50 (= $71.30 − $72.80) due to an error. The reimbursement cheque is recorded as follows:

To replenish petty cash:

$$\text{Cash required to replenish petty cash} = \text{Fund size} - \text{Cash remaining}$$

To calculate cash over/(short):

$$\text{Cash over/(short)} = \text{Total of petty cash receipts} - \text{Cash required to replenish petty cash}$$

Nov.	27			
		Office Maintenance Expenses	46.50	
		Merchandise Inventory	15.05	
		Delivery Expense	5.00	
		Office Supplies Expense	4.75	
		Cash Over and Short	1.50	
		Cash		72.80
		To reimburse petty cash.		

In the case of an overage in the petty cash fund, a credit to Cash Over and Short is recorded in the reimbursing entry.

When the reimbursement cheque is cashed and the money returned to the cash box, the total money in the box is restored to its original amount of $75.00 (= $72.80 + $2.20). The fund is now ready to begin a new cycle of operations.

Increasing or Decreasing Petty Cash Fund

A decision to increase or decrease a petty cash fund is often made when the fund is being reimbursed. To illustrate, let us assume that Demano decides to increase the petty cash fund by $25, from $75 to $100, on November 27 when it reimburses the fund. This is recorded as follows:

Nov.	27			
		Petty Cash	25.00	
		Office Maintenance Expenses	46.50	
		Merchandise Inventory	15.05	
		Delivery Expense	5.00	
		Office Supplies Expense	4.75	
		Cash Over and Short	1.50	
		Cash		97.80
		To reimburse petty cash and increase it by $25.00.		

 DECISION MAKER   Answer—End of chapter

Internal Auditor

You just graduated and have been hired as an internal audit trainee for a company. As part of your training, your supervisor has instructed you to make surprise counts of three $200 petty cash funds. You arrive at the office of one of the petty cashiers while she is on the telephone. You explain the purpose of your visit, and the petty cashier asks politely that you come back after lunch so that she can finish the business she's conducting by long distance. You agree and return after lunch. The petty cashier opens the petty cash box and shows you nine new $20 bills with consecutive serial numbers plus receipts totalling $20. Do you take further action or comment on these events in your report to your supervisor?

CHECKPOINT

4. Why are some cash payments made from a petty cash fund?
5. Why should a petty cash fund be reimbursed at the end of an accounting period?
6. What are three results of reimbursing the petty cash fund?

Do Quick Study questions: QS 7-4, QS 7-5, QS 7-6

Mid-Chapter Demonstration Problem

Castillo Company, an HR Consulting firm, established a $250 petty cash fund on February 10. On February 28, the fund had $180.14 remaining in cash and receipts for these expenditures: postage, $10.51; office supplies, $50.00; and repair expenses, $10.50. Prepare:

a. The February 10 entry to establish the fund,

b. The February 28 entry to record the fund transactions and replenish it, and

c. Independent of (b), the February 28 entry to record the fund transactions and reduce the fund to $100.

Analysis Component:

Assume that there was no receipt for the $50.00 of office supplies. Should this amount be reimbursed? Explain why or why not.

Planning the Solution

- Total petty cash receipts.
- Calculate cash required to replenish petty cash.
- Calculate cash over/(short), if any.
- Prepare journal entries as required.
- Prepare an answer to the analysis question.

SOLUTION

a.	Feb. 10	Petty Cash Fund	250.00	
		Cash		250.00
		To establish petty cash fund.		
b.	28	Postage Expense...	10.51	
		Office Supplies Expense	50.00	
		Repair Expense..	10.50	
		Cash		69.86[1]
		Cash Over and Short.		1.15[2]
		To reimburse petty cash fund.		

Calculations:

[1]Total of petty cash receipts = $10.51 + $50.00 + $10.50 = $71.01

Cash required to replenish petty cash = Fund size − Cash remaining
= $250 − $180.14
= $69.86

[2]Cash over/(short) = Receipt totals − Cash required
= $71.01 − $69.86
= $1.15

c.	28	Cash...	80.14[3]	
		Postage Expense..	10.51	
		Office Supplies Expense	50.00	
		Repair Expense...	10.50	
		Petty Cash...		150.00
		Cash Over and Short		1.15
		To reimburse petty cash fund and decrease it to $100		

Calculation:

[3]Cash required to replenish petty cash = New fund size – Cash remaining

$$= \$100.00 - \$180.14$$

$$= -\$80.14 \text{ (therefore, instead of a credit to Cash, debit Cash)}$$

Analysis Component:

The $50.00 should not be reimbursed without a receipt for two reasons. First, it is a basic internal control measure to ensure that only valid expenditures are reimbursed. If receipts were not required, individuals could request reimbursement for fictitious expenditures. Second, GAAP require that transactions be recorded based on verifiable evidence (which is related to internal controls).

Banking Activities as Controls

LO5 Explain and identify banking activities and the control features they provide.

From the first moment a business is established, the ability to efficiently make and receive payments forms the lifeblood of the business. Banks safeguard cash, provide detailed and independent records of cash transactions, and are a source of cash financing. This section highlights the key services and documents provided by banking activities that increase management's control over cash and enable businesses to transact efficiently.

BASIC BANK SERVICES

This first section outlines key bank services, including bank accounts, bank deposits, and cheques. Each of these services contributes to the control or safeguarding of cash.

Bank Account

A bank account is a record set up by a bank for a customer, permitting this customer to deposit money for safeguarding and providing the opportunity to make payments through cheque, cash, and electronic fund transfer (EFT) withdrawals. To control access to a bank account, all persons authorized to use a bank account must sign a signature card. A **signature card** includes the signature of each person authorized to sign cheques from the account. Bank employees use signature cards to verify signatures on cheques. This lowers the risk of loss from forgery for both banks and customers. Many businesses require dual signatures on cheques to strengthen control over cash payments. Many companies have more than one bank account for various reasons such as a payroll account dedicated to issuing payments for wages to employees or for special transactions.

EXHIBIT 7.4
Deposit Slip

Front

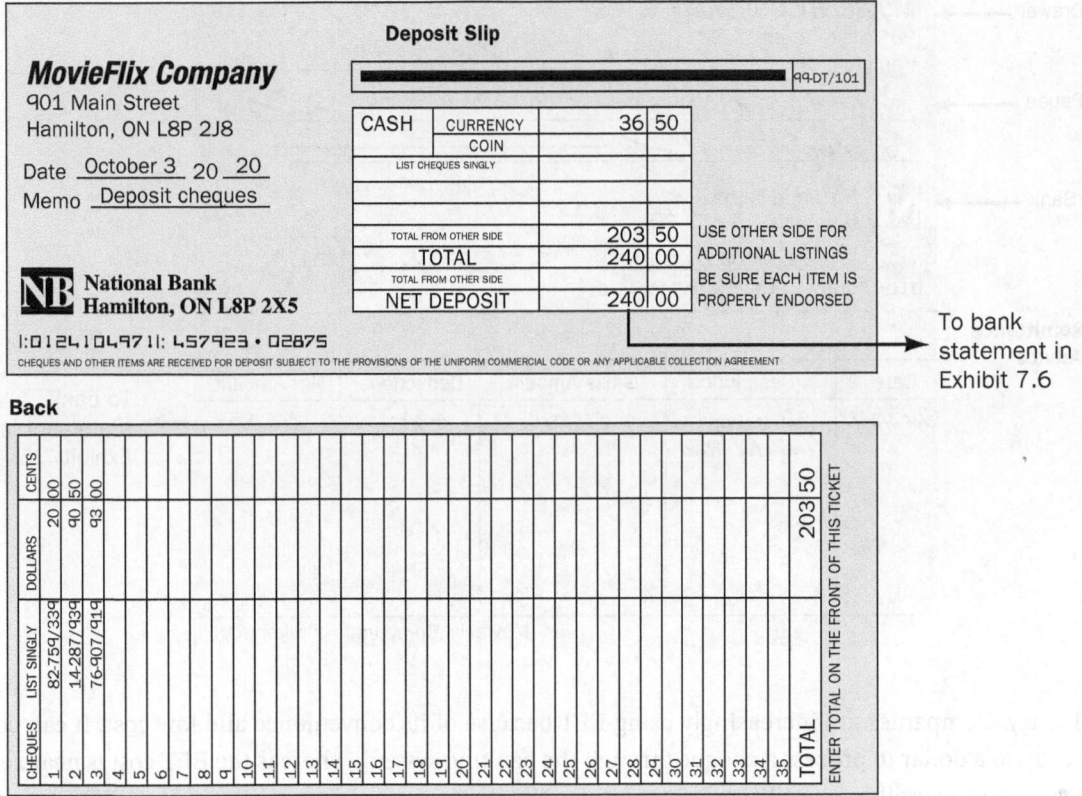

To bank statement in Exhibit 7.6

Bank Deposit

Each bank deposit is supported by a *deposit slip*. Companies use **deposit slips** to list the items such as currency, coins, and cheques included in the deposit along with each of their dollar amounts. When the deposit is brought to the bank, the company is provided a copy of the deposit slip or a deposit receipt as proof of the deposit. Exhibit 7.4 shows an example of a deposit slip.

Bank Cheque

To withdraw money from an account, a customer uses a *cheque*. A **cheque** is a document signed by the depositor instructing the bank to pay a specified amount of money to a designated recipient. Cheques are the most common method of payment used by Canadian businesses. A cheque involves three parties: a *drawer* (also referred to as payor or remitter) who signs the cheque, a *payee* who is the recipient, and a *bank* on which the cheque is drawn. The bank provides a depositor with cheques that are serially numbered and imprinted with the name and address of both the depositor and the bank. Both cheques and deposit slips are imprinted with identification codes in magnetic ink for computer processing. Exhibit 7.5 shows an example cheque. This cheque is accompanied by an optional *remittance advice* giving an explanation for the payment. When a remittance advice is unavailable, the memo line is often used for a brief explanation.

Electronic Funds Transfer

Electronic funds transfer (EFT) is the use of electronic communication to transfer cash from one party to another. No paper documents are necessary. Banks simply transfer cash from one account to another with a

EXHIBIT 7.5
Cheque with Remittance Advice

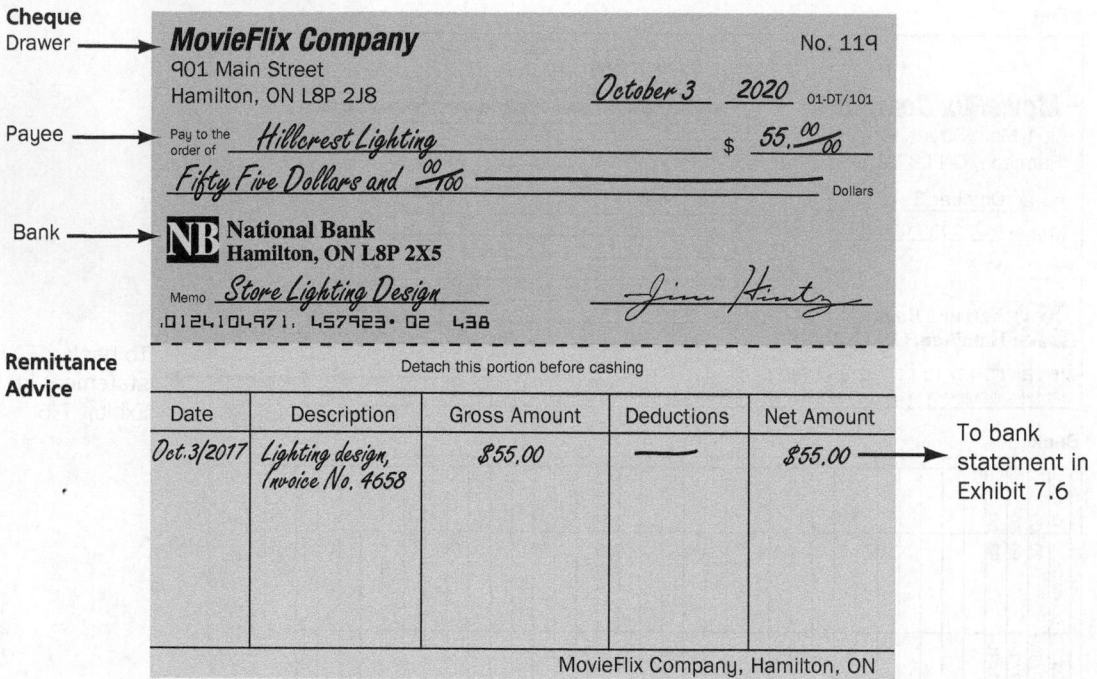

MovieFlix Company, Hamilton, ON

journal entry. Companies are increasingly using EFT because of its convenience and low cost. It can cost, for instance, up to a dollar to process a cheque through the banking system, whereas the EFT cost is near zero. We see items such as payroll, rent, utilities, insurance, and interest payments being handled by EFT. For example, Alberta Blue Cross issues more than 110,000 cheques per month, but this number is declining as more payments are being made by direct deposit. The bank statement lists cash withdrawals by EFT with cheques and other deductions. Cash receipts by EFT are listed with deposits and other additions. A bank statement is sometimes a depositor's only notice of an EFT.

Credit Card Transactions

Many companies allow customers to use credit cards such as Visa, MasterCard, or American Express to pay for purchases. The customer has the convenience of using the credit card instead of using cash or cheques. The retailer enjoys the benefits of being paid by the credit card company. The payment to the retailer normally occurs faster than if the retailer had to collect credit sales personally and the risk of credit customers who do not pay is transferred to the credit card company. The credit card company issues the customer a monthly statement detailing the customer's transactions and follows up with the customer for payment. The customer pays the credit card company directly and can be charged interest based on the credit terms on the statement.

The seller pays a fee for the services provided by the credit card company. The fee covers costs incurred by the credit card company including credit checks on credit card customers, cost of collections, and, of course, a profit margin. Therefore, when the fee is deducted, the cash received by the retailer is less than 100% of the sales value of the transaction. The fee charged by the credit card company can be calculated as a percentage of sales or it may vary depending on the volume of sales. For simplicity, we will assume in this textbook that the credit card fee is based on a percentage of the sales value.

When a credit card is used, the retailer receives cash, net of the credit card fee, immediately upon deposit of the credit card sales receipt at the bank or when the credit card is processed electronically at the point of sale. For instance, if TechCom has $100 of credit card sales with a 4% fee and cash is received immediately, the entry is (assume cost of sales is $40):

Aug.	15	Cash..	96	
		Credit Card Expense	4	
		Sales...		100
		To record credit card sales less a 4% credit card expense.		
	15	Cost of Goods Sold...	40	
		Merchandise Inventory...................................		40
		To record cost of sales.		

Some firms report credit card expense on the income statement as a type of discount deducted from sales to arrive at net sales. Other companies classify it as a selling expense or even as an administrative expense.

DECISION MAKER   Answer—End of chapter

Entrepreneur

You are the owner of a small retail store. You are considering allowing customers to purchase merchandise using credit cards. Until now, your store accepted only cash and cheques. What forms of analysis do you use to make this decision?

Debit Card Transactions

The use of **debit cards** is common and popular with consumers. Payment for a purchase is electronically transferred from the customer's bank account to the vendor's bank account immediately at the point of sale. The customer authorizes the transaction by entering their personal identification number (PIN). Normally, the bank charges the retailer a fee for this service. The entries are identical to a credit card sale. For example, assume a customer purchases a $100 service on October 1 and pays using a debit card. If the bank charges the retailer $0.40 per debit card transaction, the entry is:

Oct.	1	Cash...	99.60	
		Debit Card Expense..	0.40	
		Service Revenue...		100.00
		To record a debit card transaction.		

Interac Flash Tap and Pay Technology

Interac debit cards have evolved with the introduction of *Interac* Flash—the contactless enhancement of traditional debit that allows customers to tap and pay. Banks such as **RBC**, **Scotiabank**, and **TD Canada Trust** now issue *Interac* Flash debit cards with built-in technology that allows customers to pay using contactless debit technology. By holding an *Interac* Flash card at the contactless reader, a purchase is quickly and securely processed.

The advantages? Convenience, for one: merchants can serve customers more efficiently. The need for efficiency at the point of sale is significant because of the huge volumes of transactions now being handled electronically. In 2016, more than 80% of retailers accept contactless payments and 50% of debit cards in Canada supported contactless payments.[3]

Security is another advantage. Security is a growing concern given the increase in electronic payments and related increase in fraud. The new *Interac* Flash card is reported to enhance protection against security issues like skimming, counterfeiting, transaction replay types of fraud, and electronic pickpocketing. Controls have been put in place to limit the risk of other types of losses. For example, RBC requires that cardholders enter their PIN after every $200 of Flash purchases to validate the cardholder's identity. In terms of additional security, the *Interac* Zero Liability Policy[4] automatically protects the debit card user from unauthorized transactions.

 CHECKPOINT

7. What is a benefit to the retailer of accepting credit and debit cards?

Do Quick Study questions: QS 7-7, QS 7-8

BANK STATEMENT

At least once a month, the bank sends the depositor a bank statement showing the activity in the accounts during the month; a company can also access its banking activity online at any time. Different banks use a variety of formats for their bank statements; however, they all include the following information:

1. Beginning-of-month balance of the depositor's account.
2. Cheques and other debits decreasing the account during the month.
3. Deposits and other credits increasing the account during the month.
4. End-of-month balance of the depositor's account.

The information reported on the bank statement reflects the bank's records of the activity in the bank account during the reported month. Exhibit 7.6 shows an example bank statement for MovieFlix.

> **Important Tip:**
>
> Notice that deposits are called credits and cheques are called debits on the bank statement. This is because the bank statement reports information from the bank's point of view—*that a depositor's account is a liability on the bank's records since the money belongs to the depositor and not the bank.*

When Capri Jones, a customer of the bank, puts money into the bank, the bank debits cash and *credits* the bank's liability account to Jones. Hence, *credit memos* show the bank's increasing liability to Jones. When

---

3 https://monexgroup.com/canada-vs-world-in-contactless-payment-technology/

4 All *Interac* cardholders are protected from losses resulting from circumstances beyond their control under the *Interac* Zero Liability Policy. **Note:** *Interac, Interac* Flash, and *Interac* e-Transfer are trademarks of Interac Inc. Used under licence.

EXHIBIT 7.6
Bank Statement

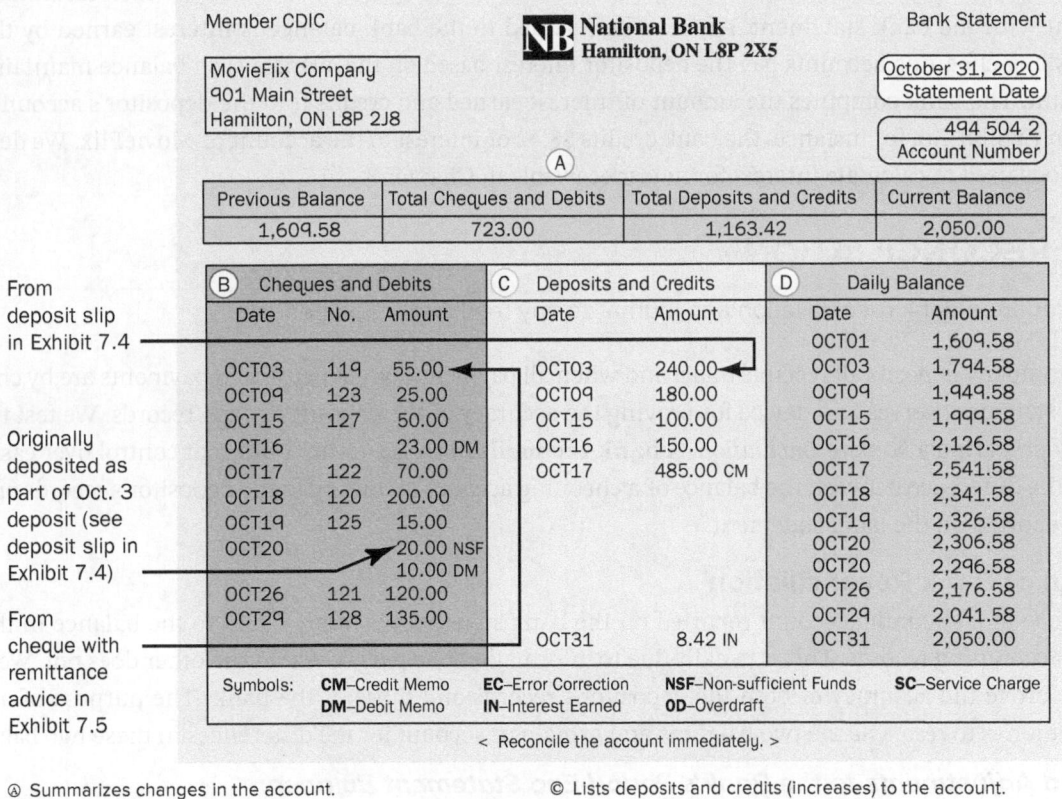

| From deposit slip in Exhibit 7.4 | Originally deposited as part of Oct. 3 deposit (see deposit slip in Exhibit 7.4) | From cheque with remittance advice in Exhibit 7.5 |

Member CDIC

NB National Bank
Hamilton, ON L8P 2X5

MovieFlix Company
901 Main Street
Hamilton, ON L8P 2J8

Bank Statement

October 31, 2020
Statement Date

494 504 2
Account Number

Ⓐ

Previous Balance	Total Cheques and Debits	Total Deposits and Credits	Current Balance
1,609.58	723.00	1,163.42	2,050.00

Ⓑ Cheques and Debits			Ⓒ Deposits and Credits		Ⓓ Daily Balance	
Date	No.	Amount	Date	Amount	Date	Amount
					OCT01	1,609.58
OCT03	119	55.00	OCT03	240.00	OCT03	1,794.58
OCT09	123	25.00	OCT09	180.00	OCT09	1,949.58
OCT15	127	50.00	OCT15	100.00	OCT15	1,999.58
OCT16		23.00 DM	OCT16	150.00	OCT16	2,126.58
OCT17	122	70.00	OCT17	485.00 CM	OCT17	2,541.58
OCT18	120	200.00			OCT18	2,341.58
OCT19	125	15.00			OCT19	2,326.58
OCT20		20.00 NSF			OCT20	2,306.58
		10.00 DM			OCT20	2,296.58
OCT26	121	120.00			OCT26	2,176.58
OCT29	128	135.00			OCT29	2,041.58
			OCT31	8.42 IN	OCT31	2,050.00

Symbols:	**CM**–Credit Memo	**EC**–Error Correction	**NSF**–Non-sufficient Funds	**SC**–Service Charge
	DM–Debit Memo	**IN**–Interest Earned	**OD**–Overdraft	

< Reconcile the account immediately. >

Ⓐ Summarizes changes in the account.
Ⓑ Lists paid cheques in date order along with other debits (or decreases).
Ⓒ Lists deposits and credits (increases) to the account.
Ⓓ Shows the daily account balances.

Jones withdraws money from the bank, the bank records it as a credit to cash and *debits* the bank's liability account for Jones. Therefore, *debit memos* reflect decreases in the bank's liability to Jones.[5]

Enclosed with a bank statement are the depositor's cancelled cheques and any debit or credit memos affecting the account. **Cancelled cheques** are cheques the bank has paid and deducted from the customer's account during the month. Other deductions also often appear on a bank statement and include (1) service charges and fees assessed by the bank, (2) customers' cheques deposited that are uncollectible, (3) corrections of previous errors, (4) withdrawals through automated teller machines (ATMs),[6] and (5) periodic payments arranged in advance by a depositor such as insurance and lease payments. Except for service charges, the bank notifies the depositor of each deduction with a debit memo when the bank reduces the balance. A copy of each debit memo is usually sent with the monthly statement.

---

5 Recall that a bank records transactions in an identical manner to any other business. For example, on October 3 the bank cashed a cheque written by MovieFlix. This was recorded by the bank as:

MovieFlix Customer Account [a liability to the bank]	55	
Cash [an asset to the bank]		55

Notice on the bank statement in Exhibit 7.6 that this cheque is reported to MovieFlix as a debit because the bank has decreased its liability to MovieFlix. As a second example, on October 3 MovieFlix deposited $240 into its bank account; this was recorded by the bank as:

Cash	240	
MovieFlix Customer Account [a liability to the bank]		240

The bank statement reports this deposit to MovieFlix as a credit because the bank's liability to MovieFlix has increased.

6 Because of a desire to make all disbursements by cheque, most business chequing accounts do not allow ATM withdrawals.

While deposits increase a depositor's bank balance, there are other transactions that increase the depositor's account. Examples are amounts the bank collects on behalf of the depositor and corrections of previous errors. Credit memos notify the depositor of all increases recorded by the bank. A copy of each credit memo is often sent with the bank statement. Another item added to the bank balance is interest earned by the depositor. Many chequing accounts pay the depositor interest based on the average cash balance maintained in the account. The bank computes the amount of interest earned and credits it to the depositor's account each month. In Exhibit 7.6, for instance, the bank credits $8.42 of interest to the account of MovieFlix. We describe the methods used to calculate interest for notes receivable in Chapter 8.

BANK RECONCILIATION

LO6 Prepare a bank reconciliation and journalize any resulting adjustment(s).

When a company deposits all receipts intact and when all payments except petty cash payments are by cheque, the bank statement serves as a device for proving the accuracy of the depositor's cash records. We test the accuracy by preparing a *bank reconciliation*. A **bank reconciliation** is a form of internal control over cash that explains the difference between the balance of a chequing account according to the depositor's records and the balance reported on the bank statement.

Purpose of Bank Reconciliation

The balance of a chequing account reported on the bank statement is rarely equal to the balance in the depositor's accounting records. This is usually due to information one party has that the other does not. We must therefore prove the accuracy of both the depositor's records and those of the bank. The purpose of a bank reconciliation is to *reconcile* the two balances and explain or account for the differences in these two balances.

Required Adjustments to the Bank's Period-End Statement Balance:

Several adjustments need to be made to the bank balance to reflect transactions that occurred in the accounting records cash balance that at year-end have not yet been reflected in the bank statement. These adjustments are due to timing differences of items being captured in the bank statement and do not require adjustments as they are already reflected in the accounting records of the company. Among the factors causing the bank statement balance to differ from the depositor's book balance are:

1. *Unrecorded deposits* (also known as *deposits in transit* or *outstanding deposits*). These are deposits made and recorded by the depositor but not yet captured on the bank statement. For example, companies often make deposits at the end of a business day, after the bank is closed. A deposit in the bank's night depository on the last day of the month is not recorded by the bank until the next business day and does not appear on the bank statement for that month.

2. *Outstanding cheques.* These are cheques written (or drawn) for outstanding payables and expenses, resulting in a decrease in the company's Cash account. The cheque has been mailed to the payee; however, the payee has not yet deposited the cheque in its bank, so the cash in the bank statement has not been reduced.

3. *Errors.* Both banks and depositors can make errors. For example, a bank error might include a cheque written by *MovieMax* Company mistakenly charged against the account of *MovieFlix* Company, or a deposit made by *MovieFlix* Company accidentally posted to the account of *Digital Access Inc.*

> **Important Tip:**
>
> We only adjust the bank balance for items that have been recorded correctly in the accounting records but by the date of the bank statement had not yet been received by the bank or paid out of the bank account. This includes outstanding cheques that have been written to suppliers/employees but have not yet been drawn out of the bank account. It also includes cash deposits in transit that were collected by the business but were not yet received by the bank.

Required Adjustments to the Cash Book Balance:

Several adjustments need to be made to the book balance to reflect transactions that occurred to the bank's record of the company's cash balance that have not yet been captured in the company's G/L cash account. These adjustments require journal entries to book the changes to the accounting records and include:

1. *Additions for collections, electronic transfers, and interest.* Banks sometimes act as collection agents for their depositors by collecting notes and other items. Banks can also receive electronic funds transfers to the depositor's account. When a bank collects an item, it adds it to the depositor's account, less any service fee. Some banks notify the company of the transaction by way of a credit memo. At the time a memo is received, it should be recorded by the depositor. Often these transactions remain unrecorded until the time of the bank reconciliation.

   Many bank accounts earn interest on the average cash balance in the account during the month. If an account earns interest, the bank statement includes a credit for the amount earned during the past month. The bank statement provides notification of earned interest.

2. *Deductions for uncollectible items and for services.* A company sometimes deposits a customer's cheque that is uncollectible. This usually is because the balance in the customer's account is not large enough to cover the cheque. This cheque is called a *non-sufficient funds (NSF)* cheque. The bank initially credited the depositor's account for the amount of the deposited cheque. When the bank learns that the cheque is uncollectible, it debits (reduces) the depositor's account for the full amount of that cheque. The bank may also charge the depositor a fee for processing an uncollectible cheque and some banks notify the depositor of the deduction by sending a debit memo. While each deduction should be recorded by the depositor when a debit memo is received, notification of the NSF cheque may not take place and an entry is sometimes not made until the bank reconciliation is prepared.

3. *Other possible bank charges* to a depositor's account reported on a bank statement include the printing of new cheques and a service charge for maintaining the account. Notification of these charges is *not* provided until the statement is mailed. All of these items must be recorded as an adjustment to the *balance per books*.

4. *Errors.* A depositor error might involve a cheque actually written for $102 but recorded in error in the cash disbursements journal as $120. These kinds of errors might not be discovered until the depositor prepares a bank reconciliation.

> **Important Tip:**
>
> We only adjust the book balance for items that showed up on the bank statement and have not yet been recorded in the G/L, such as collections of a note receivable, errors, interest earned, NSF cheques, or cheque printing charges.

Steps in Reconciling a Bank Balance

The employee who prepares the bank reconciliation should not be responsible for cash receipts, processing cheques, or maintaining cash records. This employee needs to gather information from the bank statement and from other records. A reconciliation requires this person to:

Step 1   Identify the end-of-month bank balance of the cash account as reported on the bank statement.

Step 2   Compare deposits on the bank statement with deposits in the accounting records (cash receipts journal and last month's bank reconciliation). Identify any discrepancies and determine which is correct. List any errors or unrecorded deposits.

Step 3   Identify and list any outstanding cheques through the following steps:
* Compare cancelled cheques on the bank statement with actual cheques returned with the statement. For each cheque, make sure the bank deducts the correct amount and the returned cheque is properly charged to the account. List any discrepancies or errors.
* Compare cancelled cheques on the bank statement with cheques recorded in the books (cash disbursements journal). List any outstanding cheques. Also, while companies with good internal controls would rarely write a cheque without recording it, we should inspect and list any cancelled cheques that are unrecorded in the books.
* Identify any outstanding cheques listed on the previous month's bank reconciliation that are not included in the cancelled cheques on this month's bank statement. List these cheques that remain outstanding at the end of the current month. Send the list to the cashier's office for follow-up with the payees to see if the cheques were actually received.

Step 4   Calculate the adjusted bank balance.

Step 5   Identify the company's cash balance in the General Ledger Cash Account.

Step 6   Inspect all additions (credits) on the bank statement and determine whether each is recorded in the books. These items include collections by the bank, correction of previous bank statement errors, and interest earned by the depositor. List any unrecorded items.

Step 7   Inspect all deductions (debits) to the account on the bank statement and determine whether each is recorded in the books. These include bank charges for newly printed cheques, NSF cheques, and monthly service charges. List items not yet recorded.

Step 8   Calculate the adjusted book balance.

Step 9   Check to ensure adjusted bank balance and adjusted book balance are equal. If they are not equal, investigate for mathematical accuracy and missing information.

Illustrating a Bank Reconciliation

We illustrate a bank reconciliation by preparing one for MovieFlix as of October 31. We use the guidelines listed above and follow nine specific steps. Follow each step to the corresponding Exhibits 7.6 to 7.9 to see where the information comes from and how it is shown on the bank reconciliation in Exhibit 7.10.

① Identify the bank balance of the cash account at October 31 (balance per bank).

  – *Bank balance shown on the bank statement is $2,050 (from Exhibit 7.6).*

② Identify and list any unrecorded deposits* and any bank errors.* Add them to the bank balance on the bank reconciliation.

  – *A $145 deposit was placed in the bank's night depository on October 31 and is not recorded on the bank statement (from Exhibit 7.7).*

③ Identify and list any outstanding cheques* and any bank errors.* Deduct them from the bank balance on the bank reconciliation.

  – *A comparison of cancelled cheques with the company's books showed two cheques outstanding: #124 for $150 and #126 for $200 (from Exhibit 7.8).*

④ Calculate the *adjusted bank balance*, also called *corrected or reconciled* balance.

  – *See Exhibit 7.10.*

⑤ Identify the company's balance of the cash account (book balance).

  – *Cash balance shown in the accounting records is $1,404.58 (from Exhibit 7.9).*

⑥ Identify and list any unrecorded credit memos from the bank statement, such as interest earned and errors.* Add them to the book balance on the bank reconciliation.

  ⓐ *Enclosed with the bank statement is a credit memo showing that the bank collected a note receivable for the company on October 17. The note's proceeds of $500 (minus a $15 collection fee) were credited to the company's account. This credit memo is not yet recorded by the company (from Exhibit 7.6).*

  ⓑ *The bank statement shows a credit of $8.42 for interest earned on the average cash balance in the account. There was no prior notification of this item and it is not yet recorded on the company's books (from Exhibit 7.6).*

⑦ Identify and list any unrecorded debit memos from the bank, such as service charges and errors.* Deduct them from the book balance on the bank reconciliation.

  – *Debits on the bank statement that are not recorded on the books include ⓐ a $23 charge for cheques printed by the bank, and ⓑ an NSF cheque for $20 plus ⓒ a related $10 processing fee. The NSF cheque is from a customer, Frank Heflin, and was originally included as part of the October 3 deposit (from Exhibit 7.6).*

⑧ Calculate the *adjusted book balance*, also called the *corrected* or *reconciled* balance.

  – *See Exhibit 7.10.*

⑨ Verify that the two adjusted balances from Steps 4 and 8 are equal. If so, they are reconciled. If not, check for mathematical accuracy and missing data.

  – *See Exhibit 7.10.*

*For simplicity, this example includes no errors and assumes that there were no outstanding cheques or deposits on last month's bank reconciliation. The End-of-Chapter Demonstration Problem illustrates these additional complexities.

EXHIBIT 7.6

Bank Statement (repeated from earlier page for ease of reference)

Member CDIC	National Bank Hamilton, ON L8P 2X5	Bank Statement
MovieFlix Company 901 Main Street Hamilton, ON L8P 2J8		October 31, 2020 Statement Date 494 504 2 Account Number

Previous Balance	Total Cheques and Debits	Total Deposits and Credits	Current Balance
1,609.58	723.00	1,163.42	2,050.00

Cheques and Debits			Deposits and Credits		Daily Balance	
Date	No.	Amount	Date	Amount	Date	Amount
					OCT01	1,609.58
OCT03	119	55.00	OCT03	240.00	OCT03	1,794.58
OCT09	123	25.00	OCT09	180.00	OCT09	1,949.58
OCT15	127	50.00	OCT15	100.00	OCT15	1,999.58
OCT16		23.00 DM (7a)	OCT16	150.00	OCT16	2,126.58
OCT17	122	70.00	OCT17	485.00 CM (6a)	OCT17	2,541.58
OCT18	120	200.00			OCT18	2,341.58
OCT19	125	15.00			OCT19	2,326.58
OCT20		20.00 NSF (7b)			OCT20	2,306.58
		10.00 DM (7c)			OCT20	2,296.58
OCT26	121	120.00			OCT26	2,176.58
OCT29	128	135.00			OCT29	2,041.58
			OCT31	8.42 IN (6b)	OCT31	2,050.00 (1)

Symbols:	**CM**–Credit Memo	**EC**–Error Correction	**NSF**–Non-sufficient Funds	**SC**–Service Charge
	DM–Debit Memo	**IN**–Interest Earned	**OD**–Overdraft	

< Reconcile the account immediately. >

When the reconciliation is complete, the employee sends a copy to the accounting department to record any needed journal entries. For instance, entries are needed to record any adjustments made to the balance per books to reflect items such as unrecorded debit and credit memos and any company mistakes. The entries resulting from MovieFlix's bank reconciliation are illustrated in the next section. Another copy goes to the cashier's office. This is especially important if the bank has made an error that needs correction.

Recording Adjusting Entries Identified from the Bank Reconciliation

A bank reconciliation helps locate errors by either the bank or the depositor. It also identifies unrecorded items that need recording on the company's books. In MovieFlix's reconciliation, for instance, the adjusted balance of $1,845.00 is the correct balance as of October 31. But the company's accounting records show a $1,404.58 balance. We must prepare journal entries to adjust the book balance to the correct balance. It is important to remember that only the items reconciling the book balance side require adjustment. This means that the following four entries are required for MovieFlix:

1. Collection of Note

The first entry is to record the net proceeds of MovieFlix's note receivable collected by the bank, the expense of having the bank perform that service, and the reduction in the Notes Receivable account:

Oct.	31	Cash	485.00	
		Collection Expense	15.00	
		Notes Receivable		500.00
		To record collection fee and proceeds of a note collected by the bank.		

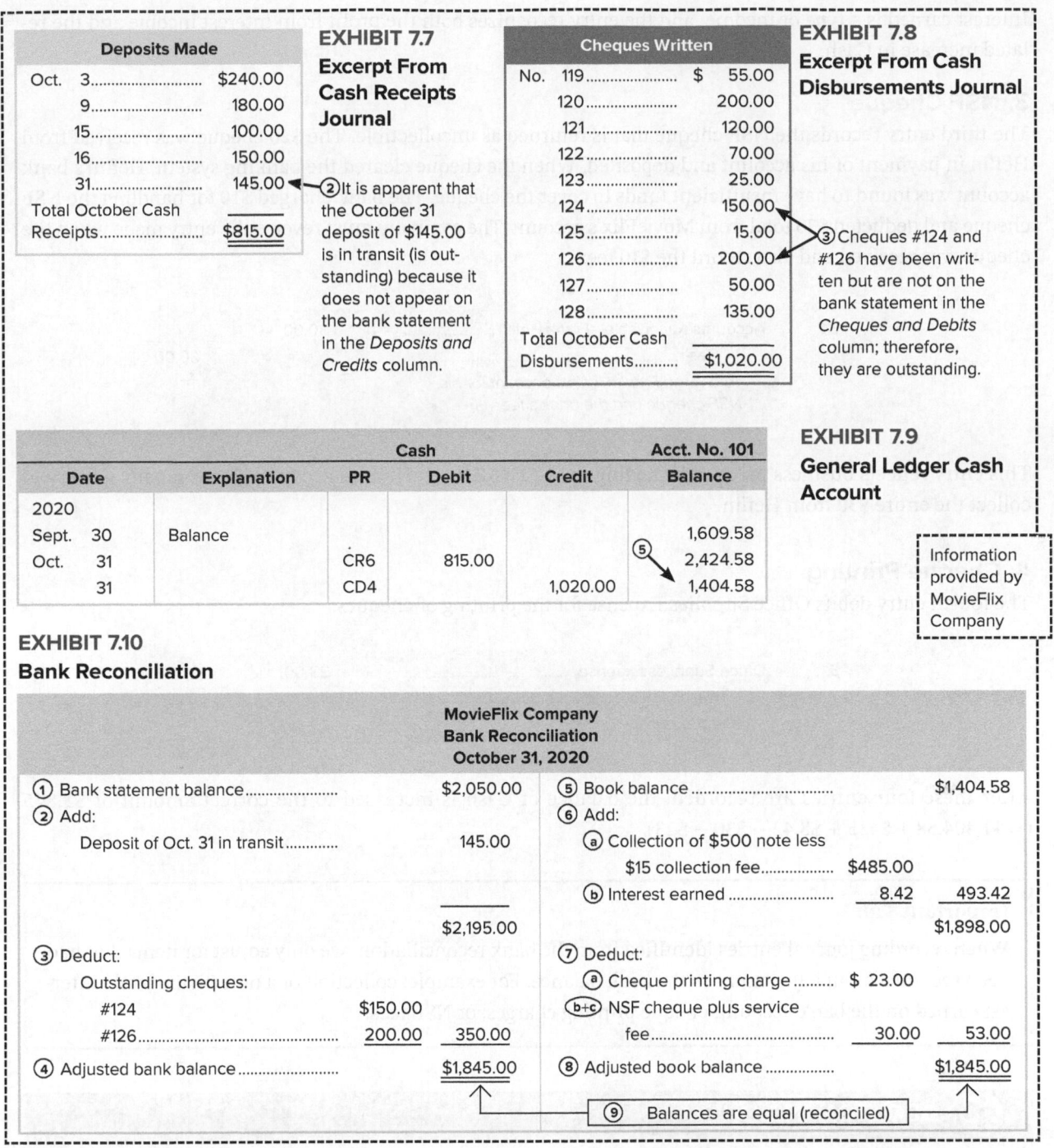

EXHIBIT 7.7
Excerpt From Cash Receipts Journal

Deposits Made	
Oct. 3	$240.00
9	180.00
15	100.00
16	150.00
31	145.00
Total October Cash Receipts	$815.00

② It is apparent that the October 31 deposit of $145.00 is in transit (is outstanding) because it does not appear on the bank statement in the *Deposits and Credits* column.

EXHIBIT 7.8
Excerpt From Cash Disbursements Journal

Cheques Written	
No. 119	$ 55.00
120	200.00
121	120.00
122	70.00
123	25.00
124	150.00
125	15.00
126	200.00
127	50.00
128	135.00
Total October Cash Disbursements	$1,020.00

③ Cheques #124 and #126 have been written but are not on the bank statement in the *Cheques and Debits* column; therefore, they are outstanding.

EXHIBIT 7.9
General Ledger Cash Account

	Cash				Acct. No. 101
Date	Explanation	PR	Debit	Credit	Balance
2020					
Sept. 30	Balance				1,609.58
Oct. 31		CR6	815.00		2,424.58
31		CD4		1,020.00	1,404.58

⑤

Information provided by MovieFlix Company

EXHIBIT 7.10
Bank Reconciliation

MovieFlix Company Bank Reconciliation October 31, 2020				
① Bank statement balance	$2,050.00	⑤ Book balance		$1,404.58
② Add:		⑥ Add:		
Deposit of Oct. 31 in transit	145.00	ⓐ Collection of $500 note less $15 collection fee	$485.00	
		ⓑ Interest earned	8.42	493.42
	$2,195.00			$1,898.00
③ Deduct:		⑦ Deduct:		
Outstanding cheques:		ⓐ Cheque printing charge	$ 23.00	
#124	$150.00	ⓑ+ⓒ NSF cheque plus service fee	30.00	53.00
#126	200.00 350.00			
④ Adjusted bank balance	$1,845.00	⑧ Adjusted book balance		$1,845.00
		⑨ Balances are equal (reconciled)		

2. Interest Earned

The second entry records the **interest income** credited to MovieFlix's account by the bank:

31	Cash	8.42	
	Interest Income		8.42
	To record interest earned on the average Cash balance in the chequing account.		

Interest earned is a type of income, and the entry recognizes both the profit from interest income and the related increase in Cash.

3. NSF Cheque

The third entry records the NSF cheque that is returned as uncollectible. The $20 cheque was received from Heflin in payment of his account and deposited. When the cheque cleared the banking system, Heflin's bank account was found to have insufficient funds to cover the cheque. The bank charged $10 for handling the NSF cheque and deducted $30 total from MovieFlix's account. The company must reverse the entry made when the cheque was received and also record the $10 fee:

31	Accounts Receivable—Frank Heflin	30.00	
	Cash..		30.00
	To charge Frank Heflin's account for his		
	NSF cheque and the bank's fee.		

This entry reflects business practice by adding the NSF $10 fee to Heflin's account. The company will try to collect the entire $30 from Heflin.

4. Cheque Printing

The fourth entry debits Office Supplies Expense for the printing of cheques:

31	Office Supplies Expense	23.00	
	Cash...		23.00
	Cheque printing charge.		

After these four entries are recorded, the balance of Cash is increased to the correct amount of $1,845 (= $1,404.58 + $485 + $8.42 − $30 − $23).

> **Important Tip:**
>
> When recording journal entries identified from the bank reconciliation, we only adjust for items that had been recorded as an adjustment to the book balance. For example: collection of a note by the bank, interest earned on the bank account, cheque printing charges, or NSF fees.

⚖ DECISION INSIGHT

What Is Cash? A Look at Today's Payment Options

Every year Canadians make approximately 24 billion payments worth more than $44 trillion, according to Lawrence Schembri, deputy governor of the Canadian Payments Association (CPA). Over the past several years Canada's payment system has undergone rapid and fundamental change. Technological innovation, convenience, and continued globalization are the key drivers behind the changes.

The CPA is mandated by Parliament to provide a leadership role in ensuring the safety and soundness of Canada's national clearing and settlement system for payments. The Minister of Finance has overall oversight of CPA activities. The association has a crucial role, as it allows millions of Canadians to conduct business transactions in a safe and efficient clearing system.

Globally, the CPA Environmental Report 2014 identifies the following trends and emerging factors:

- The digitization of payments—the replacement of cash and paper-based transactions with electronic transactions is transforming payment choices available to consumers and businesses.

- Mobile phone ownership and social and business networking (e.g., Facebook, LinkedIn) are important factors influencing payment processing platforms around the world. Mobile technology expands the reach of the Internet, and provides opportunities for cloud payments and a greater demand for cloud computing applications. Advancements in computing power are making computers more mobile on the front end, and more powerful and smarter on the back end, where improved data processing power can improve fraud mitigation and risk management controls.

- The involvement of non-banks in retail payment systems has increased substantially in recent years, with these entities introducing highly impactful technological payment innovations. New players such as Amazon Payment, Google Checkout, PayPal, and Square are using technology to transform the experience for both consumers and businesses.

Mobile device payment options are also gaining momentum with entrants such as Apple Pay, Google Wallet, and retailer-issued payment options, including the Starbucks App. These apps transmit financial data using a radio frequency referred to as "near field communications" and rely on traditional financial infrastructures for the end payment.

Cryptocurrency uses cryptographic algorithms, which combines the fields of mathematics, computer science, and electrical engineering to enable secure transactions used by ATM cards and ecurrency, such as Bitcoin and Peercoin. As ecurrency providers are not linked to domestic currency and are not monitored by central banks, many critics consider them to be high risk and highly volatile; however, consumers are embracing the flexible payments trend. Businesses need to decide how to best implement appropriate controls over cash payments and cash receipts when the currency is moving to electronic money.

As is made evident by the following charts, Canadian businesses continue to rely on cheques as the most common form of payment for transactions (based on dollar value of transactions). Schembri indicates Canadian businesses are "still among the most cheque-reliant of the major economies."

Payment Categories Proportion of Total 2011 Canadian Payments

Note: "On-Us" transactions refers to transactions conducted within the same bank. For example, a cheque written to a supplier that has a bank account at the same bank.

Video Link: To learn more about the functions of the Canadian Payments Association, take a look at the following video: https://vimeo.com/101633599

Sources: 2013 Annual Report, Canadian Payments Association; CPA Environmental Report 2014, Canadian Payments Association; http://www .bankofcanada.ca/2014/06/dual-vision-canadian-payments-system/; Canadian Payment Methods and Trends October 2012 report, Canadian Payments Association; and https://www.cdnpay.ca/imis15/pdf/pdfs_publications/examining_canadian_payment_report_2012.pdf.

CHECKPOINT

8. What is a bank statement?
9. What does it mean to reconcile a bank balance?
10. Why do we reconcile the bank statement balance of cash and the depositor's book balance of cash?
11. List items affecting the bank side of a reconciliation and indicate if the items are added or subtracted.
12. List items affecting the book side of a reconciliation and indicate if the items are added or subtracted.

Do Quick Study questions: QS 7-9, QS 7-10, QS 7-11

Financial Statement Analysis

QUICK RATIO

LO7 Calculate the quick ratio and explain its use as an indicator of a company's liquidity.

We learned in Chapter 5 that merchandise inventory often makes up a large portion of current assets for merchandising companies. We know that merchandise inventory must be sold and any resulting accounts receivable need to be collected before cash is available. This often means that a large part of current assets is not readily available for paying liabilities because it is in the form of merchandise inventory.

We explained in Chapter 4 how the current ratio, calculated as total current assets divided by total current liabilities, is useful in assessing a company's ability to pay current liabilities. Because some current assets, specifically merchandise inventories and prepaids, are not readily available as a source of payment for current liabilities, we look to a measure other than the current ratio to obtain a stricter measure of a company's ability to cover current liabilities: the *acid-test ratio*.

The *acid-test ratio* differs from the current ratio by excluding current assets that are *less liquid*, such as inventory and prepaids. The **quick ratio**, also called the **acid-test ratio**, is defined as shown in Exhibit 7.11.

EXHIBIT 7.11
Quick Ratio

$$\text{Quick ratio} = \frac{\text{Quick assets*}}{\text{Current liabilities}}$$

*Quick assets are assets that can be readily converted to cash and include cash, short-term investments, and receivables. Current asset accounts that are *excluded* from the quick ratio would include any restricted cash balances and prepaid expenses.

Exhibit 7.12 shows both the quick and current ratios of **WestJet**.

EXHIBIT 7.12
Current and Quick Ratios Compared

	At December 31,				
	2017	2016	2015	2014	2013
Current Ratio	1.04	1.21	0.97	1.29	1.085
Quick Ratio	0.87	1.08	0.82	1.06	0.95

The quick ratio is interpreted in a similar manner as the current ratio. In Exhibit 7.12, WestJet's current ratio at December 31, 2017, shows $1.04 of current assets available to cover each $1.00 of current liability as it comes due. As a stricter measure, the quick ratio tells us WestJet had $0.87 of quick assets to cover each $1.00 of current obligations at the end of 2017. A quick ratio equal to or greater than 1 is generally considered favourable (good). December 2017 saw a significant decline in the current ratio and the quick ratio for WestJet compared to prior years. WestJet's main current liabilities that increased included accounts payable and advance ticket sales. As the advance ticket sales represent an unearned revenue liability balance, for this portion of the current liabilities no real cash obligation exists, indicating the company will still be able to meet the liabilities that require cash settlement. Companies need to manage their liquid asset positions cautiously, as too much cash on hand can also signal inefficient use of company resources. Investors will want to monitor WestJet's quick and current ratios to ensure the decreasing trend does not put the company at a significant risk of failing to meet current obligations.

 CHECKPOINT

13. ABC Company had quick ratios of 1.4 and 1.6 for 2020 and 2021, respectively. Is the change in the ratio favourable or unfavourable?

Do Quick Study question: QS 7-12

CRITICAL THINKING CHALLENGE

Refer to the Critical Thinking Challenge questions at the beginning of the chapter. Compare your answers to those suggested on Connect.

IFRS AND ASPE—THE DIFFERENCES

Difference	International Financial Reporting Standards (IFRS)	Accounting Standards for Private Enterprises (ASPE)
There are no significant differences between IFRS and ASPE related to this chapter.		

A Look Ahead

Chapter 8 takes a look at accounting for customer accounts receivable and short-term notes receivable balances, specifically investigating tools such as A/R aging reports, methods to estimate bad debts, and using the accounts receivable turnover ratio and days' sales uncollected ratios to evaluate financial statements.

For further study on some topics of relevance to this chapter, please see the following Extend Your Knowledge supplements:

EYK 7-1 Voucher System of Control

EYK 7-2 Global Profiles of the Fraudster

EYK 7-3 Examples of Bank Documents (bank statement, cheque, deposit slip)

SUMMARY

LO1 Define, explain the purpose of, and identify the principles of internal control. An internal control system consists of the policies and procedures that managers use to protect assets, ensure reliable accounting, promote efficient operations, and encourage adherence to company policies. It is a key part of systems design, analysis, and performance. It can prevent avoidable losses and help managers both plan operations and monitor company and human performance. Principles of good internal control include establishing responsibilities to ensure custody, authorization, and recording of assets are performed by separate individuals. Important controls include maintaining adequate records, insuring assets and bonding employees, dividing responsibilities for related transactions, applying technological controls, and performing regular independent reviews.

LO2 Define cash and explain how it is reported. Cash consists of cash on hand and demand deposits, including currency and coins, and amounts on deposit in bank, chequing, and some savings accounts. It also includes items that are acceptable for deposit in these accounts. Cash equivalents or short-term investments are similar to cash; therefore, most companies combine them with cash as a single item on the balance sheet. Cash and cash equivalents are liquid assets because they are converted easily into other assets or used in paying for services or liabilities.

LO3 Apply internal control to cash. Internal control of cash receipts ensures that all cash received is properly recorded and deposited. Cash receipts arise from cash sales, collections of customers' accounts, receipts of interest and rent, bank loans, sale of assets, and owner investments. Good internal control for cash receipts by mail includes at least two people being assigned to open the mail and prepare a list with each sender's name, amount of money received, and explanation.

LO4 Explain and record petty cash fund transactions. To avoid writing cheques for small amounts, a company sets up one or more petty cash funds to pay for items such as postage, courier fees, repairs, and supplies. A petty cashier is responsible for safekeeping of the cash, for making payments from this fund, and for keeping receipts and records. A Petty Cash account is debited when the fund is established or increased in size. The cashier presents all paid receipts to the company's cashier for reimbursement to restore petty cash to its full amount. Petty cash disbursements are recorded whenever the fund is replenished with debits to expense accounts reflecting receipts and a credit to cash.

LO5 Explain and identify banking activities and the control features they provide. Banks offer several services—such as the bank account, the bank deposit, and chequing—that promote the control or safeguarding of cash. A bank account is set up by a bank and permits a customer to deposit money for safeguarding and cheque withdrawals. A bank deposit is money added to the account with a deposit slip as proof. A cheque is a document signed by the depositor instructing the bank to pay a specified amount of money to a designated recipient. Sales resulting from debit card and credit card transactions are usually deposited into the bank account immediately, less a fee. Electronic funds transfer (EFT) uses electronic communication to transfer cash from one party to another, and it decreases certain risks. Companies increasingly use it because of its convenience and low cost.

LO6 Prepare a bank reconciliation and journalize any resulting adjustment(s). A bank reconciliation is prepared to prove the accuracy of the depositor's and the bank's records. In completing a reconciliation, the bank statement balance is adjusted for items such as outstanding cheques and unrecorded deposits made on or before the bank statement date but not reflected on the statement. The depositor's Cash account balance also often requires adjustment. These adjustments include items such as service charges, bank collections for the depositor, and interest earned on the account balance.

LO7 Calculate the quick ratio and explain its use as an indicator of a company's liquidity. The quick ratio (also known as acid-test ratio) is calculated as quick assets (cash, short-term investments, and receivables) divided by current liabilities. It is an indicator of a company's ability to pay its current liabilities with its existing quick assets. A ratio equal to or greater than 1 is often considered adequate.

 ### Guidance Answers to DECISION MAKER

Campaign Manager

A forced vacation policy is part of a system of good internal controls. When employees are forced to take vacations, their ability to hide any fraudulent behaviour decreases. This is because someone must take on the responsibilities of the person on vacation, and the replacement employee potentially can uncover fraudulent behaviour or records. A forced vacation policy is especially important for employees in more sensitive positions of handling money or other easily transferable assets.

Internal Auditor

You inform your supervisor, who emphasizes that the purpose of the surprise visit was defeated because you allowed another employee to interfere with and influence your actions; this was a valuable first lesson! Your problem is now whether to accept the situation or to dig further to see if the petty cashier is abusing petty cash. Since you were asked to postpone your count and the fund consists of new $20 bills, you have legitimate concerns about whether money is being borrowed for personal use. You should conduct a further investigation. One result might show that the most recent reimbursement of the fund was for $180 (= 9 × $20) or more. In that case, this reimbursement can leave the fund with sequentially numbered $20 bills. But if the most recent reimbursement was for less than $180, the presence of nine sequentially numbered $20 bills suggests that the $180 of new $20 bills was obtained from a bank as replacement for bills that had been removed. Neither situation shows that the cashier is stealing money. Yet the second case indicates that the cashier "borrowed" the cash and later replaced it after the auditor showed up. In writing your report, you must not conclude that the cashier is unethical unless evidence along with your knowledge of company policies supports it. Your report must present facts according to the evidence.

Entrepreneur

Your analysis of allowing credit card sales should estimate the benefits against the costs. The primary benefit is the potential to increase sales by attracting customers who prefer the convenience of credit cards. The primary cost is the fee charged by the credit card company for providing this service to your store. Your analysis should therefore estimate the expected increase in sales dollars from allowing credit card sales and then subtract (1) the normal costs and expenses, and (2) the credit card fees associated with this expected increase in sales dollars. If your analysis shows an increase in profit from allowing credit card sales, your store should probably allow them.

 ## Guidance Answers to CHECKPOINT

1. c
2. Technology reduces processing errors, allows more extensive testing of records, limits the amount of hard evidence of processing steps, and highlights the importance of maintaining separation of duties.
3. a
4. If all cash payments are made by cheque, numerous cheques for small amounts must be written. Because this practice is expensive and time consuming, a petty cash fund is established to make small cash payments.
5. If the petty cash fund is not reimbursed at the end of an accounting period, the transactions in petty cash are not yet recorded in the accounts and the petty cash asset is overstated. But these amounts are rarely large enough to affect users' decisions based on financial statements.
6. First, when the petty cash fund is reimbursed, the petty cash transactions are recorded in their proper accounts. Second, reimbursement also gives money that allows the fund to continue being used. Third, reimbursement identifies any cash shortage or overage in the fund.
7. The retailer receives payment faster than if it had to collect credit sales, and the risk of uncollectible customer accounts is transferred to the credit card company and bank.
8. A bank statement is a detailed report prepared by the bank outlining the activities in a depositor's account over the period of time, generally monthly.
9. To reconcile a bank balance means to outline the difference between the cash balance in the depositor's accounting records and the balance on the bank statement.
10. The purpose of the bank reconciliation is to determine if any errors have been made by the bank or by the depositor and to determine if the bank has completed any transactions affecting the depositor's account that the depositor has not recorded. It is also an internal control mechanism to ensure that the company's cash system is operating properly.
11. Outstanding cheques—subtracted
    Unrecorded deposits—added
12. Bank service charges—subtracted
    Debit memos—subtracted
    NSF cheques—subtracted
    Interest earned—added
    Credit memos—added
13. Unfavourable.

DEMONSTRATION PROBLEM

Required

Consider the following information and prepare a bank reconciliation, along with any resulting journal entries, for TJ Company, an online retailer that specializes in digital device accessories, at April 30, 2020.

Analysis Component:

Assume that you are the owner of TJ Company and have just read an online article about employee accounting fraud. As a result, you have decided to review the bank reconciliation prepared for April 30. You notice that cheque #808 for $850 is not included with the cancelled cheques that are returned by the bank with the bank statement. Your office is small and is managed by one employee, Brent Wicker. When questioned, Brent cannot locate the missing cheque. What do you do, if anything? Explain.

The bank reconciliation prepared by TJ Company on March 31, 2020, follows:

TJ Company Bank Reconciliation March 31, 2020				
Bank statement balance		$7,670	Book balance	$8,590
Add:				
Deposit of March 31 in transit		1,100		
		$8,770		
Deduct:				
Outstanding cheques:				
#797	$ 60			
#804	120	180		
Adjusted bank balance		$8,590	Adjusted book balance	$8,590

The following bank statement is available for April:

Bank Statement					
To: TJ Company				April 30, 2020 Bank of Nova Scotia	
Cheques/Charges/Debits			Deposits/Credits		Balance
					7,670
#811	04/03	834	04/03	1,100	7,936
#807	04/07	375	04/07	810	8,371
#810	04/13	208	04/13	690	8,853
NSF	04/18	450	04/18	680	9,083
#808	04/23	850	04/23	355	8,588
#797	04/27	60	04/27	750	9,278
#814	04/30	550	04/30	620	9,348
#813	04/30	372	INT	47	9,023
#809	04/30	124			8,899
SC	04/30	32	04/30		8,867
NSF = Not Sufficient Funds		SC = Service Charge		INT = Interest	

A list of deposits made and cheques written during April, taken from the cash receipts journal and cash disbursements journal, is shown below:

Deposits Made			Cheques Written		
April 7	$ 810		No. 807	$ 375	
13	690		808	850	
18	680		809	124	
23	355		810	208	
27	750		811	348	
30	620		812	207	
30	770		813	372	
Total April Cash Receipts	$4,675		814	550	
			815	405	
			816	602	
			Total April Cash Disbursements...	$4,041	

General Ledger Cash Account:

		Cash			Acct. No. 101
Date	Explanation	PR	Debit	Credit	Balance
2020					
March 31	Balance				8,590
April 30		CR12	4,675		13,265
30		CD14		4,041	9,224

In reviewing cheques returned by the bank, the bookkeeper discovered that cheque #811, for delivery expense, was recorded in the cash disbursements journal incorrectly as $348. The NSF cheque for $450 was that of customer A. Hussain, deposited in April.

Planning the Solution

- Set up a schedule like Exhibit 7.10 with a bank side and a book side for the reconciliation.
- Follow the nine steps used in the chapter to prepare the bank reconciliation.
- For every reconciling item on the book side, prepare an entry, if required.
- Prepare an answer to the analysis component.

SOLUTION

TJ Company					
Bank Reconciliation					
April 30, 2020					
Bank statement balance		$8,867	Book balance		$9,224
Add:			Add:		
Deposit of April 30 in transit		770	Interest income		47
		$9,637			$9,271
Deduct:			Deduct:		
Outstanding cheques:			Error (cheque #811 for delivery exp)	$486	
#804	$120		NSF cheque	450	
#812	207		Service charge	32	968
#815	405				
#816	602	1,334			
Adjusted bank balance		$8,303	Adjusted book balance		$8,303

Required Entries

April	30	Cash..	47	
		Interest income..		47
		To record interest earned.		
	30	Delivery Expense..	486	
		Cash		486
		To correct accounting error on cheque #811.		
	30	Accounts Receivable—A. Hussain.....................	450	
		Cash		450
		To reinstate customer account due to NSF cheque.		
	30	Bank Service Charges Expense........................	32	
		Cash		32
		To record bank service charges.		

Analysis Component:

Several things need to be done. A review of prior months' bank reconciliations needs to be conducted to determine if this is an anomaly or a recurring event. The journal entry regarding cheque #808 needs to be reviewed to determine the payee. The payee, if identifiable, needs to be contacted to verify the purchase. If this cannot be done, the bank needs to be contacted to determine if its records are able to verify the payee on the cheque. Hopefully, Brent made an honest mistake and misplaced the cheque. However, in the future, the owner of TJ Company should review each bank reconciliation and ensure that the cheques being paid are scrutinized to ensure they are for business-related payments.

GLOSSARY

Acid-test ratio See *quick ratio*.

Bank reconciliation An analysis that explains the difference between the balance of a chequing account shown in the depositor's records and the balance reported on the bank statement.

Bond An insurance policy purchased by a company to protect against losses from theft by that employee.

Cancelled cheques Cheques that the bank has paid and deducted from the customer's account during the month

Cash Consists of cash on hand and demand deposits, including currency, coins, and amounts on deposit in bank chequing or savings accounts.

Cash Over and Short account An income statement account used to record cash shortages and cash overages arising from omitted petty cash receipts and from errors in making change.

Cheque A document signed by the depositor instructing the bank to pay a specified amount of money to a designated recipient.

Collusion An act in which two or more people agree to commit a fraud.

Corporate governance The mechanism by which individuals in a company, in particular the board of directors, are motivated to align their behaviours with the overall corporate good.

Debit cards Cards used at point of sale to transfer payment for a purchase immediately from the customer' to the vendor's bank account.

Deposit slip Bank document that lists the items such as currency, coins, and cheques deposited along with each of their dollar amounts.

Electronic funds transfer (EFT) The use of electronic communication to transfer cash from one party to another.

Interest income interest earned on outstanding customer notes receivable and investments in interest-bearing debt.

Internal control system All the policies and procedures managers use to protect assets, ensure reliable accounting, promote efficient operations, and urge adherence to company policies.

Liquid assets Assets such as cash that are easily converted into other types of assets or used to buy services or to pay liabilities.

Liquidity A characteristic of an asset that refers to how easily the asset can be converted into cash or another type of asset or used in paying for services or obligations.

Petty cashier Employee responsible for safekeeping of the cash, making payments from this fund, and keeping accurate records.

Principles of internal control Fundamental principles of internal control that apply to all companies requiring management to ensure transactions and activities are authorized, maintain records, insure assets, separate recordkeeping and custody of assets, establish a separation of duties, apply technological controls, and perform internal and external audits.

Quick assets Those current assets that are most liquid, specifically cash, short-term investments, and receivables.

Quick ratio A ratio used to assess a company's ability to cover its current debts with existing assets calculated as quick assets (cash, short-term investments, and receivables) divided by current liabilities; also called *acid-test ratio*.

Separation of duties An internal control principle requiring the division of responsibility for related transactions between two or more individuals or departments.

Signature card Bank document that includes the signature of each person authorized to sign cheques from the account.

Three-way match A special control over cash disbursements to prevent payment of invoices for which the goods have not yet been received or were not approved internally. Three documents—purchase order, receiving report, and invoice—must be present and the information must agree or be "matched" before any payment is made to the supplier.

KNOWLEDGE CHECK-UP

1. The following asset has the highest risk of theft:
   a. Inventory
   b. Cash
   c. Land
   d. Property, plant, and equipment

2. The fundamental principles of internal control include which of the following:
   a. Establish a separation of duties
   b. Ensure transactions are authorized
   c. Maintain records
   d. All of the above.

3. The three drivers of fraud include:
   a. Opportunity, intrinsic, and motivation
   b. Opportunity, honesty, and motivation
   c. Opportunity, rationale, and motivation
   d. None of the above.

4. Internal audits help the internal control environment by:
   a. Regularly and independently testing to make sure internal control procedures are followed
   b. Directing and training employees to follow the employee handbook
   c. Reporting results to external users of financial statements
   d. All of the above.

5. Separation of duties involves separating the following duties:
   a. Custody, authorization, and attitude of employees
   b. Custody, authorization, and recording of assets
   c. Control, access, and recording of assets
   d. Control, authorization, and receipt of assets

6. Limitations of internal control include:
   a. Human error or human neglect
   b. Human neglect and human misjudgment
   c. Human error or human fraud
   d. Human negligence and human misjudgment

7. The following procedures represent a basic guideline for handling cash:
   a. Separate handling and recordkeeping of cash
   b. Deposit cash receipts promptly in the bank
   c. Make cash disbursements by cheque
   d. All of the above.

8. The journal entry to establish a petty cash fund is the following:
   a. Dr. Petty Cash $XXX, Cr. Cash $XXX
   b. Dr. Petty Cash $XXX, Cr. Supplies $XXX
   c. Dr. Cash $XXX, Cr. Petty Cash $XXX
   d. Dr. Cash Over and Short $XXX, Cr. Petty Cash $XXX

9. Credit card transactions typically cost companies a fee. This cost is recorded as:
   a. Cost of Goods Sold
   b. Sales
   c. Credit Card Expense
   d. Merchandise Inventory

10. Outstanding cheques are _____ the _____ balance on the bank reconciliation.
    a. deducted from, bank
    b. added back to, bank
    c. deducted from, book
    d. added back to, book

CONCEPT REVIEW QUESTIONS

1. List the following assets from most liquid to least liquid: merchandise inventory, building, accounts receivable, cash.

2. Why are internal controls important in a business? List the fundamental principles of internal control.

3. Eddie works at a clothing store in the mall. He sees that his manager is very busy. At the end of the day, Eddie offers to count the cash in the cash register, deposit it at the bank, and record the accounting journal entries. What is the risk in this situation? Explain using the concept of separation of duties.

4. Internal control procedures are important in every business, but at what stage in the development of a business do they become critical?

5. The bartender at a restaurant performs a monthly inventory count for the wine, beer, and other liquor and will update the accounting records for any differences between the inventory records and the physical inventory count. Identify the weaknesses, implications, and recommendations (WIR).

6. Using the three components of the fraud triangle, explain why a student may cheat on an exam.

7. When merchandise is purchased for a large store, why are department managers not permitted to deal directly with suppliers?

8. What is a petty cash receipt? Who signs a petty cash receipt?

9. Refer to **Spin Master**'s balance sheet in Appendix III. What is its cash balance as at December 31, 2016 and December 31, 2017?

10. WestJet Airlines showed cash and cash equivalents on December 31, 2017, of $1,147,076,000. What percentage is this of total assets?

QUICK STUDY

QS 7-1 Internal control objectives LO1

You are currently part of a university work experience program. Your job placement is at the municipal transit centre. Your supervisor is responsible for the recording and distribution of monthly transit passes to authorized vendors throughout the city. The vendors pay $50 per bus pass and sell them for $55. Your work experience job is to prepare a monthly reconciliation of the transit passes including the quantity sold, the number actually distributed, the unsold passes, and the cash proceeds. You are unable to reconcile the past two months. The bus passes are sequentially numbered and, in checking the sequence, you notice that numbers 9750 to 9820, 11012 to 11750, and 22000 to 22440 cannot be accounted for. You bring this to the attention of the supervisor, who tells you that reconciliations are never done; the job was created by her superior "to give you something to do," and not to worry about it.

a. What is the main objective of internal control and how is it accomplished?

b. Why should recordkeeping for assets be separated from custody over the assets?

c. Do you report your findings?

QS 7-2 Reporting cash and other current assets LO2

Prepare the current asset section based on the following alphabetized post-closing trial balance information at March 31, 2020, for White Eagle Company:

Account	Debits	Credits
Accounts payable		$ 7,000
Accounts receivable	$ 4,500	
Accumulated depreciation		9,900
Cash	15,000	
Isaac Whiteagle, capital		25,800
Notes payable, due 2026		14,000
Petty cash	600	
Prepaid rent	3,200	
Property, plant, and equipment	8,000	
Unearned revenue		4,600

QS 7-3 Internal controls for cash LO3

The treasurer of a local not-for-profit organization was found guilty today of defrauding the organization of thousands of dollars. Among the individual's many responsibilities were the recording of cash deposits, the writing of cheques, and the preparation of the bank reconciliation. A member of the organization suspected wrongdoing when the treasurer reported total cash collections of $2,800 regarding the sale of non-sequentially numbered raffle tickets; the member submitted $1,600 to the treasurer and knew that other members had collectively sold in excess of $3,000. The police were consulted and an investigation revealed that the treasurer not only had pocketed an undisclosed amount of cash over a two-year period but also had made cash withdrawals from the bank and destroyed the debit memos returned with the bank statement.

Required Identify three weaknesses in how cash is handled. For each weakness, explain the implication of the weakness and make a recommendation to the organization for the future.

QS 7-4 Petty cash LO4

The petty cash fund of the Wee Ones Agency was established on May 1, 2020, at $75. At the end of the month, the fund contained $13 and had the following receipts: film rentals, $19; refreshments for meetings, $23 (both expenditures to be classified as Entertainment Expense); postage, $7; and printing, $13.

1. Prepare the journal entry to record the establishment of the fund.
2. Prepare a summary of the petty cash payments similar to Exhibit 7.3, and then record the reimbursement on May 31.
3. Explain when the Petty Cash account would be credited in a journal entry.

QS 7-5 Petty cash LO4

Wilson Art set up a petty cash fund of $200 on March 1, 2020. On March 17, the petty cash box contained $19 and the following receipts: $75 for printing, $48 for taxi fare, and $55 for delivery expense. Record the reimbursement of the fund on March 17.

QS 7-6 Petty cash LO4

Canmore Consulting established a $100 petty cash fund on September 1, 2020. On September 23, the petty cash box contained $7 and receipts for the following expenses: $32 for entertainment expense (lunch with a client), $45 for computer repair, and $18 for delivery expense. Record the reimbursement of the fund on September 23.

QS 7-7 Credit card transactions LO5

Journalize the following transactions (assume a perpetual inventory system):

February	1	Recorded $75,000 of sales (cost $62,000) to customers using MasterCard. Assume MasterCard charges the retailer 2.5% for credit card transactions.
February	10	Sold merchandise to customers who paid $28,000 in cash (cost $23,000).

QS 7-8 Debit card transactions LO5

Journalize the following transactions (assume a perpetual inventory system):

Oct.	1	Recorded sales of $14,000 (cost $8,000) to customers using debit cards. Assume the bank charges 0.25% for all debit card transactions.
	7	Sold merchandise to customers who paid $3,500 in cash (cost $2,800).

QS 7-9 Bank reconciliation LO6

1. Identify whether each of the following items affects the bank or book side of the reconciliation and indicate if the amount represents an addition or a subtraction:

   a. Deposits in transit.

   b. Interest on average monthly balance.

   c. Credit memos.

   d. Bank service charges.

   e. Outstanding cheques.

   f. Debit memos.

   g. NSF cheques.

2. Which of the previous items require a journal entry?

QS 7-10 Bank reconciliation LO6

Bolton Company's October 31, 2020, bank statement showed a cash balance of $15,400, while the company's general ledger Cash account for the same date showed a balance of $13,150. A bank deposit of October 31 for $1,200 does not appear on the bank statement. Cheques #150 for $980 and #169 for $2,515, both written in October, had not cleared the bank during October. Bank service charges for the month were $45. Prepare a bank reconciliation at October 31, 2020, and prepare the necessary entries.

QS 7-11 Bank reconciliation LO6

Your accountant has been asked to prepare the bank reconciliation for Ultimate Discs (UD), a store that sells frisbees.

- You log in to the online bank statement and note that the bank balance is $66,362 as at March 31, 2020. The amount of cash recorded in the accounting records (the books) is $64,800.

- You go through the online bank statement and notice an electronic fund transfer from a customer for $2,300. This customer had purchased goods on account.

- UD earned $48 of interest income, but was also charged a $25 service charge as the cash balance dropped below the minimum balance of $70,000 this month.

- The bank notified you that one of the cheques you had deposited had insufficient funds in that customer's bank account. The cheque and bank charges are $761.

Required

a. Prepare a bank reconciliation at March 31, 2020.

b. Prepare the necessary journal entries.

QS 7-12 Quick ratio LO7

Your company has a policy of granting credit only to customers whose quick ratio is greater than or equal to 1. Based on this policy, determine if the following companies would be granted credit (round to two decimal places). Why or why not?

	Company A	Company B
Cash	$1,200	$1,200
Accounts receivable	2,700	2,700
Inventory	5,000	5,000
Prepaid expenses	600	600
Accounts payable	3,100	4,750
Other current liabilities	250	950

EXERCISES

Exercise 7-1 Analyzing internal control LO1

Lombard Company is a young business that has grown rapidly. The company's bookkeeper, who was hired two years ago, left town suddenly after the company's manager discovered that a great deal of money had disappeared over the past 18 months. An audit disclosed that the bookkeeper had written and signed several cheques made payable to the bookkeeper's brother and then recorded the cheques as salaries expense. The brother, who cashed the cheques but had never worked for the company, left town with the bookkeeper. As a result, the company incurred an uninsured loss of $84,000.

Evaluate Lombard Company's internal control system and identify violations of the principles of internal control.

Exercise 7-2 Internal control objectives LO3

As a member of the city's internal audit team, you have been instructed to observe the procedures regarding the collection of coins from the municipally owned parking meters. You accompany the civic employee on the collection route. The employee uses a key to open the locked coin compartment of the meter and empties its contents into a canvas bag that closes with a drawstring. When the bag is full, the employee closes it and places it in the vehicle, which is parked along the route. At the end of the day, the civic employee delivers the bags to two individuals in a municipal office who are jointly responsible for counting the contents.

Required Write a brief report identifying three weaknesses in the above situation. For each weakness, identify the implication of the weakness and make a recommendation.

Exercise 7-3 Recommending internal control procedures LO3

What internal control procedures would you recommend in each of the following situations?

a. A concession company has one employee who sells T-shirts and sunglasses at the beach. Each day, the employee is given enough shirts and sunglasses to last through the day and enough cash to make change. The money is kept in a box at the stand.

b. An antique store has one employee who is given cash and sent to garage sales each weekend. The employee pays cash for merchandise to be resold at the antique store.

Exercise 7-4 Internal control over cash receipts LO3

Some of Fanning Co.'s cash receipts from customers are sent to the company in the mail. Fanning's bookkeeper opens the letters and deposits the cash received each day. What internal control problem do you see in this arrangement? What changes would you recommend?

Exercise 7-5 Petty cash fund LO4

Cameron Co. established a $200 petty cash fund on January 1, 2020. One week later, on January 8, the fund contained $46.85 in cash and receipts for these expenditures: postage, $51.60; transportation-in, $35.00; store supplies, $41.55; and a withdrawal of $25.00 by Jim Cameron, the owner. Cameron uses the perpetual method to account for merchandise inventory.

a. Prepare the journal entry to establish the fund on January 1.

b. Prepare a summary of the petty cash payments similar to Exhibit 7.3 and record the entry to reimburse the fund on January 8.

Analysis Component: If the January 8 entry to reimburse the fund were not recorded and financial statements were prepared for the month of January, would profit be over- or understated?

Exercise 7-6 **Petty cash fund** LO4

Willard Company established a $400 petty cash fund on September 9, 2020. On September 30, the fund had $159.40 in cash along with receipts for these expenditures: transportation-in, $32.45; office supplies, $113.55; and repairs expense, $87.60. Willard uses the perpetual method to account for merchandise inventory. The petty cashier could not account for the $7.00 shortage in the fund.

a. Prepare the September 9 entry to establish the fund.

b. Prepare a summary of the petty cash payments similar to Exhibit 7.3 and record the entry on September 30 to reimburse the fund and reduce it to $300.

Analysis Component: You are the senior marketing manager and are reviewing the unadjusted account balances for your division. You notice the $7.00 cash shortage recorded on September 30 regarding petty cash. The current petty cash custodian has been in place for three months. What should be done, if anything? Explain.

Exercise 7-7 **Petty cash fund** LO4

Conway Designs established a $250 petty cash fund on October 1, 2020. Prepare the entry to replenish the fund at the end of each of the following months of activity:

a. The petty cash box contained $28 on October 31 along with receipts for $125 for cleaning, $31 for postage, and $55 for delivery expense.

b. On November 30, the petty cash box contained only two receipts, for a $93 computer repair and a $115 entertainment expense. The petty cash custodian counted cash remaining of $50.

c. The petty cash box contained $24 on December 31 plus receipts for $48 for gas expense, $122 for office supplies, and $56 for entertainment expense. In addition to replenishing the fund, it was increased by $50.

Exercise 7-8 **Petty cash fund** LO4

Dallas Repairs completed the following petty cash transactions during July 2020:

July	5	Prepared a $250 cheque, cashed it, and turned the proceeds and the petty cash box over to Elliott Grace, the petty cash custodian.
	6	Paid $18.00 courier fees.
	12	Purchased file folders, $12.50.
	14	Reimbursed Dara Bains, the manager of the business, $34.26 for office supplies purchased.
	18	Purchased paper for printer, $42.15.
	28	Purchased stamps, $23.00
	30	Reimbursed Dara Bains $64.80 for business car expenses.
	31	Elliott Grace sorted the petty cash receipts by accounts affected and exchanged them for a cheque to reimburse the fund for expenditures. However, there was $51.04 in cash in the fund.

Required

1. Prepare a general journal entry to record establishing the petty cash fund.

2. Prepare a summary of petty cash payments similar to Exhibit 7.2 that has these categories: delivery expense, auto expense, postage expense, merchandise inventory, and office supplies.

3. Prepare the general journal entry to record the reimbursement of the fund.

Exercise 7-9 **Credit card and debit card transactions** LO5

Journalize the following transactions for Stillwater Spa Consultants:

Oct.	1	Sold services for $170,000 to customers using debit cards. Assume the bank charges 0.5% for all debit card transactions.
	7	Sold services to customers for $20,000 cash.
	8	Recorded Visa credit card sales totalling $98,000. Assume Visa applies fees of 2%.
	10	Sold $72,000 of services to Edson Community Health Clinic, terms 2/15, n/30.
	25	Collected the amount owing regarding the October 10 sale.

Exercise 7-10 Credit card and debit card transactions LO5

On January 15, Tundra Co. sold merchandise to customers for cash of $42,000 (cost $28,500). Merchandise costing $10,500 was sold to customers for $15,800 on January 17; terms 2/10, n/30. Sales totalling $296,000 (cost $198,000) were recorded on January 20 to customers using MasterCard; assume the credit card charges a 2% fee. On January 25, sales of $72,000 (cost $48,200) were made to debit card customers. The bank charges Tundra a flat fee of 0.5% on all debit card transactions.

Required Prepare journal entries for each of the transactions described (assume a perpetual inventory system).

Analysis Component: Identify the advantages and disadvantages of each type of sale: cash sale, credit sale, credit card sale, or debit card sale. Explain why Tundra would likely accept all these types of sales.

Exercise 7-11 Preparation of bank reconciliation LO6

CHECK FIGURE: 1. Adjusted book balance = $10,592

The bank reconciliation prepared by Winfield Construction on June 30, 2020, appeared as follows:

Winfield Construction Bank Reconciliation June 30, 2020			
Bank statement balance	$ 8,700	Book balance	$9,260
Add:			
Deposit of June 30 in transit	1,300		
	$10,000		
Deduct:			
Outstanding cheque #14	740		
Adjusted bank balance	$ 9,260	Adjusted book balance	$9,260

The Cash account in the general ledger appeared as follows on July 31:

		Cash			Acct. No. 101
Date	Explanation	PR	Debit	Credit	Balance
2020					
June 30	Balance				9,260
July 31		CR3	4,672		13,932
31		CD6		2,909	11,023

A list of deposits made and cheques written during July, taken from the cash receipts journal and cash disbursements journal, is shown below:

Deposits Made		Cheques Written	
July 8	$1,190	No. 52	$1,663
11	1,550	53	894
24	1,339	54	352
31	593		
Total July Cash Receipts	$4,672	Total July Cash Disbursements	$2,909

The following bank statement is available for July:

Bank Statement					
To: Winfield Construction					July 31, 2020 Bank of Montreal
Cheques/Charges			Deposits/Credits		Balance
					8,700
NSF	07/02	431	07/02	1,300	9,569
#52	07/08	1,663	07/08	1,190	9,096
#96	07/11	391	07/11	1,550	10,255
			07/24	1,339	11,594
#54	07/31	352	07/31		11,242
NSF = Not Sufficient Funds		SC = Service Charge	PMT = Principal Payment		INT = Interest

In reviewing cheques returned by the bank, the bookkeeper noted that cheque #96 written by Winburn Construction in the amount of $391 was charged against Winfield's account in error by the bank. The NSF cheque was regarding a customer account, Jim Anderson.

Required

1. Prepare a bank reconciliation at July 31.

2. Prepare the necessary journal entry to bring the general ledger Cash account into agreement with the adjusted balance on the bank reconciliation.

Analysis Component: If the journal entries in Part 2 were not recorded, what financial statement elements (profit, assets, liabilities, and equity) would be over- or understated?

Exercise 7-12 Bank reconciliation LO6

CHECK FIGURE: Adjusted book balance = $11,090

Kesler Co. deposits all receipts intact on the day received and makes all payments by cheque. On July 31, 2020, after all posting was completed, its Cash account showed a $10,932 debit balance. However, Kesler's July 31 bank statement showed only $10,077 on deposit in the bank on that day along with the following information.

a. Outstanding cheques, $2,756.

b. Included with the July cancelled cheques returned by the bank was a $30 debit memo for bank services.

c. Cheque #919, returned with the cancelled cheques, was correctly drawn for $236 in payment of the utility bill and was paid by the bank on July 15. However, it had been recorded with a debit to Utilities Expense and a credit to Cash as though it were for $326.

d. The July 31 cash receipts, $3,671, were placed in the bank's night depository after banking hours on that date and were unrecorded by the bank at the time the July bank statement was prepared.

Required

a. Prepare a bank reconciliation for Kesler Co. at July 31.

b. Give the journal entries that Kesler Co. should make as a result of having prepared the bank reconciliation in part (a).

Analysis Component: Identify whether profit, assets, liabilities, and equity would be over- or understated if the journal entries in part (b) were not recorded.

Exercise 7-13 **Bank reconciling items and required entries** LO6

Set up a table with the following headings for a bank reconciliation as of September 30:

Bank Balance		Book Balance			Not Shown on the Reconciliation
Add	Deduct	Add	Deduct	Must Adjust	

For each item that follows, place an X in the appropriate column to indicate whether the item should be added to or deducted from the book or bank balance, or whether it should not appear on the reconciliation. If the book balance is to be adjusted, place a Dr. or Cr. in the Must Adjust column to indicate whether the Cash balance should be debited or credited.

1. Interest income earned on the account.

2. Deposit made on September 30 after the bank was closed.

3. Cheques outstanding on August 31 that cleared the bank in September.

4. NSF cheque from customer returned on September 15 but not recorded by the company.

5. Cheques written and mailed to payees on September 30.

6. Deposit made on September 5 that was processed on September 8.

7. Bank service charge.

8. Cheques written and mailed to payees on October 5.

9. Cheques written by another company but charged against the company's account in error.

10. Customer payment through electronic fund transfer received in the bank but not recorded in the company's books.

11. Bank charge for collection of electronic fund transfer in Item 10.

12. Cheque written against the account and cleared by the bank; not recorded by the bookkeeper.

Exercise 7-14 **Quick ratio** LO7

Calculate the quick ratio in each of the following cases:

	Case X	Case Y	Case Z
Cash..	$ 870	$1,190	$1,520
Current investments.............................	-0-	-0-	640
Receivables...	-0-	1,340	1,080
Inventory..	2,700	1,280	5,260
Prepaid expenses	1,900	810	1,180
Total current assets..............................	$5,470	$4,620	$9,680
Current liabilities.................................	$2,900	$1,450	$4,700

Required Which case is in the best position to meet short-term obligations most easily? Explain your choice. *Round calculations to two decimal places.*

PROBLEMS

Problem 7-1A Principles of internal control LO1

For the following five scenarios, identify the principle of internal control that is violated. Next, make a recommendation as to what the business should do to ensure adherence to principles of internal control.

1. At Stratford Iron Company, Jill and Joan alternate lunch hours. Normally Jill is the petty cash custodian, but if someone needs petty cash when Jill is at lunch, Joan fills in as custodian.

2. Nadine McDonald does all the posting of patient charges and payments at the Northampton Medical Clinic. Every night, Nadine backs up the computerized accounting system to a tape and stores the tape in a locked file at her desk.

3. Jack Mawben prides himself on hiring quality workers who require little supervision. As office manager, Jack gives his employees full discretion over their tasks and has seen no reason to perform independent reviews of their work for years.

4. Bill Clark's manager has told him to "reduce overhead" no matter what! Bill decides to raise the deductible on the plant's property insurance from $5,000 to $10,000. This cuts the property insurance premium in half. In a related move, he decides that bonding of the plant's employees is really a waste of money since the company has not experienced any losses due to employee theft. Bill saves the entire amount of the bonding insurance premium by dropping the bonding insurance.

5. Catherine Young records all incoming customer cash receipts for her employer and also posts the customer payments to their accounts.

Problem 7-2A Establishing, reimbursing, and increasing the petty cash fund LO4

Halifax Fitness Consulting completed the following petty cash transactions during February 2020:

Feb.	2	Prepared a $360 cheque, cashed it, and gave the proceeds and the petty cash box to Nick Reed, the petty cashier.
	5	Purchased paper for the copier, $22
	9	Paid $38 COD charges on merchandise purchased for resale. *Assume Halifax Fitness Consulting uses the perpetual method to account for merchandise inventory.*
	12	Paid $17 postage to express mail a contract to a client.
	14	Reimbursed Kim Marin, the manager of the business, $148 for business auto expenses.
	20	Purchased stationery, $65.
	23	Paid a courier $8 to deliver merchandise sold to a customer.
	25	Paid $20 COD charges on merchandise purchased for resale.
	28	Paid $24 for stamps.
	28	Reed sorted the petty cash receipts by accounts affected and exchanged them for a cheque to reimburse the fund for expenditures. However, there was only $11 in cash in the fund. In addition, the size of the petty cash fund was increased to $500.

Required

1. Prepare a journal entry to record establishing the petty cash fund.

2. Prepare a summary of petty cash payments, similar to Exhibit 7.3 that has these categories: delivery expense, auto expense, postage expense, merchandise inventory, and office supplies. Sort the payments into the appropriate categories and total the expenditures in each category.

3. Prepare the journal entry to record the reimbursement and the increase of the fund.

Analysis Component: One of your responsibilities as an employee with Halifax Fitness is to handle the petty cash fund. You are concerned about the auto expense claims made regularly by Kim Marin, the manager who hired you: Kim tells you how much the expenditures are and you give her the cash out of petty cash. Kim has never given you receipts to substantiate her claims. The owner of the business is visiting and asks you how things are going. What should you do, if anything? Explain.

Problem 7-3A Petty cash fund reimbursement and analysis of errors LO4

Capital Irrigation has only a general journal in its accounting system and uses it to record all transactions. However, the company recently set up a petty cash fund to facilitate payments of small items. The following petty cash transactions were noted by the petty cashier as occurring during April 2020:

Apr.	1	Received a company cheque for $300 to establish the petty cash fund.
	15	Received a company cheque to replenish the fund for the following expenditures made since April 1 and to increase the fund to $400.
		a. Paid $82 for janitorial service.
		b. Purchased office supplies for $78.15.
		c. Purchased postage stamps for $25.00.
		d. Paid $92.50 to *The County Crier* for an advertisement in the newspaper.
		e. Discovered that $24.35 remained in the petty cash box.
	30	The petty cashier noted that $244.95 remained in the fund and decided that the April 15 increase in the fund was too large. Therefore, a company cheque was issued to replenish the fund for the following expenditures made since April 15 and to reduce the fund to $350.
		f. Purchased office supplies for $94.65.
		g. Reimbursed office manager for business auto, $45.60.
		h. Paid $14.80 courier charges to deliver merchandise to a customer.

Required Prepare journal entries to record the establishment of the fund on April 1 and its replenishments on April 15 and April 30.

Analysis Component: Explain how the company's financial statements would be affected if the petty cash fund were not replenished and no entry were made on April 30. *(Hint: The amount of office supplies that appears on a balance sheet is determined by a physical count of the supplies on hand.)*

Problem 7-4A Credit card and debit card transactions LO5

On September 5, Maria Smith, owner of Super Gym Personal Service, provided personal training services to customers for cash of $3,500. Services of $9,000 were billed to corporate clients, terms 2/10, n/30. In the gym Maria uses a Square card reader that attaches to her iPhone, and other services totalling $18,000 were recorded on September 20 for customers using MasterCard (assume a 3.25% fee). On September 25, sales of $7,000 were made to debit card customers, also using the Square reader on her phone. The bank charges Maria a flat fee of 0.75% on all debit card transactions.

Required Prepare journal entries for each of the transactions described.

Analysis Component: Identify the advantages and disadvantages of each type of sale: cash sale, credit sale, credit card sale, or debit card sale. Explain why Maria would likely accept all these types of payment.

Problem 7-5A Preparation of bank reconciliation and recording adjustments LO6

CHECK FIGURE: Adjusted book balance = $2,401.54

The bank reconciliation prepared by Gatz Company on May 31, 2020, appeared as follows:

Gatz Company Bank Reconciliation May 31, 2020					
Bank statement balance		$ 9,564.35	Book balance..............................		$20,056.03
Add:			Deduct:		
Deposit of May 31, in transit......		982.17	NSF cheque plus service		
		$10,546.52	charge	$11,900.50	
Deduct:			Bank service charge................	65.00	11,965.50
Outstanding cheques:			Adjusted book balance...............		$ 8,090.53
#876..	$ 655.99				
#882..	1,800.00	2,455.99			
Adjusted bank balance..................		$ 8,090.53			

The Cash account in the general ledger appeared as follows on June 30 (Gatz uses only a general journal to record transactions):

Cash					Acct. No. 101
Date	Explanation	PR	Debit	Credit	Balance
2020					
May 31	Balance				8,090.53
June 1	Cheque #883	GJ16		1,865.30	6,225.23
1	Cheque #884	GJ16		112.70	6,112.53
3	Cheque #885	GJ16		650.84	5,461.69
4	Cheque #886	GJ16		2,018.45	3,443.24
9	Deposit	GJ16	4,285.26		7,728.50
12	Cheque #887	GJ16		425.15	7,303.35
12	Cheque #888	GJ16		3,040.60	4,262.75
12	Cheque #889	GJ16		974.12	3,288.63
18	Deposit	GJ16	3,515.60		6,804.23
20	Cheque #890	GJ16		2,640.00	4,164.23
21	Cheque #891	GJ16		1,406.24	2,757.99
24	Cheque #892	GJ16		2,590.81	167.18
26	Cheque #893	GJ16		75.99	91.19
29	Deposit	GJ16	1,845.35		1,936.54

The following bank statement is available for June:

Bank Statement					
To: Gatz Company				**June 30, 2020** **Bank of Montreal**	
Cheques/Charges			**Deposits/Credits**		**Balance**
			05/31		**9,564.35**
#884	06/01	112.70	06/01	982.17	10,433.82
#883	06/04	1,865.30			8,568.52
#876	06/09	655.99	06/09	4,285.26	12,197.79
#889	06/12	974.12			11,223.67
#882	06/14	1,800.00			9,423.67
#887	06/18	245.15	06/18	3,515.60	12,694.12
#885	06/20	650.84			12,043.28
#891	06/21	1,046.24			10,997.04
#886	06/29	2,018.45			8,978.59
SC	06/30	75.00	06/30		**8,903.59**
NSF = Not Sufficient Funds		SC = Service Charge	PMT = Principal Payment		INT = Interest

Required

a. Prepare a bank reconciliation at June 30, 2020. Assume that any errors made were by the bookkeeper (cheque #887 was for office supplies; cheque #891 was for utilities expense).

b. Prepare the necessary entries resulting from the bank reconciliation.

Analysis Component: You have been employed with Gatz Company since June 1, 2020, and part of your job is writing and recording cheques as well as preparing the bank reconciliation. To your surprise, the person you replaced brought in the June bank statement as it had been mailed to her home. While preparing the June bank reconciliation, you notice that cheque #882 for $1,800 cleared the bank in June but is not among the cancelled cheques. What should you do? Explain.

Problem 7-6A Preparing a bank reconciliation and recording adjustments LO6

CHECK FIGURE: a. Adjusted book balance = $7,193

The bank reconciliation prepared by Gemma Tours on March 31, 2020, appeared as follows:

Gemma Tours Bank Reconciliation March 31, 2020					
Bank statement balance		$14,800	Book balance...		$32,710
Add:					
Deposit of March 31 in transit............		21,050			
		$35,850			
Deduct:					
Outstanding cheques:					
#79...	$1,250				
#84...	1,890	3,140			
Adjusted bank balance............................		$32,710	Adjusted book balance		$32,710

The Cash account in the general ledger appeared as follows on April 30:

			Cash			Acct. No. 101
Date	Explanation	PR	Debit	Credit		Balance
2020						
March 31	Balance					32,710.00
April 30		CR11	34,049.00			66,759.00
30		CD14		43,643.00		23,116.00

A list of deposits made and cheques written during April, taken from the cash receipts journal and cash disbursements journal, is shown below:

Deposits Made	
April 7..	$14,200
13..	850
18..	13,600
23..	945
27..	1,890
30..	2,564
Total April Cash Receipts	$34,049

Cheques Written	
No. 91..	$ 1,200
92..	5,230
93..	2,590
94..	3,452
95..	2,900
96..	1,811
97..	8,470
98..	2,900
99..	8,590
100..	6,500
Total April Cash Disbursements	$43,643

The following bank statement is available for April:

Bank Statement					
To: Gemma Tours				April 30, 2020 Bank of Montreal	
Cheques/Charges			Deposits/Credits		Balance
					14,800
#93	04/02	2,509	04/03	21,050	33,341
#92	04/07	5,230	04/07	14,200	42,311
#84	04/13	1,890	04/13	850	41,271
NSF	04/18	6,540	04/18	13,600	48,331
#95	04/23	2,900	04/23	945	46,376
#99	04/27	8,590	04/27	1,890	39,676
#96	04/30	1,811	04/30	2,564	40,429
#97	04/30	8,470	04/30	46	32,005
#94	04/30	3,452			28,553
PMT	04/30	9,420			19,133
INT	04/30	35			19,098
SC	04/30	55			19,043
NSF = Not Sufficient Funds		SC = Service Charge	PMT = Principal Payment		INT = Interest

In reviewing cheques returned by the bank, the bookkeeper discovered that cheque #93, for delivery expense, was recorded in the cash disbursements journal incorrectly as $2,590. The NSF cheque was that of customer Laura Clark, deposited in April.

Required

a. Prepare a bank reconciliation at April 30.

b. Prepare the necessary journal entries to bring the general ledger Cash account into agreement with the adjusted balance on the bank reconciliation.

Problem 7-7A Preparing a bank reconciliation and recording adjustments LO6

CHECK FIGURE: 1. Adjusted book balance = $31,984

The following information was available to reconcile Montrose Company's book balance of Cash with its bank statement balance as of October 31, 2020:

a. After all posting was completed on October 31, the company's Cash account had a $13,219 debit balance but its bank statement showed a $29,355 balance.

b. Cheques #296 for $1,334 and #307 for $12,754 were outstanding on the September 30 bank reconciliation. Cheque #307 was returned with the October cancelled cheques, but cheque #296 was not. It was also found that cheque #315 for $893 and cheque #321 for $2,000, both written in October, were not among the cancelled cheques returned with the statement.

c. In comparing the cancelled cheques returned by the bank with the entries in the accounting records, it was found that cheque #320 for the October rent was correctly written for $4,090 but was erroneously entered in the accounting records as $4,900.

d. A credit memo enclosed with the bank statement indicated that there was an electronic fund transfer related to a customer payment for $21,400. A $120 bank service charge was deducted. This transaction was not recorded by Montrose before receiving the bank statement.

e. A debit memo for $3,251 listed a $3,202 NSF cheque plus a $49 NSF charge. The cheque had been received from a customer, Jefferson Tyler. Montrose had not recorded this bounced cheque before receiving the statement.

f. Also enclosed with the statement was a $74 debit memo for bank services. It had not been recorded because no previous notification had been received.

g. The October 31 cash receipts, $6,856, were placed in the bank's night depository after banking hours on that date and this amount did not appear on the bank statement.

Required

1. Prepare a bank reconciliation for the company as of October 31, 2020.

2. Prepare the general journal entries necessary to bring the company's book balance of Cash into agreement with the reconciled balance.

Analysis Component: Assume that an October 31, 2020, bank reconciliation for the company has already been prepared and some of the items were treated incorrectly in preparing the reconciliation. For each of the following errors, explain the effect of the error on (1) the final balance that was calculated by adjusting the bank statement balance, and (2) the final balance that was calculated by adjusting the Cash account balance.

a. The company's Cash account balance of $13,219 was listed on the reconciliation as $12,319.

b. The electronic fund transfer for the collection of a customer's payment of $21,400 less the $120 collection fee was added to the bank statement balance.

Problem 7-8A Preparing a bank reconciliation and recording adjustments LO6

CHECK FIGURE: 1. Adjusted book balance, $4,871.89

Pelzer Company reconciled its bank and book statement balances of Cash on August 31 and showed two cheques outstanding at that time, #5888 for $6,220.00 and #5893 for $1,485.65.

The following information was available for the September 30, 2020, reconciliation:

From the September 30, 2020, bank statement:

Balance of previous statement on Aug. 31/20	10,674.50
6 deposits and other credits totalling	22,417.05
9 cheques and other debits totalling	26,296.05
Current balance as of Sept. 30/20	6,795.50

			Chequing Account Transactions		
Date	Amount	Transaction Description	Date	Amount	Transaction Description
Sept. 05	5,643.20	+Deposit	Sept. 25	4,230.60	+Deposit
12	2,561.45	+Deposit	30	45.00	+Interest
17	1,176.50	−NSF cheque	30	3,500.00	+Credit memo
21	6,436.80	+Deposit			

Date	Cheque No.	Amount	Date	Cheque No.	Amount
Sept. 03	5904	9,340.55	Sept. 22	5888	6,220.00
07	5901	1,450.00	24	5909	2,140.40
08	5905	338.25	28	5907	3,324.60
10	5903	1,320.15	29	5902	985.60

From Pelzer Company's accounting records:

		Cash			Acct. No. 101
Date	Explanation	PR	Debit	Credit	Balance
2020					
Aug. 31	Balance				2,968.85
Sept. 30		CR12	20,005.75		22,974.60
30		CD23		15,071.21	7,903.39

Deposits Made		Cheques Written	
Sept. 5	$ 5,643.20	No. 5901	$1,450.00
12	2,561.45	5902	985.60
21	6,436.80	5903	1,320.15
25	4,230.60	5904	3,940.55
30	1,133.70	5905	338.25
Total Sept. Cash Receipts	$20,005.75	5906	715.26
		5907	3,324.60
		5908	856.40
		5909	2,140.40
		Total Sept. Cash Disbursements	$15,071.21

- Cheque #5904 was correctly written for $9,340.55 to pay for computer equipment; however, the bookkeeper misread the amount and entered it in the accounting records with a debit to Computer Equipment and a credit to Cash as though it were for $3,940.55. The NSF cheque was originally received from a customer, Lisa Willis, in payment of her account. Its return was not recorded when the bank first notified the company.

- The credit memo resulted from an electronic fund transfer of $3,550 for a customer payment. The bank had deducted a $50 bank service charge. The collection has not been recorded.

Required

1. Prepare a September 30 bank reconciliation for the company.

2. Prepare the general journal entries needed to adjust the book balance of cash to the reconciled balance.

Analysis Component: The preceding bank statement discloses three places where the cancelled cheques returned with the bank statement are not numbered sequentially. In other words, some of the prenumbered cheques in the sequence are missing. Several possible situations would explain why the cancelled cheques returned with a bank statement might not be numbered sequentially. Describe three possible explanations.

Problem 7-9A Preparing a bank reconciliation and recording adjustments LO6

CHECK FIGURE: a. Adjusted book balance = $100,488

Stewart Recording Studio, owned by Ron Stewart, showed the following bank reconciliation at March 31:

Stewart Recording Studio Bank Reconciliation March 31, 2020				
Bank statement balance		$22,100	Book balance	$30,945
Add:				
Deposit of March 31 in transit.............		10,000		
		$32,100		
Deduct:				
Outstanding cheques:				
#14..	$840			
#22..	315	1,155		
Adjusted bank balance............................		$30,945	Adjusted book balance	$30,945

Cash					Acct. No. 101
Date	Explanation	PR	Debit	Credit	Balance
2020					
Mar. 31	Balance				30,945
Apr. 30		CR17	71,440		102,385
30		CD13		91,172	11,213

A list of deposits made and cheques written during April, taken from the cash receipts journal and cash disbursements journal, is shown below:

Deposits Made		Cheques Written	
April 7	$ 690	No. 23	$ 5,200
13	4,600	24	3,150
18	5,900	25	940
23	13,900	26	310
27	1,750	27	4,230
30	44,600	28	4,900
Total April Cash Receipts	$71,440	29	19,630
		30	41,000
		31	412
		32	11,400
		Total April Cash Disbursements	$91,172

The following bank statement is available for April:

Bank Statement					
To: Stewart Recording Studio				April 30, 2020 Bank of Canada	
Cheques/Charges			Deposits/Credits		Balance
					22,100
#31	04/03	412	04/03	10,000	31,688
#28	04/07	9,400	04/07	690	22,978
#26	04/13	310	04/13	4,600	27,268
NSF	04/18	14,200	04/18	5,900	18,968
#24	04/23	3,150	04/23	13,900	29,718
#23	04/27	5,200	04/27	1,750	26,268
#29	04/30	19,630	04/30	120,000	126,638
PMT	04/30	15,900			110,738
INT	04/30	450			110,288
SC	04/30	175			110,113
NSF = Not Sufficient Funds		SC = Service Charge	PMT = Payment of Principal on the Loan		INT = Interest on Bank Loan

- In reviewing cheques returned by the bank, the bookkeeper discovered that cheque #28, for delivery expense, was recorded in the cash disbursements journal correctly as $4,900.
- The NSF cheque for $14,200 was that of customer Oprah Winney, deposited in March.
- On the bank statement, the payment for $15,900 is regarding a note payable.
- There is also a deposit of $120,000 dated April 30. It is an investment made by the owner into the business (the bank transferred the funds electronically from the owner's personal account to his business account, which is why it was not recorded in the cash receipts journal).

Required

a. Prepare a bank reconciliation for Stewart Recording Studio at April 30.

b. Prepare the necessary journal entries to bring the general ledger Cash account into agreement with the adjusted balance on the bank reconciliation.

Problem 7-10A Preparing a bank reconciliation and recording adjustments LO6

CHECK FIGURE: a. Adjusted book balance = $82,994.99

Presented below is information related to Scuba Dive Company. The balance according to the books at October 31, 2020, was $99,657.29; cash receipts recorded during November were $64,805.69; and cash disbursements recorded for November were $76,850.30. The balance according to the bank statement on November 30, 2020, was $82,370.68.

The following cheques were outstanding at November 30:

Cheque	Amount
#920	947.29
#991	2,843.50
#1030	1,971.34
#1064	824.66

Included with the November bank statement and not recorded by the company were a bank debit memo for $32.26 covering bank charges for the month, a debit memo for $5,200.75 for a customer's cheque (Marnie Wiesen) returned and marked NSF, and a credit memo for $615.32 representing interest collected by the bank for Scuba Dive Company. Cash on hand at November 30, which has been recorded and is awaiting deposit, amounted to $7,211.10.

Required

a. Prepare a bank reconciliation at November 30, 2020.

b. Prepare any journal entries required to adjust the Cash account at November 30.

Problem 7-11A Preparing a bank reconciliation and recording adjustments LO6

CHECK FIGURE: 1. Adjusted book balance = $28,250

The following is information for Dundee Realty:

a. Balance per the bank statement dated October 31, 2020, is $26,830.

b. Balance of the Cash account on the company books as of October 31, 2020, is $5,575.

c. $14,680 of customer deposits were outstanding as of September 30; this amount had been deposited to Dundee's account in October.

d. Cheques written in October that had not cleared the bank as of October 31 were:
   #8700, $985
   #8709, $12,600
   #8801, $620
   #8815, $145.

e. The bank charged Dundee's account for a $2,350 cheque of the E-Zone Networks; the cheque was found among the cancelled cheques returned with the bank statement.

f. Bank service charges for October amount to $65.

g. A customer's cheque (Teresa Krant) for $7,050 had been deposited in the bank correctly but was recorded in the accounting records as $7,500.

h. Among the cancelled cheques is one for $260 given in payment of an account payable to Decker Company; the bookkeeper had recorded the cheque incorrectly at $620 in the company records.

i. The bank statement showed an electronic fund transfer of $22,880 for a customer payment. A bank service fee of $50 was charged.

j. A bank deposit of October 31 for $13,420 does not appear on the bank statement.

Required

1. Prepare a bank reconciliation statement as of October 31, 2020.

2. Prepare the necessary entries to make the Cash account agree with the bank reconciliation adjusted Cash balance as of October 31.

Analysis Component: Identify the effects on the income statement and balance sheet if the entries in Part 2 were not recorded.

ALTERNATE PROBLEMS

Problem 7-1B Principles of internal control LO1

For the following five scenarios, identify the principle of internal control that is violated. Next, recommend what the business should do to ensure adherence to principles of internal control.

1. Tamerick Company is a fairly small organization but has segregated the duties of cash receipts and cash disbursements. However, the employee responsible for cash disbursements also reconciles the bank account monthly.

2. Stan Spencer is the most computer literate employee in his company. His boss has recently asked him to put password protection on all the office computers. Stan's main job at the company is to process payroll. Stan has put a password in place that now allows only his boss access to the file where pay rates are changed and personnel are added or deleted from the company payroll.

3. Starlight Theatre has a computerized order-taking system for its tickets. The system is active all week and backed up every Friday night.

4. Trek There Company has two employees handling acquisitions of inventory. One employee places purchase orders and pays vendors. The second employee receives the merchandise.

5. The owner of Holiday Helper uses a cheque protector to perforate cheques, making it difficult for anyone to alter the amount of the cheque. The cheque protector sits on the owner's desk in an office that houses company cheques and is often unlocked.

Problem 7-2B Establishing, reimbursing, and increasing the petty cash fund LO4

Baby Photography completed the following petty cash transactions during July 2020:

July	5	Prepared a $500 cheque, cashed it, and turned the proceeds and the petty cash box over to Bob Stuart, the petty cashier.
	6	Paid $46 COD charges on merchandise purchased for resale. *Baby Photography uses the perpetual inventory method to account for merchandise inventory.*
	11	Paid $26 delivery charges on merchandise sold to a customer.
	12	Purchased file folders, $76
	18	Purchased paper for printer, $27.
	27	Paid $31 COD charges on merchandise purchased for resale.
	28	Purchased stamps, $60
	30	Reimbursed Collin Dodge $134 for business car expenses.
	31	Bob Stuart sorted the petty cash receipts by accounts affected and exchanged them for a cheque to reimburse the fund for expenditures. However, there was $88 in cash in the fund. In addition, the size of the petty cash fund was decreased to $400.

Required

1. Prepare a general journal entry to record establishing the petty cash fund.

2. Prepare a summary of petty cash payments similar to Exhibit 7.2 that has these categories: delivery expense, auto expense, postage expense, merchandise inventory, and office supplies.

3. Prepare the general journal entry to record the reimbursement and the decrease of the fund.

Analysis Component: You supervise Bob Stuart, the petty cashier, and while reviewing the accounts you notice that the Cash Over/Short Expense account has a balance of $300 for the seven months ended July 31, 2020. Given the size of the petty cash account, does this balance appear to be unusual? Explain and identify any concerns that you might have.

Problem 7-3B Petty cash fund reimbursement and analysis of errors LO4

The accounting system used by Dartmouth Sales and Service requires that all entries be journalized in a general journal. To facilitate payments for small items, Dartmouth established a petty cash fund. The following transactions involving the petty cash fund occurred during February 2020.

Feb.	3	A company cheque for $200 was prepared and made payable to the petty cashier to establish the petty cash fund.
	14	A company cheque was prepared to replenish the fund for the following expenditures made since February 3 and to increase the fund to $250.
		a. Purchased office supplies, $65.82.
		b. Paid $75.00 COD charges on merchandise purchased for resale. Dartmouth uses the perpetual method to account for merchandise inventory.
		c. Paid $36.40 to Data Services for minor repairs to a computer.
		d. Paid $15.23 for postage expenses.
		e. Discovered that only $5.55 remained in the petty cash box.
	28	The petty cashier noted that $39.30 remained in the fund, and decided that the February 14 increase in the fund was not large enough. A company cheque was prepared to replenish the fund for the following expenditures made since February 14, and to increase it to $300.
		f. Paid $45 to *The Smart Saver* for an advertisement in a monthly newsletter.
		g. Paid $96.35 for office supplies.
		h. Paid $69.35 to Best Movers for delivery of merchandise to a customer.

Required Prepare general journal entries to record the establishment of the fund on February 3 and its replenishment on February 14 and February 28.

Analysis Component: Explain how the company's financial statements would be affected if the petty cash fund is not replenished and no entry is made on February 28. *(Hint: The amount of Office Supplies that appears on a balance sheet is determined by a physical count of the supplies on hand.)*

Problem 7-4B Credit card and debit card transactions LO5

On July 15, Smart Vitamin Store sold merchandise to customers for cash of $22,000 (cost $13,200). Merchandise costing $12,800 was sold to Medi-Clinic for $15,480 on July 17, terms 2/10, n/30. Sales totalling $190,000 (cost $114,000) were recorded on July 20 to customers using MasterCard (assume a 2.5% fee). On July 25, sales of $102,000 (cost $61,200) were made to debit card customers. The bank charges Smart Vitamin a flat fee of 0.45% on all debit card transactions.

Required Prepare journal entries for each of the transactions described (assume a perpetual inventory system).

Analysis Component: Identify the advantages and disadvantages of each type of sale: cash sale, credit sale, credit card sale, or debit card sale. Explain why Smart Vitamin would likely accept all these types of sales.

Problem 7-5B Preparing a bank reconciliation and recording adjustments LO6

CHECK FIGURE: Adjusted book balance = $2,837.06

Mae Telford, the controller of the Baylor Company, provided the following information:

Baylor Company Bank Reconciliation October 31, 2020					
Bank statement balance		$19,687.60	Book balance.................................		$45,548.66
Add:			Deduct:		
Deposit of Oct. 31 in transit.......		4,280.45	NSF cheque plus		
		$23,968.05	service charge	$25,140.95	
Deduct:			Bank service charges..............	130.00	25,270.95
Outstanding cheques:			Adjusted book balance...............		$20,277.71
#537	$ 725,00				
#542	2,965.34	3,690.34			
Adjusted bank balance..................		$20,277.71			

The Cash account in the general ledger appeared as follows on November 30 (Baylor Company uses only a general journal to record transactions):

Date		Explanation	PR	Debit	Credit	Balance
2020						
Oct.	31	Balance				20,277.71
Nov.	1	Cheque #543	GJ5		6,505.12	13,772.59
	1	Cheque #544	GJ5		854.71	12,917.88
	1	Cheque #545	GJ5		1,156.94	11,760.94
	1	Cheque #546	GJ5		2,564.24	9,196.70
	1	Cheque #547	GJ5		1,345.68	7,851.02
	1	Cheque #548	GJ6		56.45	7,794.57
	1	Cheque #549	GJ6		564.23	7,230.34
	9	Deposit	GJ6	1,548.97		8,779.31
	9	Cheque #550	GJ6		3,457.15	5,322.16
	9	Cheque #551	GJ6		985.64	4,336.52
	18	Deposit	GJ6	5,649.85		9,986.37
	20	Cheque #552	GJ6		5,556.71	4,429.66
	27	Cheque #553	GJ6		964.25	3,465.41
	29	Deposit	GJ6	1,250.65		4,716.06

The following bank statement is available for November 2020:

Bank Statement					
To: Baylor Company				November 30, 2020	
				Bank of Canada	
Cheques/Charges			Deposits/Credits		Balance
					19,687.60
#549	11/01	564.23	11/01	4,280.45	23,403.82
#543	11/02	6,505.12			16,898.70
#537	11/07	725.00			16,173.70
#551	11/09	985.64	11/09	1,584.97	16,773.03
#542	11/12	2,965.34			13,807.69
#544	11/14	854.71			12,952.98
#547	11/18	3,145.68	11/18	5,649.85	15,457.15
#545	11/20	1,156.94			14,300.21
#546	11/29	2,564.24			11,735.97
SC	11/30	115.00	11/30		11,620.97
NSF = Not Sufficient Funds		SC = Service Charge	PMT = Principal Payment		INT = Interest

Required

a. Prepare a bank reconciliation for Baylor Company for the month of November 2020. Assume that any errors made were by the bookkeeper (cheque #547 was for advertising expense; the deposit of November 9 was regarding a credit customer, Val Pacino).

b. Prepare the necessary entries resulting from the bank reconciliation.

Analysis Component: You have been employed with Baylor Company since November 1, 2020, and part of your job is writing and recording cheques as well as preparing the bank reconciliation. In reviewing the cheques returned by the bank, you notice that the payee on cheque #543 is the employee you recently replaced. You investigate further and find that the journal entry recording cheque #543 debited Office Supplies Expense. What should you do? Explain.

Problem 7-6B Preparing a bank reconciliation and recording adjustments LO6
CHECK FIGURE: a. Adjusted book balance = $13,929

The bank reconciliation prepared by Village-on-the-Lake Condos on May 31, 2020, is shown below:

Village-on-the-Lake Condos					
Bank Reconciliation					
May 31, 2020					
Bank statement balance		$ 2,060	Book balance..		$3,910
Add:					
Deposit of May 31 in transit..............		12,500			
		$14,560			
Deduct:					
Outstanding cheques:					
#103	$6,520				
#120	4,130	10,650			
Adjusted bank balance......................		$ 3,910	Adjusted book balance		$3,910

The Cash account in the general ledger appeared as follows on June 30:

Date		Explanation	PR	Debit	Credit	Balance
			Cash			Acct. No. 101
2020						
May	31	Balance				3,910
June	30		CR21	38,680		42,590
	30		CD16		31,861	10,729

A list of deposits made and cheques written during June, taken from the cash receipts journal and cash disbursements journal, is shown below:

Deposits Made	
June 5	$ 590
10	1,120
15	5,690
20	4,510
27	7,830
30	12,600
30	6,340
Total June Cash Receipts	$38,680

Cheques Written	
No. 127	$ 2,100
128	450
129	680
130	9,750
131	196
132	6,420
133	4,550
134	6,780
135	820
136	115
Total June Cash Disbursements	$31,861

The following bank statement is available for June:

Bank Statement					
To: Village-on-the-Lake Condos				June 30, 2020 Bank of Nova Scotia	
Cheques/Charges			Deposits/Credits		Balance
					2,060
#133	06/02	4,550	06/02	12,500	10,010
#136	06/05	115	06/05	590	10,485
#129	06/10	680	06/10	1,120	10,925
#130	06/15	9,750	06/15	5,690	6,865
#103	06/20	6,520	06/20	4,510	4,855
#134	06/27	6,780	06/27	7,830	5,905
#128	06/30	450	06/30	16,200	21,655
SC	06/30	400			**21,255**
NSF = Not Sufficient Funds		SC = Service Charge	PMT = Principal Payment		INT = Interest

In reviewing deposits recorded by the bank, the bookkeeper discovered that the deposit from customer Darla Smith dated June 30, recorded in the cash receipts journal incorrectly as $12,600, was recorded by the bank correctly as $16,200.

Required

a. Prepare a bank reconciliation at June 30.

b. Prepare the necessary journal entries to bring the general ledger Cash account into agreement with the adjusted balance on the bank reconciliation.

Problem 7-7B Preparing a bank reconciliation and recording adjustments LO6

CHECK FIGURE: 1. Adjusted book balance = $35,775

The following information was available to reconcile Frogbox Moving's book Cash balance with its bank statement balance as of December 31, 2020:

a. The December 31 Cash balance according to the accounting records was $16,562, and the bank statement balance for that date was $36,780.

b. Cheque #3115 for $1,119 and cheque #3201 for $2,507, both written and entered in the accounting records in December, were not among the cancelled cheques returned. Two cheques, #3207 for $15,985 and #3221 for $1,672, were outstanding on November 30 when the bank and book statement balances were last reconciled. Cheque #3207 was returned with the December cancelled cheques, but cheque #3221 was not.

c. When the December cheques were compared with entries in the accounting records, it was found that cheque #3199 had been correctly written for $4,080 to pay for office supplies, but was erroneously entered in the accounting records as though it were written for $4,800.

d. Two debit memos were included with the returned cheques and were unrecorded at the time of the reconciliation. One of the debit memos was for $4,064 and dealt with an NSF cheque for $4,000 that had been received from a customer, Tork Industries, in payment of its account. It also assessed a $64 fee for processing. The second debit memo covered cheque printing and was for $93. These transactions had not been recorded by Frogbox before receiving the statement.

e. A credit memo indicated the receipt of an electronic fund transfer of $22,800 for a customer payment. A $150 bank service charge was deducted. This transaction was not recorded by Frogbox before receiving the statement.

f. The December 31 cash receipts of $4,293 had been placed in the bank's night depository after banking hours on that date and did not appear on the bank statement.

Required

1. Prepare a bank reconciliation for the company as of December 31.

2. Prepare the general journal entries necessary to bring the company's book balance of Cash into conformity with the reconciled balance.

Analysis Component: Explain the nature of the messages conveyed by a bank to one of its depositors when the bank sends a debit memo and a credit memo to the depositor.

Problem 7-8B Preparing a bank reconciliation and recording adjustments LO6

CHECK FIGURE: 1. Adjusted book balance = $35,201.35

Yardworx reconciled its book balance of Cash with its bank statement balance on April 30 and showed two cheques outstanding at that time, #1771 for $15,463.10 and #1780 for $955.65.

The following information is available for the May 31, 2020, reconciliation:

From the May 31, 2020, bank statement:

Balance of previous statement on Apr. 30/20	$61,045.95
5 deposits and other credits totalling..	26,088.10
9 cheques and other debits totalling...	57,005.40
Current balance as of this statement..	30,128.65

Chequing Account Transactions					
Date	Amount	Transaction Description	Date	Amount	Transaction Description
May 04	14,662.30	+Deposit	May 25	5,200.00	+Credit memo
14	849.25	+Deposit	26	4,210.10	+Deposit
18	15,600.40	−NSF cheque	31	135.00	−Service charge
22	1,166.45	+Deposit			

Date	Cheque No.	Amount	Date	Cheque No.	Amount
May 01	1784	7,600.00	May 26	1785	620.15
02	1783	1,465.80	28	1771	15,463.10
15	1787	2,334.75	29	1788	985.65
16	1782	12,800.55			

From Yardworx's accounting records:

Cash					Acct. No. 101
Date	Explanation	PR	Debit	Credit	Balance
2020					
Apr. 30	Balance				44,627.20
May 31		CR7	29,289.05		73,916.25
31		CD8		28,089.50	45,826.75

Deposits Made	
May 4..	$14,662.30
14..	849.25
22..	1,166.45
26..	4,210.10
31..	8,400.95
Total May Cash Receipts..................	$29,289.05

Cheques Written	
No. 1782...	$12,800.55
1783...	1,465.80
1784...	7,600.00
1785...	620.15
1786...	974.35
1787...	2,334.75
1788...	895.65
1789...	1,398.25
Total May Cash Disbursements.......	$28,089.50

- Cheque #1788 was correctly written for $985.65 to pay for May utilities; however, the bookkeeper misread the amount and entered it in the accounting records with a debit to Utilities Expense and a credit to Cash as though it were for $895.65. The bank paid and deducted the correct amount.

- The NSF cheque was originally received from a customer, Gertie Mayer, in payment of her account. Its return was unrecorded.

- The credit memo resulted from a $5,300 electronic fund transfer for the collection of a customer payment. The bank had deducted a $100 bank service charge fee. The collection has not been recorded in the company's books.

Required

1. Prepare a bank reconciliation for Yardworx.

2. Prepare the general journal entries needed to adjust the book balance of Cash to the reconciled balance.

Analysis Component: The preceding bank statement discloses two places where the cancelled cheques returned with the bank statement are not numbered sequentially. In other words, some of the prenumbered cheques in the sequence are missing. Several possible situations would explain why the cancelled cheques returned with a bank statement might not be numbered sequentially. Describe three possible reasons that this might occur.

Problem 7-9B Preparing a bank reconciliation and recording adjustments LO6

CHECK FIGURE: 1. Adjusted book balance = $31,532

Balloon Supply Co. reconciled its bank statement balances of Cash on October 31 and showed two cheques outstanding at that time, #1388 for $14,650 and #1393 for $9,800. The following information was available for the November 30, 2020, reconciliation:

From the November 30 bank statement:

Balance of previous statement on Oct. 31/20	106,980
6 deposits and other credits totalling	63,568
9 cheques and other debits totalling	123,873
Current balance as of November 30/20	46,675

Chequing Account Transactions					
Date	Amount	Transaction Description	Date	Amount	Transaction Description
Nov. 05	21,640	+Deposit	Nov. 25	29,008	+Deposit
12	956	+Deposit	30	250	+Interest
17	1,810	−NSF cheque	30	10,550	+Credit memo
21	1,164	+Deposit			

Date	Cheque No.	Amount	Date	Cheque No.	Amount
Nov. 03	1402	9,325	Nov. 17	1409	12,125
04	1403	11,500	20	1405	14,850
08	1388	14,650	27	1407	38,412
12	1401	18,600	29	1404	2,601

From Balloon Supply Co.'s accounting records:

			Cash			Acct. No. 101
Date		Explanation	PR	Debit	Credit	Balance
2020						
Oct	31	Balance				82,530
Nov.	30		CR12	86,145		168,675
	30		CD23		149,733	18,942

Deposits Made	
Nov 5	$21,640
12	956
21	1,164
25	29,008
30	33,377
Total November Cash Receipts	$86,145

Cheques Written	
No. 1401	$ 18,600
1402	9,325
1403	11,500
1404	6,201
1405	14,850
1406	12,980
1407	38,412
1408	25,740
1409	12,125
Total November Cash Disbursements	$149,733

- Cheque #1404 was correctly written for $2,601 to pay for computer equipment: however, the bookkeeper misread the amount and entered it in the accounting records with a debit to Computer Equipment and a credit to Cash as though it were for $6,201.

- The NSF cheque was originally received from a customer, Jerry Skyles, in payment of his account. Its return was not recorded when the bank first notified the company.

- The credit memo resulted from receiving an electronic fund transfer of $10,700 for a customer payment. The bank had deducted a $150 bank service charge fee. The collection has not been recorded in the books.

Required

1. Prepare a November 30 bank reconciliation for the company.
2. Prepare the general journal entries needed to adjust the book balance of Cash to the reconciled balance.

Problem 7-10B Preparing a bank reconciliation and recording adjustments LO6

CHECK FIGURE: 1. Adjusted book balance = $24,370

The following information was available to reconcile Shanghai Company's book balance of Cash with its bank statement balance as of February 28, 2020.

a. The bank statement at February 28 indicated a balance of $23,620. The general ledger account for Cash showed a balance at February 28 of $9,400.

b. Of the cheques issued in February, the following were still outstanding:

Cheque	Amount
#202	$ 960
#205	1,075
#213	610
#240	840

c. Two cheques, #136 for $1,036 and #200 for $2,600, were outstanding on Jan. 31 when the bank and book balances were last reconciled. Cheque #136 was returned with the February cancelled cheques but cheque #200 was not.

d. Included with the February bank statement was an NSF cheque for $6,250 that had been received from a customer, Mrs. Loni Fung, in payment of her account.

e. Cheque #219 was correctly written for $1,910 in payment for office supplies but was erroneously entered as $9,110 in the cash payments journal.

f. A debit memo for $35 was enclosed with the bank statement. This charge was for printing the chequebook for Shanghai Company.

g. Included with the bank statement was a $120 credit memo for interest earned on the bank account in February.

h. The February 28 cash receipts amounting to $6,835 had been placed in the bank's night depository after banking hours on that date and did not appear among the deposits on the February bank statement.

i. Included with the bank statement was a credit memo for an electronic fund transfer of $14,000 for the collection of a customer payment. A bank service charge of $65 was deducted.

Required

1. Prepare a bank reconciliation for the Shanghai Company as of February 28, 2020.

2. Prepare the entries needed to adjust the book balance of Cash to the reconciled balance.

Problem 7-11B Preparing a bank reconciliation and recording adjustments LO6

CHECK FIGURE: 1. Adjusted book balance = $60,580

The following is information for the Donut Holes Cafe:

a. Balance per the bank statement dated December 31, 2020, is $50,860.

b. Balance of Cash account on the company books as of December 31, 2020, is $57,285.

c. A cheque from customer Della Armstrong for $7,860 that had been deposited in the bank was erroneously recorded by the bookkeeper as $8,760.

d. A cheque made out by Neon Company for $10,140 deposited on December 21 is returned by the bank marked NSF; no entry has been made on the company records to reflect the returned cheque.

e. Among the cancelled cheques is one for $692 given in payment of an account payable to CT Financial; the bookkeeper had incorrectly recorded the cheque at $962 in the company records.

f. Bank service charges for December amount to $35.

g. The bank erroneously charged the Donut Holes Cafe account for a $5,000 cheque of HRD Company; the cheque was found among the cancelled cheques returned with the bank statement.

h. The bank had collected a $14,150 electronic fund transfer for a customer payment; $14,150 was credited to the Donut Holes Cafe's bank account; a collection fee of $50 was debited to the Donut Holes Cafe's bank account.

i. The bank deposit of December 31 for $6,860 does not appear on the bank statement.

j. Outstanding cheques as of December 31: #197, $920; #199, $1,220.

Required

1. Prepare a bank reconciliation as of December 31, 2020.

2. Prepare the necessary entries to make the Cash account agree with the bank reconciliation adjusted Cash balance as of December 31.

Analysis Component: Identify the effects on the income statement and balance sheet if the adjustments in Part 2 were not recorded.

ANALYTICAL AND REVIEW PROBLEMS

A & R Problem 7-1

CHECK FIGURE: 1. Adjusted book balance = $20,552

You are a college student and have just been hired to work part-time in the accounting department of Candy's Cleaning Services. The person you are replacing had difficulty preparing the bank reconciliation for April 30, which is shown below.

Candy's Cleaning Services Bank Reconciliation April 30, 2020					
Bank balance		$33,452	Book balance...............................		$28,934
			Add:		
Deduct:			Interest	$47	
NSF, customer Bonne.................	$ 412		Error Chq #93............................	99	146
					$29,080
Outstanding cheques:			Deduct:		
#879	2,600		Service Charge..........................		40
#100	1,400	4,412	Adjusted book balance		$29,040
Adjusted bank balance...................		$29,040			

In comparing the bank reconciliation to the Cash account in the general ledger, you notice a problem. You investigate further and come up with some additional information as follows:

a. The Cash account in the general ledger showed the following:

Cash					Acct. No. 101
Date	Explanation	PR	Debit	Credit	Balance
2020					
March 31	Balance				28,934
April 30		CR16	56,000		84,934
30		CD21		63,883	21,051

b. The error in cheque #93, for Utilities Expense, resulted from the bank incorrectly debiting our account for $99; the correct amount entered in the accounting records is $199.

c. The bank statement showed interest expense of $47; there was no other interest.

d. The bank debited our account for cheque #879 written by Candy's Hair Salon.

e. Cheque #86 for $14,000 listed as outstanding on last month's bank reconciliation was not returned with the April 30 bank statement.

Required

1. Prepare a corrected bank reconciliation for April 30, 2020.

2. Record the journal entries resulting from the corrected bank reconciliation.

A & R Problem 7-2

CHECK FIGURE: 1. Adjusted book balance = $10,014

Your assistant prepared the following bank reconciliation statement. It appears that the statement is unacceptable and the task of preparing a proper reconciliation falls upon you.

Brandon Company Bank Reconciliation May 31, 2020		
Balance per books May 31		$ 9,500
Add:		
Electronic Funds Transfer..	$1,060	
Deposit in transit...	2,455	3,515
		$13,015
Deduct:		
Bank charges..	$ 10	
NSF cheque, Rhonda Teal..	500	
Outstanding cheques...	1,800	
Error in cheque #78: correctly issued and processed by the bank for $762, but incorrectly recorded in the books as $726 (Accounts Payable–Delta Co.)...........................	36	2,346
Indicated bank balance..		$10,669
Balance per bank statement..		9,359
Discrepancy...		$ 1,310

Required

1. Prepare a proper bank reconciliation showing the true Cash balance.

2. Prepare the necessary journal entries.

A & R Problem 7-3

Wanda White acquired a sports equipment distribution business with a staff of six salespeople and two clerks. Because of the trust that Wanda had in her employees—after all, they were all her friends and just like members of the family—she believed that an honour system in regard to the operation of the petty cash fund was adequate. Consequently, Wanda placed $300 in a coffee jar, which, for convenience, was kept in a cupboard in the common room. All employees had access to the petty cash fund and withdrew amounts as required. No vouchers were required for withdrawals. As required, additional funds were placed in the coffee jar and the amount of the replenishment was charged to "miscellaneous selling expense."

Required

1. From the internal control point of view, discuss the weaknesses of the petty cash fund operation and suggest steps necessary for improvement.

2. Does the petty cash fund operation as described above violate any of the generally accepted accounting principles? If yes, which one(s), and how are the principles violated?

ETHICS CHALLENGE

EC 7-1

Marge Page, Daisy Tu, and Colleen Walker work for a dentist, Dr. Linda Thomson, who is in a private practice. Dr. Thomson is fairly knowledgeable about sound office management practices and has separated the cash receipt duties as follows. Marge opens the mail and prepares a triplicate list of money received. She sends one copy of the list to Daisy, the cashier, who deposits the receipts daily in the bank. Colleen, the recordkeeper, also receives a copy of the list and posts payments to patients' accounts. About once a month the office clerks decide to have an expensive lunch compliments of Dr. Thomson. Daisy endorses a patient's cheque in Dr. Thomson's name and cashes it at the bank. Marge destroys the remittance advice accompanying the cheque. Colleen posts the payment to the customer's account as a miscellaneous credit. The clerks justify their actions given their relatively low pay and knowing that Dr. Thomson will likely never miss the payment.

Required

1. Who would be the best person in Dr. Thomson's office to reconcile the bank statement?

2. Would a bank reconciliation detect the office fraud scheme?

3. What are some ways of uncovering this type of scheme?

4. Suggest additional internal controls that Dr. Thomson might want to implement.

FOCUS ON FINANCIAL STATEMENTS

FFS 7-1

CHECK FIGURES: Current assets = $68,190, Total assets = $112,540

Ellis Worton, the owner of Worton Consulting, showed the following unadjusted account balances at December 31, 2020, the business's year-end (accounts have been listed in alphabetical order):

Account	Account Balance*
Accounts payable	$ 31,500
Accounts receivable	46,250
Accumulated depreciation, store fixtures	61,000
Cash	19,340
Cost of goods sold	469,000
Delivery expense	11,330
Ellis Worton, capital	89,560
Ellis Worton, withdrawals	69,000
Interest expense	2,240
Notes payable (principal of $20,000 to be paid in 2021	56,000
Petty cash	350
Prepaid rent	16,200
Rent expense	11,250
Salaries expense	213,000
Salaries payable	17,750
Sales	721,400
Sales returns and allowances	6,000
Store fixtures	113,250

*Assume normal account balances.

Other information:

1. There were two reconciling items on the bank reconciliation: an outstanding cheque in the amount of $620 and an NSF cheque for $2,835.

2. A review of the Prepaid Rent account showed that the unexpired portion was $2,250.

3. Annual depreciation on the store fixtures is $7,900.

Required Prepare the December 31, 2020, classified balance sheet.

Analysis Component:

a. Calculate Worton Consulting's current ratio and quick-test ratio at December 31, 2020. Compare and comment. Round calculations to two decimal places.

b. Recalculate the current ratio and quick-test ratio assuming the current portion of the note payable was reported as part of the long-term liabilities. Compare your results to part (a) and comment. Round calculations to two decimal places.

FFS 7-2

Refer to WestJet's December 31, 2017, balance sheet in Appendix III at the end of the textbook.

Required Answer the following questions.

1. WestJet shows cash and cash equivalents on its December 31, 2017, balance sheet. Explain the meaning of cash and cash equivalents.

2. How much cash and cash equivalents did WestJet have on December 31, 2017?

3. By how much did WestJet's cash and cash equivalents increase or decrease from December 31, 2016, to December 31, 2017?

Analysis Component: Is it possible for there to be excessive cash and cash equivalents? Explain.

CRITICAL THINKING MINI CASE

You are the newly elected vice-president of campus life for the business students' association at your institution. The first big event of the year is a party that has three live bands playing from 5:00 p.m. to midnight; tickets are $20 (cash only). A number of people are helping you sell tickets during the two weeks prior to the event. At the end of each day, you collect the cash from each seller and reconcile it against the tickets sold (the tickets are sequentially numbered). You place your records and the cash in a locked filing cabinet in your office, which is always locked. In less than two weeks, all of the tickets are sold. After collecting the cash from the ticket sellers on the day of the sellout, you're feeling terrific about the success of the sales campaign you organized for the event and go to your office, unlock the door, and immediately notice that the filing cabinet has been tampered with . . . all of the money is gone . . . over $35,000!

Required Using the elements of critical thinking described on the inside front cover, comment.

CHAPTER 8

Receivables

A Look Back

Chapter 7 provides an introduction to internal control and cash with a detailed analysis of internal control guidelines, banking activities, accounting for petty cash funds, and reconciling the differences between cash reported in the bank account and cash in the company's accounting records.

A Look at This Chapter

This chapter takes a look at accounting for customer accounts receivable and short-term notes receivable, specifically investigating tools such as initial recognition of the receivables and subsequent measurement at the end of the accounting period. Valuation is assessed through methods to estimate bad debts, including the benefits of an A/R aging report, and using the accounts receivable turnover ratio and days' sales uncollected ratios to evaluate financial statements.

Used by permission of WN Pharmaceuticals

LEARNING OBJECTIVES

LO1	Describe accounts receivable and how they occur and are recorded.
LO2	Apply the allowance method to account for uncollectible accounts receivable.
LO3	Estimate uncollectible accounts receivable using approaches based on sales and accounts receivable.

LO4 Describe and record a short-term note receivable and calculate its maturity date and interest.

LO5 Calculate accounts receivable turnover and days' sales uncollected to analyze liquidity.

***Appendix 8A**

LO6 Explain how receivables can be converted to cash before maturity.

Effective Receivables Management Tools Strengthen Corporate Health

WN Pharmaceuticals is one of North America's largest manufacturers of health products and its well-known brand Webber Naturals vitamin, mineral, and herbal supplements. The company headquarters is in Coquitlam, BC. It has experienced significant growth over the past 50 years from its first product—topical vitamin E—to over 300 products today.

The company relies on leading-edge manufacturing technologies to extract the purest of nutrients for use in its products. Ingredients are sourced both domestically and globally and are rigorously tested using pharmaceutical standards for purity, potency, pesticides, contaminants, and overall quality. Natural health products are subject to strict regulations set out by government agencies in both Canada and the United States. Finished products are tested in the WN Pharmaceuticals laboratories for weight, uniformity, and potency levels to ensure all products sold meet the company's quality standards.

The company sells its vitamins to pharmacies, grocery stores, major retailers, and distributors throughout North and South America, the United Kingdom, Europe, Australia, Asia, the Middle East, and Africa. The wide range of retailers in this distribution network results in varying trade terms. These specific terms depend on the following factors:

- Risk level of the retailer based on its reputation and experience related to the country in which it operates;
- History with the company;
- Volume purchases made; and
- Special promotional campaigns.

Each customer and country requires in-depth research and analysis by the accounts receivable and credit departments to determine overall risk and whether any payment securities are required to facilitate the sales transaction. Based on this analysis, some customer terms require advance payment prior to committing to a manufacturing contract, and other negotiated terms are dependent on the risk level of the specific customer. For some customers, especially those from higher-risk regions, accounts receivable export insurance is acquired from a third-party agent, providing coverage in the event that the customer defaults on their outstanding balance. Other customers are required to have documentary letters of credit, where the risk over collecting the outstanding balance is taken on by the customer's bank, alleviating the risk of collections from WN Pharmaceuticals.

Receivables department clerks are assigned a group of customers to care for and to maintain and reconcile outstanding balances. The clerks handle questions with respect to requests for credit on promotions, issues with shipments, and invoice discrepancies. Continuous monitoring and follow-up is essential to the timely collection of claims and payment deductions, as many customers will not take the time required to research claims past 90–120 days. Detailed analysis is done on all accounts to identify the average days it takes to clear invoices, deductions, and increase the efficiency of collections.

Used by permission of WN Pharmaceuticals

(Continued)

Due to delays in claiming promotional credits by customers, the receivables department has had to come up with customized solutions and reports to ensure accurate recording of promotional spend regardless of when credit notes are issued and recognized on the general ledger. For example, if a promotion runs in January, the customer does not claim its deduction on payment until February and the receivables department isn't able to obtain backup and proof of performance along with sales rep approval until March; tying that promotional spend back to the period where expenses were incurred therefore becomes a challenge across hundreds of claims and issues regarding GAAP.

Specialized reports are created, incorporating data from sales, marketing, and accounts receivable, to monitor the promotional activity of large chain accounts and to incorporate and translate that information into cash flow forecasting and budgeting. Aging reports are used to identify possible issues or invoices that have been missed or not received by customers, and are used as collection lists for smaller chains and independent customers. The days' sales outstanding and accounts receivable turnover ratio are used by the department to determine how effectively it is managing collections. These ratios are described later in this chapter. At WN Pharmaceuticals, the receivables department is a major player in collecting and managing the cash receipts process, significantly impacting the company's overall cash flow.

Source: Interview with Sean Craig, Senior Manager of Corporate Credit, Webber Naturals, June 28, 2018.

CRITICAL THINKING CHALLENGE

Why is assessing customer credit critical to the overall success of businesses like WN Pharmaceuticals?

CHAPTER PREVIEW

Management of accounts receivable is a critical aspect of managing a company's cash resources. This chapter focuses on accounting practices for both accounts receivable and short-term notes receivable. The chapter provides a detailed description for each of these assets, identifies their use in practice, demonstrates how they are accounted for and reported in financial statements, and analyzes how to handle valuation issues and account for bad debts.

Accounts Receivable

LO1 Describe accounts receivable and how they occur and are recorded.

A *receivable* refers to an amount due from another party. The two most common receivables are accounts receivable and notes receivable. Other receivables include interest receivable, rent receivable, tax refund receivable, and amounts due from other parties such as officers and employees.

Accounts receivable are amounts due from customers and result from non-cash sales to customers. They are also referred to as **trade receivables** because they result from customers with whom we engage in *trade*. This section begins by describing how accounts receivable arise and their various sources. These sources include sales when customers use the seller's credit cards, and when a company gives credit directly to customers. When a company extends credit directly to customers, it must (1) maintain a separate account receivable for each customer and (2) account for bad debts from credit sales.

RECOGNIZING ACCOUNTS RECEIVABLE

Accounts receivable arise from credit sales to customers. Recognition of accounts receivable is directly linked to revenue recognition at the time of the sales transaction. In general, revenue from a sale of goods can be recorded when the following key criteria are met:[1]

- *Performance:* A company can recognize revenue when it transfers the product or service to the customer, meaning the customer obtains control of the specific asset purchased or receives the benefit of the service provided. This generally involves the company physically transferring the asset to the customer, meaning the customer is now responsible for the risks and rewards of ownership of the asset and the customer accepts the asset.

- *Measurement:* The amount of cash or cash equivalents it expects to receive based on the sale of the product or service can be determined. The transaction price to be recorded is determined by the customer agreement or contract.[2]

- *Collectability:* The company has an enforceable right to receive payment, as performance has been completed to date and it is probable the company will collect any outstanding balances from the customer. The enforceable right is generally linked to an agreement or formal contract with the customer.

If the above conditions are not met, the sale of the product or service cannot be recognized under generally accepted accounting principles, including the related customer's accounts receivable.

The amount of credit sales over cash sales has increased in recent years, reflecting several factors including an efficient banking system and a sound economy. Exhibit 8.1 shows the dollar amounts of accounts receivable and their percentage of total assets for seven companies. Notice how **Lululemon Athletica** has 1% of its total assets as receivables and **Amazon** has 10% of total assets as receivables.

EXHIBIT 8.1

Accounts Receivable Analysis for Selected Companies as a Percentage of Total Assets

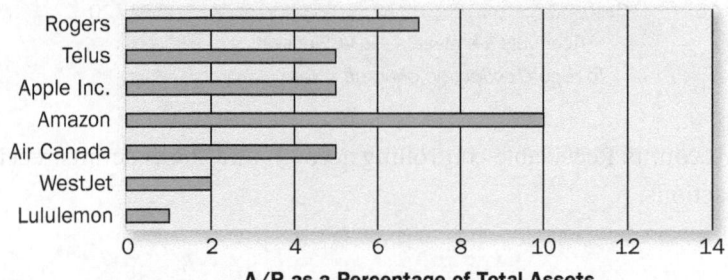

A/R as a Percentage of Total Assets

Note the above information is based on December 31, 2017, financial results for all companies except Lululemon Athletica Inc. at January 28, 2018, and Apple Inc. at September 30, 2017.

Sales on Credit

To review how accounts receivable from credit sales are recognized, we will record two transactions in the accounting records for TechCom, a small electronics wholesaler. TechCom's accounts receivable controlling account in the general ledger and accounts receivable subledger prior to recording these transactions are illustrated in Exhibit 8.2.

---

1   IFRS 2018, IAS 18, para. 14. IFRS 15 Revenue from Contracts with Customers
2   IFRS 2018, IFRS 15, para. 9, 31.

EXHIBIT 8.2

Accounts Receivable Controlling Account and the Accounts Receivable Subledger

The first transaction to be recorded on July 15 is a credit sale of $950 to CompStore (cost of sales to TechCom is $630 assuming a perpetual inventory system). The second is a collection of $720 from RDA Electronics from prior credit sales. Both transactions are reflected in Exhibit 8.3. Note that these transactions would typically be recorded in the appropriate sales and cash receipts journals. We use the general journal format here for simplicity.

EXHIBIT 8.3

Accounts Receivable Transactions

July	15	Accounts Receivable—CompStore......................	950	
		Sales...		950
		To record credit sales.		
	15	Cost of Goods Sold...	630	
		Merchandise Inventory....................................		630
		To record cost of sales.		
	15	Cash...	720	
		Accounts Receivable—RDA Electronics.......		720
		To record collection of credit sales.		

Exhibit 8.4 shows the Accounts Receivable controlling account and the accounts receivable subledger after posting these two transactions.

EXHIBIT 8.4

Accounts Receivable Controlling Account and the Accounts Receivable Subledger

Like many companies, TechCom grants credit directly to qualified customers. Many large retailers such as **Canadian Tire Corporation** and **Hudson's Bay Company** issue credit to retail customers. Once credit has been granted to approved customers, the company will earn interest on any outstanding balances. The company also avoids paying a transaction fee charged by the credit card company. Canadian Tire has a separate Financial Services segment that manages the credit granting and receivables collection process. The receivables fall under the financial statement line item "Loans Receivable" under the category of current assets. The entries in this case are the same as those above except for the possibility of added interest income. If a customer owes interest on the bill, then Canadian Tire debits Loans Receivable and credits Interest income for this amount.

 DECISION INSIGHT

Canadian Banking: Rogers Bank, a Wholly Owned Subsidiary of Rogers Communications

Rogers Bank was formed in 2011 to expand the service portfolio of **Rogers Communications**. In order to qualify to enter the banking industry, Rogers Bank needed to apply to the Minister of Finance under the federal Bank Act to obtain permission to operate as a financial institution in Canada. Rogers Bank was granted permission and entered the banking industry. According to Rogers, the decision to enter financial services markets is to provide the company with the option to issue credit cards and to have the ability to provide mobile banking opportunities with its Suretap mobile wallet to its customers in the future. Rogers Bank currently offers two options of Rogers-branded MasterCards and a Fido-branded MasterCard.

Sources: http://www.theglobeandmail.com/globe-investor/rogers-sets-sights-on-banking-/; https://www.rogersbank.com/en/compare_cards?_ga=2.96629276.2031030292.1539798703-1213399772.1539798703

 CHECKPOINT

1. Where on the balance sheet are accounts receivable reported?

Do Quick Study questions: QS 8-1 and QS 8-2

CREDIT RISK ANALYSIS ACCOUNTS RECEIVABLE

Assessing the creditworthiness of customers is an important task and has a significant impact on the company's cash resources and ability to meet expenses. Each company needs to develop its own procedures for assessing creditworthiness of its customers. It is in the company's best interest to treat the granting of credit in the form of a receivable in a similar likeness to a loan, assessing the company's history, reputation, and financial strength.

According to Canadian Tire Corporation's 2013 Annual Report, the following describes the risk management process employed by the company when extending credit to its customers:

Consumer Credit Risk

Financial Services grants credit to its customers on Canadian Tire credit cards, personal loans and lines of credit. With the granting of credit, Financial Services assumes certain risks such as the failure to accurately predict the willingness of its customers to repay debt. Financial Services manages credit risk to maintain and improve the quality of its consumer lending portfolio by:

- Employing sophisticated credit-scoring models to constantly monitor the creditworthiness of customers;
- Using the latest technology to make informed credit decisions for each customer account to limit credit risk exposure;
- Adopting technology to improve the effectiveness of the collection process; and
- Monitoring the macroeconomic environment, especially with respect to consumer debt levels, interest rates, employment levels and profit levels.

Fictitious Receivables

Accounts receivable fraud is one of the most common types of accounting fraud. "Lapping" involves intercepting and stealing a company's payment and then using subsequent payments to cover the initial theft, or using payments from a different customer to cover the theft. Another type of fraudulent receivable is sales that are recorded to fictitious customers.

Citigroup Inc. had discovered $400 million in fraudulent loans in its Mexico subsidiary. Citigroup's Mexican unit—Banco Nacional de México— had loaned Oceanografia funds based on the fact that it had millions of dollars in invoices that were expected to be collected from a Mexican state-owned oil company called Pemex. Oceanografia had allegedly falsified

Juliangvm/Pixabay.com

invoices to obtain the loan. Pemex suspended Oceanografia for 21 months and 12 days. Citigroup charged the $400 million difference to "operating expenses." In response to the fraud, Citigroup fired more than a dozen employees.

What would you do if you worked for a company that was trying to raise funds through obtaining a bank loan and you were asked to adjust the invoices to increase revenue?

Sources: https://www.thestreet.com/story/12462191/1/how-did-the-fraud-against-citis-banamex-work.html, accessed April 23, 2018 https://www.reuters.com/article/us-citigroup-mexico-fraud/citigroup-reports-fraud-in-mexico-unit-lowers-2013-results-idUSBREA1R10Q20140228, accessed April 23, 2018 https://www.reuters.com/article/us-citigroup-mexico/citigroup-fires-11-in-fraud-probe-of-banamex-unit-idUSBREA4D0FV20140514, accessed April 23, 2018

ACCOUNTS RECEIVABLE CONTROL CONSIDERATIONS

Ensuring appropriate controls are in place is essential to mitigate the risk of fraudulent activities and enable an efficient use of resources. As discussed in Chapter 7, separation of certain responsibilities in an organization can minimize the risk of misappropriation of assets. For example, it is imperative that the individuals responsible for the sales of products to customers are not also responsible for the granting of credit. It would not be in the best interest of Audi Canada if its car salespeople who get commission on vehicle sales had the final say on which customers were approved for vehicle financing; customers with weak credit and an inability to meet future car payment obligations may be approved by a salesperson interested in maximizing his or her commission.

Below are a couple of recommendations by BDO Consulting to strengthen the control environment for customer collections in its "Segregation of Duties" checklist. BDO adds a fourth element to the "CAR Principle" introduced in Chapter 7. Along with separation of duties associated with Custody, Authorization, and Recording of assets, BDO includes reconciliation of the bank statement and other records. Control considerations for customer payments include the following:

- Any employee responsible for receipt of cash should not have access to record or authorize transactions in the A/R ledger or customer accounts.

- Any employee receiving the cash or preparing the deposit should not be able to record cash transactions or prepare the bank reconciliation.

- The bank reconciliation should not be prepared by an employee who is involved in either cash receipts (collections) or disbursements (payments).

- Write-offs and adjustments to receivables should be performed by an employee who does not have the ability to record transactions.

Source: https://docplayer.net/14814964-Bdo-consulting-segregation-of-duties-checklist.html, accessed October 2018.

VALUING ACCOUNTS RECEIVABLE

When a company grants credit to its customers, there are usually a few customers who do not end up paying what they promised at the point of the sales or service transaction. The accounts of these customers are **uncollectible accounts**, commonly referred to as **bad debts**. The total amount of uncollectible accounts is an expense of selling on credit. Why do companies sell on credit if it is likely some accounts will prove uncollectible? Companies believe granting credit will substantially increase revenues and profits, which offsets the negative impact of bad debts. Also, in order to remain competitive, many companies are required to grant credit to customers, especially if it is an industry standard of practice.

Two main methods are commonly used by companies to account for uncollectible accounts: (1) allowance method, and (2) direct write-off method. Exhibit 8.5 summarizes these methods.

EXHIBIT 8.5

Methods for Writing Off Bad Debts

ALLOWANCE METHOD

LO2 Apply the allowance method to account for uncollectible accounts receivable.

The matching principle requires that expenses be reported in the same accounting period as the sales they helped produce. The **allowance method of accounting for bad debts** satisfies the matching principle by recording any estimated bad debt expense that is connected to the current period sales in the same period the related revenue is earned. How is this accomplished? Since the seller is unable to identify in advance which specific customer receivables will become uncollectible, an estimate is based on the company's past experience combined with future expectations based on both the industry and economic climates. This requires professional judgment and a big-picture perspective. As a result, an experienced accountant usually determines the end-of-period adjustment. Recording too low of an estimate for the allowance would result in an overstatement of assets and could cause users of the financial statements to make inappropriate investment decisions.

RECORDING ESTIMATED BAD DEBT EXPENSE

The allowance method estimates bad debt expense at the end of each accounting period and records it with an adjusting entry. TechCom, for instance, had credit sales of approximately $300,000 during its first year of operations. At the end of the first year, $20,000 of credit sales remained uncollected. Based on the experience of similar businesses, TechCom estimated bad debt expense to be $1,500. This estimated expense is recorded with the following adjusting entry at the end of the accounting period:

Dec.	31	Bad Debt Expense..	1,500	
		Allowance for Doubtful Accounts................		1,500
		To record estimated bad debts.		

The debit in this entry means the estimated bad debt expense of $1,500 from selling on credit is matched on the income statement with the $300,000 of sales it helped produce. The credit in this entry is to a contra asset called **Allowance for Doubtful Accounts**. A contra account is used because at the time of the adjusting entry, we do not know which customers will not pay. Because specific uncollectible accounts are not determinable at the time of the end-of-period adjusting entry, the expected amounts cannot be removed from the accounts receivable subledger. Instead, the valuation adjustment is reflected as a credit to the Allowance for Doubtful Accounts.

 DECISION INSIGHT

Payment Security

As highlighted in the chapter-opening vignette, payment securities are tools that act as insurance that a payment will be collected. They decrease the risk associated with companies not being able to collect outstanding receivables. Examples include the following:

Jan Baby/Pixabay.com

Purchase Money Security Interest—provides a priority interest in the event of bankruptcy to at least get your product back off the shelves.

Personal Guarantees—owner guarantees personal assets in the event of default of payment.

Documentary Letters of Credit—customer's bank assumes the risk of collecting the funds after shipment. These are commonly used in conducting business internationally.

Accounts Receivable Insurance—third-party insurance on accounts receivable that covers the vendor in the event of customer default.

Sale of Accounts Receivable—a third party (separate company) purchases the receivables, taking on the risk of collections and resulting in immediate collection of cash by the vendor.

Source: Interview with Sean Craig, Senior Manager of Corporate Credit, Webber Naturals, July 2018.

Bad Debts and Related Accounts in Financial Statements

Recall that TechCom has $20,000 of outstanding accounts receivable at the end of its first year of operations. After the bad debt adjusting entry is posted, TechCom's Accounts Receivable, Allowance for Doubtful Accounts, and Bad Debt Expense have balances as shown in Exhibit 8.6.

EXHIBIT 8.6

General Ledger Balances After Bad Debts Adjustment

Accounts Receivable and Allowance for Doubtful Accounts are BOTH balance sheet accounts shown under current assets.

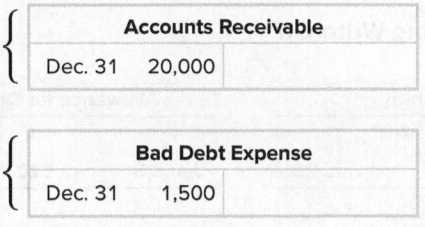

Accounts Receivable	
Dec. 31 20,000	

Allowance for Doubtful Accounts	
	1,500 Dec. 31

Bad Debt Expense is an income statement account and is normally listed as a selling expense.

Bad Debt Expense	
Dec. 31 1,500	

Although $20,000 is legally owed to TechCom by its credit customers, $18,500 (= $20,000 − $1,500) is the **realizable value**, or the estimated amount to be realized in cash collections from customers.

On the balance sheet, the Allowance for Doubtful Accounts is subtracted from Accounts Receivable to show the realizable value. This information is often reported as shown in Exhibit 8.7.

EXHIBIT 8.7

Balance Sheet Presentation of Allowance for Doubtful Accounts

Current assets:		
Accounts receivable..	$20,000	
Less: Allowance for doubtful accounts	1,500	18,500

Often the contra account to Accounts Receivable is not reported as a separate line item. This alternative presentation is shown in Exhibit 8.8.

EXHIBIT 8.8

Alternative Presentation of Allowance for Doubtful Accounts

Current assets:	
Accounts receivable (net of $1,500 estimated uncollectible accounts)	$18,500

Writing Off Bad Debt for a Specific Customer

When specific accounts receivable are identified as uncollectible, they must be removed from accounts receivable. This is done by writing these accounts off against the Allowance for Doubtful Accounts. For instance, after spending a year trying to collect from Jack Kent, TechCom finally decides that his $520 account is uncollectible and makes the following entry to write it off:

Jan.	23	Allowance for Doubtful Accounts	520	
		Accounts Receivable—Jack Kent...............		520
		To write off an uncollectible account.		

After this entry is posted, the general ledger accounts appear as shown in Exhibit 8.9.

EXHIBIT 8.9

General Ledger Balances After Posting Write-Off

Accounts Receivable					Allowance for Doubtful Accounts			
Dec. 31	20,000						1,500	Dec. 31
		520	Jan. 23		Jan. 23	520		
Balance	19,480						980	Balance

Note that the expense account is not debited, because bad debt expense is previously estimated and recorded with an adjusting entry at the end of the period in which the sale occurred. While the write-off removes the amount of the account receivable from the ledgers, it does not affect the estimated realizable value of TechCom's net accounts receivable as shown in Exhibit 8.10.

EXHIBIT 8.10

Realizable Value Before and After Write-Off

	Before Write-Off (Dec. 31)	After Write-Off (Jan. 23)
Accounts receivable..	$20,000	$19,480
Less: Allowance for doubtful accounts	1,500	980
Estimated realizable accounts receivable...	$18,500	$18,500

Neither total assets nor profit is affected by the write-off of a specific account. But both total assets and profit are affected by recognizing the year's bad debt expense in the adjusting entry.

Recovery of a Bad Debt—The Customer Makes a Payment

When a customer fails to pay and the account is written off, his or her credit standing is jeopardized. The customer sometimes chooses to pay all or part of the amount owed after the account is written off as uncollectible. This payment helps restore credit standing. When a recovery of a bad debt occurs, it is recorded in the customer's subsidiary account where this information is retained for use in future credit evaluation.

On March 11, Jack Kent pays in full his account that TechCom previously wrote off. The first entry reinstates the accounts receivable balance:

Mar.	11	Accounts Receivable—Jack Kent.........................	520	
		Allowance for Doubtful Accounts...............		520
		To reinstate the account of Jack Kent previously written off.		

The second entry reflects the cash receipt and the customer payment of the outstanding balance.

	11	Cash..	520	
		Accounts Receivable—Jack Kent...............		520
		In full payment of account.		

Jack Kent paid the entire amount previously written off, but in some cases a customer may pay only a portion of the amount owed. A question then arises of whether the entire balance of the account is returned to accounts receivable or just the amount paid. The answer is a matter of judgment. If we believe this customer will later pay in full, the entire amount owed is returned to accounts receivable. But only the amount paid is returned if we expect no further collection.

To summarize, the transactions discussed in this chapter[3] that cause changes in Accounts Receivable and Allowance for Doubtful Accounts are illustrated using T-accounts in Exhibit 8.11.

EXHIBIT 8.11

Summary of Accounts Receivable and Allowance for Doubtful Accounts Transactions

Accounts Receivable		Allowance for Doubtful Accounts	
(a) Sales on credit	(b) Collections received from credit customers		
	(c) Write-off of accounts receivable identified as uncollectible	(c) Write-off of accounts receivable identified as uncollectible	
(d) Recovery (reinstatement of accounts previously written off)	(e) Recovery (collection of reinstated accounts)		(d) Recovery (reinstatement of accounts previously written off)
			(f) Adjusting entry to estimate uncollectible accounts

CHECKPOINT

2. Why does the matching principle require that bad debt expenses be estimated?
3. What term describes the balance sheet valuation of accounts receivable less the allowance for doubtful accounts?
4. Why is estimated bad debt expense credited to a contra account rather than to the Accounts Receivable controlling account?
5. Record entries for the following transactions:

| January 10, 2020 | The $300 account of customer Cool Jam is determined to be uncollectible. |
| April 12, 2020 | Cool Jam pays in full its account that was deemed uncollectible on January 10, 2020. |

Do Quick Study questions: QS 8-3 and QS 8-4

---

3 Remember that Sales Returns and Allowances also cause Accounts Receivable to decrease.

ALTERNATIVE METHODS FOR ESTIMATING BAD DEBT

LO3 Estimate uncollectible accounts receivable using approaches based on sales and accounts receivable.

The purpose of estimating bad debt is to attempt to match bad debt expense with the related revenue that was recognized in the accounting period. There are two key approaches used by companies today to estimate bad debt expense. These methods were introduced briefly in Exhibit 8.5:

1. The percentage of receivables approach
2. The percentage of sales approach

Accounts Receivable Approach

The **accounts receivable approach**, also known as the **balance sheet approach**, uses balance sheet relationships (Accounts Receivable and the Allowance for Doubtful Accounts) to estimate bad debts. It is based on the idea that some portion of the end-of-period accounts receivable balance is not collectible. The objective for the bad debt adjusting entry is to make the Allowance for Doubtful Accounts balance equal to the portion of outstanding accounts receivable estimated to be uncollectible. To obtain this required balance for the Allowance for Doubtful Accounts account, we compare its balance before the adjustment with the required balance. The difference between the two is debited to Bad Debt Expense and credited to Allowance for Doubtful Accounts. Estimating this required balance for the allowance account is done in one of two ways:

1. By using a simple percentage estimate of uncollectible accounts from the total outstanding accounts receivable, or
2. By applying a unique percentage estimate to each category of the aged accounts receivable listing.

1. Percentage of Accounts Receivable

Estimating the required balance in the Allowance for Doubtful Accounts by using the **percentage of accounts receivable approach** assumes that a percentage of a company's outstanding receivables is uncollectible. This estimated percentage is based on past experience and is also affected by recent economic conditions and difficulties faced by customers. The total dollar amount of all outstanding receivables is multiplied by an estimated percentage to get the estimated dollar amount of uncollectible accounts. This is the amount to be reported in the balance sheet as the balance for Allowance for Doubtful Accounts. To accomplish this, we prepare the adjusting entry in the amount necessary to give us the required balance in Allowance for Doubtful Accounts.

For example, assume Modern Office, an office furniture supplier, has $50,000 of outstanding accounts receivable on December 31. Past experience suggests that 5% of outstanding receivables are uncollectible.

Therefore, we want the Allowance for Doubtful Accounts to show a $2,500 credit balance (5% of $50,000). Assume that the unadjusted balance in the Allowance for Doubtful Accounts at December 31 is currently a $500 credit.

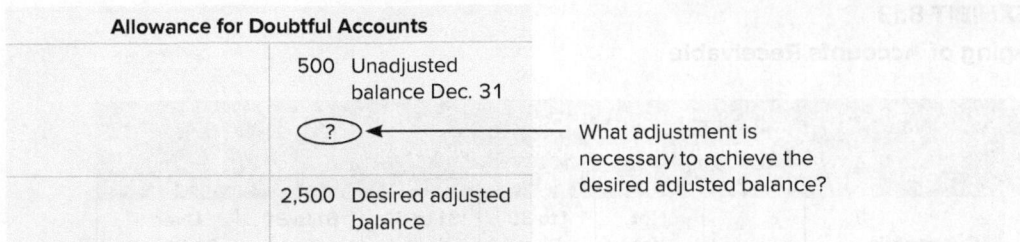

The adjusting entry to give the required $2,500 balance is:

Dec.	31	Bad Debt Expense...	2,000	
		Allowance for Doubtful Accounts..............................		2,000
		To record estimated bad debts.		

After this entry is posted, the allowance has a $2,500 credit balance as shown in Exhibit 8.12.

EXHIBIT 8.12
Allowance for Doubtful Accounts After Bad Debt Adjusting Entry

Allowance for Doubtful Accounts

	500 Unadjusted balance Dec. 31
	2,000 From Dec. 31 adjusting entry
	2,500 Adjusted balance Dec. 31

Accounts receivable would then be reported as follows on Modern Office's balance sheet:

Current assets:		
Accounts receivable...	$50,000	
Less: Allowance for doubtful accounts...	2,500	$47,500
or		
Current assets:		
Accounts receivable (net of $2,500 estimated uncollectible accounts)...		$47,500

2. Aging of Accounts Receivable

Normally, the older the account receivable outstanding is, the more likely that it will become uncollectible. An **accounts receivable aging analysis** estimates uncollectible accounts by grouping accounts receivable according to how much time has passed since they were created. The grouping categories used depend on the judgment of management but are often based on 30-day periods. Estimated rates of uncollectible amounts are applied to each class and totalled to get the required balance of the Allowance for Doubtful Accounts. This calculation is illustrated in Exhibit 8.13 for DeCor, an interior design company whose total outstanding accounts receivable at December 31 were $49,900.

EXHIBIT 8.13

Aging of Accounts Receivable

Customer's Name	Total	Not Yet Due	1 to 30 Days Past Due	31 to 60 Days Past Due	61 to 90 Days Past Due	Over 90 Days Past Due
DeCor Schedule of Accounts Receivable by Age December 31, 2020						
Chloe Arden	$ 450	$ 450				
Luca Fontana	710			$ 710		
Jasmine Kasu	500	300	$ 200			
Amy Ma	740				$ 100	$ 640
ZZ Services	1,000	810	190			
Totals	$49,900	$37,000	$6,500	$3,500	$1,900	$1,000
Percentage Uncollectible		× 2%	× 5%	× 10%	× 25%	× 40%
Estimated Uncollectible Accounts	$ 2,290	$ 740	$ 325	$ 350	$ 475	$ 400

Notice the percentage of estimated uncollectible receivables increases with the age of the accounts to reflect the increasing risk of not collecting these accounts

The total in the first column tells us the adjusted balance in DeCor's Allowance for Doubtful Accounts should be $2,290 (= $740 + $325 + $350 + $475 + $400). Because DeCor's allowance account as shown below has an unadjusted *debit balance* of $200, the required adjustment to the Allowance for Doubtful Accounts needs to be calculated as follows:

Allowance for Doubtful Accounts

Unadjusted balance Dec. 31	200	
	?	
	2,290 Desired adjusted balance Dec. 31	

What adjustment is necessary to achieve the desired adjusted balance?

DeCor records the following adjusting entry:

Dec.	31	Bad Debt Expense	2,490	
		Allowance for Doubtful Accounts		2,490
		To record estimated bad debts;		
		$2,290 + $200 = $2,490.		

On the balance sheet, DeCor's accounts receivable would be reported as follows:

Current assets:
Accounts receivable $49,900
Less: Allowance for doubtful accounts 2,290 $47,610

or

Current assets:
Accounts receivable (net of $2,290 estimated uncollectible accounts) $47,610

Percentage of Sales Approach

The **percentage of sales approach** (or **income statement approach**) uses income statement relations to estimate bad debts. It is based on the idea that a percentage of a company's credit sales for the period are uncollectible.[4] To demonstrate, assume MusicLand has credit sales of $400,000 in 2020. Based on experience, MusicLand estimates 0.6% of credit sales to be uncollectible. Using this prediction, MusicLand expects $2,400 of bad debt expense from 2020's sales ($400,000 × 0.006 = $2,400). The adjusting entry to record this estimated expense is:

Dec.	31	Bad Debt Expense..	2,400	
		Allowance for Doubtful Accounts...............		2,400
		To record estimated bad debts.		

For demonstration purposes, assume that the Allowance for Doubtful Accounts (AFDA) had an unadjusted credit balance of $200 on December 31. Bad Debt Expense and Allowance for Doubtful Accounts would appear as in Exhibit 8.14 *after* the December 31 adjustment.

EXHIBIT 8.14

Accounts Receivable and Allowance for Doubtful Accounts Balances After the December 31 Adjustment

Bad Debt Expense				Allowance for Doubtful Accounts		
					200	Unadjusted Balance Dec. 31
Dec. 31 Adjustment	2,400				2,400	Dec. 31 Adjustment
Adjusted Balance Dec. 31	2,400				2,600	Adjusted Balance Dec. 31

Note that the unadjusted balance of AFDA could be a zero balance, a credit balance, or a debit balance depending on the circumstances. If MusicLand were in its first period of operations, the AFDA would have a zero beginning balance. In the next accounting periods, if write-offs are *greater* than what had been estimated, a *debit* unadjusted balance will result. If *fewer* write-offs occur than what was estimated, as in Exhibit 8.14, a *credit* unadjusted balance will result. If the estimate for bad debts is too high or too low, the percentage used to estimate bad debts can be adjusted in future periods.

Exhibit 8.15 summarizes the principles guiding the estimation approaches and their focus of analysis.

EXHIBIT 8.15

Approaches to Estimate Bad Debts

4   Note that the focus is on credit sales. Cash sales do not produce bad debts, and they are generally not used in this estimation. But if cash sales are relatively small compared to credit sales, there is no major impact of including them.

Using an aging of receivables is the most reliable of the three calculations because it is based on a more detailed examination of the basket of outstanding receivables. In many cases, the aging analysis is supplemented with information about the current economic conditions and information about specific customers, allowing management to decide whether those accounts should be classified as uncollectible. This analysis is often best performed by the sales and credit department managers.

 CHECKPOINT

6. SnoBoard Company's end-of-period December 31, 2020, balance in the Allowance for Doubtful Accounts is a credit of $440. It estimates from an aging of accounts receivable that $6,142 is uncollectible. Prepare SnoBoard's year-end adjusting entry for bad debts.

Do Quick Study questions: QS 8-5, QS 8-6, QS 8-7, QS 8-8, and QS 8-9

Direct Write-Off Method

A third approach to writing off bad debt is referred to as the *direct write-off method*. This method is permitted only in circumstances where the total reported accounts receivable balance is insignificant to the financial statements as a whole. The **direct write-off method** records the loss from an uncollectible account receivable at the time it is determined to be uncollectible. No attempt is made to estimate uncollectible accounts or bad debt expense. For example, if TechCom determines on January 23 that it cannot collect $520 owed by an individual named Jack Kent, this loss is recognized using the direct write-off method in the following entry:

Jan.	23	Bad Debt Expense	520	
		Accounts Receivable—Jack Kent................		520
		To write off uncollectible accounts under the direct write-off method.		

The allowance method satisfies the requirement for faithful representation and matching; the direct write-off method does not.

1. An aspect of faithful representation demands that caution be exercised to prevent the overstatement of assets and profit. Overstated assets and/or profit could result in bad lending or investing decisions. By estimating uncollectible accounts, the allowance method is recognizing that less than 100% of the accounts receivable will be collected (Accounts Receivable less Allowance for Doubtful Accounts), ensuring receivables are not overstated. Under the direct write-off method, Accounts Receivable are reported on the balance sheet at 100% of the customer's outstanding balance, which is more than what will typically be collected.

2. The matching principle requires that expenses be reported in the period in which the related revenue was recorded. Often, an uncollectible account receivable is not discovered until the next accounting period. The allowance method attempts to match the expense of uncollectible accounts to the period in which the revenue was recorded by recording an estimate at the end of the period. The direct write-off method does *not* achieve matching since the expense is recorded when an account is identified as uncollectible, which is normally *not* in the period in which the revenue was recorded.

Although the direct write-off method is not in accordance with faithful representation and matching, *a business may choose to use it* instead of the allowance method. As mentioned above, this would occur when uncollectible accounts are not material. The materiality principle states that an amount can be ignored if its effect on the financial statements is unimportant to users. The materiality principle permits the matching principle to be ignored when bad debt expenses are very small in relation to a company's other financial statement items. So the direct write-off method would be used when bad debt expense is unimportant for decisions made by users of the company's financial statements.

 CHECKPOINT

7. The direct write-off method is recorded by debiting Bad Debt Expense and crediting the Allowance for Doubtful Accounts.
   a. True
   b. False

Do Quick Study question: QS 8-10

 DECISION MAKER   Answer—End of chapter

Labour Union Negotiation

You are representing your employee union in contract negotiations with management. One week prior to contract discussions, management released financial statements showing zero growth in earnings. This is far below the 10% growth predicted earlier. In your review of the financial statements, you find the company increased its "allowance for uncollectible accounts" from 1.5% to 4.5% of accounts receivable. Apart from this change, earnings would show a 9% growth. Does this information affect your negotiations?

Mid-Chapter Demonstration Problem

Maxo Industries, a distributor of electrical supplies, had outstanding accounts receivable on December 31, 2020, of $450,000 aged as follows:

Maxo Industries **Schedule of Accounts Receivable by Age** **December 31, 2020**						
Customer's Name	**Total**	**Not Yet Due**	**1 to 30 Days Past Due**	**31 to 60 Days Past Due**	**61 to 90 Days Past Due**	**Over 90 Days Past Due**
Alton Group..	$ 90,000		$ 90,000			
Filby's Electrical Service.........................	48,000			$22,000	$26,000	
GDP Servicing..	162,000	$120,000	42,000			
Parker's Electrical...................................	80,000	80,000				
Trenton Construction	15,000					$15,000
Xeon Developments	55,000	30,000	25,000			
Totals...	$450,000	$230,000	$157,000	$22,000	$26,000	$15,000
Percentage uncollectible.........................		× 1%	× 4%	× 8%	× 25%	× 60%
Estimated uncollectible accounts...............						

During the year 2020, the company had sales of $3,720,000, of which $38,000 were cash sales. The Allowance for Doubtful Accounts had an unadjusted debit balance on December 31, 2020, of $3,050.

Required

Prepare the adjusting entry to estimate uncollectible accounts on December 31, 2020, under each of the following independent assumptions, and show the resulting balance sheet presentation for accounts receivable:

a. Bad debts are estimated to be 0.6% of credit sales.

b. Bad debts are estimated to be 4% of outstanding accounts receivable.

c. Bad debts are based on an aging analysis (part of the required information is provided in the schedule above).

Analysis Component:

d. If Maxo did not record the adjusting entry to estimate uncollectible accounts receivable, what effect would this have on current assets, equity, and profit?

e. Assume Maxo's competitors report uncollectible accounts receivable of 1% of outstanding receivables. How does Maxo's experience compare?

SOLUTION

a. $0.6\% \times (\$3,720,000 - \$38,000 = \$3,682,000$ credit sales$) = \$22,092$

2020			
Dec. 31	Bad Debt Expense	22,092	
	Allowance for Doubtful Accounts...............		22,092
	To record estimated bad debts.		

Current assets:			
Accounts receivable...		$450,000	
Less: Allowance for doubtful accounts		19,042*	$430,958

or

Current assets:	
Accounts receivable (net of $19,042* estimated uncollectible accounts)...............................	$430,958

$22,092 credit adjustment – $3,050 debit balance = $19,042.

b. The required balance in the Allowance for Doubtful Accounts is $18,000 (= 4% × $450,000)

Dec. 31	Bad Debt Expense	21,050	
	Allowance for Doubtful Accounts...............		21,050
	To record estimated bad debts;		
	$18,000 + $3,050 = $21,050.		

Current assets:

Accounts receivable... $450,000

Less: Allowance for doubtful accounts 18,000 $432,000

or

Current assets:

Accounts receivable (net of $18,000 estimated uncollectible accounts)................................. $432,000

c. First, calculate total estimated uncollectible accounts by completing the bottom of the aging schedule as follows:

	Total	Not Yet Due	1–30 Days Past Due	31–60 Days Past Due	61–90 Days Past Due	Over 90 Days Past Due
Totals	$450,000	$230,000	$157,000	$22,000	$26,000	$15,000
Percentage uncollectible...................		× 1%	× 4%	× 8%	× 25%	× 60%
Estimated uncollectible accounts.....	$ 25,840	$ 2,300	$ 6,280	$ 1,760	$ 6,500	$ 9,000

Allowance for Doubtful Accounts

Unadjusted balance Dec. 31	3,050	
	?	
	25,840	Desired adjusted balance Dec. 31

What adjustment is necessary to achieve the desired adjusted balance?

Second, determine what adjustment is necessary to achieve the desired balance of $25,840 in the Allowance for Doubtful Accounts as follows:

Dec.	31	Bad Debt Expense	28,890	
		Allowance for Doubtful Accounts................		28,890
		To record estimated bad debts;		
		$25,840 + $3,050.		

Current assets:

Accounts receivable... $450,000

Less: Allowance for doubtful accounts 25,840 $424,160

or

Current assets:

Accounts receivable (net of $25,840 estimated uncollectible accounts)................................. $424,160

Analysis Component:

d. If Maxo did not record the adjusting entry to estimate uncollectible accounts receivable, current assets would be overstated, equity would be overstated, and profit would be overstated.

e. Maxo's competitors are experiencing a lower rate of uncollectible accounts receivable, which, on the surface, appears to be favourable. However, additional information is required. Perhaps Maxo has an aggressive credit policy, granting credit to a wider range of customers, which increases revenues but at the same time increases the risk of the balance not being collected but overall increases profit. It may also be that Maxo's experience is the result of weak credit policies that grant credit to riskier customers (regarding collectability).

Short-Term Notes Receivable

LO4 Describe and record a short-term note receivable and calculate its maturity date and interest.

A **promissory note**, as illustrated in Exhibit 8.16, is a written promise to pay a specified amount of money either on demand or at a definite future date. A **short-term note receivable** (or **note receivable**) is a promissory note that becomes due within the next 12 months or within the business's operating cycle if greater than 12 months.

EXHIBIT 8.16

Terminology Related to a Promissory Note

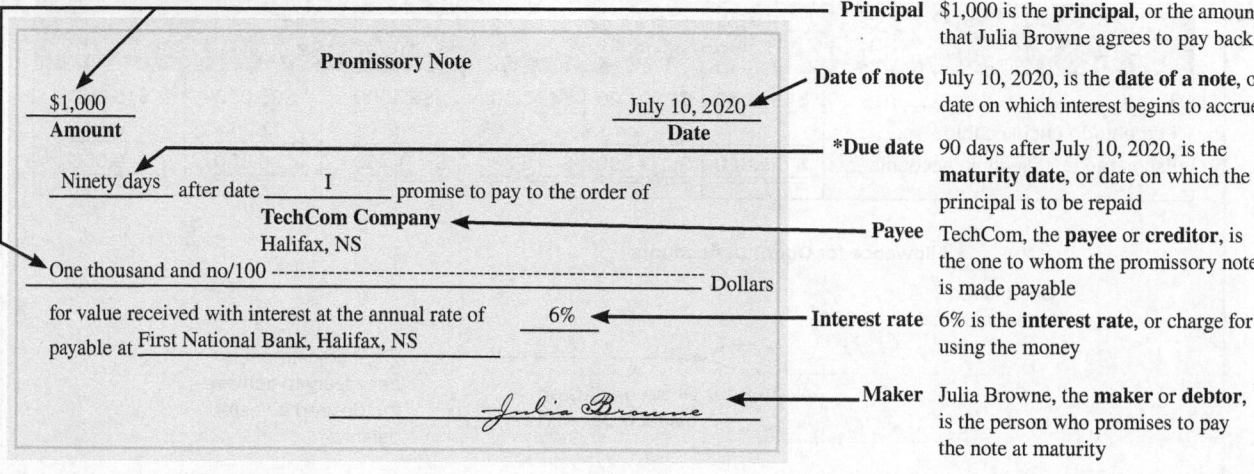

*Note: The **due date of a note** is also referred to as the *maturity date*. The **period** of this note is 90 days, the time from the date of the note to its maturity date or due date.

CALCULATIONS FOR NOTES

We need to know two calculations related to notes:

1. How to determine the maturity date, and
2. How to calculate interest.

Maturity Date

A note dated on July 10 with a specified maturity date of July 15 is a five-day note (calculated as July 15 − July 10 = 5 days). A 10-day note dated July 10 would have a maturity date of July 20 (calculated as July 10 + 10 days = July 20). The promissory note dated July 10 in Exhibit 8.16 is a 90-day note and the maturity date is calculated as shown in Exhibit 8.17.

EXHIBIT 8.17

Maturity Date Calculation

Days in July..	31
Minus date of note..	10
Days remaining in July..	21
Add days in August..	31
Add days in September..	30
Days to equal 90 days or **Maturity Date, October 8**...	8
Period of the note in days..	90

The period of a note is sometimes expressed in months or years. When months are used, the note matures and is payable in the month of its maturity on the *same day of the month* as its original date. A three-month note dated July 10, for instance, is payable on October 10. The same analysis applies when years are used.

Interest Calculation

Interest is an annual rate unless otherwise stated. The formula for calculating interest is shown in Exhibit 8.18.

EXHIBIT 8.18
Formula for Calculating Interest

$$\text{Interest} = \begin{array}{c}\text{Principal}\\\text{of the}\\\text{note}\end{array} \times \begin{array}{c}\text{Annual}\\\text{interest}\\\text{rate}\end{array} \times \begin{array}{c}\text{Time}\\\text{expressed}\\\text{in years}\end{array} \quad \text{or} \quad i = Prt$$

Interest on a $1,000, 6%, six-month note is calculated as:

$$\$1,000 \times 6\% \times \frac{6}{12} = \underline{\underline{\$30}}$$

Using the promissory note in Exhibit 8.16 where the *term of the note is in days*, interest is calculated as follows:

$$\text{Interest} = \text{Principal} \times \text{Rate} \times \frac{\text{Exact days}}{365}$$

or

$$\$1,000 \times 6\% \times \frac{90}{365} = \underline{\underline{\$14.79}}$$

> **Important Tip:**
> Unless otherwise instructed, you are to solve problems using the specific number of days and a 365-day year. Interest calculations should be rounded to the nearest whole cent.

RECEIPT OF A NOTE

To illustrate recording the receipt of a note, we use the $1,000, 90-day, 6% promissory note in Exhibit 8.16. Assume that TechCom receives this note at the time of a product sale to Julia Browne (cost of sales $630). This transaction is recorded as (assuming a perpetual inventory system):

July	10	Notes Receivable	1,000	
		Sales		1,000
		Sold merchandise in exchange for a 90-day, 6% note.		
	10	Cost of Goods Sold	630	
		Merchandise Inventory		630
		To record cost of inventory sold.		

A note receivable can also arise when a company accepts a note from an overdue customer as a way of granting a time extension on a past-due account receivable. When this occurs, a company may collect part of the past-due balance in cash. This partial payment forces a concession from the customer, reduces the customer's debt (and the seller's risk), and produces a note for a smaller amount. TechCom, for instance, agreed to accept $1,000 in cash and a $3,000, 60-day, 6% note on December 16 from Jo Cook to settle her $4,000 past-due account. TechCom made the following entry to record receipt of this cash and conversion of the remaining A/R balance to a note receivable:

Dec.	16	Cash	1,000	
		Notes Receivable	3,000	
		Accounts Receivable—Jo Cook		4,000
		Received cash and note in settlement of account.		

END-OF-PERIOD INTEREST ADJUSTMENT

When notes receivable are outstanding at the end of an accounting period, accrued interest is calculated and recorded. This recognizes both the interest income when it is earned and the added asset (interest receivable) owned by the note's holder. When TechCom's accounting period ends on December 31, $7.40 of interest accrues on the note dated December 16 ($3,000 × 6% × 15/365). The following adjusting entry records this revenue:

Dec.	31	Interest Receivable	7.40	
		Interest Income		7.40
		To record accrued interest.		

This adjusting entry means that interest income appears on the income statement of the period when it is earned. It also means that interest receivable appears on the balance sheet as a current asset.

HONOURING A NOTE—CUSTOMER PAYMENT OF NOTE

When the note dated December 16 is paid on the maturity date of February 14, the maker of the note, Jo Cook, is **honouring a note receivable**. TechCom's entry to record the cash receipt is:

Feb.	14	Cash	3,029.59	
		Interest Income		22.19
		Interest Receivable		7.40
		Notes Receivable		3,000.00
		Received payment of a note and its interest.		

Total interest earned on this note is $29.59 (= $3,000 × 6% × 60/365). On February 14, Interest Receivable is credited for $7.40 to record the collection of the interest accrued on December 31. The interest income in this period is $22.19 (= $29.59 total interest less $7.40 interest accrued on December 31) and reflects TechCom's revenue from holding the note from January 1 to February 14.

DISHONOURING A NOTE—CUSTOMER NEGLECTS TO PAY AT MATURITY

Sometimes the maker of a note does not pay the note at maturity; this is known as **dishonouring a note receivable**. The act of dishonouring does not relieve the maker of the obligation to pay. The payee should use every legitimate means to collect. Assume Julia Browne did not pay the note dated July 10 when it matured on October 8. TechCom removes the amount of the note from the Notes Receivable account and charges it back to an account receivable from its maker as follows:

Oct.	8	Accounts Receivable—Julia Browne..................	1,014.79	
		Interest Income...		14.79
		Notes Receivable...		1,000.00
		To charge the account of Julia Browne for a dishonoured note including interest; $1,000 × 6% – 90/365.		

Charging a dishonoured note back to the account of its maker serves three purposes.

1. *First,* it removes the amount of the note from the Notes Receivable account, leaving in the account only notes that have not matured, and records the dishonoured note in the maker's account.

2. *Second,* and most important, if the maker of the dishonoured note applies for credit in the future, his or her account will show all past dealings, including the dishonoured note.

3. *Third,* restoring the account also reminds the company to continue collection efforts for both principal and interest.

As accounts receivable, the customer's outstanding balance will then be included in the end-of-period A/R assessment when determining the appropriate allowance provision. If the restored account receivable is later identified as being uncollectible, it is written off as follows:

Oct.	31	Allowance for Doubtful Accounts	1,014.79	
		Accounts Receivable—Julia Browne..........		1,014.79
		To write off an uncollectible account.		

Important Tip:

Once the dishonoured note has reached maturity and has not been paid off by the customer, accrual of interest is usually no longer recorded. Interest income should be recorded only if it is determined to be collectible. In the circumstance of a dishonoured note, collectability of the underlying interest is not reasonably assured.

 CHECKPOINT

8. Brad purchases $7,000 of merchandise from Stamford Company on December 16, 2020. Stamford accepts Brad's $7,000, 90-day, 12% note as payment. Stamford's annual accounting period ends on December 31 and it doesn't make reversing entries. Prepare entries for Stamford Company on December 16, 2020, and December 31, 2020.

9. Using the information in Checkpoint 8, prepare Stamford's March 16, 2021 entry if Brad dishonours the note.

Do Quick Study questions: QS 8-11, QS 8-12, and QS 8-13

Financial Statement Analysis—Accounts Receivable Turnover and Days' Sales Uncollected

LO5 Calculate accounts receivable turnover and days' sales uncollected to analyze liquidity.

For a company selling on credit, we want to assess both the *quality* and *liquidity* of its accounts receivable to assess performance and risk. Quality of receivables refers to the likelihood of collection without loss. Experience shows that the longer receivables are outstanding beyond their due date, the lower the likelihood of collection. Liquidity of receivables refers to the speed or efficiency of collection. Therefore, tools to help monitor receivables are critical to their timely collection.

ACCOUNTS RECEIVABLE TURNOVER

The **accounts receivable turnover** is a measure of both the quality and liquidity of accounts receivable. It indicates how often, on average, receivables are received and collected during the period. Accounts receivable turnover also helps us evaluate how well management is doing in granting credit to customers in a desire to increase sales revenues. A high turnover in comparison with competitors suggests that management should consider using more liberal credit terms to increase sales. A low turnover suggests management should consider more strict credit terms and more aggressive collection efforts to avoid having its resources tied up in accounts receivable.

The formula for this ratio is shown in Exhibit 8.19.

EXHIBIT 8.19
Accounts Receivable Turnover Formula

$$\text{Accounts receivable turnover} = \frac{\text{Net sales}}{\text{Average accounts receivable}}$$

Although the numerator of this ratio is more precise if credit sales are used, total net sales are usually used by external users because information about credit sales is typically not reported. The denominator includes accounts receivable and all short-term receivables (including notes receivable) from customers. Average accounts receivable is calculated by adding the balances at the beginning and end of the period and dividing the sum by two. Some users prefer using gross accounts receivable, before subtracting the allowance for doubtful accounts, but many balance sheets report only the net amount of accounts receivable.

 DECISION MAKER   Answer—End of chapter

Private Health Care Investor

You have invested in a private diagnostic imaging clinic, so you and your fellow investors hire a health care analyst. The analyst highlights several points including the following: "Accounts receivable turnover is too low. Tighter credit policies are recommended along with discontinuing service to those most delayed payments." How do you interpret these recommendations? What actions do you take?

DAYS' SALES UNCOLLECTED

We use the number of **days' sales uncollected** (also known as **days' sales in receivables**) to assess the liquidity of receivables by estimating how much time is likely to pass before we receive cash from credit sales equal to the *current amount* of accounts receivable.[5] The formula for this ratio is shown in Exhibit 8.20.

EXHIBIT 8.20
Days' Sales Uncollected Formula

$$\text{Days' sales uncollected} = \frac{\text{Accounts receivable}}{\text{Net sales}} \times 365$$

Days' sales uncollected is more meaningful if we know the company's credit terms. A rough guideline is that days' sales uncollected should not exceed one-and-one-third times the days in its (1) credit period, if discounts are not offered, or (2) discount period, if discounts are offered.

ANALYSIS

To perform an analysis using the receivable ratios, we select data from the annual reports of two Canadian food manufacturers, **High Liner Foods Inc.** and **Maple Leaf Foods Inc.**, as shown in Exhibit 8.21.

EXHIBIT 8.21
Comparison of Accounts Receivable Turnover and Days' Sales Uncollected for High Liner Foods Inc. and Maple Leaf Foods Inc.

		($ thousands)	
		December 31, 2017	**January 1, 2017**
High Liner Foods Inc.	Accounts receivable..	$ 92,395	$ 75,190
	Net sales...	1,053,846	N/A
Maple Leaf Foods Inc.	Accounts receivable..	123,968	127,749
	Net sales...	3,522,226	N/A

Results for December 31, 2017		
	Accounts Receivable Turnover	**Days' Sales Uncollected**
High Liner	$\dfrac{\$1,053,846}{(\$92,395 + \$75,190)/2} = 12.58$ times	$\dfrac{\$92,395}{\$1,053,846} \times 365 = 30.34$ days
Maple Leaf	$\dfrac{\$3,522,226}{(\$123,968 + \$127,749)/2} = 27.99$ times	$\dfrac{\$123,968}{\$3,522,226} \times 365 = 12.85$ days

The Maple Leaf Foods accounts receivable turnover of 27.99 times tells us that in 2017 it collected receivables more than twice as fast as High Liner Foods. The days' sales uncollected ratio indicates that High Liner Foods will take 30.34 days to collect the January 1, 2017, balance in accounts receivable as compared to Maple Leaf's 12.85 days to collect its receivables balance on December 31, 2017. Although both companies are in a similar industry, their credit management appears to be significantly different based on a review of the receivables ratios.

---

5   When days' sales uncollected is calculated using *average* accounts receivable, the result tells us how many days, *on average,* it takes to collect receivables. The formula in Exhibit 8.20 tells us how many days it will take to collect the current receivables balance.

CHECKPOINT

10. WebCor reported an accounts receivable turnover of 11 at March 31, 2020. The industry average is 10 for the same date. At March 31, 2019, WebCor reported an accounts receivable turnover of 13. Did WebCor improve regarding its collection of receivables?

Do Quick Study question: QS 8-14

CRITICAL THINKING CHALLENGE

Refer to the Critical Thinking Challenge question at the beginning of the chapter. Compare your answers to those suggested on Connect.

IFRS AND ASPE—THE DIFFERENCES

Difference	International Financial Reporting Standards (IFRS)	Accounting Standards for Private Enterprises (ASPE)
There are no significant differences students need to be aware of between IFRS and ASPE related to this chapter.		

A Look Ahead

Chapter 9 investigates accounting issues for fixed assets under two major categories: property, plant, and equipment, and intangible assets. The chapter focuses on identifying all items that are included in their asset cost and analyzes options for matching their usage costs over their useful lives. Other considerations such as how to handle asset disposals, exchanges, and sales are analyzed.

SUMMARY

LO1 Describe accounts receivable and how they occur and are recorded. Accounts receivable are amounts due from customers for credit sales. The subledger lists the amounts owed by individual customers. Credit sales arise from at least two sources: (1) sales on credit and (2) non-bank credit card sales. Sales on credit refers to a company granting credit directly to customers. Non-bank credit card sales involve use of a third party issuing a credit card.

LO2 Apply the allowance method to account for uncollectible accounts receivable. Under the allowance method, bad debt expense is estimated at the end of the accounting period by debiting Bad Debt Expense and crediting the Allowance for Doubtful Accounts. This method is required under generally accepted accounting principles as it matches the expense to the associated revenue. When accounts are later identified as being uncollectible, they are written off by debiting the Allowance for Doubtful Accounts and crediting Accounts Receivable.

LO3 Estimate uncollectible accounts receivable using approaches based on sales and accounts receivable. Uncollectibles are estimated by focusing on either (a) the income statement relationship between bad debt expense and credit sales or (b) the balance sheet relationship between Accounts Receivable and the Allowance for Doubtful Accounts (AFDA). The first approach emphasizes the matching principle for the income statement. The second approach can include either a simple percentage of accounts receivable or a percentage of each category of the aged accounts receivable listing. Accounts receivable is presented net of the AFDA at its realizable value on the balance sheet. The direct write-off method debits Bad Debt Expense and credits Accounts Receivable when accounts are determined to be uncollectible. It is used when the amount of bad debt expense is immaterial.

LO4 Describe and record a short-term note receivable and calculate its maturity date and interest. A short-term note receivable is a written promise to pay a specified amount of money either on demand or at a definite future date, normally within the next 12 months or the business's operating cycle if greater than one year. The maturity date of a note is the day the note (principal and interest) must be repaid. Interest rates are typically stated in annual terms. When a note's time to maturity is more or less than one year, the amount of interest on a note is calculated by expressing time as a fraction of one year and multiplying the note's principal by this fraction and the annual interest rate. It is recorded at its principal amount by debiting the Notes Receivable account and is credited to the asset or related revenue associated with the issuance of the note. Interest earned is accrued at period-end. When a note is honoured, the payee debits the money received and credits both Notes Receivable and Interest Income. Dishonoured notes are credited to Notes Receivable and Interest Income and debited to Accounts Receivable.

LO5 Calculate accounts receivable turnover and days' sales uncollected to analyze liquidity. Accounts receivable turnover and days' sales uncollected are measures of both the quality and liquidity of accounts receivable. The accounts receivable turnover indicates how often, on average, receivables are received and collected during the period and is calculated as sales divided by average accounts receivable for the period. Days' sales uncollected is calculated as (Accounts receivable ÷ Net sales) × 365 and is used to estimate how much time is likely to pass before cash receipts from net sales are received equal to the average amount of accounts receivable. Both ratios are compared to those for other companies in the same industry, and with prior years' estimates.

 ## Guidance Answer to DECISION MAKER

Labour Union Negotiator

Yes, this information is likely to affect your negotiations. The obvious question is why the company increased the allowance to such a large extent. This major increase in allowance means a substantial increase in bad debt expense *and* a decrease in earnings. Also, this change coming immediately prior to labour contract discussions raises concerns since it reduces the union's bargaining power for increased compensation. You want to ask management for supporting documentation justifying this increase. Also, you want data for two or three prior years, and similar data from competitors. These data should give you some sense of whether the change in the allowance for uncollectibles is justified or not.

Private Health Care Investor

The recommendations are twofold. First, the analyst suggests more stringent screening of clients' credit standing. Second, the analyst suggests dropping clients who are most overdue in payments. You are likely bothered by both suggestions. They are probably financially wise recommendations but you are troubled by eliminating services to those less able to pay. One alternative is to follow a care program directed at clients less able to pay for services. This allows you to continue services to clients less able to pay and lets you discontinue services to clients able but unwilling to pay.

 ## Guidance Answers to CHECKPOINT

1. Accounts receivable are typically due within the current accounting period so would be reported on the balance sheet as a current asset.
2. Bad debt expense must be estimated to match it with the sales that gave rise to the accounts receivable. This requires that companies estimate bad debts before they learn which accounts are uncollectible.
3. Realizable value.
4. The estimated amount of bad debt expense cannot be credited to the Accounts Receivable account because the specific customer accounts that will prove uncollectible cannot be identified and removed from the accounts receivable subledger. If the controlling account were credited directly, its balance would not equal the sum of the subsidiary account balances.

5.

	2020				
	Jan.	10	Allowance for Doubtful Accounts	300	
			Accounts Receivable—Cool Jam...		300
			To record write-off of uncollectible account.		
	Apr.	12	Accounts Receivable—Cool Jam	300	
			Allowance for Doubtful Accounts...		300
			To reinstate account previously written off.		
		12	Cash..	300	
			Accounts Receivable—Cool Jam...		300
			To record collection.		

6.

	2020				
	Dec.	31	Bad Debt Expense...	5,702	
			Allowance for Doubtful Accounts...		5,702
			To record estimated bad debts; $6,142 − $440.		

7. False. The direct write-off method is recorded by debiting Bad Debt Expense and crediting Accounts Receivable.

8.

	2020				
	Dec.	16	Notes Receivable	7,000.00	
			Sales..		7,000.00
			To record 90-day, 12% note.		
		31	Interest Receivable	34.52	
			Interest Income		34.52
			To record accrued interest; $7,000 × 12% × 15/365.		

9.

	2021				
	Mar.	16	Accounts Receivable—Brad	7,207.12	
			Interest Income		172.60
			Interest Receivable...		34.52
			Notes Receivable...		7000.00
			To record dishonouring of a bad note; $7,000 × 12% × 90/365 = $207.12.		

10. At March 31, 2020, WebCor collected its receivables faster than what was reported for the industry average. However, in comparison to its performance in the previous year, WebCor's efficiency in its collection of receivables decreased.

Demonstration Problem

GardenWorks Co. had a number of transactions involving receivables during the year 2020. A description of each one follows.

Required

Prepare journal entries to record these independent transactions on the books of GardenWorks Co. GardenWorks Co.'s year-end is December 31.

a. On November 15, 2020, GardenWorks Co. agreed to accept $500 in cash and a $2,000, 90-day, 8% note from Argo Company to settle its $2,500 past-due account. Determine the maturity date and record the entry on November 15, on December 31, and on the date of maturity.

b. GardenWorks Co. held a $1,800, 6%, 45-day note of Altamira Industries. At maturity, December 15, Altamira dishonoured the note. Record the dishonouring of the Note Receivable.

c. GardenWorks Co. estimates bad debts to be 3.5% of net credit sales. During 2020, total sales were $6,200,000, of which 35% were for cash. Sales returns and allowances for the year were $128,000, all related to credit sales. Accounts receivable in the amount of $130,000 were identified as uncollectible and written off during 2020. Calculate the adjusted balance in the allowance for doubtful accounts at December 31, 2020, assuming a credit balance on January 1, 2020, of $160,000.

Analysis Component:

In (b) the note receivable was dishonoured. How should this be classified on the balance sheet?

Planning the Solution

- Examine each item to determine which accounts are affected and perform the required calculations.
- Prepare required journal entries.
- Prepare an answer to the analysis component.

SOLUTION

a.

Days in November	30
Minus date of note	15
Days remaining in November	15
Add days in December	31
	46
Add days in January	31
Days to equal 90 days or Maturity date, February 13	13
Period of the note in days	90

2020					
Nov.	15	Cash		500.00	
		Notes Receivable		2,000.00	
			Accounts Receivable—Argo Company		2,500.00
		Received cash and note in settlement of account.			
Dec.	31	Interest Receivable		20.16	
			Interest Income		20.16
		To record accrued interest; $2,000 × 46/365 × 8% = $20.16.			
2021					
Feb.	13	Cash		2,039.45	
			Interest Receivable		20.16
			Interest Income		19.29
			Notes Receivable		2,000.00
		Collected note with interest; $2,000 × 90/365 × 8% = $39.45.			

b.

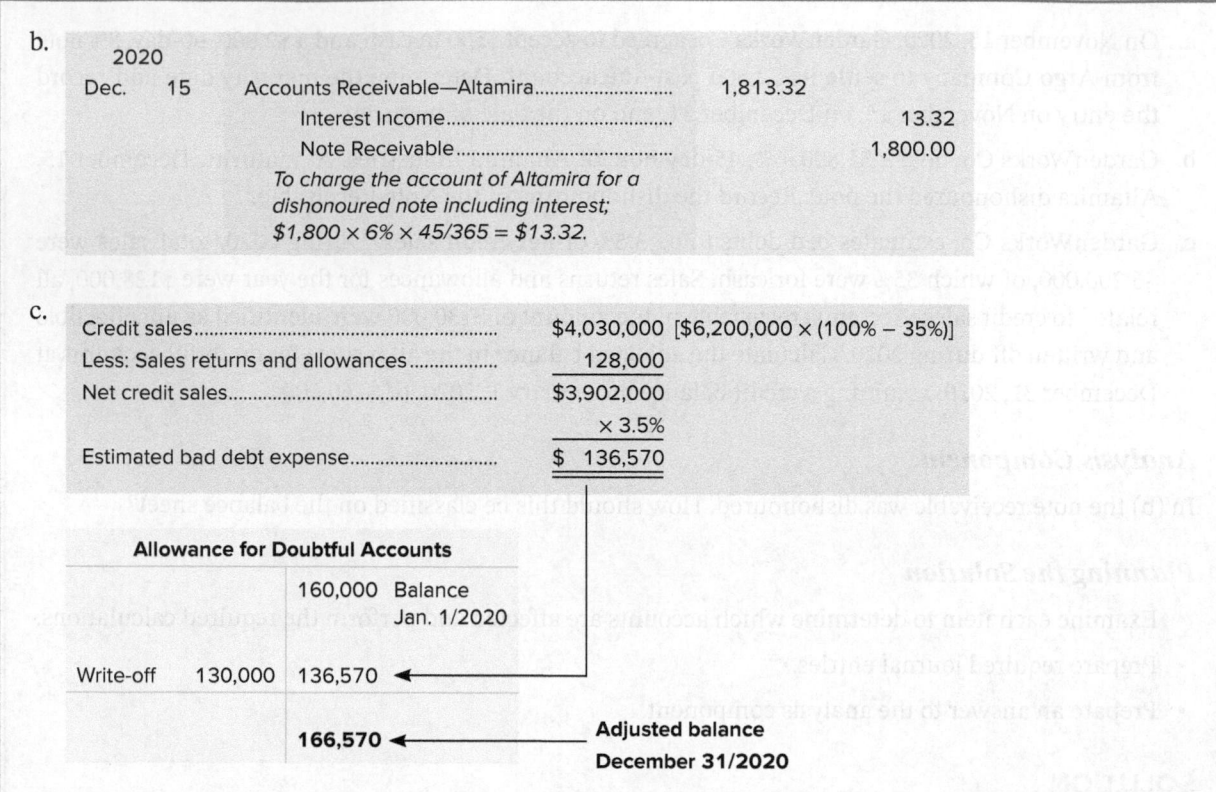

2020		
Dec. 15	Accounts Receivable—Altamira............................	1,813.32
	Interest Income...	13.32
	Note Receivable...	1,800.00
	To charge the account of Altamira for a dishonoured note including interest; $1,800 × 6% × 45/365 = $13.32.	

c.

Credit sales...	$4,030,000 [$6,200,000 × (100% − 35%)]
Less: Sales returns and allowances.................	128,000
Net credit sales...	$3,902,000
	× 3.5%
Estimated bad debt expense............................	$ 136,570

Allowance for Doubtful Accounts

		160,000	Balance Jan. 1/2020
Write-off	130,000	136,570	
		166,570	Adjusted balance December 31/2020

Analysis Component:

The dishonoured note receivable in (b) is technically recorded as a current asset on December 15. However, given the high risk of this receivable not being collected, the Allowance for Doubtful Accounts should be adjusted appropriately or the account should be written off or some other appropriate course of action should be taken to ensure that accounts receivable are not overstated at year-end because of this note.

APPENDIX 8A

Converting Receivables to Cash Before Maturity

LO6 Explain how receivables can be converted to cash before maturity.

Sometimes companies convert receivables to cash before they are due. Reasons for this include the need for cash or a desire not to be involved in collection activities. Converting receivables is usually done either (1) by selling them or (2) by using them as security for a loan. A recent survey showed that about 20% of large companies obtain cash from either the sale of receivables or the pledging of receivables as security. In some industries, such as textiles and furniture, this is common practice. Recently, this practice has spread to other industries, especially the apparel industry. Also, many small companies use sales of receivables as an immediate source of cash. This is especially the case for those selling to companies and government agencies that often delay payment.

SELLING ACCOUNTS RECEIVABLE

A company can sell its accounts receivable to a finance company or bank. The buyer, called a **factor**, charges the seller a *factoring fee* and then collects the receivables as they come due. By incurring a factoring fee, the seller receives cash earlier and passes the risk of bad debts to the factor. The seller also avoids costs of billing and accounting for the receivables.

If TechCom, for instance, sells $20,000 of its accounts receivable on August 15 and is charged a 2% factoring fee, it records this sale as:

Aug.	15	Cash..	19,600	
		Factoring Fee Expense..	400	
		Accounts Receivable......................................		20,000
		Sold accounts receivable for cash, less a 2% factoring fee.		

PLEDGING ACCOUNTS RECEIVABLE AS LOAN SECURITY

A company can also raise cash by borrowing money and then *pledging* its accounts receivable as security for the loan. Pledging receivables does not transfer the risk of bad debts to the lender. The borrower retains ownership of the receivables. But if the borrower defaults on the loan, the lender has a right to be paid from cash receipts as the accounts receivable are collected. When TechCom borrowed $35,000 and pledged its receivables as security, it recorded this transaction as:

Aug.	20	Cash..	35,000	
		Notes Payable		35,000
		Borrowed money with the note secured by pledging accounts receivable.		

Because pledged receivables are committed as security for a specific loan, the borrower's financial statements should disclose the pledging of accounts receivable. TechCom, for instance, includes the following note with its financial statements regarding its pledged receivables: "Accounts receivable in the amount of $40,000 are pledged as security for a $35,000 note payable to First National Bank."

DISCOUNTING NOTES RECEIVABLE

Notes receivable can be converted to cash before they mature. Companies that may need cash sooner to meet their obligations can discount (or sell) notes receivable at a financial institution or bank. TechCom, for instance, discounted a $3,000, 90-day, 10% note receivable at First National Bank. TechCom held the note for 50 of the 90 days before discounting it. The bank applied a 12% rate in discounting the note. TechCom received proceeds of $3,033.55 from the bank, calculated as:

Principal of Note..	$3,000.00
+ Interest from Note ($3,000 × 10% × 90/365)......................................	73.97
= Maturity Value..	$3,073.97
− Bank Discount ($3,073.97 × 12% × 40/365)...	40.42
= Proceeds..	$3,033.55

TechCom recorded the discounting of this note as:

Aug.	25	Cash..	3,033.55	
		Interest Income		33.55
		Notes Receivable...		3,000.00
		Discounted a note receivable.		

Computer programs are used in practice to calculate bank proceeds easily. Notes receivable are discounted without recourse or with recourse. When a note is discounted *without recourse*, the bank assumes the risk of a bad debt loss and the original payee does not have a *contingent liability*. A **contingent liability**[6] is a potential obligation dependent on an uncertain future event that has arisen due to a past business event (such as an employee-related lawsuit). A note discounted without recourse is like an outright sale of an asset. If a note is discounted *with recourse* and the original maker of the note fails to pay the bank when it matures, the original payee of the note must pay for it. This means a company discounting a note with recourse has a contingent liability until the bank is paid. A company should disclose contingent liabilities in notes to its financial statements. TechCom included the following note: "The Company is contingently liable for a $3,000 note receivable discounted with recourse."

FULL DISCLOSURE

The disclosure of contingent liabilities in notes is consistent with the full disclosure principle. Contingent liabilities are discussed in more detail in Chapter 10.

 CHECKPOINT

11. A company needs cash and has substantial accounts receivable. What alternatives are available for getting cash from its accounts receivable prior to receiving payments from credit customers?

Do Quick Study questions: QS 8-15 and 8-16

---

6 IFRS 2014, IAS 37, para. 10.

SUMMARY OF APPENDIX 8A

LO6 **Explain how receivables can be converted to cash before maturity.** There are three usual means to convert receivables to cash before maturity. First, a company can sell accounts receivable to a factor, which charges a factoring fee. Second, a company can borrow money by signing a note payable that is secured by pledging the accounts receivable. Third, notes receivable can be discounted at a bank, with or without recourse. The full disclosure principle requires companies to disclose the amount of receivables pledged and the contingent liability for notes discounted with recourse.

 Guidance Answers to CHECKPOINT

11. Alternatives are:
1. Selling their accounts receivable to a factor,
2. Pledging accounts receivable as loan security, and
3. Discounting notes receivable at a bank with or without recourse.

GLOSSARY

Accounts receivable Amounts due from customers for credit sales. Also referred to as *trade receivables*.

Accounts receivable approach A method of estimating bad debts using balance sheet relationships. Also known as the *balance sheet approach*.

Accounts receivable aging analysis A process of classifying accounts receivable in terms of how long they have been outstanding for the purpose of estimating the amount of uncollectible accounts.

Accounts receivable turnover A measure of both the quality and liquidity of accounts receivable; it indicates how often, on average, receivables are received and collected during the period; calculated by dividing credit sales (or net sales) by the average accounts receivable balance.

Allowance for Doubtful Accounts A contra asset account with a balance equal to the estimated amount of accounts receivable that will be uncollectible; also called the *Allowance for Uncollectible Accounts*.

Allowance method of accounting for bad debts An accounting procedure that (1) estimates and reports bad debt expense from credit sales during the period of the sales, and (2) reports accounts receivable as the amount of cash proceeds that are expected from their collection (their estimated realizable value).

Bad debts The accounts of customers who fail to pay what they have committed to pay at the time of the sale of goods or provision of service. It is the total dollar value of the unpaid accounts receivables balance. Once determined to be uncollectible, the amount is booked as bad debt expense; also called *uncollectible accounts*.

Balance sheet approach See *accounts receivable approach*.

Contingent liability A potential liability that depends on a future event arising out of a past event.

Creditor See *payee*.

Date of a note The date on which interest begins to accrue.

Days' sales uncollected A measure of the liquidity of receivables calculated by taking the balance of receivables and dividing by the credit (or net) sales over the year just completed, and then multiplying by 365 (the number of days in a year); also called *days' sales in receivables*.

Days' sales in receivables See *days' sales uncollected*.

Debtor See *maker (of a note)*.

Direct write-off method A method of accounting for bad debts that is not compliant with IFRS and ASPE. The loss from an uncollectible account receivable is recorded at the time it is determined to be uncollectible; no attempt is made to estimate uncollectible accounts or bad debt expense.

Dishonouring a note receivable When a note's maker is unable or refuses to pay at maturity.

Due date of a note See *maturity date*.

Factor The buyer of accounts receivable.

Honouring a note receivable When the maker of the note pays the note in full at maturity.

Income statement approach See *percentage of sales approach*.

Interest rate The charge for using (not paying) money until a later date.

Maker (of a note) One who signs a note and promises to pay it at maturity.

Maturity date (of a note) The date on which a note and any interest are due and payable.

Note receivable See *short-term note receivable*.

Payee (of a note) The one to whom a promissory note is made payable.

Percentage of accounts receivable approach A method of estimating bad debts that assumes a percentage of outstanding receivables is uncollectible.

Percentage of sales approach Uses income statement relations to estimate bad debts. Also known as the *income statement approach*.

Period (of a note) The time from the issue date of the note to its maturity date or due date.

Principal (of a note) The amount that the signer of a promissory note agrees to pay back when it matures, not including the interest.

Promissory note A written promise to pay a specified amount of money either on demand or at a definite future date.

Realizable value The expected proceeds from converting assets into cash.

Short-term note receivable A promissory note that becomes due within the next 12 months or within the business's operating cycle if greater than 12 months.

Trade receivables See *accounts receivable*.

Uncollectible accounts See *bad debts*.

KNOWLEDGE CHECK-UP

1. Recognition of accounts receivable is directly linked to the accounting standard for which of the following:
   a. Cash and cash equivalents
   b. Accounting for property, plant, and equipment
   c. Revenue recognition
   d. Expense recognition

2. The allowance method to account for uncollectible accounts receivable is based on which accounting principle:
   a. Matching principle
   b. Revenue recognition principle
   c. Business entity principle
   d. None of the above.

3. The estimated bad debt expense is recorded with the following adjusting entry at the end of the accounting period:
   a. Dr. Bad Debt Expense _____, Cr. Allowance for Doubtful Accounts _____
   b. Dr. Allowance for Doubtful Accounts, Cr. Bad Debt Expense _____
   c. Dr. Bad Debt Expense _____, Cr. Accounts Receivable _____
   d. Dr. Accounts Receivable _____, Cr. Cash _____

4. Recovery of a bad debt indicates which of the following:
   a. A customer refuses to pay for the outstanding balance
   b. The customer pays off all of the outstanding balance
   c. Bad debt expense is reversed
   d. None of the above.

5. The aging of accounts receivable approach is the most reliable of the three approaches to estimate bad debt by applying:
   a. a lower percentage to accounts that have been outstanding the longest.
   b. a higher percentage write-off to account balances with higher sales for the period.
   c. a higher percentage to accounts that have been outstanding the longest.
   d. None of the above.

6. The percentage of sales approach to estimate bad debt involves an income statement approach that emphasizes:
   a. matching the dollar value of credit sales for the period to the dollar value of the bad debt expense.
   b. matching the dollar value of outstanding receivables for credit sales to the dollar value of bad debt expense.
   c. recording a higher bad debt expense for accounts that have been outstanding for a longer period of time.
   d. recording the dollar value of sales for the period to the dollar value of the allowance for doubtful accounts.

7. The direct write-off method is permitted:
   a. When the percentage of uncollectible accounts is determined to be unrelated to sales volume.
   b. Only in circumstances where the total reported accounts receivable balance is insignificant to the financial statements as a whole.
   c. If the CFO determines that the aging schedule does not impact expected future collections of outstanding A/R balances.
   d. Under no circumstances under generally accepted accounting principles.

8. The maturity date on the outstanding note receivable is important for the following reason:

   a. The specific number of days the note is outstanding is important to determine interest income and interest receivable.

   b. The maturity date on the note triggers the collection of cash outstanding on the value of the note.

   c. Both A and B.

   d. None of the above.

9. When a note receivable is dishonoured, the following action is taken to adjust accounting records:

   a. The note receivable is immediately written off to bad debt expense.

   b. A percentage of the note receivable outstanding is written off to bad debt expense.

c. The dollar value of the note receivable is transferred to an accounts receivable balance.

d. The dollar value of the note receivable plus outstanding interest owed is transferred to an accounts receivable balance.

10. Accounts receivable turnover helps users of financial statements to:

    a. Measure quality of accounts receivable.

    b. Measure liquidity of accounts receivable.

    c. Both A and B.

    d. None of the above.

CONCEPT REVIEW QUESTIONS

1. Identify and explain the criteria that must be met before recording accounts receivable and revenue.

2. Identify three roles or responsibilities that should be segregated within the accounts receivable process.

3. Explain why writing off a bad debt against the allowance account does not reduce the estimated realizable value of a company's accounts receivable.

4. Why does the Bad Debt Expense account usually not have the same adjusted balance as the Allowance for Doubtful Accounts?

5. Why does the direct write-off method of accounting for bad debts commonly fail to match revenues and expenses?

6. What is the essence of the accounting principle of materiality?

7. Why might a business prefer a note receivable to an account receivable?

8. Review the balance sheet for **Spin Master** in Appendix III. Did accounts receivable increase or decrease from 2016 to 2017 and by how much?

*9. What does it mean to sell a receivable without recourse?

QUICK STUDY

QS 8-1 Entries for sale on credit and subsequent collection LO1

Journalize the following transactions for Kimmel Company (assume a perpetual inventory system):

a. On March 1, Kimmel Company sold $40,000 of merchandise costing $32,000 on credit terms of n/30 to JP Holdings.

b. On March 27, JP Holdings paid its account in full.

QS 8-2 Recognizing accounts receivable and revenue LO1

Trophy Services is in the business of selling trophies, medals, and plaques. On May 15, Central High School ordered plaques and medals to reward students with high academic and extracurricular achievement. Trophy Services shipped the goods with a cost of $450 on May 25. Central High School received the goods on June 1.

An asterisk (*) identifies assignment material based on Appendix 8A.

Upon inspecting the invoice, the order came to a price of $900 with shipping terms FOB destination and the balance is due within 30 days of receiving the goods.

a. When has Trophy Services finished delivering the products?

b. Is the related accounts receivable and revenue measurable in this transaction?

c. Is it probable that Trophy Services will collect the amount owed from Central High School?

d. Based on your analysis, conclude when Trophy Services should recognize the accounts receivable and revenue for the transaction with Central High School.

QS 8-3 Bad debts, write-off, recovery LO2

Record the following selected transactions for Allistar Company during its first two months of operations:

Mar.	4	Performed services for various customers on account; $165,000.
	15	Collected $80,000 from credit customers.
	20	Determined that Tom Williams, a credit customer, would not be paying his $5,000 account; wrote it off.
	25	Tom Williams came into an inheritance and paid Allistar the amount written off on March 20.
Apr.	2	Performed services for various customers on account; $280,000.
	9	Collected $110,000 from credit customers.
	30	Allistar estimated bad debt expense to be $8,000.

QS 8-4 Balance sheet presentation LO2

From the following alphabetized list of adjusted account balances, prepare the current asset section of Biotech's December 31, 2020, balance sheet.

Account	Debit	Credit
Accounts receivable	29,000	
Allowance for doubtful accounts		1,300
Bad debt expense	800	
Cash	10,000	
Machinery	52,000	
Office supplies	400	
Prepaid insurance	950	

QS 8-5 Adjusting entry to estimate bad debts—percentage of sales LO2, 3

Lexton Company uses the allowance method to account for uncollectible accounts receivable. At year-end, October 31, it was estimated that 0.6% of net credit sales were uncollectible based on past experience. Net sales were $690,000, of which 2/3 were on credit. Record the entry at year-end to estimate uncollectible receivables.

QS 8-6 Adjusting entry to estimate bad debts—aging of receivables LO2, 3

Dim Sum Foods has accounts receivable of $260,000 and the allowance for doubtful accounts has a credit balance of $6,000. Based on analyzing the aging of the accounts receivable, management determined that the appropriate ending balance in the allowance for doubtful accounts at year-end, December 31, should be $26,000.

a. Draw a T-account for the allowance for doubtful accounts and fill it in with all of the given information.

b. Determine the amount of bad debt expense that needs to be recorded.

c. Prepare the adjusting journal entry to record the estimated bad debts at year-end.

QS 8-7 Adjusting entry to estimate bad debts—percentage of receivables LO2, 3

Foster Company uses the allowance method to account for uncollectible accounts receivable. At year-end, December 31, the unadjusted balance in the Allowance for Doubtful Accounts was $450 credit. Based on past experience, it was estimated that 2.5% of the Accounts Receivable balance of $640,000 was uncollectible. Record the adjusting entry to estimate bad debts at December 31.

QS 8-8 Accounts receivable allowance method of accounting for bad debts LO2, 3

Duncan Company's year-end trial balance shows accounts receivable of $89,000, allowance for doubtful accounts of $500 (credit), and net credit sales of $270,000. Uncollectibles are estimated to be 1.5% of outstanding accounts receivable.

a. Prepare the December 31 year-end adjustment.

b. What amount would have been used in the year-end adjustment had the allowance account had a year-end debit balance of $200?

c. Assume the same facts, except that Duncan estimates uncollectibles as 1% of net credit sales. What amount would be used in the adjustment?

QS 8-9 Aging analysis LO2, 3

Delcom had total accounts receivable on December 31, 2020, of $160,000 aged as follows:

December 31, 2020 Accounts Receivable	Age of Accounts Receivable	Expected Percentage Uncollectible
$110,000	Not due (under 45 days)	2%
40,000	1 to 30 days past due	5%
10,000	Over 30 days past due	40%

Prepare the December 31, 2020, adjusting entry to estimate uncollectible accounts receivable assuming an unadjusted credit balance in Allowance for Doubtful Accounts of $800.

QS 8-10 Direct write-off method LO3

Winston Abbott operates Abbott Small Engine Repair on his cattle farm, greatly supplementing his farm profit. Most of his customers pay cash, so he uses the direct write-off method to account for uncollectible accounts receivable. On March 28, 2020, he determined that the $1,100 account for Jim Patterson is uncollectible. Record the write-off.

QS 8-11 Notes receivable LO4

On August 2, 2020, SLM Company received a $5,500, 90-day, 5% note from customer Will Carr as payment on his account. Determine the maturity date and prepare the August 2 and maturity date entries, assuming the note is honoured by Carr.

QS 8-12 Notes receivable LO4

Weaver Company's December 31 year-end trial balance shows an $8,000 balance in Notes Receivable. This balance is from one note dated December 1, with a term of 45 days and 4.5% interest. Determine the maturity date and prepare the December 31 and maturity date entries, assuming the note is honoured.

QS 8-13 Dishonouring of a note receivable LO4

Ajax Company had a $17,000, 7%, 30-day note from Beatrice Inc. At maturity, April 4, Beatrice dishonoured the note. Record the entry on April 4.

QS 8-14 Accounts receivable turnover and days' sales uncollected LO5

Mega Company and Holton Company are similar firms that operate within the same industry. The following information is available:

	Industry Average	Mega Company			Holton Company		
		2020	2019	2018	2020	2019	2018
Accounts receivable turnover	12	14.9	12.2	11.5	10.6	13.1	13.5
Days' sales uncollected	30	24.5	29.9	31.7	34.4	27.9	27.1

a. Which company has the *more favourable* accounts receivable turnover in 2020?

b. Which company has the *greater* number of days in uncollected accounts in 2020? Is this generally favourable or unfavourable?

c. Which company is showing an *unfavourable* trend in terms of managing accounts receivable?

*QS 8-15 Sale of accounts receivable LO6

On June 4, Maltex sold $108,000 of its accounts receivable to a collection agency, which charges a 2.5% factoring fee. Record the entry on June 4.

*QS 8-16 Discounting a note receivable LO6

Tallcrest discounted a $50,000, 45-day, 5% note receivable on August 10 at the local bank, which applies an 8% discount rate. Tallcrest had held the note for 25 days before discounting it. Record the entry on August 10.

EXERCISES

Exercise 8-1 Subledger accounts LO1

Wallace Contracting recorded the following transactions during November 2020:

Nov.	3	Accounts Receivable—ABC Shop......................	8,500	
		Sales*..		8,500
	8	Accounts Receivable—Colt Enterprises............	2,600	
		Sales*..		2,600
	11	Accounts Receivable—Red McKenzie...............	1,560	
		Sales*..		1,560
	19	Sales Returns and Allowances*.........................	214	
		Accounts Receivable—Red McKenzie.......		214
	28	Accounts Receivable—ABC Shop......................	4,980	
		Sales*..		4,980

*Cost of goods sold (or COGS) has been ignored for the purpose of maintaining focus on accounts receivable.

Required

1. Open a general ledger having T-accounts for Accounts Receivable, Sales, and Sales Returns and Allowances. Also open an accounts receivable subledger having a T-account for each customer. Post the preceding entries to the general ledger accounts and the customer accounts.

2. List the balances of the accounts in the subledger, total the balances, and compare the total with the balance of the Accounts Receivable controlling account.

An asterisk (*) identifies assignment material based on Appendix 8A.

Exercise 8-2 Recognizing accounts receivable and revenue LO1

You and your friends are taking a two-week trip to Paris, France, from June 1 to 15, 2020. On May 1, 2020, you booked and prepaid for your stay at Hotel de Paris for $300 per night for 14 nights. Based on the hotel policies, the booking is non-refundable.

1. What product or service is being sold? When does Hotel de Paris fulfill its performance of providing its product or service?

2. Can Hotel de Paris measure the amount of accounts receivable and revenue for the above transaction? Explain.

3. Is it probable that Hotel de Paris will collect payment from you and your friends for your hotel booking? Explain.

4. Based on your analysis, determine when Hotel de Paris should recognize the revenue.

Exercise 8-3 Accounts receivable control considerations LO1

Carolyn owns a small business, Snappy Frames, that sells picture frames. Carolyn says, "I let most of my employees be the CEO of their responsibilities. Trust is the key to my success!" Once customers place their order online and the products are shipped, customers will send their payment in the mail or by electronic fund transfer. Quinn, accounts receivable clerk, posts the journal entries to record the customer payments (Dr. Cash Cr. Accounts Receivable). Quinn files the payments received in the mail in the office and deposits them on a monthly basis. As Quinn helped to set up the bank account years ago, she is responsible for making deposits and withdrawals. Every month, Quinn prepares a bank reconciliation and keeps them on file. When accounts receivable are overdue by greater than 90 days, Quinn cleans up the books by writing off the accounts receivable. Carolyn recently decided to follow up on some of the greater than 90-day accounts. Oddly enough, four of the customers she called with accounts receivable accounts greater than 90 days insisted that they had paid their account in full.

1. Identify four control weaknesses. For each, explain the implication of the weakness and make a recommendation of a control that would prevent or detect error or fraud.

2. Describe what fraud may have occurred in the above situation.

Exercise 8-4 Write-off and subsequent partial recovery LO2

Kitchen Equipment Company uses the allowance method to account for uncollectibles. On October 31, it wrote off a $1,200 account of a customer, Gwen Rowe. On December 9, it received an $800 payment from Rowe.

a. Make the appropriate entry or entries for October 31.

b. Make the appropriate entry or entries for December 9.

Exercise 8-5 Write-off and subsequent partial recovery LO2

Faster Office Supply Company uses the allowance method to account for uncollectibles. On January 31, it wrote off an $8,750 account of a customer, Glass Tech Company. On July 15, it received a $5,000 payment from Glass Tech.

a. Make the appropriate entry or entries for January 31.

b. Make the appropriate entry or entries for July 15.

Exercise 8-6 Allowance for doubtful accounts LO2, 3

At the end of its annual accounting period, Midi Company estimated its bad debts as 0.70% of its $1,700,000 of credit sales made during the year. On December 31, Midi made an addition to its Allowance for Doubtful Accounts equal to that amount. On the following February 1, management decided that the $2,400 account of Catherine Hicks was uncollectible and wrote it off as a bad debt. Four months later, on June 5, Hicks unexpectedly paid the amount previously written off. Give the journal entries required to record these transactions.

Exercise 8-7 **Bad debt expense** LO2, 3

CHECK FIGURE: a. Bad Debt Expense = $7,450

At the end of each year, Dutch Supply Co. uses the simplified balance sheet approach (i.e., percentage of accounts receivable) to estimate bad debts. On December 31, 2020, it has outstanding accounts receivable of $158,000 and estimates that 3.5% will be uncollectible.

Required

a. Give the entry to record bad debt expense for 2020 under the assumption that the Allowance for Doubtful Accounts has a $1,920 debit balance before the adjustment.

b. Give the entry under the assumption that the Allowance for Doubtful Accounts has a $1,920 credit balance before the adjustment.

Exercise 8-8 **Receivables, allowance for doubtful accounts, write-off, and subsequent recovery** LO1, 2, 3

Outdoor Equipment (OE) sells camping equipment. On December 1, the accounts receivable account had a balance of $50,000, the bad debt expense account had a balance of $0, and the allowance for doubtful accounts had a credit balance of $5,000. Journalize the remaining journal entries for the 2020 year.

Dec.	2	Sold tents for $5,000 on account with a cost of $2,500.
	20	Determined that the total accounts of Rocky Co. with an accounts receivable balance of $1,200 and Grouse Co. with an accounts receivable balance of $2,500 were uncollectible and needed to be written off.
	23	Unexpectedly received payment from Grouse Co. for $2,500.
	31	Estimated that 10% of accounts receivable recorded to date would be uncollectible.

Required

1. Prepare journal entries to record the transactions. *Note:* write-off of uncollectible accounts for Rocky Co. and Grouse Co. should be posted separately.

2. Draw and fill in the T-account for accounts receivable, bad debt expense, and allowance for doubtful accounts. Determine the ending balance for each account.

Exercise 8-9 **Analyzing receivables and allowance for doubtful accounts** LO1, 2, 3

Accounts Receivable				Allowance for Doubtful Accounts		
Dec. 31/19					2,900	Dec. 31/19
Balance	83,000					Balance
	470,000	503,000			260	
		3,650		3,650	3,100	
	260	260			2,610	Dec. 31/20
Dec. 31/20						Balance
Balance	46,350					

Required Analyzing the information presented in the T-accounts above, identify the dollar value related to each of the following:

a. Credit sales during the period.

b. Collection of credit sales made during the period.

c. Write-off of an uncollectible account.

d. Recovery of the account previously written off.

e. The adjusting entry to estimate bad debts.

Exercise 8-10 Balance sheet presentation LO2, 4

From the following alphabetized list of adjusted account balances, prepare the current asset section of LisTel's March 31, 2020, balance sheet.

Account	Balance*
Accounts receivable..	$110,000
Accumulated depreciation, building	29,000
Allowance for doubtful accounts	2,350
Bad debt expense...	2,100
Building..	375,000
Cash...	19,000
Merchandise inventory	82,000
Notes receivable, due May 1, 2022..	61,000
Notes receivable, due Nov. 30, 2020..	14,300
Supplies	5,260
*Assume all balances are normal.	

Exercise 8-11 Estimating bad debt expense—percentage of sales LO3

CHECK FIGURE: d. Accounts receivable (net) = $232,700

Selected unadjusted account balances at December 31, 2020, are shown below for Demron Servicing.

Account	Debit	Credit
Accounts receivable..	$70,000	
Allowance for doubtful accounts		$ 1,100
Sales (all on credit)...		480,000
Sales discounts..	8,000	

Required

a. Demron estimates that 1.5% of net credit sales will prove to be uncollectible. Prepare the adjusting entry required on December 31, 2020, to estimate uncollectible receivables.

b. During 2021, credit sales were $620,000 (cost of sales $406,500); sales discounts of $12,000 were taken when accounts receivable of $440,000 were collected; and accounts written off during the year totalled $10,000. Prepare the entries for these transactions.

c. Record the adjusting entry required on December 31, 2021 to estimate uncollectible receivables, assuming it is based on 1.5% of net credit sales.

d. Show how accounts receivable would appear on the December 31, 2021, balance sheet.

Analysis Component: Comment on the advantages and disadvantages of using the income statement approach for estimating uncollectibles.

Exercise 8-12 Estimating bad debt expense—percentage of receivables LO3

CHECK FIGURE: d. Accounts receivable (net) = $235,200

Refer to the information in Exercise 8-11.

Required

a. Assume that Demron estimates uncollectible accounts as 2% of receivables. Prepare the adjusting entry required on December 31, 2020 to estimate uncollectible receivables.

b. During 2021, credit sales were $620,000 (cost of sales $406,500); sales discounts taken were $12,000; accounts receivable collected were $440,000; and accounts written off during the year totalled $10,000. Prepare the entries to record these transactions.

c. Record the adjusting entry required on December 31, 2021 to estimate uncollectible receivables, assuming it is based on 2% of receivables.

d. Show how accounts receivable would appear on the December 31, 2021 balance sheet.

Analysis Component: Comment on the advantages and disadvantages of using the balance sheet approach for estimating uncollectibles.

Exercise 8-13 **Aging analysis** LO3

CHECK FIGURE: c. Accounts receivable (net) = $402,400

Winfrey Designs had an unadjusted credit balance in its Allowance for Doubtful Accounts at December 31, 2020, of $2,300.

Required

a. Prepare the adjusting entry assuming that Winfrey estimates uncollectible accounts based on an aging analysis as follows:

December 31, 2020 Accounts Receivable	Age of Accounts Receivable	Expected Percentage Uncollectible
$155,000	Not due (under 30 days)	1%
45,000	1 to 30 days past due	4%
10,500	31 to 60 days past due	10%
2,500	Over 60 days past due	60%

b. During 2021, credit sales were $1,457,000; sales discounts taken were $27,000; accounts receivable collected were $1,220,000; and accounts written off during the year totalled $29,000. Prepare the adjusting entry required on December 31, 2021, to estimate uncollectible receivables assuming it is based on the following aging analysis.

December 31, 2021 Accounts Receivable	Age of Accounts Receivable	Expected Percentage Uncollectible
$290,000	Not due (under 30 days)	1%
90,000	1 to 30 days past due	4%
25,000	31 to 60 days past due	10%
16,000	Over 60 days past due	60%

c. Show how accounts receivable would appear on the December 31, 2021, balance sheet.

Analysis Component: Comment on the advantages and disadvantages of using an aging analysis for estimating uncollectible accounts.

Exercise 8-14 Direct write-off method LO3

Delores Cooper operates Cooper Garden Designs. Most of her customers pay cash so she uses the direct write-off method to account for uncollectible accounts receivable. On May 3, 2020, she determined that the $3,350 account for Wilma Benz was uncollectible. During 2020, she had total credit sales of $339,000. The December 31, 2020, balance in accounts receivable was $60,000.

Required Record the May 3 write-off using the direct write-off method.

Analysis Component: Delores wants to compare the effect of using the allowance method versus the direct write-off method for recording uncollectible accounts. If uncollectible accounts were estimated at (a) 2% of credit sales or (b) 4% of outstanding accounts receivable, prepare a comparison of the effects on profit of using the allowance methods versus the direct write-off method.

Exercise 8-15 End-of-period interest adjustment for notes receivable LO4

Outer Armour (OA) is a company that sells high quality outerwear. OA has accepted two notes receivables from customers and has a December 31, 2020 year-end.

Note Receivable A	On September 1, 2020, OA accepted a $690,000, six-month note receivable with an interest rate of 6%. Interest and the principal balance are due at maturity.
Note Receivable B	On October 31, 2020, OA accepted a $395,000 note receivable with an interest rate of 4.5%. Interest is paid the first day of each following month and the principal is due at maturity on June 30, 2021.

Required

1. Outer Armour is preparing the financial statements as at December 31, 2020. Explain why interest income needs to be recorded up to December 31 even though Notes Receivable A and B do not need to be fully paid off until 2021.

2. How many months need to be accrued for Notes Receivable A and B as of December 31, 2020?

3. Prepare the adjusting journal entries to accrue the interest for Note Receivable A and Note Receivable B as at December 31, 2020.

Exercise 8-16 Dishonouring a note LO4

Prepare journal entries to record these transactions:

Mar.	21	Accepted a $6,200, six-month, 4% note dated today from Bradley Brooks in granting a time extension on his past-due account.
Sept.	21	Brooks dishonoured his note when presented for payment.
Dec.	31	After exhausting all legal means of collection, wrote off Brooks's account against the Allowance for Doubtful Accounts.

Exercise 8-17 Honouring a note LO4

Prepare journal entries to record these transactions (round the answer to two decimal places):

Oct.	31	Accepted a $15,000, six-month, 4.5% note dated today from Leann Grimes in granting a time extension on her past-due account.
Dec.	31	Adjusted the books for the interest due on the Grimes note.
Apr.	30	Grimes honoured her note when presented for payment.

Exercise 8-18 Accounting for notes receivable transactions LO4

CHECK FIGURE: May 31, 2021: Interest income = $78.90

Following are transactions of the Barnett Company (round the answer to two decimal places):

2020		
Dec.	16	Accepted a $22,000, 60-day, 5% note dated this day in granting Carmel Karuthers a time extension on her past-due account.
	31	Made an adjusting entry to record the accrued interest on the Karuthers note.
	31	Closed the Interest income account.
2021		
Feb.	14	Received Karuthers' payment for the principal and interest on the note dated December 16.
Mar.	2	Accepted an $8,000, 4%, 90-day note dated this day in granting a time extension on the past-due account of ATW Company.
	17	Accepted a $3,200, 30-day, 4.5% note dated this day in granting Leroy Johnson a time extension on his past-due account.
May	31	Received ATW's payment for the principal and interest on the note dated March 2.

Required Prepare journal entries to record the Barnett Company's transactions.

Exercise 8-19 Accounts receivable turnover and days' sales uncollected LO5

The following information was taken from the December 31, 2020, annual report of WestCon Developments.

	($ millions)				Industry Average
	2020	2019			
Net sales.................................	$7,280	$5,410	Accounts receivable turnover		16.2
Accounts receivable..........................	598	486	Days' sales uncollected.......................................		21.0

Required

1. Calculate accounts receivable turnover and days' sales uncollected for the year 2020. (Round the answer to two decimal places.)

2. Compare your calculations in (1) to the industry average and comment on WestCon's relative performance as F (Favourable) or U (Unfavourable). (Round the answer to two decimal places.)

*Exercise 8-20 Selling and pledging accounts receivable LO6

On July 31, Konrad International had $125,900 of accounts receivable. Prepare journal entries to record the following August transactions. Also, prepare any footnotes to the August 31 financial statements that should be reported as a result of these transactions.

2020		
Aug.	2	Sold merchandise to customers on credit, $6,295. Cost of sales was $3,150.
	7	Sold $18,770 of accounts receivable to Fidelity Bank. Fidelity charges a 1.5% fee.
	15	Received payments from customers, $3,436.
	25	Borrowed $10,000 from Fidelity Bank, pledging $14,000 of accounts receivable as security for the loan.

An asterisk (*) identifies assignment material based on Appendix 8A.

*Exercise 8-21 **Discounting notes receivable LO6**

CHECK FIGURE: Feb. 19: Interest income = $487.58

Prepare journal entries to record the following transactions by Ericton Industries:

2020		
Jan.	20	Accepted a $170,000, 90-day, 9% note dated this day in granting a time extension on the past due account of Steve Stewart.
Feb.	19	Discounted the Steve Stewart note at the bank at 11.5%.

PROBLEMS

Problem 8-1A Recognizing accounts receivable and revenue LO1

A major source of revenue for Alphabet Inc. (parent company of Google Inc.) is advertising. With Google's AdWords, advertisers can pay on a cost-per-click basis. This means that the advertisers pay every time a customer clicks on one of their ads. Assume that Tech Experts creates an AdWord account with Google on October 1, 2020. Tech Experts starts advertising on a cost-per-click basis for the month of November 2020. In November, 300 users click on the Tech Experts ad at a rate of $0.30 per click. Google bills, and Tech Experts pays for, the advertising services in December 2020. Assume Google prepares financial statements on a monthly basis.

Sources: support.google.com; https://abc.xyz/investor/pdf/20171231_alphabet_10K.pdf, 2018.

Required Analyze and determine during what month Google should recognize the accounts receivable and revenue for Tech Experts using the revenue recognition criteria of performance, measurability, and collectability.

Problem 8-2A Estimating bad debt expense LO2, 3

CHECK FIGURES: 1b. Bad Debt Expense = $138,000; 2. Accounts receivable (net) = $1,962,000

On December 31, 2020, Corotel Company's year-end, the unadjusted trial balance included the following items:

Account	Debit	Credit
Accounts receivable	$2,100,000	
Allowance for doubtful accounts	33,000	
Sales ($2,850,000 cash sales)		$11,400,000

Required

1. Prepare the adjusting entry needed in Corotel's books to recognize bad debts under each of the following independent assumptions:

   a. Bad debts are estimated to be 2% of credit sales.

   b. An analysis suggests that 5% of outstanding accounts receivable on December 31, 2020, will become uncollectible.

An asterisk (*) identifies assignment material based on Appendix 8A.

2. Show how Accounts Receivable and the Allowance for Doubtful Accounts would appear on the December 31, 2020 balance sheet given the facts in requirement 1(a).

3. Show how Accounts Receivable and the Allowance for Doubtful Accounts would appear on the December 31, 2020 balance sheet given the facts in requirement 1(b).

Analysis Component: If bad debts are not adjusted for at the end of the accounting period, identify which GAAP are violated and why.

Problem 8-3A Aging accounts receivable LO2, 3 eXcel

CHECK FIGURE: 2. Bad Debt Expense = $60,205

On December 31, 2020, Toro Company's Allowance for Doubtful Accounts had an unadjusted credit balance of $31,000. The accountant for Toro has prepared a schedule of the December 31, 2020, accounts receivable by age and, on the basis of past experience, has estimated the percentage of the receivables in each age category that will become uncollectible. This information is summarized as follows:

December 31, 2020 Accounts Receivable	Age of Accounts Receivable	Expected Percentage Uncollectible
$1,500,000	Not due (under 30 days)	1.25%
708,000	1 to 30 days past due	2.00
152,000	31 to 60 days past due	6.50
98,000	61 to 90 days past due	32.75
24,000	Over 90 days past due	68.00

Required

1. Calculate the amount that should appear in the December 31, 2020, balance sheet as the Allowance for Doubtful Accounts.

2. Prepare the journal entry to record bad debt expense for 2020.

Analysis Component: On June 30, 2021, Toro Company concluded that a customer's $7,500 receivable (created in 2020) was uncollectible and that the account should be written off. What effect will this action have on Toro's 2021 profit? Explain your answer.

Problem 8-4A Aging accounts receivable LO2, 3 eXcel

CHECK FIGURE: 2. Bad Debt Expense = $83,180

On December 31, 2020, Zippy Car Company's Allowance for Doubtful Accounts had an unadjusted credit balance of $42,000. The accountant for Zippy has prepared a schedule of the December 31, 2020, accounts receivable by age and, on the basis of past experience, has estimated the percentage of the receivables in each age category that will become uncollectible. This information is summarized as follows:

December 31, 2020 Accounts Receivable	Age of Accounts Receivable	Expected Percentage Uncollectible
$2,050,000	Not due (under 30 days)	1.25%
971,000	1 to 30 days past due	2.00
207,000	31 to 60 days past due	6.50
132,000	61 to 90 days past due	33.00
34,000	Over 90 days past due	68.00

Required

1. Calculate the amount that should appear in the December 31, 2020, balance sheet as the Allowance for Doubtful Accounts.

2. Prepare the journal entry to record bad debt expense for 2020.

Analysis Component: On June 30, 2021, Zippy Car Company concluded that a customer's $10,000 receivable (created in 2020) was uncollectible and that the account should be written off. What effect will this action have on Zippy's 2021 profit? Explain your answer.

Problem 8-5A Accounts receivable transactions and bad debt adjustments LO1, 2, 3

CHECK FIGURES: 2. Bad Debt Expense = $20,460; 5. Bad Debt Expense = $7,200

Swiss Supplies showed the following selected adjusted balances at its December 31, 2019, year-end:

Accounts Receivable		Allowance for Doubtful Accounts	
Dec. 31/19 Balance 490,000			16,400 Dec. 31/19 Balance

During 2020, the following selected transactions occurred:

a. Sales totalled $2,800,000, of which 25% were cash sales (cost of sales $1,804,000).

b. Sales returns were $108,000, half regarding credit sales. The returned merchandise was scrapped.

c. An account for $24,000 was recovered.

d. Several accounts were written off: $26,000.

e. Collections from credit customers totalled $1,790,000 (excluding the recovery in (c) above).

Part A

Required

1. Journalize transactions (a) through (e). You may find it useful to post your entries to T-accounts for Accounts Receivable and Allowance for Doubtful Accounts.

Part B

Required

2. Prepare the December 31, 2020, adjusting entry to estimate bad debts assuming that uncollectible accounts are estimated to be 1% of net credit sales.

3. Show how accounts receivable will appear on the December 31, 2020, balance sheet.

4. What will bad debt expense be on the income statement for the year ended December 31, 2020?

Part C (independent of Part B)

Required

5. Prepare the December 31, 2020, adjusting entry to estimate bad debts assuming that uncollectible accounts are estimated to be 3% of outstanding receivables.

6. Show how accounts receivable will appear on the December 31, 2020, balance sheet.

7. What will bad debt expense be on the income statement for the year ended December 31, 2020?

Problem 8-6A Recording accounts receivable transactions and bad debt adjustments LO1, 2, 3

CHECK FIGURES: d. Bad Debt Expense = $47,290; h. Bad Debt Expense = $63,155

Peru Industries began operations on January 1, 2020. The company plans to use the allowance method for uncollectible accounts. During the next two years, the company completed a number of transactions involving credit sales, accounts receivable collections, and bad debts (assume a perpetual inventory system). These transactions are summarized as follows:

2020

a. Sold merchandise on credit for $2,250,000, terms n/30 (COGS = $1,240,000).

b. Wrote off uncollectible accounts receivable in the amount of $34,000.

c. Received cash of $1,330,000 in payment of outstanding accounts receivable.

d. In adjusting the accounts on December 31, concluded that 1.5% of the outstanding accounts receivable would become uncollectible.

2021

e. Sold merchandise on credit for $2,940,000, terms n/30 (COGS = $1,592,000).

f. Wrote off uncollectible accounts receivable in the amount of $53,000.

g. Received cash of $2,210,000 in payment of outstanding accounts receivable.

h. In adjusting the accounts on December 31, concluded that 1.5% of the outstanding accounts receivable would become uncollectible.

Required Prepare journal entries to record Peru's 2020 and 2021 summarized transactions and the adjusting entries to record bad debt expense at the end of each year.

Problem 8-7A Uncollectible accounts LO2, 3

CHECK FIGURES: b. Accounts receivable (net) = $126,450; d. Accounts receivable (net) = $140,600

Aaron Servicing showed the following partial unadjusted results at October 31, 2020, its year-end:

Account	Debit	Credit
Sales		$1,650,000
Accounts receivable	$148,000	
Allowance for doubtful accounts	3,200	

Part 1

Required

a. Assuming Aaron estimates bad debts to be 1.5% of sales, prepare the adjusting entry at October 31, 2020.

b. Show how accounts receivable would be shown on the October 31, 2020, balance sheet using your calculations in (a).

Part 2

Required

c. Instead of (a), assume that Aaron estimates bad debts to be 5% of outstanding accounts receivable. Prepare the adjusting entry at October 31, 2020.

d. Show how accounts receivable would be shown on the October 31, 2020, balance sheet using your calculations in (c).

Problem 8-8A Bad debt expense LO3

CHECK FIGURES: 1. Bad Debt Expense = $8,720; 2. Bad Debt Expense = $6,480

The following is information taken from the June 30, 2020, balance sheet of Tippleton Company:

Accounts receivable..	$340,000	
Less: Allowance for doubtful accounts	14,800	$325,200

Part 1

During July, Tippleton Company recorded total sales of $904,000, all on credit. There were $32,000 of sales returns and allowances. Collections during July were $982,000. Total receivables identified as being uncollectible and written off during July were $17,000. Tippleton estimates bad debts as 1% of net credit sales.

Required Prepare the adjusting entry to record estimated bad debts for July.

Part 2

During August, total sales of $957,000 were recorded, all on credit. Sales returns and allowances totalled $16,000. Collections during the month were $812,000, which included the recovery of $2,000 from a customer account written off in a previous month. No accounts were written off during August. Tippleton Company changed its method of estimating bad debts to the balance sheet approach because the new accountant said it more accurately reflected uncollectible accounts. The resulting aging analysis determined total estimated uncollectible accounts at August 31 to be $15,000.

Required Prepare the August 31 adjusting entry to record estimated bad debts for August.

Problem 8-9A Estimating bad debts LO3

CHECK FIGURE: a. Total estimated uncollectible accounts = $13,638

The following information is available regarding the outstanding accounts receivable of Mufu Contracting at September 30, 2020:

	Month of Credit Sale*				
Customer	**May**	**June**	**July**	**Aug.**	**Sept.**
B. Axley	$35,000	$ -0-	$ -0-	$ -0-	$ -0-
T. Holton	-0-	-0-	74,000	36,000	16,500
W. Nix	-0-	23,100	-0-	9,900	12,200
C. Percy	-0-	-0-	5,600	-0-	15,800
K. Willis	-0-	-0-	-0-	-0-	92,500

*All services are performed on terms of n/30. Assume all sales occurred on the last day of the month.

Mufu estimates bad debts using the following rates:

Not yet due	1 to 29 days past due	30 to 59 days past due	60 to 89 days past due	90 to 119 days past due	Over 119 days past due
0.5%	1%	4%	10%	20%	50%

Required

a. Complete a Schedule of Accounts Receivable by Age at September 30, 2020 (similar to Exhibit 8.13).

b. The Allowance for Doubtful Accounts showed an unadjusted balance on September 30, 2020, of $1,900. Record the adjusting entry at September 30, 2020, to estimate uncollectible accounts.

Problem 8-10A Uncollectible accounts LO3

CHECK FIGURE: Dec. 31, 2021: Bad debt expense = $19,560

At year-end, December 31, 2020, Corolla Sales showed unadjusted balances of $394,000 in Accounts Receivable; $13,800 debit in Allowance for Doubtful Accounts; and $1,940,000 in Sales. Uncollectible accounts are estimated to be 2.5% of sales.

Unadjusted balances at December 31, 2021, were Accounts Receivable, $514,000; Allowance for Doubtful Accounts, $1,000 credit; and Sales, $3,280,000. Corolla Sales changed the method of estimating uncollectible accounts to 4% of outstanding accounts receivable.

At December 31, 2022, the general ledger showed unadjusted balances of $460,000 in Accounts Receivable; $700 debit in Allowance for Doubtful Accounts; and $3,400,000 in Sales. Corolla prepared an aging analysis on December 31, 2022 that estimated total uncollectible accounts to be $26,500.

Required Prepare the 2020, 2021, and 2022 year-end adjusting entries to estimate uncollectible accounts.

Analysis Component: On December 31, 2020, the unadjusted balance in Allowance for Doubtful Accounts was a debit of $13,800. What is the normal balance for the Allowance for Doubtful Accounts account? What would cause Allowance for Doubtful Accounts to have an unadjusted debit balance?

Problem 8-11A Notes receivable LO4

CHECK FIGURES: d. Interest income = $454.93 e. Cash = $90,499.32

Vauxall Holdings showed the following information regarding its notes receivable:

Note	Date of Note	Principal	Interest Rate	Term	Maturity Date	Days of Accrued Interest at Dec. 31, 2020	Accrued Interest at Dec. 31, 2020*
1	Nov. 1/19	$240,000	4.0%	180 days			
2	Jan. 5/20	100,000	5.0%	90 days			
3	Nov. 20/20	90,000	4.5%	45 days			
4	Dec. 10/20	120,000	5.5%	30 days			

*Round calculations to the nearest whole cent.

Required For each note:

a. Determine the maturity date.

b. Calculate the *days* of accrued interest, if any, at December 31, 2020 (Vauxall Holdings' year-end).

c. Calculate the *amount* of accrued interest, if any, at December 31, 2020.

For Note 3:

d. Prepare the entry to record the accrued interest at December 31, 2020.

e. Prepare the entry to record the collection on the maturity date. Assume that both interest and principal are collected at maturity.

Problem 8-12A Notes receivable LO4

CHECK FIGURES: d. Interest revenue = $323.51 e. Cash = $64,355.07

Panda Distributors showed the following information regarding its notes receivable:

Note	Date of Note	Principal	Interest Rate	Term	Maturity Date	Days of Accrued Interest at July 31, 2020	Accrued Interest at July 31, 2020*
1	December 1/19	$170,000	4.0%	180 days			
2	April 5/20	71,000	5.0%	90 days			
3	June 20/20	64,000	4.5%	45 days			
4	July 10/20	85,000	5.5%	30 days			

*Round calculations to the nearest whole cent.

Required For each note:

a. Determine the maturity date.

b. Calculate the *days* of accrued interest, if any, at July 31, 2020 (Panda Distributors' year-end).

c. Calculate the *amount* of accrued interest, if any, at July 31, 2020.

For Note 3:

d. Prepare the entry to record the accrued interest at July 31, 2020.

e. Prepare the entry to record the collection on the maturity date. Assume that both interest and principal are collected at maturity.

Problem 8-13A Accrued interest calculation and dishonouring note receivable LO4

CHECK FIGURE: b. May 31, 2020

Following are transactions of the Purple Onion Company (round calculations to the nearest whole cent):

2019		
Dec.	16	Accepted a $20,000, 60-day, 5.5% note dated this day in granting Hal Krueger a time extension on his past-due account.
	31	Made an adjusting entry to record the accrued interest on the Krueger note.
	31	Closed the Interest income account.
2020		
Feb.	14	Received Krueger's payment for the principal and interest on the note dated December 16.
Mar.	2	Accepted a $15,000, 3.75%, 90-day note dated this day in granting a time extension on the past-due account of ARC Company.
	17	Accepted a $6,500, 30-day, 4% note dated this day in granting Penny Bobek a time extension on her past-due account.
Apr.	16	Bobek dishonoured her note when presented for payment.

Required

a. Prepare journal entries to record the Purple Onion's transactions.

b. Determine the maturity date of the note dated March 2. Prepare the entry on the maturity date, assuming ARC Company honours the note.

Problem 8-14A Short-term notes receivable LO4

CHECK FIGURES: d. July 14, 2020: Interest income = $783.56 e. November 1, 2020: Interest income = $989.58

Seerden Servicing monitors its accounts receivable carefully. A review determined that a customer, John Daley, was unable to pay his $130,000 past-due account. Seerden accepted a 90-day promissory note dated April 15, 2020, bearing interest of 5% in exchange for Daley's account. Another customer, ABC Drilling, signed a 4.75%, six-month note dated May 1 in place of its $50,000 past-due accounts receivable. On May 31, Seerden's year-end, accrued interest was recorded on the notes receivable. John Daley honoured his note on the maturity date. ABC Drilling dishonoured its note on the maturity date. On November 15, Seerden Servicing wrote off ABC Drilling's account as it was determined to be uncollectible.

Required Prepare Seerden Servicing's entries for each of the following dates (round calculations to the nearest whole cent):

a. April 15, 2020

b. May 1, 2020

c. May 31, 2020

d. Maturity date of John Daley's note

e. Maturity date of ABC Drilling's note

f. November 15, 2020

Analysis Component: Assuming a $4,000 debit balance in the Allowance for Doubtful Accounts on November 14, 2020, calculate the balance after posting the entry in (f) above. Comment on the adequacy of the Allowance for Doubtful Accounts.

Problem 8-15A Accounts receivable ratios LO5

Using the **Indigo** financial statements in Appendix III, calculate the following ratios for the years ended April 1, 2017, and March 31, 2018. Comment on the change.

a. Accounts receivable turnover ratio (round to two decimal places)

b. Days' sales uncollected (round to the nearest day)

*Problem 8-16A Discounting notes receivable LO6

CHECK FIGURE: Sept. 18: Interest expense = $25.00

Required Prepare entries to record the following transactions of Wipe-Out Company:

Mar.	2	Accepted a $10,240, 5%, 90-day note dated this day in granting a time extension on the past-due account of JNC Company.
Apr.	21	Discounted, with recourse, the JNC Company note at BancFirst at a cost of $50.
June	2	Received notice from BancFirst that JNC Company defaulted on the note due May 31. Paid the bank the principal plus interest due on the note. *(Hint: Create an account receivable for the maturity value of the note.)*
July	16	Received payment from JNC Company for the maturity value of its dishonoured note plus interest for 45 days beyond maturity at 5%.
Sept.	3	Accepted a $4,160, 60-day, 5% note dated this day in granting Cecile Duval a time extension on her past-due account.
	18	Discounted, without recourse, the Duval note at BancFirst at a cost of $25.

An asterisk (*) identifies assignment material based on Appendix 8A.

Analysis Component: What reporting is necessary when a business discounts notes receivable with recourse and these notes have not reached maturity by the end of the fiscal period? Explain the reason for this requirement and what accounting principle is being satisfied.

*Problem 8-17A Discounting notes receivable LO6

CHECK FIGURES: Jan. 10, 2021: Cash = $15,060.80; Mar. 29, 2021: Cash = $4,507.09

Required Prepare general journal entries to record the following transactions of Leduc Company:

2020		
Dec.	11	Accepted a $15,000, 6%, 60-day note dated this day in granting Fred Calhoun a time extension on his past-due account.
	31	Made an adjusting entry to record the accrued interest on the Fred Calhoun note.
	31	Closed the Interest income account.
2021		
Jan.	10	Discounted the Fred Calhoun note at the bank at 7%.
Feb.	10	The Fred Calhoun note was dishonoured. Paid the bank the maturity value of the note plus a $30 fee.
Mar.	5	Accepted a $4,500, 5.5%, 60-day note dated this day in granting a time extension on the past-due account of Donna Reed.
	29	Discounted the Donna Reed note at the bank at 7.5%.
May	7	The Donna Reed note had been received by the bank and paid by Donna Reed.
June	9	Accepted a $6,750, 60-day, 5% note dated this day in granting a time extension on the past-due account of Jack Miller.
Aug.	8	Received payment of the maturity value of the Jack Miller note.
	11	Accepted an $8,000, 60-day, 5% note dated this day in granting Roger Addison a time extension on his past-due account.
	31	Discounted the Roger Addison note at the bank at 6.5%.
Oct.	12	The Roger Addison note was dishonoured. Paid the bank the maturity value of the note plus a $30 fee.
Nov.	19	Received payment from Roger Addison of the maturity value of his dishonoured note, the fee, and interest on both for 40 days beyond maturity at 5%.
Dec.	23	Wrote off the Fred Calhoun account against Allowance for Doubtful Accounts.

ALTERNATE PROBLEMS

Problem 8-1B Recognizing accounts receivable and revenue LO1

A major source of revenue for Alphabet Inc. (parent company of Google Inc.) is advertising. With Google's AdSense, advertisers are required to pay for advertising services on a cost-per-impression basis. This means that advertisers pay a fixed rate each time their ads are displayed on a website. Assume that Ramen Noodle House creates an advertising account with Google on March 1, 2020. Ramen Noodle House launches an advertisement that will be displayed on a selected website three times per day at a rate of $0.50 per time the ad is displayed for the full month of April 2020. Google bills, and Ramen Noodle House pays for, the advertising services in May 2020. Assume Google prepares financial statements on a monthly basis.

Sources: support.google.com; https://abc.xyz/investor/pdf/20171231_alphabet_10K.pdf, 2018.

Required Analyze and determine when Google should recognize the accounts receivable and revenue for Ramen Noodle House using the revenue recognition criteria of performance, measurability, and collectability.

An asterisk (*) identifies assignment material based on Appendix 8A.

Problem 8-2B **Estimating bad debt expense** LO2, 3

CHECK FIGURES: 1b. Bad Debt Expense = $11,240 2. Accounts receivable (net) = $216,160

On December 31, 2020, Stilton Service Company's year-end, the unadjusted trial balance included the following items:

Account	Debit	Credit
Accounts receivable...	$239,000	
Allowance for doubtful accounts		$ 3,100
Sales ($470,000 cash sales)...		1,128,000

Required

1. Prepare the adjusting entry on the books of Stilton Service Company to estimate bad debts under each of the following independent assumptions:

   a. Bad debts are estimated to be 3% of credit sales.

   b. An analysis suggests that 6% of outstanding accounts receivable on December 31, 2020, will become uncollectible.

2. Show how Accounts Receivable and the Allowance for Doubtful Accounts would appear on the December 31, 2020, balance sheet given the facts in requirement 1(a).

3. Show how Accounts Receivable and the Allowance for Doubtful Accounts would appear on the December 31, 2020, balance sheet given the facts in requirement 1(b).

Analysis Component: Would you recommend to Stilton that it use the income statement or the balance sheet approach to estimate uncollectible accounts receivable? Explain why, identifying advantages and disadvantages for each approach.

Problem 8-3B **Aging accounts receivable** LO2, 3   e**X**cel

CHECK FIGURE: 2. Bad Debt Expense = $43,860

On December 31, 2020, RCA Company's Allowance for Doubtful Accounts had an unadjusted debit balance of $7,800. The accountant for RCA has prepared a schedule of the December 31, 2020, accounts receivable by age and, on the basis of past experience, has estimated the percentage of the receivables in each age category that will become uncollectible. This information is summarized as follows:

December 31, 2020 Accounts Receivable	Age of Accounts Receivable	Expected Percentage Uncollectible
$620,000	Not due (under 30 days)	1.75%
355,600	1 to 30 days past due	2.5
91,000	31 to 60 days past due	8.5
11,500	61 to 90 days past due	35.00
7,600	Over 90 days past due	60.00

Required

1. Calculate the amount that should appear in the December 31, 2020, balance sheet as the Allowance for Doubtful Accounts.

2. Prepare the journal entry to record bad debt expense for 2020.

Analysis Component: On July 31, 2021, RCA concluded that a customer's $4,200 receivable (created in 2020) was uncollectible and that the account should be written off. What effect will this action have on RCA's 2021 profit? Explain your answer.

Problem 8-4B Aging accounts receivable LO2, 3 ecel

CHECK FIGURE: 2. Bad Debt Expense = $97,365

On December 31, 2020, Fresh Veggie Company's Allowance for Doubtful Accounts had an unadjusted debit balance of $9,800. The accountant for Fresh has prepared a schedule of the December 31, 2020, accounts receivable by age and, on the basis of past experience, has estimated the percentage of the receivables in each age category that will become uncollectible. This information is summarized as follows:

December 31, 2020 Accounts Receivable	Age of Accounts Receivable	Expected Percentage Uncollectible
$1,510,000	Not due (under 30 days)	1.25%
715,000	1 to 30 days past due	2.00
152,000	31 to 60 days past due	6.50
97,000	61 to 90 days past due	33.00
25,000	Over 90 days past due	50.00

Required

1. Calculate the amount that should appear in the December 31, 2020, balance sheet as the Allowance for Doubtful Accounts.

2. Prepare the journal entry to record bad debt expense for 2020.

Analysis Component: On July 31, 2021, Fresh concluded that a customer's $9,200 receivable (created in 2020) was uncollectible and that the account should be written off. What effect will this action have on Fresh's 2021 profit? Explain your answer.

Problem 8-5B Accounts receivable transactions and bad debt adjustments LO1, 2, 3

CHECK FIGURES: 2. Bad Debt Expense = $118,160; 5. Bad Debt Expense = $35,940

Wondra Supplies showed the following selected adjusted balances at its December 31, 2019, year-end:

Accounts Receivable		Allowance for Doubtful Accounts	
Dec. 31/19 Balance 490,000			12,300 Dec. 31/19 Balance

During 2020, the following selected transactions occurred:

a. Sales totalled $1,800,000, of which 85% were credit sales (cost of sales $987,000).

b. Sales returns were $31,000, all regarding credit sales. The returned merchandise was scrapped.

c. An account for $29,000 was recovered.

d. Several accounts were written off, including one very large account; the total was $65,500.

e. Collected accounts receivable of $1,630,000 (excluding the recovery in (c) above). Sales discounts of $22,000 were taken.

Part A

Required

1. Journalize transactions (a) through (e). You may find it useful to post your entries to T-accounts for Accounts Receivable and Allowance for Doubtful Accounts.

Part B

Required

2. Prepare the December 31, 2020, adjusting entry to estimate bad debts, assuming uncollectible accounts are estimated to be 8% of net credit sales.

3. Show how accounts receivable will appear on the December 31, 2020, balance sheet.

4. What will bad debt expense be on the income statement for the year ended December 31, 2020?

Part C (independent of Part B)

Required

5. Prepare the December 31, 2020, adjusting entry to estimate bad debts, assuming uncollectible accounts are estimated to be 4% of outstanding receivables.

6. Show how accounts receivable will appear on the December 31, 2020, balance sheet.

7. What will bad debt expense be on the income statement for the year ended December 31, 2020?

Problem 8-6B Recording accounts receivable transactions and bad debt adjustments LO1, 2, 3

CHECK FIGURES: d. Bad Debt Expense = $12,075; h. Bad Debt Expense = $12,834

Selzer Products Co. began operations on January 1, 2020, and completed a number of transactions during 2020 and 2021 that involved credit sales, accounts receivable collections, and bad debts. Assume a perpetual inventory system. These transactions are summarized as follows:

2020

a. Sold merchandise on credit for $1,640,000, terms n/30 (COGS = $1,070,000).

b. Received cash of $1,175,000 in payment of outstanding accounts receivable.

c. Wrote off uncollectible accounts receivable in the amount of $7,500.

d. In adjusting the accounts on December 31, concluded that 1% of the outstanding accounts receivable would become uncollectible.

2021

e. Sold merchandise on credit for $1,876,000, terms n/30 (COGS = $1,224,000).

f. Received cash of $1,444,000 in payment of outstanding accounts receivable.

g. Wrote off uncollectible accounts receivable in the amount of $8,600.

h. In adjusting the accounts on December 31, concluded that 1% of the outstanding accounts receivable would become uncollectible.

Required Prepare general journal entries to record Selzer's 2020 and 2021 summarized transactions and the adjusting entries to record bad debt expense at the end of each year.

Problem 8-7B Uncollectible accounts LO2, 3

CHECK FIGURES: b. Accounts receivable (net) = $108,700; d. Accounts receivable (net) = $126,440

Littlerock Surveying showed the following partial unadjusted results at May 31, 2020, its month-end:

Account	Debit	Credit
Sales		$860,000
Accounts receivable	$132,000	
Allowance for doubtful accounts		1,800

Part 1

Required

a. Assuming Littlerock estimates bad debts to be 2.5% of sales, prepare the adjusting entry at May 31, 2020.

b. Show how accounts receivable would be shown on the May 31, 2020, balance sheet using your calculations in (a).

Part 2

Required

c. Instead of (a) above, prepare the adjusting entry at May 31, 2020, assuming that Littlerock estimates bad debts to be based on the following aging analysis.

May 31, 2020 Accounts Receivable	Age of Accounts Receivable	Expected Percentage Uncollectible
$98,000	Not due (under 30 days)	1%
27,000	1 to 30 days past due	4%
7,000	Over 60 days past due	50%

d. Show how accounts receivable would be shown on the May 31, 2020, balance sheet using your calculations in (c).

Problem 8-8B Bad debt expense LO3

CHECK FIGURES: 1. Bad Debt Expense = $8,730; 2. Bad Debt Expense = $2,820

The following is information regarding adjusted account balances for Leonardo Painters at September 30, 2020:

Accounts Receivable		Allowance for Doubtful Accounts	
235,000			13,700

Part 1

During October, Leonardo Painters recorded $1,746,000 in total revenues, all on credit. Collections during October were $1,532,000. Included in the $1,532,000 collections was the recovery of $6,100 from a customer account written off in September. Total receivables identified as being uncollectible and written off during October were $14,700. Leonardo Painters estimates bad debts to be 0.5% of net credit revenues.

Required Prepare the adjusting entry to record estimated bad debts for October.

Part 2

During November, revenues totalled $1,680,000, all on credit. Collections during the month were $1,890,000. An account for $5,400 was identified as being uncollectible and written off on November 28. It was recommended to Leonardo Painters that the method of estimating bad debts be changed to the balance sheet approach. As a result, it was estimated that 5% of the November 30 accounts receivable balance was uncollectible.

Required Prepare the adjusting entry to record estimated bad debts for November.

Problem 8-9B Estimating bad debts LO3 e**X**cel

CHECK FIGURE: a. Total estimated uncollectible accounts = $29,010

The following information is available regarding the accounts receivable of Club Fit Holdings at August 31, 2020:

	Month of Credit Sale*				
Customer	**April**	**May**	**June**	**July**	**Aug.**
A. Leslie	$ -0-	$ 24,000	$ -0-	$ 58,000	$32,000
T. Meston	52,000	-0-	-0-	-0-	-0-
P. Obrian	-0-	-0-	-0-	104,000	42,000
L. Timms	-0-	126,000	52,000	-0-	28,000
W. Victor	-0-	-0-	166,000	122,000	64,000
*All services are performed on terms of n/60. Assume all sales occurred on the last day of the month.					

Club Fit estimates uncollectability of accounts receivable using the following rates:

Not yet due	1 to 29 days past due	30 to 59 days past due	60 to 89 days past due	90 to 119 days past due	Over 119 days past due
1.5%	2%	5%	20%	35%	50%

Required

a. Complete a Schedule of Accounts Receivable by Age at August 31, 2020, similar to Exhibit 8.13.

b. The Allowance for Doubtful Accounts showed an unadjusted balance on August 31, 2020, of $9,600 (debit). Record the adjusting journal entry at August 31, 2020, to estimate uncollectible accounts.

Problem 8-10B Uncollectible accounts LO3

CHECK FIGURE: March 31, 2021: Bad debt expense = $17,290

At year-end, March 31, 2020, Waterton Contractors showed unadjusted balances of $243,000 in Accounts Receivable; $1,100 debit in Allowance for Doubtful Accounts; and $4,640,000 in Sales. Uncollectible accounts are estimated to be 0.4% of sales.

Unadjusted balances at March 31, 2021, were Accounts Receivable, $298,000; Allowance for Doubtful Accounts, $900 debit; and Sales, $3,971,000. Waterton changed the method of estimating uncollectible accounts to 5.5% of outstanding accounts receivable.

At March 31, 2022, the general ledger showed unadjusted balances of: $253,000 in Accounts Receivable; $4,600 credit in Allowance for Doubtful Accounts; and $3,750,000 in Sales. Waterton prepared an aging analysis on March 31, 2022, that estimated total uncollectible accounts to be $12,900.

Required Prepare the 2020, 2021, and 2022 year-end adjusting entries to estimate uncollectible accounts.

Analysis Component: List the adjusted balances in Allowance for Doubtful Accounts for each of March 31, 2020, 2021, and 2022. Beside each, show the respective Accounts Receivable and Sales balances. Comment on the change in Allowance for Doubtful Accounts and Accounts Receivable relative to the change in Sales.

Problem 8-11B Notes receivable LO4

CHECK FIGURES: d. Interest income = $170.96; e. Interest income = $223.56

Shostak showed the following details regarding its notes receivable:

Note	Date of Note	Principal	Interest Rate	Term	Maturity Date	Days of Accrued Interest at Dec. 31, 2020	Accrued Interest at Dec. 31, 2020
1	Sept. 20/19	$490,000	3.0%	120 days			
2	June 01/20	240,000	3.5%	45 days			
3	Nov. 23/20	164,000	4.5%	90 days			
4	Dec. 18/20	120,000	4.0%	30 days			

*Round calculations to the nearest whole cent.

Required For each note:

a. Determine the maturity date.

b. Calculate the *days* of accrued interest, if any, at December 31, 2020, Shostak's year-end.

c. Calculate the *amount* of accrued interest, if any, at December 31, 2020.

For Note 4:

d. Prepare the entry to record the accrued interest at December 31, 2020.

e. Prepare the entry to record the collection on the maturity date. Assume that interest and principal are collected at maturity.

Problem 8-12B Notes receivable LO4

CHECK FIGURES: d. Interest income = $427.19; e. Interest income = $183.08

Amber Lighting showed the following details regarding its notes receivable:

Note	Date of Note	Principal	Interest Rate	Term	Maturity Date	Days of Accrued Interest at Dec. 31, 2020	Accrued Interest at Dec. 31, 2020
1	Nov. 1/19	$370,000	3.0%	180 days			
2	Jan. 5/20	212,000	3.5%	120 days			
3	Nov. 20/20	102,000	4.5%	90 days			
4	Dec. 10/20	135,000	5.5%	30 days			

*Round calculations to the nearest whole cent.

Required For each note:

a. Determine the maturity date.

b. Calculate the *days* of accrued interest, if any, at December 31, 2020, Amber's year-end.

c. Calculate the *amount* of accrued interest, if any, at December 31, 2020.

For Note 4:

d. Prepare the entry to record the accrued interest at December 31, 2020.

e. Prepare the entry to record the collection on the maturity date. Assume that interest and principal are collected at maturity.

Problem 8-13B Accrued interest calculation and dishonouring note receivable LO4

CHECK FIGURE: b. Interest income = $484.11

Following are transactions of Rural Company (round calculations to the nearest whole cent):

2020		
Nov.	16	Accepted a $74,000, 90-day, 4% note dated this day in granting Bess Parker a time extension on her past-due account.
Dec.	31	Made an adjusting entry to record the accrued interest on the Parker note.
	31	Closed the Interest income account.
2021		
Feb.	14	Received Parker's payment for the principal and interest on the note dated November 16.
	28	Accepted a $36,000, 5.5%, 30-day note dated this day in granting a time extension on the past-due account of The Simms Co.
Mar.	1	Accepted a $62,000, 60-day, 4.75% note dated this day in granting Bedford Holmes a time extension on his past-due account.
	30	The Simms Co. dishonoured its note when presented for payment.

Required

a. Prepare journal entries to record Rural's transactions.

b. Determine the maturity date of the note dated March 1. Prepare the entry at maturity assuming Bedford Holmes honours the note.

Problem 8-14B Short-term notes receivable LO4

CHECK FIGURES: d. February 15, 2021: Interest income = $203.43; e. April 1, 2021: Interest income = $330.00

Asiatic Electroplating analyzes its accounts receivable weekly. On November 17, 2020, Asiatic accepted a 5.5%, 90-day, $90,000 note receivable from RoadWorks in exchange for its past-due account. On December 1, Ellen Huskey's $36,000 overdue account was converted to a four-month, 5.5% note receivable. On January 31, 2021, Asiatic's year-end accrued interest was recorded on the notes. RoadWorks honoured its note on the maturity date but Ellen Huskey's note was dishonoured. Huskey's account was determined to be uncollectible and written off on July 15, 2021.

Required Prepare Asiatic Electroplating's entries for each of the following dates:

a. November 17, 2020

b. December 1, 2020

c. January 31, 2021

d. Maturity date of RoadWorks' note

e. Maturity date of Huskey's note

f. July 15, 2021

Analysis Component: Assuming a $50,000 credit balance in the Allowance for Doubtful Accounts on July 14, 2021, calculate the balance after posting the entry in (f) above. Assuming no additional write-offs were made prior to year-end, comment on the adequacy of the Allowance for Doubtful Accounts.

Problem 8-15B **Accounts receivable ratios** LO5

Using the Spin Master financial statements in Appendix III, calculate the following ratios for the years ended December 31, 2017 and December 31, 2016. At December 31, 2015, Spin Master had an accounts receivable balance of $134,618,000 and net sales of $879,406,000. Comment on the change.

a. Accounts receivable turnover ratio (round to two decimal places)

b. Days' sales in inventory (round to the nearest day)

*Problem 8-16B **Discounting notes receivable** LO6

CHECK FIGURE: July 5: Interest expense = $475

Required Prepare entries to record the following transactions of Ibscon Company:

Mar.	1	Accepted a $50,000, 60-day, 4.5% note dated this day in granting Bolton Company a time extension on its past-due account.
	23	Discounted, without recourse, the Bolton note at Security Bank at a cost of $100.
June	21	Accepted a $22,000, 90-day, 5% note dated this day in granting Vince Soto a time extension on his past-due account.
July	5	Discounted, with recourse, the Soto note at Security Bank at a cost of $475.
Sept.	25	Received notice from Security Bank that the Soto note had been paid.

Analysis Component: What reporting is necessary when a business discounts notes receivable with recourse and these notes have not reached maturity by the end of the fiscal period? Explain the reason for this requirement and what accounting principle is being satisfied.

*Problem 8-17B **Discounting notes receivable** LO6

CHECK FIGURES: Mar. 28: Cash = $2,088.15; July 24: Cash = $1,304.51

Required Prepare general journal entries to record the following transactions of Billington Company.

2020		
Jan	10	Accepted a $3,000, 60-day, 6% note dated this day in granting a time extension on the past-due account of David Huerta.
Mar.	14	David Huerta dishonoured his note when presented for payment.
	19	Accepted a $2,100, 90-day, 5% note dated this day in granting a time extension on the past-due account of Rose Jones.
	28	Discounted the Rose Jones note at the bank at 8%.
Jun.	20	Received word from the bank that the Rose Jones note had been paid.
	27	Accepted $700 in cash and a $1,300, 60-day, 6% note dated this day in granting a time extension on the past-due account of Jake Thomas.
July	24	Discounted the Jake Thomas note at the bank at 7%.
Aug.	29	The Jake Thomas note was dishonoured. Paid the bank the maturity of the note plus a $10 fee.
Sept.	4	Accepted a $1,500, 60-day, 5.5% note dated this day in granting a time extension on the past-due account of Ginnie Bauer.
Oct.	13	Discounted the Ginnie Bauer note at the bank at 7%.
Nov.	6	The Ginnie Bauer note was dishonoured. Paid the bank the maturity value of the note plus a $10 fee.
Dec.	6	Received payment from Ginnie Bauer of the maturity value of her dishonoured note, the fee, and interest at 5.5% on both for 30 days beyond maturity.
	28	Decided the accounts of David Huerta and Jake Thomas were uncollectible and wrote them off against Allowance for Doubtful Accounts.

An asterisk (*) identifies assignment material based on Appendix 8A.

ANALYTICAL AND REVIEW PROBLEMS

A & R Problem 8-1

CHECK FIGURE: g. Bad Debt Expense = $18,000

Reproduced below from Farthington Supply's accounting records is the accounts receivable subledger along with selected general ledger accounts.

General Ledger								
Accounts Receivable					**Allowance for Doubtful Accounts**			
Dec. 31/19 Balance	158,500						200	Dec. 31/19 Balance
Credit sales in 2020	????	7,000 ???? 14,000	Jan. 4/20 Collections in 2020 July 15/20		July 15/20	14,000		
							????	Dec. 31/20
Dec. 31/20 Balance	????						????	Dec. 31/20 Balance

Accounts Receivable Subledger								
JenStar Company					**Indigo Developments**			
Dec. 31/19 Balance	48,000				Dec. 31/19 Balance	-0-		
		48,000	Jan. 20/20		Mar. 1/20	17,000	17,000	Mar. 20/20
Nov. 15/20	????				Nov. 28/20	39,000		
					Dec. 2/20	4,000		
Dec. 31/20 Balance	104,000				Dec. 31/20 Balance	43,000		
Lomas Industries					**PDQ Servicing**			
Dec. 31/19 Balance	????				Dec. 31/19 Balance	14,000		
		7,000	Jan. 4/20					
		????	Jan. 7/20					
Apr. 21/20	52,000	52,000	May 5/20				14,000	July 15/20
Dec. 7/20	21,000							
Dec. 31/20 Balance	21,000				Dec. 31/20 Balance	-0-		

During the year 2020, there were no recoveries of accounts previously written off. Only one account, that of PDQ Servicing, was identified as being uncollectible on July 15, 2020. On January 4, 2020, Farthington issued a $7,000 credit memo to Lomas Industries regarding damaged goods returned.

Required Analyzing the accounts, determine the following amounts:

a. The December 31, 2019, balance in Lomas Industries' account.

b. The January 7, 2020, collection from Lomas Industries.

c. The December 31, 2020, balance in the Accounts Receivable controlling account.

d. The November 15, 2020, transaction in JenStar Company's account.

e. Collections during 2020.

f. Credit sales during 2020.

g. Adjusting entry on December 31, 2020, to estimate uncollectible accounts based on a rate of 2.5% of outstanding receivables.

h. The December 31, 2020, balance in the Allowance for Doubtful Accounts.

i. Show how accounts receivable should appear on the balance sheet on December 31, 2020.

Analysis Component: Why does Farthington maintain an accounts receivable subledger? What other subledgers might the company be using and why?

A & R Problem 8-2

CHECK FIGURES: a. April 30, 2020, and Feb. 1, 2021; b. May 7, 2020, credit card expense = $710

Sullivan Equipment Sales showed the following.

2020		
Jan.	15	Sold $25,000 of merchandise for $29,000 to JanCo; terms 3/5, n/15.
	16	Wrote off Fedun's account in the amount of $15,000.
	20	Collected the amount owing from the January 15 sale.
Mar.	1	Accepted a $12,000, 60-day, 7% note dated this day in granting Parker Holdings a time extension on its past-due account.
Apr.	15	Sold merchandise costing $62,000 for $71,000 to customers who used their Visa credit cards. Assume Visa charges a 1% fee and deposits the cash electronically into the retailer's account immediately at the time of sale.
	?	Parker Holdings honoured the note dated March 1.
Nov.	1	Accepted a $24,000, three-month, 6% note dated this day in granting Grant Company a time extension on its past-due account.
Dec.	31	Sullivan's year-end. Interest was accrued on outstanding notes receivable.
	31	Bad debts are based on an aging analysis that estimated $9,700 of accounts receivable are uncollectible. Allowance for Doubtful Accounts showed an unadjusted credit balance of $1,600 on this date.
2021		
	?	Grant Company dishonoured its note dated November 1, 2020.
Mar.	5	Recovered $1,500 from Derek Holston that was previously written off.
	14	Wrote off the Grant Company account.

Required

a. Determine the maturity dates of the March 1 and November 1 notes.

b. Prepare entries as appropriate for each date.

Analysis Component: Sullivan's receivable turnovers at December 31, 2020 and 2021 were 7 and 7.5, respectively. Explain what this ratio measures and whether the change in the ratio for Sullivan was favourable or unfavourable.

ETHICS CHALLENGE

EC 8-1

Randy Meyer is the chief executive officer of a medium-sized company in Regina, Saskatchewan. Several years ago, Randy persuaded the board of directors of his company to base a percentage of his compensation on the profit the company earns each year. Each December, Randy estimates year-end financial figures in anticipation of the bonus he will receive. If the bonus is not as high as he would like, he offers several accounting recommendations to his controller for year-end adjustments. One of his favourite recommendations is for the controller to reduce the estimate of doubtful accounts. Randy has used this technique with success for several years.

1. What effect does lowering the estimate for doubtful accounts have on the income statement and balance sheet of Randy's company?

2. Do you think Randy's recommendations to adjust the allowance for doubtful accounts is within his right as CEO or do you think this action is an ethics violation? Justify your response.

3. What type of internal control might be useful for this company in overseeing the CEO's recommendations for accounting changes?

FOCUS ON FINANCIAL STATEMENTS

FFS 8-1

CHECK FIGURES: Total current assets = $61,900; Total assets = $199,900; Total current liabilities = $25,100

Clara Dover, the owner of Dover Plumbing Sales and Service, showed the following adjusted account balances for the year ended March 31, 2020 (listed alphabetically):

Account	Account Balance*
Accounts payable	$ 6,900
Accounts receivable	28,000
Accumulated depreciation, tools	11,000
Accumulated depreciation, truck	14,000
Allowance for doubtful accounts	1,800
Bad debt expense	5,600
Cash	16,000
Cash over/short expense	20**
Clara Dover, capital	248,770
Clara Dover, withdrawals	72,000
Cost of goods sold	103,000
Depreciation expense, tools	2,000
Depreciation expense, truck	5,000
Insurance expense	7,100
Interest expense	250
Merchandise inventory	9,000
Notes payable, due August 31, 2023	17,000
Notes payable, due February 1, 2021	6,000
Notes receivable, due December 1, 2022	14,000
Petty cash	400
Plumbing revenue	121,000
Prepaid insurance	3,800
Prepaid rent	6,500
Rent expense	23,000
Salaries expense	118,000
Salaries payable	3,200
Sales	124,000
Tools	82,000
Truck	67,000
Unearned plumbing revenue	9,000

*Assume all account balances are normal unless otherwise stated.
**Debit balance.

Required Prepare a classified balance sheet based on the information provided.

Analysis Component: Dover Plumbing had total *Plumbing revenue* for the year ended March 31, 2019, of $86,000 and net accounts receivable at March 31, 2019, of $21,200. Calculate and compare days' sales uncollected for March 31, 2019, and March 31, 2020. Round calculations to two decimal places.

FFS 8-2

Refer to Spin Master's balance sheet and notes in Appendix III.

Required Answer the following questions.

1. The balance sheet shows Trade and other Receivables of $369,719 at December 31, 2017, and $295,068 at December 31, 2016. What type of asset is trade and other receivables? Explain how accounts receivable arise.

2. Refer to the notes. Does the change in receivables appear to correspond to the change in total sales? Explain your answer. What is the allowance for doubtful accounts each year? What is the amount of past due accounts each year? How much was written off each year?

CRITICAL THINKING MINI CASE

You are the finance officer at a bank where the owner of Delta Designs is applying for a $600,000 loan. In reviewing the account information for the year ended June 30, 2020 you are concerned by the following selected adjusted account information:

Account	Debit	Credit
Accounts receivable*	$472,000	
Allowance for doubtful accounts		$ 7,080
Sales**		3,980,000

*85% of this balance represents receivables that are not yet due. Delta Designs offers credit terms of 2/10, n/30.
**All sales are on credit and sales occur evenly throughout the year.

Required Using the elements of critical thinking described on the inside front cover, respond.

Property, Plant, and Equipment and Intangibles

A Look Back

Chapters 7 and 8 focused on current assets: cash, cash equivalents, and receivables. We explained why they are known as liquid assets and described how companies account and report for them.

A Look at This Chapter

This chapter introduces us to non-current assets. We explain how to account for a non-current asset's initial cost, the allocation of an asset's cost to periods benefiting from it, the recording of additional costs after an asset is purchased, and the disposal of an asset.

Photo courtesy of Vancouver International Airport and Larry Goldstein

LEARNING OBJECTIVES

LO1	Describe property, plant, and equipment (PPE) and calculate their cost.
LO2	Explain, record, and calculate depreciation using the methods of straight-line, units-of-production, and double-declining-balance.
LO3	Explain and calculate depreciation for partial years.

LO4	Explain and calculate revised depreciation.
LO5	Explain and record impairment losses.
LO6	Account for asset disposal through discarding, selling, or exchanging an asset.
LO7	Account for intangible assets and their amortization.

*Appendix 9A

LO8	Explain and calculate revised depreciation when there is a betterment that creates partial-period depreciation.

Vancouver International Airport—A Canadian Leader in Customer Experience and Innovation

Vancouver Airport Authority is the community-based, not-for-profit organization that manages Vancouver International Airport (YVR).

Since its inception in 1992, Vancouver Airport Authority has experienced an incredible story of growth, innovation, and leadership along with industry excellence. YVR has become Canada's second-busiest airport, serving a record 24.2 million passengers in 2017 and connecting people and businesses to more than 127 non-stop destinations worldwide. YVR was also voted Best Airport in North America for the ninth consecutive year in the 2017 Skytrax World Airport Awards, the global benchmark of airport excellence.

As a not-for-profit organization, Vancouver Airport Authority reinvests all earnings into the operation and growth of the airport to improve facilities, enhance services, reduce costs, and support community initiatives. Vancouver Airport Authority continues to ensure airport operations are optimized through investing over $7.6 billion from 2017–2037 on major projects that will enhance the airport experience. These projects include expanding the terminal space to accommodate more aircraft and passengers, additional airside infrastructure, a new central utilities building to house YVR's heating, cooling, and backup electrical system, a new parkade, and much more.

In addition to terminal and airside improvements, Vancouver Airport Authority formed a joint venture with McArthurGlen Group to develop Greater Vancouver's first luxury designer outlet, which opened in July 2015. Since its record-breaking opening weekend nearly 10 million shoppers have visited the award-winning development, which has led to adding an additional 1.6 million square feet of retail space by 2021 for Phase 2.

YVR also recently released its latest innovation, CHECKiTXPRESS, which was developed in collaboration with New Zealand–based baggage handling solutions expert Glidepath. CHECKiTXPRESS is an innovative and user-friendly bag drop for travellers that is accessible from multiple sides. The system is designed for maximum efficiency, with ergonomic design principles that include lowering the profile of the conveyor to 10 cm off the floor and creating durable ramps to wheel bags onto the conveyor. YVR expects to expand this feature offering to other airports around the world.

Vancouver Airport Authority has developed policies and procedures to ensure the continued investment in capital assets is captured effectively in its accounting records. In its 2017 audited consolidated financial statements, Vancouver Airport Authority reported net capital assets of $1.95 billion, representing 82% of total assets. Major categories include buildings and structures, runways, rapid transit infrastructure, machinery and equipment, furniture and fixtures, computer equipment and systems, construction in progress, and the Airport Authority's impressive art collection. Based on the significant accounting policies, capital assets are amortized on a straight-line basis, at cost less estimated salvage value, over a period not exceeding the estimated useful life. Capitalized costs include the purchase price and acquisition and construction costs such as "installation costs, design and engineering fees, legal fees, survey costs, site preparation, transportation charges, labour, insurance and duties."

From new buildings to improved infrastructure and innovative services, Vancouver Airport Authority is committed to creating an airport that British Columbia can be proud of—a premier global gateway.

Sources: www.yvr.ca; https://www.newswire.ca/news-releases/mcarthurglen-vancouver-to-commence-construction-of-phase-ii-675840533.html; https://www.passengerterminaltoday.com/news/technology/vancouver-international-airport-to-deliver-worlds-most-efficient-self-service-bag-drop-system.html, accessed May 2018.

Video Link: https://www.youtube.com/watch?v=xS60bqgB8VM

CRITICAL THINKING CHALLENGE

You are asked by the CFO of YVR to evaluate one of the airport's newest capital assets additions, the Airside Operations Building, and to break it into major components for depreciation purposes. Identify at least five major components and determine an expected life for each of those components.

CHAPTER PREVIEW

Why do companies like **Facebook** and **Google** have less than 20% of total assets in PPE while other companies like **WestJet** and **Air Canada** have over 50% of total assets invested in PPE? The difference is that airlines are capital intensive and technology companies require a greater investment in research and development. Property, plant, and equipment and intangible assets are often the key areas requiring investment of capital resources for newly established businesses. Over time, the major assets held in this category require repairs, improvements, and replacement with newer, more efficient assets or more physical capacity due to expansion. As the items held in this category are material in relation to their total assets, it is essential that we are cautious to effectively capture the initial costs on the balance sheet and subsequently record the usage of these assets on the income statement as an expense, referred to as *depreciation expense*, in the period the asset is utilized.

This chapter focuses on non-current assets used in the operation of a business: *property, plant, and equipment* and *intangible assets*. Property, plant, and equipment represent a major investment for most companies and make up a large portion of assets on the balance sheet. They also affect the income statement because their costs are charged to depreciation expense, often one of the largest expenses on the income statement. This chapter will describe the purchase and use of these assets. We also explain what distinguishes property, plant, and equipment assets from other types of assets, how to determine their cost, how to allocate their costs to periods benefiting from their use, and how to record their disposal.

Property, Plant, and Equipment (PPE)

LO1   Describe property, plant, and equipment (PPE) and calculate their cost.

Non-current assets that are used in the operations of a business and have a useful life of more than one accounting period are divided into three groups:

1. Tangible assets known as property, plant, and equipment[1]
2. Intangible assets[2]
3. Goodwill[3]

Property, plant, and equipment (PPE), sometimes referred to as **capital assets** or **fixed assets**, includes land, buildings, equipment, machinery, and leasehold improvements. For instance, WestJet's $4.6 million of net PPE as at December 31, 2017, includes aircraft, ground property and equipment, spare engines and parts, buildings, and leasehold improvements as shown in the financial statements located in Appendix II.

---

1   IFRS 2015, IAS 16.

2   IFRS 2015, IAS 38.

3   Goodwill is an asset representing the future economic benefits arising from other assets acquired in a business combination that are not individually identified and separately recognized.

Intangible assets lack physical substance and include patents, copyrights, leaseholds, drilling rights, and trademarks and are discussed in a later section of this chapter.

For many businesses, PPE makes up the single largest asset category on the balance sheet. For example, on its September 30, 2017, balance sheet, the **Walt Disney Company** shows total assets of $95.8 billion with net PPE comprising $28.4 billion of this amount. **Amazon Corporation** reported $49 billion of net property, plant, and equipment at December 31, 2017, representing 37% of total assets.

PPE are set apart from other assets by two important features:

1. *These assets are used in business operations to help generate revenue.* This makes them different from *inventory*, for instance, which is an asset that is *not used* in operations but rather held for the purpose of resale. A company that purchases a computer for the purpose of selling it reports the computer on the balance sheet as inventory. But if the same company purchases this computer for use in operations, it is classified as PPE.

2. *PPE are in use and provide benefits for more than one accounting period.* This makes PPE different from *current assets* such as *supplies* that are usually consumed soon after they are placed in use. The cost of current assets is assigned to a single period as they are used.

Accounting for PPE reflects these two important features. We must initially record the cost of each PPE item (balance sheet focus) and allocate its estimated period cost to each appropriate period benefiting from its use (income statement focus) in the manner in which the asset is consumed/used.

Exhibit 9.1 shows the *three main accounting issues with PPE*. They are:

1. Calculating and accounting for the initial and subsequent costs of PPE

2. Allocating the costs of PPE against revenues for the periods they benefit in the manner in which the asset is consumed/used

3. Recording the disposal of PPE

This chapter focuses on the decisions and factors surrounding these three important issues.

EXHIBIT 9.1

Issues in Accounting for PPE

© Paha_l/Dreamstime.com/ GetStock.com

© 6thgearadvertising/Dreamstime.com/ GetStock.com

© Hartphotography/Dreamstime.com/ GetStock.com

Decline in book value over service life

Acquisition	**Use**	**Disposal**
• Calculate initial cost	• Account for subsequent costs	• Record disposal
	• Allocate cost to periods benefited	

Cost of PPE

Consistent with the *cost principle*, PPE are recorded at **cost**, which includes all normal and reasonable expenditures necessary to get the asset in place and ready for its intended use.[4] The cost of a piece of manufacturing equipment, for instance, includes the following:

1. Its invoice price, less any cash discount for early payment.

2. Freight, unpacking, and assembling costs.

3. Non-refundable sales taxes (PST).

4. All necessary costs of installing and testing the equipment before placing it in use. Examples are the costs of building a base or foundation for the equipment, of providing electrical hook-ups, and of adjusting the equipment before using it in operations.

The above example highlights several types of capital expenditures also known as *betterments*. **Betterments** represent costs of PPE that provide material benefits extending beyond the current period.[5] They are debited to PPE accounts and reported on the balance sheet.

When expenditures regarding PPE are *not* considered a normal part of getting the asset ready for its intended use, they are expensed as a current-period cost. For example, if a machine is damaged during unpacking, the **repairs** are recorded as an expense. Also, a traffic fine paid for moving heavy machinery on city streets without a proper permit is an expense and *not* part of the machinery's cost. These are **repairs and maintenance expenses**: costs that maintain an asset but do not materially increase the asset's life or productive capabilities. They are recorded as expenses and deducted from revenues in the current period's income statement. Consistent with this rule, WestJet reports:

> Major overhaul expenditures are capitalized and depreciated over the expected life between overhauls. All other costs relating to the maintenance of fleet assets are charged to the consolidated statement of earnings on consumption or as incurred.
>
> **Source:** WestJet Airlines, 2017 Annual Report

SUBSEQUENT EXPENDITURES

When PPE are acquired and put into service, additional or *subsequent* expenditures often are incurred after the acquisition to operate, maintain, repair, and improve it. In recording these subsequent expenditures, we must decide whether they are to be accounted for as betterments or as repairs and maintenance expenses. Exhibit 9.2 can be used to determine if a subsequent expenditure is a betterment or a repair and maintenance expense in nature. Examples of subsequent capital expenditures that are classified as betterments include roofing replacement, plant expansion, and major overhauls of machinery and equipment. These expenditures either extend the life of the asset or improve efficiency; therefore, they are capitalized and depreciated. Examples of expenditures that would be recorded as repair and maintenance expenses on the income statement are supplies, fuel, minor repairs, and costs relating to routine testing.

---

4   IFRS 2018, IAS 16, para. 16.

5   IFRS 2018, IAS 16, paras. 29–42, discusses the use of the cost and revaluation models of measurement after recognition of PPE. The cost model has been adopted in this chapter. The revaluation model is beyond the scope of this text and is left for discussion in a more advanced course.

EXHIBIT 9.2

Is It a Betterment or a Repairs and Maintenance Expense?

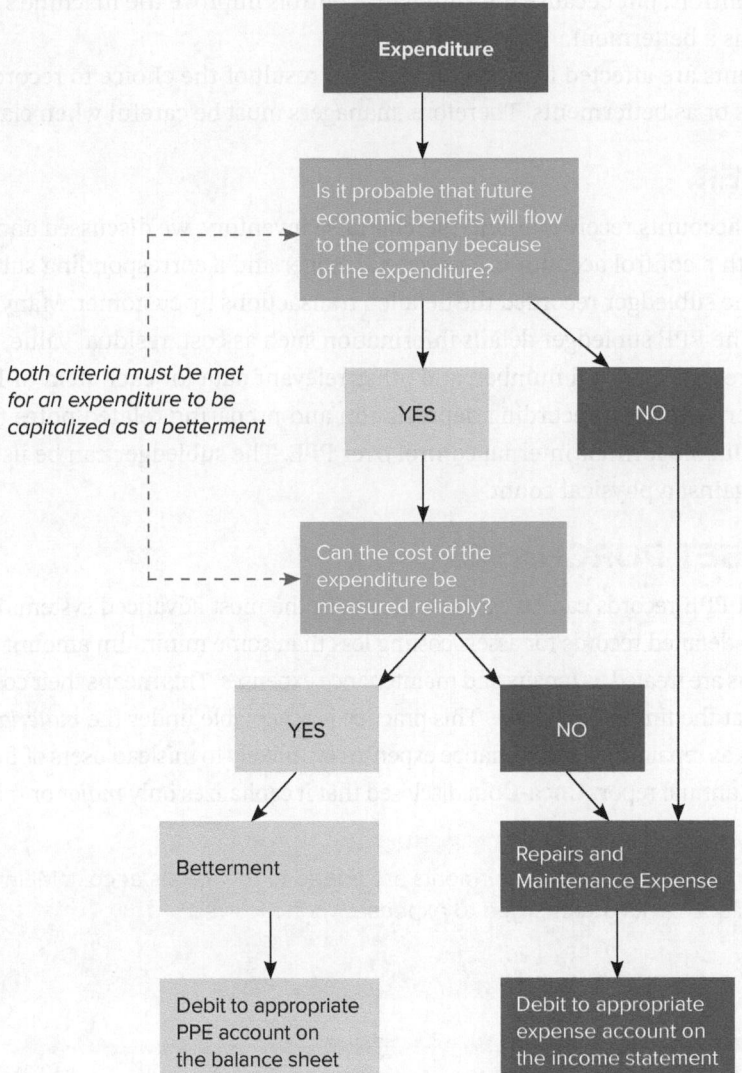

For example, consider the following expenses Dealz Wheelz, an Ontario car rental agency, incurs in its normal course of business.

1. Its 2018 Toyota Yaris experiences a battery failure and the mechanic installs a new battery to fix the problem. This would be classified as a current-period repairs and maintenance expense and is recorded as a current-period expense. Repairs and maintenance expenses like the purchase of the battery do not materially improve the future value of the economic benefits obtained from the car but help to *maintain the asset*, keeping it in good working order over its estimated useful life.

2. Dealz Wheelz had a customer drive the 2014 Ford Fusion from Toronto to Halifax in humid August weather without getting an oil change, requiring the mechanic to do a complete engine replacement upon its return to the rental depot. Replacing the engine in this situation *does* improve the future economic benefits of the car because its useful life is extended. Therefore, the new engine is recorded as a betterment and is capitalized.[6]

---

6   IFRS 2018, IAS 16, para. 13, requires the carrying amount of those parts that are replaced to be removed from the accounting records. The removal of PPE from the accounting records, also known as the disposal of PPE, is discussed in a later section of this chapter.

A betterment does not always increase an asset's useful life. An example is replacing manual controls on a machine with automatic controls to reduce labour costs. This machine will still wear out just as fast as it would with manual controls, but because the automatic controls improve the machine's efficiency in terms of labour cost savings, it is a betterment.

Financial statements are affected for several years as a result of the choice to record costs as repairs and maintenance expenses or as betterments. Therefore, managers must be careful when classifying costs.

PPE SUBLEDGER

For accounts payable, accounts receivable, and merchandise inventory, we discussed and illustrated the benefits in maintaining both a control account in the general ledger and a corresponding subledger. In the case of accounts receivable, the subledger recorded the detailed transactions by customer. Many companies also keep a subledger for PPE. The PPE subledger details information such as cost, residual value, estimated useful life, date of purchase, depreciation, serial number, and other relevant data for each item of PPE or group of PPE. This information is very useful in recording depreciation and preparing related notes to the financial statements, but is also a valuable form of internal control over PPE. The subledger can be used as an audit trail to verify recorded PPE against a physical count.

LOW-COST ASSET PURCHASES

Maintaining individual PPE records can be expensive, even in the most advanced system. For that reason, many companies do not keep detailed records for assets costing less than some minimum amount such as $100. Instead, these low-cost PPE items are treated as repairs and maintenance expenses. This means their costs are directly charged to an expense account at the time of purchase. This practice is acceptable under the *materiality principle*. Treating immaterial betterments as repairs and maintenance expenses is unlikely to mislead users of financial statements. As an example, in a recent annual report **Coca-Cola** disclosed that it capitalizes only *major* or material betterments:

> Additions and major replacements or betterments are added to the assets at cost. Maintenance and repair costs and minor replacements are charged to expense when incurred.
>
> **Source:** Coca-Cola

 DECISION MAKER   Answer—End of chapter

Restaurant Results

You are a new grad who recently opened your own restaurant. Because of a cash shortage, you are preparing financial statements in the hope of getting a short-term loan from the bank. A friend of yours suggests that you treat as many expenses as possible as betterments. What are the effects on financial statements of treating expenses as betterments? What do you think of your friend's proposal?

 CHECKPOINT

1. What is included in the cost of a PPE asset?
2. Explain the difference between repairs and maintenance expenses and betterments and how they are recorded.
3. What is a betterment and how is it recorded?

Do Quick Study questions: QS 9-1, QS 9-2, QS 9-3

In the remainder of this section we explain how to determine the capital costs for each of five types of PPE: land (property), land improvements, buildings (plant), leasehold improvements, and machinery and equipment.

LAND

When land is purchased for a building site, its cost includes the following:

- Total amount paid for the land, including any real estate commissions, fees for insuring the title, legal fees, and any accrued property taxes paid by the purchaser.
- Payments for surveying, clearing, grading, draining, and landscaping[7] are also included in the cost of land.

Other costs of land include:

- Assessments by the local government, whether incurred at the time of purchase or later, for items such as roadways, sewers, and sidewalks. These assessments are included because they permanently add to the land's value.

Land Purchased with Removal of a Building

Land purchased as a building site sometimes includes a building or other obstructions that must be removed. The total amount included in the cost of land is:

- Purchase price is capitalized under the Land account
- Any costs incurred in removing the old building, less any amounts recovered through sale of salvaged materials.

To illustrate, assume a company bought land for a retail store for $170,000. This land contains an old service garage that is removed at a net cost of $15,000 ($20,000 in costs less $5,000 proceeds from salvaged materials). Additional closing costs totalled $10,000, and consisted of brokerage fees ($8,000), legal fees ($1,500), and title costs ($500). The cost of this land is $195,000, calculated as:

Net cash price of land	$ 170,000
Net cost of service garage removal	15,000
Closing costs	10,000
Cost of land	**$195,000**

LAND IMPROVEMENTS

Because land has an unlimited life and is not consumed when used, it is not subject to depreciation. **Land improvements** include items that have limited useful lives such as:

- Parking lot surfaces
- Driveways
- Fences
- Lighting systems

While these costs increase the usefulness of the land, they are charged to a separate PPE account called Land Improvements so their costs can be allocated to the periods they benefit.

---

7 Landscaping is included in the cost of land if it is considered permanent in nature. Landscaping costs with a finite life of greater than one accounting period are charged to the Land Improvements account.

BUILDINGS

Acquired Buildings

A Building account is charged for the costs of purchasing or constructing a building when it is used in operations. When purchased, the costs of a building usually include:

- Purchase price
- Title fees
- Brokerage fees
- Legal costs
- Taxes

Its costs also include all expenditures to make it ready for its intended use, such as repairs or renovations that include:

- Wiring
- Flooring
- Lighting
- Wall coverings
- Plumbing

Constructed Buildings

When a building, or any PPE item, is constructed by a company for the company's own use, its cost includes:

- Construction-related materials and labour costs
- Heat, electricity, and other utilities consumed during construction
- A reasonable amount of depreciation expense on machinery used to construct the asset
- Design fees
- Building permits
- Interest and insurance costs applicable to the period of construction

All interest and insurance costs incurred *after* the asset is placed in use are expensed as operating expenses.

LEASEHOLD IMPROVEMENTS

Many businesses rent their facilities under a contract called a **lease**. The property's owner grants the lease and is called the **lessor**. The one who secures the right to possess and use the property is called the **lessee**. Non-current leases sometimes require the lessee to pay for alterations or improvements to the leased property—these costs are referred to as **leasehold improvements**. This category of assets includes items such as:

- Interior modifications, such as installation of walls
- Enhancements, such as installation of built-in display walls, new storefronts, updated flooring, and painting
- Plumbing, including new fixtures for restrooms
- Electrical, such as installation of updated light fixtures

Leasehold improvements become part of the property and revert to the lessor at the end of the lease. These costs are debited to a *Leasehold Improvements* account and are depreciated over either the life of the lease or the life of the improvements, whichever is shorter. In its notes to the financial statements, **Lululemon Athletica Inc.** reports net leasehold improvements at January 28, 2018, of $301 million at cost, depreciated using the straight-line method over the lower time period—the term of the lease and the estimated life of the improvement to a maximum of five years.

MACHINERY AND EQUIPMENT

The cost of machinery and equipment consists of all costs normal and necessary to purchase it and prepare it for its intended use. It includes the following items:

- Purchase price less discounts
- Non-refundable sales taxes
- Transportation charges
- Insurance while in transit
- Costs of installing, assembling, and testing of machinery and equipment

LUMP-SUM ASSET PURCHASE

A **lump-sum purchase**, also called a **basket purchase**, is the purchase of PPE in a group with a single transaction for a lump-sum price. When this occurs, we allocate the cost of the purchase among the different types of assets acquired based on their *relative values*. Their values can be estimated by appraisal or by using the tax-assessed valuations of the assets. To illustrate, assume **David's Tea** paid $630,000 cash to acquire land appraised at $210,000, land improvements appraised at $70,000, and a building appraised at $420,000. The $630,000 cost was allocated on the basis of appraised values as shown in Exhibit 9.3:

EXHIBIT 9.3

Calculating Costs in a Lump-Sum Purchase

	Appraised Value	Percent of Total	Apportioned Cost		
Land	$210,000	30	($210,000/$700,000)	$189,000	($630,000 × 30%)
Land improvements	70,000	10	($ 70,000/$700,000)	63,000	($630,000 × 10%)
Building	420,000	60	($420,000/$700,000)	378,000	($630,000 × 60%)
Totals	$700,000	100		$630,000	

Alternatively, the calculation can be done by dividing the total cost by the total appraised value ($630,000/$700,000 = 0.90 or 90%) and applying the 90% to the individual appraised values as follows:

Land	$210,000	× 90%	=	$189,000
Land improvements	70,000	× 90%	=	63,000
Building	420,000	× 90%	=	378,000

 CHECKPOINT

4. Identify the account charged for each of the following expenditures: (a) purchase price of a vacant lot, and (b) cost of paving that vacant lot.

5. What amount is recorded as the cost of a new machine given the following items related to its purchase: gross purchase price, $700,000; sales tax, $49,000; purchase discount taken, $21,000; freight to move machine to plant, $3,500; assembly costs, $3,000; cost of foundation for machine, $2,500; cost of spare parts used in maintaining machine, $4,200?

Do Quick Study question: QS 9-4

Depreciation

LO2 Explain, record, and calculate depreciation using the methods of straight-line, units-of-production, and double-declining-balance.

Because PPE (except for land) wear out or decline in usefulness as they are used, an expense must be recorded. **Depreciation**[8] is the process of matching (or allocating) the depreciable cost of an asset in a rational and systematic manner over the asset's estimated useful life.[9]

To illustrate why the allocation of an asset's cost is required, assume that a delivery van is purchased for $40,000 on January 1, 2020. It is estimated that the van will help generate $30,000 in revenues each year for four years. At the end of the four-year period, it is estimated that the van will be worthless. We could record the $40,000 as an expense in the year it was purchased, as illustrated in Exhibit 9.4. However, profit is distorted because we have not matched the expense of the delivery van over the four years that it is creating revenue. The treatment in Exhibit 9.4 is therefore *not in conformance with GAAP*.

EXHIBIT 9.4

Cost of the Delivery Van Recorded as an Expense in Year of Purchase

	2020	2021	2022	2023
Revenues	$30,000	$30,000	$30,000	$30,000
Expense	40,000	-0-	-0-	-0-
Profit (Loss)	($10,000)	$30,000	$30,000	$30,000

Estimated four-year life of the delivery van.

If instead we apply the matching principle and allocate the cost of the delivery van against the periods it generates revenue, we achieve a more accurate reflection of performance across time, as Exhibit 9.5 illustrates.

EXHIBIT 9.5

Cost of the Delivery Van Matched Against Revenues Generated Over Its Four-Year Useful Life

	2020	2021	2022	2023
Revenues	$30,000	$30,000	$30,000	$30,000
Expense	10,000*	10,000*	10,000*	10,000*
Profit (Loss)	$20,000	$20,000	$20,000	$20,000

Estimated four-year life of the delivery van.

*$40,000 ÷ 4 years = $10,000 per year.

This allocation of the delivery van's cost is *depreciation*.

Note that depreciation is a process of cost allocation, not asset valuation. *Depreciation does not measure the decline in the van's value each period.* Nor does it measure the physical deterioration of the van. Depreciation

---

8   The term "depreciation" is used to describe the allocation of the cost of a tangible asset over its useful life, and "amortization" is used to describe the allocation of the cost of an intangible asset. The amortization of intangible assets is discussed in more detail in a later section.

9   IFRS 2018, IAS 16, para. 50.

is a process of allocating an asset's cost to expense over its useful life, nothing more. Because depreciation reflects the cost of using a plant and equipment asset, we do not begin recording depreciation charges until the asset is available for use within the company.

REPORTING DEPRECIATION ON ASSETS

Both the cost and accumulated depreciation of PPE must be reported. Many companies show PPE on one line at the net amount of cost less accumulated depreciation. When this is done, the amount of accumulated depreciation is disclosed in a footnote. **Indigo Books & Music Inc.** reports $3,507,000 as the net amount of its property, plant, and equipment on its March 31, 2018, balance sheet. To satisfy the full disclosure principle,[10] it also describes its depreciation methods in Note 4 as follows:

Property, Plant, and Equipment

All items of property, plant, and equipment are initially recognized at cost, which includes any costs directly attributable to bringing the asset to the location and condition necessary for it to be capable of operating in the manner intended by the Company. Subsequent to initial recognition, property, plant and equipment assets are shown at cost less accumulated depreciation and any accumulated impairment losses.

Depreciation of an asset begins once it becomes available for use. The depreciable amount of an asset, being the cost of an asset less the residual value, is allocated on a straight-line basis over the estimated useful life of the asset. Residual value is estimated to be zero unless the Company expects to dispose of the asset at a value that exceeds the estimated disposal costs. The residual values, useful lives, and depreciation methods applied to assets are reviewed annually based on relevant market information and management considerations.

The following useful lives are applied:

Furniture, fixtures and equipment	5–10 years
Computer equipment	3–5 years
Equipment under finance leases	3–5 years
Leasehold improvements	over the shorter of useful life and lease term plus expected renewals to a maximum of 10 years

Items of property, plant, and equipment are assessed for impairment as detailed in the accounting policy note on impairment and are derecognized either upon disposal or when no future economic benefits are expected from their use. Any gain or loss arising on derecognition is included in earnings when the asset is derecognized.

Derecognized assets are removed from a company's accounting records either when they are disposed of or when the company determines that no future benefits are expected from their use. Any gain or loss arising on derecognition (removal of the asset from the accounting records) is included in earnings in the period the asset is disposed or in the period that it is determined the asset will no longer provide the company with value (referred to as future economic benefits).

10 IFRS 2018, IAS 16, para. 73.

A detailed schedule outlining the breakdown of the net book values for each category of PPE is found in Note 9 of Indigo's 2018 Annual Report, an excerpt of which is shown below.

9. Property, Plant, and Equipment

(thousands of Canadian dollars)	Furniture, fixtures, and equipment	Computer equipment	Leasehold improvements	Equipment under finance leases	Total
Gross carrying amount					
Balance, April 2, 2016	68,140	12,127	53,971	601	134,839
Additions	9,596	3,123	7,859	—	20,578
Transfers/reclassifications	—	(1,032)	997	—	(35)
Disposals	(28)	(17)	(1)	(465)	(511)
Assets with zero net book value	(4,950)	(2,038)	(6,931)	—	(13,919)
Balance, April 1, 2017	71,844	12,161	55,394	136	139,535
Additions	**16,726**	**6,439**	**13,915**	**—**	**37,080**
Disposals	**(1,534)**	**(133)**	**(362)**	**(136)**	**(2,165)**
Assets with zero net book value	**(3,825)**	**(1,924)**	**(4,446)**	**—**	**(10,195)**
Balance, March 31, 2018	**83,211**	**16,543**	**64,501**	**—**	**164,255**
Accumulated depreciation and impairment					
Balance, April 2, 2016	34,793	5,693	32,843	537	73,886
Depreciation	6,867	2,182	7,502	61	16,612
Disposals	(22)	(3)	(1)	(465)	(491)
Net impairment losses (reversals)	(384)	(4)	(575)	—	(963)
Assets with zero net book value	(4,950)	(2,038)	(6,931)	—	(13,919)
Transferred to assets held for sale	(430)	(1)	(217)	—	(648)
Balance, April 1, 2017	35,874	5,829	32,621	133	74,457
Depreciation	**7,551**	**2,458**	**9,062**	**3**	**19,074**
Disposals	**(872)**	**(73)**	**(314)**	**(136)**	**(1,395)**
Assets with zero net book value	**(3,825)**	**(1,924)**	**(4,446)**	**—**	**(10,195)**
Balance, March 31, 2018	**38,728**	**6,290**	**36,923**	**—**	**81,941**
Net carrying amount					
April 1, 2017	35,970	6,332	22,773	3	65,078
March 31, 2018	**44,483**	**10,253**	**27,578**	**—**	**82,314**

Reporting both the cost and accumulated depreciation of PPE helps balance sheet readers compare the assets of different companies. For example, a company holding assets costing $50,000 and accumulated depreciation of $40,000 is likely in a different situation than a company with new assets costing $10,000. The **book value** (original cost of the asset less its accumulated depreciation) is the same in both cases, but the first company may have more productive capacity available but is likely is facing the need to incur costs to replace older assets.

FACTORS IN CALCULATING DEPRECIATION

Three factors are relevant in determining depreciation:

1. Cost
2. Estimated residual value
3. Estimated useful (service) life.

Allocating Cost to Assets with Significant Components

The *cost* of PPE, as described earlier in this chapter, consists of all necessary and reasonable expenditures to acquire it and to prepare the asset for its intended use. Where an asset consists of major parts (or components) that are significant in relation to the total cost of the asset, each part or common group of parts is required to be depreciated separately under the IFRS.[11] To illustrate, assume an apartment building and land are purchased for a total cost of $1,650,000; $1,000,000 of the total $1,650,000 represented the cost of the land, which is not depreciated. It was determined that the remaining $650,000 could be broken down into the following significant parts and related costs: carpets, $25,000; appliances, $50,000; windows and doors, $100,000; cabinets, $75,000; roof $40,000; and the building structure, $360,000. As each of these significant parts has a different useful life, each major part must be depreciated separately. As discussed previously, it would be helpful to use a PPE subledger to record information related to assets and parts of assets.

Residual Value

Residual value is an estimate of the amount we expect to receive from selling the asset or trading it in at the end of its useful life or benefit period (also referred to as salvage value).[12] The total amount of depreciation to be expensed over an asset's benefit period equals the asset's cost minus its estimated residual value. The residual value is not depreciated, as the value is expected to be collected at the end of the asset's useful life.

For example, if the cost and estimated residual value of a forklift is $20,000 and $4,000, respectively, the total amount of depreciation to be expensed over the forklift's useful life is $16,000 (= $20,000 − $4,000). If we expect an asset to be traded in on a new asset, its residual value is the expected trade-in value.

Useful (Service) Life

The **useful life** of an asset is the length of time it is productively used in a company's operations or the estimated number of expected units of production. Useful life, also called **service life**, is not necessarily as long as the asset's total productive life. As an example, the productive life of a computer may be four years. Yet some companies trade in old computers for new ones every two years. In this case, these computers have a two-year useful life. This means the cost of these computers (less their expected trade-in value) is charged to depreciation expense over a two-year period.

Several variables often make the useful life of an asset hard to predict, such as wear and tear from use in operations, *inadequacy*, and *obsolescence*. **Inadequacy** refers to the condition where the capacity of a company's PPE is too small to meet the company's productive needs. **Obsolescence** refers to a condition where, because of new inventions and improvements, an asset is no longer useful in producing goods or services with a competitive advantage. A company usually disposes of an obsolete asset before it wears out.

For example, Silver Town, a Canadian movie theatre chain, purchases new projection equipment and expects its useful life to be 10 years. After using the projection equipment for two years, the technology changes from film-based projection to digital projection. The major production companies stop issuing the old film format and go entirely digital. The film-based equipment becomes obsolete and Silver Town needs to upgrade to digital projection to continue its operations. Obsolescence, like inadequacy, is hard to predict.

To predict the useful life of a new asset, a company uses its past experience or, when it has no experience with a type of asset, it relies on the experience of others or on engineering studies and judgment.

---

11 IFRS 2018, IAS 16, para. 43–47.
12 IFRS 2018 IAS 16, para. 6.

ETHICAL IMPACT

You are a newly graduated CPA student and recently accepted a job as a junior accountant responsible for managing the property, plant, and equipment subledger for the Bermuda Airport Authority (BAA). The controller has asked you to update the outdated PPE subledger by adjusting the following areas:

1. Hold off on recording depreciation for the new BorderXpress automatic passport control kiosks that were installed last year until there is a better idea of their expected useful life.
2. Extend the useful lives for the airport's emergency vehicles, including the fire trucks, ambulance, and security trucks, from 8 years to 15 years.
3. The building maintenance group is responsible for ensuring the airport facilities are clean and in good working condition. They recently had to deal with a major plumbing blockage and damage to one of the runways that was caused by invasive tree roots coming from a green space near the domestic terminal. The tree root removal and cleaning of the debris from the plumbing system and runway repair cost the airport $280,000. The controller has asked that you capitalize these expenses, including them in the property, plant, and equipment subledger and depreciating over 50 years with a $60,000 salvage value.
4. A storage facility that is expected to be removed next year and is currently not in use by BAA is being depreciated.

   Last week at lunch you overheard the director of finance talking to the CFO about the negotiation of a major loan to pay for a new international terminal expansion; he is concerned with the current high debt levels as a percentage of total assets. What, if any, are your concerns with each of the controller's requests? How would you handle the controller's requests? Who is impacted by your decision?

DEPRECIATION METHODS

There are many *depreciation methods* for allocating an asset's cost over the accounting periods in its useful life. Companies are required to select a method that most closely reflects the expected pattern of consumption of the benefits of the underlying asset.[13] The depreciation method chosen is applied consistently from period to period unless there is a change in use or a change in expected future benefits. Depreciation methods based on revenue produced from operations where the asset is being used are not permitted.[14]

We explain three methods in this section:

1. Straight-line depreciation (the most frequently used method)
2. Units-of-production depreciation
3. Declining-balance and double-declining-balance depreciation[15]

DECISION INSIGHT

Depreciation: A Critical Internal Process

According to Sage Advice, depreciation of fixed assets, the detailed process of tracking individual fixed assets and their related life cycle, "is one of the most important financial processes in any business or organization." For many businesses, they can be distributed in a wide range of geographic locations and have a vast range of policies to manage based on an extensive asset base with unique characteristics.

---

13 IFRS 2018, IAS 16, para. 62
14 IFRS 2018, IAS 16, para. 62A.
15 IFRS 2018, IAS 16, para. 62 uses the term *diminishing balance* instead of *declining balance*.

Sage Advice stresses that if a company doesn't have a clear picture of what fixed assets are included in their detailed accounting records, enabling the company to calculate depreciation effectively, "it will soon have a complex and time-consuming problem on its hands."

Many companies manually track their fixed assets through complex schedules in Microsoft Excel. Sage Advice recommends companies invest in fixed asset tracking software to better ensure this significant process is managed efficiently and effectively.

Source: https://www.sage.com/en-us/blog/better-fixed-asset-depreciation-process/, accessed October 19, 2018.

The calculations in this section use information from an athletic shoe manufacturer whose year-end is December 31. The term **depreciable cost** refers to the cost to be depreciated, which equals the total asset cost minus the estimated residual value. In particular, we look at equipment used for producing shoes. This equipment is used by manufacturers such as **Asics**, **Adidas**, **Nike**, **New Balance**, and **Saucony**, and its data for depreciation are shown in Exhibit 9.6.

EXHIBIT 9.6
Data for Shoe-Production Equipment

Cost..	$10,000
Estimated residual value	1,000
Depreciable cost	$ 9,000
Estimated useful life:	
Accounting periods	5 years
Units produced	36,000 shoes

Straight-Line Method

Straight-line depreciation charges the same amount to expense for each period of the asset's useful life.

The formula and calculation for straight-line depreciation of the production equipment just described is shown in Exhibit 9.7.

EXHIBIT 9.7
Straight-Line Depreciation Formula

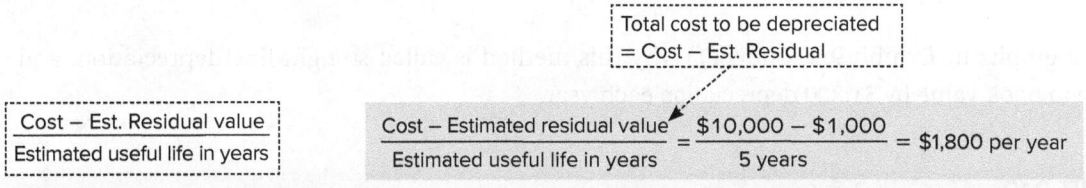

$$\frac{\text{Cost} - \text{Est. Residual value}}{\text{Estimated useful life in years}}$$

Total cost to be depreciated = Cost − Est. Residual

$$\frac{\text{Cost} - \text{Estimated residual value}}{\text{Estimated useful life in years}} = \frac{\$10,000 - \$1,000}{5 \text{ years}} = \$1,800 \text{ per year}$$

If this equipment is purchased on January 1, 2020, and used throughout its predicted useful life of five years, the straight-line method allocates an equal amount of depreciation to each of the years 2020 through 2024. We make the following adjusting entry at the end of each of these five years to record straight-line depreciation of this equipment:

Dec.	31	Depreciation Expense..	1,800	
		Accumulated Depreciation, Equipment....		1,800
		To record annual depreciation over its five-year useful life.		

The $1,800 Depreciation Expense appears on the income statement among operating expenses. This entry credits Accumulated Depreciation, Equipment, a contra account to the Equipment account under the property, plant, and equipment asset line item on the balance sheet.

The net balance sheet amounts are the asset's book values for each of those years and are calculated as the asset's original cost less its accumulated depreciation. At the end of year two, its book value is $6,400 and is reported in the PPE section of the balance sheet as shown in Exhibit 9.8:

EXHIBIT 9.8

Balance Sheet Presentation After Two Years of Depreciation

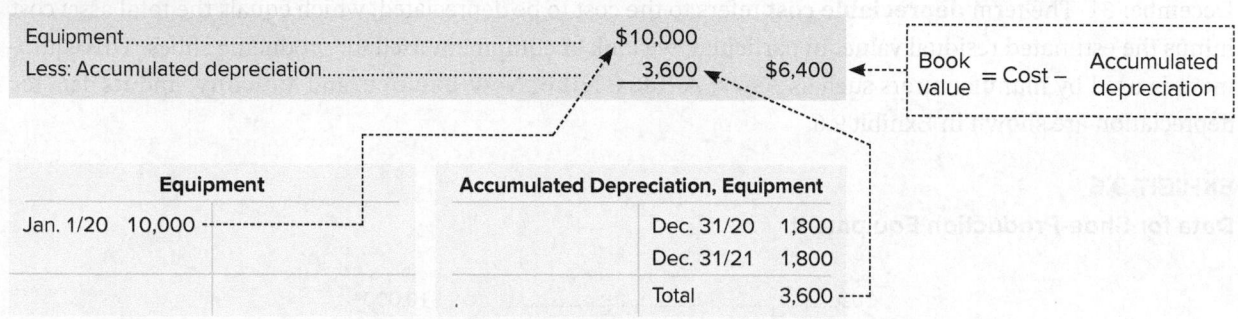

Instead of listing the cost less accumulated depreciation, many balance sheets show PPE *net* of accumulated depreciation. The *net* means *after* accumulated depreciation has been subtracted from the cost of the asset. Recall that cost less accumulated depreciation is *book value*. Exhibit 9.9 shows this alternative form of presentation for the equipment of Exhibit 9.8 (cost of $10,000 less accumulated depreciation of $3,600).

EXHIBIT 9.9

Alternative Balance Sheet Presentation

The graphs in Exhibit 9.10 show (1) why this method is called straight-line depreciation, and (2) the decline in book value by $1,800 depreciation each year.

EXHIBIT 9.10

Financial Statement Effects of Straight-Line Depreciation

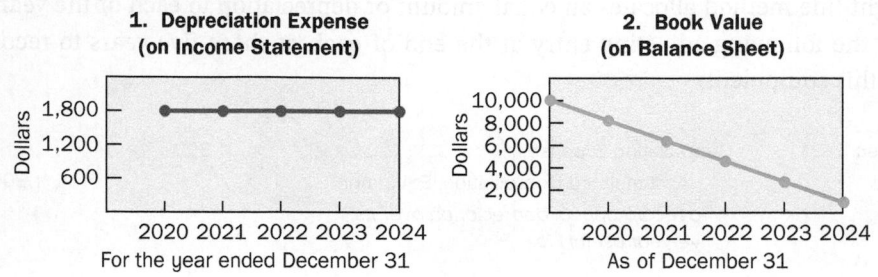

The straight-line depreciation *rate* is calculated as 100% divided by the number of periods in the asset's useful life. In the case of our shoe production equipment, this rate is 20% (100% ÷ 5 years). We use this rate and other information on the equipment to calculate the machine's *straight-line depreciation schedule* shown in Exhibit 9.11.

EXHIBIT 9.11
Straight-Line Depreciation Schedule

| | Depreciation for the Period | | | End of Period | |
Period	Cost to Be Depreciated	Depreciation Rate	Depreciation Expense	Accumulated Depreciation	Book Value
	—	—	—	—	10,000*
2020	$9,000**	20%	**$1,800**	$1,800	8,200
2021	9,000	20	**1,800**	3,600	6,400
2022	9,000	20	**1,800**	5,400	4,600
2023	9,000	20	**1,800**	7,200	2,800
2024	9,000	20	**1,800**	9,000	**1,000**

*Cost on January 1, 2020
**$10,000 − $1,000

Note the three key features of the straight-line method:

1. Depreciation expense is the same each period.
2. Accumulated depreciation is the sum of current and prior periods' depreciation expense.
3. Book value declines each period until it equals the residual value at the end of its useful life.

Straight-line is by far the most frequently applied depreciation method in financial reporting.

Units-of-Production Method

If PPE are used the same amount in each accounting period, the straight-line method produces a systematic allocation of the asset's cost over its useful life. The use of some assets varies greatly from one accounting period to the next. A builder, for instance, may use a specific piece of construction equipment for a month and then not use it again for several months.

When use of equipment varies from period to period, the units-of-production depreciation method can provide a better allocation of the asset's cost over its useful life. **Units-of-production depreciation** charges a varying amount to expense for each period of an asset's useful life directly linked to its usage.

A two-step process is used to calculate units-of-production depreciation:

1. Calculate the depreciation per unit by subtracting the asset's residual value from its total cost, and then divide by the total number of units expected to be produced during its useful life. Units of production can be expressed in units of product or in any other unit of measure such as hours used or kilometres driven. This gives us the amount of depreciation per unit of service provided by the asset.
2. Calculate depreciation expense for the period by multiplying the units used in the period by the depreciation per unit.

Exhibit 9.12 shows the formula and calculation for units-of-production depreciation for the production equipment described in Exhibit 9.6 as having an estimated production capacity of 36,000 units (assume 7,000 shoes produced in 2020).

EXHIBIT 9.12
Units-of-Production Depreciation Formula

Step 1:

$$\text{Depreciation per unit} = \frac{\text{Cost} - \text{Est. residual value}}{\text{Total est. units}} = \text{Deprec. per unit}$$

$$\text{Depreciation per unit} = \frac{\text{Cost} - \text{Estimated residual value}}{\text{Total estimated units of production}} = \frac{\$10,000 - \$1,000}{36,000 \text{ units}}$$

$$= \$0.25 \text{ per shoe}$$

Step 2:

Depreciation expense = Depreciation per unit × Units produced in period
$\$0.25$ per shoe × 7,000 shoes = **$1,750**

Using the production estimates for the equipment, we calculate the *units-of-production depreciation schedule* shown in Exhibit 9.13. If the equipment produces 7,000 shoes in 2020, its first year, depreciation for 2020 is $1,750. If the equipment produces 8,000 shoes in 2021, depreciation for 2021 is $2,000, calculated as 8,000 shoes times $0.25 per shoe.

EXHIBIT 9.13
Units-of-Production Depreciation Schedule

| | Depreciation for the Period | | | End of Period | |
Period	Number of Units	Depreciation Per Unit	Depreciation Expense	Accumulated Depreciation	Book Value
	—	—	—	—	$10,000*
2020	7,000	$0.25	**$1,750**	$1,750	8,250
2021	8,000	0.25	**2,000**	3,750	6,250
2022	9,000	0.25	**2,250**	6,000	4,000
2023	7,000	0.25	**1,750**	7,750	2,250
2024	6,000**	0.25	**1,250***	9,000	**1,000**

*Cost on January 1, 2020
**6,000 units were actually produced, but the maximum number of units on which depreciation can be calculated in 2021 is 5,000 [36,000 total estimated units less 31,000 units depreciated to date (7,000 + 8,000 + 9,000 + 7,000)]. Recall that an asset must not be depreciated below its residual value.
***5,000 × $0.25 = $1,250

Note that depreciation expense depends on unit output, that accumulated depreciation is the sum of current and prior-periods' depreciation expense, and that book value declines each period until it equals residual value at the end of the asset's useful life.

The units-of-production depreciation method is not as frequently applied as straight-line. **Suncor Energy Inc.** uses units-of-production in addition to straight-line as reported in the following excerpt of its December 31, 2017, annual report:

Exploration and Evaluation assets are not subject to depreciation, depletion and amortization. Once transferred to oil and gas properties within Property, Plant and Equipment and commercial production commences, these costs are depleted on a unit-of-production basis over proved developed reserves, with the exception of exploration and evaluation costs associated with oil sands mines, which are depreciated on a straight-line basis over the life of the mine, and property acquisition costs, which are depleted over proved reserves.

Capital expenditures are not depreciated or depleted until assets are substantially complete and ready for their intended use.

Costs to develop oil and gas properties other than certain oil sands mining assets, including costs of dedicated infrastructure, such as well pads and wellhead equipment, are depleted on a unit-of-production basis over proved developed reserves. A portion of these costs may not be depleted if they relate to undeveloped reserves.... Costs to develop and construct oil sands mines are depreciated on a straight-line basis over the life of the mine.

Major components of Property, Plant and Equipment are depreciated on a straight-line basis over their expected useful lives.

Oil sands upgraders, extraction plants and mine facilities	20 to 40 years
Oil sands mine equipment	5 to 15 years
Oil sands in situ processing facilities	30 years
Power generation and utility plants	30 to 40 years
Refineries and other processing plants	20 to 40 years
Marketing and other distribution assets	10 to 40 years

The costs of major inspection, overhaul and turnaround activities that are capitalized are depreciated on a straight-line basis over the period to the next scheduled activity, which varies from two to five years.

Depreciation, depletion and amortization rates are reviewed annually or when events or conditions occur that impact capitalized costs, reserves or estimated service lives.

Source: Suncor Energy Inc., http://www.suncor.com/investor-centre/financial-reports/annual-disclosure

Accelerated Depreciation Methods

An **accelerated depreciation method** provides higher depreciation expenses in the early years of an asset's life and lower charges in later years. While several accelerated methods are used in financial reporting, the most common is **declining-balance depreciation**, which uses depreciation rates of up to twice the straight-line rate and applies it to the asset's beginning-of-period book value. A standard percentage rate is selected and applied each year to the carrying amount of the asset at the beginning of the year. Because book value *declines* each period, the amount of depreciation also declines each period.

Double-declining-balance depreciation (DDB) or **diminishing-balance depreciation** is applied in two steps:[16]

1. Calculate the double-declining-balance rate (= 2 ÷ Estimated years of useful life), and
2. Calculate depreciation expense by multiplying the rate by the asset's beginning-of-period book value.

---

16 The double-declining-balance method is also described as being *twice the straight-line rate* because it can be alternatively applied as follows to get the same results:

1. Calculate the asset's straight-line depreciation rate (100% ÷ Estimated useful life in years),

2. Double it, and

3. Calculate depreciation expense by multiplying this doubled rate by the asset's beginning-of-period book value.

> **Important Tip:**
>
> It is important to note that unlike the straight-line and units-of-production methods, residual value is not used in these calculations. We adjust depreciation expense in the final year to depreciate the asset down to the residual value, as illustrated in Exhibit 9.15.

Returning to the shoe production equipment, we can apply the double-declining-balance method to calculate its depreciation expense. Exhibit 9.14 shows this formula and its first-year calculation for the production equipment. The abbreviated two-step process is:

1. 2 divided by the estimated useful life, and
2. Calculate annual depreciation expense as the declining-balance rate multiplied by the book value at the beginning of each period (see Exhibit 9.15).

EXHIBIT 9.14

Double-Declining-Balance Depreciation Formula

Double-declining-balance depreciation $= \text{Book value} \times \dfrac{2}{n}$,

where n = estimated useful life

Step 1:

Double-declining-balance rate $= 2 \div \text{Estimated useful life} = 2 \div 5 \text{ years} = 0.40 \text{ or } 40\%$

Step 2:

Depreciation expense $=$ Double-declining-balance rate $\times$ Beginning period book value
$= 40\% \times \$10{,}000 = \textbf{\$4{,}000}$

EXHIBIT 9.15

Double-Declining-Balance Depreciation Schedule

Period	Beginning-of-Period Book Value	Depreciation Rate	Depreciation Expense	Accumulated Depreciation	Book Value
—	—	—	—	—	$10,000*
2020	$10,000	40%	**$4,000**	$4,000	6,000
2021	6,000	40	**2,400**	6,400	3,600
2022	3,600	40	**1,440**	7,840	2,160
2023	2,160	40	**864**	8,704	1,296
2024	1,296	40	**296****	9,000**	**1,000**

*Cost on January 1, 2020
**Year 2024 depreciation is $1,296 − $1,000 = $296. This is because maximum accumulated depreciation equals cost minus residual as we depreciate the asset only up to the residual value.

The *double-declining-balance depreciation schedule* is shown in Exhibit 9.15. The schedule follows the formula except in the year 2024, when depreciation expense is $296. The $296 is calculated by subtracting the $1,000 residual value from the $1,296 book value at the beginning of the fifth year. This is done because an asset is *never* depreciated *below* its residual value. If we had used the $518.40 (40% × $1,296) for depreciation expense in 2024, then ending book value would equal $777.60, which is less than the $1,000 residual value.

> Maximum accumulated depreciation*
> = Cost − Residual
> *ALTERNATIVELY*
> Minimum book value*
> = Residual value
> *regardless of method*

Depreciation for Income Tax Reporting

The rules a company follows for financial reporting purposes are usually different from the rules it follows for income tax reporting purposes. Financial accounting aims to report useful information on financial performance and position, whereas income tax accounting reflects government-established requirements developed to raise public revenues and encourage public interests. Differences between these two bases are normal and expected. Depreciation is an example of one of these common differences between financial statement profit and taxable income.

The *Income Tax Act* requires that companies use an accelerated depreciation method for calculating the maximum *capital cost allowance* that may be claimed in any period. **Capital cost allowance (CCA)** is the term used to describe depreciation for tax purposes. CCA reduces taxable income in the early years of an asset's life because depreciation expense is greatest in the early years. The money a company saves in taxes in the early years means a company has the resources to earn additional profit. The *Income Tax Act* specifies the rates for various groups of assets. For example, a rate of 20% would be used for general machinery and equipment, and a rate of 4% for most buildings.

Comparing Depreciation Methods

Exhibit 9.16 shows depreciation expense for the shoe-production equipment under each of the three depreciation methods.

EXHIBIT 9.16

Depreciation Methods Compared: Annual Depreciation Expense

Period	Straight-Line Cost − Est. residual Est. useful life	Units-of-Production Cost − Est. residual Total est. units × Actual units of production produced in period	Double-Declining-Balance Book value × 2/n, where n = Est. useful life
2020	$ 1,800	$ 1,750	$ 4,000
2021	1,800	2,000	2,400
2022	1,800	2,250	1,440
2023	1,800	1,750	864
2024	1,800	1,250	296
	$9,000	**$9,000**	**$9,000**

While the amount of depreciation expense per period is different for different methods, *total* depreciation expense is the same ($9,000) for the machine's useful life. Each method starts with a total cost of $10,000 and ends with a residual value of $1,000. The difference is the *pattern* in depreciation expense over the useful life. This pattern is graphically represented in Exhibit 9.17. The book value of the asset when using straight-line is always greater than book value from using double-declining-balance, except at the beginning and end of an asset's useful life. Also, the straight-line method yields a steady pattern of depreciation expense, while units-of-production does not because it depends on the number of units produced. All of these methods are acceptable as they allocate cost in a rational and systematic manner.

EXHIBIT 9.17

Graphic Comparison of Depreciation Methods

CHECKPOINT

6. On January 1, 2020, Laser Renew Inc. pays $77,000 to purchase office furniture with a residual value of zero. The furniture's useful life is somewhere between 7 and 10 years. What is the 2020 straight-line depreciation on the furniture using (a) a 7-year useful life, and (b) a 10-year useful life?

7. What is the meaning of the accounting term "depreciation"?

8. Laser Renew Inc. purchases a new machine for $96,000 on January 1, 2020. Its predicted useful life is 5 years or 100,000 units of product, and its residual value is $8,000. During 2020, 10,000 units of product are produced. Calculate the book value of this machine on December 31, 2020, assuming (1) straight-line depreciation, and (2) units-of-production depreciation.

9. A specialized piece of laser therapy equipment was purchased for $340,000. Its components A, B, and C had respective costs estimated to be 20%, 50%, and 30% of the total cost. The estimated useful lives of the components were determined to be 4 years, 8 years, and 15 years, respectively. The residual value for each component was $0. Calculate the annual depreciation for each component assuming straight-line.

Do Quick Study questions: QS 9-5, QS 9-6, QS 9-7, QS 9-8, QS 9-9

PARTIAL-YEAR DEPRECIATION

LO3 Explain and calculate depreciation for partial years.

Assets are purchased and disposed of at various times during an accounting period. When an asset is purchased (or disposed of) at a time other than the beginning or end of a period, depreciation is recorded only for the part of the year the asset was in use. This is to make sure that the year of purchase or the year of disposal is charged with its appropriate share of the asset's depreciation. There are different ways to account for the depreciation for partial years. The most common method used is the nearest whole month. We are going to look at two methods:

1. Nearest whole month, and

2. Half-year convention.

Nearest Whole Month

When calculating depreciation for partial years to the nearest whole month, depreciation for a month is calculated if the asset was in use for more than half of that month. To illustrate, let's return to the athletic shoe production equipment. Assume this equipment is purchased and placed in service on April 8, 2020, and the annual accounting period ends on December 31. This equipment costs $10,000, has a useful life of five years, and has a residual value of $1,000. Because this equipment is purchased and used for more than half of April plus all of May through December, in 2020 the amount of depreciation reported is based on nine months (if the purchase date had been April 28, the depreciation would have been calculated for eight months since the asset was not in use for more than half of April). Depreciation is not calculated by taking into account specific days of use because this would imply that depreciation is precise, when in fact it is based on estimates of the useful life and residual values. Using straight-line depreciation, we calculate nine months' depreciation of $1,350 as follows:

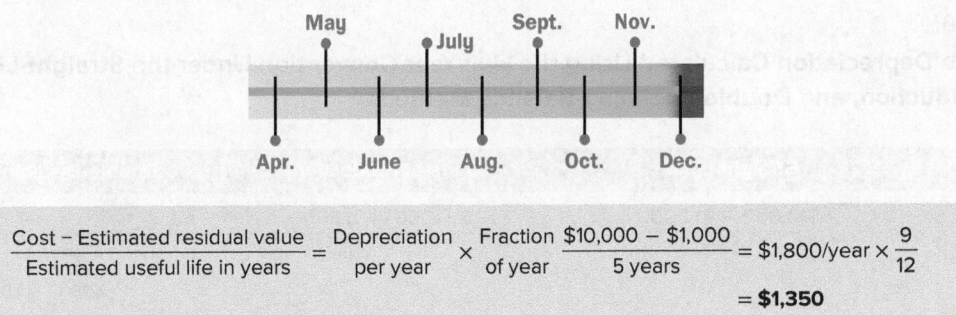

$$\frac{\text{Cost} - \text{Estimated residual value}}{\text{Estimated useful life in years}} = \frac{\text{Depreciation}}{\text{per year}} \times \frac{\text{Fraction}}{\text{of year}} \quad \frac{\$10,000 - \$1,000}{5 \text{ years}} = \$1,800/\text{year} \times \frac{9}{12}$$
$$= \mathbf{\$1,350}$$

A similar calculation is necessary when disposal of an asset occurs during a year. As an example, let's suppose the equipment described above is sold on June 4, 2024. Depreciation for 2024 is recorded for the period January 1 through June 4, or five months. Because the asset was held for less than half of June, depreciation is not calculated for June. This partial year's depreciation, calculated to the nearest whole month, is:

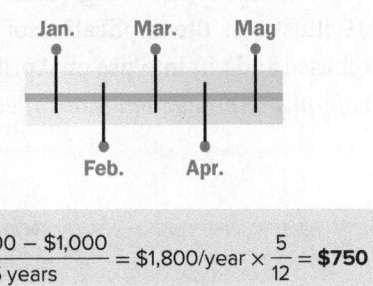

$$\frac{\$10,000 - \$1,000}{5 \text{ years}} = \$1,800/\text{year} \times \frac{5}{12} = \mathbf{\$750}$$

Exhibit 9.18 demonstrates the calculations for a partial year's depreciation to the nearest month for the units-of-production and double-declining-balance methods. *Notice that the depreciation expense calculation for units-of-production is not affected by the partial year.* This is because the units-of-production method is a function of use, not of time.

Half-Year Convention

For companies that have a large number of PPE expenditures year after year, tracking when individual assets were put into use and then calculating depreciation to the nearest month can be a costly process. Because this kind of accuracy would not necessarily increase the usefulness of information related to depreciation, the *materiality principle* allows us the flexibility to use a method more appropriate for the situation, such as the *half-year convention*. When calculating depreciation for partial years using the **half-year convention**,

EXHIBIT 9.18

Partial Year's Depreciation Calculated to Nearest Month Under the Units-of-Production and Double-Declining-Balance Methods

Date of Purchase	Units-of-Production	Double-Declining-Balance
April 8, 2020	$\dfrac{\$10,000 - \$1,000}{36,000 \text{ units}}$	Rate $= \dfrac{2}{5} = 0.40$ or 40%
		40% × $10,000
	$= \$0.25/\text{unit} \times 7,000 \text{ units} = \mathbf{\$1,750}$	$= \$4,000/\text{year } \dfrac{9}{12} = \mathbf{\$3,000}$

EXHIBIT 9.19

Partial Year's Depreciation Calculated Using the Half-Year Convention Under the Straight-Line, Units-of-Production, and Double-Declining-Balance Methods

Date of Purchase	Straight-Line	Units-of-Production	Double-Declining-Balance
April 8, 2020	$\dfrac{\$10,000 - \$1,000}{5 \text{ years}}$	$\dfrac{\$10,000 - \$1,000}{36,000 \text{ units}}$	Rate $= \dfrac{2}{5} = 0.40$ or 40%
			40% × $10,000
	$= \$1,800/\text{year} \times \dfrac{6}{12} = \mathbf{\$900}$	$= \$0.25/\text{unit} \times 7,000 \text{ units} = \mathbf{\$1,750}$	$= \$4,000/\text{year} \times \dfrac{6}{12} = \mathbf{\$2,000}$

six months' depreciation is recorded for the partial period regardless of when during the period the asset was acquired or disposed of. Exhibit 9.19 illustrates the application of the half-year convention assuming the shoe-production equipment was purchased and put into use on April 8, 2020.

Notice again that the calculation of units-of-production is not affected by partial years.

 CHECKPOINT

10. Why is depreciation for a partial year not calculated to the nearest day?

Do Quick Study questions: QS 9-10, QS 9-11, QS 9-12

REVISING DEPRECIATION RATES

LO4 Explain and calculate revised depreciation.

Depreciation is based on the original cost of an asset, estimated residual value, and estimated useful life. If the cost of the asset changes because the estimates for residual value and/or useful life are adjusted or because of a betterment, *revised depreciation* for current and future periods must be calculated.

Revising Depreciation Rates When There Is a Change in the Estimated Residual Value and/or Estimated Useful Life

Because depreciation is based on predictions of residual value and useful life, depreciation expense is an estimate. If our estimate of an asset's useful life and/or residual value changes, we use the new estimate(s) to calculate **revised depreciation** for the current and future periods. This means we calculate a new depreciation expense calculation by spreading the cost that has not yet been depreciated over the remaining useful life. This approach is used for all depreciation methods.

Let's return to our athletic shoe production equipment using straight-line depreciation. At the beginning of this asset's third year, its book value is $6,400, calculated as:

Cost..	$10,000
Less: Prior two years' accumulated depreciation (2020, 2021).......	3,600*
Book value...	$ 6,400

*Calculated as $1,800 per year as determined above using the straight-line approach for two years.

At the beginning of its third year, in 2022, the predicted number of years remaining in its useful life changes from three to four years and its estimate of residual value changes from $1,000 to $400. Depreciation for each of the equipment's four remaining years is now recalculated as shown in Exhibit 9.20.

EXHIBIT 9.20

Calculating Revised Depreciation Rates When There Is a Change in Estimated Residual Value and/or Estimated Useful Life

$$\frac{\text{Remaining book value} - \text{Revised residual value}}{\text{Revised remaining useful life}} = \frac{6,400 - 400}{4 \text{ years}} = \textbf{1,500 per year}$$

This means $1,500 of depreciation expense is recorded for the equipment at the end of 2022 through 2025 the remaining four years of its useful life.

Period	Straight-Line Method with Revised Useful Life
2020	$1,800
2021	1,800
2022	1,500
2023	1,500
2024	1,500
2025	1,500

We do not revise the previous years' depreciation expense, as these expenses reflected the best information available at the time they were recorded, based on management's estimate.

Revising estimates of the useful life or residual value of an asset is referred to as a **change in an accounting estimate**. A change in an accounting estimate results when a review of the asset shows that "expectations differ from previous estimates."[17] Accountants refer to change in an accounting estimate as being applied

---

17 IFRS 2018, IAS 16, para. 51.

prospectively. This means that it is reflected in current and future financial statements only; no adjustments are made to prior-year financial statements.[18]

Revising Depreciation Rates When There Is a Betterment

We also calculate revised depreciation if the cost of the asset changes because of a betterment, such as the installation of a new engine. Depreciation is the allocation of an asset's cost. Betterments cause the cost of an asset to change. Revised depreciation must therefore be calculated when there is a betterment.

Addition of a Component: Revise Depreciation for New Cost and Update to Useful Life/Residual Value

A betterment can be the *addition* of a component to an existing asset or the *replacement* or *overhaul* of a component. In the case where there is an addition, such as adding a computer panel to a machine to improve its efficiency, the cost of the addition is debited to the appropriate PPE account and depreciation for the asset is revised to incorporate the additional cost and any change in the estimated useful life and/or residual value.[19]

For example, on January 3, 2020, Natural Foods paid $15,000 cash for a refrigeration unit installed on its delivery van to improve the shelf life of its products upon reaching the customer. The delivery van had a book value of $32,000 at December 31, 2019, and an estimated remaining useful life of 10 years and no residual value. Assume the refrigeration unit had an estimated life of five years and no residual value and that its addition to the delivery van did not change the van's useful life or residual value. The entries to record the addition of the refrigeration unit on January 3 and revised depreciation at December 31, Natural Foods's year-end, are:

2020				
Jan.	3	Delivery Van—Refrigeration Uni............................	15,000	
		Cash		15,000
		To record addition of refrigeration unit to the van.		
Dec.	31	Depreciation Expense, Van	6,200	
		Accumulated Depreciation, Van.................		6,200
		To record revised depreciation on the van;		
		Van: $32,000 ÷ 10 yrs = $3,200;		
		Refrigeration unit: $15,000 ÷ 5 yrs		
		= $3,000; $3,200 + $3,000		
		= $6,200 total depreciation.		

Replacement of a Component: Remove Old Asset From Books + Addition of New Asset + Revised Depreciation

When a betterment results in the replacement of a component of PPE, the cost and accumulated depreciation of the replaced component must be removed from the accounting records and any resulting loss or gain must be recorded. To demonstrate the accounting entries, assume that on January 2, 2020, Natural Foods purchased equipment with several components including an engine. The engine had a cost of $50,000, an estimated useful life of five years, and a residual value of $8,000. On January 5, 2022, the engine suffered major damage and was replaced with a new one for $55,000 on account with an estimated useful life of six years and residual value of $7,000. If the old engine was scrapped (no cash was received),

---

18 IFRS 2018, IAS 8, para. 36.
19 IFRS 2018, IAS 16, para. 37

two entries are required on January 5, 2022. First, the old engine must be removed from the accounting records, which is recorded as:

2022			
Jan.	5	Accum. Deprec., Equipment—Engine................	16,800	
		Loss on Disposal..	33,200	
		Equipment—Engine (old)		50,000

To record the disposal of the old engine;
$50,000 – $8,000 = $42,000; $42,000 ÷
5 yrs = $8,400/yr deprec.; $8,400 × 2 yrs
= $16,800 accum. deprec.

> When the old engine is disposed of, the accumulated depreciation balance and cost of the old engine must both be removed from the accounting records.

Because the asset was not fully depreciated at the time of the replacement and it was scrapped, the $33,200 book value (calculated as the $50,000 cost less the $16,800 accumulated depreciation) represents a loss. Losses are reported separately from Revenue in the *Other Revenues and Expenses* section of the income statement.[20]

The purchase of the new engine on the same date must also be recorded as shown below:

2022			
Jan.	5	Equipment—Engine (new).....................................	55,000	
		Accounts Payable..		55,000

To record the new engine on the equipment.

These two entries could be combined as:

2022			
Jan.	5	Accum. Deprec., Equipment—Engine................	16,800	
		Equipment—Engine (new).................................	55,000	
		Loss on Disposal	33,200	
		Accounts Payable..		55,000
		Equipment—Engine (old)		50,000

To record the disposal of the old engine
and the acquisition of the new engine.

If we assume the old engine was sold for $5,000 cash instead of being scrapped at the time of replacement, the combined entry would be:

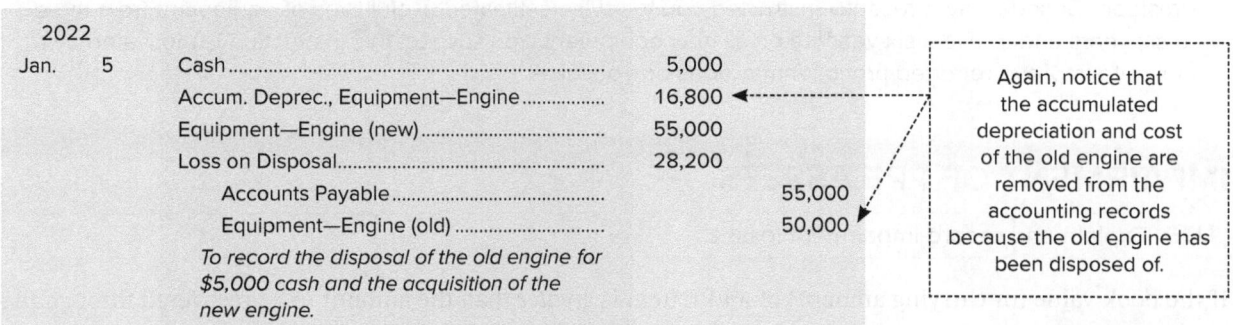

2022			
Jan.	5	Cash...	5,000	
		Accum. Deprec., Equipment—Engine................	16,800	
		Equipment—Engine (new).....................................	55,000	
		Loss on Disposal..	28,200	
		Accounts Payable..		55,000
		Equipment—Engine (old)		50,000

To record the disposal of the old engine for
$5,000 cash and the acquisition of the
new engine.

> Again, notice that the accumulated depreciation and cost of the old engine are removed from the accounting records because the old engine has been disposed of.

Notice that the $28,200 *Loss on Disposal* represents the difference between the $33,200 book value of the component being replaced and the $5,000 cash proceeds.

---

20 IFRS 2018, IAS 16, para. 68.

Depreciation on the equipment at year-end would be revised to incorporate depreciation on the replacement component. For example, depreciation on the new engine at December 31, 2022, would be:

$$\frac{\$55,000 - \$7,000}{6 \text{ years}} = \$8,000$$

When a betterment occurs partway through the accounting period, partial-period depreciation must be calculated on the component being replaced up to the time of the replacement to update the accumulated depreciation account. Revised depreciation for the year would be based on the new component for the part of the year it was in use. These calculations are illustrated in Appendix 9A.

 CHECKPOINT

11. In early January 2020, a cell phone repair shop acquires equipment at a cost of $3,800. The company estimates this equipment to have a useful life of three years and a residual value of $200. Early in 2022, the controller at the shop changes its estimate to a total four-year useful life and zero residual value. Using straight-line depreciation, what is depreciation expense on this equipment for the year ended December 31, 2022?

12. Assume the Fairmont Hotel had a desktop computer with a book value at its December 31, 2019, year-end of $5,000. The computer had an estimated remaining useful life of two years and a $500 residual value. On January 12, 2020, a second monitor costing $800 was added to the computer to enhance the booking agent's productivity. The second monitor had an estimated life of two years and no residual value. Record the addition on January 12 and the revised depreciation on the computer at December 31. Assume the second monitor was purchased on account.

Do Quick Study questions: QS 9-13, QS 9-14

 DECISION MAKER   Answer—End of chapter

Controller Constraints

Assume you are the controller for Cabinet World in the year 2020. Cabinet World has struggled financially for more than two years, losing market share to three key players in its market (IKEA, Home Depot, and Lowes) and there are no signs of improvement. The company's operations require major investments in equipment, and depreciation is a large item in calculating profit. Cabinet World normally requires frequent replacements of equipment, and equipment is typically depreciated over three years. Cabinet World's President Belinda Hayer recently instructed you to revise estimated useful lives of equipment from three to six years and to use a six-year life on all new equipment. You suspect this instruction is motivated by a desire to improve reported profit. What actions do you take?

IMPAIRMENT OF PPE ASSETS

LO5 Explain and record impairment losses.

If the book value (or carrying amount) of a PPE item is *greater* than the amount to be recovered through the asset's use or sale, the difference is recognized as an **impairment loss**, as the asset's value is impaired.[21] Impairment can result from a variety of situations that include a significant decline in an asset's market value or a major adverse effect caused by technological, economic, or legal factors. PPE must be assessed for impairment

---

21   IFRS 2018, IAS 36, para. 8.

annually to ensure that assets and profit are not overstated. When an impairment loss is recorded, revised depreciation must be calculated and recorded in future periods because of the decrease in the carrying amount of the asset caused by the impairment loss.[22]

To demonstrate, assume that on its December 31, 2020, adjusted trial balance, **Fitbit, Inc.** has specialized manufacturing equipment with a cost of $50,000 and accumulated depreciation of $27,000. As part of its December 31, 2020, year-end procedures, Fitbit, Inc. performed an annual asset impairment assessment and found that the equipment had a recoverable value of $15,000. Because the $23,000 book value of the equipment ($50,000 cost less $27,000 accumulated depreciation) is greater than the $15,000 recoverable value, the $8,000 difference is recorded as an impairment loss on December 31, 2020, as follows:

2020				
Dec.	31	Impairment Loss...	8,000	
		Equipment...		8,000
		To record impairment loss on equipment.		

At December 31, 2021, revised depreciation must be calculated and recorded on the equipment because of the impairment loss recorded in 2020. Assuming Fitbit, Inc. applies straight-line depreciation and that the remaining useful life was four years and the residual value of the equipment was zero, revised depreciation is:

2021				
Dec.	31	Depreciation Expense, Equipment.....................	3,750	
		Accum. Deprec., Equipment........................		3,750
		To record revised depreciation caused by		
		impairment loss; $50,000 − $8,000		
		= $42,000 revised cost of equipment;		
		$42,000 − $27,000 = $15,000 remaining		
		book value; $15,000 ÷ 4 years = $3,750		
		revised depreciation.		

Impairment losses may be reversed in subsequent periods if the recoverable amount of the asset exceeds the book value (or carrying amount). Reversal of impairment losses is beyond the scope of this course and is covered in more advanced courses.

◎ CHECKPOINT

13. At its December 31, 2020, year-end, Solartech Ltd. assessed its assets for impairment and found that two machines had recoverable amounts that differed from book value: Machine A and Machine B had respective book values of $107,000 and $238,000, and recoverable values of $136,000 and $92,000, respectively. Assuming the business had recorded no impairment losses in previous years, what accounting treatment is required for the impairment loss?

Do Quick Study question: QS 9-15

---

22   IFRS 2018, IAS 36, para. 63.

Mid-Chapter Demonstration Problem

Part 1

Chaps Bikes purchased manufacturing equipment for $160,000 on September 3, 2020. The estimated life of the equipment is 10 years but due to technological advances, Chaps expects to replace the equipment in five years when the residual value is estimated to be $40,000. Chaps's year-end is December 31.

Required

Complete a schedule similar to the following for each year of the asset's estimated useful life using the (a) straight-line, and (b) double-declining-balance methods (round calculations to the nearest whole dollar).

	2020	2021	2022	2023	2024	2025
Cost..						
Less: Accumulated depreciation........................						
Book value						
Depreciation expense...................................						

Analysis Component:

Which depreciation method, straight-line or double-declining-balance, will give the highest total profit over the asset's useful life? Explain your answer.

Part 2

Chaps Bikes purchased a sales vehicle for $30,000 on August 21, 2020. The company planned to use it for 100,000 km or about three years and then trade it in for $10,000. The actual kilometres driven were:

2020	10,250
2021	33,700
2022	37,980
2023	19,710

Required

Complete a schedule similar to that required in Part 1 using the units-of-production method.

Part 3

On March 21, 2018, Chaps purchased a customized paint machine for $60,000 and it was estimated to have a useful life of six years and a residual value of $15,000. During 2020, it was determined that the total useful life of the machine should be revised to eight years and the residual value decreased to $5,000.

Required

Record depreciation expense on the machine for the year ended December 31, 2020.

Part 4

As part of its December 31, 2020, year-end procedures, Chaps assessed its assets for impairment and found that a piece of its gear manufacturing equipment had a recoverable value of $14,000 and a remaining useful life of two years and residual value of zero. The December 31, 2020, adjusted trial balance showed that the equipment had a cost of $114,000 and accumulated depreciation of $62,000. Chaps recorded no impairment losses in previous years.

Required

Record the impairment loss at December 31, 2020, and the revised depreciation at December 31, 2021.

SOLUTION

Part 1

a. Straight-line

	2020	2021	2022	2023	2024	2025
Cost...	160,000	160,000	160,000	160,000	160,000	160,000
Less: Accum. deprec................................	8,000[1]	32,000[2]	56,000	80,000	104,000	120,000
Book value	152,000	128,000	104,000	80,000	56,000	40,000
Depreciation expense.............................	8,000[1]	24,000[3]	24,000	24,000	24,000	16,000[4]

[1]($160,000 − $40,000)/5 years = $24,000/year × $\frac{4}{12}$ = $8,000
[2]$8,000 + $24,000 = $32,000
[3]($160,000 − $40,000)/5 years = $24,000/year
[4]($160,000 − $40,000)/5 years = $24,000/year × $\frac{8}{12}$ = $16,000

b. Double-declining-balance

	2020	2021	2022	2023	2024	2025
Cost...	160,000	160,000	160,000	160,000	160,000	160,000
Less: Accum. deprec................................	21,333	76,800[2]	110,080	120,000	120,000	120,000
Book value	138,667	83,200	49,920	40,000	40,000	40,000
Depreciation expense.............................	21,333[3]	55,467[4]	33,280[5]	9,920[6]	-0-	-0-

[1]Double declining rate = 2/5 = 40%
[2]40% × $160,000 = $64,000 × $\frac{4}{12}$ = $21,333
[3]$21,333 + $55,467 = $76,800
[4]40% × $138,667 = $55,467
[5]40% × $83,200 = $33,280
[6]40% × $49,920 = $19,968. However, this exceeds the maximum accumulated depreciation allowed of $120,000 (cost less residual of $160,000 − $40,000). Therefore, depreciation expense in 2020 is $9,920 (= $120,000 maximum allowable accumulated depreciation less $110,080 accumulated depreciation to date).

Analysis Component:

Because both methods will have a total depreciation expense of $120,000 over the life of the asset, total profit over the asset's useful life will be identical regardless of depreciation method used. Over the life of the asset, the straight-line approach provides a consistent expense, whereas the double-declining-balance method charges more depreciation in the early years of the manufacturing equipment's life.

Part 2

	2020	2021	2022	2023
Cost..	30,000	30,000	30,000	30,000
Less: Accum. deprec.............................	2,050	8,790^2	16,386	20,000
Book value	27,950	21,210	13,614	10,000
Depreciation expense............................	2,050^1	6,740^3	7,596^4	3,614^5

^{1}($30,000 − $10,000)/100,000 km = $0.20/km; 10,250 km × $0.20/km = $2,050
^{2}$2,050 + $6,740 = $8,790
^{3}33,700 km × $0.20/km = $6,740
^{4}37,980 km × $0.20/km = $7,596
^{5}19,710 km × $0.20/km = $3,942. However, this would exceed the maximum allowed accumulated depreciation of $20,000 (= $30,000 − $10,000). Therefore, depreciation expense is limited to $3,614 (= $20,000 − $16,386).

Part 3

2020			
Dec. 31	Depreciation Expense, Equipment.....................	6,700	
	Accumulated Depreciation, Equipment....		6,700
	To record revised depreciation.		

Calculations:

1. Depreciation expense for 2018:

$$\frac{\$60,000 - \$15,000}{\text{years}} = \$7,500/\text{year} \times \frac{9}{12} = \$5,625$$

2. Accumulated depreciation at December 31, 2019:

$$\$5,625 + \$7,500 = \$13,125$$

3. Revised depreciation for 2020:

$$\frac{(\$60,000 - \$13,125) - \$5,000}{9}$$

$$8 \text{ years} - 1\frac{9}{12} \text{ years} = 6.25 \text{ years} = \$6,700$$

Part 4

2020			
Dec. 31	Impairment Loss.......................................	38,000	
	Equipment..		38,000
	To record impairment loss on equipment; $114,000 − $62,000 = $52,000 book value; $52,000 − $14,000 = $38,000		
2021			
Dec. 31	Depreciation Expense, Equipment...................	7,000	
	Accumulated Depreciation, Equipment....		7,000
	To record revised depreciation caused by impairment loss; $114,000 − $38,000 = $76,000 revised cost of equipment; $76,000 − $62,000 = $14,000 remaining book value; $14,000 ÷ 2 years = $7,000 revised depreciation.		

Disposals of PPE

LO6 Account for asset disposal through discarding, selling, or exchanging an asset.

Assets are disposed of for several reasons. Many assets eventually wear out or become obsolete. Other assets are sold because of changing business plans. Sometimes an asset is discarded or sold because it is damaged by fire or accident. Regardless of the cause, disposals of PPE occur in one of three ways: discarding, sale, or exchange. The accounting for disposals of PPE is described in Exhibit 9.21.

EXHIBIT 9.21

Accounting for Disposals of PPE

1. Calculate depreciation expense up to the date of disposal.
2. Record journal entry to record depreciation expense up to the date of disposal updating the accumulated depreciation account.
3.* Compare the asset's book value with the net amount received or paid at disposal and record any resulting gain or loss.
4.* Remove the balances of the disposed asset and related accumulated depreciation accounts. *Why? If the asset is gone, all accounts related to the asset (the asset account and its related accumulated depreciation) must be taken off the books as well.*
5.* Record any cash (and other assets) received or paid in the disposal.

Steps 3, 4, and 5 are recorded in one journal entry.

DISCARDING PPE

A PPE asset is *discarded* when it is no longer useful to the company and it has no market value. To illustrate, assume a machine costing $9,000 with accumulated depreciation of $9,000 is discarded on June 5. When accumulated depreciation equals the asset's cost, the asset is fully depreciated and the entry to record the discarding of this asset is:

June	5	Accumulated Depreciation, Machinery............	9,000	
		Machinery...		9,000
		To record the discarding of fully		
		depreciated machinery.		

This entry reflects all five steps of Exhibit 9.21. Steps 1 and 2 are not needed since the machine is fully depreciated. Since book value is zero and no cash is involved, no gain or loss is recorded in Step 3. Step 4 is shown in the debit to *Accumulated Depreciation* and credit to *Machinery*. Since no cash is involved, Step 5 is irrelevant.

How do we account for discarding an asset that is not fully depreciated or whose depreciation is not up to date? Consider equipment costing $8,000 with accumulated depreciation of $6,000 on December 31, 2020. This equipment is being depreciated using the straight-line method over eight years with zero residual value. On July 1, 2021, it is discarded. Step 1 is to calculate depreciation expense up to the date of disposal. Step 2 records depreciation expense to bring it up to date:

July	1	Depreciation Expense, Equipment.....................	500	
		Accumulated Depreciation, Equipment....		500
		To record six months' depreciation:		
		Jan. 1/21 to July 1/21; $1,000 \times \dfrac{6}{12}.$		

The July 1 balance in the Accumulated Depreciation, Equipment account after posting this entry is:

Accumulated Depreciation, Equipment					Acct. No. 168
Date	Explanation	PR	Debit	Credit	Balance
2020 Dec. 31	Balance	✓			6,000
2021 July 1		G8		500	6,500

The second and final entry reflects Steps 3–5 of Exhibit 9.21.

2021			
July 1	Accumulated Depreciation, Equipment.............................	6,500	
	Loss on Disposal of Equipment..	1,500	
	Equipment...		8,000
	To record the discarding of machinery having a $1,500 book value.		

The loss is calculated by comparing the equipment's book value of $1,500 (= $8,000 − $6,500) with the zero net cash proceeds. The loss on disposal is reported in the *Other Revenues and Expenses* section of the income statement.[23]

Gain (loss) on disposal* = Cash Proceeds − Book Value

*A gain occurs when proceeds are greater than book value; a loss occurs when proceeds are less than book value.

SELLING PPE

To illustrate the accounting for selling assets, we consider SportsWorld's April 1, 2021, sale of its delivery equipment costing $16,000 with accumulated depreciation of $12,000 on December 31, 2020. Annual depreciation on this equipment is $4,000 calculated using straight-line depreciation. The entry (Step 1) to record depreciation expense and (Step 2) update accumulated depreciation to April 1 is:

2021			
April 1	Depreciation Expense, Equipment.....................	1,000	
	Accumulated Depreciation, Equipment....		1,000
	To record three months' depreciation: Jan. 1/18 to April 1/18; $4,000 × $\frac{3}{12}$.		

The April 1 balance in the Accumulated Depreciation, Equipment account after posting this entry is:

Accumulated Depreciation, Equipment					Acct. No. 168
Date	Explanation	PR	Debit	Credit	Balance
2020 Dec. 31	Balance	✓			12,000
2021 Apr. 1		G11		1,000	13,000

---

23 IFRS 2018, IAS 16, para. 68.

The second entry to reflect Steps 3 to 5 of Exhibit 9.21 depends on the amount received in the sale. We consider three different possibilities:

| | Book Value = $16,000 − $13,000 = $3,000 | | |
Sale at Book Value (Cash Proceeds = $3,000)	Sale Above Book Value (Cash Proceeds = $7,000)	Sale Below Book Value (Cash Proceeds = $2,500)	
2021			
Apr. 1 Cash............................ 3,000	Cash.................................. 7,000	Cash............................ 2,500	
Accum. Deprec., Equip...................... 13,000	Accum. Deprec., Equip.............................. 13,000	Accum. Deprec., Equip. 13,000	
Equipment 16,000	Gain on Disposal of Equip.*................ 4,000 Equipment.................. 16,000	Loss on Disposal of Equip.................... 500 Equipment 16,000	
To record the sale of equipment for $3,000.	To record the sale of equipment for $7,000.	To record the sale of equipment for $2,500.	

*The gain on disposal is reported in the *Other Revenues and Expenses* section of the income statement (IFRS 2018, IAS 16, para. 68).

CHECKPOINT

14. A company acquires equipment on January 10, 2020, at a cost of $42,000. The CFO selected the straight-line depreciation method and assumed a five-year life and $7,000 residual value for the equipment. On June 27, 2021, the company sold this equipment for $32,000. Prepare the entry or entries for June 27, 2021.

Do Quick Study question: QS 9-16

EXCHANGING PPE

Many assets such as machinery, automobiles, and office equipment are disposed of by exchanging them (also referred to as a trade-in) for new assets. The exchange of assets is treated as both a sale of the old asset and a purchase of a new asset. Both the cost and related accumulated depreciation of the old asset must be removed from the books. The cost of the new asset will be recorded at the fair value of the asset(s) received. If the fair value cannot be reliably determined due to a transaction between related parties or lack of available information, then the new asset will be recorded at the carrying value of the asset(s) given up.[24] Any gains or losses realized on the exchange are also recorded at the time of disposal.

In a typical exchange of PPE, a trade-in allowance is received on the old asset and the balance is paid in cash. Often, the trade-in allowance offered *does not* reflect the fair value of the asset being traded in. For example, when buying a new car and trading in your old vehicle, the sales department at the dealership may decide to set the trade-in value of your car at a price higher than its fair value to make you feel they are giving you extra value in an attempt to win your business.

To illustrate, on January 2, 2020, Pizza Express trades in a 2018 Honda Accord for a 2020 Honda Pilot that has a list price of $41,000, which has been determined to be a reliable fair value. The original cost of the 2018 Accord was $30,000 and accumulated depreciation is $12,000 up to the date of the trade-in, resulting in a book

---

24 IFRS 2018, IAS 16, para. 24.

(or carrying) value of $18,000 (= $30,000 − $12,000). The dealership provides Pizza Express with a trade-in allowance of $20,000 on the Honda Accord and the $21,000 balance is to be in cash. The entry to record this transaction is as follows:

2020				
Jan.	2	Equipment: Honda Pilot...	41,000	
		Accumulated Depreciation, Equipment:		
		Honda Accord...	12,000	
		Equipment: Honda Accord..........................		30,000
		Cash		21,000
		Gain on Asset Exchange............................		2,000
		To record exchange of 2018 Honda Accord		
		and cash for 2020 Honda Pilot.		

Notice that the 2020 Honda Pilot received by Pizza Express was recorded at $41,000, the fair value of the asset received. The difference between the assets received by Pizza Express ($41,000) and the book (or carrying) value of the total assets exchanged by Pizza Express ($18,000 2018 Honda Accord + $21,000 cash) represents the gain on the exchange ($2,000).

If instead the $41,000 list price of the Honda Pilot is determined to be unreliable, as most dealers negotiate on price, the entry would be:

2020				
Jan.	2	Equipment: Honda Pilot...	39,000	
		Accumulated Depreciation, Equipment:		
		Honda Accord...	12,000	
		Equipment: Honda Accord..........................		30,000
		Cash		21,000
		To record exchange of 2018 Honda Accord		
		and cash for 2020 Honda Pilot.		

In this situation, the Honda Pilot received by Pizza Express was recorded at $39,000, the fair value of the assets given up ($18,000 + $21,000); no gain or loss is recorded.

 CHECKPOINT

15. On March 3, a local organic apple orchard trades an old truck for a new tractor. The original cost of the old truck is $30,000, and its accumulated depreciation at the time of the trade is $23,400. The new tractor has a list price of $45,000 and the trade-in allowance being offered is $5,000. Prepare entries to record the trade under two different assumptions where the list price of the new tractor is (1) representative of its fair value, or (2) not representative of its fair value.

Do Quick Study questions: QS 9-17, QS 9-18

Intangible Assets

Intangible assets are rights, privileges, and competitive advantages held by a company that are separately identifiable, have no physical substance, are non-monetary (meaning they have no fixed cash flows attached) and provide future economic benefits as a result of their use in operations. Examples are patents, copyrights, leaseholds, drilling rights, and trademarks. Lack of physical substance is not sufficient grounds for an asset to be an intangible. *Note:* Goodwill is excluded from the intangible asset category as it represents the future economic benefits that may result from the extra benefits achieved through the identifiable assets when operating together.[25] Exhibit 9.22 outlines the note disclosure for **Microsoft** from its 2017 annual report. Numbers presented are stated in millions of US dollars.

Depreciation is the systematic allocation of the cost of *plant and equipment* over its useful life.

Amortization is the systematic allocation of the cost of an *intangible asset* over its useful life.

EXHIBIT 9.22

Note 11–Intangible Assets

The components of intangible assets, all of which are finite-lived, as follows:

(in millions)	Gross Carrying Amount	Accumulated Amortization	Net Carrying Amount	Gross Carrying Amount	Accumulated Amortization	Net Carrying Amount
Year Ended June 30,			2017			2016
Technology-based (a)	$ 7,765	$(4,318)	$ 3,447	$5,970	$(3,648)	$2,322
Marketing-related	4,016	(829)	3,187	1,869	(616)	1,253
Contract-based	841	(722)	119	796	(718)	78
Customer-related	4,045	(692)	3,353	465	(385)	80
Total	$16,667(b)	$(6,561)	$10,106	$9,100	$(5,367)	$3,733

(a) Technology-based intangible assets included $59 million and $115 million as of June 30, 2017 and 2016, respectively.
(b) Includes intangible assets related to LinkedIn and other additions. See Note 9, Business Combinations, for further information.
No material impairments of intangible assets were identified during fiscal year 2017. Refer to note 11 for more information.
Source: Microsoft 2017 Annual Report: http://www.microsoft.com/investor/reports

ACCOUNTING FOR INTANGIBLE ASSETS

An intangible asset is recorded at cost when the asset is acquired.[26] Its cost must be systematically allocated to expense over its estimated useful life through the process of **amortization**.[27] The amortization period for intangible assets is estimated based on legal, regulatory, contractual, competitive, economic, or other factors that might limit its useful life. Disposal of an intangible asset is accounted for using the approach previously introduced for disposal of fixed assets. It involves removing its cost and accumulated amortization, recording any asset received, and recognizing any gain or loss for the difference.

---

25 IFRS 2018, IAS 38, para. 11, indicates that goodwill "may result from the synergy between the identifiable assets acquired or from assets that, individually, do not qualify for recognition in the financial statements."

26 IFRS 2018, IAS 38, para. 72, permits the use of either the cost model or revaluation model after recognition. The cost model is used in this text and the revaluation model is left for discussion in more advanced courses.

27 IFRS 2018, IAS 38, paras. 107–109, indicates that for intangible assets with indefinite useful lives, no amortization is recorded. Intangible assets with indefinite useful lives are assessed for impairment annually. Intangible assets with indefinite useful lives are beyond the basics of financial accounting and are left for discussion in more advanced courses.

Note that unless an intangible asset is purchased or acquired, it has no recorded value on the balance sheet. Internally generated intangible assets such as brands or trademarks are not recorded as an asset.

Intangible assets are amortized in a similar manner to fixed assets. The straight-line method is generally used *unless* another method better reflects the use of the intangible asset.[28] Intangible assets are assumed to have a residual value of zero.[29]

Intangible assets are shown on the balance sheet separately from goodwill and property, plant, and equipment. The long-term asset section of the 2017 balance sheet for Microsoft shows the following in millions of US dollars:

Property and equipment, net of accumulated depreciation of $14,793 and $12,513	23,743	18,356
Equity and other investments	6,023	10,356
Goodwill	35,122	17,872
Intangible assets, net	10,106	3,733
Other long-term assets	6,250	3,416

Intangible assets, as is the case for PPE, must be assessed annually for impairment.

PATENTS

The federal government grants patents under the federal *Patent Act* to encourage the invention of new products or processes. According to the Canadian Intellectual Property Office, to be granted a patent the intellectual property rights must relate to something that is new, inventive (non-obvious to a person of average skill in the related field) and useful. A **patent** is a legally protected exclusive right to an invention[30] that prevents others from manufacturing, selling, or unauthorized use of the invention for 20 years. When patent rights are purchased, the cost of acquiring the rights is debited to an account called *Patents*. If the owner successfully engages in lawsuits to defend a patent, the cost of lawsuits is debited to the Patents account. The costs of exploratory research and development leading to a new patent are expensed when incurred.[31]

While a patent gives its owner exclusive rights to it for 20 years, its cost is amortized over the shorter of its legal life of 20 years or estimated useful life. For example, if we purchase a patent from an independent design engineer for $25,000 with an expected useful life of 10 years, the following entries are made to record the acquisition of the patent and the annual adjusting entry over the 10-year period to amortize one-tenth of its cost:

Jan.	2	Patents	25,000	
		Cash		25,000
		To record purchase of patents.		
Dec.	31	Amortization Expense, Patents	2,500	
		Accumulated Amortization, Patents		2,500
		To write off patent cost over its 10-year useful life.		

The debit of $2,500 to Amortization Expense, Patents appears on the income statement as a cost of the product or service provided under the protection of the patent. This entry credits the Accumulated Amortization, Patents account.

---

28 IFRS 2018, IAS 38, para. 97.

29 IFRS 2018, IAS 38, para. 100.

30 http://www.ic.gc.ca/eic/site/cipointernet-internetopic.nsf/eng/wr03716.html?Open&wt_src=cipo-home, accessed February 2015.

31 IFRS 2018, IAS 38, para. 56, 57; 126–127.

COPYRIGHTS

A copyright is granted by the Canadian Intellectual Property Office of the federal government or by international agreement. A **copyright** gives its owner the exclusive right to publish and sell musical, dramatic, literary, or artistic work during the life of the creator plus 50 years.[32] Yet the useful life of most copyrights is much shorter. The costs of a copyright are amortized over its useful life. The only identifiable cost of many copyrights is the fee paid to the Copyright Office and, if immaterial, the cost is charged directly to an expense account; if material, such as the cost of purchasing the copyrights to songs by The Beatles, costs are capitalized and periodically amortized by debiting an account called *Amortization Expense, Copyrights*.

MINERAL RESOURCES

Companies like **Spry Energy Ltd.** and **Yoho Resources Inc.**, both with their head offices in Calgary, are involved in the extraction of oil and gas from the Earth. In order to engage in this activity, a company must obtain legal permissions known as **drilling rights**. Other terms related to drilling rights are mineral rights, mining rights, or oil rights. The owner of land has legal rights to the surface and perhaps to the subsurface. Often, a government body has the legal rights to the subsurface even when someone else might have legal rights to the surface. Companies wanting to drill for oil or other minerals must pay for the legal right to do so. These rights provide the company with a future economic benefit that is necessary for operating activities and, given that the rights are intangible in nature, they are accounted for as intangible assets.[33]

Oil and gas are *natural resources*. **Natural resources** include trees, mineral deposits, and water and are consumed when used. Trees are used to produce pulp and paper and lumber. **Alberta-Pacific Forest Industries Inc.**, more commonly known as **Alpac**, is one of the largest pulp and paper mills in the world and is owned by **Mitsubishi and Oji Paper Group**. Alpac purchases *timber rights*, an intangible asset, to cut trees for its operations. **Barrick Gold Corporation**, with its head office in Toronto, is the gold industry leader and reported more than $25.3 billion of total assets on its December 31, 2017, balance sheet. Of that amount, $255 million represented the book value of intangible assets relating to water rights, technology, supply contracts and exploration potential. Large volumes of water, tires, and other supplies are needed in the extraction of gold.

Property, plant, and equipment used by companies in their consumption of natural resources are depreciated.[34]

TRADEMARKS AND BRAND NAMES

Companies often adopt unique symbols or select unique names and brands in marketing their products. A **trademark** or *brand (trade) name* is a symbol, name, phrase, or jingle identified with a company, product, or service. Exhibit 9.23 outlines the World's Top 100 Most Valuable Brands as presented by Howmuch.net.

Ownership and exclusive rights to use a trademark or brand (trade) name are often established by showing that one company used it before another. But ownership is best established by registering a trademark or brand (trade) name with the Canadian Intellectual Property Office. The cost of developing, maintaining, or enhancing the value of a trademark or brand (trade) name by means such as advertising is expensed at the time the costs are incurred. If a trademark or brand (trade) name is purchased outright or as part of a business acquisition, its cost is debited to an asset account and amortized.

---

32 http://www.ic.gc.ca/eic/site/cipointernet-internetopic.nsf/eng/wr03719.html?Open&wt_src=cipo-cpyrght-main, accessed 2015

33 IFRS 2018, IFRS 6, para. 15.

34 IFRS 2018, IFRS 6, para. 16.

EXHIBIT 9.23

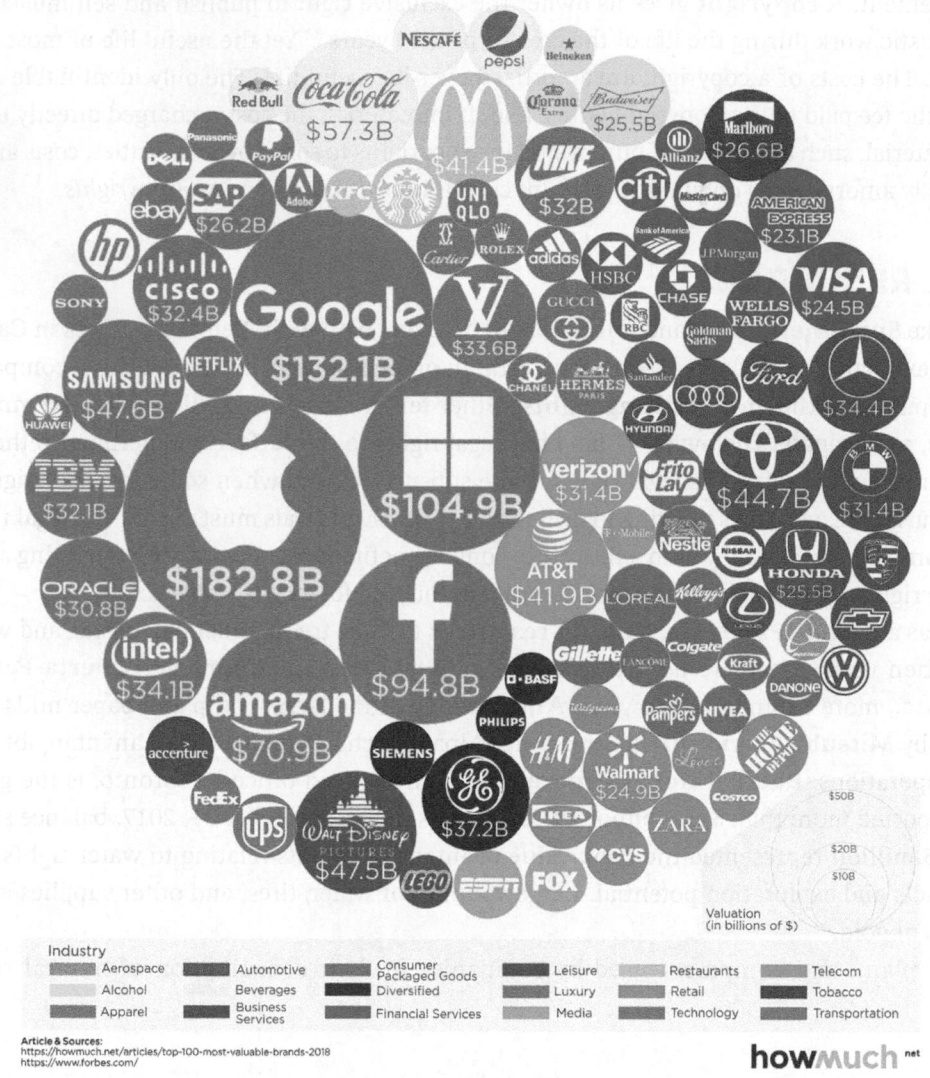

Brand Value (in billions of $)

Courtesy of HowMuch.com, a cost information website, https://howmuch.net/articles/top-100-most-valuable-brands-2018

LEASEHOLDS

A **leasehold** refers to the rights granted to the lessee to use a specific asset by the lessor in the lease. A lease-hold is an intangible asset for the lessee if a non-current lease requires the lessee to pay a bonus in advance. The resulting debit to a Leasehold account is amortized over the term of the lease by debiting Rent Expense and crediting Leaseholds.

Goodwill

Goodwill arises as a result of a business acquisition and reflects the amount paid for a business that exceeds the fair market value of the company's net assets (assets minus liabilities) if purchased separately. It is accounted for separately from other identifiable intangible assets on the financial statements. This usually implies that the company has certain valuable attributes not measured among its net assets. These can include superior management, skilled workforce, superior suppliers and customer loyalty, quality products or services, excellent location, or other competitive advantages. Goodwill is subject to a high degree of scrutiny by the acquirer, which wants to pay a reasonable amount for its acquisition. For instance, **Alphabet Inc.**, the parent company of Google, has a December 31, 2017, balance sheet of $16.7 billion.

Goodwill is recognized only when a company acquires another business.[35] Internally created goodwill is not recorded in the financial statements, due to the high level of difficulty in determining true value. Permission to do so could lead to abuse and values arrived at would lack objectivity. The amount paid by the acquirer on the acquisition date provides objective evidence that goodwill exists and sets a value to be recognized.

In 2014 **Loblaw Companies Ltd.** acquired the shares of **Shoppers Drug Mart Ltd.** with a $2,294 million addition of goodwill attributable to the newly acquired Shoppers Drug Mart. Note 17 of Loblaws 2017 annual report reveals the following breakdown of the group's carrying value of goodwill as of December 31, 2017.

Goodwill is attributable to synergies expected following the integration of Shoppers Drug Mart, improved competitive positioning in the retail market, and future growth of the company's customer base as a result of the acquisition. The goodwill arising from this acquisition is not deductible for tax purposes.

The carrying amount of goodwill attributed to each CGU grouping was as follows:

(millions of Canadian dollars)	As at Dec. 30, 2017	As at Dec. 31, 2016
Shoppers Drug Mart	$2,952	$2,925
Market	375	375
Discount	459	459
T&T Supermarket Inc	129	129
All other	7	7
Carrying amount of goodwill	$3,922	$3,895

Goodwill is not depreciated or amortized. Instead, goodwill is decreased only if its value has been determined by management to be impaired. Impairment of goodwill results when the current value of goodwill (fair value of the organization less the fair value of its net assets) is less than the carrying value of goodwill.

Causes of impairment might include ongoing past or potential cash flow losses, product obsolescence, or negative changes in variables supporting original calculations of goodwill. Testing for impairment should be done at least annually.

 CHECKPOINT

16. On January 6, 2020, assume Lego pays $120,000 for a patent with a 20-year legal life to produce a new electronic Lego product that is expected to be marketable for about three years. Prepare entries to record its acquisition and the December 31, 2020, adjustment.

Do Quick Study questions: QS 9-19, QS 9-20

---

35   IFRS 2018, IFRS 3, para. 3, 32.

CRITICAL THINKING CHALLENGE

Refer to the Critical Thinking Challenge questions at the beginning of the chapter. Compare your answers to those suggested on Connect.

IFRS AND ASPE—THE DIFFERENCES

Difference	International Financial Reporting Standards (IFRS)	Accounting Standards for Private Enterprises (ASPE)
Depreciation	• *Depreciation* is the term used to describe how costs are allocated for plant and equipment.	• The term *depreciation* or *amortization* may be used to describe how costs are allocated for plant and equipment.
Impairment of PPE and intangible assets	• Impairment must be reviewed annually. • The reversal of an impairment loss is permitted.	• Impairment is reviewed when apparent. • The reversal of an impairment loss is not permitted.
Exchange of non-monetary assets	• Non-monetary exchanges of assets are valued at the fair value of the asset received unless the fair value of the item given up is more easily determinable or the transaction lacks commercial substance.	• The new asset is recorded at the fair value of the asset given up plus any cash consideration paid (less any cash received). • If the fair value of the asset given up cannot be reliably determined, the new asset should be valued at the fair value of the asset(s) received.
Goodwill	• Impairment must be reviewed annually. • The reversal of an impairment loss is not permitted.	• Same as for PPE.

A Look Ahead

Chapter 10 in Volume 2 focuses on current liabilities. We explain how they are computed, recorded, and reported in financial statements. We also explain the accounting for company payroll and contingencies.

For further study on some topics of relevance to this chapter, please see the following Extend Your Knowledge supplement:

EYK 9-1 Presentation of Property, Plant, and Equipment and Intangibles on the Balance Sheet

SUMMARY

LO1 Describe property, plant, and equipment (PPE) and calculate their cost. PPE (1) are used in the operations of a company, and (2) have a useful life of more than one accounting period. There are three main accounting issues with PPE: (1) calculating and accounting for their initial and subsequent costs, (2) allocating their costs to the periods they benefit, and (3) recording their disposal. PPE are recorded at cost when purchased. Cost includes all normal and reasonable expenditures necessary to get the asset in place and ready for its intended use. Repairs and maintenance expenses expire in the current period and are debited to expense accounts. Betterments benefit future periods and are debited to asset accounts. The cost of a lump-sum purchase is allocated among its individual assets based on their relative values.

LO2 Explain, record, and calculate depreciation using the methods of straight-line, units-of-production, and double-declining-balance. Depreciation is the process of allocating to expense the cost of plant and equipment over the accounting periods benefiting from use of the asset. Depreciation does not measure the asset's decline in market value, nor does it measure its physical deterioration. Three factors determine depreciation: cost, residual value, and useful life. Residual value is an estimate of the asset's value at the end of its benefit period. Useful (service) life is the length of time an asset is productively used in operations.

Straight-line: $\dfrac{\text{Cost} - \text{Est. Residual value}}{\text{Estimated useful life in years}}$

Units-of-production: $\dfrac{\text{Cost} - \text{Estimated residual value}}{\text{Total estimated units}} \times \dfrac{\text{Units used}}{\text{in period}}$

Double-declining-balance: $\dfrac{\text{Book value} \times 2/n,}{\text{where } n = \text{Estimated useful life}}$

The amount of depreciation expense per period is usually different for different methods but total depreciation expense is the same. The difference is in the pattern in depreciation expense over the asset's useful life. The straight-line method yields a steady pattern of depreciation expense, while units-of-production does not because it depends on the number of units produced. DDB is an accelerated depreciation method.

LO3 **Explain and calculate depreciation for partial years.** When PPE are bought and sold throughout the year, depreciation can be calculated either to the nearest whole month *or* by applying the half-year convention.

LO4 **Explain and calculate revised depreciation.** Depreciation is revised when material changes occur in the estimated residual value and/or useful life and/or there is a betterment. Revised depreciation is calculated by spreading the *remaining* cost to be depreciated over the remaining useful life of the asset.

LO5 **Explain and record impairment losses.** If the book value of an asset is greater than its recoverable amount, an impairment loss is recorded. When an impairment loss is recorded, revised depreciation is calculated and recorded in the subsequent period because of the change in the asset's book value. Assets must be assessed annually for impairment.

LO6 **Account for asset disposal through discarding, selling, or exchanging an asset.** When PPE is discarded, sold, or exchanged, its cost and accumulated depreciation are removed from the accounts. Any cash proceeds from discarding or selling an asset are recorded and compared to the asset's book value to determine a gain or loss. When assets are exchanged, the new asset is recorded at its fair value, and any gain or loss on disposal is recognized.

LO7 **Account for intangible assets and their amortization.** An intangible asset is recorded at the cost incurred to purchase the asset. Amortization is normally recorded using the straight-line method. Intangible assets include patents, copyrights, drilling rights, leaseholds, franchises, and trademarks. Goodwill is not an intangible asset and is presented separately on the financial statements.

 Guidance Answers to DECISION MAKER

Restaurant Results

Treating an expense as a betterment results in lower reported expenses and higher profit. This is because, unlike an expense, a betterment is not expensed immediately. Instead, the cost of a betterment is spread out over the asset's life. Treating an expense as a betterment also means asset and equity totals are reported at a larger amount. This continues until the asset is fully depreciated. Your friend is probably trying to help, but the suggestion hints at unethical behaviour. You must remember that only an expenditure benefiting future periods is a betterment. If an item is truly an "expense" not benefiting future periods, then it must not be treated as a betterment.

Controller Constraints

Before you conclude that this instruction is unethical, you might tell the president of your concern that the longer estimate doesn't seem realistic in light of past experience with three-year replacements. You might ask if the change implies a new replacement plan. Depending on the president's response, such a conversation might eliminate your concern. It is possible the president's decision to change estimated useful life reflects an honest and reasonable prediction of the future. Since the company is struggling financially, the president may have concluded that the normal pattern of replacing assets every three years can't continue. Perhaps the strategy is to avoid costs of frequent replacements and stretch use of the equipment a few years longer until financial conditions improve. Even if you doubt the company will be able to use the equipment for six years, you should consider the possibility that the president has a more complete understanding of the situation and honestly believes a six-year life is a good estimate.

(Continued)

On the downside, you may be correct in suspecting that the president is acting unethically. If you conclude the president's decision is unethical, you might confront the president with your opinion that it is unethical to change the prediction just to increase profit. This is a personally risky course of action and you may want to remind the president of her own ethical responsibility. Another possibility is to wait and see if the auditor will insist on not changing the estimate. You should always insist the statements be based on reasonable estimates.

Guidance Answers to CHECKPOINT

1. Consistent with the cost principle, PPE assets are recorded at cost, which includes all normal and reasonable expenditures needed to get the asset ready for use.

2. A repairs and maintenance expense benefits only the current period and should be charged to expense of the current period. A betterment has a benefit that extends beyond the end of the current period and should be charged to an asset.

3. A betterment involves enhancing the economic benefits of an existing PPE asset, usually by replacing part of the asset with an improved or superior part. A betterment should be debited to the improved asset's account.

4. a. Land
   b. Land Improvements

5. $700,000 + $49,000 − $21,000 + $3,500 + $3,000 + $2,500 = $737,000

6. a. Straight-line with 7-year life: ($77,000/7) = $11,000
   b. Straight-line with 10-year life: ($77,000/10) = $7,700

7. Depreciation is a process of allocating and charging the cost of assets to the accounting periods that benefit from the assets' use.

8. a. Book value using straight-line depreciation:
      $96,000 − [($96,000 − $8,000)/5] = $78,400
   b. Book value using units-of-production:
      $96,000 − [($96,000 − $8,000) × (10,000/100,000)] = $87,200

9. Component A: $340,000 × 20% = $68,000 ÷ 4 years = $17,000/year;
   Component B: $340,000 × 50% = $170,000 ÷ 8 years = $21,250/year;
   Component C: $340,000 × 30% = $102,000 ÷ 15 years = $6,800/year.

10. Depreciation is based on an estimated useful life, so to calculate it to the nearest day would imply a degree of accuracy that is neither possible nor required.

11. ($3,800 − $200)/3 = $1,200
    $1,200 × 2 = $2,400
    ($3,800 − $2,400)/2 = $700

12.

2020			
Jan. 12	Computer—Monitor	800	
	Accounts Payable...		800
	To record the addition of a second monitor to the computer.		
Dec. 31	Depreciation Expense, Computer.......................	2,650	
	Accum. Deprec., Computer.........................		2,650
	To record revised depreciation on the computer caused by the addition of a second monitor; $5,000 − $500 = $4,500 ÷ 2 years = $2,250 **PLUS** *$800 ÷ 2 years = $400; Total depreciation = $2,250 + $400 = $2,650.*		

13. Machine A's book value is less than its recoverable amount so there is no impairment. There is an impairment loss of $146,000 ($238,000 book value less $92,000 recoverable amount) that must be recorded for Machine B. Additionally, revised depreciation will have to be calculated and recorded for Machine B.

14.

Jan.	27	Depreciation Expense...	3,500	
		Accum. Depreciation		3,500
	27	Cash..	32,000	
		Accum. Depreciation..	10,500	
		Gain on Sale of Equip.................................		500
		Equipment..		42,000

15. a.

Mar.	3	Tractor (new)...	45,000	
		Loss on Trade-In	1,600	
		Accum. Depreciation (old)...............................	23,400	
		Truck (old)		30,000
		Cash		40,000

b.

Mar.	3	Tractor (new)...	46,600	
		Accum. Depreciation (old)...............................	23,400	
		Truck (old)		30,000
		Cash		40,000

16.

Jan.	6	Patents...	120,000	
		Cash		120,000
Dec.	31	Amortization Expense	40,000	
		Accum. Amort., Patents...............................		40,000
		[Amortization calculation:		
		$120,000/3 = $40,000]		

Demonstration Problem

Health Smart Limited (HSL) purchased a manufacturing assembly machine for its new product launch: The Total Health Watch on March 2, 2020 for $62,000 cash. It had an estimated useful life of five years and a residual value of $14,000. On February 25, 2023, the machine was disposed of. HSL's year-end is December 31, and it calculates depreciation to the nearest whole month using straight-line depreciation.

Required

1. Prepare the entry to record the disposal under each of the following independent assumptions:
   a. The machine was sold for $26,000 cash.
   b. The machine was sold for $33,200 cash.
   c. The machine was sold for $34,180 cash.
   d. The old machine was exchanged for tools with a market value of $88,000. A trade-in allowance of $25,000 was offered on the old machine and the balance was paid in cash. Assume the $88,000 market value of the tools represents their fair value.

Additional company transaction:

2. On January 4, 2023, the company purchases with cash a patent from a biomedical engineering firm in Winnipeg for $100,000 to enable the launch of a new Total Health Watch for individuals with diabetes that incorporates glucose/insulin monitoring into the equipment. The company estimates the useful life of the patent to be 10 years. Journalize the patent acquisition and amortization for the year.

Analysis Component:

Regarding the purchase of the patent in Part 2, explain what potential adjustment might be necessary at the end of 2023 other than amortization.

Planning the Solution

- Remember that all depreciation must be recorded before removing a disposed asset from the books. Calculate and record the depreciation expense for 2020 through to 2023 using the straight-line method calculated to the nearest whole month. Record the gain/loss on the disposal as well as the removal of the asset and its related accumulated depreciation from the books.

- Record the patent as an intangible asset for its purchase price. Use straight-line amortization over the years of useful life to calculate amortization expense.

SOLUTION

1a.

2023				
Feb.	25	Depreciation Expense, Machine	1,600	
		Accumulated Depreciation, Machine..........................		1,600
		To update depreciation to date of sale.		
	25	Accumulated Depreciation, Machine[1]	28,800	
		Cash..	26,000	
		Loss on Disposal[2]..	7,200	
		Machine...		62,000
		To record sale of machine.		

1b.

Feb.	25	Depreciation Expense, Machine	1,600	
		Accumulated Depreciation, Machine..........................		1,600
		To update depreciation to date of sale.		
	25	Accumulated Depreciation, Machine...............................	28,800	
		Cash..	33,200	
		Machine...		62,000
		To record sale of machine.		

[1]2020: ($62,000 − $14,000)/5 × $\frac{10}{12}$ = $ 8,000

2021: ($62,000 − $14,000)/5 = 9,600

2022: = 9,600

2023: ($62,000 − $14,000)/5 × $\frac{2}{12}$ = 1,600

Accumulated Depreciation $28,800

[2]Gain (loss) = Proceeds − Book value

   = $26,000 − ($62,000 − $28,800) = ($7,200)

1c.

Feb.	25	Depreciation Expense, Machine		1,600	
		Accumulated Depreciation, Machine			1,600
		To update depreciation to date of sale.			
	25	Accumulated Depreciation, Machine		28,800	
		Cash		34,180	
		Machine			62,000
		Gain on Disposal[3]			980
		To record sale of machine.			

[3]Gain (loss) = $34,180 − ($62,000 − $28,800) = $\underline{\$\ 980}$

1d.

Feb.	25	Depreciation Expense, Machine		1,600	
		Accumulated Depreciation, Machine			1,600
		To update depreciation to date of exchange.			
	25	Accumulated Depreciation, Machine		28,800	
		Tools		88,000	
		Loss on Disposal[4]		8,200	
		Machine			62,000
		Cash			63,000
		To record exchange of machine.			

[4]Gain (loss) = $88,000 − [$63,000 + ($62,000 − $28,800)] = $\underline{(\$8,200)}$

2.

2023					
Jan.	4	Patent		100,000	
		Cash			100,000
		To record patent acquisition.			
Dec.	31	Amortization Expense, Patent		10,000	
		Accumulated Amortization, Patent			10,000
		To record amortization expense			
		($100,000/10 years = $10,000).			

Analysis Component:

The adjustment that might be necessary at the end of 2023 other than amortization relates to impairment. Both PPE and intangible assets must be assessed annually for impairment. If the book value (or carrying value) of the asset is greater than the recoverable amount, an impairment loss will need to be recorded. Additionally, if an impairment loss is recorded, revised amortization will need to be calculated and recorded.

Revised Depreciation When There Is a Betterment That Creates Partial-Period Depreciation

LO8 Explain and calculate revised depreciation when there is a betterment that creates partial-period depreciation.

Learning Objective 4 in the chapter discussed calculating revised depreciation when there is a change in the estimated useful life and/or estimated residual value *or* when there is a betterment. What it did not consider is the calculation of revised depreciation when a betterment occurs during the accounting period such that depreciation is for a partial period.

Calculating and recording revised depreciation involves a multi-step process when there has been a betterment partway through the accounting period. First, depreciation on the asset must be updated to the date of the betterment. Then, the betterment is recorded and, if the betterment is a replacement, the component being replaced must be removed from the books with any resulting gain or loss also recorded.[36] Finally, revised depreciation is calculated. To demonstrate, assume the following information is available regarding a piece of equipment:

Equipment:

Component	Date of Purchase	Depreciation Method*	Cost	Estimated Residual Value	Estimated Life	Accum. Dep. at Dec. 31, 2019, Year-End
Computer panel	Jan. 2/19	Straight-line	$ 16,000	-0-	8 years	$2,000
Engine	Jan. 2/19	Units-of-prod.	140,000	10,000	50,000 hrs	3,900
			$156,000			$5,900

*IFRS 2015, IAS 16, para. 45, indicates that the components of a given asset may have different depreciation methods.

On September 1, 2020, the computer panel was replaced with a new one costing $20,000 purchased on account. The new computer panel had an estimated residual value of $2,000 and an estimated useful life of six years. During 2020, the equipment had been used 1,200 hours from January 1 to August 31 and 650 hours

---

[36] IFRS 2015, IAS 16, para. 13, 67–72.

from September 1 to December 31. To record the replacement of the computer panel and record depreciation on the equipment for 2020, these steps are followed:

1. Update depreciation on the equipment to September 1, the date of the betterment.

Sept.	1	Depreciation Expense, Equipment.....................	4,453	
		Accumulated Depreciation, Equipment....		4,453
		To update depreciation on the equipment.		

Calculations:

Computer panel $16,000 cost − $0 residual = $16,000;

$16,000 ÷ 8 years = $2,000/year × $\frac{8}{12}$ = $1,333*

Engine $140,000 cost − $10,000 residual = $130,000 ÷ 50,000 hrs
= $2.60/hr; $2.60/hr × 1,200 hrs =   3,120
     $4,453

*Depreciation is rounded to the nearest whole dollar because it is based on estimates.

Notice that when depreciation is updated to September 1, *it is based on the original rates of depreciation.*

2. Record the betterment and remove the component being replaced.

Sept.	1	Equipment (new computer panel).......................	20,000	
		Accumulated Depreciation, Equipment............	3,333	
		Loss on Disposal of Equipment...........................	12,667	
		Equipment (old computer panel)................		16,000
		Accounts Payable...		20,000
		To record the replacement of the computer panel; $2,000 + $1,333 = $3,333.		

3. Calculate and record revised depreciation on the equipment from September 1 to December 31.

Dec.	31	Depreciation Expense, Equipment.....................	2,690	
		Accum. Deprec., Equipment.......................		2,690
		To record depreciation from Sept. 1 to Dec. 31.		

Calculations:

Computer panel: $20,000 cost − $2,000 residual = $18,000;

$16,000 ÷ 8 years = $3,000/year × $\frac{4}{12}$ = $1,000

Engine: $140,000 cost − $10,000 residual = $130,000;
$130,000 ÷ 50,000 hrs = $2.60/hr; $2.60/hr × 650 hrs =   1,690
     $2,690

CHECKPOINT

17. Explain the accounting treatment when a significant component of a machine is replaced by a new one.

Do Quick Study question: *QS 9-21

SUMMARY OF APPENDIX 9A

LO8 **Explain and calculate revised depreciation when there is a betterment that creates partial-period depreciation.** Depreciation is revised when there is a betterment since the book value of the asset has changed. Depreciation must be updated/recorded to the time the betterment was made. Then, if the betterment resulted in the replacement of a component, the cost and accumulated depreciation related to the replaced component must be removed from the books. Revised depreciation is then calculated based on the revised values.

 Guidance Answer to CHECKPOINT

17. When a significant component of a machine is replaced by a new one, the cost of the replacement is considered to be a betterment and debited to the machine account. Additionally, the accumulated depreciation of the component being replaced must be updated to the point in time when the replacement occurred. Then, the component being replaced must be removed from the accounting records by debiting accumulated depreciation for the updated amount and crediting the machine account for the cost of the component being replaced; any resulting gain or loss is also recorded. Finally, revised depreciation is calculated for the machine that incorporates the new component.

GLOSSARY

Accelerated depreciation method A depreciation method that produces larger depreciation charges during the early years of an asset's life and smaller charges in the later years.

Amortization A process of systematically allocating the cost of an intangible asset to expense over its estimated useful life.

Basket purchase See *lump-sum purchase.*

Betterments Costs of PPE that provide material benefits extending beyond the current period. They are debited to PPE asset accounts and reported on the balance sheet. Also referred to as a subsequent capital expenditure.

Book value The original cost of plant and equipment (or intangible asset) less its accumulated depreciation (or amortization).

Capital assets See *property, plant, and equipment.*

Capital cost allowance (CCA) The system of depreciation required by federal income tax law for federal income tax purposes.

Change in an accounting estimate A change in a calculated amount used in the financial statements that results from new information or subsequent developments and from better insight or improved judgment.

Copyright A right granted by the federal government or by international agreement giving the owner the exclusive privilege to publish and sell musical, literary, dramatic, or artistic work during the life of the creator plus 50 years.

Cost Includes all normal and reasonable expenditures necessary to get a PPE asset or intangible asset in place and ready for its intended use.

Declining-balance depreciation A depreciation method in which an asset's depreciation charge for the period is determined by applying a constant depreciation rate (up to twice the straight-line rate) each year to the asset's book value at the beginning of the year. Also known as *diminishing-balance depreciation*.

Depreciable cost The total asset cost less the residual value of the asset. Reflects the amount to be depreciated over the assets useful life.

Depreciation The process of matching (or allocating) the depreciable cost of a tangible asset in a rational and systematic manner over the asset's estimated useful life.

Derecognize Assets are removed from accounting records either upon disposal or when no future economic benefits are expected from their use. Any gain or loss arising on derecognition is included in earnings in the period the asset is disposed or void of future economic benefits.

Diminishing-balance depreciation See *double-declining-balance depreciation*.

Double-declining-balance depreciation A depreciation method in which depreciation is determined at twice the straight-line rate. It is calculated as:

Book value × 2/*n*, where *n* = Estimated useful life.

Drilling rights An intangible asset that gives the holder legal permission to extract oil and gas and/or other minerals from the subsurface. Other forms of legal permission similar to drilling rights include mineral rights, mining rights, timber rights, and water rights.

Fixed assets See *property, plant, and equipment*.

Goodwill The amount by which the value of a company exceeds the fair market value of the company's net assets if purchased separately; goodwill is *not* an intangible asset; goodwill is not amortized or depreciated but is instead subject to an annual impairment test.

Half-year convention A method of calculating depreciation for partial periods. Six months' depreciation is taken for the partial period regardless of when the asset was acquired or disposed of. Also known as the *half-year rule*.

Impairment loss Results when the book value (or carrying value) of PPE or an intangible asset is greater than its recoverable amount because of the annual impairment test.

Inadequacy A condition in which the capacity of the company's PPE is too small to meet the company's productive demands.

Intangible assets Rights, privileges, and competitive advantages to the owner of identifiable assets used in operations that have a useful life of more than one accounting period but have no physical substance; examples include patents, copyrights, drilling rights, leaseholds, franchises, and trademarks. Goodwill is not an intangible asset.

Land improvements Assets that increase the usefulness of land but that have a limited useful life and are subject to depreciation.

Lease A contract allowing property rental.

Leasehold A name for the rights granted to the lessee by the lessor in a lease.

Leasehold improvement An asset resulting from a lessee paying for alterations or improvements to the leased property.

Lessee The party to a lease that secures the right to possess and use the property.

Lessor The party to a lease that grants to another the right to possess and use property.

Lump-sum purchase Purchase of PPE in a group with a single transaction for a lump-sum price. The cost of the purchase must be allocated to individual asset accounts; also called a *basket purchase*.

Natural resources Assets that are physically consumed when used; examples include timber, mineral deposits, and oil and gas fields; also called wasting assets.

Obsolescence A condition in which, because of new inventions and improvements, a PPE item can no longer be used to produce goods or services with a competitive advantage.

Patent An exclusive right granted to its owner by the federal government to manufacture and sell a machine or device, or to use a process, for 20 years.

Property, plant, and equipment (PPE) Tangible assets used in the operations of a company that have a useful life of more than one accounting period; often abbreviated as *PPE*; sometimes referred to as *fixed assets*.

Repair and maintenance expenses Expenditures that should appear on the current income statement as expenses and be deducted from the period's revenues because they do not provide a material benefit in future periods.

Repairs Expenditures made to keep a PPE asset in normal, good operating condition; treated as a repair and maintenance expense.

Residual value Management's estimate of the amount that will be recovered at the end of a PPE item's useful life through a sale or as a trade-in allowance on the purchase of a new asset.

Revised depreciation Recalculated depreciation because of a change in cost, residual value, and/or useful life.

Service life See *useful life*.

Straight-line depreciation A method that allocates an equal portion of the total depreciation for an asset; calculated as:

$$\frac{\text{Cost} - \text{Residual value}}{\text{Estimated useful life in years}}$$

Trademark A symbol, name, phrase, or jingle identified with a company, product, or service. Also referred to as a brand (trade) name.

Units-of-production depreciation A method that charges a varying amount to expense for each period of an asset's useful life depending on its usage; expense for the period is calculated as:

$$\frac{\text{Cost} - \text{Estimated residual value}}{\text{Total estimated units of production}} \times \text{Units used in period}$$

Useful life The estimated length of time in which a PPE item or intangible asset will be productively used in the operations of the business; also called *service life*.

KNOWLEDGE CHECK-UP

1. Two features distinguishing property, plant, and equipment (PPE) from other assets are that:

   a. PPE is used in business operations to generate revenue and provides benefits for more than one accounting period.

   b. PPE is acquired through a contract and provides benefits for more than one accounting period.

   c. PPE is used in business operations to generate revenue and adds value to the organization.

   d. None of the above.

2. The cost of PPE includes which of the following:

   a. Its invoice price, less any cash discount for early payment

   b. Freight, unpacking, and assembling costs

   c. Non-refundable sales tax (PST)

   d. All of the above.

3. Which of the following costs should be capitalized as a betterment:

   a. Replacement of the engine for the company's transport truck.

   b. Installation costs for a new roof on the factory

   c. Costs to recalibrate and reprogram the factory machines to tighten quality

   d. All of the above.

4. Which of the following items qualify as repairs and maintenance expense:

   a. Costs to repair the loading dock that was recently damaged by a delivery truck

   b. Costs to fix a hole discovered in a plumbing pipe that was resulting in a leak in the vehicle showroom

   c. Costs incurred by Lawn Care Inc. to correct alignment on their fleet of Honda lawn mowers.

   d. All of the above.

5. Which of the following costs for constructed buildings should be capitalized:

   a. Interest costs incurred once the building is occupied

   b. Insurance costs incurred once the building is occupied

   c. Design fees and building permits

   d. All of the above.

6. Which of the following depreciation methods allocate the cost of the underlying asset evenly over the useful life of the asset:

   a. double-declining-balance method

   b. units-of-production method

   c. straight-line method

   d. lump-sum depreciation method

7. Which of the following depreciation methods allocates more depreciation in the early years of an asset's life and less depreciation in later years:

   a. units-of-production method

   b. double-declining-balance method

   c. straight-line method

   d. None of the above.

8. When there is a revised useful life on a depreciated asset due to more information being available or because of a subsequent capital expenditure, which of the following is adjusted:

   a. Depreciation per year is recalculated based on present value of the future cash flows expected to be received from the underlying asset.

   b. Depreciation per year remains unadjusted.

   c. Depreciation per year is recalculated based on the fair value of the asset.

   d. Depreciation per year is recalculated based on the remaining years of useful life.

9. Vegan Bites, a local restaurant, had to replace the roof of its building. Advise the new controller on how to handle the accounting adjustment for the new roof:

   a. The amount is debited to the corresponding asset account and no adjustment is made to the depreciation of the asset.

   b. The amount is debited to the corresponding asset account and depreciation is revised to incorporate the additional cost and change the estimated useful life and residual value.

   c. The cost of the original asset is removed from the accounting records and any gain or loss must be recorded; depreciation is then revised to incorporate depreciation on the replacement component.

   d. None of the above.

10. Design Inc. is an independent hardware development firm that builds computer chips that enable quick retrieval of the best information relating to the type of information the user selects as of highest importance. Design Inc. recently earned a patent on its Gen Z product and needs help on the most appropriate way to handle the development costs relating to the patent. Select the most appropriate method from the following list of options:

    a. The costs of the patent are capitalized and amortized over the shorter of its legal life of 20 years or estimated useful life.

    b. The costs are capitalized and amortized over the shorter of its legal life of 50 years or the estimated useful life.

    c. The costs of exploratory research and development leading to the new patent are expensed when incurred; none of the costs relating to development of the patent can be capitalized.

    d. The costs relating to development of the patent can be capitalized but are not subject to amortization.

CONCEPT REVIEW QUESTIONS

1. What characteristics of a property, plant, and equipment item make it different from other assets, such as accounts receivable or inventory?

2. What is the balance sheet classification of land held for future expansion? Why is the land not classified as property, plant, and equipment?

3. What are some examples of items to include in the cost of a property, plant, and equipment purchase?

4. What is the difference in how to account for land and land improvements?

5. Does the balance of the Accumulated Depreciation, Machinery account represent funds accumulated to replace the machinery when it wears out?

6. What is the difference in profit between a repairs and maintenance expense and a betterment, and how is each recorded?

7. What accounting principle justifies charging the $75 cost of PPE immediately to an expense account?

8. Refer to the statements of cash flows for **Spin Master** in Appendix II. What was the amount of depreciation and amortization for 2016 and 2017? Where will you look to find the explanation of the increase?

9. What are some of the events that might lead to disposal of PPE?

10. What are the characteristics of an intangible asset?

11. What are two types of intangible assets?

12. Refer to the balance sheet for WestJet in Appendix II. What amount did it report as intangible assets at December 31, 2017?

13. When is the only time a business can record goodwill?

14. Refer to the balance sheet for WestJet in Appendix II. What amount did it report as goodwill at December 31, 2017?

15. In the chapter-opening vignette, YVR refers to several capital initiatives that are underway. What types of construction costs can YVR capitalize for self-constructed assets such as the development of a new runway for the international terminal?

QUICK STUDY

QS 9-1 Cost of PPE LO1

Sydney Lanes, a local bowling alley, installed automatic scorekeeping equipment. The electrical work required to prepare for the installation was $18,000. The invoice price of the equipment was $180,000. Additional costs were $3,000 for delivery and $600 for insurance during transportation. During the installation, a component of the equipment was damaged because it was carelessly left on a lane and hit by the automatic lane cleaning machine. The cost of repairing the component was $2,250. What is the cost that should be capitalized of the automatic scorekeeping equipment?

QS 9-2 Costs included in PPE LO1

Fire Pizza Food Truck purchased a giant wood stove for $11,000, terms 2/10, n/60, FOB shipping point, to go on a trailer behind the food truck. Fire Pizza received an invoice for $280 for freight charges. Fire Pizza took advantage of the discount. Staff will need to wear special gloves; the gloves cost $50 a pair and staff will probably use one pair a month for the next year. The wood stove required a special steel mounting and power connections costing $815, and another $4,055 was paid to assemble the stove and get it into operation. Because a stove of this nature is so special, the insurance for the first year is $1,400. Prepare a calculation to show the cost of this machine for accounting purposes.

QS 9-3 Revenue and betterments LO1

1. Classify the following expenditures as Repairs and Maintenance Expense or Betterment:

   a. The monthly replacement cost of filters on an air conditioning system, $120.

   b. The cost of replacing a compressor for an ice cream company's refrigeration system that extends the estimated life of the system by four years, $40,000.

   c. The cost of annual tune-ups for delivery trucks, $200.

   d. The cost of $175,000 for an addition of a new wing on an office building.

2. Prepare the journal entry to record each of the above (assume all transactions occurred on March 15, 2020, and were on account).

QS 9-4 Lump-sum purchase LO1 eXcel

On April 14, 2020, Orchid Company, a new Thai restaurant, purchased land and a building for a total price of $540,000, paying cash of $85,000 and borrowing the balance from the bank. The bank appraised the land at $320,000 and the building at $180,000. Complete the following table and prepare the entry to record the purchase.

PPE Item	(a) Appraised Values	(b) Ratio of Individual Appraised Value to Total Appraised Value (a) ÷ Total Appraised Value	(c) Cost Allocation (b) × Total Actual Cost
Land			
Building			
Totals			

QS 9-5 Balance sheet presentation LO2

TechCom has provided the following selected account information, in alphabetical order, from its adjusted trial balance at October 31, 2020 (assume normal balances):

Accounts receivable..	$16,400
Accumulated depreciation, equipment..	3,800
Accumulated amortization, patent	3,100
Accumulated depreciation, vehicles...	13,800
Allowance for doubtful accounts	800
Cash..	9,000
Equipment..	25,000
Land..	48,000
Patent...	20,100
Vehicles	62,000

Prepare the asset section of the classified balance sheet at October 31, 2020.

QS 9-6 Calculating depreciation—straight-line LO2

On January 2, 2020, Crossfire acquired sound equipment for concert performances at a cost of $55,900. The rock band estimated that it would use this equipment for four years, and then sell the equipment for $1,900. Calculate depreciation for each year of the sound equipment's estimated life using the straight-line method. Crossfire's year-end is December 31.

QS 9-7 Calculating depreciation—units-of-production LO2 eXcel

Papaya, a specialty greeting card company, purchased a photocopier costing $45,000 on January 1, 2020. The equipment is expected to produce a total of 4,000,000 copies over its productive life. Its residual value at the end of its useful life is estimated to be $5,000. The equipment actually produced:

Fiscal Year	Copies Produced
2020..	650,000
2021..	798,000
2022..	424,000
2023..	935,000
2024..	1,193,000

Calculate depreciation for 2020 through to 2024 using the units-of-production method. Papaya's year-end is December 31.

QS 9-8 Calculating depreciation—double-declining-balance LO2 eXcel

Patty's Pies acquired a delivery truck on January 1, 2020, for $86,000. It is expected to last five years and then sell for about $16,000. Calculate depreciation for each year of the truck's life using the double-declining-balance method. Patty's Pies' year-end is December 31.

QS 9-9 Calculating depreciation on components LO2

Crystal Cleaners is an eco-friendly dry cleaner. The following excerpt from its PPE subledger shows the component details regarding the dry cleaning equipment:

Dry Cleaning Equipment:

Component	Depreciation Method[1]	Cost	Estimated Residual	Estimated Life
Computer panel	SL	$ 4,000	$ -0-	8 years
Dry cleaning drum	Units	70,000	5,000	400,000 garments
Stainless steel housing	SL	85,000	10,000	20 years
Miscellaneous parts	SL	26,000	-0-	2 years
		$185,000		

[1]SL = Straight-line; Units = Units-of-production.

Calculate depreciation on the dry cleaning equipment for the year ended December 31, 2020. Assume the equipment was purchased on January 2, 2020, and that 62,000 garments were dry cleaned during 2020.

QS 9-10 Calculating depreciation—partial periods LO2, 3

Equipment with an estimated life of 10 years and no expected residual value was purchased on account for $60,000 on March 6, 2020. Assuming a year-end of December 31, calculate depreciation for 2020 and 2021 using the straight-line method:

a. To the nearest whole month   **b.** Using the half-year convention

QS 9-11 Double-declining-balance—partial periods LO2, 3

Refer to the information in QS 9-10. Assume the equipment is depreciated using the double-declining-balance method. Calculate depreciation for 2020 and 2021:

a. To the nearest whole month   **b.** Using the half-year convention

QS 9-12 Units-of-production—partial periods LO2, 3

AbeCo, a luggage manufacturing company, borrowed $75,000 from the bank to purchase a machine that was estimated to produce 120,000 suitcases; its expected residual value is $15,000. During 2020 and 2021, the machine produced 20,000 and 28,000 units, respectively. Calculate depreciation for 2020 and 2021 assuming the units-of-production method is used:

a. To the nearest whole month   **b.** Using the half-year convention

QS 9-13 Revised depreciation—change in useful life and residual value LO4

On January 1, 2020, Kaldex Company purchased for $35,720 equipment with an estimated useful life of eight years and an estimated residual value at the end of its life of $4,200. Early in January 2023, it was determined that the total estimated useful life on the equipment should be 10 years with a revised estimated residual value of $1,570. Kaldex uses the straight-line method to calculate depreciation and its year-end is December 31. Calculate revised depreciation for 2023.

QS 9-14 Revised depreciation—betterment LO4

Class Act Catering Company had a deluxe, portable barbecue with a book value of $7,000 at its December 31, 2019, year-end. The barbecue had an estimated remaining useful life of five years and a $200 residual value. On January 3, 2020, a customized electronic rotisserie unit costing $1,000 was added to the barbecue to improve the quality of the barbecuing process. The rotisserie had an estimated life of five years and no residual value. Record the addition on January 3 and the revised depreciation on the barbecue at December 31. Assume cash was paid for the rotisserie and that it represents a significant expenditure.

QS 9-15 Impairment losses LO5

Phantom Company was preparing the annual financial statements and, as part of its year-end procedures, prepared the following alphabetized schedule based on adjusted values at March 31, 2020:

Asset	Cost	Accumulated Depreciation	Recoverable Amount
Building..	$1,200,000	$465,000	$735,000
Computer......................................	3,500	1,800	200
Furniture.......................................	79,000	53,000	5,000
Land..	630,000	-0-	790,000
Machine...	284,000	117,000	172,000

What, if any, impairment losses need to be accounted for? Assume Phantom Company recorded no impairment losses in previous years.

QS 9-16 Disposal of PPE LO6

Huang Furniture Company showed the following adjusted account balances on September 30, 2020:

Equipment...	$ 56,000
Accumulated depreciation, equipment..	39,000
Machinery...	109,000
Accumulated depreciation, machinery	96,000
Delivery truck...	48,000
Accumulated depreciation, delivery truck...................................	33,000
Furniture...	26,000
Accumulated depreciation, furniture	21,000

Prepare the entries to record the following on October 1, 2020:

a. Equipment was sold for cash of $17,000.

b. Machinery was sold for cash of $27,000.

c. Delivery truck was sold for cash of $11,000.

d. Furniture was given to a charity.

QS 9-17 Exchanging PPE LO6

Dean Carpet Stores owned an automobile with a $15,000 cost that had $13,500 accumulated depreciation as of December 31, 2020. Its fair value on this date was $3,000. On the same day, Dean exchanged this auto for a computer with a fair value of $5,800. Dean was required to pay an additional $2,750 cash. Prepare the entry to record this transaction for Dean.

QS 9-18 Exchanging PPE LO6

On March 1, 2020, Wallace Company purchased a new machine with a suggested retail price of $123,000. The new machine was to replace an old machine that originally cost $90,000 and had $36,000 of accumulated depreciation at the time of the exchange. The retailer was offering Wallace a trade-in allowance of $60,000. Record the exchange assuming the fair values are not known.

QS 9-19 Intangible assets and amortization LO7

On January 4, 2020, Amber's Boutique paid cash of $95,000 for a 10-year franchise. Prepare the entry to record the purchase of the franchise and the adjusting entry at December 31, 2020.

QS 9-20 Intangible assets and amortization LO7

Assume Barrick Gold Corporation purchased mineral rights for a gold mine in Peru on October 1, 2020, by paying cash of $5,000,000 and incurring a non-current note payable for the $30,000,000 balance. Barrick also paid $4,000,000 cash for water rights needed to mine the gold. Barrick is planning to mine this area for 10 years. Record the purchase of the mineral rights and water rights on October 1, 2020, and the amortization on December 31, 2020, Barrick's year-end. Assume Barrick uses the straight-line method to amortize intangibles.

*QS 9-21 Revised depreciation—betterment creating partial-period depreciation LO8

Flint Solar Energy showed the following information in its Property, Plant, and Equipment subledger regarding a machine.

Machine:						
Component	Date of Purchase	Depreciation Method	Cost	Est. Residual	Est. Life	Accum. Dep. at Dec. 31, 2019, Year-End
Motor	Jan. 1/16	Straight-line	$ 45,000	$ 5,000	10 years	$16,000
Metal housing	Jan. 1/16	Straight-line	68,000	15,000	25 years	8,480
Misc. parts	Jan. 1/16	Straight-line	15,000	-0-	5 years	12,000
			$128,000			$36,480

On September 1, 2020, the motor was replaced with a new one costing $60,000; it was purchased on account. The new motor had an estimated residual value of $10,000 and an estimated life of eight years. Calculate the *total* depreciation expense to be recorded on the machine for 2020.

EXERCISES

Exercise 9-1 Cost included in PPE LO1

CHECK FIGURE: Total acquisition costs = $30,125

Edmonton Ice Rink purchased a Zamboni ice-resurfacing machine for $28,000, terms 1/10, n/60, FOB shipping point. Edmonton Ice received a freight invoice from On-time Delivery for $450. Edmonton Ice took advantage of the discount. The Zamboni required a special steel mounting and power connections costing $985, and another $660 was paid to paint the home team colours on the Zamboni and get it into operation. In moving the Zamboni onto its steel mounting, it was banged and damaged. The repairs cost $380. Also, $310 of labour costs were incurred in calibrating (adjusting) the machine so that it would be at the right height on the ice. These adjustments were normal and were not a result of the damage. Special insurance was needed for the

---

An asterisk (*) identifies assignment material based on Appendix 9A.

new ice cleaning machine, which will cost $200 per month for the next year. Prepare a calculation to show the cost of this machine for accounting purposes.

Exercise 9-2 Recording costs of real estate—land versus building costs LO1

CHECK FIGURE: Dr. Land $1,860,000

After planning to build a new plant, Kallisto Backpack Manufacturing purchased a large lot on which a small building was located. The negotiated purchase price for this real estate was $1,200,000 for the lot plus $480,000 for the building. The company paid $75,000 to have the old building torn down and $105,000 for levelling the lot. Finally, it paid $2,880,000 in construction costs, which included the cost of a new building plus $215,000 for lighting and paving a parking lot next to the building. Present a single journal entry to record the costs incurred by Kallisto, all of which were paid in cash (assume a date of March 10, 2020, for your entry).

Exercise 9-3 Lump-sum purchase LO1 eXcel

CHECK FIGURE: Dr. Land $244,346

On April 12, 2020, Prism Ltd., a camera lens manufacturer, paid cash of $552,375 for real estate plus $29,400 cash in closing costs. The real estate included land appraised at $249,480; land improvements appraised at $83,160; and a building appraised at $261,360. Prepare a calculation similar to the table below showing the allocation of the total cost among the three purchased assets and present the journal entry to record the purchase.

PPE Asset	(a) Appraised Values	(b) Ratio of Individual Appraised Value to Total Appraised Value (a) ÷ Total Appraised Value	(c) Cost Allocation (b) × Total Actual Cost

Exercise 9-4 Lump-sum purchase LO1

CHECK FIGURE: Dr. Tools $388,800

On January 1, 2020, Bona Vista Co. purchased land, a building, equipment, and tools for a total price of $4,320,000, paying cash of $1,104,000 and borrowing the balance from the bank. The bank appraiser valued the assets as follows: $1,152,000 for the land; $1,344,000 for the building; $998,400 for the equipment; and $345,600 for the tools. Complete a table similar to above and prepare the entry to record the purchase.

Exercise 9-5 Cost of PPE, straight-line depreciation LO1, 2

CHECK FIGURE: Dr. Truck $87,000

On January 1, 2020, Land's End Construction purchased a used truck for $52,500. A new motor had to be installed to get the truck in good working order; the costs were $21,000 for the motor and $7,500 for the labour. The truck was also painted for $6,000. It was ready for use by January 4. A 12-month insurance policy costing $5,100 was purchased to cover the vehicle. The driver filled it with $225 of gas before taking it on its first trip. It is estimated that the truck has a five-year useful life and a residual value of $9,000. Land's End uses the straight-line method to depreciate all of its vehicles. Prepare the entry to record the purchase of truck, insurance, and gas, and record the depreciation at year-end, December 31, 2020.

Exercise 9-6 Alternative depreciation methods—straight-line, double-declining-balance, and units-of-production LO2

CHECK FIGURES: b. 2019 = $37,550; c. 2020 = $36,890

On January 2, 2018, Archer Company, a skateboard manufacturer, installed a computerized machine in its factory at a cost of $150,200. The machine's useful life was estimated at four years or a total of 186,000 units with a $20,000 trade-in value. Archer Company's year-end is December 31. Calculate depreciation for each year of the machine's estimated useful life under each of the following methods:

a. Straight-line

b. Double-declining-balance

c. Units-of-production, assuming actual units produced were:

Year	2018	2019	2020	2021
Units	38,400	41,300	52,700	57,000

Exercise 9-7 Calculating depreciation LO2

CHECK FIGURE: b. $122,080

Jackal Energy purchased a transport truck on January 1, 2020, for $305,200 cash. Its estimated useful life is five years or 320,000 kilometres with an estimated residual value of $52,400.

Required Calculate depreciation expense for the year ended December 31, 2020, using each of the following methods:

a. Straight-line

b. Double-declining-balance

c. Units-of-production (assume 30,000 kilometres were actually driven in 2020)

Analysis Component: Which depreciation method will produce the highest profit for Jackal in 2020?

Exercise 9-8 Alternative depreciation methods LO2

CHECK FIGURES: Deprec. exp. 2022: Straight-line = $21,250; DDB = $18,036; Units = $30,000

On January 3, 2020, Xenex Innovations purchased computer equipment for $125,250. The equipment will be used in research and development activities for five years or a total of 8,500 hours and then sold for about $19,000. Prepare a schedule with headings as shown below. Calculate depreciation and book values for each year of the equipment's life for each method of depreciation. Xenex's year-end is December 31.

	Straight-Line		Double-Declining-Balance		Units-of-Production*	
Year	Depreciation Expense	Book Value at Dec. 31	Depreciation Expense	Book Value at Dec. 31	Depreciation Expense	Book Value at Dec. 31

*Assume actual usage in hours of:

2020	2021	2022	2023	2024
1350	1,780	2,400	2,980	2,700

Analysis Component: Which method will result in the greatest:

a. Total assets being reported on the balance sheet in 2020? in 2023?

b. Operating expenses being reported on the income statement in 2020? in 2023?

Exercise 9-9 Lump-sum purchase, double-declining-balance LO1, 2

CHECK FIGURES: 2021 depreciation: Land = $0; Building = $215,040; Equipment = $60,480; Tools = $18,667

On January 1, 2020, Creative Calligraphy Inc. purchased land, building, equipment, and tools for a total of $2,520,000. An appraisal identified the fair values to be $700,000 (land), $1,120,000 (building), $210,000 (equipment), and $70,000 (tools). The estimated useful life and residual value of the building was 10 years and

$700,000; for the equipment, five years and $42,000; and for the tools, three years and $7,000. Calculate depreciation for 2020 and 2021 using the double-declining-balance method. Creative Calligraphy's year-end is December 31.

Analysis Component: Explain depreciation as it applies to land.

Exercise 9-10 Calculating depreciation LO2 eXcel

CHECK FIGURE: Depreciation expense, truck = $8,672

At December 31, 2019, Dynamic Exploration's balance sheet showed total PPE assets of $802,000 and total accumulated depreciation of $339,980 as detailed in the PPE subledger below. Dynamic calculates depreciation to the nearest whole month.

	Cost Information					Depreciation		
Description	Date of Purchase	Depreciation[1] Method	Cost[2]	Residual	Life	Balance of Accum. Deprec. Dec. 31, 2019	Depreciation Expense for 2020	Balance of Accum. Deprec. Dec. 31, 2020
Building	May 2, 2014	S/L	$650,000	$250,000	10 yr.	$226,667		
Modular furniture	May 2, 2014	S/L	72,000	-0-	6 yr.	68,000		
Truck	Jan. 25, 2017	DDB	80,000	10,000	8 yr.	45,313		

[1]S/L = Straight-line; DDB = Double-declining-balance.
[2]There have been no disposals or betterments since the date of purchase.

Required Complete the schedule by calculating depreciation expense for 2020 for each asset and then determining the balance of accumulated depreciation at December 31, 2020 (round to the nearest whole dollar).

Analysis Component: The depreciation methods used by Dynamic are not consistent among the building, modular furniture, and truck. Is this in accordance with GAAP? Explain why or why not.

Exercise 9-11 Balance sheet presentation LO2

CHECK FIGURE: Total assets = $800,020

Refer to Exercise 9-10. Assume that the only other assets at December 31, 2019, were total current assets of $338,000. Prepare the asset section of Dynamic Exploration's classified balance sheet at December 31, 2019.

Exercise 9-12 Income statement effects of alternative depreciation methods LO2

CHECK FIGURE: b. Depreciation expense, Year 3 = $60,204

Kenartha Oil recently paid $483,900 for equipment that will last five years and have a residual value of $114,000. By using the machine in its operations for five years, the company expects to earn $180,000 annually, after deducting all expenses except depreciation. Complete the schedule below assuming each of (a) straight-line depreciation and (b) double-declining-balance depreciation.

	Year 1	Year 2	Year 3	Year 4	Year 5	5-Year Totals
Profit before depreciation..............						
Depreciation expense						
Profit						

Analysis Component: If Kenartha Oil wants the Year 1 balance sheet to show the highest value possible for the equipment, which depreciation method will it choose? Explain.

Exercise 9-13 Partial-period depreciation—nearest month LO3

CHECK FIGURES: 2019 Straight-line = $23,400; Units = $42,660

VanHoutte Foods bought machinery on September 10, 2018, for $168,000. It was determined that the machinery would be used for six years or until it produced 260,000 units and then would be sold for about $27,600. Complete the schedule below by calculating annual depreciation to the nearest whole month for 2018, 2019, and 2020. VanHoutte's year-end is December 31.

	Depreciation	
Year	Straight-Line	Units-of-Production*

*Round the per unit depreciation expense to three decimal places.

Assume actual units produced of:

2018	43,000	2020	64,000
2019	79,000		

Analysis Component: If depreciation is not recorded, what is the effect on the income statement and balance sheet?

Exercise 9-14 Partial-period depreciation—half-year convention LO3

CHECK FIGURES: Straight-line, 2021 = $22,000; DDB, 2021 = $21,120

Design Pro purchased on October 1, 2019, $110,000 of furniture that was put into service on November 10, 2019. The furniture will be used for five years and then donated to a charity. Complete the schedule below by calculating annual depreciation for 2019, 2020, and 2021, applying the half-year convention for partial periods. The year-end is December 31.

	Depreciation	
Year	Straight-Line	Double-Declining-Balance

Analysis Component: What effect would it have on the 2019 financial statements if the furniture had been debited to an expense account when purchased instead of being recorded as PPE?

Exercise 9-15 Alternative depreciation methods—partial year's depreciation LO3

CHECK FIGURES: a. 2021 = $22,500; b. 2021 = $35,000

On April 1, 2020, Ice Drilling Co. purchased a trencher for $125,000. The machine was expected to last five years and have a residual value of $12,500.

Required Calculate depreciation expense for 2020 and 2021 to the nearest month, using (a) the straight-line method, and (b) the double-declining-balance method. The company has a December 31 year-end.

Exercise 9-16 Revising depreciation rates—change in useful life and residual value LO4

CHECK FIGURE: 2. $6,800

The Hilton Skating Club used straight-line depreciation for a used Zamboni ice-resurfacing machine that cost $43,500, under the assumption it would have a four-year life and a $5,000 trade-in value. After two years, the club determined that the Zamboni still had three more years of remaining useful life, after which it would have an estimated $3,850 trade-in value.

Required

1. Calculate the Zamboni's book value at the end of its second year.

2. Calculate the amount of depreciation to be charged during each of the remaining years in the Zamboni's revised useful life.

Exercise 9-17 Revising depreciation rates—change in useful life and residual value LO4

CHECK FIGURE: Revised depreciation = $7,624

On April 3, 2020, David's Chocolates purchased a machine for $71,200. It was assumed that the machine would have a five-year life and a $15,200 trade-in value. Early in January 2023, it was determined that the machine would have a seven-year useful life and the trade-in value would be $8,000. David's Chocolates uses the straight-line method to the nearest month for calculating depreciation.

Required Record depreciation at December 31, 2023, David's Chocolates' year-end. Round to the nearest whole dollar.

Exercise 9-18 Revised depreciation—betterment LO2, 4

CHECK FIGURE: 2. $14,700

At its December 31, 2019, year-end, Athletic Apparel had a warehouse with an adjusted book value of $292,500 and an estimated remaining useful life of 15 years and residual value of $90,000. Because of pick-up and delivery issues at the warehouse, a contractor was hired to construct a new door into the east wall during the week of January 5, 2020, for $25,500 on account. The estimated useful life of the door is 15 years with an estimated residual value of $7,500. Athletic uses the straight-line method to depreciate assets.

Required

1. Record the installation of the new door.

2. Record total depreciation on the warehouse at December 31, 2020.

Exercise 9-19 Impairment losses LO2, 5

Kane Biotech was preparing the annual financial statements and, as part of the year-end procedures, assessed the assets and prepared the following alphabetized schedule based on adjusted values at December 31, 2020:

Asset	Date of Purchase	Deprec. Method*	Cost	Residual Value	Useful Life	Accum. Deprec.	Recoverable Amount
Equipment	May 1/15	Units	$40,000	$ 5,000	7,000 units	$20,000	$ 8,000
Furniture	Jun. 28/15	DDB	12,000	2,000	8 yrs	9,509	2,950
Land	Apr. 5/15	N/A	85,000	N/A	N/A	N/A	101,800
Office building	Apr. 5/15	SL	77,000	17,000	15 yrs	23,000	52,500
Warehouse	Apr. 5/15	SL	55,000	10,000	20 yrs	12,938	45,100

*DDB = Double-declining-balance; SL = Straight-line; Units = Units-of-production; N/A = Not applicable

Required

1. Record any impairment losses at December 31, 2020. Assume Kane Biotech has recorded no impairment losses in previous years.

2. Record depreciation for each asset at December 31, 2021. Assume that there was no change in the residual values or useful lives regardless of any impairment losses that might have occurred. The equipment produced 1,800 units during 2021.

Exercise 9-20 Disposal of PPE LO6

CHECK FIGURES: b. Gain = $1,450; c. Loss = $950

Macho Taco sold a food truck on March 1, 2020. The accounts showed adjusted balances on February 28, 2020, as follows:

Food Truck...	$42,000
Accumulated Depreciation, Food Truck	21,850

Required Record the sale of the food truck assuming the cash proceeds were:

a. $20,150

b. $21,600

c. $19,200

d. $0 (the food truck was scrapped).

Exercise 9-21 Partial year's depreciation; disposal of PPE LO2, 3, 6

CHECK FIGURES: a. Gain = $6,000; b. Loss = $10,000

Candy Craze purchased and installed a machine on January 1, 2020, at a total cost of $296,800. Straight-line depreciation was taken each year for four years, based on the assumption of a seven-year life and no residual value. The machine was disposed of on July 1, 2021, during its fifth year of service. Candy Craze's year-end is December 31.

Required Present the entries to record the partial year's depreciation on July 1, 2021, and to record the disposal under each of the following unrelated assumptions:

a. The machine was sold for $112,000 cash.

b. Candy Craze received an insurance settlement of $96,000 resulting from the total destruction of the machine in a fire.

Exercise 9-22 Exchanging PPE LO6

CHECK FIGURE: b. Loss = $23,000

On October 6, 2020, Western Farms Co. traded in an old tractor for a new one, receiving a $68,000 trade-in allowance and paying the remaining $170,000 in cash. The old tractor cost $202,000, and straight-line depreciation of $111,000 had been recorded as of October 6, 2020. Assume the fair value of the new tractor was equal to the trade-in allowance of the old tractor plus the cash paid.

Required

a. What was the book value of the old tractor?

b. What is the gain or loss on the exchange?

c. What amount should be debited to the new Tractor account?

d. Record the exchange.

Exercise 9-23 Exchanging PPE LO6

CHECK FIGURE: b. Loss = $1,000

On November 3, 2020, Gamez 2 Go Media exchanged an old computer for a new computer that had a list price of $190,000. The original cost of the old computer was $150,000 and related accumulated depreciation was $65,000 up to the date of the exchange. Gamez 2 Go Media received a trade-in allowance of $100,000 and paid the balance in cash.

Required

a. Record the exchange assuming the fair values are unknown.

b. Assume that the fair value of the new asset was $174,000. Record the exchange.

Analysis Component: What is the dollar value that will be used to depreciate the new computer in part (b)? Explain which GAAP helped you answer the question correctly.

Exercise 9-24 Recording PPE disposal or exchange LO6

CHECK FIGURES: a. Loss = $1,050; c. Loss = $9,550; d. Gain = $4,450

On January 2, 2020, Direct Shoes Inc. disposed of a machine that cost $96,000 and had been depreciated $50,450. Present the journal entries to record the disposal under each of the following unrelated assumptions:

a. The machine was sold for $44,500 cash.

b. The machine was traded in on new tools having a $141,000 cash price. A $52,000 trade-in allowance was received, and the balance was paid in cash. Since the tools have been customized, the fair values are not known.

c. The machine plus $80,000 was exchanged for a delivery van having a fair value of $116,000.

d. The machine was traded for vacant land adjacent to the shop to be used as a parking lot. The land had a fair value of $87,000, and Direct Shoes Inc. paid $37,000 cash in addition to giving the seller the machine.

Exercise 9-25 Amortization of intangible assets LO7

CHECK FIGURE: Amortization Expense, Copyright = $14,790

Jazzy Antiques purchased the copyright on a watercolour painting for $177,480 on January 1, 2020. The copyright legally protects its owner for 19 more years. However, Jazzy plans to market and sell prints of the original for the next 12 years only. Prepare journal entries to record the purchase of the copyright and the annual amortization of the copyright on December 31, 2020. The company uses the straight-line method to amortize intangibles.

Exercise 9-26 Amortization of intangible assets LO2, 3, 7

CHECK FIGURES: 2. Timber rights, Dec. 31, 2020 = $48,000; Dec. 31, 2021 = $144,000

On September 5, 2020, Nelson Lumber purchased timber rights in Northern Quebec for $432,000, paying $96,000 cash and the balance by issuing a non-current note. Logging the area is expected to take three years, and the timber rights will have no value after that time. On September 27, 2020, Nelson Lumber purchased a patent for $148,000 for new logging equipment on account. It is expected that the patent will be technologically obsolete in 10 years. Nelson's year-end is December 31 and it uses the straight-line method to amortize intangibles.

Required

1. Record the acquisition of the timber rights and the patent.

2. Record amortization on the timber rights and the patent at December 31, 2020, and December 31, 2021.

Exercise 9-27 Balance sheet LO2, 7

CHECK FIGURE: Total assets = $302,080

Huang Resources showed the following alphabetized adjusted trial balance at October 31, 2020:

Account	Balance
Accounts payable	$ 18,400
Accounts receivable	27,200
Accumulated amortization, mineral rights	30,400
Accumulated amortization, trademark	22,400
Accumulated depreciation, building	81,600
Accumulated depreciation, equipment	110,400
Allowance for doubtful accounts	1,920
Building	147,200
Cash	9,600
Equipment	184,000
Expenses	1,443,200
Land	89,600
Mineral rights	57,600
Note payable	72,000
Revenues	1,433,600
Sally Huang, capital	221,280
Trademark	33,600

Other information:

a. All accounts have normal balances.

b. $38,000 of the note payable is due after October 31, 2021.

Required Prepare a classified balance sheet at October 31, 2020.

Exercise 9-28 Balance sheet LO2, 3, 7

CHECK FIGURE: Total assets = $87,885

Montalvo Bionics showed the following alphabetized unadjusted trial balance at April 30, 2020:

Account	Balance
Accounts payable	$ 5,080
Accounts receivable	17,300
Accumulated depreciation, furniture	10,190
Accumulated depreciation, machinery	20,200
Allowance for doubtful accounts	1,010
Cash	10,100
Expenses	89,300
Furniture	22,700
Josh Montalvo, capital	32,910
Josh Montalvo, withdrawals	83,900
Machinery	50,800
Note payable	14,600
Patent	24,900
Prepaid rent	16,260
Revenues	225,400
Unearned revenue	5,870

Other information:

a. All accounts have normal balances.

b. The furniture was depreciated using the straight-line method and had a useful life of five years and residual value of zero.

c. The machinery was depreciated using the double-declining-balance method and had a useful life of 10 years and residual value of $28,100.

d. The patent was purchased on November 2, 2019, and is expected to be used for 15 years, after which it will have no value.

e. The balance in Prepaid Rent represents rent from June 1, 2019, to May 31, 2020.

f. $6,500 of the note payable will be paid by April 30, 2021.

Required Prepare a classified balance sheet at April 30, 2020.

Exercise 9-29 Purchase equipment, depreciation, disposal of equipment LO2, 3, 6

CHECK FIGURES: 2018 deprec. oven $750; 2019 deprec. truck $8,400

Jessica Grewal decided to open a food truck business, the Samosa Shack. She encountered the following transactions in managing her equipment over the first 2 years of her business.

April 1,	2018	Purchased food truck for $48,000 and paid $6,000 to have a commercial oven installed. Other costs that she incurred are $3,600 for insurance on the truck for the first year, and $4,000 to have the truck painted with her Samosa Shack logo. Jessica estimates that the truck would last 5 years and have a $10,000 residual value. The oven is also expected to last 5 years and have a $1,000 residual value.
October 1,	2018	The oven broke down and cost $1,800 to repair.
December 31, 2018		Recorded the adjusting entry for depreciation and insurance.
April 1,	2019	Replaced all of the tires with all-season tires for $2,100 and paid another year of insurance for $3,600.
December 31, 2019		Recorded the adjusting entry for depreciation and insurance.
March 31,	2020	Jessica was exhausted from the food truck business, and decided to go back to school and sell the food truck to her friend Mark. He paid her $21,000 for the truck and oven, which included $1,000 for the oven component.

Record all the entries for the 2 years that Jessica owned the truck, including the disposal of the truck and oven. The company calculates depreciation using the straight-line method to the nearest month.

*Exercise 9-30 Revised depreciation—betterment LO2, 3, 8

CHECK FIGURES: 2. Tool carrier, Dec. 31, 2020 = $600; Dec. 31, 2021 = $1,200

Nova Scotia Telecom Company had a truck that was purchased on July 7, 2018, for $36,000. The PPE subledger shows the following information regarding the truck:

Truck:						
Component	Date of Purchase	Deprec. Method	Cost	Est. Residual	Est. Life	Accum. Dep. at Dec. 31/19
Truck body	Jul. 7/18	SL	$28,000	-0-	10 yr	$4,200
Motor	Jul. 7/18	SL	8,000	-0-	10 yr	1,200
			$36,000			$5,400

A customized tool carrier was constructed and permanently fitted to the truck on July 3, 2020, at a cost of $9,600 cash. The tool carrier adds to the economic value of the truck. It will be used for the truck's remaining

---

An asterisk (*) identifies assignment material based on Appendix 9A.

life and have a zero residual value. The useful life and residual value of the truck did not change as a result of the addition of the tool carrier.

Required

1. Record the installation of the tool carrier assuming it is a component of the truck.

2. Calculate depreciation on the truck and its new component, the tool carrier, for the company's December 31, 2020, and December 31, 2021, year-ends.

3. Calculate the book value of the truck at December 31, 2020 and 2021.

PROBLEMS

Problem 9-1A Real estate costs LO1 eXcel

CHECK FIGURE: 2. Land = $3,899,980

On March 31, 2020, Capital Investment Advisers paid $4,570,000 for land with two buildings on it. The plan was to demolish Building 1 and build a new store (Building 3) in its place. Building 2 was to be used as a company office and was appraised at a value of $1,074,790. A lighted parking lot near Building 2 had improvements (Land Improvements 1) valued at $607,490. Without considering the buildings or improvements, the tract of land was estimated to have a value of $2,990,720. Capital incurred the following additional costs:

Cost to demolish Building 1	$ 703,160
Cost of additional landscaping..	272,020
Cost to construct new building (Building 3)..	2,476,000
Cost of new land improvements near Building 2 (Land Improvements 2)............	254,600

Required

1. Prepare a schedule having the following column headings: Land, Building 2, Building 3, Land Improvements 1, and Land Improvements 2. Allocate the costs incurred by Capital to the appropriate columns and total each column.

2. Prepare a single journal entry dated March 31, 2020, to record all the incurred costs, assuming they were paid in cash on that date.

Problem 9-2A Balance sheet presentation LO2

CHECK FIGURES: 2019 Total assets = $371,920; 2020 Total assets = $443,120

The adjusted balances at December 31, 2020, for Derlak Enterprises are shown in alphabetical order below:

	2020	2019		2020	2019
Accounts payable	$ 56,800	$ 9,600	Lee Derlak, withdrawals............	$ 32,000	$ 38,400
Accumulated amortization, franchise........	19,200	11,200	Notes payable, due in 2023.....	240,000	129,600
Accumulated amortization, patent............	4,000	2,400	Office supplies............................	2,400	2,320
Accumulated depreciation, equipment.....	72,800	64,800	Operating expenses...................	780,800	571,200
Accumulated depreciation, tools...............	44,800	42,400	Patent..	16,000	16,000
Accumulated depreciation, vehicles..........	108,800	97,600	Prepaid rent................................	40,000	48,000
Cash...	12,000	28,800	Salaries payable	32,800	26,400
Equipment...	184,000	100,000	Service revenue	720,000	753,600
Franchise...	41,600	41,600	Tools	143,920	100,800
Lee Derlak, capital*....................................	206,320	62,320	Vehicles	252,800	252,800

*The owner, Lee Derlak, made no additional investments during the year.

Required Prepare a comparative classified balance sheet at December 31, 2020.

Analysis Component: Are Derlak's assets financed mainly by debt or equity in 2019? in 2020? Is the change in how assets were financed from 2019 to 2020 favourable or unfavourable? Explain.

Problem 9-3A Alternative depreciation methods—straight-line, double-declining-balance, and units-of-production LO2

CHECK FIGURES: b. 2020 = $7,000; c. 2020 = $37,940

On January 2, 2018, Country Lumber installed a computerized machine in its factory at a cost of $168,000. The machine's useful life was estimated at four years or a total of 190,000 units with a $35,000 trade-in value. Country Lumber's year-end is December 31. Calculate depreciation for each year of the machine's estimated useful life under each of the following methods:

a. Straight-line

b. Double-declining-balance

c. Units-of-production, assuming actual units produced were:

Year	2018	2019	2020	2021
Units	39,900	43,550	54,200	72,000

Problem 9-4A Calculating depreciation—partial periods LO2, 3

CHECK FIGURES: 1B. 2022 Depreciation expense = $39,000; 2A. 2022 Depreciation expense = $59,760

Yorkton Company purchased for $415,000 equipment having an estimated useful life of 10 years with an estimated residual value of $25,000. Depreciation is calculated to the nearest month. The company has a December 31 year-end.

Required Complete the following schedules (round calculations to the nearest whole dollar):

1. Assuming the purchase was made on January 1, 2020.
2. Assuming the purchase was made on July 1, 2020.

	2020	2021	2022
A. Double-declining-balance method			
Equipment	_____	_____	_____
Less: Accumulated depreciation	_____	_____	_____
Year-end book value	_____	_____	_____
Depreciation expense for the year	_____	_____	_____
B. Straight-line method			
Equipment	_____	_____	_____
Less: Accumulated depreciation	_____	_____	_____
Year-end book value	_____	_____	_____
Depreciation expense for the year	_____	_____	_____

Problem 9-5A Calculating depreciation—partial periods LO2, 3

CHECK FIGURE: DDB 2022 = $110,400

West Coast Tours runs boat tours along the West Coast of British Columbia. On March 5, 2020, it purchased, with cash, a cruising boat for $828,000, having a useful life of 10 years or 13,250 hours, with a residual value of $192,000. The company's year-end is December 31.

Required Calculate depreciation expense for the fiscal years 2020, 2021, and 2022 by completing a schedule with the following headings *(round calculations to the nearest whole dollar)*:

	Depreciation Method[1]		
Year	Straight-Line	Double-Declining-Balance	Units-of-Production[2]

[1]Depreciation is calculated to the nearest month.
[2]Assume actual hours of service were 2020, 720; 2021, 1,780; 2022, 1,535.

Analysis Component: If you could ignore the matching principle, how could you record the purchase of the boat? What impact would this have on the financial statements in the short and long term?

Problem 9-6A Calculating depreciation—partial periods LO2, 3 eXcel

CHECK FIGURE: DDB 2022 = $119,232

Refer to the information in Problem 9-5A. Redo the question assuming that depreciation for partial periods is calculated using the half-year convention.

Problem 9-7A Calculating depreciation LO2

CHECK FIGURES: 1. Dr. Depreciation Expense, Building $53,000. 1. Dr. Depreciation Expense, Equipment $77,184.
2. Total PPE = $1,144,736

Big Sky Farms Partial Balance Sheet April 30, 2020		
Property, plant and equipment:		
Land...		$ 730,000
Building[1]..	$742,000	
Less: Accumulated depreciation...	583,000	159,000
Equipment[2]...	670,000	
Less: Accumulated depreciation...	284,080	385,920
Total property, plant and equipment..		$1,274,920

[1]The building was purchased on May 3, 2009, and is depreciated to the nearest whole month using the straight-line method. Depreciation is based on a 14-year life, after which it will be demolished and replaced with a new one.

[2]The equipment was purchased on November 3, 2017, and is depreciated to the nearest whole month using the double-declining-balance method. The total estimated useful life is 10 years with a residual value of $200,000.

Required

1. Calculate *and* record depreciation for the year just ended April 30, 2021, for both the building and equipment.

2. Prepare the property, plant, and equipment section of the balance sheet at April 30, 2021.

Problem 9-8A PPE costs; partial year's depreciation; alternative methods LO1, 2, 3

CHECK FIGURES: 2. $31,320; 3. $21,000

Logic Co. recently negotiated a lump-sum purchase of several assets from a company that was going out of business. The purchase was completed on March 1, 2020, at a total cash price of $1,260,000 and included a building, land, certain land improvements, and 12 vehicles. The estimated market values of the assets were building, $652,800; land, $462,400; land improvements, $68,000; and vehicles, $176,800. The company's fiscal year ends on December 31.

Required

1. Prepare a schedule to allocate the lump-sum purchase price to the separate assets that were purchased. Also present the journal entry to record the purchase.

2. Calculate the 2020 depreciation expense on the building using the straight-line method to the nearest whole month, assuming a 15-year life and a $41,040 residual value.

3. Calculate the 2020 depreciation expense on the land improvements assuming a five-year life, $12,000 residual, and double-declining-balance depreciation calculated to the nearest whole month.

Analysis Component: Assume the assets purchased on March 1, 2020, were not put into service until May 23, 2020. Would this affect your answers in parts 2 and 3 above? Explain.

Problem 9-9A Alternative depreciation methods; partial year's depreciation LO2, 3

CHECK FIGURES: 2020 SL = $38,000; 2024 Units = $89,664; 2024 DDB = $4,500

A machine that cost $504,000, with a four-year life and an estimated $48,000 residual value, was installed in Haley Company's factory on September 1, 2020. The factory manager estimated that the machine would produce 475,000 units of product during its life. It actually produced the following units: 2020, 21,400; 2021, 122,400; 2022, 119,600; 2023, 118,200; and 2024, 102,000. The company's year-end is December 31.

Required Prepare a form with the following column headings:

Year	Straight-Line	Units-of-Production	Double-Declining-Balance

Show the depreciation for each year and the total depreciation for the machine under each depreciation method calculated to the nearest whole month. Round to the nearest whole dollar.

Problem 9-10A Calculating depreciation; partial year's depreciation LO2, 3

CHECK FIGURES: Deprec. Expense 2021: Office equip. = $3,800; Machinery = $19,638; Truck = $23,664

At December 31, 2020, Halifax Servicing's balance sheet showed capital asset information as detailed in the schedule below. Halifax calculates depreciation to the nearest whole month.

Cost Information						Depreciation		
Description	Date of Purchase	Depreciation Method	Cost[1]	Residual	Life	Balance of Accum. Deprec. Dec. 31, 2020	Depreciation Expense for 2021	Balance of Accum. Deprec. Dec. 31, 2021
Office Equip.	March 27/17	Straight-line	$ 52,000	$14,000	10 yr.			
Machinery	June 4/17	Double-declining-balance	275,000	46,000	6 yr.			
Truck	Nov. 13/20	Units-of-production	113,000	26,000	250,000 km[2]			

[1]There have been no disposals or betterments since the date of purchase.
[2]Actual kilometres driven were 2020, 14,000; 2021, 68,000.

Required Complete the schedule (round only your final answers).

Problem 9-11A Partial year's depreciation; revising depreciation rates LO1, 2, 4

CHECK FIGURE: Dec. 31, 2021 Deprec. Exp. = $21,160

NeverLate Ltd. completed the following transactions involving delivery trucks:

Mar.	26	2020	Paid cash for a new delivery truck, $92,000 plus $4,200 of freight costs. The truck was estimated to have a five-year life and a $10,000 trade-in value.
Dec.	31	2020	Recorded straight-line depreciation on the truck to the nearest whole month.
Dec.	31	2021	Recorded straight-line depreciation on the truck to the nearest whole month. However, due to new information obtained early in January, the original estimated useful life of the truck was changed from five years to four years, and the original estimated trade-in value was increased to $14,500.

Required Prepare journal entries to record the transactions.

Problem 9-12A Revising depreciation rates LO4

CHECK FIGURES: Deprec. Exp., Machinery = $95,200; Deprec. Exp., Office Furn. = $11,733

The December 31, 2020, adjusted trial balance of Maritime Manufacturing showed the following information:

Single Machinery...	$556,800
Accumulated depreciation, machinery[1]..	246,400
Office furniture..	89,600
Accumulated depreciation, office furniture[2]..	49,600

[1]Remaining useful life four years; estimated residual $64,000.
[2]Remaining useful life five years; estimated residual $11,200.

Early in 2021, the company made a decision to stop making the items produced by the machinery and buy the items instead. As a result, the remaining useful life was decreased to two years and the residual value was increased to a total of $120,000. At the beginning of 2021, it was determined that the estimated life of the office furniture should be reduced by two years and the residual value decreased by $6,400. The company calculates depreciation using the straight-line method to the nearest month.

Required Prepare the entries to record depreciation on the machinery and office furniture for the year ended December 31, 2021 (round calculations to the nearest whole dollar).

Problem 9-13A Revised depreciation—change in life/residual and betterment LO2, 3, 4

CHECK FIGURES: 1. Loss = $5,032; 2. 2020 Deprec. on Machine #5027 = $6,908

Pete's Propellers Company showed the following information in its Property, Plant, and Equipment subledger regarding Machine #5027.

Machine #5027					
Component	Date of Purchase	Depreciation Method*	Cost	Est. Residual	Est. Life
Single metal housing	Jan. 12/18	SL	$44,000	$8,000	15 yrs
Motor	Jan. 12/18	DDB	26,000	2,000	10 yrs
Blade	Jan. 12/18	SL	7,720	1,000	5 yrs
			$77,720		

*SL = Straight-line; DDB = Double-declining-balance

On January 7, 2020, the machine blade cracked and it was replaced with a new one costing $10,400 purchased for cash (the old blade was scrapped). The new blade had an estimated residual value of $1,000 and an estimated life of five years and would continue to be depreciated using the straight-line method. During 2020, it was determined that the useful life on the metal housing should be increased to a total of 20 years instead of 15 years and that the residual value should be increased to $8,600.

Required

1. Prepare the entry to record the purchase of the replacement blade.
2. Calculate the *total* depreciation expense to be recorded on Machine #5027 for 2020.

Problem 9-14A Depreciation and impairment losses LO1, 2, 3, 5

CHECK FIGURE: 2. Total assets = $271,920

Safety-First Company completed all of its October 31, 2020, adjustments in preparation for preparing its financial statements, which resulted in the following trial balance.

Account	Balance
Accounts payable	$ 11,220
Accounts receivable	19,800
Accumulated depreciation, building	79,200
Accumulated depreciation, equipment	37,400
Accumulated depreciation, furniture	20,900
Allowance for doubtful accounts	880
Building	136,400
Cash	11,000
Equipment	90,200
Expenses, including cost of goods sold	761,200
Furniture	50,600
Land	105,600
Merchandise inventory	35,200
Note payable	85,800
Sales	904,200
Tarifa Sharma, capital	62,480
Unearned revenues	7,920

Other information:

1. All accounts have normal balances.
2. $26,400 of the note payable balance is due by October 31, 2021.

The final task in the year-end process was to assess the assets for impairment, which resulted in the following schedule.

Asset	Recoverable Value
Land	$136,400
Building	105,600
Equipment	28,600
Furniture	15,400

Required

1. Prepare the entry (entries) to record any impairment losses at October 31, 2020. Assume the company recorded no impairment losses in previous years.

2. Prepare a classified balance sheet at October 31, 2020.

Analysis Component: What is the impact on the financial statements of an impairment loss?

Problem 9-15A **Partial-period depreciation; disposal of PPE** LO2, 3, 6

CHECK FIGURES: 1. GAIN = $67,350; 2. LOSS = $23,867

Endblast Productions showed the following selected asset balances on December 31, 2020:

Land...	$396,800
Building..	526,400
Accumulated depreciation, building[1]	393,600
Equipment...	171,200
Accumulated depreciation, equipment[2]	74,400

[1]Remaining estimated useful life is eight years with a residual value of $80,000; depreciated using the straight-line method to the nearest whole month.
[2]Total estimated useful life is 10 years with a residual value of $16,000; depreciated using the double-declining-balance method to the nearest whole month.

Required Prepare the entries for each of the following (round final calculations to the nearest whole dollar).

1. The land and building were sold on September 27, 2021, for $592,000 cash.

2. The equipment was sold on November 2, 2021, for $56,800 cash.

Problem 9-16A **Disposal of PPE** LO1, 2, 3, 6

CHECK FIGURES: 2. Dec. 31, 2020 = $17,080; 3a. Loss = $3,990; 3b. Gain = $2,310; 3c. Gain = $770

Vita Water purchased a used machine for $116,900 on January 2, 2020. It was repaired the next day at a cost of $4,788 and installed on a new platform that cost $1,512. The company predicted that the machine would be used for six years and would then have a $20,720 residual value. Depreciation was to be charged on a straight-line basis to the nearest whole month. A full year's depreciation was recorded on December 31, 2020. On September 30, 2025, it was retired.

Required

1. Prepare journal entries to record the purchase of the machine, the cost of repairing it, and the installation. Assume that cash was paid.

2. Prepare entries to record depreciation on the machine on December 31 of its first year and on September 30 in the year of its disposal (round calculations to the nearest whole dollar).

3. Prepare entries to record the retirement of the machine under each of the following unrelated assumptions:

   a. It was sold for $21,000.

   b. It was sold for $27,300.

   c. It was destroyed in a fire and the insurance company paid $25,760 in full settlement of the loss claim.

Problem 9-17A Partial year's depreciation; exchanging PPE LO2, 3, 6

CHECK FIGURE: Dec. 31, 2020: Deprec. Exp. = $3,236

In 2020, Staged Home Ltd. completed the following transactions involving delivery trucks:

July 5 Traded in an old truck and paid $25,600 in cash for furniture. The accounting records on July 1 showed the cost of the old truck at $36,000 and related accumulated depreciation of $6,000. The furniture was estimated to have a six-year life and a $6,268 trade-in value. The invoice for the exchange showed these items:

Price of the furniture (equal to its fair value)...	$45,100
Trade-in allowance	(19,500)
Total paid in cash	$25,600

Dec. 31 Recorded straight-line depreciation on the furniture (to nearest whole month).

Required Prepare journal entries to record the transactions.

Problem 9-18A Partial year's depreciation; alternative methods; exchange/disposal of PPE LO2, 3, 6

CHECK FIGURES: a. Machine 1550 = $6,075; Machine 1795 = $22,646; Machine BT-311 = $77,810

Zephyr Minerals completed the following transactions involving machinery.

Machine No. 1550 was purchased for cash on April 1, 2020, at an installed cost of $52,900. Its useful life was estimated to be six years with a $4,300 trade-in value. Straight-line depreciation was recorded for the machine at the ends of 2020, 2021, and 2022.

On March 29, 2023, it was traded for Machine No. 1795, with an installed cash price of $62,000. A trade-in allowance of $30,210 was received for Machine No. 1550, and the balance was paid in cash. The fair values of Machine No. 1550 and Machine No. 1795 could not be determined.

Machine No. 1795's life was predicted to be four years with a trade-in value of $8,200. Double-declining-balance depreciation on this machine was recorded each December 31. On October 2, 2024, it was traded for Machine No. BT-311, which had an installed cash price of $537,000, the machine's fair value. A trade-in allowance of $20,000 was received for Machine No. 1795, and the balance was paid in cash.

It was estimated that Machine No. BT-311 would produce 200,000 units of product during its five-year useful life, after which it would have a $35,000 trade-in value. Units-of-production depreciation was recorded for the machine for 2024, a period in which it produced 31,000 units of product. Between January 1, 2025, and August 21, 2027, the machine produced 108,000 more units. On August 21, 2027, it was sold for $81,200.

Required Round calculations to the nearest dollar and prepare journal entries to record:

a. The depreciation expense recorded to the nearest whole month on the first December 31 of each machine's life.

b. The purchase/exchange/disposal of each machine.

Problem 9-19A Intangible assets LO7

CHECK FIGURE: b. $24,000

On October 1, 2020, Kingsway Broadcasting purchased for $288,000 the copyright to publish the music composed by a local Celtic group. Kingsway expects the music to be sold over the next three years. The company uses the straight-line method to amortize intangibles.

Required Prepare entries to record:

a. The purchase of the copyright

b. The amortization for the year ended December 31, 2020, calculated to the nearest whole month

Problem 9-20A Intangible assets LO2, 3, 6, 7

CHECK FIGURES: 2. Accum. Amort., Mineral Rights = $57,200; Accum. Deprec., Equip. = $224,400; Accum. Deprec., Truck = $87,450

Copper Explorations recently acquired the rights to mine a new site. Equipment and a truck were purchased to begin mining operations at the site. Details of the mining assets follow:

Asset	Date of Purchase	Cost	Est. Residual	Est. Life
Mineral rights	Mar. 1/20	$ 62,400	$ -0-	4 yrs
Equipment	Mar. 1/20	244,800	-0-	4 yrs
Truck	Mar. 1/20	95,400	-0-	4 yrs

Copper's year-end is December 31 and it uses the straight-line method for all mining assets including intangibles.

Required

1. Record amortization and depreciation at December 31, 2020, on the mining assets, including the mineral rights.

2. Assume the mine was closed on October 31, 2023, and the assets were scrapped. Record the disposal of the assets.

*Problem 9-21A Revised depreciation—change in useful life/residual and betterment LO2, 3, 4, 8

CHECK FIGURES: 1. Loss = $9,310; 2. Total 2020 deprec. = $5,773

Ocean Fishers Ltd. had a 22-foot fishing boat with an inboard motor that was purchased on April 9, 2012, for $77,000. The PPE subledger shows the following information regarding the boat:

Fishing Boat – 22 Ft. with Inboard Motor:					
Component	Date of Purchase	Deprec. Method	Cost	Est. Residual	Est. Life
Fibreglass body	Apr. 9/12	SL	$23,800	$7,000	15 yr
Motor	Apr. 9/12	SL	53,200	-0-	10 yr
			$77,000		

On June 27, 2020, $63,000 cash was paid for a new motor to replace the old one, which was scrapped. The new motor had an estimated useful life of 12 years and a residual value of $4,200. Early in 2020, it was determined that the useful life of the boat's fibreglass body should be adjusted to a total of 20 years with no change in the residual value.

Required

1. Record the appropriate entries regarding the
   a. Purchase of the replacement motor on June 27, 2020, and
   b. Depreciation taken on the fishing boat (body plus motor) on December 31, 2020, the company's year-end.

2. Calculate *total* depreciation taken on the fishing boat (body plus motor) for the company's year ended December 31, 2020.

An asterisk (*) identifies assignment material based on Appendix 9A.

ALTERNATE PROBLEMS

Problem 9-1B Real estate costs LO1

CHECK FIGURE: 2. Dr. Land $423,600

In 2020, DelCano Properties paid $540,000 for a tract of land on which two buildings were located. The plan was to demolish Building A and build a new factory (Building C) in its place. Building B was to be used as a company office and was appraised at a value of $189,108. A lighted parking lot near Building B had improvements valued at $50,058. Without considering the buildings or improvements, the tract of land was estimated to have a value of $317,034.

The company incurred the following additional costs:

Cost to demolish Building A	$ 46,800
Cost to landscape new building site	69,000
Cost to construct new building (Building C)	542,400
Cost of new land improvements (Land Improvements C)	40,500

Required

1. Prepare a schedule having the following column headings: Land, Building B, Building C, Land Improvements B, and Land Improvements C. Allocate the costs incurred by the company to the appropriate columns and total each column.

2. Prepare a single journal entry dated June 1 to record all the incurred costs, assuming they were paid in cash on that date.

Problem 9-2B Balance sheet presentation LO2

CHECK FIGURES: 2019 Total assets = $290,610; 2020 Total assets = $453,420

The adjusted balances at September 30, 2020, for Xentel Interactive are shown in alphabetical order below:

	2020	2019
Accounts payable	$ 4,320	$ 3,150
Accounts receivable	1,800	4,320
Accumulated amortization, copyright	1,080	540
Accumulated depreciation, building	54,000	50,400
Accumulated depreciation, machinery	90,000	82,800
Building	225,000	225,000
Cash	900	2,700
Consulting revenue earned	540,000	622,800
Copyright	7,200	7,200
Land	68,400	68,400
Machinery	295,200	115,200
Mason Xentel, capital*	226,080	270,252
Mason Xentel, withdrawals	72,000	41,400
Notes payable, due October 2024	230,220	55,800
Operating expenses	558,000	625,572
Prepaid insurance	-0-	1,530
Unearned fees	82,800	5,580

*The owner, Mason Xentel, made no additional investments during the year ended September 30, 2020.

Required Prepare a comparative classified balance sheet at September 30, 2020.

Analysis Component: How were Xentel's assets mainly financed in 2019? in 2020? Has the change in how assets were financed from 2019 to 2020 *strengthened* the balance sheet? (To strengthen the balance sheet is to decrease the percentage of assets that are financed by debt as opposed to equity.)

Problem 9-3B Alternative depreciation methods—straight-line, double-declining-balance, and units-of-production LO2

CHECK FIGURES: b. 2022 = $18,300; c. 2020 = $39,560

On January 2, 2018, Wavepoint Systems, a cell phone manufacturer, installed a computerized machine in its factory at a cost of $169,200. The machine's useful life was estimated at four years or a total of 181,500 units with a $24,000 trade-in value. Wavepoint's year-end is December 31. Calculate depreciation for each year of the machine's estimated useful life and the total depreciation for all 4 years under each of the following methods:

a. Straight-line

b. Double-declining-balance

c. Units-of-production, assuming actual units produced were:

Year	2018	2019	2020	2021
Units	38,300	41,150	52,600	56,000

d. Comment on the total depreciation amounts under each method.

Problem 9-4B Calculating depreciation—partial periods LO2, 3 eXcel

CHECK FIGURES: 1B. 2022 Depreciation expense = $53,200; 2A. 2022 Depreciation expense = $84,672

LiveReel Media purchased for $588,000 machinery having an estimated useful life of 10 years with an estimated residual value of $56,000. The company's year-end is December 31. Depreciation is calculated using the half-year rule.

Required Complete the following schedules:

1. Assuming the purchase was made on January 1, 2020

2. Assuming the purchase was made on April 1, 2020

	2020	2021	2022
A. Double-declining-balance method			
Machinery	___	___	___
Less: Accumulated depreciation	___	___	___
Year-end book value	___	___	___
Depreciation expense for the year	___	___	___
B. Straight-line method			
Machinery	___	___	___
Less: Accumulated depreciation	___	___	___
Year-end book value	___	___	___
Depreciation expense for the year	___	___	___

Problem 9-5B Calculating depreciation—partial periods LO2, 3

CHECK FIGURE: DDB 2022 = $32,480

Tundra Tours runs tundra buggy expeditions in northern Manitoba for tourists to catch a glimpse of the abundant caribou, polar bears, and other wildlife. Tundra purchased a tundra buggy on October 19, 2020, for cash of $145,000. Its estimated useful life is five years or 100,000 kilometres with a residual value estimated at $25,000. Tundra Tours' year-end is December 31.

Required Calculate depreciation expense for each fiscal year of the asset's useful life by completing a schedule with the following headings *(round calculations to the nearest whole dollar)*:

	Depreciation Method[1]		
Year	Straight-Line	Double-Declining-Balance	Units-of-Production[2]

[1]Deprecation is calculated to the nearest month.
[2]Assumes actual kilometres of use were 2020, 5,800; 2021, 19,400; 2022, 22,850; 2023, 25,700; 2024, 19,980; 2025, 14,600.

Problem 9-6B **Calculating depreciation—partial periods** LO2, 3

CHECK FIGURE: DDB 2022 = $27,840

Refer to the information in Problem 9-5B. Redo the question assuming that depreciation for partial periods is calculated using the half-year convention.

Problem 9-7B **Calculating depreciation** LO2

CHECK FIGURES: 1. Dr. Depreciation Expense, Machinery $55,000; 1. Dr. Depreciation Expense, Equipment $126,667; 2. Total PPE = $241,666

Westfair Foods Partial Balance Sheet December 31, 2020		
Property, plant, and equipment:		
Machinery[1]	$ 500,000	
Less: Accumulated depreciation	330,000	$170,000
Equipment[2]	1,280,000	
Less: Accumulated depreciation	1,026,667	253,333
Total property, plant, and equipment		$423,333

[1]The machinery was purchased on January 1, 2015, and is depreciated to the nearest whole month using the straight-line method. Its total estimated useful life is eight years with a $60,000 residual value.
[2]The equipment was purchased on August 1, 2018, and is depreciated to the nearest whole month using the double-declining-balance method. The useful life is estimated to be four years with a residual value of $36,000.

Required

1. Calculate and record depreciation for the year ended December 31, 2021, for both the machinery and equipment (round calculations to the nearest whole dollar).

2. Prepare the property, plant, and equipment section of the balance sheet at December 31, 2021.

Problem 9-8B **PPE costs; partial year's depreciation; alternative methods** LO1, 2, 3

CHECK FIGURES: 2. $8,820; 3. $6,525

ID Watchdog Inc. recently negotiated a lump-sum purchase of several assets from a contractor who was planning to change locations. The purchase was completed on September 30, 2020, at a total cash price of $1,044,000, and included a building, land, certain land improvements, and a heavy general-purpose truck. The estimated market values of the assets were building, $663,300; land, $397,980; land improvements, $120,600; and truck, $24,120. The company's fiscal year ends on December 31.

CHAPTER 9 Property, Plant, and Equipment and Intangibles

Required

1. Prepare a schedule to allocate the lump-sum purchase price to the separate assets that were purchased. Also present the journal entry to record the purchase.

2. Calculate the 2020 depreciation expense on the building using the straight-line method to the nearest whole month, assuming a 15-year life and a $45,000 residual value.

3. Calculate the 2020 depreciation expense on the land improvements assuming an eight-year life, $36,000 residual, and double-declining-balance depreciation to the nearest whole month (round calculations to the nearest whole dollar).

Problem 9-9B **Alternative depreciation methods; partial year's depreciation** LO2, 3

CHECK FIGURES: 2020 SL = $31,304; 2025 Units = $21,140; 2022 DDB = $48,048

On May 2, 2020, Uniglobe Satellite Company purchased and installed a new machine that cost $273,000, with a five-year life and an estimated $38,220 residual value. Management estimated that the machine would produce 168,000 units of product during its life. Actual production of units was as follows:

2020	23,520
2021	36,960
2022	33,600
2023	31,920
2024	26,600
2025	30,940

Required Prepare a schedule with the following column headings.

Year	Straight-Line	Units-of-Production	Double-Declining-Balance

Show the depreciation for each year (calculated to the nearest whole month) and the total depreciation for the machine under each depreciation method. For units-of-production, round the depreciation charge per unit to two decimal places. The company's year-end is December 31.

Problem 9-10B **Calculating depreciation; partial year's depreciation** LO2, 3

CHECK FIGURES: Deprec. Expense: Equipment = $2,280; Machinery = $38,124; Tools = $3,432

At April 30, 2020, Hackney Building Products' year-end, the balance sheet showed PPE information as detailed in the schedule below. The company calculates depreciation for partial periods using the half-year convention.

	Cost Information					Depreciation		
Description	Date of Purchase	Depreciation Method	Cost[1]	Residual	Life	Balance of Accum. Deprec. April 30, 2020	Depreciation Expense for 2021	Balance of Accum. Deprec. April 30, 2021
Equipment	Oct. 3/17	Straight-line	$ 62,400	$ 16,800	20 yr.			
Machinery	Oct. 28/17	Units-of-production	540,000	180,000	100,000 units			
Tools	Nov. 3/17	Double-declining-balance	64,000	15,000	5 yr.			

[1]There have been no disposals or betterments since the date of purchase.
[2]Actual units produced were (for years ended April 30): 2018, 940; 2019, 10,150; 2020, 9,280; 2021, 10,590.

Required Complete the schedule.

Problem 9-11B Partial year's depreciation; revising depreciation rates LO1, 2, 4

CHECK FIGURE: Dec. 31, 2021 Deprec. Exp. = $10,600

Fab-Form Industries completed the following transactions involving the purchase of delivery equipment.

2020		
June	26	Paid cash for a new truck, $68,400 plus $3,420 in freight costs. The truck was estimated to have a four-year life and an $18,000 residual value.
	27	Paid $3,780 for special racks installed on the truck.* The racks will enhance the economic benefits flowing from the truck.
Dec.	31	Recorded straight-line depreciation on the truck to the nearest whole month.
2021		
Jan.	5	It was determined that the estimated useful life of the truck should be revised to a total of six years and the residual value changed to $10,100.
Mar.	15	Paid $660 for repairs to the truck's fender damaged when the driver backed into a loading dock.
Dec.	31	Recorded straight-line depreciation on the truck to the nearest whole month.

*Assume the special racks depreciate in an identical manner as the truck.

Required Prepare journal entries to record the transactions.

Problem 9-12B Revising depreciation rates LO4

CHECK FIGURES: Deprec. Exp., Building = $1,620; Deprec. Exp., Equip. = $7,320

The December 31, 2020, adjusted trial balance of Biomedics Inc. showed the following information:

Building	$274,800
Accumulated depreciation, building[1]	134,400
Equipment	117,600
Accumulated depreciation, equipment[2]	38,400

[1]Remaining useful life 15 years; estimated residual value $60,000.
[2]Remaining useful life 6 years; estimated residual value $18,000.

During 2021, a major increase in market demand for building space caused the company to assess the useful life and residual value of the building. It was decided that the useful life would be increased by five years and the residual value increased by $48,000. At the beginning of 2021, it was determined that the remaining estimated life of the equipment should be 10 years and the residual value $6,000. Biomedics calculates depreciation using the straight-line method to the nearest month (round calculations to the nearest whole dollar).

Required Prepare the entries to record depreciation on the building and equipment for the year ended December 31, 2021.

Problem 9-13B Revised depreciation—change in life/residual and betterment LO2, 3, 4

CHECK FIGURES: 1. Loss = $8,847; 2. 2020 Deprec. on Doors = $7,950; Total 2020 Deprec. = $28,185

Brainium Technologies showed the following information in its Property, Plant, and Equipment subledger regarding a warehouse.

Warehouse:

Component	Date of Purchase	Depreciation Method*	Cost	Est. Residual	Est. Life
Windows	Jan. 8/15	SL	$ 51,750	-0-	15 yrs
Doors	Jan. 8/15	SL	105,000	-0-	20 yrs
Roofing	Jan. 8/15	SL	43,500	-0-	10 yrs
Siding	Jan. 8/15	SL	54,000	-0-	25 yrs
Framing/walls	Jan. 8/15	SL	222,000	60,000	30 yrs
Furnace	Jan. 8/15	DDB	27,000	-0-	10 yrs
Misc.	Jan. 8/15	DDB	61,500	7,500	5 yrs
			$564,750		

*SL = Straight-line; DDB = Double-declining-balance

During 2020, it was determined that the original useful life on the warehouse doors should be reduced to a total of 12 years and that the residual value should be $23,100. On January 3, 2020, the furnace broke down unexpectedly. It was replaced the next day with a new one costing $39,000, purchased on account (the old furnace was scrapped). The new furnace had an estimated residual value of $7,500 and an estimated life of 16 years and would continue to be depreciated using the double-declining-balance method.

Required

1. Prepare the entry to record the purchase of the new furnace.
2. Calculate the *total* depreciation expense to be recorded on the warehouse for 2020.

Problem 9-14B Depreciation and impairment losses LO1, 2, 3, 5

CHECK FIGURE: 2. Total assets = $481,125

La Mancha Enterprises completed all of its March 31, 2020, adjustments in preparation for compiling its financial statements, which resulted in the following trial balance.

Account	Balance
Accounts payable..	$ 14,750
Accounts receivable..	57,500
Accumulated depreciation, computer equipment......	40,250
Accumulated depreciation, machinery........................	152,500
Accumulated depreciation, warehouse.......................	286,500
Allowance for doubtful accounts..................................	6,000
Cash..	35,000
Computer equipment..	72,500
Expenses, including cost of goods sold......................	1,246,750
Joy La Mancha, capital...	407,875
Land..	145,000
Machinery..	241,250
Mortgage payable...	93,750
Office supplies...	4,875
Revenues...	1,227,500
Salaries payable..	33,750
Warehouse..	460,000

Other information:

1. All accounts have normal balances.
2. $34,200 of the mortgage balance is due beyond March 31, 2021.

The final task in the year-end process was to assess the assets for impairment, which resulted in the following schedule.

Asset	Recoverable Value
Computer equipment..	$ 6,250
Land..	172,500
Machinery...	65,000
Warehouse..	243,750

Required

1. Prepare the entry (entries) to record any impairment losses at March 31, 2020. Assume the company recorded no impairment losses in previous years.

2. Prepare a classified balance sheet at March 31, 2020.

Analysis Component: How does the recording of an impairment loss affect equity, if at all?

Problem 9-15B Partial-period depreciation; disposal of PPE LO2, 3, 6

CHECK FIGURES: 1. Accum. Deprec. = $42,175; 2. Accum. Deprec. = $33,082; 3. Accum. Deprec. = $48,300

EveryWhere Development Co. showed the following selected PPE balances on January 31, 2020:

Van...	$ 64,400
Accumulated depreciation, van[1]...	40,600
Machinery...	128,800
Accumulated depreciation, machinery[2]..	20,440
Equipment...	75,600
Accumulated depreciation, equipment[3]..	44,800

[1]Remaining estimated useful life is 40,000 kilometres with a residual value of $9,800; depreciated using the units-of-production method.
[2]Total estimated useful life is 10 years with a residual value of $16,800; depreciated using the double-declining-balance method to the nearest whole month.
[3]Remaining estimated useful life is three years with a residual value of $5,600; depreciated using the straight-line method to the nearest whole month.

Required Prepare the entries to record the following disposals:

1. The van was sold on March 2, 2020, for cash of $17,920. It had been driven 4,500 kilometres from January 31, 2020, to the date of sale.

2. The machinery was sold on August 27, 2020, for cash of $95,718.

3. The equipment was sold on June 29, 2020, for cash of $27,720.

Problem 9-16B Disposal of PPE LO1, 2, 3, 5

CHECK FIGURES: 2. Dec. 31, 2020 = $20,604; Apr. 1, 2025 =$5,151; 3A. Loss = $21,657; 3B. Gain = $2,343; 3C. Loss = $33,657

On January 1, 2020, Ultra Green Packaging purchased a used machine for $156,000. The next day, it was repaired at a cost of $4,068 and mounted on a new platform that cost $5,760. Management estimated that the machine would be used for seven years and would then have a $21,600 residual value. Depreciation was to be charged on a straight-line basis to the nearest whole month. A full year's depreciation was charged on December 31, 2020, through to December 31, 2024, and on April 1, 2025, the machine was retired from service.

Required

1. Prepare journal entries to record the purchase of the machine, the cost of repairing it, and the installation. Assume that cash was paid.

2. Prepare entries to record depreciation on the machine on December 31, 2020, and on April 1, 2025 (round calculations to the nearest whole dollar).

3. Prepare entries to record the retirement of the machine under each of the following unrelated assumptions:

   a. It was sold for $36,000.

   b. It was sold for $60,000.

   c. It was destroyed in a fire and the insurance company paid $24,000 in full settlement of the loss claim.

Problem 9-17B Partial year's depreciation; revising depreciation; exchanging PPE LO2, 3, 4, 6

CHECK FIGURES: Aug. 31, 2020, Computer equip. = $72,600; Dec. 31, 2020, Deprec. Exp. = $7,240

During 2020, Global Designs Inc. had the following transactions.

Aug.	31	Traded in furniture with a cost of $42,000 and accumulated depreciation of $25,800 recorded in the accounting records on this date. Global paid $56,400 in cash for a computer system that was estimated to have a three-year life and a $19,200 residual value. The invoice for the exchange showed these items:

Price of the computer equipment...	$ 74,400
Trade-in allowance granted on the furniture	(18,000)
Total paid in cash	$ 56,400

Sept.	4	Paid $11,760 for upgrades to the computer equipment, which increased the economic benefits flowing from the equipment.
Dec.	31	Recorded straight-line depreciation on the computer equipment to the nearest whole month. Round calculations to the nearest whole dollar.

Required Prepare journal entries to record the transactions. Assume that the fair values were *not* known at the time of the exchange.

Problem 9-18B Partial year's depreciation; alternative methods; exchange/disposal of PPE LO2, 3, 6

CHECK FIGURES: 1. Machine 6690 = $10,800; Machine 6691 = $8,325; Machine 6711 = $7,155

Vidéotron Ltée completed the following transactions involving printing equipment.

Machine 6690 was purchased for cash on May 1, 2020, at an installed cost of $72,900. Its useful life was estimated to be four years with an $8,100 trade-in value. Straight-line depreciation was recorded for the machine at the end of 2020 and 2021.

On August 5, 2022, it was traded for Machine 6691, which had an installed cash price of $54,000. A trade-in allowance of $40,500 was received and the balance was paid in cash. The new machine's life was estimated at five years with a $9,450 trade-in value. The fair values of Machines 6690 and 6691 were not reliably determined at the time of the exchange. Double-declining-balance depreciation was recorded on each December 31 of Machine 6691's life. On February 1, 2025, it was sold for $13,500.

Machine 6711 was purchased on February 1, 2025, at an installed cash price of $79,650. It was estimated that the new machine would produce 75,000 units during its useful life, after which it would have an $8,100 trade-in value. Units-of-production depreciation was recorded on the machine for 2025, a period in which it produced 7,500 units of product. Between January 1 and October 3, 2026, the machine produced 11,250 more units. On October 3, 2026, it was sold for $54,000.

Required Prepare journal entries to record:

1. The depreciation expense recorded to the nearest whole month on the first December 31 of each machine's life (for units-of-production, round the rate per unit to three decimal places).

2. The purchase/exchange/disposal of each machine.

Problem 9-19B Intangible assets LO7

CHECK FIGURE: 2. Total PPE = $735,000

On February 3, 2020, Secure Software Group purchased the patent for a new software for cash of $220,800. The company expects the software to be sold over the next five years and uses the straight-line method to amortize intangibles.

Required

1. Prepare entries to record the:

   a. Purchase of the software patent.

   b. Straight-line amortization for the year ended December 31, 2020, calculated to the nearest whole month. Round to the nearest dollar.

2. On December 31, 2020, the company's adjusted trial balance showed the additional asset accounts shown below. Prepare the asset section of the balance sheet at December 31, 2020, including the patent purchased on February 3, 2020.

Accounts receivable...	$285,600
Accumulated depreciation, equipment...	259,200
Accumulated depreciation, building..	189,000
Allowance for doubtful accounts...	8,400
Cash..	103,200
Equipment..	477,600
Building...	595,200
Land...	110,400
Merchandise inventory...	135,600

Problem 9-20B Intangible assets LO2, 3, 6, 7

CHECK FIGURES: 2. Accum. Amort., Patent = $42,000; Accum. Deprec., Equipment = $70,560; Accum. Deprec., Computer = $63,840

RangeStar Telecommunications recently acquired a patent regarding a new telecommunications application. Additional equipment and a computer were purchased to begin making the application available to consumers. Details of the assets follow:

Asset	Date of Purchase	Cost	Est. Residual	Est. Life
Patent	Feb. 12/20	$210,000	$ -0-	20 yrs
Equipment	Feb. 12/20	320,600	56,000	15 yrs
Computer	Feb. 12/20	79,800	-0-	5 yrs

The company's year-end is December 31 and it uses the straight-line method for all production assets including intangibles, calculated to the nearest whole month.

Required

1. Record amortization and depreciation at December 31, 2020, on the production assets, including the patent.

2. Assume that because a highly superior alternative telecommunications application became available from a competitor, RangeStar's application no longer had value and was officially discontinued on January 27, 2024. The equipment was sold for $252,000 cash and the patent and computer were scrapped. Record the disposal of the assets.

*Problem 9-21B Revised depreciation—change in useful life/residual and betterment LO2, 3, 4, 8

CHECK FIGURES: 1. Gain = $4,800; 2. Total 2020 deprec. = $26,690

On August 26, 2015, Race World International purchased a piece of equipment for a total of $426,000. The PPE subledger shows the following information regarding the equipment:

Equipment					
Component	**Date of Purchase**	**Deprec. Method**	**Cost**	**Est. Residual**	**Est. Life**
Metal frame	Aug. 26/15	SL	$144,000	$36,000	20 yrs
Engine	Aug. 26/15	DDB	96,000	6,000	10 yrs
Fan	Aug. 26/15	SL	32,400	3,600	5 yrs
Conveyor system	Aug. 26/15	SL	126,000	39,600	10 yrs
Misc. parts	Aug. 26/15	DDB	27,600	4,800	5 yrs
			$426,000		

Early in 2020, it was determined that the useful life of the metal frame should be adjusted to a remaining life of 20 years with a reduction of $12,000 in the residual value. On October 3, 2020, the company paid $36,000 cash for a new fan to replace the old one, which was sold on the same day to a competitor for $8,400 cash. The new fan had an estimated useful life of five years and a residual value of $4,800.

Required

1. Record the appropriate entries regarding the:

   a. Purchase of the replacement fan on October 3, 2020, and sale of the old fan.

   b. Depreciation on the equipment on December 31, 2020, the company's year-end.

2. Calculate *total* depreciation taken on the equipment for Race World's year ended December 31, 2020.

ANALYTICAL AND REVIEW PROBLEM

A & R Problem 9-1

At the last meeting of the executive committee of Kearins Ltd., the controller was severely criticized by both the president and vice-president of production about the recognition of periodic depreciation. The president was unhappy with the fact that what he referred to as "a fictitious item" was deducted, resulting in depressed profit. In his words, "Depreciation is a fiction when the assets being depreciated are worth far more than we paid for them. What the controller is doing is unduly understating our profit. This in turn is detrimental to our shareholders because it results in the undervaluation of our shares on the market."

The vice-president was equally adamant about the periodic depreciation charges; however, she presented a different argument. She said, "Our maintenance people tell me that the level of maintenance is such that our plant and equipment will last virtually forever." She further stated that charging depreciation on top of maintenance expenses is double-counting—it seems reasonable to charge either maintenance or depreciation but not both.

The time taken by other pressing matters did not permit the controller to answer; instead, you were asked to prepare a report to the executive committee to deal with the issues raised by the president and vice-president.

Required As the controller's assistant, prepare the required report.

ETHICS CHALLENGE

Marcia Diamond is a small business owner who handles all the books for her business. Her company just finished a year in which a large amount of borrowed funds were invested into a new building addition as well as numerous equipment and fixture additions. Marcia's banker requires that she submit semiannual financial statements for his file so he can monitor the financial health of her business. He has warned her that if profit margins erode, making the loan riskier from the bank's point of view, he might raise the interest rate on the borrowed funds. Marcia knows that her profit margin is likely to decline in this current year. As she posts year-end adjusting entries, she decides to apply the following depreciation rule: All property, plant, and equipment would be depreciated using the straight-line method over 50 years with 50% of each asset's cost representing the residual value. Marcia knows that most of the assets have a useful life of less than 20 years and little or no residual value but says to herself, "I plan on being in business for the next 50 years so that's my justification."

Required

1. Identify the decisions managers like Marcia Diamond must make in applying depreciation methods.

2. Is Marcia's decision an ethical violation, or is it a legitimate decision that managers make in calculating depreciation?

3. How will Marcia's depreciation rule affect the profit margin of her business?

FOCUS ON FINANCIAL STATEMENTS

FFS 9-1

CHECK FIGURES: Deprec. Exp.—Bldg. = $46,000; Deprec. Exp.—Mach. = $31,200; Deprec. Exp.—Truck = $38,400; Deprec. Exp.—Furn. (old) = $576; Amort. Exp.—Patent = $20,760; Deprec. Exp.—Equip. = $24,429; Deprec. Exp.— Furn. (new) = $14,657; Post-closing capital balance = $661,974

Times TeleCom's PPE subledger at January 1, 2020, appeared as follows:

	Cost Information					Depreciation/Amortization	
Description	**Date of Purchase[1]**	**Deprec./ Amort. Method[2]**	**Original Cost[3]**	**Residual**	**Life**	**Accum. Balance Dec. 31, 2019**	**Expense for 2020**
Land[4]	July 3/17		$280,000				
Building[4]	July 3/17	S/L	454,000	40,000	15 yr.		
Machinery[5]	Mar 20/17	Units	150,000	30,000	250,000 units		
Truck	Mar 01/17	S/L	298,800	30,000	7 yr.		
Furniture[6,7]	Feb 18/17	DDB	24,000	3,000	5 yr.		
Patent	Nov 7/18	S/L	103,800	-0-	5 yr.		

Additional information:
[1]The company calculates depreciation and amortization to the nearest whole month.
[2]S/L = Straight-line; DDB = Double-declining-balance; Units = Units-of-production
[3]There were no disposals, revisions, or impairments prior to January 1, 2020.
[4]At the beginning of 2020, it was determined that the land and building would be used for five years less than originally estimated due to the need to expand.
[5]Actual units produced: 2017, 45,000; 2018, 55,000; 2019, 52,000; 2020, 65,000.
[6]Used office equipment and furniture were purchased on April 10, 2020, for a total of $114,000 at a bankruptcy sale. The appraised value of the office equipment was $96,000 and of the furniture $72,000. The old furniture was given to a charitable organization on April 12, 2020.
[7]The estimated useful lives and residual values of the April 10 purchases were four years and $10,000 for the office equipment, and five years and $4,000 for the furniture. These assets will be depreciated using the DDB method.

Required

a. Complete the PPE subledger; round calculations to the nearest dollar.

b. Using the information from the PPE subledger completed in part (a) and the following December 31, 2020, adjusted account balances, prepare a single-step income statement and statement of changes in equity for the year ended December 31, 2020, along with the December 31, 2020, classified balance sheet: Cash, $30,000; Accounts Receivable, $72,000; Prepaid Insurance, $15,600; Accounts Payable, $68,000; Unearned Revenue, $53,800; Notes Payable due in 2023, $284,000; Susan Times, Capital, $421,180; Susan Times, Withdrawals, $204,000; Revenue Earned, $950,000; Salaries Expense, $294,000; Insurance Expense, $30,000; Loss on disposal of furniture, $5,184. Susan Times, the owner, made no investments during 2020.

FFS 9-2

Refer to the financial statements for each of Spin Master, Indigo, and WestJet in Appendix II.

Required Answer the following questions.

Part 1

The December 31, 2017, balance sheet for Spin Master reports $32,978 (thousand) of PPE.

a. What does the $32,978 (thousand) represent (i.e., is it the cost of the PPE)?

b. Which generally accepted accounting principle (GAAP) requires that information in addition to the $32,978 (thousand) must be reported and where must it be reported?

c. What amount did Spin Master report as depreciation expense for the year ended December 31, 2017? (*Hint: Refer to the statements of cash flow in Appendix II. Alternatively, go to www.sedar.com, retrieve the complete set of audited annual financial statements, and refer to the appropriate note to the statements.*)

Part 2

a. WestJet's balance sheet reports $4,567,504 (thousand) of property and equipment on December 31, 2017. What percentage is this of its total assets?

b. Indigo's balance sheet reports $82,314 (thousand) of property and equipment at March 31, 2018. What percentage is this of its total assets?

c. Compare WestJet and Indigo's inventory, and property and equipment, each as a percentage of total assets. Why do these percentages differ between firms? *(Hint: Review the asset section of each company's balance sheet.)*

CRITICAL THINKING MINI CASE

Two years ago, on March 1, 2018, General Recycling Management Systems purchased five used trucks and debited the Trucks account for the total cost of $180,000. The estimated useful life and residual value per truck were determined to be five years and $5,000, respectively. $36,000 was paid for a two-year insurance policy covering the trucks effective March 1, 2018; this amount was also debited to the Trucks account since it related to the trucks. On February 1, 2019, new motors were installed in the trucks; parts cost $33,000, and labour was $7,000. New tires were also installed on this date at a total cost of $32,000, and each truck was given an oil change in addition to some minor brake work; the total cost was $2,500. All of these costs were debited to the Trucks account. Profit for the years ended December 31, 2019, and 2020 were $78,000 and $85,000. The manager of the business was paid a bonus equal to 15% of profit; the 2019 bonus was paid on February 1, 2020, and recorded on that date as a debit to Bonus Expense and credit to Cash; the 2020 amount was paid on February 1, 2021, and recorded on that date as a debit to Bonus Expense and credit to Cash.

Required Using the elements of critical thinking, comment on whether all of these items should have been recorded to the truck account. What would the impact be to profit if some of the items were recorded as expense? And, what would the difference be to the manager's bonus paid? What are your thoughts on the ethics involved in this situation?

Payroll Liabilities

© Lobby/Dreamstime.com/GetStock.com

LEARNING OBJECTIVES

LO1   Identify the taxes and other items frequently withheld from employees' wages.

LO2   Make the calculations necessary to prepare a payroll register and prepare the entries to record and pay payroll liabilities.

LO3   Calculate the payroll costs levied on employers and prepare the entries to record the accrual and payment of these amounts.

LO4   Calculate and record employee fringe benefit costs.

Guilty

The Canada Revenue Agency (CRA) announced that a dentist was fined $3,000 in Edmundston, New Brunswick, provincial court after pleading guilty to three charges of failing to remit over $8,000 in monies deducted and withheld from wages and salaries paid to employees.

In Montreal a director on the board of two companies was fined $541,870 and sentenced to a 12-month prison term following a CRA investigation that showed payroll deductions from the salaries of employees were not remitted to the Receiver General for Canada.

In each of the above cases, unpaid deductions had to be paid in addition to the fines. Failure to do so would result in imprisonment. The CRA takes non-payment of source deductions very seriously, as the amounts deducted from employees are deemed to be held in trust until remitted to CRA on the employees' behalf. Canadians have to be confident that the tax system is fair, and know that CRA will prosecute those individuals who cheat.

CRITICAL THINKING CHALLENGE

If payroll liabilities are not recorded, what is the effect on the financial statements?

APPENDIX PREVIEW

Wages or salaries generally amount to one of the largest expenses incurred by a business. Accounting for employees' wages and salaries is one task that is shared by almost all business entities.

Payroll accounting:

- Records cash payments to employees
- Provides valuable information regarding labour costs
- Accounts for amounts withheld from employees' pay
- Accounts for employee (fringe) benefits and payroll costs paid by the employer
- Provides the means to comply with governmental regulations on employee compensation

Student Success *Cycle*

Read the material

Apply your critical thinking skills

Do the exercises

Check your answers

As you study this appendix, you will learn the general processes that all businesses follow to account for these items.

Items Withheld from Employees' Wages

LO1 Identify the taxes and other items frequently withheld from employees' wages.

An understanding of payroll accounting and the design and use of payroll records requires some knowledge of the laws and programs that affect payrolls. Many of these require **payroll deductions**, amounts withheld from the wages of employees, and are discussed in the first portion of this appendix.

 DECISION INSIGHT

The Canadian Payroll Association (CPA) represents more than 10,000 members of the professional payroll community in Canada, the United States, and abroad. With over 18 million Canadian employees paid through CPA member companies, its mission is to provide payroll leadership through advocacy and education. The two qualifications granted through the country's only nationally recognized Payroll Management Certificate Program are Payroll Compliance Practitioner (PCP) and Certified Payroll Manager (CPM).

Source: www.payroll.ca.

WITHHOLDING EMPLOYEES' INCOME TAX

Employers are required to calculate, collect, and remit to the Receiver General for Canada the income taxes of their employees. Historically, when the first federal income tax law became effective in 1917, it applied to only a few individuals having high earnings. It was not until the Second World War that income taxes were levied on almost all wage earners. At that time, Parliament recognized that many individual wage earners could not be expected to save the money needed to pay their income taxes once each year, so Parliament began a system of pay-as-you-go withholding of taxes at the source each payday. This pay-as-you-go withholding of employee income taxes requires an employer to act as a tax-collecting agent of the federal government. Failure to cooperate results in litigation and potential criminal charges.

The amount of income taxes to be withheld from an employee's wages is determined by his or her wages and the amount of **personal tax credits**. Based on rates in effect January 1, 2018, each individual is entitled, in 2018, to some or all of the following annual amounts that are subject to tax credits (as applicable):

1. Basic Personal Amount................... $11,809[1]
2. Married or Equivalent........................ 11,809
   (with maximum earnings stipulated)

The total of each taxpayer's personal tax credits is deducted directly from income to determine the level of income tax deductions from the individual's gross pay. Additional personal credits, beyond the basic personal amount, are provided for items such as being a caregiver to dependent children, tuition dues paid, and unused personal amounts of a spouse/common-law partner. For example, based on rates effective January 1, 2018, a Saskatchewan resident with a gross weekly salary of $400 and personal tax credits of $11,809 (2018 net claim code 1[2] on the TD1 form) would have $26.70 of total income taxes withheld. Another individual with the same gross salary but with personal tax credits of $17,000 (claim code 4) would have only $3.15 withheld.

Employers withhold income tax owed by each employee every payday based on an employee's completed Personal Tax Credits Return, Form **TD1**. There are federal and provincial/territorial TD1 forms. The taxpayer must file revised TD1 forms each time the exemptions change during a year.

In determining the amounts of income taxes to be withheld from the wages of employees, employers use payroll deductions tables provided by the Canada Revenue Agency (CRA). The to-be-withheld amounts include both federal and provincial income taxes except for the province of Quebec, which levies and collects its own income tax and its own pension plan contributions. Provincial income tax rates vary from province to province. Therefore, for consistency, all examples and problems making use of tax tables in this appendix will be based on Saskatchewan's tables. Employers are required to remit the withheld taxes to the Receiver General for Canada each month.

CANADA (OR QUEBEC) PENSION PLAN (CPP OR QPP)

Every working person between the ages of 18 and 70 with few exceptions must make contributions in required amounts to the **Canada Pension Plan** (CPP) or Quebec Pension Plan (QPP).

Effective for the 2018 annual reporting period, contributions are based on earnings as follows:

Canada Pension Plan Contributions		
Effective	Employee Contributions	Employer Contributions
Rate..	4.95%*	4.95%*
Maximum...	$2,593.80	$2,593.80

*4.95% of earnings greater than $3,500 and less than $55,900.

Employers are responsible for making the proper deductions from their employees' earnings. They remit these deductions each month, together with their own contributions, to the Receiver General for Canada.

Self-employed individuals pay the combined rate for employees and employers, or 9.9% on annual earnings between $3,500 and the exempt ceiling (referred to as maximum annual pensionable earnings) of $55,900.

EMPLOYMENT INSURANCE (EI)

To assist the unemployed, the federal government began an employee/employer-financed unemployment insurance plan. Under the revised 1996 *Employment Insurance Act*, compulsory **Employment Insurance** (EI)

---

1 Source: https://www.canada.ca/content/dam/cra-arc/formspubs/pbg/td1/td1-18e.pdf

2 For more information on claim codes visit the following CRA resource: http://www.cra-arc.gc.ca/tx/bsnss/tpcs/pyrll/t4032/2015/t4032-sk-15eng.pdf

coverage was extended to all Canadian workers who are not self-employed. Over 13 million employees, including teachers, hospital workers, and top-level executives, are covered by the insurance plan.

The Employment Insurance fund from which benefits are paid is jointly financed by employees and their employers. At January 1, 2018, employers are required to deduct from their employees' wages 1.66% of insured earnings, to add a contribution of 1.4 times the amount deducted from employees' wages, and to remit both amounts to the Receiver General for Canada. The system is summarized as follows:

Employment Insurance Contributions		
Effective Jan. 1, 2018	**Employee Contributions**	**Employer Contributions**
Rate...	1.66%	1.4 times employee rate
Maximum	$858.22	$1,201.51
Note: maximum insurable earnings for 2018 are $51,700.		

Insured earnings, in most instances, refers to gross earnings. An employee may receive taxable benefits or allowances that would be included in gross earnings but would not be considered insurable earnings. However, in this text, gross earnings will be insurable earnings.

The *Employment Insurance Act* also requires that an employer complete a "record of employment" in cases of termination of employment, illness, injury, or pregnancy and keep a record for each employee that shows among other things wages subject to employment insurance and taxes withheld.

USE OF WITHHOLDING TABLES

Employers may use **wage bracket withholding tables** in determining Canada Pension Plan and Employment Insurance to be withheld from employees' gross earnings. These tables are available from CRA.

Alternatively, determining the amount of withholdings from an employee's gross wages is quite easy when the CRA Payroll Deductions Online Calculator is used. The Payroll Deductions Online Calculator can be found at https://www.canada.ca/en/revenue-agency/services/e-services/e-services-businesses/payroll-deductions-online-calculator.html.

The T4 Form

Employers are required to report wages and deductions both to each employee and to the local office of CRA. On or before the last day of February, the employer must give each employee a T4 statement that tells the employee:

- Total wages for the preceding year
- Taxable benefits received from the employer
- Income taxes withheld
- Deductions for registered pension plan
- Canada Pension Plan contributions
- Employment Insurance deductions

On or before the last day of February the employer must forward to the district taxation office copies of the employee's T4 statements plus a T4 that summarizes the information contained on the employee's T4 statements. The T4 form is shown in Exhibit AI.1. CRA publishes a guide to direct employers in filling out the T4 form. For more information refer to the CRA website: https://www.canada.ca/content/dam/cra-arc/forms-pubs/pbg/t4/t4-fill-14e.pdf.[3]

---

3   Fillable PDF forms can be found at http://www.cra-arc.gc.ca/E/pbg/tf/t4/t4-fill-14e.pdf.

EXHIBIT AI.1
2018 T4 Form

Wages, Hours, and Union Contracts

All provinces have laws establishing maximum hours of work and minimum pay rates. And, while the details vary with each province, generally employers are required to pay an employee for hours worked in excess of 40 in any one week at the employee's regular pay rate plus an overtime premium of at least one-half of his or her regular rate. In addition, employers commonly operate under contracts with their employees' union that provide even better terms.

In addition to specifying working hours and wage rates, union contracts often provide that the employer shall deduct dues from the wages of each employee and remit the amounts deducted to the union.

OTHER PAYROLL DEDUCTIONS

Employees may individually authorize additional deductions such as:

1. Deductions to pay health, accident, hospital, or life insurance premiums

2. Deductions to repay loans from the employer or the employees' credit union

3. Deductions to pay for merchandise purchased from the company

4. Deductions for donations to charitable organizations such as United Way

CHECKPOINT

1. What is the purpose of the federal Employment Insurance scheme?
2. When must T4 statements be given to employees?
3. What are other typical non-mandatory payroll deductions?

Do Quick Study question: QS AI-1

The Payroll Register

LO2 Make the calculations necessary to prepare a payroll register and prepare the entries to record and pay payroll liabilities.

Each pay period the total hours worked are summarized in a payroll register, an example of which is shown in Exhibit AI.2. The illustrated register is for a weekly pay period and shows the payroll data for each employee on a separate line.

In Exhibit AI.2, the columns under the heading Daily Time show the hours worked each day by each employee. The total of each employee's hours is entered in the column headed Total Hours. If hours include overtime hours, these are entered in the column headed O.T. Hours.

EXHIBIT AI.2

Payroll Register

Payroll Week Ended

Employees	Clock Card No.	M	T	W	T	F	S	S	Total Hours	O.T. Hours	Reg. Pay Rate	Regular Pay	O.T. Premium Pay	Gross Pay	
Auer, John	118	8	8	8	8	8			40		10.00	400.00		400.00	1
Cheung, Joen	109	0	8	8	8	8	8		40		12.00	480.00		480.00	2
Daljit, Moe	121	8	8	8	8	8	8	4	52	12	15.00	780.00	90.00	870.00	3
Lee, Shannon	104	8	8		8	8	8	4	44	4	14.00	616.00	28.00	644.00	4
Prasad, Sunil	108		8	8	8	8	4	8	44	4	15.00	660.00	30.00	690.00	5
Rupert, Allan	105	8	8	8	8	8			40		12.00	480.00		480.00	6
Totals												3,416.00	148.00	3,564.00	

Register
March 9, 2019

	Gross Pay	EI Premium	Income Taxes	Hospital Insurance	CPP	Total Deductions	Net Pay	Cheque Number	Sales Salaries	Office Salaries
1	400.00	6.64	26.70	18.00	16.47	67.81	332.19	754	400.00	
2	480.00	7.97	44.90	18.00	20.43	91.30	388.70	755	480.00	
3	870.00	14.44	137.75	24.00	39.73	215.92	654.08	756		870.00
4	644.00	10.69	84.20	18.00	28.55	141.44	502.56	757		644.00
5	690.00	11.45	95.80	24.00	30.82	162.07	527.93	758	690.00	
6	480.00	7.97	44.90	18.00	20.43	91.30	388.70	759	480.00	
	3,564.00	59.16	434.25	120.00	156.43	769.84	2,794.16		2,050.00	1,514.00

The Regular Pay Rate column shows the hourly pay rate of each employee. Total hours worked multiplied by the regular pay rate equals regular pay. Overtime hours multiplied by the overtime premium rate (50% in this case) equals overtime premium pay (O.T. Premium Pay column). And regular pay plus overtime premium pay is the **employee's gross pay**.

The amounts withheld from each employee's gross pay are recorded in the Deductions columns of the payroll register. For example, you determine the income tax deductions by matching the gross pay of each employee to the tax deduction tables and then enter the results in the tax deduction column. Income tax deductions are based on the gross pay less the amounts deducted for EI and CPP (or QPP). The tax tables allow for these adjustments and separate books are available for each province. Exhibit AI.2 assumes that income tax deductions are based on the tables provided in Exhibit AI.3 and assumes the employees reside in Saskatchewan.

For example, you can use the tables in Exhibit AI.3 to determine the appropriate CPP, EI, and income tax deductions for John Auer's $400 pay. In the CPP table, under the *Pay* column, find $400. The CPP deduction according to the table is $16.47 for the pay range $399.93–$400.12. Using the EI table, go to the *Insurable Earnings* column and find $400. The table shows that the EI deduction for the range $399.70–$400.30 is $6.64. Finally, using each of the federal and provincial tax deductions tables, go to the Pay column and find $400. Now follow the numbers across to the claim code 1 column *(assume a claim code of 1 unless otherwise specified)*. The tables show a total income tax to be deducted of $26.15[4] (federal tax of $18.90 + provincial tax of $7.25). You can use the tables to determine the CPP, EI, and income tax deductions for the remaining employees.

EXHIBIT AI.3
Excerpts from CPP, EI, and Income Tax Tables Effective January 1, 2018

Canada Pension Plan Contributions
Weekly (52 pay periods a year)

From	Pay	To	CPP	From	Pay	To	CPP	From	Pay	To	CPP	From	Pay	To	CPP
370.84	-	371.03	15.03	385.39	-	385.58	15.75	399.93	-	400.12	16.47	414.48	-	414.67	17.19
371.04	-	371.23	15.04	385.59	-	385.78	15.76	400.13	-	400.33	16.48	414.68	-	414.87	17.20
371.24	-	371.44	15.05	385.79	-	385.98	15.77	400.34	-	400.53	16.49	414.88	-	415.07	17.21
371.45	-	371.64	15.06	385.99	-	386.18	15.78	400.54	-	400.73	16.50	415.08	-	415.27	17.22
371.65	-	371.84	15.07	386.19	-	386.39	15.79	400.74	-	400.93	16.51	415.28	-	415.48	17.23
371.85	-	372.04	15.08	386.40	-	386.59	15.80	400.94	-	401.13	16.52	415.49	-	415.68	17.24
372.05	-	372.24	15.09	386.60	-	386.79	15.81	401.14	-	401.34	16.53	415.69	-	415.88	17.25
372.25	-	372.45	15.10	386.80	-	386.99	15.82	401.35	-	401.54	16.54	415.89	-	416.08	17.26
372.46	-	372.65	15.11	387.00	-	387.19	15.83	401.55	-	401.74	16.55	416.09	-	416.28	17.27
479.93	-	480.12	20.43	494.48	-	494.67	21.15	509.02	-	509.21	21.87	523.57	-	523.76	22.59
480.13	-	480.33	20.44	494.68	-	494.87	21.16	509.22	-	509.42	21.88	523.77	-	523.96	22.60
480.34	-	480.53	20.45	494.88	-	495.07	21.17	509.43	-	509.62	21.89	523.97	-	524.16	22.61
480.54	-	480.73	20.46	495.08	-	495.27	21.18	509.63	-	509.82	21.90	524.17	-	524.37	22.62
480.74	-	480.93	20.47	495.28	-	495.48	21.19	509.83	-	510.02	21.91	524.38	-	524.57	22.63
480.94	-	481.13	20.48	495.49	-	495.68	21.20	510.03	-	510.22	21.92	524.58	-	524.77	22.64
481.14	-	481.34	20.49	495.69	-	495.88	21.21	510.23	-	510.43	21.93	524.78	-	524.97	22.65
481.35	-	481.54	20.50	495.89	-	496.08	21.22	510.44	-	510.63	21.94	524.98	-	525.17	22.66
481.55	-	481.74	20.51	496.09	-	496.28	21.23	510.64	-	510.83	21.95	525.18	-	525.38	22.67
599.93	-	600.12	26.37	614.48	-	614.67	27.09	629.02	-	629.21	27.81	643.57	-	643.76	28.53
600.13	-	600.33	26.38	614.68	-	614.87	27.10	629.22	-	629.42	27.82	643.77	-	643.96	28.54
600.34	-	600.53	26.39	614.88	-	615.07	27.11	629.43	-	629.62	27.83	643.97	-	644.16	28.55
600.54	-	600.73	26.40	615.08	-	615.27	27.12	629.63	-	629.82	27.84	644.17	-	644.37	28.56
600.74	-	600.93	26.41	615.28	-	615.48	27.13	629.83	-	630.02	27.85	644.37	-	644.57	28.57
600.94	-	601.13	26.42	615.49	-	615.68	27.14	630.03	-	630.22	27.86	644.58	-	644.77	28.58
601.14	-	601.34	26.43	615.69	-	615.88	27.15	630.23	-	630.43	27.87	644.78	-	644.97	28.59
601.35	-	601.54	26.44	615.89	-	616.08	27.16	630.44	-	630.63	27.88	644.98	-	645.17	28.60
601.55	-	601.74	26.45	616.09	-	616.28	27.17	630.64	-	630.83	27.89	645.18	-	645.38	28.61

---

4 The Payroll Deductions Online Calculator produces marginally more accurate results since the table values are based on ranges vs. specific dollar amounts.

EXHIBIT AI.3

Excerpts from CPP, EI, and Income Tax Tables Effective January 1, 2018 (continued)

Canada Pension Plan Contributions

Weekly (52 pay periods a year)

Pay From		To	CPP	Pay From		To	CPP	Pay From		To	CPP	Pay From		To	CPP
823.57	-	823.76	37.44	838.11	-	838.31	38.16	852.66	-	852.85	38.88	867.20	-	867.40	39.60
823.77	-	823.96	37.45	838.32	-	838.51	38.17	852.86	-	853.05	38.89	867.41	-	867.60	39.61
823.97	-	824.16	37.46	838.52	-	838.71	38.18	853.06	-	853.25	38.90	867.61	-	867.80	39.62
824.17	-	824.37	37.47	838.72	-	838.91	38.19	853.26	-	853.46	38.91	867.81	-	868.00	39.63
824.38	-	824.57	37.48	838.92	-	839.11	38.20	853.47	-	853.66	38.92	868.01	-	868.20	39.64
824.58	-	824.77	37.49	839.12	-	839.32	38.21	853.67	-	853.86	38.93	868.21	-	868.41	39.65
824.78	-	824.97	37.50	839.33	-	839.52	38.22	853.87	-	854.06	38.94	868.42	-	868.61	39.66
824.98	-	825.17	37.51	839.53	-	839.72	38.23	854.07	-	854.26	38.95	868.62	-	868.81	39.67
825.18	-	825.38	37.52	839.73	-	839.92	38.24	854.27	-	854.47	38.96	868.82	-	869.01	39.68

Employee's maximum CPP contribution for the year 2018 is $2,593.80

Employment Insurance Premiums

Insurable Earnings From		To	EI premium	Insurable Earnings From		To	EI premium	Insurable Earnings From		To	EI premium	Insurable Earnings From		To	EI premium
347.29	-	347.89	5.77	390.67	-	391.26	6.49	434.04	-	434.63	7.21	477.41	-	478.01	7.93
347.90	-	348.49	5.78	391.27	-	391.86	6.50	434.64	-	435.24	7.22	478.02	-	478.61	7.94
348.50	-	349.09	5.79	391.87	-	392.46	6.51	435.25	-	435.84	7.23	478.62	-	479.21	7.95
349.10	-	349.69	5.80	392.47	-	393.07	6.52	435.85	-	436.44	7.24	479.22	-	479.81	7.96
349.70	-	350.30	5.81	393.08	-	393.67	6.53	436.45	-	437.04	7.25	479.82	-	480.42	7.97
350.31	-	350.90	5.82	393.68	-	394.27	6.54	437.05	-	437.65	7.26	480.43	-	481.02	7.98
350.91	-	351.50	5.83	394.28	-	394.87	6.55	437.66	-	438.25	7.27	481.03	-	481.62	7.99
351.51	-	352.10	5.84	394.88	-	395.48	6.56	438.26	-	438.85	7.28	481.63	-	482.22	8.00
352.11	-	352.71	5.85	395.49	-	396.08	6.57	438.86	-	439.45	7.29	482.23	-	482.83	8.01
352.72	-	353.31	5.86	396.09	-	396.68	6.58	439.46	-	440.06	7.30	482.84	-	483.43	8.02
353.32	-	353.91	5.87	396.69	-	397.28	6.59	440.07	-	440.66	7.31	483.44	-	484.03	8.03
353.92	-	354.51	5.88	397.29	-	397.89	6.60	440.67	-	441.26	7.32	484.04	-	484.63	8.04
354.52	-	355.12	5.89	397.90	-	398.49	6.61	441.27	-	441.86	7.33	484.64	-	485.24	8.05
355.13	-	355.72	5.90	398.50	-	399.09	6.62	441.87	-	442.46	7.34	485.25	-	485.84	8.06
355.73	-	356.32	5.91	399.10	-	399.69	6.63	442.47	-	443.07	7.35	485.85	-	486.44	8.07
356.33	-	356.92	5.92	399.70	-	400.30	6.64	443.08	-	443.67	7.36	486.45	-	487.04	8.08
356.93	-	357.53	5.93	400.31	-	400.90	6.65	443.68	-	444.27	7.37	487.05	-	487.65	8.09
357.54	-	358.13	5.94	400.91	-	401.50	6.66	444.28	-	444.87	7.38	487.66	-	488.25	8.10
553.32	-	553.92	9.19	596.69	-	597.28	9.91	640.07	-	640.66	10.63	683.44	-	684.03	11.35
553.93	-	554.51	9.20	597.29	-	597.89	9.92	640.67	-	641.26	10.64	684.04	-	684.63	11.36
554.52	-	555.12	9.21	597.90	-	598.49	9.93	641.27	-	641.86	10.65	684.64	-	685.24	11.37
555.13	-	555.72	9.22	598.50	-	599.09	9.94	641.87	-	642.46	10.66	685.25	-	685.84	11.38
555.73	-	556.32	9.23	599.10	-	599.69	9.95	642.47	-	643.07	10.67	685.85	-	686.44	11.39
556.33	-	556.93	9.24	599.70	-	600.30	9.96	643.08	-	643.67	10.68	686.45	-	687.04	11.40
556.94	-	557.53	9.25	600.31	-	600.90	9.97	643.68	-	644.27	10.69	687.05	-	687.65	11.41
557.54	-	558.13	9.26	600.91	-	601.50	9.98	644.28	-	644.87	10.70	687.66	-	688.25	11.42
558.14	-	558.73	9.27	601.51	-	602.10	9.99	644.88	-	645.48	10.71	688.26	-	688.85	11.43
558.74	-	559.33	9.28	602.11	-	602.71	10.00	645.49	-	646.08	10.72	688.86	-	689.45	11.44
559.34	-	559.93	9.29	602.72	-	603.31	10.01	646.09	-	646.68	10.73	689.46	-	690.06	11.45
559.94	-	560.54	9.30	603.32	-	603.92	10.02	646.69	-	647.28	10.74	690.07	-	690.66	11.46
560.55	-	561.14	9.31	603.93	-	604.51	10.03	647.29	-	647.89	10.75	690.67	-	691.26	11.47
561.15	-	561.74	9.32	604.52	-	605.12	10.04	647.90	-	648.49	10.76	691.27	-	691.86	11.48
561.75	-	562.34	9.33	605.13	-	605.72	10.05	648.50	-	649.09	10.77	691.87	-	692.46	11.49
562.35	-	562.95	9.34	605.73	-	606.32	10.06	649.10	-	649.69	10.78	692.47	-	693.07	11.50
562.96	-	563.55	9.35	606.33	-	606.93	10.07	649.70	-	650.30	10.79	693.08	-	693.67	11.51
563.56	-	564.15	9.36	606.94	-	607.53	10.08	650.31	-	650.90	10.80	693.68	-	694.27	11.52

EXHIBIT AI.3

Excerpts from CPP, EI, and Income Tax Tables Effective January 1, 2018 (continued)

Employment Insurance Premiums

Insurable Earnings From	To	EI premium	Insurable Earnings From	To	EI premium	Insurable Earnings From	To	EI premium	Insurable Earnings From	To	EI premium
867.78	- 868.37	14.41	911.15	- 911.74	15.13	954.52	- 955.12	15.85	997.90	- 998.49	16.57
868.38	- 868.97	14.42	911.75	- 912.34	15.14	955.13	- 955.72	15.86	998.50	- 999.09	16.58
868.98	- 869.57	14.43	912.35	- 912.95	15.15	955.73	- 956.32	15.87	999.10	- 999.69	16.59
869.58	- 870.18	14.44	912.96	- 913.55	15.16	956.33	- 956.92	15.88	999.70	- 1000.30	16.60
870.19	- 870.78	14.45	913.56	- 914.15	15.17	956.93	- 957.53	15.89	1000.31	- 1000.90	16.61
870.79	- 871.38	14.46	914.16	- 914.75	15.18	957.54	- 958.13	15.90	1000.91	- 1001.50	16.62
871.39	- 871.98	14.47	914.76	- 915.36	15.19	958.14	- 958.73	15.91	1001.51	- 1002.10	16.63
871.99	- 872.59	14.48	915.37	- 915.96	15.20	958.74	- 959.33	15.92	1002.11	- 1002.71	16.64
872.60	- 873.19	14.49	915.97	- 916.56	15.21	959.34	- 959.93	15.93	1002.72	- 1003.31	16.65

Yearly maximum insurable earnings are $51,700
Yearly maximum employee premiums are $858.22
The premium rate for 2018 is 1.66%

(1) **Note**

For insurable earnings above this amount, determine the employee's EI premium as follows:

(1) Enter the employee's insurable remuneration payable now (including, for example, insurable taxable benefits, bonuses, overtime, accumulated overtime, retroactive pay increases and other insurable earnings)... $ _____

(2) Multiply by:

the premium rate for the year 0.0166

(3) EI Premium for the pay period,

step 1 times step 2 .... $ _____

The maximum premium is $858.22. Stop deducting EI premiums when the employee reaches the maximum premium for the year.

Federal tax deductions
Effective January 1, 2018
Weekly (52 pay periods a year)
Also look up the tax deductions in the provincial table

Pay From	Less Than	CC 0	CC 1	CC 2	CC 3	CC 4	CC 5	CC 6	CC 7	CC 8	CC 9	CC 10
393	- 397	52.40	18.30	15.05	8.55	2.05						
397	- 401	52.95	18.90	15.65	9.10	2.60						
401	- 405	53.50	19.45	16.20	9.70	3.15						
405	- 409	54.05	20.00	16.75	10.25	3.75						
409	- 413	54.65	20.55	17.30	10.80	4.30						
473	- 477	63.60	29.55	26.25	19.75	13.25	6.75	0.25				
477	- 481	64.15	30.10	26.85	20.35	13.80	7.30	0.80				
481	- 485	64.70	30.65	27.40	20.90	14.40	7.85	1.35				
485	- 489	65.25	31.20	27.95	21.45	14.95	8.45	1.95				
489	- 493	65.85	31.75	28.50	22.00	15.50	9.00	2.50				
633	- 641	86.30	52.20	48.95	42.45	35.95	29.45	22.95	16.45	9.90	3.40	
641	- 649	87.40	53.25	50.10	43.60	37.05	30.55	24.05	17.55	11.05	4.55	
649	- 657	88.55	54.40	51.20	44.70	38.80	38.20	25.20	18.65	12.15	5.65	
657	- 665	89.65	55.50	52.35	45.80	39.90	39.30	26.30	19.80	13.30	6.80	.25
665	- 673	90.75	56.60	53.45	46.95	41.00	40.45	27.40	20.90	14.40	7.90	1.40
833	- 841	114.30	80.25	77.00	70.50	63.95	57.45	50.95	44.45	37.95	31.45	24.90
841	- 849	115.40	81.35	78.10	71.60	65.10	58.60	52.10	45.55	39.05	32.55	26.05
849	- 857	116.55	82.50	79.25	72.70	66.20	59.70	53.20	46.70	40.20	33.65	27.15
857	- 865	117.65	83.60	80.35	73.85	67.35	60.80	54.30	47.80	41.30	34.80	28.30
865	- 873	118.80	84.70	81.45	74.95	68.45	55.45	55.45	48.95	42.40	35.90	29.40

EXHIBIT AI.3

Excerpts from CPP, EI, and Income Tax Tables Effective January 1, 2018 (continued)

Saskatchewan provincial tax deductions
Effective January 1, 2018
Weekly (52 pay periods a year)
Also look up the tax deductions in the federal table

Pay From	Less Than	CC 0	CC 1	CC 2	CC 3	CC 4	CC 5	CC 6	CC 7	CC 8	CC 9	CC 10
396	398	39.30	6.85	4.75	.60							
398	400	39.50	7.05	4.95	.80							
400	402	39.65	7.25	5.15	.95							
402	404	39.85	7.45	5.35	1.15							
404	406	40.05	7.60	5.55	1.35							
476	480	47.20	14.80	12.70	8.50	4.35	.20					
480	484	47.60	15.20	13.10	8.90	4.75	.55					
484	488	48.00	15.55	13.50	9.30	5.15	.95					
488	492	48.40	15.95	13.85	9.70	5.55	1.35					
492	496	48.80	16.35	14.25	10.10	5.90	1.75					
636	640	62.90	30.45	28.40	24.20	20.05	15.85	11.70	7.50	3.35		
640	644	63.30	30.85	28.80	24.60	20.45	16.25	12.10	7.90	3.75		
644	648	63.70	31.25	29.15	25.00	20.80	16.65	12.50	8.30	4.15		
648	652	64.10	31.65	29.55	25.40	21.20	17.05	12.85	8.70	4.50	.35	
652	656	64.50	32.05	29.95	25.80	21.60	17.45	13.25	9.10	4.90	.75	
656	664	65.05	32.65	30.55	26.35	22.20	18.00	13.85	9.65	5.50	1.35	
664	672	65.85	33.40	31.35	27.15	23.00	18.80	14.65	10.45	6.30	2.10	
672	680	66.65	34.20	32.10	27.95	23.75	19.60	15.40	11.25	7.05	2.90	
680	688	67.40	35.00	32.90	28.70	24.55	20.40	16.20	12.05	7.85	3.70	
688	696	68.20	35.75	33.70	29.50	25.35	21.15	17.00	12.80	8.65	4.45	.30
856	864	84.70	52.25	50.15	46.00	41.80	37.65	33.45	29.30	25.10	20.95	16.75
864	872	85.45	53.05	50.95	46.75	42.60	38.40	34.25	30.05	25.90	21.70	17.55
872	880	86.35	53.95	51.85	47.65	43.50	39.30	35.15	30.95	26.80	22.60	18.45
880	888	87.30	54.85	52.80	48.60	44.45	40.25	36.10	31.90	27.75	23.55	19.40
888	896	88.25	55.80	53.75	49.55	45.40	41.20	37.05	32.85	28.70	24.50	20.35

> **Important Tip:**
>
> For the purposes of simplifying the learning process for payroll, we will focus all of our examples using employees that live in the province of Saskatchewan. Also, when using the federal and provincial tax tables assume the question refers to claim code 1 unless otherwise specified.

The column headed Hospital Insurance in Exhibit AI.2 shows the amounts withheld to pay for hospital insurance for the employees and their families. The total withheld from all employees is a current liability of the employer until paid to the insurance company. Likewise, the total withheld for employees' union dues is a current liability until paid to the union.

Additional columns may be added to the payroll register for any other deductions that occur sufficiently often to warrant special columns. For example, a company that regularly deducts amounts from its employees' pay for Canada Savings Bonds may add a special column for this deduction.

An employee's gross pay less total deductions is the **employee's net pay** and is entered in the Net Pay column. The total of this column is the amount the employees are to be paid. The numbers of the cheques used to pay the employees are entered in the column headed Cheque Number.

The Distribution columns are used to classify the various salaries in terms of different kinds of expense. Here you enter each employee's gross salary in the proper column according to the type of work performed. The column totals then indicate the amounts to be debited to the salary expense accounts.

RECORDING THE PAYROLL

The entry to record the payroll shown in Exhibit AI.2 is:

March 10	Sales Salaries Expense	2,050.00	
	Office Salaries Expense	1,514.00	
	EI Payable		59.16
	Employees' Income Taxes Payable		434.25
	Employees' Hospital Insurance Payable		120.00
	CPP Payable		156.43
	Salaries Payable		2,794.16
	To record the March 10 payroll.		

The debits of the entry were taken from the payroll register's distribution column totals. They charge the employees' gross earnings to the proper salary expense accounts. The credits to EI Payable, Employees' Income Taxes Payable, Employees' Hospital Insurance Payable, and CPP Payable record these amounts as current liabilities. The credit to Salaries Payable (also called Payroll Payable, Wages Payable, or Accrued Salaries Payable, etc.) records as a liability the net amount to be paid to the employees.

 CHECKPOINT

4. What constitutes the employee's gross pay?
5. What is the employee's net pay?

Do Quick Study questions: QS AI-2, QS AI-3, QS AI-4, QS AI-5, QS AI-6

PAYING THE EMPLOYEES

Almost every business pays its employees by cheque or through electronic funds transfer (EFT). Employers give each employee an earnings statement each payday showing the hours worked, gross pay, deductions, and net pay, as shown in Exhibit AI.4.

EXHIBIT AI.4

A Payroll Cheque

John Auer	40		10.00	400.00		400.00	6.64	26.70	16.47	18.00	67.81	332.19
Employee	Total Hours	O.T. Hours	Reg. Pay Rate	Regular Pay	O.T. Prem. Pay	Gross Pay	EI Premium	Income Taxes	CP Plan	Hosp. Ins.	Total Deductions	Net Pay

STATEMENT OF EARNINGS AND DEDUCTIONS FOR EMPLOYEE'S RECORDS—DETACH BEFORE CASHING CHEQUE

GRASSLAND INDUSTRIES
Loon Lake, Saskatchewan

No. 1517

PAY TO THE
ORDER OF ___John Auer_____   Date _March 6, 2017_ $ __332.19__

Three hundred and thirty two dollars and nineteen cents – – – – – – – – – –

Lloydminster Credit Union
Lloydminster, Saskatchewan

GRASSLAND INDUSTRIES

Jane R. Morris

EMPLOYEE'S INDIVIDUAL EARNINGS RECORD

An **employee's individual earnings record**, as shown in Exhibit AI.5, provides for each employee, in one record, a full year's summary of the employee's working time, gross earnings, deductions, and net pay. In addition, it accumulates information that:

1. Serves as a basis for the employer's payroll tax returns.

2. Indicates when an employee's earnings have reached the maximum amounts for CPP and EI deductions.

3. Supplies data for the T4 slip, which must be given to the employee at the end of the year.

The payroll information on an employee's individual earnings record is posted from the payroll register. Note the last column of the record. It shows an employee's earnings to date and is used to determine when the earnings reach maximum amounts and are no longer subject to the various deductions such as CPP and EI.

EXHIBIT AI.5

Employee's 2018 Individual Earnings Record

Employee's Name __John Auer__ SIN No. __123-456-789__ Employee No. __114__

Home Address __Box 68, Loon Lake__ Notify in Case of Emergency __Margaret Auer__ Phone No. __555-964-9834__

Employed __May 15, 1999__ Date of Termination ____ Reason ____

Date of Birth __June 6, 1972__ Date Becomes 65 __June 6, 2037__ Male (X) Female ( ) Married ( ) Single (X) Number of Exemptions __0__ Pay Rate __$10.00__

Occupation __Clerk__ Place __Warehouse__

Date			Time Lost		Time Worked											
Per. Ends	Paid	Hrs.	Rea-son	Total	O.T. Hours	Reg. Pay	O.T. Pay	Gross Pay	EI Prem	Income Taxes	Hosp. Ins.	CPP	Total Deduc-tions	Net Pay	Cheque No.	Cumu-lative Earnings
6-Jan	6-Jan			40		400.00		400.00	6.64	26.70	18.00	16.47	67.81	332.19		400.00
13-Jan	13-Jan			40		400.00		400.00	6.64	26.70	18.00	16.47	67.81	332.19		800.00
20-Jan	20-Jan			40		400.00		400.00	6.64	26.70	18.00	16.47	67.81	332.19		1,200.00
27-Jan	27-Jan	4	Sick	36		360.00		360.00	5.98	16.50	18.00	14.49	54.97	305.03		1,560.00
3-Feb	3-Feb			40		400.00		400.00	6.64	26.70	18.00	16.47	67.81	332.19		1,960.00
10-Feb	10-Feb			40		400.00		400.00	6.64	26.70	18.00	16.47	67.81	332.19		2,360.00
25-May	25-May			40		400.00		400.00	6.64	26.70	18.00	16.47	67.81	332.19		8,360.00

 DECISION MAKER   Answer—End of appendix

Landscape Maintenance Technician

You take a summer job working for a family friend who runs a small landscaping service. When the time arrives for your first paycheque, the owner slaps you on the back, gives you full payment in cash, winks, and adds: "No need to pay those high taxes, eh?" What are your responsibilities in this case? Do you take any action?

CHECKPOINT

> **6.** What is the purpose of the employee's individual earnings record?
>
> **Do Quick Study questions: QS AI-7, QS AI-8**

Mid-Appendix Demonstration Problem

On January 27, the end of its fourth weekly pay period in 2018, Moosejaw Micro Brew Co.'s payroll record showed that its one office employee and two sales employees had earned $481 (claim code 2), $645 (claim code 4), and $868 (claim code 4), respectively. Each employee has $40 of hospital insurance premiums withheld plus $15 of union dues.

Required

a. Prepare a schedule similar to the register in Exhibit AI.2 to summarize deductions by employee and in total. Use the tables in Exhibit AI.3 to determine the appropriate CPP, EI, and income tax to be withheld.

b. Give the journal entry to record the payroll on January 27.

Analysis Component: What effect does the entry in part (b) have on the balance sheet?

SOLUTION

a.

| | | Deductions | | | | | | Payment | | | Distribution | |
| | A | | | | | | | B | = A − B | | | |
CC	Gross Pay	EI Premium	Income Taxes	Hospital Insurance	CPP	Union Dues	Total Deductions	Net Pay	Cheque Number	Sales Salaries	Office Salaries
2	481.00	7.98	39.95	40.00	20.48	15.00	123.41	357.59	754	481.00	
4	645.00	10.71	57.85	40.00	28.60	15.00	152.16	492.84	758		645.00
4	868.00	14.41	111.05	40.00	39.63	15.00	220.09	647.91	759		868.00
	1,994.00	33.10	208.85	120.00	88.71	45.00	495.66	1,498.34		481.00	1,513.00

b.

January 27	Office Salaries Expense...	481.00	
	Sales Salaries Expense..	1,513.00	
	EI Payable...		33.10
	Employees' Income Taxes Payable............		208.85
	Employees' Hospital Insurance Payable ..		120.00
	CPP Payable..		88.71
	Employees' Union Dues Payable		45.00
	Salaries Payable..		1,498.34
	To record payroll deductions for pay period ending January 27.		

Analysis Component: The entry in part (b) will cause liabilities, specifically current liabilities, to increase and equity to decrease.

Payroll Deductions Required of the Employer

LO3 Calculate the payroll costs levied on employers and prepare the entries to record the accrual and payment of these amounts.

Under the previous discussion of the Canada (or Quebec) Pension Plan (CPP or QPP), it was pointed out that pension deductions are required in like amounts on both employed workers and their employers. A covered employer is required by law to deduct from the employees' pay the amounts of their CPP (or QPP), but in addition, the employer must pay an amount equal to the sum of the employees' CPP (or QPP). Commonly, the amount deducted by the employer is recorded at the same time as the payroll to which it relates is recorded. Also, since both the employees' and employer's shares are reported on the same form and are paid in one amount, the liability for both is normally recorded in the same liability account, the CPP (or QPP) Payable account.

An employer is also required to pay Employment Insurance (EI) that is 1.4 times the sum of the employees' EI deductions. Most employers record both of these payroll deductions with a journal entry that is made at the time of recording the payroll to which they relate. For example, the entry to record the employer's amounts on the payroll in Exhibit AI.2 is:

March 10	EI Expense (1.4 × $59.16)	82.82	
	CPP (or QPP) Expense	156.43	
	EI Payable		82.82
	CPP (or QPP) Payable		156.43
	To record the employer's payroll taxes.		

The debit in the entry records as an expense the payroll taxes levied on the employer, and the credits record the liabilities for the taxes.

PAYING THE PAYROLL DEDUCTIONS

Income tax, EI, and CPP (or QPP) amounts withheld each payday from the employees' pay plus the employer's portion of EI and CPP (or QPP) are current liabilities until paid to the Receiver General for Canada. The normal method of payment is to pay the amounts due at any chartered bank or remit them directly to the Receiver General for Canada. Payment of these amounts is usually required to be made before the 15th of the month following the month that deductions were made from the earnings of the employees. Large employers are required to remit on the 10th and 25th of each month.

For simplicity, we assume the payment of the March 10 amounts recorded above is made the following day. Recall, however, that the employer must remit the amounts withheld from the employee as determined in Exhibit AI.2 *plus* the employer's portion recorded above. The following T-accounts summarize all of these amounts:

EI Payable	
	59.16*
	82.82**
	141.98

Employees' Income Taxes Payable	
	434.25*

CPP (or QPP) Payable	
	156.43*
	156.43*
	312.86

Hospital Insurance Payable	
	120.00*

*Employees' portion per Exhibit AI.2
** Employer's portion

The entry to record remittance to the Receiver General for Canada is then:

March 11	EI Payable...	141.98	
	Employees' Income Taxes Payable	434.25	
	CPP (or QPP) Payable..	312.86	
	Cash		889.09
	To record the remittance of payroll liabilities to the Receiver General for Canada.		

The entry to record remittance to the hospital insurance plan authority is then:

March 11	Employment Hospital Insurance Payable	120.00	
	Cash		120.00
	To record the remittance of employees' hospital insurance premiums.		

Notice that the payment of payroll liabilities is recorded in the same manner as payment of any other liabilities.

ACCRUING PAYROLL DEDUCTIONS ON WAGES

Mandatory payroll deductions are levied *only on wages actually paid.* Accrued wages are not subject to payroll deductions until they are paid. However, to satisfy the matching principle, both accrued wages and the related accrued deductions should be recorded at the end of an accounting period. In reality, because the amounts of such deductions vary little from one accounting period to the next and often are small in amount, many employers apply the materiality principle and do not accrue payroll deductions.

 CHECKPOINT

7. When are the payments for employee deductions due to the Receiver General for Canada?

Do Quick Study questions: QS AI-9, QS AI-10

Employee (Fringe) Benefit Costs

LO4 Calculate and record employee fringe benefit costs.

Many companies pay for a variety of benefits called **employee fringe benefits** in addition to the wages earned by employees and the related amounts paid by the employer. For example, an employer may pay for part (or all) of the employees' medical insurance, life insurance, and disability insurance. Another typical employee benefit involves employer contributions to a retirement income plan. Workers' compensation and vacation pay are required to be paid by employers according to the legislation in each province.

WORKERS' COMPENSATION

Legislation is in effect in all provinces for payments to employees for an injury or disability arising out of or in the course of their employment. Under the provincial workers' compensation acts, employers are required to insure their employees against injury or disability that may arise as a result of employment. Premiums are normally based on (1) accident experience of the industrial classification to which each business is assigned and (2) the total payroll.

Procedures for payment are as follows:

1. At the beginning of each year, every covered employer is required to submit to the Workers' Compensation Board[5] an estimate of the expected payroll for the coming year.

2. Provisional premiums are then established by the board relating estimated requirements for disability payments to estimated payroll. Provisional premium notices are then sent to all employers.

3. Provisional premiums are normally payable in three to six installments during the year.

4. At the end of each year, actual payrolls are submitted to the board, and final assessments are made based on actual payrolls and actual payments. Premiums are normally between 1% and 3% of gross payroll and are borne by the employer.

EMPLOYER CONTRIBUTIONS TO EMPLOYEE INSURANCE AND RETIREMENT PLANS

The entries to record employee benefits costs depend on the nature of the benefit. Some employee retirement plans are quite complicated and involve accounting procedures that are too complex for discussion in this introductory course. In other cases, however, the employer simply makes periodic cash contributions to a retirement fund for each employee and records the amounts contributed as expense. Other employee benefits that require periodic cash payments by the employer include employer payments of insurance premiums for employees.

In the case of employee benefits that simply require the employer to make periodic cash payments, the entries to record the employer's obligations are similar to those used for payroll deductions.[6] For example, assume that an employer with five employees has agreed to pay medical insurance premiums of $40 per month for each employee. The employer will also contribute 10% of each employee's salary to a retirement program. If each employee earns $2,500 per month, the entry to record these employee benefits for the month of March is:

March 31	Benefits Expense	1,450	
	Employees' Medical Insurance Payable		200
	Employees' Retirement Program Payable		1,250
	To record employee benefits;		
	($2,500 × 5) × 10% = $1,250.		

5 In Ontario, the Workers' Compensation Board is called the Workplace Safety and Insurance Board (WSIB). In BC, it is called WorkSafeBC.

6 Some payments of employee benefits must be added to the gross salary of the employee for the purpose of calculating income tax, CPP, and EI payroll deductions. However, in this chapter and in the problems at the end of the chapter, the possible effect of employee benefit costs on payroll taxes is ignored to avoid undue complexity in the introductory course.

VACATION PAY

Employers are required to allow their employees paid vacation time (at a minimum rate of 4% of gross earnings) as a benefit of employment. For example, many employees receive two weeks' vacation in return for working 50 weeks each year. The effect of a two-week vacation is to increase the employer's payroll expenses by 4% (2/50 = 0.04). After five years of service, most employees are entitled to a three-week vacation (i.e., 3/49 = 6.12%). However, new employees often do not begin to accrue vacation time until after they have worked for a period of time, perhaps as much as a year. The employment contract may say that no vacation is granted until the employee works one year, but if the first year is completed, the employee receives the full two weeks. Contracts between the employer and employee may allow for vacation pay in excess of the 4% minimum.

To account for vacation pay, an employer should estimate and record the additional expense during the weeks the employees are working and earning the vacation time. For example, assume that a company with a weekly payroll of $20,000 grants two weeks' vacation after one year's employment. The entry to record the estimated vacation pay is:

Date	Benefits Expense..	800	
	Estimated Vacation Pay Liability.................		800
	To record estimated vacation pay;		
	$20,000 × 0.04 = $800.		

As employees take their vacations and receive their vacation pay, the entries to record the vacation payroll take the following general form:

Date	Estimated Vacation Pay Liability........................	xxx	
	EI and CPP (or QPP) Payable.......................		xxx
	Employees' Income Taxes Payable............		xxx
	Other Withholding Liability Accounts		
	Such as Employees' Hospital		
	Insurance Payable..		xxx
	Salaries Payable...		xxx
	To record payroll.		

Mandatory payroll deductions and employee benefits costs are often a major category of expense incurred by a company. They may amount to well over 25% of the salaries earned by employees.

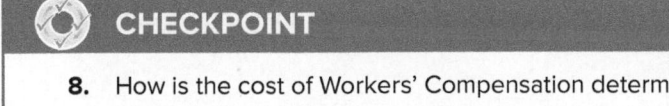

CHECKPOINT

8. How is the cost of Workers' Compensation determined?

Do Quick Study question: QS AI-11

CRITICAL THINKING CHALLENGE

Refer to the Critical Thinking Challenge question at the beginning of the appendix. Compare your answers to those suggested on Connect.

SUMMARY

LO1 **Identify the taxes and other items frequently withheld from employees' wages.** Amounts withheld from employees' wages include federal income taxes, Canada (or Quebec) Pension Plan (CPP or QPP), and Employment Insurance (EI). Payroll costs levied on employers include EI and CPP (or QPP). An employee's gross pay may be the employee's specified wage rate multiplied by the total hours worked plus an overtime premium rate multiplied by the number of overtime hours worked. Alternatively, it may be the given periodic salary of the employee. Taxes withheld and other deductions for items such as union dues, insurance premiums, and charitable contributions are subtracted from gross pay to determine the net pay.

LO2 **Make the calculations necessary to prepare a payroll register and prepare the entries to record and pay payroll liabilities.** A payroll register is used to summarize all employees' hours worked, regular and overtime pay, payroll deductions, net pay, and distribution of gross pay to expense accounts during each pay period. It provides the necessary information for journal entries to record the accrued payroll and to pay the employees.

LO3 **Calculate the payroll costs levied on employers and prepare the entries to record the accrual and payment of these amounts.** When a payroll is accrued at the end of each pay period, payroll deductions and levies should also be accrued with debits and credits to the appropriate expense and liability accounts.

LO4 **Calculate and record employee fringe benefit costs.** Fringe benefit costs that involve simple cash payments by the employer should be accrued with an entry similar to the one used to accrue payroll levies. Legislated employee benefits related to Workers' Compensation and vacation pay are paid for by the employer.

 Guidance Answer to DECISION MAKER

Landscape Maintenance Technician

You need to be concerned about being an accomplice to unlawful payroll activities. Not paying federal and provincial taxes on wages earned is unlawful and unethical. Such payments won't provide CPP and EI contributions. The best course of action is to request payment by cheque. If this fails to change the owner's payment practices, you must consider quitting this job.

 Guidance Answers to CHECKPOINT

1. Employment Insurance is designed to alleviate hardships caused by interruptions in earnings through unemployment.
2. On or before the last day in February.
3. Deductions for Canada Savings Bonds, health or life insurance premiums, loan repayments, and donations to charitable organizations.
4. Regular pay plus overtime pay.
5. Gross pay less all the deductions.
6. An employee's individual earnings record serves as a basis for the employer's tax returns, indicates when the maximum CPP (or QPP) and EI deductions have been reached, and supplies the data for the employees' T4 slips.
7. Normally by the 15th of the following month; large employers must remit on the 10th and 25th of each month.
8. Premiums are based on the accident experience in the specific industry and on the size of the employer's payroll.

Demonstration Problem

Presented below are various items of information for three part-time employees of the Saskatchewan Consulting Company for the week ending March 30, 2018.

	Billings	Dephir	Singe
Wage rate (per hour)	$ 75.00	$ 60.00	$ 18.00
Overtime premium (when >40 hours)..............	50%	50%	50%
Annual vacation...	2.5 weeks	2.5 weeks	2.5 weeks
Cumulative wages as of March 30, 2018:	$28,500.00	$58,600.00	$10,800.00
For the week (pay period) ended March 30, 2018:			
Hours worked..	8	22	48
Medical insurance:			
Employer's contribution..........................	$ 25.00	$ 25.00	$ 25.00
Withheld from employee.........................	18.00	18.00	18.00
Union dues withheld....................................	50.00	70.00	50.00
Income tax withheld	77.80	298.35	165.80
Employment Insurance withheld..............	9.96	—	15.54
Canada Pension withheld	26.37	—	43.00
Payroll deduction rates:			
Employment Insurance.....................................	1.66% to an annual maximum of $858.22		
Canada Pension Plan...	4.95% less annual exemption of $3,500; maximum per year is $2,593.80		

Required In solving the following requirements, round all amounts to the nearest whole penny. Prepare schedules that determine, for each employee and for all employees combined, the following information:

1. Wages earned for the week, total overtime pay (if any), and gross wages.

2. Vacation pay accrued for the week.

3. Costs imposed on the employer.

4. Employees' net pay for the week.

5. Employer's total payroll-related cost (wages, mandatory deductions, and fringe benefits).

Present journal entries to record the following:

6. Payroll expense.

7. Payroll deductions and employees' benefits expense.

8. Remittance to the Receiver General for Canada on April 15.

Analysis Component: What percentage of the total payroll-related cost to the employer represents deductions and fringe benefits versus gross pay? Round your answers to two decimal places.

Planning the Solution

- Calculate the gross pay for each employee.
- Calculate the amounts deducted for all employees and their net pay.
- Calculate the employer's share of payroll deductions.
- Prepare the necessary journal entries.
- Address the analysis component.

SOLUTION

1. The gross wages (including overtime) for the week:

	Billings	Dephir	Singe	Total
Regular wage rate.............................	$ 75.00	$ 60.00	$ 18.00	
Regular hours...................................	× 8	× 22	× 48	
Regular pay......................................	$600.00	$1,320.00	$864.00	$2,784.00
Overtime premium.............................	$ 37.50	$ 30.00	$ 9.00	
Overtime hours.................................	-0-	× -0-	× 8	
Total overtime pay	$ -0-	$ -0-	$ 72.00	$ 72.00
Gross wages.....................................	$600.00	$1,320.00	$936.00	$2,856.00

2. The vacation pay accrued for the week:

	Billings	Dephir	Singe	Total
Annual vacation..	2.5 weeks	2.5 weeks	2.5 weeks	
Weeks worked in year..............................	49.5 weeks	49.5 weeks	49.5 weeks	
Vacation pay as a percentage of regular pay	5.05%	5.05%	5.05%	
Regular pay this week	× $600.00	× $1,320.00	× $936.00	
Vacation pay this week	$ 30.30	$ 66.66	$ 47.27	$144.23

The information in the following table is needed for part 3:

			Earnings Subject to	
Employees	Earnings Through March 30	Earnings This Week	CPP	Employment Insurance
Billings..................................	$28,500.00	$ 600.00	$ 532.69[3]	$ 600.00
Dephir[1].................................	58,600.00	1,320.00	—	—
Singe[2]..................................	10,800.00	936.00	868.69[3]	936.00
Totals		$2,856.00	$1,402.00	$1,536.00

[1] Dephir's earnings have exceeded the CPP maximum of $55,900 and EI maximum of $51,700 and the maximum deductions of $2,593.80 (CPP) and $858.22 (EI). Therefore, neither CPP nor EI is deducted.

[2] Deductions would cease when the yearly maximum deduction of $930.60 was reached.

[3] Recall that the first $3,500 of income is exempt from CPP. This represents $67.31/week (= $3,500/52 weeks).

3. The costs imposed on the employer.

	Billings	Dephir	Singe	Total
CPP (1.0)	$26.37	—	$43.00	$ 69.37
Employment Insurance (1.4)	13.94	—	21.76	35.70
Totals	$40.31	—	$64.76	$105.07

4. The net amount paid to the employees:

	Billings	Dephir	Singe	Total
Regular pay	$600.00	$1,320.00	$864.00	$2,784.00
Overtime pay	-0-	-0-	72.00	72.00
Gross pay	$600.00	$1,320.00	$936.00	$2,856.00
Withholdings:				
Income tax withholding	$ 73.15	$ 280.75	$157.20	$ 511.10
CPP withholding	26.37	—	43.00	69.37
EI withholding	9.96	—	15.54	25.50
Medical insurance	18.00	18.00	18.00	54.00
Union dues	50.00	70.00	50.00	170.00
Total withholdings	$177.48	$ 368.75	$283.74	$ 829.97
Net pay to employees	$422.52	$ 951.25	$652.26	$2,026.03

5. The total payroll-related cost to the employer.

	Billings	Dephir	Singe	Total
Regular pay	$600.00	$1,320.00	$ 864.00	$2,784.00
Overtime pay	-0-	-0-	72.00	72.00
Gross pay	$600.00	$1,320.00	$ 936.00	$2,856.00
Deductions and fringe benefits:				
CPP	$ 26.37	$ —	$ 43.00	$ 69.37
EI	13.94	—	21.76	35.70
Vacation	30.30	66.66	47.27	144.23
Medical insurance	25.00	25.00	25.00	75.00
Total deductions and fringe benefits	$ 95.61	$ 91.66	$ 137.03	$ 324.30
Total payroll-related cost	$695.61	$1,411.66	$1,073.03	$3,180.30

6. Journal entry for payroll expense:

2018			
March 27	Salary Expense	2,856.00	
	Employees' Income Taxes Payable		511.10
	CPP Payable		69.37
	EI Payable		25.50
	Employees' Medical Insurance Payable		54.00
	Employees' Union Dues Payable		170.00
	Salaries Payable		2,026.03
	To record payroll expense.		

7. Journal entry for payroll deductions and employees' benefit expense:

2018			
March 27	CPP Expense...	69.37	
	EI Expense...	35.70	
	Benefits Expense...	219.23	
	CPP Payable..		69.37
	EI Payable...		35.70
	Accrued Vacation Pay Payable.................		144.23
	Employees' Medical Insurance Payable...		75.00
	To record employer's share of payroll *deductions and benefits expense.*		

8. Journal entry to record the remittance to the Receiver General for Canada:

2018			
Apr. 15	EI Payable[1]	61.20	
	CPP Payable[2]...	138.74	
	Employees' Income Taxes Payable	511.10	
	Cash		711.04
	Calculations:		
	1. $25.50 (Employees' Portion) +$35.70 *(Employer's Portion) = $61.20*		
	2. $69.37 (Employees' Portion) + $69.37 *(Employer's Portion) = $138.74*		

Analysis Component: Deductions and fringe benefits represent 10.20% (= $324.30/$3,180.30) of total payroll-related costs, and gross pay is 89.80% (= $2,856.00/$3,180.30).

GLOSSARY

Canada Pension Plan A national contributory retirement pension scheme.

Employee fringe benefits Payments by an employer, in addition to wages and salaries, that are made to acquire employee benefits such as insurance coverage and retirement income.

Employee's gross pay The amount an employee earns before any deductions for taxes or other items such as union dues or insurance premiums.

Employee's individual earnings record A record of an employee's hours worked, gross pay, deductions, net pay, and certain personal information about the employee.

Employee's net pay The amount an employee is paid, determined by subtracting from gross pay all deductions for taxes and other items that are withheld from the employee's earnings.

Employment Insurance An employee/employer–financed unemployment insurance plan.

Payroll deductions Amounts deducted from an employee's pay, usually based on the amount of an employee's gross pay.

Personal tax credits Amounts that may be deducted from an individual's income taxes and that determine the amount of income taxes to be withheld.

TD1 A form, known as the Personal Tax Credit Return, that determines how much income tax is to be withheld by the employer based on the employee's exemptions.

Wage bracket withholding table A table showing the amounts to be withheld from employees' wages at various levels of earnings.

CONCEPT REVIEW QUESTIONS

1. Who pays the contributions to the Canada Pension Plan?

2. Who pays premiums under the Workers' Compensation laws?

3. Who pays federal Employment Insurance? What is the rate?

4. What are the objectives of Employment Insurance laws?

5. To whom and when are payroll deductions remitted?

6. What determines the amount that must be deducted from an employee's wages for income taxes?

7. What is a tax withholding table?

8. What is the Canada Pension Plan deduction rate for self-employed individuals?

9. What information is accumulated on an employee's individual earnings record? Why must this information be accumulated? For what purposes is the information used?

10. What payroll charges are levied on the employer? What amounts are deducted from the wages of an employee?

11. What are employee fringe benefits? Name some examples.

Note: For consistency, assume all companies used in the questions are based in Saskatchewan. All questions making use of tax tables in this appendix will be based on Saskatchewan's tables.

QUICK STUDY

QS AI-1 Payroll expenses LO1

A company deducts $260 in Employment Insurance and $205 in Canada Pension from the weekly payroll of its employees. How much is the company's expense for these items for the week?

QS AI-2 Preparing payroll journal entries LO2

Trax Ltd. has six employees, each of whom earns $3,000 per month. Income taxes are 20% of gross pay and the company deducts EI and CPP. Prepare the March 31 journal entry to record payroll for the month.

QS AI-3 Paying employees LO2

Use the information in QS AI-2 to record the payment of the wages to the employees for March.

QS AI-4 Completing a payroll register LO2 eXcel

Employee	Gross Pay	EI Premium	Income Taxes	CPP	Total Deductions	Net Pay	Office Salaries	Sales Salaries
			Deductions			Pay	Distribution	
Johnson, S.	1,200.00	19.92	241.15	56.07				
Waverley, N.	530.00	8.80	57.25	22.90				
Zender, B.	675.00	11.21	92.05	30.08				
Totals	2,405.00	39.93	390.45	109.05				

Required Prairie Rigging's three employees are paid weekly. Waverley works in the office and Johnson and Zender are sales representatives. Complete the payroll register above for the week ended March 9, 2018.

QS AI-5 Completing a payroll register using tables LO2 eXcel

Employee	Gross Pay	EI Premium	Income Taxes	CPP	Total Deductions	Net Pay	Salaries Expense
			Deductions			Pay	
Bentley, A.	2,010.00						
Craig, T.	2,115.00						
Totals	4,125.00						

Required Meadow Lake Groceries has two employees who are paid monthly. Using the monthly payroll deduction tables link at the end of the appendix, complete the payroll register above for the month ended March 31, 2018, assuming both employees' TD1 claim code is 1. For the complete CPP, EI, and federal and provincial tax deduction tables, please go to Connect.

QS AI-6 Completing a payroll register by calculating deductions LO2 eXcel

	Deductions					Pay	Distribution	
Employee	Gross Pay	EI Premium	Income Taxes	CPP	Total Deductions	Net Pay	Office Salaries	Sales Salaries
Withers, S.	2,500.00						2,500.00	
Volt, C.	1,800.00							1,800.00
Totals								

Required Maidstone Plumbing Services' two employees are paid biweekly. Assuming a tax rate of 30%, complete the payroll register above for the two-week period ended February 24, 2018.

QS AI-7 Payroll journal entry LO2

Games Co. has eight employees, each of whom earns $3,500 per month. Income taxes are 20% of gross pay and the company deducts EI and CPP. Prepare the March 31, 2018, journal entry to record Games Co.'s salaries expenses for the month.

QS AI-8 Payroll journal entry LO2

Chandler Tailors pays its three part-time employees monthly. The following information is available for the February 2018 payroll:

	Deductions					Pay	Distribution	
Employee	Gross Pay	EI Premium	Income Taxes	CPP	Total Deductions	Net Pay	Office Salaries	Sales Salaries
Berkley, M.	575.00	9.55	0.00	14.03	23.58	551.42	575.00	
Chandler, O.	840.00	13.94	0.00	27.14	41.08	798.92		840.00
Meister, P.	1,020.00	16.93	0.00	36.05	52.98	967.02		1,020.00
Totals	2,435.00	40.42	0.00	77.22	117.64	2,317.36	575.00	1,860.00

Required Prepare the journal entry to record payroll expenses for the month.

QS AI-9 Recording employer's payroll deductions LO3

Refer to the information in QS AI-8. Prepare a journal entry to record Chandler Tailors' share of payroll deductions.

QS AI-10 Payment of payroll deductions LO3

Refer to the information in QS AI-8 and QS AI-9. Prepare a journal entry to record payment by Chandler Tailors to the Receiver General for Canada on March 15.

QS AI-11 Recording fringe benefit costs LO4

Games Co. (see QS AI-7) contributes 8% of an employee's salary to a retirement program, pays medical insurance premiums of $60 per employee, and pays vacation allowance equivalent to 5% of the employee's salary. Prepare a journal entry to record the fringe benefit costs for March.

EXERCISES

Exercise AI-1 Calculating gross and net pay LO2

CHECK FIGURE: Net pay = $1,863.51

Julie Leung, an employee of the Import Company, worked 172 hours during the month of January 2018. Her pay rate is $12.50 per hour, and her wages are subject to no deductions other than income taxes, EI, and CPP. The overtime premium is 50% and is applicable to any time greater than 160 hours per month. Calculate her regular pay, overtime premium pay, gross pay, total deductions, and net pay (assume claim code 1). For the complete CPP, EI, and federal and provincial tax deduction tables, please go to Connect.

Exercise AI-2 Calculating payroll deductions and recording the payroll LO2 eXcel

CHECK FIGURE: Total EI withholding = $64.09

The following information as to earnings and deductions for the weekly pay period ended March 9 was taken from a company's payroll records:

Employees' Names	Weekly Gross Pay	Earnings to End of Previous Week	Income Taxes	Health Insurance Deductions
Hellen Craig....................	$ 720	$12,510	$101.55	$ 24.00
Joseph Lim......................	610	10,320	76.60	24.00
Dino Patelli.....................	830	15,500	128.20	36.00
Sharleen McFee.............	1,700	29,500	407.90	24.00
	$3,860		$714.25	$108.00

Required Calculate the amounts paid to each employee, and the employees' EI and CPP withholdings, and prepare a general journal entry to record the payroll. Assume all employees work in the office.

Exercise AI-3 Completing a payroll register LO2 eXcel

CHECK FIGURE: Total deductions = $2,386.79

Lendrum Servicing's four employees are paid every two weeks. Atkins runs the office and the remaining employees are sales representatives.

		Deductions					Pay	Distribution	
Employee	Gross Pay	EI Premium	Income Taxes	United Way	CPP	Total Deductions	Net Pay	Admin. Salaries	Sales Salaries
Atkins, D.	1,900.00	31.54	322.25	80.00	87.39				
Nesbitt, M.	1,260.00	20.92	161.35	50.00	55.71				
Trent, F.	1,680.00	27.89	261.60	40.00	76.50				
Vallot, M.	3,000.00	49.80	680.00	300.00	141.84				
Totals	7,840.00	130.15	1,425.20	470.00	361.44				

Required Complete the payroll register above for the biweekly period ended March 16, 2018.

Exercise AI-4 Completing a payroll register using tables LO2

CHECK FIGURE: Total EI premiums = $136.45   e**X**cel

D&D Stockyards' four employees are paid monthly. Each employee donates 5% of gross pay to United Way through payroll deductions. Crimson and Peterson purchase Canada Savings Bonds through monthly payroll deductions of $150 and $200, respectively.

		Deductions							Pay	Distribution	
Employee	Gross Pay	EI Premium	Income Taxes	Canada Saving Bonds	CPP	United way	Total Deductions	Net Pay		Office Salaries	Sales Salaries
Crimson, L.	1,995.00									1,995.00	
Long, M.	2,040.00										2,040.00
Morris, P.	2,000.00										2,000.00
Peterson, B.	2,280.00										2,280.00
Totals											

Required Using the payroll tables, complete the payroll register above for the monthly pay period ended February 29, 2018, assuming the following TD1 claim codes for each employee: Crimson (2), Long (1), Morris (1), and Peterson (3). For the complete CPP, EI, and federal and provincial tax deduction tables, please go to Connect.

Exercise AI-5 Completing a payroll register by calculating deductions LO2   e**X**cel

CHECK FIGURE: Total deductions = $1,547.64

		Deductions							Pay	Distribution	
Employee	Gross Pay	EI Premium	Income Taxes	Medical Ins.	CPP	United way	Total Deductions	Net Pay		Office Salaries	Guide Salaries
Wynn, L.	1,200.00			65.00		40.00					1,200.00
Short, M.	950.00			65.00		100.00				950.00	
Pearl, P.	1,150.00			65.00		-0-					1,150.00
Quincy, B.	875.00			65.00		50.00					875.00
Totals											

Required Piperel Lake Resort's four employees are paid weekly. Assume an income tax rate of 20%. Complete the payroll register above for the month ended January 31, 2018.

Exercise AI-6 Other payroll deductions LO2

CHECK FIGURE: Monthly United Way contribution = $34.77

Sharon Von Hatton is the only employee of a self-employed businessperson. She earned a monthly salary of $2,050 in February 2018, her first month of employment. In response to a citywide effort to obtain charitable contributions to the local United Way programs, Von Hatton has requested that her employer withhold 2% of her salary (after CPP, EI, and income taxes have been deducted).

Required Prepare the journal entry to record payroll expenses for the month of February 2018. Use the tables to determine CPP, EI, and income tax deductions (assume claim code 1). For the complete CPP, EI, and federal and provincial tax deduction tables, please go to Connect.

Exercise AI-7 Payroll journal entry LO2

Paradise Hills Berry Farm has 25 employees who are paid biweekly. The payroll register showed the following payroll deductions for the pay period ending March 23, 2018.

Gross Pay	EI Premium	Income Taxes	CPP	Medical Ins.	United Way
65,950.00	1,094.77	9,095.00	3,097.93	1,150.00	1,319.00

Required Using the information provided, prepare the journal entry to record the payroll expenses.

Exercise AI-8 Recording employer's payroll deductions LO3

Refer to the information in Exercise AI-7. Prepare a journal entry to record the employer's share of payroll deductions.

Exercise AI-9 Payment of payroll deductions LO3

Refer to the information in Exercise AI-7 and Exercise AI-8. Prepare a journal entry to record payment by the employer to the Receiver General for Canada on April 15.

Exercise AI-10 Calculating and recording payroll deductions LO3, 4

Use the information provided in Exercise AI-2 to complete the following requirements:

1. Prepare a general journal entry to record the employer's payroll costs resulting from the payroll.

2. Prepare a general journal entry to record the following employee benefits incurred by the company: (a) health insurance costs equal to the amounts contributed by each employee and (b) contributions equal to 10% of gross pay for each employee's retirement income program.

Exercise AI-11 Analyzing total labour costs LO2, 3, 4

CHECK FIGURE: Total CPP contributions = $12,092.85

O'Riley Company's payroll costs and fringe benefit expenses include the normal CPP and EI contributions, retirement fund contributions of 10% of total earnings, and health insurance premiums of $120 per employee per month. Given the following list of employees' projected 2018 annual salaries, payroll costs and fringe benefits are what percentage of salaries?

Doherty	$ 52,000
Fane	61,000
Kahan	59,000
Martin	49,000
Leung	76,000
Total	$297,000

Exercise AI-12 Calculating and recording payroll costs (using tables) LO2, 3, 4

Milly's Drive-In's 12 employees earn a gross pay of $2,050 each per month. Milly's Drive-In contributes 8% of gross pay to a retirement program for employees and pays an extended medical insurance premium of $50 per month per employee.

Required Prepare the entries to record the employer's payroll costs for the month of March 2018. Use the payroll tables to determine CPP, EI, and income tax deductions (assume claim code 1). For the complete CPP, EI, and federal and provincial tax deduction tables, please go to Connect.

Exercise AI-13 Calculating fringe benefits costs LO4

Bellward Company grants vacation time of two weeks to those employees who have worked for the company one complete year. After 10 years of service, employees receive four weeks of vacation. The monthly payroll for January totals $320,000, of which 70% is payable to employees with 10 or more years of service. On January 31, record the January expense arising from the vacation policy of the company. Round calculations to the nearest whole dollar.

PROBLEMS

Problem AI-1A Payroll register and payroll deductions LO2, 3

CHECK FIGURE: Total deductions = $2,281.70

The payroll records of Brownlee Company provided the following information for the weekly pay period ended March 23, 2018:

			Payroll Week Ended March 23, 2018									
Employees	Employee No.	Daily Time						Pay Rate	Hospital Insurance	Union Dues	Earnings to End of Previous Week
		M	T	W	T	F	S	S				
Ray Loran	11	8	8	8	8	8	4	0	40.00	40.00	16.00	43,000
Kathy Sousa	12	7	8	6	7	8	4	0	36.00	40.00	15.00	46,000
Gary Smith	13	8	8	0	8	8	4	4	32.00	40.00	14.00	21,000
Nicole Parton	14	8	8	8	8	8	0	0	40.00	40.00	16.00	32,000
Diana Wood	15	0	6	6	6	6	8	8	36.00	40.00	16.00	36,000
Totals										200.00	77.00	

Required

1. Enter the relevant information in the proper columns of a payroll register and complete the register; calculate CPP and EI deductions. Charge the wages of Kathy Sousa to Office Wages Expense and the wages of the remaining employees to Service Wages Expense. Calculate income tax deductions at 20% of gross pay. Employees are paid an overtime premium of 50% for all hours in excess of 40 per week.

2. Prepare general journal entries to record the payroll register information, including the employer's expenses.

Problem AI-2A Payroll register and journal entries LO2, 3

On January 13, at the end of the second weekly pay period of the year, a company's payroll register showed that its 30 employees had earned $19,570 of sales salaries and $6,230 of office salaries. Assume withholdings from the employees' salaries were to include $428.28 of EI, $1,177.14 of CPP, $5,310 of income taxes, $930 of hospital insurance, and $420 of union dues.

Required

1. Prepare the general journal entry to record the January 13 payroll.

2. Prepare a general journal entry to record the employer's payroll expenses resulting from the January 13 payroll.

Problem AI-3A Journal entries—payroll taxes, and employee fringe benefits LO2, 3, 4

A company showed the following information in its payroll register for the week ended March 16, 2018:

			Deductions					Pay		Distribution	
EI Premium	Income Taxes	Medical Insurance	CPP	Union Dues	Total Deductions	Net Pay		Sales Salaries Expense	Office Salaries Expense	Shop Salaries Expense	
19.92	241.15	47.50	56.07	90.00	454.64	745.36		1,200.00			
23.24	308.50	52.50	65.97	105.00	555.21	844.79				1,400.00	
28.22	407.90	25.00	80.82	127.50	669.44	1,030.56				1,700.00	
17.43	193.70	35.00	48.64	78.75	373.52	676.48			1,050.00		
88.81	1,151.25	160.00	251.50	401.25	2,052.81	3,297.19		1,200.00	1,050.00	3,100.00	

1. Prepare a general journal entry to record the payroll register information.
2. Prepare a general journal entry to record the employer's payroll expenses resulting from the payroll.
3. Prepare general journal entries to accrue employee fringe benefit costs for the week. Assume that the company matches the employees' payments for medical insurance and contributes an amount equal to 8% of each employee's gross pay to a retirement program. Also, each employee accrues vacation pay at the rate of 6% of the wages and salaries earned. The company estimates that all employees eventually will be paid their vacation pay.

Problem AI-4A Journal entries for payroll transactions LO2, 3, 4

A company has three employees, each of whom has been employed since January 1, earns $2,600 per month, and is paid on the last day of each month. On March 1, the following accounts and balances appeared in its ledger.

a. Employees' Income Taxes Payable, $1,006.05 (liability for February).
b. EI Payable, $310.75 (liability for February).
c. CPP Payable, $685.56 (liability for February).
d. Employees' Medical Insurance Payable, $1,560.00 (liability for January and February).

During March and April, the company completed the following related to payroll.

Mar.	17	Issued cheque #320 payable to the Receiver General for Canada. The cheque was in payment of the February employee income taxes, EI, and CPP amounts due.
	31	Prepared a general journal entry to record the March payroll register, which had the following column totals:

	EI	Income Taxes	CPP	Medical Insurance	Total Deductions	Net Pay	Office Salaries	Shop Salaries
	$129.48	$1,006.05	$342.78	$390.00	$1,885.47	$5,914.53	$2,600	$5,200

	31	Recorded the employer's $390.00 liability for its 50% contribution to the medical insurance plan of employees and 6% vacation pay accrued to the employees.
	31	Prepared a general journal entry to record the employer's costs resulting from the March payroll.
Apr.	17	Issued cheque #375 payable to the Receiver General for Canada in payment of the March mandatory deductions.
	17	Issued cheque #376 payable to All Canadian Insurance Company in payment of the employee medical insurance premiums for the first quarter.

Required Prepare the entries to record the transactions.

ALTERNATE PROBLEMS

Problem AI-1B Payroll register and payroll deductions LO2, 3

CHECK FIGURE: Total deductions = $1,988.99

The payroll records of Wailee Company provided the following information for the weekly pay period ended March 23, 2018:

| | | | | | | | | | | | | Payroll |
| | | | | | | | | | | | | Week Ended March 23, 2018 |

Employees	Employee No.	M	T	W	T	F	S	S	Pay Rate	Hospital Insurance	Union Dues	Earnings to End of Previous Week
		Daily Time										
Ben Amoko	31	8	8	8	8	8	0	0	34.00	30.00	12.00	43,000
Auleen Carson	32	7	8	8	7	8	4	0	36.00	30.00	12.00	42,100
Mark Cheng	33	8	8	0	8	8	4	4	36.00	30.00	12.00	28,000
Gene Deszca	34	8	8	8	8	8	0	0	30.00	30.00	12.00	32,000
Ysong Tan	35	0	6	6	6	6	8	8	30.00	30.00	12.00	36,000
Totals										150.00	60.00	

Required

1. Enter the relevant information in the proper columns of a payroll register and complete the register; calculate CPP and EI deductions. Charge the wages of Auleen Carson to Office Wages Expense and the wages of the remaining employees to Service Wages Expense. Calculate income tax deductions at 20% of gross pay. Employees are paid an overtime premium of 50% for all hours in excess of 40 per week.

2. Prepare general journal entries to record the payroll register information, including the employer's expenses.

Problem AI-2B Payroll register and journal entries LO2, 3

On January 13, at the end of the second weekly pay period of the year, a company's payroll register showed that its 45 employees had earned $23,400 of sales salaries and $5,820 of office salaries. Assume withholdings from the employees' salaries were to include $485.05 of EI, $1,296.46 of CPP, $6,180 of income taxes, $920 of hospital insurance, and $490 of union dues.

Required

1. Prepare the general journal entry to record the January 13 payroll.

2. Prepare a general journal entry to record the employer's payroll expenses resulting from the January 13 payroll.

Problem AI-3B Journal entries—payroll taxes, and employee fringe benefits LO2, 3, 4

A company showed the following information in its payroll register for the week ended March 16, 2018:

			Deductions					Pay		Distribution	
EI Premium	Income Taxes	Medical Insurance	CPP	Union Dues	Total Deductions	Net Pay	Sales Salaries Expense	Office Salaries Expense	Shop Salaries Expense
24.07	324.35	47.50	68.44	90.00	554.36	895.64	1,450.00		
32.87	507.35	52.50	94.68	105.00	792.40	1,187.60			1,760.00
29.22	428.75	25.00	83.79	127.50	694.26	1,065.74			1,760.00
28.55	412.70	35.00	81.81	78.75	636.81	1,083.19		1,720.00	
114.71	1673.15	160.00	328.72	401.25	2,677.83	4,232.17	1,450.00	1,720.00	3,740.00

1. Prepare a general journal entry to record the payroll register information.

2. Prepare a general journal entry to record the employer's payroll expenses resulting from the payroll.

3. Prepare general journal entries to accrue employee fringe benefit costs for the week. Assume that the company matches the employees' payments for medical insurance and contributes an amount equal to 8% of each employee's gross pay to a retirement program. Also, each employee accrues vacation pay at the rate of 6% of the wages and salaries earned. The company estimates that all employees eventually will be paid their vacation pay.

Problem AI-4B Journal entries for payroll transactions LO2, 3, 4

A company has three employees, each of whom has been employed since January 1, earns $3,000 per month, and is paid on the last day of each month. On March 1, the following accounts and balances appeared in its ledger.

a. Employees' Income Taxes Payable, $1,298.25 (liability for February).

b. EI Payable, $358.56 (liability for February).

c. CPP Payable, $804.36 (liability for February).

d. Employees' Medical Insurance Payable, $1,380.00 (liability for January and February).

During March and April, the company completed the following related to payroll:

Mar. 17 Issued cheque #635 payable to the Receiver General for Canada. The cheque was in payment of the February employee income taxes, EI, and CPP amounts due.

31 Prepared a general journal entry to record the March payroll register, which had the following column totals:

EI	Income Taxes	CPP	Medical Insurance	Total Deductions	Net Pay	Office Salaries	Shop Salaries
$149.40	$1,298.25	$402.18	$345.00	$2,214.63	$6,785.37	$3,000	$6,000

31 Recorded the employer's $345.00 liability for its 50% contribution to the medical insurance plan of employees and 6% vacation pay accrued to the employees.

31 Prepared a general journal entry to record the employer's payroll costs resulting from the March payroll.

Apr. 14 Issued cheque #764 payable to the Receiver General for Canada in payment of the March mandatory deductions.

14 Issued cheque #765 payable to National Insurance Company in payment of the employee medical insurance premiums for the first quarter.

Required Prepare the entries to record the transactions.

ANALYTICAL AND REVIEW PROBLEMS

A & R Problem AI-1

Using the current year's withholding tables for Canada Pension Plan, Employment Insurance, and income tax, update the payroll register of Exhibit A.2. In calculating income tax withholdings, state your assumption as to each employee's personal deductions. Assume that hospital insurance deductions continue at the same amounts as in Exhibit A.2.

A & R Problem AI-2

The following data were taken from the payroll register of Eastcoastal Company:

Gross Salary	xxx
Employees' Income Tax Deductions	xxx
EI Deductions	xxx
CPP Deductions	xxx
Hospital Insurance Deductions	xxx
Union Dues Deductions	xxx

Eastcoastal contributes an equal amount to the hospital insurance plan, in addition to the statutory payroll taxes, and 6% of the gross salaries to a pension retirement program.

Required Record in general journal form the payroll, payment of the employees, and remittance to the appropriate persons amounts owing in connection with the payroll. (*Note:* All amounts are to be indicated as xxx.)

ETHICS CHALLENGE

EC AI-1

Moe Daljit is the accountant for Valley Sales Company, which is currently experiencing a cash shortage because its Pacific Rim customers have not been paying their accounts on a timely basis. The owner has been unable to arrange adequate bank financing to cover the cash shortage and has suggested that Moe delay sending the amounts withheld from employees to the Receiver General for Canada for a few months, "until things clear up." Then he adds, "After all, we will be sending the money to the Receiver General eventually."

Required

1. What are the company's responsibilities with respect to amounts withheld from employees' wages and salaries?
2. What are the ethical factors in this situation?
3. Would you recommend that Moe follow the owner's "suggestion"?
4. What alternatives might be available to the owner if Moe does not delay sending the amounts to the Receiver General for Canada?

CRITICAL THINKING MINI CASE

Delta Yard Maintenance offers a variety of services to its customers, including lawn and garden care, tree pruning, exterior painting, fence building/installation, eavestrough cleaning, snow removal, and other miscellaneous tasks. Delta employs five full-time salaried individuals and 15 to 20 part-time wage employees. During the year just ended, $194,392 was paid in cash to the part-time employees "under the table," meaning that cash was paid to the employees and no payroll deductions were withheld. The part-time wage employees would not have paid income tax on the cash received because Delta would not have issued T4 slips. To cover up these payments, Delta claimed $194,392 in various other expenses that were not supported by documentation. You have just been hired by Delta as one of the five full-time individuals—the office manager. One of your many duties will be to keep the accounting records, including payroll.

Required Using the elements of critical thinking described on the inside front cover, comment.

For the complete CPP, EI, and Federal and Provincial tax deduction tables, please see the Course-wide Content on Connect.

Accounting Information Systems

The Accounting Information Systems Appendix can be accessed online through Connect.

Financial Statement Information

This appendix includes financial statement information from Spin Master Corporation, WestJet Airlines Ltd., Indigo Books & Music Inc., and Telus Corporation. All of this information is taken from their annual reports. An annual report is a summary of the financial results of a company's operations for the year and its future plans. It is directed at external users of financial information, but also affects actions of internal users.

An annual report is also used by a company to showcase itself and its products. Many include attractive pictures, diagrams, and illustrations related to the company. But the financial section is its primary objective. This section communicates much information about a company, with most data drawn from the accounting information system.

The layout of the annual reports' financial sections that are included in this appendix for Spin Master and WestJet are:

- Management's report
- Auditor's report
- Financial statements
- Notes to financial statements

In addition, selected portions of the Indigo and Telus annual reports have also been incorporated. These include the following:

- Auditor's report
- Financial statements
- Weblink to the notes to financial statements

There are questions at the end of each chapter that refer to information in this appendix. We encourage readers to spend extra time with these questions as they are especially useful in reinforcing and showing the relevance and diversity of financial reporting.

More current financial information about these and other Canadian corporations can be found online at www.sedar.com.

SPIN MASTER CORP.
2017 ANNUAL REPORT

Deloitte.

Deloitte LLP
Bay Adelaide East
8 Adelaide Street West
Suite 200
Toronto ON M5H 0A9
Canada

Tel: 416-601-6150
Fax: 416-601-6151
www.deloitte.ca

Independent Auditor's Report

To the Shareholders of
Spin Master Corp.

We have audited the accompanying consolidated financial statements of Spin Master Corp., which comprise the consolidated statements of financial position as at December 31, 2017 and December 31, 2016, and the consolidated statements of operations and comprehensive income, consolidated statements of changes in equity and consolidated statements of cash flows for the years then ended, and a summary of significant accounting policies and other explanatory information.

Management's Responsibility for the Consolidated Financial Statements

Management is responsible for the preparation and fair presentation of these consolidated financial statements in accordance with International Financial Reporting Standards, and for such internal control as management determines is necessary to enable the preparation of consolidated financial statements that are free from material misstatement, whether due to fraud or error.

Auditor's Responsibility

Our responsibility is to express an opinion on these consolidated financial statements based on our audits. We conducted our audits in accordance with Canadian generally accepted auditing standards. Those standards require that we comply with ethical requirements and plan and perform the audit to obtain reasonable assurance about whether the consolidated financial statements are free from material misstatement.

An audit involves performing procedures to obtain audit evidence about the amounts and disclosures in the consolidated financial statements. The procedures selected depend on the auditor's judgment, including the assessment of the risks of material misstatement of the consolidated financial statements, whether due to fraud or error. In making those risk assessments, the auditor considers internal control relevant to the entity's preparation and fair presentation of the consolidated financial statements in order to design audit procedures that are appropriate in the circumstances, but not for the purpose of expressing an opinion on the effectiveness of the entity's internal control. An audit also includes evaluating the appropriateness of accounting policies used and the reasonableness of accounting estimates made by management, as well as evaluating the overall presentation of the consolidated financial statements. We believe that the audit evidence we have obtained in our audits is sufficient and appropriate to provide a basis for our audit opinion.

Opinion

In our opinion, the consolidated financial statements present fairly, in all material respects, the financial position of Spin Master Corp. as at December 31, 2017 and December 31, 2016, and its financial performance and its cash flows for the years then ended in accordance with International Financial Reporting Standards.

Deloitte LLP

Chartered Professional Accountants
Licensed Public Accountants
March 7, 2018

Spin Master Corp.

Consolidated statements of financial position as at December 31, 2017 and December 31, 2016

(In thousands of United States dollars)	Notes	2017	2016
Assets			
Current assets			
Cash		117,262	99,416
Trade and other receivables	9	369,719	295,068
Inventories	10	120,329	79,924
Prepaid expenses		20,500	21,398
		627,810	495,806
Non-current assets			
Advances on royalties		5,000	11,695
Property, plant and equipment	11	32,978	26,996
Intangible assets	12	145,165	130,390
Goodwill	13	105,487	91,707
Deferred tax assets	8	21,945	19,002
		310,575	279,790
Total assets		938,385	775,596
Liabilities			
Current liabilities			
Trade payables and other liabilities	14	350,757	228,935
Loans and borrowings	15	531	158,107
Deferred revenues		10,472	5,500
Provisions	16	25,398	26,454
Interest payable		45	6
Income tax payable	8	37,290	12,331
		424,493	431,333
Non-current liabilities			
Loans and borrowings	15	—	38
Provisions	16	5,735	12,025
Other long-term liabilities			110
Deferred tax liabilities	8	8,075	6,411
		13,810	18,584
Total liabilities		438,303	449,917
Shareholders' equity			
Share capital	17	681,310	670,115
Accumulated deficit		(247,340)	(408,406)
Contributed surplus		20,323	21,436
Accumulated other comprehensive income		45,789	42,534
Total shareholders' equity		500,082	325,679
Total liabilities and shareholders' equity		938,385	775,596

Approved by the Board of Directors on March 7, 2018.

The accompanying notes on pages 5 to 45 are an integral part of these consolidated financial statements.

Spin Master Corp.

Consolidated statements of operations and comprehensive income

For the year ended December 31

(In thousands of United States dollars, except share data)	Notes	2017	2016
Revenue	4	1,551,324	1,154,454
Cost of sales		750,868	557,712
Gross profit		800,456	596,742
Expenses			
Selling, marketing, distribution and product development	7	312,186	243,689
Administrative expenses	7	262,066	201,008
Other expenses	5	6,700	35
Foreign exchange (gain) loss		(11,370)	5,530
Finance costs	6	10,445	8,601
Income before income tax expense		220,429	137,879
Income tax expense	8	59,363	38,364
Net income		161,066	99,515
Items that may be subsequently reclassified to net income or loss			
Currency translation adjustment		3,255	(863)
Other comprehensive income (loss)		3,255	(863)
Total comprehensive income		164,321	98,652
Earnings per share			
Basic and diluted	18	1.58	0.99
Weighted average number of common shares outstanding			
Basic	18	101,675,906	100,647,133
Diluted	18	101,846,680	100,702,757

The accompanying notes on pages 5 to 45 are an integral part of these consolidated financial statements.

Spin Master Corp.
Consolidated statements of changes in equity

(In thousands of United States dollars)	Note	Share capital	Accumulated deficit	Contributed surplus	Accumulated other comprehensive income	Total
Balance at January 1, 2016		589,263	(507,921)	31,580	43,397	156,319
Net income		—	99,515	—	—	99,515
Currency translation adjustment		—	—	—	(863)	(863)
Share-based compensation	17	—	—	20,943	—	20,943
Issuance of subordinate shares, net of transaction costs	17	48,394	—	—	—	48,394
Shares released from equity participation	17	32,458	—	(31,087)	—	1,371
Balance at December 31, 2016		670,115	(408,406)	21,436	42,534	325,679
Balance at January 1, 2017		670,115	(408,406)	21,436	42,534	325,679
Net income		—	161,066	—	—	161,066
Currency translation adjustment		—	—	—	3,255	3,255
Share-based compensation	17	—	—	10,082	—	10,082
Shares released from equity participation	17	11,195	—	(11,195)	—	—
Balance at December 31, 2017		681,310	(247,340)	20,323	45,789	500,082

The accompanying notes on pages 5 to 45 are an integral part of these consolidated financial statements.

Spin Master Corp.
Consolidated statements of cash flows

For the year ended December 31 (In thousands of United States dollars)	Notes	2017	2016
Operating activities			
Net income		161,066	99,515
Adjustments to reconcile net income to net cash provided by operating activities			
Income tax expense	8	59,363	38,364
Interest expense	6	3,357	2,833
Depreciation and amortization	7, 11, 12	44,908	30,490
Amortization of fair value increments to inventories acquired in business combinations		2,805	—
Accretion expense	6	2,559	2,868
Amortization of financing costs	6	879	602
Impairment of non-current assets	5	9,693	265
Share-based compensation expense	17	10,082	20,943
Changes in net working capital	19	16,782	(87,220)
Changes in contingent consideration liabilities		(6,290)	3,567
Income taxes paid		(34,878)	(33,233)
Interest paid		(2,921)	(5,956)
Cash provided by operating activities		**267,405**	**73,038**
Investing activities			
Capital expenditures - property, plant and equipment	11	(25,918)	(24,036)
Capital expenditures - intangible assets	12	(31,264)	(17,542)
Disposal of property, plant and equipment		—	10
Business acquisitions, net of cash acquired	23	(24,416)	(130,705)
Cash used in investing activities		**(81,598)**	**(172,273)**
Financing activities			
Proceeds from borrowings	15	25,791	204,000
Repayment of borrowings	15	(187,276)	(96,242)
Issuance of subordinate voting shares, net of transaction costs	17	—	47,709
Cash (used in) provided by financing activities		**(161,485)**	**155,467**
Effect of foreign currency exchange rate changes on cash		(6,476)	(2,529)
Net increase in cash during the year		**17,846**	**53,703**
Cash, beginning of year		99,416	45,713
Cash, end of year		**117,262**	**99,416**

The accompanying notes on pages 5 to 45 are an integral part of these consolidated financial statements.

Spin Master Corp.

Consolidated financial statements for the years ended December 31, 2017 and December 31, 2016

1. Description of business

Spin Master Corp., (the "Company"), formerly SML Investments Inc., was incorporated on June 9, 2004, under the laws of the Province of Ontario, Canada. Spin Master Ltd., which was incorporated on May 9, 1994, under the laws of the Province of Ontario, Canada, is a subsidiary of the Company. The Company, through Spin Master Ltd. and its subsidiaries, is a children's entertainment company engaged in the design, marketing and sale of entertainment products for children. The Company's principal place of business is 121 Bloor Street East, Toronto, Canada, M4W 1A9.

The Company has three reportable operating segments: North America, Europe and Rest of World (see Note 25). The North American segment is comprised of the United States and Canada. The European segment is comprised of the United Kingdom, France, Italy, the Benelux, Germany, Austria, Switzerland and Poland. The Rest of World segment is primarily comprised of Hong Kong, China, Australia and Mexico, as well as all other areas of the world serviced by the Company's distribution network.

2. Summary of Significant accounting policies

(A) Statement of compliance and basis of preparation and measurement

The consolidated financial statements have been prepared in accordance with International Financial Reporting Standards ("IFRS"). All financial information is presented in thousands of United States dollars ("USD"), except as otherwise indicated.

These consolidated financial statements were approved and authorized for issuance by the Board of Directors on March 7, 2018.

The consolidated financial statements have been prepared on the historical cost basis except for certain financial instruments that are measured at fair value, as explained in the accounting policies below. Historical cost is measured on the fair value of the consideration provided in exchange for goods and services.

(B) Application of new and revised IFRS

Amendments to International Accounting Standard ("IAS") 7 - Statement of Cash Flows

The amendments to IAS 7 Statement of Cash Flows are part of the International Accounting Standards Board's ("IASB") Disclosure Initiative and help users of financial statements better understand changes in an entity's debt. The amendments require entities to provide disclosures about changes in their liabilities arising from financing activities, including both changes arising from cash flows and non-cash changes (such as foreign exchange gains or losses). On initial application of the amendment, entities are not required to provide comparative information for preceding periods.

The amendment was adopted on January 1, 2017. The amendment does not have a significant impact on the Company's consolidated financial statements for the year ended December 31, 2017.

Amendments to IAS 12 - Recognition of deferred tax assets for unrealized losses

The IASB issued the amendments to IAS 12 Income Taxes to clarify the accounting for deferred tax assets for unrealized losses on debt instruments measured at fair value. The amendments clarify that an entity needs to consider whether tax law restricts the sources of taxable profits against which it may make deductions on the reversal of that deductible temporary difference. Furthermore, the amendments provide guidance on how an entity should determine future taxable profits and explain the circumstances in which taxable profit may include the recovery of some assets for more than their carrying amount.

Entities are required to apply the amendments retrospectively. However, on initial application of the amendments, the change in the opening equity of the earliest comparative period may be recognized in opening retained earnings (or in another component of equity, as appropriate), without allocating the change between opening retained earnings and other components of equity. Entities applying this relief must disclose that fact.

The amendment was adopted on January 1, 2017, and there is no impact to the Company's consolidated financial statements.

(C) Basis of preparation

The consolidated financial statements incorporate the financial statement accounts of the Company and entities controlled by the Company and its subsidiaries (the "Group"). Control is achieved when the Company:

- has power over the investee;

Spin Master Corp.

Consolidated financial statements for the years ended December 31, 2017 and December 31, 2016

2. Significant accounting policies (continued)

(C) Basis of preparation (continued)

- is exposed, or has rights, to variable returns from its involvement with the investee; and
- has the ability to use its power to affect its returns.

The Company reassesses whether or not it controls an investee if facts and circumstances indicate that there are changes to one or more of the three elements of control listed above.

Consolidation of a subsidiary begins when the Company obtains control over the subsidiary and ceases when the Company loses control of the subsidiary. Specifically, income and expenses of a subsidiary acquired or disposed of during the year are included in the consolidated statement of operations and other comprehensive income from the date the Company gains control until the date when the Company ceases to control the subsidiary.

When necessary, adjustments are made to the financial statements of subsidiaries to bring their accounting policies into line with the Group's accounting policies.

All intragroup assets and liabilities, equity, income, expenses and cash flows relating to transactions between members of the Group are eliminated in full on consolidation.

The Company has reclassified certain sales tax receivable and sales tax payable balances for the comparative period in the statement of financial position, in order to reflect the appropriate netting of sales tax receivable and payable accounts, in accordance with IAS 12 "Income Taxes". The impact of the reclassification was an increase of $22,164 in trade and other receivables and a corresponding increase in trade payables and other liabilities as at December 31, 2016.

(D) Business combinations

Acquisitions of businesses are accounted for using the acquisition method. The consideration transferred in a business combination is measured at fair value, which is calculated as the sum of the acquisition-date fair values of the assets transferred by the Company, liabilities incurred by the Company to the former owners of the acquiree and the equity interests issued by the Company in exchange for control of the acquiree. Acquisition-related costs are recognized in profit or loss as incurred.

When the consideration transferred by the Group in a business combination includes assets or liabilities resulting from a contingent consideration arrangement, the contingent consideration is measured at its acquisition-date fair value and included as part of the consideration transferred in a business combination. Changes in the fair value of the contingent consideration that qualify as measurement period adjustments are adjusted retrospectively, with corresponding adjustment against goodwill. Measurement period adjustments are adjustments that arise from additional information obtained during the "measurement period" (which cannot exceed one year from the acquisition date) about facts and circumstances that existed at the acquisition date.

All other subsequent changes in the fair value of contingent consideration classified as an asset or liability are accounted for in accordance with the relevant policy. Changes in the fair value of contingent consideration classified as equity are not recognized.

If the initial accounting for a business combination is incomplete by the end of the reporting period in which the combination occurs, the Group reports provisional amounts for the items for which the accounting is incomplete. Those provisional amounts are adjusted during the measurement period (see above), or additional assets or liabilities are recognized, to reflect new information obtained about facts and circumstances that existed at the acquisition date that, if known would have affected the amounts recognized at that time.

At the acquisition date, the identifiable assets acquired and the liabilities assumed are recognized at their fair value.

Goodwill arising on an acquisition of a business is carried at cost as established at the date of acquisition of the business less accumulated impairment losses, if any. Goodwill is measured as the excess of the sum of the consideration transferred, over the net of the acquisition-date amounts of the identifiable assets acquired and the liabilities assumed. For the purposes of impairment testing, goodwill is allocated to each of the Company's Cash-Generating Units ("CGUs") (or groups of CGUs) that are expected to benefit from the combination.

Spin Master Corp.
Consolidated financial statements for the years ended December 31, 2017 and December 31, 2016

2. Significant accounting policies (continued)

(E) Goodwill

A CGU to which goodwill has been allocated is tested for impairment annually, or more frequently when there is an indication that the unit may be impaired. If the recoverable amount of the CGU is less than its carrying amount, the impairment loss is allocated first to reduce the carrying amount of any goodwill allocated to the unit and then to the other assets of the unit pro-rata based on the carrying amount of each asset in the unit.

Any impairment loss for goodwill is recognized directly in profit or loss, and an impairment loss recognized for goodwill is not reversed in subsequent periods. On disposal of the relevant CGU, the attributed amount of goodwill is included in the determination of the profit or loss on disposal.

(F) Revenue recognition

Sale of goods

The majority of the Company's revenue is derived from the sales of toys and related products to retail customers and distributors in select international markets.

Revenue represents the fair value of the sale of goods excluding value added tax and after deduction of estimates for defective products and sales allowances relating to the sale.

Estimates for defective products and allowances to customers are made as a reduction against revenue in the period in which the related sales are recorded. Estimates are made based on contractual terms and conditions and historical data.

Revenues from the sale of goods are recognized when all the following conditions have been met and control over the goods has been transferred to the buyer:

- Significant risks and rewards of ownership of the goods have been transferred to the buyer;
- The revenues can be measured reliably;
- It is probable that the economic benefits associated with the transaction will flow to the Company; and
- Costs incurred or to be incurred in respect of the transaction can be measured reliably.

These conditions are typically met at the time the risks and rewards of ownership of the product pass to the customer.

Television distribution, royalty & license sales

Television distribution sales as well as royalty and licensing revenues which allow others to use the Company's brands are recognized on an accrual basis in accordance with the substance of the relevant agreements. Revenue is measured at the fair value of the consideration received or receivable when it is probable the economic benefits associated with the transaction will flow to the Company and the amount of revenue can be measured reliably.

These conditions are typically met in the period in which the royalty or licensing period has commenced unless there are future performance obligations that must be met or upon the delivery of the programs to the broadcaster for television distribution sales.

Customer advances on contracts, licensing and/or television distribution, are recorded in deferred revenue until all of the foregoing revenue recognition conditions have been met.

(G) Leases

Leases are classified as finance leases whenever the terms of the lease transfer substantially all the risks and rewards of ownership to the lessee. All other leases are classified as operating leases.

Operating lease payments are recognized as an expense on a straight-line basis over the lease term. Contingent rentals arising under operating leases are recognized as an expense in the period in which they are incurred.

In the event that lease incentives are received to enter into operating leases, such incentives are recognized as a liability. The aggregate benefit of incentives is recognized as a reduction of rental expense on a straight-line basis, except where another systematic basis is more representative of the time pattern in which economic benefits from the leased asset are consumed.

Spin Master Corp.
Consolidated financial statements for the years ended December 31, 2017 and December 31, 2016

2. Significant accounting policies (continued)

(H) Foreign currencies

The Company reports its financial results in USD; however, the functional currency of the Company is the Canadian dollar.

The assets and liabilities of foreign operations that have a functional currency different from that of the Company, including goodwill and fair value adjustments arising on acquisition, are translated into the Company's functional currency of Canadian dollars using exchange rates prevailing at the end of each reporting period. Income and expense items are translated at the average exchange rates for the period, unless exchange rates fluctuate significantly during that period, in which case the exchange rates at the dates of the transactions are used. Exchange differences arising, if any, are recognized in the foreign currency translation adjustment as part of other comprehensive income.

In preparing the financial statements of each individual Group entity, transactions in currencies other than the Group entity's functional currency are recognized at the rates of exchange prevailing at the dates of the transactions. At the end of each reporting period, monetary items denominated in foreign currencies are retranslated at the rates prevailing at that date. Non-monetary items carried at fair value that are denominated in foreign currencies are retranslated at the rates prevailing when the fair value was determined. Non-monetary items that are measured in terms of historical cost in a foreign currency are not retranslated. The resulting foreign currency exchange gains or losses are recognized in net income or loss.

For the purposes of presenting these consolidated financial statements, the assets and liabilities of the Group's foreign operations are translated into USD using exchange rates prevailing at the end of each reporting period. Income and expense items are translated in the same manner as above with exchange differences impacting other comprehensive income and accumulated in equity.

At December 31, 2017 and 2016, the functional currencies of the Groups subsidiaries included the Canadian dollar, the Euro, the Great Britain pound, the Hong Kong dollar, the Mexican peso, the Chinese yuan, the Swedish krona and the Australian dollar.

(I) Earnings per share

Basic earnings per share ("EPS") is calculated by dividing net income by the weighted average number of shares outstanding during the period. Diluted earnings per share is calculated by dividing net income by the weighted average number of common shares outstanding, if all the convertible securities were exercised during the period. Convertible securities refer to all outstanding stock options.

(J) Income taxes

Income tax expense represents the sum of the taxes currently payable and deferred taxes.

Current tax

For each entity in the Group, the tax currently payable is based on taxable income for the year. Taxable income differs from "income before income tax expense" as reported on the consolidated statement of operations and comprehensive income because of items of income or expense that are taxable or deductible in other years and items that are never taxable or deductible. The Company's current tax is calculated using tax rates that have been enacted or substantively enacted by the end of the reporting period.

Deferred tax

Deferred tax is recognized on temporary differences between the carrying amount of assets and liabilities in the consolidated financial statements and the corresponding tax basis used in the computation of taxable income. Deferred tax liabilities are recognized for taxable temporary differences. Deferred tax assets are recognized for deductible temporary differences to the extent that it is probable that taxable profits will be available against which those deductible temporary differences can be utilized.

Deferred tax assets and liabilities are not recognized if the temporary difference arises from the initial recognition (other than a business combination) of assets and liabilities in a transaction that does not affect either taxable income or net income before taxes. In addition, deferred tax liabilities are not recognized if the temporary difference arises from the initial recognition of goodwill.

The carrying amount of deferred tax assets is reviewed at the end of each reporting period and reduced to the extent that it is no longer probable that sufficient taxable income will be available to allow all or part of the asset to be recovered.

Spin Master Corp.

Consolidated financial statements for the years ended December 31, 2017 and December 31, 2016

2. Significant accounting policies (continued)

(J) Income taxes (continued)

Deferred tax liabilities and assets are measured at the tax rates that are expected to apply in the period in which the liability is expected to be settled or the asset realized, based on tax rates (and tax laws) that have been enacted or substantively enacted at the end of the reporting period, reflecting the tax consequences that would follow from the manner in which the Company expects, at the end of the reporting period, to recover or settle the carrying amount of its assets and liabilities.

Current and deferred tax for the period

Current and deferred tax are recognized in profit or loss, except when they relate to items that are recognized in other comprehensive income or directly in equity, in which case the current and deferred tax are also recognized in other comprehensive income or directly in equity, respectively. Where current tax or deferred tax arises from the initial accounting for a business combination, the tax effect is included in the accounting for the business combination.

(K) Cash

Cash includes cash on hand and in banks, net of outstanding bank overdrafts.

(L) Property, plant and equipment

Property, plant and equipment are stated at cost, net of accumulated depreciation and accumulated impairment losses, if any.

Repair and maintenance costs are recognized in profit or loss as incurred. Depreciation is recognized so as to write off the cost or valuation of assets less their residual values over their useful lives, using the straight-line method or declining balance method.

The estimated useful lives, residual values and depreciation method are reviewed at the end of each reporting period, with the effect of any changes in estimate accounted for on a prospective basis.

The following are the estimated useful lives for the major classes of property, plant and equipment:

Land	Not depreciated
Buildings	30 years
Moulds, dies and tools	2 years
Office equipment	3 years
Leasehold improvements	Lesser of lease term or 5 years
Computer hardware	3 years
Machinery and equipment	30% declining balance

An item of property, plant and equipment is derecognized upon disposal or when no future economic benefits are expected to arise from the continued use of the asset. Any gain or loss arising on the disposal or retirement of an item of property, plant and equipment is determined as the difference between the sales proceeds and the carrying amounts of the asset and is recognized in profit or loss.

(M) Intangible assets

The following are the estimated useful lives for the major classes of intangible assets:

Brands	Indefinite
Character trademarks	5 years
Customer lists	5 years
Intellectual property	10 years
Non-competition agreements	1 year
Content development	1-5 years
Computer software	1 year

Spin Master Corp.

Consolidated financial statements for the years ended December 31, 2017 and December 31, 2016

2. Significant accounting policies (continued)

(M) Intangible Assets (continued)

Intangible assets acquired separately

Intangible assets with finite useful lives that are acquired separately are carried at cost less accumulated amortization and accumulated impairment losses, if any.

Amortization is recognized on a straight-line basis over the estimated useful life of the intangible assets. The estimated useful life and amortization method are reviewed at the end of each reporting period, with the effect of any changes in estimate being accounted for on a prospective basis.

Intangible assets with indefinite useful lives, such as brands and trademarks that are acquired separately are carried at cost less accumulated impairment losses.

Intangible assets acquired in a business combination

Intangible assets acquired in a business combination and recognized separately from goodwill are initially recognized at their fair value at the acquisition date (which is regarded as their initial cost).

Subsequent to initial recognition, intangible assets acquired in business combinations are reported at cost less accumulated amortization if applicable and accumulated impairment losses, on the same basis as intangible assets that are acquired separately.

Internally-generated intangible assets - research and development expenditures

Expenditures on research activities are recognized as incurred. An internally-generated intangible asset arising from development (or from the development phase of an internal project) is recognized only if all of the following have been demonstrated:

- the technical feasibility of completing the intangible asset so that it will be available for use or sale;
- the intention to complete the intangible asset for use or sale;
- the ability to use or sell the intangible asset;
- how the intangible asset will generate probable future economic benefits;
- the availability of adequate technical, financial and other resources to complete the development and to use or sell the intangible asset; and
- the ability to measure reliably the expenditure attributable to the intangible asset during its development.

The amount initially recognized for internally-generated intangible assets is the sum of the expenditure incurred from the date when the intangible asset first meets the recognition criteria listed above. Where no internally-generated intangible asset can be recognized, development expenditures are recognized in profit or loss in the period in which they are incurred.

Subsequent to initial recognition, internally-generated intangible assets are reported at cost less accumulated amortization and accumulated impairment losses, on the same basis as intangible assets that are acquired separately.

Television production assets

Television production assets are a component of intangible assets, and are recorded at cost under Content Development. Capitalized costs net of anticipated federal and provincial tax credits are charged to amortization expense as completed episodes are delivered on a pro-rata basis over the total number of episodes for the season. The federal and provincial tax credits are not recognized until there is reasonable assurance that the Company will comply with the conditions attaching to them and that the tax credits will be received.

Deferred revenue related to television production assets arises as a result of consideration received in advance of the Company fulfilling its obligation.

Impairment of tangible and intangible assets other than goodwill

At the end of each reporting period, the Company reviews the carrying amounts of its tangible and intangible assets to determine whether there is any indication that those assets are impaired. If any such indication exists, the recoverable amount of the asset is estimated in order to determine the extent of the impairment loss (if any).

When it is not possible to estimate the recoverable amount of an individual asset, the Company estimates the recoverable amount of the CGU to which the asset belongs. When a reasonable and consistent basis

Spin Master Corp.

Consolidated financial statements for the years ended December 31, 2017 and December 31, 2016

2. **Significant accounting policies** *(continued)*

(M) Intangible Assets (continued)

of allocation can be identified, corporate assets are also allocated to individual CGUs, or otherwise they are allocated to the smallest group of CGUs for which a reasonable and consistent allocation basis can be identified.

Intangible assets with indefinite useful lives and intangible assets not yet available for use are tested for impairment at least annually as part of year-end procedures, and whenever there is an indication that the asset may be impaired.

Recoverable amount is the higher of fair value less costs to sell and value in use. In assessing value in use, the estimated future cash flows are discounted to their present value using a pre-tax discount rate that reflects current market assessments of the time value of money and the risks specific to the asset for which the estimates of future cash flows have not been adjusted.

If the recoverable amount of an asset (or CGU) is estimated to be less than its carrying amount, the carrying amount of the asset (or CGU) is reduced to its recoverable amount. An impairment loss equal to the difference between the carrying and recorded amounts is recognized immediately in profit or loss.

When an impairment loss subsequently reverses, the carrying amount of the asset (or a CGU) is increased to the revised estimate of its recoverable amount, provided that the increased carrying amount does not exceed the carrying amount that would have been determined had no impairment loss been recognized for the asset (or CGU) in prior years. A reversal of an impairment loss is recognized immediately in profit or loss.

(N) Advances on royalties

The Company enters into license agreements with inventors and licensors for the use of their intellectual properties in its products. These agreements may call for payment in advance or future payment of minimum guaranteed amounts. Amounts paid in advance are initially recorded as an asset and subsequently expensed to net income or loss as revenue from the related products is recognized. If all, or a portion of an advance, does not appear to be recoverable through future use of the rights obtained under license, the non-recoverable portion is written-off and recognized immediately in profit or loss.

(O) Inventories

Inventories are stated at the lower of cost and net realizable value. Cost is determined on a standard cost basis, and includes the purchase price and other costs, such as import duties, taxes and transportation costs. Trade discounts and rebates are deducted from the purchase price. Net realizable value represents the estimated selling price for inventories in the ordinary course of business, less all estimated costs of completion and costs necessary to make the sale. Reserves for excess and obsolete inventory are based upon quantities on hand, projected volumes from demand forecast and net realizable value. The impact of changes in inventory reserves is reflected in cost of sales.

(P) Provisions

A provision is a liability of uncertain timing or amount. Provisions are recognized when the Company has a present legal or constructive obligation as a result of past events, it is probable that an outflow of resources will be required to settle the obligation and the amount can be reliably estimated. Provisions are measured at the present value of the amount expected to be required to settle the obligation and are re-measured each reporting date.

Future royalty obligations

Where the Company is committed to pay royalties on sales of acquired brands, the future royalty obligation is measured based on the Company's estimate of the related brands future sales, discounted based on the timing of the expected payments and recorded as a provision.

Provision for defectives

Defectives refer to when the end consumer returns defective goods to the Company's customers. Customers without a fixed allowance for defectives are eligible for a credit for the cost of the product if returned as defective by the end consumer. The estimate of defectives is made based on the class and nature of the product and is recorded as a reduction to revenue in the consolidated statements of operations and comprehensive income.

Spin Master Corp.

Consolidated financial statements for the years ended December 31, 2017 and December 31, 2016

2. **Significant accounting policies** *(continued)*

(P) Provisions (continued)

Supplier obligations

Supplier obligations represent the estimated compensation to be paid to suppliers for lower than expected volumes purchased, resulting in the supplier having excess raw material and finished goods inventory. While payments are not contractually required, the Company regularly compensates suppliers to maintain supplier relationships, which represents a constructive obligation due to past practices. The supplier obligation is based on an estimate of the cost of the supplier's excess raw material and finished goods inventory.

Share-based payments

As part of the Company's Initial Public Offering (the "Initial Offering"), employees were granted subordinate voting shares under two arrangements; the settlement of equity participation agreements and the issuance of restricted stock units ("RSUs"). The Initial Offering price multiplied by the number of shares that an employee was entitled to receive is recognized as an expense in administrative expenses, with a corresponding increase in contributed surplus over the period, at the end of which, the employees become unconditionally entitled to shares. The amount expensed is adjusted for forfeitures as required.

The Company has one share option plan for key employees, which forms part of their long-term incentive compensation plan. Under the plan, the exercise price of each option equals the market price of the Company's share on the date of grant and the options have a maximum term of ten years. Options vest between zero and four years.

(Q) Financial instruments

Financial assets and financial liabilities are recognized when the Company becomes a party to the contractual provisions of the respective instrument.

Financial assets and financial liabilities are initially measured at fair value. Transaction costs that are directly attributable to the acquisition or issue of financial assets and financial liabilities (other than financial assets and financial liabilities at fair value through profit or loss) are included in the initial carrying value of the related instrument and are amortized using the effective interest method. Transaction costs directly attributable to the acquisition of financial assets or financial liabilities at fair value through profit or loss are recognized immediately in profit or loss.

Fair value estimates are made at the consolidated statement of financial position date based on relevant market information and information about the financial instrument. All financial instruments are classified into one of the following categories: fair value through profit or loss ("FVTPL"), held-to-maturity, loans and receivables, available-for-sale financial assets or other liabilities.

The Company has made the following classifications:

Cash	Loans and receivables
Trade and other receivables	Loans and receivables
Loans to related parties	Loans and receivables
Other long-term assets	Loans and receivables
Trade payables and other liabilities	Other liabilities
Borrowings	Other liabilities
Interest payable	Other liabilities
Loans from related parties	Other liabilities
Other long-term liabilities	Other liabilities
Foreign exchange forward contracts	FVTPL

(R) Financial assets

The classification of financial assets depends on the nature and purpose of the financial assets and is determined at the time of initial recognition.

Spin Master Corp.

Consolidated financial statements for the years ended December 31, 2017 and December 31, 2016

2.   **Significant accounting policies** *(continued)*

(R) Financial Assets (continued)

Financial Assets at FVTPL

Financial assets are classified as FVTPL when the financial asset is either held for trading or it is designated as FVTPL. A financial asset is classified as held for trading if:

- it has been acquired principally for the purpose of selling it in the near term; or
- on initial recognition it is part of a portfolio of identified financial instruments that the Company manages together and has a recent actual pattern of short-term profit-taking; or
- it is a derivative that is not designated and effective as a hedging instrument.

Loans and receivables

Loans and receivables are non-derivative financial assets with fixed or determinable payments that are not quoted in an active market. Loans and receivables are initially measured at fair value plus any attributable transaction costs. Subsequent to initial recognition, loans and receivables are measured at amortized cost using the effective interest method, less any impairment.

Impairment of financial assets

Financial assets, other than those classified as FVTPL, are assessed for indicators of impairment at the end of each reporting period. Financial assets are considered to be impaired when there is objective evidence that, as a result of one or more events that occurred after the initial recognition of the financial asset, the estimated future cash flows of the investment have been affected.

The carrying amount of the financial asset is reduced by the impairment loss directly for all financial assets with the exception of trade receivables, where the carrying amount is reduced through the use of an allowance account.

When a trade receivable is considered uncollectible, it is written off against the allowance account. Subsequent recoveries of amounts previously written off are offset against the allowance account. Changes in the carrying amount of the allowance account are recognized in profit or loss.

For financial assets measured at amortized cost, if, in a subsequent period, the amount of the impairment loss decreases and the decrease can be related objectively to an event occurring after the impairment was recognized, the previously recognized impairment loss is reversed through profit or loss to the extent that the carrying amount of the investment at the date the impairment is reversed does not exceed what the amortized cost would have been had the impairment not been recognized.

(S) Financial liabilities and equity instruments

Classification as debt or equity

Debt and equity instruments issued by the Company are classified as either financial liabilities or as equity in accordance with the substance of the contractual arrangements and the definitions of a financial liability and an equity instrument.

Equity instruments

An equity instrument is any contract that evidences a residual interest in the assets of an entity after deducting all of its liabilities. Equity instruments issued by the Company are recognized as the proceeds received, net of direct issue costs.

Other financial liabilities

Other financial liabilities (including borrowings and trade and other payables) are initially measured at fair value, net of transaction costs. Subsequently, other financial liabilities are measured at amortized cost using the effective interest method.

The effective interest method is a method of calculating the amortized cost of a financial liability and of allocating interest expense over the relevant period. The effective interest rate is the rate that exactly discounts estimated future cash payments (including all fees and points paid or received that form an integral part of the effective interest rate, transaction costs and other premiums or discounts) through the expected life of the financial liability, or (where appropriate) a shorter period, to the net carrying amount on initial recognition.

Spin Master Corp.

Consolidated financial statements for the years ended December 31, 2017 and December 31, 2016

2.   **Significant accounting policies** *(continued)*

(T) Derivative financial instruments

The Company enters into foreign exchange forward contracts to manage its exposure to foreign exchange rate risks.

Derivatives are initially recognized at fair value at the date the derivative contracts are entered into and are subsequently re-measured to their fair value at the end of each reporting period. The resulting gain or loss is recognized in profit or loss.

(U) Fair value hierarchy and liquidity risk disclosure

Fair value measurements are classified using a fair value hierarchy that reflects the significance of the inputs used in making the measurements. The fair value hierarchy has the following levels:

- Level 1 - valuation based on quoted prices (unadjusted) in active markets for identical assets or liabilities;
- Level 2 - valuation techniques based on inputs other than quoted prices included in Level 1 that are observable for the asset or liability, either directly (i.e. as prices) or indirectly (i.e. derived from prices); and
- Level 3 - valuation techniques using inputs for the asset or liability that are not based on observable market data (unobservable inputs).

The fair value of short-term financial instruments approximates their carrying amounts due to the relatively short period to maturity. These include cash, trade and other receivables, as well as trade payables and accrued liabilities and provisions. Fair value amounts represent point-in-time estimates and may not reflect fair value in the future.

(V) Accounting standards issued but not yet adopted

IFRS 15 Revenue from Contracts with Customers

In May 2014, the IASB issued IFRS 15, "Revenue from Contracts with Customers", which replaces IAS 11 - Construction Contracts, IAS 18 - Revenue and International Financial Reporting Interpretations Committee 13 - Customer Loyalty Programs ("IFRIC 13"), as well as various other interpretations regarding revenue. IFRS 15 outlines a single comprehensive model for entities to use in accounting for revenue arising from contracts with customers; except for contracts that are within the scope of the standards on leases, non-monetary transactions, insurance contracts, and financial instruments. IFRS 15 also contains enhanced disclosure requirements. The standard is effective for annual periods beginning on or after January 1, 2018.

In April 2016, the IASB published clarifications to IFRS 15 which addressed three topics (identifying performance obligations, principal versus agent considerations, and licensing) and provides some transition relief for modified contracts and completed contracts. The amendments are effective for annual periods beginning on or after January 1, 2018.

The guidance permits two methods of adoption: retrospectively to each prior reporting period restated (full retrospective method), or retrospectively with the cumulative effect of initially applying the guidance recognized at the date of initial application (modified retrospective method). The Company will adopt the standard using the full retrospective method to restate each prior reporting period presented.

In preparation for adoption of the standard, the Company has completed the review of relevant contracts and has concluded there will be no material transitional adjustment upon adoption and no material changes in the timing of revenue recognition is expected once adopted.

IFRS 9 Financial Instruments

In July 2014, the IASB issued the final version of IFRS 9, "Financial Instruments". The new standard includes revised guidance on the classification and measurement of financial assets, including impairment, as well as new hedge accounting principles.

IFRS 9 will replace IAS 39 Financial Instruments: Recognition and Measurement. Under IFRS 9, all recognized financial assets that are currently within the scope of IAS 39 will be measured at either amortized cost, fair value through other comprehensive income ("FVOCI") or fair value. The basis of classification will depend on the business model and the contractual cash flow characteristics of the financial asset. All equity instruments will be measured at fair value or FVOCI. A debt instrument that has cash flows which represent solely payments of principal and interest is measured at amortized cost only if it is held to collect the contractual cash flows or FVOCI if it is held to collect and sale contractual cash flows. Otherwise it is measured at FVTPL. For financial liabilities designated as at FVTPL, the change in the fair value attributable to

Spin Master Corp.

Consolidated financial statements for the years ended December 31, 2017 and December 31, 2016

2. Significant accounting policies (continued)

(V) Accounting standards issued but not yet adopted (continued)

changes in the liability's credit risk is recognized in other comprehensive income ("OCI") unless it gives rise to an accounting mismatch in profit or loss.

IFRS 9 introduces a new expected credit loss ("ECL") model for all financial assets in scope of the impairment requirements. The new ECL will result in an allowance for credit losses being recorded on financial assets regardless of whether there has been an actual loss event.

In preparation for adoption of the standard, the Company has completed its assessment of the implications of implementing the new standard and has concluded there will be no material transitional adjustment upon adoption and no material changes are expected once adopted.

IFRS 2 Share Based Payments

The IASB issued amendments to IFRS 2 "Share Based Payments". The amendment is intended to clarify the estimation of the fair value of cash settled share based payments. The amendments are effective for annual reporting periods beginning on or after January 1, 2018. The Company is evaluating the impact on its financial statements.

IFRIC 22 Foreign Currency Transactions and Advance Consideration

IFRIC 22 clarifies the accounting for transactions that include the receipt or payment of advance consideration in a foreign currency. The interpretation addresses how to determine the date of the transaction for the purpose of determining the exchange rate to use on initial recognition of the related asset, expense or income (or part of it) on the derecognition of a non-monetary asset or non-monetary liability arising from the payment or receipt of advance consideration in a foreign currency. The IASB has reached the consensus that the date of the transaction, for the purpose of determining the exchange rate, is the date of initial recognition of the non-monetary prepayment asset or deferred income liability. If there are multiple payments or receipts in advance, a date of transaction is established for each payment or receipt. IFRIC 22 is effective for annual reporting periods beginning on or after January 1, 2018. The Company is evaluating the impact on its financial statements.

IFRIC 23 Uncertainty Over Income Tax Treatments

In June 2017, the IASB issued IFRIC 23 to clarify how the requirements of IAS 12 Income Taxes should be applied when there is uncertainty over income tax treatments. The interpretation specifically addresses:

- Whether an entity considers uncertain tax treatments separately;
- The assumptions an entity makes about the examination of tax treatments by taxation authorities;
- How and entity determine taxable profit (or loss), tax bases, unused tax losses, unused tax credits and tax rates; and
- How an entity considers changes in facts and circumstances.

The interpretation is effective for annual periods beginning on or after January 1, 2019, with modified retrospective or retrospective application. The Company is currently evaluating the impact of IFRIC 23 on its financial statements.

IFRS 16 Leases

In January 2016, the IASB issued a new Lease Standard, IFRS 16. IFRS 16 sets out the principles for the recognition, measurement, presentation and disclosure of leases for both parties to a contract (the customer ('lessee') and the supplier ('lessor')). IFRS 16 is effective from January 1, 2019. A company can choose to apply IFRS 16 before that date but only if it also applies IFRS 15 Revenue from Contracts with Customers. IFRS 16 completes the IASB's project to improve the financial reporting of leases and replaces the previous leases Standard, IAS 17 Leases, and related Interpretations. The standard is effective for annual periods beginning on or after January 1, 2019. The Company is evaluating the impact on its financial statements.

3. Significant accounting judgments and estimates

In the application of the Company's accounting policies, management is required to make judgments, estimates and assumptions about the carrying amounts of assets and liabilities that are not readily apparent from other sources. These estimates and associated assumptions are based on historical experience and other factors that are considered to be relevant, and actual results may differ. The estimates and underlying assumptions are reviewed on an ongoing

Spin Master Corp.

Consolidated financial statements for the years ended December 31, 2017 and December 31, 2016

3. Significant accounting judgments and estimates (continued)

basis, and adjustments are recognized in the period in which the estimate is revised if the revision affects only that period, or in the period of the revision and future periods if the revision affects both current and future periods.

Critical judgments in applying accounting policies

The Company has identified the following judgments, apart from estimates, which management has made in the process of applying the Company's accounting policies, and which have the most significant effect on the amounts recognized in the consolidated financial statements.

(A) Determination of CGUs

A CGU is defined as is the smallest identifiable group of assets that generates cash inflows that are largely independent of the cash inflows from other assets or groups of assets. Determining the impact of impairment requires significant judgment in identifying which assets or groups of assets are CGUs of the Company.

(B) Functional currency

Transactions in foreign currencies are translated to the respective functional currencies of Group entities at exchange rates as of the dates the transactions occur. Monetary assets and liabilities denominated in foreign currencies at the reporting date are retranslated to the functional currency at the exchange rate at that date.

Determining the appropriate functional currencies for entities in the Group requires analysis of various factors, including the currencies and country-specific factors that mainly influence sales prices, and the currencies that mainly influence labour, materials and other costs of providing goods or services.

Significant estimates and assumptions

The Company has identified the following accounting policies under which significant judgments, estimates and assumptions are made, where actual results may differ from these estimates under different assumptions and conditions, and which may materially affect financial results or the financial position in future periods.

(A) Useful life of property, plant and equipment and intangible assets with finite useful lives

The Company employs significant estimates to determine the estimated useful lives of property, plant and equipment and intangible assets with finite useful lives, considering industry trends such as technological advancements, past experience, expected use and review of asset lives.

Components of an item of property, plant and equipment may have different useful lives. The Company makes estimates when determining depreciation methods, depreciation rates and asset useful lives, which requires taking into account industry trends and company-specific factors. The Company reviews depreciation methods, useful lives and residual values annually or when circumstances change and adjusts its depreciation methods and assumptions prospectively.

(B) Impairment testing of goodwill and indefinite life intangible assets

Goodwill and indefinite life intangible assets are assessed for impairment at least annually, and whenever there is an indication that the asset may be impaired. The Company determines the fair value of its CGU groupings and indefinite life intangible assets using discounted cash flow models corroborated by other valuation techniques.

The process of determining these fair values requires the Company to make estimates and assumptions of a long term nature regarding discount rates, projected revenues, royalty rates and margins, as applicable, derived from past experience, actual operating results and budgets. These estimates and assumptions may change in the future due to uncertain competitive and economic market conditions or changes in business strategies.

(C) Provision for inventory

Inventories are stated at the lower of cost and estimated net realizable value. The Company estimates net realizable value as the amount at which inventories are expected to be sold, taking into consideration fluctuations in retail prices due to seasonality less estimated costs required to sell. Inventories are written down to net realizable value when the cost of inventories is estimated to be unrecoverable due to obsolescence, damage or declining selling prices.

(D) Sales allowances

A sales allowance is established to reflect credits requested by customers relating to contractual discounts, negotiated discounts, customer audits, defective products and costs incurred by customers to sell the Company's products. The

Spin Master Corp.
Consolidated financial statements for the years ended December 31, 2017 and December 31, 2016

3. Significant accounting judgments and estimates (continued)

allowance is based on specific reserves based upon the Company's evaluation of the likelihood of the outcome of sales allowance claims.

(E) Income and other taxes

The calculation of current and deferred income taxes requires the Company to make estimates and assumptions and to exercise judgment regarding the carrying values of assets and liabilities which are subject to accounting estimates inherent in those balances, the interpretation of income tax legislation across various jurisdictions, expectations about future operating results, the timing of reversal of temporary differences and possible audits of income tax filings by the tax authorities.

Changes or differences in underlying estimates or assumptions may result in changes to the current or deferred income tax balances on the consolidated statements of financial position, a charge or credit to income tax expense in the consolidated statement of earnings and may result in cash payments or receipts. All income, capital and commodity tax filings are subject to audits and reassessments. Changes in interpretations or judgments may result in a change in the Company's income, capital or commodity tax provisions in the future. The amount of such a change cannot be reasonably estimated.

4. Revenue

The Company earns revenue from the following primary sources:

- Sales of toys and related products; and
- Royalties and licensing fees earned for the use of intellectual property, application revenues and the distribution of television programs ("Other revenue")

Year ended December 31	2017	2016
Revenue from sale of goods	1,465,532	1,106,514
Other revenue	85,792	47,940
Total revenue	1,551,324	1,154,454

5. Other (income) expenses

Year ended December 31	2017	2016
Impairment of non-current assets (see Notes 11,12)	9,693	265
Revaluation of provisions	–	(222)
Other	(2,993)	(8)
Total other expenses	6,700	35

6. Finance costs

Year ended December 31	2017	2016
Interest on bank loans	3,357	2,833
Bank fees	3,650	2,228
Accretion expense	2,559	2,868
Amortization of financing costs	879	602
Other	–	70
Total finance costs	10,445	8,601

7. Costs included within expenses

Included within expenses are the following: research and development costs, depreciation expense and employee benefit expenses.

Spin Master Corp.
Consolidated financial statements for the years ended December 31, 2017 and December 31, 2016

7. Costs included within expenses (continued)

Research and development costs

Year ended December 31	2017	2016
Research and development costs	23,365	22,017
Total research and development costs	23,365	22,017

Depreciation and amortization expense

Year ended December 31	2017	2016
Depreciation and amortization included in cost of sales	34,679	23,680
Depreciation and amortization included in administrative expenses	10,229	6,810
Total depreciation and amortization expense	44,908	30,490

Employee benefits expenses

Year ended December 31	2017	2016
Salaries, wages and bonuses	2,671	3,856
Other employee benefits	955	683
Total employee benefits expenses in cost of sales	3,626	4,539
Salaries, wages and bonuses	129,684	99,473
Share-based compensation	10,082	20,943
Termination benefits	1,680	1,823
Other employee benefits	28,509	14,236
Total employee benefits expenses in administrative expenses	169,955	136,475
Total employee benefits expenses	173,581	141,014

Selling, marketing, distribution and product development

Year ended December 31	2017	2016
Selling	106,471	77,102
Marketing	128,713	112,339
Distribution	53,637	32,231
Product development	23,365	22,017
Total selling, marketing, distribution and product development	312,186	243,689

Administrative expenses

Year ended December 31	2017	2016
Staff costs	169,955	136,474
Technology	8,382	5,131
Professional services	23,696	19,482
Property and operations	31,246	22,496
Depreciation of property, plant and equipment (excluding tooling)	10,229	6,896
Other	18,558	10,529
Total administrative expenses	262,066	201,008

Spin Master Corp.
Consolidated financial statements for the years ended December 31, 2017 and December 31, 2016

8. Income taxes

Income tax recognized in profit or loss

Year ended December 31	2017	2016
Current tax expense	59,838	28,354
Deferred tax expense	(475)	10,010
Total income tax expense	**59,363**	**38,364**

Reconciliations of the income tax expense for the year at the statutory tax rate with the amounts presented in the consolidated statements of operations are as follows:

Year ended December 31	2017	2016
Net income before income taxes	220,429	137,879
Statutory tax rate (26.5%)	58,414	36,538
Adjustments		
Effect of expenses that are not deductible in determining taxable income	1,112	1,471
Effect of unused tax losses and tax offsets not recognized as deferred tax assets	480	277
Effect of previously unrecognized unused tax losses and deductible temporary differences now recognized as deferred tax assets	(510)	(187)
Effect of different tax rates of subsidiaries operating in other jurisdictions	(6,782)	(3,976)
Effect of tax rate changes	2,528	—
Effect of tax settlement with the Canada Revenue Agency on transfer pricing matter	—	(153)
Other	4,121	4,394
Total income tax expense	**59,363**	**38,364**

The tax rates used for the reconciliations above is the Canadian statutory tax rate of the parent payable by corporate entities in the Group, on taxable profits under tax law in the respective jurisdictions in which the Company operates.

Current tax assets and liabilities

Year ended December 31	2017	2016
Income tax payable	37,290	12,331
Total income tax payable	**37,290**	**12,331**

Deferred tax balances

The following is the analysis of deferred tax assets and liabilities presented in the consolidated statements of financial position:

Year ended December 31	2017	2016
Deferred tax assets	21,945	19,002
Deferred tax liabilities	(8,075)	(6,411)
Net deferred tax asset	**13,870**	**12,591**

Spin Master Corp.
Consolidated financial statements for the years ended December 31, 2017 and December 31, 2016

8. Income taxes (continued)

Recognized deferred tax assets and liabilities

As at December 31	2016	Recognized in profit or loss	Recognized in equity	2017
Deferred tax assets (liabilities) in relation to:				
Property, plant and equipment	1,104	(560)	70	614
Intangible assets	(3,990)	(276)	(242)	(4,508)
Provisions	5,021	2,834	317	8,172
Allowance for doubtful accounts	260	79	16	355
	2,395	2,077	161	4,633
Tax losses	9,538	(2,786)	602	7,354
Other	658	1,184	41	1,883
Total deferred tax	**12,591**	**475**	**804**	**13,870**

Unrecognized deductible temporary differences and unused tax losses

Year ended December 31	2017	2016
Tax losses	2,604	1,919
Other	—	2,139
Total deductible temporary difference and unused tax losses	**2,604**	**4,058**

Unused tax losses of $1,077 will expire beyond 2027 and $1,527 may be carried forward indefinitely.

Unrecognized taxable temporary differences associated with investments

The aggregate amount of temporary differences associated with investments in subsidiaries for which deferred tax liabilities were not recognized as at December 31, 2017, is $228,749 (2016 - $182,708).

9. Trade and other receivables

As at	December 31, 2017	December 31, 2016
Trade receivables	393,617	307,051
Provisions for sales allowances	(120,547)	(79,261)
Allowance for doubtful accounts	(2,789)	(2,684)
	270,281	225,106
Other receivables	99,438	69,962
Total net trade and other receivables	**369,719**	**295,068**

Trade receivables disclosed above include amounts that are past due as at the end of the reporting period for which the Company has not recognized an allowance because there has not been a significant change in credit quality and the amounts are still considered recoverable.

Trade receivables past due but not impaired

As at	December 31, 2017	December 31, 2016
60-90 days	9,697	7,077
91-120 days	7,229	3,031
> 120 days	35,771	34,244
Total trade receivables past due but not impaired	**52,697**	**44,352**

Spin Master Corp.
Consolidated financial statements for the years ended December 31, 2017 and December 31, 2016

9.   Trade and other receivables (continued)

Movement in the allowance for doubtful accounts

As at	December 31, 2017	December 31, 2016
Balance at the beginning of the year	2,684	1,245
Impairment losses recognized on receivables	8,060	2,058
Amounts written off during the year as uncollectible	(7,636)	(409)
Impairment losses reversed	(424)	(237)
Foreign currency translation	105	27
Balance as at December 31, 2017	**2,789**	**2,684**

In determining the recoverability of a trade receivable, the Company considers any change in the credit quality of the trade receivable from the date credit was initially granted up to the end of the reporting period.

10.   Inventories

As at	December 31, 2017	December 31, 2016
Raw materials	10,931	9,114
Finished goods	109,398	70,810
Total inventories	**120,329**	**79,924**

The cost of inventories recognized as an expense in cost of sales during the year was $670,621 (2016 - $501,551).

During 2017, $6,114 of inventories were written down to net realizable value (2016 - $4,048). This charge is included within cost of sales in the consolidated statements of operations and comprehensive income.

Spin Master Corp.
Consolidated financial statements for the years ended December 31, 2017 and December 31, 2016

11.   Property, plant and equipment

	Moulds, dies and tools	Equipment	Property, land and building	Computer hardware	Total
Cost					
Balance at December 31, 2015	80,161	6,789	6,420	7,893	101,263
Additions	19,574	2,470	1,517	475	24,036
Asset retirements	(1,317)	(2)	(27)	(19)	(1,365)
Asset impairments	(854)	(343)	(230)	(150)	(1,577)
Assets recognized upon acquisition	1,205	6,548	1,930	244	9,927
Foreign currency translation	(2,885)	(61)	(157)	(28)	(3,131)
Total at December 31, 2016	**95,884**	**15,401**	**9,453**	**8,415**	**129,153**
Additions	19,505	2,134	2,954	1,325	25,918
Asset retirements	(6,341)	(127)	(127)	(447)	(7,042)
Asset impairments	(660)	–	–	–	(660)
Foreign currency translation	3,916	706	590	470	5,682
Total at December 31, 2017	**112,304**	**18,114**	**12,870**	**9,763**	**153,051**

	Moulds, dies and tools	Equipment	Property, land and building	Computer hardware	Total
Accumulated depreciation					
Balance at December 31, 2015	(67,771)	(5,718)	(4,938)	(6,740)	(85,167)
Depreciation	(11,417)	(1,644)	(299)	(446)	(13,806)
Asset retirements	1,312	2	22	19	1,355
Asset impairments	616	338	209	149	1,312
Assets recognized upon acquisition	(80)	(4,124)	(1,359)	(52)	(5,615)
Foreign currency translation	321	(82)	(45)	(430)	(236)
Total at December 31, 2016	**(77,019)**	**(11,228)**	**(6,410)**	**(7,500)**	**(102,157)**
Depreciation	(17,445)	(1,555)	(1,080)	(655)	(20,735)
Asset retirements	6,341	82	52	400	6,875
Foreign currency translation	(2,631)	(564)	(355)	(506)	(4,056)
Total at December 31, 2017	**(90,754)**	**(13,265)**	**(7,793)**	**(8,261)**	**(120,073)**
Net carrying amount					
Total at December 31, 2016	**18,865**	**4,173**	**3,043**	**915**	**26,996**
Total at December 31, 2017	**21,550**	**4,849**	**5,077**	**1,502**	**32,978**

For the year ended December 31, 2017, the Company recorded $660 (2016 - $265) of impairment losses in respect of 4 CGUs (2016 - 8). Impairment losses are recorded where the carrying amount of the CGU exceeds its recoverable amount. The recoverable amount was based the CGU's value in use.

Spin Master Corp.
Consolidated financial statements for the years ended December 31, 2017 and December 31, 2016

12. Intangible assets

	Brands - indefinite	Trademarks, licenses & customer lists - definite	Content development	Computer software	Total
Cost					
Balance, December 31, 2015	33,951	13,500	42,722	18,484	108,657
Additions	–	62	15,390	2,090	17,542
Disposals	–	–	–	(288)	(288)
Asset acquisitions via business combinations	44,480	20,747	852	–	66,079
Foreign currency translation	1,542	195	1,979	477	4,193
Total at December 31, 2016	**79,973**	**34,504**	**60,943**	**20,763**	**196,183**
Additions	–	–	30,109	1,155	31,264
Asset impairments	(5,734)	(3,045)	(859)	(5,288)	(14,926)
Asset acquisitions via business combinations	6,300	4,400	–	–	10,700
Foreign currency translation	2,463	124	4,487	1,517	8,591
Total at December 31, 2017	**83,002**	**35,983**	**94,680**	**18,147**	**231,812**
Balance, December 31, 2015	–	(402)	(29,688)	(16,197)	(46,287)
Amortization	–	(2,713)	(12,263)	(1,708)	(16,684)
Disposals	–	–	–	288	288
Foreign currency translation	–	(277)	(1,935)	(898)	(3,110)
Total at December 31, 2016	**–**	**(3,392)**	**(43,886)**	**(18,515)**	**(65,793)**
Amortization	–	(3,180)	(19,173)	(1,820)	(24,173)
Asset impairment	–	1,074	129	4,690	5,893
Foreign currency translation	–	(320)	(978)	(1,276)	(2,574)
Total at December 31, 2017	**–**	**(5,818)**	**(63,908)**	**(16,921)**	**(86,647)**
Net carrying amount					
Balance at December 31, 2016	**79,973**	**31,112**	**17,057**	**2,248**	**130,390**
Balance at December 31, 2017	**83,002**	**30,165**	**30,772**	**1,226**	**145,165**

Indefinite life intangibles have been allocated for impairment testing purposes to the following CGUs determined by brands:

- The 'Wild Planet' brand has been allocated to the 'Spy Gear' CGU;
- The 'Meccano' brand has been allocated to the 'Meccano Brand' CGU;
- The 'Imagination Games', 'Head Bandz', 'Boom Boom Balloon' 'Catch a Bubble', 'Bellz', 'EG Games', 'Cardinal', 'Marbles' and 'Perplexus' brands have been allocated to the 'Games and Puzzles' CGU;
- The 'Swimways' and 'Aerobie' brands have been allocated to the 'Swimways' CGU;
- The 'Toca Boca' and 'Sago Mini' brands have been allocated to the 'Toca Boca' CGU; and
- The 'Etch A Sketch' brand has been allocated to the 'Etch A Sketch' CGU.

Impairment losses

For the year ended December 31, 2017, the Company recorded $9,033 (2016 - $nil) of impairment losses in respect of 3 CGUs (2016 - nil). Impairment losses are recorded where the carrying amount of the CGU exceeds its recoverable amount. The recoverable amount was based on the CGU's value in use.

The recoverable amount of the CGUs is determined based on a value in use calculation which uses cash flow projections based on financial budgets approved by management covering a five-year period and a pre-tax discount rate of 11.5% per annum (2016: 11.1% per annum).

Spin Master Corp.
Consolidated financial statements for the years ended December 31, 2017 and December 31, 2016

12. Intangible assets (continued)

Cash flow projections during the budget period are based on the same expected gross margins and raw materials price inflation throughout the budget period. The cash flows beyond the five-year period have been extrapolated using a steady 1.0% (2016: 1.0%) per annum growth rate which is the projected long-term average growth rate. Management believes that any reasonable possible change in the key assumptions on which the recoverable amount is based would not cause the aggregate carrying amount to exceed the aggregate recoverable amount of the CGUs.

The carrying amount of indefinite life intangible assets, comprised of brands and trademarks, was allocated to CGUs as follows:

As at	December 31, 2017	December 31, 2016
Spy Gear	5,047	7,577
Meccano Brand	2,221	2,221
Games and Puzzles	27,313	25,695
Swimways	27,790	24,690
Toca Boca	13,000	13,000
Etch A Sketch	7,631	6,790
Total	**83,002**	**79,973**

13. Goodwill

As at	December 31, 2017	December 31, 2016
Balance, beginning of year	91,707	36,130
Additions during the year	13,123	55,806
Foreign currency translation	657	(229)
Total goodwill	**105,487**	**91,707**

Goodwill has been allocated for impairment testing purposes to the following CGUs:

- The 'Feva' business has been allocated to the 'Spin Master UK' CGU;
- The 'Meccano' business has been allocated to the 'Meccano Brand' CGU;
- The 'X Concepts (Tech Deck)' business has been allocated to the 'Tech Deck' CGU;
- The 'Cardinal', 'EG Games', 'Marbles' and 'Perplexus' businesses have been allocated to the 'Games and Puzzles' CGU;
- The 'Etch A Sketch' business has been allocated to the 'Etch A Sketch' CGU;
- The 'Toca Boca' business has been allocated to the 'Toca Boca' CGU; and
- The 'Swimways' and 'Aerobie' businesses have been allocated to the 'Swimways' CGU.

The carrying amount of goodwill was allocated to these CGUs as follows:

As at December 31	2017	2016
Spin Master UK	215	215
Meccano Brand	2,145	2,145
Tech Deck	1,206	1,206
Games and Puzzles	44,223	35,264
Etch A Sketch	4,148	3,933
Toca Boca	11,492	11,492
Swimways	42,058	37,452
Total goodwill	**105,487**	**91,707**

There have been no impairment losses recognized with respect to goodwill during 2017 (2016 - $nil).

Spin Master Corp.

Consolidated financial statements for the years ended December 31, 2017 and December 31, 2016

14. Trade payables and other liabilities

As at	December 31, 2017	December 31, 2016
Trade payables	155,519	92,171
Accrued liabilities	195,238	136,764
Total trade payables and other liabilities	**350,757**	**228,935**

15. Loans and borrowings

As at	December 31, 2017	December 31, 2016
Unsecured debt (at amortized cost)		
Loans from third parties (i)	44	215
	44	215
Secured debt (at amortized cost)		
Bank facilities (ii) and (iii)	532	160,831
	576	161,046
Less:		
Financing costs	45	2,901
Total loans and borrowings	**531**	**158,145**
Current	531	158,107
Non-current	–	38
Total loans and borrowings	**531**	**158,145**

(i) Fixed rate loans with Région Nord-Pas de Calais, Cap Calais and OSEO related to Meccano operations in France, with remaining maturity periods not exceeding 1 year (2016 - 3 years). The weighted average effective interest rate on the loans is 1.27% per annum (2016 - 1.06% per annum).

(ii) Variable rate secured facility with maximum borrowings of $905 to finance television production. The interest rate on amounts drawn under the facility bear interest at a variable rate referenced to the lending institution's Canadian dollar prime rate.

The obligation under the facility is secured through a general security agreement over the production company's assets and by a guarantee by the parent company of the production company.

As at December 31, 2017, the Company had $532 outstanding (December 31, 2016 - $1,640) on the obligation.

On March 6, 2017 the Company entered into a Revolving Credit Facility (the "Production Facility") with a limit of $31,867 to finance television and film production. The interest rate on amounts drawn under the Production Facility bear interest at a variable rate referenced to the lending institution's Canadian dollar prime rate. As at December 31, 2017, nil was drawn on the Production Facility.

(iii) On December 21, 2016, the Company's Revolving Credit Facility and Term Credit Facility were restructured into a single five-year secured revolving facility (the "Facility"), and the total capital available was increased from $280,000 to $510,000. The new maturity date of the Facility is December 2021. Advances under the Facility may be used for general corporate purposes including refinancing existing indebtedness, funding working capital requirements, permitted acquisitions and permitted distributions.

Available borrowing options under the Facility include:

- Prime Rate Loans;
- Base Rate Loans;
- Bankers' Acceptances from BA Lenders with a maturity of thirty (30), sixty (60), ninety (90) or one hundred and eighty (180) days, subject to availability;

Spin Master Corp.

Consolidated financial statements for the years ended December 31, 2017 and December 31, 2016

15. Loans and borrowings (continued)

- BA Equivalent Loans from the Non-BA Lenders with a maturity of thirty (30)), sixty (60), ninety (90) or one hundred and eighty (180) days, subject to availability;
- LIBOR Loans with an Interest Period of one (1), two (2), three (3) or six (6) months, subject to availability;
- Swing Loans; or
- Letters of Credit

The obligation under the Facility is secured by a general security and pledge agreement in respect of all present and future personal property, assets and undertaking of the credit parties. This facility is subject to the maintenance of the following financial covenants:

- Total leverage ratio, defined as the ratio of (a) Total debt at such time, to (b) EBITDA for the applicable twelve-month period, is calculated on a quarterly basis, of 3.00 to 1.00 or less, provided that, in the event the borrower used proceeds of a borrowing to complete a single permitted acquisition with aggregate consideration greater than $100 million during any two consecutive fiscal quarters falling within the twelve-month reporting period immediately following such permitted acquisition, the borrower must only maintain the total leverage ratio 3.50 to 1.00 or less; and

- Interest coverage ratio, calculated on a consolidated, rolling four quarter basis, at 3.00:1.00 or greater.

The Company was in compliance with the total leverage and interest coverage ratio covenants as at December 31, 2017 and December 31, 2016.

As at December 31, 2017, the Company had utilized $545 (December 31, 2016 - $160,912) of its Facility: nil (December 31, 2016 - $159,190) drawn in LIBOR Loans, nil drawn in Swing Line loans and $545 (December 31, 2016 - $1,722) drawn in letters of credit.

16. Provisions and contingent liabilities

As at December 31	2017	2016
Defectives (i)	8,956	10,943
Royalties (ii)	–	29
Supplier liabilities (iii)	5,826	5,202
Contingent consideration, acquisitions (iv)	16,351	22,305
Total provisions	**31,133**	**38,479**
Current	25,398	26,454
Non-current	5,735	12,025
Total provisions	**31,133**	**38,479**

	Defectives	Royalties	Supplier liabilities	Contingent consideration, acquisitions	Total
As at December 31, 2015	**6,038**	**584**	**3,493**	**8,458**	**18,573**
Provisions recognized	10,943	–	1,709	11,892	24,544
Accretion recognized	–	–	–	2,868	2,868
Reductions arising from payments	(6,038)	(334)	–	(861)	(7,233)
Revaluation of provisions	–	(221)	–	(52)	(273)
As at December 31, 2016	**10,943**	**29**	**5,202**	**22,305**	**38,479**
As at December 31, 2016	**10,943**	**29**	**5,202**	**22,305**	**38,479**
Provisions recognized	14,936	–	1,616	1,539	18,091
Accretion recognized	–	–	–	2,559	2,559
Reductions arising from payments	(16,923)	(29)	(992)	(6,773)	(24,688)
Revaluation of provisions	–	–	–	(3,279)	(3,308)
As at December 31, 2017	**8,956**	**–**	**5,826**	**16,351**	**31,133**

Spin Master Corp.
Consolidated financial statements for the years ended December 31, 2017 and December 31, 2016

16. Provisions and contingent liabilities (continued)

Provisions

(i)   Defectives refer to when the end consumer returns faulty goods to the Company's customers. Customers without a fixed allowance for defectives are eligible for a credit for the cost of the product if returned as defective by the end consumer. The estimate of defectives is made based on the class and nature or the product and reduces the net sales figure on the statements of operations and comprehensive income.

(ii) During 2012, the Company acquired a number of brands in an asset acquisition. As part of the purchase price, the Company committed to pay royalties on sales of those brands until November 21, 2016. The future royalty obligation was estimated based on the Company's estimate of the related brands' future sales.

(iii) Supplier obligations represent the estimated compensation to be paid to suppliers for lower than expected volumes purchased, resulting in the supplier having excess raw material and finished goods inventory. While payments are not legally required, the Company will regularly compensate suppliers to maintain supplier relationships. The supplier obligation is based on the Company's estimate of the cost of the supplier's excess raw material and finished goods inventory. The provision for supplier obligations is recorded in Cost of Sales on the consolidated statements of operations and comprehensive income.

(iv) The Company took part in several business combinations as described in Note 23 which includes an earn-out payable over the next five calendar years. The fair value of the total contingent consideration on December 31, 2017 was $16,351 (2016 - $22,305) and is based on the achievement of certain financial performance criteria. The accretion of the earn-out is recorded in other (income) expense in the consolidated statements of operations and comprehensive income.

The Company is involved in various routine legal proceedings incidental to the ordinary course of its business. The Company believes that the outcome of all pending legal proceedings in the aggregate is not reasonably likely to have a material adverse effect on the Company's business, financial condition and/or its results of operations. However, in light of the uncertainties involved in legal proceedings generally, the ultimate outcome of a particular matter could be material to the Company's operating results for a particular period depending on, among other things, the size of the loss or the nature of the liability imposed and the level of the Company's income for that particular period.

17. Share capital

(a) Authorized as at December 31, 2017 and December 31, 2016

Unlimited number of Multiple voting shares;

Unlimited number of Subordinate voting shares; and

Unlimited number of Preferred shares issuable in series.

As at	December 31, 2017	December 31, 2016
Multiple voting shares	375,115	406,595
Subordinate voting shares	306,195	263,520
Total share capital issued and outstanding	**681,310**	**670,115**

	Number of shares	Number of shares
Multiple voting shares	73,549,812	77,230,812
Subordinate voting shares	28,126,094	24,445,309
Total share capital issued and outstanding	**101,675,906**	**101,676,121**

Spin Master Corp.
Consolidated financial statements for the years ended December 31, 2017 and December 31, 2016

17. Share capital (continued)

Issued and outstanding

On May 24, 2017 the three founders of the Company closed an offering of 3,681,000 subordinate voting shares of the Company at a price of $30.21 per share, for aggregate gross proceeds to the selling shareholders of $111,203. To satisfy the sale, the selling shareholders converted in aggregate 3,681,000 multiple voting shares into subordinate voting shares on a one-for-one basis. The Company did not receive any proceeds from the sale of subordinate voting shares associated with this offering.

On June 6, 2016, the Company closed the public offering of 4,900,000 subordinate voting shares at a price of $20.69 per subordinate voting share (the "Secondary Offering"). The Secondary Offering included a treasury offering of 2,450,000 subordinate voting shares by the Company for gross proceeds of $50,691 and a secondary offering of 2,450,000 subordinate voting shares, satisfied by the exchange of multiple voting shares by the founders of the Company. The Company incurred $2,587 of issuance costs, which is deducted from share capital in accordance with IAS 32, Financial instruments: Presentation.

(b) Share-based plans

Participation arrangements

The Company had equity participation arrangements ("Participation Arrangements") with nine senior employees and one former employee pursuant to which they were entitled to receive a cash payment and shares on the Initial Public Offering (the "Initial Offering") of the Company. The Participation Arrangements served to reward past service and encourage retention. The terms of the Participation Arrangements differ between participants with vested participants being entitled to some or all of their shares between six months and six years following the Initial Offering.

The Company satisfied the participants' entitlements by making a one-time cash payment to participants and by issuing an aggregate of 4,790,178 Subordinate voting shares immediately prior to the closing of the Initial Offering. The compensation expense for the Participation Arrangements is calculated based on the fair value of each Participation Arrangement, as determined by the value of the Company at the closing of the Initial Offering, less the value of the cash settlement. The Company recognizes compensation expense over the vesting period of the Participation Arrangements, which is between six months and six years.

As at December 31, 2017, 2,473,228 Subordinate voting shares have vested with a fair value of $106,439 (December 31, 2016 - $59,229).

Restricted Share Units ("RSUs")

In connection with the Initial Offering, the Company issued RSUs at a value of $10,500 to all of its current employees (other than the participants under the Participation Arrangements and employees in China).

The RSUs served to reward past service of the employees and align their interests with those of the Company. The RSUs were settled with Subordinate voting shares that fully vested on the first anniversary of the closing of the Initial Offering. Upon vesting of the RSUs, the Company issued approximately 693,057 Subordinate voting shares. Only employees that were employed on the settlement date received Subordinate voting shares.

The RSUs were accounted for as equity instruments as the Company had the ability and intent to settle the awards with Subordinate voting shares. The compensation expense for RSUs was calculated based on the fair value of each RSU as determined by the closing value of the Company's Subordinate voting shares on the business day of the grant date. The Company recognized compensation expense over the vesting period of the RSU.

Share Purchase Options ("Options")

The Company has one share option plan for key employees, which forms part of their long-term incentive compensation plan. Under the plan, the exercise price of each option equals the market price of the Company's share on the date of grant and the options have a maximum term of ten years. Options vest between zero and four years.

Spin Master Corp.

Consolidated financial statements for the years ended December 31, 2017 and December 31, 2016

17. Share capital (continued)

The expense recognized for employee services received during the year is shown in the following table:

	Year ended December 31,	
	2017	2016
Expense arising from equity-settled "Participation Agreement" transactions	8,689	14,270
Expense arising from equity-settled "RSU" transactions	—	5,949
Expense arising from share options	1,393	724
Total share-based compensation expense	10,082	20,943

Compensation expense of $10,082 (2016 - $20,943) is recorded in administrative expenses in the consolidated statement of operations and comprehensive income. A corresponding amount was recorded in contributed surplus.

In 2017, the Company incurred compensation expense of nil its financial results for RSU equity awards granted (2016 - $5,949).

There was no activity for Participation Arrangements and RSUs since December 31, 2016 as shown below:

	Participation Agreement		RSUs	
	Number	Weighted average grant date fair value	Number	Weighted average grant date fair value
Balance as at December 31, 2016	4,739,038	65,174	747,521	10,280
Balance as at December 31, 2017	4,739,038	65,174	747,521	10,280

The weighted average remaining contractual life for Participation Arrangements outstanding as at December 31, 2017 is 24 months.

The following is a summary of the activity of the outstanding share purchase options:

	Number of options	Weighted average exercise price (CAD)
Balance as at December 31, 2016	346,148	$22.94
Granted during the period	206,551	$37.64
Balance as at December 31, 2017	552,699	$28.43

18. Earnings per share

Details of the calculations of earnings per share are set out below:

	2017		2016	
	Weighted average number of shares	Per common share amount ($)	Weighted average number of shares	Per common share amount ($)
Basic	101,675,906	1.58	100,647,133	0.99
Diluted	101,846,680	1.58	100,702,757	0.99

The Participation Arrangements and RSUs issued to employees as Subordinate voting shares resulted in the issuance of fewer multiple voting shares to the principal shareholders. As these share issuances are anti-dilutive, they are not included in the computation of diluted earnings per share.

Spin Master Corp.

Consolidated financial statements for the years ended December 31, 2017 and December 31, 2016

19. Changes in net working capital

	Year ended December 31,	
	2017	2016
(Increase) decrease in:		
Trade and other receivables	(136,594)	(150,612)
Inventories	(42,384)	(39,205)
Prepaid expenses	1,005	(6,731)
Advances on royalties	5,160	(10,140)
	(172,813)	(206,688)
Increase (decrease) in:		
Trade payables and other liabilities	186,668	90,484
Deferred revenues	4,972	(1,265)
Provisions	(2,596)	30,249
Other	550	—
	189,594	119,468
Total changes in net working capital	16,782	(87,220)

20. Related party transactions

Balances and transactions between the Company and its subsidiaries, which are related parties of the Company, have been eliminated on consolidation and are not disclosed in this note.

There were no related party transactions included in consolidated financial statements of the Company as at December 31, 2017 and December 31, 2016.

Compensation of key management personnel

The remuneration of directors and other key management personnel during the year was as follows:

Year ended December 31	2017	2016
Salaries, wages and bonuses	5,230	5,293
Other employee benefits	340	1,548
Share-based compensation	1,037	9,155
Total compensation of key management personnel	6,607	15,996

21. Operating leases

Operating leases relate primarily to the leasing of offices and related office equipment, and have been entered into with lease terms of between two and ten years in length.

Payments recognized as an expense

Year ended December 31	2017	2016
Minimum lease payments	10,539	7,099
Total minimum lease payments	10,539	7,099

22. Commitments for expenditures

As at December 31, 2017, the Company had minimum guarantees to licensors of approximately $47,331 (2016 - $32,092).

Spin Master Corp.

Consolidated financial statements for the years ended December 31, 2017 and December 31, 2016

22. Commitments for expenditures (continued)

Non-cancellable operating lease commitments

As at December 31	2017	2016
No later than 1 year	6,832	6,784
Later than 1 year and no later than 5 years	40,859	16,097
Later than 5 years	16,231	—
Total lease commitments	**63,922**	**22,881**

23. Business combinations

Acquisition of Perplexus

On November 30, 2017 the Company acquired certain assets related to the Perplexus product, co-invented in 2001 by Michael McGinnis and Kiltsner Industrial Design Group of San Francisco and manufactured by Busy Life LLC.

Pursuant to the terms set forth in the agreement, the Company acquired control of Perplexus through the acquisition of certain assets, for a total purchase consideration of $9,861 less an escrow for possible adjustments. In addition, the Company has agreed to pay an earn-out of up to $2,000 per year based on Perplexus sales over a five year term, commencing January 1, 2018.

Included in the total purchase consideration of $9,861 is $815 related to the estimated fair value of the future earn-out payments as at the acquisition date. The total purchase consideration has been initially allocated to the identifiable intangible assets based on its estimated fair values of $2,000 (related to the trade name), and $7,861 of goodwill acquired. The assets are included in the games and puzzles product category, belonging to the North America segment effective November 30, 2017. The pro forma and actual results of operations for this acquisition have not been presented and are immaterial. The Company incurred $90 in transactions related costs which have all been included in administrative expenses in the consolidated statements of operations and comprehensive income for the year ended December 31, 2017.

Assets acquired at the date of acquisition

	Fair Value as at November 30, 2017
Assets acquired	
Intangible assets	2,000
Fair value of identifiable assets acquired	**2,000**

Goodwill arising on acquisition

	Total
Consideration transferred	9,861
Fair value of identifiable assets acquired	2,000
Goodwill arising from transaction	**7,861**

Goodwill relates to the benefit of expected synergies, revenue growth and future market development. These benefits are not recognized separately from goodwill as they do not meet the recognition criteria for identifiable intangible assets. As at the date of acquisition, $7,861 of goodwill is expected to be deductible for income tax purposes and is being amortized for tax purposes over 15 years.

Net cash outflow on acquisition

	Total
Consideration paid in cash	9,046
Net cash outflow	**9,046**

Spin Master Corp.

Consolidated financial statements for the years ended December 31, 2017 and December 31, 2016

23. Business combinations (continued)

Acquisition of Aerobie Inc. ("Aerobie")

On July 28, 2017 the Company acquired certain assets of Aerobie, a privately held Company headquartered in Palo Alto, California. Aerobie is a manufacturer of outdoor flying disks and sports toys, which will complement the Company's existing products in the outdoor segment. Pursuant to the terms set forth in the agreement, the Company acquired control of Aerobie through the acquisition of certain assets, for total purchase consideration of $11,418, less an escrow for possible adjustments. Additionally, the Company has agreed to pay additional consideration in the form of a royalty, calculated in each quarterly period of a three year royalty term, commencing January 1, 2018.

Included in the total purchase consideration of $11,418 is $724 related to the estimated fair value of the future royalty payments as at the acquisition date. The total purchase consideration has been initially allocated to identifiable intangible assets based on their estimated fair values of $6,100 (related to brands and customer relationships), $4,606 of goodwill acquired and $712 of inventory acquired. The assets are included in the Outdoor product category, belonging to the North America segment effective July 28, 2017. The pro forma and actual results of operations for this acquisition have not been presented and are immaterial. The Company incurred $200 in transaction related costs which have been included in administrative expenses in the consolidated statement of operations and comprehensive income for the year ended December 31, 2017.

Assets acquired at the date of acquisition

	Fair Value as at July 28, 2017
Assets acquired	
Inventories	712
Intangible assets	6,100
Fair value of identifiable assets acquired	**6,812**

Goodwill arising on acquisition

	Total
Consideration transferred	11,418
Fair value of identifiable assets acquired	(6,812)
Goodwill arising from transaction	**4,606**

Goodwill relates to the benefit of expected synergies, revenue growth and future market development. These benefits are not recognized separately from goodwill as they do not meet the recognition criteria for identifiable intangible assets. As at the date of acquisition, $4,606 of goodwill is expected to be deductible for income tax purposes and is being amortized for tax purposes over 15 years.

Net cash outflow on acquisition

	Total
Consideration paid in cash	10,694
Net cash outflow	**10,694**

Acquisition of Marbles Corporation

On April 28, 2017, the Company acquired Marbles Holdings, LLC ("Marbles"), a privately held Company headquartered in Chicago, Illinois, pursuant to an asset purchase agreement. Marbles is a leader in brain-building and high-quality games, gifts and gadgets for all ages. The acquisition will complement the Company's existing products and builds upon the Company's substantial presence and will strengthen its position as a leader in the Games market. The Company obtained control of the Marbles business through the acquisition of brand-related patents, trademarks and inventory for the brands for total cash consideration of $4,675.

Spin Master Corp.
Consolidated financial statements for the years ended December 31, 2017 and December 31, 2016

23. Business combinations (continued)

Acquisition of Marbles Corporation (continued)

The acquired assets were sold through a bankruptcy court approved sale process and include all of Marbles' proprietary and licensed games, warehoused inventory and the Marbles name and website. Spin Master submitted a bid for the assets and subsequently emerged as the successful bidder at the conclusion of the open auction sale process on April 24, 2017. The court overseeing the Marbles bankruptcy case issued an order approving the sale to Spin Master on April 26, 2017. The Company closed the acquisition of Marbles on April 28, 2017.

The total purchase consideration has been allocated to identifiable intangible assets based on their estimated fair values of $2,600 (related to brands, trademarks and customer relationships). Additionally $1,419 of net tangible assets were acquired. The assets are included in the Games & Puzzles product category, belonging to the North America segment effective April 28, 2017. The pro forma and actual results of operations for this acquisition have not been presented and are immaterial. The Company incurred $1,218 in transaction related costs, $262 of which have been included in administrative expenses and $956 of which have been included in other expenses in the consolidated statement of operations and comprehensive income for the year ended December 31, 2017.

Assets acquired and liabilities recognized at the date of acquisition

	Fair Value as at April 28, 2017
Assets acquired	
Inventories	983
Prepaid expenses	450
Intangible assets	2,600
	4,033
Liabilities assumed	
Royalties payable	14
	14
Fair value of identifiable net assets acquired	**4,019**

Goodwill arising on acquisition

	Total
Consideration transferred	4,675
Fair value of identifiable net assets acquired	(4,019)
Goodwill arising from transaction	**656**

Goodwill relates to the benefit of expected synergies, revenue growth and future market development. These benefits are not recognized separately from goodwill as they do not meet the recognition criteria for identifiable intangible assets. As at the date of acquisition, $656 of goodwill is expected to be deductible for income tax purposes and is being amortized for tax purposes at 5% declining balance.

Net cash outflow on acquisition

	Total
Consideration paid in cash	4,675
Net cash outflow	**4,675**

Prior year acquisitions

Acquisition of Swimways Corporation ("Swimways")

On August 2, 2016, the Company acquired Swimways, a privately held Company headquartered in Virginia Beach, Virginia with offices in Guangzhou, China and a manufacturing and distribution facility in Tarboro, North Carolina. Swimways has a diverse portfolio of toys, games, and sporting goods for the pool, beach and backyard which will

Spin Master Corp.
Consolidated financial statements for the years ended December 31, 2017 and December 31, 2016

23. Business combinations (continued)

Acquisition of Swimways Corporation ("Swimways") (continued)

complement the Company's existing products and drive sales throughout the year, outside of the seasonality traditionally associated with toys and games. Pursuant to the terms set forth in the agreement, the Company acquired control of Swimways through the acquisition of 100% of the shares of Swimways for total cash consideration of $85 million on closing, less an escrow for possible adjustments. In addition, the Company agreed to pay an earn-out of up to $8.5 million based on Swimways sales growth over four years. The potential payments for the first two years of the earn-out are included in the total purchase consideration, whereas the payments related to the latter two years of the earn-out are recognized separately from the business combination transaction because they are contingent upon the continued employment with the acquired entity.

Where the deferred consideration is contingent upon continued employment, it is recognized separately from the business combination transaction and treated as remuneration within administrative expenses in the period of performance. At each balance sheet date, the contingent deferred consideration balance comprises of the accrual for unsettled remuneration which has been recognized as at that date. For the period ended December 31, 2016, the Company recorded $466 in administrative expenses and a corresponding liability related to deferred consideration for post-acquisition services.

Included in the total purchase consideration of $91,376 is $5,220 related to the estimated fair value of the deferred payments included in the earn-out which are not contingent upon continuing employment. The total purchase consideration has been allocated to identifiable intangible assets based on their estimated fair values of $33,800 (related to brands and intellectual property), $37,452 of goodwill acquired and $20,124 of net tangible assets acquired.

The Company incurred $800 in transaction related costs which have all been included in administrative expenses in the consolidated statement of operations and comprehensive income for the year ended December 31, 2016.

Assets acquired and liabilities recognized at the date of acquisition

Assets acquired	
Cash	760
Trade and other receivables	13,205
Inventories	6,345
Prepaid expenses	687
Property, plant and equipment	3,059
Intangible assets	33,800
Other assets	273
	58,129
Liabilities assumed	
Trade payables and accrued liabilities	4,205
	4,205
Fair value of identifiable net assets acquired	**53,924**

The trade and other receivables acquired (which principally comprised trade receivables) in this transaction with a fair value of $13,205 had gross contractual amounts of $13,205.

Goodwill arising on acquisition

	Total
Consideration transferred, including deferred payments	91,376
Fair value of identifiable net assets acquired	(53,924)
Goodwill arising from transaction	**37,452**

Spin Master Corp.
Consolidated financial statements for the years ended December 31, 2017 and December 31, 2016

23.   Business combinations (continued)

Acquisition of Swimways Corporation ("Swimways") (continued)

Goodwill arose on the acquisition of Swimways because the consideration paid for the combination effectively included amounts in relation to the benefit of expected synergies, revenue growth and future market development. These benefits are not recognized separately from goodwill because they do not meet the recognition criteria for identifiable intangible assets. As at the date of acquisition, $37,452 of goodwill is expected to be deductible for income tax purposes and is amortized over 15 years.

The consideration transferred includes $5,220 in deferred payments. The deferred payment is payable to the vendor upon the achievement of key performance indicators over a two year period. The potential undiscounted amount of all future payments that the Company could be required to make under the contingent consideration arrangement is between $0 and $5,500.

Net cash outflow on acquisition

	Total
Consideration paid in cash	89,332
Less: receivable relating to closing net debt and working capital	(3,176)
Less: cash balance acquired	(760)
Net cash outflow	**85,396**

Impact of acquisition on the results of the Company

Included in the Company's financial results for the year ended December 31, 2016 is $16,870 in revenues and $2,450 in net losses, attributable to the Swimways acquisition. On a proforma basis (unaudited), had this acquisition been completed on January 1, 2016, the Company's total revenue and net loss for the year would have amounted to $1,239,244 and $100,658, respectively. Management considers these 'pro-forma' estimates to represent an approximate measure of the performance of the combined Company on an annualized basis.

Acquisition of Toca Boca and Sago Mini companies ("Toca Boca")

On May 2, 2016, the Company acquired Toca Boca, a privately held Company with offices in Stockholm, San Francisco, New York and Toronto, from Bonnier Group of Sweden, pursuant to a share purchase agreement. Toca Boca, is a play studio that makes digital toys and creates mobile applications for kids aged 2-9, focusing on the pre-school segment. The acquisition will allow the Company to develop a leadership position in the mobile application space for kids. Pursuant to the terms set forth in the agreement, the Company obtained control of Toca Boca through the acquisition of 100% of the shares of Toca Boca for total cash consideration of $30,839.

Included in the total purchase consideration of $32,098 is $833 of deferred payments and $426 of working capital adjustments. The total purchase consideration of $32,098 has been allocated to identifiable intangible assets based on their estimated fair values of $23,202 (related to brands and trademarks), $7,184 of goodwill acquired and $453 of net tangible assets acquired.

The determination of the final values of the assets acquired and liabilities assumed may result in adjustments to the values presented and a corresponding adjustment to goodwill. The pro forma and actual results of operations for this acquisition have not been presented and are immaterial. The Company incurred $500 in transaction related costs which have all been included in administrative expense in the consolidated statement of operations and comprehensive income for the year ended December 31, 2016.

Spin Master Corp.
Consolidated financial statements for the years ended December 31, 2017 and December 31, 2016

23.   Business combinations (continued)

Acquisition of Toca Boca and Sago Mini companies ("Toca Boca") (continued)

Assets acquired and liabilities recognized at the date of acquisition

	Fair value as at May 2, 2016
Assets acquired	
Trade and other receivables	1,072
Inventories	251
Prepaid expenses	283
Property, plant and equipment	467
Intangible assets	23,202
Deferred tax assets	1,193
Other assets	163
	26,631
Liabilities assumed	
Trade payables and accrued liabilities	733
Other liabilities	984
	1,717
Fair value of identifiable net assets acquired	**24,914**

The trade and other receivables acquired (which principally comprised trade receivables) in this transaction with a fair value of $1,072 had gross contractual amounts of $1,072.

Goodwill arising on acquisition

	Total
Consideration transferred, including deferred payments	32,098
Fair value of identifiable net assets acquired	(24,914)
Goodwill arising from transaction	**7,184**

Goodwill arose on the acquisition of Toca Boca because the consideration paid for the combination effectively included amounts in relation to the benefit of expected synergies, revenue growth and future market development. These benefits are not recognized separately from goodwill because they do not meet the recognition criteria for identifiable intangible assets. As at the date of acquisition, $7,184 of the goodwill is expected to be deductible for income tax purposes and is amortized over 15 years.

The consideration transferred includes $833 related to the estimated fair value of the deferred payments as at the acquisition date. The deferred payment is payable to the vendor upon the achievement of key performance indicators over a five year period. The potential undiscounted amount of all future payments the Company could be required to make under the contingent consideration arrangement is between $0 and $4,000.

Net cash outflow on acquisition

	Total
Consideration paid in cash	30,839
Net cash outflow	**30,839**

Acquisition of assets of Editrice Giochi SRL ("EG Games")

On March 11, 2016, the Company acquired EG Games, a privately held company headquartered in Italy, pursuant to a share purchase agreement. EG Games specializes in producing and selling board games. The acquisition builds upon the Company's substantial presence and will strengthen its position as a leader in the Games market in Europe.

Spin Master Corp.
Consolidated financial statements for the years ended December 31, 2017 and December 31, 2016

23. **Business combinations (continued)**

Acquisition of assets of Editrice Giochi SRL ("EG Games") (continued)

Pursuant to the terms set forth in the agreement, the Company obtained control of EG Games through the acquisition of 100% of the net assets of EG Games for total cash consideration of $5,000, of which $2,900 was due on closing, including an indemnity escrow amount of $435 held for 3 years after closing and $2,100 in Deferred Payments. Deferred Payments are to be paid into escrow quarterly over the next 7 years based on 6.5% of Gross Sales up to a maximum payment of $2,100 and is to be paid to the vendor on the 7th anniversary of the Closing date subject to set-off rights. In addition, the Company agreed to pay additional cash consideration of $500 if the aggregate gross sales during the five year period commencing from the acquisition date reaches a specified target.

Included in the total purchase consideration of $5,111 is $1,671 relating to the estimated fair value of the deferred payments and $310 related to the estimated fair value of the additional cash consideration as at the acquisition date. The total purchase consideration has been initially allocated to identifiable intangible assets based on their estimated fair values of $1,983 (related to brands and trademarks), and $2,700 of goodwill acquired. Additionally, $428 of net tangible assets were acquired. These assets are included in the Activities, Games & Puzzles, and Fun Furniture product category, belonging to the Europe segment effective March 11, 2016. The pro forma and actual results of operations for this acquisition have not been presented and are immaterial. The Company incurred $199 in transaction related costs which have all been included in administrative expenses in the consolidated statement of operations and comprehensive income for the year-ended December 31, 2016.

Assets acquired and liabilities recognized at the date of acquisition

	Fair value as at March 11, 2016
Assets acquired	
Cash	105
Trade and other receivables	138
Inventories	671
Intangible assets	1,983
	2,897
Liabilities assumed	
Trade payables and accrued liabilities	486
	486
Fair value of identifiable net assets acquired	2,411

The trade and other receivables acquired (which principally comprised trade receivables) in this transaction with a fair value of $138 had gross contractual amounts of $138.

Goodwill arising on acquisition

	Total
Consideration transferred, including deferred payments	5,111
Fair value of identifiable net assets acquired	(2,411)
Goodwill arising from transaction	2,700

Goodwill arose on the acquisition of EG Games because the cost of the combination effectively included amounts in relation to the benefit of expected synergies, revenue growth and future market development. These benefits are not recognized separately from goodwill because they do not meet the recognition criteria for identifiable intangible assets. Goodwill recognized is not expected to be deductible for income tax purposes.

Spin Master Corp.
Consolidated financial statements for the years ended December 31, 2017 and December 31, 2016

23. **Business combinations (continued)**

Acquisition of assets of Editrice Giochi SRL ("EG Games") (continued)

Net cash outflow on acquisition

	Total
Consideration paid in cash	3,144
Cash balances acquired	(105)
Net cash outflow	3,039

Acquisition of assets of Etch A Sketch

On February 11, 2016, the Company acquired the rights to the brands of Etch A Sketch and Doodle Sketch ("Etch A Sketch"), pursuant to an asset purchase agreement with the Ohio Art Company. The acquisition will complement the Company's existing products and builds on its reputation for acquiring legacy brands and infusing them with unexpected innovation. The Company obtained control of Etch A Sketch through the acquisition of all brand-related patents, trademarks, and inventory for the brands for total cash consideration of $8,950, including an indemnity escrow amount of $850. In addition, the Company agreed to pay a royalty between 2-4% based on future revenues for 8 years from the date of closing up with a minimum royalty payment of $3,150 up to a maximum of $8,150.

Included in the total purchase consideration of $11,074 is $2,124 related to the estimated fair value of the future royalty payments as at the acquisition date. The total purchase consideration has been initially allocated to identifiable intangible assets based on their estimated fair values of $6,790 (related to brands and trademarks), and $3,712 of goodwill acquired. Additionally, $572 of net tangible assets were acquired. These assets are included in the Activities, Games & Puzzles, and Fun Furniture product category effective February 11, 2016.

The pro forma and actual results of operations for this acquisition have not been presented because they are not material. The Company incurred $57 in transaction related costs which have all been included in administrative expenses in the consolidated statement of operations and comprehensive income for the year ended December 31, 2016.

Assets acquired at the date of acquisition

	Fair value as at February 11, 2016
Assets acquired	
Inventories	572
Intangible assets	6,790
Fair value of identifiable net assets acquired	7,362

Goodwill arising on acquisition

	Total
Consideration transferred, including present value of royalty payments	11,074
Fair value of identifiable net assets acquired	(7,362)
Post-closing purchase price adjustment	275
Goodwill arising from transaction	3,987

Goodwill arose on the acquisition of the Etch A Sketch brand because the consideration paid for the combination effectively included amounts in relation to the benefit of expected synergies, revenue growth and future market development. These benefits are not recognized separately from goodwill because they do not meet the recognition criteria for identifiable intangible assets. As at the date of acquisition, $3,987 of the goodwill is expected to be deductible for income tax purposes and is amortized at 7% declining balance.

Spin Master Corp.
Consolidated financial statements for the years ended December 31, 2017 and December 31, 2016

23. Business combinations (continued)

Acquisition of assets of Etch A Sketch (continued)

Net cash outflow on acquisition

	Total
Consideration paid in cash	8,950
Net cash outflow	**8,950**

24. Financial instruments and risk management

Capital management

Management includes the following items in its definition of capital:

As at	2017	2016
Capital components		
Short-term borrowings	531	158,107
Non-current borrowings	–	38
Total debt	**531**	**158,145**
Share capital	681,310	670,115
Contributed surplus	20,323	21,436
Accumulated deficit	(247,340)	(408,406)
Total capital	**454,824**	**441,290**

The Company makes adjustments to its' capital based on the funds available to the Company, in order to support the operations of the business and in order to ensure that the entities in the Company will be able to continue as going concerns, while maximizing the return to stakeholders through the optimization of the debt and equity balances.

The Company manages its capital structure, and makes adjustments to it in light of changes in economic conditions. In order to maintain or modify the capital structure, the Company may arrange new debt with existing or new lenders, or obtain additional financing through other means.

Management reviews its capital management approach on an ongoing basis and believes that this approach is reasonable. There were no changes in the Company's approach to capital management during the year ended December 31, 2017.

The Company is subject to capital requirements under the credit facility agreement, as described in Note 15. As at December 31, 2017, the Company was in compliance with all financial covenants.

Financial risk management objectives

Management's objective is to protect the Company and its subsidiaries on a consolidated basis against material economic exposures and the variability of results from various financial risks that include foreign currency risk, interest rate risk, credit risk and liquidity risk.

Market risk

Foreign currency risk

Due to the nature of the Company's international operations, it is exposed to foreign currency risk driven by fluctuations in exchange rates. Risk arises because the value of monetary assets, liabilities, revenues and expenditures arising from transactions denominated in foreign currencies may vary due to changes in exchange rates ("transaction exposures") and because the non-US dollar denominated financial statements of the Company's subsidiaries may vary on translation into the US dollar presentation currency ("translation exposures"). These exposures could impact the Company's earnings and cash flows.

The Company uses derivative financial instruments such as foreign exchange forward contracts to manage foreign currency risk.

24. Financial instruments and risk management (continued)

As at December 31, 2017, the Company is committed under outstanding foreign exchange contracts to purchase USD, representing total purchase commitments of approximately $48,060 (2016 - $162,777).

The consolidated statements of financial position include the following amounts (by denomination) presented in USD:

As at December 31	2017	2016
Financial Assets		
USD	335,123	161,090
CAD	19,248	10,027
Euros	56,173	91,696
Pound	25,881	39,598
Peso	40,392	21,266
Yen	19	–
Australian dollar	9,634	–
Total Assets	**486,470**	**323,677**
Financial Liabilities		
USD	85,569	293,838
CAD	145,330	58,687
Euros	38,863	8,183
Pound	9,402	7,366
Peso	14,750	2,537
Yen	99	–
Australian dollar	3,365	–
Total Liabilities	**297,378**	**370,611**

Foreign currency risk - sensitivity analysis

The Company is consistently exposed to the Canadian dollar, the Peso, the British Pound and the Euro. A sensitivity rate of 5% is used when reporting foreign currency risk internally to key management personnel, and represents management's assessment of the reasonably possible change in foreign exchange rates to which the Company is exposed.

For the year ended December 31, 2017, a 5% strengthening of the above currencies against the USD would have resulted in a decrease to net assets of $3,508 (2016 - an increase to net assets of $4,517).

The sensitivity analysis includes only outstanding foreign currency denominated monetary assets and liabilities, and adjusts their translation as at the end of the reporting period for a 5% change in foreign currency rates.

Interest rate risk - management

Interest rate risk is the risk that the Company's financial assets and liabilities will increase or decrease in value due to a change in interest rates. The Company is exposed to interest rate risk as its loan facility bears interest at a variable rate.

Interest rate risk - sensitivity analysis

The Company is exposed to interest rate risk on financial instruments. A sensitivity rate of 50 basis points is used when reporting interest rate risk internally to key management personnel, and represents management's assessment of the reasonably possible change in interest rates to which the Company is exposed.

For the year ended December 31, 2017, with all other variables held constant, a 50 basis point increase in interest rates would have resulted in no impact to net income for the year (2016 - a decrease to net income of $600).

Spin Master Corp.
Consolidated financial statements for the years ended December 31, 2017 and December 31, 2016

24. Financial instruments and risk management (continued)

Credit risk

As the Company usually grants credit to customers on an unsecured basis, credit risk arises from the possibility that customers may experience financial difficulty and may be unable to fulfill their financial obligations.

This risk is managed through the establishment of credit limits and payment terms based on an evaluation of the customer's financial performance, ability to generate cash, financing availability and liquidity status. These factors are reviewed at least annually, with more frequent reviews performed as necessary.

In addition, the Company uses a variety of financial arrangements to ensure collectability of trade receivables, including requiring letters of credit, cash in advance of shipment and through the purchase of insurance on material customer receivables.

As at December 31, 2017, approximately 33% (2016 - 43%) of the Company's trade receivables are from three major retail customers which represent approximately 48% of gross product sales for the year ended December 31, 2017 (2016 - 52%). The Company's credit insurance provides coverage for all of these customers.

The Company mitigates credit risk on its cash balance by ensuring all deposits are with financial institutions with high credit-ratings assigned by international credit-rating agencies.

Liquidity risk

The following details the Company's remaining contractual maturities for its financial liabilities with contractual repayment periods. The tables reflect the undiscounted cash flows of financial liabilities based on the earliest date on which the Company can be required to pay, including both interest and principal.

To the extent that interest rates are floating, the undiscounted amount is derived from interest rate curves at the end of the reporting period. The contractual maturity is based on the earliest date on which the Company may be required to pay.

The Company's contractual maturities are as follows:

	Less than 1 year	1 year to 5 years	Greater than 5 years	2017 Total
Trade payables and other liabilities	350,757	–	–	350,757
Loans and borrowings	531	–	–	531
Provisions	25,398	5,735	–	31,133
Total as at December 31	**376,686**	**5,735**	**–**	**382,421**

	Less than 1 year	1 year to 5 years	Greater than 5 years	2016 Total
Trade payables and other liabilities	228,935	–	–	228,935
Other long-term liabilities	–	110	–	110
Loan and borrowings	158,107	38	–	158,145
Provisions	26,454	12,025	–	38,479
Total as at December 31	**413,496**	**12,173**	**–**	**425,669**

Financing facilities

As at December 31,	2017	2016
Secured bank loan facilities		
Amount used	531	160,831
Amount unused	510,373	343,450
Total as at December 31	**510,904**	**504,281**

24. Financial instruments and risk management (continued)

Fair value measurements

With the exception of foreign exchange forward contracts, the Company does not currently record any financial assets or liabilities at fair value in the financial statements and their carrying amounts approximate their fair values.

The fair value of foreign exchange forward contracts represented an asset as at December 31, 2017 of $971 and is recorded in other assets (2016 - liability $78 and is recorded in other liabilities). These fair values are categorized within Level 2 of the fair value hierarchy. The fair value of foreign exchange contracts is estimated based on forward exchange rates observable at the end of the reporting period and contract forward rates.

25. Segment information

Spin Master's portfolio includes children's products, brands and entertainment properties which are grouped into five major product categories as follows:

(i) Activities, games and puzzles and fun furniture
(ii) Remote control and interactive characters
(iii) Boys action and high-tech construction
(iv) Pre-school and girls
(v) Outdoor

Information reported to the Chief Operating Decision Maker ("CODM") for the purposes of resource allocation and assessment of segment performance focuses on geographical areas rather than product category. The directors of the Company have chosen to organize the Company around the 3 operating segments as follows: (i) North America, (ii) Europe, and (iii) Rest of World. Factors considered in determining the operating segments include the nature of the Company's business activities, the management structure directly accountable to the CODM, availability of discrete financial information and strategic priorities within the organizational structure.

Segment revenue and results

The following table shows the Company's revenue and results from continuing operations by reportable segment:

	Year ended December 31	
	2017	2016
Revenue by segment		
North America	1,082,709	847,278
Europe	368,009	271,130
Rest of world	206,310	136,150
Gross product sales	**1,657,028**	**1,254,558**
Other revenue and sales allowances	(105,704)	(100,104)
Total consolidated revenue	**1,551,324**	**1,154,454**
Segment income		
North America	189,973	65,023
Europe	19,647	65,455
Rest of world	19,806	44,314
Total segment income	**229,426**	**174,792**
Corporate and other	(8,997)	(36,913)
Income before income tax expense	**220,429**	**137,879**

Revenues for North America include revenues attributable to Canada of $142,707 (2016 - $122,350) for the period ended December 31, 2017.

Revenue reported by segment above represents revenue generated from external customers. There were no inter-segment sales in the current year (2016 - $nil). The Company does not include sales adjustments such as trade discounts and other allowances in reporting revenue by segment ("referred to as gross product sales").

Spin Master Corp.
Consolidated financial statements for the years ended December 31, 2017 and December 31, 2016

25. Segment information (continued)

The accounting policies of the reportable segments are the same as the Company's accounting policies described in Note 2. Segment income represents income before income tax expense earned by each segment without allocation of other expenses, foreign exchange (gain) loss and finance costs. This is the measure reported to the CODM for the purposes of resource allocation and assessment of segment performance.

Segment assets

As at December 31	2017	2016
Assets		
North America	489,390	571,267
Europe	99,819	105,561
Rest of world	138,087	37,596
Total segment assets	**727,296**	**714,424**
Corporate and other	211,089	61,172
Total consolidated assets	**938,385**	**775,596**

A breakdown of non-current assets by location of assets are detailed as follows:

As at December 31	2017	2016
Non-current assets		
North America	204,136	140,880
Europe	12,741	10,519
Rest of world	9,665	6,042
Total segment non-current assets	**226,542**	**157,441**
Corporate and other	84,033	122,349
Total consolidated non-current assets	**310,575**	**279,790**

Non-current assets for North America include non-current assets attributable to Canada of $82,862 (2016 - $68,902) for the periods ending December 31, 2017.

Segment liabilities

As at December 31	2017	2016
Liabilities		
North America	295,313	220,317
Europe	60,619	25,116
Rest of world	55,335	15,518
Total segment liabilities	**411,267**	**260,951**
Corporate and other	27,036	188,966
Total consolidated liabilities	**438,303**	**449,917**

For the purposes of monitoring segment performance and allocating resources between segments:

- all assets are allocated to reportable segments other than deferred tax assets, other long-term assets and computer software. Goodwill is allocated to CGUs. Assets used jointly by reportable segments are allocated on the basis of the revenues earned by individual reportable segments; and

- all liabilities are allocated to reportable segments other than royalties payable (included within trade payables and other liabilities) and deferred tax liabilities. Liabilities for which reportable segments are jointly liable are allocated in proportion to segment assets.

Spin Master Corp.
Consolidated financial statements for the years ended December 31, 2017 and December 31, 2016

25. Segment information (continued)

Depreciation and amortization by segment

Year ended December 31	2017	2016
Depreciation and amortization by segment		
North America	33,681	24,193
Europe	5,207	3,100
Rest of world	3,216	1,808
Total segment depreciation and amortization	**42,104**	**29,101**
Corporate and other	2,804	1,389
Total consolidated depreciation and amortization	**44,908**	**30,490**

In addition to the depreciation and amortization reported above, impairment losses of $9,693 (2016 - $265) were recognized in respect of property, plant and equipment and intangible assets, for the year ended December 31, 2017. These impairment losses were attributable to the following reportable segments:

Year ended December 31	2017	2016
Impairment losses		
North America	9,033	–
Rest of world	660	265
Total impairment losses	**9,693**	**265**

Revenue from major product categories

The following is an analysis of the Company's worldwide revenues from continuing operations based on its major product categories:

Year ended December 31	2017	2016
Revenue from product categories		
Activities, games and puzzles, and fun furniture	365,378	337,768
Remote control and interactive characters	593,355	282,777
Boys action and high-tech construction	112,102	154,454
Pre-school and girls	493,069	460,484
Outdoor	93,124	19,075
Gross product sales	**1,657,028**	**1,254,558**
Other revenues and sales allowances	(105,704)	(100,104)
Total revenues	**1,551,324**	**1,154,454**

Major customers

Sales to the Company's largest customers accounted for 48.1% and 52.0% of consolidated gross product sales for 2017 and 2016 respectively. Sales to single customers of the company that contributed 10% or more to gross product sales include three customers. The largest customer contributed $363,674 (2016 - $303,952) while the second and third largest customers each contributed $230,696 (2016 - $193,343) and $203,425 (2016 - $154,119), respectively. No other single customer contributed 10% or more to gross product sales of the company for 2017 and 2016.

26. Events after the reporting period

On February 28, 2018, the Company signed an agreement to acquire certain assets relating to the Gund line of business from Enesco LLC for $79.1 million. Gund is a manufacturer and distributor of plush toys and is best known for its line of teddy bears. Established in 1898, Gund has a 120-year history as a market leader and toy industry pioneer widely known for its high quality and innovative design. Headquartered in Edison, New Jersey, Gund distributes product throughout the United States, Canada, Europe, Japan, Australia and South America. The acquisition will allow Spin Master to build a stable platform for expansion into the infant toy and specialty gift categories and further grow the business internationally. Gund will be included in the Activities, Games and Puzzles and Fun Furniture business segment. The purchase consideration will be funded from internally generated cash resources and the Company's existing Credit Facility. The acquisition is expected to close on April 1, 2018.

2017 Annual Report

Stretching our wings

MANAGEMENT'S REPORT TO THE SHAREHOLDERS

The consolidated financial statements have been prepared by management in accordance with International Financial Reporting Standards. When a choice between accounting methods exists, management has chosen those they deem most appropriate in the circumstances. Financial statements will, by necessity, include certain amounts based on judgments and estimates. Management has determined such amounts on a reasonable basis so that the consolidated financial statements are presented fairly in all material respects. All information in this report is the responsibility of management.

Management has established systems of internal control, including disclosure controls and procedures and internal controls over financial reporting, which are designed and operated to provide reasonable assurance that financial and non-financial information is disclosed in a timely, complete, relevant and accurate manner. These systems of internal control also serve to safeguard the Corporation's assets. The systems of internal control are monitored by management and are further supported by an internal audit department whose functions include reviewing internal controls and their applications.

The Board of Directors is responsible for the overall stewardship and governance of the Corporation, including obtaining reasonable assurance management fulfills its responsibilities for financial reporting and internal control, and reviewing and approving the consolidated financial statements. The Board carries out these responsibilities principally through its Audit Committee.

The Audit Committee of the Board of Directors, composed of independent Directors, meets regularly with management, the internal auditors and the external auditors to satisfy itself that each is properly discharging its responsibilities and to review the consolidated financial statements and management's discussion and analysis. The Audit Committee reports its findings to the Board of Directors prior to the approval of the consolidated financial statements and management's discussion and analysis for issuance to the shareholders. The Audit Committee also recommends, for review by the Board of Directors and approval of shareholders, the reappointment of the external auditors. The internal and external auditors have full and free access to the Audit Committee.

The consolidated financial statements have been audited by KPMG LLP, the independent external auditors, in accordance with Canadian Generally Accepted Auditing Standards on behalf of the shareholders. The auditors' report outlines the scope of their examination and sets forth their opinion.

Gregg Saretsky
President and
Chief Executive Officer

Harry Taylor
Executive Vice-President, Finance and
Chief Financial Officer

February 5, 2018
Calgary, Canada

INDEPENDENT AUDITORS' REPORT

To the Shareholders of WestJet Airlines Ltd.

We have audited the accompanying consolidated financial statements of WestJet Airlines Ltd., which comprise the consolidated statements of financial position at December 31, 2017 and December 31, 2016, the consolidated statements of earnings, changes in equity, cash flows and comprehensive income for the years then ended, and notes, comprising a summary of significant accounting policies and other explanatory information.

Management's Responsibility for the Consolidated Financial Statements

Management is responsible for the preparation and fair presentation of these consolidated financial statements in accordance with International Financial Reporting Standards and for such internal controls as management determines are necessary to enable the preparation of consolidated financial statements that are free from material misstatement, whether due to fraud or error.

Auditors' Responsibility

Our responsibility is to express an opinion on these consolidated financial statements based on our audits. We conducted our audits in accordance with Canadian Generally Accepted Auditing Standards. Those standards require that we comply with ethical requirements and plan and perform the audit to obtain reasonable assurance about whether the consolidated financial statements are free from material misstatement.

An audit involves performing procedures to obtain audit evidence about the amounts and disclosures in the consolidated financial statements. The procedures selected depend on our judgment, including the assessment of the risks of material misstatement of the consolidated financial statements, whether due to fraud or error. In making those risk assessments, we consider internal controls relevant to the entity's preparation and fair presentation of the consolidated financial statements in order to design audit procedures that are appropriate in the circumstances, but not for the purpose of expressing an opinion on the effectiveness of the entity's internal controls. An audit also includes evaluating the appropriateness of accounting policies used and the reasonableness of accounting estimates made by management as well as evaluating the overall presentation of the consolidated financial statements.

We believe that the audit evidence we have obtained in our audits is sufficient and appropriate to provide a basis for our audit opinion.

Opinion

In our opinion, the consolidated financial statements present fairly, in all material respects, the consolidated financial position of WestJet Airlines Ltd. at December 31, 2017 and December 31, 2016, and its consolidated financial performance and its consolidated cash flows for the years then ended in accordance with International Financial Reporting Standards.

KPMG LLP

Chartered Professional Accountants

February 5, 2018
Calgary, Canada

WESTJET

Consolidated Statement of Earnings
For the years ended December 31
(Stated in thousands of Canadian dollars, except per share amounts)

	Note	2017	2016
Revenue:			
Guest		3,822,045	3,556,941
Other		680,275	565,918
		4,502,320	4,122,859
Operating expenses:			
Aircraft fuel		950,043	765,867
Salaries and benefits		935,145	854,056
Rates and fees		644,763	617,573
Depreciation and amortization	6	403,021	350,484
Sales and marketing		384,452	356,745
Maintenance		203,227	209,226
Aircraft leasing		165,902	178,445
Other		330,014	291,024
Employee profit share		46,793	59,342
		4,063,360	3,682,762
Earnings from operations		438,960	440,097
Non-operating income (expense):			
Finance income		19,626	16,618
Finance cost	14	(53,710)	(49,074)
Gain (loss) on foreign exchange		(4,877)	7,402
Gain (loss) on disposal of property and equipment		6,562	(3,314)
Gain (loss) on derivatives		(2,426)	4,504
		(34,825)	(23,864)
Earnings before income tax		404,135	416,233
Income tax expense (recovery):			
Current	10	58,645	133,055
Deferred	10	61,912	(12,280)
		120,557	120,775
Net earnings		283,578	295,458
Earnings per share:			
Basic	13	2.44	2.46
Diluted	13	2.42	2.45

The accompanying notes are an integral part of the consolidated financial statements.

WESTJET

Consolidated Statement of Financial Position
At December 31
(Stated in thousands of Canadian dollars)

	Note	2017	2016
Assets			
Current assets:			
Cash and cash equivalents	4	1,147,076	1,520,822
Marketable securities	4	226,090	-
Total cash, cash equivalents and marketable securities		1,373,166	1,520,822
Restricted cash	5	109,700	102,649
Accounts receivable	18	129,648	127,785
Prepaid expenses, deposits and other	18	138,676	181,070
Inventory	18	43,045	33,535
		1,794,235	1,965,861
Non-current assets:			
Property and equipment	6	4,567,504	4,036,880
Intangible assets	7	59,517	66,187
Other assets	18	78,584	95,368
Total assets		6,499,840	6,164,296
Liabilities and shareholders' equity			
Current liabilities:			
Accounts payable and accrued liabilities	18	549,844	547,490
Advance ticket sales		695,111	626,635
Deferred rewards program		203,433	155,567
Non-refundable guest credits		43,288	42,942
Current portion of maintenance provisions	8	82,129	103,571
Current portion of long-term debt	9	153,149	145,128
		1,726,954	1,621,333
Non-current liabilities:			
Maintenance provisions	8	270,347	262,663
Long-term debt	9	1,895,898	1,901,530
Other liabilities	18	19,171	8,374
Deferred income tax	10	374,946	309,694
Total liabilities		4,287,316	4,103,594
Shareholders' equity:			
Share capital	11	548,977	555,716
Equity reserves		97,514	93,039
Hedge reserves		(1,902)	(11,003)
Retained earnings		1,567,935	1,422,950
Total shareholders' equity		2,212,524	2,060,702
Total liabilities and shareholders' equity		6,499,840	6,164,296

The accompanying notes are an integral part of the consolidated financial statements.

On behalf of the Board:

Gregg Saretsky, Director   Hugh Bolton, Director

WESTJET

Consolidated Statement of Cash Flows
For the years ended December 31
(Stated in thousands of Canadian dollars)

	Note	2017	2016
Operating activities:			
Net earnings		283,578	295,458
Items not involving cash:			
Depreciation and amortization		403,021	350,484
Change in maintenance provisions		65,372	82,564
Amortization of transaction costs		4,807	5,092
Amortization of hedge settlements		–	833
(Gain) loss on derivatives		4,059	(2,472)
(Gain) loss on disposal of property and equipment		(6,562)	3,314
Share-based payment expense	11	19,050	18,432
Deferred income tax expense (recovery)		61,912	(12,280)
Unrealized foreign exchange (gain) loss		2,496	(4,498)
Change in non-cash working capital		237,663	40,384
Change in restricted cash		(7,051)	(34,076)
Change in other assets		(1,296)	7,129
Change in other liabilities		6,379	(2,486)
Purchase of shares pursuant to compensation plans		(4,784)	(7,197)
Maintenance provision settlements		(56,571)	(36,094)
		1,012,073	704,587
Investing activities:			
Aircraft additions		(881,069)	(847,718)
Aircraft disposals		9,511	4,660
Other property and equipment and intangible additions and disposals		(48,855)	(76,996)
Purchases of marketable securities		(231,293)	–
Change in non-cash working capital		(16,009)	(22,288)
		(1,167,715)	(942,342)
Financing activities:			
Increase in long-term debt	11	186,796	998,715
Repayment of long-term debt	12	(154,249)	(157,193)
Shares repurchased		(90,317)	(126,152)
Dividends paid		(64,886)	(66,967)
Cash interest paid		(63,188)	(56,046)
Change in non-cash working capital		(14,597)	(14,026)
		(200,441)	578,331
Cash flow from/(used in) operating, investing and financing activities		(356,083)	340,576
Effect of foreign exchange on cash and cash equivalents		(17,663)	(3,551)
Net change in cash and cash equivalents		(373,746)	337,025
Cash and cash equivalents, beginning of year		1,520,822	1,183,797
Cash and cash equivalents, end of year		1,147,076	1,520,822
Supplemental disclosure of operating cash flows			
Cash interest received		17,634	16,148
Cash taxes paid, net		(97,911)	(118,014)

The accompanying notes are an integral part of the consolidated financial statements.

WESTJET

Consolidated Statement of Changes in Equity
For the years ended December 31
(Stated in thousands of Canadian dollars)

	Note	2017	2016
Share capital:			
Balance, beginning of year	11	555,716	582,796
Issuance of shares pursuant to compensation plans	11	10,131	1,146
Shares repurchased	11	(16,870)	(28,226)
		548,977	555,716
Equity reserves:			
Balance, beginning of year		93,039	82,713
Share-based payment expense	11	19,050	18,432
Issuance of shares pursuant to compensation plans		(14,575)	(8,106)
		97,514	93,039
Hedge reserves:			
Balance, beginning of year		(11,003)	1,903
Other comprehensive income (loss)		9,101	(12,906)
		(1,902)	(11,003)
Retained earnings:			
Balance, beginning of year		1,422,950	1,292,581
Dividends declared	12	(64,886)	(66,967)
Shares repurchased	11	(260)	(196)
Purchase of shares pursuant to compensation plans		283,578	295,458
Net earnings		1,567,935	1,422,950
Total shareholders' equity		2,212,524	2,060,702

The accompanying notes are an integral part of the consolidated financial statements.

WestJet

Consolidated Statement of Comprehensive Income

For the years ended December 31
(Stated in thousands of Canadian dollars)

	2017	2016
Net earnings	283,578	295,458
Items that are or may be reclassified to net earnings:		
Other comprehensive income (loss), net of tax:		
Amortization of hedge settlements to aircraft leasing	–	833
Net unrealized loss on foreign exchange derivatives[(i)]	(10,336)	(6,042)
Reclassification of net realized (gain) loss on foreign exchange derivatives[(ii)]	5,385	(3,683)
Net unrealized gain on interest rate derivatives[(iii)]	5,181	1,037
Reclassification of net realized loss on interest rate derivatives[(iv)]	2,009	2,838
Net unrealized gain (loss) on cross-currency swap derivatives[(v)]	6,903	(7,718)
Reclassification of net realized gain on cross-currency swap derivatives[(vi)]	(41)	(171)
	9,101	(12,906)
Total comprehensive income	292,679	282,552

(i) Net of income taxes of $3,814 (2016 – $2,219).
(ii) Net of income taxes of $(1,985) (2016 – $1,352).
(iii) Net of income taxes of $(1,913) (2016 – $(374)).
(iv) Net of income taxes of $(737) (2016 – $(1,044)).
(v) Net of income taxes of $(2,534) (2016 – $2,837).
(vi) Net of income taxes of $15 (2016 – $63).

The accompanying notes are an integral part of the consolidated financial statements.

WestJet

Notes to Consolidated Financial Statements

As at and for the years ended December 31, 2017 and 2016
(Stated in thousands of Canadian dollars, except percentage, ratio, share and per share amounts)

1. Statement of significant accounting policies

The annual consolidated financial statements of WestJet Airlines Ltd. (the Corporation) for the years ended December 31, 2017 and 2016 were authorized for issue by the Board of Directors on February 5, 2018. The Corporation is a public company incorporated and domiciled in Canada. The Corporation provides airline service and travel packages. The Corporation's shares are publicly traded on the Toronto Stock Exchange (TSX) under the symbol WJA. The principal business address is 22 Aerial Place N.E., Calgary, Alberta, T2E 3J1 and the registered office is Suite 2400, 525 - 8 Avenue S.W., Calgary, Alberta, T2P 1G1.

(a) Basis of presentation

These annual consolidated financial statements and the notes hereto have been prepared in accordance with International Financial Reporting Standards (IFRS) as issued by the International Accounting Standards Board (IASB).

These annual consolidated financial statements have been prepared on an historical cost basis except for certain financial assets and liabilities, including derivative financial instruments that are measured at fair value. Where applicable, these differences have been described in the notes hereto.

Amounts presented in these annual consolidated financial statements and the notes hereto are in Canadian dollars, the Corporation's reporting currency, unless otherwise stated. The Corporation's functional currency is the Canadian dollar.

(b) Principles of consolidation

The accompanying consolidated financial statements include the accounts of the Corporation and its subsidiaries. Subsidiaries consist of entities over which the Corporation is exposed to, or has rights to, variable returns as well as the ability to affect those returns through the power to direct the relevant activities of the entity. A description of the Corporation's subsidiaries is provided in Note 17. All intercompany balances and transactions between the Corporation and its subsidiaries have been eliminated.

(c) Seasonality

The airline industry is sensitive to general economic conditions and the seasonal nature of air travel. The Corporation experiences increased domestic travel in the summer months and more demand for transborder and international travel over the winter months, thus reducing the effects of seasonality on net earnings.

(d) Revenue recognition

(i) Guest

Guest revenue, including the air component of vacation packages, is recognized when air transportation is provided. Tickets sold but not yet used are reported in the consolidated statement of financial position as advance ticket sales.

(ii) Other

Other revenue includes items such as net revenue from the sale of the land component of vacation packages, ancillary fees as well as cargo and charter revenue.

Revenue for the land component of vacation packages is generated from providing agency services equal to the amount paid by the guest for products and services, less payment to the travel supplier, and is reported at the net amount received. Revenue from the land component is deferred as advance ticket sales and recognized in earnings on departure of the vacation.

Ancillary revenue is recognized when the services and products are provided to the guest. Ancillary revenues include items such as fees associated with guest itinerary changes or cancellations. Plus upgrades, baggage fees, buy-on-board sales, pre-reserved seating fees and breakage from the WestJet Rewards Program relating to partner funded credits.

Notes to Consolidated Financial Statements
As at and for the years ended December 31, 2017 and 2016
(Stated in thousands of Canadian dollars, except percentage, ratio, share and per share amounts)

1. Statement of significant accounting policies (continued)

(d) Revenue recognition (continued)

(iii) WestJet Rewards Program

The Corporation has a rewards program that allows guests to accumulate credits based on their WestJet travel spend to be used towards future flights and vacation packages. Revenue received in relation to credits issued is deferred as a liability until the credit is utilized and air transportation is provided, at which time it is recognized in guest revenue. Revenue associated with WestJet issued credits expected to expire (breakage) is recognized in guest revenue at the time the credit is issued.

The Corporation also has a co-branded MasterCard with the Royal Bank of Canada (RBC). RBC issues and funds reward credits to cardholders as a percentage of their total retail spend. The Corporation records a receivable and liability for reward credits issued and funded by RBC for cardholder retail spend. Revenue related to reward credits redeemed is deferred as advance ticket sales at the time of booking and subsequently recognized in guest revenue at the time of travel. Revenue related to new credit cards issued is recognized in other revenue immediately upon activation.

(iv) Non-refundable guest credits

The Corporation issues future travel credits to guests for flight changes and cancellations. Where appropriate, travel credits are also issued for flight delays, missing baggage and other inconveniences. All credits are non-refundable and have expiry dates dependent upon the nature of the credit. The Corporation records a liability at face value for credits issued for flight changes and cancellations. Revenue related to flight changes and cancellations is recorded in guest revenue when air transportation is provided. When the Corporation provides travel credits related to flight delays, missing baggage or other inconveniences as goodwill gestures, a performance obligation is not created until such time as the guest utilizes the credit to book a flight. These credits are recorded as a reduction to guest revenue to offset any revenue generated from the booking.

(e) Adoption of IFRS 9 – Financial instruments

The Corporation has early adopted IFRS 9 *Financial Instruments* issued in July 2014 (IFRS 9), with a date of initial application of January 1, 2017. IFRS 9 introduces new requirements for the classification and measurement of financial assets, amends the requirements related to hedge accounting, and introduces a forward-looking expected loss impairment model. The adoption of this standard has not had a material impact on the Corporation's financial statements.

IFRS 9 contains three classification categories for financial assets: measured at amortized cost, fair value through other comprehensive income (FVOCI) and fair value through profit or loss (FVTPL). The classification of financial assets under IFRS 9 is based on the business model in which a financial asset is managed and its contractual cash flow characteristics. The standard eliminates the previous IAS 39 categories of held to maturity, loans and receivables and available for sale. Most of the requirements in IAS 39 for classification and measurement of financial liabilities were carried forward in IFRS 9 and the adoption of IFRS 9 has not had an impact on the Corporations accounting policies for financial liabilities.

The following table summarizes the classification and measurement changes for each class of the Corporation's financial assets and financial liabilities upon adoption at January 1, 2017.

Financial Asset (Liability)	IAS 39		IFRS 9	
	Category	Measurement	Category	Measurement
Cash	FVTPL	Fair value	Assets at amortized cost	Amortized cost
Cash equivalents	FVTPL	Fair value	Assets at amortized cost	Amortized cost
Restricted cash	FVTPL	Fair value	Assets at amortized cost	Amortized cost
Accounts receivable	Loans and receivables	Amortized cost	Assets at amortized cost	Amortized cost
Deposits	FVTPL	Fair value	Assets at amortized cost	Amortized cost
Foreign exchange derivatives	FVTPL	Fair value	FVTPL	Fair value
Cross currency interest rate swap derivatives	FVTPL	Fair value	FVTPL	Fair value
Interest rate derivatives	FVTPL	Fair value	FVTPL	Fair value
Accounts payable and accrued liabilities	Other financial liabilities	Amortized cost	Financial liabilities at amortized cost	Amortized cost
Long-term debt	Other financial liabilities	Amortized cost	Financial liabilities at amortized cost	Amortized cost

Notes to Consolidated Financial Statements
As at and for the years ended December 31, 2017 and 2016
(Stated in thousands of Canadian dollars, except percentage, ratio, share and per share amounts)

1. Statement of significant accounting policies (continued)

(e) Adoption of IFRS 9 – Financial instruments (continued)

As a result of adopting IFRS 9, certain financial assets were reclassified from fair value through profit and loss to assets at amortized cost. The change in classification category did not result in an adjustment to the carrying amount of the related assets. In accordance with the transition provisions of IFRS 9, the financial assets and liabilities held at January 1, 2017 were reclassified based on the characteristics of each financial instrument at January 1, 2017.

The Corporation has adopted the new general hedge accounting model in IFRS 9. The adoption of IFRS 9 did not result in any changes in the eligibility of existing hedge relationships, the accounting for derivative financial instruments designated as effective hedging instruments or the line items in which they are included in the statement of financial position. In accordance with the transitional provisions of IFRS 9, changes to hedge accounting policies have been applied prospectively.

Changes in accounting policies resulting from the adoption of IFRS 9 have been applied retrospectively, except assessments relating to the determination of the business model within which a financial asset is held, which have been made on the basis of the facts and circumstances that existed at the date of initial application. Additionally, for financial assets with a low credit risk at the date of initial application of IFRS 9, the Corporation has concluded that the credit risk on the asset had not increased significantly since its initial recognition, due to the nature and term of the financial assets.

(f) Financial instruments

Financial assets are initially measured at fair value. On initial recognition, the Corporation classifies its financial assets as subsequently measured at either amortized cost or fair value, depending on its business model for managing the financial assets and the contractual cash flow characteristics of the financial assets. Financial assets are not reclassified subsequent to their initial recognition, unless the Corporation changes its business model for managing financial assets.

A financial asset is measured at amortized cost if it meets both of the following conditions and is not designated as FVTPL:

(i) The asset is held within a business model whose objective is to hold assets to collect contractual cash flows; and

(ii) The contractual terms of the financial asset give rise on specified dates to cash flows that are solely payments of principal and interest on the principal amount outstanding.

All other financial assets are subsequently measured at their fair values with changes in fair value, including any interest or dividend income, recognized in profit or loss.

The Corporation uses the "expected credit loss" model for calculating impairment and recognizes expected credit losses as a loss allowance for assets measured at amortized cost. The Corporations trade and other receivables are typically short-term with payments received within a 12-month period, and do not have a significant financing component. Therefore, the Corporation recognizes an amount equal to the lifetime expected credit losses based on the Corporation's historical experience and including forward-looking information. The carrying amount of these assets in the consolidated statement of financial position is net of any loss allowance. As a result of the adoption of IFRS 9, no additional provision for impairment was required.

When financial assets and liabilities are designated as part of a hedging relationship and qualify for hedge accounting, they are classified and accounted for as either cash flow hedges, fair value hedges or a hedge of a net investment. The Corporation's policy is not to utilize derivative financial instruments for trading or speculative purposes. At inception of designated hedging relationships, the Corporation documents the risk management objective and strategy for undertaking the hedge. The Corporation also documents the economic relationship between the hedged item and the hedging instrument, including whether the changes in cash flows of the hedged item and hedging instrument are expected to offset each other.

(g) Cash flow hedges

The Corporation uses forward foreign exchange contracts to hedge the variability in cash flows arising from changes in foreign exchange rates relating to U.S. dollar operating expenditures, including aircraft lease payments and the non-air component of vacation packages. Additionally, the Corporation also uses interest rate swaps to hedge the variability in cash flows resulting from fluctuations in interest rates on variable rate debt. The Corporation has elected to designate these instruments in their entirety as hedging instruments for hedge accounting purposes, including both the spot and forward elements of the contract in the valuation of the instrument. The Corporation has established a hedge ratio of 1:1 for all its hedging relationships.

Under cash flow hedge accounting, the effective portion of the change in the fair value of the hedging instrument is recognized in other comprehensive income (OCI) and presented within shareholders' equity as hedge reserves. The ineffective portion of the change in fair value is recognized in non-operating income (expense). Upon maturity of the hedged instrument, the effective gains and losses previously accumulated in hedge reserves are recorded in net earnings under the same caption as the hedged item.

Notes to Consolidated Financial Statements
As at and for the years ended December 31, 2017 and 2016
(Stated in thousands of Canadian dollars, except percentage, ratio, share and per share amounts)

1. Statement of significant accounting policies (continued)

(g) Cash flow hedges (continued)

With respect to hedges of foreign currency exposure, the Corporation determines the existence of an economic relationship between the hedging instrument and hedged item based on the currency, amount and timing of their respective cash flows. The Corporation assesses whether the derivative designated in each hedging relationship is expected to be and has been effective in offsetting changes in cash flows of the hedged item using the hypothetical derivative method. In these hedge relationships, the main sources of ineffectiveness are the effect of the counterparty and the Corporation's own credit risk on the fair value of the forward foreign exchange contracts, which is not reflected in the change in the fair value of the hedged item, and the presence of embedded derivative features in the hedged item that are not included in the terms of the related hedging instrument, such as early redemption features.

For hedges of interest rate risk exposure, the Corporation determines the existence of an economic relationship between the hedging instrument and hedged item based on the reference interest rates, repricing dates and maturities and the notional amounts. The Corporation assesses whether the derivative designated in each hedging relationship is expected to be effective in offsetting changes in cash flows of the hedged item using the hypothetical derivative method. With respect to these hedging relationships, the main source of ineffectiveness relates to the effect of the counterparty and the Corporations credit risk on the fair value of the swaps, which is not reflected in the change in the fair value of the hedged cash flows.

If the hedging relationship ceases to qualify for cash flow hedge accounting, then hedge accounting is discontinued prospectively and any change in fair value of the instrument from the point it ceases to qualify is recorded in non-operating income (expense). Amounts previously accumulated in hedge reserves will remain in shareholders' equity until the hedged item is settled, at which time, the amount is recorded in net earnings under the same caption as the hedged item. If the transaction is no longer expected to occur, amounts previously accumulated in hedge reserves will be reclassified to non-operating income (expense).

(h) Foreign currency

Monetary assets and liabilities, denominated in foreign currencies, are translated into Canadian dollars at the rate of exchange in effect at the consolidated statement of financial position date, with any resulting gain or loss recognized in net earnings. Non-monetary assets, non-monetary liabilities, revenue and expenses arising from transactions denominated in foreign currencies are translated into Canadian dollars at the rates prevailing at the time of the transaction.

(i) Cash and cash equivalents

Cash and cash equivalents consist of cash and short-term investments that are highly liquid in nature and have maturity dates of up to three months.

(j) Marketable securities

Marketable securities consist of investments with maturity dates of greater than three months but less than twelve months. All marketable securities are classified as amortized cost with interest earned reflected in finance income in the consolidated statement of earnings.

(k) Inventory

Inventories are valued at the lower of cost and net realizable value, with cost being determined on a first-in, first-out basis and a specific item basis depending on the nature of the inventory. The Corporation's inventory balance consists of aircraft fuel, deicing fluid and aircraft expendables.

Notes to Consolidated Financial Statements
As at and for the years ended December 31, 2017 and 2016
(Stated in thousands of Canadian dollars, except percentage, ratio, share and per share amounts)

1. Statement of significant accounting policies (continued)

(l) Property and equipment

Property and equipment is stated at cost and depreciated to its estimated residual value. Expected useful lives and depreciation methods are reviewed annually.

Asset class	Basis	Rate
Aircraft, net of estimated residual value	Straight-line	15 to 20 years
Engine, airframe and landing gear overhaul	Straight-line	3 to 12 years
Ground property and equipment	Straight-line	3 to 25 years
Spare engines and rotables, net of estimated residual value	Straight-line	15 to 20 years
Buildings	Straight-line	40 years
Leasehold improvements	Straight-line	5 years/Term of lease

Estimated residual values of the Corporation's aircraft range between $2,500 and $8,700 per aircraft. Spare engines have an estimated average residual value equal to 10% of the original purchase price. Residual values, where applicable, are reviewed annually against prevailing market rates at the consolidated statement of financial position date.

Major overhaul expenditures are capitalized and depreciated over the expected life between overhauls. All other costs relating to the maintenance of fleet assets are charged to the consolidated statement of earnings on consumption or as incurred.

Rotable parts are purchased, depreciated and disposed of on a pooled basis. When parts are purchased, the cost is added to the pool and depreciated over its useful life of 15 to 20 years. The cost to repair rotable parts is recognized in maintenance expense as incurred.

(m) Intangible assets

Included in intangible assets are costs related to software, landing rights and other. Software and landing rights are carried at cost less accumulated amortization and are amortized on a straight-line basis over their respective useful lives of five to 20 years. Expected useful lives and amortization methods are reviewed annually.

(n) Impairment

Property and equipment and intangible assets are grouped into cash generating units (CGU) and reviewed for impairment when events or changes in circumstances indicate that the carrying value of the CGU may not be recoverable. When events or circumstances indicate that the carrying amount of the CGU may not be recoverable, the long-lived assets are tested for recoverability by comparing the recoverable amounts, defined as the greater of the CGU's fair value less cost to sell or value-in-use, with the carrying amount of the CGU. Fair value is defined as the amount an asset could be exchanged, or a liability settled, between consenting parties, in an arm's length transaction. Value-in-use is defined as the present value of the cash flows expected from the future use or eventual sale of the asset at the end of its useful life. If the carrying value of the CGU exceeds the greater of the fair value less cost to sell and value-in-use, an impairment loss is recognized in net earnings for the difference. Impairment losses may subsequently be reversed and recognized in earnings due to changes in events and circumstances, but only to the extent of the original carrying amount of the asset, net of depreciation or amortization, had the original impairment not been recognized.

(o) Maintenance

(i) Provisions

Provisions are made when it is probable that an outflow of economic benefits will be required to settle a present legal or constructive obligation in respect of a past event and where the amount of the obligation can be reliably estimated.

The Corporation's aircraft operating lease agreements require leased aircraft to be returned to the lessor in a specified operating condition. This obligation requires the Corporation to record a maintenance provision liability for certain return conditions specified in the operating lease agreements. Certain obligations are based on aircraft usage and the passage of time, while others are fixed amounts. Expected future costs are estimated based on contractual commitments and company-specific history. Each period, the Corporation recognizes additional maintenance expense based on increased aircraft usage, the passage of time and any changes to judgments or estimates, including discount rates and expected timing and cost of maintenance activities. The unwinding of the discounted present value is recorded as a finance cost on the consolidated statement of earnings. The discount rate used by the Corporation is the current pre-tax risk-free rate approximated by the corresponding term of a US or Canadian government bond to the remaining term until cash outflow. Any difference between the provision recorded and the actual amount incurred at the time the maintenance activity is performed is recorded to maintenance expense.

Notes to Consolidated Financial Statements
As at and for the years ended December 31, 2017 and 2016
(Stated in thousands of Canadian dollars, except percentage, ratio, share and per share amounts)

1.   Statement of significant accounting policies (continued)

(o)   Maintenance (continued)

(ii) Reserves

A certain number of aircraft leases also require the Corporation to pay a maintenance reserve to the lessor. Payments are based on aircraft usage. The purpose of these deposits is to provide the lessor with collateral should an aircraft be returned in an operating condition that does not meet the requirements stipulated in the lease agreement. Maintenance reserves are refunded to the Corporation when qualifying maintenance is performed, or if not refunded, act to reduce the end of lease obligation payments arising from the requirement to return leased aircraft in a specified operating condition. Where the amount of maintenance reserves paid exceeds the estimated amount recoverable from the lessor, the non-recoverable amount is recorded as maintenance expense in the period it is incurred. Non-recoverable amounts previously recorded as maintenance expense may be recovered and capitalized based on changes to expected overhaul costs and recoverable amounts over the term of the lease.

(iii) Power-by-the-hour maintenance contracts

The Corporation is party to certain power-by-the-hour aircraft maintenance agreements, whereby the Corporation makes payments to maintenance providers based on flight hours flown. Payments are capitalized when they relate to qualifying capital expenditures such as major overhauls, otherwise, payments are recorded to maintenance expense on the consolidated statement of earnings when incurred.

(p)   Leases

The determination of whether an arrangement is, or contains, a lease is made at the inception of the arrangement based on the substance of the arrangement and whether (i) fulfillment of the arrangement is dependent on the use of a specific asset and (ii) whether the arrangement conveys a right to use the asset.

Operating leases do not result in the transfer of substantially all risks and rewards incidental to ownership. Non-contingent lease payments are recognized as an expense in the consolidated statement of earnings on a straight-line basis over the term of the lease. The Corporation has a variety of operating leases including, but not limited to, those for aircraft, land, hangar space and airport operations.

(q)   Income taxes

Current tax assets and liabilities are recognized based on amounts receivable from or payable to a tax authority within the next 12 months. A current tax asset is recognized for a benefit relating to an unused tax loss or unused tax credit that can be carried back to recover current tax of a previous period.

Deferred tax assets and liabilities are recognized for temporary differences between the tax and accounting bases of assets and liabilities on the consolidated statement of financial position using the tax rates that are expected to apply in the period in which the deferred tax asset or liability is expected to settle. The tax rates that are expected to be applied in future periods are based on the enacted or substantively enacted rates known at the end of the reporting period. Deferred tax assets are only recognized to the extent that it is probable that a taxable profit will be available when the deductible temporary differences can be utilized. A deferred tax asset is also recognized for any unused tax losses and unused tax credits to the extent that it is probable that future taxable profit will be available for use against the unused tax losses and unused tax credits. Deferred tax assets and liabilities are not discounted.

Current and deferred tax benefit or expense is recognized in the same period as the related transaction or event is recognized in net earnings. Current and deferred tax benefit or expense related to transactions or events in OCI or equity are recognized directly in those accounts.

Current tax assets and liabilities are offset on the consolidated statement of financial position to the extent the Corporation has a legally enforceable right to offset and the amounts are levied by the same taxation authority or when the Corporation has the right to offset and intends to settle on a net basis or realize the asset and settle the liability simultaneously. Deferred tax assets and liabilities are classified as long-term.

Notes to Consolidated Financial Statements
As at and for the years ended December 31, 2017 and 2016
(Stated in thousands of Canadian dollars, except percentage, ratio, share and per share amounts)

1.   Statement of significant accounting policies (continued)

(r)   Share-based payment plans

Equity-settled share-based payments to employees are measured at the fair value of the equity instrument granted. An option valuation model is used to fair value stock options issued to employees on the date of grant. The market value of the Corporation's voting shares on the date of the grant is used to determine the fair value of the equity-based share units issued to employees.

The initial fair value of equity-settled share-based payments is recognized as compensation expense with a corresponding increase in equity reserves over the related service period provided to the Corporation. When the service period commences prior to the grant date, compensation expense is recognized at the beginning of the service period subject to specific vesting conditions and the best estimate of equity instruments expected to vest. Estimates related to vesting conditions are reviewed regularly with any adjustments recorded to compensation expense. On the vesting date, the Corporation revises, if necessary, the estimate to equal the number of equity instruments ultimately vested and adjusts the corresponding compensation expense and equity reserves accordingly.

Market conditions attached to certain equity-settled share-based payments are taken into account when estimating the fair value of the equity instruments granted.

Upon exercise or settlement of equity-based instruments, consideration received, if any, together with amounts previously recorded in the equity reserves, are recorded as an increase in share capital.

Cash-settled share-based payments are measured based on the fair value of the cash liability. The amount determined is recorded as compensation expense at the date of grant. The liability is remeasured each period with a corresponding adjustment to the related compensation expense until the date of settlement.

(s)   Earnings per share

Basic earnings per share is calculated by dividing net earnings attributable to equity holders by the weighted average number of voting shares outstanding during the period, accounting for any changes to the number of voting shares outstanding, except those transactions affecting the number of voting shares outstanding without a corresponding change in resources.

Diluted earnings per share is calculated by dividing net earnings attributable to equity holders by the weighted average number of voting shares outstanding adjusted for the effects of all potentially dilutive voting shares. Potentially dilutive voting shares are only those shares that would result in a decrease to earnings per share or increase to loss per share. The calculation of potentially dilutive voting shares assumes the exercise of all dilutive instruments, both vested and unvested, at the average market price during the period with the expected proceeds received from exercise assumed to reduce the number of dilutive voting shares otherwise issued.

(t)   Critical accounting judgments and estimates

The preparation of these consolidated financial statements in conformity with IFRS requires management to make judgments and estimates that could materially affect the amounts recognized in the consolidated financial statements. By their nature, judgments and estimates may change in light of new facts and circumstances in the internal and external environment. The following judgments and estimates are those deemed by management to be material to the Corporation's consolidated financial statements.

Judgments

(i) Componentization

The componentization of the Corporation's assets, namely aircraft, are based on management's judgment of what components constitute a significant cost in relation to the total cost of an asset and whether these components have similar or dissimilar patterns of consumption and useful lives for purposes of calculating depreciation and amortization. These judgments are made at the time the aircraft is acquired and do not change for the life of the aircraft. Management has considered market values, depreciation rates and industry practices in determining the level of componentization.

(ii) Depreciation and amortization

Depreciation and amortization methods for aircraft and related components as well as other property and equipment and intangible assets are based on management's judgment of the most appropriate method to reflect the pattern of an asset's future economic benefit expected to be consumed by the Corporation. Among other factors, these judgments are based on industry standards, manufacturers' guidelines and company-specific history and experience.

Notes to Consolidated Financial Statements
As at and for the years ended December 31, 2017 and 2016
(Stated in thousands of Canadian dollars, except percentage, ratio, share and per share amounts)

1. Statement of significant accounting policies (continued)

(t) Critical accounting judgments and estimates (continued)

Judgments (continued)

(iii) Impairment

Assessment of impairment triggers are based on management's judgment of whether there are sufficient internal and external factors that would indicate an asset or CGU is impaired. The determination of a CGU is also based on management's judgment and is an assessment of the smallest group of assets that generate cash inflows independently of other assets. Management has assessed WestJet as one CGU and considered factors such as whether an active market exists for the output produced by the asset or group of assets as well as how management monitors and makes decisions about the Corporation's operations. Management has concluded there are no triggers of impairment at December 31, 2017.

(iv) Lease classification

Assessing whether a lease is a finance lease or an operating lease is based on management's judgment of the criteria applied in IAS 17 – Leases. The most prevalent leases of the Corporation are those for aircraft. Management has determined that all of the Corporation's leased aircraft are operating leases.

(v) Unconsolidated structured entities

The classification of the Corporation's participation in 10 Canadian Fuel Facility Corporations (FFCs), eight US FFCs and three Canadian De-Icing Facility Corporations (DFCs) as interests in unconsolidated structured entities is based on management's judgment of each entity including contractual relationships and power over the relevant decisions. Management considered the restricted, narrow and well-defined objectives and activities of each FFC and DFC, the financial dependence of each FFC and DFC on the contracting airlines, and the contractual terms of each FFC and DFC preventing any single airline from having control or significant influence. Refer to Note 17 for additional disclosures of the Corporation's interest in unconsolidated structured entities.

(vi) Operating and reportable segments

The assessment of the Corporation as one operating and reportable segment is based on management's judgment that resource allocation decisions and performance assessments are done at a consolidated company and fleet level with a view that the Corporation manages an integrated network of markets with a consolidated fleet of different sized aircraft.

Estimates

(vii) Depreciation and amortization

Depreciation and amortization are calculated to write-off the cost, less estimated residual value, of assets on a systematic and rational basis over their expected useful lives. Estimates of residual value and useful lives are based on data and information from various sources including vendors, industry publications, and company-specific history. Expected useful lives and residual values are reviewed annually for any change to judgments and estimates.

(viii) Maintenance provisions

The Corporation has a legal obligation to adhere to certain maintenance conditions set out in its aircraft operating lease agreements relating to the condition of the aircraft at lease return. To fulfill these obligations, a provision is made during the lease term. Estimates related to the maintenance provision include the likely utilization of the aircraft, the expected future cost of the maintenance, the point in time at which maintenance is expected to occur, the discount rate used to present value the future cash flows, the lifespan of life-limited parts and assumptions of lease extension terms. These estimates are based on data and information obtained from various sources including the lessor, current maintenance schedules and fleet plans, contracted costs with maintenance service providers, other vendors and company-specific history.

(ix) Income taxes

Deferred tax assets and liabilities contain estimates about the nature and timing of future permanent and temporary differences as well as the future tax rates that will apply to those differences. Changes in tax laws and rates as well as changes to the expected timing of reversals may have a significant impact on the amounts recorded for deferred tax assets and liabilities. Management closely monitors current and potential changes to tax law and bases its estimates on the best available information at each reporting date.

Notes to Consolidated Financial Statements
As at and for the years ended December 31, 2017 and 2016
(Stated in thousands of Canadian dollars, except percentage, ratio, share and per share amounts)

2. New accounting standards and interpretations

The IASB and International Financial Reporting Interpretations Committee (IFRIC) have issued the following standards that have not been applied in preparing these consolidated financial statements as their effective dates fall within annual periods beginning subsequent to the current reporting period.

Proposed standards	Description	Previous standard	Effective date
IFRS 15 – Revenue from Contracts with Customers	A new standard on revenue recognition that contains a single model that applies to contracts with customers and two approaches to recognizing revenue; at a point in time or over time.	IAS 11 - Construction contracts; IAS 18 – Revenue; IFRIC 13 - Customer Loyalty Programmes; IFRIC 15 - Agreements for the Construction of Real Estate; IFRIC 18 - Transfers of Assets from Customers; SIC-31 - Revenue - Barter Transactions Involving Advertising Services	Effective for annual periods beginning on or after January 1, 2018. Early adoption is permitted.
IFRS 16 - Leases	A new standard on lease accounting that results in substantially all lessee leases being recorded on the statement of financial position.	IAS 17 – Leases	Effective for annual periods beginning on or after January 1, 2019. Early adoption is permitted.

IFRS 15 – Revenue from Contracts with Customers

In May 2014, the IASB issued IFRS 15 Revenue from Contracts with Customers (IFRS 15) which provides a single revenue recognition model aimed at providing greater comparability across industries and companies. The revised IFRS standard will replace existing revenue recognition guidance and is effective for annual and interim reporting periods beginning on or after January 1, 2018. The Corporation has adopted this standard on the required effective date, using the full retrospective transition method. In addition, the Corporation has elected to make use of the following practical expedients:

- The Corporation applies the practical expedient in paragraph 94 of IFRS 15 and contract costs incurred related to contracts with an amortization period of less than one year will be been expensed as incurred.
- The Corporation applies the practical expedient in paragraph 121 of IFRS 15 and does not disclose information about remaining performance obligations that have original expected durations of one year or less.
- The Corporation applies the practical expedient C5(c) of IFRS 15 and for contracts that were modified before the beginning of the earliest period presented, the Corporation does not separately evaluate the effect of the contract modification before the beginning of the earlier period presented.
- The Corporation also applies the practical expedient in paragraph C5(d) of IFRS and does not disclose the amount of the transaction price allocated to the remaining performance obligations and an explanation of when the Corporation expects to recognize that amount as revenue for the year ended December 31, 2016.

The corporation has assessed the impact of IFRS 15 and the differences are summarized below:

Passenger and ancillary breakage

The Corporation has concluded that revenue will be recognized at flight date as tickets are invalid after flight date per the Corporation's flight tariffs. Currently, breakage related to passenger tickets and ancillary fees are deferred for a period of 18 months. This change has an impact of approximately $36.1 million increase, net of tax to January 1, 2017 opening retained earnings and an approximately $49.5 million decrease to advance ticket sales.

Consideration Payable

The Corporation issues future travel credits and WestJet dollars related to flight delays, missing baggage, or other inconveniences as goodwill gestures. The current accounting policy is to record the travel credit when it is used to book a subsequent flight. Under IFRS 15, consideration payable to a customer will be recorded as a reduction to revenue and an increase to non-refundable guest credits when the travel credit is issued. This has an impact of approximately $7.8 million, net of tax reduction to January 1, 2017 opening retained earnings and an approximately $10.7 million increase to non-refundable guest credits.

Notes to Consolidated Financial Statements
As at and for the years ended December 31, 2017 and 2016
(Stated in thousands of Canadian dollars, except percentage, ratio, share and per share amounts)

3. Capital management

The Corporation's policy is to maintain a strong capital base in order to maintain investor, creditor and market confidence and to sustain the future development of the airline. The Corporation manages its capital structure and makes adjustments in light of changes in economic conditions and the risk characteristics of the underlying assets.

In order to manage the capital structure, the Corporation may, from time to time, purchase shares for cancellation pursuant to normal course issuer bids, issue new shares, pay dividends and adjust current and projected debt levels.

In the management of capital, the Corporation includes shareholders' equity (excluding hedge reserves), long-term debt, cash and cash equivalents and the Corporation's off-balance-sheet obligations related to its aircraft operating leases, all of which are presented in detail below.

The Corporation monitors its capital structure on a number of bases, including cash to trailing 12 months revenue, adjusted debt-to-equity and adjusted net debt to earnings before net finance cost, taxes, depreciation and amortization and aircraft leasing (EBITDAR). EBITDAR is a non-GAAP financial measure commonly used in the airline industry to evaluate results by excluding differences in tax jurisdictions and in the method an airline finances its aircraft. In addition, the Corporation will adjust EBITDAR for non-operating gains and losses on derivatives and foreign exchange. The calculation of EBITDAR is a measure that does not have a standardized meaning prescribed under IFRS and therefore may not be comparable to similar measures presented by other issuers. The Corporation adjusts debt to include its off-balance-sheet aircraft operating leases. To derive a present-value debt equivalent, common industry practice is to multiply the trailing 12 months of aircraft leasing expense by a multiplier. The Corporation uses a multiplier of 7.5. The Corporation defines adjusted net debt as adjusted debt less cash and cash equivalents. The Corporation defines equity as total shareholders' equity, excluding hedge reserves.

	2017	2016	Change
Cash to trailing 12 months revenue			
Cash, cash equivalents and marketable securities	1,373,166	1,520,822	(147,656)
Trailing 12 months revenue	4,502,320	4,122,859	379,461
Cash to trailing 12 months revenue[iv]	30.5%	36.9%	(6.4 pts)
Adjusted debt-to-equity			
Long-term debt[i]	2,049,047	2,046,658	2,389
Off-balance-sheet aircraft leases[ii]	1,244,265	1,338,338	(94,073)
Adjusted debt	3,293,312	3,384,996	(91,684)
Total shareholders' equity	2,212,524	2,060,702	151,822
Add: Hedge reserves	1,902	11,003	(9,101)
Adjusted equity	2,214,426	2,071,705	142,721
Adjusted debt-to-equity[iv]	1.49	1.63	(8.6%)
Adjusted net debt to EBITDAR			
Adjusted debt (as above)	3,293,312	3,384,996	(91,684)
Less: Cash, cash equivalents and marketable securities	(1,373,166)	(1,520,822)	147,656
Adjusted net debt	1,920,146	1,864,174	55,972
Net earnings	283,578	295,458	(11,880)
Add:			
Net finance cost[iii]	34,084	32,456	1,628
Taxes	120,557	120,775	(218)
Depreciation and amortization	403,021	350,484	52,537
Aircraft leasing	165,902	178,445	(12,543)
Other[iv]	7,303	(11,906)	19,209
EBITDAR	1,014,445	965,712	48,733
Adjusted net debt to EBITDAR[v]	1.89	1.93	(2.1%)

(i)   At December 31, 2017, long-term debt includes the current portion of long-term debt of $153,149 (December 31, 2016 – $145,128) and long-term debt of $1,895,898 (December 31, 2016 – $1,901,530).

(ii) Off-balance-sheet aircraft leases is calculated by multiplying the trailing 12 months of aircraft leasing expense by 7.5. At December 31, 2017, the trailing 12 months of aircraft leasing costs totaled $165,902 (December 31, 2016 – $178,445).

(iii) At December 31, 2017, net finance cost includes the trailing 12 months of finance income of $19,626 (December 31, 2016 – $16,618) and the trailing 12 months of finance cost of $53,710 (December 31, 2016 – $49,074).

(iv) At December 31, 2017, other includes the trailing 12 months foreign exchange loss of $4,877 (December 31, 2016 – gain of $7,402) and trailing 12 months non-operating loss on derivatives of $2,426 (December 31, 2016 – gain of $4,504).

(v)   The Corporation has internal guidelines for cash to trailing 12 months revenue of approximately 30%, an adjusted debt-to-equity measure of no more than 2.5 and an adjusted net debt to EBITDAR measure of no more than 2.5. The Corporation's internal guidelines are not related to any covenants.

Notes to Consolidated Financial Statements
As at and for the years ended December 31, 2017 and 2016
(Stated in thousands of Canadian dollars, except percentage, ratio, share and per share amounts)

2. New accounting standards and interpretations (continued)

Cancel fees

Similarly to change fees, the Corporation has concluded that cancel fees, which are currently recognized at the date of ticket cancellation and credit for future travel is issued, will be treated as a contract modification and would not be a distinct performance obligation from the guest's subsequent flight and will be deferred until the flight occurs and presented in Guest revenue. This has an impact of approximately $4.1 million, net of tax reduction to January 1, 2017 opening retained earnings and an approximately $5.7 million increase to advance ticket sales

Change fees

The Corporation has concluded that change fees, which are currently recognized at the date of the ticket change and presented in Other revenue, will be treated as a contract modification and would not be a distinct performance obligation from the guest's subsequent flight and will be deferred until the flight occurs and presented in Guest revenue. This has an impact of approximately $3.1 million, net of tax reduction to January 1, 2017 opening retained earnings and an approximately $4.3 million increase to advance ticket sales.

Reclass of certain ancillary services

The Corporation has concluded that the majority of ancillary services, currently presented within Other revenue, will no longer be considered distinct from the guest's associated flight and therefore, will be presented within Guest revenue. This change has no impact to January 1, 2017 opening retained earnings.

WestJet Rewards

Although the Corporation will continue to defer the revenue related to WestJet rewards received by guests until they are used towards the purchase of a new flight, the allocation methodology of how to apportion the airfare between the flight segments and WestJet rewards will change. The Corporation has evaluated the change in the allocation methodology to be immaterial and therefore there is no impact to January 1, 2017 opening retained earnings. The Corporation has also concluded that tier status is considered a marketing expense and therefore no revenue will be deferred related to the guest benefits associated with tier status.

WestJet Co-Brand MasterCard

The Corporation has assessed the impact of IFRS 15 on the WestJet MasterCard Co-Brand agreement with the Royal Bank of Canada (RBC) and have identified the following performance obligations: brand, WestJet dollars, and companion vouchers. The Corporation is in the process of finalizing the valuation of each of the performance obligations identified in order to allocate the consideration received on a relative stand-alone selling price basis. The Corporation anticipates that there will be a deferral of revenue as a result of IFRS 15, as the Corporation currently does not defer any revenue related to companion vouchers.

The Corporation will also continue drafting illustrative disclosures to the quarterly and annual 2018 financial statements. The Corporation will also continue to implement new business processes and internal controls required to adopt this standard.

IFRS 16 – Leases

In January 2016, the IASB issued IFRS 16 Leases (IFRS 16), effective for annual and interim reporting periods beginning on or after January 1, 2019. This standard eliminates the classification of leases as either operating leases or finance leases for a lessee, and instead, all leases are capitalized by recognizing the present value of lease payments and presenting them as either lease assets or together with property and equipment. It also allows for the service component of a lease agreement to be separated from the value of the asset and thus not reported on the statement of financial position. The Corporation anticipates the adoption of IFRS 16 will have a material impact on the statement of financial position as all aircraft operating leases will be capitalized with a corresponding lease liability. In addition to the aircraft operating leases, the Corporation must identify and review potential contracts that may contain a lease arrangement prior to quantifying the impact of IFRS 16. As at December 31, 2017, the Corporation has completed a scoping exercise to identify the potential number and types of contracts that may contain leases within the company and does not anticipate early adoption of this standard.

Notes to Consolidated Financial Statements
As at and for the years ended December 31, 2017 and 2016
(Stated in thousands of Canadian dollars, except percentage, ratio, share and per share amounts)

4. Cash, cash equivalents and marketable securities

	December 31 2017	December 31 2016
Bank balances(i)	238,858	261,408
Short-term investments(ii)	908,218	1,259,414
Total cash and cash equivalents	1,147,076	1,520,822
Marketable securities(iii)	226,090	-
	1,373,166	1,520,822

(i) Included in these balances, at December 31, 2017, the Corporation has US-dollar cash and cash equivalents totaling US $46,641 (December 31, 2016 – US $102,823).
(ii) Included in these balances, at December 31, 2017, the Corporation has US-dollar short-term investments totaling US $151,696 (December 31, 2016 – US $125,884).
(iii) Included in these balances, at December 31, 2017, the Corporation has US-dollar marketable securities totaling US$100,000 (December 31, 2016 – US $nil).

5. Restricted cash

	December 31 2017	December 31 2016
Cash held in trust for WestJet Vacations Inc.	76,389	70,080
Security on facilities for letters of guarantee	32,234	31,013
Passenger facility charges	1,077	1,556
	109,700	102,649

6. Property and equipment

	January 1 2017	Net Additions	Depreciation	Transfers	December 31 2017
Aircraft(i)	3,125,040	46,416	(337,285)	645,568	3,479,739
Ground property and equipment	73,911	12,718	(18,945)	5,262	72,946
Spare engines and rotables	186,092	12,988	(25,089)	21,938	195,929
Deposits on aircraft	492,376	752,368	-	(594,257)	650,487
Buildings	102,833	-	(3,524)	-	99,309
Leasehold improvements	14,180	3,648	(4,329)	4,071	17,570
Assets under development	42,448	91,658	-	(82,582)	51,524
	4,036,880	919,796	(389,172)	-	4,567,504

	January 1 2016	Net additions	Depreciation	Transfers	December 31 2016
Aircraft(i)	2,741,974	120,764	(290,733)	553,035	3,125,040
Ground property and equipment	72,176	17,922	(18,166)	1,979	73,911
Spare engines and rotables	167,446	32,562	(19,772)	5,856	186,092
Deposits on aircraft	319,019	640,098	-	(466,741)	492,376
Buildings	106,364	-	(3,531)	-	102,833
Leasehold improvements	10,374	5,742	(3,159)	1,223	14,180
Assets under development	55,909	81,891	-	(95,352)	42,448
	3,473,262	898,979	(335,361)	-	4,036,880

(i) Aircraft includes (a) aircraft (b) engine, airframe and landing gear core components (c) engine, airframe and landing gear overhaul components, and (d) inflight entertainment systems. For the year ended December 31, 2017, total aircraft depreciation expense for overhaul components was $153,660 (December 31, 2016 – $130,114).

Notes to Consolidated Financial Statements
As at and for the years ended December 31, 2017 and 2016
(Stated in thousands of Canadian dollars, except percentage, ratio, share and per share amounts)

6. Property and equipment (continued)

December 31, 2017	Cost	Accumulated depreciation	Net book value
Aircraft	5,078,004	(1,598,265)	3,479,739
Ground property and equipment	169,946	(97,000)	72,946
Spare engines and rotables	307,594	(111,665)	195,929
Deposits on aircraft	650,487	-	650,487
Buildings	136,781	(37,472)	99,309
Leasehold improvements	31,641	(14,071)	17,570
Assets under development	51,524	-	51,524
	6,425,977	(1,858,473)	4,567,504

December 31, 2016	Cost	Accumulated depreciation	Net book value
Aircraft	4,439,579	(1,314,539)	3,125,040
Ground property and equipment	198,083	(124,172)	73,911
Spare engines and rotables	278,863	(92,771)	186,092
Deposits on aircraft	492,376	-	492,376
Buildings	136,783	(33,950)	102,833
Leasehold improvements	27,431	(13,251)	14,180
Assets under development	42,448	-	42,448
	5,615,563	(1,578,683)	4,036,880

The net book value of the property and equipment pledged as collateral for the Corporation's long-term debt was $1,446,554 at December 31, 2017 (December 31, 2016 – $1,471,441).

7. Intangible assets

	January 1 2017	Net additions	Amortization	Transfers	December 31 2017
Software	33,429	1,148	(12,869)	13,208	34,916
Landing rights	13,766	-	(892)	-	12,874
Other	5,521	-	(88)	-	5,433
Assets under development	13,471	6,031	-	(13,208)	6,294
	66,187	7,179	(13,849)	-	59,517

	January 1 2016	Net additions	Amortization	Transfers	December 31 2016
Software	29,641	4,698	(14,141)	13,231	33,429
Landing rights	14,595	65	(894)	-	13,766
Other	5,609	-	(88)	-	5,521
Assets under development	13,704	12,998	-	(13,231)	13,471
	63,549	17,761	(15,123)	-	66,187

Notes to Consolidated Financial Statements
As at and for the years ended December 31, 2017 and 2016
(Stated in thousands of Canadian dollars, except percentage, ratio, share and per share amounts)

7. Intangible assets (continued)

December 31, 2017	Cost	Accumulated amortization	Net book value
Software	90,377	(55,461)	34,916
Landing rights	17,845	(4,971)	12,874
Other	5,836	(403)	5,433
Assets under development	6,294	-	6,294
	120,352	(60,835)	59,517

December 31, 2016	Cost	Accumulated amortization	Net book value
Software	90,943	(57,514)	33,429
Landing rights	17,847	(4,081)	13,766
Other	5,836	(315)	5,521
Assets under development	13,471	-	13,471
	128,097	(61,910)	66,187

8. Maintenance provisions and reserves

The Corporation's operating aircraft lease agreements require leased aircraft to be returned to the lessor in a specified operating condition. The maintenance provision liability represents the present value of the expected future cost. A maintenance expense is recognized over the term of the provision based on aircraft usage and the passage of time, while the unwinding of the present value discount is recognized as a finance cost. The majority of the Corporation's maintenance provision liabilities are recognized and settled in US dollars. Where applicable, all amounts have been converted to Canadian dollars at the period end foreign exchange rate.

	December 31 2017	December 31 2016
Opening balance	366,234	329,033
Additions	45,682	72,900
Change in estimate[i]	16,544	7,560
Foreign exchange	(22,559)	(9,269)
Accretion[ii]	3,146	2,104
Settled	(56,571)	(36,094)
Ending balance	352,476	366,234
Current portion	(82,129)	(103,571)
Long-term portion	270,347	262,663

(i) Reflects changes to the timing and scope of maintenance activities and the discount rate used to present value the liability.

(ii) At December 31, 2017, the Corporation's aircraft lease maintenance provisions are discounted using a weighted average risk-free rate of approximately 1.61% (December 31, 2016 – 0.96%) to reflect the weighted average remaining term of approximately 40 months (December 31, 2016 – 23 months) until cash outflow.

A certain number of operating aircraft leases also require the Corporation to pay a maintenance reserve to the lessor. Maintenance reserves are either refunded when qualifying maintenance is performed or offset against end of lease obligations for returning leased aircraft in a specified operating condition. Where the amount of maintenance reserves paid exceeds the estimated amount recoverable from the lessor, the non-recoverable amount is recorded as maintenance expense in the period it is incurred. Non-recoverable amounts previously recorded as maintenance expense may be recovered and capitalized based on changes to expected overhaul costs and recoverable amounts over the term of the lease. The Corporation's maintenance reserves are recognized and settled in US dollars. All amounts have been converted to Canadian dollars at the period end foreign exchange rate.

At December 31, 2017, the current portion of maintenance reserves included in prepaid expenses, deposits and other is $16,281 (December 31, 2016 – $13,727) and the long-term portion of maintenance reserves included in other assets is $13,761 (December 31, 2016 – $16,823).

Notes to Consolidated Financial Statements
As at and for the years ended December 31, 2017 and 2016
(Stated in thousands of Canadian dollars, except percentage, ratio, share and per share amounts)

9. Long-term debt

	December 31 2017	December 31 2016
Term loans – purchased aircraft[i]	59,770	128,697
Term loans – purchased aircraft[ii]	156,929	177,606
Term loans – purchased aircraft[iii]	645,501	510,067
Senior unsecured notes[iv]	399,139	398,612
Non-revolving facility[v]	288,196	299,182
USD senior unsecured notes[vi]	499,512	532,494
Ending balance	2,049,047	2,046,658
Current portion	(153,149)	(145,128)
Long-term portion	1,895,898	1,901,530

(i) 19 individual term loans, amortized over a 12-year term, repayable in quarterly principal instalments totaling $13,505, at an effective weighted average fixed rate of 6.05%, maturing between 2017 and 2020. These facilities are guaranteed by the Export-Import Bank of the United States (Ex-Im Bank) and secured by 19 Boeing 737 Next Generation aircraft. At December 31, 2016 – 25 individual term loans, amortized over a 12-year term, repayable in quarterly principal instalments totaling $17,952, at an effective weighted average fixed rate of 5.95%, maturing between 2017 and 2020. There are no financial covenants related to these term loans.

(ii) Seven individual term loans, amortized over a 12-year term, repayable in quarterly principal instalments totaling $5,576, in addition to a floating rate of interest at the three-month Canadian Dealer Offered Rate plus a basis point spread, with an effective weighted average floating interest rate of 2.96% at December 31, 2017, maturing between 2024 and 2025. The Corporation has fixed the rate of interest on these seven term loans, at a weighted average rate of 3.20%, using interest rate swaps. These facilities are guaranteed by Ex-Im Bank and secured by seven Boeing 737 Next Generation aircraft. No change from December 31, 2016, other than the weighted average floating interest rate of 2.48%. There are no financial covenants related to these term loans.

(iii) 43 individual term loans, amortized over a 12-year term, repayable in quarterly principal instalments totaling $14,643, at an effective weighted average fixed rate of 3.18%, maturing between 2025 and 2029. Each term loan is secured by one Q400 aircraft. At December 31, 2016 – 34 individual term loans, amortized over a 12-year term, repayable in quarterly principal instalments totaling $10,971, at an effective weighted average fixed rate of 3.10%, maturing between 2025 and 2028. There are no financial covenants related to these term loans.

(iv) 3.287% Senior Unsecured Notes with semi-annual interest payments and an effective interest rate of 3.43%, at December 31, 2017, with principal due upon maturity in July 2019. The notes rank equally in right of payment with all other existing and future unsubordinated debt of the Corporation, but are effectively subordinate to all of the Corporation's existing and future secured debt to the extent of the value of the assets securing such debt. No change from December 31, 2016. There are no financial covenants related to these senior unsecured notes.

(v) Non-revolving, unsecured term loan repayable in quarterly principal instalments of $3,750 that commenced on March 31, 2017, increasing annually, with an effective weighted average floating interest rate of 3.00% at December 31, 2017, maturing in 2020. The Corporation has fixed the rate of interest on the term loan, at a weighted average rate of 2.51%, using interest rate swaps. At December 31, 2016 – effective weighted average floating interest rate of 2.49%. The credit facility contains two financial covenants: (i) minimum pooled asset coverage ratio of 1.5 to 1, and (ii) minimum fixed charge coverage ratio of 1.25 to 1 measurable on a quarterly basis. At December 31, 2017 the Corporation has met both covenants.

(vi) Senior unsecured notes denominated in US Dollars with semi-annual interest payments and a fixed effective rate of 3.78% at December 31, 2017, with principal due upon maturity in June 2021. The notes rank equally in right of payment with all other existing and future unsubordinated debt of the Corporation, but are effectively subordinate to all of the Corporation's existing and future secured debt to the extent of the value of the assets securing such debt. There are no financial covenants related to these senior unsecured notes. No change from December 31, 2016.

Future scheduled principal and interest repayments of long-term debt at December 31, 2017 are as follows:

Within 1 year	218,572
1 – 3 years	943,602
4 – 5 years	716,274
Over 5 years	409,399
	2,287,847

The Corporation has an unsecured, revolving syndicated credit facility to borrow up to $300,000. The credit facility is available for general corporate purposes, including the funding of future aircraft acquisitions, and matures in June 2020 with an option to extend the three-year term on an annual basis. Funds from the revolving credit facility can be drawn by way of: (i) Canadian dollar prime loans, (ii) US dollar base rate loans, (iii) US dollar LIBOR loans, (iv) Canadian dollar bankers' acceptances, and (v) Canadian or US dollar fronted letters of credit. Interest is calculated by reference to the applicable base rate plus an applicable pricing margin based on the Corporation's debt rating. The Corporation also pays a standby fee for the undisbursed portion of the revolving credit facility. At December 31, 2017, the Corporation has $nil (December 31, 2016 – $nil) drawn on the facility. The credit facility contains two financial covenants: (i) minimum pooled asset coverage ratio of 1.5 to 1, and (ii) minimum fixed charge coverage ratio of 1.25 to 1. At December 31, 2017, the Corporation has met both covenants.

Notes to Consolidated Financial Statements
As at and for the years ended December 31, 2017 and 2016
(Stated in thousands of Canadian dollars, except percentage, ratio, share and per share amounts)

9. Long-term debt (continued)

The Corporation has an $820,000 loan agreement with Export Development Canada for the future purchase of Bombardier Q400 NextGen aircraft. The Corporation is charged a non-refundable commitment fee of 0.2 per cent per annum on the undisbursed portion of the loan. The undisbursed portion of the loan at December 31, 2017, is $47,575 (December 31, 2016 – $234,371). Availability of any undrawn amount expires on December 31, 2018. The expected amount available for each aircraft is up to 80 per cent of the net price with a term to maturity of up to 12 years, repayable in quarterly instalments, including interest at a floating or fixed rate, determined at the inception of the loan.

10. Income taxes

(a) Reconciliation of total income tax expense

The effective rate on the Corporation's earnings before income tax differs from the expected amount that would arise using the combined Canadian federal and provincial statutory income tax rates. A reconciliation of the difference is as follows:

	2017	2016
Earnings before income tax	404,135	416,233
Combined Canadian federal and provincial income tax rate	26.92%	26.93%
Expected income tax provision	108,793	112,092
Add (deduct):		
Non-deductible expenses	6,042	5,310
Non-deductible share-based payment expense	3,835	3,021
Effect of tax rate changes	2,082	645
Other	(195)	(293)
Actual income tax provision	120,557	120,775
Effective tax rate	29.83%	29.02%

The increase in the effective tax rate is due to increased non-deductible expenses as well as the general corporate income tax rate increase in British Columbia, from 11% to 12%. The rate increase in British Columbia becomes effective January 1, 2018 and while the 2017 statutory rate is not adjusted, the deferred tax liability is revalued at the increased rate.

(b) Deferred tax

Components of the net deferred tax liability are as follows:

	2017	2016
Deferred tax liability:		
Property and equipment	(462,814)	(404,012)
Deferred tax asset:		
Maintenance provision	87,164	90,273
Net unrealized loss on derivatives designated in a hedging relationship	704	4,045
	(374,946)	(309,694)

	2017	2016
Deferred tax liability at December 31, 2016:	309,694	327,028
Deferred income tax expense (recovery), period ended December 31, 2017	61,912	(12,280)
Tax impact of net unrealized(gain) loss on effective portion of derivatives designated in a hedging relationship	3,340	(5,054)
Deferred tax liability at December 31, 2017	374,946	309,694

Notes to Consolidated Financial Statements
As at and for the years ended December 31, 2017 and 2016
(Stated in thousands of Canadian dollars, except percentage, ratio, share and per share amounts)

11. Share capital

(a) Authorized

Unlimited number of common voting shares

The common voting shares may be owned and controlled only by Canadians and shall confer the right to one vote per common voting share at all meetings of shareholders of the Corporation.

If a common voting share becomes beneficially owned or controlled by a person who is not a Canadian, such common voting share shall be converted into one variable voting share automatically and without any further act of the Corporation or the holder.

Unlimited number of variable voting shares

The variable voting shares may be beneficially owned and controlled only by a person who is not Canadian and are entitled to one vote per variable voting share unless (i) the number of issued and outstanding variable voting shares exceed 25% of the total number of all issued and outstanding variable voting shares and common voting shares collectively, including securities currently convertible into such a share and currently exercisable options and rights to acquire such shares (or any higher percentage the Governor in Council may specify pursuant to the Canada Transportation Act) or (ii) the total number of votes cast by, or on behalf of, the holders of variable voting shares at any meeting exceeds 25% (or any higher percentage the Governor in Council may specify pursuant to the Canada Transportation Act) of the total number of votes cast that may be cast at such meeting.

If either of the thresholds described in the paragraph above is surpassed at any time, the vote attached to each variable voting share will decrease automatically and without further act or formality to equal the maximum permitted vote per variable voting share. In the circumstance described in (i) in the paragraph above, the variable voting shares as a class cannot carry more than 25% (or any higher percentage the Governor in Council may specify pursuant to the Canada Transportation Act) of the aggregate votes attached to all variable voting shares and common voting shares collectively, including securities currently convertible into such a share and currently exercisable options and rights to acquire such shares. In the circumstance described in (ii) in the paragraph above, the variable voting shares as a class cannot, for a given shareholders' meeting, carry more than 25% (or any higher percentage the Governor in Council may specify pursuant to the Canada Transportation Act) of the total number of votes that can be exercised at the meeting.

Each issued and outstanding variable voting share shall be automatically converted into one common voting share without any further intervention on the part of the Corporation or of the holder if (i) the variable voting share is or becomes owned and controlled by a Canadian or if (ii) the provisions contained in the Canada Transportation Act relating to foreign ownership restrictions are repealed and not replaced with other similar provisions in applicable legislation.

Unlimited number of non-voting shares and unlimited number of non-voting first, second and third preferred shares

The non-voting shares and non-voting preferred shares may be issued, from time to time in one or more series, each series consisting of such number of non-voting shares and non-voting preferred shares as determined by the Corporation's Board of Directors who may also fix the designations, rights, privileges, restrictions and conditions attached to the shares of each series of non-voting shares and non-voting preferred shares. There are no non-voting shares or non-voting preferred shares issued and outstanding.

(b) Issued and outstanding

	2017		2016	
	Number	Amount	Number	Amount
Common and variable voting shares:				
Balance, beginning of year	117,200,439	555,716	123,086,477	582,796
Issuance of shares pursuant to compensation plans	376,047	10,131	68,911	1,146
Shares repurchased	(3,523,597)	(16,870)	(5,954,949)	(28,226)
Balance, end of year	114,052,889	548,977	117,200,439	555,716

At December 31, 2017, the number of common voting shares outstanding was 76,918,114 (December 31, 2016 – 93,972,416) and the number of variable voting shares was 37,134,775 (December 31, 2016 – 23,228,023).

Notes to Consolidated Financial Statements
As at and for the years ended December 31, 2017 and 2016
(Stated in thousands of Canadian dollars, except percentage, ratio, share and per share amounts)

11. Share capital (continued)

(b) Issued and outstanding (continued)

On May 16, 2016, the Corporation filed a notice with the TSX to make a normal course issuer bid to purchase outstanding shares on the open market. As approved by the TSX, the Corporation was authorized to purchase up to 4,000,000 common voting shares and variable voting shares (representing approximately 3.3 per cent of the Corporation's issued and outstanding shares as of April 30, 2016) during the period May 18, 2016 to May 17, 2017 (the 2016 bid), or until such time as the bid is completed or terminated at the Corporation's option. Any shares purchased under this bid are purchased on the open market through the facilities of the TSX at the prevailing market price at the time of the transaction. Common voting shares and variable voting shares acquired under this bid are cancelled. The 2016 bid expired on May 17, 2017, with the Corporation purchasing and cancelling all 4,000,000 of the shares it was authorized.

On August 1, 2017, the Corporation filed a notice with the TSX to make a normal course issuer bid to purchase outstanding shares on the open market. As approved by the TSX, the Corporation is authorized to purchase up to 5,856,671 common voting shares and variable voting shares (representing approximately five per cent of the Corporation's issued and outstanding shares as of July 20, 2017) during the period August 3, 2017 to August 2, 2018 (the 2017 bid), or until such time as the bid is completed or terminated at the Corporation's option. Any shares purchased under this bid are purchased on the open market through the facilities of the TSX at the prevailing market price at the time of the transaction. Common voting shares and variable voting shares acquired under this bid are cancelled. At December 31, 2017, 3,330,425 shares have been repurchased under this bid with 2,526,246 remaining.

During the year ended December 31, 2017, the Corporation purchased and cancelled a total of 3,523,597 shares (December 31, 2016 – 5,954,949) for total consideration of $90,317 (December 31, 2016 – $126,152). The average book value of the shares repurchased was $4.79 per share (December 31, 2016 – $4.74) and was charged to share capital. The excess of the market price over the average book value, including transaction costs, was $73,447 (December 31, 2016 – $97,926) and was charged to retained earnings.

(c) Stock option plan

The Corporation has a stock option plan, whereby at December 31, 2017, 11,664,318 (2016 – 11,040,365) voting shares were reserved for issuance to officers and employees of the Corporation, subject to the following limitations:

(i) the number of voting shares reserved for issuance to any one optionee will not exceed 5% of the issued and outstanding voting shares at any time;

(ii) the number of voting shares reserved for issuance to insiders shall not exceed 10% of the issued and outstanding voting shares; and

(iii) the number of voting shares issuable under the stock option plan, which may be issued within a one-year period, shall not exceed 10% of the issued and outstanding voting shares at any time.

Stock options are granted at a price equal to the five-day weighted average market value of the Corporation's voting shares preceding the date of grant and vest completely or on a graded basis on the first, second and third anniversary from the date of grant. Stock options expire no later than seven years from the date of grant.

The fair value of options granted and the assumptions used in their determination are as follows:

	2017	2016
Weighted average fair value per option	3.77	3.58
Expected life of options (years)	3.6	3.7
Weighted average risk-free interest rate	1.0%	0.6%
Weighted average expected volatility	26.9%	27.9%
Weighted average dividend yield	2.2%	1.9%

Notes to Consolidated Financial Statements
As at and for the years ended December 31, 2017 and 2016
(Stated in thousands of Canadian dollars, except percentage, ratio, share and per share amounts)

11. Share capital (continued)

(c) Stock option plan (continued)

Changes in the number of options, with their weighted average exercise prices, are summarized below:

	2017 Number of options	2017 Weighted average exercise price	2016 Number of options	2016 Weighted average exercise price
Stock options outstanding, beginning of year	8,622,779	22.91	5,706,547	24.40
Granted	3,567,702	22.07	3,562,396	20.07
Exercised	(2,530,385)	21.57	(261,890)	16.32
Forfeited	(83,382)	21.45	(258,856)	22.78
Expired	(146,888)	23.59	(125,418)	23.90
Stock options outstanding, end of year	9,429,826	22.95	8,622,779	22.91
Exercisable, end of year	5,196,596	23.67	4,676,301	24.63

Under the terms of the Corporation's stock option plan, with the approval of the Corporation, option holders can either (i) elect to receive shares by delivering cash to the Corporation in the amount of the exercise price of the options, or (ii) choose a cashless settlement alternative, whereby they can elect to receive a number of shares equivalent to the market value of the options over the exercise price. For the year ended December 31, 2017, option holders exercised 2,526,630 options (2016 – 259,158 options) on a cashless basis and received 372,292 shares (2016 – 66,179 shares). For the year ended December 31, 2017, 3,755 options were exercised on a cash basis (2016 – 2,732 options).

Options outstanding and exercisable at December 31, 2017:

	Outstanding options			Exercisable options	
Range of exercise price	Number outstanding	Weighted average remaining life (years)	Weighted average exercise price	Number exercisable	Weighted average exercise prices
14.73-20.00	60,775	1.84	15.43	54,452	15.36
20.01-23.00	5,866,890	3.77	21.33	1,851,033	20.29
23.01-26.00	1,370,288	1.73	23.83	1,291,134	23.83
26.01-31.16	2,131,873	1.94	26.92	1,999,977	26.93
	9,429,826	3.05	22.95	5,196,596	23.67

(d) Key employee plan

The Corporation has a key employee plan (KEP), whereby restricted share units (RSU) are issued to senior management and pilots of the Corporation. The fair market value of the RSUs at the time of grant is equal to the weighted average trading price of the Corporation's voting shares for the five trading days immediately preceding the date of grant. Each RSU entitles the employee to receive payment upon vesting in the form of voting shares of the Corporation. The Corporation intends to settle all RSUs with shares either through the purchase of voting shares on the open market or the issuance of new shares from treasury; however, wholly at its own discretion, the Corporation may settle the units in cash. The RSU's time vest at the end of a two or three-year period, with compensation expense being recognized in net earnings over the service period. At December 31, 2017, 944,738 (2016 – 944,738) voting shares of the Corporation were reserved for issuance under the KEP plan. For the year ended December 31, 2017, the Corporation settled 96,068 RSUs through the open market and nil RSUs with shares issued from treasury (December 31, 2016 – 158,995 and nil, respectively).

Changes in the number of units, with their weighted average fair value, are summarized below:

	2017 Number of units	2017 Weighted average fair value	2016 Number of units	2016 Weighted average fair value
Units outstanding, beginning of year	238,381	22.50	278,140	24.09
Granted	96,697	22.21	122,919	19.96
Units, in lieu of dividends	5,584	24.75	6,415	21.78
Settled	(96,068)	23.57	(158,995)	23.21
Forfeited	(12,954)	21.60	(10,098)	23.72
Units outstanding, end of year	231,640	22.04	238,381	22.50

Notes to Consolidated Financial Statements
As at and for the years ended December 31, 2017 and 2016
(Stated in thousands of Canadian dollars, except percentage, ratio, share and per share amounts)

11. Share capital (continued)

(e) Executive share unit plan

The Corporation has an equity-based executive share unit (ESU) plan, whereby RSUs and performance share units (PSU) may be issued to senior executive officers. At December 31, 2017, 1,011,927 (2016 – 1,011,927) voting shares of the Corporation were reserved for issuance under the ESU plan.

The fair market value of the RSUs and PSUs at the time of grant is equal to the weighted average trading price of the Corporation's voting shares for the five trading days immediately preceding the grant date.

Each RSU entitles the senior executive officers to receive payment upon vesting in the form of voting shares of the Corporation. RSUs time vest over a period of up to three years, with compensation expense being recognized in net earnings over the service period.

Each PSU entitles the senior executive officers to receive payment upon vesting in the form of voting shares of the Corporation. PSUs time vest over a period of up to three years and incorporate performance criteria established at the time of grant. Compensation expense is recognized in net earnings over the service period based on the number of units expected to vest.

The Corporation intends to settle all RSUs and PSUs with shares either through the purchase of voting shares on the open market or the issuance of new shares from treasury; however, wholly at its own discretion, the Corporation may settle the units in cash. For the year ended December 31, 2017, the Corporation settled 62,364 RSUs and 66,063 PSUs through the purchase of shares on the open market and nil through the issuance from treasury (December 31, 2016 – 83,389 and 64,619 and nil, respectively).

Changes in the number of units, with their weighted average fair value, are summarized below:

| | 2017 | | | | 2016 | | | |
| | RSUs | | PSUs | | RSUs | | PSUs | |
	Number of units	Weighted fair value	Number of units	Weighted fair value	Number of units	Weighted fair value	Number of units	Weighted fair value
Units outstanding, beginning of year	197,865	22.80	336,718	22.78	222,720	24.04	02,887	24.79
Granted	118,392	22.25	207,755	22.19	100,798	20.35	203,666	20.12
Units, in lieu of dividends	5,779	24.84	10,042	24.90	5,864	21.78	9,007	21.87
Settled	(62,364)	23.37	(66,063)	23.89	(83,389)	22.65	(64,619)	22.10
Forfeited					(48,128)	23.55	(114,223)	23.72
Units outstanding, end of year	259,672	22.46	488,452	22.42	197,865	22.80	336,718	22.78

(f) Share-based payment expense

The following table summarizes share-based payment expense for the Corporation's equity-based plans:

	2017	2016
Stock option plan	13,498	12,536
Key employee plan	2,109	2,341
Executive share unit plan	3,443	3,555
Total share-based payment expense	19,050	18,432

Notes to Consolidated Financial Statements
As at and for the years ended December 31, 2017 and 2016
(Stated in thousands of Canadian dollars, except percentage, ratio, share and per share amounts)

11. Share capital (continued)

(g) Deferred share units

The Corporation has a cash-settled deferred share unit (DSU) plan as an alternative form of compensation for independent members of the Corporation's Board of Directors. Each DSU entitles a participant to receive cash upon settlement equal to the market value of the equivalent number of shares of the Corporation. The number of DSUs granted is determined based on the closing price of the Corporation's common shares on the trading day immediately prior to the date of grant. Total compensation expense is recognized at the time of grant. Fluctuations in the market value are recognized to compensation expense in the period in which the fluctuations occur. For the year ended December 31, 2017, 44,576 (2016 – 51,494) DSUs were granted, with $2,222 (2016 – $1,992) of expense included in salaries and benefits. During the year ended December 31, 2017, the Corporation settled 5,355 DSUs (2016 – 32,873). The carrying amount of the liability, included in accounts payable and accrued liabilities, relating to the cash-settled DSUs at December 31, 2017 is $5,784 (2016 – $4,150). At December 31, 2017, 219,411 (2016 – 180,125) DSUs are vested and outstanding. DSUs are redeemable upon the Director's retirement from the Board.

(h) Employee share purchase plan

The Corporation has an employee share purchase plan (ESPP), whereby the Corporation matches the contributions made by employees. Under the terms of the ESPP, employees may, dependent on their employment agreement, contribute up to a maximum of 10%, 15% or 20% of their gross salary to acquire voting shares of the Corporation at the current fair market value. The contributions are matched by the Corporation and are required to be held within the ESPP for a period of one year. Employees may offer to sell ESPP shares, which have not been held for at least one year, to the Corporation, at a purchase price equal to 50% of the weighted average trading price of the Corporation's voting shares for the five trading days immediately preceding the employee's notice to the Corporation, to a maximum of four times per year.

Under the terms of the ESPP, the Corporation acquires voting shares on behalf of employees through open market purchases. The Corporation's share of the contributions in 2017 amounted to $96,945 (2016 – $92,284) and is recorded as compensation expense within salaries and benefits.

12. Dividends

During the year ended December 31, 2017, the Corporation's Board of Directors declared quarterly cash dividends of $0.14 per common voting share and variable voting share. For the year ended December 31, 2017, the Corporation paid dividends totaling $64,886 (2016 – $66,967).

13. Earnings per share

The following reflects the share data used in the computation of basic and diluted earnings per share:

	2017	2016
Weighted average number of shares outstanding – basic	116,295,497	120,257,581
Employee stock options	707,201	54,520
Key employee-RSUs	176,167	159,984
Executive-RSUs	141,135	81,976
Executive-PSUs	44,926	56,643
Weighted average number of shares outstanding – diluted	117,364,926	120,610,704

For the year ended December 31, 2017, 2,544,013 employee stock options (2016 – 7,124,866 options) were not included in the calculation of dilutive potential shares as the result would have been anti-dilutive.

14. Finance cost

	2017	2016
Interest on long-term debt	73,126	65,768
Capitalized interest[i]	(19,825)	(18,798)
Accretion on maintenance provisions	409	2,104
	53,710	49,074

(i) Relates to interest capitalized on deposits paid for Boeing and Bombardier aircraft yet to be delivered using a weighted average interest rate of 3.27%. Of the total amount capitalized for the twelve months ended December 31, 2016, $8,197 relates to prior periods.

Notes to Consolidated Financial Statements
As at and for the years ended December 31, 2017 and 2016
(Stated in thousands of Canadian dollars, except percentage, ratio, share and per share amounts)

15. Financial instruments and risk management

(a) Fair value of financial assets and financial liabilities

The Corporation's financial assets and liabilities consist primarily of cash and cash equivalents, marketable securities, restricted cash, accounts receivable, derivatives, other interest-bearing deposits, accounts payable and accrued liabilities and long-term debt. The following tables set out the Corporation's classification and carrying amount, together with the fair value, for each type of financial asset and financial liability at December 31, 2017 and 2016:

December 31, 2017	Fair value Through profit or loss	Amortized cost Financial assets	Financial liabilities	Total Carrying amount	Fair value
Asset (liability):					
Cash and marketable securities⁽ⁱ⁾		1,482,866		1,482,866	1,482,866
Accounts receivable		129,648		129,648	129,648
Foreign exchange derivatives⁽ⁱⁱ⁾	(4,525)			(4,525)	(4,525)
Interest rate derivatives⁽ⁱⁱⁱ⁾	2,168			2,168	2,168
Cross-currency interest rate swap derivatives⁽ⁱᵛ⁾	(9,309)			(9,309)	(9,309)
Other deposits⁽ᵛ⁾		82,655		82,655	81,709
Accounts payable and accrued liabilities⁽ᵛⁱ⁾			(542,640)	(542,640)	(542,640)
Long-term debt⁽ᵛⁱⁱ⁾			(2,049,047)	(2,049,047)	(1,906,152)
	(11,666)	1,695,169	(2,591,687)	(908,184)	(766,235)

December 31, 2016	Fair value Through profit or loss	Amortized cost Loans and receivables	Other financial liabilities	Total Carrying amount	Fair value
Cash⁽ⁱ⁾	1,623,471			1,623,471	1,623,471
Accounts receivable		127,785		127,785	127,785
Foreign exchange derivatives⁽ⁱⁱ⁾	6,534			6,534	6,534
Interest rate derivatives⁽ⁱⁱⁱ⁾	(7,672)			(7,672)	(7,672)
Cross-currency interest rate swap derivatives⁽ⁱᵛ⁾	15,158			15,158	15,158
Other deposits⁽ᵛ⁾	84,466			84,466	83,568
Accounts payable and accrued liabilities⁽ᵛⁱ⁾			(543,014)	(543,014)	(543,014)
Long-term debt⁽ᵛⁱⁱ⁾			(2,046,658)	(2,046,658)	(1,971,965)
	1,721,957	127,785	(2,589,672)	(739,930)	(666,135)

(i) Includes restricted cash of $109,700 (December 31, 2016 – $102,649) and marketable securities of $226,090 (December 31, 2016 - nil).

(ii) Includes $820 (December 31, 2016 – $7,725) classified in prepaid expenses, deposits and other, and $5,345 (December 31, 2016 – $1,191) classified in accounts payable and accrued liabilities.

(iii) Includes $2,067 (December 31, 2016 – $nil) classified in prepaid expenses, deposits and other, $1,299 (December 31, 2016 – $3,285) classified in accounts payable and accrued liabilities, $2,814 (December 31, 2016 – $1,359) classified in other long-term assets, and $1,414 classified in other long-term liabilities (December 31, 2016 – $5,746).

(iv) Includes $nil (December 31, 2016 – $601) classified in prepaid expenses, deposits and other, $560 (December 31, 2016 – $nil) classified in accounts payable and accrued liabilities, $nil (December 31, 2016 – $14,557) classified in other long-term assets and $8,749 classified in other long-term liabilities (December 31, 2016 – $nil).

(v) Includes $36,189 (December 31, 2016 – $36,723) classified in prepaid expenses, deposits and other, and $46,466 (December 31, 2016 – $48,090) classified in other long-term assets. The fair value of the long-term aircraft deposits is determined by discounting the future contractual cash flows using an average rate of 1.49% (December 31, 2016 – 0.89%) for an average term of 2.42 years (December 31, 2016 – 2.88 years).

(vi) Excludes foreign exchange derivative liabilities of $5,345 (December 31, 2016 – $1,191), interest rate derivative liabilities of $1,299 (December 31, 2016 – $3,285) and cross-currency interest rate swap derivative liabilities of $560 (December 31, 2016 - $nil).

(vii) Includes current portion of long-term debt of $153,149 (December 31, 2016 – $145,128) and long-term debt of $1,895,898 (December 31, 2016 – $1,901,530). The fair value of the long-term debt is determined by discounting the future contractual cash flows of principal and interest under the current financing arrangements using the Corporation's December 31, 2017 implied Corporate BBB- rate of 4.85% (December 31, 2016 – 3.69%) for a 5.07 year term (December 31, 2016 – 5.45 year term), equal to the weighted average remaining term of the Corporation's long term debt at December 31, 2017.

Notes to Consolidated Financial Statements
As at and for the years ended December 31, 2017 and 2016
(Stated in thousands of Canadian dollars, except percentage, ratio, share and per share amounts)

15. Financial instruments and risk management (continued)

(a) Fair value of financial assets and financial liabilities (continued)

The following items shown in the consolidated statement of financial position at December 31, 2017 and 2016, are measured at fair value on a recurring basis and classified using level 1 or level 2 inputs. Level 1 inputs are defined as quoted prices in active markets while level 2 is defined as significant other observable inputs. There are no financial assets or liabilities classified as level 3 (significant unobservable inputs) in the fair value hierarchy.

December 31, 2017	Level 1	Level 2	Total
Asset (liability):			
Foreign exchange derivatives	–	(4,525)	(4,525)
Interest rate derivatives	–	2,168	2,168
Cross-currency interest rate swap derivatives	–	(9,309)	(9,309)
		(11,666)	(11,666)

December 31, 2016	Level 1	Level 2	Total
Asset (liability):			
Cash and cash equivalents	1,623,471	–	1,623,471
Foreign exchange derivatives	–	6,534	6,534
Interest rate derivatives	–	(7,672)	(7,672)
Cross-currency interest rate swap derivatives	–	15,158	15,158
Other deposits	84,466		84,466
	1,707,937	14,020	1,721,957

During the years ended December 31, 2017 and 2016, there were no transfers between level 1, level 2 and level 3 financial assets and liabilities measured at fair value.

Cash and cash equivalents: Classified as level 1 at December 31, 2016, these consist of bank balances and short-term investments, primarily highly liquid instruments, with terms up to 91 days. Interest income is recorded in the consolidated statement of earnings as finance income. Due to its short-term nature, the carrying value of cash and cash equivalents approximates its fair value.

Foreign exchange derivatives: Classified as level 2, these consist of foreign exchange forward contracts where the fair value of the forward contracts is measured based on the difference between the contracted rate and the current forward price. At December 31, 2017, to fix the exchange rate on a portion of the Corporation's US dollar aircraft lease payments and hotel costs for the next twelve months, the Corporation has entered into foreign exchange contracts with an average monthly notional of US $19,013 (December 31, 2016 – US $21,078) for a total of US $228,155 (2016 – US $252,934) at a weighted average contracted rate on the forward contracts of 1.2745 (December 31, 2016 – 1.3150) Canadian dollars to one US dollar, and the weighted average forward rate used in determining the fair value was 1.2547 (December 31, 2016 – 1.3414) Canadian dollars to one US dollar. At December 31, 2017, a portion of the change in the fair value of foreign exchange derivatives amounting to $399 (December 31, 2016- $nil) was recognized within gain (loss) on derivatives in the consolidated statement of earnings as hedge ineffectiveness.

Interest rate derivatives: Classified as level 2, these consist of interest rate swap contracts that exchange a floating rate of interest with a fixed rate of interest. The fair value of the interest rate swaps is determined by measuring the difference between the fixed contracted rate and the forward curve for the applicable floating interest rates. At December 31, 2017, the Corporation's swap contracts have an outstanding notional value of $441,831 with a weighted average fixed interest rate of 1.61% (December 31, 2016 – 1.69%). The December 31, 2017 weighted average floating forward inter-est rate was 2.09% (December 31, 2016 – 1.32%).

Cross-currency interest rate swap derivatives: Classified as level 2, these consist of fixed US dollar to fixed Canadian dollar uncollateralized cross-currency interest rate swap agreements to mitigate exposure to fluctuations in future cash flows that are attributable to foreign currency risk resulting from the issuance of US denominated long-term debt. The USD $400,000 notional at 3.50% interest per annum was exchanged for CAD $511,110 at a 3.56% weighted average interest per annum through the terms of the swaps, which match the 5-year maturity of the USD senior unsecured notes. The fair value of the cross-currency interest rate swap contracts was determined by discounting the difference between the contracted prices and market based yield curves.

Other deposits: Classified as level 1, these consist of deposits related to certain leased aircraft as well as airport operations.

Notes to Consolidated Financial Statements

As at and for the years ended December 31, 2017 and 2016
(Stated in thousands of Canadian dollars, except percentage, ratio, share and per share amounts)

15. Financial instruments and risk management (continued)

(a) Fair value of financial assets and financial liabilities (continued)

The following table represents the maturity of derivative financial instruments by risk category:

(notional in 000's)	Currency	Total	Within 1 year	1–5 years	Over 5 years
Foreign currency risk:					
Foreign exchange derivatives	USD	228,155	228,155	–	–
Cross-currency interest rate swap derivatives	USD	400,000	–	400,000	–
		628,155	228,155	400,000	–
Interest rate risk:					
Interest rate derivatives	CAD	441,831	29,804	145,468	266,559

(b) Risk management related to financial instruments

The Corporation is exposed to market, credit and liquidity risks associated with its financial assets and liabilities. From time to time, the Corporation may use various financial derivatives to reduce exposures from changes in foreign exchange rates, interest rates and jet fuel prices. The Corporation does not hold or use any derivative instruments for trading or speculative purposes.

The Corporation's Board of Directors has responsibility for the establishment and approval of the Corporation's overall risk management policies, including those related to financial instruments. Management performs continuous assessments so that all significant risks related to financial instruments are reviewed and addressed in light of changes to market conditions and the Corporation's operating activities.

Market risk

Market risk is the risk that the fair value or future cash flows of a financial instrument will fluctuate due to changes in market prices. The Corporation's significant market risks relate to fuel price risk, foreign exchange risk and interest rate risk.

(i) Fuel price risk

The airline industry is inherently dependent upon jet fuel to operate and, therefore, the Corporation is exposed to the risk of volatile fuel prices. Fuel prices are impacted by a host of factors outside the Corporation's control, such as significant weather events, geopolitical tensions, refinery capacity, and global demand and supply.

The Corporation estimates that a one-cent change in the value of the Canadian dollar versus the US dollar will have an approximate impact of $7.4 million on fuel costs and that a change of one US-dollar per barrel of West Texas Intermediate (WTI) crude oil will have an approximate impact of US $9.7 million on fuel costs. For the year ended December 31, 2017, aircraft fuel expense represented approximately 23% (2016 – 21%) of the Corporation's total operating expenses.

(ii) Foreign exchange risk

The Corporation is exposed to foreign exchange risks arising from fluctuations in exchange rates on its US-dollar-denominated monetary assets and liabilities and its US-dollar operating expenditures, mainly aircraft fuel, aircraft leasing expense, the land component of vacations packages, aircraft purchases and depreciation and certain maintenance and airport operation costs.

US dollar monetary assets and liabilities

The gain or loss on foreign exchange included in the Corporation's consolidated statement of earnings is mainly attributable to the changes and settlements in the value of the Corporation's US-dollar-denominated monetary assets and liabilities. At December 31, 2017, US-dollar-denominated net monetary assets totaled approximately US $61,574 (2016 – liability of US $19,423).

The Corporation estimates that a one-cent change in the value of the US dollar versus the Canadian dollar at December 31, 2017, totaled $14,584 (2016 – $14,584). A reasonable change in market interest rates at December 31, 2017, would have increased or decreased net earnings for the year ended December 31, 2017, by $433 (2016 – $138), as a result of the Corporation's US-dollar-denominated net monetary asset balance.

US-dollar aircraft leasing and vacation package hotel costs

The Corporation has foreign exchange forward contracts to fix the foreign exchange rate on a portion of US-dollar hotel costs that form part of the Corporation's vacation packages and to fix the US-dollar cost of aircraft leasing. All foreign exchange forward contracts are governed by the Corporation's Foreign Currency Risk Management Policy. The Corporation applies cash flow hedge accounting for certain foreign exchange hedges.

Notes to Consolidated Financial Statements

As at and for the years ended December 31, 2017 and 2016
(Stated in thousands of Canadian dollars, except percentage, ratio, share and per share amounts)

15. Financial instruments and risk management (continued)

(b) Risk management related to financial instruments (continued)

Market risk (continued)

The following table presents the financial impact and statement presentation of the Corporation's foreign exchange derivatives on the consolidated statement of financial position:

	Statement presentation	2017	2016
Fair value	Prepaid expenses, deposits and other	820	7,725
Fair value	Accounts payable and accrued liabilities	(5,345)	(1,191)
Unrealized gain (loss)	Hedge reserves (before tax)	(4,305)	2,476

The following table presents the financial impact and statement presentation of the Corporation's foreign exchange derivatives on the consolidated statement of earnings:

	Statement presentation	2017	2016
Realized gain (loss)	Aircraft leasing	(2,182)	5,534
Realized loss	Other revenue	(5,188)	(500)
Realized and unrealized gain (loss)	Gain (loss) on derivatives	(2,426)	4,504

The following table presents the financial impact and statement presentation of the Corporation's cross-currency swaps on the consolidated statement of financial position:

	Statement presentation	2017	2016
Fair value	Prepaid expenses, deposits and other	–	601
Fair value	Accounts payable and accrued liabilities	(560)	–
Fair value	Other assets	–	14,557
Fair value	Other liabilities	(8,749)	–
Unrealized gain (loss)	Hedge reserves (before tax)	(9,309)	15,158

The following table presents the financial impact and statement presentation of the Corporation's cross-currency swaps on the consolidated statement of earnings:

	Statement presentation	2017	2016
Realized gain	Finance cost	56	234

A one-cent change in the US-dollar exchange rate for the year ended December 31, 2017, would impact hedge reserves, net of taxes, by $1,586 (2016 – $877) and gain on derivatives, net of taxes, by $79 (2016 – $973) as a result of the Corporation's foreign exchange derivatives.

(iii) Interest rate risk

Interest rate risk is the risk that the value or future cash flows of a financial instrument will fluctuate as a result of changes in market interest rates.

Cash, cash equivalents and marketable securities

The Corporation is exposed to interest rate fluctuations on its short-term investments, included in cash, cash equivalents and marketable securities. A change of 50 basis points in the market interest rate would have an approximate impact on net earnings of $3,673 (2016 – $2,753) as a result of the Corporation's short-term investment activities.

Deposits

The Corporation is exposed to interest rate fluctuations on interest-bearing deposits related to airport operations, which, at December 31, 2017, totaled $14,584 (2016 – $14,584). A reasonable change in market interest rates at December 31, 2017, would not have significantly impacted the Corporation's net earnings due to the small size of these deposits.

Long-term debt

The Corporation is exposed to interest rate risks arising from fluctuations in market interest rates on its variable-rate debt. The fixed-rate debt and interest rate swaps on the Corporation's long-term debt mitigate the majority of the impacts of interest rate fluctuations over the term of the outstanding debt and therefore a change in interest rates at December 31, 2017, would not impact net earnings.

Notes to Consolidated Financial Statements

As at and for the years ended December 31, 2017 and 2016
(Stated in thousands of Canadian dollars, except percentage, ratio, share and per share amounts)

15. Financial instruments and risk management (continued)

(b) Risk management related to financial instruments (continued)

Market risk (continued)

At December 31, 2017, the Corporation has entered into interest rate swaps with a weighted-average term of 6.7 years and a weighted-average fixed contracted rate was 1.61%, inclusive of a basis point spread. The Corporation applies cash flow hedge accounting to certain interest rate swaps.

The following table presents the financial impact and statement presentation of the Corporation's interest rate derivatives on the consolidated statement of financial position:

	Statement presentation	2017	2016
Fair value	Prepaid expenses, deposits and other	2,067	–
Fair value	Other assets	2,814	1,359
Fair value	Accounts payable and accrued liabilities	(1,299)	(3,285)
Fair value	Other liabilities	(1,414)	(5,746)
Unrealized loss	Hedge reserves (before tax)	(3,106)	(6,734)

The following table presents the financial impact and statement presentation of the Corporation's interest rate derivatives on the consolidated statement of earnings:

	Statement presentation	2017	2016
Realized loss	Finance cost	(2,746)	(3,882)

A change of 50 basis points in market interest rates at December 31, 2017, would impact hedge reserves, net of taxes, by $3,368 (2016 – $5,583) and loss on derivatives, net of taxes, by $nil (2016 – $nil) as a result of the Corporation's interest rate derivatives.

Credit risk

Credit risk is the risk that one party to a financial instrument will cause a financial loss for the other party by failing to discharge an obligation. At December 31, 2017, the Corporation's credit exposure consists primarily of the carrying amounts of cash, cash equivalents and marketable securities, restricted cash, accounts receivable, other deposits and the fair value of derivative financial assets.

The Corporation's maximum exposure to credit risk is represented by the balances in the aforementioned accounts:

	2017	2016
Cash, cash equivalents and marketable securities[i]	1,373,166	1,520,822
Restricted cash[i]	109,700	102,649
Accounts receivable[ii]	129,648	127,785
Other deposits[iii]	82,655	84,466
Derivative financial assets[iv]	5,701	24,242

(i) Consist of bank balances, short-term investments with terms of up to 91 days and marketable securities with terms up to 365 days. Credit risk associated with cash, cash equivalents, marketable securities and restricted cash is minimized substantially by ensuring that these financial assets are invested primarily in debt instruments with highly rated financial institutions, some with provincial-government-backed guarantees. The Corporation manages its exposure by assessing the financial strength of its counterparties and by limiting the total exposure to any one individual counterparty.

(ii) All significant counterparties, both current and new, are reviewed and approved for credit on a regular basis under the Corporation's credit management processes. The Corporation does not hold any collateral as security, however, in some cases the Corporation requires guaranteed letters of credit with certain of its counterparties. Trade receivables are generally settled within 30 to 60 days. Industry receivables are generally settled in less than 30 days.

(iii) The Corporation is exposed to counterparty credit risk on its deposit relating to certain leased aircraft and airport operations, however it considers this risk to be remote because of the nature and size of the counterparties.

(iv) Derivative financial assets consist of foreign exchange forward contracts and interest rate swaps. The Corporation reviews the size and credit rating of both current and any new counterparties in addition to limiting the total exposure to any one counterparty.

There were no new bad debts recorded for the year ended December 31, 2017 (2016 – $nil).

Notes to Consolidated Financial Statements

As at and for the years ended December 31, 2017 and 2016
(Stated in thousands of Canadian dollars, except percentage, ratio, share and per share amounts)

15. Financial instruments and risk management (continued)

(b) Risk management related to financial instruments (continued)

Liquidity risk

Liquidity risk is the risk that the Corporation will encounter difficulty in meeting obligations associated with financial liabilities. The Corporation maintains a strong liquidity position and sufficient financial resources to meet its obligations as they fall due.

The table below presents a maturity analysis of the Corporation's undiscounted contractual cash flows for its non-derivative and derivative financial liabilities at December 31, 2017. The analysis is based on foreign exchange and interest rates in effect at the consolidated statement of financial position date, and includes both principal and interest cash flows for long-term debt.

	Total	Within 1 year	1–3 years	4–5 years	Over 5 years
Accounts payable and accrued liabilities[i]	542,640	542,640	–	–	–
Derivative financial liabilities[ii]	17,367	7,204	10,163	–	–
Long-term debt and interest	2,287,847	218,572	943,602	716,274	409,399
	2,847,854	768,416	953,765	716,274	409,399

(i) Excludes foreign exchange derivative liabilities of $5,345, interest rate derivative liabilities of $1,299 and cross-currency swap derivative liabilities of $560.
(ii) Derivative financial liabilities consist of foreign exchange forward contracts of $5,345, interest rate derivative contracts of $2,713 and cross-currency swap derivative contracts of $9,309. The Corporation reports interest rate derivatives at their net position.

A portion of the Corporation's cash and cash equivalents balance relates to cash collected with respect to advance ticket sales, for which the balance at December 31, 2017, was $695,111 (2016 – $626,635). The Corporation has cash and cash equivalents on hand to have sufficient liquidity to meet its liabilities, when due, under both normal and stressed conditions.

The Corporation aims to maintain a current ratio, defined as current assets over current liabilities, of approximately 1.00 or greater with the understanding that point-in-time fluctuations may periodically bring the ratio below 1.00. At December 31, 2017, the Corporation's current ratio was 1.04 (2016 – 1.21).

At December 31, 2017, the Corporation has not been required to post collateral with respect to any of its outstanding derivative contracts.

Notes to Consolidated Financial Statements
As at and for the years ended December 31, 2017 and 2016
(Stated in thousands of Canadian dollars, except percentage, ratio, share and per share amounts)

16. Commitments

(a) Purchased aircraft and spare engines

At December 31, 2017, the Corporation is committed to purchase 10 787-9 Dreamliner aircraft for delivery between 2019 and 2021 and 51 737 MAX aircraft for delivery between 2018 and 2027. The Corporation is also committed to purchase two Q400 NextGen aircraft for delivery in 2018 and a total of 10 Boeing and Bombardier spare engines for delivery between 2018 and 2026.

The remaining estimated deposits and delivery payments for the 63 aircraft and 10 spare engines are presented in the table below. Where applicable, US dollar commitments are translated at the period end foreign exchange rate.

Within 1 year	510,686
1 – 3 years	1,389,839
4 – 5 years	1,379,643
Over 5 years	1,478,190
	4,758,358

(b) Leases and contractual commitments

The Corporation has entered into leases and other contractual commitments for aircraft, land, buildings, equipment, computer hardware, software licenses and inflight entertainment. At December 31, 2017, the future payments under these commitments are presented in the table below. Where applicable, US dollar commitments are translated at the period end foreign exchange rate.

Within 1 year	273,587
1 – 3 years	347,978
4 – 5 years	167,563
Over 5 years	88,507
	877,635

(c) Letters of guarantee

At December 31, 2017, the Corporation has a revolving letter of credit facility totaling $50,000 (December 31, 2016 – $50,000). The facility requires funds to be assigned and held in cash security for the full value of letters of guarantee issued by the Corporation. At December 31, 2017, $32,234 (December 31, 2016 – $31,013) letters of guarantee were issued under the facility by assigning restricted cash.

Notes to Consolidated Financial Statements
As at and for the years ended December 31, 2017 and 2016
(Stated in thousands of Canadian dollars, except percentage, ratio, share and per share amounts)

17. Related parties

(a) Interests in subsidiaries

The consolidated financial statements of WestJet Airlines Ltd., the parent company, include the accounts of the Corporation and its following five directly wholly-owned subsidiaries incorporated in Canada, as well as an indirectly wholly-owned Alberta partnership:

WestJet Investment Corp. (WIC)
WestJet Operations Corp. (WOC)
WestJet Vacations Inc. (WVI)
WestJet Encore Ltd. (Encore)
Swoop Inc. (Swoop)
WestJet, An Alberta Partnership (Partnership)

The Partnership is the primary operating entity of the Corporation. WIC, WOC, WVI, Encore and Swoop were created for legal, tax and marketing purposes and do not operate independently of the Partnership. Their relationship is such that they depend critically on the Partnership for a variety of resources including financing, human resources and systems and technology. There are no legal or contractual restrictions on the Corporation's and subsidiaries' ability to access or use assets or settle liabilities of the consolidated group.

(b) Interests in consolidated structured entities

The Corporation also controls and consolidates three structured entities in which the Corporation has no equity ownership but controls and has power over all relevant activities and is exposed to and has rights to variable returns by means of contractual relationships. These entities were established for legal purposes to facilitate the financing of aircraft. These entities do not conduct any operations except to hold legal title to specific aircraft and their related debt obligations. Through these contractual relationships, the Corporation is required to fund all of the aircraft debt obligations of these entities. There are no legal or contractual restrictions between the Corporation and these entities that limit the access or use of assets or the settlement of liabilities. The full amount of the aircraft debt obligations are reported as long-term debt on the Corporation's consolidated statement of financial position. The nature of the risks associated with these entities is limited to specific tax legislation in Canada and the U.S. Although considered remote by Management, the potential for future changes to Canadian and U.S. tax legislation affecting these entities could have potential adverse tax effects on the Corporation.

(c) Interests in unconsolidated structured entities

The Corporation is a party to 18 Fuel Facility Corporations (FFCs) and three De-icing Facility Corporations (DFCs) for the purpose of obtaining cost effective into-plane fuel services and aircraft de-icing services at select Canadian and US airports. These operating costs are recorded in aircraft fuel and other expenses, respectively, on the consolidated statement of earnings. At December 31, 2017, the Corporation has $2,318 in operating deposits with the FFCs and DFCs classified in prepaids, deposits and other on the consolidated statement of financial position. The Corporation has no equity ownership and no control or significant influence in the FFCs or DFCs. The financing and operating costs of these entities are shared amongst numerous contracting airlines based on a variety of contractual terms including fuel volume consumption and qualifying flights. The Corporation classifies its monthly operating cost obligations to the FFCs and DFCs as other financial liabilities and these obligations are included in accounts payable and accrued liabilities on the consolidated statement of financial position. The 18 FFCs and three DFCs have combined total assets of approximately $898,696 and liabilities of approximately $897,752 based on the most recent information received. In the event any or all contracting airlines default and withdraw from the FFCs and DFCs and no amounts are recovered through legal recourse, the Corporation and any remaining contracting airlines are liable for the outstanding obligations of the FFCs and DFCs. These obligations represent the Corporation's maximum exposure to loss from the FFCs and DFCs.

(d) Key management personnel

The Corporation has defined key management personnel as Senior Executive Officers and the Board of Directors, as they have the collective authority and responsibility for planning, directing and controlling the activities of the Corporation. The following table outlines the total compensation expense for key management personnel for the years ended December 31, 2017 and 2016.

	2017	2016
Salaries, benefits and other compensation[i]	7,840	5,860
Share-based payment expense[ii]	6,802	6,530
	14,642	12,390

(i) Other compensation includes the employee share purchase plan, profit share, cash compensation paid to the Board of Directors, payments under the Corporation's short-term incentive plan to Senior Executive Officers and amounts paid on departure.

(ii) Includes amounts expensed pursuant to the stock option plan, executive share unit plan and deferred share unit plan.

Notes to Consolidated Financial Statements
As at and for the years ended December 31, 2017 and 2016
(Stated in thousands of Canadian dollars, except percentage, ratio, share and per share amounts)

18. Additional financial information

(a) Assets

	Note	2017	2016
Accounts receivable:			
Trade and industry[i]		120,518	119,375
Other		11,427	10,707
Allowance		(2,297)	(2,297)
		129,648	127,785
Prepaid expenses, deposits and other:			
Prepaid expenses[ii]		81,667	122,072
Short-term deposits[iii]		36,189	36,723
Maintenance reserves – current portion	8	16,281	13,727
Derivatives	15	2,887	8,326
Other		1,652	222
		138,676	181,070
Inventory:			
Fuel		20,649	14,892
Aircraft expendables		21,483	17,810
De-icing fluid		380	484
Other		533	349
		43,045	33,535
Other Assets:			
Aircraft deposits[iv]		39,968	41,173
Maintenance reserves – long term	8	13,761	16,823
Derivatives	15	2,814	15,916
Other[v]		22,041	21,456
		78,584	95,368

(i) Trade receivables include receivables relating to airport operations, fuel rebates, marketing programs and ancillary revenue products and services. Industry receivables include receivables relating to travel agents, interline agreements with other airlines and partnerships. Significant counterparties are reviewed and approved for credit on a regular basis. Trade receivables are generally settled in 30 to 60 days. Industry receivables are generally settled in less than 30 days.

(ii) Includes prepaid expenses for insurance, vacation package vendors, maintenance services on owned and leased aircraft and other operating costs.

(iii) Includes deposits relating to aircraft fuel, airport operations, deposits on leased aircraft and other operating costs.

(iv) Includes long-term deposits with lessors for leased aircraft.

(v) Includes long-term deposits for airport operations and long-term prepaid financing costs.

(b) Liabilities

	Note	2017	2016
Accounts payable and accrued liabilities:			
Trade and industry		478,836	450,249
Taxes payable		23,394	63,198
Derivatives	15	7,204	4,476
Other		40,410	29,567
		549,844	547,490
Other liabilities:			
Deferred contract incentives[i]		9,008	2,628
Derivatives	15	10,163	5,746
		19,171	8,374

(i) Deferred contract incentives relate to discounts received on aircraft related items as well as the net effect of rent free periods and cost escalations on land leases. Incentives, rent free periods and cost escalations are recognized on a straight-line basis over the terms of the related contracts.

Corporate information

Board of Directors

Clive Beddoe,
Chair of the Board

Brad Armitage,
WEA Chair

Hugh Bolton,
Director

Ron Brenneman,
Director

Christopher Burley,
Vice Chair of the Board

Brett Godfrey,
Director

Allan Jackson,
Director

S. Barry Jackson,
Director

L. Jacques Ménard,
Director

Janice Rennie,
Director

Karen Sheriff,
Director

Edward Sims,
President and Chief Executive Officer

Executive team

Edward Sims,
President and Chief Executive Officer

Harry Taylor,
Executive Vice-President, Finance and Chief Financial Officer

Bob Cummings,
Executive Vice-President, Strategy

Mark Porter,
Executive Vice-President, People and Culture

Barbara Munroe,
Executive Vice-President, Corporate Services and General Counsel

Cameron Kenyon,
Executive Vice-President, Operations

Craig Maccubbin,
Executive Vice-President and Chief Information Officer

Charles Duncan,
Executive Vice-President and President, WestJet Encore

Steven Greenway,
Executive Vice-President and President, Swoop

Stock exchange listing
Shares in WestJet stock are publicly traded on the Toronto Stock Exchange under the symbol WJA.

Investor relations contact information
Phone: 1-877-493-7853
Email: investor_relations@westjet.com

WestJet headquarters
22 Aerial Place NE
Calgary, Alberta T2E 3J1
Phone: 403-444-2600
Toll-free: 888-293-7853

Annual meeting
WestJet Airlines Ltd.'s annual meeting will be held at 10 a.m. (MT) on Tuesday, May 8, 2018, at WestJet's headquarters at 22 Aerial Place NE Calgary, Alberta T2E 3J1

Auditors
KPMG LLP, Calgary, Alberta

Transfer agent and registrar
AST Trust Company (Canada) www.astfinancial.com
Toll-free in North America: 1-800-387-0825

the future is friendly®

stronger together

2017 ANNUAL REPORT

Management's discussion and analysis

Caution regarding forward-looking statements

This document contains forward-looking statements about expected events and the financial and operating performance of TELUS Corporation. The terms *TELUS, the Company, we, us* and *our* refer to TELUS Corporation and, where the context of the narrative permits or requires, its subsidiaries.

Forward-looking statements include any statements that do not refer to historical facts. They include, but are not limited to, statements relating to our objectives and our strategies to achieve those objectives, our targets, outlook, updates, and our multi-year dividend growth program. Forward-looking statements are typically identified by the words *assumption, goal, guidance, objective, outlook, strategy, target* and other similar expressions, or future or conditional verbs such as *aim, anticipate, believe, could, expect, intend, may, plan, predict, seek, should, strive* and *will*.

By their nature, forward-looking statements are subject to inherent risks and uncertainties and are based on assumptions, including assumptions about future economic conditions and courses of action. These assumptions may ultimately prove to have been inaccurate and, as a result, our actual results or events may differ materially from expectations expressed in or implied by the forward-looking statements. Our general outlook and assumptions for 2018 are presented in *Section 9 General trends, outlook and assumptions* in this Management's discussion and analysis (MD&A).

Risks and uncertainties that could cause actual performance or events to differ materially from the forward-looking statements made herein and in other TELUS filings include, but are not limited to, the following:

* Competition including: our ability to continue to retain customers through an enhanced customer service experience, including through the deployment and operation of evolving wireless and wireline networks; the ability of industry competitors to successfully launch their respective platforms and to combine a mix of residential local voice over Internet protocol (VoIP), long distance, high-speed Internet access (HSIA) and, in some cases, wireless services under one bundled and/or discounted monthly rate, along with their existing broadcast or satellite-based TV services; the success of new products, new services and supporting systems, such as Internet of Things (IoT) services for Internet-connected devices; continued intense rivalry across all services among wireless and wireline telecommunications companies, cable-TV providers, other communications companies and over-the-top (OTT) services, which, among other things, places pressures on current and future average revenue per subscriber unit per month (ARPU), cost of acquisition, cost of retention and churn rate for all services, as do customer usage patterns, flat-rate pricing trends for voice and data, inclusive rate plans for voice and data and availability of Wi-Fi networks for data; mergers and acquisitions of industry competitors; pressures on high-speed Internet and TV ARPU and churn rate resulting from market conditions, government actions and customer usage patterns; residential and business network access line (NAL) losses; subscriber additions and retention volumes, and associated costs for wireless, TV and high-speed Internet services; and our ability to obtain and offer content on a timely basis across multiple devices on wireless and TV platforms at a reasonable cost.
* Technological substitution including: reduced utilization and increased commoditization of traditional wireline voice local and long distance services from impacts of OTT applications and wireless substitution, a declining overall market for paid TV services, including as a result of content piracy and signal theft and as a result of a rise in OTT direct to consumer video offerings and virtual multichannel video programming distribution platforms; the increasing number of households that have only wireless and/or Internet-based telephone services; potential wireless ARPU declines as a result of, among other factors, substitution to messaging and OTT applications; substitution to increasingly available

Wi-Fi services; and disruptive technologies such as OTT IP services, including Network as a Service in the business market, that may displace or re-rate our existing data services.
* Technology including: subscriber demand for data that may challenge wireless networks and spectrum capacity levels in the future and may be accompanied by increases in delivery cost; our reliance on information technology and our need to streamline our legacy systems; technology options, evolution paths and roll-out plans for video distribution platforms and telecommunications networks (including broadband initiatives, such as fibre to the premises (FTTP), wireless small-cell deployment, 5G wireless and availability of resources and ability to build out adequate broadband capacity); our reliance on wireless network access agreements, which have facilitated our deployment of wireless technologies; choice of suppliers and those suppliers' ability to maintain and service their product lines, which could affect the success of upgrades to, and evolution of, technology that we offer; supplier concentration and market power for network equipment, TELUS TV and wireless handsets; the performance of wireless technology; our expected long-term need to acquire additional spectrum capacity through future spectrum auctions and from third parties to address increasing demand for data; deployment and operation of new wireline broadband networks at a reasonable cost and availability and success of new products and services to be rolled out on such networks; network reliability and change management; self-learning tools and automation that may change the way we interact with customers; and uncertainties around our strategy to replace certain legacy wireline networks, systems and services to reduce operating costs.
* Capital expenditure levels and potential outlays for spectrum licences in spectrum auctions or from third parties, due to: our broadband initiatives, including connecting more homes and businesses directly to fibre; our ongoing deployment of newer wireless technologies, including wireless small cells to improve coverage and capacity and prepare for a more efficient and timely evolution to 5G wireless services; utilizing acquired spectrum; investments in network resiliency and reliability; subscriber demand for data; evolving systems and business processes; implementing efficiency initiatives; supporting large complex deals; and future wireless spectrum auctions held by Innovation, Science and Economic Development Canada (ISED). Our capital expenditure levels could be impacted if we do not achieve our targeted operational and financial results.
* Regulatory decisions and developments including: the potential of government intervention to further increase wireless competition; the CRTC wireless wholesale services review, in which it was determined that the CRTC will regulate wholesale GSM-based domestic roaming rates and the setting of such rates charged to wireless service providers (WSPs); the Governor in Council's order to the CRTC to reconsider whether Wi-Fi networks should be considered a home network for WSPs seeking mandated roaming; future spectrum auctions and spectrum policy determinations, including the recently announced repurposing of 600 MHz spectrum (and including limitations on established wireless providers, proposed spectrum set-aside that favours certain carriers and other advantages provided to new and foreign participants, and the amount and cost of spectrum acquired); restrictions on the purchase, sale and transfer of spectrum licences; the impact of the CRTC's wireline wholesale services review, with a formal review of rates for wholesale FTTP access still to be commenced for TELUS; disputes with certain municipalities regarding rights-of-way bylaws; and other potential threats to unitary federal regulatory authority over telecommunications, including provincial wireless legislation; the potential impacts of the CRTC's decision to require pro-rated refunds when customers terminate their services; the

CRTC's proposed phase-out of the local service subsidy regime and corresponding establishment of a broadband funding regime to support the enhancement of high-speed Internet services focusing on underserved areas in Canada; the impact of the review of the Minister of Canadian Heritage's new Creative Canada policy framework announced on September 28, 2017; the CRTC's consultation and report on distribution models of the future; vertical integration in the broadcasting industry resulting in competitors owning broadcast content services, and timely and effective enforcement of related regulatory safeguards; the review of the *Copyright Act* scheduled to begin in early 2018; the federal government's stated intention to review the *Broadcasting Act* and *Telecommunications Act* as announced in the March 22, 2017 federal budget; TELUS' applications for renewal of its broadcasting distribution licences; the North American Free Trade Agreement renegotiation; and restrictions on non-Canadian ownership and control of TELUS Common Shares and the ongoing monitoring and compliance with such restrictions.

- Human resource matters including: recruitment, retention and appropriate training in a highly competitive industry, and the level of employee engagement.

- Operational performance and business combination risks including: our reliance on legacy systems and ability to implement and support new products and services and business operations in a timely manner; our ability to implement effective change management for system replacements and upgrades, process redesigns and business integrations (such as our ability to successfully integrate acquisitions, complete divestitures or establish partnerships in a timely manner, and realize expected strategic benefits, including those following compliance with any regulatory orders); the implementation of complex large enterprise deals that may be adversely impacted by available resources, system limitations and degree of co-operation from other service providers; our ability to successfully manage operations in foreign jurisdictions; information security and privacy breaches, including data loss or theft of data; intentional threats to our infrastructure and business operations; and real estate joint venture re-development risks.

- Business continuity events including: our ability to maintain customer service and operate our networks in the event of human error or human-caused threats, such as cyberattacks and equipment failures that could cause various degrees of network outages; supply chain disruptions; natural disaster threats; epidemics; pandemics; political instability in certain international locations; and the completeness and effectiveness of business continuity and disaster recovery plans and responses.

- Ability to successfully implement cost reduction initiatives and realize planned savings, net of restructuring and other costs, without losing customer service focus or negatively affecting business operations. Examples of these initiatives are: our operating efficiency and effectiveness program to drive improvements in financial results, including the future benefits of the immediately vesting transformative compensation initiative; business integrations; business product simplification; business process outsourcing; offshoring and reorganizations, including any full-time equivalent (FTE) employee reduction programs; procurement initiatives; and real estate rationalization. Additional revenue and cost efficiency and effectiveness initiatives will continue to be assessed and implemented.

- Financing and debt requirements including: our ability to carry out financing activities, and our ability to maintain investment grade credit ratings in the range of BBB+ or the equivalent.

- Ability to sustain our dividend growth program through 2019. This program may be affected by factors such as the competitive environment, economic performance in Canada, our earnings and free cash flow, our levels of capital expenditures and spectrum licence purchases, acquisitions, the management of our capital structure, and regulatory decisions and developments. Quarterly dividend decisions are subject to assessment and determination by our Board of Directors (Board) based on the Company's financial position and outlook. Shares may be purchased under our normal course issuer bid (NCIB) when and if we consider it opportunistic, based on the Company's financial position and outlook, and the market price of TELUS shares. There can be no assurance that our dividend growth program or any NCIB will be maintained, not changed and/or completed through 2019.

- Taxation matters including: interpretation of complex domestic and foreign tax laws by the tax authorities that may differ from our interpretations; the timing of income and deductions, such as tax depreciation and operating expenses; changes in tax laws, including tax rates; tax expenses being materially different than anticipated, including the taxability of income and deductibility of tax attributes; elimination of income tax deferrals through the use of different tax year-ends for operating partnerships and corporate partners; and tax authorities adopting more aggressive auditing practices, for example, tax reassessments or adverse court decisions impacting the tax payable by us.

- Litigation and legal matters including: our ability to successfully respond to investigations and regulatory proceedings; our ability to defend against existing and potential claims and lawsuits, including intellectual property infringement claims and class actions based on consumer claims, data, privacy or security breaches and secondary market liability; and the complexity of legal compliance in domestic and foreign jurisdictions, including compliance with anti-bribery and foreign corrupt practices laws.

- Health, safety and the environment including: lost employee work time resulting from illness or injury, public concerns related to radio frequency emissions, environmental issues affecting our business including climate change, waste and waste recycling, risks relating to fuel systems on our properties, and changing government and public expectations regarding environmental matters and our responses.

- Economic growth and fluctuations including: the state of the economy in Canada, which may be influenced by economic and other developments outside of Canada, including potential outcomes of yet unknown policies and actions of foreign governments; future interest rates; inflation; unemployment levels; effects of fluctuating oil prices; effects of low business spending (such as reducing investments and cost structure); pension investment returns, funding and discount rates; and Canadian dollar: U.S. dollar exchange rates.

These risks are described in additional detail in *Section 9 General trends, outlook and assumptions and Section 10 Risks and risk management* in this MD&A. Those descriptions are incorporated by reference in this cautionary statement but are not intended to be a complete list of the risks that could affect the Company.

Many of these factors are beyond our control or our current expectations or knowledge. Additional risks and uncertainties not currently known to us or that we currently deem to be immaterial may also have a material adverse effect on our financial position, financial performance, cash flows, business or reputation. Except as otherwise indicated in this document, the forward-looking statements made herein do not reflect the potential impact of any non-recurring or special items or any mergers, acquisitions, dispositions or other business combinations or transactions that may be announced or that may occur after the date of this document.

Readers are cautioned not to place undue reliance on forward-looking statements. Forward-looking statements in this document describe our expectations and are based on our assumptions as at the date of this document and are subject to change after this date. Except as required by law, we disclaim any intention or obligation to update or revise any forward-looking statements.

This cautionary statement qualifies all of the forward-looking statements in this MD&A.

Report of management on internal control over financial reporting

Management of TELUS Corporation (TELUS, or the Company) is responsible for establishing and maintaining adequate internal control over financial reporting and for its assessment of the effectiveness of internal control over financial reporting.

TELUS' President and Chief Executive Officer and Executive Vice-President and Chief Financial Officer have assessed the effectiveness of the Company's internal control over financial reporting as of December 31, 2017, in accordance with the criteria established in *Internal Control – Integrated Framework (2013)* issued by the Committee of Sponsoring Organizations of the Treadway Commission. Internal control over financial reporting is a process designed by, or under the supervision of, the President and Chief Executive Officer and the Executive Vice-President and Chief Financial Officer and effected by the Board of Directors, management and other personnel to provide reasonable assurance regarding the reliability of financial reporting and the preparation of financial statements for external purposes in accordance with generally accepted accounting principles.

Due to its inherent limitations, internal control over financial reporting may not prevent or detect misstatements on a timely basis. Also, projections of any evaluation of the effectiveness of internal control over financial reporting to future periods are subject to the risk that the controls may become inadequate because of changes in conditions, or that the degree of compliance with the policies or procedures may deteriorate.

Based on the assessment referenced in the preceding paragraph, management has determined that the Company's internal control over financial reporting is effective as of December 31, 2017. In connection with this assessment, no material weaknesses in the Company's internal control over financial reporting were identified by management as of December 31, 2017.

Deloitte LLP, an Independent Registered Public Accounting Firm, audited the Company's Consolidated financial statements for the year ended December 31, 2017, and as stated in the Report of Independent Registered Public Accounting Firm, they have expressed an unqualified opinion on the effectiveness of the Company's internal control over financial reporting as of December 31, 2017.

Doug French
Executive Vice-President
and Chief Financial Officer
February 8, 2018

Darren Entwistle
President and
Chief Executive Officer
February 8, 2018

Report of independent registered public accounting firm

To the Board of Directors and Shareholders of TELUS Corporation

Opinion on the Consolidated Financial Statements

We have audited the accompanying consolidated financial statements of TELUS Corporation and subsidiaries (the Company), which comprise the consolidated statements of financial position as at December 31, 2017 and December 31, 2016, the consolidated statements of income and other comprehensive income, consolidated statements of changes in owners' equity and consolidated statements of cash flows for the years then ended, and the related notes, including a summary of significant accounting policies and other explanatory information (collectively referred to as the financial statements).

In our opinion, the financial statements present fairly, in all material respects, the financial position of the Company as at December 31, 2017 and December 31, 2016, and its financial performance and its cash flows for the years then ended, in accordance with International Financial Reporting Standards as issued by the International Accounting Standards Board.

Report on Internal Control over Financial Reporting

We have also audited, in accordance with the standards of the Public Company Accounting Oversight Board (United States) (PCAOB), the Company's internal control over financial reporting as of December 31, 2017, based on criteria established in *Internal Control – Integrated Framework (2013)* issued by the Committee of Sponsoring Organizations of the Treadway Commission and our report dated February 8, 2018, expressed an unqualified opinion on the Company's internal control over financial reporting.

Basis for Opinion

Management's Responsibility for the Financial Statements

Management is responsible for the preparation and fair presentation of these financial statements in accordance with International Financial Reporting Standards as issued by the International Accounting Standards Board, and for such internal control as management determines is necessary to enable the preparation of financial statements that are free from material misstatement, whether due to fraud or error.

Auditor's Responsibility

Our responsibility is to express an opinion on these financial statements based on our audits. We conducted our audits in accordance with Canadian generally accepted auditing standards and the standards of the PCAOB. Those standards require that we plan and perform the audit to obtain reasonable assurance about whether the financial statements are free from material misstatement, whether due to fraud or error. Those standards also require that we comply with ethical requirements. We are a public accounting firm registered with the PCAOB and are required to be independent with respect to the Company in accordance with the U.S. federal securities laws and the applicable rules and regulations of the Securities and Exchange Commission and the PCAOB. Further, we are required to be independent of the Company in accordance with the ethical requirements that are relevant to our audit of the financial statements in Canada and to fulfill our other ethical responsibilities in accordance with these requirements.

An audit includes performing procedures to assess the risks of material misstatement of the financial statements, whether due to fraud or error, and performing procedures that respond to those risks. Such procedures include examining, on a test basis, evidence regarding the amounts and disclosures in the financial statements. The procedures selected depend on our judgment, including the assessment of the risks of material misstatement of the financial statements, whether due to fraud or error. In making those risk assessments, we consider internal control relevant to the Company's preparation and fair presentation of the financial statements in order to design audit procedures that are appropriate in the circumstances. An audit also includes evaluating the appropriateness of accounting policies and principles used and the reasonableness of accounting estimates made by management, as well as evaluating the overall presentation of the financial statements.

We believe that the audit evidence we have obtained in our audits is sufficient and appropriate to provide a reasonable basis for our audit opinion.

Deloitte LLP

Deloitte LLP
Chartered Professional Accountants
Vancouver, Canada
February 8, 2018

We have served as the Company's auditor since 2002.

Report of independent registered public accounting firm

To the Board of Directors and Shareholders of TELUS Corporation

Opinion on Internal Control over Financial Reporting
We have audited the internal control over financial reporting of TELUS Corporation and subsidiaries (the Company) as of December 31, 2017, based on criteria established in *Internal Control – Integrated Framework (2013)* issued by the Committee of Sponsoring Organizations of the Treadway Commission (COSO). In our opinion, the Company maintained, in all material respects, effective internal control over financial reporting as of December 31, 2017, based on criteria established in *Internal Control – Integrated Framework (2013)* issued by COSO.

We have also audited, in accordance with the standards of the Public Company Accounting Oversight Board (United States) (PCAOB) and Canadian generally accepted auditing standards, the consolidated financial statements as of and for the year ended December 31, 2017, of the Company and our report dated February 8, 2018, expressed an unmodified/unqualified opinion on those financial statements.

Basis for Opinion
The Company's management is responsible for maintaining effective internal control over financial reporting and for its assessment of the effectiveness of internal control over financial reporting, included in the accompanying Report of Management on Internal Control over Financial Reporting. Our responsibility is to express an opinion on the Company's internal control over financial reporting based on our audit. We are a public accounting firm registered with the PCAOB and are required to be independent with respect to the Company in accordance with the U.S. federal securities laws and the applicable rules and regulations of the Securities and Exchange Commission and the PCAOB.

We conducted our audit in accordance with the standards of the PCAOB. Those standards require that we plan and perform the audit to obtain reasonable assurance about whether effective internal control over financial reporting was maintained in all material respects. Our audit included obtaining an understanding of internal control over financial reporting, assessing the risk that a material weakness exists, testing and evaluating the design and operating effectiveness of internal control based on the assessed risk, and performing such other procedures as we considered necessary in the circumstances. We believe that our audit provides a reasonable basis for our opinion.

Definition and Limitations of Internal Control over Financial Reporting
A company's internal control over financial reporting is a process designed to provide reasonable assurance regarding the reliability of financial reporting and the preparation of financial statements for external purposes in accordance with International Financial Reporting Standards as issued by the International Accounting Standards Board. A company's internal control over financial reporting includes those policies and procedures that (1) pertain to the maintenance of records that, in reasonable detail, accurately and fairly reflect the transactions and dispositions of the assets of the company; (2) provide reasonable assurance that transactions are recorded as necessary to permit preparation of financial statements in accordance with International Financial Reporting Standards as issued by the International Accounting Standards Board, and that receipts and expenditures of the company are being made only in accordance with authorizations of management and directors of the company; and (3) provide reasonable assurance regarding prevention or timely detection of unauthorized acquisition, use, or disposition of the company's assets that could have a material effect on the financial statements.

Because of its inherent limitations, internal control over financial reporting may not prevent or detect misstatements. Also, projections of any evaluation of effectiveness to future periods are subject to the risk that controls may become inadequate because of changes in conditions, or that the degree of compliance with the policies or procedures may deteriorate.

Deloitte LLP

Deloitte LLP
Chartered Professional Accountants
Vancouver, Canada
February 8, 2018

Consolidated statements of income and other comprehensive income

Years ended December 31 (millions except per share amounts)	Note	2017	2016
Operating Revenues			
Service		$12,478	$12,000
Equipment		724	725
Revenues arising from contracts with customers		13,202	12,725
Other operating income	7	102	74
		13,304	12,799
Operating Expenses			
Goods and services purchased		5,935	5,631
Employee benefits expense	8	2,595	2,939
Depreciation	17	1,617	1,564
Amortization of intangible assets	18	552	483
		10,699	10,617
Operating Income		2,605	2,182
Financing costs	9	573	520
Income Before Income Taxes		2,032	1,662
Income taxes	10	553	426
Net Income		1,479	1,236
Other Comprehensive Income	11		
Items that may subsequently be reclassified to income			
Change in unrealized fair value of derivatives designated as cash flow hedges		19	(20)
Foreign currency translation adjustment arising from translating financial statements of foreign operations		5	5
Change in unrealized fair value of available-for-sale financial assets		(11)	—
		13	(15)
Item never subsequently reclassified to income			
Employee defined benefit plans re-measurements		(172)	—
		(159)	(15)
Comprehensive Income		$ 1,320	$ 1,221
Net Income Attributable to:			
Common Shares		$ 1,460	$ 1,223
Non-controlling interests		19	13
		$ 1,479	$ 1,236
Comprehensive Income Attributable to:			
Common Shares		$ 1,297	$ 1,206
Non-controlling interests		23	15
		$ 1,320	$ 1,221
Net Income Per Common Share	12		
Basic		$ 2.46	$ 2.06
Diluted		$ 2.46	$ 2.06
Total Weighted Average Common Shares Outstanding			
Basic		593	592
Diluted		593	593

The accompanying notes are an integral part of these consolidated financial statements.

Consolidated statements of financial position

As at December 31 (millions)	Note	2017	2016
Assets			
Current assets			
Cash and temporary investments, net		$ 509	$ 432
Accounts receivable	6	1,623	1,471
Income and other taxes receivable		96	9
Inventories	1(p)	378	318
Prepaid expenses		260	233
Current derivative assets	4(h)	18	11
		2,884	2,474
Non-current assets			
Property, plant and equipment, net	17	11,368	10,464
Intangible assets, net	18	10,658	10,364
Goodwill, net	18	4,217	3,787
Other long-term assets	20	421	640
		26,664	25,255
		$29,548	$27,729
Liabilities and Owners' Equity			
Current liabilities			
Short-term borrowings	22	$ 100	$ 100
Accounts payable and accrued liabilities	23	2,460	2,330
Income and other taxes payable		34	37
Dividends payable	13	299	284
Advance billings and customer deposits	24	782	737
Provisions	25	78	124
Current maturities of long-term debt	26	1,404	1,327
Current derivative liabilities	4(h)	33	12
		5,190	4,951
Non-current liabilities			
Provisions	25	492	395
Long-term debt	26	12,256	11,604
Other long-term liabilities	27	847	736
Deferred income taxes	10(b)	2,500	2,107
		16,095	14,842
Liabilities		21,285	19,793
Owners' equity			
Common equity	28	8,221	7,917
Non-controlling interests		42	19
		8,263	7,936
		$29,548	$27,729
Contingent Liabilities	29		

The accompanying notes are an integral part of these consolidated financial statements.

Approved by the Directors:

W. A. MacKinnon
William A. MacKinnon
Director

R.H. Auchinleck
Director

Consolidated statements of changes in owners' equity

(millions)	Note	Common Shares (Note 28) Number of shares	Share capital	Contributed surplus	Retained earnings	Accumulated other comprehensive income	Total	Non-controlling interests	Total
			Equity contributed		Common equity				
Balance as at January 1, 2016		594	$5,050	$135	$2,428	$59	$7,672	$–	$7,672
Net income		–	–	–	1,223	–	1,223	13	1,236
Other comprehensive income	11	–	–	–	–	(17)	(17)	2	(15)
Dividends	13	–	–	–	(1,091)	–	(1,091)	–	(1,091)
Treasury shares acquired	14(a), 28(b)	(1)	(45)	–	–	–	(45)	–	(45)
Shares settled from Treasury	14(a), 28(b)	1	44	–	(3)	–	41	–	41
Share option award net-equity settlement feature	14(a)	–	2	(2)	–	–	–	–	–
Normal course issuer bid purchase of Common Shares		(4)	(36)	–	(129)	–	(165)	–	(165)
Reversal of opening liability for automatic share purchase plan commitment pursuant to normal course issuer bids for Common Shares	28(b)	–	14	–	46	–	60	–	60
Change in ownership interests of subsidiary	1(a), 31(b)	–	–	239	–	–	239	4	243
Balance as at December 31, 2016		590	$5,029	$372	$2,474	$42	$7,917	$19	$7,936
Balance as at January 1, 2017		590	$5,029	$372	$2,474	$42	$7,917	$19	$7,936
Net income		–	–	–	1,460	–	1,460	19	1,479
Other comprehensive income	11	–	–	–	(172)	9	(163)	4	(159)
Dividends	13	–	–	–	(1,167)	–	(1,167)	–	(1,167)
Dividends reinvested and optional cash payments		2	71	–	–	–	71	–	71
Share option award net-equity settlement feature	14(a)	1	2	(2)	–	–	–	–	–
Issue of shares in business combination		2	100	–	–	–	100	–	100
Other		–	3	–	–	–	3	–	3
Balance as at December 31, 2017		595	$5,205	$370	$2,595	$51	$8,221	$42	$8,263

The accompanying notes are an integral part of these consolidated financial statements.

Link to Full 2017 Annual Report: https://assets.ctfassets.net/rz9m1rynx8pv/t4ESxjDOBE0qKoOiU8YmQ/416fb9b2cfbf87be4cfee491ff16eae7/TELUS_2017_annual_report-for_online.pdf.

CONSOLIDATED FINANCIAL STATEMENTS

Consolidated statements of cash flows

Years ended December 31 (millions)	Note	2017	2016
Operating Activities			
Net income		$1,479	$1,236
Adjustments to reconcile net income to cash provided by operating activities:			
Depreciation and amortization		2,169	2,047
Deferred income taxes	10	430	(42)
Share-based compensation expense, net	14(a)	17	(2)
Net employee defined benefit plans expense	15(b),(g)	82	93
Employer contributions to employee defined benefit plans		(67)	(71)
Other		(21)	29
Net change in non-cash operating working capital	31(a)	(142)	(71)
Cash provided by operating activities		3,947	3,219
Investing Activities			
Cash payments for capital assets, excluding spectrum licences	31(a)	(3,081)	(2,752)
Cash payments for spectrum licences		–	(145)
Cash payments for acquisitions, net	18(b)	(564)	(90)
Real estate joint ventures advances and contributions	21(c)	(26)	(33)
Real estate joint ventures receipts	21(c)	18	103
Proceeds on dispositions		28	3
Other		(18)	(9)
Cash used by investing activities		(3,643)	(2,923)
Financing Activities			
Dividends paid to holders of Common Shares	31(b)	(1,082)	(1,070)
Purchases of Common Shares for cancellation	28(b)	–	(179)
Long-term debt issued	26	6,367	5,726
Redemptions and repayment of long-term debt	26	(5,502)	(4,843)
Issue of shares by subsidiary to non-controlling interests	1(a)	(1)	294
Other		(9)	(15)
Cash used by financing activities		(227)	(87)
Cash Position			
Increase in cash and temporary investments, net		77	209
Cash and temporary investments, net, beginning of period		432	223
Cash and temporary investments, net, end of period		$509	$432
Supplemental Disclosure of Operating Cash Flows			
Interest paid		$(539)	$(510)
Interest received		$7	$4
Income taxes paid, net		$(191)	$(600)

The accompanying notes are an integral part of these consolidated financial statements.

"THE FUTURE BELONGS TO
THOSE WHO BELIEVE IN THE
BEAUTY OF THEIR DREAMS

– ELEANOR ROOSEVELT

ANNUAL REPORT
FOR THE 52-WEEK PERIOD
ENDED MARCH 31, 2018

Independent Auditors' Report

To the Shareholders of Indigo Books & Music Inc.

We have audited the accompanying consolidated financial statements of Indigo Books & Music Inc., which comprise the consolidated balance sheets as at March 31, 2018 and April 1, 2017, and the consolidated statements of earnings and comprehensive earnings, changes in equity, and cash flows for the 52-week period ended March 31, 2018 and the 52-week period ended April 1, 2017, and a summary of significant accounting policies and other explanatory information.

Management's responsibility for the consolidated financial statements

Management is responsible for the preparation and fair presentation of these consolidated financial statements in accordance with International Financial Reporting Standards, and for such internal control as management determines is necessary to enable the preparation of consolidated financial statements that are free from material misstatement, whether due to fraud or error.

Auditors' responsibility

Our responsibility is to express an opinion on these consolidated financial statements based on our audits. We conducted our audits in accordance with Canadian generally accepted auditing standards. Those standards require that we comply with ethical requirements and plan and perform the audit to obtain reasonable assurance about whether the consolidated financial statements are free from material misstatement.

An audit involves performing procedures to obtain audit evidence about the amounts and disclosures in the consolidated financial statements. The procedures selected depend on the auditors' judgment, including the assessment of the risks of material misstatement of the consolidated financial statements, whether due to fraud or error. In making those risk assessments, the auditors consider internal control relevant to the entity's preparation and fair presentation of the consolidated financial statements in order to design audit procedures that are appropriate in the circumstances, but not for the purpose of expressing an opinion on the effectiveness of the entity's internal control. An audit also includes evaluating the appropriateness of accounting policies used and the reasonableness of accounting estimates made by management, as well as evaluating the overall presentation of the consolidated financial statements.

We believe that the audit evidence we have obtained in our audits is sufficient and appropriate to provide a basis for our audit opinion.

Opinion

In our opinion, the consolidated financial statements present fairly, in all material respects, the financial position of Indigo Books & Music Inc. as at March 31, 2018 and April 1, 2017, and its financial performance and its cash flows for the 52-week period ended March 31, 2018 and for the 52-week period ended April 1, 2017 in accordance with International Financial Reporting Standards.

Ernst & Young LLP

Toronto, Canada
May 29, 2018

Chartered Professional Accountants
Licensed Public Accountants

Consolidated Balance Sheets

(thousands of Canadian dollars)

	As at March 31, 2018	As at April 1, 2017
ASSETS		
Current		
Cash and cash equivalents (note 6)	150,256	130,438
Short-term investments (note 6)	60,000	100,000
Accounts receivable	6,747	7,448
Inventories (note 7)	264,586	231,576
Prepaid expenses	4,124	11,706
Derivative assets (note 8)	1,439	266
Assets held for sale (note 11)	—	1,037
Total current assets	487,152	482,471
Property, plant, and equipment (note 9)	82,314	65,078
Intangible assets (note 10)	24,215	15,272
Equity investments (note 22)	4,330	1,800
Deferred tax assets (note 12)	35,563	43,981
Total assets	633,574	608,602
LIABILITIES AND EQUITY		
Current		
Accounts payable and accrued liabilities (note 21)	176,479	170,611
Unredeemed gift card liability	44,218	50,396
Provisions (note 13)	166	110
Deferred revenue	8,807	12,852
Income taxes payable	152	360
Derivative liabilities (note 8)	327	—
Total current liabilities	230,149	234,329
Long-term accrued liabilities (note 21)	2,283	2,378
Long-term provisions (note 13)	45	51
Total liabilities	232,477	236,758
Equity		
Share capital (note 15)	221,854	215,971
Contributed surplus (note 16)	11,621	10,671
Retained earnings	166,807	145,007
Accumulated other comprehensive income (note 8)	815	195
Total equity	401,097	371,844
Total liabilities and equity	633,574	608,602

See accompanying notes

On behalf of the Board:

Heather Reisman
Director

Michael Kirby
Director

Consolidated Statements of Earnings and Comprehensive Earnings

(thousands of Canadian dollars, except per share data)

	52-week period ended March 31, 2018	52-week period ended April 1, 2017
Revenue (note 17)	1,079,425	1,019,845
Cost of sales	(604,094)	(565,640)
Gross profit	475,331	454,205
Operating, selling, and administrative expenses (notes 9, 10 and 17)	(448,909)	(428,981)
Operating profit	26,422	25,224
Net interest income	3,010	2,196
Share of earnings from equity investments (note 22)	1,049	1,617
Earnings before income taxes	30,481	29,037
Income tax expense (note 12)		
Current	(489)	(335)
Deferred	(8,192)	(7,784)
Net earnings	21,800	20,918
Other comprehensive income (note 8)		
Items that are or may be reclassified subsequently to net earnings:		
Net change in fair value of cash flow hedges [net of taxes of 897; 2017 – (496)]	(2,648)	1,357
Reclassification of net realized (gain) loss [net of taxes of (1,194); 2017 – 425]	3,268	(1,162)
Other comprehensive income	620	195
Total comprehensive income	22,420	21,113
Net earnings per common share (note 18)		
Basic	$0.81	$0.79
Diluted	$0.80	$0.78

See accompanying notes

Consolidated Statements of Changes in Equity

(thousands of Canadian dollars)	Share Capital	Contributed Surplus	Retained Earnings	Accumulated Other Comprehensive Income	Total Equity
Balance, April 2, 2016	209,318	10,591	124,089	–	343,998
Net earnings	–	–	20,918	–	20,918
Exercise of options (notes 15 and 16)	5,983	(1,017)	–	–	4,966
Directors' deferred share units converted (note 15)	670	(670)	–	–	–
Share-based compensation (notes 15 and 16)	–	1,400	–	–	1,400
Directors' compensation (note 16)	–	367	–	–	367
Other comprehensive income (note 8)	–	–	–	195	195
Balance, April 1, 2017	215,971	10,671	145,007	195	371,844
Balance, April 1, 2017	215,971	10,671	145,007	195	371,844
Net earnings	–	–	21,800	–	21,800
Exercise of options (notes 15 and 16)	5,883	(979)	–	–	4,904
Share-based compensation (notes 15 and 16)	–	1,588	–	–	1,588
Directors' compensation (note 16)	–	341	–	–	341
Other comprehensive income (note 8)	–	–	–	620	620
Balance, March 31, 2018	**221,854**	**11,621**	**166,807**	**815**	**401,097**

See accompanying notes

Consolidated Statements of Cash Flows

(thousands of Canadian dollars)	52-week period ended March 31, 2018	52-week period ended April 1, 2017
CASH FLOWS FROM OPERATING ACTIVITIES		
Net earnings	21,800	20,918
Adjustments to reconcile net earnings to cash flows from operating activities		
Depreciation of property, plant, and equipment (note 9)	19,074	16,612
Amortization of intangible assets (note 10)	7,922	8,573
Net reversal of capital assets (notes 9 and 10)	776	(963)
Loss on disposal of capital assets (notes 9 and 10)	–	2,770
Share-based compensation (note 16)	1,588	1,400
Directors' compensation (note 16)	341	367
Deferred tax assets (note 12)	8,192	7,784
Disposal of assets held for sale (note 11)	1,037	(1,037)
Other	1,042	147
Net change in non-cash working capital balances (note 19)	(29,335)	(17,196)
Interest expense	10	36
Interest income	(3,020)	(2,232)
Income taxes received	–	51
Share of earnings from equity investments (note 22)	(1,049)	(1,617)
Cash flows from operating activities	**28,378**	**35,613**
CASH FLOWS FROM INVESTING ACTIVITIES		
Purchase of property, plant, and equipment (note 9)	(37,080)	(19,774)
Addition of intangible assets (note 10)	(16,871)	(10,089)
Change in short-term investments (note 6)	40,000	(100,000)
Distribution from equity investments (note 22)	1,233	1,238
Interest received	2,872	1,190
Investment in associate (note 22)	(2,714)	–
Cash flows used for investing activities	**(12,560)**	**(127,435)**
CASH FLOWS FROM FINANCING ACTIVITIES		
Repayment of long-term debt	–	(53)
Interest paid	–	(28)
Proceeds from share issuances (note 15)	4,904	4,966
Cash flows from financing activities	**4,904**	**4,885**
Effect of foreign currency exchange rate changes on cash and cash equivalents	(904)	887
Net increase (decrease) in cash and cash equivalents during the period	**19,818**	**(86,050)**
Cash and cash equivalents, beginning of period	130,438	216,488
Cash and cash equivalents, end of period	150,256	130,438

See accompanying notes

Link to the Full 2018 Annual Report: https://static.indigoimages.ca/2018/corporate/Indigo_Annual-Report_2018.pdf.

Chart of Accounts

Note: The blanks in the account names below allow students to specify account names.

Assets

CURRENT ASSETS

101 Cash
102 Petty cash
103 Investments
104 _____ investments
106 Accounts receivable
107 Allowance for doubtful accounts
108 GST receivable
109 Interest receivable
110 Rent receivable
111 Notes receivable
119 Merchandise inventory
120 _____ inventory
124 Office supplies
125 Store supplies
126 _____ supplies
128 Prepaid insurance
129 Prepaid _____
131 Prepaid rent

NON-CURRENT INVESTMENTS

141 Investment in _____ shares
142 Investment in _____ bonds
144 Investment in _____

PROPERTY, PLANT, AND EQUIPMENT (PPE)

151 Automobiles/car/vehicle
152 Accumulated depreciation, automobiles/car/vehicle
153 Trucks
154 Accumulated depreciation, trucks
159 Library

160 Accumulated depreciation, library
161 Furniture
162 Accumulated depreciation, furniture
163 Office equipment
164 Accumulated depreciation, office equipment
165 Store equipment
166 Accumulated depreciation, store equipment
167 _____ equipment
168 Accumulated depreciation, _____ equipment
169 Machinery
170 Accumulated depreciation, machinery
173 Building _____
174 Accumulated depreciation, building _____
175 Land
176 Leasehold improvements
179 Land improvements, _____
180 Accumulated depreciation, land improvements _____

INTANGIBLE ASSETS

191 Patents
192 Accumulated amortization, patents
193 Leasehold
194 Accumulated amortization, leasehold
195 Franchise
196 Accumulated amortization, franchise
197 Copyright

198 Accumulated amortization, copyright
199 Brand name

GOODWILL

200 Goodwill

Liabilities

CURRENT LIABILITIES

201 Accounts payable
202 Insurance payable
203 Interest payable
204 Legal fees payable
205 Short-term notes payable
206 Rent payable
207 Salaries payable
208 Wages payable
209 Estimated warranty liability
210 Income taxes payable
211 Common dividends payable
212 Preferred dividends payable
213 EI payable
214 CPP payable
215 Employees' medical insurance payable
216 PST payable
217 GST payable
218 _____ payable

UNEARNED REVENUES

230 Unearned consulting revenue
231 Unearned revenue
232 Unearned _____ / Unearned _____ revenue

LONG-TERM LIABILITIES

250 Long-term notes payable
251 Long-term lease liability

252 Bonds payable
253 Discount on bonds payable
254 Premium on bonds payable

Equity

301 _____, capital
302 _____, withdrawals

CORPORATE CONTRIBUTED CAPITAL

307 Common shares
310 Common share dividends distributable
313 Contributed capital from the retirement of common shares
315 Preferred shares

RETAINED EARNINGS

318 Retained earnings
319 Cash dividends
320 Share dividends

REVENUES

401 _____ revenue
403 _____ services revenue
405 Commission revenue
406 Rent revenue
407 Dividends income
408 Earnings from investment in _____
409 Interest income
413 Sales
414 Sales returns and allowances
415 Sales discounts

EXPENSES
COST OF SALES

500 Cost of goods sold
501 Purchases

502 Purchases returns and allowances
503 Purchases discounts
504 Transportation-in/freight-in

DEPRECIATION/ AMORTIZATION

600 Depreciation expense, automobiles/car/vehicle
602 Depreciation expense, _____
603 Amortization expense, copyrights
604 Amortization expense, _____

EMPLOYEE-RELATED EXPENSE

620 Office salaries expense
621 Sales salaries expense
622 Salaries expense
623 _____ wages expense
624 Employees' benefits expense

FINANCIAL EXPENSES

630 Cash over and short
633 Interest expense
634 Transaction fees

INSURANCE EXPENSES

636 Insurance expense, building
637 Insurance expense, _____

RENTAL EXPENSES

640 Rent expense
641 Rent expense, office space
642 Rent expense, _____

SUPPLIES EXPENSE

650 Office supplies expense
651 _____ supplies expense

OTHER EXPENSES

655 Advertising expense
656 Bad debts expense
659 Collection expense
661 Debit card expense
662 Credit card expense
663 Delivery expense/freight-out expense
667 Equipment expense
668 Food and drinks expense
671 Gas and oil expense
673 Janitorial expense
674 Legal fees expense
676 Mileage expense
682 Postage expense
683 Property taxes expense
684 Repairs expense, _____
688 Telephone/cell phone expense
689 Travel and entertaining expense
690 Utilities expense
691 Warranty expense
695 Income taxes expense
696 _____ expense

OTHER INCOME AND LOSSES

701 Gain on retirement of bonds
702 Gain on sale of machinery
703 Investment income
705 Gain on _____
805 Loss on retirement of bonds
806 Loss on sale of investments
807 Loss on sale of machinery
809 Loss on _____

CLEARING ACCOUNTS

901 Income summary

Index

Note: Page numbers followed by *e* or *n* represent exhibits or notes, respectively.

A

Abercrombie & Fitch, 5
Abnormal balance, 103
Accelerated depreciation methods, 618, 623–625
Account
  abnormal balance, 103
  asset accounts, 81–82
  balance of account, 85
  chart of accounts, 89
  debits and credits, 85
  defined, 81
  double-entry accounting, 85–88
  equity accounts, 83
  liability accounts, 82–83
  normal balance, 88
  T-account, 84
  zero balance, 103
Account balance, 85
Account form balance sheet, 176
Accountant
  opportunities in, 9–10
  professional certification, 11
  salaries, 9*e*
Accounting. *See also* Accounting information
  defined, 3–4
  ethics and, 8, 11–14
  financial accounting, 9–10
  GAAP and, 14–15, 16*e*
  managerial accounting, 9, 9*e*, 10
  opportunities in, 9–10
  professional certification, 11
  recordkeeping, 4
  reporting, 4
  social responsibility and, 14
  standards, 14–15, 16*e*
  taxation, 9, 9*e*, 10
Accounting cycle
  closing process, 243–249
  defined, 80–81
  exhibit of, 90*e*, 156*e*
  journal entries, 90–94
  summary of steps in, 250*e*

transaction analysis, 25–31
trial balance, 103–107
Accounting equation
  analysis example, 100–101
  defined, 24–25
  double-entry accounting and, 86
  transaction analysis, 25–26
  transaction example, 26–31
Accounting ethics, 12–14
Accounting information
  external users of, 7–8
  internal users of, 7*e*, 8
Accounting periods, 158–159
Accounting Standards Board (AcSB), 14–15
Accounting Standards for Private Enterprises (ASPE)
  adjusting entries, 178
  depreciation, 646
  depreciation vs. amortization, 178, 261
  exchange of non-monetary assets, 646
  expense classification, 342
  expenses vs. IFRS, 107
  financial statements, 35
  GAAP framework and, 16*e*
  goodwill, 646
  impairment, 646
  internal controls, 499
  merchandise inventory, 425
  public vs. private enterprises and, 14–15
Accounts payable
  accounting equation and, 81
  defined, 22, 82
  partial payment of, 97
  purchases on credit, 95
Accounts receivable
  aging analysis, 551–552, 553*e*
  bad debts. *See* Bad debts
  control, 544
  credit risk analysis, 543
  defined, 21, 82, 540
  discounting, 570
  loan security, as, 569–570
  recognizing, 541
  sales on credit, 541–543
  selling for cash, 569

Accounts receivable aging analysis, 551–552
Accounts receivable approach (bad debt estimation)
  aging analysis, 551–552
  defined, 550
  methods summary, 545*e*
  percentage of accounts receivable, 550–551
Accounts receivable insurance, 546
Accounts receivable turnover, 562, 563
Accrual basis accounting
  cash basis vs., 159–160
  defined, 156
Accrued expenses
  adjusting entries, 167–170, 172*e*
  defined, 167
  reversing entries, 266–267
Accrued interest expense, 167–168
Accrued interest income, 171
Accrued revenues
  adjusting entries, 170–171, 172*e*
  defined, 170
Accrued salaries expense, 168–170
Accrued services revenue, 170–171
Acid-test ratio, 498
AcSB. *See* Accounting Standards Board (AcSB)
Adjusted trial balance
  closing process and, 245*e*
  defined, 175
  financial statements and, 176–177
  perpetual inventory system, 334–336
  worksheet and, 238–240
Adjusting entry
  accrual vs. cash basis accounting, 159–160
  accrued expenses, 167–170, 172*e*
  accrued revenues, 170–171, 172*e*
  after allowance for doubtful accounts, 551*e*
  balance sheet and, 172*e*
  bank reconciliation and, 490–491, 495–496
  defined, 156, 161
  depreciation, 164–165, 172*e*

SUMMARY OF FOCUS ON FINANCIAL STATEMENT ONLINE COMPANIES—VOLUME 1

EXTEND YOUR KNOWLEDGE (EYK) INDEX—VOLUME 1